FEDERALISM

ASPEN ELECTIVE SERIES

FEDERALISM

Anthony J. Bellia Jr.
Professor of Law and Notre Dame Presidential Fellow
University of Notre Dame

Wolters Kluwer
Law & Business

AUSTIN   BOSTON   CHICAGO   NEW YORK   THE NETHERLANDS

Aspen Publishers
Attn: Permissions Department
76 Ninth Avenue, 7th Floor
New York, NY 10011-5201

To contact Customer Care, e-mail customer.care@aspenpublishers.com, call 1-800-234-1660, fax 1-800-901-9075, or mail correspondence to:

Aspen Publishers
Attn: Order Department
PO Box 990
Frederick, MD 21705

Printed in the United States of America.

1 2 3 4 5 6 7 8 9 0

ISBN 978-0-7355-8921-6

Library of Congress Cataloging-in-Publication Data

Bellia, Anthony J., Jr.
    Federalism / Anthony J. Bellia, Jr.
       p. cm.
    ISBN 978-0-7355-8921-6 (perfectbound : alk. paper)
    1. Federal government—United States. 2. Constitutional history—United States. I. Title.

KF4600.B45 2010
320.473'049—dc22

                                                                2010046666

This book contains paper from well-managed forests to SFI standards.

About Wolters Kluwer Law & Business

Wolters Kluwer Law & Business is a leading provider of research information and workflow solutions in key specialty areas. The strengths of the individual brands of Aspen Publishers, CCH, Kluwer Law International and Loislaw are aligned within Wolters Kluwer Law & Business to provide comprehensive, in-depth solutions and expert-authored content for the legal, professional and education markets.

CCH was founded in 1913 and has served more than four generations of business professionals and their clients. The CCH products in the Wolters Kluwer Law & Business group are highly regarded electronic and print resources for legal, securities, antitrust and trade regulation, government contracting, banking, pension, payroll, employment and labor, and healthcare reimbursement and compliance professionals.

Aspen Publishers is a leading information provider for attorneys, business professionals and law students. Written by preeminent authorities, Aspen products offer analytical and practical information in a range of specialty practice areas from securities law and intellectual property to mergers and acquisitions and pension/benefits. Aspen's trusted legal education resources provide professors and students with high-quality, up-to-date and effective resources for successful instruction and study in all areas of the law.

Kluwer Law International supplies the global business community with comprehensive English-language international legal information. Legal practitioners, corporate counsel and business executives around the world rely on the Kluwer Law International journals, loose-leafs, books and electronic products for authoritative information in many areas of international legal practice.

Loislaw is a premier provider of digitized legal content to small law firm practitioners of various specializations. Loislaw provides attorneys with the ability to quickly and efficiently find the necessary legal information they need, when and where they need it, by facilitating access to primary law as well as state-specific law, records, forms and treatises.

Wolters Kluwer Law & Business, a unit of Wolters Kluwer, is headquartered in New York and Riverwoods, Illinois. Wolters Kluwer is a leading multinational publisher and information services company.

For my parents

Tony

and

Maureen

who exemplify the first principles of good governance

SUMMARY OF CONTENTS

TABLE OF CONTENTS

PREFACE

"The erection of a new government, whatever care or wisdom may distinguish the work, cannot fail to originate questions of intricacy and nicety; and these may in a particular manner be expected to flow from the establishment of a constitution founded upon the total or partial incorporation of a number of distinct sovereignties."

Alexander Hamilton
THE FEDERALIST No. 82

Hamilton was right. More than two hundred years after he wrote these words, judges and other public officials continue to struggle with "questions of intricacy and nicety" stemming from "the total or partial incorporation of a number of distinct sovereignties." Indeed, they still debate the nature of incorporation and its consequences for governance in the United States.

The Constitution of the United States establishes a federal government of limited and enumerated powers. Articles I, II, and III define federal legislative, executive, and judicial powers, respectively. The Tenth Amendment, in turn, provides that "[t]he powers not delegated to the United States by the Constitution, nor prohibited by it to the States, are reserved to the States respectively, or to the people." The Supreme Court of the United States has long insisted that, in these provisions, the Constitution recognizes a system of "dual sovereignty." In 1819, in *McCullough v. Maryland*, 17 U.S. (4 Wheat.) 316, 410 (1819), Chief Justice John Marshall wrote, "In America, the powers of sovereignty are divided between the government of the Union, and those of the States. They are each sovereign, with respect to the objects committed to it, and neither sovereign with respect to the objects committed to the other."

In concept, this principle is straightforward. In application, it is complex and contested. Hamilton was not the only prominent member of the Founding generation to foresee that the Constitution would long generate complex questions regarding the relationship between the federal government and the states. James Madison "brought with him into the [Federal] Convention [of 1787] a strong bias in favor of an enumeration and definition of the powers necessary to be exercised by the national Legislature; but [he] . . . also brought doubts concerning its practicability." 1 THE RECORDS OF THE FEDERAL CONVENTION OF 1787, at 53 (Max Farrand ed., rev. ed. 1966) (Notes of James Madison). In *McCullough*, Chief Justice Marshall observed that the federal "government is acknowledged by all, to be one of enumerated powers. . . . But the question respecting the extent of the powers actually granted, is perpetually arising, and will probably continue to arise, so long as our system shall exist." 17 U.S. (4 Wheat.) at 405.

Since the Founding, public officials in the United States have struggled to understand and define the relationship between the national government and the states. Constitutional questions involving that relationship have arisen from the earliest days of the Union — and foundational questions surrounding that relationship remain contested today. Such questions involve not only the relative constitutional powers of the federal government and the states, but also the constitutional responsibilities of various institutions to resolve disputes about those powers.

I wrote this book because U.S. federalism is a subject that deserves its own book-length treatment. Several law school courses consider aspects of federalism — courses such as constitutional law, civil procedure, and federal courts. But given the breadth of other topics that these courses must cover, certain federalism-related topics may fall through the cracks or receive only cursory treatment. These topics include important recurring practical questions, such as the scope of federal preemption. They include defining moments in American constitutional development, such as the nineteenth-century contest over slavery or the rejection of federal general common law in *Erie Railroad Co. v. Tompkins*, 304 U.S. 64 (1938). They include questions of U.S. federalism intensely debated among academics, such as the place of customary international law in the federal system. This book considers federalism-related topics that students may not encounter or may encounter only piecemeal across various courses. Its purpose is to enable students to understand better the nature of U.S. federalism and to analyze critically various premises underlying constitutional discourse about federalism.

This book provides ample materials for a stand-alone course on U.S. federalism. It also provides a base of materials for use in courses in constitutional law, or more specialized courses in federalism, such as the history of federalism, the theory of federalism, topics in federalism, comparative federalism, and judicial federalism, to name just some. The book's website — www.aspen lawschool.com-books-bellia_federalism — contains additional materials that might prove useful supplements in a variety of courses.

In addressing questions of federalism, courts, other public officials, and scholars have relied heavily on historical practice, constitutional structure, and political theory. Accordingly, this book is designed to enable students to study constitutional doctrine in light of the events, practices, and principles that continue to shape it.

Part I — Framing American Federalism — lays the foundation for serious engagement with constitutional doctrine surrounding the relationship between the federal government and the states. It explores Founding-era conceptions of federalism, antebellum and Reconstruction contests over federalism, normative political theories of federalism, and the political safeguards of federalism. The materials address the relationship between federal and state power under the Constitution and how disputes over that power should be resolved. The Supreme Court has relied on various sources presented in Part I in resolving federalism questions throughout U.S. history. By reading these primary materials, students will be better equipped to understand and critique present-day judicial analyses of federalism.

Part II — National and State Power to Regulate — considers constitutional doctrines surrounding the relative powers of the federal government and the states. It addresses several enumerated powers of Congress, including its powers under the Commerce Clause, the General Welfare Clause, and §5 of the Fourteenth Amendment. Additionally, it considers doctrines of state sovereignty that have operated as limits on some or all of these powers. Finally, it considers federal limits on state power, including implied constitutional limits under the Commerce Clause and foreign relations powers, and preemption of state law by federal regulatory schemes.

Part III — Judicial Federalism and Rules of Decision — examines the relationship between judicial rules of decision and the federal constitutional structure. It traces jurisprudential shifts in the sources of law that federal courts have applied from the Founding era to the present, exploring questions of federalism that different sources of law have generated along the way. In particular, it considers the relationship between the federal constitutional structure and federal common law, customary international law, and general law as rules of decision in federal courts.

This book presents students with extensive historical, theoretical, and judicial materials involving the U.S. federal structure. It is not intended, however, to serve as a research compendium. Its goal is to engage students deeply in the materials presented rather than to offer a comprehensive synthesis of constitutional doctrine. Before each set of materials, the book poses a series of questions for the reader's consideration. Following each set, the book refers back to those questions with a series of "points for discussion." In crafting these points, I have attempted to avoid both overwhelming the reader with questions and leaving the reader with too little guidance as to which points warrant further consideration.

This book brings historical practice, structural principle, political theory, and contemporary doctrine to bear on many discrete questions involving the U.S. federal structure. The student who seriously engages these materials should achieve a deeper understanding of the structure of governance in the United States, and greater competence to resolve the problems of governance that are "perpetually arising, and will probably continue to arise, so long as our system shall exist."

A.J. Bellia
November 2010

ACKNOWLEDGMENTS

First and foremost, I am grateful to my wife, Tricia Bellia, without whose support I could not have written this book. She gave me the time — and, more than that, the peace of mind — to write it. Her substantive contributions pervade the book.

I also am grateful to many colleagues — too numerous to mention — whose comments and writings contributed to this book. In particular, however, I thank my friend and sometime co-author, Brad Clark, for countless insights and critiques that helped shape this book.

I also thank Carol McGeehan of Aspen Publishers for encouraging me to pursue this project and John Devins for advice and counsel that significantly improved it in many ways throughout the editorial process. In that process, several anonymous reviewers provided comments on various chapters. These comments were invaluable, inspiring revisions that dramatically improved the book. I am very grateful for the generosity of each of these reviewers.

In addition, I thank the Notre Dame Law School for generous research support — and for its commitment to the study of constitutional structure.

I received outstanding research assistance as I prepared this book. Notre Dame research librarian Patti Ogden provided exceptional research support. Having studied some of these materials with me in class, she also provided very helpful substantive suggestions. For all of her contributions, I thank her. I also thank Notre Dame law students Nick Curcio, Katie Hammond, J. D. Lindermuth, Jake Lombardo, Meghan Sweeney, and Carolyn Wendel, who provided excellent research assistance.

Finally, I thank the many Notre Dame law students who have studied federalism with me through the years. In many ways, this book reflects their insights and questions.

A Note on Sources. I have indicated omissions from excerpted materials with ellipses or brackets, except at the beginning of excerpts or sections within excerpts. I generally have not indicated the omission of citations or footnotes. Numbered footnotes are from original sources. In parts, I have joined portions of edited text into new paragraphs to improve readability.

I am grateful to the following sources for their permission to reprint excerpts of published work:

Robert B. Ahdieh, *Dialectical Regulation*, 38 Connecticut Law Review 863, 863-868, 871-872 (2006). Copyright © 2006 by the Connecticut Law Review. Reprinted by permission of the Connecticut Law Review and Robert B. Ahdieh.

Bernard Bailyn, The Ideological Origins of the American Revolution (1967). Reprinted by permission of the publisher of THE IDEOLOGICAL ORIGINS OF THE AMERICAN REVOLUTION by Bernard Bailyn, pp. 198, 200-205, 208-210, 223, 228-229, Cambridge, Mass.: The Belknap Press of Harvard University Press, Copyright © 1967, 1992 by the President and Fellows of Harvard College.

Anthony J. Bellia Jr. and Bradford R. Clark, *The Federal Common Law of Nations*, 109 Columbia Law Review 1, 5-9, 47-48, 53-55 (2009). Reprinted with permission of Bradford R. Clark.

Bradford R. Clark, *Separation of Powers as a Safeguard of Federalism*, 79 Texas Law Review 1321, 1323-1325, 1328-1331, 1342-1343, 1403, 1412-1419 (2001). © Copyright 2001, Texas Law Review Association. Reprinted by permission of the Texas Law Review Association and Bradford R. Clark.

William A. Fletcher, *The General Common Law and Section 34 of the Judiciary Act of 1789: The Example of Marine Insurance*, 97 Harvard Law Review 1513, 1517-1520, 1523-1525 (1984). Reprinted by permission of William A. Fletcher.

John Harrison, *Reconstructing the Privileges or Immunities Clause*, 101 Yale Law Journal 1385, 1397-1410 (1992). Copyright © 1992 by the Yale Law Journal Company, Inc. Reprinted by permission of the Yale Law Journal Company, Inc., from *The Yale Law Journal*, Vol. 101, pp. 1385, and by permission of John Harrison.

Harold Hongju Koh, *Is International Law Really State Law?*, 111 Harvard Law Review 1824, 1824-1826, 1830-1835 (1998). Reprinted by permission of Harold Hongju Koh.

Larry D. Kramer, *Putting the Politics Back into the Political Safeguards of Federalism*, 100 Columbia Law Review 215, 220-227, 278-279, 282-293 (2000). Reprinted by permission of the Columbia Law Review Association and Larry D. Kramer.

Michael W. McConnell, *Federalism: Evaluating the Founders' Design*, 54 University of Chicago Law Review 1484, 1484, 1492-1496, 1498-1512 (1987). © 1987 by Michael McConnell. Reprinted by permission of Michael McConnell.

Caleb Nelson, *Preeemption*, 86 Virginia Law Review 225, 232, 234-242, 245-247, 250-252, 254-256, 260-262, 303-305 (2000). Copyright © 2000 by the Virginia Law Review Association. Reprinted by permission of the Virginia Law Review Association and Caleb Nelson.

Caleb Nelson, *The Persistance of General Law*, 106 Columbia Law Review 503, 503-505 (2006). Reprinted by permission of the Columbia Law Review Association and Caleb Nelson.

Saikrishna B. Prakash & John C. Yoo, *Questions for the Critics of Judicial Review*, 72 George Washington Law Review 354, 354-358, 360-361, 368, 377 (2003). Copyright © 2003 by The George Washington Law Review. Reprinted by permission of the George Washington Law Review, and Saikrishna B. Prakash and John C. Yoo.

Edward L. Rubin & Malcolm Feeley, *Federalism: Some Notes on a National Neurosis*, 41 UCLA Law Review 903, 906-908, 910-911, 913-928, 931-934, 948 (1994). Reprinted by permission of Edward L. Rubin and Malcolm Feeley.

Joshua Sarnoff, *Cooperative Federalism, the Delegation of Federal Power, and the Constitution*, 39 Arizona Law Review 205, 212-218, 220 (1997). Copyright © 1997 by the Arizona Board of Regents. Reprinted by permission of the Arizona Law Review and Joshua Sarnoff.

Robert A. Schapiro, *Toward a Theory of Interactive Federalism*, 91 Iowa Law Review 243, 248-249, 285-296 (2005). Reprinted by permission of the Iowa Law Review and Robert A. Schapiro.

Herbert J. Storing, What the Anti-Federalists Were For 15-21 (1981). © 1981 by the University of Chicago. Reprinted by permission of the University of Chicago Press.

Herbert Wechsler, *The Political Safeguards of Federalism: The Role of the States in the Composition and Selection of the National Government*, 54 Columbia Law Review 543, 543-550, 552-553, 557-559 (1954). Copyright, 1954 by the Trustees of the Columbia Law Review. Reprinted by permission of the Columbia Law Review.

Louise Weinberg, *Federal Common Law*, 83 Northwestern University Law Review 805, 805-806, 809-816 (1989). Copyright © 1989 by Louise Weinberg. Reprinted by permission of Louis Weinberg.

Phillip J. Weiser, *Towards a Constitutional Architecture for Cooperative Federalism*, 79 North Carolina Law Review 663, 665-666, 668-674, 700-701 (2001). Copyright © 2001 by The North Carolina Law Review Association. Reprinted by permission of the North Carolina Law Review and Phillip J. Weiser.

Gordon S. Wood, The Creation of the American Republic 1776-1787, 382-383, 388-389 (1969). From THE CREATION OF THE AMERICAN REPUBLIC, 1778-1787 by Gordon S. Wood. Published for the Omohundro Institute of Early American History and Culture. Copyright © 1970 by the University of North Carolina Press; new preface copyright © 1998 by the University of North Carolina Press. Used by permission of the publisher.

Ernest A. Young, *Sorting Out the Debate Over Customary International Law*, 42 Virginia Journal of International Law 365, 366-369, 372, 374-375, 377-378, 382-384, 392-394, 400-404, 406-409, 413, 415-419, 421-423, 432-434 (2002). Copyright © 2002 Virginia Journal of International Law Association. Reprinted by permission of the Virginia Journal of International Law via Copyright Clearance Center and by Ernest A. Young.

THE CONSTITUTION OF THE UNITED STATES OF AMERICA

We the People of the United States, in Order to form a more perfect Union, establish Justice, insure domestic Tranquility, provide for the common defence, promote the general Welfare, and secure the Blessings of Liberty to ourselves and our Posterity, do ordain and establish this Constitution for the United States of America.

ARTICLE I

Section 1. All legislative Powers herein granted shall be vested in a Congress of the United States, which shall consist of a Senate and House of Representatives.

Section 2. The House of Representatives shall be composed of Members chosen every second Year by the People of the several States, and the Electors in each State shall have the Qualifications requisite for Electors of the most numerous Branch of the State Legislature.

No Person shall be a Representative who shall not have attained to the Age of twenty five Years, and been seven Years a Citizen of the United States, and who shall not, when elected, be an Inhabitant of that State in which he shall be chosen.

[Representatives and direct Taxes shall be apportioned among the several States which may be included within this Union, according to their respective Numbers, which shall be determined by adding to the whole Number of free Persons, including those bound to Service for a Term of Years, and excluding Indians not taxed, three fifths of all other Persons.]* The actual Enumeration shall be made within three Years after the first Meeting of the Congress of the United States, and within every subsequent Term of ten Years, in such Manner as they shall by Law direct. The Number of Representatives shall not exceed one for every thirty Thousand, but each State shall have at Least one Representative; and until such enumeration shall be made, the State of New Hampshire shall be entitled to chuse three, Massachusetts eight, Rhode Island and Providence Plantations one, Connecticut five, New York six, New Jersey four, Pennsylvania eight, Delaware one, Maryland six, Virginia ten, North Carolina five, South Carolina five and Georgia three.

When vacancies happen in the Representation from any State, the Executive Authority thereof shall issue Writs of Election to fill such Vacancies.

The House of Representatives shall chuse their Speaker and other Officers; and shall have the sole Power of Impeachment.

Section 3. The Senate of the United States shall be composed of two Senators from each State, chosen [by the Legislature thereof,]** for six Years; and each Senator shall have one Vote.

Immediately after they shall be assembled in Consequence of the first Election, they shall be divided as equally as may be into three Classes. The

---

* Amended by §2 of the Fourteenth Amendment.
** Amended by the Seventeenth Amendment.

Seats of the Senators of the first Class shall be vacated at the Expiration of the second Year, of the second Class at the Expiration of the fourth Year, and of the third Class at the Expiration of the sixth Year, so that one third may be chosen every second Year; [and if Vacancies happen by Resignation, or otherwise, during the Recess of the Legislature of any State, the Executive thereof may make temporary Appointments until the next Meeting of the Legislature, which shall then fill such Vacancies.]*

No person shall be a Senator who shall not have attained to the Age of thirty Years, and been nine Years a Citizen of the United States, and who shall not, when elected, be an Inhabitant of that State for which he shall be chosen.

The Vice President of the United States shall be President of the Senate, but shall have no Vote, unless they be equally divided.

The Senate shall chuse their other Officers, and also a President pro tempore, in the absence of the Vice President, or when he shall exercise the Office of President of the United States.

The Senate shall have the sole Power to try all Impeachments. When sitting for that Purpose, they shall be on Oath or Affirmation. When the President of the United States is tried, the Chief Justice shall preside: And no Person shall be convicted without the Concurrence of two thirds of the Members present.

Judgment in Cases of Impeachment shall not extend further than to removal from Office, and disqualification to hold and enjoy any Office of honor, Trust or Profit under the United States: but the Party convicted shall nevertheless be liable and subject to Indictment, Trial, Judgment and Punishment, according to Law.

Section 4. The Times, Places and Manner of holding Elections for Senators and Representatives, shall be prescribed in each State by the Legislature thereof; but the Congress may at any time by Law make or alter such Regulations, except as to the Place of chusing Senators.

The Congress shall assemble at least once in every Year, and such Meeting shall be [on the first Monday in December,]** unless they shall by Law appoint a different Day.

Section 5. Each House shall be the Judge of the Elections, Returns and Qualifications of its own Members, and a Majority of each shall constitute a Quorum to do Business; but a smaller number may adjourn from day to day, and may be authorized to compel the Attendance of absent Members, in such Manner, and under such Penalties as each House may provide.

Each House may determine the Rules of its Proceedings, punish its Members for disorderly Behavior, and, with the Concurrence of two thirds, expel a Member.

Each House shall keep a Journal of its Proceedings, and from time to time publish the same, excepting such Parts as may in their Judgment require Secrecy; and the Yeas and Nays of the Members of either House on any

---

* Amended by the Seventeenth Amendment.
** Amended by §2 of the Twentieth Amendment.

question shall, at the Desire of one fifth of those Present, be entered on the Journal.

Neither House, during the Session of Congress, shall, without the Consent of the other, adjourn for more than three days, nor to any other Place than that in which the two Houses shall be sitting.

Section 6. The Senators and Representatives shall receive a Compensation for their Services, to be ascertained by Law, and paid out of the Treasury of the United States. They shall in all Cases, except Treason, Felony and Breach of the Peace, be privileged from Arrest during their Attendance at the Session of their respective Houses, and in going to and returning from the same; and for any Speech or Debate in either House, they shall not be questioned in any other Place.

No Senator or Representative shall, during the Time for which he was elected, be appointed to any civil Office under the Authority of the United States which shall have been created, or the Emoluments whereof shall have been increased during such time; and no Person holding any Office under the United States, shall be a Member of either House during his Continuance in Office.

Section 7. All bills for raising Revenue shall originate in the House of Representatives; but the Senate may propose or concur with Amendments as on other Bills.

Every Bill which shall have passed the House of Representatives and the Senate, shall, before it become a Law, be presented to the President of the United States; If he approve he shall sign it, but if not he shall return it, with his Objections to that House in which it shall have originated, who shall enter the Objections at large on their Journal, and proceed to reconsider it. If after such Reconsideration two thirds of that House shall agree to pass the Bill, it shall be sent, together with the Objections, to the other House, by which it shall likewise be reconsidered, and if approved by two thirds of that House, it shall become a Law. But in all such Cases the Votes of both Houses shall be determined by yeas and Nays, and the Names of the Persons voting for and against the Bill shall be entered on the Journal of each House respectively. If any Bill shall not be returned by the President within ten Days (Sundays excepted) after it shall have been presented to him, the Same shall be a Law, in like Manner as if he had signed it, unless the Congress by their Adjournment prevent its Return, in which Case it shall not be a Law.

Every Order, Resolution, or Vote to which the Concurrence of the Senate and House of Representatives may be necessary (except on a question of Adjournment) shall be presented to the President of the United States; and before the Same shall take Effect, shall be approved by him, or being disapproved by him, shall be repassed by two thirds of the Senate and House of Representatives, according to the Rules and Limitations prescribed in the Case of a Bill.

Section 8. The Congress shall have Power To lay and collect Taxes, Duties, Imposts and Excises, to pay the Debts and provide for the common Defence and general Welfare of the United States; but all Duties, Imposts and Excises shall be uniform throughout the United States;

To borrow Money on the credit of the United States;

To regulate Commerce with foreign Nations, and among the several States, and with the Indian Tribes;

To establish an uniform Rule of Naturalization, and uniform Laws on the subject of Bankruptcies throughout the United States;

To coin Money, regulate the Value thereof, and of foreign Coin, and fix the Standard of Weights and Measures;

To provide for the Punishment of counterfeiting the Securities and current Coin of the United States;

To establish Post Offices and Post Roads;

To promote the Progress of Science and useful Arts, by securing for limited Times to Authors and Inventors the exclusive Right to their respective Writings and Discoveries;

To constitute Tribunals inferior to the supreme Court;

To define and punish Piracies and Felonies committed on the high Seas, and Offenses against the Law of Nations;

To declare War, grant Letters of Marque and Reprisal, and make Rules concerning Captures on Land and Water;

To raise and support Armies, but no Appropriation of Money to that Use shall be for a longer Term than two Years;

To provide and maintain a Navy;

To make Rules for the Government and Regulation of the land and naval Forces;

To provide for calling forth the Militia to execute the Laws of the Union, suppress Insurrections and repel Invasions;

To provide for organizing, arming, and disciplining the Militia, and for governing such Part of them as may be employed in the Service of the United States, reserving to the States respectively, the Appointment of the Officers, and the Authority of training the Militia according to the discipline prescribed by Congress;

To exercise exclusive Legislation in all Cases whatsoever, over such District (not exceeding ten Miles square) as may, by Cession of particular States, and the acceptance of Congress, become the Seat of the Government of the United States, and to exercise like Authority over all Places purchased by the Consent of the Legislature of the State in which the Same shall be, for the Erection of Forts, Magazines, Arsenals, dock-Yards, and other needful Buildings; And

To make all Laws which shall be necessary and proper for carrying into Execution the foregoing Powers, and all other Powers vested by this Constitution in the Government of the United States, or in any Department or Officer thereof.

Section 9. The Migration or Importation of such Persons as any of the States now existing shall think proper to admit, shall not be prohibited by the Congress prior to the Year one thousand eight hundred and eight, but a tax or duty may be imposed on such Importation, not exceeding ten dollars for each Person.

The privilege of the Writ of Habeas Corpus shall not be suspended, unless when in Cases of Rebellion or Invasion the public Safety may require it.

No Bill of Attainder or ex post facto Law shall be passed.

No capitation, or other direct, Tax shall be laid, [unless in Proportion to the Census or Enumeration herein before directed to be taken.]*

No Tax or Duty shall be laid on Articles exported from any State.

No Preference shall be given by any Regulation of Commerce or Revenue to the Ports of one State over those of another: nor shall Vessels bound to, or from, one State, be obliged to enter, clear, or pay Duties in another.

No Money shall be drawn from the Treasury, but in Consequence of Appropriations made by Law; and a regular Statement and Account of the Receipts and Expenditures of all public Money shall be published from time to time.

No Title of Nobility shall be granted by the United States: And no Person holding any Office of Profit or Trust under them, shall, without the Consent of the Congress, accept of any present, Emolument, Office, or Title, of any kind whatever, from any King, Prince or foreign State.

Section 10. No State shall enter into any Treaty, Alliance, or Confederation; grant Letters of Marque and Reprisal; coin Money; emit Bills of Credit; make any Thing but gold and silver Coin a Tender in Payment of Debts; pass any Bill of Attainder, ex post facto Law, or Law impairing the Obligation of Contracts, or grant any Title of Nobility.

No State shall, without the Consent of the Congress, lay any Imposts or Duties on Imports or Exports, except what may be absolutely necessary for executing it's inspection Laws: and the net Produce of all Duties and Imposts, laid by any State on Imports or Exports, shall be for the Use of the Treasury of the United States; and all such Laws shall be subject to the Revision and Controul of the Congress.

No State shall, without the Consent of Congress, lay any duty of Tonnage, keep Troops, or Ships of War in time of Peace, enter into any Agreement or Compact with another State, or with a foreign Power, or engage in War, unless actually invaded, or in such imminent Danger as will not admit of delay.

ARTICLE II

Section 1. The executive Power shall be vested in a President of the United States of America. He shall hold his Office during the Term of four Years, and, together with the Vice President chosen for the same Term, be elected, as follows:

Each State shall appoint, in such Manner as the Legislature thereof may direct, a Number of Electors, equal to the whole Number of Senators and Representatives to which the State may be entitled in the Congress: but no Senator or Representative, or Person holding an Office of Trust or Profit under the United States, shall be appointed an Elector.

[The Electors shall meet in their respective States, and vote by Ballot for two Persons, of whom one at least shall not be an Inhabitant of the same State with

---

* See the Sixteenth Amendment.

themselves. And they shall make a List of all the Persons voted for, and of the Number of Votes for each; which List they shall sign and certify, and transmit sealed to the Seat of the Government of the United States, directed to the President of the Senate. The President of the Senate shall, in the Presence of the Senate and House of Representatives, open all the Certificates, and the Votes shall then be counted. The Person having the greatest Number of Votes shall be the President, if such Number be a Majority of the whole Number of Electors appointed; and if there be more than one who have such Majority, and have an equal Number of Votes, then the House of Representatives shall immediately chuse by Ballot one of them for President; and if no Person have a Majority, then from the five highest on the List the said House shall in like Manner chuse the President. But in chusing the President, the Votes shall be taken by States, the Representation from each State having one Vote; a quorum for this Purpose shall consist of a Member or Members from two thirds of the States, and a Majority of all the States shall be necessary to a Choice. In every Case, after the Choice of the President, the Person having the greatest Number of Votes of the Electors shall be the Vice President. But if there should remain two or more who have equal Votes, the Senate shall chuse from them by Ballot the Vice President.]*

The Congress may determine the Time of chusing the Electors, and the Day on which they shall give their Votes; which Day shall be the same throughout the United States.

No person except a natural born Citizen, or a Citizen of the United States, at the time of the Adoption of this Constitution, shall be eligible to the Office of President; neither shall any Person be eligible to that Office who shall not have attained to the Age of thirty-five Years, and been fourteen Years a Resident within the United States.

[In Case of the Removal of the President from Office, or of his Death, Resignation, or Inability to discharge the Powers and Duties of the said Office, the same shall devolve on the Vice President, and the Congress may by Law provide for the Case of Removal, Death, Resignation or Inability, both of the President and Vice President, declaring what Officer shall then act as President, and such Officer shall act accordingly, until the Disability be removed, or a President shall be elected.]**

The President shall, at stated Times, receive for his Services, a Compensation, which shall neither be increased nor diminished during the Period for which he shall have been elected, and he shall not receive within that Period any other Emolument from the United States, or any of them.

Before he enter on the Execution of his Office, he shall take the following Oath or Affirmation: — "I do solemnly swear (or affirm) that I will faithfully execute the Office of President of the United States, and will to the best of my Ability, preserve, protect and defend the Constitution of the United States."

---

* Amended by the Twelfth Amendment.
** Amended by the Twenty-fifth Amendment.

Section 2. The President shall be Commander in Chief of the Army and Navy of the United States, and of the Militia of the several States, when called into the actual Service of the United States; he may require the Opinion, in writing, of the principal Officer in each of the executive Departments, upon any subject relating to the Duties of their respective Offices, and he shall have Power to Grant Reprieves and Pardons for Offenses against the United States, except in Cases of Impeachment.

He shall have Power, by and with the Advice and Consent of the Senate, to make Treaties, provided two thirds of the Senators present concur; and he shall nominate, and by and with the Advice and Consent of the Senate, shall appoint Ambassadors, other public Ministers and Consuls, Judges of the supreme Court, and all other Officers of the United States, whose Appointments are not herein otherwise provided for, and which shall be established by Law: but the Congress may by Law vest the Appointment of such inferior Officers, as they think proper, in the President alone, in the Courts of Law, or in the Heads of Departments.

The President shall have Power to fill up all Vacancies that may happen during the Recess of the Senate, by granting Commissions which shall expire at the End of their next Session.

Section 3. He shall from time to time give to the Congress Information of the State of the Union, and recommend to their Consideration such Measures as he shall judge necessary and expedient; he may, on extraordinary Occasions, convene both Houses, or either of them, and in Case of Disagreement between them, with Respect to the Time of Adjournment, he may adjourn them to such Time as he shall think proper; he shall receive Ambassadors and other public Ministers; he shall take Care that the Laws be faithfully executed, and shall Commission all the Officers of the United States.

Section 4. The President, Vice President and all civil Officers of the United States, shall be removed from Office on Impeachment for, and Conviction of, Treason, Bribery, or other high Crimes and Misdemeanors.

ARTICLE III

Section 1. The judicial Power of the United States, shall be vested in one supreme Court, and in such inferior Courts as the Congress may from time to time ordain and establish. The Judges, both of the supreme and inferior Courts, shall hold their Offices during good Behavior, and shall, at stated Times, receive for their Services a Compensation which shall not be diminished during their Continuance in Office.

Section 2. The judicial Power shall extend to all Cases, in Law and Equity, arising under this Constitution, the Laws of the United States, and Treaties made, or which shall be made, under their Authority; to all Cases affecting Ambassadors, other public Ministers and Consuls; to all Cases of admiralty and maritime Jurisdiction; to Controversies to which the United States shall be a Party; to Controversies between two or more States; [between a State and

Citizens of another State,]* between Citizens of different States, between Citizens of the same State claiming Lands under Grants of different States, [and between a State, or the Citizens thereof, and foreign States, Citizens or Subjects.]**

In all Cases affecting Ambassadors, other public Ministers and Consuls, and those in which a State shall be Party, the supreme Court shall have original Jurisdiction. In all the other Cases before mentioned, the supreme Court shall have appellate Jurisdiction, both as to Law and Fact, with such Exceptions, and under such Regulations as the Congress shall make.

The Trial of all Crimes, except in Cases of Impeachment, shall be by Jury; and such Trial shall be held in the State where the said Crimes shall have been committed; but when not committed within any State, the Trial shall be at such Place or Places as the Congress may by Law have directed.

Section 3. Treason against the United States, shall consist only in levying War against them, or in adhering to their Enemies, giving them Aid and Comfort. No Person shall be convicted of Treason unless on the Testimony of two Witnesses to the same overt Act, or on Confession in open Court.

The Congress shall have power to declare the Punishment of Treason, but no Attainder of Treason shall work Corruption of Blood, or Forfeiture except during the Life of the Person attainted.

ARTICLE IV

Section 1. Full Faith and Credit shall be given in each State to the public Acts, Records, and judicial Proceedings of every other State. And the Congress may by general Laws prescribe the Manner in which such Acts, Records and Proceedings shall be proved, and the Effect thereof.

Section 2. The Citizens of each State shall be entitled to all Privileges and Immunities of Citizens in the several States.

A Person charged in any State with Treason, Felony, or other Crime, who shall flee from Justice, and be found in another State, shall on demand of the executive Authority of the State from which he fled, be delivered up, to be removed to the State having Jurisdiction of the Crime.

[No Person held to Service or Labour in one State, under the Laws thereof, escaping into another, shall, in Consequence of any Law or Regulation therein, be discharged from such Service or Labour, But shall be delivered up on Claim of the Party to whom such Service or Labour may be due.]***

Section 3. New States may be admitted by the Congress into this Union; but no new States shall be formed or erected within the Jurisdiction of any other State; nor any State be formed by the Junction of two or more States, or

---

* See the Eleventh Amendment.
** See the Eleventh Amendment.
*** Amended by the Thirteenth Amendment.

parts of States, without the Consent of the Legislatures of the States concerned as well as of the Congress.

The Congress shall have Power to dispose of and make all needful Rules and Regulations respecting the Territory or other Property belonging to the United States; and nothing in this Constitution shall be so construed as to Prejudice any Claims of the United States, or of any particular State.

Section 4. The United States shall guarantee to every State in this Union a Republican Form of Government, and shall protect each of them against Invasion; and on Application of the Legislature, or of the Executive (when the Legislature cannot be convened) against domestic Violence.

ARTICLE V

The Congress, whenever two thirds of both Houses shall deem it necessary, shall propose Amendments to this Constitution, or, on the Application of the Legislatures of two thirds of the several States, shall call a Convention for proposing Amendments, which, in either Case, shall be valid to all Intents and Purposes, as part of this Constitution, when ratified by the Legislatures of three fourths of the several States, or by Conventions in three fourths thereof, as the one or the other Mode of Ratification may be proposed by the Congress; Provided that no Amendment which may be made prior to the Year One thousand eight hundred and eight shall in any Manner affect the first and fourth Clauses in the Ninth Section of the first Article; and that no State, without its Consent, shall be deprived of its equal Suffrage in the Senate.

ARTICLE VI

All Debts contracted and Engagements entered into, before the Adoption of this Constitution, shall be as valid against the United States under this Constitution, as under the Confederation.

This Constitution, and the Laws of the United States which shall be made in Pursuance thereof; and all Treaties made, or which shall be made, under the Authority of the United States, shall be the supreme Law of the Land; and the Judges in every State shall be bound thereby, any Thing in the Constitution or Laws of any State to the Contrary notwithstanding.

The Senators and Representatives before mentioned, and the Members of the several State Legislatures, and all executive and judicial Officers, both of the United States and of the several States, shall be bound by Oath or Affirmation, to support this Constitution; but no religious Test shall ever be required as a Qualification to any Office or public Trust under the United States.

ARTICLE VII

The Ratification of the Conventions of nine States, shall be sufficient for the Establishment of this Constitution between the States so ratifying the Same.

AMENDMENTS TO THE CONSTITUTION OF THE UNITED STATES OF AMERICA

AMENDMENT I (1791)

Congress shall make no law respecting an establishment of religion, or prohibiting the free exercise thereof; or abridging the freedom of speech, or of the press; or the right of the people peaceably to assemble, and to petition the Government for a redress of grievances.

AMENDMENT II (1791)

A well regulated Militia, being necessary to the security of a free State, the right of the people to keep and bear Arms, shall not be infringed.

AMENDMENT III (1791)

No Soldier shall, in time of peace be quartered in any house, without the consent of the Owner, nor in time of war, but in a manner to be prescribed by law.

AMENDMENT IV (1791)

The right of the people to be secure in their persons, houses, papers, and effects, against unreasonable searches and seizures, shall not be violated, and no Warrants shall issue, but upon probable cause, supported by Oath or affirmation, and particularly describing the place to be searched, and the persons or things to be seized.

AMENDMENT V (1791)

No person shall be held to answer for a capital, or otherwise infamous crime, unless on a presentment or indictment of a Grand Jury, except in cases arising in the land or naval forces, or in the Militia, when in actual service in time of War or public danger; nor shall any person be subject for the same offense to be twice put in jeopardy of life or limb; nor shall be compelled in any criminal case to be a witness against himself, nor be deprived of life, liberty, or property, without due process of law; nor shall private property be taken for public use, without just compensation.

AMENDMENT VI (1791)

In all criminal prosecutions, the accused shall enjoy the right to a speedy and public trial, by an impartial jury of the State and district wherein the crime shall have been committed, which district shall have been previously ascertained by law, and to be informed of the nature and cause of the accusation; to be confronted with the witnesses against him; to have compulsory process for obtaining witnesses in his favor, and to have the assistance of counsel for his defence.

AMENDMENT VII (1791)

In Suits at common law, where the value in controversy shall exceed twenty dollars, the right of trial by jury shall be preserved, and no fact tried by a jury, shall be otherwise re-examined in any Court of the United States, than according to the rules of the common law.

AMENDMENT VIII (1791)

Excessive bail shall not be required, nor excessive fines imposed, nor cruel and unusual punishments inflicted.

AMENDMENT IX (1791)

The enumeration in the Constitution, of certain rights, shall not be construed to deny or disparage others retained by the people.

AMENDMENT X (1791)

The powers not delegated to the United States by the Constitution, nor prohibited by it to the States, are reserved to the States respectively, or to the people.

AMENDMENT XI (1798)

The Judicial power of the United States shall not be construed to extend to any suit in law or equity, commenced or prosecuted against one of the United States by Citizens of another State, or by Citizens or Subjects of any Foreign State.

AMENDMENT XII (1804)

The Electors shall meet in their respective states, and vote by ballot for President and Vice President, one of whom, at least, shall not be an inhabitant of the same state with themselves; they shall name in their ballots the person voted for as President, and in distinct ballots the person voted for as Vice President, and they shall make distinct lists of all persons voted for as President, and of all persons voted for as Vice President and of the number of votes for each, which lists they shall sign and certify, and transmit sealed to the seat of the government of the United States, directed to the President of the Senate; — The President of the Senate shall, in the presence of the Senate and House of Representatives, open all the certificates and the votes shall then be counted; — The person having the greatest number of votes for President, shall be the President, if such number be a majority of the whole number of Electors appointed; and if no person have such majority, then from the persons having the highest numbers not exceeding three on the list of those voted for as President, the House of Representatives shall choose immediately, by ballot, the President. But in choosing the President, the votes shall be taken by states, the representation from each state having one vote; a quorum for this purpose shall consist of a member or members from two-thirds of the states, and a majority of all the states shall be necessary to a choice. [And if the House of

Representatives shall not choose a President whenever the right of choice shall devolve upon them, before the fourth day of March next following, then the Vice President shall act as President, as in the case of the death or other constitutional disability of the President. —]* The person having the greatest number of votes as Vice President, shall be the Vice President, if such number be a majority of the whole number of Electors appointed, and if no person have a majority, then from the two highest numbers on the list, the Senate shall choose the Vice President; a quorum for the purpose shall consist of two-thirds of the whole number of Senators, and a majority of the whole number shall be necessary to a choice. But no person constitutionally ineligible to the office of President shall be eligible to that of Vice President of the United States.

AMENDMENT XIII (1865)

Section 1. Neither slavery nor involuntary servitude, except as a punishment for crime whereof the party shall have been duly convicted, shall exist within the United States, or any place subject to their jurisdiction.

Section 2. Congress shall have power to enforce this article by appropriate legislation.

AMENDMENT XIV (1868)

Section 1. All persons born or naturalized in the United States, and subject to the jurisdiction thereof, are citizens of the United States and of the State wherein they reside. No State shall make or enforce any law which shall abridge the privileges or immunities of citizens of the United States; nor shall any State deprive any person of life, liberty, or property, without due process of law; nor deny to any person within its jurisdiction the equal protection of the laws.

Section 2. Representatives shall be apportioned among the several States according to their respective numbers, counting the whole number of persons in each State, excluding Indians not taxed. But when the right to vote at any election for the choice of electors for President and Vice President of the United States, Representatives in Congress, the Executive and Judicial officers of a State, or the members of the Legislature thereof, is denied to any of the male inhabitants of such State, being twenty-one years of age, and citizens of the United States, or in any way abridged, except for participation in rebellion, or other crime, the basis of representation therein shall be reduced in the proportion which the number of such male citizens shall bear to the whole number of male citizens twenty-one years of age in such State.

Section 3. No person shall be a Senator or Representative in Congress, or elector of President and Vice President, or hold any office, civil or military, under the United States, or under any State, who, having previously taken an oath, as a member of Congress, or as an officer of the United States, or as a member of any State legislature, or as an executive or judicial officer of any

---

* Superseded by §3 of the Twentieth Amendment.

State, to support the Constitution of the United States, shall have engaged in insurrection or rebellion against the same, or given aid or comfort to the enemies thereof. But Congress may by a vote of two-thirds of each House, remove such disability.

Section 4. The validity of the public debt of the United States, authorized by law, including debts incurred for payment of pensions and bounties for services in suppressing insurrection or rebellion, shall not be questioned. But neither the United States nor any State shall assume or pay any debt or obligation incurred in aid of insurrection or rebellion against the United States, or any claim for the loss or emancipation of any slave; but all such debts, obligations and claims shall be held illegal and void.

Section 5. The Congress shall have power to enforce, by appropriate legislation, the provisions of this article.

AMENDMENT XV (1870)

Section 1. The right of citizens of the United States to vote shall not be denied or abridged by the United States or by any State on account of race, color, or previous condition of servitude.

Section 2. The Congress shall have power to enforce this article by appropriate legislation.

AMENDMENT XVI (1913)

The Congress shall have power to lay and collect taxes on incomes, from whatever source derived, without apportionment among the several States, and without regard to any census or enumeration.

AMENDMENT XVII (1913)

The Senate of the United States shall be composed of two Senators from each State, elected by the people thereof, for six years; and each Senator shall have one vote. The electors in each State shall have the qualifications requisite for electors of the most numerous branch of the State legislatures.

When vacancies happen in the representation of any State in the Senate, the executive authority of such State shall issue writs of election to fill such vacancies: *Provided*, That the legislature of any State may empower the executive thereof to make temporary appointments until the people fill the vacancies by election as the legislature may direct.

This amendment shall not be so construed as to affect the election or term of any Senator chosen before it becomes valid as part of the Constitution.

AMENDMENT XVIII (1919)

Section 1. After one year from the ratification of this article the manufacture, sale, or transportation of intoxicating liquors within, the importation thereof into, or the exportation thereof from the United States and all territory subject to the jurisdiction thereof for beverage purposes is hereby prohibited.

Section 2. The Congress and the several States shall have concurrent power to enforce this article by appropriate legislation.

Section 3. This article shall be inoperative unless it shall have been ratified as an amendment to the Constitution by the legislatures of the several States, as provided in the Constitution, within seven years from the date of the submission hereof to the States by the Congress.

AMENDMENT XIX (1920)

The right of citizens of the United States to vote shall not be denied or abridged by the United States or by any State on account of sex.

Congress shall have power to enforce this article by appropriate legislation.

AMENDMENT XX (1933)

Section 1. The terms of the President and Vice President shall end at noon on the 20th day of January, and the terms of Senators and Representatives at noon on the 3d day of January, of the years in which such terms would have ended if this article had not been ratified; and the terms of their successors shall then begin.

Section 2. The Congress shall assemble at least once in every year, and such meeting shall begin at noon on the 3d day of January, unless they shall by law appoint a different day.

Section 3. If, at the time fixed for the beginning of the term of the President, the President elect shall have died, the Vice President elect shall become President. If a President shall not have been chosen before the time fixed for the beginning of his term, or if the President elect shall have failed to qualify, then the Vice President elect shall act as President until a President shall have qualified; and the Congress may by law provide for the case wherein neither a President elect nor a Vice President elect shall have qualified, declaring who shall then act as President, or the manner in which one who is to act shall be selected, and such person shall act accordingly until a President or Vice President shall have qualified.

Section 4. The Congress may by law provide for the case of the death of any of the persons from whom the House of Representatives may choose a President whenever the right of choice shall have devolved upon them, and for the case of the death of any of the persons from whom the Senate may choose a Vice President whenever the right of choice shall have devolved upon them.

Section 5. Sections 1 and 2 shall take effect on the 15th day of October following the ratification of this article.

Section 6. This article shall be inoperative unless it shall have been ratified as an amendment to the Constitution by the legislatures of three-fourths of the several States within seven years from the date of its submission.

AMENDMENT XXI (1933)

Section 1. The eighteenth article of amendment to the Constitution of the United States is hereby repealed.

Section 2. The transportation or importation into any State, Territory, or possession of the United States for delivery or use therein of intoxicating liquors, in violation of the laws thereof, is hereby prohibited.

Section 3. The article shall be inoperative unless it shall have been ratified as an amendment to the Constitution by conventions in the several States, as provided in the Constitution, within seven years from the date of the submission hereof to the States by the Congress.

AMENDMENT XXII (1951)

Section 1. No person shall be elected to the office of the President more than twice, and no person who has held the office of President, or acted as President, for more than two years of a term to which some other person was elected President shall be elected to the office of the President more than once. But this Article shall not apply to any person holding the office of President, when this Article was proposed by the Congress, and shall not prevent any person who may be holding the office of President, or acting as President, during the term within which this Article becomes operative from holding the office of President or acting as President during the remainder of such term.

Section 2. This article shall be inoperative unless it shall have been ratified as an amendment to the Constitution by the legislatures of three-fourths of the several States within seven years from the date of its submission to the States by the Congress.

AMENDMENT XXIII (1961)

Section 1. The District constituting the seat of Government of the United States shall appoint in such manner as the Congress may direct: A number of electors of President and Vice President equal to the whole number of Senators and Representatives in Congress to which the District would be entitled if it were a State, but in no event more than the least populous State; they shall be in addition to those appointed by the States, but they shall be considered, for the purposes of the election of President and Vice President, to be electors appointed by a State; and they shall meet in the District and perform such duties as provided by the twelfth article of amendment.

Section 2. The Congress shall have power to enforce this article by appropriate legislation.

AMENDMENT XXIV (1964)

Section 1. The right of citizens of the United States to vote in any primary or other election for President or Vice President, for electors for President or Vice President, or for Senator or Representative in Congress, shall not be denied or abridged by the United States or any State by reason of failure to pay any poll tax or other tax.

Section 2. The Congress shall have power to enforce this article by appropriate legislation.

AMENDMENT XXV (1967)

Section 1. In case of the removal of the President from office or of his death or resignation, the Vice President shall become President.

Section 2. Whenever there is a vacancy in the office of the Vice President, the President shall nominate a Vice President who shall take office upon confirmation by a majority vote of both Houses of Congress.

Section 3. Whenever the President transmits to the President pro tempore of the Senate and the Speaker of the House of Representatives his written declaration that he is unable to discharge the powers and duties of his office, and until he transmits to them a written declaration to the contrary, such powers and duties shall be discharged by the Vice President as Acting President.

Section 4. Whenever the Vice President and a majority of either the principal officers of the executive departments or of such other body as Congress may by law provide, transmit to the President pro tempore of the Senate and the Speaker of the House of Representatives their written declaration that the President is unable to discharge the powers and duties of his office, the Vice President shall immediately assume the powers and duties of the office as Acting President.

Thereafter, when the President transmits to the President pro tempore of the Senate and the Speaker of the House of Representatives his written declaration that no inability exists, he shall resume the powers and duties of his office unless the Vice President and a majority of either the principal officers of the executive department or of such other body as Congress may by law provide, transmit within four days to the President pro tempore of the Senate and the Speaker of the House of Representatives their written declaration that the President is unable to discharge the powers and duties of his office. Thereupon Congress shall decide the issue, assembling within forty-eight hours for that purpose if not in session. If the Congress, within twenty-one days after receipt of the latter written declaration, or, if Congress is not in session, within twenty-one days after Congress is required to assemble, determines by two-thirds vote of both Houses that the President is unable to discharge the powers and duties of his office, the Vice President shall continue to discharge the same as Acting President; otherwise, the President shall resume the powers and duties of his office.

AMENDMENT XXVI (1971)

Section 1. The right of citizens of the United States, who are eighteen years of age or older, to vote shall not be denied or abridged by the United States or by any State on account of age.

Section 2. The Congress shall have power to enforce this article by appropriate legislation.

AMENDMENT XXVII (1992)

No law, varying the compensation for the services of the Senators and Representatives, shall take effect, until an election of representatives shall have intervened.

PART

FRAMING QUESTIONS OF AMERICAN FEDERALISM

CHAPTER 1

FRAMING AMERICAN FEDERALISM

"This government is acknowledged by all, to be one of enumerated powers. The principle, that it can exercise only the powers granted to it . . . is now universally admitted. But the question respecting the extent of the powers actually granted, is perpetually arising, and will probably continue to arise, so long as our system shall exist."

John Marshall, Chief Justice of the United States
McCullough v. Maryland, 17 U.S. (4 Wheat.) 316, 405 (1819)

On July 4, 1776, the Continental Congress of the 13 British colonies in North America declared that the colonies were no longer part of the British Empire. After reciting "a long train of abuses and usurpations" by King George III against the colonies, the Declaration of Independence concluded:

> We, therefore, the Representatives of the united States of America, in General Congress, Assembled, appealing to the Supreme Judge of the world for the rectitude of our intentions, do, in the Name, and by Authority of the good People of these Colonies, solemnly publish and declare, That these United Colonies are, and of Right ought to be Free and Independent States, that they are Absolved from all Allegiance to the British Crown, and that all political connection between them and the State of Great Britain, is and ought to be totally dissolved; and that as Free and Independent States, they have full Power to levy War, conclude Peace, contract Alliances, establish Commerce, and to do all other Acts and Things which Independent States may of right do. — And for the support of this Declaration, with a firm reliance on the protection of divine Providence, we mutually pledge to each other our Lives, our Fortunes and our sacred Honor.

The following year, on November 15, 1777, the Continental Congress voted to adopt the Articles of Confederation and Perpetual Union, a plan to establish "a firm league of friendship" among the states. In 1781, all 13 states had ratified this plan.

A first principle of the Articles was that "[e]ach state retains its sovereignty, freedom, and independence, and every Power, Jurisdiction, and right, which is not by this Confederation expressly delegated to the United States, in Congress assembled." Under the Articles, each state appointed its own delegates, and each state delegation had one vote in Congress. Moreover, states reserved the power to recall delegates. The Articles limited the authority of states to act in certain foreign affairs matters (such as making war, entering treaties, or receiving ambassadors) without the consent of Congress. Correspondingly, the Articles empowered Congress to act in such matters. Congressional action required the votes of a majority of the states, and Congress depended on the states to raise the revenue necessary to fund any measures it enacted. The Articles concluded that they "shall be inviolably observed by every State, and the union shall be perpetual; nor shall any alteration at any time hereafter be made in any of them; unless such alteration be agreed to in a Congress of the United States, and be afterwards confirmed by the legislatures of every State."

Defects in the Articles became evident in the years that followed their ratification. States pursued divergent interests, and the Confederation Congress, dependent on states for revenue, was powerless to serve common interests effectively. Notably, under the Articles, Congress was incapable of regulating commerce among the states, and states thwarted common foreign policy interests by disregarding treaty obligations of the United States.

> There were . . . many defects in the Articles of Confederation that had become obvious by the 1780s. Lacking the powers to tax and to regulate the nation's commerce, the Confederation Congress could neither pay off the debts the United States had incurred during the Revolution nor retaliate against the mercantilist trade policies of the European states, particularly Great Britain. At the same time, the new republican confederacy was hard-pressed to maintain its independence in a world of hostile monarchical empires. Britain refused to send a minister to the United States and ignored its treaty obligations to evacuate from American territory in the Northwest. In the Southwest Spain refused to recognize American claims to the territory between Florida and the Ohio River and was trying to use its ability to close the Mississippi to American trade to bring American settlers moving into Kentucky and Tennessee under its control. By 1786 all these problems, both domestic and international, had created mounting pressures to reform the Articles.

GORDON S. WOOD, EMPIRE OF LIBERTY: A HISTORY OF THE EARLY REPUBLIC, 1789-1815, at 15 (2009).

As the 1780s progressed, advocates of stronger central authority among the states grew increasingly concerned that state legislatures were acting irresponsibly and without regard for the common good.

To address problems of interstate commerce that arose under the Articles, a convention was held in Annapolis, Maryland, in 1786. Only five state delegations (of 13 states) participated in the Annapolis Convention, an insufficient number to form an agreement. Nonetheless, the convention produced a report, finding "[t]hat there are important defects in the system of the Federal Government," and calling for a meeting "at Philadelphia on the second Monday in May next, to take into consideration the situation of the United States, [and] to devise such further provisions as shall appear to them necessary to render the constitution of the Federal Government adequate to the exigencies of the Union." The Confederation Congress agreed in principle to such a convention. This convention was the Federal Convention of 1787.

The Federal Convention lasted from May 25, 1787, until September 17, 1787. Participants included several of the most prominent members of the Founding generation, including Benjamin Franklin, Alexander Hamilton, James Madison, and George Washington. (Notably absent were John Adams and Thomas Jefferson, who were in Europe during the Convention.) Although the purpose of the Convention was to remedy defects in the Articles of Confederation, certain delegates undertook from the outset to structure a new system of government. The challenge was to devise a government capable of serving the common interests of the states — and the interests of a new nation — while respecting state authority over matters appropriate for local governance.

Several famous debates and compromises occurred during the Convention. Four resolutions of the Convention are central to understanding the system of government that the delegates devised: the delegates (1) prescribed how the people and the states would participate in constituting a federal government, (2) enumerated and otherwise limited the powers of the federal government, (3) provided procedures for the making of federal law, and (4) provided procedures for the enforcement of federal law.

1. *Constituting a Federal Government.* First, the delegates structured how the people and the states would participate in constituting a federal government. The federal government would have a legislative, an executive, and a judicial branch. By various means, the people and the states would exert control over the selection process for members of Congress, the President, and federal judges.

The legislative branch would consist of two houses — a House of Representatives and a Senate. Representation in the House would be apportioned by population. By proportional representation, "the people of the several States" would choose the members of the House of Representatives. U.S. Const. art. I, §2. Moreover, the states would determine voter qualifications for the House, as the Constitution provided that "the Electors in each State shall have the Qualifications requisite for Electors of the most numerous Branch of the State Legislature." *Id.* In the Senate, the states would have equal representation, two senators per state. State legislatures would elect the Senate. *See id.* art. I, §3. (The Seventeenth Amendment, ratified in 1913, provides for the direct election of senators by the people of a state.) By controlling voter qualifications and electing senators, states would exert control over the membership of Congress. Moreover, with equal representation in the Senate, smaller states would wield a stronger voice than if representation were according to population.

The delegates vested executive power in the President of the United States. Electors, not the people directly, would select the President: "Each State shall appoint, in such Manner as the Legislature thereof may direct, a Number of Electors, equal to the whole Number of Senators and Representatives to which the State may be entitled in the Congress." *Id.* art. II, §1. In other words, a state would control the manner in which its electors were to be selected. Furthermore, smaller states would enjoy a number of electors disproportionate to their respective populations (because each state had equal representation in the Senate and an elector for each senator). If, upon vote of the electors, no single candidate commanded a majority, the House of Representatives would select the President, each state delegation having one vote. *Id.* art. II, §1. By controlling the manner of appointment of electors, states would exert control over the election of the President. Moreover, by having the number of electors determined, in part, by Senate representation and exercising an equal vote should the election of a President go to the House, smaller states maintained a voice in presidential elections disproportionate to their respective populations.

The delegates vested the judicial power of the United States "in one supreme Court, and in such inferior Courts as the Congress may from time to time ordain and establish." *Id.* art. III, §1. Judges would occupy the federal bench upon nomination by the President and confirmation by the Senate. *See id.* art. II, §2. Thus, to the extent states controlled the selection of the President and enjoyed equal representation in the Senate, they indirectly influenced the appointment of federal judges.

2. *Enumerating Federal Powers.* In addition to structuring how the people and the states would constitute a federal government, the delegates limited and enumerated the powers federal institutions could exercise. Article I enumerated the powers of Congress. Notably, it empowered Congress to regulate interstate commerce, "provide for the common Defence and general Welfare of the United States," and legislate on various matters pertaining to foreign relations. *Id.* art. I, §8. It also empowered Congress "[t]o make all Laws which shall be necessary and proper for carrying into Execution the foregoing Powers." *Id.* art. I, §8, cl.18. Article II specified certain powers of the President, including serving as commander-in-chief of the armed forces, granting pardons, receiving ambassadors, and making treaties and appointing various officials by and with the advice and consent of the Senate. *See id.* art. II, §2. Article III enumerated limited categories of cases and controversies within the federal judicial power, including cases arising under federal law, admiralty and maritime cases, controversies involving various forms of diversity of citizenship and state involvement, and other cases and controversies implicating the foreign relations of the United States. *See id.* art. III, §2.

3. *Specifying Federal Lawmaking Procedures.* The Constitution provided specific procedures for the making of federal law. For the United States to enact a statute, both houses of Congress must pass a bill (bicameralism), and the President must sign it (presentment). Should the President veto a bill, Congress may override the veto by a two-thirds vote of both houses. *See id.* art. I, §7. For the United States to enter into a treaty, the President must make it, with the ratification of two-thirds of senators present. *See id.* art. II, §2. For the Constitution to be amended, two-thirds of both houses of Congress must propose an amendment (or call a convention for proposing amendments upon the application of two-thirds of state legislatures), and the legislatures or conventions of three-fourths of the states must ratify it. *See id.* art. V. For any of these forms of federal law to take effect, the Senate — the branch deemed most responsive at the time to the interests of the states — must assent. (For an analysis of how the role of the Senate in federal lawmaking factored in the Constitution's drafting, see Bradford R. Clark, *Separation of Powers as a Safeguard of Federalism*, 79 Tex. L. Rev. 1321, 1357-1372 (2001).)

4. *Enforcing Federal Law Against States.* Finally, the Constitution provided certain mechanisms for the enforcement of federal law against the states. At the Federal Convention, delegates proposed various means to ensure that states did not thwart prerogatives of the Union. Proposals included a congressional negative on state laws, the use of force against recalcitrant states, and a requirement that state officials take an oath to uphold the Constitution. Ultimately, the delegates settled upon judicial mechanisms to enforce federal prerogatives. First, the Supremacy Clause required state courts to enforce validly enacted federal laws in cases within their jurisdiction:

> This Constitution, and the Laws of the United States which shall be made in Pursuance thereof; and all Treaties made, or which shall be made, under the Authority of the United States, shall be the supreme Law of the Land; and the Judges in every State shall be bound thereby, any Thing in the Constitution or Laws of any State to the Contrary notwithstanding.

U.S. CONST. art. VI.

Second, Article III extended the judicial power of the United States "to all Cases, in Law and Equity, arising under this Constitution, the Laws of the United States, and Treaties made, or which shall be made, under their Authority." *Id.* art. III, §2. In this provision, the delegates empowered Congress to give federal courts jurisdiction to enforce the three forms of federal law — the Constitution, laws, and treaties of the United States — over demands of conflicting state law.

The delegates resolved that "[t]he Ratification of the Conventions of nine States, shall be sufficient for the Establishment of this Constitution between the States so ratifying the Same." *Id.* art. VII. After the Constitution was submitted to the states, vigorous debates ensued about whether states should ratify it. Regarding federalism, these debates concerned (1) the nature and purposes of the federal system proposed and (2) the relative responsibilities of various institutions to uphold it.

As you read the materials in this book, keep in mind each of these four aspects of the Constitution, and consider the following questions that they implicate:

- *First*, the Founders propounded that state governments would exert significant control over who served in the political branches (the legislative and executive) of the federal government. Today, do states exert the kind of political control over the federal government that the Founders envisioned? Whether, and to what extent, states exert political control over the composition of the federal government factors significantly in present-day debates over how, if at all, the Supreme Court should police congressional powers.
- *Second*, the Constitution enumerates a specific list of congressional powers. Over time, political, social, and economic forces have exerted pressure on those limitations. How should the powers of Congress be understood today? What role, if any, should courts or other institutions

play in policing congressional exercises of those powers? To what extent should courts defer to the judgment of Congress that a particular regulation is necessary to serve one of the enumerated objects of its powers? Judges, other public officials, and scholars continue to debate such questions.

- *Third*, the Constitution provides specific procedures for the making of federal law. Over time, federal judges have developed areas of "federal common law" — non-enacted federal law providing rules of decision for cases in federal and state courts. How, if at all, is such law consistent with the Constitution's provision of detailed federal lawmaking procedures? This question, too, has important present-day implications.
- *Fourth*, the Constitution provides judicial mechanisms to ensure that state law does not obstruct the proper enforcement of federal law in federal and state courts. Courts have long struggled to determine when federal law "preempts" state law. How should courts make such determinations? This remains one of the most difficult yet practically important questions of federal-state relations in the U.S. constitutional system.

You will explore each of these questions — and many related ones — as you study the materials in this book.

A. THE NATURE AND PURPOSES OF AMERICAN FEDERALISM

The materials in this section explore how members of the Founding generation understood the nature and purposes of the Constitution's federal structure. Specifically, the materials explore three broad questions. First, how did members of the Founding generation understand the concept of *sovereignty*, and how did their understandings differ from concepts of sovereignty that prevailed in English thought at the time? To appreciate how proponents and opponents of the Constitution understood the relationship between the federal government and the states, it is necessary first to appreciate how they understood the concept of sovereignty. Second, what was the nature of the objections to the system of government that the Constitution proposed? You will better understand the original import of the Constitution if you appreciate the views of those who opposed it. Finally, how did proponents of the Constitution defend its governmental structure? You will read some of the most enduring writings about American federalism and political theory that emerged from the Founding era.

As you read the materials in this section, consider the following questions:

- What is *federalism*?
- How can the structure of government that the Constitution originally established be said to be a *federal* one?
- What is *sovereignty* in the federal system that the Constitution establishes?
- What *value*, if any, lies in the federal nature of this system?

1. THE CONCEPT OF SOVEREIGNTY

In eighteenth-century England, ultimate governmental sovereignty—or absolute governing power in a state—rested with Parliament. The "people" had their voice in one part of Parliament, namely the House of Commons, but the formal authority of the people did not transcend the authority of Parliament. The federal structure of the U.S. Constitution differs from England's parliamentary structure in two important respects. First, whereas in England unitary sovereignty rested in Parliament, the Constitution recognized a "dual sovereignty" between the federal government and the states, each with its own sphere of sovereign authority. Second, whereas in England the people were *part* of the ultimate governmental sovereign authority, the Constitution recognized "the People" as the *whole* of that governing authority.

The following two excerpts describe the origins of these two ideas. These ideas have long influenced—and continue to influence—understandings of the U.S. constitutional structure. The Supreme Court has often described the federal structure as one of "dual sovereignty" between the federal government and the states. Moreover, the Justices continue to maintain that ultimate sovereignty rests with the people. The Justices have invoked these ideas in resolving various questions about the Constitution's federal structure. You will see both of these ideas—that the Constitution recognizes dual sovereignty and that the people hold ultimate sovereignty—emerge throughout the materials in this book. As you read the following excerpts, consider these questions:

- What does it mean for a government or a people to be *sovereign*?
- As a practical matter, is it possible to divide sovereignty between governments?
- Is the idea of dual sovereignty between the federal government and the states consistent with the idea that ultimate sovereignty rests with the people?

BERNARD BAILYN, THE IDEOLOGICAL ORIGINS OF THE
AMERICAN REVOLUTION

198, 200-205, 208-210, 223, 228-229 (1967)

[O]f all the intellectual problems the colonists faced, one was absolutely crucial: . . . it was over this issue that the Revolution was fought. On the pivotal question of sovereignty, which is the question of the nature and location of the ultimate power in the state, American thinkers attempted to depart sharply from one of the most firmly fixed points in eighteenth-century political thought. . . .

The idea of sovereignty current in the English-speaking world of the 1760's . . . was composed essentially of two elements. The first was the notion that there must reside somewhere in every political unit a single, undivided, final power, higher in legal authority than any other power, subject to no law, a law unto itself. . . .

Final, unqualified, indivisible power was, however, only one part of the notion of sovereignty as it was understood by Englishmen on the eve of the

American Revolution. The other concerns its location. Who, or what body, was to hold such powers? . . .

Parliament [was the] body absolute and arbitrary in its sovereignty; the creator and interpreter, not the subject, of law; the superior and master of all other rights and powers within the state. It was this conception of Parliamentary sovereignty that triumphed in the Glorious Revolution; and it was this conception, justified in the end by the theory of an ultimate supremacy of the people — a supremacy, that is, normally dormant and exercised only at moments of rebellion against tyrannical government — that was carried on into the eighteenth century and into the debates that preceded the American Revolution. . . .

By the mid-eighteenth century this Whig conception of a sovereign Parliament had hardened into orthodoxy. . . . [I]t was given its classic formulation by Blackstone, who wrote in his *COMMENTARIES* that "there is and must be in all [forms of government] a supreme, irresistible, absolute, uncontrolled authority, in which the *jura summi imperii*, or the rights of sovereignty, reside," and that in England this "sovereignty of the British constitution" was lodged in Parliament, the aggregate body of King, Lords, and Commons, whose actions "no power on earth can undo."[44] . . .

[I]f in England the concept of sovereignty was not only logical but realistic, it was far from that in the colonies. From the beginning of settlement, circumstances in America had run directly counter to the exercise of unlimited and undivided sovereignty. Despite the efforts that had been made by the English government in the late seventeenth century to reduce the areas of local jurisdiction in the colonies, local provincial autonomy continued to characterize American life. Never had Parliament or the crown, or both together, operated in actuality as theory indicated sovereign powers should. They had exercised authority, of course. The crown had retained the final power of legalizing or annulling actions of the colonial legislatures and of the colonial courts; it had made appointments to high office; it had laid down rules and policies for its colonial officials to follow; it had held in its own hand major decisions, civil and military, affecting relations with other nations; and it had continued to claim control of, if not actually to control, vast areas of wild land in the west as well as certain settled territories in the east. Similarly, Parliament had created the colonial postal system, regulated naturalization, and laid down rules for certain economic activities in the colonies, of which the laws of trade and navigation were the most important. But these were far from total powers; together they did not constitute governance in depth, nor did they exclude the exercise of real power by lesser bodies or organs of government. They touched only the outer fringes of colonial life; they dealt with matters obviously beyond the competence of any lesser authority; they concerned the final review of actions initiated and sustained by colonial authorities. All other powers were enjoyed, in fact if not in constitutional theory, by local, colonial organs of government. This area of residual authority, constituting the "internal police" of the community, included most of the substance of everyday life. . . .

------

44. [CHARLES H. MCILWAIN, CONSTITUTIONALISM AND THE CHANGING WORLD 63-64 (1939).]

The condition of British America by the end of the Seven Years' War was therefore anomalous: extreme decentralization of authority within an empire presumably ruled by a single, absolute, undivided sovereign. And anomalous it had been known to be at the time. . . . But since . . . no sustained effort had been made to alter the situation, the colonists found themselves . . . with a challenge to their settled way of life — a way of life that had been familiar in some places for a century or more. The arguments the colonists put forward against Parliament's claims to the right to exercise sovereign power in America were efforts to express in logical form, to state in the language of constitutional theory, the truth of the world they knew. They were at first, necessarily, fumbling and unsure efforts, for there were no arguments — there was no vocabulary — to resort to: the ideas, the terminology, had to be invented.

How was this to be done? What arguments, what words, could be used to elevate to the status of constitutional principle the divisions of authority that had for so long existed and which the colonists associated with the freedom they had enjoyed? . . .

[L]eading colonial writers were attacking the problem of sovereignty in a different way — a more realistic and pragmatic way. Tacitly acknowledging that by accepted definition sovereignty was both absolute and arbitrary, but convinced nevertheless that there were things that Parliament could not rightly do, they set out, silent on the metaphysics of the problem, to locate pragmatically a line of separation between powers of Parliament that were valid when exercised in America and those that were not. It was only later and gradually, when challenged by informed and articulate opponents, that they faced up to the implications of what they had been doing, and acknowledged that they were in effect calling "sovereignty itself into question" and attempting to reconceive the basic principles of state authority. . . .

For . . . any effort to restrict Parliament's power assumed that sovereignty was in some sense divisible; and to search deliberately for the actual seams along which the fabric of power might be divided was to grope toward a political order in which "powers of government are separated and distinguished and in which these powers are distributed among governments, each government having its quota of authority and each its distinct sphere of activity."[51] But the awareness of this fact was slow in developing: the discussion began at the level of specific distinctions in the powers of Parliament, and it progressed to more general grounds only after it was shown that these distinctions could not be maintained.

The first distinction advanced in the effort to express in constitutional language the limitations on Parliament's power familiar to the colonists, was extemporized casually by the simple expedient of applying to this constitutional problem one of the most common pairs of antonyms in the English language. No distinction could be more obvious or fundamental than that between things "internal" and things "external." Not only did it appear to separate out conveniently the powers that had been exercised for so long by the colonists' own Assemblies and those that had been exercised by

---

51. Andrew C. McLaughlin, "The Background of American Federalism," *American Political Science Review*, 12 (1918), 215. . . .

Parliament, but it did so echoing the words of some of the most respected authorities on questions of government. An ordinary distinction already drawn into theoretical discussions, used in all sorts of ways in everyday speech, it quickly drifted into the discussion of Anglo-American relations. It was used loosely throughout the pre-Revolutionary years, applied generally to spheres of government, and it was specified by some to the problem of taxation. . . .

Leading Americans . . . continued to insist . . . that "the sovereignty over the colonies must be limited," that "a line there must be," in principle as well as in fact, setting off Parliament's powers from those of the colonial legislatures, and that this line gave to the English government control of the commerce and foreign affairs of the colonies and to the colonial Assemblies "exclusive right of internal legislation," including taxing. But the response was as adamant, . . . rigidly secured to the traditional conception of sovereignty. . . . Spokesmen for England repeated, with what appears to have been an almost obsessive and ritualistic regularity, that if the colonial legislatures were not in principle "subordinate to the supreme sovereign authority of the nation . . . there is *imperium in imperio*: two sovereign authorities in the same state; which is a contradiction." Arguments to the contrary, Joseph Galloway wrote, were nothing but "unintelligible jargon and horrid nonsense"; an independent unit of government within the territory of the principal state, he explained, "is a *monster*, a thing *out of nature*"; what the Revolutionaries had taken into their "*learned* heads, philosophers-like," to do was to "conceive that the supreme legislative authority, which is indivisible in its nature, was, like matter, divisible *ad infinitum*; and under this profound mistake, you began with splitting and dividing it, until by one slice after another, you have hacked and pared it away to less than an atom."[62] . . .

The course of intellectual, as well as of political and military, events had brought into question the entire concept of a unitary, concentrated, and absolute governmental sovereignty. It had been challenged, implicitly or explicitly, by all those who had sought constitutional grounds for limiting Parliament's power in America. In its place had come the sense, premised on the assumption that the ultimate sovereignty — ultimate yet still real and effective — rested with the people, that it was not only conceivable but in certain circumstances salutary to divide and distribute the attributes of governmental sovereignty among different levels of institutions. The notion had proved unacceptable as a solution of the problem of Anglo-American relations, but it was acted upon immediately and instinctively in forming the new union of sovereign states. The problems, intellectual and political, inherent in such an arrangement would persist; some were scarcely glimpsed when the nation was formed. . . .

But the federalist tradition, born in the colonists' efforts to state in constitutional language the qualification of Parliament's authority they had known — to comprehend, systematize, and generalize the unplanned circumstance of colonial life — nevertheless survived, and remains, to justify the distribution of absolute power among governments no one of which can claim to

---

62. Dickinson, *Essay on the Constitutional Power of Great-Britain*, in *Pennsylvania Archives*, 2d ser., III, 603, 569-589. . . .

be total, and so to keep the central government from amassing "a degree of energy, in order to sustain itself, dangerous to the liberties of the people."[68]

GORDON S. WOOD, THE CREATION OF THE
AMERICAN REPUBLIC **1776-1787**

382-383, 388-389 (1969)

If sovereignty had to reside somewhere in the state — and the best political science of the eighteenth century said that it did — then many Americans concluded that it must reside only in the people-at-large. The legislatures could never be sovereign; no set of men, representatives or not, could "set themselves up against the general voice of the people." "The community, [. . .] however represented, ought to remain the supreme authority and ultimate judicature." In the people alone "that plenary power rests and abides which all agree should rest somewhere."[64] . . .

To someone steeped in British legal thought this explicit retention of legal sovereignty in the people was preposterous. It could only signify a repudiation of the concept and an eventual breakdown of all governmental order. But developments in America since 1776 had infused an extraordinary meaning into the idea of the sovereignty of the people. The Americans were not simply making the people a nebulous and unsubstantial source of all political authority. The new conception of a constitution, the development of extralegal conventions [such as the Federal Convention of 1787], the reliance on instructions [from the people to their legislative representatives], the participation of the people in politics out-of-doors, the clarification of the nature of representation, the never-ending appeals to the people by competing public officials — all gave coherence and reality, even a legal reality, to the hackneyed phrase, the sovereignty of the people. . . .

The people no longer actually shared in a part of the government (as, for example, the people of England participated in their government through the House of Commons), but they remained outside the entire government, watching, controlling, pulling the strings for all their agents in every branch or part of the government. They embraced the whole government, and no branch or part could speak with the complete authority of the people. Indeed, not even all parts of the government collectively incorporated the full powers of the people. . . . Conventions, assemblies, senates, magistry were all agents of the people for certain limited purposes. Only such a conception of representation made sense of the developments of the Confederation period — the use of instructions, the electioneering, and the extra-legislative organizations, in particular the special constituting conventions creating a superior law ratifiable by the people themselves in their sovereign capacity and hence unalterable by the people's provisional agents in the legislatures. . . . Yet neither the

---

68. [Anon., *Concise View*, in Jedediah Morse, ANNALS OF THE AMERICAN REVOLUTION 394 (New York, Kennikat Press 1824).]

64. ["Philodemus" [Thomas Tudor Tucker], *Conciliatory Hints* (1784) reprinted in AMERICAN POLITICAL WRITING DURING THE FOUNDING ERA, 1760-1805 at 619 (1983); Anon., *Rudiments of Law and Government, Deduced from the Law of Nature* (1783) reprinted in AMERICAN POLITICAL WRITING DURING THE FOUNDING ERA, 1760-1805 at 585 (1983).]

convention nor the assembly possessed the total authority of the people. . . . The power of the people outside of the government was always absolute and untrammeled; that of their various delegates in the government could never be. . . .

These were the revolutionary ideas that had unfolded rapidly in the decade after Independence, but not deliberately or evenly. Men were always only half aware of where their thought was going, for these new ideas about politics were not the products of extended reasoned analysis but were rather numerous responses of different Americans to a swiftly changing reality, of men involved in endless polemics compelled to contort and draw out from the prevailing assumptions the latent logic few had foreseen. Rarely before 1787 were these new thoughts comprehended by anyone as a whole. They were bits and pieces thrown up by the necessities of argument and condition, without broad design or significance. But if crystallized by sufficient pressures they could result in a mosaic of an entirely new conception of politics to those who would attempt to describe it.

POINTS FOR DISCUSSION

1. What does it mean for the federal government and the states each to have a share of sovereignty? As you will read, some have distinguished *federalism* from *decentralization*. Decentralization, it is argued, is a system in which one government, which holds ultimate governing authority, devolves authority, in its discretion, to lower levels of government. Federalism, in contrast, is a system in which each level of government derives its respective governing authority from a source independent of the other and has ultimate authority with respect to the matters within its sphere of authority. Under these definitions, is a system of dual sovereignty between the federal government and the states, with ultimate sovereignty residing with the people, a system of federalism or decentralization?

2. The dual sovereignty system that Professor Bailyn describes divides governing authority over different objects, perhaps between *internal* and *external* objects. Bailyn observes that "problems, intellectual and political, inherent in such an arrangement would persist," and indeed "some were scarcely glimpsed when the nation was formed." To what problems is he referring? Is it possible, as a practical matter, to divide ultimate governing authority between different units of government over the same territory and persons? Throughout this book, you will see judges and other public officials attempt to define the relative governing authority of the federal government and the states. For example, you will see how the Supreme Court has employed various approaches over time to delineate the bounds of Congress's Article I, §8 power to regulate interstate commerce — and you will assess how successful these approaches have been.

2. ANTI-FEDERALIST CONCERNS

In the following pages, you will read several descriptions of the nature and purpose of the Constitution's federal structure. Proponents of the Constitution offered most of these descriptions in arguing for the Constitution's adoption. Some of these selections extol the virtues of strengthening the powers of the Union while minimizing the Constitution's effect upon the governing authority of the states. To better understand these selections, it is useful to appreciate what they were *arguing against*. The following excerpt describes fundamental tenets of Anti-Federalists — those who favored the primacy of state governments relative to the breadth of new powers that the Constitution would bestow upon the Union.

As you read this excerpt, consider the following questions:

- How persuasive were Anti-Federalist arguments in favor of state primacy?
- What, if any, were the downsides of state primacy? Conversely, what were the benefits of a stronger Union?

HERBERT J. STORING, WHAT THE ANTI-FEDERALISTS WERE FOR

15-21 (1981)

The Anti-Federalists' defense of federalism and of the primacy of the states rested on their belief that there was an inherent connection between the states and the preservation of individual liberty, which is the end of any legitimate government. . . . The governments instituted to secure the rights spoken of by the Declaration of Independence are the state governments. They do the primary business that governments are supposed to do. The Government of the Union supplements the state governments, especially by giving them an external strength that none of them could manage on its own. But in principle the general government is subordinate to the state governments.

Why must the essential business of government be done by governmental units like the states? Primarily this was, in the Anti-Federalist view, a question of size. It was thought to have been demonstrated, historically and theoretically, that free, republican governments could extend only over a relatively small territory with a homogeneous population. . . . One problem is that in large, diverse states, many significant differences in condition, interest, and habit have to be ignored for the sake of uniform administration. . . . A national government would be compelled to impose a crude uniform rule on American diversity, which would in fact result in hardship and inequity for many parts of the country.

Behind the administrative defects of a large republic lie three fundamental considerations, bearing on the kind of government needed in a free society. Only a small republic can enjoy a voluntary attachment of the people to the government and a voluntary obedience to the laws. Only a small republic can secure a genuine responsibility of the government to the people. Only a small republic can form the kind of citizens who will maintain republican government. These claims are central to the Anti-Federalist position. . . .

The dependence of any republican government on the confidence of the people was one of the reasons given by the nationalists in the Constitutional Convention . . . for resting the general government directly on the people. . . . But the Anti-Federalists denied that the simple expedient of having the people elect federal representatives was enough to secure their attachment. . . . Both reason and experience prove, Richard Henry Lee wrote, that so extensive and various a territory as the United States "cannot be governed in freedom" except in a confederation of states. Within each state, "opinion founded on the knowledge of those who govern, procures obedience without force. But remove the opinion, which must fall with a knowledge of characters in so widely extended a country, and force then becomes necessary to secure the purposes of civil government. . . ." The general rule is that government must exist, if not by persuasion, then by force. In a large empire standing armies are necessary "to cure the defect of the laws" and to take the place of popular confidence in and respect for the government.

The second characteristic of the small republic is its capacity to ensure a strict responsibility of the government to the people. In a direct democracy, responsibility is ensured by the absence of much differentiation between the people and their government. However, most of the Anti-Federalists admitted the need, under American conditions at least, for a system of representation as a substitute for the meeting together of all the citizens. The problem, then, was to keep the representatives responsible, in the rather narrow meaning of that term, that is, directly answerable to and dependent on their constituents. . . . Effective and thoroughgoing responsibility is to be found only in a likeness between the representative body and the citizens at large. . . . This describes the state legislatures reasonably well, it was claimed, but the federal legislature could not even come close to being representative in this genuine sense, at least not without a sharp increase in its number. Federal elections will present the voters with a choice among representatives of the well-known few, or the "natural aristocracy" as the Anti-Federalists often called them. . . .

No great talents are necessary for government, and the men of great abilities are, on the whole, a danger rather than a benefit to a republic. If, however, the Anti-Federalists distrusted "great abilities," they were willing to admit that "sameness" in a representative body is not literally possible. Every representative body is more aristocratic than the body of the people by whom it is chosen, and any representative body covering the whole United States would inevitably be highly selective. Here the argument shifts from the desirability of the small republic to the mitigation of the evils of the large one. Given the need, especially in the general government, for some considerable compromise of the principle of sameness, the Anti-Federalists' secondary, more practical goal was a representation large enough to secure a substantial (if not proportionate) representation of the middling classes, in particular the sturdy yeomanry. . . .

An adequate representation of the middling classes serves, then, as a practical and effective substitute for a full representation of the people; for it does not require an excessively large body, and yet in pursuing their own interests the middling classes tend to pursue the interests of the public at large. . . .

The third part of the Anti-Federalists defense of the small republic concerned the kind of citizens a free republic needs. The Anti-Federalists emphasized repeatedly that the character of a people is affected by government and laws, but that that relation had been dangerously ignored in the framing of the proposed Constitution. . . .

A republican citizenry must be free and independent-minded, but it must also be homogeneous. . . . Only within the relatively small communities formed by the individual states could such homogeneity be found. . . .

Homogeneity implied, for the Anti-Federalists, not only likeness but likeness of a certain kind: a society in which there are no extremes of wealth, influence, education, or anything else—the homogeneity of a moderate, simple, sturdy, and virtuous people. Republican government depends on civic virtue, on a devotion to fellow citizens and to country so deeply instilled as to be almost as automatic and powerful as the natural devotion to self-interest. . . . [T]he small republic . . . offers little inducement or opportunity for the exercise of divisive and corrupting talents and . . . daily reminds each man of the benefits derived from and the duties owed to his little community.

Wherever they looked in the new Constitution the Anti-Federalists saw threats to civic virtue. The federal city provided for would breed monarchical institutions and courtly habits. . . . The standing army would be not only a potential instrument of oppression but a source of moral corruption. . . . Commerce itself, the benefits of which were one of the major reasons for the American Union, seemed to threaten republican simplicity and virtue. Commerce is the vehicle of distinctions in wealth, of foreign influence, and of the decline of morals. . . . Anti-Federalists constantly complained of America's hankering after European luxury. . . .

Implicit in all of these opinions relating to republican citizenship is a concern with civic education, broadly conceived. . . . More often the Anti-Federalist thought of the whole organization of the polity as having an educative function. The small republic was seen as a school of citizenship as much as a scheme for government. An important part—much more important than we are today likely to remember—of their argument for a federal bill of rights was the educative function of such a document in reminding the citizen of the ends of civil government and in strengthening his attachment to it. . . .

POINTS FOR DISCUSSION

1. How persuasive are the advantages that Anti-Federalists believed state primacy held over greater Union powers?

2. What, if any, were the disadvantages of state primacy or, conversely, the advantages of greater Union power?

3. *THE FEDERALIST*

The Federalist is a series of 85 articles written by Alexander Hamilton, John Jay, and James Madison in support of ratification of the Constitution. New York newspapers serially published these articles beginning on October 27, 1787, under the pen name "Publius." The series began with articles arguing that the Articles of Confederation were inadequate to serve the needs of the United States; later articles described the form of government that the delegates had framed at the Federal Convention.

In *Cohens v. Virginia*, 19 U.S. (6 Wheat.) 264, 418-419 (1821), Chief Justice John Marshall wrote for the Supreme Court:

> The opinion of the *Federalist* has always been considered as of great authority. It is a complete commentary on our constitution; and is appealed to by all parties in the questions to which that instrument has given birth. Its intrinsic merit entitles it to this high rank; and the part two of its authors [Hamilton and Madison] performed in framing the constitution, put it very much in their power to explain the views with which it was framed. These essays having been published while the constitution was before the nation for adoption or rejection, and having been written in answer to objections founded entirely on the extent of its powers, and on its diminution of State sovereignty, are entitled to the more consideration where they frankly avow that the power objected to is given, and defend it.

James Madison addressed several subjects in the excerpts of *The Federalist* that follow. In *The Federalist No. 10*, Madison famously argued that the Union, as a large republic, would better control the ill effects of faction than the states alone. In *The Federalist No. 44*, Madison described how the Constitution expressly limits state power, including how the Supremacy Clause obliges state judges to enforce validly enacted federal law. In *The Federalist No. 45* and *The Federalist No. 46*, Madison explained why the people should not fear the Union exerting undue power relative to states.

As you read the following papers, consider these questions:

- How does Madison describe the Constitution's dual sovereign structure? How does he justify it?
- How does Madison minimize the effect that the Constitution would have on pre-existing state regulatory authority?
- How does the idea that the people hold ultimate sovereignty relate to the Constitution's federal structure?
- How does Madison gear his writing toward overcoming Anti-Federalist objections?

In *The Federalist No. 10*, Madison defends the size and republican nature of the government that the Constitution would establish. He argues that the Union — a large, republican government — would counteract the pernicious effects of faction while maintaining the virtues of state authority over "local" matters. Thus, he asserts that the Constitution's federal structure would better serve the public good than individual states could alone.

THE FEDERALIST NO. 10 (JAMES MADISON)

"The Union as a Safeguard Against Domestic Faction and Insurrection"
To the People of the State of New York:

AMONG the numerous advantages promised by a well-constructed Union, none deserves to be more accurately developed than its tendency to break and control the violence of faction. . . .

By a faction, I understand a number of citizens, whether amounting to a majority or a minority of the whole, who are united and actuated by some common impulse of passion, or of interest, adversed to the rights of other citizens, or to the permanent and aggregate interests of the community.

There are two methods of curing the mischiefs of faction: the one, by removing its causes; the other, by controlling its effects.

There are again two methods of removing the causes of faction: the one, by destroying the liberty which is essential to its existence; the other, by giving to every citizen the same opinions, the same passions, and the same interests.

It could never be more truly said than of the first remedy, that it was worse than the disease. Liberty is to faction what air is to fire, an aliment without which it instantly expires. But it could not be less folly to abolish liberty, which is essential to political life, because it nourishes faction, than it would be to wish the annihilation of air, which is essential to animal life, because it imparts to fire its destructive agency.

The second expedient is as impracticable as the first would be unwise. As long as the reason of man continues fallible, and he is at liberty to exercise it, different opinions will be formed. As long as the connection subsists between his reason and his self-love, his opinions and his passions will have a reciprocal influence on each other; and the former will be objects to which the latter will attach themselves. The diversity in the faculties of men, from which the rights of property originate, is not less an insuperable obstacle to a uniformity of interests. The protection of these faculties is the first object of government. From the protection of different and unequal faculties of acquiring property, the possession of different degrees and kinds of property immediately results; and from the influence of these on the sentiments and views of the respective proprietors, ensues a division of the society into different interests and parties.

The latent causes of faction are thus sown in the nature of man; and we see them everywhere brought into different degrees of activity, according to the different circumstances of civil society. A zeal for different opinions concerning religion, concerning government, and many other points, as well of speculation as of practice; an attachment to different leaders ambitiously contending for pre-eminence and power; or to persons of other descriptions whose fortunes have been interesting to the human passions, have, in turn, divided mankind into parties, inflamed them with mutual animosity, and rendered them much more disposed to vex and oppress each other than to co-operate for their common good. So strong is this propensity of mankind to fall into mutual animosities, that where no substantial occasion presents itself, the most frivolous and fanciful distinctions have been sufficient to kindle their unfriendly passions and excite their most violent conflicts. But the most common and durable source of factions has been the various and unequal distribution of property. Those who hold and those who are without property have ever formed distinct interests in society. Those who are creditors, and those who are debtors, fall under a like discrimination. A landed interest, a manufacturing interest, a mercantile interest, a moneyed interest, with many lesser interests, grow up of necessity in civilized nations, and divide them into different classes, actuated by different sentiments and views. The regulation of these various and interfering interests forms the principal task of modern legislation, and involves the spirit of party and faction in the necessary and ordinary operations of the government. . . .

It is in vain to say that enlightened statesmen will be able to adjust these clashing interests, and render them all subservient to the public good. Enlightened statesmen will not always be at the helm. Nor, in many cases, can such an adjustment be made at all without taking into view indirect and remote considerations, which will rarely prevail over the immediate interest which one party may find in disregarding the rights of another or the good of the whole.

The inference to which we are brought is, that the CAUSES of faction cannot be removed, and that relief is only to be sought in the means of controlling its EFFECTS.

If a faction consists of less than a majority, relief is supplied by the republican principle, which enables the majority to defeat its sinister views by regular vote. It may clog the administration, it may convulse the society; but it will be unable to execute and mask its violence under the forms of the Constitution. When a majority is included in a faction, the form of popular government, on the other hand, enables it to sacrifice to its ruling passion or interest both the public good and the rights of other citizens. To secure the public good and private rights against the danger of such a faction, and at the same time to preserve the spirit and the form of popular government, is then the great object to which our inquiries are directed. . . .

By what means is this object attainable? Evidently by one of two only. Either the existence of the same passion or interest in a majority at the same time must be prevented, or the majority, having such coexistent passion or interest, must be rendered, by their number and local situation, unable to concert and carry into effect schemes of oppression. If the impulse and the opportunity be suffered to coincide, we well know that neither moral nor religious motives can be relied on as an adequate control. They are not found to be such on the injustice and violence of individuals, and lose their efficacy in proportion to the number combined together, that is, in proportion as their efficacy becomes needful.

From this view of the subject it may be concluded that a pure democracy, by which I mean a society consisting of a small number of citizens, who assemble and administer the government in person, can admit of no cure for the mischiefs of faction. A common passion or interest will, in almost every case, be felt by a majority of the whole; a communication and concert result from the form of government itself; and there is nothing to check the inducements to sacrifice the weaker party or an obnoxious individual. Hence it is that such democracies have ever been spectacles of turbulence and contention; have ever been found incompatible with personal security or the rights of property; and have in general been as short in their lives as they have been violent in their deaths. Theoretic politicians, who have patronized this species of government, have erroneously supposed that by reducing mankind to a perfect equality in their political rights, they would, at the same time, be perfectly equalized and assimilated in their possessions, their opinions, and their passions.

A republic, by which I mean a government in which the scheme of representation takes place, opens a different prospect, and promises the cure for which we are seeking. Let us examine the points in which it varies from pure democracy, and we shall comprehend both the nature of the cure and the efficacy which it must derive from the Union.

The two great points of difference between a democracy and a republic are: first, the delegation of the government, in the latter, to a small number of citizens elected by the rest; secondly, the greater number of citizens, and greater sphere of country, over which the latter may be extended.

The effect of the first difference is, on the one hand, to refine and enlarge the public views, by passing them through the medium of a chosen body of citizens, whose wisdom may best discern the true interest of their country, and whose patriotism and love of justice will be least likely to sacrifice it to temporary or partial considerations. Under such a regulation, it may well happen that the public voice, pronounced by the representatives of the people, will be more consonant to the public good than if pronounced by the people themselves, convened for the purpose. On the other hand, the effect may be inverted. Men of factious tempers, of local prejudices, or of sinister designs, may, by intrigue, by corruption, or by other means, first obtain the suffrages, and then betray the interests, of the people. The question resulting is, whether small or extensive republics are more favorable to the election of proper guardians of the public weal; and it is clearly decided in favor of the latter by two obvious considerations:

In the first place, it is to be remarked that, however small the republic may be, the representatives must be raised to a certain number, in order to guard against the cabals of a few; and that, however large it may be, they must be limited to a certain number, in order to guard against the confusion of a multitude. Hence, the number of representatives in the two cases not being in proportion to that of the two constituents, and being proportionally greater in the small republic, it follows that, if the proportion of fit characters be not less in the large than in the small republic, the former will present a greater option, and consequently a greater probability of a fit choice.

In the next place, as each representative will be chosen by a greater number of citizens in the large than in the small republic, it will be more difficult for unworthy candidates to practice with success the vicious arts by which elections are too often carried; and the suffrages of the people being more free, will be more likely to centre in men who possess the most attractive merit and the most diffusive and established characters.

It must be confessed that in this, as in most other cases, there is a mean, on both sides of which inconveniences will be found to lie. By enlarging too much the number of electors, you render the representatives too little acquainted with all their local circumstances and lesser interests; as by reducing it too much, you render him unduly attached to these, and too little fit to comprehend and pursue great and national objects. The federal Constitution forms a happy combination in this respect; the great and aggregate interests being referred to the national, the local and particular to the State legislatures.

The other point of difference is, the greater number of citizens and extent of territory which may be brought within the compass of republican than of democratic government; and it is this circumstance principally which renders factious combinations less to be dreaded in the former than in the latter. The smaller the society, the fewer probably will be the distinct parties and interests composing it; the fewer the distinct parties and interests, the more frequently will a majority be found of the same party; and the smaller the number of individuals composing a majority, and the smaller the compass within which they are placed, the more easily will they concert and execute their plans of oppression. Extend the sphere, and you take in a greater variety of parties and interests; you make it less probable that a majority of the whole will have a common motive to invade the rights of other citizens; or if such a common motive exists, it will be more difficult for all who feel it to discover their own strength, and to act in unison with each other. Besides other impediments, it may be remarked that, where there is a consciousness of unjust or dishonorable purposes, communication is always checked by distrust in proportion to the number whose concurrence is necessary.

Hence, it clearly appears, that the same advantage which a republic has over a democracy, in controlling the effects of faction, is enjoyed by a large over a small republic, — is enjoyed by the Union over the States composing it. Does the advantage consist in the substitution of representatives whose enlightened views and virtuous sentiments render them superior to local prejudices and schemes of injustice? It will not be denied that the representation of the Union will be most likely to possess these requisite endowments. Does it consist in the greater security afforded by a greater variety of parties, against the event of any one party being able to outnumber and oppress the rest? In an equal degree does the increased variety of parties comprised within the Union, increase this security. Does it, in fine, consist in the greater obstacles opposed to the concert and accomplishment of the secret wishes of an unjust and interested majority? Here, again, the extent of the Union gives it the most palpable advantage.

The influence of factious leaders may kindle a flame within their particular States, but will be unable to spread a general conflagration through the other States. A religious sect may degenerate into a political faction in a part of the Confederacy; but the variety of sects dispersed over the entire face of it must secure the national councils against any danger from that source. A rage for paper money, for an abolition of debts, for an equal division of property, or for any other improper or wicked project, will be less apt to pervade the whole body of the Union than a particular member of it; in the same proportion as such a malady is more likely to taint a particular county or district, than an entire State.

In the extent and proper structure of the Union, therefore, we behold a republican remedy for the diseases most incident to republican government. And according to the degree of pleasure and pride we feel in being republicans, ought to be our zeal in cherishing the spirit and supporting the character of Federalists.

PUBLIUS.

POINTS FOR DISCUSSION

1. Madison argued that a large republican form of government would counteract the ill effects of faction. First, representatives in that government would be less "of fractious tempers." Moreover,

> Extend the sphere, and you take in a greater variety of parties and interests; you
> make it less probable that a majority of the whole will have a common motive

to invade the rights of other citizens; or if such a common motive exists, it will be more difficult for all who feel it to discover their own strength, and to act in unison with each other.

How do these arguments resonate, if at all, with your understanding of federal governance today?

2. Madison argued that good government should take "into view indirect and remote considerations, which will rarely prevail over the immediate interest which one party may find in disregarding the rights of another or the good of the whole." As you read the materials in this book, you will observe ongoing tension between "immediate interest[s]" and "indirect and remote considerations." For example, Supreme Court Justices, in reviewing the constitutionality of federal laws, have attached differing importance to the immediate pragmatic need for federal legislation and the indirect benefits of ensuring that Congress does not exceed its enumerated powers. What might those indirect benefits be? Be mindful of how public officials and scholars have described those benefits in the materials throughout this book.

In *The Federalist No. 44*, Madison describes limits that the Constitution imposes on the states — and why he believes that such limits are reasonable. At the Federal Convention, Madison proposed that the Constitution give Congress a negative on state laws contravening federal prerogatives. Ultimately, the delegates rejected this proposal. Nonetheless, through other means, the Constitution limited the power of states to thwart national prerogatives.

First, the Constitution *expressly* limited the authority of states to engage in certain acts. Article I, §10 of the Constitution provides:

> No State shall enter into any Treaty, Alliance, or Confederation; grant Letters of Marque and Reprisal; coin Money; emit Bills of Credit; make any Thing but gold and silver Coin a Tender in Payment of Debts; pass any Bill of Attainder, ex post facto Law, or Law impairing the Obligation of Contracts, or grant any Title of Nobility.
>
> No State shall, without the Consent of the Congress, lay any Imposts or Duties on Imports or Exports, except what may be absolutely necessary for executing it's inspection Laws: and the net Produce of all Duties and Imposts, laid by any State on Imports or Exports, shall be for the Use of the Treasury of the United States; and all such Laws shall be subject to the Revision and Controul of the Congress.
>
> No State shall, without the Consent of Congress, lay any Duty of Tonnage, keep Troops, or Ships of War in time of Peace, enter into any Agreement or Compact with another State, or with a foreign Power, or engage in War, unless actually invaded, or in such imminent Danger as will not admit of delay.

These provisions were geared in part toward enabling the Union to act with one voice in foreign relations and international commerce.

Moreover, as you will study in Chapter 7, the Supreme Court has held that certain enumerated federal powers, such as the powers to regulate interstate commerce and conduct foreign relations, *implicitly* prohibit the states from enacting certain regulations in those fields.

In addition to limiting state regulatory power in these ways, the Constitution provides judicial mechanisms to ensure the proper enforcement of federal law. The Supremacy Clause of Article VI provides:

> This Constitution, and the Laws of the United States which shall be made in Pursuance thereof; and all Treaties made, or which shall be made, under the Authority of the United States, shall be the supreme Law of the Land; and the Judges in every State shall be bound thereby, any Thing in the Constitution or Laws of any State to the Contrary notwithstanding.

Moreover, Article III, §2 of the Constitution authorizes Congress to give federal courts jurisdiction over all cases "arising under this Constitution, the Laws of the United States, and Treaties made, or which shall be made, under their Authority. . . ." In Chapter 7, you will study how courts, in fulfilling their obligations under these provisions, have struggled to determine when the Constitution and federal regulatory schemes preempt state law.

Finally, Article VI provides that federal and state officials alike must, "by Oath or Affirmation," support the Constitution: "The Senators and Representatives before mentioned, and the Members of the several State Legislatures, and all executive and judicial Officers, both of the United States and of the several States, shall be bound by Oath or Affirmation, to support this Constitution. . . ."

In the following passage, Madison describes the reasonableness, in his view, of both the Supremacy Clause and the Oaths Clause.

THE FEDERALIST NO. 44 (JAMES MADISON)

"Restrictions on the Authority of the Several States"
To the People of the State of New York:
"This Constitution and the laws of the United States which shall be made in pursuance thereof, and all treaties made, or which shall be made, under the authority of the United States, shall be the supreme law of the land, and the judges in every State shall be bound thereby, any thing in the constitution or laws of any State to the contrary notwithstanding." The indiscreet zeal of the adversaries to the Constitution has betrayed them into an attack on this part of it also, without which it would have been evidently and radically defective. To be fully sensible of this, we need only suppose for a moment that the supremacy of the State constitutions had been left complete by a saving clause in their favor. In the first place, as these constitutions invest the State legislatures with absolute sovereignty, in all cases not excepted by the existing articles of Confederation, all the authorities contained in the proposed Constitution, so far as they exceed those enumerated in the Confederation, would have been annulled, and the new Congress would have been reduced to the same impotent condition with their predecessors. In the next place, as the constitutions of some of the States do not even expressly and fully recognize the existing powers of the Confederacy, an express saving of the supremacy of the former would, in such States, have brought into question every power

contained in the proposed Constitution. In the third place, as the constitutions of the States differ much from each other, it might happen that a treaty or national law, of great and equal importance to the States, would interfere with some and not with other constitutions, and would consequently be valid in some of the States, at the same time that it would have no effect in others. In fine, the world would have seen, for the first time, a system of government founded on an inversion of the fundamental principles of all government; it would have seen the authority of the whole society every where subordinate to the authority of the parts; it would have seen a monster, in which the head was under the direction of the members. 3. "The Senators and Representatives, and the members of the several State legislatures, and all executive and judicial officers, both of the United States and the several States, shall be bound by oath or affirmation to support this Constitution." It has been asked why it was thought necessary, that the State magistracy should be bound to support the federal Constitution, and unnecessary that a like oath should be imposed on the officers of the United States, in favor of the State constitutions. Several reasons might be assigned for the distinction. I content myself with one, which is obvious and conclusive. The members of the federal government will have no agency in carrying the State constitutions into effect. The members and officers of the State governments, on the contrary, will have an essential agency in giving effect to the federal Constitution. The election of the President and Senate will depend, in all cases, on the legislatures of the several States. And the election of the House of Representatives will equally depend on the same authority in the first instance; and will, probably, forever be conducted by the officers, and according to the laws, of the States. . . .

PUBLIUS.

POINTS FOR DISCUSSION

1. Madison argued that it is reasonable for the Constitution to provide that validly enacted federal law is the supreme law of the land. He did not explain here, however, the circumstances in which a federal law should be held to preempt state law. Must state law directly conflict with federal law to be preempted? Or must it merely obstruct the purposes of federal law to be preempted? Or, to be preempted, must state law simply fall within a field that Congress has chosen to regulate? Are the answers to these questions obvious? You will consider these questions and others in Chapter 7.

2. In discussing the Oaths Clause, Madison explained:

> The members and officers of the State governments . . . will have an essential agency in giving effect to the federal Constitution. The election of the President and Senate will depend, in all cases, on the legislatures of the several States. And the election of the House of Representatives will equally depend on the same authority in the first instance; and will, probably, forever be conducted by the officers, and according to the laws, of the States.

In this passage, does Madison mean that state officials will have an obligation to enforce federal law against individuals if Congress directs them to do so? Or does he mean that state officials necessarily must participate in determining the composition of the federal government? Or does he mean both? Supreme Court Justices have described this first question as the "oldest question of constitutional law." *New York v. United States*, 505 U.S. 144, 149 (1992). You will study this question in Chapter 6.

Article I establishes the legislative branch of the federal government. It defines how the House of Representatives and Senate shall be structured and constituted and also confers a list of enumerated powers on Congress. Article II establishes the executive branch. It defines how the President shall be elected and specifies certain executive powers. Review Articles I and II. Anti-Federalists objected to the nature and scope of the political powers they conferred. In *The Federalist No. 45* and *The Federalist No. 46*, Madison argues that the powers the Constitution confers upon the Union are necessary — and not to be feared as unduly subsuming state authority.

THE FEDERALIST NO. 45 (JAMES MADISON)

"The Alleged Danger From the Powers of the Union to the State Governments Considered"

To the People of the State of New York:

HAVING shown that no one of the powers transferred to the federal government is unnecessary or improper, the next question to be considered is, whether the whole mass of them will be dangerous to the portion of authority left in the several States. The adversaries to the plan of the convention, instead of considering in the first place what degree of power was absolutely necessary for the purposes of the federal government, have exhausted themselves in a secondary inquiry into the possible consequences of the proposed degree of power to the governments of the particular States. But if the Union, as has been shown, be essential to the security of the people of America against foreign danger; if it be essential to their security against contentions and wars among the different States; if it be essential to guard them against those violent and oppressive factions which embitter the blessings of liberty, and against those military establishments which must gradually poison its very fountain; if, in a word, the Union be essential to the happiness of the people of America, is it not preposterous, to urge as an objection to a government, without which the objects of the Union cannot be attained, that such a government may derogate from the importance of the governments of the individual States? Was, then, the American Revolution effected, was the American Confederacy formed, was the precious blood of thousands spilt, and the hard-earned substance of millions lavished, not that the people of America should enjoy peace, liberty, and safety, but that the government of the individual States, that particular municipal establishments, might enjoy a certain extent of power, and be arrayed with certain dignities and attributes of sovereignty? We have heard of the impious doctrine in the Old World, that the people were made for kings, not kings for the people. Is the same doctrine to be revived in the New, in another shape that the solid happiness of the people is to be sacrificed to the views of political institutions of a different form? It is too early for politicians to presume on our forgetting that the public good, the real welfare of the great body of the people, is the supreme object to be pursued; and that no form of government whatever has any other value than as it may be fitted for the attainment of this object. Were the plan of the convention adverse to the public happiness, my voice would be, Reject the plan. Were the Union itself inconsistent with the public happiness, it would be, Abolish the Union. In like manner, as far as the sovereignty of the States cannot be reconciled to the happiness of the people, the voice of every good citizen must be, Let the former be sacrificed to the latter. How far the sacrifice is necessary, has been shown. How far the unsacrificed residue will be endangered, is the question before us. Several important considerations have been touched in the course of these papers, which discountenance the supposition that the operation of the federal government will by degrees prove fatal to the State governments. The more I revolve the subject, the more fully I am persuaded that the balance is much more likely to be disturbed by the preponderancy of the last than of the first scale. . . .

The State government will have the advantage of the Federal government, whether we compare them in respect to the immediate dependence of the one on the other; to the weight of personal influence which each side will possess; to the powers respectively vested in them; to the predilection and probable support of the people; to the disposition and faculty of resisting and frustrating the measures of each other. The State governments may be regarded as constituent and essential parts of the federal government; whilst the latter is nowise essential to the operation or organization of the former. Without the intervention of the State legislatures, the President of the United States cannot be elected at all. They must in all cases have a great share in his appointment, and will, perhaps, in most cases, of themselves determine it. The Senate will be elected absolutely and exclusively by the State legislatures. Even the House of Representatives, though drawn immediately from the people, will be chosen very much under the influence of that class of men, whose influence over the people obtains for themselves an election into the State legislatures. Thus, each of the principal branches of the federal government will owe its existence more or less to the favor of the State governments, and must consequently feel a dependence, which is much more likely to beget a disposition too obsequious than too overbearing towards them. On the other side, the component parts of the State governments will in no instance be indebted for their appointment to the direct agency of the federal government, and very little, if at all, to the local influence of its members. The number of individuals employed under the Constitution of the United States will be much smaller than the number employed under the particular States.

There will consequently be less of personal influence on the side of the former than of the latter. The members of the legislative, executive, and judiciary departments of thirteen and more States, the justices of peace, officers of militia, ministerial officers of justice, with all the county, corporation, and town officers, for three millions and more of people, intermixed, and having particular acquaintance with every class and circle of people, must exceed, beyond all proportion, both in number and influence, those of every description who will be employed in the administration of the federal system. Compare the members of the three great departments of the thirteen States, excluding from the judiciary department the justices of peace, with the members of the corresponding departments of the single government of the Union; compare the militia officers of three millions of people with the military and marine officers of any establishment which is within the compass of probability, or, I may add, of possibility, and in this view alone, we may pronounce the advantage of the States to be decisive. If the federal government is to have collectors of revenue, the State governments will have theirs also. And as those of the former will be principally on the seacoast, and not very numerous, whilst those of the latter will be spread over the face of the country, and will be very numerous, the advantage in this view also lies on the same side. . . .

The powers delegated by the proposed Constitution to the federal government are few and defined. Those which are to remain in the State governments are numerous and indefinite. The former will be exercised principally on external objects, as war, peace, negotiation, and foreign commerce. . . . The powers reserved to the several States will extend to all the objects which, in the ordinary course of affairs, concern the lives, liberties, and properties of the people, and the internal order, improvement, and prosperity of the State. The operations of the federal government will be most extensive and important in times of war and danger; those of the State governments, in times of peace and security. As the former periods will probably bear a small proportion to the latter, the State governments will here enjoy another advantage over the federal government. The more adequate, indeed, the federal powers may be rendered to the national defense, the less frequent will be those scenes of danger which might favor their ascendancy over the governments of the particular States. If the new Constitution be examined with accuracy and candor, it will be found that the change which it proposes consists much less in the addition of NEW POWERS to the Union, than in the invigoration of its ORIGINAL POWERS. The regulation of commerce, it is true, is a new power; but that seems to be an addition which few oppose, and from which no apprehensions are entertained. The powers relating to war and peace, armies and fleets, treaties and finance, with the other more considerable powers, are all vested in the existing Congress by the articles of Confederation. The proposed change does not enlarge these powers; it only substitutes a more effectual mode of administering them. . . .

PUBLIUS.

THE FEDERALIST NO. 46 (JAMES MADISON)

"The Influence of the State and Federal Governments Compared"
To the People of the State of New York:
RESUMING the subject of the last paper, I proceed to inquire whether the federal government or the State governments will have the advantage with

regard to the predilection and support of the people. Notwithstanding the different modes in which they are appointed, we must consider both of them as substantially dependent on the great body of the citizens of the United States.

I assume this position here as it respects the first, reserving the proofs for another place. The federal and State governments are in fact but different agents and trustees of the people, constituted with different powers, and designed for different purposes. The adversaries of the Constitution seem to have lost sight of the people altogether in their reasonings on this subject; and to have viewed these different establishments, not only as mutual rivals and enemies, but as uncontrolled by any common superior in their efforts to usurp the authorities of each other. These gentlemen must here be reminded of their error. They must be told that the ultimate authority, wherever the derivative may be found, resides in the people alone, and that it will not depend merely on the comparative ambition or address of the different governments, whether either, or which of them, will be able to enlarge its sphere of jurisdiction at the expense of the other. Truth, no less than decency, requires that the event in every case should be supposed to depend on the sentiments and sanction of their common constituents. Many considerations, besides those suggested on a former occasion, seem to place it beyond doubt that the first and most natural attachment of the people will be to the governments of their respective States.

Into the administration of these a greater number of individuals will expect to rise. From the gift of these a greater number of offices and emoluments will flow. By the superintending care of these, all the more domestic and personal interests of the people will be regulated and provided for. With the affairs of these, the people will be more familiarly and minutely conversant. And with the members of these, will a greater proportion of the people have the ties of personal acquaintance and friendship, and of family and party attachments; on the side of these, therefore, the popular bias may well be expected most strongly to incline. Experience speaks the same language in this case. The federal administration, though hitherto very defective in comparison with what may be hoped under a better system, had, during the war, and particularly whilst the independent fund of paper emissions was in credit, an activity and importance as great as it can well have in any future circumstances whatever.

It was engaged, too, in a course of measures which had for their object the protection of everything that was dear, and the acquisition of everything that could be desirable to the people at large. It was, nevertheless, invariably found, after the transient enthusiasm for the early Congresses was over, that the attention and attachment of the people were turned anew to their own particular governments; that the federal council was at no time the idol of popular favor; and that opposition to proposed enlargements of its powers and importance was the side usually taken by the men who wished to build their political consequence on the prepossessions of their fellow-citizens. If, therefore, as has been elsewhere remarked, the people should in future become more partial to the federal than to the State governments, the change can only result from such manifest and irresistible proofs of a better administration, as will overcome all their antecedent propensities. And in that case, the people ought not surely to be precluded from giving most of their confidence where they may discover it to be most due; but even in that case the State governments could have little to apprehend, because it is only within a certain sphere that the federal power can, in the nature of things, be advantageously administered. The remaining points on which I propose to compare the federal and State governments, are the disposition and the faculty they may respectively possess, to resist and frustrate the measures of each other. It has been already proved that the members of the federal will be more dependent on the members of the State governments, than the latter will be on the former. It has appeared also, that the prepossessions of the people, on whom both will depend, will be more on the side of the State governments, than of the federal government. So far as the disposition of each towards the other may be influenced by these causes, the State governments must clearly have the advantage.

But in a distinct and very important point of view, the advantage will lie on the same side. The prepossessions, which the members themselves will carry into the federal government, will generally be favorable to the States; whilst it will rarely happen, that the members of the State governments will carry into the public councils a bias in favor of the general government. A local spirit will infallibly prevail much more in the members of Congress, than a national spirit will prevail in the legislatures of the particular States. Every one knows that a great proportion of the errors committed by the State legislatures proceeds from the disposition of the members to sacrifice the comprehensive and permanent interest of the State, to the particular and separate views of the counties or districts in which they reside. And if they do not sufficiently enlarge their policy to embrace the collective welfare of their particular State, how can it be imagined that they will make the aggregate prosperity of the Union, and the dignity and respectability of its government, the objects of their affections and consultations? For the same reason that the members of the State legislatures will be unlikely to attach themselves sufficiently to national objects, the members of the federal legislature will be likely to attach themselves too much to local objects. The States will be to the latter what counties and towns are to the former. Measures will too often be decided according to their probable effect, not on the national prosperity and happiness, but on the prejudices, interests, and pursuits of the governments and people of the individual States. What is the spirit that has in general characterized the proceedings of Congress? A perusal of their journals, as well as the candid acknowledgments of such as have had a seat in that assembly, will inform us, that the members have but too frequently displayed the character, rather of partisans of their respective States, than of impartial guardians of a common interest; that where on one occasion improper sacrifices have been made of local considerations, to the aggrandizement of the federal government, the great interests of the nation have suffered on a hundred, from an undue attention to the local prejudices, interests, and views of the particular States. I mean not by these reflections to insinuate, that the new federal government will not embrace a more enlarged plan of policy than the existing government may have pursued; much less, that its views will be as confined as those of the State legislatures; but only that it will partake sufficiently of the spirit of both, to be disinclined to invade the rights of the individual States, or the prerogatives of their governments. The motives on the part of the State governments, to augment their prerogatives by defalcations from the federal government, will be overruled by no reciprocal predispositions in the members. Were it admitted, however, that the Federal government may feel an equal disposition with the State governments to extend its power beyond the due limits, the latter would still have the advantage in the means of defeating such encroachments. If an act of a particular State, though unfriendly to the national government, be generally popular in that State and should not too grossly violate the oaths of the State officers, it is executed immediately and, of course, by means on the spot and depending on the State alone. The opposition of the federal government, or the interposition of federal officers, would but inflame the zeal of all parties on the side of the State, and the evil could not be prevented or repaired, if at all, without the employment of means which must always be resorted to with reluctance and difficulty.

On the other hand, should an unwarrantable measure of the federal government be unpopular in particular States, which would seldom fail to be the case, or even a warrantable measure be so, which may sometimes be the case, the means of opposition to it are powerful and at hand. The disquietude of the people; their repugnance and, perhaps, refusal to co-operate with the officers of the Union; the frowns of the executive magistracy of the State; the embarrassments created by legislative devices, which would often be added on such occasions, would oppose, in any State, difficulties not to be despised; would form, in a large State, very serious impediments; and where the sentiments of several adjoining States happened to be in unison, would present obstructions which the federal government would hardly be willing to encounter. But ambitious encroachments of the federal government, on the authority of the State governments, would not excite the opposition of a single State, or of a few States only. They would be signals of general alarm. Every government would espouse the common cause. A correspondence would be opened. Plans of resistance would be concerted. One spirit would animate and conduct the whole. The same combinations, in short, would result from an apprehension of the federal, as was produced by the dread of a foreign, yoke; and unless the projected innovations should be voluntarily renounced, the same appeal to a trial of force would be made in the one case as was made in the other. But what degree of madness could ever drive the federal government to such an extremity. In the contest with Great Britain, one part of the empire was employed against the other.

The more numerous part invaded the rights of the less numerous part. The attempt was unjust and unwise; but it was not in speculation absolutely chimerical. But what would be the contest in the case we are supposing? Who would be the parties? A few representatives of the people would be opposed to the people themselves; or rather one set of representatives would be contending against thirteen sets of representatives, with the whole body of their common constituents on the side of the latter. The only refuge left for those who prophesy the downfall of the State governments is the visionary supposition that the federal government may previously accumulate a military force for the projects of ambition. The reasonings contained in these papers must have been employed to little purpose indeed, if it could be necessary now to disprove the reality of this danger. That the people and the States should, for a sufficient period of time, elect an uninterupted succession of men ready to betray both; that the traitors should, throughout this period, uniformly and systematically pursue some fixed plan for the extension of the military establishment; that the governments and the people of the States should silently and patiently behold the gathering storm, and continue to supply the materials, until it should be prepared to burst on their own heads, must appear to every one more like the incoherent dreams of a delirious jealousy, or the misjudged exaggerations of a counterfeit zeal, than like the sober apprehensions of genuine patriotism.

Extravagant as the supposition is, let it however be made. Let a regular army, fully equal to the resources of the country, be formed; and let it be entirely at the devotion of the federal government; still it would not be going too far to say, that the State governments, with the people on their side, would be able to repel the danger. The highest number to which, according to the best computation, a standing army can be carried in any country, does not exceed one hundredth part of the whole number of souls; or one twenty-fifth part of the number able to bear arms. This proportion would not yield, in the United States, an army of more than twenty-five or thirty thousand men. To these would be opposed a militia amounting to near half a million of citizens with arms in their hands, officered by men chosen from among themselves, fighting for their common liberties, and united and conducted by governments possessing their affections and confidence. It may well be doubted, whether a militia thus circumstanced could ever be conquered by such a proportion of regular troops. Those who are best acquainted with the last successful resistance of this country against the British arms, will be most inclined to deny the possibility of it. Besides the advantage of being armed, which the Americans possess over the people of almost every other nation, the existence of subordinate governments, to which the people are attached, and by which the militia officers are appointed, forms a barrier against the enterprises of ambition, more insurmountable than any which a simple government of any form can admit of. Notwithstanding the military establishments in the several kingdoms of Europe, which are carried as far as the public resources will bear, the governments are afraid to trust the people with arms. And it is not certain, that with this aid alone they would not be able to shake off their yokes. But were the people to possess the additional advantages of local governments chosen by themselves, who could collect the national will and direct the national force, and of officers appointed out of the militia, by these governments, and attached both to them and to the militia, it may be affirmed with the greatest assurance, that the throne of every tyranny in Europe would be speedily overturned in spite of the legions which surround it. Let us not insult the free and gallant citizens of America with the suspicion, that they would be less able to defend the rights of which they would be in actual possession, than the debased subjects of arbitrary power would be to rescue theirs from the hands of their oppressors. Let us rather no longer insult them with the supposition that they can ever reduce themselves to the necessity of making the experiment, by a blind and tame submission to the long train of insidious measures which must precede and produce it. The argument under the present head may be put into a very concise form, which appears altogether conclusive. Either the mode in which the federal government is to be constructed will render it sufficiently dependent on the people, or it will not. On the first supposition, it will be restrained by that dependence from forming schemes obnoxious to their constituents. On the other supposition, it will not possess the confidence of the people, and its schemes of usurpation will be easily defeated by the State governments, who will be supported by the people. On summing up the considerations stated in this and the last paper, they seem to amount to the most convincing evidence, that the powers proposed to be lodged in the federal government are as little formidable to those reserved to the individual States, as they are indispensably necessary to accomplish the purposes of the Union; and that all those alarms which have been sounded, of a meditated and consequential annihilation of the State governments, must, on the most favorable interpretation, be ascribed to the chimerical fears of the authors of them.

Publius.

POINTS FOR DISCUSSION

1. In *The Federalist No. 45*, Madison attempted to delineate the respective spheres of the federal and state governments:

> The powers delegated by the proposed Constitution to the federal government are few and defined. Those which are to remain in the State governments are numerous and indefinite. The former will be exercised principally on external objects, as war, peace, negotiation, and foreign commerce. . . .
>
> The powers reserved to the several States will extend to all the objects which, in the ordinary course of affairs, concern the lives, liberties, and properties of the people, and the internal order, improvement, and prosperity of the State.

Is it possible to draw a bright line between the internal and external objects of governance? In 1784, Alexander Hamilton wrote, with reference to the powers of Congress under the Articles of Confederation:

> Congress, say our political jugglers, have no right to meddle with our internal police. . . . The truth is . . . it is impossible for Congress to do a single act which will not, directly or indirectly, affect the internal police of every State. In short, if nothing was to be done by Congress that would affect our internal police . . . would not all the powers of the Confederation be annihilated, and the Union dissolved?

Alexander Hamilton, *A Letter from Phocion to the Considerate Citizens of New York* (Jan. 1784), reprinted in 3 The Papers of Alexander Hamilton 485 (Harold C. Syrett and Jacob E. Cooke eds., 1962).

Is Hamilton correct? If so, is dual sovereignty possible?

2. In *The Federalist No. 45*, Madison argued that "[t]he State government will have the advantage of the Federal government." For one, he argued that

"[t]he State governments may be regarded as constituent and essential parts of the federal government. . . ." For another, he contended in *The Federalist No. 46* that "the first and most natural attachment of the people will be to the governments of their respective States." Should these observations have assuaged Anti-Federalist concerns that the federal government would assume undue regulatory authority relative to the states? Do Madison's observations resonate with your understanding of how the U.S. federal system operates at present?

3. In *The Federalist No. 46*, Madison argued that "ultimate authority, wherever the derivative may be found, resides in the people alone. . . ." The "ultimate authority" of "the people," Madison contended, will restrain the federal government "from forming schemes obnoxious to their constituents" and enable federal "schemes of usurpation" to be "easily defeated by the State governments." By what means under the Constitution may "the people" exercise such "ultimate authority"? If the people exercise ultimate sovereignty, how can it be said that the Constitution establishes a system of dual sovereignty?

4. Note Madison's argument in *The Federalist No. 45* that "[t]he regulation of commerce, it is true, is a new power; but that seems to be an addition which few oppose, and from which no apprehensions are entertained." Given the fears of federal ascendancy over states that existed during the Founding period, why would few have opposed the commerce power in the late 1780s? As you will study in Chapter 5, the commerce power emerged in the twentieth century as the primary source of federal regulatory power in a range of areas, including business, labor, the environment, and civil rights. Why was this so? Did its emergence represent an unjustified expansion of federal power — realizing Anti-Federalist fears — or a proper adaptation of federal power to political, social, and economic conditions in the twentieth century? Keep in mind these questions as you study the powers of Congress.

B. THE RESPONSIBILITY TO SAFEGUARD THE FEDERAL STRUCTURE

As you have read, members of the Founding generation discussed the nature and scope of federal regulatory power under the Constitution. They also addressed another foundational question: Should disputes arise about the relative powers of the federal and state governments, what institution or institutions would have authority to resolve them? For instance, public officials debated whether Congress had power under the Constitution to establish a Bank of the United States. What institution (or institutions) had authority to resolve that constitutional question? There are several possibilities. Congress, as a body representative of the people, might have authority to discern the bounds of its own power. Courts, through judicial review, might determine whether acts of Congress comply with its enumerated powers. The President, in executing the law, might refrain from enforcing certain provisions. The states, acting individually or collectively, might resist Congress's assertion of power. Members of the Founding generation took seriously this question, which the materials in this section address.

The question is not merely of historical significance. Judges, other public officials, and scholars continue to debate what institutions have authority to resolve disputes over the relative powers of the federal government and the states under the Constitution. In recent decades, Supreme Court Justices have squarely debated what role, if any, the judiciary should play in reviewing congressional legislation on federalism grounds. Likewise, scholars have debated the role of federal lawmaking procedures and the electoral process in maintaining the federal structure. You will study these matters in later chapters.

Here, you will examine how public officials addressed this question in ratification debates and early constitutional controversies, and how the Supreme Court addressed it during the first few decades after ratification. As you read these materials, consider the following questions:

- What institutions are responsible for maintaining the Constitution's federal structure? Specifically, what are the respective roles of Congress, the courts, and state institutions in safeguarding the federal structure?
- What role do the people play in resolving disputes over federal-state power?
- Is authority to resolve disputes over the relative powers of the federal government and the states an authority to define the federal system itself?

1. DEBATING VARIOUS ENFORCEMENT MECHANISMS

In this section, you will read various ratification-era selections on how, if at all, the Constitution provides checks on congressional power relative to the states. As you read each selection, note the specific check or checks the author identifies and the arguments for or against each check.

OLIVER ELLSWORTH, DEBATE IN THE CONNECTICUT CONVENTION

7 January 1788

If the general legislature should at any time overleap their limits, the judicial department is a constitutional check. If the United States go beyond their powers, if they make a law which the Constitution does not authorize, it is void; and the judicial power, the national judges, who to secure their impartiality are to be made independent, will declare it to be void. On the other hand, if the states go beyond their limits, if they make a law which is a usurpation of the general government, the law is void; and upright independent judges will declare it to be so. Still, however, if the United States and the individual states will quarrel, if they want to fight, they may do it, and no frame of government can possibly prevent it. It is sufficient for this Constitution that, so far from laying them under a necessity of contending, it provides every reasonable check against it. But perhaps, at some time or other, there will be a contest; the states may rise againt the general government. If this does take place, if all the states combine, if all oppose, the whole will not eat up the members, but the measure which is opposed to the sense of the people will prove abortive. In republics, it is a fundamental principle that the majority govern, and that the minority comply with the general voice. How contrary, then, to republican principles, how humiliating, is our present situation! A single state can rise up, and put a *veto* upon the most important public measures. We have seen this actually take place. A single state has controlled the general voice of the Union; a minority, a very small minority has governed us. So far is this from being consistent with republican principles, that it is, in effect, the worst species of monarchy.

Hence we see how necessary for the Union is a coercive principle. No man pretends the contrary: we all see and feel this necessity. The only question is, Shall it be a coercion of law, or a coercion of arms? There is no other possible alternative. Where will those who oppose a coercion of law come out? Where will they end? A necessary consequence of their principles is a war of the states one against another. I am for coercion by law, — that coercion which acts only upon delinquent individuals. This Constitution does not attempt to coerce sovereign bodies, states, in their political capacity. No coercion is applicable to such bodies, but that of an armed force. If we should attempt to execute the laws of the Union by sending an armed force against a delinquent state, it would involve the good and bad, the innocent and guilty, in the same calamity.

But this legal coercion singles out the guilty individual, and punishes him for breaking the laws of the Union. All men will see the reasonableness of this; they will acquiesce, and say, Let the guilty suffer.

How have the morals of the people been depraved for the want of an efficient government, which might establish justice and righteousness! For the want of this, iniquity has come in upon us like an overflowing flood. If we wish to prevent this alarming evil, if we wish to protect the good citizen in his right, we must lift up the standard of justice; we must establish a national government to be enforced by the equal decisions of law, and the peaceable arm of the magistrate.

JOHN MARSHALL, DEBATE IN THE VIRGINIA RATIFYING CONVENTION

20 June 1788

Has the Government of the United States power to make laws on every subject? . . . Can they make laws affecting the mode of transferring property, or contracts, or claims, between citizens of the same State? Can they go beyond the delegated powers? If they were to make a law not warranted by any of the powers enumerated, it would be considered by the judges as an infringement of the Constitution which they are to guard. They would not consider such a law as coming under their jurisdiction. — They would declare it void.

JAMES MADISON, OBSERVATIONS ON JEFFERSON'S DRAFT OF A CONSTITUTION FOR VIRGINIA

15 October 1788

In the State Constitutions & indeed in the Fedl. one also, no provision is made for the case of a disagreement in expounding them; and as the Courts are generally the last in making their decision, it results to them, by refusing or not refusing to execute a law, to stamp it with its final character. This makes the Judiciary Dept paramount in fact to the Legislature, which was never intended, and can never be proper. . . .

THE FEDERALIST NO. 39 (JAMES MADISON)

"The Conformity of the Plan to Republican Principles"
To the People of the State of New York:

The difference between a federal and national government, as it relates to the OPERATION OF THE GOVERNMENT, is supposed to consist in this, that in the former the powers operate on the political bodies composing the Confederacy, in their political capacities; in the latter, on the individual citizens composing the nation, in their individual capacities. On trying the Constitution by this criterion, it falls under the NATIONAL, not the FEDERAL character; though perhaps not so completely as has been understood. In several cases, and particularly in the trial of controversies to which States may be parties, they must be viewed and proceeded against in their collective and political capacities only. So far the national countenance of the government on this side seems to be disfigured by a few federal features. But this blemish is perhaps unavoidable in any plan; and the operation of the government on the people, in their individual capacities, in its ordinary and most essential proceedings, may, on the whole, designate it, in this relation, a NATIONAL government.

But if the government be national with regard to the OPERATION of its powers, it changes its aspect again when we contemplate it in relation to the EXTENT of its powers. The idea of a national government involves in it, not only an authority over the individual citizens, but an indefinite supremacy over all persons and things, so far as they are objects of lawful government. Among a people consolidated into one nation, this supremacy is completely vested in the national legislature. Among communities united for particular purposes, it is vested partly in the general and partly in the municipal legislatures. In the former case, all local authorities are subordinate to the supreme; and may be controlled, directed, or abolished by it at pleasure. In the latter, the local or municipal authorities form distinct and independent portions of the supremacy, no more subject, within their respective spheres, to the general authority, than the general authority is subject to them, within its own sphere. In this relation, then, the proposed government cannot be deemed a NATIONAL one; since its jurisdiction extends to certain enumerated objects only, and leaves to the several States a residuary and inviolable sovereignty over all other objects. It is true that in controversies relating to the boundary between the two jurisdictions, the tribunal which is ultimately to decide, is to be established under the general government. But this does not change the principle of the case. The decision is to be impartially made, according to the rules of the Constitution; and all the usual and most effectual precautions are taken to secure this impartiality. Some such tribunal is clearly essential to prevent an appeal to the sword and a dissolution of the compact; and that it ought to be established under the general rather than under the local governments, or, to speak more properly, that it could be safely established under the first alone, is a position not likely to be combated.

If we try the Constitution by its last relation to the authority by which amendments are to be made, we find it neither wholly NATIONAL nor wholly FEDERAL. Were it wholly national, the supreme and ultimate authority would reside in the MAJORITY of the people of the Union; and this authority would be competent at all times, like that of a majority of every national society, to alter or abolish its established government. Were it wholly federal, on the other hand, the concurrence of each State in the Union would be essential to every alteration that would be binding on all. The mode provided by the plan of the convention is not founded on either of these principles. In requiring more than a majority, and particularly in computing the proportion by STATES, not by CITIZENS, it departs from the NATIONAL and advances towards the FEDERAL character; in rendering the concurrence of less than the whole number of States sufficient, it loses again the FEDERAL and partakes of the NATIONAL character.

The proposed Constitution, therefore, is, in strictness, neither a national nor a federal Constitution, but a composition of both. In its foundation it is federal, not national; in the sources from which the ordinary powers of the government are drawn, it is partly federal and partly national; in the operation of these powers, it is national, not federal; in the extent of them, again, it is federal, not national; and, finally, in the authoritative mode of introducing amendments, it is neither wholly federal nor wholly national.

THE FEDERALIST No. 44 (JAMES MADISON)

"Restrictions on the Authority of the Several States"
To the People of the State of New York:

If it be asked what is to be the consequence, in case the Congress shall misconstrue this part of the Constitution, and exercise powers not warranted by its true meaning, I answer, the same as if they should misconstrue or enlarge any other power vested in them; as if the general power had been reduced to particulars, and any one of these were to be violated; the same, in short, as if the State legislatures should violate the irrespective constitutional authorities. In the first instance, the success of the usurpation will depend on the executive and judiciary departments, which are to expound and give effect to the legislative acts; and in the last resort a remedy must be obtained from the people who can, by the election of more faithful representatives, annul the acts of the usurpers. The truth is, that this ultimate redress may be more confided in against unconstitutional acts of the federal than of the State legislatures, for this plain reason, that as every such act of the former will be an invasion of the rights of the latter, these will be ever ready to mark the innovation, to sound the alarm to the people, and to exert their local influence in effecting a change of federal representatives. There being no such intermediate body between the State legislatures and the people interested in watching the conduct of the former, violations of the State constitutions are more likely to remain unnoticed and unredressed. . . .

THE FEDERALIST NO. 78 (ALEXANDER HAMILTON)

"The Judiciary Department"
To the People of the State of New York:
WE PROCEED now to an examination of the judiciary department of the proposed government. . . .

The complete independence of the courts of justice is peculiarly essential in a limited Constitution. By a limited Constitution, I understand one which contains certain specified exceptions to the legislative authority; such, for instance, as that it shall pass no bills of attainder, no ex-post-facto laws, and the like. Limitations of this kind can be preserved in practice no other way than through the medium of courts of justice, whose duty it must be to declare all acts contrary to the manifest tenor of the Constitution void. Without this, all the reservations of particular rights or privileges would amount to nothing.

Some perplexity respecting the rights of the courts to pronounce legislative acts void, because contrary to the Constitution, has arisen from an imagination that the doctrine would imply a superiority of the judiciary to the legislative power. It is urged that the authority which can declare the acts of another void, must necessarily be superior to the one whose acts may be declared void. As this doctrine is of great importance in all the American constitutions, a brief discussion of the ground on which it rests cannot be unacceptable.

There is no position which depends on clearer principles, than that every act of a delegated authority, contrary to the tenor of the commission under which it is exercised, is void. No legislative act, therefore, contrary to the Constitution, can be valid. To deny this, would be to affirm, that the deputy is greater than his principal; that the servant is above his master; that the representatives of the people are superior to the people themselves; that men acting by virtue of powers, may do not only what their powers do not authorize, but what they forbid.

If it be said that the legislative body are themselves the constitutional judges of their own powers, and that the construction they put upon them is conclusive upon the other departments, it may be answered, that this cannot be the natural presumption, where it is not to be collected from any particular provisions in the Constitution. It is not otherwise to be supposed, that the Constitution could intend to enable the representatives of the people to substitute their WILL to that of their constituents. It is far more rational to suppose, that the courts were designed to be an intermediate body between the people and the legislature, in order, among other things, to keep the latter within the limits assigned to their authority. The interpretation of the laws is the proper and peculiar province of the courts. A constitution is, in fact, and must be regarded by the judges, as a fundamental law. It therefore belongs to them to ascertain its meaning, as well as the meaning of any particular act proceeding from the legislative body. If there should happen to be an irreconcilable variance between the two, that which has the superior obligation and validity ought, of course, to be preferred; or, in other words, the Constitution ought to be preferred to the statute, the intention of the people to the intention of their agents.

Nor does this conclusion by any means suppose a superiority of the judicial to the legislative power. It only supposes that the power of the people is superior to both; and that where the will of the legislature, declared in its statutes, stands in opposition to that of the people, declared in the Constitution, the judges ought to be governed by the latter rather than the former. They ought to regulate their decisions by the fundamental laws, rather than by those which are not fundamental.

This exercise of judicial discretion, in determining between two contradictory laws, is exemplified in a familiar instance. It not uncommonly happens, that there are two statutes existing at one time, clashing in whole or in part with each other, and neither of them containing any repealing clause or expression. In such a case, it is the province of the courts to liquidate and fix their meaning and operation. So far as they can, by any fair construction, be reconciled to each other, reason and law conspire to dictate that this should be done; where this is impracticable, it becomes a matter of necessity to give effect to one, in exclusion of the other. The rule which has obtained in the courts for determining their relative validity is, that the last in order of time shall be preferred to the first. But this is a mere rule of construction, not derived from any positive law, but from the nature and reason of the thing. It is a rule not enjoined upon the courts by legislative provision, but adopted by themselves, as consonant to truth and propriety, for the direction of their conduct as interpreters of the law. They thought it reasonable, that between the interfering acts of an EQUAL authority, that which was the last indication of its will should have the preference.

But in regard to the interfering acts of a superior and subordinate authority, of an original and derivative power, the nature and reason of the thing indicate the converse of that rule as proper to be followed. They teach us that the prior act of a superior ought to be preferred to the subsequent act of an inferior and subordinate authority; and that accordingly, whenever a particular statute contravenes the Constitution, it will be the duty of the judicial tribunals to adhere to the latter and disregard the former.

It can be of no weight to say that the courts, on the pretense of a repugnancy, may substitute their own pleasure to the constitutional intentions of the legislature. This might as well happen in the case of two contradictory statutes; or it might as well happen in every adjudication upon any single statute. The courts must declare the sense of the law; and if they should be disposed to exercise WILL instead of JUDGMENT, the consequence would equally be the substitution of their pleasure to that of the legislative body. The observation, if it prove any thing, would prove that there ought to be no judges distinct from that body.

If, then, the courts of justice are to be considered as the bulwarks of a limited Constitution against legislative encroachments, this consideration will afford a strong argument for the permanent tenure of judicial offices, since nothing will contribute so much as this to that independent spirit in the judges which must be essential to the faithful performance of so arduous a duty. . . .

To avoid an arbitrary discretion in the courts, it is indispensable that they should be bound down by strict rules and precedents, which serve to define and point out their duty in every particular case that comes before them; and it will readily be conceived from the variety of controversies which grow out of the folly and wickedness of mankind, that the records of those precedents must unavoidably swell to a very considerable bulk, and must demand long and laborious study to acquire a competent knowledge of them. Hence it is, that there can be but few men in the society who will have sufficient skill in the laws to qualify them for the stations of judges. And making the proper deductions for the ordinary depravity of human nature, the number must be still smaller of those who unite the requisite integrity with the requisite knowledge. These considerations apprise us, that the government can have no great option between fit character; and that a temporary duration in office, which would naturally discourage such characters from quitting a lucrative line of practice to accept a seat on the bench, would have a tendency to throw the administration of justice into hands less able, and less well qualified, to conduct it with utility and dignity. . . .

Upon the whole, there can be no room to doubt that the convention acted wisely in copying from the models of those constitutions which have established GOOD BEHAVIOR as the tenure of their judicial offices, in point of duration. . . .

PUBLIUS.

In the preceding passage, Alexander Hamilton argued that judicial review was a necessary check on congressional power under the Constitution. In so arguing, Hamilton rejected the idea that judicial review would make the judiciary superior to Congress. The following excerpt argues that such judicial review is inappropriate in a system of representative government. The author of this paper, "Brutus," is presumed to have been Robert Yates, a New York judge, delegate to the Federal Convention, and Anti-Federalist. As you read this passage, consider the alternative check upon congressional power that Brutus defends.

THE ANTI-FEDERALIST NOS. 78-79

"The Power of the Judiciary"

[T]he supreme court under this constitution would be exalted above all other power in the government, and subject to no controul. . . . I question whether the world ever saw, in any period of it, a court of justice invested with such immense powers, and yet placed in a situation so little responsible. . . .

The judges in England, it is true, hold their offices during their good behaviour, but then their determinations are subject to correction by the house of lords; and their power is by no means so extensive as that of the proposed supreme court of the union. — I believe they in no instance assume the authority to set aside an act of parliament under the idea that it is inconsistent with their constitution. They consider themselves bound to decide according to the existing laws of the land, and never undertake to controul them by adjudging that they are inconsistent with the constitution—much less are they vested with the power of giving an *equitable* construction to the constitution.

The judges in England are under the controul of the legislature, for they are bound to determine according to the laws passed by them. But the judges under this constitution will controul the legislature, for the supreme court are authorised in the last resort, to determine what is the extent of the powers of the Congress; they are to give the constitution an explanation, and there is no power above them to set aside their judgment. The framers of this constitution appear to have followed that of the British, in rendering the judges independent, by granting them their offices during good behaviour, without following the constitution of England, in instituting a tribunal in which their errors may be corrected; and without adverting to this, that the judicial under this system have a power which is above the legislative, and which indeed transcends any power before given to a judicial by any free government under heaven.

I do not object to the judges holding their commissions during good behaviour. I suppose it a proper provision provided they were made properly responsible. But I say, this system has followed the English government in this, while it has departed from almost every other principle of their jurisprudence, under the idea, of rendering the judges independent; which, in the British constitution, means no more than that they hold their places during good behaviour, and have fixed salaries . . . [the Constitution's drafters] have made the judges *independent*, in the fullest sense of the word. There is no power above them, to controul any of their decisions. There is no authority that can remove them, and they cannot be controuled by the laws of the legislature. In short, they are independent of the people, of the legislature, and of every power under heaven. Men placed in this situation will generally soon feel themselves independent of heaven itself. . . .

1st. There is no power above them that can correct their errors or controul their decisions.—The adjudications of this court are final and irreversible, for there is no court above them to which appeals can lie, either in error or on the merits. In this respect it differs from the courts in England, for there the house of lords is the highest court, to whom appeals, in error, are carried from the highest of the courts of law.

2d. They cannot be removed from office or suffer a diminution of their salaries, for any error in judgment or want of capacity.

It is expressly declared by the constitution,—"That they shall at stated times receive a compensation for their services which shall not be diminished during their continuance in office."

The only clause in the constitution which provides for the removal of the judges from office, is that which declares, that "the president, vice-president, and all civil officers of the United States, shall be removed from office, on impeachment for, and conviction of treason, bribery, or other high crimes and misdemeanors." By this paragraph, civil officers, in which the judges are included, are removable only for crimes. Treason and bribery are named, and the rest are included under the general terms of high crimes and misdemeanors.—Errors in judgment, or want of capacity to discharge the duties of the office, can never be supposed to be included in these words, *high crimes and misdemeanors.* A man may mistake a case in giving judgment, or manifest that he is incompetent to the discharge of the duties of a judge, and yet give no evidence of corruption or want of integrity. To support the charge, it will be necessary to give in evidence some facts that will shew, that the judges committed the error from wicked and corrupt motives.

3d. The power of this court is in many cases superior to that of the legislature. . . . [T]his court will be authorised to decide upon the meaning of the constitution, and that, not only according to the natural and ob[vious] meaning of the words, but also according to the spirit and intention of it. In the exercise of this power they will not be subordinate to, but above the legislature. For all the departments of this government will receive their powers, so far as they are expressed in the constitution, from the people immediately, who are the source of power. The legislature can only exercise such powers as are given them by the constitution, they cannot assume any of the rights annexed to the judicial, for this plain reason, that the same authority which vested the legislature with their powers, vested the judicial with theirs. — Both are derived from the same source, both therefore are equally valid, and the judicial hold their powers independently of the legislature, as the legislature do of the judicial. — The supreme court then have a right, independent of the legislature, to give a construction to the constitution and every part of it, and there is no power provided in this system to correct their construction or do it away. If, therefore, the legislature pass any laws, inconsistent with the sense the judges put upon the constitution, they will declare it void; and therefore in this respect their power is superior to that of the legislature. In England the judges are not only subject to have their decisions set aside by the house of lords, for error, but in cases where they give an explanation to the laws or constitution of the country contrary to the sense of the parliament, though the parliament will not set aside the judgment of the court, yet, they have authority, by a new law, to explain the former one, and by this means to prevent a reception of such decisions. But no such power is in the legislature. The judges are supreme — and no law, explanatory of the constitution, will be binding on them. . . .

When great and extraordinary powers are vested in any man, or body of men, which in their exercise, may operate to the oppression of the people, it is of high importance that powerful checks should be formed to prevent the abuse of it.

Perhaps no restraints are more forcible, than such as arise from responsibility to some superior power. — Hence it is that the true policy of a republican government is, to frame it in such manner, that all persons who are concerned in the government, are made accountable to some superior for their conduct in office. — This responsibility should ultimately rest with the People. To have a government well administered in all its parts, it is requisite the different departments of it should be separated and lodged as much as may be in different hands. The legislative power should be in one body, the executive in another, and the judicial in one different from either. — But still each of these bodies should be accountable for their conduct. Hence it is impracticable, perhaps, to maintain a perfect distinction between these several departments. — For it is difficult, if not impossible, to call to account the several officers in government, without in some degree mixing the legislative and judicial. The legislature in a free republic are chosen by the people at stated periods, and their responsibility consists, in their being amenable to the people. When the term, for which they are chosen, shall expire, who will then have opportunity to displace them if they disapprove of their conduct—but it would be improper that the judicial should be elective, because their business requires that they should possess a degree of law knowledge, which is acquired only by a regular education, and besides it is fit that they should be placed, in a certain degree in an independent situation, that they may maintain firmness and steadiness in their decisions. As the people therefore ought not to elect the judges, they cannot be amenable to them immediately, some other mode of amenability must therefore be devised for these, as well as for all other officers which do not spring from the immediate choice of the people: this is to be effected by making one court subordinate to another, and by giving them cognizance of the behaviour of all officers, but on this plan we at last arrive at some supreme, over whom there is no power to controul but the people themselves. This supreme controling power should be in the choice of the people, or else you establish an authority independent, and not amenable at all, which is repugnant to the principles of a free government. Agreeable to these principles I suppose the supreme judicial ought to be liable to be called to account, for any misconduct, by some body of men, who depend upon the people for their places; and so also should all other great officers in the State, who are not made amenable to some superior officers. . . .

Brutus.

POINTS FOR DISCUSSION

1. These readings suggest mechanisms for maintaining or safeguarding the federal structure that the Constitution establishes. These mechanisms include the political process, judicial review, and executive enforcement of the law. What are the benefits and detriments of each of these possible safeguards?

2. In these excerpts, "the people" figure prominently. Oliver Ellsworth, for instance, stated that "the measure which is opposed to the sense of the people will prove abortive." What are the various ways in which the people may act as a check on congressional authority relative to the states?

Hamilton ("Publius") and Yates ("Brutus") disputed whether judges should review whether federal legislative acts are within the constitutional powers of Congress. Yates rejected judicial review on the ground that governing "responsibility should ultimately rest with the People." Hamilton embraced judicial review on the ground that it can serve to vindicate "the power of the people." How does each of these writers define *the people*? Given how each defines *the people*, which institution is the proper agent of the people's authority in this context—Congress or the courts?

3. In his *Observations on Jefferson's Draft of a Constitution for Virginia*, Madison stated that judicial review "makes the Judiciary Dept paramount in fact to the Legislature, which was never intended, and can never be proper."

In *The Federalist No. 39* and *The Federalist No. 44*, however, Madison suggested that, in exercising their constitutional responsibilities, courts should police the boundaries of federal and state power. Are Madison's *Observations* consistent with his views in *The Federalist*? Assume that Madison was only addressing the Virginia Constitution in his *Observations*, whereas *The Federalist* addressed the U.S. Constitution: On what ground might Madison have believed that judicial review was inappropriate under the Virginia Constitution, but appropriate under the U.S. Constitution?

2. THE RESPONSIBILITY OF STATES

The 1790s were a politically tumultuous decade in the United States. Two parties emerged, Federalists and the Republicans. Federalist Congresses, with George Washington and then John Adams as President, enacted various measures to strengthen the federal government, such as creating a Bank of the United States. These measures engendered intense political opposition. Opponents challenged Congress's constitutional power to enact them. They contended that the constitutional powers of Congress should be strictly construed. In particular, they argued that the Necessary and Proper Clause — which empowers Congress "[t]o make all Laws which shall be necessary and proper for carrying into Execution" Congress's enumerated powers — requires a strict necessity. They claimed that establishing a national bank was not strictly necessary to carry into execution Congress's enumerated powers. Proponents of these measures, on the other hand, argued that congressional powers should be broadly construed. Alexander Hamilton, for instance, argued in 1791 in his *Opinion on the Constitutionality of the Bank* that:

> [the] criterion of what is constitutional, and of what is not so . . . is the end, to which the measure relates as a mean. If the end be clearly comprehended within any of the specified powers, and if the measure have an obvious relation to that end, and is not forbidden by any particular provision of the constitution — it may safely be deemed to come within the compass of the national authority. There is also this further criterion which may materially assist the decision: Does the proposed measure abridge a pre-existing right of any State, or of any individual? If it does not, there is a strong presumption in favour of its constitutionality; and slighter relations to any declared object of the constitution may be permitted to turn the scale.

Alexander Hamilton, Opinion on the Constitutionality of the Bank (Feb. 23, 1791), in 3 THE FOUNDERS' CONSTITUTION 250 (Philip B. Kurland and Ralph Lerner eds., 1987). In other words, Hamilton claimed that congressionally chosen means to serve the enumerated ends of congressional power were entitled to a strong presumption of constitutionality. He did not believe that Congress's powers should be strictly construed. Amid intense political conflicts, Republican-sympathizing newspapers launched vehement attacks against Federalists.

U.S. foreign policy, including its attitude toward France, also generated political conflict at this time. In the 1790s, the United States pursued a strict policy of neutrality in foreign wars, including the war between England and France. Involvement in foreign wars threatened the existence of the still fragile Union. Although Republicans did not necessarily disagree with neutrality, many expressed sympathy for the ideals of the French Revolution. As Thomas Jefferson expressed to James Madison, "I fear that a fair neutrality [in the conflict between England and France] will prove a disagreeable pill to our friends, tho' necessary to keep out of the calamities of war." Letter from Thomas Jefferson to James Madison, Apr. 28, 1793, reprinted in VI The Writings of Thomas Jefferson 232 (Paul L. Ford ed. 1892-1899).

In 1798, the Federalist Congress enacted the so-called Alien and Sedition Acts. The Federalists, believing war with France was imminent, feared that French citizens and other immigrants in the United States might serve as agents for enemy nations. Federalists countered this perceived threat, in part, by enacting the Alien Friends Act of 1798. This act authorized the President to expel, without a hearing or statement of reasons, any alien whom the President believed to be "dangerous to the peace and safety of the United States." Act of June 25, 1798, ch. 58, 1 Stat. 570. Moreover, in response to attacks in the press, Federalists enacted the Sedition Act of 1798. The First Amendment of the Bill of Rights protected freedom of the press: "Congress shall make no law . . . abridging the freedom of . . . the press. . . ." U.S. Const. amend. 1. Under English common law, however, which many believed the Constitution's freedom of press incorporated, the government could prosecute a publisher for seditious libel for bringing public officials into disrepute. The Sedition Act made it a crime to

> write, print, utter or publish . . . any false, scandalous, and malicious writing or writings against the Government of the United States, or either House of the Congress of the United States, with intent to defame the said government, or either house of the said Congress, or the President, or to bring them . . . into contempt or disrepute, or to excite against them, or either or any of them, the hatred of the good people of the United States.

Act of July 14, 1798, ch. 74, 1 Stat. 596. Some argued that the Sedition Act allowed more speech than common law seditious libel did, for the Act provided that truth was a defense to seditious libel, whereas English common law did not recognize that defense. The Alien Act was set to expire two years after its enactment, and the Sedition Act was set to expire on March 3, 1801, the last day of the Adams administration.

Republicans intensely opposed these measures. In response to them, the Kentucky Legislature and the Virginia Assembly passed resolutions known as the Kentucky and Virginia Resolutions, respectively. These Resolutions argued that the Constitution did not give the federal government unlimited power; rather, it established a compact by which specific powers were delegated to the federal government and the remainder reserved to the states. The Kentucky Resolutions of 1798, attributed to Jefferson, asserted that a state had a right of nullification — the right to judge whether the federal government had exceeded its authority under the Constitution. The Virginia Resolutions, attributed to Madison, asserted that states had the right to maintain their authority against clear congressional overreaching. The Virginia Resolutions appealed to other states to cooperate to protect state authority against federal intrusion. In 1799, the Kentucky Legislature passed additional resolutions. Taken together, these Resolutions argued that the constitutional powers of Congress should be strictly construed and that states had some role to play in checking overexertions of congressional power.

No other state legislature concurred in either the Virginia or Kentucky Resolutions. Nonetheless, various questions "have made the Resolutions a continued object of interest. One concerns the extensive use to which the Resolutions, as text and example, were put by states-rights spokesman in the South throughout the entire anti-bellum era, long after the specific occasion for them had ceased to be an issue." STANLEY ELKINS & ERIC MCKITRICK, THE AGE OF FEDERALISM: THE EARLY AMERICAN REPUBLIC, 1788-1800, 719 (1993). Indeed, the "principles of '98" became a "rallying cry" of advocates of the nullification movement and "would be a bible of state-rights particularism down to the Civil War, with Jefferson as its prophet." *Id.* at 721. Another question of interest has been "how the Resolutions are to be read as statements of constitutional doctrine, and how compatible they are with the idea of a federal national state." *Id.* at 719.

As you read these materials, consider the following questions:

- How do the Resolutions envision a state or states providing a check on federal power?
- How do the Resolutions differ from each other?
- How do the Resolutions relate to the idea that the people hold ultimate sovereignty?

VIRGINIA RESOLUTIONS OF 1798

Resolved, That the General Assembly of Virginia doth unequivocally express a firm resolution to maintain and defend the Constitution of the United States, and the Constitution of this state, against every aggression, either foreign or domestic; and that they will support the government of the United States in all measures warranted by the former.

That this Assembly most solemnly declares a warm attachment to the union of the states, to maintain which it pledges its powers; and that, for this end, it is their duty to watch over and oppose every infraction of those principles which constitute the only basis of that union, because a faithful observance of them can alone secure its existence and the public happiness.

That this Assembly doth explicitly and peremptorily declare, that it views the powers of the federal government as resulting from the compact to which the states are parties, as limited by the plain sense and intention of the instrument constituting that compact, as no further valid than they are authorized by the grants enumerated in that compact; and that, in case of a deliberate, palpable, and dangerous exercise of other powers, not granted by the said compact, the states, who are parties thereto, have the right, and are in duty bound, to interpose, for arresting the progress of the evil, and for maintaining, within their respective limits, the authorities, rights and liberties, appertaining to them.

That the General Assembly doth also express its deep regret, that a spirit has, in sundry instances, been manifested by the federal government to enlarge it powers by forced constructions of the constitutional charter which defines them; and that indications have appeared of a design to expound certain general phrases (which, having been copied from the very limited grant of powers in the former Articles of Confederation, were the less liable to be misconstrued) so as to destroy the meaning and effect of the particular enumeration which necessarily explains and limits the general phrases, and so as to consolidate the states, by degrees, into one sovereignty, the obvious tendency and inevitable result of which would be, to transform the present republican system of the United States into an absolute, or, at best, a mixed monarchy.

That the General Assembly doth particularly PROTEST *against the palpable and alarming infractions of the Constitution, in the two late cases of the "Alien and Sedition Acts," passed at the last session of Congress; the first of which exercises a power nowhere delegated to the federal government, and which, by uniting legislative and judicial powers to those of executive, subverts the general principles of free government, as well as the particular organization and positive provisions of the Federal Constitution; and the other of which acts exercises, in like manner, a power not delegated by the Constitution, but, on the contrary, expressly and positively forbidden by one of the amendments thereto, — a power which, more than any other, ought to produce universal alarm, because it is levelled against the right of freely examining public characters and measures, and of free communication among the people thereon, which has ever been justly deemed the only effectual guardian of every other right.*

That this state having, by its Convention, which ratified the Federal Constitution, expressly declared that, among other essential rights, "the liberty of conscience and the press cannot be cancelled, abridged, restrained, or modified, by any authority of the United States," and from its extreme anxiety to guard these rights from every possible attack of sophistry and ambition, having, with other states, recommended an amendment for that purpose, which amendment was, in due time, annexed to the Constitution, — it would mark a reproachful inconsistency, and criminal degeneracy, if an indifference were now shown to the most palpable violation of one of the rights thus declared and secured, and to the establishment of a precedent which may be fatal to the other.

That the good people of this commonwealth, having ever felt, and continuing to feel, the most sincere affection for their brethren of the other states; the truest anxiety for establishing and perpetuating the union of all; and the most scrupulous fidelity to that Constitution, which is the pledge of mutual friendship, and the instrument of mutual happiness, — the General Assembly doth solemnly appeal to the like dispositions in the other states, in confidence that they will concur with this commonwealth in declaring, as it does hereby declare, that the acts aforesaid are unconstitutional; and that the necessary and proper measures will be taken *by each* for coöperating with this state, in maintaining unimpaired the authorities, rights, and liberties, reserved to the states respectively, or to the people.

That the governor be desired to transmit a copy of the foregoing resolutions to the executive authority of each of the other states, with a request that the same may be communicated to the legislature thereof; and that a copy be furnished to each of the senators and representatives representing this state in the Congress of the United States.

KENTUCKY RESOLUTIONS OF 1798

1. *Resolved*, That the several states composing the United States of America are not united on the principle of unlimited submission to their general government; but that, by compact, under the style and title of a Constitution for the United States, and of amendments thereto, they constituted a general government for special purposes, delegated to that government certain definite powers, reserving, each state to itself, the residuary mass of right to their own self-government; and that whensoever the general government assumes undelegated powers, its acts are unauthoritative, void, and of no force; that to this compact each state acceded as a state, and is an integral party; that this government, created by this compact, was not made the exclusive or final judge of the extent of the powers delegated to itself, since that would have made its discretion, and not the Constitution, the measure of its powers; but that, as in all other cases of compact among parties having no common judge, *each party has an equal right to judge for itself, as well of infractions as of the mode and measure of redress.*

2. *Resolved*, That the Constitution of the United States having delegated to Congress a power to punish treason, counterfeiting the securities and current coin of the United States, piracies and felonies committed on the high seas, and offences against the laws of nations, and no other crimes whatever; and it being true, as a general principle, and one of the amendments to the Constitution having also declared "that the powers not delegated to the United States by the Constitution, nor prohibited by it to the states, are reserved to the states respectively, or to the people," — therefore . . . all [acts of Congress] . . . which assume to create, define, or punish crimes other than those enumerated in the Constitution, . . . are altogether void, and of no force; and that the power to create, define, and punish, such other crimes is reserved, and of right appertains, solely and exclusively, to the respective states, each within its own territory.

3. *Resolved*, That it is true, as a general principle, and is also expressly declared by one of the amendments to the Constitution, that "the powers not delegated to the United States by the Constitution, nor prohibited by it to the states, are reserved to the states respectively, or to the people;" and that, no power over the freedom of religion, freedom of speech, or freedom of the press, being delegated to the United States by the Constitution, nor prohibited by it to the states, all lawful powers respecting the same did of right remain, and were reserved to the states, or to the people; that thus was manifested their determination to retain to themselves the right of judging how far the licentiousness of speech, and of the press, may be abridged without lessening their useful freedom, and how far those abuses which cannot be separated from their

use, should be tolerated rather than the use be destroyed; and thus also they guarded against all abridgment, by the United States, of the freedom of religious principles and exercises, and retained to themselves the right of protecting the same, as this, stated by a law passed on the general demand of its citizens, had already protected them from all human restraint or interference; and that, in addition to this general principle and express declaration, another and more special provision has been made by one of the amendments to the Constitution, which expressly declares, that "Congress shall make no laws respecting an establishment of religion, or prohibiting the free exercise thereof, or abridging the freedom of speech, or of the press," thereby guarding, in the same sentence, and under the same words, the freedom of religion, of speech, and of the press, insomuch that whatever violates either throws down the sanctuary which covers the others, — and that libels, falsehood, and defamation, equally with heresy and false religion, are withheld from the cognizance of federal tribunals. That therefore the [Sedition Act,] which does abridge the freedom of the press, is not law, but is altogether void, and of no force.

4. *Resolved*, That alien friends are under the jurisdiction and protection of the laws of the state wherein they are; that no power over them has been delegated to the United States, nor prohibited to the individual states, distinct from their power over citizens; and it being true, as a general principle, and one of the amendments to the Constitution having also declared, that "the powers not delegated to the United States by the Constitution, nor prohibited to the states, are reserved to the states, respectively, or to the people," the [Alien Friend Act,] which assumes power over alien friends not delegated by the Constitution, is not law, but is altogether void and of no force.

5. *Resolved*, That, in addition to the general principle, as well as the express declaration, that powers not delegated are reserved, another and more special provision inserted in the Constitution from abundant caution, has declared, "that the migration or importation of such persons as any of the states now existing shall think proper to admit, shall not be prohibited by the Congress prior to the year 1808." That this commonwealth does admit the migration of alien friends described as the subject of the said act concerning aliens; that a provision against prohibiting their migration is a provision against all acts equivalent thereto, or it would be nugatory; that to remove them, when migrated, is equivalent to a prohibition of their migration, and is, therefore, contrary to the said provision of the Constitution, and *void*.

6. *Resolved*, That the imprisonment of a person under the protection of the laws of this commonwealth, on his failure to obey the simple order of the President to depart out of the United States, as is undertaken by [the Alien Friends Act], one amendment in which has provided, that "no person shall be deprived of liberty without due process of law;" and that another having provided, "that, in all criminal prosecutions, the accused shall enjoy the right of a public trial by an impartial jury, to be informed as to the nature and cause of the accusation, to be confronted with the witnesses against him, to have compulsory process for obtaining witnesses in his favor, and to have assistance of counsel for his defence," the same act undertaking to authorize the President to remove a person out of the United States who is under the protection of the law, on his own suspicion, without jury, without public trial, without

confrontation of the witnesses against him, without having witnesses in his favor, without defence, without counsel — contrary to these provisions also of the Constitution — is therefore not law, but utterly void, and of no force.

That transferring the power of judging any person who is under the protection of the laws, from the courts to the President of the United States, as is undertaken by the same act concerning aliens, is against the article of the Constitution which provides, that "the judicial power of the United States shall be vested in the courts, the judges of which shall hold their office during good behavior," and that the said act is void for that reason also; and it is further to be noted that this transfer of judiciary power is to that magistrate of the general government who already possesses all the executive, and a qualified negative in all the legislative powers.

7. *Resolved*, That the construction applied by the general government (as is evident by sundry of their proceedings) to those parts of the Constitution of the United States which delegate to Congress power to lay and collect taxes, duties, imposts, excises; to pay the debts, and provide for the common defence and general welfare, of the United States, and to make all laws which shall be necessary and proper for carrying into execution the powers vested by the Constitution in the government of the United States, or any department thereof, goes to the destruction of all the limits prescribed to their power by the Constitution; that words meant by that instrument to be subsidiary only to the execution of the limited powers, ought not to be so construed as themselves to give unlimited powers, nor a part so to be taken as to destroy the whole residue of the instrument; that the proceedings of the general government, under color of those articles, will be a fit and necessary subject for revisal and correction at a time of greater tranquillity, while those specified in the preceding resolutions call for immediate redress.

8. *Resolved*, That the preceding resolutions be transmitted to the senators and representatives in Congress from this commonwealth, who are enjoined to present the same to their respective houses, and to use their best endeavors to procure, at the next session of Congress, a repeal of the aforesaid unconstitutional and obnoxious acts.

9. *Resolved*, lastly, That the governor of this commonwealth be, and is, authorized and requested to communicate the preceding resolutions to the legislatures of the several states, to assure them that this commonwealth considers union for special national purposes, and particularly for those specified in their late federal compact, to be friendly to the peace, happiness, and prosperity, of all the states; that, faithful to that compact, according to the plain intent and meaning in which it was understood and acceded to by the several parties, it is sincerely anxious for its preservation; that it does also believe, that, to take from the states all the powers of self-government, and transfer them to a general and consolidated government, without regard to the special government, and reservations solemnly agreed to in that compact, is not for the peace, happiness, or prosperity of these states; and that, therefore, this commonwealth is determined, as it doubts not its co-states are, to submit to undelegated and consequently unlimited powers in no man, or body of men, on earth; that, if the acts before specified should stand, these conclusions would flow from them — that the general government may place any act they think

proper on the list of crimes, and punish it themselves, whether enumerated or not enumerated by the Constitution as cognizable by them; that they may transfer its cognizance to the President, or any other person, who may himself be the accuser, counsel, judge, and jury, whose suspicions may be the evidence, his order the sentence, his officer the executioner, and his breast the sole record of the transaction; that a very numerous and valuable description of the inhabitants of these states, being, by this precedent, reduced, as outlaws, to absolute dominion of one man, and the barriers of the Constitution thus swept from us all, no rampart now remains against the passions and the power of a majority of Congress, to protect from a like exportation, or other grievous punishment, the minority of the same body, the legislatures, judges, governors, and counsellors of the states, nor their other peaceable inhabitants, who may venture to reclaim the constitutional rights and liberties of the states and people, or who, for other causes, good or bad, may be obnoxious to the view, or marked by the suspicions, of the President, or be thought dangerous to his or their elections, or other interests, public or personal; that the friendless alien has been selected as the safest subject of a first experiment; but the citizen will soon follow, or rather has already followed; for already has a Sedition Act marked him as a prey: That these and successive acts of the same character, unless arrested on the threshold, may tend to drive these states into revolution and blood, and will furnish new calumnies against republican governments, and new pretexts for those who wish it to be believed that man cannot be governed but by a rod of iron; that it would be a dangerous delusion were a confidence in the men of our choice to silence our fears for the safety of our rights; that confidence is every where the parent of despotism; free government is founded in jealousy, and not in confidence; it is jealousy, and not confidence, which prescribes limited constitutions to bind down those whom we are obliged to trust with power; that our Constitution has accordingly fixed the limits to which, and no farther, our confidence may go; and let the honest advocate of confidence read the Alien and Sedition Acts, and say if the Constitution has not been wise in fixing limits to the government it created, and whether we should be wise in destroying those limits; let him say what the government is, if it be not a tyranny, which the men of our choice have conferred on the President, and the President of our choice has assented to and accepted, over the friendly strangers, to whom the mild spirit of our country and its laws had pledged hospitality and protection; that the men of our choice have more respected the bare suspicions of the President than the solid rights of innocence, the claims of justification, the sacred force of truth, and the forms and substance of law and justice.

In questions of power, then, let no more be said of confidence in man, but bind him down from mischief by the chains of the Constitution. That this commonwealth does therefore call on its co-states for an expression of their sentiments on the acts concerning aliens, and for the punishment of certain crimes herein before specified, plainly declaring whether these acts are or are not authorized by the federal compact. And it doubts not that their sense will be so announced as to prove their attachment to limited government, whether general or particular, and that the rights and liberties of their co-states will be exposed to no dangers by remaining embarked on a common bottom with their own; but they will concur with this commonwealth in considering the said acts as so palpably against the Constitution as to amount to an undisguised declaration, that the compact is not meant to be the measure of the powers of the general government, but that it will proceed in the exercise over these states of all powers whatsoever. That they will view this as seizing the rights of the states, and consolidating them in the hands of the general government, with a power assumed to bind the states, not merely in cases made federal, but in all cases whatsoever, by laws made, not with their consent, but by others against their consent; that this would be to surrender the form of government we have chosen, and live under one deriving its powers from its own will, and not from our authority; and that the co-states, recurring to their natural rights not made federal, will concur in declaring these void and of no force, and will each unite with this commonwealth in requesting their repeal at the next session of Congress.

KENTUCKY RESOLUTIONS OF **1799**

The representatives of the good people of this commonwealth, in General Assembly convened, having maturely considered the answers of sundry states in the Union to their resolutions, passed the last session, respecting certain unconstitutional laws of Congress, commonly called the Alien and Sedition Laws, would be faithless, indeed, to themselves, and to those they represent, were they silently to acquiesce in the principles and doctrines attempted to be maintained in all those answers, that of Virginia only excepted. To again enter the field of argument, and attempt more fully or forcibly to expose the unconstitutionality of those obnoxious laws, would, it is apprehended, be as unnecessary as unavailing. We cannot, however, but lament that, in the discussion of those interesting subjects by sundry of the legislatures of our sister states, unfounded suggestions and uncandid insinuations, derogatory to the true character and principles of this commonwealth, have been substituted in place of fair reasoning and sound argument. Our opinions of these alarming measures of the general government, together with our reasons for those opinions, were detailed with decency and with temper, and submitted to the discussion and judgment of our fellow-citizens throughout the Union. Whether the like decency and temper have been observed in the answers of most of those states who have denied, or attempted to obviate, the great truths contained in those resolutions, we have now only to submit to a candid world. Faithful to the true principles of the federal Union, unconscious of any designs to disturb the harmony of that Union, and anxious only to escape the fangs of despotism, the good people of this commonwealth are regardless of censure or calumniation. Lest, however, the silence of this commonwealth should be construed into an acquiescence in the doctrines and principles advanced, and attempted to be maintained, by the said answers; or at least those of our fellow-citizens, throughout the Union, who so widely differ from us on those important subjects, should be deluded by the expectation that we shall be deterred from what we conceive our duty, or shrink from the principles contained in those resolutions, — therefore,

Resolved, That this commonwealth considers the federal Union, upon the terms and for the purposes specified in the late compact, conducive to the liberty and happiness of the several states: That it does now unequivocally declare its attachment to the Union, and to that compact, agreeably to its obvious and real intention, and will be among the last to seek its dissolution: That, if those who administer the general government be permitted to transgress the limits fixed by that compact, by a total disregard to the special delegations of power therein contained, an annihilation of the state governments, and the creation, upon their ruins, of a general consolidated government, will be the inevitable consequence: That the principle and construction, contended for by sundry of the state legislatures, that the general government is the exclusive judge of the extent of the powers delegated to it, stop not short of *despotism* — since the discretion of those who administer the government, and not the *Constitution*, would be the measure of their powers: That the several states who formed that instrument, being sovereign and independent, have the unquestionable right to judge of the infraction; and, *That a nullification, by those sovereignties, of all unauthorized acts done under color of that instrument, is the rightful remedy*: That this commonwealth does, under the most deliberate reconsideration, declare, that the said Alien and Sedition Laws are, in their opinion, palpable violations of the said Constitution; and, however cheerfully it may be disposed to surrender its opinion to a majority of its sister states, in matters of ordinary or doubtful policy, yet, in momentous regulations like the present, which so vitally wound the best rights of the citizen, it would consider a silent acquiescence as highly criminal: That, although this commonwealth, as a party to the federal compact, will bow to the laws of the Union, yet it does, at the same time, declare, that it will not now, or ever hereafter, cease to oppose, in a constitutional manner, every attempt, at what quarter soever offered, to violate that compact: And finally, in order that no pretext or arguments may be drawn from a supposed acquiescence, on the part of this commonwealth, in the constitutionality of those laws, and be thereby used as precedents for similar future violations of the federal compact, this commonwealth does now enter against them its solemn PROTEST.

JAMES MADISON, REPORT ON THE VIRGINIA RESOLUTIONS (1800)

The resolution declares, *first*, that "it views the powers of the federal government as resulting from the compact to which the states are parties;" in other words, that the federal powers are derived from the Constitution; and that the Constitution is a compact to which the states are parties. . . .

[I]n all the contemporary discussions and comments which the Constitution underwent, it was constantly justified and recommended on the ground that the powers not given to the government were withheld from it; and that, if any doubt could have existed on this subject, under the original text of the Constitution, it is removed, as far as words could remove it, by the . . . amendment, now a part of the Constitution, which expressly declares, "that the powers not delegated to the United States by the Constitution, nor prohibited by it to the states, are reserved to the states respectively, or to the people."

The other position involved in this branch of the resolution, namely, "that the states are parties to the Constitution," or compact, is, in the judgment of the committee, equally free from objection. It is indeed true that the term "states" is sometimes used in a vague sense, and sometimes in different senses, according to the subject to which it is applied. Thus it sometimes means the separate sections of territory occupied by the political societies within each; sometimes the particular governments established by those societies; sometimes those societies as organized into those particular governments; and lastly, it means the people composing those political societies, in their highest sovereign capacity. Although it might be wished that the perfection of language admitted less diversity in the signification of the same words, yet little inconvenience is produced by it, where the true sense can be collected with certainty from the different applications. In the present instance, whatever different construction of the term "states," in the resolution, may have been entertained, all will at least concur in that last mentioned; because in that sense the Constitution was submitted to the "states;" in that sense the "states" ratified it; and in that sense of the term "states," they are consequently parties to the compact from which the powers of the federal government result.

The next position is, that the General Assembly views the powers of the federal government "as limited by the plain sense and intention of the instrument constituting that compact," and "as no further valid than they are authorized by the grants therein enumerated." It does not seem possible that any just objection can lie against either of these clauses. The first amounts merely to a declaration that the compact ought to have the interpretation plainly intended by the parties to it; the other, to a declaration that it ought to have the execution and effect intended by them. If the powers granted be valid, it is solely because they are granted; and if the granted powers are valid because granted, all other powers not granted must not be valid.

The resolution, having taken this view of the federal compact, proceeds to infer, "That, in case of a deliberate, palpable, and dangerous exercise of other powers, not granted by the said compact, the states, who are parties thereto, have the right, and are in duty bound, to interpose for arresting the progress of the evil, and for maintaining, within their respective limits, the authorities, rights, and liberties, appertaining to them."

It appears . . . to be a plain principle, founded in common sense, illustrated by common practice, and essential to the nature of compacts, that, where resort can be had to no tribunal superior to the authority of the parties, the parties themselves must be the rightful judges, in the last resort, whether the bargain made has been pursued or violated. The Constitution of the United States was formed by the sanction of the states, given by each in its sovereign capacity. It adds to the stability and dignity, as well as to the authority, of the Constitution, that it rests on this legitimate and solid foundation. The states, then, being the parties to the constitutional compact, and in their sovereign capacity, it follows of necessity that there can be no tribunal, above their authority, to decide, in the last resort, whether the compact made by them be violated; and consequently, that, as the parties to it, they must themselves decide, in the last resort, such questions as may be of sufficient magnitude to require their interposition.

It does not follow, however, because the states, as sovereign parties to their constitutional compact, must ultimately decide whether it has been violated, that such a decision ought to be interposed either in a hasty manner or on doubtful and inferior occasions. Even in the case of ordinary conventions between different nations, where, by the strict rule of interpretation, a breach of a part may be deemed a breach of the whole, — every part being deemed a condition of every other part, and of the whole, — it is always laid down that the breach must be both wilful and material, to justify an application of the rule. But in the case of an intimate and constitutional union, like that of the United States, it is evident that the interposition of the parties, in their sovereign capacity, can be called for by occasions only deeply and essentially affecting the vital principles of their political system.

The resolution has, accordingly guarded against any misapprehension of its object, by expressly requiring, for such an interposition, "the case of a deliberate, palpable, and dangerous breach of the Constitution, by the exercise of powers not granted by it." It must be a case not of a light and transient nature, but of a nature dangerous to the great purposes for which the Constitution was established. It must be a case, moreover, not obscure or doubtful in its construction, but plain and palpable. Lastly, it must be a case not resulting from a partial consideration or hasty determination, but a case stamped with a final consideration and deliberate adherence. It is not necessary, because the resolution does not require, that the question should be discussed, how far the exercise of any particular power, ungranted by the Constitution, would justify the interposition of the parties to it. As cases might easily be stated, which none would contend ought to fall within that description, — cases, on the other hand, might, with equal ease, be stated, so flagrant and so fatal as to unite every opinion in placing them within the description. . . .

From this view of the resolution, it would seem inconceivable that it can incur any just disapprobation from those who, laying aside all momentary impressions, and recollecting the genuine source and object of the Federal Constitution, shall candidly and accurately interpret the meaning of the General Assembly. If the deliberate exercise of dangerous powers, palpably withheld by the Constitution, could not justify the parties to it in interposing even so far as to arrest the progress of the evil, and thereby to preserve the Constitution itself, as well as to provide for the safety of the parties to it, there would be an end to all relief from usurped power, and a direct subversion of the rights specified or recognized under all the state constitutions, as well as a plain denial of the fundamental principle on which our independence itself was declared.

But it is objected, that the judicial authority is to be regarded as the sole expositor of the Constitution in the last resort; and it may be asked for what reason the declaration by the General Assembly, supposing it to be theoretically true, could be required at the present day, and in so solemn a manner.

On this objection it might be observed, first, that there may be instances of usurped power, which the forms of the Constitution would never draw within the control of the judicial department; secondly, that, if the decision of the judiciary be raised above the authority of the sovereign parties to the Constitution, the decisions of the other departments, not carried by the forms of the Constitution before the judiciary, must be equally authoritative and final with the decisions of that department. But the proper answer to the objection is, that the resolution of the General Assembly relates to those great and extraordinary cases, in which all the forms of the Constitution may prove ineffectual against infractions dangerous to the essential rights of the parties to it. The resolution supposes that dangerous powers, not delegated, may not only be usurped and executed by the other departments, but that the judicial department, also, may exercise or sanction dangerous powers beyond the grant of the Constitution; and, consequently, that the ultimate right of the parties to the Constitution, to judge whether the compact has been dangerously violated, must extend to violations by one delegated authority as well as by another — by the judiciary as well as by the executive, or the legislature.

However true, therefore, it may be, that the judicial department is, in all questions submitted to it by the forms of the Constitution, to decide in the last resort, this resort must necessarily be deemed the last in relation to the authorities of the other departments of the government; not in relation to the rights of the parties to the constitutional compact, from which the judicial, as well as the other departments, hold their delegated trusts. On any other hypothesis, the delegation of judicial power would annul the authority delegating it; and the concurrence of this department with the others in usurped powers, might subvert forever, and beyond the possible reach of any rightful remedy, the very Constitution which all were instituted to preserve. . . .

The authority of constitutions over governments, and of the sovereignty of the people over constitutions, are truths which are at all times necessary to be kept in mind; and at no time, perhaps, more necessary than at present. . . .

It cannot be forgotten that, among the arguments addressed to those who apprehended danger to liberty from the establishment of the general government over so great a country, the appeal was emphatically made to the intermediate existence of the state governments between the people and that government, to the vigilance with which they would descry the first symptoms of usurpation, and to the promptitude with which they would sound the alarm to the public. This argument was probably not without its effect; and if it was a proper one then to recommend the establishment of a constitution, it must be a proper one now to assist in its interpretation.

POINTS FOR DISCUSSION

1. How do the Virginia and Kentucky Resolutions differ from each other in describing a role for states in checking federal power?

2. Are the respective roles that these Resolutions envisioned for states in checking federal power consistent with Madison's proposition that ultimate authority resides in the people?

3. In his *Report*, Madison explained that, under the Virginia Resolutions, only in "the case of a deliberate, palpable, and dangerous breach of the

Constitution, by the exercise of powers not granted by it," would the states impose their authority to determine whether the Constitution had been violated. What would make a breach of the Constitution "deliberate, palpable, and dangerous"? On what grounds are the states more appropriately situated to make that determination than courts? On what grounds are courts more appropriately situated?

4. In later materials, you will see courts rely on various kinds of historical materials to resolve disputes over the relative power of the federal government and the states under the Constitution. In the last paragraph of Madison's *Report*, he asserted that an argument made during the Constitution's ratification process can be "a proper one now to assist in its interpretation." On what basis, in Madison's view, is it proper to consider ratification debates in interpreting the Constitution? Are there any limitations on the value of ratification debates as a guide to constitutional interpretation?

3. THE MARSHALL COURT AND JUDICIAL REVIEW

This section focuses on the early practice of judicial review as a safeguard of the federal structure. Judicial review as a safeguard of federalism may assume one of two forms. First, courts may review the lawfulness of *state* laws in light of federal prerogatives. At the Federal Convention, the delegates considered various mechanisms for ensuring the supremacy of federal prerogatives, including the use of force and a congressional negative on state laws. After rejecting other means, the delegates adopted judicial review as an enforcement mechanism. The Supremacy Clause (Article VI) and Arising Under Clause (Article III) provide this mechanism.

The Supremacy Clause provides:

> This Constitution, and the Laws of the United States which shall be made in Pursuance thereof; and all Treaties made, or which shall be made, under the Authority of the United States, shall be the supreme Law of the Land; and the Judges in every State shall be bound thereby, any Thing in the Constitution or Laws of any State to the contrary notwithstanding.

In other words, state courts must enforce validly enacted federal laws, notwithstanding state laws to the contrary.

The Arising Under Clause provides that "[t]he judicial power shall extend to all cases, in law and equity, arising under this Constitution, the laws of the United States, and treaties made, or which shall be made, under their authority. . . ." This Clause authorizes Congress to employ federal court jurisdiction as an additional means of ensuring the supremacy of validly enacted federal laws:

> At the Federal Convention, delegates apparently extended federal judicial power to cases "arising under" the Constitution, laws, and treaties of the United States as a means — more limited than other means, such as a congressional negative [on state laws, or the use of force] — of ensuring the supremacy of federal law. In ratification debates, those who attempted to give "arising under" jurisdiction any meaningful import described it to encompass cases involving the enforcement of a federal law or a dispute over the meaning of

a federal law. They argued that "arising under" jurisdiction was necessary to ensure the proper enforcement and uniformity of federal laws.

Anthony J. Bellia Jr., *The Origins of Article III "Arising Under" Jurisdiction*, 57 DUKE L. J. 263, 343 (2007). The Framers devised a *"judicial* review devise" to take the "place of federal *legislative* review of state laws for consistency with national law." James S. Liebman & William F. Ryan, *"Some Effectual Power": The Quantity and Quality of Decisionmaking Required of Article III Courts,"* 98 COLUM. L. REV. 696, 733 (1998).

In addition to judicial review of state laws, courts have reviewed whether *federal* laws comply with constitutional limits on federal power. In other words, courts have reviewed whether acts of Congress exceeded Congress's constitutionally authorized powers. In *Marbury v. Madison*, 5 U.S. (1 Cranch) 137 (1803), the Court engaged in such judicial review. The *Marbury* Court interpreted the Judiciary Act of 1789 to give the Supreme Court original jurisdiction to issue writs of mandamus. The Court held, however, that that this jurisdiction exceeded the bounds of the Court's original jurisdiction provided in Article III of the Constitution. Because Congress lacked power to give the Court jurisdiction that Article III did not provide, the Court declined to exercise jurisdiction over the writ of mandamus before it:

> [I]f a law be in opposition to the constitution; if both the law and the constitution apply to a particular case, so that the court must either decide that case conformably to the law, disregarding the constitution; or conformably to the constitution, disregarding the law; the court must determine which these conflicting rules governs the case. This is of the very essence of judicial duty.
>
> If then, the courts are to regard the constitution, and the constitution is superior to any ordinary act of the legislature, the constitution, and not such ordinary act, must govern the case to which they both apply.

Id. at 178.

Judges and scholars vigorously debate whether and how courts should determine if an act of Congress exceeds its enumerated constitutional powers or otherwise violates a reserved power of the states. You will consider this debate in detail in Chapter 4 and subsequent chapters. Some argue that the Constitution's primary check on congressional power relative to the states is the political process, which is structured to protect state interests and state regulatory autonomy. On this view, courts should play a limited role, if any, in reviewing federal legislation on federalism grounds. Others argue that the political process is an inadequate—or at least non-exclusive—check on congressional power and that judicial review is an important, if not essential, additional check.

If some form of judicial review of federal acts is appropriate, how broadly or narrowly should courts construe congressional power? Jefferson claimed in the Kentucky Resolutions of 1798 that the Constitution should be strictly construed against assertions of federal power. St. George Tucker, a lawyer and legal scholar who published a famous edition of *Blackstone's Commentaries* in 1803, echoed Jefferson's view, advocating a rule of "strict construction":

> The American revolution seems to have given birth to [a] new political phenomenon: in every state a written constitution was framed, and adopted by the

people, both in their individual and sovereign capacity, and character. By this means, the just distinction between the sovereignty, and the government, was rendered familiar to every intelligent mind; the former was found to reside in the people, and to be unalienable from them; the latter in their servants and agents: by this means, also, government was reduced to its elements; its object was defined, it's principles ascertained; its powers limited, and fixed; its structure organized; and the functions of every part of the machine so clearly designated, as to prevent any interference, so long as the limits of each were observed. The same reasons operated in behalf of similar restrictions in the federal constitution, whether considered as the act of the body politic of the several states, or, of the people of the states, respectively, or, of the people of the United States, collectively. Accordingly we find the structure of the government, its several powers and jurisdictions, and the concessions of the several states, generally, pretty accurately defined, and limited. But to guard against encroachments on the powers of the several states, in their politic character, and of the people, both in their individual and sovereign capacity, an amendatory article was added, immediately after the government was organized, declaring; that the powers not delegated to the United States, by the constitution; nor prohibited by it to the states, are reserved to the states, respectively, or to the people. And, still further, to guard the people against constructive usurpations and encroachments on their rights, another article declares; that the enumeration of certain rights in the constitution, shall not be construed to deny, or disparage, others retained by the people. The sum of all which appears to be, that the powers delegated to the federal government, are, in all cases, to receive the *most strict construction* that the instrument will bear, where the rights of a state or of the people, either collectively, or individually, may be drawn in question.

The advantages of a written constitution, considered as the original contract of society must immediately strike every reflecting mind; power, when undefined, soon becomes unlimited; and the disquisition of social rights where there is no text to resort to, for their explanation, is a task, equally above ordinary capacities, and incompatable with the ordinary pursuits, of the body of the people. . . . But where the sovereignty is, confessedly, vested in the people, government becomes a subordinate power, and is the mere creature of the people's will: it ought therefore to be so constructed, that its operations may be the subject of constant observation, and scrutiny.

1 ST. GEORGE TUCKER, BLACKSTONE'S COMMENTARIES app. note D, at 153-155 (reprint 1969) (Phila., William Young Birch & Abraham Small 1803) (emphasis added).

Several opinions of the Marshall Court stand in contrast to the rule of strict construction that Tucker advocated. As you read the opinions that follow, bear in mind that when John Marshall became Chief Justice in 1801, the United States was still a fledgling nation. The powers of Congress were unsettled and controversial. The possibility of war threatened the fragile existence of the Union. The authority of the Supreme Court—including to review state court judgments and to engage in judicial review—had yet to be accepted. The Marshall Court, over Republican objections, upheld contested assertions of national power, construing Congress's powers more broadly than Jefferson or Tucker would have allowed. In doing so, the Marshall Court laid the foundation for the United States to have a strong national government, as many Federalists envisioned.

Nonetheless, debates over how courts should construe the powers of Congress endure to the present day. Pay close attention to the methods of interpretation that the Marshall Court employed in upholding various federal powers in these cases. The Court continues to employ — and debate — such methods in resolving disputes over federal-state power.

As you read the cases in this section, consider the following questions:

- What role did the Marshall Court envision for the judiciary in checking state and federal power under the Constitution?
- How does the Marshall Court's manner of construing congressional power differ from the rule of strict construction that Tucker advocated?
- How much deference, if any, should the Court afford Congress in determining whether Congress has exceeded its constitutional powers?
- What specific modalities of interpretation does the Court employ in construing congressional power?

On February 25, 1791, Congress issued a charter for the First Bank of the United States, effective until 1811. The lawfulness of this charter was the subject of intense disagreement. A key question was how broadly or narrowly Congress should understand its powers under the Necessary and Proper Clause of Article I. That Clause provides that Congress has power "[t]o make all Laws which shall be necessary and proper for carrying into Execution the foregoing Powers, and all other Powers vested by this Constitution in the Government of the United States, or in any Department or Officer thereof." Alexander Hamilton and James Madison stood at the center of this debate. Hamilton, the first Secretary of the Treasury, had proposed the Bank as part of his overall financial plan for the United States. He believed that the Bank was necessary to establish the financial stability of and financial credit for the United States. He urged a broad understanding of the Necessary and Proper Clause. Madison, a member of the House of Representatives from Virginia, opposed the Bank in part because he believed its benefits would inure primarily to northern commercial interests. Madison argued that the Necessary and Proper Clause did not empower Congress to create the Bank.

Speaking to the House in early February 1791, after the Senate had passed the first bank bill, Madison reminded his fellow congressmen that the Federal Convention had not provided that Congress should have a power to charter such a corporation. Given the "limited and enumerated" nature of congressional powers, he contended, Congress could not act without an express or implied grant of authority. Madison argued that neither the power to tax nor "to borrow Money on the credit of the United States," U.S. CONST. art. 1, §8, empowered Congress to charter a Bank.

Madison then directed his attention to the Necessary and Proper Clause. In Madison's view, the Clause did nothing more than reinforce those powers elsewhere provided in the Constitution; it was "merely declaratory of what would have resulted by unavoidable implication." 2 ANNALS OF CONG. 1898 (1791) (statement of Rep. Madison). If the Clause were interpreted as an affirmative grant of additional powers, "[t]he essential characteristic of the government, as composed of limited and enumerated powers, would be destroyed." *Id.* He feared that Congress, under the cover of the Necessary and Proper Clause, might appropriate any of a number of powers rightfully belonging to the states by asserting some tenuous link to one of the powers it rightfully enjoyed. "If implications, thus remote and thus multiplied, can be linked together," he cautioned, "a chain may be formed that will reach every object of legislation, every object within the whole compass of political economy." *Id.* at 1899. (In the present day, courts might characterize this as a *structural* argument — showing how, if Congress's powers were understood in a particular way, a core aspect of the structure of government that the Constitution established would be undermined. Here, the argument is that if Congress has authority to charter the Bank, the limited nature of Congress's powers would be undermined because no meaningful limitation would exist on its authority.) Madison expressed concerns that the precedent of establishing the Bank would imperil specific state prerogatives. Just as Congress had found the Bank to "be conducive to the successful conducting of the national finances," Congress might find an exclusive, federal power to tax similarly convenient. *Id.* In short, Madison argued that interpreting the Constitution to support the Bank's charter would lead "to the subversion of every power whatever in the several States." *Id.* at 1958.

Notwithstanding Madison's opposition, the bill passed. Before signing it, President Washington sought the opinions of cabinet members on the bill's constitutionality. Secretary of State Thomas Jefferson and Attorney General Edmund Randolph believed, as had Madison, that the Bank was beyond Congress's powers. Hamilton, however, who had proposed the Bank, defended its constitutionality.

Hamilton believed the Bank to be "an expedient essential to our safety and success," Letter from Alexander Hamilton to Robert Morris, Apr. 30, 1781, reprinted in 3 THE WORKS OF ALEXANDER HAMILTON 360 (Henry Cabot Lodge ed., 1904), and understood the Necessary and Proper Clause to empower Congress to enact such measures. Hamilton relied on the "grammatical" and "popular" understandings of "necessary" in interpreting the provision. He argued that "necessary . . . often means no more than *needful, requisite, incidental, useful*, or *conducive to*." Alexander Hamilton, Opinion on the Constitutionality of the Bank (Feb. 23, 1791), reprinted in 3 THE FOUNDERS' CONSTITUTION 249 (Philip B. Kurland and Ralph Lerner eds., 1987). (In the present day, courts might characterize this as a *textual* argument — demonstrating the most reasonable meaning that, in context, a text conveys to the reader.) This reading of the Necessary and Proper Clause comported with Hamilton's position on the sovereign nature of governmental power. Hamilton claimed "that every power vested in a Government is in its nature *sovereign*, and includes by *force* of the *term*, a right to employ all the *means* requisite, and fairly *applicable* to the attainment of the *ends* of such power." *Id.* at 248. Accordingly, the Necessary and Proper Clause confirmed that Congress had any power that bore a "natural relation" to the fulfillment of an express power. *Id.* Hamilton feared that a more restrictive reading would render the enumerated powers of Congress ineffective.

Hamilton prevailed when, on February 25, 1791, President Washington signed into law the bill creating the First Bank of the United States. The Bank operated until 1811, when its original charter expired. Congress narrowly rejected the Bank's renewal. For the next four years, the United States operated without a national bank. In 1815, Congress revisited the issue, passing a bill to re-charter the Bank. Now-President James Madison vetoed the bill, not on constitutional grounds, but because he believed the legislation was not well-suited to serve its intended purpose:

> Waiving the question of the constitutional authority of the Legislature to establish an incorporated bank as being precluded in my judgment by repeated recognitions under varied circumstances of the validity of such an institution in acts of the legislative, executive, and judicial branches of the Government, accompanied by indications, in different modes, of a concurrence of the general will of the nation, the proposed bank does not appear to be calculated to answer the purposes of reviving the public credit, of providing a national medium of circulation, and of aiding the Treasury by facilitating the indispensable anticipations of the revenue and by affording to the public more durable loans.

James Madison, Veto Message (Jan. 30, 1815), reprinted in 8 THE WRITINGS OF JAMES MADISON 327 (Gaillard Hunt ed., 1908). (In the present day, courts might describe Madison's argument that, on the basis of past practice, the constitutionality of the Bank was a closed question as an argument of *historical practice*—identifying a course of action by public officials or institutions operating under the Constitution to demonstrate or establish constitutional meaning.)

In December 1815, Madison encouraged Congress to work toward establishing a second bank. Congress passed a bill establishing the Second Bank of the United States in January 1816, and Madison signed it into law. Although Madison considered history to have answered the constitutional questions that surrounded the Bank for 25 years, others challenged its constitutionality. The Supreme Court took up these challenges in 1819 in *McCullough v. Maryland*, 17 U.S. (4 Wheat.) 316 (1819).

McCULLOUGH v. MARYLAND

17 U.S. (4 Wheat.) 316 (1819)

[John James brought this action of debt, on behalf of himself and the State of Maryland, against James McCullough, cashier of the Baltimore branch of the Bank of the United States. He sought to recover penalties that a Maryland statute imposed on the Bank for failing pay taxes that Maryland had assessed against the Bank.]

MARSHALL, CH. J., delivered the opinion of the Court.

In the case now to be determined, the defendant, a sovereign state, denies the obligation of a law enacted by the legislature of the Union, and the plaintiff, on his part, contests the validity of an act which has been passed by the legislature of that state. The constitution of our country, in its most interesting and vital parts, is to be considered; the conflicting powers of the government of the Union and of its members, as marked in that constitution, are to be discussed; and an opinion given, which may essentially influence the great operations of the government. No tribunal can approach such a question without a deep sense of its importance, and of the awful responsibility involved in its decision. But it must be decided peacefully, or remain a source of hostile legislation, perhaps, of hostility of a still more serious nature; and if it is to be so decided, by this tribunal alone can the decision be made. On the supreme court of the United States has the constitution of our country devolved this important duty.

The first question made in the cause is — has congress power to incorporate a bank? It has been truly said, that this can scarcely be considered as an open question, entirely unprejudiced by the former proceedings of the nation respecting it. The principle now contested was introduced at a very early period of our history, has been recognised by many successive legislatures, and has been acted upon by the judicial department, in cases of peculiar delicacy, as a law of undoubted obligation.

It will not be denied, that a bold and daring usurpation might be resisted, after an acquiescence still longer and more complete than this. But it is conceived, that a doubtful question, one on which human reason may pause, and the human judgment be suspended, in the decision of which the great principles of liberty are not concerned, but the respective powers of those who are equally the representatives of the people, are to be adjusted; if not put at rest by the practice of the government, ought to receive a considerable impression from that practice. An exposition of the constitution, deliberately established by legislative acts, on the faith of which an immense property has been advanced, ought not to be lightly disregarded.

The power now contested was exercised by the first congress elected under the present constitution. The bill for incorporating the Bank of the United States did not steal upon an unsuspecting legislature, and pass unobserved. Its principle was completely understood, and was opposed with equal zeal and ability. After being resisted, first, in the fair and open field of debate, and afterwards, in the executive cabinet, with as much persevering talent as any measure has ever experienced, and being supported by arguments which convinced minds as pure and as intelligent as this country can boast, it became a law. The original act was permitted to expire; but a short experience of the embarrassments to which the refusal to revive it exposed the government, convinced those who were most prejudiced against the measure of its necessity, and induced the passage of the present law. It would require no ordinary share of intrepidity, to assert that a measure adopted under these circumstances, was a bold and plain usurpation, to which the constitution gave no countenance. These observations belong to the cause; but they are not made under the impression, that, were the question entirely new, the law would be found irreconcilable with the constitution.

In discussing this question, the counsel for the state of Maryland have deemed it of some importance, in the construction of the constitution, to consider that instrument, not as emanating from the people, but as the act of sovereign and independent states. The powers of the general government, it has been said, are delegated by the states, who alone are truly sovereign; and must be exercised in subordination to the states, who alone possess supreme dominion. It would be difficult to sustain this proposition. The convention which framed the constitution was indeed elected by the state legislatures. But the instrument, when it came from their hands, was a mere proposal, without obligation, or pretensions to it. It was reported to the then existing congress of the United States, with a request that it might "be submitted to a convention of delegates, chosen in each state by the people thereof, under the recommendation of its legislature, for their assent and ratification." This mode of proceeding was adopted; and by the convention, by congress, and by the state legislatures, the instrument was submitted to the *people*. They acted upon it in the only manner in which they can act safely, effectively and wisely, on such a subject, by assembling in convention. It is true, they assembled in their several states — and where else should they have assembled? No political dreamer was ever wild enough to think of breaking down the lines which separate the states, and of compounding the American people into one common mass. Of consequence, when they act, they act in their states. But the measures they adopt do not, on that account, cease to be the measures of the people themselves, or become the measures of the state governments.

From these conventions, the constitution derives its whole authority. The government proceeds directly from the people; is "ordained and established," in the name of the people; and is declared to be ordained, "in order to form a more perfect union, establish justice, insure domestic tranquillity, and secure the blessings of liberty to themselves and to their posterity." The assent of the states, in their sovereign capacity, is implied, in calling a convention, and thus submitting that instrument to the people. But the people were at perfect liberty to accept or reject it; and their act was final. It required not the affirmance, and could not be negatived, by the state governments. The constitution, when thus adopted, was of complete obligation, and bound the state sovereignties. . . .

The government of the Union, then (whatever may be the influence of this fact on the case), is, emphatically and truly, a government of the people. In form, and in substance, it emanates from them. Its powers are granted by them, and are to be exercised directly on them, and for their benefit.

This government is acknowledged by all, to be one of enumerated powers. The principle, that it can exercise only the powers granted to it . . . is now universally admitted. But the question respecting the extent of the powers actually granted, is perpetually arising, and will probably continue to arise, so long as our system shall exist. In discussing these questions, the conflicting powers of the general and state governments must be brought into view, and the supremacy of their respective laws, when they are in opposition, must be settled.

If any one proposition could command the universal assent of mankind, we might expect it would be this — that the government of the Union, though limited in its powers, is supreme within its sphere of action. This would seem to result, necessarily, from its nature. It is the government of all; its powers are delegated by all; it represents all, and acts for all. Though any one state may be willing to control its operations, no state is willing to allow others to control them. The nation, on those subjects on which it can act, must necessarily bind its component parts. But this question is not left to mere reason: the people have, in express terms, decided it, by saying, "this constitution, and the laws of the United States, which shall be made in pursuance thereof," "shall be the supreme law of the land," and by requiring that the members of the state legislatures, and the officers of the executive and judicial departments of the states, shall take the oath of fidelity to it. . . .

Among the enumerated powers, we do not find that of establishing a bank or creating a corporation. But there is no phrase in the instrument which, like the articles of confederation, excludes incidental or implied powers; and which requires that everything granted shall be expressly and minutely described. Even the 10th amendment, which was framed for the purpose of quieting the excessive jealousies which had been excited, omits the word "expressly," and declares only, that the powers "not delegated to the United States, nor prohibited to the states, are reserved to the states or to the people;" thus leaving the question, whether the particular power which may become the subject of contest, has been delegated to the one government, or prohibited to the other, to depend on a fair construction of the whole instrument. The men who drew and adopted this amendment had experienced the embarrassments resulting from the insertion of this word in the articles of confederation, and probably omitted it, to avoid those embarrassments. A constitution, to contain an accurate detail of all the subdivisions of which its great powers will admit, and of all the means by which they may be carried into execution, would partake of the prolixity of a legal code, and could scarcely be embraced by the human mind. It would, probably, never be understood by the public. Its nature, therefore, requires, that only its great outlines should be marked, its important objects designated, and the minor ingredients which compose those objects, be deduced from the nature of the objects themselves. That this idea was entertained by the framers of the American constitution, is not only to be inferred from the nature of the instrument, but from the language. Why else were some of the limitations, found in the 9th section of the 1st article, introduced? It is also, in some degree, warranted, by their having omitted to use any restrictive term which might prevent its receiving a fair and just interpretation. In considering this question, then, we must never forget that it is a *constitution* we are expounding.

Although, among the enumerated powers of government, we do not find the word "bank" or "incorporation," we find the great powers, to lay and collect taxes; to borrow money; to regulate commerce; to declare and conduct a war; and to raise and support armies and navies. The sword and the purse, all the external relations, and no inconsiderable portion of the industry of the nation, are intrusted to its government. It can never be pretended, that these vast powers draw after them others of inferior importance, merely because they are inferior. Such an idea can never be advanced. But it may with great reason be contended, that a government, intrusted with such ample powers, on the due execution of which the happiness and prosperity of the nation so vitally depends, must also be intrusted with ample means for their execution. The power being given, it is the interest of the nation to facilitate its execution. It can never be their interest, and cannot be presumed to have been their intention, to clog and embarrass its execution, by withholding the most appropriate means. . . . Can we adopt that construction (unless the words imperiously require it), which would impute to the framers of that instrument, when granting these powers for the public good, the intention of impeding their exercise, by withholding a choice of means? . . .

It is not denied, that the powers given to the government imply the ordinary means of execution. That, for example, of raising revenue, and applying it to national purposes, is admitted to imply the power of conveying money from place to place, as the exigencies of the nation may require, and of employing the usual means of conveyance. . . .

But the constitution of the United States has not left the right of congress to employ the necessary means, for the execution of the powers conferred on the government, to general reasoning. To its enumeration of powers is added, that of making "all laws which shall be necessary and proper, for carrying into execution the foregoing powers, and all other powers vested by this constitution, in the government of the United States, or in any department thereof." The counsel for the state of Maryland have urged various arguments, to prove that this clause, though, in terms, a grant of power, is not so, in effect; but is really restrictive of the general right, which might otherwise be implied, of selecting means for executing the enumerated powers. . . .

[T]he argument on which most reliance is placed, is drawn from that peculiar language of this clause. Congress is not empowered by it to make all laws, which may have relation to the powers confered on the government, but such only as may be *"necessary and proper"* for carrying them into execution. The word *"necessary"* is considered as controlling the whole sentence, and as limiting the right to pass laws for the execution of the granted powers, to such as are indispensable, and without which the power would be nugatory. That it excludes the choice of means, and leaves to congress, in each case, that only which is most direct and simple.

Is it true, that this is the sense in which the word "necessary" is always used? Does it always import an absolute physical necessity, so strong, that one thing to which another may be termed necessary, cannot exist without that other? We think it does not. If reference be had to its use, in the common affairs of the world, or in approved authors, we find that it frequently imports no more than that one thing is convenient, or useful, or essential to another. To employ the means necessary to an end, is generally understood as employing any means calculated to produce the end, and not as being confined to those single means, without which the end would be entirely unattainable. . . . The word "necessary" . . . has not a fixed character, peculiar to itself. . . . A thing may be necessary, very necessary, absolutely or indispensably necessary. To no mind would the same idea be conveyed by these several phrases. The comment on the word is well illustrated by the passage cited at the bar, from the 10th section of the 1st article of the constitution. It is, we think, impossible to compare the sentence which prohibits a state from laying "imposts, or duties on imports or exports, except what may be *absolutely* necessary for executing its inspection laws," with that which authorizes congress "to make all laws which shall be necessary and proper for carrying into execution" the powers of the general government, without feeling a conviction, that the convention understood itself to change materially the meaning of the word "necessary," by prefixing the word "absolutely." This word, then, like others, is used in various senses; and, in its construction, the subject, the context, the intention of the person using them, are all to be taken into view.

Let this be done in the case under consideration. The subject is the execution of those great powers on which the welfare of a nation essentially depends. It must have been the intention of those who gave these powers, to insure, so far as human prudence could insure, their beneficial execution. This could not be done, by confiding the choice of means to such narrow limits as not to leave it in the power of congress to adopt any which might be appropriate, and which were conducive to the end. This provision is made in a constitution, intended to endure for ages to come, and consequently, to be adapted to the various *crises* of human affairs. To have prescribed the means by which government should, in all future time, execute its powers, would have been to change, entirely, the character of the instrument, and give it the properties of a legal code. It would have been an unwise attempt to provide, by immutable rules, for exigencies which, if foreseen at all, must have been seen dimly, and which can be best provided for as they occur. To have declared, that the best means shall not be used, but those alone, without which the power given would be nugatory, would have been to deprive the legislature of the capacity to avail itself of experience, to exercise its reason, and to accommodate its legislation to circumstances. If we apply this principle of construction to any of the powers of the government, we shall find it so pernicious in its operation that we shall be compelled to discard it.

So, with respect to the whole penal code of the United States: whence arises the power to punish, in cases not prescribed by the constitution? All admit, that the government may, legitimately, punish any violation of its laws; and yet, this is not among the enumerated powers of congress. The right to enforce the observance of law, by punishing its infraction, might be denied, with the more plausibility, because it is expressly given in some cases. Congress is empowered "to provide for the punishment of counterfeiting the securities and current coin of the United States," and "to define and punish piracies and felonies committed on the high seas, and offences against the law of nations." The several powers of congress may exist, in a very imperfect state, to be sure, but they may exist and be carried into execution, although no punishment should be inflicted, in cases where the right to punish is not expressly given.

Take, for example, the power "to establish post-offices and post-roads." This power is executed, by the single act of making the establishment. But, from this has been inferred the power and duty of carrying the mail along the post-road, from one post-office to another. And from this implied power, has again been inferred the right to punish those who steal letters from the post-office, or rob the mail. It may be said, with some plausibility, that the right to carry the mail, and to punish those who rob it, is not indispensably necessary to the establishment of a post-office and post-road. This right is indeed essential to the beneficial exercise of the power, but not indispensably necessary to its existence. So, of the punishment of the crimes of stealing or falsifying a record or process of a court of the United States, or of perjury in such court. To punish these offences, is certainly conducive to the due administration of justice. But courts may exist, and may decide the causes brought before them, though such crimes escape punishment.

The baneful influence of this narrow construction on all the operations of the government, and the absolute impracticability of maintaining it, without rendering the government incompetent to its great objects, might be illustrated by numerous examples drawn from the constitution, and from our laws. . . .

[T]he argument which most conclusively demonstrates the error of the construction contended for by the counsel for the state of Maryland, is founded on the intention of the convention, as manifested in the whole clause. To waste time and argument in proving that, without it, congress might carry its powers into execution, would be not much less idle, than to hold a lighted taper to the sun. As little can it be required to prove, that in the absence of this clause, congress would have some choice of means. That it might employ those which, in its judgment, would most advantageously effect the object to be accomplished. That any means adapted to the end, any means which tended directly to the execution of the constitutional powers of the government, were in themselves constitutional. This clause, as construed by the state of Maryland, would abridge, and almost annihilate, this useful and necessary right of the legislature to select its means. That this could not be intended, is, we should think, had it not been already controverted, too apparent for controversy.

We think so for the following reasons: 1st. The clause is placed among the powers of congress, not among the limitations on those powers. 2d. Its terms purport to enlarge, not to diminish the powers vested in the government. It purports to be an additional power, not a restriction on those already granted. No reason has been, or can be assigned, for thus concealing an intention to narrow the discretion of the national legislature, under words which purport to enlarge it. . . .

The result of the most careful and attentive consideration bestowed upon this clause is, that if it does not enlarge, it cannot be construed to restrain the powers of congress, or to impair the right of the legislature to exercise its best judgment in the selection of measures to carry into execution the constitutional powers of the government. If no other motive for its insertion can be suggested, a sufficient one is found in the desire to remove all doubts respecting the right to legislate on that vast mass of incidental powers which must be involved in the constitution, if that instrument be not a splendid bauble.

We admit, as all must admit, that the powers of the government are limited, and that its limits are not to be transcended. But we think the sound construction of the constitution must allow to the national legislature that discretion, with respect to the means by which the powers it confers are to be carried into execution, which will enable that body to perform the high duties assigned to it, in the manner most beneficial to the people. Let the end be legitimate, let it be within the scope of the constitution, and all means which are appropriate, which are plainly adapted to that end, which are not prohibited, but consist with the letter and spirit of the constitution, are constitutional. . . .

If a corporation may be employed, indiscriminately with other means, to carry into execution the powers of the government, no particular reason can be assigned for excluding the use of a bank, if required for its fiscal operations. To use one, must be within the discretion of congress, if it be an appropriate mode of executing the powers of government. That it is a convenient, a useful, and essential instrument in the prosecution of its fiscal operations, is not now a subject of controversy. All those who have been concerned in the administration of our finances, have concurred in representing its importance and necessity; and so strongly have they been felt, that statesmen of the first class, whose previous opinions against it had been confirmed by every circumstance which can fix the human judgment, have yielded those opinions to the exigencies of the nation. Under the confederation, congress, justifying the measure by its necessity, transcended, perhaps, its powers, to obtain the advantage of a bank; and our own legislation attests the universal conviction of the utility of this measure. The time has passed away, when it can be necessary to enter into any discussion, in order to prove the importance of this instrument, as a means to effect the legitimate objects of the government.

But were its necessity less apparent, none can deny its being an appropriate measure; and if it is, the decree of its necessity, as has been very justly observed, is to be discussed in another place. Should congress, in the execution of its powers, adopt measures which are prohibited by the constitution; or should congress, under the pretext of executing its powers, pass laws for the accomplishment of objects not intrusted to the government; it would become the painful duty of this tribunal, should a case requiring such a decision come before it, to say, that such an act was not the law of the land. But where the law is not prohibited, and is really calculated to effect any of the objects intrusted to the government, to undertake here to inquire into the decree of its necessity, would be to pass the line which circumscribes the judicial department, and to tread on legislative ground. This court disclaims all pretensions to such a power. . . .

It being the opinion of the court, that the act incorporating the bank is constitutional; and that the power of establishing a branch in the state of Maryland might be properly exercised by the bank itself, we proceed to inquire—

2. Whether the state of Maryland may, without violating the constitution, tax that branch? That the power of taxation is one of vital importance; that it is retained by the states; that it is not abridged by the grant of a similar power to the government of the Union; that it is to be concurrently exercised by the two governments—are truths which have never been denied. But such is the paramount character of the constitution, that its capacity to withdraw any subject from the action of even this power, is admitted. The states are expressly forbidden to lay any duties on imports or exports, except what may be absolutely necessary for executing their inspection laws. If the obligation of this prohibition must be conceded—if it may restrain a state from the exercise of its taxing power on imports and exports—the same paramount character would seem to restrain, as it certainly may restrain, a state from such other exercise of this power, as is in its nature incompatible with, and repugnant to, the constitutional laws of the Union. A law, absolutely

repugnant to another, as entirely repeals that other as if express terms of repeal were used.

On this ground, the counsel for the bank place its claim to be exempted from the power of a state to tax its operations. There is no express provision for the case, but the claim has been sustained on a principle which so entirely pervades the constitution, is so intermixed with the materials which compose it, so interwoven with its web, so blended with its texture, as to be incapable of being separated from it, without rending it into shreds. This great principle is, that the constitution and the laws made in pursuance thereof are supreme; that they control the constitution and laws of the respective states, and cannot be controlled by them. From this, which may be almost termed an axiom, other propositions are deduced as corollaries, on the truth or error of which, and on their application to this case, the cause has been supposed to depend. These are, 1st. That a power to create implies a power to preserve: 2d. That a power to destroy, if wielded by a different hand, is hostile to, and incompatible with these powers to create and to preserve: 3d. That where this repugnancy exists, that authority which is supreme must control, not yield to that over which it is supreme. . . .

That the power of taxing it by the states may be exercised so as to destroy it, is too obvious to be denied. But taxation is said to be an absolute power, which acknowledges no other limits than those expressly prescribed in the constitution, and like sovereign power of every other description, is intrusted to the discretion of those who use it. But the very terms of this argument admit, that the sovereignty of the state, in the article of taxation itself, is subordinate to, and may be controlled by the constitution of the United States. How far it has been controlled by that instrument, must be a question of construction. In making this construction, no principle, not declared, can be admissible, which would defeat the legitimate operations of a supreme government. It is of the very essence of supremacy, to remove all obstacles to its action within its own sphere, and so to modify every power vested in subordinate governments, as to exempt its own operations from their own influence. This effect need not be stated in terms. It is so involved in the declaration of supremacy, so necessarily implied in it, that the expression of it could not make it more certain. We must, therefore, keep it in view, while construing the constitution. . . .

The sovereignty of a state extends to everything which exists by its own authority, or is introduced by its permission; but does it extend to those means which are employed by congress to carry into execution powers conferred on that body by the people of the United States? We think it demonstrable, that it does not. Those powers are not given by the people of a single state. They are given by the people of the United States, to a government whose laws, made in pursuance of the constitution, are declared to be supreme. Consequently, the people of a single state cannot confer a sovereignty which will extend over them. . . .

We find, then, on just theory, a total failure of this original right to tax the means employed by the government of the Union, for the execution of its powers. The right never existed, and the question whether it has been surrendered, cannot arise. . . .

If we apply the principle for which the state of Maryland contends, to the constitution, generally, we shall find it capable of changing totally the character of that instrument. We shall find it capable of arresting all the measures of the government, and of prostrating it at the foot of the states. . . . If the states may tax one instrument, employed by the government in the execution of its powers, they may tax any and every other instrument. . . . This was not intended by the American people. They did not design to make their government dependent on the states. . . .

It has also been insisted, that, as the power of taxation in the general and state governments is acknowledged to be concurrent, every argument which would sustain the right of the general government to tax banks chartered by the states, will equally sustain the right of the states to tax banks chartered by the general government. But the two cases are not on the same reason. The people of all the states have created the general government, and have conferred upon it the general power of taxation. The people of all the states, and the states themselves, are represented in congress, and, by their representatives, exercise this power. When they tax the chartered institutions of the states, they tax their constituents; and these taxes must be uniform. But when a state taxes the operations of the government of the United States, it acts upon institutions created, not by their own constituents, but by people over whom they claim no control. It acts upon the measures of a government created by others as well as themselves, for the benefit of others in common with themselves. The difference is that which always exists, and always must exist, between the action of the whole on a part, and the action of a part on the whole — between the laws of a government declared to be supreme, and those of a government which, when in opposition to those laws, is not supreme.

But if the full application of this argument could be admitted, it might bring into question the right of congress to tax the state banks, and could not prove the rights of the states to tax the Bank of the United States. . . .

[T]he states have no power, by taxation or otherwise, to retard, impede, burden, or in any manner control, the operations of the constitutional laws enacted by congress to carry into execution the powers vested in the general government. . . .

POINTS FOR DISCUSSION

1. The *McCullough* Court famously stated: "Let the end be legitimate, let it be within the scope of the constitution, and all means which are appropriate, which are plainly adapted to that end, which are not prohibited, but consist with the letter and spirit of the constitution, are constitutional." Contrast this approach with Tucker's principle of strict construction. What values underlie these different interpretive approaches?

2. In *McCullough*, Chief Justice Marshall commented: "So, with respect to the whole penal code of the United States: whence arises the power to punish, in cases not prescribed by the constitution? All admit, that the government may, legitimately, punish any violation of its laws; and yet, this is not among the enumerated powers of congress." In contrast, in the second resolution of the Kentucky Resolutions of 1798, Jefferson expressed:

> [T]he Constitution of the United States, having delegated to Congress a power to punish treason, counterfeiting the securities and current coin of the United States, piracies, and felonies committed on the high seas, and offenses against the law of nations, and no other crimes, whatsoever . . . , the power to create, define, and punish such other crimes is reserved, and, of right, appertains solely and exclusively to the respective States, each within its own territory.

What accounts for these differing understandings of Congress's power to define and punish crimes?

3. The *McCullough* Court also engaged in judicial review of Maryland's act of taxing the Bank. In holding that Maryland could not tax the Bank — in other words, that this act was preempted — the Court explained: "It is of the very essence of supremacy, to remove all obstacles to its action within its own sphere, and so to modify every power vested in subordinate governments, as to exempt its own operations from their own influence." Does *McCullough* establish that the Constitution preempts any state law that obstructs Congress's ability to act within its enumerated powers? How must a state act obstruct the Constitution or a federal statute in order for the state law to be preempted? You will return to this subject in Chapter 7, which considers various forms of implied constitutional and statutory preemption.

4. In *McCullough*, the Court employed various modalities to interpret the Necessary and Proper Clause, including the following:

- *Text*. The Court analyzed, in context, the meaning of the word "necessary."
- *Historical Practice*. The Court drew analogies between the Bank of the United States and other means that Congress had used since the Founding to carry enumerated powers into execution. It also explained that "the respective powers of those who are equally the representatives of the people, . . . if not put at rest by the practice of the government, ought to receive a considerable impression from that practice."
- *Structure*. The Court explained that, without congressional power to select the means necessary to achieve enumerated ends, the structure of federal governance would be ineffective.
- *Purpose*. The Court explained that the purpose, or motive, of the Necessary and Proper Clause was to give Congress incidental powers necessary to make its enumerated powers effective.

You will see the Court continue to employ each of these modalities of interpretation — and others — in present-day federalism cases. What is the value of each of these modalities of constitutional interpretation? How might Tucker have critiqued how the Court employed them in light of his rule of strict construction?

As *McCullough v. Maryland* illustrates, judicial review can assume one of two forms: review of whether a federal statute comports with the Constitution, or review of whether a state law is preempted by the Constitution or another form of supreme federal law. In *McCullough*, the Court exercised judicial review both to assess whether a federal statute was within Congress's constitutional powers and to protect the supremacy of constitutionally enacted federal law against state legislation.

In subsequent cases, the Marshall Court addressed another important aspect of federal judicial enforcement of supreme federal law, namely Supreme Court review of state court judgments. Section 25 of the Judiciary Act of 1789 authorized the Supreme Court to review "a final judgment or decree in any suit, in the highest court of law or equity of a State in which a decision in the suit could be had" if the state court denied a right asserted under the Constitution, laws, or treaties of the United States. Act of Sept. 24, 1789, ch. 20, §25, 1 Stat. 73, 85. In *Martin v. Hunter's Lessee*, 14 U.S. (1 Wheat.) 304 (1816), the Court asserted its power under section 25 to review a state court judgment that denied a claimed federal right.

The case involved a dispute over lands that Thomas Lord Fairfax, a British loyalist, had owned in Virginia. During the Revolutionary War, Virginia seized the land. Thomas Martin subsequently inherited Lord Fairfax's interests in the land. Virginia assigned a tract of the land to David Hunter. The Fairfax interests claimed that Virginia had violated its obligations under the Paris Peace Treaty of 1783 and the Jay Treaty of 1794, which afforded some protection to Loyalist land interests. Accordingly, Martin sued to recover the land in Virginia state court. Ultimately, the Virginia courts ruled in favor of Hunter, denying the rights that the Fairfax interests asserted under the treaties. Martin appealed to the Supreme Court. In *Fairfax's Devisee v. Hunter's Lessee*, 11 U.S. (7 Cranch) 603 (1813), Justice Joseph Story, writing for the Court, upheld the Fairfax interests pursuant to the treaties. (Chief Justice Marshall had recused himself on grounds of a conflict of interest.)

On remand, however, the Virginia Court of Appeals (its highest court) refused to enter judgment in favor of the Fairfax interests. *Hunter v. Martin*, 18 Va. (4 Munf.) 1 (1815). Many Virginians viewed the Court's mandated reversal of a decision passed down from the state's highest tribunal as an impermissible infringement of state sovereignty. The Virginia Court of Appeals maintained that §25 of the Judiciary Act was unconstitutional. The Court of Appeals observed that Article III of the Constitution grants Congress the power to "ordain and establish" inferior federal courts. Article III also extends the judicial power of the United States to cases "arising under" the Constitution, laws, and treaties of the United States. Accordingly, the Court of Appeals claimed that the constitutional means for Congress to ensure the proper enforcement of federal law was to establish inferior federal courts and give them original jurisdiction over cases "arising under" federal law. By enacting §25, Congress had bypassed those means, subjecting the highest tribunals of the sovereign states to the indignity of appellate scrutiny.

The case was again appealed to the Supreme Court. In *Martin v. Hunter's Lessee*, the Court held that the Constitution does allow the Supreme Court to review state court determinations of federal law. Justice Story explained for the Court that the Constitution does not leave the states entirely independent of the federal government. He relied on both the Supremacy Clause and the Arising Under Clause to uphold the constitutionality of §25.

The Supremacy Clause — which provides that state judges shall be bound to the Constitution, laws, and treaties of the United States as the supreme law of the land, U.S. CONST. art. VI — presumes that state tribunals would entertain federal questions in their ordinary jurisdiction. And the Arising Under Clause — which extends the federal judicial power to "*all* Cases, in Law and equity, arising under this Constitution, the Laws of the United States, and Treaties made, or which shall be made, under their Authority," U.S. CONST. art. III, §2 (emphasis added) — presumes that the Supreme Court could exercise its appellate jurisdiction to review state court decisions on questions of federal law. Thus, the Court concluded, Congress properly authorized such review in §25.

In the following case, *Cohens v. Virginia*, 19 U.S. (6 Wheat.) 264 (1821), the Supreme Court confirmed the holding of *Hunter's Lessee* that the Court may review state court decisions on questions of federal law — even when, as in *Cohens*, the state is a party to the controversy. A Virginia criminal law prohibited selling out-of-state lottery tickets in Virginia. Philip and Mendes Cohen were arrested and convicted for selling Grand National Lottery tickets in violation of this law. They claimed that an act of Congress protected their activities. Virginia viewed Supreme Court review of a state court judgment to which a state was a party (*Cohens* was a state criminal case) as an even greater affront to state sovereignty than review in *Hunter's Lessee* had been.

COHENS V. VIRGINIA

19 U.S. (6 Wheat.) 264 (1821)

Mr. CHIEF JUSTICE MARSHALL delivered the opinion of the Court.

This is a writ of error to a judgment rendered in the Court of Hustings for the borough of Norfolk, on an information for selling lottery tickets, contrary to an act of the Legislature of Virginia. In the State Court, the defendant claimed the protection of an act of Congress. . . .

Judgment was rendered against the defendants; and the Court in which it was rendered being the highest Court of the State in which the cause was cognizable, the record has been brought into this Court by writ of error. . . .

The defendant in error moves to dismiss this writ, for want of jurisdiction. . . .

1st. The first question to be considered is, whether the jurisdiction of this Court is excluded by the character of the parties, one of them being a State, and the other a citizen of that State?

The second section of the third article of the constitution defines the extent of the judicial power of the United States. Jurisdiction is given to the Courts of the Union in two classes of cases. In the first, their jurisdiction depends on the character of the cause, whoever may be the parties. This class comprehends "all cases in law and equity arising under this constitution, the laws of the United States, and treaties made, or which shall be made, under their authority." This clause extends the jurisdiction of the Court to all the cases described, without making in its terms any exception whatever, and without any regard to the condition of the party. If there by any exception, it is to be implied against the express words of the article.

In the second class, the jurisdiction depends entirely on the character of the parties. In this are comprehended "controversies between two or more States, between a State and citizens of another State," "and between a State and foreign States, citizens or subjects." If these be the parties, it is entirely unimportant what may be the subject of controversy. Be it what it may, these parties have a constitutional right to come into the Courts of the Union. . . .

A case in law or equity consists of the right of the one party, as well as of the other, and may truly be said to arise under the constitution or a law of the United States, whenever its correct decision depends on the construction of either. Congress seems to have intended to give its own construction of this part of the constitution in the 25th section of the judiciary act, and we perceive no reason to depart from that construction.

The jurisdiction of the Court, then, being extended by the letter of the constitution to all cases arising under it, or under the laws of the United States, it follows that those who would withdraw any case of this description from that jurisdiction, must sustain the exemption they claim on the spirit and true meaning of the constitution, which spirit and true meaning must be so apparent as to overrule the words which its framers have employed.

The counsel for the defendant in error have undertaken to do this; and have laid down the general proposition, that a sovereign independent State is not suable, except by its own consent.

This general proposition will not be controverted. But its consent is not requisite in each particular case. It may be given in a general law. And if a State has surrendered any portion of its sovereignty, the question whether a liability to suit be a part of this portion, depends on the instrument by which the surrender is made. If, upon a just construction of that instrument, it shall appear that the State has submitted to be sued, then it has parted with this sovereign right of judging in every case on the justice of its own pretensions, and has entrusted that power to a tribunal in whose impartiality it confides.

The American States, as well as the American people, have believed a close and firm Union to be essential to their liberty and to their happiness. They have been taught by experience, that this Union cannot exist without a government for the whole; and they have been taught by the same experience that this government would be a mere shadow, that must disappoint all their hopes, unless invested with large portions of that sovereignty which belongs to independent States. Under the influence of this opinion, and thus instructed by experience, the American people, in the conventions of their respective States, adopted the present constitution.

If it could be doubted, whether from its nature, it were not supreme in all cases where it is empowered to act, that doubt would be removed by the declaration, that "this constitution, and the laws of the United States, which shall be made in pursuance thereof, and all treaties made, or which shall be made, under the authority of the United States, shall be the supreme law of the land; and the judges in every State shall be bound thereby; any thing in the constitution or laws of any State to the contrary notwithstanding."

This is the authoritative language of the American people, and, if gentlemen please, of the American States. It marks, with lines too strong to be mistaken, the characteristic distinction between the government of the Union, and those of the States. The general government, though limited as to its objects, is supreme with respect to those objects. This principle is a part of the constitution; and if there be any who deny its necessity, none can deny its authority. . . .

With the ample powers confided to this supreme government, for these interesting purposes, are connected many express and important limitations on the sovereignty of the States, which are made for the same purposes. The powers of the Union, on the great subjects of war, peace, and commerce, and on many others, are in themselves limitations of the sovereignty of the States, but in addition to these, the sovereignty of the States is surrendered in many instances where the surrender can only operate to the benefit of the people, and, where, perhaps, no other power is conferred on Congress than a conservative power to maintain the principles established in the constitution. The maintenance of these principles in their purity, is certainly among the great duties of the government. One of the instruments by which this duty may be peaceably performed, is the judicial department. It is authorized to decide all cases of every description, arising under the constitution or laws of the United States. From this general grant of jurisdiction, no exception is made of those cases in which a State may be a party. When we consider the situation of the government of the Union and of a State, in relation to each other, the nature of our constitution, the subordination of the State governments to that constitution; the great purpose for which jurisdiction over all cases arising under the constitution and laws of the United States, is confided to the judicial department; are we at liberty to insert in this general grant, an exception of those cases in which a State may be a party? Will the spirit of the constitution justify this attempt to control its words? We think it will not. We think a case arising under the constitution or laws of the United States, is cognizable in the Courts of the Union, whoever may be the parties to that case. . . .

We think, then, that, as the constitution originally stood, the appellate jurisdiction of this Court, in all cases arising under the constitution, laws, or treaties of the United States, was not arrested by the circumstance that a State was a party.

This leads to a consideration of the 11th amendment.

It is in these words: "The judicial power of the United States shall not be construed to extend to any suit in law or equity commenced or prosecuted against one of the United States, by citizens of another State, or by citizens or subjects of any foreign State."

It is a part of our history, that, at the adoption of the constitution, all the States were greatly indebted; and the apprehension that these debts might be prosecuted in the federal Courts, formed a very serious objection to that instrument. Suits were instituted; and the Court maintained its jurisdiction. The alarm was general; and, to quiet the apprehensions that were so extensively entertained, this amendment was proposed in Congress, and adopted by the State legislatures. That its motive was not to maintain the sovereignty of a State from the degradation supposed to attend a compulsory appearance before the tribunal of the nation, may be inferred from the terms of the amendment. It does not comprehend controversies between two or more States, or between a State and a foreign State. The jurisdiction of the Court still extends to these cases: and in these a State may still be sued. We must ascribe the amendment, then, to some other cause than the dignity of a State. There is no difficulty in finding this cause. Those who were inhibited from commencing a suit against a State, or from prosecuting one which might be commenced before the adoption of the amendment, were persons who might probably be its creditors. There was not much reason to fear that foreign or sister States would be creditors to any considerable amount, and there was reason to retain the jurisdiction of the Court in those cases, because it might be essential to the preservation of peace. The amendment, therefore, extended to suits commenced or prosecuted by individuals, but not to those brought by States.

The first impression made on the mind by this amendment is, that it was intended for those cases, and for those only, in which some demand against a State is made by an individual in the Courts of the Union. If we consider the causes to which it is to be traced, we are conducted to the same conclusion. A general interest might well be felt in leaving to a State the full power of consulting its convenience in the adjustment of its debts, or of other claims upon it, but no interest could be felt in so changing the relations between the whole and its parts, as to strip the government of the means of protecting, by the instrumentality of its Courts, the constitution and laws from active violation. . . .

[T]he effect of a writ of error is simply to bring the record into Court, and submit the judgment of the inferior tribunal to re-examination. It does not in any manner act upon the parties, it acts only on the record. It removes the record into the supervising tribunal. Where, then, a State obtains a judgment against an individual, and the Court, rendering such judgment, overrules a defence set up under the constitution or laws of the United States, the transfer of this record into the Supreme Court, for the sole purpose of inquiring whether the judgment violates the constitution or laws of the United States, can, with no propriety, we think, be denominated a suit commenced or prosecuted against the State whose judgment is so far re-examined. . . .

[T]he defendant who removes a judgment rendered against him by a State Court into this Court, for the purpose of re-examining the question, whether that judgment be in violation of the constitution or laws of the United States, does not commence or prosecute a suit against the State, whatever may be its opinion where the effect of the writ may be to restore the party to the possession of a thing which he demands.

But should we in this be mistaken, the error does not affect the case now before the Court. If this writ of error be a suit in the sense of the 11th amendment, it is not a suit commenced or prosecuted "by a citizen of another State, or by a citizen or subject of any foreign State." It is not then within the amendment, but is governed entirely by the constitution as originally framed, and we have already seen, that in its origin, the judicial power was extended to all cases arising under the constitution or laws of the United States, without respect to parties.

2d. The second objection to the jurisdiction of the Court is, that its appellate power cannot be exercised, in any case, over the judgment of a State Court. . . .

That the United States form, for many, and for most important purposes, a single nation, has not yet been denied. In war, we are one people. In making peace, we are one people. In all commercial regulations, we are one and the same people. In many other respects, the American people are one, and the government which is alone capable of controlling and managing their interests in all these respects, is the government of the Union. It is their government, and in that character they have no other. America has chosen to be, in many respects, and to many purposes, a nation, and for all these purposes, her government is complete; to all these objects, it is competent. The people have declared, that in the exercise of all powers given for these objects, it is supreme. It can, then, in effecting these objects, legitimately control all individuals or governments within the American territory. The constitution and laws of a State, so far as they are repugnant to the constitution and laws of the United States, are absolutely void. These States are constituent parts of the United States. They are members of one great empire—for some purposes sovereign, for some purposes subordinate.

In a government so constituted, is it unreasonable that the judicial power should be competent to give efficacy to the constitutional laws of the legislature? That department can decide on the validity of the constitution or law of a State, if it be repugnant to the constitution or to a law of the United States. Is it unreasonable that it should also be empowered to decide on the judgment of a State tribunal enforcing such unconstitutional law? Is it so very unreasonable as to furnish a justification for controlling the words of the constitution?

We think it is not. We think that in a government acknowledgedly supreme, with respect to objects of vital interest to the nation, there is nothing inconsistent with sound reason, nothing incompatible with the nature of government, in making all its departments supreme, so far as respects those objects, and so far as is necessary to their attainment. The exercise of the appellate power over those judgments of the State tribunals which may contravene the constitution or laws of the United States, is, we believe, essential to the attainment of those objects. . . .

[T]he words of the Constitution . . . give to the Supreme Court appellate jurisdiction in all cases arising under the constitution, laws, and treaties of the United States. The words are broad enough to comprehend all cases of this description, in whatever Court they may be decided. In expounding them, we may be permitted to take into view those considerations to which Courts have always allowed great weight in the exposition of laws.

The framers of the constitution would naturally examine the state of things existing at the time, and their work sufficiently attests that they did so. All acknowledge that they were convened for the purpose of strengthening the confederation by enlarging the powers of the government, and by giving efficacy to those which it before possessed, but could not exercise. They inform us themselves, in the instrument they presented to the American public, that one of its objects was to form a more perfect union. Under such circumstances, we certainly should not expect to find, in that instrument, a diminution of the powers of the actual government.

Previous to the adoption of the confederation, Congress established Courts which received appeals in prize causes decided in the Courts of the respective States. This power of the government, to establish tribunals for these appeals, was thought consistent with, and was founded on, its political relations with the States. These Courts did exercise appellate jurisdiction over those cases decided in the State Courts, to which the judicial power of the federal government extended.

The confederation gave to Congress the power "of establishing Courts for receiving and determining finally appeals in all cases of captures."

This power was uniformly construed to authorize those Courts to receive appeals from the sentences of State Courts, and to affirm or reverse them. State tribunals are not mentioned, but this clause in the confederation necessarily comprises them. Yet the relation between the general and State governments was much weaker, much more lax, under the confederation than under the present constitution; and the States being much more completely sovereign, their institutions were much more independent.

The Convention which framed the constitution, on turning their attention to the judicial power, found it limited to a few objects, but exercised, with respect to some of those objects, in its appellate form, over the judgments of the State Courts. They extend it, among other objects, to all cases arising under the constitution, laws, and treaties of the United States; and in a subsequent clause declare, that in such cases, the Supreme Court shall exercise appellate jurisdiction. Nothing seems to be given which would justify the withdrawal of a judgment rendered in a State Court, on the constitution, laws, or treaties of the United States, from this appellate jurisdiction.

Great weight has always been attached, and very rightly attached, to contemporaneous exposition. No question, it is believed, has arisen to which this principle applies more unequivocally than to that now under consideration.

The opinion of the *Federalist* has always been considered as of great authority. . . . In discussing the extent of the judicial power, the *Federalist* says, "Here another question occurs: what relation would subsist between the national and State Courts in these instances of concurrent jurisdiction? I answer, that an appeal would certainly lie from the latter, to the Supreme Court of the United States. The constitution in direct terms gives an appellate jurisdiction to the Supreme Court in all the enumerated cases of federal cognizance in which it is not to have an original one, without a single expression to confine its operation to the inferior federal Courts. The objects of appeal, not the tribunals from which it is to be made, are alone contemplated. From this circumstance, and from the reason of the thing, it ought to be construed to extend to the State tribunals. Either this must be the case, or the local Courts must be excluded from a concurrent jurisdiction in matters of national concern, else the judicial authority of the Union may be eluded at the pleasure of every plaintiff or prosecutor. Neither of these consequences ought, without evident necessity, to be involved, the latter would be entirely inadmissible, as it would defeat some of the most important and avowed purposes of the proposed government, and would essentially embarrass its measures. Nor do I perceive any foundation for such a supposition. Agreeably to the remark already made, the national and State systems are to be regarded as ONE WHOLE. The Courts of the latter will of course be natural auxiliaries to the execution of the laws of the Union, and an appeal from them will as naturally lie to that tribunal which is destined to unite and assimilate the principles of natural justice, and the rules of national decision. The evident aim of the plan of the national convention is, that all the causes of the specified classes shall, for weighty public reasons, receive their original or final determination in the Courts of the Union. To confine, therefore, the general expressions which give appellate jurisdiction to the Supreme Court, to appeals from the subordinate federal Courts, instead of allowing their extension to the State Courts, would be to abridge the latitude of the terms, in subversion of the intent, contrary to every sound rule of interpretation."

A contemporaneous exposition of the constitution, certainly of not less authority than that which has been just cited, is the judiciary act itself. We know that in the Congress which passed that act were many eminent members of the Convention which formed the constitution. Not a single individual, so far as is known, supposed that part of the act which gives the Supreme Court appellate jurisdiction over the judgments of the State Courts in the cases therein specified, to be unauthorized by the constitution.

While on this part of the argument, it may be also material to observe that the uniform decisions of this Court on the point now under consideration, have been assented to, with a single exception, by the Courts of every State in the Union whose judgments have been revised. It has been the unwelcome duty of this tribunal to reverse the judgments of many State Courts in cases in which the strongest State feelings were engaged. Judges, whose talents and character would grace any bench, to whom a disposition to submit to jurisdiction that is usurped, or to surrender their legitimate powers, will certainly not be imputed, have yielded without hesitation to the authority by which their judgments were reversed, while they, perhaps, disapproved the judgment of reversal.

This concurrence of statesmen, of legislators, and of judges, in the same construction of the constitution, may justly inspire some confidence in that construction. . . .

Let the nature and objects of our Union be considered; let the great fundamental principles, on which the fabric stands, be examined, and we think the result must be, that there is nothing so extravagantly absurd in giving to the Court of the nation the power of revising the decisions of local tribunals on questions which affect the nation, as to require that words which import this power should be restricted by a forced construction. The question then must depend on the words themselves. [O]n their construction we shall be the more readily excused for not adding to the observations already made, because the subject was fully discussed and exhausted in the case of *Martin v. Hunter.* . . .

After having bestowed upon this question the most deliberate consideration of which we are capable, the Court is unanimously of opinion, that the objections to its jurisdiction are not sustained, and that the motion ought to be overruled. . . .

POINTS FOR DISCUSSION

1. In *Cohens*, the Court determined that Article III courts not only may enforce validly enacted federal laws in the face of conflicting state laws, but also may review state court judgments that fail to uphold asserted federal rights. Is the role that Marshall envisioned for the Supreme Court consistent with the ideas of dual sovereignty and/or that ultimate sovereignty rests with the people?

2. The *Cohens* Court also considered whether it lacked jurisdiction because a state was party to the controversy. In particular, the Court addressed whether the Eleventh Amendment precluded the Court from exercising jurisdiction. How does the Eleventh Amendment relate to this case? On what grounds did Chief Justice Marshall hold that the Eleventh Amendment did not preclude the Court from exercising appellate jurisdiction in this case? Among the most contested federalism questions of the present day is whether, in light of the Eleventh Amendment and principles of state sovereign immunity, private individuals may sue states in federal courts. You will examine this question in detail in Chapter 6.

3. In determining whether Article III "judicial Power" extended to the case before it, the *Cohens* Court considered, *inter alia*:

- "the words" of Article III;
- the Framers' "purpose of strengthening the confederation by enlarging the powers of the government, and by giving efficacy to those which it before possessed, but could not exercise";
- "contemporaneous exposition," such as *The Federalist* and the Judiciary Act; and
- the "concurrence of statesmen, of legislators, and of judges, in the same construction of the constitution."

What relevance, if any, does each of these sources have to the Constitution's meaning? Assuming these sources contain conflicting evidence regarding the Constitution's meaning, to which source or sources should courts attach greater weight? As you will see in subsequent chapters, the Supreme Court continues to refer to such sources in resolving constitutional federalism disputes. As you read the cases in this book, be mindful of how the Court uses the following sources:

- *Text*—what meaning the words of the Constitution convey.
- *Historical Practice*—what meaning the actions of public officials and institutions operating under the Constitution evince.
- *Structure*—what meaning the Constitution's structure of government (separation of powers and federalism) implies.
- *Purpose*—what meaning the purposes of constitutional provisions reveal.

In 1823, in the aftermath of *Cohens*, Thomas Jefferson and James Madison exchanged correspondence on several topics of public interest. In June 1823, they corresponded on the relative authority of federal and state governments—and who should resolve disputes about that authority. On June 13, Jefferson sent Madison a copy of a letter that Jefferson had sent to Justice William Johnson, a Jefferson appointee to the Supreme Court of the

United States. Jefferson's letter to Johnson and Madison's reaction to it are reproduced in part as follows.

As you read these letters, consider the differing views of Jefferson and Madison on how constitutional disputes over federal-state power should be resolved. Jefferson rejects federal judicial review in his letter to Johnson. Recall how, in the Kentucky Resolutions of 1798, Jefferson asserted state authority to nullify unconstitutional federal laws. In this letter, Jefferson argues that the "ultimate arbiter" of the Constitution is "the people of the Union." Madison, in response, considers various means of resolving federal-state disputes, concluding, as he had in *The Federalist No. 39*, that judicial review is constitutionally prescribed and is a peaceable means of resolving disputes over federal-state power.

LETTER FROM THOMAS JEFFERSON TO WILLIAM JOHNSON

12 June 1823

The capital and leading object of the Constitution was to leave with the States all authorities which respected their own citizens only, and to transfer to the United States those which respected citizens of foreign or other States: to make us several as to ourselves, but one as to all others. In the latter case, then, constructions should lean to the general jurisdiction, if the words will bear it; and in favor of the States in the former, if possible to be so construed. . . .

Can it be believed, that under the jealousies prevailing against the General Government, at the adoption of the Constitution, the States meant to surrender the authority of preserving order, of enforcing moral duties and restraining vice, within their own territory? And this is the present case, that of Cohen being under the ancient and general law of gaming. Can any good be effected by taking from the States the moral rule of their citizens, and subordinating it to the general authority or their corporations, which may justify forcing the meaning of words, hunting after possible constructions, and hanging inference on inference, from heaven to earth, like Jacob's ladder? Such an intention was impossible, and such a licentiousness of construction and inference, if exercised by both governments, as may be done with equal right, would equally authorize both to claim all power, general and particular, and break up the foundations of the Union. Laws are made for men of ordinary understanding, and should, therefore, be construed by the ordinary rules of common sense. Their meaning is not to be sought for in metaphysical subtleties, which may make anything mean everything or nothing, at pleasure. . . . The States supposed that by their tenth amendment, they had secured themselves against constructive powers. . . . I ask for no straining of words against the General Government, nor yet against the States. I believe the States can best govern our home concerns, and the General Government our foreign ones. . . .

But the Chief Justice says, "there must be an ultimate arbiter somewhere." True, there must; but does that prove it is either party? The ultimate arbiter is the people of the Union, assembled by their deputies in convention, at the call of Congress, or of two-thirds of the States. Let them decide to which they mean to give an authority claimed by two of their organs. And it has been the peculiar wisdom and felicity of our Constitution, to have provided this peaceable appeal, where that of other nations is at once to force.

LETTER FROM JAMES MADISON TO THOMAS JEFFERSON

27 June 1823

[A]fter surmounting the difficulty in tracing the boundary between the General & State Govts. the problem remains for maintaining it in practice; particularly in cases of Judicial cognizance. To refer every point of disagreement to the people in Conventions would be a process too tardy, too troublesome, & too expensive; besides its tendency to lessen a salutary veneration for an instrument so often calling for such explanatory interpositions. A paramount or even a definitive Authority in the individual States, would soon make the Constitution & laws different in different States, and thus destroy that equality & uniformity of rights & duties which form the essence of the Compact; to say nothing of the opportunity given to the States individually of involving by their decisions the whole Union in foreign Contests. To leave conflicting decisions to be settled between the Judicial parties could not promise a happy result. The end must be a trial of strength between the Posse headed by the Marshal and the Posse headed by the Sheriff. Nor would the issue be safe if left to a compromise between the two Govts. the case of a disagreement between different Govts. being essentially different from a disagreement between branches of the same Govts. In the latter case neither party being able to consummate its will without the concurrence of the other, there is a necessity on both to consult and to accommodate. No so, with different Govts. each possessing every branch of power necessary to carry its purpose into compleat effect. It here becomes a question between Independent Nations, with no other *dernier* resort than physical force. Negotiation might indeed in some instances avoid this extremity; but how often would it happen, among so many States, that an unaccommodating spirit in some would render that resource unavailing.

We arrive at the agitated question whether the Judicial Authority of the U.S. be the constitutional resort for determining the line between the federal & State jurisdictions. Believing as I do that the General Convention regarded a provision within the Constitution for deciding in a peaceable & regular mode all cases arising in the course of its operation, as essential to an adequate System of Govt. that it intended the Authority vested in the Judicial Department as a final resort in relation to the States, for cases resulting to it in the exercise of its functions, (the concurrence of the Senate chosen by the State Legislatures, in appointing the Judges, and the oaths & official tenures of these, with the surveillance of public Opinion, being relied on as guarantying their impartiality); and that this intention is expressed by the articles declaring that the federal Constitution & laws shall be the supreme law of the land, and that the Judicial Power of the U.S. shall extend to all cases arising under them: Believing moreover that this was the prevailing view of the subject when the Constitution was adopted & put into execution; that it has so continued thro' the long period which has elapsed; and that even at this time an appeal to a national decision would prove that no general change has taken place: thus believing I have never yielded my original opinion indicated in the "Federalist" No. 39. . . .

I am not unaware that the Judiciary career has not corresponded with what was anticipated. At one period the Judges perverted the Bench of Justice into a rostrum for partizan harangues. And latterly the Court, by some of its decisions, still more by extrajudicial reasonings & dicta, has manifested a propensity to enlarge the general authority in derogation of the local, and to amplify its own jurisdiction, which has justly incurred the public censure. And if no remedy of the abuse be practicable under the forms of the Constitution, I should prefer a resort to the Nation for an amendment of the Tribunal itself, to continual appeals from its controverted decisions to that Ultimate Arbiter.

POINTS FOR DISCUSSION

1. In his letter, Madison assessed various mechanisms for resolving federal-state power disputes. How does his assessment of the relative merits of these mechanisms differ from Jefferson's assessment?

2. Consider Jefferson's argument that the ultimate arbiter of the Constitution is the people. Is judicial review necessarily inconsistent with that claim? Recall Hamilton's argument in *The Federalist No. 78* that judicial review effectuates the will of the people in establishing the Constitution. Does Jefferson's claim that the people are the ultimate arbiter support the state nullification power that he asserted in the Kentucky Resolutions of 1798? Recall Yates's argument in *The Anti-Federalist* that Congress represents the will of the people. Does ultimate sovereignty of the people resolve the question of how, under the Constitution, disputes over federal and state power should be resolved?

3. Madison's endorsement of judicial review in this letter arguably lies in tension with his assertion of state authority to resolve some constitutional disputes in the Virginia Resolutions of 1798. What accounts for this tension? Did Madison adjust his views according to the political exigencies and practical realities of the times? If so, should he have?

The last case in this chapter is *Gibbons v. Ogden*, 22 U.S. (9 Wheat.) 1 (1824). It is an appropriate case with which to conclude, for it involves each key issue that you have studied thus far:

- *The Scope of Federal and State Power. Gibbons* considers the relative authority of the federal government and the states. Specifically, it addresses the scope of Congress's power to regulate interstate commerce and how that power affects state regulatory power.
- *Resolving Disputes over Federal and State Power. Gibbons* employs judicial review as a mechanism for resolving a dispute over federal and state

regulatory authority under the Constitution. The *Gibbons* Court examines both (a) whether an act of Congress falls within Congress's enumerated powers under the Constitution and (b) whether a state may enforce its law in the face of conflicting federal law.

- *Constitutional Interpretation. Gibbons* rejects the strict construction of congressional powers that Jefferson and Tucker advocated. Moreover, *Gibbons* illustrates the use of important modalities of constitutional interpretation, including text, historical practice, structure, and purpose.

Additionally, *Gibbons* foreshadows the development of three important doctrines that you will study in this book:

- *The Commerce Clause.* From *Gibbons* to the present day, the Court has attempted to define Congress's enumerated power to regulate interstate commerce. Over the last century, the Commerce Clause developed into a primary font of federal regulatory schemes in a broad array of areas. The Court has heard many challenges to federal authority under the Commerce Clause and continues to do so today. Indeed, in the 1990s and 2000s, the Court heard a flurry of such cases, striking down two acts of Congress as exceeding its power to regulate interstate commerce in *United States v. Lopez*, 514 U.S. 549 (1995), and *United States v. Morrison*, 529 U.S. 598 (2000). *Gibbons* has factored prominently in such cases, not only for how it defines the commerce power but also for how it suggests courts should evaluate the constitutionality of congressional acts under the Commerce Clause.
- *The Negative Commerce Clause.* In *Gibbons*, the Court did not resolve whether the Constitution's conferral of power on Congress to regulate interstate commerce implicitly precludes the states from regulating acts that fall within Congress's commerce power. The Court did, however, acknowledge the issue. In the twentieth century, the Court developed a so-called *negative* or *dormant* Commerce Clause jurisprudence, holding that the Commerce Clause implicitly preempts certain state laws relating to interstate commerce. The line that divides allowable from prohibited state regulation has proven, in some cases, difficult to draw.
- *Statutory Preemption.* In *Gibbons*, the Court explained that a state may not enforce a law that conflicts with a validly enacted federal statute. In other words, federal law preempts conflicting state law. The Court has struggled, over time, to define the contours of federal preemption of state law. Justices have vigorously debated the scope of preemption, and preemption remains one of the most important and contested issues in U.S. federalism.

As you read *Gibbons v. Ogden*, consider how the Court's opinion reflects upon the issues of federalism that you have considered in this chapter. Think too, at least preliminarily, about the kinds of issues the Court might face after *Gibbons* about the scope of the commerce power, the implied preemption of state law under the Commerce Clause, and federal statutory preemption of state law.

GIBBONS V. OGDEN

22 U.S. (9 Wheat.) 1 (1824)

[The New York Legislature granted Robert Livingston and Robert Fulton exclusive rights to operate steamboats in waters of New York. Livingston and Fulton assigned rights to Aaron Ogden to run a ferry between New York and New Jersey. Thomas Gibbons operated a steamboat service that competed with Ogden's ferry. Under an act of Congress, Gibbons' ferries were licensed as "vessels to be employed in the coasting trade." Ogden sued in New York courts to enjoin Gibbons from operating his vessels in New York waters. The New York courts granted the injunction, and Gibbons appealed.]

Mr. CHIEF JUSTICE MARSHALL delivered the opinion of the Court. . . .

As preliminary to the very able discussions of the constitution, which we have heard from the bar, and as having some influence on its construction, reference has been made to the political situation of these States, anterior to its formation. It has been said, that they were sovereign, were completely independent, and were connected with each other only by a league. This is true. But, when these allied sovereigns converted their league into a government, when they converted their Congress of Ambassadors, deputed to deliberate on their common concerns, and to recommend measures of general utility, into a Legislature, empowered to enact laws on the most interesting subjects, the whole character in which the States appear, underwent a change, the extent of which must be determined by a fair consideration of the instrument by which that change was effected.

This instrument contains an enumeration of powers expressly granted by the people to their government. It has been said, that these powers ought to be construed strictly. But why ought they to be so construed? Is there one sentence in the constitution which gives countenance to this rule? In the last of the enumerated powers, that which grants, expressly, the means for carrying all others into execution, Congress is authorized "to make all laws which shall be necessary and proper" for the purpose. But this limitation on the means which may be used, is not extended to the powers which are conferred; nor is there one sentence in the constitution, which has been pointed out by the gentlemen of the bar, or which we have been able to discern, that prescribes this rule. We do not, therefore, think ourselves justified in adopting it. What do gentlemen mean, by a strict construction? If they contend only against that enlarged construction, which would extend words beyond their natural and obvious import, we might question the application of the term, but should not controvert the principle. If they contend for that narrow construction which, in support or some theory not to be found in the constitution, would deny to the government those powers which the words of the grant, as usually understood, import, and which are consistent with the general views and objects of the instrument; for that narrow construction, which would cripple the government, and render it unequal to the object for which it is declared to be instituted, and to which the powers given, as fairly understood, render it competent; then we cannot perceive the propriety of this strict construction, nor adopt it as the rule by which the constitution is to be expounded. As men, whose intentions require no concealment, generally employ the words which most directly and aptly express the ideas they intend to convey, the enlightened patriots who framed our constitution, and the people who adopted it, must be understood to have employed words in their natural sense, and to have intended what they have said. If, from the imperfection of human language, there should be serious doubts respecting the extent of any given power, it is a well settled rule, that the objects for which it was given, especially when those objects are expressed in the instrument itself, should have great influence in the construction. We know of no reason for excluding this rule from the present case. The grant does not convey power which might be beneficial to the grantor, if retained by himself, or which can enure solely to the benefit of the grantee; but is an investment of power for the general advantage, in the hands of agents selected for that purpose; which power can never be exercised by the people themselves, but must be placed in the hands of agents, or lie dormant. We know of no rule for construing the extent of such powers, other than is given by the language of the instrument which confers them, taken in connexion with the purposes for which they were conferred.

The words are, "Congress shall have power to regulate commerce with foreign nations, and among the several States, and with the Indian tribes."

The subject to be regulated is commerce; and our constitution being . . . one of enumeration, and not of definition, to ascertain the extent of the power, it becomes necessary to settle the meaning of the word. The counsel for the appellee would limit it to traffic, to buying and selling, or the interchange of commodities, and do not admit that it comprehends navigation. This would restrict a general term, applicable to many objects, to one of its significations. Commerce, undoubtedly, is traffic, but it is something more: it is intercourse. It describes the commercial intercourse between nations, and parts of nations, in all its branches, and is regulated by prescribing rules for carrying on that intercourse. The mind can scarcely conceive a system for regulating commerce between nations, which shall exclude all laws concerning navigation, which shall be silent on the admission of the vessels of the one nation into the ports of the other, and be confined to prescribing rules for the conduct of individuals, in the actual employment of buying and selling, or of barter.

If commerce does not include navigation, the government of the Union has no direct power over that subject, and can make no law prescribing what shall constitute American vessels, or requiring that they shall be navigated by American seamen. Yet this power has been exercised from the commencement of the government, has been exercised with the consent of all, and has been understood by all to be a commercial regulation. All America understands, and has uniformly understood, the word "commerce," to comprehend navigation. It was so understood, and must have been so understood, when the constitution was framed. The power over commerce, including navigation, was one of the primary objects for which the people of America adopted their government, and must have been contemplated in forming it. The convention must have used the word in that sense, because all have understood it in that sense; and the attempt to restrict it comes too late. . . .

The word used in the constitution, then, comprehends, and has been always understood to comprehend, navigation within its meaning; and a power to regulate navigation, is as expressly granted, as if that term had been added to the word "commerce."

To what commerce does this power extend? The constitution informs us, to commerce "with foreign nations, and among the several States, and with the Indian tribes."

It has, we believe, been universally admitted, that these words comprehend every species of commercial intercourse between the United States and foreign nations. No sort of trade can be carried on between this country and any other, to which this power does not extend. It has been truly said, that commerce, as the word is used in the constitution, is a unit, every part of which is indicated by the term.

If this be the admitted meaning of the word, in its application to foreign nations, it must carry the same meaning throughout the sentence, and remain a unit, unless there be some plain intelligible cause which alters it.

The subject to which the power is next applied, is to commerce "among the several States." The word "among" means intermingled with. A thing which is among others, is intermingled with them. Commerce among the States, cannot stop at the external boundary line of each State, but may be introduced into the interior.

It is not intended to say that these words comprehend that commerce, which is completely internal, which is carried on between man and man in a State, or between different parts of the same State, and which does not extend to or affect other States. Such a power would be inconvenient, and is certainly unnecessary.

Comprehensive as the word "among" is, it may very properly be restricted to that commerce which concerns more States than one. The phrase is not one which would probably have been selected to indicate the completely interior traffic of a State, because it is not an apt phrase for that purpose; and the enumeration of the particular classes of commerce, to which the power was to be extended, would not have been made, had the intention been to extend the power to every description. The enumeration presupposes something not enumerated; and that something, if we regard the language or the subject of the sentence, must be the exclusively internal commerce of a State. The genius and character of the whole government seem to be, that its action is to be applied to all the external concerns of the nation, and to those internal concerns which affect the States generally; but not to those which are completely within a particular State, which do not affect other States, and with which it is not necessary to interfere, for the purpose of executing some of the general powers of the government. The completely internal commerce of a State, then, may be considered as reserved for the State itself. . . .

We are now arrived at the inquiry — What is this power?

It is the power to regulate; that is, to prescribe the rule by which commerce is to be governed. This power, like all others vested in Congress, is complete in itself, may be exercised to its utmost extent, and acknowledges no limitations, other than are prescribed in the constitution. These are expressed in plain terms, and do not affect the questions which arise in this case, or which have been discussed at the bar. If, as has always been understood, the sovereignty of Congress, though limited to specified objects, is plenary as to those objects, the power over commerce with foreign nations, and among the several States, is vested in Congress as absolutely as it would be in a single government, having in its constitution the same restrictions on the exercise of the power as are found in the constitution of the United States. The wisdom and the discretion of Congress, their identity with the people, and the influence which their constituents possess at elections, are, in this, as in many other instances, as that, for example, of declaring war, the sole restraints on which they have relied, to secure them from its abuse. They are the restraints on which the people must often rely solely, in all representative governments.

The power of Congress, then, comprehends navigation, within the limits of every State in the Union; so far as that navigation may be, in any manner, connected with "commerce with foreign nations, or among the several States, or with the Indian tribes." It may, of consequence, pass the jurisdictional line of New York, and act upon the very waters to which the prohibition now under consideration applies.

But it has been urged with great earnestness, that, although the power of Congress to regulate commerce with foreign nations, and among the several States, be co-extensive with the subject itself, and have no other limits than are prescribed in the constitution, yet the States may severally exercise the same power, within their respective jurisdictions. In support of this argument, it is said, that they possessed it as an inseparable attribute of sovereignty, before the formation of the constitution, and still retain it, except so far as they have surrendered it by that instrument; that this principle results from the nature of the government, and is secured by the tenth amendment; that an affirmative grant of power is not exclusive, unless in its own nature it be such that the continued exercise of it by the former possessor is inconsistent with the grant, and that this is not of that description.

The appellant . . . contends, that full power to regulate a particular subject, implies the whole power, and leaves no residuum; that a grant of the whole is incompatible with the existence of a right in another to any part of it. . . .

In discussing the question, whether this power is still in the States, in the case under consideration, we may dismiss from it the inquiry, whether it is surrendered by the mere grant to Congress, or is retained until Congress shall exercise the power. We may dismiss that inquiry, because it has been exercised, and the regulations which Congress deemed it proper to make, are now in full operation. The sole question is, can a State regulate commerce with foreign nations and among the States, while Congress is regulating it? . . .

It is obvious, that the government of the Union, in the exercise of its express powers, that, for example, of regulating commerce with foreign nations and among the States, may use means that may also be employed by a State, in the exercise of its acknowledged powers; that, for example, of regulating commerce within the State. If Congress license vessels to sail from one port to another, in the same State, the act is supposed to be, necessarily, incidental to the power expressly granted to Congress, and implies no claim of a direct power to regulate the purely internal commerce of a State, or to act directly on its system of police. So, if a State, in passing laws on subjects acknowledged to be within its control, and with a view to those subjects, shall adopt a measure of the same character with one which Congress may adopt, it does not derive its authority from the particular power which has been granted, but from some other, which remains with the State, and may be executed by the same means. All experience shows, that the same measures, or measures scarcely distinguishable from each other, may flow from distinct powers; but this does not prove that the powers themselves are identical. Although the means used in their execution may sometimes approach each other so nearly as to be confounded, there are other situations in which they are sufficiently distinct to establish their individuality.

In our complex system, presenting the rare and difficult scheme of one general government, whose action extends over the whole, but which possesses only certain enumerated powers; and of numerous State governments, which retain and exercise all powers not delegated to the Union, contests respecting power must arise. . . .

Since . . . in exercising the power of regulating their own purely internal affairs, whether of trading or police, the States may sometimes enact laws, the validity of which depends on their interfering with, and being contrary to, an act of Congress passed in pursuance of the constitution, the Court will enter upon the inquiry, whether the laws of New York, as expounded by the highest tribunal of that State, have, in their application to this case, come into collision with an act of Congress, and deprived a citizen of a right to which that act entitles him. Should this collision exist, it will be immaterial whether those laws were passed in virtue of a concurrent power "to regulate commerce with foreign nations and among the several States," or, in virtue of a power to regulate their domestic trade and police. In one case and the other, the acts of New York must yield to the law of Congress; and the decision sustaining the privilege they confer, against a right given by a law of the Union, must be erroneous.

This opinion has been frequently expressed in this Court, and is founded, as well on the nature of the government as on the words of the constitution. In argument, however, it has been contended, that if a law passed by a State, in the exercise of its acknowledged sovereignty, comes into conflict with a law passed by Congress in pursuance of the constitution, they affect the subject, and each other, like equal opposing powers.

But the framers of our constitution foresaw this state of things, and provided for it, by declaring the supremacy not only of itself, but of the laws made in pursuance of it. The nullity of any act inconsistent with the constitution, is produced by the declaration, that the constitution is the supreme law. The appropriate application of that part of the clause which confers the same supremacy on laws and treaties, is to such acts of the State Legislatures as do not transcend their powers, but, though enacted in the execution of acknowledged State powers, interfere with, or are contrary to the laws of Congress, made in pursuance of the constitution, or some treaty made under the authority of the United States. In every such case, the act of Congress, or the treaty, is supreme; and the law of the State, though enacted in the exercise of powers not controverted, must yield to it. . . .

[The Court determined that New York's grant of a steamboat monopoly to Livingston and Fulton conflicted with Acts of Congress providing for coastal licenses.]

Mr. JUSTICE JOHNSON.

The "power to regulate commerce," here meant to be granted, was that power to regulate commerce which previously existed in the States. But what was that power? The States were, unquestionably, supreme; and each possessed that power over commerce, which is acknowledged to reside in every sovereign State. The definition and limits of that power are to be sought among the features of international law; and, as it was not only admitted, but insisted on by both parties, in argument, that, *"unaffected by a state of war, by treaties, or by municipal regulations, all commerce among independent States was legitimate,"* there is no necessity to appeal to the oracles of the *jus commune* for the correctness of that doctrine. The law of nations, regarding man as a social animal, pronounces all commerce legitimate in a state of peace, until prohibited by positive law. The power of a sovereign state over commerce, therefore, amounts to nothing more than a power to limit and restrain it at pleasure. And since the power to prescribe the limits to its freedom, necessarily implies the power to determine what shall remain unrestrained, it follows, that the power must be exclusive; it can reside but in one potentate; and hence, the grant of this power carries with it the whole subject, leaving nothing for the State to act upon. . . .

It has been contended, that the grants of power to the United States over any subject, do not, necessarily, paralyze the arm of the States, or deprive them of the capacity to act on the same subject. . . .

It is no objection to the existence of distinct, substantive powers, that, in their application, they bear upon the same subject. The same bale of goods, the same cask of provisions, or the same ship, that may be the subject of commercial regulation, may also be the vehicle of disease. And the health laws that require them to be stopped and ventilated, are no more intended as regulations on commerce, than the laws which permit their importation, are intended to innoculate the community with disease. Their different purposes mark the distinction between the powers brought into action; and while frankly exercised, they can produce no serious collision. . . .

It would be in vain to deny the possibility of a clashing and collision between the measures of the two governments. The line cannot be drawn with sufficient distinctness between the municipal powers of the one, and the commercial powers of the other. In some points they meet and blend so as scarcely to admit of separation. Hitherto the only remedy has been applied which the case admits of; that of a frank and candid co-operation for the general good. Witness the laws of Congress requiring its officers to respect the inspection laws of the States, and to aid in enforcing their health laws; that which surrenders to the States the superintendence of pilotage, and the many laws passed to permit a tonnage duty to be levied for the use of their ports. Other instances could be cited, abundantly to prove that collision must be sought to be produced; and when it does arise, the question must be decided how far the powers of Congress are adequate to put it down. Wherever the powers of the respective governments are frankly exercised, with a distinct view to the ends of such powers, they may act upon the same object, or use the same means, and yet the powers be kept perfectly distinct. A resort to the same means, therefore, is no argument to prove the identity of their respective powers. . . .

POINTS FOR DISCUSSION

1. In *Gibbons*, the Court defined "commerce" to be commercial intercourse, including navigation. Moreover, Chief Justice Marshall explained that the commerce power

> is complete in itself, may be exercised to its utmost extent, and acknowledges no limitations, other than are prescribed in the constitution. These are expressed in plain terms, and do not affect the questions which arise in this case, or which have been discussed at the bar. If, as has always been understood, the sovereignty of Congress, though limited to specified objects, is plenary as to those objects, the power over commerce with foreign nations, and among the several States, is vested in Congress as absolutely as it would be in a single government, having in its constitution the same restrictions on the exercise of the power as are found in the constitution of the United States. The wisdom and the discretion of Congress, their identity with the people, and the influence which their constituents possess at elections, are, in this, as in many other instances, as that, for example, of declaring war, the sole restraints on which they have relied, to secure them from abuse. They are the restraints on which the people must often rely solely, in all representative governments.

Supreme Court Justices have debated the meaning of this passage. Some argue that it means that courts must afford Congress great deference in determining whether a regulation falls within its commerce power. On this view, the primary safeguard of state interests and regulatory autonomy against congressional overreaching is the political process, not the courts. Others argue that this passage means only that Congress's power to regulate interstate commerce may not be restrained if Congress, in fact, is regulating interstate commerce. On this view, courts may scrutinize whether an act of Congress is, in fact, a regulation of interstate commerce. Which reading of this passage is more compelling?

2. The *Gibbons* Court refrained from deciding whether the Commerce Clause itself preempts state regulation of interstate commerce in the absence of federal regulation. As you will study in Chapter 7, Justices have disputed whether and when the Commerce Clause implicitly preempts state regulation relating to interstate commerce. Before you read these cases, consider when, if ever, courts should hold the Commerce Clause to implicitly preempt state regulation absent congressional action.

3. The *Gibbons* Court held, under the Supremacy Clause, that an act of Congress preempts conflicting state law. To be preempted, must state law actually conflict with federal law? What if state law obstructs a purpose of federal law but does not conflict with its actual commands? Recall that in *McCullough v. Maryland*, 17 U.S. (4 Wheat.) 316 (1819), the Court explained: "It is of the very essence of supremacy, to remove all obstacles to its action within its own sphere, and so to modify every power vested in subordinate governments, as to exempt its own operations from their own influence." *Id.* at 427. Imagine that New York, rather than granting exclusive navigation rights, had imposed strict safety and inspection requirements upon vessels engaged in navigation — requirements that made federally licensed navigation more expensive to perform. Should the Court have held such a state law unconstitutional, not because it conflicted with federal law, but because it obstructed an important purpose of a federal law, namely to encourage commercial navigation? In Chapter 7, when you study federal preemption of state law in more detail, you will see how the Justices have dealt with such questions.

2

CONTESTING AND RECONSTRUCTING AMERICAN FEDERALISM

This chapter considers various federalism questions that arose during the antebellum and Reconstruction periods. As you studied in the last chapter, the Virginia and Kentucky Resolutions of 1798 and 1799 asserted some state authority to counteract unconstitutional federal laws. No other states adopted these resolutions, and the Supreme Court, under Chief Justice John Marshall, upheld contested assertions of federal power in several cases. In ensuing years, advocates of state power to nullify federal law invoked the Virginia and Kentucky Resolutions as authority. The Supreme Court continued to address controversial questions of federal power into the mid-nineteenth century — including in the context of slavery. After the secession of southern states and Civil War, the Reconstruction Amendments to the Constitution abolished slavery (Thirteenth Amendment), guaranteed certain individual rights against states (Fourteenth Amendment), and forbade states from denying U.S. citizens the right to vote (Fifteenth Amendment). Each of these amendments empowered Congress to enforce its provisions by appropriate legislation. These amendments recalibrated, in some measure, the relative powers of the federal government and the states.

This chapter explores the nullification and secession crisis that preceded the Civil War, constitutional questions of federal power that slavery generated, and the postwar Reconstruction Amendments to the Constitution. The extent to which the Reconstruction Amendments changed the balance of federal and state power under the Constitution remains to be worked out fully even to the present day.

As you read the materials in this chapter, consider the following questions:

- Was nullification a constitutional check on congressional power?
- How did the Court's treatment of federal power relating to slavery differ, if at all, from Marshall Court treatments of federal power? How did values about slavery as an institution factor in the Court's decisions?

- How did the Reconstruction Amendments affect the relationship between the federal government and the states?
- How should the judiciary responsibly discharge its duty to decide cases involving the relative powers of the federal government and the states?

A. THE CONSTITUTIONALITY OF NULLIFICATION

This section addresses the question of nullification—whether a state has the power to hold an act of Congress unconstitutional and without force within the state's territorial jurisdiction. Proponents of nullification invoked the Virginia and Kentucky Resolutions of 1798 and 1799, which you studied in the last chapter.

Federal tariff acts precipitated the nullification controversy. In 1828, Congress enacted a tariff designed to protect industries in the United States from European competition by increasing the price of goods imported from Europe. The tariff met opposition in Southern states because of its effect on their interests: Among other things, British demand for U.S. cotton, produced in the South, diminished in response to the tariff, and the price at which manufactured goods were available in Southern states increased. Members of the South Carolina legislature asked then–Vice President John C. Calhoun to write a report on the tariff. (Notably, Calhoun had previously been a nationalist and supporter of protective tariffs.) Calhoun obliged, drafting what became known as the "South Carolina Exposition." In the *Exposition*, Calhoun set forth and defended a doctrine of nullification. He relied on both the Virginia Resolutions of 1798 and Madison's 1800 *Report on the Virginia Resolutions*. Eventually, in 1832, a South Carolina state convention declared the federal tariff acts unconstitutional and unenforceable in South Carolina.

In this section, you will read two selections—excerpts of (1) Calhoun's 1828 *Exposition,* as reported to the South Carolina House of Representatives, and (2) a letter from James Madison to Edward Everett, dated August 28, 1830. Calhoun provides a theory in favor of nullification, and Madison argues against it. According to Calhoun, a state could nullify a federal law, subject to override by three-fourths of the states. These selections complement each other well because both not only discuss the constitutional legitimacy of nullification but also engage Madison's 1798 Virginia Resolutions and 1800 *Report* on them.

As you read these selections, keep in mind the following questions:

- What is the nature of Calhoun and Madison's disagreement regarding judicial review as an authoritative means of resolving constitutional disputes over federal-state power?
- What is the nature of Calhoun and Madison's disagreement over the constitutionality of state nullification of federal law?
- Who, Calhoun or Madison, more accurately describes the import of the Virginia Resolutions of 1798?

THE SOUTH CAROLINA EXPOSITION

1828

[In the S.C. House of Representatives, December 19, 1828.] . . . [T]he Act of Congress of the last session, with the whole system of legislation imposing duties on imports, not for revenue, but for the protection of one branch of industry, at the expense of others, is unconstitutional, unequal and oppressive; calculated to corrupt the public morals, and to destroy the liberty of the country. . . .

The General Government is one of specific powers, and it can rightfully exercise only the powers expressly granted, and those that may be "necessary and proper" to carry them into effect; all others being reserved expressly to the States, or to the people. It results necessarily, that those who claim to exercise a power under the Constitution, are bound to shew, that it is expressly granted, or that it is necessary and proper, as a means to some of the granted powers. The advocates of the Tariff have offered no such proof. . . .

It would be weakness to attempt to disguise the fact . . . that different and opposing interests do, and must ever exist in this country, against the danger of which *representation* affords not the slightest protection. . . . Thus to prevent rulers from abusing their trust, constituents must controul them through elections; and so to prevent the major from oppressing the minor interests of society, the constitution must provide . . . a check founded on the same principle, and equally efficacious. . . . Those governments only, which provide checks, which limit and restrain within proper bounds the power of the majority, have had a prolonged existence, and been distinguished for virtue, power and happiness. . . .

In drawing the line between the General and State Governments, the great difficulty consisted in determining correctly to which the various political powers belonged. This difficult duty was however performed with so much success, that to this day there is an almost uniform acquiescence in the correctness with which it was executed. It would be extraordinary if a system thus based, with profound wisdom, on the diversity of geographical interest, should make no provision against the danger of their conflict. The framers of our constitution[] have not exposed themselves to the imputations of such weakness. When their work is fairly examined it will be found, that they have provided, with admirable skill, the most effective remedy, and that if it has not prevented the approach of the dangers, the fault is not theirs, but ours, in neglecting to make the proper application of it. The powers of the General Government are particularly enumerated, and specifically delegated; all others are expressly reserved to the States and the people. Those of the General Government are intended to act uniformly on all the parts, the residue are left to the States, by whom alone from the nature of these powers, they can be justly and fairly exercised.

Our system, then consists of two distinct and independent sovereignties. The general powers conferred on the General Government, are subject to its sole and separate control, and the States cannot, without violating the Constitution, interpose their authority to check, or in any manner counteract its movements, so long, as they are confined to its proper sphere; so also the peculiar and local powers, reserved to the States, are subject to their exclusive control, nor can the General Government interfere with them, without on its part, also violating the Constitution. In order to have a full and clear conception of our institutions, it will be proper to remark, that there is in our system a striking distinction between the government and the sovereign power. Whatever may be the true doctrine in regard to the sovereignty of the States individually, it is unquestionably clear that while the government of the union is vested in its legislative, executive and political departments, the actual sovereign power, resides in the several States, who created it, in their separate and distinct political character. But by an express provision of the Constitution it may be amended or changed, by three-fourths of the States; and each State by assenting to the Constitution with this provision, has surrendered its original rights as a sovereign, which made its individual consent necessary to any change in its political condition, and has placed this important power in the hands of three-fourths of the States; in which the sovereignty of the union under the Constitution does now actually reside. Not the least portion of this high sovereign authority, resides in Congress or any of the departments of the General Government. They are but the creatures of the Constitution, appointed, but to execute its provisions, and therefore, any attempt in all or any of the departments to exercise any power definitely, which in its consequences may alter the nature of the instrument or change the condition of the parties to it, would be an act of the highest political usurpation. It is thus, that our political system, recognizing the opposition of geographical interests in the community, has provided the most efficient check against its dangers. . . . [T]he Constitution has made us a community only to the extent of our common interest, leaving the States distinct and independent, as to their peculiar interests, and has drawn the line of separation with consummate skill. The great question however is, what means are provided by our system for the purpose of enforcing this fundamental provision: If we look to the practical operation of the system, we will find, on the side of the States, not a solitary constitutional means resorted to, in order to protect their reserved rights, against the encroachment of the General Government, while the latter has from the beginning, adopted the most efficient, to prevent that of the States on their authority. The 25th section of the Judiciary Act, passed in 1789, provides an appeal from the State[] Courts to the Supreme Court of the United States, in all cases in the decision of which the construction of the Constitution, the laws of Congress, or treaties of the United States may be involved; thus giving to that high tribunal the right of final interpretation, and the power in reality of nullifying the Acts of the State Legislatures, whenever in their opinion they may conflict with the power delegated to the General Government. A more ample and complete protection against the encroachments of the States by their Legislatures cannot be imagined; and for this purpose, this high power may be considered indispensable and constitutional; but by a strange misconception of the nature of our system, in fact, of the nature of government, it has been regarded, not only as affording protection to the General Government against the States, but also to the States against the General Government; and as the only means provided by the

Constitution of restraining the State and General Government within their respective spheres; and consequently of deciding on the extent of the powers of each, even where a State in its highest sovereign capacity, is at issue with the General Government on the question, whether a particular power be delegated, or not. Such a construction of the powers of the Federal Court, which would raise one of the departments of the General Government, above the sovereign parties, who created the Constitution, would enable it in practice to alter at pleasure the relative powers of the States and General Government. This most erroneous and dangerous doctrine, in regard to the powers of the Federal Court, has been . . . ably refuted by Mr. Madison in his report to the Virginia Legislature, in 1800. . . . Speaking of the rights of the State to interpret the Constitution for itself in the last resort he says: "that it has been objected that the judicial authority is to be regarded, as the sole expositor of the Constitution; on this objection it might be observed — 1st. That there may be instances of usurped power," (the case of the Tariff is a striking illustration of its truth,) "which the forms of the Constitution could never draw within the control of the judicial department: *secondly,* that if the decision of the judiciary, be raised above the authority of the sovereign parties to the Constitution, the decisions of the other departments, not carried by the forms of the Constitution before the judiciary, must be equally authoritative and final with the decision of that department. But the proper answer to the objection is, that the resolution of the General Assembly, relates to those, great and extraordinary cases, in which all the forms of the Constitution may prove ineffectual against infractions, dangerous to the essential rights of the parties to it. The resolution supposes, that dangerous powers not delegated, may not only be usurped and executed by the other departments, but that the judicial department also may exercise, or sanction dangerous powers beyond the grant of the Constitution, and consequently, that the ultimate right of the parties to the Constitution, to judge, whether the compact has been dangerously violated, must extend to violations by one delegated authority as well as by another — by the judiciary as well by the Executive, or the Legislature. . . ."

A government like ours of divided powers, must necessarily give great importance to a proper system of construction [of the Constitution through judicial review], but it is perfectly clear that no system of the kind, however perfect, can prescribe bounds to the encroachment of power. They constitute in fact, but an appeal by the minority to the justice of the majority, and if such appeals were sufficient to restrain the avarice, and ambition of those, who are invested with power, then would a system of technical construction be sufficient. But on such a supposition, reason and justice might alone be relied on, without the aid of any constitutional or artificial restraint whatever. Universal experience, in all ages and countries however, teaches that power can only be met by power, and not by reason and justice, and that all restrictions on authority, unsustained by an equal antagonist power, must forever prove wholly insufficient in practice. . . . [C]onstruction [of the Constitution through the power of judicial review,] on which reliance is placed, to preserve the rights of the States, has been wielded, as it ever will and must be if not checked, to destroy those rights. . . . But that protection, which the minor interest ever fails to find, in any technical system of construction, where alone in practice it has heretofore been sought, it may find in the reserved rights of the States themselves, if they be properly called into action; and there only will it ever be found of sufficient efficacy. The constitutional power to protect their rights as members of the confederacy, results necessarily, by the most simple and demonstrable arguments, from the very nature of the relation subsisting between the States and General Government. If it be conceded, as it must by every one who is the least conversant with our institutions, that the sovereign power is divided between the States and General Government, and that the former holds its reserved rights, in the same high sovereign capacity, which the latter does its delegated rights; it will be impossible to deny to the States the right of deciding on the infraction of their rights, and the proper remedy to be applied for the correction. The right of judging, in such cases, is an essential attribute of sovereignty of which the States cannot be divested, without losing their sovereignty itself; and being reduced to a subordinate corporate condition. In fact, to divide power, and to give to one of the parties the exclusive right of judging of the portion allotted to each, is in reality not to divide at all; and to reserve such exclusive right to the General Government, (it matters not by what department it be exercised,) is in fact to constitute it one great consolidated government, with unlimited powers, and to reduce the States to mere corporations. . . . [T]he existence of the right of judging of their powers, clearly established from the sovereignty of the States, as clearly implies a veto, or controul on the action of the General Government on contested points of authority; and this very controul is the remedy, which the Constitution has provided to prevent the encroachment of the General Government on the reserved right of the States; and by the exercise of which, the distribution of power between the General and State Governments, may be preserved forever inviolate, as is established by the Constitution; and thus afford effectual protection to the great minor interest of the community, against the oppression of the majority. . . .

LETTER FROM JAMES MADISON TO EDWARD EVERETT

28 August 1830

[DEAR] SIR—I have duly [received] your letter in [which] you refer to the "nullifying doctrine," advocated as a constitutional right by some of our distinguished fellow citizens; and to the proceedings of the [Virginia] legislature in 98 & 99, as appealed to in behalf of that doctrine; and you express a wish for my ideas on those subjects. . . .

In order to understand the true character of the Constitution of the U.S. the error, not uncommon, must be avoided, of viewing it through the medium either of a consolidated Government or of a confederated [Government] whilst it is neither the one nor the other, but a mixture of both. . . .

[T]he characteristic peculiarities of the Constitution are 1. The mode of its formation, 2. The division of the supreme powers of [Government] between the States in their united capacity and the States in their individual capacities.

1. It was formed, not by the Governments of the component States, as the Federal [Government] for which it was substituted was formed; nor was it formed by a majority of the people of the U.S. as a single community in the manner of a consolidated Government.

It was formed by the States — that is by the people in each of the States, acting in their highest sovereign capacity; and formed, consequently by the same authority which formed the State Constitutions.

Being thus derived from the same source as the Constitutions of the States, it has within each State, the same authority as the Constitution of the State; and is as much a Constitution, in the strict sense of the term, within its prescribed sphere, as the Constitutions of the States are within their respective spheres; but with this obvious & essential difference, that being a compact among the States in their highest sovereign capacity, and constituting the people thereof one people for certain purposes, it cannot be altered or annulled at the will of the States individually, as the Constitution of a State may be at its individual will.

2. And that it divides the supreme powers of [Government] between the [Government] of the United States, & the [Government] of the individual States, is stamped on the face of the instrument; the powers of war and taxation, of commerce & of treaties, and other enumerated powers vested in the [Government] of the U.S. being of as high & sovereign a character as any of the powers reserved to the State [Governments].

Nor is the [Government] of the U.S. created by the Constitution, less a [Government] in the strict sense of the term, within the sphere of its powers, than the [Government] created by the constitutions of the States are within their several spheres. It is like them organized into Legislative, Executive, & Judiciary Departments. It operates like them, directly on persons & things. And, like them, it has at command a physical force for executing the powers committed to it. The concurrent operation in certain cases is one of the features marking the peculiarity of the system.

Between these different constitutional [Governments] — the one operating in all the States, the others operating separately in each, with the aggregate powers of [Government] divided between them, it could not escape attention that controversies would arise concerning the boundaries of jurisdiction; and that some provision ought to be made for such occurrences. A political system that does not provide for a peaceable & authoritative termination of occurring controversies, would not be more than the shadow of a [Government]; the object & end of a real [Government] being the substitution of law & order for uncertainty[,] confusion, and violence.

That to have left a final decision in such cases to each of the States, then 13 & already 24, could not fail to make the [Constitution and] laws of the U.S. different in different States was obvious; and not less obvious, that this diversity of independent decisions, must altogether distract the [Government] of the Union & speedily put an end to the Union itself. A uniform authority of the laws, is in itself a vital principle. . . .

To have made the decisions under the authority of the individual States, co-ordinate in all cases with decisions under the authority of the U.S. would unavoidably produce collisions incompatible with the peace of society, & with that regular & efficient administration which is the essence of free [Government]. Scenes could not be avoided in which a ministerial officer of the U.S. and the correspondent officer of an individual State, would have rencounters in executing conflicting decrees, the result of which would depend on the comparative force of the local posse attending them, and that a casualty depending on the political opinions and party feelings in different States.

To have referred every clashing decision under the two authorities for a final decision to the States as parties to the Constitution, would be attended with delays, with inconveniences, and with expenses amounting to a prohibition of the expedient, not to mention its tendency to impair the salutary veneration for a system requiring such frequent interpositions, nor the delicate questions which might present themselves as to the form of stating the appeal, and as to the Quorum for deciding it.

To have trusted to negotiation, for adjusting disputes between the [Government] of the U.S. and the State [Governments] as between independent & separate sovereignties, would have lost sight altogether of a Constitution & Government for the Union; and opened a direct road from a failure of that resort, to the ultima ratio between nations wholly independent of and alien to each other. . . . Although the issue of negociation might sometimes avoid this extremity, how often would it happen among so many States, that an unaccommodating spirit in some would render that resource unavailing? A contrary supposition would not accord with a knowledge of human nature or the evidence of our own political history.

The Constitution, not relying on any of the preceding modifications for its safe & successful operation, has expressly declared on the one hand; 1. "That the Constitution, and the laws made in pursuance thereof, and all Treaties made under the authority of the U.S. shall be the supreme law of the land; 2. That the judges of every State shall be bound thereby, anything in the [Constitution] or laws of any State to the contrary notwithstanding; 3. That the judicial power of the U.S. shall extend to all cases in law & equity arising under the Constitution, the laws of the U.S. and Treaties made under their authority &c."

On the other hand, as a security of the rights & powers of the States in their individual capacities, [against] an undue preponderance of the powers granted to the Government over them in their united capacity, the Constitution has relied on, 1. The responsibility of the Senators and Representatives in the Legislature of the U.S. to the Legislatures & people of the States. 2. The responsibility of the President to the people of the U. States; & 3. the liability of the [Executive] and Judiciary functionaries of the U.S. to impeachment by the Representatives of the people of the States, in one branch of the Legislature of the U.S. and trial by the Representatives of the States, in the other branch; the State functionaries, Legislative, Executive, & judiciary, being at the same time in their appointment & responsibility, altogether independent of the agency or authority of the U. States.

How far this structure of the [Government] of the U.S. be adequate & safe for its objects, time alone can absolutely determine. Experience seems to have shown that whatever may grow out of future stages of our national career, there is as yet a sufficient controul in the popular will over the Executive &

Legislative Departments of the [Government]. When the Alien & Sedition laws were passed in contravention to the opinions and feelings of the community, the first elections that ensued put an end to them. . . .

With respect to the Judicial power of the U.S. and the authority of the Supreme Court in relation to the boundary of jurisdiction between the Federal & the State [Governments] I may be permitted to refer to the [thirty-ninth] number of the "Federalist" for the light in which the subject was regarded by its writer, at the period when the Constitution was depending; and it is believed that the same was the prevailing view then taken of it, that the same view has continued to prevail, and that it does so at this time notwithstanding the eminent exceptions to it.

But it is perfectly consistent with the concession of this power to the Supreme Court, in cases falling within the course of its functions, to maintain that the power has not always been rightly exercised. To say nothing of the period, happily a short one, when judges in their seats did not abstain from intemperate & party harangues, equally at variance with their duty and their dignity, there have been occasional decisions from the Bench which have incurred serious & extensive disapprobation. Still it would seem that, with but few exceptions, the course of the judiciary has been hitherto sustained by the predominant sense of the nation. . . .

Should the provisions of the Constitution as here reviewed be found not to secure the [Government] & rights of the States [against] usurpations & abuses on the part of the U.S. the final resort within the purview of the [Constitution] lies in an amendment of the [Constitution] according to a process applicable by the States.

And in the event of a failure of every constitutional resort, and an accumulation of usurpations & abuses, rendering passive obedience & non-resistance a greater evil, than resistance & revolution, there can remain but one resort, the last of all, an appeal from the cancelled obligations of the constitutional compact, to original rights & the law of self-preservation. This is the ultima ratio under all [Government] whether consolidated, confederated, or a compound of both; and it cannot be doubted that a single member of the Union, in the extremity supposed, but in that only would have a right, as an extra & ultra constitutional right, to make that appeal.

This brings us to the expedient lately advanced, which claims for a single State a right to appeal [against] an exercise of power by the [Government] of the U.S. decided by the State to be unconstitutional, to the parties of the Const. compact; the decision of the State to have the effect of nullifying the act of the [Government] of the U.S. unless the decision of the State be reversed by three-fourths of the parties. . . .

[I]t is understood that the nullifying doctrine imports that the decision of the State is to be presumed valid, and that it overrules the law of the U.S. unless overruled by ¾ of the States.

Can more be necessary to demonstrate the inadmissibility of such a doctrine than that it puts it in the power of the smallest fraction over ¼ of the U.S. — that is, of 7 States out of 24 — to give the law and even the [Constitution] to 17 States, each of the 17 having as parties to the [Constitution] an equal right with each of the 7 to expound it & to insist on the exposition. . . . [T]o establish a positive &

permanent rule giving such a power to such a minority over such a majority, would overturn the first principle of free [Government] and in practice necessarily overturn the [Government] itself.

It is to be recollected that the Constitution was proposed to the people of the States as a *whole*, and unanimously adopted by the States as a *whole*, it being a part of the Constitution that not less than ¾ of the States should be competent to make any alteration in what had been unanimously agreed to. So great is the caution on this point, that in two cases when peculiar interests were at stake, a proportion even of ¾ is distrusted, and unanimity required to make an alteration.

When the Constitution was adopted as a whole, it is certain that there were many parts which if separately proposed would have been promptly rejected. It is far from impossible, that every part of the Constitution might be rejected by a majority, and yet, taken together as a whole be unanimously accepted. Free constitutions will rarely if ever be formed without reciprocal concessions; without articles conditioned on & balancing each other. . . .

What the fate of the Constitution of the U.S. would be if a small proportion of States could expunge parts of it particularly valued by a large majority, can have but one answer. . . .

The reply to all such suggestions seems to be unavoidable and irresistible, that the Constitution is a compact; that its text is to be expounded according to the provision for expounding it, making a part of the compact; and that none of the parties can rightfully renounce the expounding provision more than any other part. When such a right accrues, as it may accrue, it must grow out of abuses of the compact releasing the sufferers from their fealty to it.

In favour the nullifying claim for the States individually, it appears, as you observe, that the proceedings of the Legislature of [Virginia] in 98 and 99 [against] the Alien and Sedition Acts are much dwelt upon. . . .

[T]he Resolutions of Virginia, as vindicated in the Report on them, will be found entitled to an exposition, showing a consistency in their parts and an inconsistency of the whole with the doctrine under consideration.

That the Legislature [could] not have intended to sanction such a doctrine is to be inferred from the debates in the House of Delegates, and from the address of the two Houses to their constituents on the subject of the resolutions. The tenor of the debates [which] were ably conducted and are understood to have been revised for the press by most, if not all, of the speakers, discloses no reference whatever to a constitutional right in an individual State to arrest by force the operation of a law of the U.S. Concert among the States for redress against the alien & sedition laws, as acts of usurped power, was a leading sentiment, and the attainment of a concert the immediate object of the course adopted by the Legislature, which was that of inviting the other States "to *concur* in declaring the acts to be unconstitutional, and to *co-operate* by the necessary & proper measures in maintaining unimpaired the authorities rights & liberties reserved to the States respectively & to the people." That by the necessary and proper measures to be *concurrently* and co-operatively taken, were meant measures known to the Constitution, particularly the ordinary controul of the people and Legislatures of the States over the

[Government] of the U.S. cannot be doubted; and the interposition of this controul as the event showed was equal to the occasion.

POINTS FOR DISCUSSION

1. Calhoun and Madison both analyzed judicial review, the political process, and nullification as means for resolving disputes over the relative powers of the federal government and the states under the Constitution. Calhoun concluded that nullification is necessary and constitutionally legitimate; Madison concluded that it is illegitimate. Contrast Calhoun's and Madison's respective treatments of judicial review and the political process as checks on federal power. Identify their points of disagreement regarding the (a) efficacy and (b) finality of judicial review as a check on congressional power. How should their points of disagreement be resolved?

2. What is the key point of disagreement between Calhoun and Madison on the constitutionality of nullification? How should this point of disagreement be resolved?

3. Madison and Calhoun both engaged the Virginia Resolutions of 1798 and Madison's 1800 *Report* on them in explaining their respective positions on nullification. How did they treat these materials differently? Whose characterization of the Resolutions and *Report*, if either, more fairly described their import? How much weight, if any, should the fact that Madison drafted the Resolutions and *Report* carry in determining whether he or Calhoun more fairly described them?

B. FEDERALISM AND SLAVERY

Several antebellum Supreme Court cases involving slavery addressed important questions of federalism. The best known of them is *Dred Scott v. Sandford*, 60 U.S. (19 How.) 393 (1857). As Professor Paul Finkelman has explained:

> Federalism, as it developed in the 19th century and as it has evolved since, was greatly influenced by slavery. Some aspects of Constitutional law, including the notion of state police powers and the preemption doctrine, were deeply rooted in slavery. So too, was much of the fear of a central government that led to the enactment of the Tenth Amendment. Obviously states' rights theory, as it developed in the 19th century and as it has been used ever since, was deeply rooted in debates over slavery. As early as 1790, southern states began to articulate claims of states' rights in controversies involving slavery. By the end of the antebellum period, both southern and northern states had made assertions of states' rights in the context of slavery. Modern states' rights arguments, sometimes framed in Tenth Amendment jurisprudence, are often a recycling of these older arguments relating to slavery. Similarly, much of our modern Commerce Clause jurisprudence, including such important concepts as the dormant Commerce Clause and the state police powers exception to federal commerce power, developed, at least in part, because of slavery. Thus, in the antebellum period slavery was often the connecting link between Commerce Clause jurisprudence and the development of states' rights theory. . . . [W]e live with the results of this linkage. . . .

Paul Finkelman, *Teaching Slavery in American Constitutional Law*, 34 Akron L. Rev. 261, 263 (2000) (footnotes omitted).

In the cases in this section, the Supreme Court addressed several important questions about federalism that it continues to confront:

- What are Congress's powers under the Commerce Clause and the Necessary and Proper Clause?
- How, if at all, do traditional state regulatory prerogatives limit the enumerated powers of Congress?
- How, if at all, does the Commerce Clause implicitly preempt state regulation?
- What is the scope of federal statutory preemption of state law?
- What power does Congress have, if any, to use state officials to carry federal regulatory schemes into execution?

Keep these questions in mind as you read the cases in this section.

1. THE FUGITIVE SLAVE ACT AND FEDERAL ENFORCEMENT POWER

The Constitution of the United States expressly addressed the issue of fugitive slaves in Article IV, §2 (later amended by the Thirteenth Amendment): "No Person held to Service or Labour in one State, under the Laws thereof, escaping into another, shall, in Consequence of any Law or Regulation therein, be discharged from such Service or Labour, but shall be delivered up on Claim of the Party to whom such Service or Labour may be due." In 1793, Congress enacted the so-called Fugitive Slave Act. The Act provided that a slave owner could seize a slave who had escaped into another state and obtain a certificate from a federal judge or state magistrate allowing the slave owner to remove the slave to the state from which the slave had fled:

> [W]hen a person held to labour in any of the United States, or in either of the territories on the northwest or south of the river Ohio, under the laws thereof, shall escape into any other part of the said states or territory, the person to whom such labour or service may be due, his agent or attorney, is hereby empowered to seize or arrest such fugitive from labour, and to take him or her before any judge of the circuit or district courts of the United States, residing or being within the state, or before any magistrate of a county, city or town corporate, wherein such seizure or arrest shall be made, and upon proof to the satisfaction of such judge or magistrate, either by oral testimony or affidavit taken before and certified by a magistrate of any such state or territory, that the person so seized or arrested, doth, under the laws of the state or territory from which he or she fled, owe service or labour to the person claiming him or her, it shall be the duty of such judge or magistrate to give a certificate thereof to such claimant, his agent, or attorney, which shall be sufficient warrant for removing the said fugitive from labour to the state or territory from which he or she fled.

Act of Feb. 12, 1793, ch. 7, §3, 1 Stat. 302-05 (repealed 1864).

In the first decades of the nineteenth century, Pennsylvanians increasingly came to oppose helping out-of-state slaveholders obtain the return of fugitive slaves. In 1826, Pennsylvania passed a law making it a crime to remove any person out of the state into slavery. Slave catcher Edward Prigg was indicted for violating this statute when he abducted Margaret Morgan and took her into Maryland to sell her as a slave. In defense, Prigg claimed that the 1826 Pennsylvania law was unconstitutional. Justice Story, writing for the Court, reversed Prigg's conviction, holding that Pennsylvania could not enforce its statute under the Constitution. As you read this case, consider these questions:

- How does the Court describe Congress's power to carry the Fugitive Slave Clause of Article IV into execution? Does its description follow from *McCullough v. Maryland*, 17 U.S. (4 Wheat.) 316 (1819)?
- What power, if any, does the Court hold Congress to have to enlist states to carry the Fugitive Slave Clause into execution?
- On what grounds does the Court hold that the Fugitive Slave Clause preempts the 1826 Pennsylvania statute?
- On what grounds does the Court hold that the Fugitive Slave Act of 1793 preempts the 1826 Pennsylvania statute?

PRIGG V. PENNSYLVANIA

41 U.S. (16 Pet.) 539 (1842)

STORY, JUSTICE, delivered the opinion of the court.

The plaintiff in error was indicted in the court of Oyer and Terminer for York county, for having, with force and violence, taken and carried away from that county, to the state of Maryland, a certain negro woman, named Margaret Morgan, with a design and intention of selling and disposing of, and keeping her as a slave or servant for life, contrary to a statute of Pennsylvania, passed on the 26th of March 1826. That statute in the first section, in substance, provides, that if any person or persons shall from and after the passing of the act, by force and violence take and carry away, or cause to be taken and carried away, and shall by fraud or false pretense, seduce, or cause to be seduced, or shall attempt to take, carry away, or seduce, any negro or mulatto from any part of that commonwealth, with a design and intention of selling and disposing of, or causing to be sold, or of keeping and detaining, or of causing to be kept and detained, such negro or mulatto as a slave or servant for life, or for any term whatsoever; every such person or persons, his or their aiders or abettors, shall, on conviction thereof, be deemed guilty of felony[.] . . .

The question arising in the case [is] as to the constitutionality of the statute of Pennsylvania[.] . . . [T]he second section of the fourth article [of the Constitution provides]: . . .

"No person held to service or labour in one state under the laws thereof, escaping into another, shall, in consequence of any law or regulation therein, be discharged from such service or labor; but shall be delivered up, on claim of the party to whom such service or labour may be due." . . .

Historically, it is well known, that the object of this clause was to secure to the citizens of the slave-holding states the complete right and title of ownership in their slaves, as property, in every state in the Union into which they might escape from the state where they were held in servitude. The full recognition of this right and title was indispensable to the security of this species of property in all the slave holding states; and, indeed, was so vital to the preservation of their domestic interests and institutions, that it cannot be doubted that it constituted a fundamental article, without the adoption of which the Union could not have been formed. Its true design was, to guard against the doctrines and principles prevalent in the non-slave-holding states, by preventing them from intermeddling with, or obstructing, or abolishing the rights of the owners of slaves. . . .

How, then, are we to interpret the language of the clause? The true answer is, in such a manner, as, consistently with the words, shall fully and completely effectuate the whole objects of it. If by one mode of interpretation the right must become shadowy and unsubstantial, and without any remedial power adequate to the end; and by another mode it will attain its just end and secure its manifest purpose; it would seem, upon principles of reasoning, absolutely irresistible, that the latter ought to prevail: No Court of justice can be authorized so to construe any clause of the Constitution as to defeat its obvious ends, when another construction, equally accordant with the words and sense thereof, will enforce and protect them.

The clause manifestly contemplates the existence of a positive, unqualified right on the part of the owner of the slave, which no state law or regulation can in any way qualify, regulate, control, or restrain. The slave is not to be discharged from service or labour, in consequence of any state law or regulation. . . .

If this be so, then all the incidents to that right attach also; the owner must, therefore, have the right to seize and repossess the slave, which the local laws of his own state confer upon him as property; and we all know that this right of seizure and recaption is universally acknowledged in all the slave holding states. . . .

But . . . [m]any cases must arise in which, if the remedy of the owner were confined to the mere right of seizure and recaption, he would be utterly without any adequate redress. . . .

And this leads us to the consideration of the other part of the clause, which implies at once a guaranty and duty. It says, "But he (the slave) shall be delivered up on claim of the party to whom such service or labour may be due." Now, we think it exceedingly difficult, if not impracticable, to read this language and not to feel that it contemplated some further remedial redress than that which might be administered at the hands of the owner himself. . . .

If, indeed, the Constitution guarantees the right, and if it requires the delivery upon the claim of the owner, (as cannot well be doubted,) the natural inference certainly is, that the national government is clothed with the appropriate authority and functions to enforce it. The fundamental principle applicable to all cases of this sort, would seem to be, that where the end is required, the means are given; and where the duty is enjoined, the ability to perform it is contemplated to exist on the part of the functionaries to whom it is intrusted. The clause is found in the national Constitution, and not in that of any state. It does not point out any state functionaries, or any state action to carry its provisions into effect. The states cannot, therefore, be compelled to enforce them; and it might well be deemed an unconstitutional exercise of the power of interpretation, to insist that the states are bound to provide means to carry into effect the duties of the national government, nowhere delegated or intrusted to them by the constitution. On the contrary, the natural, if not the necessary conclusion is, that the national government, in the absence of all positive provisions to the contrary, is bound, through its own proper departments, legislative, judicial, or executive, as the case may require, to carry into effect all the rights and duties imposed upon it by the Constitution. . . .

[T]he act of the 12th of February 1793, ch. 51, . . . after having, in the first and second sections, provided for the case of fugitives from justice by a demand to be made of the delivery through the executive authority of the state where they are found, proceeds, in the third section, to provide, that [a slave owner (or agent) may seize a fugitive slave and obtain a certificate from a federal judge or state magistrate warranting that the owner may remove the slave to the state from which the slave fled.] . . .

[U]pon just principles of construction, . . . the legislation of Congress, if constitutional, must supersede all state legislation upon the same subject; and by necessary implication prohibit it. For if Congress have a constitutional power to regulate a particular subject, and they do actually regulate it in a given manner, and in a certain form; it cannot be, that the state legislatures have a right to interfere, and . . . to prescribe additional regulations, and what they may deem auxiliary provisions for the same purpose. In such a case, the legislation of Congress, in what it does prescribe, manifestly indicates that it does not intend that there shall be any farther legislation to act upon the subject-matter. Its silence as to what it does not do, is as expressive of what its intention is as the direct provisions made by it. . . .

But it has been argued, that the act of Congress is unconstitutional, because it does not fall within the scope of any of the enumerated powers of legislation confided to that body; and therefore, it is void. . . . No one has ever supposed that congress could, constitutionally, by its legislation, exercise powers, or enact laws beyond the powers delegated to it by the constitution; but it has, on various occasions, exercised powers which were necessary and proper as means to carry into effect rights expressly given, and duties expressly enjoined thereby. The end being required, it has been deemed a just and necessary implication, that the means to accomplish it are given also; or, in other words, that the power flows as a necessary means to accomplish the end. . . .

We hold the act to be clearly constitutional in all its leading provisions, and, indeed, with the exception of that part which confers authority upon state magistrates, to be free from reasonable doubt and difficulty upon the grounds already stated. As to the authority so conferred upon state magistrates, while a difference of opinion has existed, and may exist still on the point, in different states, whether state magistrates are bound to act under it; none is entertained by this Court, that state magistrates may, if they choose, exercise that authority, unless prohibited by state legislation.

The remaining question is, whether the power of legislation upon this subject is exclusive in the national government, or concurrent in the states, until it is exercised by Congress. In our opinion, it is exclusive[.] . . .

The doctrine stated by this court, in *Sturgis v. Crowninshield*, 4 Wheat. Rep. 122, 193, contains the true, although not the sole rule or consideration, which is applicable to this particular subject. "Wherever," said Mr. Chief Justice Marshall, in delivering the opinion of the Court, "the terms in which a power is granted to Congress, or the nature of the power require that it should be exercised exclusively by Congress, the subject is as completely taken from the state legislatures, as if they had been forbidden to act." The nature of the power, and the true objects to be attained by it, are then as important to be weighed, in considering the question of its exclusiveness, as the words in which it is granted.

In the first place, . . . the right to seize and retake fugitive slaves, and the duty to deliver them up, in whatever state of the Union they may be found, and of course the corresponding power in Congress to use the appropriate means to enforce the right and duty, derive their whole validity and obligation exclusively from the Constitution of the United States, and are there, for the first time, recognised and established in that peculiar character. Before the adoption of the Constitution, no state had any power whatsoever over the subject, except within its own territorial limits, and could not bind the sovereignty or the legislation of other states. Whenever the right was acknowledged, or the duty enforced in any state, it was as a matter of comity and favour, and not as a matter of strict moral, political, or international obligation or duty. Under the Constitution it is recognised as an absolute, positive, right and duty, pervading the whole Union with an equal and supreme force, uncontrolled and uncontrollable by state sovereignty or state legislation. It is, therefore, in a just sense a new and positive right, independent of comity, confined to no territorial limits, and bounded by no state institutions or policy. The natural inference deductible from this consideration certainly is, in the absence of any positive delegation of power to the state legislatures, that it belongs to the legislative department of the national government, to which it owes its origin and establishment. It would be a strange anomaly, and forced construction, to suppose that the national government meant to rely for the due fulfilment of its own proper duties and the rights it intended to secure, upon state legislation; and not upon that of the Union. A fortiori, it would be more objectionable to suppose that a power, which was to be the same throughout the Union, should be confided to state sovereignty, which could not rightfully act beyond its own territorial limits.

In the next place, the nature of the provision and the objects to be attained by it, require that it should be controlled by one and the same will, and act uniformly by the same system of regulations throughout the Union. If, then, the states have a right, in the absence of legislation by Congress, to act upon the subject, each state is at liberty to prescribe just such regulations as suit its own policy, local convenience and local feelings. . . .

It is scarcely conceivable that the slaveholding states would have been satisfied with leaving to the legislation of the non-slaveholding states, a power of regulation, in the absence of that of Congress, which would or might practically amount to a power to destroy the rights of the owner. . . .

[W]e hold the power of legislation on this subject to be exclusive in Congress. To guard, however, against any possible misconstruction of our views, it is proper to state, that we are by no means to be understood in any manner whatsoever to doubt or to interfere with the police power belonging to the states in virtue of their general sovereignty. That police power extends over all subjects within the territorial limits of the states; and has never been conceded to the United States. It is wholly distinguishable from the right and duty secured by the provision now under consideration; which is exclusively derived from and secured by the Constitution of the United States, and owes its whole efficacy thereto. We entertain no doubt whatsoever, that the states, in virtue of their general police power, possess full jurisdiction to arrest and restrain runaway slaves, and remove them from their borders, and otherwise to secure themselves against their depredations and evil example, as they certainly may do in cases of idlers, vagabonds, and paupers. The rights of the owners of fugitive slaves are in no just sense interfered with, or regulated by such a course; and in many cases, the operations of this police power, although designed essentially for other purposes, for the protection, safety, and peace of the state, may essentially promote and aid the interests of the owners. But such regulations can never be permitted to interfere with or to obstruct the just rights of the owner to reclaim his slave, derived from the Constitution of the United States; or with the remedies prescribed by Congress to aid and enforce the same.

Upon these grounds, we are of opinion that the act of Pennsylvania upon which this indictment is founded, is unconstitutional and void. It purports to punish as a public offence against that state, the very act of seizing and removing a slave by his master, which the Constitution of the United States was designed to justify and uphold. . . .

TANEY, CH. J.

I concur in the opinion pronounced by the Court, that the law of Pennsylvania, under which the plaintiff in error was indicted, is unconstitutional and void[.] . . .

But, as I understand the opinion of the Court, it goes further, and decides that the power to provide a remedy for this right is vested exclusively in Congress; and that all laws upon the subject passed by a state, since the adoption of the Constitution of the United States, are null and void; even although they were intended, in good faith, to protect the owner in the exercise of his rights of property, and do not conflict in any degree with the act of Congress.

I do not consider this question as necessarily involved in the case before us[.] . . .

I think, the states are not prohibited; and that, on the contrary, it is enjoined upon them as a duty to protect and support the owner, when he is endeavouring to obtain possession of his property found within their respective territories. . . .

I dissent, therefore, . . . from that part of the opinion of the Court which denies the obligation and the right of the state authorities to protect the master, when he is endeavouring to seize a fugitive from his service, in pursuance of the right given to him by the Constitution of the United States;— provided the state law is not in conflict with the remedy provided by Congress.

THOMPSON, JUSTICE.

I concur in the judgment given by the Court in this case. . . . But I cannot concur in that part of the opinion of the Court, which asserts that the power of legislation by Congress is exclusive; and that no state can pass any law to carry into effect the constitutional provision on this subject; although Congress had passed no law in relation to it.

Mr. JUSTICE BALDWIN, Concurred with the Court in reversing the judgment of the Supreme Court of Pennsylvania, on the ground that the act of the legislature was unconstitutional; inasmuch as the slavery of the person removed was admitted, the removal could not be kidnapping. But he dissented from the principles laid down by the Court as the grounds of their opinion.

DANIEL, JUSTICE.

Concurring entirely as I do with the majority of the Court, in the conclusions they have reached relative to the effect and validity of the statute of Pennsylvania now under review, it is with unfeigned regret that I am constrained to dissent from some of the principles and reasonings which that majority in passing to our common conclusions, have believed themselves called on to affirm. . . .

Whilst I am free to admit the powers which are exclusive in the federal government, some of them became so denominated by the express terms of the Constitution; some because they are prohibited to the states; and others because their existence, and much more their practical exertion by the two governments, would be repugnant, and would neutralize if they did not conflict with and destroy each other: I cannot regard the third clause of the fourth article as falling either within the definition or meaning of an exclusive power. . . .

McLEAN, JUSTICE.

I differ on one point from the opinion of the Court[.] . . . It seems to be taken as a conceded point in the argument, that Congress had no power to impose duties on state officers, as provided in the above act. As a general principle this is true; but does not the case under consideration form an exception? Congress can no more regulate the jurisdiction of the state tribunals, than a state can define the judicial power of the Union. The officers of each government are responsible only to the respective authorities under which they are commissioned. But do not the clauses in the Constitution in regard to fugitives from labour, and from justice, give Congress a power over state officers, on these subjects? The power in both the cases is admitted or proved to be exclusively in the federal government.

The clause in the Constitution preceding the one in relation to fugitives from labour, declares that, "A person charged in any state with treason, felony, or other crime, who shall flee from justice, and be found in another state, shall, on demand of the executive authority of the state from which he fled, be delivered up to be removed to the state having jurisdiction of the crime."

In the first section of the act of 1793, Congress have provided that on demand being made as above, "it shall be the duty of the executive authority to cause the person demanded to be arrested, &c.["]

The constitutionality of this law, it is believed, has never been questioned. It has been obeyed by the governors of states, who have uniformly acknowledged its obligation. . . .

Now, if Congress may by legislation, require this duty to be performed by the highest state officer, may they not on the same principle require appropriate duties in regard to the surrender of fugitives from labour, by other state officers. Over these subjects the constitutional power is the same. . . .

If the constitution was designed, in this respect, to require, not a negative but a positive duty on the state and the people of the state where the fugitive from labour may be found; of which, it would seem, there can be no doubt, it must be equally clear that Congress may prescribe in what manner the claim and surrender shall be made. I am therefore brought to the conclusion that, although, as a general principle, Congress cannot impose duties on state officers, yet in the cases of fugitives from labour and from justice, they have the power to do so. . . .

POINTS FOR DISCUSSION

1. The Necessary and Proper Clause provides that Congress has power "[t]o make all Laws which shall be necessary and proper for carrying into Execution the foregoing Powers, and all other Powers vested by this Constitution in the Government of the United States, or in any Department or Officer thereof." In *McCullough v. Maryland*, 17 U.S. (4 Wheat.) 316 (1819), Chief Justice Marshall described the scope of the Clause as follows: "Let the end be legitimate, let it be within the scope of the constitution, and all means which are appropriate, which are plainly adapted to that end, which are not prohibited, but consist with the letter and spirit of the constitution, are constitutional." *Id.* at 421. The *Prigg* Court, in describing Congress's power to carry the Fugitive Slave Clause of Article IV into execution, wrote that Congress may exercise powers that are "necessary and proper as means to carry into effect rights expressly given, and duties expressly enjoined" by the Constitution. "The end being required, it has been deemed a just and necessary implication, that the means to accomplish it are given also; or, in other words, that the power flows as a necessary means to accomplish the end." Does *Prigg*'s description of congressional power necessarily follow from *McCullough*? In other words, should the Necessary and Proper Clause be held to empower Congress to carry into execution not only its enumerated powers, but also rights that the Constitution confers upon individuals?

2. Although the *Prigg* Court held that Congress had power to carry the Fugitive Slave Clause of Article IV into execution, it suggested an important limitation on that power: Congress may not require the states to carry it into execution. Justice Story explained that "the national government . . . is bound, through its own proper departments, legislative, judicial, or executive, as the case may require, to carry into effect all the rights and duties imposed upon it by the Constitution." The Fugitive Slave Act of 1793, however, provided that a slave owner could obtain a fugitive slave removal certificate from either a federal judge or *state* magistrate. "As to the authority so conferred upon state magistrates," Justice Story explained, such magistrates "may, if they choose, exercise that authority, unless prohibited by state legislation." The Court suggested here that Congress could not require state magistrates to issue such certificates if state law prohibited them from doing so.

In dissent, Justice McLean recognized that "[a]s a general principle," Congress has "no power to impose duties on state officers." He thought, however, that the Fugitive Slave Clause of Article IV authorized an exception to this principle.

Justice Story and others claimed that *Prigg* was an anti-slavery opinion insofar as it recognized state authority to refuse to enforce the Fugitive Slave Act of 1793. If Congress had broad authority under the Necessary and Proper Clause to enforce the Fugitive Slave Clause of Article IV, what precluded Congress from requiring state magistrates to enforce it? As you will study in Chapter 6, Supreme Court Justices continue to debate whether Congress may require state officials to carry federal regulatory schemes into execution.

3. The *Prigg* Court also determined that Congress's power to carry the Fugitive Slave Clause of Article IV into execution is "exclusive" of state legislation. On what grounds should courts determine that a congressional power is exclusive of state regulation rather than concurrent with it?

Consider, for example, Congress's Article I, §8 power to "declare War." Should congressional power to declare war be held exclusive of state power or concurrent with it? What about Congress's Article I, §8 power to "lay and collect Taxes"? Should that power be held exclusive of or concurrent with state power?

As Congress's power to regulate interstate commerce has expanded in the twentieth century, and as states' power to affect foreign relations has increased with advances in transportation and communication, the Court continues to face difficult questions of implied constitutional preemption. How, if at all, does Congress's power to regulate interstate commerce implicitly preempt state regulation in that field? How, if at all, do Congress's foreign relations powers implicitly preempt state regulation touching foreign relations? You will study these issues in Chapter 7.

4. Justice Story explained for the Court that "if Congress have a constitutional power to regulate a particular subject, and they do actually regulate it in a given manner, and in a certain form; it cannot be that the state legislatures have a right to interfere; and . . . to prescribe additional regulations, and what they may deem auxiliary provisions for the same purpose." This passage describes a form of federal statutory preemption of state law. You saw the Marshall Court describe two different forms of preemption in the last chapter. In *Gibbons v. Ogden*, 22 U.S. (9 Wheat.) 1 (1824), the Court held, under the Supremacy Clause, that an act of Congress preempts conflicting state law. Today, the Supreme Court refers to this as *conflict* preemption. In *McCullough v. Maryland, supra*, the Court suggested that federal law may preempt state law that stands as an obstacle to a federal regulatory purpose. Today, the Supreme Court refers to this as *obstacle* preemption. How does the kind of preemption that Justice Story described in *Prigg* differ from conflict or obstacle preemption? Today, the Supreme Court refers to the kind of preemption described in *Prigg* as *field* preemption — reflecting the idea that Congress has occupied a field of regulation. You will study these various forms of federal statutory preemption of state law in Chapter 7.

2. THE MISSOURI COMPROMISE AND LIMITS ON FEDERAL POWER

In 1787 Congress, operating under the Articles of Confederation, passed the Northwest Ordinance: "There shall be neither slavery nor involuntary servitude" in territories north and west of the Ohio River. Much of the territory purchased from France in the Louisiana Purchase of 1803, which included Missouri, lay north and west of the Ohio River. When Missouri sought admission to the Union as a slave state in 1819, the balance of power in Congress on the issue of slavery was at stake. Northern states argued that Missouri should be admitted as a free state because it lay north and west of the Ohio River and therefore was within the territory covered by the Northwest Ordinance. Southern states argued that the Northwest Ordinance did not apply to territories obtained through the Louisiana Purchase. In the end, Congress passed the so-called Missouri Compromise in 1820, consisting of three parts: (1) Maine (previously part of Massachusetts) entered the Union as a free state; (2) Missouri entered the Union as a slave state; and (3) in all territories north and west of Missouri, slavery was permanently abolished. Regarding the third part, the Missouri Compromise specifically provided, "That in all territory ceded by France to the United States, under the name of Louisiana, which lies north of thirty-six degrees and thirty minutes north latitude, not included within the limits of [Missouri] . . . slavery and involuntary servitude . . . shall be, and is hereby, forever prohibited." Act of Mar. 6, 1820, ch. 22, §8, 3 Stat. 545, 548 (1820). Opponents of the Missouri Compromise's prohibitions on slavery claimed that it violated the Constitution by disallowing slaveholders from entering such territories with their slaves—property, they claimed, the Constitution protected.

States also enacted regulations of slavery that slaveholders and others challenged as unconstitutional. In 1832, Mississippi adopted a constitutional provision prohibiting the importation of slaves as commercial merchandise. The Supreme Court heard a constitutional challenge to this provision in *Groves v. Slaughter*, 40 U.S. 449 (1841). There, it was argued that Congress's constitutional power to regulate interstate commerce precluded states from enacting such a prohibition. The Court avoided the constitutional question by holding that the Mississippi Constitution's provision required legislative implementation to take effect and thus did not bar the sale of slaves of its own force. Individual Justices, nonetheless, expressed opinions on whether the Mississippi provision was unconstitutional in light of Congress's power to regulate interstate commerce.

Justice McLean addressed whether Congress's power to regulate interstate commerce implicitly precluded states from enacting laws such as Mississippi's. He also considered whether Congress's power to regulate interstate commerce included commercial regulations of slavery. If Congress's power to regulate interstate commerce did not extend to slavery, it would not implicitly preempt state regulations of slavery. Justice McLean's discussion presaged two present-day disputed questions of congressional power: (1) whether, and to what extent, the Commerce Clause implicitly preempts state regulation and (2) whether traditional prerogatives of state governance may limit Congress's power to regulate interstate commerce.

In a separate opinion, Justice Baldwin described slaves as "property." In light of Congress's power to regulate interstate commerce, he asserted, states could not regulate the interstate movement of such property. Moreover, he contended that the Due Process Clause of the Fifth Amendment protected such property from congressional deprivation. Under the Due Process Clause, "[n]o person shall . . . be deprived of life, liberty, or property, without due process of law." Justice Baldwin argued that the Due Process Clause prohibited Congress from depriving a slave owner of the property right in a slave. In characterizing slaves as property protected by the Due Process Clause of the Fifth Amendment, Justice Baldwin foreshadowed Justice Taney's infamous analysis in *Dred Scott v. Sandford*, 60 U.S. (19 How.) 393 (1857), which you will read later in this section.

As you read the opinions in *Groves*, consider the following questions:

- On what ground does Justice McLean contend that the Commerce Clause itself preempts state regulation?
- On what grounds do the Justices contend that Congress's power to regulate interstate commerce is limited by state regulatory prerogatives?

GROVES V. SLAUGHTER

40 U.S. 449 (1841)

[In 1838, Slaughter sued defendants in U.S. Circuit Court to recover on a promissory note that he received in 1836 as consideration for the transfer of slaves. The slaves had been imported into Mississippi for sale as merchandise. Defendants argued that the promissory note was unenforceable because it rested upon an illegal consideration. Specifically, they argued that the note was unenforceable under following article of the constitution of Mississippi, adopted in 1832:

> The introduction of slaves into this state, as merchandise, or for sale, shall be prohibited, from and after the first day of May, 1833: provided, the actual settler or settlers, shall not be prohibited from purchasing slaves in any state in this Union, and bringing them into this state for their own individual use, until the year 1845.

The circuit court gave judgment for Slaughter.]

THOMPSON, JUSTICE, delivered the opinion of the court.

The question arising under the constitution of Mississippi is, whether this prohibition, per se, interdicts the introduction of slaves as merchandise, or for sale, after a given time; or is only directory to the legislature, and requiring their action in order to bring it into full operation, and render unlawful the introduction of the slaves for sale at any time prior to the act of the 13th of May, 1837. . . .

[T]his article [of the Mississippi Constitution] does not, per se, operate as a prohibition to the introduction of slaves, as merchandise, but required legislative action to bring it into complete operation. . . .

The judgment of the Circuit Court is accordingly affirmed. And this view of the case makes it unnecessary to inquire whether this article in the constitution of Mississippi is repugnant to the Constitution of the United States; and indeed, such inquiry is not properly in the case, as the decision has been placed entirely upon the construction of the constitution of Mississippi.

McLean, Justice.

[A]lthough the question I am to consider, is not necessary to a decision of the case; yet, it is so intimately connected with it, and has been so elaborately argued, that under existing circumstances I deem it fit and proper to express my opinion upon it.

The second section of the constitution of Mississippi, adopted the 26th of October, 1832, declares that the introduction of slaves into that state, as merchandise, or for sale, shall be prohibited from and after the 1st day of May, 1833: provided, that the actual settlers shall not be prohibited from purchasing slaves in any state in the Union, and bringing them into that state for their own individual use, until the year 1845: and the question is, whether this provision is in conflict with that part of the constitution of the United States, which declares that congress shall have power "to regulate commerce with foreign nations, and among the several states."

In the case of *Gibbons v. Ogden*, 9 Wheat. 186, this Court decided, that the power to regulate commerce is exclusively vested in Congress, and that no part of it can be exercised by a state.

The necessity of a uniform commercial regulation, more than any other consideration, led to the adoption of the federal Constitution. And, unless the power be not only paramount, but exclusive, the Constitution must fail to attain one of the principal objects of its formation.

It has been contended that a state may exercise a commercial power, if the same has not been exercised by Congress. And that this power of the state ceased, when the federal authority was exerted over the same subject matter.

This argument is founded upon the supposition that a state may exercise a power which is expressly given to the federal government, if it shall not exert the power in all the modes, and over all the subjects to which it can be applied.

If this rule of construction were generally adopted and practically enforced, it would be as fatal to the spirit of the constitution, as it is opposed to its letter. If a commercial power may be exercised by a state because it has not been exercised by Congress, the same rule must apply to other powers expressly delegated to the federal government.

It is admitted that the power of taxation is common to the state and federal governments; but this is not in its nature or effect a repugnant power; and its exercise is vital to both governments.

A power may remain dormant, though the expediency of its exercise has been fully considered. It is often wiser and more politic to forbear, than to exercise a power.

A state regulates its own internal commerce, may pass inspection and police laws, designed to guard the health and protect the rights of its citizens. But these laws must not be extended so as to come in conflict with a power expressly given to the federal government.

It is enough to say that the commercial power, as it regards foreign commerce, and commerce among the several states, has been decided by this Court to be exclusively vested in Congress. . . . The transportation of slaves from a foreign country, before the abolition of that traffic, was subject to this commercial power. This would seem to be admitted in the Constitution, as it provides "the importation of such persons as any of the states, now existing, shall think proper to admit, shall not be prohibited by Congress prior to the year eighteen hundred and eight: but a tax or duty, may be imposed on such importation, not exceeding ten dollars for each person."

An exception to a rule is said to prove the existence of the rule; and this exception to the exercise of the commercial power, may well be considered as a clear recognition of the power in the case stated. . . .

Can the transfer and sale of slaves from one state to another, be regulated by Congress, under the commercial power?

If a state may admit or prohibit slaves at its discretion, this power must be in the state, and not in Congress. The Constitution seems to recognise the power to be in the states. The importation of certain persons, meaning slaves, which was not to be prohibited before eighteen hundred and eight, was limited to such states, then existing, as shall think proper to admit them. Some of the states at that time prohibited the admission of slaves, and their right to do so was as strongly implied by this provision as the right of other states that admitted them. . . .

In all the old states, at the time of the Revolution, slavery existed in a greater or less degree. By more than one-half of them, including those that have been since admitted into the Union, it has been abolished or prohibited. And in these states, a slave cannot be brought as merchandise, or held to labour, in any of them, except as a transient person.

The constitution of Ohio declares that there shall be neither slavery nor involuntary servitude in the state, except for the punishment of crimes. Is this provision in conflict with the power in Congress to regulate commerce? It goes much further than the constitution of Mississippi. That prohibits only the introduction of slaves into the state by the citizens of other states, as merchandize; but the constitution of Ohio not only does this, but it declares that slavery shall not exist in the state. Does not the greater power include the lesser. If Ohio may prohibit the introduction of slaves into it altogether, may not the state of Mississippi regulate their admission?

The Constitution of the United States operates alike on all the states: and one state has the same power over the subject of slavery as every other state. If it be constitutional in one state to abolish or prohibit slavery, it cannot be unconstitutional in another, within its discretion, to regulate it.

Could Ohio, in her constitution, have prohibited the introduction into the state, of the cotton of the south, or the manufactured articles of the north? If a state may exercise this power, it may establish a non-intercourse with the other states. This, no one will pretend, is within the power of a state. Such a measure would be repugnant to the Constitution, and it would strike at the foundation of the Union. The power vested in Congress to regulate commerce among the several states, was designed to prevent commercial conflicts among them. But, whilst Ohio could not proscribe the productions of the south, nor the fabrics of the north, no one doubts its power to prohibit slavery. And what can more unanswerably establish the doctrine that a state may prohibit slavery, or, in its discretion, regulate it, without trenching upon the commercial power of Congress?

The power over slavery belongs to the states respectively. It is local in its character, and in its effects; and the transfer or sale of slaves cannot be separated from this power. It is, indeed, an essential part of it.

Each state has a right to protect itself against the avarice and intrusion of the slave dealer; to guard its citizens against the inconveniences and dangers of a slave population.

The right to exercise this power, by a state, is higher and deeper than the constitution. The evil involves the prosperity, and may endanger the existence of a state. Its power to guard against, or to remedy the evil, rests upon the law of self-preservation; a law vital to every community, and especially to a sovereign state.

TANEY, CH. J.

In my judgment, the power over this subject is exclusively with the several states; and each of them has a right to decide for itself, whether it will or will not allow persons of this description to be brought within its limits, from another state, either for sale, or for any other purpose; and, also, to pre-scribe the manner and mode in which they may be introduced, and to deter-mine their condition and treatment within their respective territories: and the action of the several states upon this subject, cannot be controlled by Con-gress, either by virtue of its power to regulate commerce, or by virtue of any power conferred by the Constitution of the United States. . . .

BALDWIN, Justice.

That the power of congress "to regulate commerce among the several states," is exclusive of any interference by the states, has been, in my opinion, conclusively settled by the solemn opinions of this Court, in *Gibbons v. Ogden.* . . .

Cases may, indeed, arise, wherein there may be found difficulty in discrim-inating between regulations of "commerce among the several states," and the regulations of "the internal police of a state;" but the subject-matter of such regulations, of either description, will lead to the true line which separates them, when they are examined with a disposition to avoid a collision between the powers granted to the federal government, by the people of the several states, and those which they have reserved exclusively to themselves. "Com-merce among the states," as defined by this Court, is "trade," "traffic," "inter-course," and dealing in articles of commerce between states, by its citizens or others, and carried on in more than one state. Police, relates only to the inter-nal concerns of one state, and commerce, within it, is purely a matter of internal regulation, when confined to those articles which have become so distributed as to form items in the common mass of property. It follows, that any regulation which affects the commercial intercourse between any two or more states, referring solely thereto, is within the powers granted exclusively to Congress; and that those regulations which affect only the commerce carried on within one state, or which refer only to subjects of internal police, are within the powers reserved. . . . [T]he clause of the constitution of Mississippi, which has been under our consideration . . . does not purport to be a regulation of police, for any defined object connected with the internal tranquility of the state, the health, or morals of the people: it is general in its terms: it is aimed at the introduction of slaves as merchandise, from other states, not with the intention of excluding diseased, convicted, or insurgent slaves, or such as may be otherwise dangerous to the peace or welfare of the state. . . . If we adopt the construction contended for by the plaintiffs in error, that it operates by its own force, the constitution of Mississippi must be taken to be a law of that state in relation to the regulation of the traffic or dealing in slaves brought there for the purpose of sale; in other words, a regulation of commerce among the several states, if slaves are the subjects of such commerce, according to the true meaning of the constitution of the United States, as expounded by this Court. . . .

I feel bound to consider slaves as property, by the law of the states before the adoption of the Constitution, and from the first settlement of the colonies; that this right of property exists independently of the Constitution, which does not create, but recognises and protects it from violation, by any law or regulation of any state, in the cases to which the Constitution applies. . . .

Being property by the law of any state, the owners are protected from any violations of the rights of property by Congress, under the fifth amendment of the Constitution; these rights do not consist merely in ownership, the right of disposing of property of all kinds, is incident to it, which Congress cannot touch. . . .

Any reasoning or principle which would authorize any state to interfere with such transit of a slave, would equally apply to a bale of cotton, or cotton goods; and thus leave the whole commercial intercourse between the states liable to interruption to extinction by state laws, or constitutions. It is fully within the power of any state to entirely prohibit the importation of slaves of all descriptions, or of those who are diseased, convicts, or of dangerous or immoral habits or conduct; this is a regulation of police, for purposes of internal safety to the state, or the health and morals of its citizens, or to effectuate its system of policy in the abolition of slavery. But where no object of police is discernible in a state law or constitution, nor any rule of policy, other than that which gives to its own citizens a "privilege," which is denied to citizens of other states, it is wholly different. The direct tendency of all such laws is partial, antinational, subversive of the harmony which should exist among the states, as well as inconsistent with the most sacred principles of the constitution. . . . For these reasons, my opinion is, that had the contract in question been invalid by the constitution of Mississippi, it would be valid by the constitution of the United States. These reasons are drawn from those principles on which alone this government must be sustained; the leading one of which is, that wherever slavery exists by the laws of a state, slaves are property in every constitutional sense, and for every purpose, whether as subjects of taxation, as the basis of representation, as articles of commerce, or fugitives from service. To consider them as persons merely, and not property, is, in my settled opinion, the first step towards state of things to be avoided only by a firm adherence to the fundamental principles of the state and federal governments, in relation to this species of property. If the first step taken is a mistaken one, the successive ones will be fatal to the whole system. I have taken my stand on the only position which, in my judgment, is impregnable; and feel confident in its strength, however it may be assailed in public opinion, here or elsewhere. . . .

POINTS FOR DISCUSSION

1. Justice McLean explained that "the power to regulate commerce is exclusively vested in Congress, and that no part of it can be exercised by a state." Thus, state law "must not be extended so as to come in conflict with a power expressly given to the federal government." Did the Supreme Court decide this in *Gibbons v. Ogden*, 22 U.S. (9 Wheat.) 1 (1824), as Justice McLean represented that it did? In Chapter 7, you will further explore the idea that the Commerce Clause, in its dormant state, may preempt state law.

2. Although Justice McLean believed that Congress's commerce power may, in its dormant state, preempt state law, he found that the commerce power did not extend to slavery. His analysis rested upon the idea that there exist certain state regulatory prerogatives that limit Congress's power under the Commerce Clause. Justice Taney claimed as well that "the power over this subject is exclusively with the several states." Justice Baldwin understood states to have power to make regulations "of police, for purposes of internal safety to the state, or the health and morals of its citizens, or to effectuate its system of policy in the abolition of slavery." Are these ideas — that certain areas of state regulation fall outside Congress's power to regulate interstate commerce — consistent with Chief Justice Marshall's statement in *Gibbons v. Ogden*, *supra*, that Congress's power to regulate interstate commerce, "like all others vested in Congress, is complete in itself, may be exercised to its utmost extent, and acknowledges no limitations, other than are prescribed in the constitution," 22 U.S. (9 Wheat.) at 196? As you will study in subsequent chapters, an important present-day federalism debate among Supreme Court Justices has been whether state regulatory prerogatives operate to define or limit Congress's power to regulate interstate commerce.

The most infamous antebellum slavery case — indeed one of the most infamous cases in U.S. constitutional law — is *Dred Scott v. Sandford*, 60 U.S. (19 How.) 393 (1857). The court considered whether Dred Scott, a slave who had been removed to free territory, was entitled, upon being returned to a slave state, to sue for his freedom. The opinion of Chief Justice Roger Taney addressed several issues involving slavery and federalism. It is helpful, as you read his opinion, to keep the following issues distinct:

- Was Dred Scott a citizen of the United States, such that he had standing to bring a lawsuit in a court of the United States?
- Under Article IV, §3, which empowers Congress "to dispose of and make all needful Rules and Regulations respecting the Territory or other Property belonging to the United States," did Congress have power to make regulations for territories acquired *after* the Constitution was adopted?
- Under Article IV, §3, which further provides that "[n]ew States may be admitted by the Congress into this Union," did Congress have power to make regulations for territories acquired *after* the Constitution was adopted?
- Did the Due Process Clause of the Fifth Amendment, which provides that "[n]o person shall . . . be deprived of life, liberty, or property, without due process of law," forbid Congress from outlawing slaveholding in territories of the United States?

You should be aware of several debates that Justice Taney's consideration of these issues prompted. First, some argue that *Dred Scott* is the Court's first use of the controversial doctrine of *substantive due process*. Under this doctrine, certain liberty interests or property rights are so fundamental that due process requirements forbid the government from depriving individuals of them. Although the doctrine of substantive due process is beyond the scope of this book, you should be aware of this issue. Second, some charge that *Dred Scott* illustrates dangers of originalism—a theory of interpretation arguing that courts should understand the Constitution according to the original intent of those who framed it or, as is more commonly argued, the original public meaning of the Constitution. Consider this charge as you read the case. Finally, some argue that most of Justice Taney's opinion in *Dred Scott* is dicta. As you will read, the Court's first determination was that Dred Scott lacked the privilege of bringing a lawsuit in a court of the United States because he was not a citizen thereof. Today, it might be said that the Court determined that Dred Scott lacked *standing*. If the Court had no power to hear the case because Dred Scott lacked standing to bring it, the Court had no power to resolve any of the issues that the case involved. Moreover, controversy surrounds whether a majority of Justices supported most of Justice Taney's opinion. All Justices wrote separate opinions in the case, and scholars have argued that a majority of Justices never explicitly supported his conclusions. Although the following excerpt does not include the concurring opinions (all told, the opinions in the case total more than 200 pages), you should be aware of this controversy.

Following *Dred Scott*, you will read two excerpts of speeches by Frederick Douglass, a leader in the abolitionist movement, who had himself escaped from slavery. Douglass criticized Justice Taney's methodology and conclusions. As you read *Dred Scott* and Douglass's critique of it, keep in mind the following questions:

- Does Justice Taney's analysis of congressional power under the Constitution qualitatively differ from analyses of congressional power by the Marshall Court?

- How does Justice Taney's analysis of original constitutional meaning differ from Douglass's?
- What values, if any, lie in upholding limitations on congressional power in the face of compelling needs for national congressional action?

DRED SCOTT V. SANDFORD

60 U.S. (19 How.) 393 (1857)

[Dred Scott was a slave who belonged to Dr. Emerson, a United States army surgeon. In 1834, Emerson took Scott from the State of Missouri to the Rock Island military post in the State of Illinois. In 1836, Dr. Emerson took Scott from Rock Island to Fort Snelling in the Wisconsin Territory, a free territory under the Missouri Compromise. While there, Dred Scott married Harriett Robinson, another slave, with Emerson's consent. The Scotts had two children, Eliza and Lizzie. In 1838, Dr. Emerson took the Scotts from Fort Snelling to the State of Missouri. Emerson left the Scotts, upon his death, to his wife, Irene Sanford. Scott sued for his freedom in Missouri state court on the ground that his family had resided in a territory where slavery was prohibited. The state court ruled for Scott, but the Supreme Court of Missouri reversed. Scott also filed a trespass action against Sanford in U.S. Circuit Court, where Sanford prevailed. The case came to the Supreme Court of the United States on a writ of error from the Circuit Court. (Sanford's name was misrecorded in court documents as "Sandford.")]

Mr. CHIEF JUSTICE TANEY delivered the opinion of the court.

[I]

The question is simply this: Can a negro, whose ancestors were imported into this country, and sold as slaves, become a member of the political community formed and brought into existence by the Constitution of the United States, and as such become entitled to all the rights, and privileges, and immunities, guarantied by that instrument to the citizen? One of which rights is the privilege of suing in a court of the United States in the cases specified in the Constitution. . . .

The words "people of the United States" and "citizens" are synonymous terms, and mean the same thing. They both describe the political body who, according to our republican institutions, form the sovereignty, and who hold the power and conduct the Government through their representatives. They are what we familiarly call the "sovereign people," and every citizen is one of this people, and a constituent member of this sovereignty. The question before us is, whether the class of persons described in the plea in abatement compose a portion of this people, and are constituent members of this sovereignty? We think they are not, and that they are not included, and were not intended to be included, under the word "citizens" in the Constitution, and can therefore claim none of the rights and privileges which that instrument provides for and secures to citizens of the United States. On the contrary, they were at that time considered as a subordinate and inferior class of beings, who had been subjugated by the dominant race, and, whether emancipated or not, yet remained subject to their authority, and had no rights or privileges but such as those who held the power and the Government might choose to grant them.

It is not the province of the court to decide upon the justice or injustice, the policy or impolicy, of these laws. The decision of that question belonged to the political or law-making power; to those who formed the sovereignty and framed the Constitution. The duty of the court is, to interpret the instrument they have framed, with the best lights we can obtain on the subject, and to administer it as we find it, according to its true intent and meaning when it was adopted.

In discussing this question, we must not confound the rights of citizenship which a State may confer within its own limits, and the rights of citizenship as a member of the Union. It does not by any means follow, because he has all the rights and privileges of a citizen of a State, that he must be a citizen of the United States. He may have all of the rights and privileges of the citizen of a State, and yet not be entitled to the rights and privileges of a citizen in any other State. . . . It is very clear . . . that no State can, by any act or law of its own, passed since the adoption of the Constitution, introduce a new member into the political community created by the Constitution of the United States. . . .

The question then arises, whether the provisions of the Constitution, in relation to the personal rights and privileges to which the citizen of a State should be entitled, embraced the negro African race, at that time in this country, or who might afterwards be imported, who had then or should afterwards be made free in any State; and to put it in the power of a single State to make him a citizen of the United States, and endue him with the full rights of citizenship in every other State without their consent? Does the Constitution of the United States act upon him whenever he shall be made free under the laws of a State, and raised there to the rank of a citizen, and immediately clothe him with all the privileges of a citizen in every other State, and in its own courts? . . .

It becomes necessary . . . to determine who were citizens of the several States when the Constitution was adopted. . . .

In the opinion of the court, the legislation and histories of the times, and the language used in the Declaration of Independence, show, that neither the class of persons who had been imported as slaves, nor their descendants, whether they had become free or not, were then acknowledged as a part of the people, nor intended to be included in the general words used in that memorable instrument. . . .

The language of the Declaration of Independence is . . . conclusive:

It begins by declaring that, "when in the course of human events it becomes necessary for one people to dissolve the political bands which have connected them with another, and to assume among the powers of the earth the separate and equal station to which the laws of nature and nature's God entitle them, a decent respect for the opinions of mankind requires that they should declare the causes which impel them to the separation."

It then proceeds to say: "We hold these truths to be self-evident: that all men are created equal; that they are endowed by their Creator with certain unalienable rights; that among them is life, liberty, and the pursuit of happiness; that to secure these rights, Governments are instituted, deriving their just powers from the consent of the governed."

The general words above quoted would seem to embrace the whole human family, and if they were used in a similar instrument at this day would be so understood. But it is too clear for dispute, that the enslaved African race were not intended to be included, and formed no part of the people who framed and adopted this declaration; for if the language, as understood in that day, would embrace them, the conduct of the distinguished men who framed the Declaration of Independence would have been utterly and flagrantly inconsistent with the principles they asserted; and instead of the sympathy of mankind, to which they appealed, they would have deserved and received universal rebuke and reprobation.

Yet the men who framed this declaration were great men—high in literary acquirements—high in their sense of honor, and incapable of asserting principles inconsistent with those on which they were acting. They perfectly understood the meaning of the language they used, and how it would be understood by others; and they knew that it would not in any part of the civilized world be supposed to embrace the negro race, which, by common consent, had been excluded from civilized Governments and the family of nations, and doomed to slavery. They spoke and acted according to the then established doctrines and principles, and in the ordinary language of the day, and no one misunderstood them. . . .

This state of public opinion had undergone no change when the Constitution was adopted, as is equally evident from its provisions and language.

The brief preamble sets forth by whom it was formed, for what purposes, and for whose benefit and protection. It declares that it is formed by the *people* of the United States; that is to say, by those who were members of the different political communities in the several States; and its great object is declared to be to secure the blessings of liberty to themselves and their posterity. It speaks in general terms of the *people* of the United States, and of *citizens* of the several States, when it is providing for the exercise of the powers granted or the privileges secured to the citizen. It does not define what description of persons are intended to be included under these terms, or who shall be regarded as a citizen and one of the people. It uses them as terms so well understood, that no further description or definition was necessary.

But there are two clauses in the Constitution which point directly and specifically to the negro race as a separate class of persons, and show clearly that they were not regarded as a portion of the people or citizens of the Government then formed.

One of these clauses reserves to each of the thirteen States the right to import slaves until the year 1808, if it thinks proper. . . . And by the other provision the States pledge themselves to each other to maintain the right of property of the master, by delivering up to him any slave who may have escaped from his service, and be found within their respective territories. . . .

If any of [the Constitution's] provisions are deemed unjust, there is a mode prescribed in the instrument itself by which it may be amended; but while it remains unaltered, it must be construed now as it was understood at the time of its adoption. It is not only the same in words, but the same in meaning, and delegates the same powers to the Government, and reserves and secures the same rights and privileges to the citizen; and as long as it continues to exist in its present form, it speaks not only in the same words, but with the same meaning and intent with which it spoke when it came from the hands of its framers, and was voted on and adopted by the people of the United States. Any other rule of construction would abrogate the judicial character of this court, and make it the mere reflex of the popular opinion or passion of the day. . . .

[U]pon a full and careful consideration of the subject, the court is of opinion, that, upon the facts stated in the plea in abatement, Dred Scott was not a citizen of Missouri within the meaning of the Constitution of the United States, and not entitled as such to sue in its courts; and, consequently, that the Circuit Court had no jurisdiction of the case, and that the judgment on the plea in abatement is erroneous. . . .

[II]

It is true that the result either way, by dismissal or by a judgment for the defendant, makes very little, if any, difference in a pecuniary or personal point of view to either party. But the fact that the result would be very nearly the same to the parties in either form of judgment, would not justify this court in sanctioning an error in the judgment which is patent on the record, and which, if sanctioned, might be drawn into precedent, and lead to serious mischief and injustice in some future suit.

We proceed, therefore, to inquire whether the facts relied on by the plaintiff entitled him to his freedom. . . .

The act of Congress, upon which the plaintiff relies, declares that slavery and involuntary servitude, except as a punishment for crime, shall be forever prohibited in all that part of the territory ceded by France, under the name of Louisiana, which lies north of thirty-six degrees thirty minutes north latitude, and not included within the limits of Missouri. And the difficulty which meets us at the threshold of this part of the inquiry is, whether Congress was authorized to pass this law under any of the powers granted to it by the Constitution; for if the authority is not given by that instrument, it is the duty of this court to declare it void and inoperative. . . .

[A]

The counsel for the plaintiff has laid much stress upon that article in the Constitution which confers on Congress the power "to dispose of and make all needful rules and regulations respecting the territory or other property belonging to the United States;" but, in the judgment of the court, that provision has no bearing on the present controversy, and the power there given, whatever it may be, is confined, and was intended to be confined, to the territory which at that time belonged to, or was claimed by, the United States, and was within their boundaries as settled by the treaty with Great Britain, and can have no influence upon a territory afterwards acquired from a foreign Government. . . .

[Under the Constitution, the federal] Government was to be carefully limited in its powers, and to exercise no authority beyond those expressly granted by the Constitution, or necessarily to be implied from the language of the instrument, and the objects it was intended to accomplish; . . . it was obvious that some provision was necessary to give the new Government sufficient power to enable it to carry into effect the objects for which [the states had ceded unsettled land to the Confederation Congress], and the compacts and agreements which the States had made with each other in the exercise of their powers of sovereignty. It was necessary that the lands should be sold to pay the war debt; that a Government and system of jurisprudence should be maintained in it, to protect the citizens of the United States who should migrate to the territory, in their rights of person and of property. . . . And, moreover, there were many articles of value besides this property in land, such as arms, military stores, munitions, and ships of war, which were the common property of the States, when acting in their independent characters as confederates, which neither the new Government nor any one else would have a right to take possession of, or control, without authority from them; and it was to place these things under the guardianship and protection of the new Government, and to clothe it with the necessary powers, that the clause was inserted in the Constitution which gives Congress the power "to dispose of and make all needful rules and regulations respecting the territory or other property belonging to the United States." It was intended for a specific purpose, to provide for the things we have mentioned. It was to transfer to the new Government the property then held in common by the States, and to give to that Government power to apply it to the objects for which it had been destined by mutual agreement among the States before their league was dissolved. It applied only to the property which the States held in common at that time, and has no reference whatever to any territory or other property which the new sovereignty might afterwards itself acquire. . . .

The words "rules and regulations" are usually employed in the Constitution in speaking of some particular specified power which it means to confer on the Government, and not, as we have seen, when granting general powers of legislation. . . .

[W]e think it clear, that [this clause] applies only to the particular territory of which we have spoken, and cannot, by any just rule of interpretation, be extended to territory which the new Government might afterwards obtain from a foreign nation. . . .

[B]

This brings us to examine by what provision of the Constitution the present Federal Government, under its delegated and restricted powers, is authorized to acquire territory outside of the original limits of the United States, and what powers it may exercise therein over the person or property of a citizen of the United States, while it remains a Territory, and until it shall be admitted as one of the States of the Union.

There is certainly no power given by the Constitution to the Federal Government . . . to acquire a Territory to be held and governed permanently in that character. . . .

[H]owever, . . . [t]he power to expand the territory of the United States by the admission of new States is plainly given; and in the construction of this power by all the departments of the Government, it has been held to authorize the acquisition of territory, not fit for admission at the time, but to be admitted as soon as its population and situation would entitle it to admission. It is acquired to become a State, and not to be held as a colony and governed by Congress with absolute authority; and as the propriety of admitting a new State is committed to the sound discretion of Congress, the power to acquire territory for that purpose, to be held by the United States until it is in a suitable condition to become a State upon an equal footing with the other States, must rest upon the same discretion. It is a question for the political department of the Government, and not the judicial; and whatever the political department of the Government shall recognise as within the limits of the United States, the judicial department is also bound to recognise, and to administer in it the laws of the United States, so far as they apply, and to maintain in the Territory the authority and rights of the Government, and also the personal rights and rights of property of individual citizens, as secured by the Constitution. All we mean to say on this point is, that, as there is no express regulation in the Constitution defining the power which the General Government may exercise over the person or property of a citizen in a Territory thus acquired, the court must necessarily look to the provisions and principles of the Constitution, and its distribution of powers, for the rules and principles by which its decision must be governed.

Taking this rule to guide us, it may be safely assumed that citizens of the United States who migrate to a Territory belonging to the people of the United States, cannot be ruled as mere colonists, dependent upon the will of the General Government, and to be governed by any laws it may think proper to impose. The principle upon which our Governments rest, and upon which alone they continue to exist, is the union of States, sovereign and independent within their own limits in their internal and domestic concerns, and bound together as one people by a General Government, possessing certain enumerated and restricted powers, delegated to it by the people of the several States, and exercising supreme authority within the scope of the powers granted to it, throughout the dominion of the United States. A power, therefore, in the General Government to obtain and hold colonies and dependent territories, over which they might legislate without restriction, would be inconsistent with its own existence in its present form. Whatever it acquires, it acquires for the benefit of the people of the several States who created it. It is their trustee acting for them, and charged with the duty of promoting the interests of the whole people of the Union in the exercise of the powers specifically granted.

At the time when the Territory in question was obtained by cession from France, it contained no population fit to be associated together and admitted as a State; and it therefore was absolutely necessary to hold possession of it, as a Territory belonging to the United States, until it was settled and inhabited by a civilized community capable of self-government, and in a condition to be admitted on equal terms with the other States as a member of the Union. . . .

But until that time arrives, it is undoubtedly necessary that some Government should be established, in order to organize society, and to protect the inhabitants in their persons and property; and as the people of the United

States could act in this matter only through the Government which represented them, . . . it was not only within the scope of its powers, but it was its duty to pass such laws and establish such a Government as would enable those by whose authority they acted to reap the advantages anticipated from its acquisition, and to gather there a population which would enable it to assume the position to which it was destined among the States of the Union. The power to acquire necessarily carries with it the power to preserve and apply to the purposes for which it was acquired. The form of government to be established necessarily rested in the discretion of Congress. . . .

But the power of Congress over the person or property of a citizen can never be a mere discretionary power under our Constitution and form of Government. . . . The Territory being a part of the United States, the Government and the citizen both enter it under the authority of the Constitution, with their respective rights defined and marked out; and the Federal Government can exercise no power over his person or property, beyond what that instrument confers, nor lawfully deny any right which it has reserved.

A reference to a few of the provisions of the Constitution will illustrate this proposition.

For example, no one, we presume, will contend that Congress can make any law in a Territory respecting the establishment of religion, or the free exercise thereof, or abridging the freedom of speech or of the press, or the right of the people of the Territory peaceably to assemble, and to petition the Government for the redress of grievances.

Nor can Congress deny to the people the right to keep and bear arms, nor the right to trial by jury, nor compel any one to be a witness against himself in a criminal proceeding.

These powers, and others, in relation to rights of person, which it is not necessary here to enumerate, are, in express and positive terms, denied to the General Government; and the rights of private property have been guarded with equal care. Thus the rights of property are united with the rights of person, and placed on the same ground by the fifth amendment to the Constitution, which provides that no person shall be deprived of life, liberty, and property, without due process of law. And an act of Congress which deprives a citizen of the United States of his liberty or property, merely because he came himself or brought his property into a particular Territory of the United States, and who had committed no offence against the laws, could hardly be dignified with the name of due process of law. . . .

The powers over person and property of which we speak are not only not granted to Congress, but are in express terms denied, and they are forbidden to exercise them. And this prohibition is not confined to the States, but the words are general, and extend to the whole territory over which the Constitution gives it power to legislate, including those portions of it remaining under Territorial Government, as well as that covered by States. It is a total absence of power everywhere within the dominion of the United States, and places the citizens of a Territory, so far as these rights are concerned, on the same footing with citizens of the States, and guards them as firmly and plainly against any inroads which the General Government might attempt, under the plea of implied or incidental powers. And if Congress itself cannot do this—if it is beyond the powers conferred on the Federal Government—it will be admitted, we presume, that it could not authorize a Territorial Government to exercise them. It could confer no power on any local Government, established by its authority, to violate the provisions of the Constitution.

It seems, however, to be supposed, that there is a difference between property in a slave and other property, and that different rules may be applied to it in expounding the Constitution of the United States. . . .

[But] if the Constitution recognises the right of property of the master in a slave, and makes no distinction between that description of property and other property owned by a citizen, no tribunal, acting under the authority of the United States, whether it be legislative, executive, or judicial, has a right to draw such a distinction, or deny to it the benefit of the provisions and guarantees which have been provided for the protection of private property against the encroachments of the Government.

Now, as we have already said in an earlier part of this opinion, upon a different point, the right of property in a slave is distinctly and expressly affirmed in the Constitution. The right to traffic in it, like an ordinary article of merchandise and property, was guaranteed to the citizens of the United States, in every State that might desire it, for twenty years. And the Government in express terms is pledged to protect it in all future time, if the slave escapes from his owner. This is done in plain words—too plain to be misunderstood. And no word can be found in the Constitution which gives Congress a greater power over slave property, or which entitles property of that kind to less protection than property of any other description. The only power conferred is the power coupled with the duty of guarding and protecting the owner in his rights.

Upon these considerations, it is the opinion of the court that the act of Congress which prohibited a citizen from holding and owning property of this kind in the territory of the United States north of the line therein mentioned, is not warranted by the Constitution, and is therefore void; and that neither Dred Scott himself, nor any of his family, were made free by being carried into this territory; even if they had been carried there by the owner, with the intention of becoming a permanent resident. . . .

Mr. JUSTICE McLEAN dissenting.

[I]

[T]he plea which raises the question of jurisdiction, in my judgment, is radically defective. The gravamen of the plea is this: "That the plaintiff is a negro of African descent, his ancestors being of pure African blood, and were brought into this country, and sold as negro slaves."

There is no averment in this plea which shows or conduces to show an inability in the plaintiff to sue in the Circuit Court. It does not allege that the plaintiff had his domicil in any other State, nor that he is not a free man in Missouri. He is averred to have had a negro ancestry, but this does not show that he is not a citizen of Missouri, within the meaning of the act of Congress authorizing him to sue in the Circuit Court. It has never been held necessary, to constitute a citizen within the act, that he should have the qualifications of an elector. Females and minors may sue in the Federal courts, and so may any individual who has a permanent domicil in the State under whose laws his rights are protected, and to which he owes allegiance.

Being born under our Constitution and laws, no naturalization is required, as one of foreign birth, to make him a citizen. The most general and appropriate definition of the term citizen is "a freeman." Being a freeman, and having his domicil in a State different from that of the defendant, he is a citizen within the act of Congress, and the courts of the Union are open to him. . . .

The pleader has not the boldness to allege that the plaintiff is a slave, as that would assume against him the matter in controversy, and embrace the entire merits of the case in a plea to the jurisdiction. But beyond the facts set out in the plea, the court, to sustain it, must assume the plaintiff to be a slave, which is decisive on the merits. This is a short and an effectual mode of deciding the cause; but I am yet to learn that it is sanctioned by any known rule of pleading. . . .

No injustice can result to the master, from an exercise of jurisdiction in this cause. Such a decision does not in any degree affect the merits of the case; it only enables the plaintiff to assert his claims to freedom before this tribunal. If the jurisdiction be ruled against him, on the ground that he is a slave, it is decisive of his fate. . . .

On the question of citizenship, it must be admitted that we have not been very fastidious. Under the late treaty with Mexico, we have made citizens of all grades, combinations, and colors. The same was done in the admission of Louisiana and Florida. No one ever doubted, and no court ever held, that the people of these Territories did not become citizens under the treaty. They have exercised all the rights of citizens, without being naturalized under the acts of Congress. . . .

In the formation of the Federal Constitution, care was taken to confer no power on the Federal Government to interfere with this institution in the States. In the provision respecting the slave trade, in fixing the ratio of representation, and providing for the reclamation of fugitives from labor, slaves were referred to as persons, and in no other respect are they considered in the Constitution.

We need not refer to the mercenary spirit which introduced the infamous traffic in slaves, to show the degradation of negro slavery in our country. This system was imposed upon our colonial settlements by the mother country, and it is due to truth to say that the commercial colonies and States were chiefly engaged in the traffic. But we know as a historical fact, that James Madison, that great and good man, a leading member in the Federal Convention, was solicitous to guard the language of that instrument so as not to convey the idea that there could be property in man.

I prefer the lights of Madison, Hamilton, and Jay, as a means of construing the Constitution in all its bearings, rather than to look behind that period, into a traffic which is now declared to be piracy, and punished with death by Christian nations. I do not like to draw the sources of our domestic relations from so dark a ground. Our independence was a great epoch in the history of freedom; and while I admit the Government was not made especially for the colored race, yet many of them were citizens of the New England States, and exercised, the rights of suffrage when the Constitution was adopted, and it was not doubted by any intelligent person that its tendencies would greatly ameliorate their condition.

Many of the States, on the adoption of the Constitution, or shortly afterward, took measures to abolish slavery within their respective jurisdictions; and it is a well-known fact that a belief was cherished by the leading men, South as well as North, that the institution of slavery would gradually decline, until it would become extinct. The increased value of slave labor, in the culture of cotton and sugar, prevented the realization of this expectation. Like all other communities and States, the South were influenced by what they considered to be their own interests.

But if we are to turn our attention to the dark ages of the world, why confine our view to colored slavery? On the same principles, white men were made slaves. All slavery has its origin in power, and is against right.

[II]

The power of Congress to establish Territorial Governments, and to prohibit the introduction of slavery therein, is the next point to be considered. . . .

[I]n providing for the Government of a Territory, to some extent, the combined powers of the Federal and State Governments are necessarily exercised. . . . If Congress may establish a Territorial Government in the exercise of its discretion, it is a clear principle that a court cannot control that discretion. This being the case, I do not see on what ground the act is held to be void. It did not purport to forfeit property, or take it for public purposes. It only prohibited slavery; in doing which, it followed the ordinance of 1787.

[III]

I will now consider . . . "The effect of taking slaves into a State or Territory, and so holding them, where slavery is prohibited."

If the principle laid down in the case of *Prigg v. The State of Pennsylvania* is to be maintained, and it is certainly to be maintained until overruled, as the law of this court, there can be no difficulty on this point. In that case, the court says: "The state of slavery is deemed to be a mere municipal regulation, founded upon and limited to the range of the territorial laws." If this be so, slavery can exist nowhere except under the authority of law, founded on usage having the force of law, or by statutory recognition. . . .

It is said the Territories are common property of the States, and that every man has a right to go there with his property. This is not controverted. But the court say a slave is not property beyond the operation of the local law which makes him such. Never was a truth more authoritatively and justly uttered by man. Suppose a master of a slave in a British island owned a million of property in England; would that authorize him to take his slaves with him to England? The Constitution, in express terms, recognises the *status* of slavery as founded on the municipal law: "No person held to service or labor in one State, *under the laws thereof*, escaping into another, shall," &c. Now, unless the fugitive escape from a place where, by the municipal law, he is held to labor, this provision affords no remedy to the master. What can be more conclusive than this? Suppose a slave escape from a Territory where slavery is not authorized by law, can he be reclaimed?

In this case, a majority of the court have said that a slave may be taken by his master into a Territory of the United States, the same as a horse, or any other kind of property. It is true, this was said by the court, as also many other things, which are of no authority. Nothing that has been said by them, which has not a direct bearing on the jurisdiction of the court, against which they decided, can be considered as authority. I shall certainly not regard it as such. The question of jurisdiction, being before the court, was decided by them authoritatively, but nothing beyond that question. A slave is not a mere chattel. He bears the impress of his Maker, and is amenable to the laws of God and man; and he is destined to an endless existence. . . .

Mr. JUSTICE CURTIS dissenting.

[I]

The first section of the second article of the Constitution uses the language, "a citizen of the United States at the time of the adoption of the Constitution." One mode of approaching this question is, to inquire who were citizens of the United States at the time of the adoption of the Constitution.

Citizens of the United States at the time of the adoption of the Constitution can have been no other than citizens of the United States under the Confederation. . . . [I]t may safely be said that the citizens of the several States were citizens of the United States under the Confederation.

That Government was simply a confederacy of the several States, possessing a few defined powers over subjects of general concern, each State retaining every power, jurisdiction, and right, not expressly delegated to the United States in Congress assembled. And no power was thus delegated to the Government of the Confederation, to act on any question of citizenship, or to make any rules in respect thereto. The whole matter was left to stand upon the action of the several States, and to the natural consequence of such action, that the citizens of each State should be citizens of that Confederacy into which that State had entered, the style whereof was, "The United States of America."

To determine whether any free persons, descended from Africans held in slavery, were citizens of the United States under the Confederation, and consequently at the time of the adoption of the Constitution of the United States, it is only necessary to know whether any such persons were citizens of either of the States under the Confederation, at the time of the adoption of the Constitution.

Of this there can be no doubt. At the time of the ratification of the Articles of Confederation, all free native-born inhabitants of the States of New Hampshire, Massachusetts, New York, New Jersey, and North Carolina, though descended from African slaves, were not only citizens of those States, but such of them as had the other necessary qualifications possessed the franchise of electors, on equal terms with other citizens. . . .

The fourth of the fundamental articles of the Confederation was as follows: "The free inhabitants of each of these States, paupers, vagabonds, and fugitives from justice, excepted, shall be entitled to all the privileges and immunities of free citizens in the several States." . . .

[I]t is clear, that under the Confederation, and at the time of the adoption of the Constitution, free colored persons of African descent might be, and, by reason of their citizenship in certain States, were entitled to the privileges and immunities of general citizenship of the United States.

Did the Constitution of the United States deprive them or their descendants of citizenship?

That Constitution was ordained and established by the people of the United States, through the action, in each State, of those persons who were qualified by its laws to act thereon, in behalf of themselves and all other citizens of that State. In some of the States, as we have seen, colored persons were among those qualified by law to act on this subject. These colored persons were not only included in the body of "the people of the United States," by whom the Constitution was ordained and established, but in at least five of the States they had the power to act, and doubtless did act, by their suffrages, upon the question of its adoption. It would be strange, if we were to find in that instrument anything which deprived of their citizenship any part of the people of the United States who were among those by whom it was established.

I can find nothing in the Constitution which, *proprio vigore*, deprives of their citizenship any class of persons who were citizens of the United States at the time of its adoption, or who should be native-born citizens of any State after its adoption; nor any power enabling Congress to disfranchise persons born on the soil of any State, and entitled to citizenship of such State by its Constitution and laws. And my opinion is, that, under the Constitution of the United States, every free person born on the soil of a State, who is a citizen of that State by force of its Constitution or laws, is also a citizen of the United States. . . .

Among the powers unquestionably possessed by the several States, was that of determining what persons should and what persons should not be citizens. . . .

"The citizens of each State shall be entitled to all the privileges and immunities of citizens of the several States." Nowhere else in the Constitution is there anything concerning a general citizenship; but here, privileges and immunities to be enjoyed throughout the United States, under and by force of the national compact, are granted and secured. In selecting those who are to enjoy these national rights of citizenship, how are they described? As citizens of each State. It is to them these national rights are secured. The qualification for them is not to be looked for in any provision of the Constitution or laws of the United States. They are to be citizens of the several States, and, as such, the privileges and immunities of general citizenship, derived from and guaranteed by the Constitution, are to be enjoyed by them. . . .

[A]s free colored persons were then citizens of at least five States, and so in every sense part of the people of the United States, they were among those for whom and whose posterity the Constitution was ordained and established. . . .

I dissent, therefore, from that part of the opinion of the majority of the court, in which it is held that a person of African descent cannot be a citizen of the United States[.] . . .

[II]

I regret I must go further, and dissent both from what I deem their assumption of authority to examine the constitutionality of the act of Congress commonly called the Missouri compromise act, and the grounds and conclusions announced in their opinion. . . .

I confess myself unable to perceive any difference whatever between my own opinion of the general extent of the power of Congress and the opinion of the majority of the court, save that I consider it derivable from the express language of the Constitution, while they hold it to be silently implied from the power to acquire territory. Looking at the power of Congress over the Territories as of the extent just described, what positive prohibition exists in the Constitution, which restrained Congress from enacting a law in 1820 to prohibit slavery north of thirty-six degrees thirty minutes north latitude?

The only one suggested is that clause in the fifth article of the amendments of the Constitution which declares that no person shall be deprived of his life, liberty, or property, without due process of law. . . .

Slavery, being contrary to natural right, is created only by municipal law. This is not only plain in itself, and agreed by all writers on the subject, but is inferable from the Constitution, and has been explicitly declared by this court. The Constitution refers to slaves as "persons held to service in one State, under the laws thereof." Nothing can more clearly describe a *status* created by municipal law. In *Prigg v. Pennsylvania*, this court said: "The state of slavery is deemed to be a mere municipal regulation, founded on and limited to the range of territorial laws." . . .

Is it conceivable that the Constitution has conferred the right on every citizen to become a resident on the territory of the United States with his slaves, and there to hold them as such, but has neither made nor provided for any municipal regulations which are essential to the existence of slavery?

Is it not more rational to conclude that they who framed and adopted the constitution were aware that persons held to service under the laws of a State are property only to the extent and under the conditions fixed by those laws; that they must cease to be available as property, when their owners voluntarily place them permanently within another jurisdiction, where no municipal laws on the subject of slavery exist; and that, being aware of these principles, and having said nothing to interfere with or displace them, or to compel Congress to legislate in any particular manner on the subject, and having empowered Congress to make all needful rules and regulations respecting the territory of the United States, it was their intention to leave to the discretion of Congress what regulations, if any, should be made concerning slavery therein? Moreover, if the right exists, what are its limits, and what are its conditions? . . .

It was certainly understood by the Convention which framed the Constitution, and has been so understood ever since, that, under the power to regulate commerce, Congress could prohibit the importation of slaves; and the exercise of the power was restrained till 1808. . . .

FREDERICK DOUGLASS, SPEECH ON THE DRED SCOTT DECISION

1857

This infamous decision of the Slaveholding wing of the Supreme Court maintains that slaves are within the contemplation of the Constitution of the United States, property; that slaves are property in the same sense that horses, sheep, and swine are property; that the old doctrine that slavery is a creature of local law is false; that the right of the slaveholder to his slave does not depend upon the local law, but is secured wherever the Constitution of the United States extends; that Congress has no right to prohibit slavery anywhere; that slavery may go in safety anywhere under the star-spangled banner; that colored persons of African descent have no rights that white men are bound to respect; that colored men of African descent are not and cannot be citizens of the United States. . . .

The Supreme Court of the United States is not the only power in this world. It is very great, but the Supreme Court of the Almighty is greater. Judge Taney can do many things, but he cannot perform impossibilities. He cannot bale out the ocean, annihilate the firm old earth, or pluck the silvery star of liberty from our Northern sky. He may decide, and decide again; but he cannot reverse the decision of the Most High. He cannot change the essential nature of things — making evil good, and good evil. . . .

Your fathers have said that man's right to liberty is self-evident. There is no need of argument to make it clear. The voices of nature, of conscience, of reason, and of revelation, proclaim it as the right of all rights, the foundation of all trust, and of all responsibility. Man was born with it. It was his before he comprehended it. The deed conveying it to him is written in the center of his soul, and is recorded in Heaven. . . . To decide against this right in the person of Dred Scott, or the humblest and most whip-scarred bondman in the land, is to decide against God. . . .

In one point of view, we, the abolitionists and colored people, should meet this decision, unlooked for and monstrous as it appears, in a cheerful spirit. This very attempt to blot out forever the hopes of an enslaved people may be one necessary link in the chain of events preparatory to the downfall and complete overthrow of the whole slave system. . . .

But I come now to the great question as to the constitutionality of slavery. . . .

When I admit that slavery is constitutional, I must see slavery recognized in the Constitution. I must see that it is there plainly stated that one man of a certain description has a right of property in the body and soul of another man of a certain description. There must be no room for a doubt. In a matter so important as the loss of liberty, everything must be proved beyond all reasonable doubt.

The well known rules of legal interpretation bear me out in this stubborn refusal to see slavery where slavery is not, and only to see slavery where it is.

The Supreme Court has, in its day, done something better than make slaveholding decisions. It has laid down rules of interpretation which are in harmony with the true idea and object of law and liberty.

It has told us that the intention of legal instruments must prevail; and that this must be collected from its words. It has told us that language must be construed strictly in favor of liberty and justice.

It has told us where rights are infringed, where fundamental principles are overthrown, where the general system of the law is departed from, the Legislative intention must be expressed with irresistible clearness, to induce a court of justice to suppose a design to effect such objects.

These rules are as old as law. They rise out of the very elements of law. It is to protect human rights, and promote human welfare. Law is in its nature opposed to wrong, and must everywhere be presumed to be in favor of the right. . . .

Besides there is another rule of law as well of common sense, which requires us to look to the ends for which a law is made, and to construe its details in harmony with the ends sought.

Now let us approach the Constitution from the standpoint thus indicated, and instead of finding in it a warrant for the stupendous system of robbery, comprehended in the term slavery, we shall find it strongly against that system. . . .

Neither in the preamble nor in the body of the Constitution is there a single mention of the term slave or slave holder, slave master or slave state, neither is there any reference to the color, or the physical peculiarities of any part of the people of the United States. Neither is there anything in the Constitution standing alone, which would imply the existence of slavery in this country.

"We, the people" — not we, the white people — not we, the citizens, or the legal voters — not we, the privileged class, and excluding all other classes but we, the people; not we, the horses and cattle, but we the people — the men and women, the human inhabitants of the United States, do ordain and establish this Constitution, &c.

I ask, then, any man to read the Constitution, and tell me where, if he can, in what particular that instrument affords the slightest sanction of slavery?

Where will he find a guarantee for slavery? Will he find it in the declaration that no person shall be deprived of life, liberty, or property, without due process of law? Will he find it in the declaration that the Constitution was established to secure the blessing of liberty? . . .

These . . . strike at the root of slavery, and . . . faithfully carried out, would put an end to slavery in every State in the American Union. . . .

How is the constitutionality of slavery made out, or attempted to be made out?

First, by discrediting and casting away as worthless the most beneficent rules of legal interpretation; by disregarding the plain and common sense reading of the instrument itself; by showing that the Constitution does not mean what it says, and says what it does not mean, by assuming that the written Constitution is to be interpreted in the light of a secret and unwritten understanding of its framers, which understanding is declared to be in favor of slavery. It is in this mean, contemptible, underhand method that the Constitution is pressed into the service of slavery.

They do not point us to the Constitution itself, for the reason that there is nothing sufficiently explicit for their purpose; but they delight in supposed intentions — intentions nowhere expressed in the Constitution, and everywhere contradicted in the Constitution.

Judge Taney lays down this system of interpreting . . . :

> The general words above quoted would seem to embrace the whole human family, and, if they were used in a similar instrument at this day, would be so understood. But it is too clear for dispute that the enslaved African race were not intended to be included, and formed no part of the people who framed and adopted this declaration; for if the language, as understood in that day, would embrace them, the conduct of the distinguished men who framed the Declaration of Independence would have been utterly and flagrantly inconsistent with the principles they asserted; and instead of the sympathy of mankind, to which they appealed, they would have deserved and received universal rebuke and reprobation. . . .

The argument here is, that the Constitution comes down to us from a slaveholding period and a slaveholding people; and that, therefore, we are bound to suppose that the Constitution recognizes colored persons of African descent, the victims of slavery at that time, as debarred forever from all participation in the benefit of the Constitution and the Declaration of Independence, although the plain reading of both includes them in their beneficent range. . . .

It is a fact, a great historic fact, that at the time of the adoption of the Constitution, the leading religious denominations in this land were antislavery, and were laboring for the emancipation of the colored people of African descent.

The church of a country is often a better index of the state of opinion and feeling than is even the government itself. . . .

The testimony of the church, and the testimony of the founders of this Republic, from the declaration downward, prove Judge Taney false; as false to history as he is to law.

Washington and Jefferson, and Adams, and Jay, and Franklin, and Rush, and Hamilton, and a host of others, held no such degrading views on the subject of slavery as are imputed by Judge Taney to the Fathers of the Republic.

All, at that time, looked for the gradual but certain abolition of slavery, and shaped the Constitution with a view to this grand result.

George Washington can never be claimed as a fanatic, or as the representative of fanatics. The slaveholders impudently use his name for the base purpose of giving respectability to slavery. Yet, in a letter to Robert Morris, Washington uses this language — language which, at this day, would make him a terror of the slaveholders, and the natural representative of the Republican party.

> There is not a man living, who wishes more sincerely than I do, to see some plan adopted for the abolition of slavery; but there is only one proper and effectual mode by which it can be accomplished, and that is by Legislative authority; and this, as far as my suffrage will go, shall not be wanting.

Washington only spoke the sentiment of his times. There were, at that time, Abolition societies in the slave States — Abolition societies in Virginia, in North Carolina, in Maryland, in Pennsylvania, and in Georgia — all slave-holding States. . . .

In the light of these facts, the Constitution was framed, and framed in conformity to it. . . .

It may be said that it is quite true that the Constitution was designed to secure the blessings of liberty and justice to the people who made it, and to the posterity of the people who made it, but was never designed to do any such thing for the colored people of African descent.

This is Judge Taney's argument, . . . but it is not the argument of the Constitution. . . .

The Constitution knows all the human inhabitants of this country as "the people." It makes, as I have said before, no discrimination in favor of, or against, any class of the people, but is fitted to protect and preserve the rights of all, without reference to color, size, or any physical peculiarities. Besides, . . . in eleven out of the old thirteen States, colored men were legal voters at the time of the adoption of the Constitution.

In conclusion, let me say, all I ask of the American people is, that they live up to the Constitution, adopt its principles, imbibe its spirit, and enforce its provisions. . . .

Frederick Douglass, The Constitution of the United States: Is It Pro-Slavery or Anti-Slavery?

1860

The . . . question . . . may be fairly stated thus: . . . Does the United States Constitution guarantee to any class or description of people in that country the right to enslave, or hold as property, any other class or description of people in that country? . . .

Before we examine into the disposition, tendency, and character of the Constitution, I think we had better ascertain what the Constitution itself is. Before looking for what it means, let us see what it is. Here, too, there is much dust to be cleared away. What, then, is the Constitution? I will tell you. . . . [I]t is a plainly written document . . . in English, beginning with a preamble, filled out with articles, sections, provisions, and clauses, defining the rights, powers, and duties to be secured, claimed, and exercised under its authority. It is not even like the British Constitution, which is made up of enactments of Parliament, decisions of Courts, and the established usages of the Government. The American Constitution is a written instrument full and complete in itself. No Court in America, no Congress, no President, can add a single word thereto, or take a single word thereto. It is a great national enactment done by the people, and can only be altered, amended, or added to by the people. . . . Again, it should be borne in mind that the mere text, and only the text, and not any commentaries or creeds written by those who wished to give the text a meaning apart from its plain reading, was adopted as the Constitution of the United States. It should also be borne in mind that the intentions of those who framed the Constitution, be they good or bad, for slavery or against slavery, are so respected so far, and so far only, as we find those intentions plainly stated in the Constitution. . . .

It so happens that no such words as "African slave trade," no such words as "slave insurrections," are anywhere used in that instrument. . . . Here then are several provisions of the Constitution to which reference has been made. I read them word for word just as they stand in the paper, called the United States Constitution, Art. I, sec. 2. "Representatives and direct taxes shall be apportioned among the several States which may be included in this Union, according to their respective numbers, which shall be determined by adding to the whole number of free persons, including those bound to service for a term years, and excluding Indians not taxed, three-fifths of all other persons; Art. I, sec. 9. The migration or importation of such persons as any of the States now existing shall think fit to admit, shall not be prohibited by the Congress prior to the year one thousand eight hundred and eight, but a tax or duty may be imposed on such importation, not exceeding tend dollars for each person; . . . Art. I, sec. 8. To provide for calling for the militia to execute the laws of the Union, suppress insurrections, and repel invasions." . . . Let us look at them just as they stand, one by one. Let us grant, for the sake of the argument, that the first of these provisions, referring to the basis of representation and taxation, does refer to slaves. . . . It is a downright disability laid upon the slaveholding States; one which deprives those States of two-fifths of their natural basis of representation. A black man in a free State is worth just two-fifths more than a black man in a slave State, as a basis of political power under the Constitution. Therefore, instead of encouraging slavery, the Constitution encourages freedom by giving an increase of "two-fifths" of political power to free over slave States. So much for the three-fifths clause; taking it at its worst, it still leans to freedom, not slavery; for, be it remembered that the Constitution nowhere forbids a coloured man to vote. I come to the next, that which it is said guaranteed the continuance of the African slave trade for twenty years. . . . [T]his part of the Constitution, so far as the slave trade is concerned, became a dead letter more than 50 years ago, and now binds no man's conscience for the continuance of any slave trade whatsoever. . . . The abolition of the slave trade was supposed to be the certain death of slavery. Cut off the stream, and the pond will dry up, was the common notion at the time. . . .

[T]he American statesmen, in providing for the abolition of the slave trade, thought they were providing for the abolition of the slavery. This view is quite consistent with the history of the times. All regarded slavery as an expiring and doomed system, destined to speedily disappear from the country. But, again, it should be remembered that this very provision, if made to refer to the African slave trade at all, makes the Constitution anti-slavery rather than for slavery, for it says to the slave States, the price you will have to pay for coming into the American Union is, that the slave trade, which you would carry on indefinitely out of the Union, shall be put an end to in twenty years if you come into the Union. Secondly, if it does apply, it expired by its own limitation more than fifty years ago. Thirdly, it is anti-slavery, because it looked to the abolition of slavery rather than to its perpetuity. Fourthly, it showed that the intentions of the framers of the Constitution were good, not bad. I think this is quite enough for this point. I go to the "slave insurrection" clause, though, in truth, there is no such clause. The one which is called so has nothing whatever to do with slaves or slaveholders any more than your laws for suppression of popular outbreaks has to do with making slaves of you and your children. It is only a law for suppression of riots or insurrections. But I will be generous here, as well as elsewhere, and grant that it applies to slave insurrections. . . . The right to put down an insurrection carries with it the right to determine the means by which it shall be put down. If it should turn out that slavery is a source of insurrection, that there is no security from insurrection while slavery lasts, why, the Constitution would be best obeyed by putting an end to slavery, and an anti-slavery Congress would do the very same thing. Thus, you see, the so-called slave-holding provisions of the American Constitution, which a little while ago looked so formidable, are, after all, no defence or guarantee for slavery whatever. . . .

POINTS FOR DISCUSSION

1. Justice Taney evaluated congressional power to regulate slavery in federal territories under Congress's Article 4, §3 powers to make "needful Rules and Regulations respecting" territories of the United States and to admit new states into the Union. Does his evaluation of congressional power qualitatively differ from Marshall Court analyses of congressional power?

2. Justice Taney explained that "[t]he duty of the court is, to interpret the instrument [the Framers] have framed, with the best lights we can obtain on the subject, and to administer it as we find it, according to its true intent and meaning when it was adopted." Douglass contended, however, that "the intentions of those who framed the Constitution, be they good or bad, for slavery or against slavery, are so respected so far, and so far only, as we find those intentions plainly stated in the Constitution." Identify and critically evaluate the different methods of interpretation that Taney and Douglass employed. As you will see in Chapters 5 and 6, the Justices have relied heavily upon original understandings in ascertaining what constitutional limits exist on congressional power. You will see the methodological differences between Taney and Douglass reemerge in present-day disputes over congressional power.

3. In analyzing the issues before the Court in *Dred Scott*, Justice Taney asserted that "[i]t is not the province of the court to decide upon the justice or injustice, the policy or impolicy, of these laws" concerning slavery. Douglass, however, characterized Taney as attempting to "perform impossibilities":

> Your fathers have said that man's right to liberty is self-evident. There is no need of argument to make it clear. The voices of nature, of conscience, of reason, and of revelation, proclaim it as the right of all rights, the foundation of all trust, and of all responsibility. Man was born with it. It was his before he comprehended it. The deed conveying it to him is written in the center of his soul, and is recorded in Heaven. . . . To decide against this right in the person of Dred Scott, or the humblest and most whip-scarred bondman in the land, is to decide against God. . . .

Consider the following passage, in which Professor John Finnis criticizes juristic analysis that "does not have as its primary or any concern the interests and well-being of this or any person." John Finnis, *The Priority of Persons*, in Oxford Essays in Jurisprudence 1, 7 (Series No. 4, Jeremy Horder ed., 2000).

> Among the most striking examples [of judicial abdication from concern with the interests and well-being of real people] is the justly infamous judgment of the Supreme Court of the United States in *Scott v. Sandford* (1857), holding that members of 'the African race' imported into or born in the United States . . . were not citizens of the United States, and could never be made citizens by Congress. . . . The decision rested on the fact that, at the time of the Declaration of Independence (1776) and the founding of the Constitution (1789), public opinion — real enough though the Court vastly exaggerates its unanimity — considered that 'the negro might justly and lawfully be reduced to slavery' as 'beings of an inferior order.' At the time of the framing and adoption of the Constitution, 'neither the class of persons who had been imported as slaves, nor their descendants, whether they had become free' had any 'rights or privileges but such as those who held the power and the Government might choose to grant them.' And 'the duty of the court is . . . to administer [the instrument they have framed] as we find it, according to its true intent and meaning when it was adopted.' The Court's radical failure, then, was to approach its duty of doing justice according to law without recognizing that law, the whole legal enterprise, is for the sake of persons, and that the founders' intentions were therefore to be interpreted — not, as the Court did, so as to promote their background prejudices (from which the Court dissociated itself) against the people they wished to treat as mere property, but rather — in favour of the basic interests and well-being of every person within the jurisdiction so far as was possible without contradicting the Constitution's provisions.

Id. at 7-8. Was it possible for the *Dred Scott* Court to serve "the basic interests and well-being" of persons "without contradicting the Constitution's provisions"?

Imagine that the Constitution expressly forbade Congress from enacting any regulations of slavery in territories of the United States. In 1857, should the Court have upheld such a constitutional provision against a congressional regulation prohibiting slavery in the territories? What values would upholding such an express limit on congressional power advance?

In present-day cases that you will read in this book, you will see Justices discern constitutional limitations on congressional power and uphold those limitations against legislation that certain Justices describe as necessary and expedient as a policy matter. For instance, in *New York v. United States*, 505 U.S. 144 (1992), which you will read in Chapter 6, the Court held that Congress may not require state legislatures to enact legislation implementing a federal program regulating radioactive waste disposal. In dissent, Justice White argued that Congress had enacted a sound solution to a problem warranting national action. Granted, *New York* does not pit the values of upholding limitations on federal power against such a basic affront to human dignity as slavery. Nonetheless, in such a case as *New York*, what value is served by upholding limits on congressional power in the face of legislation that, in a judge's opinion, represents sound national policy? Do excerpts of *The Federalist* that you read in Chapter 1 suggest any answers to this question? Keep this question in mind as you study the values of federalism in Chapter 3 and present-day federalism disputes in Chapters 5 and 6.

C. FEDERALISM AND SECESSION

Upon the election of Republican Abraham Lincoln as President in 1860, but before his inauguration in March 1861, seven states seceded from the Union: South Carolina, Mississippi, Florida, Alabama, Georgia, Louisiana, and Texas. Republicans charged that secession was an unlawful act of rebellion. In February 1861, Jefferson Davis became provisional president of the Confederate States of America. In his inaugural address of February 18, 1861, Davis defended secession against the charge that it was an act of revolution:

> Our present political position has been achieved in a manner unprecedented in the history of nations. It illustrates the American idea that governments rest on the consent of the governed, and that it is the right of the people to alter or abolish them at will whenever they become destructive of the ends for which they were established. The declared purpose of the compact of the Union from which we have withdrawn was to "establish justice, insure domestic tranquillity, provide for the common defense, promote the general welfare, and secure the blessings of liberty to ourselves and our posterity;" and when, in the judgment of the sovereign States composing this Confederacy, it has been perverted from the purposes for which it was ordained, and ceased to answer the ends for which it was established, a peaceful appeal to the ballot box declared that, so far as they are concerned, the Government created by that compact should cease to exist. In this they merely asserted the right which the Declaration of Independence of July 4, 1776, defined to be "inalienable." Of the time and occasion of its exercise they as sovereigns were the final judges, each for itself. . . .
>
> The right solemnly proclaimed at the birth of the United States, and which has been solemnly affirmed and reaffirmed in the Bills of Rights of the States subsequently admitted into the Union of 1789, undeniably recognizes in the people the power to resume the authority delegated for the purposes of government. Thus the sovereign States here represented have proceeded to form this Confederacy; and it is by abuse of language that their act has been denominated a revolution. They formed a new alliance, but within each State its government has remained; so that the rights of person and property have not been disturbed. The agent through which they communicated with foreign nations is changed, but this does not necessarily interrupt their international relations. Sustained by the consciousness that the transition from the former Union to the present Confederacy has not proceeded from a disregard on our part of just obligations, or any failure to perform every constitutional duty, moved by no interest or passion to invade the rights of others, anxious to cultivate peace and commerce with all nations, if we may not hope to avoid war, we may at least expect that posterity will acquit us of having needlessly engaged in it.

Lincoln declared secession an unlawful act of rebellion in his First Inaugural Address of March 4, 1861, and in his message of July 4, 1861, to a special session of Congress. By this time, the Supreme Court had decided *Dred Scott v. Sandford*, 60 U.S. (19 How.) 393 (1857), determining, among other things, that Congress had no authority to prohibit slavery in federal territories—a decision that outraged Republicans. In his First Inaugural Address, Lincoln aspired both to strengthen his base in the North and to avoid further disunion in the South. As you read Lincoln's words, consider the following questions:

- What are Lincoln's specific points of disagreement with Davis as to the lawfulness of secession?
- What does Lincoln declare to be the respective roles of the states, Congress, courts, and the people in upholding the federal structure that the Constitution established? Which writings that you have read from the Founding period and Marshall Court does Lincoln echo? Which are in tension with his views?

First Inaugural Address of Abraham Lincoln

March 4, 1861

Fellow-Citizens of the United States:

In compliance with a custom as old as the Government itself, I appear before you to address you briefly and to take in your presence the oath prescribed by the Constitution of the United States to be taken by the President "before he enters on the execution of this office." . . .

Apprehension seems to exist among the people of the Southern States that by the accession of a Republican Administration their property and their peace and personal security are to be endangered. There has never been any reasonable cause for such apprehension. Indeed, the most ample evidence to the contrary has all the while existed and been open to their inspection. It is found in nearly all the published speeches of him who now addresses you. I do but quote from one of those speeches when I declare that—

> I have no purpose, directly or indirectly, to interfere with the institution of slavery in the States where it exists. I believe I have no lawful right to do so, and I have no inclination to do so.

Those who nominated and elected me did so with full knowledge that I had made this and many similar declarations and had never recanted them; and more than this, they placed in the platform for my acceptance, and as a law to themselves and to me, the clear and emphatic resolution which I now read:

> *Resolved*, That the maintenance inviolate of the rights of the States, and especially the right of each State to order and control its own domestic institutions according to its own judgment exclusively, is essential to that balance of power on which the perfection and endurance of our political fabric depend; and we denounce the lawless invasion by armed force of the soil of any State or Territory, no matter what pretext, as among the gravest of crimes.

I now reiterate these sentiments, and in doing so I only press upon the public attention the most conclusive evidence of which the case is susceptible that the property, peace, and security of no section are to be in any wise endangered by the now incoming Administration. I add, too, that all the protection which, consistently with the Constitution and the laws, can be given will be cheerfully given to all the States when lawfully demanded, for whatever cause — as cheerfully to one section as to another.

There is much controversy about the delivering up of fugitives from service or labor. The clause I now read is as plainly written in the Constitution as any other of its provisions:

> No person held to service or labor in one State, under the laws thereof, escaping into another, shall in consequence of any law or regulation therein be discharged from such service or labor, but shall be delivered up on claim of the party to whom such service or labor may be due.

It is scarcely questioned that this provision was intended by those who made it for the reclaiming of what we call fugitive slaves; and the intention of the lawgiver is the law. All members of Congress swear their support to the whole Constitution — to this provision as much as to any other. To the proposition, then, that slaves whose cases come within the terms of this clause "shall be delivered up" their oaths are unanimous. Now, if they would make the effort in good temper, could they not with nearly equal unanimity frame and pass a law by means of which to keep good that unanimous oath?

There is some difference of opinion whether this clause should be enforced by national or by State authority, but surely that difference is not a very material one. If the slave is to be surrendered, it can be of but little consequence to him or to others by which authority it is done. And should anyone in any case be content that his oath shall go unkept on a merely unsubstantial controversy as to *how* it shall be kept?

Again: In any law upon this subject ought not all the safeguards of liberty known in civilized and humane jurisprudence to be introduced, so that a free man be not in any case surrendered as a slave? And might it not be well at the same time to provide by law for the enforcement of that clause in the Constitution which guarantees that "the citizens of each State shall be entitled to all privileges and immunities of citizens in the several States"?

I take the official oath to-day with no mental reservations and with no purpose to construe the Constitution or laws by any hypercritical rules; and while I do not choose now to specify particular acts of Congress as proper to be enforced, I do suggest that it will be much safer for all, both in official and private stations, to conform to and abide by all those acts which stand unrepealed than to violate any of them trusting to find impunity in having them held to be unconstitutional. . . .

I hold that in contemplation of universal law and of the Constitution the Union of these States is perpetual. Perpetuity is implied, if not expressed, in the fundamental law of all national governments. It is safe to assert that no government proper ever had a provision in its organic law for its own termination. Continue to execute all the express provisions of our National Constitution, and the Union will endure forever, it being impossible to destroy it except by some action not provided for in the instrument itself.

Again: If the United States be not a government proper, but an association of States in the nature of contract merely, can it, as a contract, be peaceably unmade by less than all the parties who made it? One party to a contract may violate it—break it, so to speak—but does it not require all to lawfully rescind it?

Descending from these general principles, we find the proposition that in legal contemplation the Union is perpetual confirmed by the history of the Union itself. The Union is much older than the Constitution. It was formed, in fact, by the Articles of Association in 1774. It was matured and continued by the Declaration of Independence in 1776. It was further matured, and the faith of all the then thirteen States expressly plighted and engaged that it should be perpetual, by the Articles of Confederation in 1778. And finally, in 1787, one of the declared objects for ordaining and establishing the Constitution was *"to form a more perfect Union."*

But if destruction of the Union by one or by a part only of the States be lawfully possible, the Union is *less* perfect than before the Constitution, having lost the vital element of perpetuity.

It follows from these views that no State upon its own mere motion can lawfully get out of the Union; that *resolves* and *ordinances* to that effect are legally void, and that acts of violence within any State or States against the authority of the United States are insurrectionary or revolutionary, according to circumstances.

I therefore consider that in view of the Constitution and the laws the Union is unbroken, and to the extent of my ability, I shall take care, as the Constitution itself expressly enjoins upon me, that the laws of the Union be faithfully executed in all the States. Doing this I deem to be only a simple duty on my part, and I shall perform it so far as practicable unless my rightful masters, the American people, shall withhold the requisite means or in some authoritative manner direct the contrary. I trust this will not be regarded as a menace, but only as the declared purpose of the Union that it *will* constitutionally defend and maintain itself. . . .

Before entering upon so grave a matter as the destruction of our national fabric, with all its benefits, its memories, and its hopes, would it not be wise to ascertain precisely why we do it? Will you hazard so desperate a step while there is any possibility that any portion of the ills you fly from have no real existence? Will you, while the certain ills you fly to are greater than all the real ones you fly from, will you risk the commission of so fearful a mistake?

All profess to be content in the Union if all constitutional rights can be maintained. Is it true, then, that any right plainly written in the Constitution has been denied? I think not. Happily, the human mind is so constituted that no party can reach to the audacity of doing this. Think, if you can, of a single instance in which a plainly written provision of the Constitution has ever been denied. If by the mere force of numbers a majority should deprive a minority of any clearly written constitutional right, it might in a moral point of view justify revolution; certainly would if such right were a vital one. But such is not our case. All the vital rights of minorities and of individuals are so plainly assured to them by affirmations and negations, guaranties and prohibitions, in the Constitution that controversies never arise concerning them. But no organic law can ever be framed with a provision specifically applicable to every question which may occur in practical administration. No foresight can anticipate nor any document of reasonable length contain express provisions for all possible questions. Shall fugitives from labor be surrendered by national or by State authority? The Constitution does not expressly say. *May* Congress prohibit slavery in the Territories? The Constitution does not expressly say. *Must* Congress protect slavery in the Territories? The Constitution does not expressly say.

From questions of this class spring all our constitutional controversies, and we divide upon them into majorities and minorities. If the minority will not acquiesce, the majority must, or the Government must cease. There is no other alternative, for continuing the Government is acquiescence on one side or the other. If a minority in such case will secede rather than acquiesce, they make a precedent which in turn will divide and ruin them, for a minority of their own will secede from them whenever a majority refuses to be controlled by such minority. For instance, why may not any portion of a new confederacy a year or two hence arbitrarily secede again, precisely as portions of the present Union now claim to secede from it? All who cherish disunion sentiments are now being educated to the exact temper of doing this.

Is there such perfect identity of interests among the States to compose a new union as to produce harmony only and prevent renewed secession?

Plainly the central idea of secession is the essence of anarchy. A majority held in restraint by constitutional checks and limitations, and always changing easily with deliberate changes of popular opinions and sentiments, is the only true sovereign of a free people. Whoever rejects it does of necessity fly to anarchy or to despotism. Unanimity is impossible. The rule of a minority, as a permanent arrangement, is wholly inadmissible; so that, rejecting the majority principle, anarchy or despotism in some form is all that is left.

I do not forget the position assumed by some that constitutional questions are to be decided by the Supreme Court, nor do I deny that such decisions must be binding in any case upon the parties to a suit as to the object of that suit, while they are also entitled to very high respect and consideration in all parallel cases by all other departments of the Government. And while it is obviously possible that such decision may be erroneous in any given case, still the evil effect following it, being limited to that particular case, with the chance that it may be overruled and never become a precedent for other cases, can better be borne than could the evils of a different practice. At the same time, the candid citizen must confess that if the policy of the Government upon vital questions affecting the whole people is to be irrevocably fixed by decisions of the Supreme Court, the instant they are made in ordinary litigation between parties in personal actions the people will have ceased to be their own rulers, having to that extent practically resigned their Government into the hands of that eminent tribunal. Nor is there in this view any assault upon the court or the judges. It is a duty from which they may not shrink to decide cases properly brought before them, and it is no fault of theirs if others seek to turn their decisions to political purposes.

One section of our country believes slavery is *right* and ought to be extended, while the other believes it is *wrong* and ought not to be extended. This is the only substantial dispute. The fugitive-slave clause of the Constitution and the law for the suppression of the foreign slave trade are each as well enforced, perhaps, as any law can ever be in a community where the moral sense of the people imperfectly supports the law itself. The great body of the people abide by the dry legal obligation in both cases, and a few break over in each. This, I think, can not be perfectly cured, and it would be worse in both cases *after* the separation of the sections than before. The foreign slave trade, now imperfectly suppressed, would be ultimately revived without restriction in one section, while fugitive slaves, now only partially surrendered, would not be surrendered at all by the other.

Physically speaking, we can not separate. We can not remove our respective sections from each other nor build an impassable wall between them. A husband and wife may be divorced and go out of the presence and beyond the reach of each other, but the different parts of our country can not do this. They can not but remain face to face, and intercourse, either amicable or hostile, must continue between them. Is it possible, then, to make that intercourse more advantageous or more satisfactory *after* separation than *before*? Can aliens make treaties easier than friends can make laws? Can treaties be more faithfully enforced between aliens than laws can among friends? Suppose you go to war, you can not fight always; and when, after much loss on both sides and no gain on either, you cease fighting, the identical old questions, as to terms of intercourse, are again upon you.

This country, with its institutions, belongs to the people who inhabit it. Whenever they shall grow weary of the existing Government, they can exercise their *constitutional* right of amending it or their *revolutionary* right to dismember or overthrow it. I can not be ignorant of the fact that many worthy and patriotic citizens are desirous of having the National Constitution amended. While I make no recommendation of amendments, I fully recognize the rightful authority of the people over the whole subject, to be exercised in either of the modes prescribed in the instrument itself; and I should, under existing circumstances, favor rather than oppose a fair opportunity being afforded the people to act upon it. I will venture to add that to me the convention mode seems preferable, in that it allows amendments to originate with the people themselves, instead of only permitting them to take or reject propositions originated by others, not especially chosen for the purpose, and which might not be precisely such as they would wish to either accept or refuse. I understand a proposed amendment to the Constitution — which amendment, however, I have not seen — has passed Congress, to the effect that the Federal Government shall never interfere with the domestic institutions of the States, including that of persons held to service. To avoid misconstruction of what I have said, I depart from my purpose not to speak of particular amendments so far as to say that, holding such a provision to now be implied constitutional law, I have no objection to its being made express and irrevocable.

The Chief Magistrate derives all his authority from the people, and they have referred none upon him to fix terms for the separation of the States. The people themselves can do this if also they choose, but the Executive as such has nothing to do with it. His duty is to administer the present Government as it came to his hands and to transmit it unimpaired by him to his successor.

Why should there not be a patient confidence in the ultimate justice of the people? Is there any better or equal hope in the world? In our present differences, is either party without faith of being in the right? If the Almighty Ruler of Nations, with His eternal truth and justice, be on your side of the North, or on yours of the South, that truth and that justice will surely prevail by the judgment of this great tribunal of the American people. . . .

ABRAHAM LINCOLN, MESSAGE TO CONGRESS IN SPECIAL SESSION

July 4, 1861

[T]he question [is] whether a constitutional republic, or democracy—a government of the people by the same people—can, or cannot, maintain its territorial integrity, against its own domestic foes. It presents the question, whether discontented individuals, too few in numbers to control administration, according to organic law, in any case, can always, upon the pretences made in this case, or on any other pretences, or arbitrarily, without any pretence, break up their Government, and thus practically put an end to free government upon the earth. . . .

This sophism derives much—perhaps the whole—of its currency, from the assumption, that there is some omnipotent, and sacred supremacy, pertaining to a *State*—to each State of our Federal Union. Our States have neither more, nor less power, than that reserved to them, in the Union, by the Constitution—no one of them ever having been a State *out* of the Union. The original ones passed into the Union even *before* they cast off their British colonial dependence; and the new ones each came into the Union directly from a condition of dependence, excepting Texas. And even Texas, in its temporary independence, was never designated a State. The new ones only took the designation of States, on coming into the Union, while that name was first adopted for the old ones, in, and by, the Declaration of Independence. Therein the "United Colonies" were declared to be "Free and Independent States"; but, even then, the object plainly was not to declare their independence of *one another*, or of the *Union*; but directly the contrary, as their mutual pledge, and their mutual action, before, at the time, and afterward, abundantly show. The express plighting of faith, by each and all of the original thirteen, in the Articles of Confederation, two years later, that the Union shall be perpetual, is most conclusive. Having never been States, either in substance, or in name, *outside* of the Union, whence this magical omnipotence of "State Rights," asserting a claim of power to lawfully destroy the Union itself? Much is said about the "sovereignty" of the States; but the word, even, is not in the national Constitution, nor, as is believed, in any of the State constitutions. What is "sovereignty," in the political sense of the term? Would it be far wrong to define it "A political community, without a political superior"? Tested by this, no one of our States, except Texas, ever was a sovereignty. And even Texas gave up the character on coming into the Union; by which act she acknowledged the Constitution of the United States, and the laws and treaties of the United States made in pursuance of the Constitution, to be, for her, the supreme law of the land. The States have their *status* IN the Union, and they have no other *legal status*. If they break from this, they can only do so against law, and by revolution. The Union, and not themselves separately, procured their independence, and their liberty. By conquest, or purchase, the Union gave each of them, whatever of independence, and liberty, it has. The Union is older than any of the States; and, in fact, it created them as States. Originally, some dependent colonies made the Union; and, in turn, the Union threw off their old dependence, for them, and made them States, such as they are. Not one of them ever had a State constitution, independent of the Union. Of course, it is not forgotten that all the new States framed their constitutions, before they entered the Union; nevertheless, dependent upon, and preparatory to, coming into the Union.

Unquestionably the States have the powers, and rights, reserved to them in, and by the National Constitution; but among these, surely, are not included all conceivable powers, however mischievous, or destructive; but, at most, such only as were known in the world, at the time, as governmental powers; and certainly, a power to destroy the government itself, had never been known as a governmental—as a merely administrative power. This relative matter of National power, and State rights, as a principle, is no other than the principle of *generality*, and *locality*. Whatever concerns the whole, should be confided to the whole—to the general government; while whatever concerns *only* the State, should be left exclusively, to the State. This is all there is of original principle about it. Whether the National Constitution, in defining boundaries between the two, has applied the principle with exact accuracy, is not to be questioned. We are all bound by that defining, without question.

What is now combatted, is the position that secession is *consistent* with the Constitution—is *lawful* and *peaceful*. It is not contended that there is any express law for it; and nothing should ever be implied as law, which leads to unjust, or absurd consequences. The nation purchased, with money, the countries out of which several of these States were formed. Is it just that they shall go off without leave, and without refunding? The nation paid very large sums, (in the aggregate, I believe, nearly a hundred millions) to relieve Florida of the aboriginal tribes. Is it just that she shall now be off without consent, or without making any return? The nation is now in debt for money applied to the benefit of these so-called seceding States, in common with the rest. Is it just, either that creditors shall go unpaid, or the remaining States pay the whole? A part of the present national debt was contracted to pay the old debts of Texas. Is it just that she shall leave, and pay no part of this herself?

Again, if one State may secede, so may another; and when all shall have seceded, none is left to pay the debts. Is this quite just to creditors? Did we notify them of this sage view of ours, when we borrowed their money? If we now recognize this doctrine, by allowing the seceders to go in peace, it is difficult to see what we can do, if others choose to go, or to extort terms upon which they will promise to remain.

The seceders insist that our Constitution admits of secession. They have assumed to make a national constitution of their own, in which, of necessity, they have either *discarded*, or *retained*, the right of secession, as they insist, it exists in ours. If they have discarded it, they thereby admit that, on principle, it ought not to be in ours. If they have retained it, by their own construction of ours they show that to be consistent they must secede from one another, whenever they shall find it the easiest way of settling their debts, or effecting any other selfish, or unjust object. The principle itself is one of disintegration, and upon which no government can possibly endure.

If all the States, save one, should assert the power to *drive* that one out of the Union, it is presumed the whole class of seceder politicians would at once deny the power, and denounce the act as the greatest outrage upon State rights. But suppose that precisely the same act, instead of being called "driving the one out," should be called "the seceding of the others from that one," it would be exactly what the seceders claim to do, unless, indeed, they make the point, that the one, because it is a minority, may rightfully do, what the others, because they are a majority, may not rightfully do. These politicians are subtle, and profound, on the rights of minorities. They are not partial to that power which made the Constitution, and speaks from the preamble, calling itself "We, the People." . . .

The Constitution provides, and all the States have accepted the provision, that "the United States shall guarantee to every State in this Union a republican form of government." But if a State may lawfully go out of the Union, having done so, it may also discard the republican form of government; so that to prevent its going out, is an indispensable *means*, to the *end*, of maintaining the guaranty mentioned; and when an end is lawful and obligatory, the indispensable means to it, are also lawful, and obligatory. . . .

POINTS FOR DISCUSSION

1. What are Lincoln's specific points of disagreement with Davis as to the lawfulness of secession? Is secession constitutional?

2. What, according to Lincoln, are the respective roles of the states, Congress, courts, and the people in upholding the federal structure that the Constitution established? Consider Lincoln's views in light of materials you have read from the Founding period and Marshall Court. For instance, regarding judicial review, Lincoln asserted that although Supreme Court decisions are binding upon the parties to a case, "if the policy of the Government upon vital questions affecting the whole people is to be irrevocably fixed by decisions of the Supreme Court, . . . the people will have ceased to be their own rulers." Which writings from the Founding period and the Marshall Court does Lincoln echo? Which are in tension with his views? Should we understand Lincoln — or members of the Founding generation — as expressing constitutional under-standings shorn from the political context of the day?

D. THE RECONSTRUCTION AMENDMENTS

On April 9, 1865, Confederate General Robert E. Lee surrendered his army to Union General Ulysses S. Grant. On April 14, President Lincoln was assassinated, and Vice President Andrew Johnson became President. As part of his Reconstruction plan, President Johnson urged the former Confederate states to adopt the Thirteenth Amendment to the Constitution as a condition for regaining seats in Congress. By December 1865, the states had ratified the Thirteenth Amendment:

> Section 1. Neither slavery nor involuntary servitude, except as a punishment for crime whereof the party shall have been duly convicted, shall exist within the United States, or any place subject to their jurisdiction.
>
> Section 2. Congress shall have power to enforce this article by appropriate legislation.

The Thirteenth Amendment completed the legal abolition of slavery, which had begun in 1863 with the Emancipation Proclamation.

Still, states and localities enacted "black codes" discriminating against and limiting the liberty of freed slaves. In January 1866, Senator Lyman Trumbull introduced a Civil Rights Bill in Congress, explaining:

> Since the abolition of slavery, the Legislatures which have assembled in the insurrectionary States have passed laws relating to the freedmen, and in nearly all the States, they have discriminated against them. They deny them certain rights, subject them to severe penalties, and still impose upon them the very restrictions which were imposed upon them in consequence of the existence of slavery, and before it was abolished. The purpose of the bill under consideration is to destroy all these discriminations, and to carry into effect the constitutional amendment.

CONG. GLOBE, 39th Cong., 1st Sess. 474 (1866). In April 1866, Congress enacted the Civil Rights Act of 1866, which guaranteed certain civil rights to freed slaves. It provided:

> [A]ll persons born in the United States and not subject to any foreign power, excluding Indians not taxed, are hereby declared to be citizens of the United States; and such citizens, of every race and color, without regard to any previous condition of slavery or involuntary servitude, except as a punishment for crime whereof the party shall have been duly convicted, shall have the same right, in every State and Territory in the United States, to make and enforce contracts, to sue, be parties, and give evidence, to inherit, purchase, lease, sell, hold, and convey real and personal property, and to full and equal benefit of all laws and proceedings for the security of person and property, as is enjoyed by white citizens, and shall be subject to like punishment, pains, and penalties, and to none other, any law, statute, ordinance, regulation, or custom, to the contrary notwithstanding.

Civil Rights Act of 1866, ch. 31, §1, 14 Stat. 27, 27 (1866).

Opponents of this Act claimed that Congress lacked the power to enact it. They characterized it as a congressional attempt to remake, among other things, state contract and property law, in violation of the constitutional principle of limited federal powers. Proponents of the Act responded that it only concerned racial equality—that states could regulate local affairs however they pleased so long as they afforded all citizens equal rights.

President Johnson vetoed the bill on the ground that Congress lacked the power to enact it, but Congress overrode his veto.

In light of constitutional concerns about the Civil Rights Act of 1866, Congress proposed the Fourteenth Amendment in June 1866, and three-fourths of the states ratified it by 1868. Sections 1 and 5 of the Fourteenth Amendment provide:

> Section 1. All persons born or naturalized in the United States and subject to the jurisdiction thereof, are citizens of the United States and of the State wherein they reside. No State shall make or enforce any law which shall abridge the privileges or immunities of citizens of the United States; nor shall any State deprive any person of life, liberty, or property, without due process of law; nor deny to any person within its jurisdiction the equal protection of the laws. . . .
>
> Section 5. The Congress shall have power to enforce, by appropriate legislation, the provisions of this article.

Moreover, in 1870, the Fifteenth Amendment, which protects a political right to vote, was ratified:

> Section 1. The right of citizens of the United States to vote shall not be denied or abridged by the United States or by any State on account of race, color, or previous condition of servitude.
>
> Section 2. The Congress shall have power to enforce this article by appropriate legislation.

This section of the chapter focuses on the Fourteenth Amendment and its implications for the relative authority of the federal government and the states.

Judges, other public officials, and scholars have long questioned the extent to which the Fourteenth Amendment altered the relationship between the federal government and the states. Section 1 of the Fourteenth Amendment includes several important provisions. First, the Citizenship Clause, rejecting the holding of *Dred Scott v. Sandford*, 60 U.S. (19 How.) 393 (1857), recognizes that "[a]ll persons born or naturalized in the United States, and subject to the jurisdiction thereof, are citizens of the United States and of the State wherein they reside." Second, the Privileges or Immunities Clause provides that "[n]o State shall make or enforce any law which shall abridge the privileges or immunities of citizens of the United States. . . ." The meaning of the Privileges or Immunities Clause has attracted significant scholarly attention. In the *Slaughter-House Cases*, 83 U.S. (16 Wall.) 36 (1872), which you will read, the Court interpreted the Clause more narrowly than scholars have argued its words and context warranted. In doing so, the Court left the Due Process and Equal Protection Clauses to do much of the equal rights work that the Fourteenth Amendment was meant to accomplish.

In the following passage, Professor John Harrison provides an account of the framing of the Privileges and Immunities Clause. This background will help you appreciate the *Slaughter-House Cases*, current debates over the scope of the Privileges or Immunities Clause, and the predominant role that the Due Process and Equal Protection Clauses have assumed in U.S. constitutional jurisprudence.

JOHN HARRISON, RECONSTRUCTING THE PRIVILEGES OR IMMUNITIES CLAUSE

101 Yale L.J. 1385, 1397-1410 (1992)

This [excerpt] describes the events leading to the drafting of the Fourteenth Amendment and the legal doctrines that the Amendment's drafters employed. . . .

A. The Comity Clause

The concept of privileges and immunities was not new in 1866. Article IV, Section 2 of the original United States Constitution begins: "The Citizens of each State shall be entitled to all Privileges and Immunities of Citizens in the several States." This clause forbids the states from giving unfavorable treatment to visiting out-of-state Americans with respect to the body of rights that constitutes the privileges and immunities of state citizenship. From this reading comes the provision's usual name, the Comity Clause.

Two features of the clause as usually understood deserve attention. First, its protections extend only to citizens of American states who are temporarily in other states, but who have retained citizenship in their home state. It has no effect, either substantive or equality-based, on the treatment a state gives its own citizens. Second, the Comity Clause does not impose a complete ban on unfavorable treatment of visiting Americans. Rather, it applies only to the privileges and immunities of citizens, whatever those privileges and immunities may be.

The limitation to privileges and immunities came up in the most famous Comity Clause case of all, one that was often quoted in 1866: *Corfield v. Coryell*.[39] Plaintiff Corfield, apparently a citizen of Delaware, owned a fishing boat called the *Hiram*, which was leased and then subleased to a fisherman, who took her to rake oysters in a part of Delaware Bay claimed by New Jersey. During the fishing expedition, the *Hiram* was seized by an armed New Jersey vessel, taken up the Maurice River to Leesburg, New Jersey, and sold as prize.

Corfield brought a federal diversity action for trespass against Coryell, who had acted as prize master. Coryell claimed that his action was justified under a New Jersey statute that prohibited any person not an "actual inhabitant and resident" of New Jersey from raking for oysters in New Jersey waters from a boat not wholly owned by a New Jersey citizen. Corfield replied that the New Jersey statute was invalid under the Commerce Clause and the Comity Clause. . . .

Justice Bushrod Washington, sitting on circuit, held for the defendant. He rejected Corfield's Commerce Clause argument, holding that the statute was not a regulation of commerce but an allocation of property rights. . . . Justice Washington began his discussion of Corfield's Article IV claim with a now-famous description of the privileges and immunities of citizens[:]

[The inquiry is, what are the privileges and immunities of citizens in the several states? We feel no hesitation in confining these expressions to those privileges and immunities which are, in their nature, fundamental; which belong, of

---

39. 6 F. Cas. 546 (C.C.E.D. Pa. 1823) (No. 3230).

right, to the citizens of all free governments; and which have, at all times, been enjoyed by the citizens of the several states which compose this Union, from the time of their becoming free, independent, and sovereign. What these fundamental principles are, it would perhaps be more tedious than difficult to enumerate. They may, however, be all comprehended under the following general heads: Protection by the government; the enjoyment of life and liberty, with the right to acquire and possess property of every kind, and to pursue and obtain happiness and safety; subject nevertheless to such restraints as the government may justly prescribe for the general good of the whole. The right of a citizen of one state to pass through, or to reside in any other state, for purposes of trade, agriculture, professional pursuits, or otherwise; to claim the benefit of the writ of habeas corpus; to institute and maintain actions of any kind in the courts of the state; to take, hold and dispose of property, either real or personal; and an exemption from higher taxes or impositions than are paid by the other citizens of the state; may be mentioned as some of the particular privileges and immunities of citizens, which are clearly embraced by the general description of privileges deemed to be fundamental: to which may be added, the elective franchise, as regulated and established by the laws or constitution of the state in which it is to be exercised. These, and many others which might be mentioned, are, strictly speaking, privileges and immunities, and the enjoyment of them by the citizens of each state, in every other state, was manifestly calculated (to use the expressions of the preamble of the corresponding provision in the old articles of confederation) "the better to secure and perpetuate mutual friendship and intercourse among the people of the different states of the Union."]

Corfield, however, involved not some well-known fundamental right, but oysters, and Justice Washington found that citizens enjoyed commonly owned oysters as property, not privileges or immunities. Thus, the Privileges and Immunities Clause did not provide any basis for Corfield's claim.

In the first half of the nineteenth century, various understandings of the Comity Clause and the concept of privileges and immunities were put forward. The interstate comity reading was very prominent and appears to have been the mainstream interpretation. Under it, the clause requires states to give out-of-state Americans at least the same privileges and immunities that their own citizens enjoy. The interstate comity reading assumes that privileges and immunities constitute a substantial part of the content of a state's law, especially its basic law of private civil capacity, such as the right to make contracts and to own property.

B. The Thirty-ninth Congress

The Thirty-eighth Congress adjourned on March 3, 1865. The following month General Lee surrendered, Lincoln was assassinated, and Andrew Johnson became President. Under Johnson's "Presidential Reconstruction," most of the former Confederate states formed new governments, ratified the Thirteenth Amendment, and elected Senators and Representatives to the Thirty-ninth Congress, which convened on December 4, 1865. The two Houses refused to seat the Southern Senators and Representatives and created a Joint Committee on Reconstruction in order to formulate their own approach to the postwar crisis of the Union. The nation was given a new fundamental legal rule, and Congress a new power, when on December 18th the Secretary of State proclaimed that the Thirteenth Amendment, with its ban on slavery and congressional enforcement provision, had been ratified.

To understand the origins of the Fourteenth Amendment, we must focus on three aspects of the work of the Thirty-ninth Congress: the Civil Rights Act of 1866, which was introduced in January and passed over the President's veto in April; a proposed constitutional amendment relating to civil rights that was reported by the Joint Committee in February but never voted on in either House; and the Fourteenth Amendment itself. The theme linking these three was equality or, as we might put it today, antidiscrimination.

1. The Civil Rights Act of 1866

As the Thirty-ninth Congress organized itself, the provisionally reconstructed Southern States were passing the Black Codes, which limited the rights of blacks and freed slaves. Largely in response to these developments, on January 5, 1866, Senator Lyman Trumbull of Illinois, Chairman of the Senate Judiciary Committee, introduced the Civil Rights Bill. The bill was designed to secure equality between blacks and whites in the enjoyment of certain rights basic to ordinary life. Section 1 formed the heart of the bill. In its original form, this section mandated equality with respect to both civil rights in general and as specifically listed.

Senator Trumbull specifically stated that he designed the bill to override discriminatory state laws like the Black Codes. He explained:

> Since the abolition of slavery, the Legislatures which have assembled in the insurrectionary States have passed laws relating to the freedmen, and in nearly all the States they have discriminated against them. They deny them certain rights, subject them to severe penalties, and still impose upon them the very restrictions which were imposed upon them in consequence of the existence of slavery, and before it was abolished. The purpose of the bill under consideration is to destroy all these discriminations, and to carry into effect the constitutional amendment.

He maintained that the Thirteenth Amendment empowered Congress to pass the bill because legal race discrimination constituted a badge of servitude and thus violated the Thirteenth Amendment. More broadly, he stated that the freedom that the Thirteenth Amendment was designed to protect necessarily included equal enjoyment of the basic legal capacities of contract and property and the basic protections of government.

The claim that Congress had such power provoked heated controversy. The Civil Rights Bill, whatever its primary object may have been, was not limited to protecting freed slaves and was not even limited to the states in which slavery had formerly existed. According to its opponents, the new national rule of equal civil rights was nothing but an attempt by Congress to rewrite the states' domestic laws of property, contract, personal security, and so forth. State law, they argued, created citizens' rights; if Congress could legislate upon all matters of state law, it could pass national laws on all those subjects, thereby overthrowing the principle of enumerated powers on which American federalism rested.

Advocates of the Civil Rights Bill responded that it was limited to racial equality and did not represent federal interference with the substance of state law. The states would remain free to create whatever rights they pleased, as long as they gave them to all citizens. Their argument relied on the realization that congressional power to require equality did not necessarily have to rest on a claim of plenary federal power to make private law. A power limited to requiring equality would be enough to authorize the bill.

One Republican who shared the doubts about the adequacy of Congress' constitutional power was Representative John Bingham of Ohio, a member of the Joint Committee and the principal drafter of Section 1 of the Fourteenth Amendment. Bingham, a firm abolitionist, favored the policy of the Civil Rights Bill but thought that Congress lacked the power to enact it. These doubts may have been shared by President Johnson, who said that he vetoed the bill on the grounds that it exceeded Congress' power.

These constitutional arguments did not sway the Republican majority. Over the President's veto, they made the bill the Civil Rights Act of 1866. Section 1 provided:

> [A]ll persons born in the United States and not subject to any foreign power, excluding Indians not taxed, are hereby declared to be citizens of the United States; and such citizens, of every race and color, without regard to any previous condition of slavery or involuntary servitude, except as a punishment for crime whereof the party shall have been duly convicted, shall have the same right, in every State and Territory in the United States, to make and enforce contracts, to sue, be parties, and give evidence, to inherit, purchase, lease, sell, hold, and convey real and personal property, and to full and equal benefit of all laws and proceedings for the security of person and property, as is enjoyed by white citizens, and shall be subject to like punishment, pains, and penalties, and to none other, any law, statute, ordinance, regulation, or custom, to the contrary notwithstanding.

2. The Joint Committee's First Proposed Amendment

The concerns regarding congressional power led Bingham to suggest, and the Joint Committee to report, a constitutional amendment designed to give Congress the power to adopt civil rights legislation. Bingham's draft, submitted on February 13, 1866, while the Civil Rights Bill was under consideration, would have amended the Constitution to provide:

> The Congress shall have power to make all laws which shall be necessary and proper to secure to the citizens of each State all privileges and immunities of citizens in the several States, and to all persons in the several States equal protection in the rights of life, liberty, and property.

The amendment was debated in the House and postponed.

Bingham did not explain precisely what the amendment would accomplish, nor did he explicate the text so as to make clear why it would do whatever it did. We can, however, divine two things about his understanding of the proposal with as much confidence as is possible where Bingham is concerned. First, however many purposes the amendment may have had, equality was its animating principle. Bingham began his concluding speech by approvingly quoting President Johnson's statement that "the American system rests on the assertion of the equal right of every man to life, liberty, and the pursuit of happiness." That speech's finale, too, was a paean to equality. More specifically, although Bingham's proposal (like Section 1 of the Fourteenth Amendment) never mentioned race, the elimination of race discrimination was very much on his mind. In an exchange with Representative Robert Hale, Republican of New York, Bingham explained that his proposal was not limited to the late Confederate States; rather, it would give Congress power to eliminate race discrimination throughout the country.

Second, it is likely that Bingham thought that *both* clauses of his proposal gave Congress power to forbid discrimination. He regularly ran together the two constitutional provisions from which his proposal derived, the Privileges and Immunities Clause of Article IV and the Due Process Clause of the Fifth Amendment. He praised "these great canons of the supreme law, securing to all the citizens in every State all the privileges and immunities of citizens, and to all people all the sacred rights of persons." Indeed, he included them together when he referred to the "bill of rights." Bingham said that his equal protection language was about forbidding discrimination, and probably about that alone. He never distinguished the other clause by saying that it had nothing to do with discrimination.

Bingham also made reference to equal rights in discussing the privileges and immunities language of his amendment. In his second and concluding speech on the proposal, Bingham asked: "What does the word immunity in your Constitution mean? Exemption from unequal burdens. Ah! say gentlemen who oppose this amendment, we are not opposed to equal rights; we are not opposed to the bill of rights that all shall be protected alike in life, liberty, and property. . . ." A few moments later, in response to Representative Hale's objections of the previous day, Bingham said: "The gentleman did not utter a word against the equal right of all citizens of the United States in every State to all privileges and immunities of citizens. . . ." Apparently, Bingham thought that his proposal would enable Congress to mandate equal privileges and immunities of citizenship in the states.

The House's reaction to Bingham's proposal confirms that it was understood as requiring equal rights among citizens. When debate concluded, Roscoe Conkling of New York, a member of the Joint Committee, moved that the amendment be postponed. In support of Conkling's motion, Republican Giles Hotchkiss of New York explained that Bingham's proposal was not properly designed to achieve its goal, which was "to provide that no State shall discriminate between its citizens and give one class of citizens greater rights than it confers upon another." Hotchkiss wished to revise the language because Bingham's draft, which gave a new power to Congress but did not impose a self-executing limitation on the states, could not be regarded as "permanently securing those rights."

Hotchkiss explained to Bingham:

> [I]f the gentleman's object is, as I have no doubt it is, to provide against a discrimination to the injury or exclusion of any class of citizens in any State from the privileges which other classes enjoy, the right should be incorporated

into the Constitution. It should be a constitutional right that cannot be wrested from any class of citizens, or from the citizens of any State by mere legislation.

The Joint Committee decided that it would have to try again.

3. The Fourteenth Amendment

That second try became the Fourteenth Amendment. The Amendment was an omnibus proposal that dealt simultaneously with four of the leading problems of Reconstruction: the status of the Civil Rights Bill, apportionment of representatives, suffrage, and eligibility of former rebels for state and federal office. Section 1 of the Amendment addressed the first of those questions.

What is now the second sentence of Section 1 of the Fourteenth Amendment emerged as the result of a rather disorienting series of votes in the Joint Committee. Apparently the committee had some trouble choosing between a straightforward ban on race discrimination (proposed by Pennsylvania Republican Thaddeus Stevens) and the more delphic language (proposed by Bingham) that eventually was incorporated in the Amendment. While we do not know the exact rationale for the committee's decision, it seems fairly clear that they understood both provisions as incorporating the Civil Rights Act into the Constitution.

The second sentence of Section 1 was approved and ratified as it emerged from the Joint Committee. The congressional discussions of Section 1 show that the provision was designed to require equal civil rights, but no one explained precisely how the language would yield that result. Thaddeus Stevens, chairman for the House of the Joint Committee, introduced the proposal in that chamber. He said that Section 1 would put the Civil Rights Act into the Constitution, but did not explain how, and in particular which part of, the language did the job.

The introductory speech in the Senate was delivered by Jacob Howard of Michigan, who was filling in for the ill William Fessenden of Maine, chairman of the Joint Committee for the Senate. Howard provided by far the most detailed discussion of Section 1, saying that the Privileges or Immunities Clause, insofar as he understood it, protected a wide variety of rights, including those listed in *Corfield* and the first eight amendments to the federal Constitution. He said that the Equal Protection Clause would abolish all caste legislation, and stressed that Section 1 would not deal with suffrage. It remained to be seen exactly what would be made of the Amendment.

———

In the *Slaughter-House Cases*, 83 U.S. (16 Wall) 36 (1872), which follow, the Supreme Court read the Privileges or Immunities Clause narrowly, leaving the Due Process and Equal Protection Clauses to fulfill the equal rights aspirations of the Reconstruction era.

The Court's jurisprudence under the Due Process Clause — which in specifics is beyond the scope of this book — has been controversial for at least two reasons. First, over time, the Court has selectively incorporated most, but not all, of the provisions of the Bill of Rights to apply to the states through the Due

Process Clause of the Fourteenth Amendment. Before the Fourteenth Amendment was ratified in 1868, the Supreme Court understood the Bill of Rights to operate as a limitation only upon federal, not state, power. *Barron v. Baltimore*, 32 U.S. 243 (1833). After the Fourteenth Amendment was ratified, the Supreme Court began to consider, case by case, what provisions of the Bill of Rights the Due Process Clause might incorporate. (For a summary of incorporation, see Chapter 7.) Scholars have questioned whether this process of selective incorporation comports with the original understanding of the Fourteenth Amendment.

Second, over time, the Court has found the Due Process Clause to protect certain substantive rights not included in the Bill of Rights against state interference. Scholars and judges have debated whether the Due Process Clause, which speaks in terms of *procedural* rights (a state may not "deprive any person of life, liberty, or property, without due process of law"), protects certain *substantive* rights from governmental interference regardless of the process given. Some reject the doctrine of "substantive due process" altogether. Others dispute the nature of the substantive rights the Supreme Court has found the Due Process Clause to protect.

The Privileges or Immunities Clause of the Fourteenth Amendment has attracted widespread attention because some scholars believe that it was originally understood to do some of the work that the Due Process Clause came to do in U.S. constitutional jurisprudence. Scholars have examined whether the Privileges or Immunities Clause was originally understood to incorporate the Bill of Rights to apply against the states. In an influential 1949 article, Professor Charles Fairman argued that the Privileges or Immunities Clause was not originally understood to incorporate the Bill of Rights against the states. Charles Fairman, *Does the Fourteenth Amendment Incorporate the Bill of Rights? The Original Understanding*, 2 Stan. L. Rev. 5 (1949). More recently, however, scholars have argued that the Privileges or Immunities Clause was originally understood, at a minimum, to incorporate the provisions of the Bill of Rights against the states. Professor Richard Aynes, for instance, has argued that there now is a consensus that the Privileges or Immunities Clause was meant to incorporate the Bill of Rights to apply against the states. Richard L. Aynes, *Ink Blot or Not: The Meaning of Privileges and/or Immunities*, 11 U. Pa. J. Const. L. 1295, 1309 (2009). Moreover, some scholars have argued that the Privileges or Immunities Clause provides a more satisfactory framework for assessing claims of unenumerated individual rights against the states. To appreciate the importance of these debates and the prominence of the Due Process Clause in U.S. constitutional jurisprudence, you must understand how the Supreme Court interpreted the Privileges or Immunities Clause in the *Slaughter-House Cases*.

You also must understand the *Slaughter-House Cases* to appreciate the practical effect the Reconstruction Amendments have had on the relationship between the federal government and the states. As you read the Justices' opinions, consider the following questions:

- What interpretive methodology(ies) does the Court bring to bear on the Fourteenth Amendment?

- Had the Court accepted the plaintiffs' assertion of right, how would its decision have affected the relationship between the federal government and the states?

SLAUGHTER-HOUSE CASES

83 U.S. (16 Wall.) 36 (1872)

Mr. JUSTICE MILLER delivered the opinion of the court.

The statute . . . assailed as unconstitutional . . . forbids the landing or slaughtering of animals whose flesh is intended for food, within the city of New Orleans and other parishes and boundaries named and defined, or the keeping or establishing any slaughter-houses or *abattoirs* within those limits except by the corporation thereby created, which is also limited to certain places afterwards mentioned. Suitable penalties are enacted for violations of this prohibition.

[The statute] declares that the company . . . shall have the sole and exclusive privilege of conducting and carrying on the live-stock landing and slaughter-house business within the limits and privilege granted by the act, and that all such animals shall be landed at the stock-landings and slaughtered at the slaughter-houses of the company, and nowhere else. . . .

This statute is denounced not only as creating a monopoly and conferring odious and exclusive privileges upon a small number of persons at the expense of the great body of the community of New Orleans, but it is asserted that it deprives a large and meritorious class of citizens — the whole of the butchers of the city — of the right to exercise their trade, the business to which they have been trained and on which they depend for the support of themselves and their families; and that the unrestricted exercise of the business of butchering is necessary to the daily subsistence of the population of the city. . . .

Unless . . . it can be maintained that the exclusive privilege granted by this charter to the corporation, is beyond the power of the legislature of Louisiana, there can be no just exception to the validity of the statute. . . .

The proposition is . . . reduced to these terms: Can any exclusive privileges be granted to any of its citizens, or to a corporation, by the legislature of a State? . . .

The plaintiffs in error accepting this issue, allege that the statute is a violation of the Constitution of the United States in these several particulars:

> That it creates an involuntary servitude forbidden by the thirteenth article of amendment;
> That it abridges the privileges and immunities of citizens of the United States;
> That it denies to the plaintiffs the equal protection of the laws; and,
> That it deprives them of their property without due process of law; contrary to the provisions of the first section of the fourteenth article of amendment.

This court is thus called upon for the first time to give construction to these articles. . . .

The most cursory glance at these articles discloses a unity of purpose, when taken in connection with the history of the times, which cannot fail to have an important bearing on any question of doubt concerning their true meaning. Nor can such doubts, when any reasonably exist, be safely and rationally solved without a reference to that history; for in it is found the occasion and the necessity for recurring again to the great source of power in this country, the people of the States, for additional guarantees of human rights; additional powers to the Federal government; additional restraints upon those of the States. Fortunately that history is fresh within the memory of us all, and its leading features, as they bear upon the matter before us, free from doubt. . . .

[The Court discusses the history of the adoption of the Thirteenth, Fourteenth, and Fifteenth Amendments.]

We repeat, then, in the light of this recapitulation of events, almost too recent to be called history, but which are familiar to us all; and on the most casual examination of the language of these amendments, no one can fail to be impressed with the one pervading purpose found in them all, lying at the foundation of each, and without which none of them would have been even suggested; we mean the freedom of the slave race, the security and firm establishment of that freedom, and the protection of the newly-made freeman and citizen from the oppressions of those who had formerly exercised unlimited dominion over him. It is true that only the fifteenth amendment, in terms, mentions the negro by speaking of his color and his slavery. But it is just as true that each of the other articles was addressed to the grievances of that race, and designed to remedy them as the fifteenth.

We do not say that no one else but the negro can share in this protection. Both the language and spirit of these articles are to have their fair and just weight in any question of construction. Undoubtedly while negro slavery alone was in the mind of the Congress which proposed the thirteenth article, it forbids any other kind of slavery, now or hereafter. If Mexican peonage or the Chinese coolie labor system shall develop slavery of the Mexican or Chinese race within our territory, this amendment may safely be trusted to make it void. And so if other rights are assailed by the States which properly and necessarily fall within the protection of these articles, that protection will apply, though the party interested may not be of African descent. But what we do say, and what we wish to be understood is, that in any fair and just construction of any section or phrase of these amendments, it is necessary to look to the purpose which we have said was the pervading spirit of them all, the evil which they were designed to remedy, and the process of continued addition to the Constitution, until that purpose was supposed to be accomplished, as far as constitutional law can accomplish it.

The first section of the fourteenth article, to which our attention is more specially invited, opens with a definition of citizenship — not only citizenship of the United States, but citizenship of the States. No such definition was previously found in the Constitution, nor had any attempt been made to define it by act of Congress. It had been the occasion of much discussion in the courts, by the executive departments, and in the public journals. It had been said by eminent judges that no man was a citizen of the United States, except as he was a citizen of one of the States composing the Union. Those, therefore, who had been born and resided always in the District of Columbia or in the Territories, though within the United States, were not citizens. Whether this proposition was sound or not had never been judicially decided. But it had been held by this court, in the celebrated Dred Scott case, only a few years before the outbreak of the civil war, that a man of African descent, whether a slave or not, was not and could not be a citizen of a State or of the United States. This decision, while it met the condemnation of some of the ablest statesmen and constitutional lawyers of the country, had never been overruled; and if it was to be accepted as a constitutional limitation of the right of citizenship, then all the negro race who had recently been made freemen, were still, not only not citizens, but were incapable of becoming so by anything short of an amendment to the Constitution.

To remove this difficulty primarily, and to establish a clear and comprehensive definition of citizenship which should declare what should constitute citizenship of the United States, and also citizenship of a State, the first clause of the first section was framed.

> "All persons born or naturalized in the United States, and subject to the jurisdiction thereof, are citizens of the United States and of the State wherein they reside."

The first observation we have to make on this clause is, that it puts at rest both the questions which we stated to have been the subject of differences of opinion. It declares that persons may be citizens of the United States without regard to their citizenship of a particular State, and it overturns the Dred Scott decision by making *all persons* born within the United States and subject to its jurisdiction citizens of the United States. That its main purpose was to establish the citizenship of the negro can admit of no doubt. The phrase, "subject to its jurisdiction" was intended to exclude from its operation children of ministers, consuls, and citizens or subjects of foreign States born within the United States.

The next observation is more important in view of the arguments of counsel in the present case. It is, that the distinction between citizenship of the United States and citizenship of a State is clearly recognized and established. Not only may a man be a citizen of the United States without being a citizen of a State, but an important element is necessary to convert the former into the latter. He must reside within the State to make him a citizen of it, but it is only necessary that he should be born or naturalized in the United States to be a citizen of the Union.

It is quite clear, then, that there is a citizenship of the United States, and a citizenship of a State, which are distinct from each other, and which depend upon different characteristics or circumstances in the individual.

We think this distinction and its explicit recognition in this amendment of great weight in this argument, because the next paragraph of this same section, which is the one mainly relied on by the plaintiffs in error, speaks only of privileges and immunities of citizens of the United States, and does not speak of those of citizens of the several States. The argument, however, in favor of the plaintiffs rests wholly on the assumption that the citizenship is the same, and the privileges and immunities guaranteed by the clause are the same.

The language is, "No State shall make or enforce any law which shall abridge the privileges or immunities of citizens of the *United States*." It is a little remarkable, if this clause was intended as a protection to the citizen of a State against the legislative power of his own State, that the word citizen of the State should be left out when it is so carefully used, and used in contradistinction to citizens of the United States, in the very sentence which precedes it. It is too clear for argument that the change in phraseology was adopted understandingly and with a purpose.

Of the privileges and immunities of the citizen of the United States, and of the privileges and immunities of the citizen of the State, and what they respectively are, we will presently consider; but we wish to state here that it is only the former which are placed by this clause under the protection of the Federal Constitution, and that the latter, whatever they may be, are not intended to have any additional protection by this paragraph of the amendment.

If, then, there is a difference between the privileges and immunities belonging to a citizen of the United States as such, and those belonging to the citizen of the State as such the latter must rest for their security and protection where they have heretofore rested; for they are not embraced by this paragraph of the amendment.

The first occurrence of the words "privileges and immunities" in our constitutional history, is to be found in the fourth of the articles of the old Confederation.

It declares "that the better to secure and perpetuate mutual friendship and intercourse among the people of the different States in this Union, the free inhabitants of each of these States, paupers, vagabonds, and fugitives from justice excepted, shall be entitled to all the privileges and immunities of free citizens in the several States; and the people of each State shall have free ingress and regress to and from any other State, and shall enjoy therein all the privileges of trade and commerce, subject to the same duties, impositions, and restrictions as the inhabitants thereof respectively."

In the Constitution of the United States, which superseded the Articles of Confederation, the corresponding provision is found in section two of the fourth article, in the following words: "The citizens of each State shall be entitled to all the privileges and immunities of citizens of the several States."

There can be but little question that the purpose of both these provisions is the same, and that the privileges and immunities intended are the same in each. In the article of the Confederation we have some of these specifically mentioned, and enough perhaps to give some general idea of the class of civil rights meant by the phrase.

Fortunately we are not without judicial construction of this clause of the Constitution. The first and the leading case on the subject is that of *Corfield v. Coryell*, decided by Mr. Justice Washington in the Circuit Court for the District of Pennsylvania in 1823.

"The inquiry," he says, "is, what are the privileges and immunities of citizens of the several States? We feel no hesitation in confining these expressions to those privileges and immunities which are *fundamental*; which belong of right to the citizens of all free governments, and which have at all times been enjoyed by citizens of the several States which compose this Union, from the

time of their becoming free, independent, and sovereign. What these fundamental principles are, it would be more tedious than difficult to enumerate.
They may all, however, be comprehended under the following general heads:
protection by the government, with the right to acquire and possess property
of every kind, and to pursue and obtain happiness and safety, subject, nevertheless, to such restraints as the government may prescribe for the general
good of the whole." . . .

It would be the vainest show of learning to attempt to prove by citations
of authority, that up to the adoption of the recent amendments, no claim or
pretence was set up that those rights depended on the Federal government for
their existence or protection, beyond the very few express limitations which
the Federal Constitution imposed upon the States — such, for instance, as the
prohibition against ex post facto laws, bills of attainder, and laws impairing
the obligation of contracts. But with the exception of these and a few other
restrictions, the entire domain of the privileges and immunities of citizens of
the States, as above defined, lay within the constitutional and legislative
power of the States, and without that of the Federal government. Was it
the purpose of the fourteenth amendment, by the simple declaration that
no State should make or enforce any law which shall abridge the privileges
and immunities of *citizens of the United States*, to transfer the security and
protection of all the civil rights which we have mentioned, from the States
to the Federal government? And where it is declared that Congress shall have
the power to enforce that article, was it intended to bring within the power of
Congress the entire domain of civil rights heretofore belonging exclusively to
the States?

All this and more must follow, if the proposition of the plaintiffs in error be
sound. For not only are these rights subject to the control of Congress
whenever in its discretion any of them are supposed to be abridged by State
legislation, but that body may also pass laws in advance, limiting and restricting the exercise of legislative power by the States, in their most ordinary and
usual functions, as in its judgment it may think proper on all such subjects.
And still further, such a construction followed by the reversal of the judgments
of the Supreme Court of Louisiana in these cases, would constitute this court a
perpetual censor upon all legislation of the States, on the civil rights of their
own citizens, with authority to nullify such as it did not approve as consistent
with those rights, as they existed at the time of the adoption of this amendment. The argument we admit is not always the most conclusive which is
drawn from the consequences urged against the adoption of a particular construction of an instrument. But when, as in the case before us, these consequences are so serious, so far-reaching and pervading, so great a departure from
the structure and spirit of our institutions; when the effect is to fetter and
degrade the State governments by subjecting them to the control of Congress,
in the exercise of powers heretofore universally conceded to them of the most
ordinary and fundamental character; when in fact it radically changes the
whole theory of the relations of the State and Federal governments to each
other and of both these governments to the people; the argument has a force
that is irresistible, in the absence of language which expresses such a purpose
too clearly to admit of doubt.

We are convinced that no such results were intended by the Congress which proposed these amendments, nor by the legislatures of the States which ratified them.

Having shown that the privileges and immunities relied on in the argument are those which belong to citizens of the States as such, and that they are left to the State governments for security and protection, and not by this article placed under the special care of the Federal government, we may hold ourselves excused from defining the privileges and immunities of citizens of the United States which no State can abridge, until some case involving those privileges may make it necessary to do so.

But lest it should be said that no such privileges and immunities are to be found if those we have been considering are excluded, we venture to suggest some which own their existence to the Federal government, its National character, its Constitution, or its laws.

One of these is well described in the case of *Crandall v. Nevada*[, 73 U.S. (6 Wall.) 35, 36 (1867).] . . . It is said to be the right of the citizen of this great country, protected by implied guarantees of its Constitution, "to come to the seat of government to assert any claim he may have upon that government, to transact any business he may have with it, to seek its protection, to share its offices, to engage in administering its functions. He has the right of free access to its seaports, through which all operations of foreign commerce are conducted, to the subtreasuries, land offices, and courts of justice in the several States." . . .

Another privilege of a citizen of the United States is to demand the care and protection of the Federal government over his life, liberty, and property when on the high seas or within the jurisdiction of a foreign government. Of this there can be no doubt, nor that the right depends upon his character as a citizen of the United States. The right to peaceably assemble and petition for redress of grievances, the privilege of the writ of *habeas corpus*, are rights of the citizen guaranteed by the Federal Constitution. The right to use the navigable waters of the United States, however they may penetrate the territory of the several States, all rights secured to our citizens by treaties with foreign nations, are dependent upon citizenship of the United States, and not citizenship of a State. One of these privileges is conferred by the very article under consideration. It is that a citizen of the United States can, of his own volition, become a citizen of any State of the Union by a *bonâ fide* residence therein, with the same rights as other citizens of that State. To these may be added the rights secured by the thirteenth and fifteenth articles of amendment, and by the other clause of the fourteenth, next to be considered.

But it is useless to pursue this branch of the inquiry, since we are of opinion that the rights claimed by these plaintiffs in error, if they have any existence, are not privileges and immunities of citizens of the United States within the meaning of the clause of the fourteenth amendment under consideration. . . .

The argument has not been much pressed in these cases that the defendant's charter deprives the plaintiffs of their property without due process of law, or that it denies to them the equal protection of the law. The first of these paragraphs has been in the Constitution since the adoption of the fifth amendment, as a restraint upon the Federal power. It is also to be found in some form of expression in the constitutions of nearly all the States, as a restraint upon the power of the States. . . .

We are not without judicial interpretation, therefore, both State and National, of the meaning of this clause. And it is sufficient to say that under no construction of that provision that we have ever seen, or any that we deem admissible, can the restraint imposed by the State of Louisiana upon the exercise of their trade by the butchers of New Orleans be held to be a deprivation of property within the meaning of that provision. . . .

In the light of the history of these amendments, and the pervading purpose of them, . . . it is not difficult to give a meaning to this clause. The existence of laws in the States where the newly emancipated negroes resided, which discriminated with gross injustice and hardship against them as a class, was the evil to be remedied by this clause, and by it such laws are forbidden. . . .

We doubt very much whether any action of a State not directed by way of discrimination against the negroes as a class, or on account of their race, will ever be held to come within the purview of this provision. It is so clearly a provision for that race and that emergency, that a strong case would be necessary for its application to any other. . . .

In the early history of the organization of the government, its statement seem to have divided on the line which should separate the powers of the National government from those of the State governments, and though this line has never been very well defined in public opinion, such a division has continued from that day to this.

The adoption of the first eleven amendments to the Constitution so soon after the original instrument was accepted, shows a prevailing sense of danger at that time from the Federal power. And it cannot be denied that such a jealousy continued to exist with many patriotic men until the breaking out of the late civil war. It was then discovered that the true danger to the perpetuity of the Union was in the capacity of the State organizations to combine and concentrate all the powers of the State, and of contiguous States, for a determined resistance to the General Government.

Unquestionably this has given great force to the argument, and added largely to the number of those who believe in the necessity of a strong National government.

But, however pervading this sentiment, and however it may have contributed to the adoption of the amendments we have been considering, we do not see in those amendments any purpose to destroy the main features of the general system. Under the pressure of all the excited feeling growing out of the war, our statesmen have still believed that the existence of the State with powers for domestic and local government, including the regulation of civil rights — the rights of person and of property — was essential to the perfect working of our complex form of government, though they have thought proper to impose additional limitations on the States, and to confer additional power on that of the Nation.

But whatever fluctuations may be seen in the history of public opinion on this subject during the period of our national existence, we think it will be found that this court, so far as its functions required, has always held with a steady and an even hand the balance between State and Federal power, and we trust that such may continue to be the history of its relation to that subject so long as it shall have duties to perform which demand of it a construction of the Constitution, or of any of its parts. . . .

Mr. JUSTICE FIELD, dissenting:

I am unable to agree with the majority of the court in these cases, and will proceed to state the reasons of my dissent from their judgment. . . .

The provisions of the fourteenth amendment, which is properly a supplement to the thirteenth, cover, in my judgment, the case before us, and inhibit any legislation which confers special and exclusive privileges like these under consideration. The amendment was adopted to obviate objections which had been raised and pressed with great force to the validity of the Civil Rights Act, and to place the common rights of American citizens under the protection of the National government. . . .

The amendment . . . assumes that there are such privileges and immunities which belong of right to citizens as such, and ordains that they shall not be abridged by State legislation. . . . What, then, are the privileges and immunities which are secured against abridgment by State legislation? . . .

The terms, privileges and immunities, are not new in the amendment; they were in the Constitution before the amendment was adopted. They are found in the second section of the fourth article, which declares that "the citizens of each State shall be entitled to all privileges and immunities of citizens in the several States," and they have been the subject of frequent consideration in judicial decisions. . . . In all these cases there is a recognition of the equality of right among citizens in the pursuit of the ordinary avocations of life, and a declaration that all grants of exclusive privileges, in contravention of this equality, are against common right, and void.

This equality of right, with exemption from all disparaging and partial enactments, in the lawful pursuits of life, throughout the whole country, is the distinguishing privilege of citizens of the United States. To them, everywhere, all pursuits, all professions, all avocations are open without other restrictions than such as are imposed equally upon all others of the same age, sex, and condition. The State may prescribe such regulations for every pursuit and calling of life as will promote the public health, secure the good order and advance the general prosperity of society, but when once prescribed, the pursuit or calling must be free to be followed by every citizen who is within the conditions designated, and will conform to the regulations. This is the fundamental idea upon which our institutions rest, and unless adhered to in the legislation of the country our government will be a republic only in name. The fourteenth amendment, in my judgment, makes it essential to the validity of the legislation of every State that this equality of right should be respected. How widely this equality has been departed from, how entirely rejected and trampled upon by the act of Louisiana, I have already shown. And it is to me a matter of profound regret that its validity is recognized by a majority of this court, for by it the right of free labor, one of the most sacred and imprescriptible rights of man, is violated. . . .

Mr. JUSTICE BRADLEY, also dissenting:

I concur in the opinion . . . by Mr. Justice Field; but desire to add a few observations. . . .

The question is now settled by the fourteenth amendment itself, that citizenship of the United States is the primary citizenship in this country; and that State citizenship is secondary and derivative, depending upon citizenship of the United States and the citizen's place of residence. . . .

Every citizen, then, being primarily a citizen of the United States, and, secondarily, a citizen of the State where he resides, what, in general, are the privileges and immunities of a citizen of the United States? Is the right, liberty, or privilege of choosing any lawful employment one of them? . . .

[I]n my judgment, the right of any citizen to follow whatever lawful employment he chooses to adopt (submitting himself to all lawful regulations) is one of his most valuable rights, and one which the legislature of a State cannot invade, whether restrained by its own constitution or not.

The right of a State to regulate the conduct of its citizens is undoubtedly a very broad and extensive one, and not to be lightly restricted. But there are certain fundamental rights which this right of regulation cannot infringe. It may prescribe the manner of their exercise, but it cannot subvert the rights themselves. . . . The privileges and immunities of Englishmen were established and secured by long usage and by various acts of Parliament. . . .

[T]he Declaration of Independence . . . lays the foundation of our National existence upon this broad proposition: "That all men are created equal; that they are endowed by their Creator with certain inalienable rights; that among these are life, liberty, and the pursuit of happiness." Here again we have the great threefold division of the rights of freemen, asserted as the rights of man. Rights to life, liberty, and the pursuit of happiness are equivalent to the rights of life, liberty, and property. These are the fundamental rights which can only be taken away by due process of law, and which can only be interfered with, or the enjoyment of which can only be modified, by lawful regulations necessary or proper for the mutual good of all; and these rights, I contend, belong to the citizens of every free government.

For the preservation, exercise, and enjoyment of these rights the individual citizen, as a necessity, must be left free to adopt such calling, profession, or trade as may seem to him most conducive to that end. Without this right he cannot be a freeman. This right to choose one's calling is an essential part of that liberty which it is the object of government to protect; and a calling, when chosen, is a man's property and right. Liberty and property are not protected where these rights are arbitrarily assailed. . . .

Is a monopoly or exclusive right, given to one person, or corporation, to the exclusion of all others, to keep slaughter-houses in a district of nearly twelve hundred square miles, for the supply of meat for a great city, a reasonable regulation of that employment which the legislature has a right to impose?

The keeping of a slaughter-house is part of, and incidental to, the trade of a butcher — one of the ordinary occupations of human life. To compel a butcher, or rather all the butchers of a large city and an extensive district, to slaughter their cattle in another person's slaughter-house and pay him a toll therefor, is such a restriction upon the trade as materially to interfere with its prosecution. . . .

The granting of monopolies, or exclusive privileges to individuals or corporations, is an invasion of the right of others to choose a lawful calling, and an infringement of personal liberty. . . .

If my views are correct with regard to what are the privileges and immunities of citizens, it follows conclusively that any law which establishes a sheer monopoly, depriving a large class of citizens of the privilege of pursuing a lawful employment, does abridge the privileges of those citizens.

The amendment also prohibits any State from depriving any person (citizen or otherwise) of life, liberty, or property, without due process of law.

In my view, a law which prohibits a large class of citizens from adopting a lawful employment, or from following a lawful employment previously adopted, does deprive them of liberty as well as property, without due process of law. Their right of choice is a portion of their liberty; their occupation is their property. Such a law also deprives those citizens of the equal protection of the laws, contrary to the last clause of the section. . . .

[G]reat fears are expressed that this construction of the amendment will lead to enactments by Congress interfering with the internal affairs of the States, and establishing therein civil and criminal codes of law for the government of the citizens, and thus abolishing the State governments in everything but name; or else, that it will lead the Federal courts to draw to their cognizance the supervision of State tribunals on every subject of judicial inquiry, on the plea of ascertaining whether the privileges and immunities of citizens have not been abridged.

In my judgment no such practical inconveniences would arise. Very little, if any, legislation on the part of Congress would be required to carry the amendment into effect. . . . The point would be regularly raised, in a suit at law, and settled by final reference to the Federal court. As the privileges and immunities protected are only those fundamental ones which belong to every citizen, they would soon become so far defined as to cause but a slight accumulation of business in the Federal courts. Besides, the recognized existence of the law would prevent its frequent violation. But even if the business of the National courts should be increased, Congress could easily supply the remedy by increasing their number and efficiency. The great question is, What is the true construction of the amendment? When once we find that, we shall find the means of giving it effect. The argument from inconvenience ought not to have a very controlling influence in questions of this sort. The National will and National interest are of far greater importance. . . .

Mr. Justice Swayne, dissenting:

I concur in the dissent in these cases and in the views expressed by my brethren, Mr. Justice Field and Mr. Justice Bradley. I desire, however, to submit a few additional remarks.

The first eleven amendments to the Constitution were intended to be checks and limitations upon the government which that instrument called into existence. They had their origin in a spirit of jealousy on the part of the

States, which existed when the Constitution was adopted. . . . The thirteenth [and] fourteenth . . . amendments are a new departure, and mark an important epoch in the constitutional history of the country. They trench directly upon the power of the States, and deeply affect those bodies. They are, in this respect, at the opposite pole from the first eleven.

Fairly construed these amendments may be said to rise to the dignity of a new Magna Charta. The thirteenth blotted out slavery and forbade forever its restoration. It struck the fetters from four millions of human beings and raised them at once to the sphere of freemen. This was an act of grace and justice performed by the Nation. Before the war it could have been done only by the States where the institution existed, acting severally and separately from each other. The power then rested wholly with them. In that way, apparently, such a result could never have occurred. The power of Congress did not extend to the subject, except in the Territories. . . .

The first section of the fourteenth amendment is alone involved in the consideration of these cases. No searching analysis is necessary to eliminate its meaning. Its language is intelligible and direct. Nothing can be more transparent. Every word employed has an established signification. There is no room for construction. There is nothing to construe. Elaboration may obscure, but cannot make clearer, the intent and purpose sought to be carried out. . . .

A citizen of a State is *ipso facto* a citizen of the United States. No one can be the former without being also the latter; but the latter, by losing his residence in one State without acquiring it in another, although he continues to be the latter, ceases for the time to be the former. "The privileges and immunities" of a citizen of the United States include, among other things, the fundamental rights of life, liberty, and property, and also the rights which pertain to him by reason of his membership of the Nation. The citizen of a State has the same fundamental rights as a citizen of the United States, and also certain others, local in their character, arising from his relation to the State, and in addition, those which belong to the citizen of the United States, he being in that relation also. There may thus be a double citizenship, each having some rights peculiar to itself. It is only over those which belong to the citizen of the United States that the category here in question throws the shield of its protection. . . .

In the next category, obviously *ex industriâ*, to prevent, as far as may be, the possibility of misinterpretation, either as to persons or things, the phrases "citizens of the United States" and "privileges and immunities" are dropped, and more simple and comprehensive terms are substituted. The substitutes are "any person," and "life," "liberty," and "property," and "the equal protection of the laws." Life, liberty, and property are forbidden to be taken "without due process of law," and "equal protection of the laws" is guaranteed to all. Life is the gift of God, and the right to preserve it is the most sacred of the rights of man. Liberty is freedom from all restraints but such as are justly imposed by law. Beyond that line lies the domain of usurpation and tyranny. Property is everything which has an exchangeable value, and the right of property includes the power to dispose of it according to the will of the owner. Labor is property, and as such merits protection. The right to make it available is next in importance to the rights of life and liberty. It lies to a large extent at the foundation of most other forms of property, and of all solid individual and national prosperity. "Due process of law" is the application of the law as it exists in the fair and regular course of administrative procedure. "The equal protection of the laws" places all upon a footing of legal equality and gives the same protection to all for the preservation of life, liberty, and property, and the pursuit of happiness. . . .

(1.) Does the act of the legislature creating the monopoly in question abridge the privileges and immunities of the plaintiffs in error as citizens of the United States?

(2.) Does it deprive them of liberty or property without due process of law, or deny them the equal protection of the laws of the State . . .? . . .

Both these inquiries I remit for their answer as to the facts to the opinions of my brethren, Mr. Justice Field and Mr. Justice Bradley. . . .

These amendments are all consequences of the late civil war. The prejudices and apprehension as to the central government which prevailed when the Constitution was adopted were dispelled by the light of experience. The public mind became satisfied that there was less danger of tyranny in the head than of anarchy and tyranny in the members. The provisions of this section are all eminently conservative in their character. They are a bulwark of defence, and can never be made an engine of oppression. The language employed is unqualified in its scope. There is no exception in its terms, and there can be properly none in their application. By the language "citizens of the United States" was meant *all* such citizens; and by "any person" was meant *all* persons within the jurisdiction of the State. No distinction is intimated on account of race or color. This court has no authority to interpolate a limitation that is neither expressed nor implied. Our duty is to execute the law, not to make it. The protection provided was not intended to be confined to those of any particular race or class, but to embrace equally all races, classes, and conditions of men. . . . The construction adopted by the majority of my brethren is, in my judgment, much too narrow. It defeats, by a limitation not anticipated, the intent of those by whom the instrument was framed and of those by whom it was adopted. To the extent of that limitation it turns, as it were, what was meant for bread into a stone. By the Constitution, as it stood before the war, ample protection was given against oppression by the Union, but little was given against wrong and oppression by the States. That want was intended to be supplied by this amendment. . . .

POINTS FOR DISCUSSION

1. Note the different interpretive presumptions that Justice Miller and Justice Swayne employ in their opinions. Justice Miller argued that the Court should not accept an interpretation of the Privileges or Immunities Clause that "radically changes the whole theory of the relations of the State and Federal governments to each other and of both these governments to the people . . . in the absence of language which expresses such a purpose too clearly to admit of doubt." Justice Swayne, in dissent, argued that the text of the Fourteenth Amendment is "intelligible and direct" and that "[t]he construction adopted by the majority . . . is . . . much too narrow. It defeats, by a limitation not anticipated, the intent of those by whom the instrument was framed and of those by whom it was adopted." How does this interpretive dispute relate to that between Justice Taney and Frederick Douglass regarding *Dred Scott v. Sandford*, 83 U.S. (16 Wall) 36 (1872)? Between St. George Tucker's rule of strict construction and the Marshall Court's descriptions of federal power? What competing values underlie these disputes?

Justice Miller applied what today might be called a "clear statement rule" of interpretation. In Chapter 6, you will see how the Court has applied clear statement rules in present times in interpreting federal statutes. In *Gregory v. Ashcroft*, 501 U.S. 452 (1991), the Court refused to read an act of Congress to interfere with certain traditional state regulatory prerogatives in the absence of a clear statement of congressional intent to do so. Moreover, in Chapter 7, you will see how the Court has applied a "presumption against preemption" — requiring courts to read acts of Congress to preempt state laws only if Congress expressed a clear intent to preempt them. The Justices dispute whether such interpretive presumptions are appropriate. When you read these disputes, consider how they relate, if at all, to prior disputes about interpretive presumptions in U.S. constitutional history.

2. The *Slaughter-House* majority expressed concern that a broad interpretation of the Privileges or Immunities Clause would radically change the relationship between the federal government and the states. How specifically would it change it? Is the concern that it would increase the powers of Congress? Of federal courts? Of both? Section 5 of the Fourteenth Amendment provides that "Congress shall have power to enforce, by appropriate legislation, the provisions of this article." Do the answers to these questions depend on the scope of power that §5 of the Fourteenth Amendment confers on Congress? You will study the scope of §5 in the next case and in Chapter 5.

In the aftermath of the Civil War, former Confederate soldiers and others organized resistance to Reconstruction in Southern states. Violence against freed slaves and white Republicans was endemic. From 1866 to 1875, Congress passed several statutes intended to enforce the Thirteenth and Fourteenth Amendments. One such law, the Civil Rights Act of 1870, forbade conspiracies to "prevent or hinder [a person's] free exercise and enjoyment of any right or privilege granted or secured to him by the constitution or laws of the United States. . . ." Act of May 31, 1870, ch. 114, 16 Stat. 140 §6 (1870). In *United States v. Cruikshank*, 92 U.S. 542 (1875), Cruikshank and other defendants were indicted under this Act for lynching two black men when a white militia attacked a group of Republican blacks who had taken a courthouse in Colfax, Louisiana, over a disputed election. The defendants were charged with violating various rights of the victims, including to assemble peaceably and bear arms. The Court held, among other things, that the Due Process and Equal Protection Clauses of the Fourteenth Amendment do not protect the rights of one citizen against another:

> The Fourteenth Amendment prohibits a State from depriving any person of life, liberty, or property, without due process of law; but this adds nothing to the rights of one citizen as against another. It simply furnishes an additional

guaranty against any encroachment by the States upon the fundamental rights which belong to every citizen as a member of society. . . .

The Fourteenth Amendment prohibits a State from denying to any person within its jurisdiction the equal protection of the laws; but this provision does not . . . add any thing to the rights which one citizen has under the Constitution against another. The equality of the rights of citizens is a principle of republicanism. Every republican government is in duty bound to protect all its citizens in the enjoyment of this principle, if within its power. That duty was originally assumed by the States; and it still remains there. The only obligation resting upon the United States is to see that the States do not deny the right. This the amendment guarantees, but no more. The power of the national government is limited to the enforcement of this guaranty.

Id. at 554-55.

The Civil Rights of 1875 was the last civil rights statute that the Republican Congress enacted after the Civil War. It prohibited public accommodations (such as inns, public transportation, and theaters) from discriminating on the basis of race — providing "[t]hat all persons within the jurisdiction of the United States shall be entitled to the full and equal enjoyment of the accommodations, advantages, facilities, and privileges of inns, public conveyances on land or water, theaters, and other places of public amusement." Civil Rights Act of 1875, ch. 114, §1, 18 Stat. 335, 335-336. The Act provided both criminal penalties and civil redress for victims of discrimination. The law was rarely enforced by federal officials before the Supreme Court considered its constitutionality in the *Civil Rights Cases*, 109 U.S. 3 (1883). Relying in part on *Cruikshank*, the Court held that Congress's §5 power to enforce the Fourteenth Amendment does not extend to private acts of discrimination. As you read the *Civil Rights Cases*, consider the following questions:

- What is the scope of Congress's power to enforce the Fourteenth Amendment?
- What power, if any, does Congress have to prohibit private discrimination under the Commerce Clause?
- What interpretive presumptions and methods do the Justices apply in this case?

CIVIL RIGHTS CASES

109 U.S. 3 (1883)

BRADLEY, J.

These cases are all founded on the first and second sections of the Act of Congress known as the Civil Rights Act, passed March 1, 1875, entitled "An Act to protect all citizens in their civil and legal rights." Two of the cases, those against Stanley and Nichols, were indictments for denying to persons of color the accommodations and privileges of an inn or hotel; two of them, those against Ryan and Singleton, were, one on information, the other an indictment, for denying to individuals the privileges and accommodations of a theater, the information against Ryan being for refusing a colored person a seat in the dress circle of Maguire's theater in San Francisco; and the indictment against Singleton was for denying to another person, whose color was not stated, the full enjoyment of the accommodations of the theater known as the Grand Opera House in New York, "said denial not being made for any reasons by law applicable to citizens of every race and color, and regardless of any previous condition of servitude." The case of Robinson and wife against the Memphis & Charleston R.R. Company was an action brought in the Circuit Court of the United States for the Western District of Tennessee, to recover the penalty of five hundred dollars given by the second section of the act; and the gravamen was the refusal by the conductor of the railroad company to allow the wife to ride in the ladies' car, for the reason, as stated in one of the counts, that she was a person of African descent. . . .

It is obvious that the primary and important question in all the cases is the constitutionality of the law: for if the law is unconstitutional none of the prosecutions can stand. . . .

[I]t is the purpose of the law to declare that, in the enjoyment of the accommodations and privileges of inns, public conveyances, theaters, and other places of public amusement, no distinction shall be made between citizens of different race or color, or between those who have, and those who have not, been slaves. Its effect is to declare that in all inns, public conveyances, and places of amusement, colored citizens, whether formerly slaves or not, and citizens of other races, shall have the same accommodations and privileges in all inns, public conveyances, and places of amusement as are enjoyed by white citizens; and *vice versa*. The second section makes it a penal offense in any person to deny to any citizen of any race or color, regardless of previous servitude, any of the accommodations or privileges mentioned in the first section.

Has Congress constitutional power to make such a law? Of course, no one will contend that the power to pass it was contained in the Constitution before the adoption of the last three amendments. The power is sought, first, in the Fourteenth Amendment, and the views and arguments of distinguished Senators, advanced whilst the law was under consideration, claiming authority to pass it by virtue of that amendment, are the principal arguments adduced in favor of the power. . . .

The first section of the Fourteenth Amendment . . . after declaring who shall be citizens of the United States, and of the several States, is prohibitory in its character, and prohibitory upon the States. It declares . . . :

> "No state shall make or enforce any law which shall abridge the privileges or immunities of citizens of the United States; nor shall any State deprive any person of life, liberty, or property without due process of law; nor deny to any person within its jurisdiction the equal protection of the laws."

It is State action of a particular character that is prohibited. Individual invasion of individual rights is not the subject-matter of the amendment. It has a deeper and broader scope. It nullifies and makes void all State legislation, and State action of every kind, which impairs the privileges and immunities of citizens of the United States, or which injures them in life, liberty or property without due process of law, or which denies to any of them the equal protection of the laws. It not only does this, but, in order that the national will, thus declared, may not be a mere *brutum fulmen*, the last section of the amendment invests Congress with power to enforce it by appropriate legislation. To enforce what? To enforce the prohibition. To adopt appropriate legislation for correcting the effects of such prohibited State law and State acts, and thus to render them effectually null, void, and innocuous. This is the legislative power conferred upon Congress, and this is the whole of it. It does not invest Congress with power to legislate upon subjects which are within the domain of State legislation; but to provide modes of relief against State legislation, or State action, of the kind referred to. It does not authorize Congress to create a code of municipal law for the regulation of private rights; but to provide modes of redress against the operation of State laws, and the action of State officers executive or judicial, when these are subversive of the fundamental rights specified in the amendment. Positive rights and privileges are undoubtedly secured by the Fourteenth Amendment; but they are secured by way of prohibition against State laws and State proceedings affecting those rights and privileges, and by power given to Congress to legislate for the purpose of carrying such prohibition into effect; and such legislation must necessarily be predicated upon such supposed State laws or State proceedings, and be directed to the correction of their operation and effect. A quite full discussion of this aspect of the amendment may be found in *U.S. v. Cruikshank*, 92 U.S. 542. . . .

And so in the present case, until some State law has been passed, or some State action through its officers or agents has been taken, adverse to the rights of citizens sought to be protected by the Fourteenth Amendment, no legislation of the United States under said amendment, nor any proceeding under such legislation, can be called into activity: for the prohibitions of the amendment are against State laws and acts done under State authority. Of course, legislation may, and should be, provided in advance to meet the exigency when it arises; but it should be adapted to the mischief and wrong which the amendment was intended to provide against; and that is, State laws, or State action of some kind, adverse to the rights of the citizen secured by the amendment. Such legislation cannot properly cover the whole domain of rights appertaining to life, liberty and property, defining them and providing for their vindication. That would be to establish a code of municipal law regulative of all private rights between man and man in society. It would be to make Congress take the place of the State legislatures and to supersede them. It is absurd to affirm that, because the rights of life, liberty and property (which include all civil rights that men have), are by the amendment sought to be protected against invasion on the part of the State without due process of law, Congress may therefore provide due process of law for their vindication in every case; and that, because the denial by a State to any persons, of the equal protection of the laws, is prohibited by the amendment, therefore Congress may establish laws for their equal protection. In fine, the legislation which Congress is authorized to adopt in this behalf is not general legislation upon the rights of the citizen, but corrective legislation, that is, such as may be necessary and proper for counteracting such laws as the States may adopt or enforce, and which, by the amendment, they are prohibited from making or enforcing, or such acts and proceedings as the states may commit or take, and which, by the amendment, they are prohibited from committing or taking. It is not necessary for us to state, if we could, what legislation would be proper for Congress to adopt. It is sufficient for us to examine whether the law in question is of that character.

An inspection of the law shows that it makes no reference whatever to any supposed or apprehended violation of the Fourteenth Amendment on the part of the States. . . . In other words, it steps into the domain of local jurisprudence, and lays down rules for the conduct of individuals in society towards each other, and imposes sanctions for the enforcement of those rules, without referring in any manner to any supposed action of the State or its authorities.

If this legislation is appropriate for enforcing the prohibitions of the amendment, it is difficult to see where it is to stop. Why may not Congress with equal show of authority enact a code of laws for the enforcement and vindication of all rights of life, liberty, and property? If it is supposable that the States may deprive persons of life, liberty, and property without due process of law (and the amendment itself does suppose this), why should not Congress proceed at once to prescribe due process of law for the protection of every one of these fundamental rights, in every possible case, as well as to prescribe equal privileges in inns, public conveyances, and theaters? The truth is that the implication of a power to legislate in this manner is based upon the assumption that if the States are forbidden to legislate or act in a particular way on a particular subject, and power is conferred upon Congress to enforce the prohibition, this gives Congress power to legislate generally upon that subject, and not merely power to provide modes of redress against such State legislation or action. The assumption is certainly unsound. It is repugnant to the Tenth Amendment of the Constitution, which declares that powers not delegated to the United States by the Constitution, nor prohibited by it to the States, are reserved to the States respectively or to the people. . . .

Of course, these remarks do not apply to those cases in which Congress is clothed with direct and plenary powers of legislation over the whole subject, accompanied with an express or implied denial of such power to the States, as in the regulation of commerce with foreign nations, among the several States, and with the Indian tribes, the coining of money, the establishment of post offices and post roads, the declaring of war, etc. In these cases Congress has power to pass laws for regulating the subjects specified in every detail, and the conduct and transactions of individuals in respect thereof. But where a subject is not submitted to the general legislative power of Congress, but is only submitted thereto for the purpose of rendering effective some prohibition against particular State legislation or State action in reference to that subject, the power given is limited by its object, and any legislation by Congress in the matter must necessarily be corrective in its character, adapted to counteract and redress the operation of such prohibited State laws or proceedings of State officers.

If the principles of interpretation which we have laid down are correct, as we deem them to be . . . it is clear that the law in question cannot be sustained by any grant of legislative power made to Congress by the Fourteenth Amendment. . . . Whether it would not have been a more effective protection of the rights of citizens to have clothed Congress with plenary power over the whole subject, is not now the question. What we have to decide is, whether such plenary power has been conferred upon Congress by the Fourteenth Amendment; and, in our judgment, it has not.

We have discussed the question presented by the law on the assumption that a right to enjoy equal accommodations and privileges in all inns, public conveyances, and places of public amusement, is one of the essential rights of the citizen which no State can abridge or interfere with. Whether it is such a right, or not, is a different question which, in the view we have taken of the validity of the law on the ground already stated, it is not necessary to examine. . . .

And whether Congress, in the exercise of its power to regulate commerce amongst the several States, might or might not pass a law regulating rights in public conveyances passing from one State to another, is also a question which is not now before us, as the sections in question are not conceived in any such view. . . .

On the whole we are of opinion, that no countenance of authority for the passage of the law in question can be found in . . . the . . . Fourteenth Amendment of the Constitution; . . . it must . . . be declared void, at least so far as its operation in the several States is concerned.

HARLAN, J., dissenting.

The opinion in these cases proceeds, as it seems to me, upon grounds entirely too narrow and artificial. . . . [T]he substance and spirit of the recent amendments of the Constitution have been sacrificed by a subtle and ingenious verbal criticism. "It is not the words of the law but the internal sense of it that makes the law: the letter of the law is the body; the sense and reason of the law is the soul." Constitutional provisions, adopted in the interest of liberty, and for the purpose of securing, through national legislation, if need be, rights inhering in a state of freedom, and belonging to American citizenship, have been so construed as to defeat the ends the people desired to accomplish, which they attempted to accomplish, and which they supposed they had accomplished by changes in their fundamental law. By this I do not mean that the determination of these cases should have been materially controlled by considerations of mere expediency or policy. I mean only, in this form, to express an earnest conviction that the court has departed from the familiar rule requiring, in the interpretation of constitutional provisions, that full effect be given to the intent with which they were adopted. . . .

[W]hen, under what circumstances, and to what extent, may Congress, by means of legislation, exert its power to enforce the provisions of [the Fourteenth] amendment? . . .

The assumption that this amendment consists wholly of prohibitions upon State laws and State proceedings in hostility to its provisions, is unauthorized by its language. . . .

It is . . . a grave misconception to suppose that the fifth section of the amendment has reference exclusively to express prohibitions upon State laws or State action. If any right was created by that amendment, the grant of power, through appropriate legislation, to enforce its provisions, authorizes Congress, by means of legislation, operating throughout the entire Union, to guard, secure, and protect that right.

It is, therefore, an essential inquiry what, if any, right, privilege or immunity was given, by the nation to colored persons, when they were made citizens of the State in which they reside? Did the constitutional grant of State citizenship to that race, of its own force, invest them with any rights, privileges and immunities whatever? That they became entitled, upon the adoption of the Fourteenth Amendment, "to all privileges and immunities of citizens in the several States," within the meaning of section 2 of article 4 of the Constitution, no one, I suppose, will for a moment question. What are the privileges and immunities to which, by that clause of the Constitution, they became entitled? To this it may be answered, generally, upon the authority of the adjudged cases, that they are those which are fundamental in citizenship in a free republican government, such as are "common to the citizens in the latter States under their constitutions and laws by virtue of their being citizens." . . .

But what was secured to colored citizens of the United States — as between them and their respective States — by the national grant to them of state citizenship? With what rights, privileges, or immunities did this grant invest them? There is one, if there be no other — exemption from race discrimination in respect of any civil right belonging to citizens of the white race in the same State. That, surely, is their constitutional privilege when within the jurisdiction of other States. And such must be their constitutional right, in their own State, unless the recent amendments be splendid baubles, thrown out to delude those who deserved fair and generous treatment at the hands of the nation. Citizenship in this country necessarily imports at least equality of civil rights among citizens of every race in the same State. It is fundamental in American citizenship that, in respect of such rights, there shall be no discrimination by the State, or its officers, or by individuals or corporations exercising public functions or authority, against any citizen because of his race or previous condition of servitude. . . .

If, then, exemption from discrimination, in respect of civil rights, is a new constitutional right, secured by the grant of State citizenship to colored citizens of the United States, . . . why may not the nation, by means of its own legislation of a primary direct character, guard, protect and enforce that right? It is a right and privilege which the nation conferred. It did not come from the States in which those colored citizens reside. It has been the established doctrine of this court during all its history, accepted as vital to the national supremacy, that Congress, in the absence of a positive delegation of power to the State legislatures, may, by its own legislation, enforce and protect any right derived from or created by the national Constitution. . . .

It is said that any interpretation of the Fourteenth Amendment different from that adopted by the majority of the court, would imply that Congress has authority to enact a municipal code for all the States, covering every matter affecting the life, liberty, and property of the citizens of the several States. Not so. Prior to the adoption of that amendment the constitutions of the several States, without perhaps an exception, secured all *persons* against deprivation of life, liberty, or property, otherwise than by due process of law, and, in some form, recognized the right of all *persons* to the equal protection of the laws. Those rights, therefore, existed before that amendment was proposed or adopted. . . . If, by reason of that fact, it be assumed that protection in these rights of persons still rests primarily with the States, and that Congress may not interfere except to enforce, by means of corrective legislation, the prohibitions upon State laws or State proceedings inconsistent with those rights, it does not at all follow, that privileges which have been *granted by the nation*, may not be protected by primary legislation upon the part of Congress. The personal rights and immunities recognized in the prohibitive clauses of the amendment were, prior to its adoption, under the protection, primarily, of the States, while rights, created by or derived from the United States, have always been, and, in the nature of things, should always be, primarily, under the protection of the general government. Exemption from race discrimination in respect of the civil rights which are fundamental in *citizenship* in a republican government, is, as we have seen, a new right, created by the nation, with express power in Congress, by legislation, to enforce the constitutional provision from which it is derived. . . .

To-day, it is the colored race which is denied, by corporations and individuals wielding public authority, rights fundamental in their freedom and citizenship. At some future time, it may be that some other race will fall under the ban of race discrimination. If the constitutional amendments be enforced, according to the intent with which, as I conceive, they were adopted, there cannot be, in this republic, any class of human beings in practical subjection to another class, with power in the latter to dole out to the former just such privileges as they may choose to grant. The supreme law of the land has decreed that no authority shall be exercised in this country upon the basis of discrimination, in respect of civil rights, against freemen and citizens because of their race, color, or previous condition of servitude. To that decree — for the due enforcement of which, by appropriate legislation, Congress has been invested with express power — every one must bow, whatever may have been, or whatever now are, his individual views as to the wisdom or policy, either of the recent changes in the fundamental law, or of the legislation which has been enacted to give them effect. . . .

POINTS FOR DISCUSSION

1. In the *Civil Rights Cases*, the Court held that Congress's power under §5 of the Fourteenth Amendment does not extend to private (as opposed to state) acts:

> [U]ntil some State law has been passed, or some State action through its officers or agents has been taken, adverse to the rights of citizens sought to be protected by the Fourteenth Amendment, no legislation of the United States under said amendment, nor any proceeding under such legislation, can be called into activity: for the prohibitions of the amendment are against State laws and acts done under State authority.

The Supreme Court continues to apply this precedent in the present day. For instance, as you will read in Chapter 5, the Court held in *United States v. Morrison*, 529 U.S. 598 (2000), that the §5 power does not authorize Congress to provide a civil remedy for private acts of sexual violence.

The Supreme Court has recently addressed Congress's power under §5 to enact "prophylactic" legislation against states — legislation that proscribes lawful state action as a means of correcting or preventing unlawful state action under the Fourteenth Amendment. The Court expressed a few thoughts in the *Civil Rights Cases* on Congress's power to counteract prospective state violations of the Fourteenth Amendment:

> Of course, legislation may, and should be, provided in advance to meet the exigency when it arises; but it should be adapted to the mischief and wrong which the amendment was intended to provide against; and that is, State laws, or State action of some kind, adverse to the rights of the citizen secured by the amendment. . . .
>
> In fine, the legislation which Congress is authorized to adopt in this behalf is not general legislation upon the rights of the citizen, but corrective legislation, that is, such as may be necessary and proper for counteracting such laws as the States may adopt or enforce, and which, by the amendment, they are prohibited from making or enforcing, or such acts and proceedings as the states may commit or take, and which, by the amendment, they are prohibited from committing or taking. It is not necessary for us to state, if we could, what legislation would be proper for Congress to adopt.

From your reading of the *Civil Rights Cases*, how would you begin to define Congress's power under §5 to proscribe state acts that do not violate the Fourteenth Amendment as a means of correcting or preventing state acts that do violate the Fourteenth Amendment? You will consider the Court's treatment of this question in Chapter 5.

2. The Court explained in the *Civil Rights Cases* that "no one will contend that the power [of Congress] to pass [the Civil Rights Act's prohibition on private discrimination] was contained in the Constitution before the adoption of" the Reconstruction Amendments. Additionally,

> whether Congress, in the exercise of its power to regulate commerce amongst the several States, might or might not pass a law regulating rights in public conveyances passing from one State to another, is also a question which is not now before us, as the sections in question are not conceived in any such view.

In these passages, did the Court determine that Congress lacks power under the Commerce Clause generally to outlaw private discrimination? As you will read in Chapter 5, the Court held in the 1960s that the Commerce Clause did authorize Congress to enact laws akin to the Civil Rights Act of 1875 prohibiting private discrimination. See *Heart of Atlanta Motel Inc. v. United States*, 379 U.S. 241 (1964); *Katzenbach v. McClung*, 379 U.S. 294 (1964).

3. In dissent in the *Civil Rights Cases*, Justice Harlan argued that "in the interpretation of constitutional provisions, . . . full effect [should] be given to the intent with which they were adopted." How does this interpretive approach relate to the interpretive dispute between Justice Taney and Frederick Douglass regarding *Dred Scott v. Sandford*? Between Tucker's rule of strict construction and Marshall Court assessments of federal power?

CHAPTER 3

FRAMING THEORIES OF FEDERALISM

In Chapters 1 and 2, you read various historical accounts of the U.S. federal structure. This chapter presents more recent analyses of U.S. federalism. Constitutional analyses of federalism questions have drawn heavily upon history and political theory. It is important, then, to appreciate historical and present-day accounts of the structure, practice, and values of U.S. federalism. This chapter considers three paradigms of U.S. federalism that courts and scholars have invoked: (1) dual federalism, (2) cooperative federalism, and (3) dynamic federalism.

As you read the materials in this chapter, take care to distinguish several kinds of questions about the U.S. federal structure. First, keep in mind two questions about the Constitution's original structural design:

- What *is* the federal structure that the Constitution establishes?
- What *values* was the federal structure *meant* to advance?

Moreover, in light of the Constitution's original design, consider how the structure of government in the United States has come to *work in practice*. Finally, as you read these materials, consider why government structures matter—and what values, if any, courts and other constitutional decision-makers should try to promote in resolving constitutional questions:

- What *values* do courts (and other constitutional decision makers) advance (or hinder) by (a) attempting to enforce the federal structure as established by the Constitution, or (b) adapting the structure to present-day political realities?
- By what measure should courts and other authoritative actors define the relationship between the federal government and the states?

Theories of dual, cooperative, and dynamic federalism provide different answers to these questions. The *dual federalism* paradigm understands federal and state governments to operate in different spheres of authority. The Supreme Court has endorsed and implemented this paradigm on many occasions. From this paradigm, judges and scholars have examined what the Constitution's federal structure *is*, what *values* that structure was *originally meant* to serve, and what *values* that structure *in fact* promotes. This chapter presents a defense and a critique of dual federalism.

Cooperative federalism envisions the federal and state governments cooperatively sharing regulatory authority to serve certain policy ends. In the paradigmatic cooperative federalism program, the federal government establishes a national policy, and states work to implement it in ways that account for local needs. Cooperative federalism is not necessarily incompatible with dual federalism. On one level, cooperative federalism provides an account of how dual federalism may work *in practice*. On another level, however, cooperative federalism may lie in tension with dual federalism. Some argue that dual federalism unnecessarily constrains the authority of the federal government to shape valuable cooperative programs, such as those that would *compel* states to cooperate in implementing federal programs. (Invoking dual federalism, the Supreme Court has held, as you will study in Chapter 6, that Congress may not compel state officials to implement a federal regulatory program. *Printz v. United States*, 521 U.S. 898 (1997).) These scholars argue that courts and other constitutional decision makers should understand the Constitution to allow such programs because, in practice, they advance worthwhile values. This chapter presents both sympathetic and critical accounts of cooperative federalism.

Finally, theories of *dynamic federalism* envision that federal and state governments have overlapping authority to design and implement policy in most, if not all, regulatory areas. Proponents argue that dynamic federalism promotes pluralism and fosters dialogue in ways that other federalism paradigms do not. Accordingly, proponents contend that courts and other constitutional decision makers should understand the Constitution to accommodate dynamic governmental interactions that advance those values. Proponents reject dual federalism to the extent that it impedes those values. This chapter provides excerpts explaining the theory of dynamic federalism.

As you read the materials in this section, consider these questions:

- What values do dual, cooperative, and dynamic theories of federalism, respectively, purport to advance?
- What, if any, judicial response does each theory warrant? Are the reasons offered in support of each theory reasons that judges should adopt in resolving constitutional federalism questions?
- Is each theory in fact a theory of federalism? What is federalism?
- How do dual, cooperative, and dynamic accounts of federalism relate to the Founding-era accounts of federalism that you read in Chapter 1 and the antebellum and Reconstruction accounts that you read in Chapter 2?

A. DUAL FEDERALISM: A DEFENSE AND CRITIQUE

The following excerpts present a defense and critique of dual federalism. As mentioned, the Supreme Court has endorsed and implemented dual federalism in many cases. You will read several of these cases in Chapters 5 and 6.

As you read the following excerpts as prelude to these cases, carefully consider these questions:

- How should the authors' points of disagreement about dual federalism be resolved?
- Should judges resolve constitutional federalism issues on the basis of dual federalism?
- How does the theory of dual federalism discussed in the following excerpts relate to Founding-era, antebellum, and Reconstruction accounts of federalism that you read in Chapters 1 and 2?

MICHAEL W. MCCONNELL, FEDERALISM:
EVALUATING THE FOUNDERS' DESIGN

54 U. Chi. L. Rev. 1484, 1492-1496, 1498-1512 (1987)

[W]hy forego national measures, thought to promote the peace, liberty, and safety of the people, merely because they intrude upon the [power] traditionally reserved to the governments of the individual States? Why do we care about federalism? . . .

During the debates over the drafting and ratification of the Constitution, supporters and opponents alike came to articulate complex and sophisticated theories of federalism. . . . The "natural attachment" of the people in 1787 to their states was augmented by practical arguments about how the new system of dual sovereignty would promote three complementary objectives: (1) "to secure the public good," (2) to protect "private rights," and (3) "to preserve the spirit and form of popular government." Achievement of these ends, according to Madison, was the "great object" of the Constitution. To understand the "founders' design" we must look again at those arguments. . . . [W]e must look at them in light of modern experience and knowledge about political decision making. The arguments of 1787 stand up remarkably well.

A. To "Secure the Public Good"

Rejecting both pure confederation and consolidation, the "Federal Farmer" (the ablest and most influential of the anti-federalist pamphleteers) argued that a "partial consolidation" is the only system "that can secure the freedom and happiness of this people." He reasoned that "one government and general legislation alone, never can extend equal benefits to all parts of the United States: Different laws, customs, and opinions exist in the different states, which by a uniform system of laws would be unreasonably invaded."[35] The framers sought, the Federal Farmer concluded, to preserve decentralized decision making because smaller units of government are better able to further the interests and general welfare of the people.

Three important advantages of decentralized decision making emerge from an examination of the founders' arguments and the modern literature. First, decentralized decision making is better able to reflect the diversity of interests and preferences of individuals in different parts of the nation.

---

35. [Herbert J. Storing, 2 The Complete Anti-Federalist] 2.8.13-14 [(1981)].

Second, allocation of decision making authority to a level of government no larger than necessary will prevent mutually disadvantageous attempts by communities to take advantage of their neighbors. And third, decentralization allows for innovation and competition in government.

1. *Responsiveness to Diverse Interests and Preferences.* The first, and most axiomatic, advantage of decentralized government is that local laws can be adapted to local conditions and local tastes, while a national government must take a uniform — and hence less desirable — approach. So long as preferences for government policies are unevenly distributed among the various localities, more people can be satisfied by decentralized decision making than by a single national authority. This was well understood by the founding generation. A noted pamphleteer, "The Impartial Examiner," put the point this way: "For being different societies, though blended together in legislation, and having as different interests; no uniform rule for the whole seems to be practicable."[36]

For example, assume that there are only two states, with equal populations of 100 each. Assume further that 70 percent of State A, and only 40 percent of State B, wish to outlaw smoking in public buildings. The others are opposed. If the decision is made on a national basis by a majority rule, 110 people will be pleased, and 90 displeased. If a separate decision is made by majorities in each state, 130 will be pleased, and only 70 displeased. The level of satisfaction will be still greater if some smokers in State A decide to move to State B, and some anti-smokers in State B decide to move to State A. In the absence of economies of scale in government services, significant externalities, or compelling arguments from justice, this is a powerful reason to prefer decentralized government. States are preferable governing units to the federal government, and local government to states. Modern public choice theory provides strong support for the framers' insight on this point.

2. *Destructive Competition for the Benefits of Government.* A second consideration in designing a federal structure is more equivocal. The unit of decision making must be large enough so that decisions reflect the full costs and benefits, but small enough that destructive competition for the benefits of central government action is minimized. In economic language, this is the problem of "externalities."

Externalities present the principal countervailing consideration in favor of centralized government: if the costs of government action are borne by the citizens of State C, but the benefits are shared by the citizens of States D, E, and F, State C will be unwilling to expend the level of resources commensurate with the full social benefit of the action. This was the argument in *Federalist* 25 for national control of defense. Since an MX missile in Pennsylvania will deter a Soviet attack on Connecticut and North Carolina as well as Pennsylvania, optimal levels of investment in MX's require national decisions and national taxes. Or, similarly, since expenditures on water pollution reduction in Kentucky will benefit riparians all the way to New Orleans, it makes sense to nationalize decisions about water pollution regulation and treatment. Thus,

---

36. Storing, 5 Complete Anti-Federalist at 5.14.6. . . .

as James Wilson explained to the Pennsylvania ratifying convention, "[w]hatever the object of government extends, in its operation, *beyond the bounds* of a particular state, should be considered as belonging to the government of the United States" . . . (emphasis in original).

That significant external effects of this sort provide justification for national decisions is well understood—hence federal funding of defense, interstate highways, national parks, and medical research, and federal regulation of interstate commerce, pollution, and national labor markets. It is less well understood that nationalizing decisions where the impact is predominantly local has an equal and opposite effect. The framers' awareness that ill consequences flow as much from excessive as from insufficient centralization is fundamental to their insistence on enumerating and thus limiting the powers of the federal government. Hence the other half of Wilson's explanation: "Whatever object of government is confined in its operation and effect, *within the bounds* of a particular State, should be considered as belonging to the government of that State" . . . (emphasis in original). This stands in marked contrast to the modern tendency to resolve all doubts in favor of federal control.

The point is quite general. It applies to lawmaking and regulation no less than to taxing and spending. A major effect of regulation is to shift burdens from one region or locality to another. Familiar examples are environmental laws that protect eastern "dirty" coal from competition from western "clean" coal and railroad regulation that enables low density areas to maintain service at the expense of other traffic. But the effect is especially obvious in the case of federal spending. If the national treasury is seen as a common pool resource for financing schemes of predominantly local benefit, it will be oversubscribed. Current budgetary woes are largely attributable to this fiscal "tragedy of the commons."

Where the benefits of government action are predominantly local but financing is national, each community can be expected to pursue projects even where total cost exceeds the actual benefit. Local decision makers will take into account only the local portion of the cost, since the national portion will be effectively "free."

Nobel laureate James Buchanan has demonstrated mathematically that centralized decision making about projects of localized impact will result in excessive spending—excessive meaning more than any of the individual communities involved would freely choose. Each community would be better off if they could agree in advance (as they thought they did in the Constitution) to confine federal attention to issues of predominantly interstate consequence. . . .

3. *Innovation and Competition in Government.* A final reason why federalism has been thought to advance the public good is that state and local governmental units will have greater opportunity and incentive to pioneer useful changes. A consolidated national government has all the drawbacks of a monopoly: it stifles choice and lacks the goad of competition.

Lower levels of government are more likely to depart from established consensus simply because they are smaller and more numerous. Elementary statistical theory holds that a greater number of independent observations will produce more instances of deviation from the mean. If innovation is desirable, it follows that decentralization is desirable. This statistical proposition is strengthened, moreover, by the political reality that a smaller unit of government is more likely to have a population with preferences that depart from the majority's. It is, therefore, more likely to try an approach that could not command a national majority.

Perhaps more important is that smaller units of government have an incentive, beyond the mere political process, to adopt popular policies. If a community can attract additional taxpayers, each citizen's share of the overhead costs of government is proportionately reduced. Since people are better able to move among states or communities than to emigrate from the United States, competition among governments for taxpayers will be far stronger at the state and local than at the federal level. Since most people are taxpayers, this means that there is a powerful incentive for decentralized governments to make things better for most people. In particular, the desire to attract taxpayers and jobs will promote policies of economic growth and expansion.

It is well known, for example, that families often choose a community on the basis of the school system; a better school system encourages development and raises property values. Competition among communities is therefore likely to result in superior education (as well as more cost-effective ways of providing it). This is especially likely given the strong business support for education. Because of the need for a well-educated work force, businesses often choose to locate in communities with a superior educational system and push for improved education in communities where they already have facilities. . . .

To be sure, the results of competition among states and localities will not always be salutary. State-by-state determination of the laws of incorporation likely results in the most efficient forms of corporate organization, but state-by-state determination of the law of products liability seems to have created a liability monster. This is because each state can benefit in-state plaintiffs by more generous liability rules, the costs being exported to largely out-of-state defendants; while no state can do much to protect its in-state manufacturers from suits by plaintiffs in the other states. Thus, competition among the states in this arena leads to one-sidedly pro-plaintiff rules of law.

The most important example of this phenomenon is the effect of state-by-state competition on welfare and other redistributive policies. In most cases, immigration of investment and of middle-to-upper income persons is perceived as desirable, while immigration of persons dependent on public assistance is viewed as a drain on a community's finances. Yet generous welfare benefits paid by higher taxes will lead the rich to leave and the poor to come. This creates an incentive, other things being equal, against redistributive policies. Indeed, it can be shown that the level of redistribution in a decentralized system is likely to be lower even if there is virtually unanimous agreement among the citizens that higher levels would be desirable. Where redistribution is the objective, therefore, advocates should and do press for federal programs, or at least for minimum federal standards.

Thus, the competition among states has an uncertain effect: often salutary but sometimes destructive. There are races to the bottom as well as races to the top. Often one's view of the allocation of authority for specific issues will depend on a prediction as to substantive outcomes rather than a general theory of federalism.

B. To Protect "Private Rights"

The most important reason offered by the defenders of state sovereignty was that state and local governments are better protectors of liberty. Patrick Henry went to the heart of the matter when he told the Virginia ratifying convention:

> You are not to inquire how your trade may be increased, nor how you are to become a great and powerful people, but how your liberties can be secured; for liberty ought to be the direct end of your Government.[67]

The most eloquent of the opponents of the Constitution, Henry stated flatly that in the "alarming transition, from a Confederacy to a consolidated Government," the "rights and privileges" of Americans were "endangered."[68] He was far from alone in this fear.

At a distance of 200 years, it is this aspect of the founders' thought that is most difficult for us to understand. After *Brown v. Board of Education*[71] and the various civil rights acts, after the revolution in criminal procedure fostered by federal law and federal courts, after the imposition of uniform federal standards for basic liberties under the Bill of Rights, and after the proliferation of novel statutory "rights" arising from the interventions of the welfare-regulatory state, it is the federal government, not the states, that appears to be our system's primary protector of individual liberties. This seems to be the premise of the Fourteenth Amendment and of much of New Deal legislation. The view at the founding, however, was much more divided and ambivalent.

Madison's most important contribution to the debate over ratification is his challenging argument that individual liberties, such as property rights and freedom of religion, are better protected at the national than the state level. The argument, presented principally in *Federalist* 10, is familiar to all, but is no less controversial for being familiar. . . .

Madison's argument, greatly simplified, is that the most serious threat to individual liberty is the tyranny of a majority faction. Since any given faction is more likely to be concentrated in a particular locality, and to be no more than a small minority in the nation as a whole, it follows that factional tyranny is more likely in the state legislatures than in the Congress of the United States. This argument is supplemented by others, based on the "proper structure of the Union"[74] — deliberative representation, separation of powers, and checks and balances — that also suggest that the federal government is a superior protector of rights. Here I shall concentrate on the argument from the "extent . . . of the Union."[75] Madison's argument blunted the anti-federalists'

---

67. Storing, 5 Complete Anti-Federalist at 5.16.2. . . .
68. Id.
71. 347 U.S. 483 (1954).
74. *Federalist* 10 (Madison).
75. Id.

appeal to state sovereignty as the guarantor of liberty. It was, however, only partially successful. Why?

Modern public choice theory has cast some doubt on elements of Madison's theory. In particular, Madison's assumption that the possibility of minority tyranny is neutralized by majority vote requirements and that minority factions are inherently vulnerable to majority tyranny is undermined by studies showing that a small, cohesive faction intensely interested in a particular outcome can exercise disproportionate influence in the political arena. Madison underestimated both the dangers of minority rule and the defensive resources of minority groups. Moreover, some observers have suggested that the conditions of modern federal politics—especially the balkanized, issue-oriented conjunction of bureaucratic agencies and committee staffs—is especially susceptible to factional politics. . . . Proponents of greater state sovereignty in 1787-89 may have been rightly skeptical of Madison's claims that there would be less danger of factional oppression at the federal level.

But even taking Madison's fundamental insight as correct—and surely it has much to commend it—the argument on its own terms cautions against total centralization of authority in Washington. It points instead to a hybrid system in which states retain a major role in the protection of individual liberties. There are three basic reasons.

1. *Liberty Through Mobility.* Madison's argument demonstrates that factional oppression is more likely to occur in the smaller, more homogenous jurisdictions of individual states. But it does not deny that oppression at the federal level, when it occurs, is more dangerous. The lesser likelihood must be balanced against the greater magnitude of the danger. The main reason oppression at the federal level is more dangerous is that it is more difficult to escape. If a single state chose, for example, to prohibit divorce, couples seeking a divorce could move (or perhaps merely travel) to other states where their desires can be fulfilled. Oppressive measures at the state level are easier to avoid. Important recent examples of this phenomenon are the migration of homosexuals to cities like San Francisco, where they received official toleration, and the migration of individuals from Massachusetts to New Hampshire to escape high rates of taxation. A more contentious example is the regulation of abortion. If the power to regulate abortion is returned to the states, there is little likelihood of effective enforcement of anti-abortion laws, since permissive jurisdictions would attract business from more restrictive states. On the other hand, a nationwide rule—either voted by Congress or adopted by the courts as a construction of the due process clause—would have far more dramatic consequences.

Recognition of this feature of decentralized decision making does not depend on any particular understanding of the substantive content of "liberty." For these purposes, liberty need not be equated with government inaction. "States' rights" does not imply minimalist government. Under a regime of decentralized decision making, it is more, not less, likely that communities will adopt a radical, controversial from of social organization. Santa Monica, California, for example, can adopt a form of socialism that is unlikely to command majority support in any state or the nation at large. To some,

Santa Monica will be a beacon of (a particular form of) liberty; to others, it is a petty tyranny. Indianapolis can (or could, if the courts would allow it) adopt anti-pornography legislation more stringent than national norms. To some (a curious alliance of feminists and social conservatives) this protects their freedom from a pornography-ridden society; to others, this is a violation of freedom of expression. The liberty that is protected by federalism is not the liberty of the apodictic solution, but the liberty that comes from diversity coupled with mobility.

2. *Self-Interested Government.* Madison held that there are two different and distinct dangers inherent in republican government: the "oppression of [the] . . . rulers" and the "injustice" of "one part of the society against . . . the other part."[81] The first concern is that government officials will rule in their own interest instead of the interest of the people. The second is that some persons, organized in factions, will use the governmental powers to oppress others. Significantly, while Madison argued that the danger of faction is best met at the federal level (for the reasons summarized above), he conceded that the danger of self-interested representation is best tackled at the state level. "As in too small a sphere oppressive combinations may be too easily formed ag[ainst] the weaker party; so in too extensive a one, a defensive concert may be rendered too difficult against the oppression of those entrusted with the administration."[82] Consequently, while powers most likely to be abused for factional advantage ought to be vested in the federal government, powers that are most likely to be abused by self-aggrandizing officials should be left in the states, where direct popular control is stronger.

3. *Diffusion of Power.* Madison himself did not view his argument as establishing the superiority of a consolidated national government; rather, he presented his famous arguments about the tyranny of factions in favor of the intermediate, federalist solution of dual sovereignty. In *Federalist* 51, he underscored that "the rights of the people" are best protected in a system in which "two distinct governments," federal and state, "will control each other." The diffusion of power, in and of itself, is protective of liberty. In Tocqueville's evocative words, "Municipal bodies and county administrations are like so many hidden reefs retarding or dividing the flood of the popular will."[84]

That the framers and ratifiers of the Constitution were not wholly persuaded that individual liberties are safer in the hands of the central government is evident from their provision of explicit protections for certain cherished liberties in the Bill of Rights. An instructive example is the freedom of religion. If Madison's theory of factions is correct, it suggests that governmental authority over religion is more safely lodged in the federal government, where the multiplicity of religious sects will guarantee against oppression, than in the states, where a single religious denomination often enjoys majority support. Indeed, Madison used the example of religious sects to demonstrate his point in *Federalist* 10 and 51.

---

81. Federalist 51. . . .
82. James Madison to Thomas Jefferson, Oct. 24, 1787, in 10 The Papers of James Madison 214 (Robert A. Rutland, ed., 1977).
84. [Alexis de] Tocqueville, Democracy in America 263 [(J.P. Mayer ed., 1969)].

The actual treatment of religious freedom in the Constitution is, however, diametrically opposed to the Madisonian model. State authority over religion was left intact. Madison proposed an amendment that "No State shall violate the equal right of conscience,"[87] even stating that this (along with speech, press, and jury trial rights against the states) was "the most valuable" of his proposed amendments to the Constitution.[88] Notwithstanding his plea, the proposal was rejected by the Senate. By contrast, the federal government was forbidden to pass any law "respecting an establishment of religion"—that is, either establishing or disestablishing a religion—or prohibiting the "free exercise thereof."[90] This was the "states' rights" approach to the religion question; it left decisions "respecting" the establishment of religion wholly to the states.

This decision was understandable. While it was more likely that individual states would erect a religious establishment (indeed, at that time, five of the thirteen states had an establishment of some sort), a national establishment would have been far more threatening to religious liberty. Religious dissenters were free to travel to more tolerant states, and did; moreover, the example of the more tolerant states generated pressure on the more restrictive states to modify their policies. By 1834, the last state establishment was repealed. A national establishment would have been far more difficult to eradicate. Moreover, religious minorities are more likely to have influence in an individual state where they are concentrated, and thus more likely to have their rights respected, than at the national level. As "Philadelphiensis" said of these Quakers who feared the loss of their religious exemption from compulsory military service if control over the military were vested in Congress instead of the state legislature: "Their influence in the state of Pennsylvania is fully sufficient to save them from suffering very materially on this account; but in the great vortex of the whole continent it can have no weight."[92]

The religious freedom example illustrates that, right or wrong, the framers of the Constitution and Bill of Rights believed that state governments were, in some vital respects, safer repositories of power over individual liberties than the federal government. It is thus no accident that the "police power"—the protection of public health, safety, and morals—was left to the states, with the federal government entrusted with less sensitive powers like those over interstate and foreign commerce. . . . Given the diversity of views about issues of morality, and the potential for oppression, it is natural that lovers of liberty would be inclined toward decentralized decision making.

At this point, an important qualification is in order. The arguments from the "public good" and from "private rights" make sense only if one presupposes that the decision in question is appropriate to democratic decision making at *some* level, be it state or federal. Some issues are so fundamental to basic justice that they must be taken out of majoritarian control altogether. This is why both state and federal governments are prohibited, for example, from passing ex post facto laws and bills of attainder. These issues are thus subject

---

87. 1 Annals of Cong. 452 (June 8, 1789) (J. Gales, ed. 1834). . . .
88. Id. at 458.
90. U.S. Const. amend. I.
92. Storing, 3 Complete Anti-Federalist at 3.9.12.

to a single national rule; the reason, however, has nothing to do with federalism. Federalism is a system for allocation of democratic decision making power. For those few but important matters on which democracy itself cannot be trusted, neither the "public good" nor the "private rights" argument for state autonomy can hold sway.

Obviously, different people will assign wider or narrower latitude to majoritarian institutions. The alternative to democracy in our system is not utopia but judicial rule, which is not immune to abuse and which unavoidably conflicts with the ideals of republicanism. . . . The conclusion that states should retain a high degree of decision making autonomy is stronger on the humble assumption that most governmental decisions are fairly debatable — that is, that there is no single compelling just answer to many questions of government.

Even as to compelling matters of justice, however, federalism remains important as a tactical consideration, at least until a just national consensus emerges. Prior to a national majority against slavery, abolitionists would prefer state-by-state decision making, since there would be at least some free states. Upon emergence of an anti-slavery national majority, abolitionists would prefer national legislative power. Once a substantial national consensus developed — manifested in two-thirds of both Houses of Congress and three-quarters of the states — it became time to take the issue out of democratic politics. But these judgments would not be principled decisions about federalism; they would be tactical judgments about abolitionism. (On this analysis, the Constitution's allocation of power with respect to slavery was precisely what tactically-minded abolitionists should have wanted given the political circumstances. I therefore believe critics of the framers' work as supportive of slavery are mistaken.)

C. To Preserve "the Spirit and Form of Popular Government"

It was an article of faith among advocates of state autonomy that republicanism could survive only in a small jurisdiction. As stated by the prominent anti-federalist essayist, "Brutus," "a free republic cannot succeed over a country of such immense extent, containing such a number of inhabitants, and these increasing in such rapid progression as that of the whole United States."[96] They believed consolidated national government would lead to aristocratic or despotic rule. Their reasons may be reduced to three major themes: (1) enforcement of laws, (2) nature of representation, and (3) cultivation of public spiritedness.

1. *Enforcement of Laws.* Obedience to the law can arise from two different sources: fear of punishment and voluntary compliance. A republican government, which has a minimal coercive apparatus, must rely predominantly upon the latter. As Brutus explained, in a free republic "the government must rest for its support upon the confidence and respect which the people have for their government and laws."[97] To the advocates of decentralized government, this

---

96. Storing, 2 Complete Anti-Federalist at 2.9.11. . . .
97. Id. at 2.9.18. See also Gordon S. Wood, The Creation of the American Republic, 1776-1787, 66 (1969).

necessarily implied that the units of government must be small and close to the people. "The confidence which the people have in their rulers, in a free republic," according to Brutus, "arises from their knowing them, from their being responsible to them for their conduct, and from the power they have of displacing them when they misbehave."[98] Unfortunately, this confidence is impossible in a country the size of the United States.

> The different parts of so extensive a country could not possibly be made acquainted with the conduct of their representatives, nor be informed of the reasons upon which measures were founded. The consequence will be, they will have no confidence in their legislature, suspect them of ambitious views, be jealous of every measure they adopt, and will not support the laws they pass.[99]

This proposition finds support in the folklore of the small town, which in contrast to the big city is an oasis of law abidingness and community good feeling. It also seems consistent with public choice theory, since in a smaller setting it is more likely that a strategy of cooperation will overcome the "prisoner's dilemma," which in this context holds that the optimal strategy for each citizen is to violate the law while all others abide by it. In a smaller jurisdiction, there is greater likelihood of monitoring and of stigmatization or retaliation, hence greater incentive to abide by legal and other ethical norms.

2. Nature of Representation. One of the principal arguments for substantial state autonomy was that representatives in a smaller unit of government will be closer to the people. Patrick Henry, for example, warned in the Virginia ratifying convention that "throwing the country into large districts . . . will destroy that connection that ought to subsist between the electors and the elected."[101] Assuming representative bodies of roughly the same number, any given representative will have fewer constituents and a smaller district at the state or local level. Each citizen's influence on his representative, therefore, will be proportionately greater, and geographically concentrated minorities are more likely to achieve representation.

Because federal electoral districts must of necessity be larger and more populous, representation is likely to be skewed in favor of the well-known few — what were known at the time as the "aristocratic" element. The Federal Farmer argued that increasing the number of representatives would make the nation "more democratical and secure, strengthen the confidence of the people in it, and thereby render it more nervous and energetic."[103] However, the sheer size of the United States makes it impossible to increase the number of representatives sufficiently, without turning the Congress into what Madison called "the confusion of a multitude."[104]

Moreover, if representatives to the national government are required to spend much of their time at the distant national capital, they are likely to lose touch with the sentiments of their constituents, and instead come to identify

---

98. [Id.]
99. Id.
101. Storing, 5 Complete Anti-Federalist at 5.16.27. . . .
103. Id. at 2.8.158.
104. Federalist 10 (Madison). . . .

themselves with the interests of the central governmental apparatus. Even Madison realized that "within a small sphere, this voice [of the people] could be most easily collected, and the public affairs most accurately managed."[106]

3. *Public Spiritedness.* Critics of governmental centralization warned that public spiritedness — then called "public virtue"[107] — could be cultivated only in a republic of small dimensions. Republicanism, it was thought, depended to an extraordinary degree on the willingness of each citizen to submerge his own passions and interests for the common good. The only substitute for public virtue was an unacceptable degree of coercion, compatible only with nonrepublican forms of government.

There were two reasons to believe that a centralized government would undermine republican virtue. First, public spiritedness is a product of participation in deliberation over the public good. If the citizens are actively engaged in the public debate they will have more of a stake in the community. The federal government is too distant and its compass too vast to permit extensive participation by ordinary citizens in its policy formulations. By necessity, decision making will be delegated to agents. But as they are cut off from active participation in the commonwealth, the citizens will become less attached to it and more inclined to attend to their private affairs.

Second, the natural sentiment of benevolence, which lies at the heart of public spiritedness, is weaker as the distance grows between the individual and the objects of benevolence. An individual is most likely to sacrifice his private interests for the good of his family, and then for his neighbors and, by extension, his community. He is unlikely to place great weight upon the well-being of strangers hundreds of miles away. It is unlikely, therefore, that citizens of a nation as large as the United States will assume an attitude of republican virtue toward national affairs. . . .

The argument for substantial state and local autonomy was powerful at the time of the founding, and remains so. . . . Whatever our chosen theory of interpretation, it is good to cast our minds back to the time of the founding, when popular attention was directed, uniquely in our history, to the issues of self-government. It is the only way to recall, and perhaps recapture, what we may have lost.

EDWARD L. RUBIN & MALCOLM FEELEY, FEDERALISM:
SOME NOTES ON A NATIONAL NEUROSIS

---

41 UCLA L. Rev. 903, 906-908, 910-911, 913-928, 931-934, 948 (1994)

The concept of federalism, it appears, certainly has staying power once it gets into your system. We Americans love federalism or, as the Court has called it, "Our Federalism."[26] It conjures up images of Fourth of July parades down Main Street, drugstore soda fountains, and family farms with tire swings in the front yard. Imagery aside, a number of appealing arguments have been

---

106. 10 Papers of James Madison at 212 (cited in note 82).
107. See Wood, Creation of the American Republic at 68 (cited in note 97).
26. Younger v. Harris, 401 U.S. 37, 44 (1971).

made on its behalf. . . . . Federalism, Justice O'Connor states, "increases opportunity for citizen involvement in democratic processes," it "makes government more responsive by putting the States in competition for a mobile citizenry," and "it allows for more innovation and experimentation in government."[27] But its principal virtue is that it constitutes "a check on abuses of government power" by diffusing power among separate sovereigns.[28] Justice O'Connor thus invoked all the familiar themes regularly cited by legal scholars in support of federalism. . . .

In our view, federalism in America achieves none of the beneficial goals that the Court claims for it. . . .

In fact, federalism is America's neurosis. We have a federal system because we began with a federal system; the new nation consisted of a group of self-governing units that had to relinquish some of their existing powers to a central government. We began with a federal system because of some now uninteresting details of eighteenth century British colonial administration. We carry this system with us, like any neurosis, because it is part of our collective psychology, and we proclaim its virtues out of the universal desire for self-justification. But our political culture is essentially healthy, and we do not let our neuroses control us. Instead, we have been trying to extricate ourselves from federalism for at least the last 130 years. When federalism is raised as an argument against some national policy, we generally reject it by whatever means are necessary, including, in one case, killing its proponents.[35] This Article describes that process, and asserts that, on grounds of political morality, it has been exactly the right thing to do. . . .

I. Federalism and Decentralization

A. The Difference Between Federalism and Decentralization

"Federalism," like most broad political or legal terms, can mean many different things, but any definition that would justify judicial enforcement, to say nothing of the emotional freight that we Americans attach to it, must distinguish federalism from decentralization. Decentralization is a managerial concept; it refers to the delegation of centralized authority to subordinate units of either a geographic or a functional character. Setting aside the political context for the moment, and focusing on the concept of decentralization as a matter of organization or systems theory, the main reason to decentralize is to achieve effective management. Very often, an administrator who is relatively close to the subject matter will be more knowledgeable, more responsive, and more involved than a higher ranking person ensconced in some distant central office. An industrial corporation might decentralize authority to factory managers, or a state university system might decentralize authority to the head of each constituent campus. The Israeli army employs decentralization as a military strategy; while Egyptian and Syrian field commanders are expected to follow detailed instructions, an Israeli commander in the field possesses virtually complete autonomy.

---

27. [Gregory v. Ashcroft, 501 U.S. 452, 458 (1991).]
28. [Id. at 459.]
35. The Civil War.

But none of this has anything to do with federalism. All these decentralized systems are hierarchically organized and the leaders at the top or center have plenary power over the other members of the organization. Decentralization represents a deliberate policy that the leaders select, or at least approve, based on their view of the best way to achieve their goals. A decentralized system can be, and often is, the product of a purely managerial decision by a centralized authority.

The essence of federalism, as a coherent political concept, is quite different. To be sure, federal systems share certain structural features with decentralized ones. The most basic is that, within a single system of governance, decisions are made by subsidiary units and the central authority defers to those decisions. But in a federal system, the subordinate units possess prescribed areas of jurisdiction that cannot be invaded by the central authority, and leaders of the subordinate units draw their power from sources independent of that central authority. Federalism is not a managerial decision by the central decision-maker, as decentralization can be, but a structuring principle for the system as a whole. . . .

Clearly, only federalism can operate as a bar to national policy, and only federalism can justify the imposition of that bar by the judiciary. Decentralization, being an instrumental, managerial strategy, is no different in degree from any other policy; like cost or administrative convenience, it is simply one factor that political decision-makers should take into account. Their failure to do so could lead to the charge that they are unwise, but everyone agrees that such debates over policy alternatives are consigned to the ordinary political process. To place a policy beyond the power of the central government, and to enforce that policy by judicial action, requires the assertion that a right has been infringed. That right, in the case of federalism, is the right of states to act independently, in furtherance of goals the national government does not share. The notion that an admittedly valid national policy is best implemented by decentralizing its administration cannot support either the rhetoric of federalism or the remedy of judicial intervention.

B. Decentralization in Federalist Clothes: Public Participation, Citizen Choice, State Competition, and Experimentation

Once we recognize the distinction between federalism and decentralization, we can see that many standard arguments advanced for federalism are clearly nothing more than policy arguments for decentralization. These are the claims that some nationally-defined policy is best achieved by permitting regional variation. The point is not simply that federalism is unnecessary for implementing such policies, that it represents an unnecessary use of constitutional artillery. Rather, federalism is absolutely antithetical to these policies because it allows the wrong kinds of variation. Implementing a national policy through a decentralized system means that the permitted variations will be those that contribute to achieving the designated policy. In contrast, federalism allows the states to vary as they choose, pursuing their own policies instead of the national one. This can be justified only by arguments favoring a variety of policies, not by arguments favoring the implementation of a single policy by a variety of methods.

Of the standard arguments for federalism, four are really arguments that specific national policies are best implemented by decentralized decision-making; these are public participation, effectuating citizen choice through competition among jurisdictions, achieving economic efficiency through competition among jurisdictions, and encouraging experimentation. All four reflect policies that are applicable to the American political context; while questions can certainly be raised about their desirability, they are at least plausible strategies for governing our country. They are national strategies, however, linked to federalism only by confusing that concept with decentralization, and by the airy, flag-waving-in-the-breeze rhetoric that characterizes the entire subject.

1. Public Participation

The public participation argument is the most complex of the four. . . . Here, the claim is that locating various decisions at the regional or local level will enable more people to participate in these decisions. As the Court stated in *Gregory* [*v. Ashcroft*], federalism "increases opportunity for citizen involvement in democratic processes."

Participation of this sort may not be as unambiguous a benefit as the Court and many commentators imply. In our present political context, participation, generally a middle and upper-middle class activity, is as likely to exclude and disadvantage less fortunate citizens as it is to help them. Certainly, the story of participation in state and local government regularly features low voter turn-outs, entrenched elites, and narrow-minded policies. Nonetheless, many people speak well of local participation, and we can certainly concede that it is superior to some alternatives.

If one wants to implement a program of ensuring and increasing local participation, decentralized decisions may well be a valid way to proceed. This would be a national policy, however, because the goal would be to encourage participation in every state or locality. Federalism does not necessarily increase participation; it simply authorizes a set of specified political sub-units — states in our case — to decide for themselves how much participation is desirable. Some might choose to encourage participation but others might choose to suppress it. There are, moreover, a variety of other methods for achieving the same goal, such as hiring community organizers, funding local organizations, and requiring approvals for government decisions from different sectors of the population. None of these have anything to do with federalism, but if participation is a real, rather than an excuse for favoring federalism, they should be given equal consideration.

One might argue that the states, being "closer to the people" than the federal government, are more likely to foster local participation. This is one of many unproven assumptions that fester in this field without either theoretical or empirical support. As a matter of theory, there is simply no reason why an intermediate political unit would be more favorable to local units than the nation's central authority. Actual alignments are likely to depend on the correspondence of substantive policies. For example, the white-dominated governments of the southern states undoubtedly fostered the autonomy of white-dominated towns against federal intervention; on the other hand, the federal government was correspondingly more solicitous of black communities, at least during the Reconstruction and Civil Rights eras. As an empirical matter, support for urban planning generally, or for specific city functions such as schools or police, has often come from the federal government, not from the states.

It is also argued that federalism fosters public participation by enabling citizens to choose their own rulers. But this merely combines decentralization and the independent norm of electoral politics, without involving federalism at all. In a truly federal regime, some states might opt for elections, while others might not; it is the Guarantee Clause, a nationalizing provision, that probably requires states to choose their leadership by election. As a practical matter, elections are deeply ingrained in our political culture. We do not need the Guarantee Clause because every state, no matter how much normative latitude it is given, grants its citizens the power to choose their own leaders by election, at the local level as well as the state level. This phenomenon cannot possibly be attributed to federalism, since federalism does not protect the political systems of localities. Indeed, it has the reverse effect, for it subjects these localities to the plenary control of state government and precludes or limits the ability of the national government to set standards for local politics. Thus, if the electoral principle were under attack in certain states, and Americans decided at a national level that we needed to make sure that every locality held elections, federalism would constitute a barrier to the implementation of this policy.

2. Citizen Choice

A second standard argument, again in the words of the *Gregory* opinion, is that federalism "assures a decentralized government that will be more sensitive to the diverse needs of a heterogeneous society" and that it "makes government more responsive by putting the states in competition for a mobile citizenry." On its face, these statements seem contradictory, because they elide the familiar distinction between voice and exit. Responsiveness is generally regarded as allied to voice; a government, for example, responds when those within its jurisdiction express their dissatisfaction with its policies. Competition for a mobile citizenry, on the other hand, seems allied to exit; the government attracts those dissatisfied with other jurisdictions, while accepting, or celebrating, the departure of those dissatisfied with its own policies. These arguments can be reconciled, however, through an understanding of exit and voice as alternative ways in which individuals relate to organizations. Individuals will seek organizations that are responsive to their needs, or voice; if their present organization fails to respond, they can exercise their exit option to locate a more responsive one. Conversely, an organization can generate a self-selected membership by resisting some divergent voices, and will then be more responsive to those who have remained or entered.

The precise claim . . . is that a group of government jurisdictions can offer varying packages of government services with varying means of funding those services and varying costs to their citizens. Citizens can then choose among these jurisdictions, so that they come to rest in one that matches their personal preferences, or utility function. This argument has found much favor in the law and economics literature. There is something a bit fanciful in the image of people choosing a place to live the way shoppers choose their favorite breakfast cereal, and critics have pointed out that the transaction costs of obtaining information and transplanting one's life may well overwhelm the utility gains from the selection process, particularly for people with limited resources. But there is also much truth to the argument considering our mobile, restless society.

Nonetheless, this argument is unrelated, or only tangentially related, to the concept of federalism. The package of government services and costs that a particular jurisdiction offers is only one element in its overall appeal to potential citizens. Climate, size, location, employment opportunities, and a variety of other factors are likely to loom larger in the utility function of our wandering citizen, even apart from considerations that discourage mobility, like family ties, nostalgia, and local loyalty. In addition, government service packages involve a number of factors, such as education, police protection, social welfare, and recreation, all of which can vary, and all of which can be funded by a variety of mechanisms that produce differential impacts on people in different economic positions. The net result, in economic terms, is that the supply of jurisdictions from which citizens can choose is likely to be less than perfectly elastic.

This difficulty can be partially resolved if there is a large number of such jurisdictions, and indeed, if there is a large number in each region of the nation. Thus, the concept of government service packages applies better to localities, like counties, cities, and towns. States are too large to produce the necessary range of choices; telling wheat farmers in Kansas that they can obtain the kinds of schools they want by moving to New Jersey is unlikely to provide an increase in their overall utility function. What would help them, assuming the entire concept makes sense, is a choice of jurisdictions with different educational policies within their own region or city. . . .

But federalism only protects the autonomy of states, not the autonomy or variability of local governments. Indeed, the very essence of American federalism is that the national government is forbidden to interfere with state policies for managing and controlling local governments. Consequently, federalism does not secure the kind of governmental variability that would provide any realistic choice for citizens; its principal effect in this area is to create a legal barrier against the imposition of such variability as a matter of national policy. If we are truly serious about providing people with the exit option of choice, or the voice option of participation, we should provide those options universally, through a national, decentralized program, rather than by relying on the adventitious impact of a tangentially-related policy like federalism.

Given the variations in local government that in fact exist in the United States, concern about the need for a national policy to encourage competition might seem abstract or fanciful. But the universality of local variation only indicates . . . [t]hat we have a national political culture, and no state is likely to take advantage of the normative independence that serves as federalism's raison d'etre to suppress local variation. In addition, however, we should not be overly smug about the level of variation that our nation provides. Most people cannot freely choose a community that values education and provides high quality schools in exchange for higher taxes. There is a rather distressing correspondence between quality education, for example, and high-income communities. True citizen choice might be enhanced through a national policy to encourage the development of realistic options in each section of the country. That would involve decentralization, but it is the very antithesis of federalism.

3. State Competition

A third argument for federalism, closely related to the preceding one, is based on competition among jurisdictions rather than on choice by citizens. The idea is that jurisdictions will compete for productive assets, such as factories, and desirable people, such as chemical engineers, by creating a favorable economic climate. Asset managers and individuals will then choose among jurisdictions, voting with their well-heeled feet in favor of the most efficient states, thus ensuring the efficiency of the nation as a whole. This argument, unlike the argument regarding citizen choice, does apply to states. Firms, unlike individuals, have a relatively simple utility function based on profit maximization. They do not need to consider their preference for a particular climate, size of community or community location, to say nothing of family ties or local loyalty. These factors only affect the individuals within the firm, and they only matter to the firm, as a decision-making entity, to the extent that they affect the firm's single criterion of profitability. As a result, America's fifty-three jurisdictions may be enough to provide the requisite variation for inter-jurisdictional competition. To be sure, the competition argument leaves open an interesting question about the fate of undesirable facilities, like radioactive waste dumps, and of undesirable people—chemical dependents rather than chemical engineers. Nonetheless, a central authority might well choose to decentralize certain aspects of the economy to generate this salutary competition.

Once again, however, the arguments cannot really be viewed as favoring federalism, because federalism allows a multiplicity of norms and not simply a multiplicity of rules. In a truly federal system, some sub-units might not be interested in economic efficiency or social welfare at all; they might be primarily motivated by the desire to preserve an agrarian lifestyle, to protect the environment, or to encourage individual spirituality. These particular sub-units might lose out in the competition for factories and chemical engineers, as the economic analysis predicts. But rather than perceiving their losses as a chastening lesson that induces them to change their laws, they might regard them as a necessary cost or as a positive advantage. Clearly, this would not achieve the single goal that the proponents of efficiency desire. What they really want is a unitary system, devoted to efficiency, which delegates instrumental decisions to decentralized sub-units, but which retains normative control to make sure that every sub-unit is committed to the general goal.

To put the argument more generally, true federalism cannot be regarded as a means of favoring any specific, first-order norm because its essence is to permit a multiplicity of norms. It favors only the second-order norm that no first-order norm should dominate the polity. In practice, a federal regime may turn out to be a means of achieving a specific, first-order norm such as participation, citizen choice, or economic efficiency. This will occur when that norm is so widely shared that every sub-unit will adopt it, even if left to its own normative devices. The United States, despite its federal structure and its self-image as a vast and variegated nation, is in fact a heavily homogenized culture with high levels of normative consensus. It displays less regional variation than Great Britain or Italy, to say nothing of China, India, or the former Soviet Union; the more appropriate comparisons might be Finland or Venezuela. In political structure, the states are now virtually identical. There is one state (Nebraska) with a unicameral legislature, one state (Hawaii) with a unitary finance system, and one state (Minnesota) that refers to the Democratic and Republican Parties by funny names, but that is the limit of the variation. In economic structure, every state has the same general goal of maximizing material welfare, and has chosen the same mixed free enterprise economy for doing so. This is why the Guarantee Clause can be safely declared non-justiciable. If some American state were to establish a monarchy or adopt Communism, national institutions, in particular the United States Marine Corps, would respond quickly, and the Supreme Court would approve that response.

Thus, the Supreme Court and the commentators can argue in favor of federalism when they mean decentralization because the general absence of normative variation in the United States has made the two concepts functionally equivalent. If our federal system in fact provides opportunities for voice, options for exit, or economic efficiency, the reason is that every sub-unit of our federal system shares that goal. But this lack of variation makes federalism vestigial; it is simply decentralization in fancy clothes, and the rights that it grants to each state protect little more than their own continued existence.

4. Experimentation

A final and somewhat different instrumental argument for federalism refers to a technique, not a policy: that federalism gives the states an opportunity to experiment with different programs. Presumably, this is desirable, not because of an abiding national commitment to pure research, but because the variations may ultimately provide information about a number of governmental programs and enable us to choose the best one. To quote Justice Brandeis: "It is one of the happy incidents of the federal system that a single courageous State may, if its citizens choose, serve as a laboratory; and try novel social and economic experiments without risk to the rest of the country."[76] This has a certain ring to it, but on further examination experimentation turns out to be a happy incident of managerial decentralization, not of federalism.

In a unitary system, the central authority will generally have a single goal, but it may be uncertain which of several policies will best achieve that goal. To resolve this uncertainty, it could order different sub-units to experiment with different strategies until the best way to achieve the goal emerges. Experimentation of this sort is an instrumental concept, useful only when the sub-units share a single goal. It is not particularly relevant to sub-units whose goals are different from each other. But true federalism allows governmental

---

76. New State Ice. Co. v. Liebmann, 285 U.S. 262, 311 (1932) (Brandeis, J., dissenting).

sub-units to choose different goals, not to experiment with different mechanisms for achieving a single one.

The experimentation argument for federalism, therefore, is an effort to justify a normative regime by invoking the appeal of an instrumental one. The instinct to do so is understandable in this instrumental age, but the argument for experimentation, like the argument for participation, citizen choice, or competition, supports only managerial decentralization. A unitary manager can experiment with different policies for achieving the same goal, just as it can encourage different sub-units to compete against each other in pursuit of that goal. But these arguments would be inapplicable to federalism if our country consisted of sub-units with truly different goals. Consider, for example, precisely what experiment one would design to tell the French Canadians whether they should retain their language. The experimentation argument, like the competition argument, seems applicable to federalism only when there is no normative disagreement among sub-units so that federalism merges into administrative decentralization. The fact that this is true in the United States today is what gives this argument its surface plausibility.

In fact, even decentralization creates problems for the kind of experimentation that is needed to select policies in a highly regulated administrative state. To experiment with different approaches for achieving a single, agreed-upon goal, one sub-unit must be assigned an option that initially seems less desirable, either because that option requires changes in existing practices, or because it offers lower, although still-significant chances of success. Allowed to choose their own strategies, as they are in a decentralized system, no sub-units would choose these unappealing options; they must be forced or encouraged to do so by the centralized authority. Economic theory underscores this conclusion. Experiments are likely to be public goods; once produced, their products are available to all states regardless of each state's investment. As a result, individual states will have no incentive to invest in experiments that involve any substantive or political risk, but will prefer to wait for other states to generate them; this will, of course, produce relatively few experiments.

The standard solution to this dilemma is either coercion or coordination through some inclusive entity, such as the central government. Assuming that the decentralized states are rational actors who desire to experiment (a heroic assumption, but certainly one that is required for the entire states-as-laboratories argument), they might agree among themselves to share the costs of such experiments. More typically, they might agree to subject themselves to coercive discipline to overcome the free rider problem, just as a patriotic citizenry that supports strong national defense might opt for a military draft and a system of taxation, rather than a volunteer army supported by individual contributions. In either case, the natural consequence of their agreement would be centralization. It is thus hardly surprising, even given the most favorable assumptions about the rationality and conscientiousness of state governments, that most significant "experimental" programs in recent years have in fact been organized and financed by the national government. The effect of federalism, to the extent that it is still operative, has not been to encourage experimental state programs or state-sponsored coordinating agencies, but simply to keep some truly innovative national efforts limited, tentative, and vaguely apologetic.

Finally, even if decentralized states establish a mechanism by which they can coerce themselves to experiment, they will need to collect massive amounts of data if proper choices are to be made; in technical areas particularly, the virtues of a specific policy are unlikely to be self-evident. Decentralized states, acting on their own, will have little incentive to generate this information; they may be motivated to articulate politically palatable justifications for their policies, but they are unlikely to gather data directed to its replication or modification. And if the information is gathered and assimilated, it will not be helpful unless the original policy choices are coordinated by a centralized authority. Even in the absence of normative, truly federalist variations, state-initiated experiments are unlikely to be truly useful to other states because of more specific, technical variations. The tall smokestacks developed by one state may not work under the climatic conditions of another, or may conflict with a policy of installing scrubbing devices that the other state has already instituted. Of course, data and experience developed for one set of conditions can be applied to another, but such applications require information and analysis that no state is likely to undertake on behalf of others. Thus, centralization is not only necessary to initiate the experimental process, but also to implement that process in any reasonably effective fashion.

All of this is implicit in the imagery of scientific experimentation, once that imagery is taken seriously. Experiments generally involve variations among subsets of a total population, but those variations are carefully and minutely prescribed by the researcher — a centralized authority if ever there was one. In medical research, for example, it would be unusual for the researcher to authorize her subjects to follow whatever course of treatment they desire, even if all the subjects agree on the general goal of finding a medical cure. The more common practice is for the researcher to prescribe the treatment for each group. This allows the use of therapies that would not otherwise be chosen, and provides usable data regarding their effects.

II. Federalism and the Diffusion of Power

Concern about the concentration of power was one of the guiding forces in the design of our entire political system. The Founders of our nation, according to the current view, were motivated by their commitment to liberty and defined themselves as revolutionaries because of their opposition to the unchecked authority that Britain exercised over their lives. Federalism can be seen as responding to this basic concern because it insulates certain decisions from the power of the central government. By doing so, the argument goes, power is diffused among different governmental entities; in particular, the central government is disabled from imposing norms upon the states, at least in certain subject areas. The enormous growth of the national government during the course of the last century is thus seen as a threat to liberty, a threat that can be counteracted by the principle of federalism.

This argument can be viewed in either formal or functional terms. The formal version is that the dispersion of power among the states is required by the Tenth Amendment. But the language of the Tenth Amendment is too opaque to support such an interpretation. This conclusion is not based on a general opposition to using the intent of the Framers to determine the meaning of the constitutional text. Intentionalism has been subject to a blistering attack by legal scholars, although it continues to be popular in governmental circles. But even those who believe that the intent of the Framers should control must acknowledge that our ability to discern that intent varies from one clause to another. The Tenth Amendment stands at the bottom of any list of comprehensibility; it employs no recognized language and invokes no established concepts. It was adopted without discussion and thus lacks the legislative history that the main body of the document possesses. . . .

The functional argument regarding the dispersion of power is that it secures liberty by protecting the populace from the unconstrained control of a single governmental actor. . . .

The image that seems to underlie this concept is that there exists some fixed amount of power — administrative power in this case — which can either be concentrated in the central government or spread between the central government and the states. In fact, there is no fixed supply of administrative power such that increases in federal power necessarily cause decreases in state power through a zero sum exchange. Rather, the power of government at all levels has been steadily increasing in our culture for a substantial period of time. One hundred years ago, the workplace was essentially unregulated other than by judicial enforcement of individual contracts. Now, a formidable panoply of labor, health, and safety regulations emanates from both the federal government and the states. Similarly, the government's involvement in environmental matters once consisted essentially of selling off the environment in hundred-acre parcels; now, governments at all levels monitor the quality of air and water, and regulate the emissions of factories which once spewed their fumes into the air with laissez-faire abandon.

One cannot even be certain that this increasing power of government at all levels has necessarily led to a reduction in the power of private entities. The power of human beings in general has increased immeasurably in our modern age. We have changed the physical features of our planet, which for so long, under the designation "nature," were assumed to be predominant and immutable . . . , raising the Earth's temperature, punching photo-chemical holes through its ozone layer, transforming large lakes into porridges of synthetic substances, and covering the landscape with vast networks of asphalt and plastic. To this may be added the less concrete phenomena that Weber noted, whereby control of economic behavior has been transferred from ritual and tradition to self-conscious, bureaucratic enterprises. Thus, there is much more human activity for governments to govern, and it is entirely conceivable that the power of the federal government, of the state governments that complain about its usurpations, and of the private enterprises that complain about them both, are all increasing at a rapid and roughly proportional rate.

But even if we assume that the administrative power of the federal government is growing at the direct expense of states and private enterprises, we cannot conclude that this growth reduces the dispersion of governmental control over the people, and thereby threatens liberty. The crucial question is not the gross aggregation of power, but the way power is exercised in each area of human life. Once we focus on particular areas, it becomes apparent that the growth of the national government often increases the diffusion of administrative power by adding a second decision-maker to the previously comprehensive power of the state. . . .

[F]ederal intervention generally means that two governmental hierarchies will be involved in a particular area of governance instead of one. This is sometimes described as cooperative federalism. . . . Of course, the federal government can preempt state authority in its entirety, but this is not the typical pattern; more often, federal action alters state governance, or simply adds to it. Whether one regards our political system as cooperative, competitive, or simply a mess — whether it resembles marble cake or mush — there is little doubt that state and national powers overlap, and that national policy is regularly implemented by state officials. All the advantages associated with power dispersion can flow from this intervention. The second decision-maker can introduce new standards, subject old ones to debate, increase popular awareness, decrease arbitrary power, restrain corruption and thereby expand liberty — the liberty of individuals from excessive or inappropriate government control.

To be sure, the federal government might take complete control of a particular area, thus transferring exclusive jurisdiction from the state to itself. This would mean that federal intervention neither increased nor decreased the dispersion of power. In our system, however, federal intervention has almost always resulted in increased dispersion, because the expansion of federal power into areas that were previously the exclusive province of the states has generally involved the sharing of power between federal and state officials. Even congressional action follows this pattern; federal courts are still more securely committed to it. Thus, diffusion of power virtually never provides a rationale for courts to stay their hand or to strike down national legislation.

Perhaps it could be argued that the aggregation of federal power across a broad range of governmental areas represents a dangerous concentration of power, even if its effect, in individual areas, is to disperse power among multiple authorities. But this assumes the point at issue — whether federalism has moral force that justifies its invocation as a constraint on governmental action. If one wants to argue this point, rather than asserting it, one must show that federal aggrandizement impinges on some independent value, such as individual liberty. As indicated, however, federal intervention tends to increase liberty in each area of governance, and thus with respect to each group of people. . . .

[C]laims of federalism are often nothing more than strategies to advance substantive positions, or alternatively, . . . people declare themselves federalists when they oppose national policy, and abandon that commitment when they favor it. This is true precisely because the United States has a unitary political consciousness and lacks subsidiary political communities. Disagreements among states, or between the states and the national government, are limited to their own terms, and all alignments shift when the next issue arises. Consequently, there is nothing for federalism to protect, aside from the states' ability to disagree about the particular issue at hand. The term "states" or "federalism" becomes a code word for particular substantive positions, because that is what we really care about. . . .

In essence, therefore, federalism protects nothing but itself; it is a sort of endangered species act for political ideas. That may have a certain charm, a quality that evokes small-town America and its homespun values, although not, one hopes, the languid life of the antebellum plantation, with the wind whispering through the magnolias and the slaves singing happily in the fields. Even at its best, sappy imagery of this sort provides no valid basis for constraining national policy. If "we" — the political community of the United States — decide upon a particular course of action, federalism should not constrain its implementation. . . .

POINTS FOR DISCUSSION

1. In his article, Professor McConnell asks: "[W]hy forego national measures, thought to promote the peace, liberty, and safety of the people, merely because they intrude upon the 'certain extent of power' traditionally reserved to the governments of the individual States?" Carefully identify each point of disagreement between Professor McConnell and Professors Rubin and Feeley regarding this question. How should each point of disagreement be resolved?

2. Professor McConnell argues that a system of federalism encourages greater participation by individuals in matters of governance. Professors Rubin and Feeley respond that a decentralized system is better equipped to achieve this goal, assuming it to be worthy one. These competing claims implicate the principle of "subsidiarity." Consider the following passage by Professor John Finnis:

> '[S]ubsidiarity' . . . affirms that the proper function of association is to help the participants in the association to help themselves or, more precisely, to constitute themselves through the individual initiatives of choosing commitments (including commitments to friendship and other forms of association) and of realizing these commitments through personal inventiveness and effort in projects (many of which will, of course, be co-operative in execution and even communal in purpose). And since in large organizations the process of decision-making is more remote from the initiative of most of those many members who will carry out the decision, the same principle requires that larger associations should not assume functions which can be performed efficiently by small associations.
>
> What is the source of this principle? . . . Human good requires not only that one *receive* and *experience* benefits or desirable states; it requires that one *do* certain things, that one should *act*, with integrity and authenticity; if one can obtain the desirable objects and experiences through one's own action, so much the better. Only in action . . . does one fully participate in human goods. No one can spend all his time, in all his associations, leading and taking initiatives; but one who is never more than a cog in big wheels turned by others is denied participation in one important aspect of human well-being.

JOHN FINNIS, NATURAL LAW AND NATURAL RIGHTS 146-147 (1980). How does the principle of subsidiarity as described by Professor Finnis relate to the concept of federalism? Does the principle of subsidiarity require federalism?

3. Professor McConnell and Professors Rubin and Feeley dispute whether dual federalism effectively promotes certain *values* — many of which, according to Professor McConnell, the Framers designed the Constitution to serve.

Is the question whether dual federalism effectively promotes particular values relevant to how courts should decide constitutional federalism questions? Critically evaluate the following possibilities, which cases that you will read in subsequent chapters suggest:

a. Whether dual federalism effectively promotes certain values is *irrelevant* to judicial decision making because judicial review of federal regulation on federalism grounds should proceed on other grounds, such as text, historical practice, structure, and precedent. See *New York v. United States*, 505 U.S. 144, 157 (1992) ("Our task would be the same even if one could prove that federalism secured no advantages to anyone. It consists not of devising our preferred system of government, but of understanding and applying the framework set forth in the Constitution.").

b. Whether dual federalism effectively promotes certain values is mostly *irrelevant* to judicial decision making because the Constitution generally does not authorize judicial review of federal regulation on federalism grounds. See *Garcia v. San Antonio Metro. Transit Auth.*, 469 U.S. 528, 550 (1985) ("[T]he principal means chosen by the Framers to ensure the role of the States in the federal system lies in the structure of the Federal Government itself.").

c. Whether dual federalism effectively promotes certain values is *relevant* to judicial decision making if those values are ones that the federal structure was originally designed to promote. See *Gregory v. Ashcroft*, 501 U.S. 452, 458 (1991) ("Perhaps the principal benefit of the federalist system is a check on abuses of government power. The constitutionally mandated balance of power between the States and the Federal Government was adopted by the Framers to ensure the protection of our fundamental liberties.") (internal quotation marks and citations omitted).

d. Whether dual federalism effectively promotes certain values is *relevant* to judicial decision making insofar as courts should functionally assess what allocation of power best promotes values that judges determine a government structure *ought* to promote, regardless of whether the Constitution was originally designed to promote them. *Cf. New York v. United States*, 505 U.S. 144, 211 (1992) (Stevens, J., dissenting) ("Nor does the structure of the constitutional order or the values of federalism mandate . . . a formal rule" that Congress may not require state legislatures to enact laws.)

4. Professors Rubin and Feeley contend that "claims of federalism are often nothing more than strategies to advance substantive positions, or alternatively, . . . people declare themselves federalists when they oppose national policy, and abandon that commitment when they favor it." As you read the cases in this book, consider whether this is true. If it is true, why do judges rely on federalism claims in their reasoning rather than on the merits of the policy outcomes that their decisions produce? Should judges provide an honest account of their reasons for decision?

5. How does Professor McConnell's defense of dual federalism relate to Founding-era, antebellum, and Reconstruction accounts of federalism that you read in Chapters 1 and 2?

B. COOPERATIVE FEDERALISM: A DEFENSE AND CRITIQUE

Cooperative federalism envisions the federal government and the states working together to serve national policy ends in ways that account for differing local circumstances:

> It is commonplace to observe that "dual federalism" is dead, replaced by something variously called "cooperative federalism," "intergovernmental relations," or "marble-cake federalism." According to this conventional wisdom, state and local officials do not enforce merely their own laws in their distinct policymaking sphere. Rather, . . . state and local governments also cooperate with the federal government in many policymaking areas, ranging from unemployment insurance to historic preservation. These nonfederal governments help implement federal policy in a variety of ways: by submitting implementation plans to federal agencies, by promulgating regulations, and by bringing administrative actions to enforce federal statutes. Thus, cooperative federalism offers us a vision of independent governments working together to implement federal policy.

Roderick M. Hills, Jr., *The Political Economy of Cooperative Federalism: Why State Autonomy Makes Sense and "Dual Sovereignty" Doesn't*, 96 Mich. L. Rev. 813, 815 (1998) (footnotes omitted).

Judges and scholars typically characterize two kinds of federal regulatory schemes as reflecting cooperative federalism — (1) conditional grants to states and (2) conditional preemption of state law:

> *Conditional grants* are exercises of Congress's spending power. . . . Congress provides funds to the states on the condition that the state spend the funds in accordance with federal priorities. . . . Congress enacts legislation defining the purposes of the grant, establishing the criteria for getting the money, any matching requirements, and so on. . . . Congress may impose various substantive conditions on both the federal grant money and preexisting state funds to ensure the federal grant is spent for specified classes of beneficiaries or specified federal purposes. . . .
>
> Congress can also "hire" the states to carry out federal programs through the use of *conditional preemption.* Under this system, Congress enacts a general regulatory scheme, delegating implementation to the states on the condition that the states submit an acceptable implementation plan to the federal government. . . . So, for example, the national government may enact a statute providing that, unless the state governments submit an acceptable plan for reducing airborne pollutants, the administrator of the Environmental Protection Agency will promulgate and enforce a purely federal plan that will preempt any inconsistent state law.

Id. at 859-860, 866 (emphasis added) (footnotes omitted).

The Supreme Court has recognized the concept of cooperative federalism in several cases. As Professor Robert Glickman has explained:

> [T]he rhetoric of "cooperative federalism" is routinely invoked by the courts in a variety of regulatory and other contexts. During the last thirty years, the Supreme Court has characterized as "cooperative federalism" endeavors such

as educational programs for handicapped children, financial aid for needy families with dependent children, telecommunications facility siting requirements, health insurance, financial security in old age, interstate efforts to fight crime, and . . . environmental law. . . .

In a recent opinion, Justice Breyer identified some of the attributes of a typical cooperative federalism program, regarding it as one that rejects a nationally uniform approach to problem solving in which Congress preempts state authority, and that instead allows state and local authorities to make at least some decisions, subject to minimum federal standards. In an earlier environmental case, the Court described a "program of cooperative federalism" as one "that allows the States, within limits established by federal minimum standards, to enact and administer their own regulatory programs, structured to meet their own particular needs." Similarly, in . . . 1992 . . . the Court used the term "program of cooperative federalism" to describe instances in which, although "Congress has the authority to regulate private activity under the Commerce Clause," it has chosen "to offer States the choice of regulating that activity according to federal standards or having state law pre-empted by federal regulation." In the same opinion, it swept within the rubric of cooperative federalism statutory programs that "anticipat[e] a partnership between the States and the Federal Government, animated by a shared objective" or that employ "any other permissible method of encouraging a State to conform to federal policy choices."

Robert L. Glickman, *From Cooperative to Inoperative Federalism*, 41 Wake Forest L. Rev. 719, 725-727 (2006) (footnotes omitted).

In this section, you will read two accounts of cooperative federalism — one sympathetic and one critical. As you read these accounts, consider these questions:

- How does cooperative federalism relate to dual federalism?
- How should the idea of cooperative federalism inform judicial resolution of constitutional federalism questions?
- To what extent is cooperative federalism, in fact, federalism?

PHILIP J. WEISER, TOWARDS A CONSTITUTIONAL ARCHITECTURE FOR COOPERATIVE FEDERALISM

79 N.C. L. Rev. 663, 665-666, 668-674, 700-701 (2001)

The rhetoric of a "dual federalism" characterizes many of the Supreme Court's recent statements on the constitutional law of federalism. In short, this vision of federal-state relations views each jurisdiction as a separate entity that regulates in its own distinct sphere of authority without coordinating with the other. In reality, however, Congress continues to enact "cooperative federalism" regulatory programs that invite state agencies to implement federal law. In contrast to a dual federalism, cooperative federalism envisions a sharing of regulatory authority between the federal government and the states that allows states to regulate within a framework delineated by federal law. In particular, modern regulatory programs put in place across a variety of fields ranging from nearly all environmental programs to telecommunications regulation to health care . . . all embrace a unified federal structure that includes a role for state implementation. Significantly, these programs neither leave state authority unconstrained within its domain, as would a dual federalism program, nor displace such authority entirely with a unitary federal program, as would a preemptive federalism. Preemptive federalism, like dual federalism, views the federal government and the states as two separate spheres, but instead of leaving room for state regulation, it preempts all state authority and supplants it with a unitary federal regime. By crafting a middle ground solution between the extremes of dual federalism and preemptive federalism, Congress continues to outstrip existing constitutional rhetoric, which envisions a separation that does not exist in practice.

Future debates over federalism will increasingly confront the tension between the constitutional rhetoric and political reality of federalism. . . .

Although there is no precise definition for which regimes fit the cooperative federalism model, the Supreme Court has suggested that this term best describes those instances in which a federal statute provides for state regulation or implementation to achieve federally proscribed policy goals. In such instances, Congress either allows states to regulate in compliance with federal standards or preempts state law with federal regulation. In a variation of this model, such as that adopted in the Medicaid Act, Congress relies on a federal regulatory agency to develop certain standards for the state agencies to follow when implementing the federal statutory scheme that provides federal funding to the states. . . .

The New Deal programs that marked the rise of the modern administrative state called for state implementation of federal programs mostly to distribute federal benefits — such as unemployment insurance and Aid to Families with Dependent Children (AFDC) — as opposed to the implementation of federal economic regulation. Although these programs involved the sharing of funding, as opposed to regulatory authority, they put the concept of a cooperative federalism on the map. The Supreme Court described AFDC, for example, as "a scheme of cooperative federalism . . . [that is] financed largely by the Federal Government, on a matching fund basis, and is administered by the States."[15] Such programs insisted on a certain level of uniformity (i.e., compliance with federal requirements), but also left important discretion with state agencies to implement the programs within federal requirements.

Beginning most notably with the environmental statutes enacted in the late 1960s and early 1970s, the federal government began to rely on state agencies to implement federal regulatory requirements. . . . In the case of the Clean Air Act, for example, the statute provided for certain uniform federal standards, but left the states with considerable flexibility in addressing the statute's objectives. . . .

Contrary to the suggestion of some commentators, the movement in favor of a cooperative federalism regulatory regime does not necessarily entail a "concentration of political powers in the national government."[23] Rather, while recognizing the need for a federal framework, these regimes rely on existing state agencies to administer and implement federal law. In viewing

---

15. King v. Smith, 392 U.S. 309, 316 (1968).
23. Joseph F. Zimmerman, Contemporary American Federalism 1 (1992).

the enactment of such a federal regulatory regime as a power grab, commentators fail to appreciate that the real authority under such regimes often rests with the states which ultimately exercise considerable discretion in making and implementing policy. Thus, even where a federal regime theoretically sets the policy, its reliance on the states to implement the law means that the states will be very influential in practice because they are afforded considerable discretion in translating broad goals into reality. This power is significant in that, by the federal government's own admission, it is almost always unwilling and/or unable to take back the power to implement cooperative federalism programs.

The federal government's increasing willingness to allow states to superintend the implementation of federal law stems from at least two key factors. First, state governments have become increasingly competent in economic regulation and public administration. Second, the New Deal's ideological commitment to centralization began to deteriorate, as Presidents Johnson through Clinton each stressed (albeit for different reasons and with different emphasis) the important role that the states play in our federal system. . . .

[T]he benefits of state implementation of federal law could not simply be accomplished through decentralizing federal authority. . . . [T]he federal government lacks the political and/or fiscal will to incur the tremendous transaction costs necessary to replace state agencies with local field offices. Moreover, such field offices would invariably be less accountable to local interests than a formally elected, autonomous governmental unit. . . .

A central question concerning the role of state agencies in implementing cooperative federalism initiatives is under what circumstances, if any, a cooperative federalism regulatory program can justify state agency implementation of a federal law in a manner not specifically authorized under existing state law. Due to the relatively recent emergence of cooperative federalism regulatory (as opposed to funding) programs, courts and commentators have yet to pay particularly close attention to this issue or to develop a stable constitutional architecture for cooperative federalism.

Ultimately, states must decide whether to endorse cooperative federalism as a regulatory strategy. In particular, state courts will have the final say on whether state charters designed for different historical circumstances — i.e., an era of dual federalism — should be interpreted to facilitate state agency participation in federal regulatory programs. In short, the challenge for states (or federal courts predicting how state courts would act) is to decide how, if at all, to justify state agency action necessary to implement cooperative federalism regulatory programs that lie outside those actions specifically authorized by state law. . . .

[T]he Supreme Court . . . would do well to . . . treat[] federalism as a flexible principle that appreciates the importance of the states as laboratories as well as partners with the federal government in regulating interstate commerce. . . . In so doing, the Court would avoid two extremes, both of which bode poorly for the role of states in the federal scheme: a situation where the federal government must nationalize an area in order to be an effective regulator or one where the states are merely "branch offices" of the federal government. In a world where commerce is increasingly becoming international, thereby providing another important rationale for federal legislative involvement, it is critical that the Court develop a law of federalism that provides a sustainable role for the states. . . .

JOSHUA D. SARNOFF, COOPERATIVE FEDERALISM, THE DELEGATION OF FEDERAL POWER, AND THE CONSTITUTION

39 Ariz. L. Rev. 205, 212-218, 220 (1997)

Congress may enact cooperative federalism statutes for many reasons. Federal legislators elected by state citizens may feel obliged to preserve and protect traditional state regulatory roles because state citizens prefer state regulation. As a result, political obstacles may prevent Congress from raising revenue and from creating, imposing, and maintaining a national regulatory police force even if federal legislators would prefer federal regulation and a federal bureaucracy.

The constitutional structure of political representation further assures that Congress will rely upon state regulation or implementation. The composition and voting rules of the United States Senate allow the representatives of a small minority of the nation's population to block federal legislation. State regulation or implementation thus may be the quid pro quo for federal legislators to enact statutes that preempt state regulatory prerogatives.

Federal legislators also may believe that state regulation or state implementation of federal policies provides better results than the federal equivalents. First, Congress may believe that state regulation or implementation will result in resource savings and economies of scale. State bureaucracies may already exist, allowing Congress to rely upon existing resources and regulatory expertise. Similarly, state agencies may be more familiar with the regulatory problem or more able to coordinate specific regulatory policies with other activities such as zoning and planning.

Second, Congress may believe that state regulation and implementation will result in better and more efficient policies that maximize social welfare. State officials may be better situated than federal bureaucrats to assess local conditions and citizen preferences. State regulation and implementation thus may more efficiently tailor regulatory requirements. . . . States also may experiment with different regulatory approaches, leading to adoption of more efficient and effective policies.

Third, Congress may believe that state regulation and implementation will result in decisionmaking at a level of government that is more accountable to the citizenry. State and local political processes may provide greater opportunities for citizen participation. Cooperative federalism thus fosters democratic participation in governance. It also improves accountability by minimizing federal and state regulation that duplicates regulatory costs and causes confusion over the level of government responsible for policy.

These beliefs, however, are highly questionable as generic or irrebuttable presumptions. First, federal bureaucratic regulation may be more efficient and may result in greater resource savings. The federal government may obtain economies of scale by avoiding the repetitive costs incurred by states in research, standard setting, control-measure selection, implementation, and enforcement. Federal bureaucracies may be more able than states to develop or retain expertise over time. They also may be more able to transfer experience from or to impose more cost-effective regulatory strategies. Economies of scale also may be realized if the "network effects" of conforming to uniform federal regulations are significant.

Second, federal regulation and implementation may be more likely to maximize social welfare than their state equivalents. Absent federal coercion, states may be unwilling to experiment. States also may be less able than the federal government to identify problems or to share information efficiently among jurisdictions. Uniform federal standards also may be efficient if the costs of tailoring requirements to local conditions or to local preferences exceed the benefits. . . .

Third, the federal government may be more accountable to citizens than particular state governments. The federal government is clearly more accountable than state governments to the citizens of other states, who do not vote for state officials.

In sum, Congress often enacts cooperative federalism statutes based on debatable beliefs that state regulation or implementation is more efficient, results in better decisionmaking or renders government more accountable than the federal equivalents. These beliefs are likely to be true, if at all, only on a retail basis. Nevertheless, political factors often dictate wholesale federal legislative reliance on state regulation and implementation. Congress thus enacts and maintains cooperative federalism statutes even when theoretical justification is lacking.

Further, Congress normally specifies the presumptive choice of federal or state regulation without serious consideration of relative institutional competence and delegates to federal agencies the task of performing comparative analyses. The criteria that Congress imposes to delineate intergovernmental relations, moreover, may not match the results of such analyses. . . .

Congress also may enact cooperative federalism statutes to promote constitutional values of federalism. In particular, cooperative federalism may be thought to advance the Constitution's preferences for local governance and for local values. "Devolving" power to states thus furthers values that federal legislators are sworn to uphold.

The Constitution, however, does not contain a preference for local decision-making or for local values. The Framers of the Constitution did not view state regulation or state implementation of policy as necessarily better or more efficient than the federal equivalents. James Madison, the principal architect of American federalism, indicated that "the evils issuing from [state governmental] sources contributed more to . . . the [Constitutional] Convention . . . than . . . the inadequacy of the Confederation. . . ."[66] The Constitution thus gave Congress the power to tax, to spend, and to regulate private conduct. These new powers avoided the need to rely upon states. . . .

Further, states lack inherent moral attributes or needs and thus may possess "rights" only to the extent created or preserved by the Constitution. The Constitution rejected any broad conception of states rights by enacting the

---

66. 5 THE WRITINGS OF JAMES MADISON 27 (G. Hunt ed., 1901) (letter to Thomas Jefferson).

Supremacy Clause and by failing to require that the federal government treat states equally. . . .

The Framers of the Constitution, moreover, contemplated that intergovernmental competition rather than cooperation would best assure good policy. Federalism could secure and protect individual freedom and liberty only if each level of government would help to control the other. Justice Kennedy, who appears to hold the pivotal vote in current federalism cases, clearly understands this point. To be effective, federalism must provide "two distinct and discernible lines of political accountability: one between the citizens and the Federal Government; the second between the citizens and the States."[87] In turn, citizens: (1) must be "loyal" to both levels of government; (2) must not place their primary allegiance in only one of the levels; and (3) must respect both the "universalist" moral principles to which our nation is committed and the "value-pluralism" necessary to respect the integrity of states as political entities.

But federal legislation may preempt state power and thus state values. Citizens routinely, albeit ambivalently, have to choose their primary loyalty. Citizens may pick the issues on which to support federal values or a plurality of values. But they cannot simultaneously support preemptive federal legislation and conflicting state values and regulatory prerogatives.

Judicial, legislative, and academic debates over federalism are thus political battles for the hearts and minds of the citizenry on questions of morality. Sadly, the answers to interjurisdictional moral disputes are not self-evident. . . .

POINTS FOR DISCUSSION

1. How does cooperative federalism relate to dual federalism? How, if at all, are the two paradigms compatible? How, if at all, are they incompatible?

2. Professor Weiser and Professor Sarnoff dispute whether cooperative federalism programs advance certain values. Professor Weiser argues that cooperative federalism programs maintain local policy discretion in regulatory implementation, save administrative resources, and preserve government accountability to local interests. Professor Sarnoff disagrees that, in aggregate, cooperative federalism programs advance any of these values. Should the Supreme Court resolve whether a cooperative federalism program is constitutional on the basis of whether the program in fact advances these values? In recent times, the Supreme Court has considered the constitutionality of conditional spending and other cooperative programs. For example, in *South Dakota v. Dole*, 483 U.S. 203 (1987), which you will read in Chapter 5, the Court considered whether Congress may condition a state's receipt of federal highway funds on its agreement to raise its drinking age to 21. In *Printz v. United States*, 521 U.S. 898 (1997), the Supreme Court addressed whether Congress may *compel* state law enforcement officials to implement a federal regulatory scheme. How, if at all, should the functional value of a federal regulatory program factor in a judicial analysis of whether the program is constitutional?

---

87. United States v. Lopez, 115 S. Ct. 1624, 1638 (1995) (Kennedy, J., concurring).

On what other grounds, if any, should courts resolve such constitutional questions?

3. Professors Rubin and Feeley distinguish federalism from decentralization. In what sense, if any, is cooperative federalism a theory of federalism as they define it? In what sense, if any, is cooperative federalism a theory of decentralization?

C. DYNAMIC FEDERALISM

In recent years, certain scholars have propounded a theory of "dynamic" federalism. Scholars also have referred to this theory as "adaptive," "polyphonic," or "interactive" federalism, among other names. Professors J.B. Ruhl and James Salzman describe dynamic federalism as follows:

> Under Dynamic Federalism, federal and state governments function as alternative centers of power and any matter is presumptively within the authority of both the federal and state governments. The theory is not radical — it does not suggest overhauling the basic federal-state-local structure of governance. Rather, it explicitly calls for overlapping federal and state (and, through states, local) jurisdictions. Scholars of Dynamic Federalism reject the . . . model in which there is a particular allocation of at least primary regulatory authority between the states and the federal government, replacing it with one in which multiple levels of government interact in the regulatory process. . . .
>
> [T]he key point . . . is the theory's overlapping, flexible distribution of authority between federal, state, and local agencies. . . . [W]hile it may appear inefficient to have several agencies whittling away at the same [problem], the built-in redundancy of Dynamic Federalism can provide significant benefits. . . . It allows governance adaptation to transpire more quickly and with less political jockeying than static, exclusive jurisdiction models. . . . Having multiple agencies working within overlapping scales can also promote synergy between the agencies. . . .

J.B. Ruhl & James Salzman, *Climate Change, Dead Zones, and Massive Problems in the Administrative State: A Guide for Whittling Away*, 98 Cal. L. Rev. 59, 103-05 (2010) (internal quotation marks and citations omitted).

Professor Kirsten Engel describes dynamic federalism as "the recognition, and even celebration, of the real-world overlap and dynamic relationship between state and federal authority." Kirsten Engel, *Harnessing the Benefits of Dynamic Federalism in Environmental Law*, 56 Emory L.J. 159, 176 (2006). Dynamic federalism, she argues, encourages more appropriate levels of government to respond to given problems, combines governmental resources to better address social ills, prevents excessive influence of interest groups, and allows for more innovative regulation. *Id.* at 177-179.

The following two excerpts address the idea of dynamic federalism. In the first, Professor Robert Ahdieh describes the reality of intersystemic regulation from which theories of dynamic federalism proceed. In the second, Professor Robert Schapiro propounds a theory of dynamic federalism, with implications for judicial resolution of federalism disputes.

As you read these excerpts, consider the following questions:

- How does dynamic federalism relate to dual and cooperative federalism?
- How should the idea of dynamic federalism inform judicial analyses of constitutional federalism questions?
- To what extent is dynamic federalism, in fact, federalism?

ROBERT B. AHDIEH, DIALECTICAL REGULATION

38 Conn. L. Rev. 863, 863-868, 871-872 (2006)

From the emergence of the New Deal state, through the rise of civil rights and risk regulation in the 1960s and 1970s, to the present day, the mass of public regulation—and the number of regulators charged with its design and implementation—has grown explosively over the 20th century. With this growth has come a concomitant increase in the engagement of regulatory institutions across jurisdictional lines. Independent regulatory authorities—federal and state environmental agencies, U.S. and foreign banking regulators, and tribunals convened under the North American Free Trade Agreement (NAFTA) and Mississippi state law, among other examples—today engage one another in pursuit of their respective mandates. In the face of advances in communication technologies, the increased ease and decreased cost of long-distance travel, and the expanded and extended scope of economic and industrial activity, regulators today face the undeniable reality of a small, small world.

In its most commonly acknowledged—but least controversial—form, such cross-jurisdictional interaction among regulatory entities is purely dialogic. In such cases, regulatory institutions with related missions engage one another to exchange information, share ideas, and otherwise learn from each other. . . .

For the most part, such voluntary patterns of engagement have met little resistance in the study of regulation. Less welcome—if even acknowledged—has been a universe of cross-jurisdictional interactions motivated by jurisdictional "overlap." In these cases, independent public agencies enjoy regulatory authority over the same individuals or institutions, with regard to the same or related issues. . . . [T]he conventional account finds little wisdom—and much to fear—in such overlap.

Even less appreciated, in both senses of the word, have been interactions in which the relevant institutional dynamic produces both jurisdictional overlap *and* a degree of what I will term regulatory "dependence." In these cases, engagement among regulators is even less voluntary in nature than in cases of overlap alone. Rather, in this growing universe of regulatory interactions, each agency's pursuit of its mandate is shaped—in a non-trivial fashion—by the other entity's acts of commission or omission. Each entity is reliant on the other, in one way or another. As a result, there emerges a regulatory regime characterized by increased interaction, of a more recurrent nature, and by a close intermingling of regulatory conflict and cooperation. Ultimately, rather than increased regulatory cooperation supporting each agency's pursuit of its own mission, we may even see something akin to joint, or intertwined, regulation of relevant individuals, institutions, or subject-matter. In such regimes, discrete sets of regulatory rules may collapse into a collective whole. . . .

[S]uch patterns of regulatory engagement, which I characterize as "intersystemic regulation," can be observed across an array of fields. Under the No Child Left Behind Act, federal and state education officials depend on one another's regulatory initiatives, mandates, and funding commitments in pursuit of their own education goals. . . . Perhaps the very best examples of intersystemic regulation can be found in environmental law, where the federal Environmental Protection Agency and state environmental regulators find themselves caught in complex—and expanding—patterns of interdependence.

For the most part, patterns of intersystemic regulatory interaction combining overlap and dependence have not been emphasized in the regulatory literature. Notwithstanding the unavoidable familiarity with such patterns on the ground, theoretical accounts have inadequately grappled with them. Even where acknowledged, such regulatory engagement is commonly disputed in one way or another. The extent of overlap, some would insist, is overstated; lines of jurisdiction are sufficiently clear. Even when overlap is self-evident, the presence of meaningful dependence may be disputed, with challenges to the actual power of one or the other regulatory authority to assert itself. Even when overlap and dependence are undeniable, finally, there is the standard dualist response: In the face of overlap and dependence, our normative task is to more effectively delimit each entity's jurisdiction and authority, and thereby eliminate the relevant overlap and dependence. The dualist paradigm of the federalism literature, with its single-minded commitment to the project of jurisdictional line-drawing, is suggestive in this regard.

Such reactions are hardly surprising. At heart, they reflect some visceral sense of law's project as one of categorization, clear definition, and line-drawing. . . .

Yet such devotion to certainty and clarity—whatever its general utility—has minimized our appreciation, let alone embrace, of selective overlap and dependence in the interaction of regulatory entities across jurisdictional lines. A constrained mental map of potential patterns of regulatory design has caused us to overlook the presence of the divergent patterns described above. . . .

Thus, while theories of regulation abound, a theory of intersystemic regulation is lacking. . . . [A]nalysis of intersystemic regulatory interactions can and should shift from the margins of regulation theory to its center. . . .

Across a variety of subjects—among them some of the most contentious topics in law today— . . . a shift toward greater awareness and appreciation of intersystemic regulation may be invaluable. Minimally, it may enhance our insight into the dynamic at work in these areas; at best, it may suggest alternative approaches to thorny challenges. Ongoing debates over federalism, for example, seem trapped in unnecessarily binary conceptions of the vertical allocation of power. Yet, a third way for the resolution of federalism questions—and one more closely comporting with the realities of day-to-day governance—might well be found in the overlap and dependence of intersystemic and dialectical regulation. . . .

In negotiating the overlap of regulatory authority across jurisdictional lines, the traditional lawyerly task has been one of line-drawing. Practitioners and scholars of law have seen their comparative advantage in the definition of clear bounds between the jurisdiction of independent regulatory authorities. Most commonly, they have done so by denying the existence of overlap; where this proves inadequate, they have sought to define jurisdiction so as to eliminate what overlap might exist. In a shrinking world, however, such responses may be neither viable nor wise.

A more resonant project might therefore be that of the poet. This project lies not in line-drawing, distinguishing, or simplifying. To the contrary, it explores — and even encourages — overlap, interdependence, and attendant complexity. From this distinct regulatory perspective, the goal is not to identify the single regulatory actor best suited or most appropriately charged with responsibility for a given entity or subject matter. Rather, multiple regulators are embraced as having a shared — if both competing and cooperating — place in a more inclusive and all encompassing regulatory regime.

Robert A. Schapiro, Toward a Theory of
Interactive Federalism

---

91 Iowa L. Rev. 243, 248-249, 285-296 (2005)

Defenders of federalism cite several benefits that federalism supposedly promotes, including efficient and responsive governance, participatory self-government, and protection against tyranny. Critics note that federalism actually can impede the realization of these goals and can endanger other values as well. . . .

Scholars have attempted to develop coherent replacements for dualist visions of federalism, but have not succeeded. . . . [T]he concept of cooperative federalism . . . offers a more accurate description of the actual interaction of federal and state governments. The concept of cooperative federalism, however, has generated little normative legal doctrine. The theory emphasizes voluntary interaction; cooperative federalism does not prescribe the resolution of state-federal conflicts. . . .

In the contemporary United States, the core achievements of federalism, I argue, result from the joint operation of state and national authority. The key to understanding the promise of federalism lies in considering state and national power not in isolation, but in interconnection. Dualism thus provides the wrong conceptual framework. By focusing on defining boundaries, rather than exploiting overlap, courts and commentators miss the full potential of contemporary federalism.

The concept of polyphony, I contend, presents a better model for understanding federalism. The states and the federal government represent independent voices of authority. However, it is the dynamic interaction among states and the national government that forms the true sound of federalism. Unlike a purely cooperative model of federalism, a polyphonic conception recognizes an important role for competition among states and between states and the federal government. The relationship of the states and the federal government may indeed be confrontational rather than cooperative. Polyphony accepts a substantial role for dissonance as well as harmony. . . .

In the polyphonic conception, federalism is characterized by the existence of multiple, independent sources of political authority. The scope of this political authority is defined by territory, not by subject matter. No kind of conduct is categorically beyond the boundaries of state or federal jurisdiction. The federal and state governments function as alternative centers of power. In the first instance, any matter is presumptively within the authority of the federal government and of a state government. Full concurrent power is the norm. A polyphonic conception of federalism thus resists the idea of defining enclaves of state power protected from federal intrusion. . . . [P]olyphonic federalism rejects the dualist vestiges of dual federalism. . . .

Whereas dualist federalisms insist on dividing state and federal realms of authority, the key elements of polyphonic federalism are the protection of the institutional integrity of multiple sources of power and the promotion of the dynamic interaction of those centers of authority. Rather than asking whether some activity belongs on the state or federal side of a line, polyphonic federalism asks how the overlapping power of the state and federal governments can best address a particular issue. . . .

The polyphonic conception remains federalist. As in dualist conceptions of federalism, the allocation of authority between the states and the national government has constitutional status. That allocation differs between the polyphonic and dualist approach, but the constitutional recognition of independent state and federal authority remains.

Neither the federal government nor the states can eliminate the independent lawmaking authority of the other. Though its powers are broad, Congress cannot destroy the institutional integrity of states. . . . The continued functioning of the state political apparatus receives constitutional protection. Congress cannot prevent a state legislature from meeting and enacting laws. Congress cannot eliminate the state judiciary and its function of interpreting and enforcing those laws. . . . The federal government would violate constitutional principles of federalism if it assumed control over the state governmental process.

Although the state political process enjoys constitutional protection, the particular outputs of that process do not. From the polyphonic perspective, no state legislation is immunized from the potentially preemptive effects of federal enactments. Congress does not face limits on the subject matter of its authority. In no areas of regulation can the states be assured of supremacy. Congress could enact laws effectively federalizing a domain, preventing state legislation in that realm from having effect. . . .

Given polyphonic federalism's embrace of concurrent state and federal jurisdiction, the management of overlapping state and federal authority constitutes a central concern. . . . [T]he values associated with dualist federalism do not offer much guidance in addressing co-extensive authority. Dualist federalism advances the values of choice, self-governance, and preventing tyranny by dividing state and federal power. Polyphonic federalism focuses on a different set of values. In emphasizing the interconnection of state and federal power, the polyphonic conception supports plurality, dialogue, and redundancy. These gains come at some cost. The intermingling of state and federal authority may impair the goals of uniformity, finality, and hierarchical accountability. . . .

1. Plurality, Dialogue, Redundancy

With the overlap of federal and state power comes the possibility of multiple approaches to a particular problem. State and federal governments operate within different institutional frameworks, which give them varying perspectives. Their different geographical scope also may endow them with divergent strengths and weaknesses. Some solutions may work better when imposed nationally, while others function more efficiently on a local scale. The states and the federal government may attempt differing approaches to addressing issues. For example, many methods exist for trying to ensure environmental protection and workplace safety. The federal government may seek to impose some firm national baselines, while the states may experiment with additional safeguards or alternative implementation schemes. Complex problems can benefit from a variety of approaches.

In addition simply to increasing the opportunities for legal protection, the concurrence of federal and state authority provides a valuable opportunity for dialogue. The states and the federal government can attempt alternative means of preventing employment discrimination or defining the fundamental right to privacy. The different governments can learn from each other. They can sharpen their understanding of how best to define and to implement important governmental safeguards. . . .

Indeed, even if Congress mandates a uniform policy denying effect to state legislation, state action may nevertheless have a valuable role to play in a federalist system. State enactments that conflict with federal law may constitute important symbols of opposition. Even if a state policy cannot become legally binding, the existence of a potential alternative system reminds officials and citizens of the possibility of choosing other solutions. A state law can provide an important protest—a powerful criticism of the federal approach. That kind of officially stated opposition can, in time, help to produce a change in federal policy. That change might take the form of adopting a state alternative, or the federal government might simply allow local variance.

The overlap of federal and state authority produces a related benefit as well. State and federal law may provide alternative forms of relief. To a large extent, redundant protection currently constitutes the norm. . . . The United States Supreme Court, for example, has often stated that the main federal civil rights cause of action under 28 U.S.C. §1983 stands as a supplement, not as a replacement, for state-law remedies. State and federal constitutions both safeguard fundamental rights.

The potential regulatory redundancy constitutes a fail-safe mechanism—an additional source of protection if one or the other government should fail to offer adequate safeguards. . . .

2. Counter-Values: Uniformity, Finality, and Hierarchical Accountability

If two regulatory heads are better than one, it may still be the case that sometimes too many regulatory chefs spoil the broth. Overlap has its costs. Concurrent jurisdiction may threaten significant principles of uniformity, finality, and hierarchical accountability.

Uniformity in law serves as an important value. To the extent that state and federal law both apply, parties may be subject to conflicting duties. Certainly their lives become more complicated. Keeping track of multiple obligations may tax individuals and firms, especially those operating in more than one state. The problem of multijurisdictional transactions is endemic to federalism itself, but a polyphonic regime expands the possibility for federal and state conflict within a single state. Complicated issues of federal preemption may arise.

A related concern is the finality of legal proceedings. Finality constitutes a crucial legal value. A definite and certain resolution of regulatory disputes enables individuals and firms to continue to lead their lives, free from legal uncertainty. Dialogue between state and federal actors represents suspension of finality. . . . If federal and state regulations both apply, federal and state authorities may each seek to enforce the laws in separate, uncoordinated proceedings.

When the United States Supreme Court has sought to justify dividing state and federal realms, it has concentrated less on problems of uniformity and finality and more on potential issues of accountability. . . . Members of the Court have asserted that the failure to protect a realm of state autonomy creates confusion among the citizenry. The overlap of state and federal authority prevents citizens from understanding where ultimate responsibility lies. When citizens object to government policies, should they direct their ire at their state capital or at Washington, D.C.? Justices have asserted that this blurring of lines of accountability becomes particularly acute with regard to areas that traditionally have been subject primarily to state rather than federal regulation, such as family law, education, and crime. . . .

[T]he dualist attempt to draw lines between state and federal authority does not represent an effective means of guaranteeing accountability. A polyphonic account asks how states and the national government might best work together to promote political accountability, consistent with the other values of polyphony.

The challenge for a polyphonic account of federalism is how and when to promote the values of plurality, dialogue, and redundancy without undermining important concerns for uniformity, finality, and hierarchical accountability. That challenge may be difficult, but the polyphonic account at least identifies the proper values for managing the overlap of federal and state power. . . .

3. The Role of Courts

Judicial administrability serves as one of the chief justifications for the Court's attempt to construct a [dualist] categorical approach [to federalism]. One suspects that this concern for judicially applicable rules helps to explain the persistence of dualist notions of federalism in the courts, while cooperative federalism long has been the norm in the administrative relations of the states and the national government. Drawing lines is something that courts can do, and applying categorical distinctions seems well-suited to the judicial role. . . . It may be that active judicial supervision can succeed only with relatively rigid, if not arbitrary, lines. If that analysis is correct, however, it is the active judicial intervention that must cease. The polyphonic conception of federalism rejects drawing lines between state and federal power. Polyphony ends the search for the "truly local" and the "truly national." It substitutes the functional considerations of plurality, dialogue, and redundancy, along with the countervailing concerns for uniformity, finality, and accountability. The substitution of functional for formal criteria entails a diminished role for courts. Legislatures can do a much better job than courts in trying to sort out the relevant considerations. Courts must defer to this legislative calculus. . . .

In the polyphonic conception, courts should apply a background presumption that state power and federal power can coexist. In the absence of evidence to the contrary, courts should not strike down state laws because they operate in the same field as federal law. . . . Courts should not be in the business of eliminating state regulatory plans in the name of creating uniform federal regulatory policy. The existence of multiple overlapping regimes of regulation represents one of the important consequences of federalism. Such concurrence promotes plurality, dialogue, and redundancy. The presumption of concurrence would decrease implied preemption of state laws that stand as an "obstacle" to the achievement of federal purposes. . . .

The presumption of concurrence would leave large areas of preemption . . . doctrine unchanged. Congress could expressly preempt state law. . . . In the absence of congressional guidance, though, the presumption would lead the courts toward a greater acceptance of concurrent state regulation.

The values of polyphonic federalism . . . correspond to deferential review when Congress clearly has decided to regulate an area. In conditions of less certainty, such as preemption . . . , the courts would be more accommodating of state action. State and federal courts also can serve as active participants in realizing the promise of the polyphonic conception, rather than just as referees.

POINTS FOR DISCUSSION

1. Professors David Adelman and Kirsten Engel have described how dual, cooperative, and dynamic federalism theories relate to each other in the following terms:

> [The dynamic federalism] movement began as a response to a dualist model of federalism premised on preserving state sovereignty by delimiting spheres of state authority immune from federal interference. Finding the task as difficult as it is fruitless, early scholars have advocated strong, overlapping state and federal jurisdiction. . . .

Cooperative federalism is at odds with both the classical [dual] and dynamic schools of federalism, although the incongruity is most pronounced with the former. Among advocates of [dual federalism,] cooperative federalism unjustifiably expands the role of the federal government by sanctioning federal intervention irrespective of whether an environmental problem is wholly intrastate. . . . Although states can largely control the regulatory programs delegated to them, most of the costs of the programs are fixed by immutable federal standards. . . . The devolutionist wing of the classical [dual] school is particularly incensed by the "federalizing" of local issues. . . .

A cooperative framework fares somewhat better with the dynamic school. The overlapping authority, although asymmetric, at least has the trappings of a dynamic system. Cooperative federalism nonetheless falls short from the point of view of the dynamic school. The federal laws and regulations are often, but not always, so comprehensive as to exclude for all practical purposes alternative approaches by the states. Viewed from the perspective of either classical or dynamic theory, cooperative federalism entails misconceived compromises that sacrifice either too much efficiency or too much diversity and innovation.

David E. Adelman & Kirsten H. Engel, *Adaptive Federalism: The Case Against Reallocating Environmental Regulatory Authority*, 92 Minn. L. Rev. 1796, 1812-1813 (2008). Critically evaluate this account of how dual, cooperative, and dynamic theories of federalism interrelate.

2. Professor Schapiro argues that dynamic, or polyphonic, federalism has implications for judicial review:

The values of polyphonic federalism . . . correspond to deferential review when Congress clearly has decided to regulate an area. In conditions of less certainty, such as preemption . . . , the courts would be more accommodating of state action. State and federal courts also can serve as active participants in realizing the promise of the polyphonic conception, rather than just as referees.

He derives these implications from values that he contends interactive regulation promotes. How does judicial review, as he envisions it, differ, if at all, from judicial review as envisioned by the Marshall Court—in practice and/or justification?

3. In what sense, if any, is dynamic federalism a theory of federalism, as Professors Rubin and Feeley define that term? In what sense, if any, is it a theory of decentralization?

4. How do dual, cooperative, and dynamic accounts of federalism relate to the Founding-era, antebellum, and Reconstruction accounts of federalism that you read in Chapters 1 and 2?

CHAPTER 4

THE POLITICAL SAFEGUARDS OF FEDERALISM

In *The Federalist No. 45*, James Madison argued that the political process would protect the states from federal overreaching under the Constitution. He claimed that the federal government would be responsive to states because states had equal suffrage in the Senate, set voter qualifications for the House of Representatives, and controlled aspects of the process for electing the President. These features of the federal system — and others — have come to be known as the "political safeguards of federalism." The political safeguards of federalism figure prominently in debates over the place of judicial review in the U.S. federal system.

This chapter describes the political safeguards of federalism, examines how effectively they protect state interests and autonomy, and explores their relationship to judicial review as a safeguard of federalism. The political safeguards warrant independent treatment in this chapter because of the central role they have played in historical and present-day federalism debates.

This chapter first presents the most influential twentieth-century work on the political safeguards of federalism — Herbert Wechsler, *The Political Safeguards of Federalism: The Role of the States in the Composition and Selection of the National Government*, 54 Colum. L. Rev.543 (1954). It then presents critiques of this work. These selections explore, among other things, whether courts should consider the political safeguards of federalism to be the exclusive safeguards of federalism or, rather, whether courts should exercise some form of judicial review of national legislation. Next, this chapter presents two Supreme Court cases that set the stage for judicial debates about the political safeguards and judicial review that you will encounter throughout this book — *National League of Cities v. Usery*, 426 U.S. 833 (1976), and *Garcia v. San Antonio Metropolitan Transit Authority*, 469 U.S. 528 (1985). Having already read important historical and judicial materials that the Justices invoke in these cases, you should be well positioned to critically evaluate the opinions. *Usery* and *Garcia* did not put an end to debates over the political safeguards, and you will revisit these debates in subsequent chapters. This chapter concludes with *U.S. Term Limits, Inc. v. Thornton*, 514 U.S. 779 (1995), in which the Court considered the constitutionality of state-imposed term limits on members of Congress. The Court addressed, in part, how far a state may go in structuring the political process to influence national governance.

As you read the materials in this chapter, consider what aspects of federalism, if any, the political safeguards of federalism in fact protect. Bear in mind the distinction between state *autonomy* and state *interests*. The political process may or may not protect one or the other or both, but they are distinct concepts. State *autonomy* is a state's authority to regulate free from federal control. State autonomy may or may not reflect a state's *interests*. A state may have an interest in maintaining its own regulatory autonomy, but it also may have an interest in national regulation, regardless of its effect on state autonomy. In other words, a state may prefer that the federal government, rather than the states, regulate a certain area.

Moreover, consider the following questions as you read the materials in this chapter:

- How effectively does the political process actually protect state interests or autonomy? Has its effectiveness changed over time?
- What is the relationship between the political process and judicial review as safeguards of federalism? Are political safeguards of federalism exclusive safeguards, or do political safeguards and judicial review both protect state autonomy in the federal system?
- How far may states go in using the political process to safeguard their own interests or autonomy? Does the Constitution limit the ability of states to structure the political process to serve their own interests or autonomy?

A. THE POLITICAL SAFEGUARDS AND JUDICIAL REVIEW

The readings in this section identify and analyze various political safeguards of federalism. Taken together, these articles address three key questions:

- What do the political safeguards of federalism safeguard—state regulatory interests or state autonomy?
- How effectively do the political safeguards protect state interests or autonomy?
- What is the relationship between political and judicial safeguards of federalism?

HERBERT WECHSLER, THE POLITICAL SAFEGUARDS OF FEDERALISM: THE ROLE OF THE STATES IN THE COMPOSITION AND SELECTION OF THE NATIONAL GOVERNMENT

54 Colum. L. Rev. 543 (1954)

I

Our constitution makers established a central government authorized to act directly upon individuals through its own agencies — and thus they formed a nation capable of function and of growth. To serve the ends of federalism they employed three main devices:

> They preserved the states as separate sources of authority and organs of administration—a point on which they hardly had a choice.
>
> They gave the states a role of great importance in the composition and selection of the central government.
>
> They undertook to formulate a distribution of authority between the nation and the states, in terms which gave some scope at least to legal processes for its enforcement.

Scholarship—not only legal scholarship—has given most attention to the last of these enumerated mechanisms, perhaps because it has been fascinated by the Supreme Court and its interpretations of the power distribution clauses of the Constitution. The continuous existence of the states as governmental entities and their strategic role in the selection of the Congress and the President are so immutable a feature of the system that their importance tends to be ignored. Of the Framers' mechanisms, however, they have had and have today the larger influence upon the working balance of our federalism. The actual extent of central intervention in the governance of our affairs is determined far less by the formal power distribution than by the sheer existence of the states and their political power to influence the action of the national authority.

The fact of the continuous existence of the states, with general governmental competence unless excluded by the Constitution or valid Act of Congress, set the mood of our federalism from the start. The first Congress did not face the problem of building a legal system from the ground up; it started with the premise that the standing *corpus juris* of the country was provided by the states. . . .

National action has thus always been regarded as exceptional in our polity, an intrusion to be justified by some necessity, the special rather than the ordinary case. This point of view cuts even deeper than the concept of the central government as one of granted, limited authority, articulated in the Tenth Amendment. National power may be quite unquestioned in a given situation; those who would advocate its exercise must none the less answer the preliminary question why the matter should not be left to the states. Even when Congress acts, its tendency has been to frame enactments on an *ad hoc* basis to accomplish limited objectives, supplanting state-created norms only so far as may be necessary for the purpose. Indeed, with all the centralizing growth throughout the years, federal law is still a largely interstitial product, rarely occupying any field completely, building normally upon legal relationships established by the states. . . . As a state legislature views the common law as something to be left alone unless a need for change has been established, so Congress has traditionally viewed the governance of matters by the states.

The tradition plainly serves the values of our federalism in so far as it maintains a burden of persuasion on those favoring national intervention. New York, for example, faced the need for rent control after the need was deemed to have passed in most parts of the country. Should a national program have been continued when New York and every other state was competent to launch a program of its own, adapted to its special needs? Under such circumstances national action has consequences that are plainly undesirable. On the one hand, it is likely to impose control in areas where the politically dominant local judgment finds control unnecessary. On the other hand, it is likely to attenuate the rigor of control in areas where it is really needed. For if the need is not severe the country over, the terms of national legislation will be shaped by a Congress in which the hostile sentiment has a large influence, rather than by a legislature more generally sensitive to the need. This was, of course, the actual experience with federal control of rent throughout the later post-war years.

The political logic of federalism thus supports placing the burden of persuasion on those urging national action. Though the explanation is the same, it is more difficult to find support for the commonly fragmentary quality of many national enactments, with their resultant ambiguity as to how far they supersede state law entirely and how far they call for integration with it. . . . [T]he existence of the states as governmental entities and as the sources of the standing law is in itself the prime determinant of our working federalism, coloring the nature and the scope of our national legislative processes from their inception.

II

If I have drawn too much significance from the mere fact of the existence of the states, the error surely will be rectified by pointing also to their crucial role in the selection and the composition of the national authority. More is involved here than that aspect of the compromise between the larger and the smaller states that yielded their equality of status in the Senate. Representatives no less than Senators are allotted by the Constitution to the states, although their number varies with state population as determined by the census. Though the House was meant to be the "grand depository of the democratic principle of the government,"[6] as distinguished from the Senate's function as the forum of the states, the people to be represented with due deference to their respective numbers were *the people of the states*. And with the President, as with Congress, the crucial instrument of the selection — whether through electors or, in the event of failure of majority, by the House voting as state units — is again the states. The consequence, of course, is that the states are the strategic yardsticks for the measurement of interest and opinion, the special centers of political activity, the separate geographical determinants of national as well as local politics.

Despite the rise of national parties, the shift to popular election of the Senate and the difficulty of appraising the precise impact of such provisions on the legislative process, Madison's analysis has never lost its thrust:

> The State governments may be regarded as constituent and essential parts of the federal government; whilst the latter is nowise essential to the operation or organization of the former.[7]

---

6. George Mason in the Convention, 5 ELLIOT'S DEBATES 136 (1876).
7. THE FEDERALIST, No. 45 at 288 (Lodge ed., 1888).

> A local spirit will infallibly prevail much more in the members of Congress, than a national spirit will prevail in the legislatures of the particular States.[8]
>
> Even the House of Representatives, though drawn immediately from the people, will be chosen very much under the influence of that class of men, whose influence over the people obtains for themselves an election into the State legislatures.[9]

To the extent that federalist values have real significance they must give rise to local sensitivity to central intervention; to the extent that such a local sensitivity exists, it cannot fail to find reflection in the Congress. Indeed, the problem of the Congress is and always has been to attune itself to national opinion and produce majorities for action called for by the voice of the entire nation. It is remarkable that it should function thus as well as it does, given its intrinsic sensitivity to any insular opinion that is dominant in a substantial number of the states.

III

The point is so clear in the Senate that, as Madison observed of the equality accorded to the states, "it does not call for much discussion." The forty-nine votes that will determine Senate action, even with full voting, could theoretically be drawn from twenty-five states, of which the combined population does not reach twenty-nine millions, a bare 19% of all state residents. The one-third plus one that will defeat a treaty or a resolution of amendment could, equally theoretically, be drawn from seventeen states with a total population little over twelve millions, less than that of New York. I say theoretically since, short of a combination to resist an effort to impair state equality within the Senate (which the Constitution purports to place beyond amendment) or to diminish the political power of the smaller states in other ways, a coalition in these terms is quite unthinkable. The fact remains that in more subtle ways the Senate cannot fail to function as the guardian of state interests as such, when they are real enough to have political support or even to be instrumental in attaining other ends. And if account is taken of the operation of seniority within the Senate, of the opportunity of Senators to marshal individual authority, not to speak of the possibility of filibuster, this power of negation, vested in the states without regard to population, multiplies in many ways. Given a controversy that has any sectional dimension, it is not long before the impact of this power is perceived. . . .

[T]he composition of the Senate is intrinsically calculated to prevent intrusion from the center on subjects that dominant state interests wish preserved for state control.

IV

Even the House is slanted somewhat in the same direction, though the incidence is less severe. This is not due appreciably to the one seat reserved for every state regardless of its population, nor to the mechanics or the

---

8. *Id.*, No. 46 at 294.
9. *Id.*, No. 45 at 288-89.

mathematics of Congressional apportionment, though they present their problems. It is due rather to the states' control of voters' qualifications, on the one hand, and of districting, on the other.

The position with respect to voters' qualifications derives from the constitutional provision that fixes the electorate of Representatives (and of Senators as well since the Seventeenth Amendment) as those persons who "have the qualifications requisite for electors of the most numerous branch of the State Legislature."[16] Subject, then, to the prohibition of the denial of franchise because of color, race or sex, embodied in the Fifteenth and Nineteenth Amendments and the radiations of the equal protection clause of the Fourteenth, the states determine — indirectly it is true — the electorate that chooses Representatives. The consequences of contracting the electorate by such devices as a poll-tax are, of course, incalculable, but they tend to buttress what traditionally dominant state interests conceive to be their special state position; that is the point of the contraction. This sentiment, reflected in the Representatives that these constituencies send to Congress, is not ordinarily conducive to support for an adventurous expansion of the national authority, though there have been exceptions, to be sure. . . .

State control of congressional districting derives from the constitutional provision that "the times, places and manner of holding elections for Senators and Representatives, shall be prescribed in each State by the Legislature thereof."[20] The same clause provides, however, that "Congress may at any time by law make or alter such regulations. . . ." Though the matter has been disputed, it seems plain that state control thus rests entirely on the tolerance of Congress. . . . The district system . . . rests wholly upon state initiative at the present time. More important, the delineation of the districts rests entirely with the states. . . .

V

If Congress, from its composition and the mode of its selection, tends to reflect the "local spirit" predicted by Madison, the prime organ of a compensating "national spirit" is, of course, the President — both as the Chief Executive and as the leader of his party. Without the unifying power of the highest office, derived from the fixed tenure gained by his election and the sense that the President speaks for and represents the full national constituency, it would be difficult to develop the centripetal momentum so essential to the total federal scheme. No modern President can doubt that one of his essential functions is to balance the localism and the separatism of the Congress by presenting programs that reflect the needs of the entire nation, building the best coalitions that he can for their enactment, using the prerogatives and prestige of his office to that end. . . .

Familiar though they are, the constitutional provisions governing our presidential choices should be noted. The electors, in whom the initial choice is vested, are appointed by the states in the manner provided by each state's legislature. Their number reflects the compromise concerning representation

---

16. U.S. CONST. Art. I, §2.
20. *Id.*, Art. I, §4.

in Congress, being determined by the number of Representatives allotted to the state on the apportionment plus the two Senators that each state is assured. A majority of all the votes is necessary for election by electors. If it is not obtained by any candidate, the choice among the three who lead in electoral votes devolves upon the House of Representatives voting not as individuals but by states, with each state granted equal voice and a majority of all required for election.

Had these provisions worked out as the Framers contemplated, with the electors as an independent agency of choice, it is hard to think that there would often have been an electoral majority; the electors would have functioned merely as a nominating body, with selection falling mainly to the House voting under the rule of state equality. It is not comfortable to conjecture how far this result might have reduced the President to a mere agent of the states, exacerbating the intrinsic localism of the Congress, losing the unifying thrust for which the Presidency stands. It is uncomfortable also to reflect that only the rise and success of the two-party system, buttressed by the general ticket method of selecting the electors (under which a state's votes are cast as a unit), prevents that result today. . . .

Federalist considerations . . . play an important part even in the selection of the President, although a lesser part than many of the Framers must have contemplated. A presidential candidacy must be pointed towards the states of largest population in so far as they are doubtful. It must balance this direction by attention to the other elements of the full coalition that is looked to for an electoral majority. Both major parties have a strong incentive to absorb protest movements of such sectional significance that their development in strength would throw elections to the House. Both must give some attention to the organized minorities that may approach balance of power status in important states, without, however, making promises that will outrun the tolerance of other necessary elements of their required strength. Both parties recognize that they must appeal to some total combination of allegiance, choice or interest that will yield sufficient nation-wide support to win elections and make possible effective government.

The most important element of party competition in this framework is the similarity of the appeal that each must make. This is a constant affront to those who seek purity of ideology in politics; it is the clue, however, to the success of our politics in the elimination of extremists — and to the tolerance and basic unity that is essential if our system is to work.

The President must be, as I have said above, the main repository of "national spirit" in the central government. But both the mode of his selection and the future of his party require that he also be responsive to local values that have large support within the states. And since his programs must, in any case, achieve support in Congress — in so far as they involve new action — he must surmount the greater local sensitivity of Congress before anything is done.

VI

If this analysis is correct, the national political process in the United States — and especially the role of the states in the composition and selection of the central government — is intrinsically well adapted to retarding or restraining new intrusions by the center on the domain of the states. Far from a national authority that is expansionist by nature, the inherent tendency in our system is precisely the reverse, necessitating the widest support before intrusive measures of importance can receive significant consideration, reacting readily to opposition grounded in resistance within the states. Nor is this tendency effectively denied by pointing to the size or scope of the existing national establishment. However useful it may be to explore possible contractions in specific areas, such evidence points mainly to the magnitude of unavoidable responsibility under the circumstances of our time.

It is in light of this inherent tendency, reflected most importantly in Congress, that the governmental power distribution clauses of the Constitution gain their largest meaning as an instrument for the protection of the states. Those clauses, as is well known, have served far more to qualify or stop intrusive legislative measures in the Congress than to invalidate enacted legislation in the Supreme Court.

This does not differ from the expectation of the Framers quite as markedly as might be thought. For the containment of the national authority Madison did not emphasize the function of the Court; he pointed to the composition of the Congress and to the political processes. So in his letter to Everett, written in 1830, he summarized the views that he had often stated:

> as a security of the rights and powers of the states in their individual capacities ag[ainst] an undue preponderance of the powers granted to the Government over them in their united capacity, the Constitution has relied on 1. The responsibility of the Senators and Representatives in the Legislature of the U.S. to the Legislatures & peoples of the States. 2. The responsibility of the President to the people of the U. States; & 3. The liability of the Ex. and Judiciary functionaries of the U.S. to impeachment by the Representatives of the people of the States, in one branch of the legislature of the U.S. and trial by the Representatives of the States, in the other branch; the State functionaries, Legislative, Executive & judiciary, being at the same time in their appointment & responsibility, altogether independent of the agency or authority of the U. States.[53]

The prime function envisaged for judicial review — in relation to federalism — was the maintainance of national supremacy against nullification or usurpation by the individual states, the national government having no part in their composition or their councils. This is made clear by the fact that reliance on the courts was substituted, apparently on Jefferson's suggestion, for the earlier proposal to give Congress a veto of state enactments deemed to trespass on the national domain. And . . . it is mainly in the realm of such policing of the states that the Supreme Court has in fact participated in determining the balances of federalism. This is not to say that the Court can decline to measure national enactments by the Constitution when it is called upon to face the question in the course of ordinary litigation; the supremacy clause governs there as well. It is rather to say that the Court is on weakest ground when it opposes its interpretation of the Constitution to that of Congress in the interest of the states, whose representatives control the

---

53. 9 WRITINGS OF JAMES MADISON 383, 395-396 (Hunt ed., 1910).

legislative process and, by hypothesis, have broadly acquiesced in sanctioning the challenged Act of Congress.

Federal intervention as against the states is thus primarily a matter for congressional determination in our system as it stands. . . .

LARRY D. KRAMER, PUTTING THE POLITICS BACK INTO THE POLITICAL SAFEGUARDS OF FEDERALISM

100 Colum. L. Rev. 215 (2000)

I. The Political Safeguards of Federalism Are Dead!

Wechsler's thesis was that "the existence of the states as governmental entities and as the sources of the standing law is in itself the prime determinant of our working federalism, coloring the nature and the scope of our national legislative processes from their inception." The states do not need judicial review to protect them from Congress, and the Supreme Court is, in fact, "on weakest ground when it opposes its interpretation of the Constitution to that of Congress in the interest of the states." Wechsler adduced a number of arguments to support this thesis, arguments that have seldom received a careful reading from the scholars and judges who accept his conclusion.

A. The American Political Tradition

The first and most important device safeguarding state interests, according to Wechsler, is a political "tradition" that imposes "a burden of persuasion on those favoring national intervention." The existence of national power may be unquestioned, but still "those who would advocate its exercise must none the less answer the preliminary question why the matter should not be left to the states." This is purely a product of history, Wechsler says, and of the fact of the states' continuous existence, which "set the mood of our federalism from the start." Because of this "mood," federal law remains "a largely interstitial product," with national action "regarded as exceptional in our polity, an intrusion to be justified by some necessity, the special rather than the ordinary case."

Far be it from me to suggest that Congress no longer hesitates before displacing state law. It unquestionably does. Indeed, by comparison with other developed nations, the most striking fact about government in the United States is how much authority is still exercised at the state and local level. Even apart from the big social welfare programs—administered for the most part by state officials, but under federal guidelines and in ways that make questions of control difficult to sort out—almost all private law (tort, contract, property) is state law, as is most of the law respecting crime, education, voting, domestic relations, commercial transactions, corporations, insurance, health care, trusts and estates, land use, occupational licensing and regulation, and more. The federal government has, to be sure, regulated some aspects of each of these fields. But most governing in America—including almost everything that really matters to people in their daily lives—is still done by state officials.

Yet while the enduring importance of the states is clear, so too is the fact that one cannot explain it by reference to some self-sustaining tradition or ideology that makes federal law the exception and state law the rule. Traditions and ideologies are not self-sustaining. They can develop momentum, sometimes weighty enough to perpetuate themselves long after the conditions that brought them into being have disappeared. But if there is pressure to change, as has been true from the start with respect to the "exceptional" and "interstitial" nature of federal law, they will eventually die—unless, that is, some structural or cultural mechanism exists to replenish their vitality. If we observe that states remain important elements of American government, even if we choose to describe this state of affairs in terms of a "tradition" of relying first on state government, we must ask: what institutions or political devices have produced this outcome? The existence of the tradition Wechsler described is the fact to be explained, and cannot itself provide a source of solace to those concerned about unchecked federal growth.

B. Structural Safeguards

Wechsler plainly understood this concern. "If I have drawn too much significance from the mere fact of the existence of the states," he urged, "the error surely will be rectified by pointing also to their crucial role in the selection and the composition of the national authority." According to Wechsler, the Framers designed the federal government's political departments to give states a say in national politics and to ensure that national lawmakers would be responsive to "local sensitivity to central intervention." "The consequence, . . ." Wechsler concluded, "is that states are the strategic yardsticks for the measurement of interest and opinion, the special centers of political activity, the separate geographical determinants of national as well as local politics."

1. *State Interests Versus State Institutions.* —Note how this last sentence conflates two rather different concerns, only one of which ultimately matters to advocates of federalism: ensuring that national lawmakers are responsive to geographically narrow *interests*, and protecting the governance prerogatives of state and local *institutions*. So far as I am aware, no one defends federalism on the ground that it makes national representatives sensitive to private interests organized along state or local lines. Rather, federalism is meant to preserve the regulatory authority of state and local institutions to legislate policy choices.

This distinction matters enormously. Preferences in Congress are aggregated on a nationwide basis: However sensitive federal legislators may be to state or local interests, if interests in an area represented by a majority of these legislators concur, interests in the rest of the country will be subordinated. The whole point of federalism (or at least the best reason to care about it) is that, because preferences for governmental policy are unevenly distributed among the states and regions of the nation, more people can be satisfied by decentralized decision making. Federalism is a way to capture this advantage, by assuring that federal policymakers leave suitable decisions to be made in the first instance by state politicians in state institutions.

It is, of course, theoretically possible today to accommodate differences in local needs or sensibilities through non-uniform federal legislation or decentralized federal administrative agencies. Partly for this reason, some commentators have urged that federalism is obsolete. But while the argument is not without force, it overlooks important differences between a federal system, in which state and local representatives derive their political authority independently of the central government, and a unitary one, in which the central government delegates authority to subaltern officials. Even if national representatives respond to state and local concerns, they will predictably be less responsive than representatives elected to serve in formally autonomous state or local governments: National representatives will worry about local interests only so far as necessary within a worldview that remains fundamentally nationalistic. It is simply naive to imagine that federal lawmakers will routinely be willing to accommodate the full range of local differences or to permit federal regulators to treat some states completely differently than others. . . .

Federalism must be understood as a means rather than an end: an institutional strategy formulated to assure a greater degree of decentralization than is ever likely to be seen in a unitary system. Hence its advocates' focus on preserving the governance prerogatives of state and local institutions.

2. *The Failure of Structural Safeguards.* — With this distinction between state interests and state institutions in mind, the weakness and/or immateriality of the structural devices Wechsler invokes in support of his thesis becomes clear. Most are mechanisms that (possibly) give state and local interests a greater voice in national politics, but in ways that do not necessarily protect state and local institutions. Wechsler observes, for instance, that representatives in both houses of Congress are allotted by state, which, he says, ensures that the people will be represented as "the people of the states." But while allocating representation on this basis may enhance the power of geographically-defined interests at the federal level, it does so in a way that is likely, if anything, to diminish the institutional role of state government. For if we assume that members of Congress elected on the basis of geography respond to state and local *interests*, does this not, in turn, give them an incentive to reduce or minimize the role of state *government*? Federal politicians will want to earn the support and gratitude of local constituents by providing desired services themselves — through the federal government — rather than giving or sharing credit with state officials. State officials are rivals, not allies, a fact the Framers anticipated and among the reasons they originally made Senators directly beholden to state legislators. . . .

Wechsler turns next to the Senate, which he argues protects state interests through its provisions for equal representation by states. This allocation enables a majority of states, comprising less than a majority of the population, to block legislative action. . . . But while this may be so, just why it counts as protecting states is baffling. To the extent that Senators respond to popular pressure from constituents — a product of the Seventeenth Amendment's elimination of the one feature of the Senate that really might have protected states, the power of state legislators to choose Senators — the equal representation of each state distorts democratic decisionmaking. But however objectionable it may be to permit less than a majority of the people to hijack the legislative process, this in no way means that federal lawmakers will choose not to preempt state law or not to displace the political authority of state institutions.

The same confusion between protecting state interests and protecting state institutions explains why Wechsler's reliance on the Electoral College also will not do as a political safeguard for federalism. The Electoral College was originally proposed in part as an *anti*-state's-rights device by nationalists at the Convention who wanted to keep the selection of a chief magistrate out of the states' hands without, at the same time, making him beholden to Congress. Still, the power of state legislators to pick electors could have given the states considerable leverage over the chief executive had the Electoral College stayed true to its original design. But the emergence of the popular canvass and winner-take-all rule have deprived the College of most of its significance. It still affects presidential campaigns, of course, by forcing candidates to look for votes in enough states to win a majority of the electors. But while this geographical dispersion may have benefits (and costs) when the President sits down to define a national mandate, it does nothing to help state governments fend off preemptive federal legislation.

Wechsler . . . offers the College's tendency to force presidential candidates to worry about constructing a national coalition as evidence that "[f]ederalist considerations . . . play an important part even in the selection of the President." There might be something to this point if by "federalism" we meant the need for national politicians to worry about the whole nation. But insofar as we are concerned with protecting the integrity and authority of state political institutions, it is hard to see that the Electoral College helps or matters much.

The only political safeguards Wechsler identifies that do not suffer from this conflating of state interests and state institutions are those he attaches to the House of Representatives, which he says are "the states' control of voters' qualifications, on the one hand, and of districting, on the other." Inasmuch as these are powers actually exercised by state legislatures, they could theoretically provide a mechanism to protect the states' political authority. In practice, neither power has any impact on federalism.

As Wechsler recognizes, the power to decide who votes for members of Congress can be exercised only indirectly—by limiting the electorate in state elections. Even in theory, then, this power never provided more than the most attenuated control. What little control it may once have afforded—through, say, poll taxes or the exclusion of racial minorities—has been eradicated by five constitutional amendments (Section 2 of the Fourteenth Amendment, as well as the Fifteenth, Nineteenth, Twenty-Fourth, and Twenty-Sixth Amendments), federal voting rights legislation, and the Supreme Court's Equal Protection cases. It is, in fact, impossible to think of anything a state could do to protect itself with this power today that would not be either unlawful or ineffective.

The same thing is true of the states' power to draw congressional districts—a power that exists only at the sufferance of Congress. . . . Districting is always hotly contested, of course, but these are fights among competing local interests in which representing or protecting the states' political institutions in Washington is never an issue. . . . Subsequent federal statutes and Supreme Court decisions have mopped up any lingering significance for federalism that this power might once have had. . . .

III. Federalism American Style

A. The Real "Political Safeguards" of Federalism

The political system of federalism into which the United States stumbled during the first decades has proved to be remarkably durable and effective. For most of our history, the decentralized American party systems completely dominated the scene and protected the states by making national officials politically dependent upon state and local party organizations. These organizations provided the institutional framework for managing politics at every level of government, and, by linking the fortunes of officeholders at different levels, they fostered a mutual dependency that induced federal lawmakers to defer to the desires of state officials and state parties. . . .

Two critical features of American parties, both relatively constant across historical party systems, have shaped the parties' role in federalism. First, American parties are not especially programmatic, which is to say they are more concerned with getting people elected than with getting them elected for any specific purpose. Party platforms are seldom taken seriously, and successful candidates abandon or ignore controversial planks with relative ease. The parties must stand for something, of course, because otherwise they would have no appeal whatsoever for voters. But what they stand for is broad enough and flexible enough to leave room for enormous disagreement, and when ideology conflicts with electoral success, it is usually ideology that yields. Second, American parties are basically non-centralized: confederations of national, state, and local cadres whose most conspicuous features are flabby organization and slack discipline. . . .

This curious combination of characteristics — traits that make American parties unique in the world — has created a political culture in which members of local, state, and national networks are encouraged, indeed expected, to work for the election of candidates at every level. This, in turn, promotes relationships and establishes obligations among officials that cut across governmental planes. The expectation of aid and support exists even in the face of quite serious disagreements about policy, which the party encourages setting aside in the interest of winning. Nor does the obligation to support party candidates end on election day, for staying in power constrains successful candidates to work with their counterparts at other levels. A member of Congress, even a President, will need to help state officials either as a matter of party fellowship or in order to shore up the willingness of state officials to offer support in the future; the same thing is true in reverse. The whole process is one of elaborate, if diffuse, reciprocity: of mutual dependency among party and elected officials at different levels; of one hand washing the other. It is this party-fostered system of mutual dependency that explains the success of American federalism despite the historical absence of judicial protection and the failure of other constitutional devices meant to protect state institutions. . . .

The parties influenced federalism by establishing a framework for politics in which officials at different levels were dependent upon each other to get, and stay, elected. Candidates may need the parties somewhat less than they used to; state parties may be somewhat less powerful than they were formerly;

but there is no doubt that political parties continue to play a crucial role in forging links between officials at the state and federal level. The political dependency of state and federal officials on each other remains among the most notable facts of American government.

Moreover, while the parties' effectiveness in safeguarding state government may have been compromised to some degree by twentieth-century developments, these same developments have yielded new "political" safeguards that assure and in some respects may even strengthen the states' voice in national politics. The New Deal weakened the parties, but it also spawned a bureaucratic structure that plays a prominent supporting role in federalism. We have long recognized how the interdependence of the legislative and administrative processes gives administrators a voice and a role in lawmaking. Because the federal government depends on state administrators to oversee or implement so many of its programs, states have been able to use their position in the administrative system to protect state institutional interests in Congress.

Obviously, the federal government is senior partner in this joint venture, and many scholars have therefore assumed that state and local officials have no real power—that they participate as lowly functionaries subject to unrestricted supervision (or funding withdrawal) from federal superiors. Realistically, however, Congress can neither abandon politically popular programs nor "fire" the states and have federal bureaucrats assume full responsibility for them. The federal government needs the states as much as the reverse, and this mutual dependency guarantees state officials an influential voice in the lawmaking and budgetary processes.

The interlocking nature of both the political parties and the administrative bureaucracy has, in addition, contributed to the development of a broader political culture that in various ways favors the states in national politics. State governments did not sit idly by while organized private interest groups and lobbies proliferated after World War II; they formed associations of their own to lend weight and focus to the states' voice in politics. The influence of this "intergovernmental lobby" is, in fact, widely acknowledged and respected in Washington.

More important, states have remained the primary training ground for federal officials. A very high percentage of employees in all three branches of the federal government began their careers working for states. Many rose to elected positions high in state government before moving to the federal system. Fully half of the members of the House of Representatives, for example, began their careers as state legislators, and men and women recruited and trained at the state level are found throughout the federal bureaucracy. With views shaped by this background and experience, these former state officials remain aware of and sympathetic to the concerns of state institutions—a feeling undoubtedly reinforced by continuing ties to friends and former colleagues still in the state system. This sort of connection, for example, probably accounts for the intergovernmental lobby's record of success.

In measuring the overall effectiveness of these numerous safeguards—political parties, the administrative bureaucracy, the intergovernmental lobby, states as recruiting and training grounds, etc.—it is important to recognize the extent to which they overlap and reinforce one another. Recruitment for state government is accomplished primarily through state and local parties; the men and women thus enlisted make connections and establish friendships with others inside and outside the party administering both state and federal programs. State politicians can earn reputations in the party by doing work for intergovernmental lobbies or favors for congressmen and other federal officials. Ambitious bureaucrats seek advancement through the party as well as within civil service ranks. And so on. Each facet of the system is intertwined with others, creating an intricate web whose tangled threads join to ensure its long-term durability, and in which states remain a powerful locus of political and lawmaking authority.

The Founders envisioned a political system that was, by modern standards (though not by the standards of their own century), exceedingly simple. When it came to federalism, they expected Congress to be kept in check through the direct political agency of the states, using the same techniques that had been successfully employed against Parliament and the Continental Congress. What they got instead was a system reliant on parties to serve as a kind of political circulatory system, connecting and breathing life into the skeletal framework created in the Constitution. Yet as much as this system differed from the one conceived by the men who wrote and ratified the new frame of government, it preserved one crucial property: It protected the states by ensuring their ability to influence national politics. Two centuries of evolution have made the system vastly more complicated still, but this indispensable attribute has endured. The states remain safe within a political system that is fundamentally structured to ensure their long-term political vitality. . . .

American federalism "works" . . . because it is able to channel power up or down, as the people choose. The states do not need an untouchable domain of judicially protected jurisdiction; they need only the capacity to compete effectively for political authority, something the structure of American politics guarantees.

In *The Federalist No. 46*, Madison wrote:

> If therefore, as has been elsewhere remarked, the people should in future become more partial to the federal than to the State governments, the change can only result, from such manifest and irresistible proofs of a better administration, as will overcome all their antecedent propensities. And in that case, the people ought not surely to be precluded from giving most of their confidence where they may discover it to be most due.

And so, too, the opposite case: If the people prefer, they should equally be able to "give their confidence" to their state governments. And so they have, as both history and recent events confirm; for "the people" have changed their mind on this issue from time to time, and the political system has responded—without any help from the courts, though sometimes over their interfering opposition.

B. The Supreme Court's Game of Blind Man's Bluff

So what should the Supreme Court do about federalism? To begin with, in thinking about the Court's proper role, we should avoid the mistake of speaking about "the" doctrine of judicial review, as if there were only one. We seem predisposed to think of judicial review in monolithic terms, as if courts either do or do not exercise review, and as if exercising review always means interpreting the Constitution to strike down any laws that the Justices believe are inconsistent with its provisions. This is a key argument for advocates of judicially enforced federalism, who invariably note that the Court aggressively reviews laws when it comes to separation of powers or individual rights, and say there is no reason to treat federalism as an "exception" subject to "second-class status."

It takes only a moment, however, to realize that there is no single doctrine of judicial review. . . . The Framers of the Constitution expected, and may even have hoped, that judges would be active in reviewing the constitutionality of state legislation without at the same time anticipating a similar role for judges when it came to acts of Congress. The same thing was true in other areas as well: Thomas Jefferson told Madison that he favored a Bill of Rights partly because of "the legal check which it puts into the hands of the judiciary," though Jefferson neither favored judicial review in general nor expected to see it in other areas. Such disparate expectations for what courts should do when it came to different sorts of questions naturally shaped the early practice, which in turn affected subsequent developments. As in every area of doctrine, different traditions and conventions evolved, and independent lines of authority branched and diverged. We need to recognize that there is nothing unusual or exceptional about this fact, which means, however, that the scope of judicial review in areas like separation of powers or individual rights may have little relevance when it comes to assessing the Court's practice in the historically distinct domain of federalism.

The current Supreme Court seems determined to become actively and aggressively involved in setting limits on Congress's power vis-à-vis the states. Thus, in recent decisions on a wide range of issues, the Court has apparently made protecting the states from Congress one of its top priorities, a trend that shows no signs of abating. The question is, why? . . .

The answer undoubtedly turns first on the legal philosophies and ideological predispositions of the Justices — but in this case, we are dealing with philosophies and ideologies fortified by misperceptions about history. . . .

[A] majority of the Justices seem genuinely to believe that the Framers of the Constitution wanted and expected them to protect the states from an overreaching national legislature, that the Court took this responsibility seriously for the first century-and-a-half of its existence, and that the present Court is thus merely resurrecting and restoring a legal duty that it erroneously abandoned in the years after 1937. . . .

Active judicial intervention to protect the states from Congress is consistent with neither the original understanding nor with more than two centuries of practice. It is a posture, a pose, backed by nothing except formal adherence to a fictitious concept of monolithic judicial review that is wholly abstract and that does not square with the original practice, reason, or subsequent experience. . . .

The stakes are high. So far, the Justices have managed to avoid provoking a constitutional crisis by confining their activities to the peripheries of congressional power. But that could change quickly if the Court continues along its present course. With due respect, I think the Justices have little idea what they are doing when they intrude this way—no clear picture how their decisions affect governmental operations beyond the particular statutes they invalidate, no hint whether they have made government better or worse. When the Court strikes down a law, at least when it does so in a high-profile case, it does much more than merely invalidate a particular statute. It sends a pulse into the law-making process that can have pervasive effects on a wide range of legislation, and it creates a rhetorical tool that can be used to great effect by ideologically motivated politicians and legislators. The judges who do this, and those who support their decisions, may think the Court is doing a good thing by reining in Congress. But matters are not so simple, for the effects of judicial intervention can be unpredictable. . . .

One might be willing to tolerate such decisions, for better or worse, were there a clear constitutional mandate demanding judicial intercession. But there is no such mandate, and more than two centuries of successful federalism without the aid of an aggressive judiciary suggests that no such intercession is needed. . . .

The specific limits of federal power envisaged by the Founders in 1789 are gone, and any effort to roll back federal power to what it meant at the Founding would be foolish as well as utterly impractical. Even the harshest critics of New Deal jurisprudence acknowledge that changes in society, culture, and the economy require a different kind of national authority today, both practically and as an interpretive matter. Hence, notwithstanding any purported claims of fidelity to original intent, the limits on Congress proposed by today's advocates of judicially-enforced federalism in fact look nothing like any limits that existed when the Constitution was adopted. The question thus becomes, which process should determine the appropriate revised allocation of authority between the federal government and the states: constitutional politics or judicial edict? Mesmerized by the mantra "our Federal government is one of limited powers," the Justices assume that it necessarily falls on them to define new limits—some limits, any limits, even if those limits bear no resemblance to anything imagined by the Founders or observed in the past. But imposing novel judicially-defined limits just for the sake of having judicially-defined limits is an ill-conceived formalism. In a world of global markets and cultural, economic, and political interdependency, the proper reach of federal power is necessarily fluid, and it may well be that it is best defined through politics. Certainly, as we have seen, this is more consistent with the original design than the Court's new made-up limits-for-the-sake-of-limits. Embracing the hurly-burly of politics while paying attention to how states protect themselves in that domain is a much "truer" interpretation of our Constitution.

Put another way, many theories of federalism make the mistake of assuming an underlying ideal, permanent division of authority between the national government and the states: a substantive allocation that stands apart from and independent of the process by which this division is to be implemented. The judicial review question is thus cast as an inquiry into whether courts or politics is "better" at preserving this predetermined allocation. Most modern theorists are willing to concede that the fixed boundaries of federal power, whatever they may be, leave a large field for legislative discretion, and so would confine the scope of judicial intervention to what they view as relatively extreme and obvious cases. Nevertheless, they insist, there are boundaries out there, boundaries abstractly fixed and permanent.

In fact, the substantive content of any normative theory of federalism can never be other than open-ended and contestable. All we have are a set of broadly-defined powers and a set of very general principles that, in any given context at any given time, can lead reasonable people to reach very different conclusions about the proper limits of federal authority. Hubris may be the greatest peril when it comes to federalism, for it is too easy to assume that one's intuitions about what "obviously" goes too far are indisputable. They never are. A proper normative theory of federalism must necessarily incorporate a procedural component: a judgment about *to whom* arguments over the limits of Congress's powers should be addressed. For the Founders, this was an easy call: such arguments were to be addressed to the people, through politics. And the wisdom of their judgment in this respect has been ratified in practice throughout more than two centuries of American history — leaving as the real puzzle here just why these judges feel compelled to countermand that decision and substitute their own.

SAIKRISHNA B. PRAKASH & JOHN C. YOO, QUESTIONS FOR THE CRITICS OF JUDICIAL REVIEW

72 Geo. Wash. L. Rev. 354 (2003)

[W]e profoundly disagree with Professor Kramer's controversial claims that the Constitution, as originally understood, never authorized judicial review, and that the Founders regarded popular constitutional methods as the *exclusive* means of safeguarding the Constitution. . . .

Perhaps the most serious flaw with Professor Kramer's argument is its surprising failure to consider constitutional text and structure. After all, Professor Kramer makes both historical *and* legal claims. To make the latter type of claim, one must at least attempt to make sense of constitutional text and structure. . . .

Professor Kramer's argument fails to consider the meaning of several important constitutional provisions. First, Article III, section 2, states that the "judicial Power shall extend to all Cases, in Law and Equity, arising under this Constitution." This phrase gives federal courts jurisdiction to hear cases that challenge the constitutionality of governmental actions. Cases involving federal statutes that conflict with the Constitution fall within this grant. In deciding such cases, federal courts have to choose between the Constitution and a federal law, and presumably would choose the written Constitution — especially because nothing in the Constitution instructs a federal court to treat federal statutes on par with the Constitution. Nonetheless, Professor Kramer fails to interpret this provision at all. . . .

There is no textual exception to the "arising under" jurisdiction that would allow suits challenging the constitutionality of state law, but not federal law. Nor are federal courts ever directed either automatically to uphold the constitutionality of federal law, or to ignore arguments on the constitutionality of a federal law. . . . In enacting the Judiciary Act of 1789, the first Congress certainly did not read the language in this manner when it confirmed that the Supreme Court enjoyed the authority to affirm or reverse state court decisions that had found a federal statute to be unconstitutional. After all, if the Supreme Court was to affirm a state decision striking down a federal law, it would first have to interpret and enforce the Constitution.

Second, Kramer's argument against judicial review implicitly (but necessarily) relies upon an unsatisfying reading of the Supremacy Clause. The Supremacy Clause provides that:

> This Constitution, and the Laws of the United States which shall be made in Pursuance thereof; and all Treaties made, or which shall be made, under the Authority of the United States, shall be the supreme Law of the Land; and the Judges in every State shall be bound thereby, any Thing in the Constitution or Laws of any State to the Contrary notwithstanding.

By limiting supreme-law status to those federal statutes "made in Pursuance" of the Constitution, the Supremacy Clause establishes that the Constitution is superior to unconstitutional federal statutes. The Clause also vests a limited power of judicial review in state judges. When there is a conflict between the supreme law and state constitutions or laws, state judges are to enforce the supreme federal law. . . .

The Clause, by making only those federal statutes "made in Pursuance" of the Constitution part of the Supreme Law of the Land, indicates that not all federal statutes are Supreme Law. Judging which federal statutes comprise part of the Supreme Law of the Land (and are thus entitled to trump contrary state law) necessarily requires judicial review of the constitutionality of federal statutes. Hence, if state judges are to enforce the Supreme Law of the Land, they must occasionally determine the constitutionality of federal statutes, if only to determine which of these federal statutes must be allowed to trump state law. . . .

Professor Kramer's problems with the constitutional text are compounded by his failure to account for the constitutional structure. As Chief Justice Marshall suggested in *Marbury v. Madison*, the structure of the federal government itself dictates the existence of judicial review. Judicial review arises from two fundamental constitutional principles: the limited authority of the federal government under a written Constitution, and the coordinate status of the judiciary within the separation of powers. In other words, constitutional structure requires the federal courts to refuse to enforce unconstitutional laws in the course of performing their function of deciding Article III cases or controversies. . . .

The contrary view — that the Constitution forbids judicial review — would disregard these basic constitutional principles. First, the anti-judicial review position would undermine the limited nature of the Constitution by removing one of the checks on the powers of the other branches. The Founders were concerned that the legislature would become the judge of its own powers, which they believed would lead Congress to exercise unwarranted and potentially unlimited powers. This is not to say that the political process does not operate to protect federalism; we agree with Professor[] Wechsler . . . that the composition of the Senate and the structure of the elections for the House of

Representatives and the president favor state interests. But, nowhere does the constitutional text and structure compel the conclusion that the political safeguards of federalism are the *exclusive* protections for federalism. By embedding protections for federalism in the structure of the political process and by establishing judicial review, the Founders simply created a double safeguard to protect against an overweening central government.

Second, the anti-judicial review position singles out federalism for disfavored treatment, when there is no justification for such a result in the constitutional text or structure. Professor[] Kramer . . . , for example, believe[s] that judicial review must exist to protect individual rights but not federalism. Nothing in the constitutional text, however, establishes that judicial review extends to some parts of the Constitution but not to others. In fact, given Professor Kramer's claim that the Framers did not originally understand judicial review to even exist, it seems utterly contradictory to then claim, as he does, that judicial review should continue as a means of protecting individual rights. If judicial review is conceded to exist, then it must exist over federalism questions as well as individual rights — there is no textual exception for federalism questions. Indeed, for the first few years of the Republic there was no bill of rights, and hence judicial review must have extended primarily to questions about the limits of the powers of the federal government.

Third, the arguments of Professor Kramer and others single out the judiciary as the one branch (indeed, the one entity) that cannot interpret and enforce the higher law of the Constitution. No one disputes that the president may veto bills that he believes to be unconstitutional, nor does anyone argue that Congress cannot reject bills it believes to be unconstitutional. . . . Yet, under his anti-judicial review thesis, federal judges are burdened with a unique disability, compelled to enforce unconstitutional laws when their colleagues in the coordinate branches are not. It is far from obvious why it is acceptable for the executive to second-guess the legislature (when deciding to veto a bill or enforce a statute) and thus act as an *"interloper,"* but impermissible for judges to play the same role. In both situations, one agent of the people checks another. Nothing in the constitutional text or structure mandates such a perverse, asymmetrical allocation of power. Indeed, such an allocation would damage the separation of powers by undermining the independence of the judiciary and its ability to resist the encroachments of the other branches. . . .

If we are to believe Professor Kramer, we must conclude that quite a few of the best lawyers and most prominent statesmen of the Founding era were absolutely wrong when they read the Constitution as authorizing judicial review of federal statutes. And we must believe that the opposite view — that the Constitution did not authorize judicial review — was the more conventional view even though no one apparently voiced it. In other words, Kramer's arguments suggest the existence of a silent majority of Founders who, though confronted with numerous claims that the Constitution authorized judicial review, apparently never uttered a peep in dissent. Needless to say, we think all of this is rather unlikely. . . .

We have no quarrel with the notion that the people were the ultimate check on unconstitutional governmental action. Instead, our disagreement stems from Professor Kramer's attempt to transform the final safeguard into the only safeguard. Professor Kramer refuses to acknowledge that the discussions of popular constitutionalism as a constitutional safeguard do not compel the conclusion that all other forms of constitutional enforcement were excluded. . . .

POINTS FOR DISCUSSION

1. At various points in his article, Professor Wechsler describes the political safeguards of federalism as protecting state *interests*. Professor Kramer, on the other hand, argues that federalism is about protecting state *institutions* or *autonomy*. He further argues that the political safeguards Professor Wechsler identifies are ill-suited for protecting state autonomy. Does Professor Kramer identify the appropriate concern: whether the political safeguards of federalism protect state autonomy?

2. As you read in Chapter 1, James Madison argued that state control over the election of federal officials would protect states from federal overreaching. As Professor Kramer observes, however, constitutional amendments and adjudication have diluted the strength of such controls. Do the state controls that Madison identifies — and Wechsler more fully explores — safeguard federalism in any meaningful way today? Are the political safeguards of federalism that Professor Kramer identifies any better suited to protect state autonomy (in contrast to state interests) than those Professor Wechsler considers?

3. The excerpts in this section debate whether courts should review federal legislation for compliance with constitutional limitations on federal power. Professor Wechsler does not categorically reject judicial review as a safeguard of federalism, but he argues that "the Court is on weakest ground when it opposes its interpretation of the Constitution to that of Congress in the interests of the States, whose representatives control the legislative process and, by hypothesis, have broadly acquiesced in sanctioning the challenged Act of Congress." Professor Kramer, on the other hand, categorically rejects judicial review as a safeguard of federalism: "*Active judicial intervention to protect the states from Congress is consistent with neither the original understanding nor with more than two centuries of practice.*" Professors Prakash and Yoo disagree with Professor Kramer, arguing that constitutional text and structure demonstrate that judicial review was meant to complement the political process in protecting state autonomy from federal intrusion. How should this disagreement be resolved? In considering this question, be mindful of the evaluative methodology you are employing. To what extent are you drawing upon constitutional text, structure, and historical practice? Are you considering the relative functional effectiveness of political and judicial safeguards? Why are you using the evaluative criteria that you are using?

B. THE *USERY* AND *GARCIA* DEBATE

The questions explored in the last section are not merely academic. They arose in two cases before the Supreme Court in the 1970s and 1980s — *National League of Cities v. Usery*, 426 U.S. 833 (1976), and *Garcia v. San Antonio*

Metropolitan Transit Authority, 469 U.S. 528 (1985). As you read these cases, continue to keep in mind these questions:

- What do the political safeguards of federalism safeguard — state regulatory interests or autonomy?
- How effectively do the political safeguards protect state interests or autonomy?
- What is the relationship between political and judicial safeguards of federalism?

In *Usery* and *Garcia*, the Justices took positions on certain of these questions. Having read some of the historical and judicial writings that the Justices invoke, you should critically evaluate their analyses. You also should note how the Justices weigh constitutional text, structure, historical practice, and the functional efficacy of political and judicial safeguards of federalism in their opinions. *Usery* and *Garcia* did not end debates about the relationship between political and judicial safeguards of federalism, which you will explore throughout this book.

NATIONAL LEAGUE OF CITIES v. USERY

426 U.S. 833 (1976)

Mr. JUSTICE REHNQUIST delivered the opinion of the Court.

Nearly 40 years ago Congress enacted the Fair Labor Standards Act, and required employers covered by the Act to pay their employees a minimum hourly wage . . . and to pay them at one and one-half times their regular rate of pay for hours worked in excess of 40 during a workweek. . . . This Court unanimously upheld the Act as a valid exercise of congressional authority under the commerce power in *United States v. Darby*, 312 U.S. 100 (1941). . . .

The original Fair Labor Standards Act passed in 1938 specifically excluded the States and their political subdivisions from its coverage. In 1974, however, Congress . . . extended the minimum wage and maximum hour provisions to almost all public employees employed by the States and by their various political subdivisions. Appellants in these cases include individual cities and States, the National League of Cities, and the National Governors' Conference; . . . [t]hey assert[] in effect that when Congress sought to apply the Fair Labor Standards Act provisions virtually across the board to employees of state and municipal governments it "infringed a constitutional prohibition" running in favor of the States *as States*. . . .

It is established beyond peradventure that the Commerce Clause of Art. I of the Constitution is a grant of plenary authority to Congress. That authority is, in the words of Mr. Chief Justice Marshall in *Gibbons v. Ogden*, 9 Wheat. 1 (1824), "the power to regulate; that is, to prescribe the rule by which commerce is to be governed." *Id.*, at 196.

When considering the validity of asserted applications of this power to wholly private activity, the Court has made it clear that:

"[e]ven activity that is purely intrastate in character may be regulated by Congress, where the activity, combined with like conduct by others similarly situated, affects commerce among the States or with foreign nations." *Fry v. United States*, 421 U.S. 542, 547 (1975).

Congressional power over areas of private endeavor, even when its exercise may pre-empt express state-law determinations contrary to the result which has commended itself to the collective wisdom of Congress, has been held to be limited only by the requirement that "the means chosen by (Congress) must be reasonably adapted to the end permitted by the Constitution." *Heart of Atlanta Motel v. United States*, 379 U.S. 241, 262 (1964). . . .

Congressional enactments which may be fully within the grant of legislative authority contained in the Commerce Clause may nonetheless be invalid because found to offend against the right to trial by jury contained in the Sixth Amendment or the Due Process Clause of the Fifth Amendment. Appellants' essential contention is that the 1974 amendments to the Act, while undoubtedly within the scope of the Commerce Clause, encounter a similar constitutional barrier because they are to be applied directly to the States and subdivisions of States as employers. . . .

This Court has never doubted that there are limits upon the power of Congress to override state sovereignty, even when exercising its otherwise plenary powers to tax or to regulate commerce which are conferred by Art. I of the Constitution. . . . It is one thing to recognize the authority of Congress to enact laws regulating individual businesses necessarily subject to the dual sovereignty of the government of the Nation and of the State in which they reside. It is quite another to uphold a similar exercise of congressional authority directed, not to private citizens, but to the States as States. We have repeatedly recognized that there are attributes of sovereignty attaching to every state government which may not be impaired by Congress, not because Congress may lack an affirmative grant of legislative authority to reach the matter, but because the Constitution prohibits it from exercising the authority in that manner. . . .

One undoubted attribute of state sovereignty is the States' power to determine the wages which shall be paid to those whom they employ in order to carry out their governmental functions, what hours those persons will work, and what compensation will be provided where these employees may be called upon to work overtime. The question we must resolve here, then, is whether these determinations are "functions essential to separate and independent existence," . . . *Lane County v. Oregon, supra*, 7 Wall. at 76, so that Congress may not abrogate the States' otherwise plenary authority to make them.

In their complaint appellants advanced estimates of substantial costs which will be imposed upon them by the 1974 amendments.

Judged solely in terms of increased costs in dollars, these allegations show a significant impact on the functioning of the governmental bodies involved. . . .

Increased costs are not, of course, the only adverse effects which compliance with the Act will visit upon state and local governments, and in turn upon the citizens who depend upon those governments. In its complaint in intervention, for example, California asserted that it could not comply with the overtime costs (approximately $750,000 per year) which the Act required to be paid to California Highway Patrol cadets during their academy training program. California reported that it had thus been forced to reduce its academy training program from 2,080 hours to only 960 hours, a compromise undoubtedly of substantial importance to those whose safety and welfare may depend upon the preparedness of the California Highway Patrol. . . .

Quite apart from the substantial costs imposed upon the States and their political subdivisions, the Act displaces state policies regarding the manner in which they will structure delivery of those governmental services which their citizens require. The Act, speaking directly to the States *qua States*, requires that they shall pay all but an extremely limited minority of their employees the minimum wage rates currently chosen by Congress. It may well be that as a matter of economic policy it would be desirable that States, just as private employers, comply with these minimum wage requirements. But it cannot be gainsaid that the federal requirement directly supplants the considered policy choices of the States' elected officials and administrators as to how they wish to structure pay scales in state employment. The State might wish to employ persons with little or no training, or those who wish to work on a casual basis, or those who for some other reason do not possess minimum employment requirements, and pay them less than the federally prescribed minimum wage. It may wish to offer part-time or summer employment to teenagers at a figure less than the minimum wage, and if unable to do so may decline to offer such employment at all. But the Act would forbid such choices by the States. The only "discretion" left to them under the Act is either to attempt to increase their revenue to meet the additional financial burden imposed upon them by paying congressionally prescribed wages to their existing complement of employees, or to reduce that complement to a number which can be paid the federal minimum wage without increasing revenue. . . .

This dilemma presented by the minimum wage restrictions may seem not immediately different from that faced by private employers, who have long been covered by the Act and who must find ways to increase their gross income if they are to pay higher wages while maintaining current earnings. The difference, however, is that a State is not merely a factor in the "shifting economic arrangements" of the private sector of the economy, *Kovacs v. Cooper*, 336 U.S. 77, 95 (1949) (Frankfurt, J., concurring), but is itself a coordinate element in the system established by the Framers for governing our Federal Union. . . .

Our examination of the effect of the 1974 amendments, as sought to be extended to the States and their political subdivisions, satisfies us that both the minimum wage and the maximum hour provisions will impermissibly interfere with the integral governmental functions of these bodies. . . . [T]heir application will . . . significantly alter or displace the States' abilities to structure employer-employee relationships in such areas as fire prevention, police protection, sanitation, public health, and parks and recreation. . . . [I]t is functions such as these which governments are created to provide, services such as these which the States have traditionally afforded their citizens. If Congress may withdraw from the States the authority to make those fundamental employment decisions upon which their systems for performance of these functions must rest, we think there would be little left of the States' "separate and independent existence." . . . We hold that insofar as the challenged amendments operate to directly displace the States' freedom to structure integral operations in areas of traditional governmental functions, they are not within the authority granted Congress by Art. I, §8, cl. 3. . . .

Mr. Justice Blackmun, concurring.

In my view, the result with respect to the statute under challenge here is necessarily correct. I may misinterpret the Court's opinion, but it seems to me that it adopts a balancing approach, and does not outlaw federal power in areas such as environmental protection, where the federal interest is demonstrably greater and where state facility compliance with imposed federal standards would be essential. . . .

Mr. Justice Brennan, with whom Mr. Justice White and Mr. Justice Marshall join, dissenting.

[One hundred and fifty-two] years ago Mr. Chief Justice Marshall enunciated that principle to which, until today, his successors on this Court have been faithful.

> "[T]he power over commerce . . . is vested in Congress as absolutely as it would be in a single government, having in its constitution the same restrictions on the exercise of the power as are found in the constitution of the United States. *The wisdom and the discretion of Congress, their identity with the people, and the influence which their constituents possess at elections, are . . . the sole restraints on which they have relied, to secure them from its abuse. They are the restraints on which the people must often rely solely, in all representative governments."* *Gibbons v. Ogden*, 9 Wheat. 1, 197 (1824). . . .

My Brethren do not successfully obscure today's patent usurpation of the role reserved for the political process by their purported discovery in the Constitution of a restraint derived from sovereignty of the States on Congress' exercise of the commerce power. Mr. Chief Justice Marshall recognized that limitations "prescribed in the constitution," *Gibbons v. Ogden, supra*, at 196, restrain Congress' exercise of the power. . . . Thus laws within the commerce power may not infringe individual liberties protected by the First Amendment, . . . or the Sixth Amendment. . . . But there is no restraint based on state sovereignty requiring or permitting judicial enforcement anywhere expressed in the Constitution; our decisions over the last century and a half have explicitly rejected the existence of any such restraint on the commerce power. . . .

The reliance of my Brethren upon the Tenth Amendment as "an express declaration of [a state sovereignty] limitation" . . . must astound scholars of the Constitution. . . . [E]arly decisions, *Gibbons v. Ogden*, 9 Wheat., at 196; *McCulloch v. Maryland, supra*, 4 Wheat. [316,] 404-407 [(1819)]; and *Martin v. Hunter's Lessee*, 1 Wheat. 304, 324-325 (1816), hold that nothing in the Tenth Amendment constitutes a limitation on congressional exercise of powers delegated by the Constitution to Congress. . . . [Moreover], as the Tenth Amendment's significance was more recently summarized:

> "The amendment states but a truism that all is retained which has not been surrendered. *There is nothing in the history of its adoption to suggest that it was more*

than declaratory of the relationship between the national and state governments as it had been established by the Constitution before the amendment or that its purpose was other than to allay fears that the new national government might seek to exercise powers not granted, and that the states might not be able to exercise fully their reserved powers. . . .

"From the beginning and for many years the amendment has been construed as not depriving the national government of authority to resort to all means for the exercise of a granted power which are appropriate and plainly adapted to the permitted end." *United States v. Darby*, 312 U.S. [100,] 124 [(1941)] (emphasis added). . . .

[D]evoid of meaningful content is my Brethren's argument that the 1974 amendments "displac[e] State policies." The amendments neither impose policy objectives on the States nor deny the States complete freedom to fix their own objectives. My Brethren boldly assert that the decision as to wages and hours is an "undoubted attribute of state sovereignty," and then never say why. . . .

Certainly the paradigm of sovereign action — action *qua State* — is in the enactment and enforcement of state laws. Is it possible that my Brethren are signaling abandonment of the heretofore unchallenged principle that Congress "can, if it chooses, entirely displace the States to the full extent of the far-reaching Commerce Clause"? *Bethlehem Steel Co. v. New York State Board*, 330 U.S. 767, 780 (1947) (opinion of Frankfurter, J.). Indeed, that principle sometimes invalidates state laws regulating subject matter of national importance even when Congress has been silent. *Gibbons v. Ogden*, 9 Wheat. 1 (1824). . . . In either case the ouster of state laws obviously curtails or prohibits the States' prerogatives to make policy choices respecting subjects clearly of greater significance to the "State *qua State*" than the minimum wage paid to state employees. The Supremacy Clause dictates this result under "the federal system of government embodied in the Constitution."

My Brethren do more than turn aside longstanding constitutional jurisprudence that emphatically rejects today's conclusion. More alarming is the startling restructuring of our federal system, and the role they create therein for the federal judiciary. This Court is simply not at liberty to erect a mirror of its own conception of a desirable governmental structure. . . .

It is unacceptable that the judicial process should be thought superior to the political process in this area. Under the Constitution the Judiciary has no role to play beyond finding that Congress has not made an unreasonable legislative judgment respecting what is "commerce." . . .

Judicial restraint in this area merely recognizes that the political branches of our Government are structured to protect the interests of the States, as well as the Nation as a whole, and that the States are fully able to protect their own interests in the premises. Congress is constituted of representatives in both the Senate and House *elected from the States*. *The Federalist No. 45*, pp. 311-312 (J. Cooke ed. 1961) (J. Madison); *The Federalist No. 46*, pp. 317-318 (J. Cooke ed. 1961) (J. Madison). Decisions upon the extent of federal intervention under the Commerce Clause into the affairs of the States are in that sense decisions of the States themselves. Judicial redistribution of powers granted the National Government by the terms of the Constitution violates the fundamental tenet of our federalism that the extent of federal intervention into the States' affairs in the exercise of delegated powers shall be determined by the States' exercise of political power through their representatives in Congress. See Wechsler, The Political Safeguards of Federalism: The Role of the States in the Composition and Selection of the National Government, 54 Col[um]. L. Rev. 543 (1954). . . .

We are left then with a catastrophic judicial body blow at Congress' power under the Commerce Clause. Even if Congress may nevertheless accomplish its objectives — for example, by conditioning grants of federal funds upon compliance with federal minimum wage and overtime standards, ... there is an ominous portent of disruption of our constitutional structure implicit in today's mischievous decision.

Mr. Justice Stevens, dissenting.

[I]t is unwise for the Federal Government to exercise its power in the ways described in the Court's opinion. . . . My disagreement with the wisdom of this legislation may not, of course, affect my judgment with respect to its validity. On this issue there is no dissent from the proposition that the Federal Government's power over the labor market is adequate to embrace these employees. Since I am unable to identify a limitation on that federal power that would not also invalidate federal regulation of state activities that I consider unquestionably permissible, I am persuaded that this statute is valid. . . .

Garcia v. San Antonio Metropolitan Transit Authority

469 U.S. 528 (1985)

Justice Blackmun delivered the opinion of the Court.

We revisit in these cases an issue raised in *National League of Cities v. Usery*, 426 U.S. 833 (1976). In that litigation, this Court, by a sharply divided vote, ruled that the Commerce Clause does not empower Congress to enforce the minimum-wage and overtime provisions of the Fair Labor Standards Act (FLSA) against the States "in areas of traditional governmental functions." *Id.*, at 852. Although *National League of Cities* supplied some examples of "traditional governmental functions," it did not offer a general explanation of how a "traditional" function is to be distinguished from a "nontraditional" one. Since then, federal and state courts have struggled with the task, thus imposed, of identifying a traditional function for purposes of state immunity under the Commerce Clause.

In the present cases, a Federal District Court concluded that municipal ownership and operation of a mass-transit system is a traditional governmental function and thus, under *National League of Cities*, is exempt from the obligations imposed by the FLSA. . . .

Our examination of this "function" standard applied in these and other cases over the last eight years now persuades us that the attempt to draw the boundaries of state regulatory immunity in terms of "traditional governmental function" is not only unworkable but is also inconsistent with established principles of federalism and, indeed, with those very federalism principles on which *National League of Cities* purported to rest. That case, accordingly, is overruled. . . .

I

[The] San Antonio Metropolitan Transit Authority (SAMTA) . . . is the major provider of transportation in the San Antonio metropolitan area. . . . The present controversy concerns the extent to which SAMTA may be subjected to the minimum-wage and overtime requirements of the FLSA. . . .

II

[I]t long has been settled that Congress' authority under the Commerce Clause extends to intrastate economic activities that affect interstate commerce. . . . Were SAMTA a privately owned and operated enterprise, it could not credibly argue that Congress exceeded the bounds of its Commerce Clause powers in prescribing minimum wages and overtime rates for SAMTA's employees. Any constitutional exemption from the requirements of the FLSA therefore must rest on SAMTA's status as a governmental entity. . . .

[U]nder *National League of Cities* . . . , four conditions must be satisfied before a state activity may be deemed immune from a particular federal regulation under the Commerce Clause. First, it is said that the federal statute at issue must regulate "the 'States as States.' " Second, the statute must "address matters that are indisputably 'attribute[s] of state sovereignty.' " Third, state compliance with the federal obligation must "directly impair [the States'] ability 'to structure integral operations in areas of traditional governmental functions.' " Finally, the relation of state and federal interests must not be such that "the nature of the federal interest . . . justifies state submission." [*Hodel v. Virginia Surface Mining & Recl. Assn.*, 452 U.S. 264, 287-288, and n. 29 (1981) (quoting *National League of Cities*, 426 U.S., at 845, 852, 854).] . . .

The controversy in the present cases has focused on the third . . . requirement — that the challenged federal statute trench on "traditional governmental functions." The District Court voiced a common concern: "Despite the abundance of adjectives, identifying which particular state functions are immune remains difficult." Just how troublesome the task has been is revealed by the results reached in other federal cases. Thus, courts have held that regulating ambulance services, licensing automobile drivers, operating a municipal airport, performing solid waste disposal, and operating a highway authority are functions protected under *National League of Cities*. At the same time, courts have held that issuance of industrial development bonds, regulation of intrastate natural gas sales, regulation of traffic on public roads, regulation of air transportation, operation of a telephone system, leasing and sale of natural gas, operation of a mental health facility, and provision of in-house domestic services for the aged and handicapped are *not* entitled to immunity. We find it difficult, if not impossible, to identify an organizing principle that places each of the cases in the first group on one side of a line and each of the cases in the second group on the other side. The constitutional distinction between licensing drivers and regulating traffic, for example, or between operating a highway authority and operating a mental health facility, is elusive at best. . . .

We believe, however, that there is a more fundamental problem at work here. . . . Any rule of state immunity that looks to the "traditional," "integral," or "necessary" nature of governmental functions inevitably invites an unelected federal judiciary to make decisions about which state policies it favors and which ones it dislikes.

We . . . now reject, as unsound in principle and unworkable in practice, a rule of state immunity from federal regulation that turns on a judicial appraisal of whether a particular governmental function is "integral" or "traditional." Any such rule leads to inconsistent results at the same time that it disserves principles of democratic self-governance, and it breeds inconsistency precisely because it is divorced from those principles. If there are to be limits on the Federal Government's power to interfere with state functions — as undoubtedly there are — we must look elsewhere to find them. We accordingly return to the underlying issue that confronted this Court in *National League of Cities* — the manner in which the Constitution insulates States from the reach of Congress' power under the Commerce Clause.

III

The central theme of *National League of Cities* was that the States occupy a special position in our constitutional system and that the scope of Congress' authority under the Commerce Clause must reflect that position. Of course, the Commerce Clause by its specific language does not provide any special limitation on Congress' actions with respect to the States. See *EEOC v. Wyoming*, 460 U.S. 226, 248 (1983) (concurring opinion). It is equally true, however, that the text of the Constitution provides the beginning rather than the final answer to every inquiry into questions of federalism, for "[b]ehind the words of the constitutional provisions are postulates which limit and control." *Monaco v. Mississippi*, 292 U.S. 313, 322 (1934). *National League of Cities* reflected the general conviction that the Constitution precludes "the National Government [from] devour[ing] the essentials of state sovereignty." *Maryland v. Wirtz*, 392 U.S. [183,] 205 [(1968)] (dissenting opinion). In order to be faithful to the underlying federal premises of the Constitution, courts must look for the "postulates which limit and control." . . .

We doubt that courts ultimately can identify principled constitutional limitations on the scope of Congress' Commerce Clause powers over the States merely by relying on *a priori* definitions of state sovereignty. In part, this is because of the elusiveness of objective criteria for "fundamental" elements of state sovereignty, a problem we have witnessed in the search for "traditional governmental functions." There is, however, a more fundamental reason: the sovereignty of the States is limited by the Constitution itself. A variety of sovereign powers, for example, are withdrawn from the States by Article I, §10. Section 8 of the same Article works an equally sharp contraction of state sovereignty by authorizing Congress to exercise a wide range of legislative powers and (in conjunction with the Supremacy Clause of Article VI) to displace contrary state legislation. By providing for final review of questions of federal law in this Court, Article III curtails the sovereign power of the States' judiciaries to make authoritative determinations of law. See *Martin v. Hunter's*

Lessee, 1 Wheat. 304 (1816). Finally, the developed application, through the Fourteenth Amendment, of the greater part of the Bill of Rights to the States limits the sovereign authority that States otherwise would possess to legislate with respect to their citizens and to conduct their own affairs.

The States unquestionably do "retai[n] a significant measure of sovereign authority." *EEOC v. Wyoming*, 460 U.S., at 269 (Powell, J., dissenting). They do so, however, only to the extent that the Constitution has not divested them of their original powers and transferred those powers to the Federal Government. In the words of James Madison to the Members of the First Congress: "Interference with the power of the States was no constitutional criterion of the power of Congress. If the power was not given, Congress could not exercise it; if given, they might exercise it, although it should interfere with the laws, or even the Constitution of the States." 2 Annals of Cong. 1897 (1791). Justice Field made the same point in the course of his defense of state autonomy in his dissenting opinion in *Baltimore & Ohio R. Co. v. Baugh*, 149 U.S. 368, 401 (1893), a defense quoted with approval in *Erie R. Co. v. Tompkins*, 304 U.S. 64, 78-79 (1938):

> "[T]he Constitution of the United States . . . recognizes and preserves the autonomy and independence of the States—independence in their legislative and independence in their judicial departments. [Federal] [s]upervision over either the legislative or the judicial action of the States is in no case permissible except as to matters by the Constitution specifically authorized or delegated to the United States. Any interference with either, except as thus permitted, is an invasion of the authority of the State and, to that extent, a denial of its independence."

As a result, to say that the Constitution assumes the continued role of the States is to say little about the nature of that role. Only recently, this Court recognized that the purpose of the constitutional immunity recognized in *National League of Cities* is not to preserve "a sacred province of state autonomy." *EEOC v. Wyoming*, 460 U.S., at 236. With rare exceptions, like the guarantee, in Article IV, §3, of state territorial integrity, the Constitution does not carve out express elements of state sovereignty that Congress may not employ its delegated powers to displace. James Wilson reminded the Pennsylvania ratifying convention in 1787: "It is true, indeed, sir, although it presupposes the existence of state governments, yet this Constitution does not suppose them to be the sole power to be respected." 2 Debates in the Several State Conventions on the Adoption of the Federal Constitution 439 (J. Elliot 2d ed. 1876) (Elliot). The power of the Federal Government is a "power to be respected" as well, and the fact that the States remain sovereign as to all powers not vested in Congress or denied them by the Constitution offers no guidance about where the frontier between state and federal power lies. In short, we have no license to employ freestanding conceptions of state sovereignty when measuring congressional authority under the Commerce Clause.

When we look for the States' "residuary and inviolable sovereignty," The Federalist No. 39, p. 285 (B. Wright ed. 1961) (J. Madison), in the shape of the constitutional scheme rather than in predetermined notions of sovereign power, a different measure of state sovereignty emerges. Apart from the limitation on federal authority inherent in the delegated nature of Congress' Article I powers, the principal means chosen by the Framers to ensure the role of the States in the federal system lies in the structure of the Federal Government itself. It is no novelty to observe that the composition of the Federal Government was designed in large part to protect the States from overreaching by Congress. The Framers thus gave the States a role in the selection both of the Executive and the Legislative Branches of the Federal Government. The States were vested with indirect influence over the House of Representatives and the Presidency by their control of electoral qualifications and their role in Presidential elections. U.S. Const., Art. I, §2, and Art. II, §1. They were given more direct influence in the Senate, where each State received equal representation and each Senator was to be selected by the legislature of his State. Art. I, §3. The significance attached to the States' equal representation in the Senate is underscored by the prohibition of any constitutional amendment divesting a State of equal representation without the State's consent. Art. V.

The extent to which the structure of the Federal Government itself was relied on to insulate the interests of the States is evident in the views of the Framers. James Madison explained that the Federal Government "will partake sufficiently of the spirit [of the States], to be disinclined to invade the rights of the individual States, or the prerogatives of their governments." The Federalist No. 46, p. 332 (B. Wright ed. 1961). Similarly, James Wilson observed that "it was a favorite object in the Convention" to provide for the security of the States against federal encroachment and that the structure of the Federal Government itself served that end. 2 Elliot, at 438-439. Madison placed particular reliance on the equal representation of the States in the Senate, which he saw as "at once a constitutional recognition of the portion of sovereignty remaining in the individual States, and an instrument for preserving that residuary sovereignty." The Federalist No. 62, p. 408 (B. Wright ed. 1961). He further noted that "the residuary sovereignty of the States [is] implied *and secured* by that principle of representation in one branch of the [federal] legislature" (emphasis added). The Federalist No. 43, p. 315 (B. Wright ed. 1961). *See also McCulloch v. Maryland*, 4 Wheat. 316, 435 (1819). In short, the Framers chose to rely on a federal system in which special restraints on federal power over the States inhered principally in the workings of the National Government itself, rather than in discrete limitations on the objects of federal authority. State sovereign interests, then, are more properly protected by procedural safeguards inherent in the structure of the federal system than by judicially created limitations on federal power. . . .

We realize that changes in the structure of the Federal Government have taken place since 1789, not the least of which has been the substitution of popular election of Senators by the adoption of the Seventeenth Amendment in 1913, and that these changes may work to alter the influence of the States in the federal political process. Nonetheless, against this background, we are convinced that the fundamental limitation that the constitutional scheme imposes on the Commerce Clause to protect the "States as States" is one of process rather than one of result. Any substantive restraint on the exercise of Commerce Clause powers must find its justification in the procedural nature of this basic limitation, and it must be tailored to compensate for possible failings in the national political process rather than to dictate a "sacred province of state autonomy." *EEOC v. Wyoming*, 460 U.S., at 236.

Insofar as the present cases are concerned, then, we need go no further than to state that we perceive nothing in the overtime and minimum-wage requirements of the FLSA, as applied to SAMTA, that is destructive of state sovereignty or violative of any constitutional provision. SAMTA faces nothing more than the same minimum-wage and overtime obligations that hundreds of thousands of other employers, public as well as private, have to meet. . . .

JUSTICE POWELL, with whom THE CHIEF JUSTICE, JUSTICE REHNQUIST, and JUSTICE O'CONNOR join, dissenting. . . .

I

A unique feature of the United States is the *federal* system of government guaranteed by the Constitution and implicit in the very name of our country. Despite some genuflecting in the Court's opinion to the concept of federalism, today's decision effectively reduces the Tenth Amendment to meaningless rhetoric when Congress acts pursuant to the Commerce Clause. . . .

To leave no doubt about its intention, the Court renounces its decision in *National League of Cities* because it "inevitably invites an unelected federal judiciary to make decisions about which state policies it favors and which ones it dislikes." In other words, the extent to which the States may exercise their authority, when Congress purports to act under the Commerce Clause, henceforth is to be determined from time to time by political decisions made by members of the Federal Government, decisions the Court says will not be subject to judicial review. I note that it does not seem to have occurred to the Court that *it*—an unelected majority of five Justices—today rejects almost 200 years of the understanding of the constitutional status of federalism. In doing so, there is only a single passing reference to the Tenth Amendment. Nor is so much as a dictum of any court cited in support of the view that the role of the States in the federal system may depend upon the grace of elected federal officials, rather than on the Constitution as interpreted by this Court. . . .

II

. . .

A

Much of the Court's opinion is devoted to arguing that it is difficult to define *a priori* "traditional governmental functions." *National League of Cities* neither engaged in, nor required, such a task. The Court discusses and condemns as standards "traditional governmental functions," "purely historical" functions, "'uniquely' governmental functions," and "'necessary' governmental services." But nowhere does it mention that *National League of Cities* adopted a familiar type of balancing test for determining whether Commerce Clause enactments transgress constitutional limitations imposed by the federal nature of our system of government. . . .

B

Today's opinion does not explain how the States' role in the electoral process guarantees that particular exercises of the Commerce Clause power will not infringe on residual state sovereignty. Members of Congress are elected from the various States, but once in office they are Members of the Federal Government. Although the States participate in the Electoral College, this is hardly a reason to view the President as a representative of the States' interest against federal encroachment. We noted recently "[t]he hydraulic pressure inherent within each of the separate Branches to exceed the outer limits of its power. . . ." *INS v. Chadha*, 462 U.S. 919, 951 (1983). The Court offers no reason to think that this pressure will not operate when Congress seeks to invoke its powers under the Commerce Clause, notwithstanding the electoral role of the States. . . .

More troubling than the logical infirmities in the Court's reasoning is the result of its holding, *i.e.*, that federal political officials, invoking the Commerce Clause, are the sole judges of the limits of their own power. This result is inconsistent with the fundamental principles of our constitutional system. See, *e.g.*, The Federalist No. 78 (Hamilton). At least since *Marbury v. Madison*, 1 Cranch 137, 177 (1803), it has been the settled province of the federal judiciary "to say what the law is" with respect to the constitutionality of Acts of Congress. In rejecting the role of the judiciary in protecting the States from federal overreaching, the Court's opinion offers no explanation for ignoring the teaching of the most famous case in our history.

III

A

In our federal system, the States have a major role that cannot be pre-empted by the National Government. As contemporaneous writings and the debates at the ratifying conventions make clear, the States' ratification of the Constitution was predicated on this understanding of federalism. Indeed, the Tenth Amendment was adopted specifically to ensure that the important role promised the States by the proponents of the Constitution was realized.

Much of the initial opposition to the Constitution was rooted in the fear that the National Government would be too powerful and eventually would eliminate the States as viable political entities. This concern was voiced repeatedly until proponents of the Constitution made assurances that a Bill of Rights, including a provision explicitly reserving powers in the States, would be among the first business of the new Congress. . . .

Antifederalists raised these concerns in almost every state ratifying convention. See generally 1-4 Debates in the Several State Conventions on the Adoption of the Federal Constitution (J. Elliot 2d. ed. 1876). As a result, eight States voted for the Constitution only after proposing amendments to be adopted after ratification. All eight of these included among their recommendations some version of what later became the Tenth Amendment. *Ibid.* So strong was the concern that the proposed Constitution was seriously defective without a specific bill of rights, including a provision reserving powers to the States, that in order to secure the votes for ratification, the Federalists eventually conceded that such provisions were necessary. See 1 B. Schwartz, The Bill of Rights: A Documentary History 505 and *passim* (1971). It was thus generally agreed that consideration of a bill of rights would be among the first business of the new Congress. See generally 1 Annals of Cong. 432-437 (1789) (remarks of James Madison). Accordingly, the 10 Amendments that we know as the Bill of Rights were proposed and adopted early in the first session of the First Congress. 2 Schwartz, The Bill of Rights, *supra*, at 983-1167.

This history, which the Court simply ignores, documents the integral role of the Tenth Amendment in our constitutional theory. It exposes as well, I believe, the fundamental character of the Court's error today. Far from being "unsound in principle," judicial enforcement of the Tenth Amendment is essential to maintaining the federal system so carefully designed by the Framers and adopted in the Constitution.

B

The Framers had definite ideas about the nature of the Constitution's division of authority between the Federal and State Governments. In The Federalist No. 39, for example, Madison explained this division by drawing a series of contrasts between the attributes of a "national" government and those of the government to be established by the Constitution. While a national form of government would possess an "indefinite supremacy over all persons and things," the form of government contemplated by the Constitution instead consisted of "local or municipal authorities [which] form distinct and independent portions of the supremacy, no more subject within their respective spheres to the general authority, than the general authority is subject to them, within its own sphere." *Id.*, at 256 (J. Cooke ed. 1961). Under the Constitution, the sphere of the proposed government extended to jurisdiction of "certain enumerated objects only, . . . leav[ing] to the several States a residuary and inviolable sovereignty over all other objects." *Ibid.*

Madison elaborated on the content of these separate spheres of sovereignty in The Federalist No. 45:

> "The powers delegated by the proposed Constitution to the Federal Government, are few and defined. Those which are to remain in the State Governments are numerous and indefinite. The former will be exercised principally on external objects, as war, peace, negociation, and foreign commerce. . . . The powers reserved to the several States will extend to all the objects, which, in the ordinary course of affairs, concern the lives, liberties and properties of the people; and the internal order, improvement, and prosperity of the State." *Id.*, at 313 (J. Cooke ed. 1961).

Madison considered that the operations of the Federal Government would be "most extensive and important in times of war and danger; those of the State Governments in times of peace and security." *Ibid.* As a result of this division of powers, the state governments generally would be more important than the Federal Government. *Ibid.*

The Framers believed that the separate sphere of sovereignty reserved to the States would ensure that the States would serve as an effective "counterpoise" to the power of the Federal Government. The States would serve this essential role because they would attract and retain the loyalty of their citizens. The roots of such loyalty, the Founders thought, were found in the objects peculiar to state government. For example, Hamilton argued that the States "regulat[e] all those personal interests and familiar concerns to which the sensibility of individuals is more immediately awake . . . ." The Federalist No. 17, p. 107 (J. Cooke ed. 1961). Thus, he maintained that the people would perceive the States as "the immediate and visible guardian of life and property," a fact which "contributes more than any other circumstance to impressing upon the minds of the people affection, esteem and reverence towards the government." *Ibid.* Madison took the same position, explaining that "the people will be more familiarly and minutely conversant" with the business of state governments, and "with the members of these, will a greater proportion of the people have the ties of personal acquaintance and friendship, and of family and party attachments. . . ." The Federalist No. 46, p. 316 (J. Cooke ed. 1961). Like Hamilton, Madison saw the States' involvement in the everyday concerns of the people as the source of their citizens' loyalty. *Ibid.*

Thus, the harm to the States that results from federal overreaching under the Commerce Clause is not simply a matter of dollars and cents. *National League of Cities*, 426 U.S., at 846-851. Nor is it a matter of the wisdom or folly of certain policy choices. Rather, by usurping functions traditionally performed by the States, federal overreaching under the Commerce Clause undermines the constitutionally mandated balance of power between the States and the Federal Government, a balance designed to protect our fundamental liberties.

C

The emasculation of the powers of the States that can result from the Court's decision is predicated on the Commerce Clause as a power "delegated to the United States" by the Constitution. The relevant language states: "Congress shall have power . . . To regulate Commerce with foreign Nations, and among the several States, and with the Indian Tribes." Art. I, §8, cl. 3. Section eight identifies a score of powers, listing the authority to lay taxes, borrow money on the credit of the United States, pay its debts, and provide for the common defense and the general welfare *before* its brief reference to "Commerce." It is clear from the debates leading up to the adoption of the Constitution that the commerce to be regulated was that which the States themselves lacked the practical capability to regulate. Indeed, the language of the Clause itself focuses on activities that only a National Government could regulate: commerce with foreign nations and Indian tribes and "*among*" the several States.

To be sure, this Court has construed the Commerce Clause to accommodate unanticipated changes over the past two centuries. As these changes have occurred, the Court has had to decide whether the Federal Government has exceeded its authority by regulating activities beyond the capability of a single State to regulate or beyond legitimate federal interests that outweighed the authority and interests of the States. In so doing, however, the Court properly has been mindful of the essential role of the States in our federal system.

The opinion for the Court in *National League of Cities* was faithful to history in its understanding of federalism. The Court observed that "our federal system of government imposes definite limits upon the authority of Congress to regulate the activities of States as States by means of the commerce power." 426 U.S., at 842. The Tenth Amendment was invoked to prevent Congress from exercising its "power in a fashion that impairs the States' integrity or their ability to function effectively in a federal system." *Id.*, at 842-843. . . .

D

In contrast, the Court today propounds a view of federalism that pays only lipservice to the role of the States. Although it says that the States "unquestionably do 'retai[n] a significant measure of sovereign authority,'" it fails to recognize the broad, yet specific areas of sovereignty that the Framers intended the States to retain. Indeed, the Court barely acknowledges that the Tenth Amendment exists. That Amendment states explicitly that "[t]he powers not delegated to the United States . . . are reserved to the States." The Court recasts this language to say that the States retain their sovereign powers "only to the extent that the Constitution has not divested them of their original powers and transferred those powers to the Federal Government." This rephrasing is not a distinction without a difference; rather, it reflects the Court's unprecedented view that Congress is free under the Commerce Clause to assume a State's traditional sovereign power, and to do so without judicial review of its action. Indeed, the Court's view of federalism appears to relegate the States to precisely the trivial role that opponents of the Constitution feared they would occupy.

In *National League of Cities*, we spoke of fire prevention, police protection, sanitation, and public health as "typical of [the services] performed by state and local governments in discharging their dual functions of administering the public law and furnishing public services." 426 U.S., at 851. Not only are these activities remote from any normal concept of interstate commerce, they are also activities that epitomize the concerns of local, democratic self-government. In emphasizing the need to protect traditional governmental functions, we identified the kinds of activities engaged in by state and local governments that affect the everyday lives of citizens. These are services that people are in a position to understand and evaluate, and in a democracy, have the right to oversee.[18] . . . [T]he States and local governments are better able than the National Government to perform them. 426 U.S., at 851.

The Court maintains that the standard approved in *National League of Cities* "disserves principles of democratic self-governance." In reaching this conclusion, the Court looks myopically only to persons elected to positions in the Federal Government. It disregards entirely the far more effective role of democratic self-government at the state and local levels. One must compare

---

18. . . . Moreover, we have witnessed in recent years the rise of numerous special interest groups that engage in sophisticated lobbying, and make substantial campaign contributions to some Members of Congress. These groups are thought to have significant influence in the shaping and enactment of certain types of legislation. Contrary to the Court's view, a "political process" that functions in this way is unlikely to safeguard the sovereign rights of States and localities.

realistically the operation of the state and local governments with that of the Federal Government. Federal legislation is drafted primarily by the staffs of the congressional committees. In view of the hundreds of bills introduced at each session of Congress and the complexity of many of them, it is virtually impossible for even the most conscientious legislators to be truly familiar with many of the statutes enacted. Federal departments and agencies customarily are authorized to write regulations. Often these are more important than the text of the statutes. As is true of the original legislation, these are drafted largely by staff personnel. The administration and enforcement of federal laws and regulations necessarily are largely in the hands of staff and civil service employees. These employees may have little or no knowledge of the States and localities that will be affected by the statutes and regulations for which they are responsible. In any case, they hardly are as accessible and responsive as those who occupy analogous positions in state and local governments.

In drawing this contrast, I imply no criticism of these federal employees or the officials who are ultimately in charge. The great majority are conscientious and faithful to their duties. My point is simply that members of the immense federal bureaucracy are not elected, know less about the services traditionally rendered by States and localities, and are inevitably less responsive to recipients of such services, than are state legislatures, city councils, boards of supervisors, and state and local commissions, boards, and agencies. It is at these state and local levels — not in Washington as the Court so mistakenly thinks — that "democratic self-government" is best exemplified.

IV

. . . In overruling *National League of Cities*, today's opinion apparently authorizes federal control, under the auspices of the Commerce Clause, over the terms and conditions of employment of all state and local employees. Thus, for purposes of federal regulation, the Court rejects the distinction between public and private employers that had been drawn carefully in *National League of Cities*. The Court's action reflects a serious misunderstanding, if not an outright rejection, of the history of our country and the intention of the Framers of the Constitution.

I return now to the balancing test approved in *National League of Cities*. . . . The Court does not find in these cases that the "federal interest is demonstrably greater." 426 U.S., at 856 (Blackmun, J., concurring). No such finding could have been made, for the state interest is compelling. The financial impact on States and localities of displacing their control over wages, hours, overtime regulations, pensions, and labor relations with their employees could have serious, as well as unanticipated, effects on state and local planning, budgeting, and the levying of taxes. As we said in *National League of Cities*, federal control of the terms and conditions of employment of state employees also inevitably "displaces state policies regarding the manner in which [States] will structure delivery of those governmental services that citizens require." *Id.*, at 847.

The Court emphasizes that municipal operation of an intracity mass transit system is relatively new in the life of our country. It nevertheless is a classic example of the type of service traditionally provided by local government. It is *local* by definition. It is indistinguishable in principle from the traditional services of providing and maintaining streets, public lighting, traffic control, water, and sewerage systems. Services of this kind are precisely those with which citizens are more "familiarly and minutely conversant." The Federalist No. 46, p. 316 (J. Cooke ed. 1961). State and local officials of course must be intimately familiar with these services and sensitive to their quality as well as cost. Such officials also know that their constituents and the press respond to the adequacy, fair distribution, and cost of these services. It is this kind of state and local control and accountability that the Framers understood would insure the vitality and preservation of the federal system that the Constitution explicitly requires. *See National League of Cities*, 426 U.S. at 847-852.

V

Although the Court's opinion purports to recognize that the States retain some sovereign power, it does not identify even a single aspect of state authority that would remain when the Commerce Clause is invoked to justify federal regulation. In *Maryland v. Wirtz*, 392 U.S. 183 (1968), overruled by *National League of Cities* and today reaffirmed, the Court sustained an extension of the FLSA to certain hospitals, institutions, and schools. Although the Court's opinion in *Wirtz* was comparatively narrow, Justice Douglas, in dissent, wrote presciently that the Court's reading of the Commerce Clause would enable "the National Government [to] devour the essentials of state sovereignty, though that sovereignty is attested by the Tenth Amendment." 392 U.S. at 205. Today's decision makes Justice Douglas' fear once again a realistic one.

As I view the Court's decision today as rejecting the basic precepts of our federal system and limiting the constitutional role of judicial review, I dissent. . . .

POINTS FOR DISCUSSION

1. How do the various opinions in these cases relate the political safeguards of federalism to judicial review? Consider the following statements:

a. Justice Rehnquist for the Court in *Usery*:

> We hold that insofar as the challenged amendments operate to directly displace the States' freedom to structure integral operations in areas of traditional governmental functions, they are not within the authority granted Congress by Art. I, §8, cl. 3.

b. Justice Brennan in dissent in *Usery*:

> Judicial restraint in this area merely recognizes that the political branches of our Government are structured to protect the interests of the States, as well as the Nation as a whole, and that the States are fully able to protect their own interests in the premises. . . . Decisions upon the extent of federal intervention under the Commerce Clause into the affairs of the States are in that sense decisions of the States themselves. Judicial redistribution of powers granted the National

Government by the terms of the Constitution violates the fundamental tenet of our federalism that the extent of federal intervention into the States' affairs in the exercise of delegated powers shall be determined by the States' exercise of political power through their representatives in Congress.

c. Justice Blackmun for the Court in *Garcia*:

[T]he principal means chosen by the Framers to ensure the role of the States in the federal system lies in the structure of the Federal Government itself. It is no novelty to observe that the composition of the Federal Government was designed in large part to protect the States from overreaching by Congress. . . .

[W]e are convinced that the fundamental limitation that the constitutional scheme imposes on the Commerce Clause to protect the "States as States" is one of process rather than one of result.

d. Justice Powell in dissent in *Garcia*:

Today's opinion does not explain how the States' role in the electoral process guarantees that particular exercises of the Commerce Clause power will not infringe on residual state sovereignty. . . . We noted recently "[t]he hydraulic pressure inherent within each of the separate Branches to exceed the outer limits of its power. . . ." *INS v. Chadha*, 462 U.S. 919, 951 (1983). The Court offers no reason to think that this pressure will not operate when Congress seeks to invoke its powers under the Commerce Clause, notwithstanding the electoral role of the States. . . .

More troubling than the logical infirmities in the Court's reasoning is the result of its holding, *i.e.*, that federal political officials, invoking the Commerce Clause, are the sole judges of the limits of their own power. This result is inconsistent with the fundamental principles of our constitutional system. At least since *Marbury v. Madison*, 1 Cranch 137, 177 (1803), it has been the settled province of the federal judiciary "to say what the law is" with respect to the constitutionality of Acts of Congress.

What importance does each Justice ascribe in these passages to constitutional text, structure, historical practice, and the functional efficacy of political and judicial safeguards of federalism? How should their disagreements be resolved? As you answer this question, be mindful of the importance you are ascribing to each of these modalities of interpretation and why you are doing so.

2. In Chapters 5 and 6, you will revisit the *Usery/Garcia* dispute over whether Congress may exercise its enumerated powers to regulate certain traditional areas of state governance. For now, consider the relationship between Congress's Article I powers and the Tenth Amendment. In *Usery*, Justice Rehnquist stated:

We have repeatedly recognized that there are attributes of sovereignty attaching to every state government which may not be impaired by Congress, not because Congress may lack an affirmative grant of legislative authority to reach the matter, but because the Constitution prohibits it from exercising the authority in that manner.

Accordingly, the *Usery* Court addressed whether the act of Congress at issue, "while undoubtedly within the scope of the Commerce Clause, encounter[ed] a . . . constitutional barrier" under the Tenth Amendment. May an act of Congress within the scope of the Commerce Clause be nonetheless unconstitutional because it exercises a power reserved to the states under the Tenth Amendment?

In dissent in *Usery*, Justice Brennan, quoting *United States v. Darby*, 312 U.S. 100 (1941), argued that the Tenth Amendment "states but a truism that all is retained which has not been surrendered." In *New York v. United States*, 505 U.S. 144 (1992), which you will study in Chapter 6, Justice O'Connor, writing for the Court, described the inquiries of "whether an Act of Congress is authorized by one of the powers delegated to Congress in Article I" and "whether an Act of Congress invades the province of state sovereignty reserved by the Tenth Amendment" as "mirror images of each other": "If a power is delegated to Congress in the Constitution, the Tenth Amendment expressly disclaims any reservation of that power to the States; if a power is an attribute of state sovereignty reserved by the Tenth Amendment, it is necessarily a power the Constitution has not conferred on Congress." *Id.* at 155-156. How does this description of the relationship between Article I and the Tenth Amendment differ from Justice Rehnquist's in *Usery*? Is there any practical difference between the two descriptions? You will consider these questions in more detail in Chapter 6.

C. LIMITATIONS ON POLITICAL SAFEGUARDS

In the next case — *U.S. Term Limits, Inc. v. Thornton*, 514 U.S. 779 (1995) — the Supreme Court held that Arkansas lacked power under the Constitution to impose term limits upon members of the U.S. House of Representatives and Senate elected from that state. In so holding, the Court asserted two significant propositions: (1) representatives in the national government "owe primary allegiance not to the people of a State, but to the people of the Nation," and (2) "[p]ermitting individual states to formulate diverse qualifications for their representatives would . . . undermin[e] the uniformity and the national character that that the Framers envisioned and sought to ensure." As you read this case, consider how these propositions relate to the process-based theory of federalism espoused by the Court in *Garcia*.

U.S. TERM LIMITS, INC. V. THORNTON

514 U.S. 779 (1995)

JUSTICE STEVENS delivered the opinion of the Court.

The Constitution sets forth qualifications for membership in the Congress of the United States. Article I, §2, cl. 2, which applies to the House of Representatives, provides:

> "No Person shall be a Representative who shall not have attained to the Age of twenty five Years, and been seven Years a Citizen of the United States, and who

shall not, when elected, be an Inhabitant of that State in which he shall be chosen."

Article I, §3, cl. 3, which applies to the Senate, similarly provides:

"No Person shall be a Senator who shall not have attained to the Age of thirty Years, and been nine Years a Citizen of the United States, and who shall not, when elected, be an Inhabitant of that State for which he shall be chosen."

Today's cases present a challenge to an amendment to the Arkansas State Constitution that prohibits the name of an otherwise-eligible candidate for Congress from appearing on the general election ballot if that candidate has already served three terms in the House of Representatives or two terms in the Senate. The Arkansas Supreme Court held that the amendment violates the Federal Constitution. We agree with that holding. Such a state-imposed restriction is contrary to the "fundamental principle of our representative democracy," embodied in the Constitution, that "the people should choose whom they please to govern them." *Powell v. McCormack*, 395 U.S. 486, 547 (1969) (internal quotation marks omitted). Allowing individual States to adopt their own qualifications for congressional service would be inconsistent with the Framers' vision of a uniform National Legislature representing the people of the United States. If the qualifications set forth in the text of the Constitution are to be changed, that text must be amended. . . .

Powell . . . involved the power of the House to exclude a Member pursuant to Art. I, §5. . . . Our conclusion [in *Powell*] that Congress may not alter or add to the qualifications in the Constitution was integral to our analysis and outcome. . . .

Our reaffirmation of *Powell* does not necessarily resolve the specific questions presented in these cases. For petitioners argue that whatever the constitutionality of additional qualifications for membership imposed by Congress, the historical and textual materials discussed in *Powell* do not support the conclusion that the Constitution prohibits additional qualifications imposed by States. In the absence of such a constitutional prohibition, petitioners argue, the Tenth Amendment and the principle of reserved powers require that States be allowed to add such qualifications. . . .

We disagree for two independent reasons. First, we conclude that the power to add qualifications is not within the "original powers" of the States, and thus is not reserved to the States by the Tenth Amendment. Second, even if States possessed some original power in this area, we conclude that the Framers intended the Constitution to be the exclusive source of qualifications for Members of Congress, and that the Framers thereby "divested" States of any power to add qualifications.

The "plan of the convention" as illuminated by the historical materials, our opinions, and the text of the Tenth Amendment draws a basic distinction between the powers of the newly created Federal Government and the powers retained by the pre-existing sovereign States. As Chief Justice Marshall explained, "it was neither necessary nor proper to define the powers retained by the States. These powers proceed, not from the people of America, but from the people of the several States; and remain, after the adoption of the constitution, what they were before, except so far as they may be abridged by that instrument." *Sturges v. Crowninshield,* 4 Wheat. 122, 193 (1819).

This classic statement by the Chief Justice endorsed Hamilton's reasoning in The Federalist No. 32 that the plan of the Constitutional Convention did not contemplate "[a]n entire consolidation of the States into one complete national sovereignty," but only a partial consolidation in which "the State governments would clearly retain all the rights of sovereignty which they before had, and which were not, by that act, *exclusively* delegated to the United States." The Federalist No. 32. The text of the Tenth Amendment unambiguously confirms this principle:

> "The powers not delegated to the United States by the Constitution, nor prohibited by it to the States, are reserved to the States respectively, or to the people."

As we have frequently noted, "[t]he States unquestionably do retain a significant measure of sovereign authority. They do so, however, *only to the extent that the Constitution has not divested them of their original powers* and transferred those powers to the Federal Government." *Garcia v. San Antonio Metropolitan Transit Authority,* 469 U.S. 528, 549, (1985) (internal quotation marks and citation omitted) (emphasis added); see also *New York v. United States,* 505 U.S. 144, 155-156 (1992). . . .

Contrary to petitioners' assertions, the power to add qualifications is not part of the original powers of sovereignty that the Tenth Amendment reserved to the States. Petitioners' Tenth Amendment argument misconceives the nature of the right at issue because that Amendment could only "reserve" that which existed before. As Justice Story recognized, "the states can exercise no powers whatsoever, which exclusively spring out of the existence of the national government, which the constitution does not delegate to them. . . . No state can say, that it has reserved, what it never possessed." 1 Story[, Commentaries on the Constitution of the United States] §627.

Justice Story's position thus echoes that of Chief Justice Marshall in *McCulloch v. Maryland,* 4 Wheat. 316 (1819). In *McCulloch,* the Court rejected the argument that the Constitution's silence on the subject of state power to tax corporations chartered by Congress implies that the States have "reserved" power to tax such federal instrumentalities. As Chief Justice Marshall pointed out, an "original right to tax" such federal entities "never existed, and the question whether it has been surrendered, cannot arise." *Id.,* at 430. In language that presaged Justice Story's argument, Chief Justice Marshall concluded: "This opinion does not deprive the States of any resources which they originally possessed." 4 Wheat., at 436.

With respect to setting qualifications for service in Congress, no such right existed before the Constitution was ratified. The contrary argument overlooks the revolutionary character of the Government that the Framers conceived. Prior to the adoption of the Constitution, the States had joined together under the Articles of Confederation. In that system, "the States retained most of their sovereignty, like independent nations bound together only by treaties." *Wesberry v. Sanders,* 376 U.S. 1, 9 (1964). After the Constitutional Convention convened, the Framers were presented with, and eventually adopted a variation of, "a plan not merely to amend the Articles of Confederation but to create an entirely new National Government with a National Executive, National Judiciary, and a National Legislature." *Id.,* at 10. In adopting that plan, the Framers envisioned a uniform national system, rejecting the notion that the Nation was a collection of States, and instead creating a direct link between the National Government and the people of the United States. In that National Government, representatives owe primary allegiance not to the people of a State, but to the people of the Nation. As Justice Story observed, each Member of Congress is "an officer of the union, deriving his powers and qualifications from the constitution, and neither created by, dependent upon, nor controllable by, the states. . . . Those officers owe their existence and functions to the united voice of the whole, not of a portion, of the people." 1 Story §627. Representatives and Senators are as much officers of the entire Union as is the President. States thus "have just as much right, and no more, to prescribe new qualifications for a representative, as they have for a president. . . . It is no original prerogative of state power to appoint a representative, a senator, or president for the union." *Ibid. . . .*

In short, as the Framers recognized, electing representatives to the National Legislature was a new right, arising from the Constitution itself. The Tenth Amendment thus provides no basis for concluding that the States possess reserved power to add qualifications to those that are fixed in the Constitution. Instead, any state power to set the qualifications for membership in Congress must derive not from the reserved powers of state sovereignty, but rather from the delegated powers of national sovereignty. In the absence of any constitutional delegation to the States of power to add qualifications to those enumerated in the Constitution, such a power does not exist. . . .

Our conclusion that States lack the power to impose qualifications vindicates the same "fundamental principle of our representative democracy" that we recognized in *Powell,* namely, that "the people should choose whom they please to govern them." *Id.,* at 547. . . .

[W]e believe that state-imposed qualifications, as much as congressionally imposed qualifications, would undermine the second critical idea recognized in *Powell:* that an aspect of sovereignty is the right of the people to vote for whom they wish. Again, the source of the qualification is of little moment in assessing the qualification's restrictive impact. . . .

[S]tate-imposed restrictions, unlike the congressionally imposed restrictions at issue in *Powell,* violate a third idea central to this basic principle: that the right to choose representatives belongs not to the States, but to the people. From the start, the Framers recognized that the "great and radical vice" of the Articles of Confederation was "the principle of LEGISLATION for STATES or GOVERNMENTS, in their CORPORATE or COLLECTIVE CAPACITIES, and as contradistinguished from the INDIVIDUALS of whom they consist." The Federalist No. 15, at 108 (Hamilton). Thus the Framers, in perhaps their most important contribution, conceived of a Federal Government directly responsible to the people, possessed of direct power over the people, and chosen directly, not by States, but by the people. The Framers implemented this ideal most clearly in the provision, extant from the beginning of the Republic, that calls for the Members of the House of Representatives to be "chosen every second Year by the

People of the several States." Art. I, §2, cl. 1. Following the adoption of the Seventeenth Amendment in 1913, this ideal was extended to elections for the Senate. The Congress of the United States, therefore, is not a confederation of nations in which separate sovereigns are represented by appointed delegates, but is instead a body composed of representatives of the people. As Chief Justice John Marshall observed: "The government of the Union, then, . . . is, emphatically, and truly, a government of the people. In form and in substance it emanates from them. Its powers are granted by them, and are to be exercised directly on them, and for their benefit." *McCulloch v. Maryland,* 4 Wheat., at 404-405. Ours is a "government of the people, by the people, for the people." A. Lincoln, Gettysburg Address (1863). . . .

The Framers deemed this principle critical when they discussed qualifications. . . . Permitting individual States to formulate diverse qualifications for their representatives would result in a patchwork of state qualifications, undermining the uniformity and the national character that the Framers envisioned and sought to ensure. Cf. *McCulloch v. Maryland,* 4 Wheat., at 428-429 ("Those means are not given by the people of a particular State, not given by the constituents of the legislature, . . . but by the people of all the States. They are given by all, for the benefit of all — and upon theory, should be subjected to that government only which belongs to all."). Such a patchwork would also sever the direct link that the Framers found so critical between the National Government and the people of the United States. . . .

Petitioners argue that, even if States may not add qualifications, Amendment 73 is constitutional because it is not such a qualification, and because Amendment 73 is a permissible exercise of state power to regulate the "Times, Places and Manner of holding Elections." We reject these contentions.

Unlike §§1 and 2 of Amendment 73, which create absolute bars to service for long-term incumbents running for state office, §3 merely provides that certain Senators and Representatives shall not be certified as candidates and shall not have their names appear on the ballot. They may run as write-in candidates and, if elected, they may serve. . . .

In our view, Amendment 73 is an indirect attempt to accomplish what the Constitution prohibits Arkansas from accomplishing directly. As the plurality opinion of the Arkansas Supreme Court recognized, Amendment 73 is an "effort to dress eligibility to stand for Congress in ballot access clothing," because the "intent and the effect of Amendment 73 are to disqualify congressional incumbents from further service." 316 Ark., at 266. We must, of course, accept the state court's view of the purpose of its own law: We are thus authoritatively informed that the sole purpose of §3 of Amendment 73 was to attempt to achieve a result that is forbidden by the Federal Constitution. . . .

Moreover, petitioners' broad construction of the Elections Clause is fundamentally inconsistent with the Framers' view of that Clause. The Framers intended the Elections Clause to grant States authority to create procedural regulations, not to provide States with license to exclude classes of candidates from federal office. . . . [T]he Framers understood the Elections Clause as a grant of authority to issue procedural regulations, and not as a source of power to dictate electoral outcomes, to favor or disfavor a class of candidates, or to evade important constitutional restraints.

We are . . . firmly convinced that allowing the several States to adopt term limits for congressional service would effect a fundamental change in the constitutional framework. Any such change must come not by legislation adopted either by Congress or by an individual State, but rather — as have other important changes in the electoral process — through the amendment procedures set forth in Article V. The Framers decided that the qualifications for service in the Congress of the United States be fixed in the Constitution and be uniform throughout the Nation. That decision reflects the Framers' understanding that Members of Congress are chosen by separate constituencies, but that they become, when elected, servants of the people of the United States. They are not merely delegates appointed by separate, sovereign States; they occupy offices that are integral and essential components of a single National Government. In the absence of a properly passed constitutional amendment, allowing individual States to craft their own qualifications for Congress would thus erode the structure envisioned by the Framers, a structure that was designed, in the words of the Preamble to our Constitution, to form a "more perfect Union." . . .

JUSTICE KENNEDY, concurring.

Federalism was our Nation's own discovery. The Framers split the atom of sovereignty. It was the genius of their idea that our citizens would have two political capacities, one state and one federal, each protected from incursion by the other. The resulting Constitution created a legal system unprecedented in form and design, establishing two orders of government, each with its own direct relationship, its own privity, its own set of mutual rights and obligations to the people who sustain it and are governed by it. It is appropriate to recall these origins, which instruct us as to the nature of the two different governments created and confirmed by the Constitution.

A distinctive character of the National Government, the mark of its legitimacy, is that it owes its existence to the act of the whole people who created it. . . . As James Madison explained, the House of Representatives "derive[s] its powers from the people of America," and "the operation of the government on the people in their individual capacities" makes it "a national government," not merely a federal one. *Id.*, No. 39, at 244, 245 (emphasis deleted). The Court confirmed this principle in *McCulloch v. Maryland,* 4 Wheat. 316, 404-405, (1819), when it said: "The government of the Union, then, . . . is, emphatically, and truly, a government of the people. In form and in substance it emanates from them. Its powers are granted by them, and are to be exercised directly on them, and for their benefit." . . .

In one sense it is true that "the people of each State retained their separate political identities," for the Constitution takes care both to preserve the States and to make use of their identities and structures at various points in organizing the federal union. It does not at all follow from this that the sole political identity of an American is with the State of his or her residence. It denies the dual character of the Federal Government which is its very foundation to assert that the people of the United States do not have a political identity as well, one independent of, though consistent with, their identity as citizens of the State of their residence. . . .

It might be objected that because the States ratified the Constitution, the people can delegate power only through the States or by acting in their capacities as citizens of particular States. But in *McCulloch v. Maryland,* the Court set forth its authoritative rejection of this idea. . . .

The political identity of the entire people of the Union is reinforced by the proposition, which I take to be beyond dispute, that, though limited as to its objects, the National Government is, and must be, controlled by the people without collateral interference by the States. *McCulloch* affirmed this proposition as well, when the Court rejected the suggestion that States could interfere with federal powers. . . . The States have no power, reserved or otherwise, over the exercise of federal authority within its proper sphere. That the States may not invade the sphere of federal sovereignty is as incontestable, in my view, as the corollary proposition that the Federal Government must be held within the boundaries of its own power when it intrudes upon matters reserved to the States. . . .

The arguments for term limitations (or ballot restrictions having the same effect) are not lacking in force; but the issue, as all of us must acknowledge, is not the efficacy of those measures but whether they have a legitimate source, given their origin in the enactments of a single State. There can be no doubt, if we are to respect the republican origins of the Nation and preserve its federal character, that there exists a federal right of citizenship, a relationship between the people of the Nation and their National Government, with which the States may not interfere. Because the Arkansas enactment intrudes upon this federal domain, it exceeds the boundaries of the Constitution.

JUSTICE THOMAS, with whom THE CHIEF JUSTICE, JUSTICE O'CONNOR, and JUSTICE SCALIA join, dissenting.

Nothing in the Constitution deprives the people of each State of the power to prescribe eligibility requirements for the candidates who seek to represent them in Congress. The Constitution is simply silent on this question. And where the Constitution is silent, it raises no bar to action by the States or the people. . . .

Because the majority fundamentally misunderstands the notion of "reserved" powers, I start with some first principles. Contrary to the majority's suggestion, the people of the States need not point to any affirmative grant of power in the Constitution in order to prescribe qualifications for their representatives in Congress, or to authorize their elected state legislators to do so. . . .

Our system of government rests on one overriding principle: All power stems from the consent of the people. To phrase the principle in this way, however, is to be imprecise about something important to the notion of "reserved" powers. The ultimate source of the Constitution's authority is the consent of the people of each individual State, not the consent of the undifferentiated people of the Nation as a whole.

The ratification procedure erected by Article VII makes this point clear. The Constitution took effect once it had been ratified by the people gathered in convention in nine different States. But the Constitution went into effect only "between the States so ratifying the same," Art. VII; it did not bind the people of North Carolina until they had accepted it. In Madison's words, the popular consent upon which the Constitution's authority rests was "given by the people, not as individuals composing one entire nation, but as composing the distinct and independent States to which they respectively belong." The Federalist No. 39, p. 243 (C. Rossiter ed. 1961). . . .

When they adopted the Federal Constitution, of course, the people of each State surrendered some of their authority to the United States (and hence to entities accountable to the people of other States as well as to themselves). They affirmatively deprived their States of certain powers, see, *e.g.,* Art. I, §10, and they affirmatively conferred certain powers upon the Federal Government, see, *e.g.,* Art. I, §8. Because the people of the several States are the only true source of power, however, the Federal Government enjoys no authority beyond what the Constitution confers: The Federal Government's powers are limited and enumerated. . . .

In each State, the remainder of the people's powers — "[the powers not delegated to the United States by the Constitution, nor prohibited by it to the States," Amdt. 10 — are either delegated to the state government or retained by the people. The Federal Constitution does not specify which of these two possibilities obtains; it is up to the various state constitutions to declare which powers the people of each State have delegated to their state government. As far as the Federal Constitution is concerned, then, the States can exercise all powers that the Constitution does not withhold from them. The Federal Government and the States thus face different default rules: Where the Constitution is silent about the exercise of a particular power — that is, where the Constitution does not speak either expressly or by necessary implication — the Federal Government lacks that power and the States enjoy it.

These basic principles are enshrined in the Tenth Amendment, which declares that all powers neither delegated to the Federal Government nor prohibited to the States "are reserved to the States respectively, or to the people." With this careful last phrase, the Amendment avoids taking any position on the division of power between the state governments and the people of the States: It is up to the people of each State to determine which "reserved" powers their state government may exercise. But the Amendment does make clear that powers reside at the state level except where the Constitution removes them from that level. All powers that the Constitution neither delegates to the Federal Government nor prohibits to the States are controlled by the people of each State.

To be sure, when the Tenth Amendment uses the phrase "the people," it does not specify whether it is referring to the people of each State or the people of the Nation as a whole. But the latter interpretation would make the Amendment pointless: There would have been no reason to provide that where the Constitution is silent about whether a particular power resides at the state level, it might or might not do so. In addition, it would make no sense to speak of powers as being reserved to the undifferentiated people of the Nation as a whole, because the Constitution does not contemplate that those people will either exercise power or delegate it. The Constitution simply does not recognize any mechanism for action by the undifferentiated people of the Nation. Thus, the amendment provision of Article V calls for amendments to be ratified not by a convention of the national people, but by conventions of the people in each State or by the state legislatures elected by those people. Likewise, the Constitution calls for Members of Congress to be chosen State by State, rather than in nationwide elections. Even the selection of the President — surely the most national of national figures — is accomplished by an electoral college made up of delegates chosen by the various States, and candidates can lose a Presidential election despite winning a majority of the votes cast in the Nation as a whole.

In short, the notion of popular sovereignty that undergirds the Constitution does not erase state boundaries, but rather tracks them. The people of each State obviously did trust their fate to the people of the several States when they consented to the Constitution; not only did they empower the governmental institutions of the United States, but they also agreed to be bound by constitutional amendments that they themselves refused to ratify. See Art. V (providing that proposed amendments shall take effect upon ratification by three-quarters of the States). At the same time, however, the people of each State retained their separate political identities. As Chief Justice Marshall put it, "[n]o political dreamer was ever wild enough to think of breaking down the lines which separate the States, and of compounding the American people into one common mass." *McCulloch v. Maryland,* 4 Wheat. 316, 403 (1819). . . .

Any ambiguity in the Tenth Amendment's use of the phrase "the people" is cleared up by the body of the Constitution itself. Article I begins by providing that the Congress of the United States enjoys "[a]ll legislative Powers herein granted," §1, and goes on to give a careful enumeration of Congress' powers, §8. It then concludes by enumerating certain powers that are *prohibited* to the States. The import of this structure is the same as the import of the Tenth Amendment: If we are to invalidate Arkansas' Amendment 73, we must point to something in the Federal Constitution that deprives the people of Arkansas of the power to enact such measures. . . .

The majority is . . . quite wrong to conclude that the people of the States cannot authorize their state governments to exercise any powers that were unknown to the States when the Federal Constitution was drafted. . . .

In an effort to defend its position, the majority points to language in *Garcia v. San Antonio Metropolitan Transit Authority,* 469 U.S. 528, 549 (1985), which it takes to indicate that the Tenth Amendment covers only "the original powers of [state] sovereignty." But *Garcia* dealt with an entirely different issue: the extent to which principles of state sovereignty implicit in our federal system curtail Congress' authority to exercise its enumerated powers. When we are asked to decide whether a congressional statute that appears to have been authorized by Article I is nonetheless unconstitutional because it invades a protected sphere of state sovereignty, it may well be appropriate for us to inquire into what we have called the "traditional aspects of state sovereignty." See *National League of Cities v. Usery,* 426 U.S. 833, 841, 849 (1976). The question raised by the present case, however, is not whether any principle of state sovereignty implicit in the Tenth Amendment bars congressional action that Article I appears to authorize, but rather whether Article I bars state action that it does not appear to forbid. The principle necessary to answer this question is express on the Tenth Amendment's face: Unless the Federal Constitution affirmatively prohibits an action by the States or the people, it raises no bar to such action. . . .

The majority also seeks support for its view of the Tenth Amendment in *McCulloch v. Maryland,* 4 Wheat. 316, (1819). But this effort is misplaced. *McCulloch* did make clear that a power need not be "expressly" delegated to the United States or prohibited to the States in order to fall outside the Tenth Amendment's reservation; delegations and prohibitions can also arise by necessary implication. True to the text of the Tenth Amendment, however, *McCulloch* indicated that all powers as to which the Constitution does not speak (whether expressly or by necessary implication) are "reserved" to the state level. . . . *McCullough* seemed to assume that the people had "conferred on the general government the power contained in the constitution, and on the States the whole residuum of power." *Id.,* at 410. . . .

For the past 175 years, *McCulloch* has been understood to rest on the proposition that the Constitution affirmatively barred Maryland from imposing its tax on the bank's operations. . . . For the majority, however, *McCulloch* apparently turned on the fact that before the Constitution was adopted, the States had possessed no power to tax the instrumentalities of the governmental institutions that the Constitution created. This understanding of *McCulloch* makes most of Chief Justice Marshall's opinion irrelevant; according to the majority, there was no need to inquire into whether federal law deprived Maryland of the power in question, because the power could not fall into the category of "reserved" powers anyway. . . .

Despite the majority's citation of *Garcia* and *McCullough,* the only true support for its view of the Tenth Amendment comes from Joseph Story's 1833 treatise on constitutional law. See 2 J. Story, Commentaries on the Constitution of the United States §§623-628. Justice Story was a brilliant and accomplished man, and one cannot casually dismiss his views. On the other hand, he was not a member of the Founding generation, and his Commentaries on the Constitution were written a half century after the framing. Rather than representing the original understanding of the Constitution, they represent only his own understanding. In a range of cases concerning the federal/state relation, moreover, this Court has deemed positions taken in Story's commentaries to be more nationalist than the Constitution warrants. In this case too, Story's position that the only powers reserved to the States are those that the States enjoyed before the framing conflicts with both the plain language of the Tenth Amendment and the underlying theory of the Constitution. . . .

The majority . . . asserts that because Congress as a whole is an institution of the National Government, the individual Members of Congress "owe primary allegiance not to the people of a State, but to the people of the Nation." . . .

Political scientists can debate about who commands the "primary allegiance" of Members of Congress once they reach Washington. From the framing to the present, however, the *selection* of the Representatives and Senators from each State has been left entirely to the people of that State or to their state legislature. The very name "congress" suggests a coming together of representatives from distinct entities. In keeping with the complexity of our federal system, once the representatives chosen by the people of each State assemble in Congress, they form a national body and are beyond the control of the individual States until the next election. But the selection of representatives in Congress is indisputably an act of the people of each State, not some abstract people of the Nation as a whole. . . .

I take it to be established, then, that the people of Arkansas do enjoy "reserved" powers over the selection of their representatives in Congress. Purporting to exercise those reserved powers, they have agreed among themselves that the candidates covered by §3 of Amendment 73 — those whom they have already elected to three or more terms in the House of Representatives or to two or more terms in the Senate — should not be eligible to appear on the ballot for reelection, but should nonetheless be returned to Congress if enough voters are sufficiently enthusiastic about their candidacy to write in their names. Whatever one might think of the wisdom of this arrangement, we may not override the decision of the people of Arkansas unless something in the Federal Constitution deprives them of the power to enact such measures. . . .

[W]hile the majority is correct that the Framers expected the selection process to create a "direct link" between Members of the House of Representatives and the people, the link was between the Representatives from each State and the people of that State. . . .

The majority settles on "the Qualifications Clauses" as the constitutional provisions that Amendment 73 violates. Because I do not read those provisions to impose any unstated prohibitions on the States, it is unnecessary for me to decide whether the majority is correct to identify Arkansas' ballot-access restriction with laws fixing true term limits or otherwise prescribing "qualifications" for congressional office. . . . [T]he Qualifications Clauses are merely straightforward recitations of the minimum eligibility requirements that the Framers thought it essential for every Member of Congress to meet. They restrict state power only in that they prevent the States from *abolishing* all eligibility requirements for membership in Congress.

Because the text of the Qualifications Clauses does not support its position, the majority turns instead to its vision of the democratic principles that animated the Framers. But the majority's analysis goes to a question that is not before us: whether Congress has the power to prescribe qualifications for its own members. . . . The democratic principles that contributed to the Framers' decision to withhold this power from Congress do not prove that the Framers also deprived the people of the States of their reserved authority to set eligibility requirements for their own representatives. . . .

I agree with the majority that Congress has no power to prescribe qualifications for its own Members. This fact, however, does not show that the Qualifications Clauses contained a hidden exclusivity provision. The reason for Congress' incapacity is not that the Qualifications Clauses deprive Congress of the authority to set qualifications, but rather that nothing in the Constitution grants Congress this power. In the absence of such a grant, Congress may not act. But deciding whether the Constitution denies the qualification-setting power to the States and the people of the States requires a fundamentally different legal analysis. . . .

When the people of a State themselves decide to restrict the field of candidates whom they are willing to send to Washington as their representatives, they simply have not violated the principle that "the people should choose whom they please to govern them." See [2 Debates in the Several State Conventions on the Adoption of the Federal Constitution 257 (J. Elliot 2d ed. 1876)] (remarks of Alexander Hamilton at the New York Convention). . . .

In fact, the authority to narrow the field of candidates in this way may be part and parcel of the right to elect Members of Congress. That is, the right to choose may include the right to winnow. . . .

It is radical enough for the majority to hold that the Constitution implicitly precludes the people of the States from prescribing any eligibility requirements for the congressional candidates who seek their votes. This holding, after all, does not stop with negating the term limits that many States have seen fit to impose on their Senators and Representatives. Today's decision also means that no State may disqualify congressional candidates whom a court has found to be mentally incompetent, who are currently in prison, or who have past vote-fraud convictions. Likewise, after today's decision, the people of each State must leave open the possibility that they will trust someone with their vote in Congress even though they do not trust him with *a* vote in the election for Congress. . . .

The majority's opinion . . . does not itself suggest any principled stopping point. No matter how narrowly construed, however, today's decision reads the Qualifications Clauses to impose substantial implicit prohibitions on the States and the people of the States. I would not draw such an expansive negative inference from the fact that the Constitution requires Members of Congress to be a certain age, to be inhabitants of the States that they represent, and to have been United States citizens for a specified period. Rather, I would read the Qualifications Clauses to do no more than what they say.

POINTS FOR DISCUSSION

1. The *U.S. Term Limits* Court explained that "[p]ermitting individual states to formulate diverse qualifications for their representatives would result in a patchwork of state qualifications, undermining the uniformity and the national character that the Framers envisioned and sought to ensure." In *Garcia*, however, the Court relied in part upon individual state "control of electoral qualifications" to hold that "[s]tate sovereign interests . . . are more properly protected by procedural safeguards inherent in the structure of the federal system than by judicially created limitations on federal power." Is there any basis upon which to distinguish state control of voter qualifications (a recognized safeguard of federalism in *Garcia v. San Antonio Metropolitan Transit Authority*, 469 U.S. 528 (1985)) from state control of candidate qualifications (a rejected state power in *U.S. Term Limits*)?

2. In *U.S. Term Limits*, the Court observed that "[i]n that National government, representatives owe primary allegiance not to the people of a

State, but to the people of the Nation." Is this statement consistent with the idea that the political safeguards of federalism are effective safeguards of federalism?

3. The Constitution expressly provides the political safeguards of federalism upon which the *Garcia* Court relied in declining to exercise judicial review — equal state representation in the Senate, state control of voter qualifications, and the Electoral College system. The *U.S. Term Limits* Court rejected another potential political safeguard of federalism — state authority to regulate the qualifications of candidates for Congress. Does the Court's reasoning foreclose states from regulating the political process in any way that the Constitution does not expressly authorize?

PART II

NATIONAL AND STATE POWER TO REGULATE

5

THE ENUMERATED POWERS OF CONGRESS

This chapter considers the enumerated powers of Congress under the Constitution. Article I, §1 of the Constitution provides that "[a]ll legislative Powers herein granted shall be vested in a Congress of the United States, which shall consist of a Senate and House of Representatives." Article I, §8 proceeds to grant Congress a list of enumerated powers, including powers (1) "[t]o regulate Commerce . . . among the several States," and (2) "[t]o lay and collect Taxes, Duties, Imposts and Excises, . . . and provide for the . . . general Welfare of the United States. . . ." In addition, Article I, §8 grants Congress power "[t]o make all Laws which shall be necessary and proper for carrying into Execution the foregoing powers. . . ." This chapter considers these important powers.

The Constitution's conferral of powers upon Congress, however, is not limited to Article I, §8. The Reconstruction Amendments—the Thirteenth, Fourteenth, and Fifteenth Amendments—empower Congress to enforce their provisions through appropriate legislation. This chapter addresses Congress's power to enforce the Fourteenth Amendment. Section 1 of the Fourteenth Amendment provides, in part, that a state shall not "deprive any person of life, liberty, or property, without due process of law; nor deny to any person within its jurisdiction the equal protection of the laws." The Court has held that the Due Process Clause of §1 incorporates most of the Bill of Rights against the States. Section 5 of the Fourteenth Amendment provides that "[t]he Congress shall have power to enforce, by appropriate legislation, the provisions of this article." This chapter examines the power of Congress under §5 to enforce the Fourteenth Amendment and the rights that it incorporates.

As you read the materials in this and subsequent chapters, you will see the Court draw upon some of the historical, judicial, and academic materials that you studied in Part I. Review those materials, and carefully evaluate how the Justices use them in constitutional analysis. One question that runs through most of the opinions in this chapter is how much deference courts should afford Congress in determining the constitutionality of federal statutes. Note how the Court answers this question in each case—and how the Justices draw upon the historical debates, political theory, and constitutional safeguards of federalism that you studied in Part I.

A. THE COMMERCE POWER

Article I, §8 of the Constitution empowers Congress "[t]o regulate Commerce with foreign Nations, and among the several States, and with the Indian Tribes." In *The Federalist No. 45*, James Madison stated that "[t]he regulation of commerce, it is true, is a new power; but that seems to be an addition which few oppose, and from which no apprehensions are entertained." Over time, the Commerce Clause has become one of the most important and controversial enumerated powers of Congress. In the last century, the Supreme Court relied on the Commerce Clause to uphold legislative programs of the New Deal and civil rights eras. Congress has enacted many important economic, environmental, criminal, and social regulatory schemes under the Commerce Clause.

The Supreme Court has struggled with several questions relating to the Commerce Clause. First, what is the scope of Congress's commerce power? The Court repeatedly has addressed the question of what legislation the Commerce Clause empowers Congress to enact. Through the twentieth century, the Court has adopted, rejected, and modified several definitions of the commerce power.

Second, how much deference should the Court afford Congress in determining whether a statute qualifies as a constitutional regulation of interstate commerce? Over time, the Court has provided definitions of the commerce power that, in application, require empirical or factual determinations. For example, in several cases, the Court has explained that the Commerce Clause empowers Congress to regulate certain intrastate activities that, in aggregate with other such activities, have a "substantial effect" on interstate commerce. Whether a set of regulated activities substantially affects interstate commerce is partly a factual question. To what extent should the Court defer to congressional determinations, actual or presumed, that regulated activities substantially affect interstate commerce? To what extent should the Court make such determinations itself? Justices continue to debate these questions in the present day.

Third, in determining whether an act of Congress is constitutional under the Commerce Clause, should the Court consider Congress's actual purpose in enacting the law? If a regulation bears a sufficient connection to commerce to qualify as a regulation of interstate commerce under Article I, should the fact that Congress's *actual purpose* in enacting the regulation was unrelated to interstate commerce defeat the statute's constitutionality? The role of congressional purpose in judicial analyses of the commerce power has shifted over time.

Consider the first Supreme Court case to hold that an act of Congress exceeded the commerce and other federal powers — *United States v. Dewitt*, 76 U.S. 41 (1869). In *Dewitt*, the Court considered whether Congress had power to prohibit the sale of certain lamp oils. The Court's brief opinion involved each of the questions identified above.

First, the opinion attempted to define the scope of the commerce power: Article I's "grant of power to regulate commerce among the States has always been understood . . . as a virtual denial of any power to interfere with the internal trade and business of the separate States." *Id.* at 44. The Court distinguished between a regulation of interstate commerce and a regulation of a state's "internal trade." Does this distinction directly follow from the Commerce Clause? Is it a workable distinction?

Second, the opinion addressed the question of judicial deference to Congress. The Court explained that Congress may regulate the internal trade of a state only "as a necessary and proper means for carrying into execution some other power expressly granted or vested." *Id.* The United States argued that Congress's regulation was "necessary and proper" to support a tax on other lamp oils. The government's theory was that, by outlawing the lamp oil at issue, Congress would increase production and sale of other, federally taxable lamp oils — thereby generating greater federal tax revenue. The Court rejected this theory on the ground that the consequences of increasing production and sale of taxed oils were "too remote and uncertain" to sustain the regulation under the Necessary and Proper Clause. *Id.* To what extent should courts make such determinations? To what extent should courts defer to Congress regarding such judgments?

Third, the *Dewitt* Court's opinion examined the actual purpose of Congress in enacting the regulation. In assessing whether the act was a necessary and proper means for carrying into execution Congress's powers to tax, the Court found "no reason for saying that it was regarded by Congress as such a means." *Id.* Should courts consider actual congressional purposes in determining whether Congress had constitutional authority to enact a regulation? Are courts competent to discern actual congressional purposes?

This section presents the general course of the Supreme Court's Commerce Clause jurisprudence from the turn of the twentieth century to the present day. As you read the materials in this section, consider the following questions:

- How have the Court's understandings of the commerce power shifted over time? Why have they shifted?
- What specific definitions of the commerce power has the Court articulated? How has the Court derived each? How judicially workable is each?
- What deference should the Court afford Congress in determining whether a regulation is a constitutional regulation of interstate commerce?
- What role have actual congressional purposes played in judicial Commerce Clause analyses? What role should they play?

1. THE PROGRESSIVE ERA

The Progressive Era is commonly defined as a period of political reform extending from the 1890s until the 1920s. During this time, Congress enacted economic and social reforms under the Commerce Clause, including antitrust, lottery, and child labor regulations. The Supreme Court addressed constitutional challenges to such regulations in various cases. Although the Supreme Court sustained many Progressive-Era reforms, scholars have long described the Court's rejection of certain progressive programs under the Commerce Clause as part of a broader theory of *laissez-faire* constitutionalism. Roughly speaking, scholars claim that certain Justices restricted congressional power under the Commerce Clause because they preferred to allow free reign to markets and opposed governmental regulation generally.

The following three cases addressed the constitutionality of federal restrictions on (1) anticompetitive activities, (2) the interstate movement of lottery tickets, and (3) the interstate transportation of the products of child labor. As you read these cases, keep the following questions in mind:

- How does the Court define congressional power to regulate interstate commerce? What values do these definitions advance?
- To what extent do the Justices defer to Congress's judgment that a regulation is necessary and proper to carry the commerce power into execution?

UNITED STATES V. E. C. KNIGHT CO.

156 U.S. 1 (1895)

[The United States filed a bill charging that several sugar refineries, including E. C. Knight Company, violated the 1890 Sherman Antitrust Act. The Act provided that "[e]very contract, combination in the form of trust or otherwise, or conspiracy, in restraint of trade or commerce among the several states or with foreign nations is . . . illegal." Act of July 2, 1890, ch. 647, 26 Stat. 209. The Act also provided criminal penalties for its violation.

The United States alleged that the American Sugar Refining Company had entered into a scheme to purchase the assets of four refineries, including E. C. Knight, "in order that the American Sugar Refining Company might obtain complete control of the price of sugar in the United States," and "for the purpose of restraining the trade thereof with other States as theretofore carried on independently by said defendants." The United States further alleged that "the American Sugar Refining Company combined and conspired with the other defendants to restrain trade and commerce in refined sugar among the several states and foreign nations."]

Mr. CHIEF JUSTICE FULLER . . . delivered the opinion of the court.

By the purchase of the stock of the four Philadelphia refineries, with shares of its own stock, the American Sugar Refining Company acquired nearly complete control of the manufacture of refined sugar within the United States. The bill charged that the contracts under which these purchases were made constituted combinations in restraint of trade, and that in entering into them the defendants combined and conspired to restrain the trade and commerce in refined sugar among the several States and with foreign nations, contrary to the act of Congress of July 2, 1890. . . .

The fundamental question is, whether conceding that the existence of a monopoly in manufacture is established by the evidence, that monopoly can be directly suppressed under the act of Congress in the mode attempted by this bill.

It cannot be denied that the power of a State to protect the lives, health, and property of its citizens, and to preserve good order and the public morals, "the power to govern men and things within the limits of its dominion," is a power originally and always belonging to the States, not surrendered by them to the general government, nor directly restrained by the Constitution of the United States, and essentially exclusive. The relief of the citizens of each State from the burden of monopoly and the evils resulting from the restraint of trade among such citizens was left with the States to deal with . . . On the other hand, the power of Congress to regulate commerce among the several States is also exclusive. The Constitution does not provide that interstate commerce shall be free, but, by the grant of this exclusive power to regulate it, it was left free except as Congress might impose restraints. Therefore it has been determined that the failure of Congress to exercise this exclusive power in any case is an expression of its will that the subject shall be free from restrictions or impositions upon it by the several States, and if a law passed by a State in the exercise of its acknowledged powers comes into conflict with that will, the Congress and the State cannot occupy the position of equal opposing sovereignties, because the Constitution declares its supremacy and that of the laws passed in pursuance thereof, and that which is not supreme must yield to that which is supreme. "Commerce, undoubtedly, is traffic," said Chief Justice Marshall, "but it is something more, it is intercourse. It describes the commercial intercourse between nations and parts of nations in all its branches, and is regulated by prescribing rules for carrying on that intercourse." That which belongs to commerce is within the jurisdiction of the United States, but that which does not belong to commerce is within the jurisdiction of the police power of the State. *Gibbons v. Ogden*, 9 Wheat. 1, 189, 210.

The argument is that the power to control the manufacture of refined sugar is a monopoly over a necessary of life, to the enjoyment of which by a large part of the population of the United States interstate commerce is indispensable, and that, therefore, the general government in the exercise of the power to regulate commerce may repress such monopoly directly and set aside the instruments which have created it. But this argument cannot be confined to necessaries of life merely, and must include all articles of general consumption. Doubtless the power to control the manufacture of a given thing involves in a certain sense the control of its disposition, but this is a secondary and not the primary sense, and although the exercise of that power may result in bringing the operation of commerce into play, it does not control it, and affects it only incidentally and indirectly. Commerce succeeds to manufacture, and is not a part of it. The power to regulate commerce is the power to prescribe the rule by which commerce shall be governed, and is a power independent of the power to suppress monopoly. But it may operate in repression of monopoly whenever that comes within the rules by which commerce is governed or whenever the transaction is itself a monopoly of commerce.

It is vital that the independence of the commercial power and of the police power, and the delimitation between them, however sometimes perplexing, should always be recognized and observed, for while the one furnishes the strongest bond of union, the other is essential to the preservation of the autonomy of the states as required by our dual form of government, and acknowledged evils, however grave and urgent they may appear to be, had better be borne, than the risk be run, in the effort to suppress them, of more serious consequences by resort to expedients of even doubtful constitutionality.

It will be perceived how far-reaching the proposition is that the power of dealing with a monopoly directly may be exercised by the general government whenever interstate or international commerce may be ultimately affected. The regulation of commerce applies to the subjects of commerce and not to matters of internal police. Contracts to buy, sell, or exchange goods to be transported among the several States, the transportation and its instrumentalities, and articles bought, sold, or exchanged for the purposes of such transit among the States, or put in the way of transit, may be regulated, but this is because they form part of interstate trade or commerce. The fact that an article is manufactured for export to another State does not of itself make it an article of interstate commerce, and the intent of the manufacturer does not determine the time when the article or product passes from the control of the State and belongs to commerce. . . .

Slight reflection will show that if the national power extends to all contracts and combinations in manufacture, agriculture, mining, and other productive industries, whose ultimate result may affect external commerce, comparatively little of business operations and affairs would be left for state control. . . .

Mr. JUSTICE HARLAN, dissenting.

The court holds it to be vital in our system of government to recognize and give effect to both the commercial power of the nation and the police powers of the States, to the end that the Union be strengthened, and the autonomy of the States preserved. In this view I entirely concur. Undoubtedly, the preservation of the just authority of the States is an object of deep concern to every lover of his country. No greater calamity could befall our free institutions than the destruction of that authority, by whatever means such a result might be accomplished. . . . But it is equally true that the preservation of the just authority of the General Government is essential as well to the safety of the States as to the attainment of the important ends for which that government was ordained by the People of the United States, and the destruction of *that* authority would be fatal to the peace and well-being of the American people. The Constitution which enumerates the powers committed to the nation for objects of interest to the people of all the States, should not, therefore, be subjected to an interpretation so rigid, technical, and narrow, that those objects cannot be accomplished. . . .

Congress is invested with power to regulate commerce with foreign nations and among the several States. The power to regulate is the power to prescribe the rule by which the subject regulated is to be governed. It is one that must be exercised whenever necessary throughout the territorial limits of the several states. *Cohens v. Virginia*, 6 Wheat. 264, 413. The power to make these regulations "is complete in itself, may be exercised to its utmost extent, and acknowledges no limitations, other than are prescribed in the Constitution." It is plenary because vested in congress "as absolutely as it would be in a single government having in its constitution the same restrictions on the exercise of the power as are found in the Constitution of the United States." It may be exercised "whenever the subject exists." *Gibbons v. Ogden*, 9 Wheat. 1, 195, 196. . . .

[T]here is a trade among the several States which is distinct from that carried on within the territorial limits of a State. The regulation and control of the former are committed by the national Constitution to Congress. Commerce among the States, as this court has declared, is a unit, and in respect of *that* commerce this is one country, and we are one people. It may be regulated by rules applicable to every part of the United States, and state lines and state jurisdiction cannot interfere with the enforcement of such rules. The jurisdiction of the general government extends over every foot of territory within the United States. Under the power with which it is invested, Congress may remove unlawful obstructions, of whatever kind, to the free course of trade among the states. In so doing it would not interfere with the "autonomy of the States," because the power thus to protect interstate commerce is expressly given by the people of all the States. . . . Any combination, therefore, that disturbs or unreasonably obstructs freedom in buying and selling articles manufactured to be sold to persons in other States or to be carried to other States . . . affects, not incidentally, but directly, the people of all the States, and the remedy for such an evil is found only in the exercise of powers confided to a government which, this court has said, was the government of all, exercising powers delegated by all, representing all, acting for all. *McCulloch v. Maryland*, 4 Wheat. 316, 405. . . .

In committing to Congress the control of commerce with foreign nations and among the several States, the Constitution did not define the means that may be employed to protect the freedom of commercial intercourse and traffic established for the benefit of all the people of the Union. It wisely forbore to impose any limitations upon the exercise of that power except those arising from the general nature of the government, or such as are embodied in the fundamental guaranties of liberty and property. It gives to Congress, in express words, authority to enact all laws necessary and proper for carrying into execution the power to regulate commerce, and whether an act of Congress, passed to accomplish an object to which the general government is competent, is within the power granted, must be determined by the rule announced through Chief Justice Marshall three-quarters of a century ago, and which has been repeatedly affirmed by this court. That rule is: "The sound construction of the Constitution must allow to the national legislature the discretion with respect to the means by which the powers it confers are to be carried into execution, which will enable that body to perform the high duties assigned to it in the manner most beneficial to the people. Let the end be legitimate, let it be within the scope of the Constitution; and all means which are appropriate, which are plainly adapted to that end, which are not prohibited, but consistent with the letter and spirit of the constitution, are constitutional." *McCulloch v. Maryland*, 4 Wheat. 316, 421. The end proposed to be accomplished by the act of 1890 is the protection of trade and commerce among the States against unlawful restraints. Who can say that that end is not legitimate or is not within the scope of the Constitution? The means employed are the suppression, by legal proceedings, of combinations, conspiracies, and monopolies, which by their inevitable and admitted tendency, improperly restrain trade and commerce among the States. Who can say that such means are not appropriate to attain the end of freeing commercial intercourse among the States from burdens and exactions imposed upon it by combinations which, under principles long recognized in this country as well as at the common law, are illegal and dangerous to the public welfare? What clause of the Constitution can be referred to which prohibits the means thus prescribed in the act of Congress? . . .

To the general government has been committed the control of commercial intercourse among the States, to the end that it may be free at all times from any restraints except such as Congress may impose or permit for the benefit of the whole country[.] The common government of all the people is the only one that can adequately deal with a matter which directly and injuriously affects the entire commerce of the country, which concerns equally all the people of the Union, and which, it must be confessed, cannot be adequately controlled by any one State. Its authority should not be so weakened by construction that it cannot reach and eradicate evils that, beyond all question, tend to defeat an object which that government is entitled, by the Constitution, to accomplish. . . .

CHAMPION v. AMES (LOTTERY CASE)

188 U.S. 321 (1903)

The general question arising upon this appeal involves the constitutionality of . . . "An Act for the Suppression of Lottery Traffic through National and Interstate Commerce . . ." [The Act prohibited, under criminal penalty, carrying a lottery ticket from one state into another. Champion was charged with conspiracy to violate this statute — specifically, conspiring to carry lottery tickets of the Pan-American Lottery Company from Texas to California.]

[Champion] sued out the present writ of habeas corpus upon the theory that the act . . . was void, under the Constitution of the United States.

Mr. JUSTICE HARLAN . . . delivered the opinion of the court:

The appellant insists that the carrying of lottery tickets from one State to another State by an express company engaged in carrying freight and packages from State to State, although such tickets may be contained in a box or package, does not constitute, and cannot by any act of Congress be legally made to constitute, *commerce* among the States within the meaning of the clause of the Constitution of the United States providing that Congress shall have power "to regulate commerce with foreign nations, and among the several States, and with the Indian tribes;" consequently, that Congress cannot make it an offence to cause such tickets to be carried from one State to another. . . .

What is the import of the word "commerce" as used in the Constitution? It is not defined by that instrument. Undoubtedly, the carrying from one State to another by independent carriers of things or commodities that are ordinary subjects of traffic, and which have in themselves a recognized value in money, constitutes interstate commerce. But does not commerce among the several States include something more? Does not the carrying from one state to another, by independent carriers, of lottery tickets that entitle the holder to the payment of a certain amount of money therein specified also constitute commerce among the States? . . .

The leading case under the commerce clause of the Constitution is *Gibbons v. Ogden*, 9 Wheat. 1, 189, 194. Referring to that clause, Chief Justice Marshall said: "The subject to be regulated is commerce; and our Constitution being, as was aptly said at the bar, one of enumeration, and not of definition, to ascertain the extent of the power it becomes necessary to settle the meaning of the word. . . . Commerce, undoubtedly, is traffic, but it is something more; it is intercourse. It describes the commercial intercourse between nations and parts of nations, in all its branches, and is regulated by prescribing rules for carrying on that intercourse . . ."

[P]rior adjudications . . . show that commerce among the States embraces navigation, intercourse, communication, traffic, the transit of persons, and the transmission of messages by telegraph. They also show that the power to regulate commerce among the several States is vested in Congress as absolutely as it would be in a single government, having in its constitution the same restrictions on the exercise of the power as are found in the Constitution of the United States; that such power is plenary, complete in itself, and may be exerted by Congress to its utmost extent, subject *only* to such limitations as the Constitution imposes upon the exercise of the powers granted by it; and that in determining the character of the regulations to be adopted Congress has a large discretion which is not to be controlled by the courts, simply because, in their opinion, such regulations may not be the best or most effective that could be employed. . . .

We are of opinion that lottery tickets are subjects of traffic and therefore are subjects of commerce, and the regulation of the carriage of such tickets from State to State, at least by independent carriers, is a regulation of commerce among the several States.

But it is said that the statute in question does not regulate the carrying of lottery tickets from State to State, but by punishing those who cause them to be so carried Congress in effect prohibits such carrying; that in respect of the carrying from one State to another of articles or things that are, in fact, or according to usage in business, the subjects of commerce, the authority given Congress was not to *prohibit*, but only to *regulate*. . . .

It is to be remarked that the Constitution does not define what is to be deemed a legitimate regulation of interstate commerce. In *Gibbons v. Ogden* it was said that the power to regulate such commerce is the power to prescribe the rule by which it is to be governed. But this general observation leaves it to be determined, when the question comes before the court, whether Congress in prescribing a particular rule has exceeded its power under the Constitution. While our Government must be acknowledged by all to be one of enumerated powers, *McCulloch v. Maryland*, 4 Wheat. 316, 405, 407, the Constitution does not attempt to set forth all the means by which such powers may be carried into execution. It leaves to Congress a large discretion as to the means that may be employed in executing a given power. The sound construction of the Constitution, this court has said, "must allow to the national legislature that discretion, with respect to the means by which the powers it confers are to be carried into execution, which will enable that body to perform the high duties assigned to it, in the manner most beneficial to the people. Let the end be legitimate, let it be within the scope of the Constitution, and all means which are appropriate, which are plainly adapted to that end, which are not prohibited, but consist with the letter and spirit of the Constitution, are constitutional." 4 Wheat. 421.

We have said that the carrying from State to State of lottery tickets constitutes interstate commerce, and that the regulation of such commerce is within the power of Congress under the Constitution. Are we prepared to say that a provision which is, in effect, a *prohibition* of the carriage of such articles from State to State is not a fit or appropriate mode for the *regulation* of that particular kind of commerce? If lottery traffic, *carried on through interstate commerce*, is a matter of which Congress may take cognizance and over which its power may be exerted, can it be possible that it must tolerate the traffic, and simply regulate the manner in which it may be carried on? Or may not Congress, for the protection of the people of all the States, and under the power to regulate interstate commerce, devise such means, within the scope of the Constitution, and not prohibited by it, as will drive that traffic out of commerce among the States? . . .

If a State, when considering legislation for the suppression of lotteries within its own limits, may properly take into view the evils that inhere in the raising of money, in that mode, why may not Congress, invested with the power to regulate commerce among the several States, provide that such commerce shall not be polluted by the carrying of lottery tickets from one state to another? In this connection it must not be forgotten that the power of Congress to regulate commerce among the States is plenary, is complete in itself, and is subject to no limitations except such as may be found in the Constitution. . . .

If it be said that the [A]ct . . . is inconsistent with the Tenth Amendment, reserving to the States respectively or to the people, the powers not delegated to the United States, the answer is that the power to regulate commerce among the States has been expressly delegated to Congress.

Besides, Congress, by that act, does not assume to interfere with traffic or commerce in lottery tickets carried on exclusively within the limits of any State, but has in view only commerce of that kind among the several States. It has not assumed to interfere with the completely internal affairs of any State, and has only legislated in respect of a matter which concerns the people of the United States. As a State may, for the purpose of guarding the morals of its own people, forbid all sales of lottery tickets within its limits, so Congress, for the purpose of guarding the people of the United States against the "widespread pestilence of lotteries" and to protect the commerce which concerns all the States, may prohibit the carrying of lottery tickets from one State to another. . . . If the carrying of lottery tickets from one State to another be interstate commerce, and if Congress is of opinion that an effective regulation for the suppression of lotteries, carried on through such commerce, is to make it a criminal offense to cause lottery tickets to be carried from one State to another, we know of no authority in the courts to hold that the means thus devised are not appropriate and necessary to protect the country at large against a species of interstate commerce which, although in general use and somewhat favored in both national and state legislation in the early history of the country, has grown into disrepute and has become offensive to the entire people of the Nation. It is a kind of traffic which no one can be entitled to pursue as of right. . . .

It is said, however, that if, in order to suppress lotteries carried on through interstate commerce, Congress may exclude lottery tickets from such commerce, that principle leads necessarily to the conclusion that Congress may arbitrarily exclude from commerce among the States any article, commodity, or thing, of whatever kind or nature, or however useful or valuable, which it may choose, no matter with what motive, to declare shall not be carried from one State to another. It will be time enough to consider the constitutionality of such legislation when we must do so. The present case does not require the court to declare the full extent of the power that Congress may exercise in the regulation of commerce among the States. We may, however, repeat, in this connection, what the court has heretofore said, that the power of Congress to regulate commerce among the States, although plenary, cannot be deemed arbitrary, since it is subject to such limitations or restrictions as are prescribed by the Constitution. This power, therefore, may not be exercised so as to infringe rights secured or protected by that instrument. It would not be difficult to imagine legislation that would be justly liable to such an objection as that stated, and be hostile to the objects for the accomplishment of which Congress was invested with the general power to regulate commerce among the several States. But, as often said, the possible abuse of a power is not an argument against its existence. There is probably no governmental power that may not be exerted to the injury of the public. If what is done by Congress is manifestly in excess of the powers granted to it, then upon the courts will rest the duty of adjudging that its action is neither legal nor binding upon the people. But if what Congress does is within the limits of its power, and is simply unwise or injurious, the remedy is that suggested by Chief Justice Marshall in *Gibbons v. Ogden*, when he said: "The wisdom and the discretion of Congress, their identity with the people, and the influence which their constituents possess at elections, are, in this, as in many other instances, as that, for example, of declaring war, the sole restraints on which they have relied, to secure them from its abuse. They are the restraints on which the people must often rely solely, in all representative governments."

The whole subject is too important, and the questions suggested by its consideration are too difficult of solution, to justify any attempt to lay down a rule for determining in advance the validity of every statute that may be enacted under the commerce clause. We decide nothing more in the present case than that lottery tickets are subjects of traffic among those who choose to sell or buy them; that the carriage of such tickets by independent carriers from one State to another is therefore interstate commerce; that under its power to regulate commerce among the several States Congress — subject to the limitations imposed by the Constitution upon the exercise of the powers granted — has plenary authority over such commerce, and may prohibit the carriage of such tickets from State to State; and that legislation to that end, and of that character, is not inconsistent with any limitation or restriction imposed upon the exercise of the powers granted to Congress. . . .

Mr. CHIEF JUSTICE FULLER, with whom concur Mr. JUSTICE BREWER, Mr. JUSTICE SHIRAS, and Mr. JUSTICE PECKHAM, dissenting:

[The] question is whether the prohibition by Congress of the carriage of lottery tickets from one State to another by means other than the mails is within the powers vested in that body by the Constitution of the United States. That the purpose of Congress in this enactment was the suppression of lotteries cannot reasonably be denied. That purpose is avowed in the title of the act, and is its natural and reasonable effect, and by that its validity must be tested.

The power of the State to impose restraints and burdens on persons and property in conservation and promotion of the public health, good order and prosperity is a power originally and always belonging to the States, not surrendered by them to the General Government nor directly restrained by the Constitution of the United States, and essentially exclusive, and the suppression of lotteries as a harmful business falls within this power, commonly called, of police. . . .

[T]his act cannot be brought within the power to regulate commerce among the several States, unless lottery tickets are articles of commerce, and, therefore, when carried across state lines, of interstate commerce; or unless the power to regulate interstate commerce includes the absolute and exclusive power to prohibit the transportation of anything or anybody from one State to another. . . .

It cannot be successfully contended that either Congress or the States can, by their own legislation, enlarge their powers, and the question of the extent and limit of the powers of either is a judicial question under the fundamental law.

If a particular article is not the subject of commerce, the determination of Congress that it is, cannot be so conclusive as to exclude judicial inquiry. . . .

Is the carriage of lottery tickets from one State to another commercial intercourse?

The lottery ticket purports to create contractual relations, and to furnish the means of enforcing a contract right.

This is true of insurance policies, and both are contingent in their nature. Yet this court has held that the issuing of fire, marine, and life insurance policies, in one State, and sending them to another, to be there delivered to the insured on payment of premium, is not interstate commerce. . . .

If a lottery ticket is not an article of commerce, how can it become so when placed in an envelope or box or other covering, and transported by an express company? To say that the mere carrying of an article which is not an article of commerce in and of itself nevertheless becomes such the moment it is to be transported from one State to another, is to transform a non-commercial article into a commercial one simply because it is transported. I cannot conceive that any such result can properly follow.

It would be to say that everything is an article of commerce the moment it is taken to be transported from place to place, and of interstate commerce if from State to State.

An invitation to dine, or to take a drive, or a note of introduction, all become articles of commerce under the ruling in this case, by being deposited with an express company for transportation. This in effect breaks down all the differences between that which is, and that which is not, an article of commerce, and the necessary consequence is to take from the States all jurisdiction over the subject so far as interstate communication is concerned. It is a long step in the direction of wiping out all traces of state lines, and the creation of a centralized government.

Does the grant to Congress of the power to regulate interstate commerce import the absolute power to prohibit it? . . .

[T]he power . . . to regulate interstate commerce . . . was intended to secure equality and freedom in commercial intercourse as between the States, not to permit the creation of impediments to such intercourse . . .

[T]he right of passage of persons and property from one state to another cannot be prohibited by Congress. . . .

HAMMER v. DAGENHART

247 U.S. 251 (1918)

Mr. JUSTICE DAY delivered the opinion of the Court.

A bill was filed in the United States District Court for the Western District of North Carolina by a father in his own behalf and as next friend of his two minor sons, one under the age of fourteen years and the other between the ages of fourteen and sixteen years, employees in a cotton mill at Charlotte, North Carolina, to enjoin the enforcement of the act of Congress intended to prevent interstate commerce in the products of child labor. Act of Sept. 1, 1916, c. 432, 39 Stat. 675. . . .

The controlling question for decision is: Is it within the authority of Congress in regulating commerce among the States to prohibit the transportation in interstate commerce of manufactured goods, the product of a factory in which, within thirty days prior to their removal therefrom, children under the age of fourteen have been employed or permitted to work, or children between the ages of fourteen and sixteen years have been employed or permitted to work more than eight hours in any day, or more than six days in any week, or after the hour of seven o'clock P.M., or before the hour of 6 o'clock A.M.?

The power essential to the passage of this act, the Government contends, is found in the commerce clause of the Constitution which authorizes Congress to regulate commerce with foreign nations and among the States.

In *Gibbons v. Ogdon*, 9 Wheat. 1, Chief Justice Marshall, speaking for this court, and defining the extent and nature of the commerce power, said, "It is the power to regulate; that is, to prescribe the rule by which commerce is to be governed." In other words, the power is one to control the means by which commerce is carried on, which is directly the contrary of the assumed right to forbid commerce from moving and thus destroying it as to particular commodities. But it is insisted that adjudged cases in this court establish the doctrine that the power to regulate given to Congress incidentally includes the authority to prohibit the movement of ordinary commodities. . . .

The first of these cases is *Champion v. Ames*, 188 U.S. 321, the so-called *Lottery Case*, in which it was held that Congress might pass a law having the effect to keep the channels of commerce free from use in the transportation of tickets used in the promotion of lottery schemes. . . .

In each of these instances the use of interstate transportation was necessary to the accomplishment of harmful results. In other words, although the power over interstate transportation was to regulate, that could only be accomplished by prohibiting the use of the facilities of interstate commerce to effect the evil intended.

This element is wanting in the present case. The thing intended to be accomplished by this statute is the denial of the facilities of interstate commerce to those manufacturers in the States who employ children within the prohibited ages. The act in its effect does not regulate transportation among the States, but aims to standardize the ages at which children may be employed in mining and manufacturing within the States. The goods shipped are of themselves harmless. The act permits them to be freely shipped after thirty days from the time of their removal from the factory. When offered for shipment, and before transportation begins, the labor of their production is over, and the mere fact that they were intended for interstate commerce transportation does not make their production subject to federal control under the commerce power. . . .

Over interstate transportation, or its incidents, the regulatory power of Congress is ample, but the production of articles, intended for interstate commerce, is a matter of local regulation.

When the commerce begins is determined, not by the character of the commodity, nor by the intention of the owner to transfer it to another state for sale, nor by his preparation of it for transportation, but by its actual delivery to a common carrier for transportation, or the actual commencement of its transfer to another state. . . .

If it were otherwise, all manufacture intended for interstate shipment would be brought under federal control to the practical exclusion of the authority of the States, a result certainly not contemplated by the framers of the Constitution when they vested in Congress the authority to regulate commerce among the States. . . .

The grant of power of Congress over the subject of interstate commerce was to enable it to regulate such commerce, and not to give it authority to control the States in their exercise of the police power over local trade and manufacture.

The grant of authority over a purely federal matter was not intended to destroy the local power always existing and carefully reserved to the States in the Tenth Amendment to the Constitution.

Police regulations relating to the internal trade and affairs of the States have been uniformly recognized as within such control. . . . That there should be limitations upon the right to employ children in mines and factories in the interest of their own and the public welfare, all will admit. . . . It may be desirable that such laws be uniform, but our Federal Government is one of enumerated powers . . . .

To sustain this statute would not be in our judgment a recognition of the lawful exertion of congressional authority over interstate commerce, but would sanction an invasion by the federal power of the control of a matter purely local in its character, and over which no authority has been delegated to Congress in conferring the power to regulate commerce among the States.

We have neither authority nor disposition to question the motives of Congress in enacting this legislation. The purposes intended must be attained consistently with constitutional limitations and not by an invasion of the powers of the States. This court has no more important function than that which devolves upon it the obligation to preserve inviolate the constitutional limitations upon the exercise of authority, federal and state, to the end that each may continue to discharge, harmoniously with the other, the duties entrusted to it by the Constitution.

In our view the necessary effect of this act is, by means of a prohibition against the movement in interstate commerce of ordinary commercial commodities, to regulate the hours of labor of children in factories and mines within the States, a purely state authority. Thus the act in a twofold sense is repugnant to the Constitution. It not only transcends the authority delegated to Congress over commerce but also exerts a power as to a purely local matter to which the federal authority does not extend. The far reaching result of upholding the act cannot be more plainly indicated than by pointing out that if Congress can thus regulate matters entrusted to local authority by prohibition of the movement of commodities in interstate commerce, all freedom of commerce will be at an end, and the power of the States over local matters may be eliminated, and thus our system of government be practically destroyed. . . .

Mr. JUSTICE HOLMES, dissenting.

The objection urged against the power is that the States have exclusive control over their methods of production and that Congress cannot meddle with them, and taking the proposition in the sense of direct intermeddling I agree to it and suppose that no one denies it. But if an act is within the powers specifically conferred upon Congress, it seems to me that it is not made any less constitutional because of the indirect effects that it may have, however obvious it may be that it will have those effects, and that we are not at liberty upon such grounds to hold it void. . . .

Regulation means the prohibition of something, and when interstate commerce is the matter to be regulated I cannot doubt that the regulation may prohibit any part of such commerce that Congress sees fit to forbid. At all events it is established by the *Lottery Case* and others that have followed it that a law is not beyond the regulative power of Congress merely because it prohibits certain transportation out and out. *Champion v. Ames*, 188 U. S. 321, 355, 359, *et seq.* . . .

[T]he power to regulate commerce and other constitutional powers could not be cut down or qualified by the fact that it might interfere with the carrying out of the domestic policy of any State. . . . [I]f there is any matter upon which civilized countries have agreed . . . it is the evil of premature and excessive child labor. I should have thought that if we were to introduce our own moral conceptions where in my opinion they do not belong, this was preëminently a case for upholding the exercise of all its powers by the United States.

But I had thought that the propriety of the exercise of a power admitted to exist in some cases was for the consideration of Congress alone and that this Court always had disavowed the right to intrude its judgment upon questions of policy or morals. It is not for this Court to pronounce when prohibition is necessary to regulation if it ever may be necessary. . . .

The act does not meddle with anything belonging to the States. They may regulate their internal affairs and their domestic commerce as they like. But when they seek to send their products across the State line they are no longer within their rights. If there were no Constitution and no Congress their power to cross the line would depend upon their neighbors. Under the Constitution such commerce belongs not to the States but to Congress to regulate. It may carry out its views of public policy whatever indirect effect they may have upon the activities of the States. . . .

Mr. Justice McKenna, Mr. Justice Brandeis, and Mr. Justice Clarke concur in this opinion.

POINTS FOR DISCUSSION

1. In *United States v. E. C. Knight Co.*, the Court distinguished "manufacture" from "commerce." On what basis did the Court derive this distinction? Is it a workable distinction? In this and other cases, the Court has attempted to define meaningful limits on the commerce power in order to prevent the federal government from having, in effect, unlimited regulatory power. Does the distinction between "manufacture" and "commerce" effectively serve this structural interest?

2. In *Champion v. Ames*, the Court held that the Commerce Clause empowered Congress to prohibit the interstate transportation of lottery tickets. Justice Fuller argued in dissent that the Court's reasoning would empower Congress to prohibit the transportation of any article in interstate commerce. In response, the Court expressly refrained from holding that Congress has power to exclude any article from interstate commerce. In *Hammer v. Dagenhart*, the Court held that Congress lacked power under the Commerce Clause to prohibit the interstate transportation of goods produced through child labor. How did the Court distinguish the regulation at issue in *Dagenhart* from the prohibition of interstate lottery ticket transportation at issue in *Champion*? What values, if any, does the distinction advance?

3. Each of these cases implicates the question of how much deference courts should afford Congress in determining whether a regulation is necessary and proper for carrying the commerce power into execution. Consider Justice Harlan's views. In *E. C. Knight*, Justice Harlan rhetorically asked in dissent, "Who can say that [antitrust regulations] are not appropriate to attain the end of freeing commercial intercourse among the States from burdens and exactions imposed upon it by combinations which . . . are illegal and dangerous to the public welfare?" In *Champion*, Justice Harlan wrote for the Court:

> If the carrying of lottery tickets from one State to another be interstate commerce, and if Congress is of opinion that an effective regulation for the suppression of lotteries, carried on through such commerce, is to

make it a criminal offense to cause lottery tickets to be carried from one State to another, we know of no authority in the courts to hold that the means thus devised are not appropriate and necessary to protect the country at large against a species of interstate commerce which . . . has grown into disrepute. . . .

How much deference should courts afford Congress in determining whether a regulation is necessary and proper for carrying an enumerated power into execution? Do Justice Harlan's views in fact accord with those of Chief Justice Marshall in *McCullough v. Maryland*, 17 U.S. (4 Wheat.) 316 (1819)? Are there any drawbacks to courts giving Congress the deference that Justice Harlan advocated?

2. THE NEW DEAL

In response to the Great Depression, Congress enacted various economic programs—known as the New Deal—from 1933 to 1936 during President Franklin Delano Roosevelt's first term of office. The Supreme Court held several of these programs unconstitutional in light of such cases as *United States v. E. C. Knight Co.*, 156 U.S. 1 (1895), and *Hammer v. Dagenhart*, 247 U.S. 251 (1918). A long-standing account of the Court's initial treatment of New Deal legislation was that four conservative Justices devoted to laissez-faire economics—Pierce Butler, James McReynolds, George Sutherland, and Willis Van Devanter (described as the "Four Horsemen")—thwarted the New Deal with the acquiescence of two moderate Justices, Charles Evans Hughes and Owen Roberts.

In time, however, the Court came to uphold most New Deal legislation. Some have believed that certain members of the Court switched their votes in response to President Roosevelt's plan to increase the size of the Court and "pack" it with Justices sympathetic to New Deal programs. As Professor Barry Cushman has summarized this belief, "[f]earing institutional evisceration, the moderates, in an act spurred by a mixture of cowardice, 'statesmanship,' and newfound constitutional enlightenment, decide[d] to switch rather than fight." BARRY CUSHMAN, RETHINKING THE NEW DEAL COURT 3 (1998). The phrase "the switch in time that saved nine" charged Justice Roberts with switching his vote in *West Coast Hotel Co. v. Parrish*, 300 U.S. 379 (1937), which upheld state minimum-wage legislation, thereby marking the end of the Court's efforts to thwart economic regulation.

In his influential book, *Rethinking the New Deal Court* (and related articles), Professor Cushman demonstrated the errors of this account. He explained that the Court experienced not a spontaneous "switch" prompted by external political pressures but rather a slow and subtle shift that began before the 1936 election and 1937 court-packing plan announcement. Professor Cushman argued that, for various reasons, the Justices had good reason to doubt that Roosevelt's court-packing plan was politically viable. Moreover, the Justices' conference vote in *West Coast Hotel* preceded President Roosevelt's announcement of the court-packing plan. According to Professor Cushman, the jurisprudential shift, which began before 1936, was gradual and, at least doctrinally, maintained some limits on congressional power from the

Progressive Era. Professor Cushman argued that those limits largely disappeared with the Court's decision in *Wickard v. Filburn*, 317 U.S. 111 (1942). This gradual shift resulted in part, Professor Cushman argued, from the increasing unworkability of certain Progressive Era precedents in light of developing economic circumstances:

> With economic development and integration, some of the system's premises ceased to be persuasive descriptive accounts of the world. These changing conditions prompted the Court to reassess and revise those premises. . . .
>
> [A]s the Court elaborated doctrine in cases presenting fact patterns that challenged the underlying premises of the system, the system lost its appearance of coherence and symmetry, becoming unwieldy. Some businesses were affected with a public interest, others were not; some economic activities affected interstate commerce directly, others only indirectly. The problem was that there were an increasing number of cases in which one could not predict the outcome ex ante. Moreover, the system began to generate paradoxical outcomes: the Court held that Congress could regulate lottery tickets . . . but not interstate commerce in goods made by child labor. . . . Such paradoxes made the system appear increasingly indeterminate and politically charged, and fueled external academic critiques that sought further to undermine the system's plausibility. . . . [S]uch paradoxes and asymmetries . . . played a role in prompting such synthetic opinions as . . . *NLRB v. Jones & Laughlin Steel Corp.* . . .
>
> The story of the New Deal Court, then, is not a simple tale of how "laissez-faire" constitutionalism was summarily jettisoned for political reasons in the course of a couple of months in the spring of 1937. It is instead the more complex story of how a structurally interdependent system of thought gradually unraveled over the first forty years of the twentieth century and how, after it had unraveled so far as to become completely unserviceable, it was abandoned by a generation of jurists with no stake in salvaging its remains. . . .

Barry Cushman, *Rethinking the New Deal Court*, 80 Va. L. Rev. 201, 258-260 (1994).

As you read the following cases—all decided after 1937—consider the following questions:

- How does the Court define the commerce power in each case? How do these definitions depart from *E. C. Knight* and *Dagenhart*? What values do they advance?
- What role, if any, does the motive or purpose of Congress play in the Court's analyses of whether the Commerce Clause authorized the regulations at issue?
- How much deference does the Court give Congress in determining whether it had power to enact the regulations at issue?

NLRB v. Jones & Laughlin Steel Corp.

301 U.S. 1 (1937)

Mr. CHIEF JUSTICE HUGHES delivered the opinion of the Court.

In a proceeding under the National Labor Relations Act of 1935 the National Labor Relations Board found that the respondent, Jones & Laughlin

Steel Corporation, had violated the act by engaging in unfair labor practices affecting commerce. . . . The unfair labor practices charged were that the corporation was discriminating against members of the union with regard to hire and tenure of employment, and was coercing and intimidating its employees in order to interfere with their self-organization. . . .

The scheme of the National Labor Relations Act . . . may be briefly stated. The first section sets forth findings with respect to the injury to commerce resulting from the denial by employers of the right of employees to organize and from the refusal of employers to accept the procedure of collective bargaining. There follows a declaration that it is the policy of the United States to eliminate these causes of obstruction to the free flow of commerce. The Act then defines the terms it uses, including the terms "commerce" and "affecting commerce." It creates the National Labor Relations Board and prescribes its organization. It sets forth the right of employees to self-organization and to bargain collectively through representatives of their own choosing. It defines "unfair labor practices." It lays down rules as to the representation of employees for the purpose of collective bargaining. The Board is empowered to prevent the described unfair labor practices affecting commerce and the Act prescribes the procedure to that end. . . .

[T]he Jones & Laughlin Steel Corporation . . . is organized under the laws of Pennsylvania and has its principal office at Pittsburgh. It is engaged in the business of manufacturing iron and steel in plants situated in Pittsburgh and nearby Aliquippa, Pennsylvania. It manufactures and distributes a widely diversified line of steel and pig iron, being the fourth largest producer of steel in the United States. With its subsidiaries — nineteen in number — it is a completely integrated enterprise, owning and operating ore, coal and limestone properties, lake and river transportation facilities and terminal railroads located at its manufacturing plants. It owns or controls mines in Michigan and Minnesota. It operates four ore steamships on the Great Lakes, used in the transportation of ore to its factories. It owns coal mines in Pennsylvania. It operates towboats and steam barges used in carrying coal to its factories. It owns limestone properties in various places in Pennsylvania and West Virginia. It owns the Monongahela connecting railroad which connects the plants of the Pittsburgh works and forms an interconnection with the Pennsylvania, New York Central and Baltimore and Ohio Railroad systems. It owns the Aliquippa and Southern Railroad Company which connects the Aliquippa works with the Pittsburgh and Lake Erie, part of the New York Central system. Much of its product is shipped to its warehouses in Chicago, Detroit, Cincinnati and Memphis, — to the last two places by means of its own barges and transportation equipment. In Long Island City, New York, and in New Orleans it operates structural steel fabricating shops in connection with the warehousing of semi-finished materials sent from its works. Through one of its wholly-owned subsidiaries it owns, leases and operates stores, warehouses, and yards for the distribution of equipment and supplies for drilling and operating oil and gas wells and for pipe lines, refineries and pumping stations. It has sales offices in twenty cities in the United States and a wholly-owned subsidiary which is devoted exclusively to distributing its product in Canada. Approximately 75 per cent. of its product is shipped out of Pennsylvania. . . .

The act specifically defines the "commerce" to which it refers:

"The term 'commerce' means trade, traffic, commerce, transportation, or communication among the several States, or between the District of Columbia or any Territory of the United States and any State or other Territory, or between any foreign country and any State, Territory, or the District of Columbia, or within the District of Columbia or any Territory, or between points in the same State but through any other State or any Territory or the District of Columbia or any foreign country."

There can be no question that the commerce thus contemplated by the act (aside from that within a Territory or the District of Columbia) is interstate and foreign commerce in the constitutional sense. The act also defines the term "affecting commerce":

"The term 'affecting commerce' means in commerce, or burdening or obstructing commerce or the free flow of commerce, or having led or tending to lead to a labor dispute burdening or obstructing commerce or the free flow of commerce."

This definition . . . does not purport to extend to the relationship between all industrial employees and employers. Its terms do not impose collective bargaining upon all industry regardless of effects upon interstate or foreign commerce. It purports to reach only what may be deemed to burden or obstruct that commerce and, thus qualified, it must be construed as contemplating the exercise of control within constitutional bounds. It is a familiar principle that acts which directly burden or obstruct interstate or foreign commerce, or its free flow, are within the reach of the congressional power. Acts having that effect are not rendered immune because they grow out of labor disputes. It is the effect upon commerce, not the source of the injury, which is the criterion. Whether or not particular action does affect commerce in such a close and intimate fashion as to be subject to federal control, and hence to lie within the authority conferred upon the Board, is left by the statute to be determined as individual cases arise. . . .

[T]he power to regulate commerce is . . . plenary and may be exerted to protect interstate commerce "no matter what the source of the dangers which threaten it." *Second Employers' Liability Cases*, [223 U.S. 1, 51.] Although activities may be intrastate in character when separately considered, if they have such a close and substantial relation to interstate commerce that their control is essential or appropriate to protect that commerce from burdens and obstructions, Congress cannot be denied the power to exercise that control. Undoubtedly the scope of this power must be considered in the light of our dual system of government and may not be extended so as to embrace effects upon interstate commerce so indirect and remote that to embrace them, in view of our complex society, would effectually obliterate the distinction between what is national and what is local and create a completely centralized government. The question is necessarily one of degree. . . .

The close and intimate effect which brings the subject within the reach of federal power may be due to activities in relation to productive industry although the industry when separately viewed is local. . . .

[T]he stoppage of [the steel company's] operations by industrial strife would have a most serious effect upon interstate commerce. In view of respondent's far-flung activities, it is idle to say that the effect would be indirect or remote. It is obvious that it would be immediate and might be catastrophic. We are asked to shut our eyes to the plainest facts of our national life and to deal with the question of direct and indirect effects in an intellectual vacuum. Because there may be but indirect and remote effects upon interstate commerce in connection with a host of local enterprises throughout the country, it does not follow that other industrial activities do not have such a close and intimate relation to interstate commerce as to make the presence of industrial strife a matter of the most urgent national concern. When industries organize themselves on a national scale, making their relation to interstate commerce the dominant factor in their activities, how can it be maintained that their industrial labor relations constitute a forbidden field into which Congress may not enter when it is necessary to protect interstate commerce from the paralyzing consequences of industrial war? We have often said that interstate commerce itself is a practical conception. It is equally true that interferences with that commerce must be appraised by a judgment that does not ignore actual experience. . . .

The act has been criticised as one-sided in its application; that it subjects the employer to supervision and restraint and leaves untouched the abuses for which employees may be responsible; that it fails to provide a more comprehensive plan, — with better assurances of fairness to both sides and with increased chances of success in bringing about, if not compelling, equitable solutions of industrial disputes affecting interstate commerce. But we are dealing with the power of Congress, not with a particular policy or with the extent to which policy should go. We have frequently said that the legislative authority, exerted within its proper field, need not embrace all the evils within its reach. . . .

Mr. JUSTICE MCREYNOLDS delivered the following dissenting opinion. . . .

Mr. Justice Van Devanter, Mr. Justice Sutherland, Mr. Justice Butler and I are unable to agree with the decisions just announced.

[T]he power of Congress under the commerce clause does not extend to relations between employers and their employees engaged in manufacture. . . .

With striking lucidity, fifty years ago, *Kidd v. Pearson*, 128 U.S. 1, 21, declared: "If it be held that the term [commerce with foreign nations and among the several states] includes the regulation of all such manufactures as are intended to be the subject of commercial transactions in the future, it is impossible to deny that it would also include all productive industries that contemplate the same thing. The result would be that Congress would be invested, to the exclusion of the States, with the power to regulate, not only manufacture, but also agriculture, horticulture, stockraising, domestic fisheries, mining — in short, every branch of human industry." This doctrine found full approval in *United States v. E. C. Knight Co.*, 156 U.S. 1, 12, 13. . . .

Any effect on interstate commerce by the discharge of employees shown here, would be indirect and remote in the highest degree. . . .

The Constitution still recognizes the existence of states with indestructible powers; the Tenth Amendment was supposed to put them beyond controversy. . . .

There is no ground on which reasonably to hold that refusal by a manufacturer, whose raw materials come from states other than that of his factory and whose products are regularly carried to other states, to bargain collectively with employees in his manufacturing plant, directly affects interstate commerce. In such business, there is not one but two distinct movements or streams in interstate transportation. The first brings in raw material and there ends. Then follows manufacture, a separate and local activity. Upon completion of this and not before, the second distinct movement or stream in interstate commerce begins and the products go to other states. Such is the common course for small as well as large industries. It is unreasonable and unprecedented to say the commerce clause confers upon Congress power to govern relations between employers and employees in these local activities. . . .

It is gravely stated that experience teaches that if an employer discourages membership "in any organization of any kind" "in which employees participate, and which exists for the purpose in whole or in part of dealing with employers concerning grievances, labor disputes, wages, rates of pay, hours of employment or conditions of work," discontent may follow and this in turn may lead to a strike, and as the outcome of the strike there may be a block in the stream of interstate commerce. Therefore Congress may inhibit the discharge! Whatever effect any cause of discontent may ultimately have upon commerce is far too indirect to justify congressional regulation. Almost anything — marriage, birth, death — may in some fashion affect commerce. . . .

That Congress has power by appropriate means, not prohibited by the Constitution, to prevent direct and material interference with the conduct of interstate commerce is settled doctrine. But the interference struck at must be direct and material, not some mere possibility contingent on wholly uncertain events. . . .

UNITED STATES v. DARBY

312 U.S. 100 (1941)

Mr. JUSTICE STONE delivered the opinion of the Court.

The two principal questions raised . . . are, *first*, whether Congress has constitutional power to prohibit the shipment in interstate commerce of lumber manufactured by employees whose wages are less than a prescribed minimum or whose weekly hours of labor at that wage are greater than a prescribed maximum, and, *second*, whether it has power to prohibit the employment of workmen in the production of goods "for interstate commerce" at other than prescribed wages and hours. . . .

The Fair Labor Standards Act set up a comprehensive legislative scheme for preventing the shipment in interstate commerce of certain products and commodities produced in the United States under labor conditions as respects wages and hours which fail to conform to standards set up by the Act. Its purpose . . . is to exclude from interstate commerce goods produced for the commerce and to prevent their production for interstate commerce, under conditions detrimental to the maintenance of the minimum standards of living necessary for health and general well-being; and to prevent the use of interstate commerce as the means of competition in the distribution of goods so produced, and as the means of spreading and perpetuating such substandard labor conditions among the workers of the several states. . . .

[The Act] prohibits . . . the shipment in interstate commerce, of goods produced for interstate commerce by employees whose wages and hours of employment do not conform to the requirements of the Act. . . . [T]he only question arising under the commerce clause with respect to such shipments is whether Congress has the constitutional power to prohibit them.

While manufacture is not of itself interstate commerce, the shipment of manufactured goods interstate is such commerce and the prohibition of such shipment by Congress is indubitably a regulation of the commerce. The power to regulate commerce is the power "to prescribe the rule by which commerce is to be governed." *Gibbons v. Ogden*, 9 Wheat. 1, 196. It extends not only to those regulations which aid, foster and protect the commerce, but embraces those which prohibit it. . . . *Lottery Case* (*Champion v. Ames*), 188 U.S. 321. . . . It is conceded that the power of Congress to prohibit transportation in interstate commerce includes noxious articles, *Lottery Case, supra* . . . , stolen articles . . . , kidnapped persons . . . , and articles such as intoxicating liquor or convict made goods, traffic in which is forbidden or restricted by the laws of the state of destination. . . .

The power of Congress over interstate commerce "is complete in itself, may be exercised to its utmost extent, and acknowledges no limitations, other than are prescribed in the Constitution." *Gibbons v. Ogden, supra*, 196. That power can neither be enlarged nor diminished by the exercise or nonexercise of state power. Congress, following its own conception of public policy concerning the restrictions which may appropriately be imposed on interstate commerce, is free to exclude from the commerce articles whose use in the states for which they are destined it may conceive to be injurious to the public health, morals or welfare, even though the state has not sought to regulate their use. *Lottery Case, supra*. . . .

Such regulation is not a forbidden invasion of state power merely because either its motive or its consequence is to restrict the use of articles of commerce within the states of destination; and is not prohibited unless by other Constitutional provisions. It is no objection to the assertion of the power to regulate interstate commerce that its exercise is attended by the same incidents which attend the exercise of the police power of the states. . . .

The motive and purpose of the present regulation are plainly to make effective the Congressional conception of public policy that interstate commerce should not be made the instrument of competition in the distribution of goods produced under substandard labor conditions, which competition is injurious to the commerce and to the states from and to which the commerce flows. The motive and purpose of a regulation of interstate commerce are matters for the legislative judgment upon the exercise of which the Constitution places no restriction and over which the courts are given no control. . . . Whatever their motive and purpose, regulations of commerce which do not infringe some constitutional prohibition are within the plenary power conferred on Congress by the Commerce Clause. . . . [W]e conclude that the prohibition of the shipment interstate of goods produced under the forbidden substandard labor conditions is within the constitutional authority of Congress.

In the more than a century which has elapsed since the decision of *Gibbons v. Ogden*, these principles of constitutional interpretation have been so long and repeatedly recognized by this Court as applicable to the Commerce Clause, that there would be little occasion for repeating them now were it not for the decision of this Court twenty-two years ago in *Hammer v. Dagenhart*, 247 U.S. 251. In that case it was held by a bare majority of the Court over the powerful and now classic dissent of Mr. Justice Holmes setting forth the fundamental issues involved, that Congress was without power to exclude the products of child labor from interstate commerce. The reasoning and conclusion of the Court's opinion there cannot be reconciled with the conclusion which we have reached, that the power of Congress under the Commerce Clause is plenary to exclude any article from interstate commerce subject only to the specific prohibitions of the Constitution.

Hammer v. Dagenhart has not been followed. The distinction on which the decision was rested that Congressional power to prohibit interstate commerce is limited to articles which in themselves have some harmful or deleterious property — a distinction which was novel when made and unsupported by any provision of the Constitution — has long since been abandoned. The thesis of the opinion that the motive of the prohibition or its effect to control in some measure the use or production within the states of the article thus excluded from the commerce can operate to deprive the regulation of its constitutional authority has long since ceased to have force.

The conclusion is inescapable that *Hammer v. Dagenhart*, was a departure from the principles which have prevailed in the interpretation of the Commerce Clause both before and since the decision and that such vitality, as a precedent, as it then had has long since been exhausted. It should be and now is overruled. . . .

The power of Congress over interstate commerce is not confined to the regulation of commerce among the states. It extends to those activities intrastate which so affect interstate commerce or the exercise of the power of Congress over it as to make regulation of them appropriate means to the attainment of a legitimate end, the exercise of the granted power of Congress to regulate interstate commerce. See *McCulloch v. Maryland*, 4 Wheat. 316, 421. . . .

The means adopted by [the Act] for the protection of interstate commerce by the suppression of the production of the condemned goods for interstate commerce is so related to the commerce and so affects it as to be within the reach of the commerce power. Congress, to attain its objective in the suppression of nationwide competition in interstate commerce by goods produced under substandard labor conditions, has made no distinction as to the volume or amount of shipments in the commerce or of production for commerce by any particular shipper or producer. It recognized that in present day industry, competition by a small part may affect the whole and that the total effect of the competition of many small producers may be great. The legislation aimed at a whole embraces all its parts.

Our conclusion is unaffected by the Tenth Amendment which provides: "The powers not delegated to the United States by the Constitution, nor prohibited by it to the States, are reserved to the States respectively, or to the people." The amendment states but a truism that all is retained which has not been surrendered. There is nothing in the history of its adoption to suggest that it was more than declaratory of the relationship between the national and state governments as it had been established by the Constitution before the amendment or that its purpose was other than to allay fears that the new national government might seek to exercise powers not granted, and that the states might not be able to exercise fully their reserved powers.

From the beginning and for many years the amendment has been construed as not depriving the national government of authority to resort to all means for the exercise of a granted power which are appropriate and plainly adapted to the permitted end. *Martin v. Hunter's Lessee*, 1 Wheat. 304, 324, 325; *McCulloch v. Maryland*, *supra*, 4 Wheat. 405, 406; *Lottery Case*, *supra*. . . .

WICKARD v. FILBURN

317 U.S. 111 (1942)

Mr. JUSTICE JACKSON delivered the opinion of the Court.

The appellee for many years past has owned and operated a small farm in Montgomery County, Ohio, maintaining a herd of dairy cattle, selling milk, raising poultry, and selling poultry and eggs. It has been his practice to raise a small acreage of winter wheat, sown in the Fall and harvested in the following July; to sell a portion of the crop; to feed part to poultry and livestock on the farm, some of which is sold; to use some in making flour for home consumption; and to keep the rest for the following seeding. . . .

In July of 1940, pursuant to the Agricultural Adjustment Act of 1938, as then amended, there were established for the appellee's 1941 crop a wheat acreage allotment of 11.1 acres and a normal yield of 20.1 bushels of wheat an acre. He was given notice of such allotment in July of 1940, before the Fall planting of his 1941 crop of wheat, and again in July of 1941, before it was harvested. He sowed, however, 23 acres, and harvested from his 11.9 acres of excess acreage 239 bushels, which under the terms of the Act . . . constituted farm marketing excess, subject to a penalty of 49 cents a bushel, or $117.11 in all. . . .

The general scheme of the Agricultural Adjustment Act of 1938 as related to wheat is to control the volume moving in interstate and foreign commerce in order to avoid surpluses and shortages and the consequent abnormally low or high wheat prices and obstructions to commerce. Within prescribed limits and by prescribed standards the Secretary of Agriculture is directed to ascertain and proclaim each year a national acreage allotment for the next crop of wheat, which is then apportioned to the states and their counties, and is eventually broken up into allotments for individual farms. . . .

It is urged that under the Commerce Clause . . . , Congress does not possess the power it has in this instance sought to exercise. The question would merit little consideration since our decision in *United States v. Darby*, 312 U.S. 100, sustaining the federal power to regulate production of goods for commerce, except for the fact that this Act extends federal regulation to production not intended in any part for commerce but wholly for consumption on the farm. . . . Penalties do not depend upon whether any part of the wheat, either within or without the quota, is sold or intended to be sold. . . .

Appellee says that this is a regulation of production and consumption of wheat. Such activities are, he urges, beyond the reach of Congressional power under the Commerce Clause, since they are local in character, and their effects upon interstate commerce are at most "indirect." . . .

At the beginning Chief Justice Marshall described the federal commerce power with a breadth never yet exceeded. *Gibbons v. Ogden*, 9 Wheat. 1, 194-195. He made emphatic the embracing and penetrating nature of this power by warning that effective restraints on its exercise must proceed from political rather than from judicial processes. . . .

Whether the subject of the regulation in question was "production," "consumption," or "marketing" is . . . not material for purposes of deciding the question of federal power before us. . . . [E]ven if appellee's activity be local and though it may not be regarded as commerce, it may still, whatever its nature, be reached by Congress if it exerts a substantial economic effect on interstate commerce, and this irrespective of whether such effect is what might at some earlier time have been defined as "direct" or "indirect." . . .

The wheat industry has been a problem industry for some years. Largely as a result of increased foreign production and import restrictions, annual exports of wheat and flour from the United States during the ten-year period ending in 1940 averaged less than 10 per cent of total production, while during the 1920's they averaged more than 25 per cent. The decline in the export trade has left a large surplus in production which, in connection with an abnormally large supply of wheat and other grains in recent years, caused congestion in a number of markets; tied up railroad cars; and caused elevators in some instances to turn away grains, and railroads to institute embargoes to prevent further congestion.

Many countries, both importing and exporting, have sought to modify the impact of the world market conditions on their own economy. Importing countries have taken measures to stimulate production and self-sufficiency. The four large exporting countries of Argentina, Australia, Canada, and the United States have all undertaken various programs for the relief of growers. Such measures have been designed in part at least to protect the domestic price received by producers. Such plans have generally evolved towards control by the central government. . . .

The effect of consumption of home-grown wheat on interstate commerce is due to the fact that it constitutes the most variable factor in the disappearance of the wheat crop. Consumption on the farm where grown appears to vary in an amount greater than 20 per cent of average production. The total amount of wheat consumed as food varies but relatively little, and use as seed is relatively constant.

The maintenance by government regulation of a price for wheat undoubtedly can be accomplished as effectively by sustaining or increasing the demand as by limiting the supply. The effect of the statute before us is to restrict the amount which may be produced for market and the extent as well to which one may forestall resort to the market by producing to meet his own needs. That appellee's own contribution to the demand for wheat may be trivial by itself is not enough to remove him from the scope of federal regulation where, as here, his contribution, taken together with that of many others similarly situated, is far from trivial.

It is well established by decisions of this Court that the power to regulate commerce includes the power to regulate the prices at which commodities in that commerce are dealt in and practices affecting such prices. One of the primary purposes of the Act in question was to increase the market price of wheat, and to that end to limit the volume thereof that could affect the market. It can hardly be denied that a factor of such volume and variability as home-consumed wheat would have a substantial influence on price and market conditions. This may arise because being in marketable condition such wheat overhangs the market and if induced by rising prices tends to flow into the market and check price increases. But if we assume that it is never marketed, it supplies a need of the man who grew it which would otherwise be reflected by purchases in the open market. Home-grown wheat in this sense competes with wheat in commerce. The stimulation of commerce is a use of the regulatory function quite as definitely as prohibitions or restrictions thereon. This record leaves us in no doubt that Congress may properly have considered that wheat consumed on the farm where grown if wholly outside the scheme of regulation, would have a substantial effect in defeating and obstructing its purpose to stimulate trade therein at increased prices.

It is said, however, that this Act, forcing some farmers into the market to buy what they could provide for themselves, is an unfair promotion of the markets and prices of specializing wheat growers. It is of the essence of regulation that it lays a restraining hand on the self-interest of the regulated and that advantages from the regulation commonly fall to others. The conflicts of economic interest between the regulated and those who advantage by it are wisely left under our system to resolution by the Congress under its more flexible and responsible legislative process. Such conflicts rarely lend themselves to judicial determination. And with the wisdom, workability, or fairness, of the plan of regulation we have nothing to do. . . .

POINTS FOR DISCUSSION

1. In *NLRB v. Jones & Laughlin Steel*, the Court held that the commerce power extends to activities that "have such a close and substantial relation to interstate commerce that their control is essential or appropriate to protect that commerce from burdens and obstructions." In *United States v. Darby*, the Court explained that the commerce power "extends to those activities intrastate which so affect interstate commerce . . . as to make regulation of them appropriate means . . . to regulate interstate commerce." Do these formulations impose any meaningful limitations on the commerce power? If so, how workable are these limitations?

2. In *Wickard v. Filburn*, the Court rejected *Jones & Laughlin Steel*'s distinction between "direct" and "indirect" effects upon commerce. Instead, it applied a "substantial effects" test and adopted an "aggregation" principle: (1) in regulating the interstate wheat market, Congress may regulate intrastate activities that exert "a substantial economic effect on interstate commerce," and (2) in determining whether such a substantial economic effect exists, the Court may consider the aggregate effect of regulated activities on interstate commerce (here, the effect of Filburn's homegrown wheat consumption in aggregate with the consumption of other farmers). Do these standards impose any meaningful judicially enforceable limitations on congressional power? Do these standards lie in tension with the structural constitutional principle emphasized in *Jones & Laughlin Steel* that the distinction between what is national and what is local should not be obliterated?

In *Gonzales v. Raich*, 545 U.S. 1 (2005), which you will read later in this chapter, the Justices discussed the reasoning of *Wickard*, suggesting two distinct readings: (1) that Congress may regulate *any* intrastate activities that, in the aggregate, have a substantial economic effect on interstate commerce; or (2) that Congress may regulate intrastate activities only if such activities are "economic," or if the regulation of intrastate activities is a necessary part of a broader regulation of an interstate market, such as the Agricultural Adjustment Act. Which reading better describes *Wickard*?

3. The *Darby* Court recognized that policy concerns over substandard labor conditions motivated Congress to enact the Fair Labor Standards Act. The Court explained, however, that

> [t]he motive and purpose of a regulation of interstate commerce are matters for the legislative judgment upon the exercise of which the Constitution places no restriction and over which the courts are given no control. . . . Whatever their motive and purpose, regulations of commerce which do not infringe some constitutional prohibition are within the plenary power conferred on Congress by the Commerce Clause.

Note how this analysis departs from *Hammer v. Dagenhart*, 247 U.S. 251 (1918), in which the Court concluded that Congress's motive to regulate manufacture and trade undermined the regulation's constitutionality under the Commerce Clause. Should courts consider congressional motive and purpose in assessing whether Congress has power to enact legislation under the Commerce Clause?

4. In *Wickard* the Court stated that the "record leaves us in no doubt that Congress may properly have considered that wheat consumed on the farm where grown if wholly outside the scheme of regulation would have a substantial effect in defeating and obstructing its purpose to stimulate trade therein at increased prices." Did the *Wickard* Court afford Congress an appropriate level of deference in determining that homegrown wheat consumption, in aggregate, had a substantial effect on the interstate wheat market?

3. THE CIVIL RIGHTS ERA

Recall that in the *Civil Rights Cases*, 109 U.S. 3 (1883), the Supreme Court held that Congress lacked authority under §5 of the Fourteenth Amendment to prohibit private discrimination in public accommodations. Section 5 provides that "[t]he Congress shall have power to enforce, by appropriate legislation, the provisions of this article." The Court reasoned in the *Civil Rights Cases* that a Fourteenth Amendment violation requires state action; absent state action, Congress has no violation against which to enforce the Fourteenth Amendment.

In the Civil Rights Act of 1964, Congress again proscribed private discrimination in public accommodations. In the following two cases, *Heart of Atlanta Motel v. United States*, 379 U.S. 241 (1964), and *Katzenbach v. McClung*, 379 U.S. 294 (1964), the Court considered whether Congress has power to prohibit private discrimination under the Commerce Clause. As you read these cases, consider the following questions:

- How does the Court define Congress's power to regulate interstate commerce?
- How much deference does the Court afford Congress in determining the constitutionality of the regulations at issue?
- What role, if any, does the Necessary and Proper Clause play in the Justices' analyses?

HEART OF ATLANTA MOTEL V. UNITED STATES

379 U.S. 241 (1964)

Mr. JUSTICE CLARK delivered the opinion of the Court.

Appellant owns and operates the Heart of Atlanta Motel which has 216 rooms available to transient guests. The motel . . . is readily accessible to interstate highways. . . . Appellant solicits patronage from outside the State of Georgia through various national advertising media, including magazines of national circulation; it maintains over 50 billboards and highway signs within the State, soliciting patronage for the motel; it accepts convention trade from outside Georgia and approximately 75% of its registered guests are from out of State. Prior to passage of the [Civil Rights Act of 1964] the motel had followed a practice of refusing to rent rooms to Negroes. . . .

The appellant contends that Congress in passing this Act exceeded its power to regulate commerce. . . .

[In relevant part, Title II of the Act] provides that:

> "All persons shall be entitled to the full and equal enjoyment of the goods, services, facilities, privileges, advantages, and accommodations of any place of public accommodation, as defined in this section, without discrimination or segregation on the ground of race, color, religion, or national origin."

There are listed . . . four classes of business establishments, each of which "serves the public" and "is a place of public accommodation . . . if its operations affect commerce, or if discrimination or segregation by it is supported by State action." The covered establishments are:

> "(1) any inn, hotel, motel, or other establishment which provides lodging to transient guests, other than an establishment located within a building which contains not more than five rooms for rent or hire and which is actually occupied by the proprietor of such establishment as his residence;
> "(2) any restaurant, cafeteria . . . (not here involved);
> "(3) any motion picture house . . . (not here involved). . . ."

[The Act] defines the phrase "affect commerce" as applied to the above establishments. It first declares that "any inn, hotel, motel, or other establishment which provides lodging to transient guests" affects commerce *per se*. Restaurants, cafeterias, etc., in class two affect commerce only if they serve or offer to serve interstate travelers or if a substantial portion of the food which they serve or products which they sell have "moved in commerce." Motion picture houses and other places listed in class three affect commerce if they customarily present films, performances, etc., "which move in commerce." . . .

A person aggrieved may bring suit. . . .

It is admitted that the operation of the motel brings it within the provisions of . . . the Act and that appellant refused to provide lodging for transient Negroes because of their race or color and that it intends to continue that policy unless restrained.

The sole question posed is, therefore, the constitutionality of the Civil Rights Act of 1964 as applied to these facts. The legislative history of the Act indicates that Congress based the Act on §5 and the Equal Protection Clause of the Fourteenth Amendment as well as its power to regulate interstate commerce. . . .

The Senate Commerce Committee made it quite clear that the fundamental object of Title II was to vindicate "the deprivation of personal dignity that surely accompanies denials of equal access to public establishments." At the same time, however, it noted that such an objective has been and could be readily achieved "by congressional action based on the commerce power of the Constitution." Our study of the legislative record, made in the light of prior cases, has brought us to the conclusion that Congress possessed ample power in this regard, and we have therefore not considered the other grounds relied upon. This is not to say that the remaining authority upon which it acted was not adequate, a question upon which we do not pass, but merely that since the commerce power is sufficient for our decision here we have considered it alone. . . .

In light of our ground for decision, it might be well at the outset to discuss the *Civil Rights Cases*, [109 U.S. 3 (1883),] which declared provisions of the Civil Rights Act of 1875 unconstitutional. We think that decision inapposite, and without precedential value in determining the constitutionality of the present Act. Unlike . . . the present legislation, the 1875 Act broadly proscribed discrimination in "inns, public conveyances on land or water, theaters, and other places of public amusement," without limiting the categories of affected businesses to those impinging upon interstate commerce. In contrast, the applicability of Title II is carefully limited to enterprises having a direct and substantial relation to the interstate flow of goods and people. . . . Further, the fact that certain kinds of businesses may not in 1875 have been sufficiently involved in interstate commerce to warrant bringing them within the ambit of the commerce power is not necessarily dispositive of the same question today. Our populace had not reached its present mobility, nor were facilities, goods and services circulating as readily in interstate commerce as they are today. Although the principles which we apply today are those first formulated by Chief Justice Marshall in *Gibbons v. Ogden*, 9 Wheat. 1 (1824), the conditions of transportation and commerce have changed dramatically, and we must apply those principles to the present state of commerce. The sheer increase in volume of interstate traffic alone would give discriminatory practices which inhibit travel a far larger impact upon the Nation's commerce than such practices had on the economy of another day. Finally, there is language in the *Civil Rights Cases* which indicates that the Court did not fully consider whether the 1875 Act could be sustained as an exercise of the commerce power. . . .

We, therefore, conclude that the *Civil Rights Cases* have no relevance to the basis of decision here where the Act explicitly relies upon the commerce power, and where the record is filled with testimony of obstructions and restraints resulting from the discriminations found to be existing. . . .

While the Act as adopted carried no congressional findings the record of its passage through each house is replete with evidence of the burdens that discrimination by race or color places upon interstate commerce. . . . This testimony included the fact that our people have become increasingly mobile with millions of people of all races traveling from State to State; that Negroes in particular have been the subject of discrimination in transient accommodations, having to travel great distances to secure the same; that often they have been unable to obtain accommodations and have had to call upon friends to put them up overnight, and that these conditions had become so acute as to require the listing of available lodging for Negroes in a special guidebook which was itself "dramatic testimony to the difficulties" Negroes encounter in travel. These exclusionary practices were found to be nationwide, the Under Secretary of Commerce testifying that there is "no question that this discrimination in the North still exists to a large degree" and in the West and Midwest as well. This testimony indicated a qualitative as well as quantitative effect on interstate travel by Negroes. The former was the obvious impairment of the Negro traveler's pleasure and convenience that resulted when he continually was uncertain of finding lodging. As for the latter, there was evidence that this uncertainty stemming from racial discrimination had the effect of discouraging travel on the part of a substantial portion of the Negro community. This was the conclusion not only of the Under Secretary of Commerce but also of the Administrator of the Federal Aviation Agency who wrote the Chairman of the Senate Commerce Committee that it was his "belief that air commerce is adversely affected by the denial to a substantial segment of the traveling public of adequate and desegregated public accommodations." We shall not burden this opinion with further details since the voluminous testimony presents overwhelming evidence that discrimination by hotels and motels impedes interstate travel. . . .

The power of Congress to deal with these obstructions depends on the meaning of the Commerce Clause. Its meaning was first enunciated 140 years ago by the great Chief Justice John Marshall in *Gibbons v. Ogden*, 9 Wheat. 1 (1824), in these words:

> "The subject to be regulated is commerce; and the meaning of the word . . . is intercourse. . . .
>
> "To what commerce does this power extend? The constitution informs us, to commerce 'with foreign nations, and among the several States, and with the Indian tribes.' . . .
>
> "We are now arrived at the inquiry—What is this power?

"It is the power to regulate; that is, to prescribe the rule by which commerce is to be governed. This power, like all others vested in Congress, is complete in itself, may be exercised to its utmost extent, and acknowledges no limitations, other than are prescribed in the constitution. . . . If, as has always been understood, the sovereignty of Congress . . . is plenary as to those objects [specified in the Constitution], the power over commerce . . . is vested in Congress as absolutely as it would be in a single government, having in its constitution the same restrictions on the exercise of the power as are found in the constitution of the United States. The wisdom and the discretion of Congress, their identity with the people, and the influence which their constituents possess at elections, are, in this, as in many other instances, as that, for example, of declaring war, the sole restraints on which they have relied, to secure them from its abuse. They are the restraints on which the people must often rely solely, in all representative governments."

In short, the determinative test of the exercise of power by the Congress under the Commerce Clause is simply whether the activity sought to be regulated is "commerce which concerns more States than one" and has a real and substantial relation to the national interest. Let us now turn to this facet of the problem.

That the "intercourse" of which the Chief Justice spoke included the movement of persons through more States than one was settled as early as 1849, in the *Passenger Cases*, 7 How. 283, where Mr. Justice McLean stated: "That the transportation of passengers is a part of commerce is not now an open question." At 401. . . . The . . . interest in protecting interstate commerce . . . led Congress . . . to extend the exercise of its power to gambling, *Lottery Case*, 188 U.S. 321 (1903); . . . to wages and hours, *United States v. Darby*, 312 U.S. 100 (1941); to members of labor unions, [*NLRB*] *v. Jones & Laughlin Steel Corp.*, 301 U.S. 1 (1937); [and] to crop control, *Wickard v. Filburn*, 317 U.S. 111 (1942) . . . .

That Congress was legislating against moral wrongs in many of these areas rendered its enactments no less valid. In framing Title II of this Act Congress was also dealing with what it considered a moral problem. But that fact does not detract from the overwhelming evidence of the disruptive effect that racial discrimination has had on commercial intercourse. It was this burden which empowered Congress to enact appropriate legislation, and, given this basis for the exercise of its power, Congress was not restricted by the fact that the particular obstruction to interstate commerce with which it was dealing was also deemed a moral and social wrong.

It is said that the operation of the motel here is of a purely local character. But . . . [a]s Chief Justice Stone put it in *United States v. Darby*:

"The power of Congress over interstate commerce is not confined to the regulation of commerce among the states. It extends to those activities intrastate which so affect interstate commerce or the exercise of the power of Congress over it as to make regulation of them appropriate means to the attainment of a legitimate end, the exercise of the granted power of Congress to regulate interstate commerce."

Thus the power of Congress to promote interstate commerce also includes the power to regulate the local incidents thereof, including local activities in both the States of origin and destination, which might have a substantial and harmful effect upon that commerce. One need only examine the evidence which we have discussed above to see that Congress may—as it has—prohibit racial discrimination by motels serving travelers, however "local" their operations may appear. . . .

Mr. JUSTICE BLACK, concurring.*

It requires no novel or strained interpretation of the Commerce Clause to sustain Title II as applied in either of these cases. At least since *Gibbons v. Ogden*, decided in 1824 in an opinion by Chief Justice John Marshall, it has been uniformly accepted that the power of Congress to regulate commerce among the States is plenary, "complete in itself, may be exercised to its utmost extent, and acknowledges no limitations, other than are prescribed in the constitution." 9 Wheat., at 196. Nor is "Commerce" as used in the Commerce Clause to be limited to a narrow, technical concept. It includes not only, as Congress has enumerated in the Act, "travel, trade, traffic, commerce, transportation, or communication," but also all other unitary transactions and activities that take place in more States than one. That some parts or segments of such unitary transactions may take place only in one State cannot, of course, take from Congress its plenary power to regulate them in the national interest. The facilities and instrumentalities used to carry on this commerce, such as railroads, truck lines, ships, rivers, and even highways are also subject to congressional regulation, so far as is necessary to keep interstate traffic upon fair and equal terms.

Furthermore, it has long been held that the Necessary and Proper Clause . . . adds to the commerce power of Congress the power to regulate local instrumentalities operating within a single State if their activities burden the flow of commerce among the States. . . .

I recognize that every remote, possible, speculative effect on commerce should not be accepted as an adequate constitutional ground to uproot and throw into the discard all our traditional distinctions between what is purely local, and therefore controlled by state laws, and what affects the national interest and is therefore subject to control by federal laws. . . . But in deciding the constitutional power of Congress in cases like the two before us we do not consider the effect on interstate commerce of only one isolated, individual, local event, without regard to the fact that this single local event when added to many others of a similar nature may impose a burden on interstate commerce by reducing its volume or distorting its flow. *Wickard v. Filburn*, 317 U.S. 111, at 127-128; *United States v. Darby*, 312 U.S. 100, at 123. . . . Measuring, as this Court has so often held is required, by the aggregate effect of a great number of such acts of discrimination, I am of the opinion that Congress has constitutional power under the Commerce and Necessary and Proper Clauses to protect interstate commerce from the injuries bound to befall it from these discriminatory practices.

---

*This opinion applies also to . . . *Katzenbach v. McClung*, [379 U.S. 294 (1964)]. . . .

Mr. JUSTICE DOUGLAS, concurring.[*]

Though I join the Court's opinions, I am somewhat reluctant here . . . to rest solely on the Commerce Clause. My reluctance is not due to any conviction that Congress lacks power to regulate commerce in the interests of human rights. . . . [Rather,] I would prefer to rest on the assertion of legislative power contained in §5 of the Fourteenth Amendment which states: "The Congress shall have power to enforce, by appropriate legislation, the provisions of this article." . . .

A decision based on the Fourteenth Amendment would have a more settling effect, making unnecessary litigation over whether a particular restaurant or inn is within the commerce definitions of the Act or whether a particular customer is an interstate traveler. . . .

Mr. JUSTICE GOLDBERG, concurring.[*]

I join in the opinions and judgments of the Court, since I agree "that the action of the Congress in the adoption of the Act as applied here . . . is within the power granted it by the Commerce Clause of the Constitution, as interpreted by this Court for 140 years." . . .

KATZENBACH v. MCCLUNG

379 U.S. 294 (1964)

Mr. JUSTICE CLARK delivered the opinion of the Court.

This case was argued with . . . *Heart of Atlanta Motel v. United States*, decided this date, in which we upheld the constitutional validity of Title II of the Civil Rights Act of 1964 against an attack of hotels, motels, and like establishments. This complaint for injunctive relief against appellants attacks the constitutionality of the Act as applied to a restaurant.

Ollie's Barbecue is a family-owned restaurant in Birmingham, Alabama, specializing in barbecued meats and homemade pies, with a seating capacity of 220 customers. It is located on a state highway 11 blocks from an interstate one and a somewhat greater distance from railroad and bus stations. The restaurant caters to a family and white-collar trade with a take-out service for Negroes. It employs 36 persons, two-thirds of whom are Negroes.

In the 12 months preceding the passage of the Act, the restaurant purchased locally approximately $150,000 worth of food, $69,683 or 46% of which was meat that it bought from a local supplier who had procured it from outside the State. The District Court expressly found that a substantial portion of the food served in the restaurant had moved in interstate commerce. The restaurant has refused to serve Negroes in its dining accommodations since its original opening in 1927, and since July 2, 1964, it has been operating in violation of the Act. The court below concluded that if it were required to serve Negroes it would lose a substantial amount of business. . . .

The basic holding in *Heart of Atlanta Motel*, answers many of the contentions made by the appellees. There we outlined the overall purpose and

---

[*]This opinion applies also to . . . *Katzenbach v. McClung*, [379 U.S. 294 (1964)]. . . .

operations plan of Title II and found it a valid exercise of the power to regulate interstate commerce insofar as it requires hotels and motels to serve transients without regard to their race or color. In this case we consider its application to restaurants which serve food a substantial portion of which has moved in commerce. . . . Title II commands that all persons shall be entitled to the full and equal enjoyment of the goods and services of any place of public accommodation without discrimination or segregation on the ground of race, color, religion, or national origin; and . . . place[s] any "restaurant . . . principally engaged in selling food for consumption on the premises" under the Act "if it serves or offers to serve interstate travelers or a substantial portion of the food which it serves . . . has moved in commerce."

Ollie's Barbecue admits that it is covered by these provisions of the Act. The Government makes no contention that the discrimination at the restaurant was supported by the State of Alabama. There is no claim that interstate travelers frequented the restaurant. The sole question, therefore, narrows down to whether Title II, as applied to a restaurant annually receiving about $70,000 worth of food which has moved in commerce, is a valid exercise of the power of Congress. . . .

[B]oth Houses of Congress conducted prolonged hearings on the Act. [W]hile no formal findings were made, which of course are not necessary, it is well that we make mention of the testimony at these hearings the better to understand the problem before Congress and determine whether the Act is a reasonable and appropriate means toward its solution. The record is replete with testimony of the burdens placed on interstate commerce by racial discrimination in restaurants. A comparison of per capita spending by Negroes in restaurants, theaters, and like establishments indicated less spending, after discounting income differences, in areas where discrimination is widely practiced. This condition, which was especially aggravated in the South, was attributed in the testimony of the Under Secretary of Commerce to racial segregation. This diminutive spending springing from a refusal to serve Negroes and their total loss as customers has, regardless of the absence of direct evidence, a close connection to interstate commerce. The fewer customers a restaurant enjoys the less food it sells and consequently the less it buys. In addition, the Attorney General testified that this type of discrimination imposed "an artificial restriction on the market" and interfered with the flow of merchandise. In addition, there were many references to discriminatory situations causing wide unrest and having a depressant effect on general business conditions in the respective communities.

Moreover there was an impressive array of testimony that discrimination in restaurants had a direct and highly restrictive effect upon interstate travel by Negroes. This resulted, it was said, because discriminatory practices prevent Negroes from buying prepared food served on the premises while on a trip, except in isolated and unkempt restaurants and under most unsatisfactory and often unpleasant conditions. This obviously discourages travel and obstructs interstate commerce for one can hardly travel without eating. Likewise, it was said, that discrimination deterred professional, as well as skilled, people from moving into areas where such practices occurred and thereby caused industry to be reluctant to establish there.

We believe that this testimony afforded ample basis for the conclusion that established restaurants in such areas sold less interstate goods because of the discrimination, that interstate travel was obstructed directly by it, that business in general suffered and that many new businesses refrained from establishing there as a result of it. . . .

It goes without saying that, viewed in isolation, the volume of food purchased by Ollie's Barbecue from sources supplied from out of state was insignificant when compared with the total foodstuffs moving in commerce. But, as our late Brother Jackson said for the Court in *Wickard v. Filburn*, 317 U.S. 111 (1942):

> "That appellee's own contribution to the demand for wheat may be trivial by itself is not enough to remove him from the scope of federal regulation where, as here, his contribution, taken together with that of many others similarly situated, is far from trivial." At 127-128.

[The Commerce Clause] confers upon Congress the power "[t]o regulate Commerce . . . among the several States" and [the Necessary and Proper Clause] grants it the power "[t]o make all Laws which shall be necessary and proper for carrying into Execution the foregoing Powers. . . ." This grant . . . "extends to those activities intrastate which so affect interstate commerce, or the exertion of the power of Congress over it, as to make regulation of them appropriate means to the attainment of a legitimate end, the effective execution of the granted power to regulate interstate commerce." *United States v. Wrightwood Dairy Co.*, 315 U.S. 110, 119 (1942). Much is said about a restaurant business being local but "even if appellee's activity be local and though it may not be regarded as commerce, it may still, whatever its nature, be reached by Congress if it exerts a substantial economic effect on interstate commerce. . . ." *Wickard v. Filburn*, supra, at 125. The activities that are beyond the reach of Congress are "those which are completely within a particular State, which do not affect other States, and with which it is not necessary to interfere, for the purpose of executing some of the general powers of the government." *Gibbons v. Ogden*, 9 Wheat. 1, 195 (1824). . . .

The appellees contend that Congress has arbitrarily created a conclusive presumption that all restaurants meeting the criteria set out in the Act "affect commerce." Stated another way, they object to the omission of a provision for a case-by-case determination — judicial or administrative — that racial discrimination in a particular restaurant affects commerce.

But Congress' action in framing this Act was not unprecedented. In *United States v. Darby*, 312 U.S. 100, 657 (1941), this Court held constitutional the Fair Labor Standards Act of 1938. There Congress determined that the payment of substandard wages to employees engaged in the production of goods for commerce, while not itself commerce, so inhibited it as to be subject to federal regulation. The appellees in that case argued, as do the appellees here, that the Act was invalid because it included no provision for an independent inquiry regarding the effect on commerce of substandard wages in a particular business. But the Court rejected the argument. . . .

Here, as there, Congress has determined for itself that refusals of service to Negroes have imposed burdens both upon the interstate flow of food and upon the movement of products generally. Of course, the mere fact that Congress has said when particular activity shall be deemed to affect commerce does not preclude further examination by this Court. But where we find that the legislators, in light of the facts and testimony before them, have a rational basis for finding a chosen regulatory scheme necessary to the protection of commerce, our investigation is at an end. The only remaining question — one answered in the affirmative by the court below — is whether the particular restaurant either serves or offers to serve interstate travelers or serves food a substantial portion of which has moved in interstate commerce.

The appellees urge that Congress, in passing the Fair Labor Standards Act and the National Labor Relations Act, made specific findings which were embodied in those statutes. Here, of course, Congress had included no formal findings. But their absence is not fatal to the validity of the statute, see *United States v. Carolene Products Co.*, 304 U.S. 144, 152 (1938), for the evidence presented at the hearings fully indicated the nature and effect of the burdens on commerce which Congress meant to alleviate.

Confronted as we are with the facts laid before Congress, we must conclude that it had a rational basis for finding that racial discrimination in restaurants had a direct and adverse effect on the free flow of interstate commerce. Insofar as the sections of the Act here relevant are concerned, . . . Congress prohibited discrimination only in those establishments having a close tie to interstate commerce, *i.e.*, those, like the McClungs', serving food that has come from out of the State. We think in so doing that Congress acted well within its power to protect and foster commerce in extending the coverage of Title II only to those restaurants offering to serve interstate travelers or serving food, a substantial portion of which has moved in interstate commerce. . . .

The power of Congress in this field is broad and sweeping; where it keeps within its sphere and violates no express constitutional limitation it has been the rule of this Court, going back almost to the founding days of the Republic, not to interfere. The Civil Rights Act of 1964, as here applied, we find to be plainly appropriate in the resolution of what the Congress found to be a national commercial problem of the first magnitude. We find it in no violation of any express limitations of the Constitution and we therefore declare it valid. . . .

[The concurring opinions of JUSTICE BLACK, JUSTICE DOUGLAS, and JUSTICE GOLDBERG appear in *Heart of Atlanta Motel, Inc., v. United States*, 379 U.S. 241 (1964).]

POINTS FOR DISCUSSION

1. In *Heart of Atlanta Motel*, the Court stated that "the determinative test of the exercise of power by the Congress under the Commerce Clause is simply whether the activity sought to be regulated is 'commerce which concerns more States than one' and has a real and substantial relation to the national interest." Is this the same test that the Court applied in *Darby*? In *Wickard*? If not, how does it differ? Would the case come out the same under the "substantial effects" test as articulated in *Wickard*?

2. In *McClung*, the Court explained that "where we find that the legislators, in light of the facts and testimony before them, have a rational basis for finding a chosen regulatory scheme necessary to the protection of commerce, our investigation is at an end." Under this "rational basis" test, what is the role of the Court in determining the constitutionality of acts of Congress? Where

Congress makes factual findings, must courts defer to those findings? Where Congress makes no findings but develops a record of facts and testimony, must courts defer to those facts and testimony? Keep these questions in mind as you read the cases in the next section.

3. In *Heart of Atlanta Motel*, the Court explained,

> That Congress was legislating against moral wrongs in many of these areas rendered its enactments no less valid. In framing Title II of this Act Congress was also dealing with what it considered a moral problem. But that fact does not detract from the overwhelming evidence of the disruptive effect that racial discrimination has had on commercial intercourse.

How does this treatment of legislative purpose relate to the Court's treatment of legislative purpose in *Dagenhart* and *Darby*? How should the Court treat legislative purpose in this context?

4. In his concurring opinion in *Heart of Atlanta Motel* and *McClung*, Justice Black observed "that the Necessary and Proper Clause . . . adds to the commerce power of Congress the power to regulate local instrumentalities operating within a single State if their activities burden the flow of commerce among the States." In *McClung*, the Court cited the Necessary and Proper Clause explicitly. Did the introduction of the Necessary and Proper Clause add anything to the Court's analysis under the Commerce Clause? Keep the role of the Necessary and Proper Clause in mind as you read the cases in the next section.

4. THE REHNQUIST COURT

In 1995 the Supreme Court held that a federal statute exceeded congressional power under the Commerce Clause for the first time since the New Deal era. In the ensuing decade, the Court, under Chief Justice William Rehnquist, considered many cases of congressional power. You will read several of these cases in this chapter and the next. In this section you will read three Rehnquist Court opinions addressing the Commerce Clause: *United States v. Lopez*, 514 U.S. 549 (1995); *United States v. Morrison*, 529 U.S. 598 (2000); and *Gonzales v. Raich*, 545 U.S. 1 (2005).

In *Lopez* and *Morrison*, the Court invalidated acts of Congress under the Commerce Clause. As you read these two cases, consider these questions:

- How does the Court define the scope of the commerce power?
- How much deference does the Court afford Congress in determining whether a statute is constitutional under the Commerce Clause?
- How do the Justices understand the relationship between the political safeguards of federalism and judicial review?

UNITED STATES V. LOPEZ

514 U.S. 549 (1995)

CHIEF JUSTICE REHNQUIST delivered the opinion of the Court.

In the Gun-Free School Zones Act of 1990, Congress made it a federal offense "for any individual knowingly to possess a firearm at a place that

the individual knows, or has reasonable cause to believe, is a school zone."
18 U.S.C. §922(q)(1)(A). . . .

We start with first principles. The Constitution creates a Federal Government of enumerated powers. See Art. I, §8. As James Madison wrote: "The powers delegated by the proposed Constitution to the federal government are few and defined. Those which are to remain in the State governments are numerous and indefinite." The Federalist No. 45, pp. 292-293 (C. Rossiter ed. 1961). This constitutionally mandated division of authority "was adopted by the Framers to ensure protection of our fundamental liberties." *Gregory v. Ashcroft,* 501 U.S. 452, 458 (1991) (internal quotation marks omitted). "Just as the separation and independence of the coordinate branches of the Federal Government serve to prevent the accumulation of excessive power in any one branch, a healthy balance of power between the States and the Federal Government will reduce the risk of tyranny and abuse from either front." *Ibid.*

The Constitution delegates to Congress the power "[t]o regulate Commerce with foreign Nations, and among the several States, and with the Indian Tribes." Art. I, §8, cl. 3. The Court, through Chief Justice Marshall, first defined the nature of Congress' commerce power in *Gibbons v. Ogden,* 9 Wheat. 1, 189-190 (1824):

> "Commerce, undoubtedly, is traffic, but it is something more: it is intercourse.
> It describes the commercial intercourse between nations, and parts of nations,
> in all its branches, and is regulated by prescribing rules for carrying on that
> intercourse."

The commerce power "is the power to regulate; that is, to prescribe the rule by which commerce is to be governed. This power, like all others vested in congress, is complete in itself, may be exercised to its utmost extent, and acknowledges no limitations, other than are prescribed in the constitution." *Id.,* at 196. The *Gibbons* Court, however, acknowledged that limitations on the commerce power are inherent in the very language of the Commerce Clause.

> "It is not intended to say that these words comprehend that commerce, which
> is completely internal, which is carried on between man and man in a State, or
> between different parts of the same State, and which does not extend to or
> affect other States. Such a power would be inconvenient, and is certainly
> unnecessary.
>
> "Comprehensive as the word 'among' is, it may very properly be restricted
> to that commerce which concerns more States than one. . . . The enumeration
> presupposes something not enumerated; and that something, if we regard the
> language, or the subject of the sentence, must be the exclusively internal commerce of a State." *Id.,* at 194-195.

For nearly a century thereafter, the Court's Commerce Clause decisions dealt but rarely with the extent of Congress' power, and almost entirely with the Commerce Clause as a limit on state legislation that discriminated against interstate commerce. . . . Under this line of precedent, the Court held that certain categories of activity such as "production," "manufacturing," and "mining" were within the province of state governments, and thus were beyond the power of Congress under the Commerce Clause.

In 1887, Congress enacted the Interstate Commerce Act, 24 Stat. 379, and in 1890, Congress enacted the Sherman Antitrust Act, 26 Stat. 209, as amended, 15 U.S.C. §1 *et seq.* These laws ushered in a new era of federal regulation under the commerce power. When cases involving these laws first reached this Court, we imported from our negative Commerce Clause cases the approach that Congress could not regulate activities such as "production," "manufacturing," and "mining." See, *e.g., United States v. E. C. Knight Co.,* 156 U.S. 1, 12 (1895) ("Commerce succeeds to manufacture, and is not part of it"). Simultaneously, however, the Court held that, where the interstate and intrastate aspects of commerce were so mingled together that full regulation of interstate commerce required incidental regulation of intrastate commerce, the Commerce Clause authorized such regulation.

In *A.L.A. Schechter Poultry Corp. v. United States,* 295 U.S. 495, 550 (1935), the Court struck down regulations that fixed the hours and wages of individuals employed by an intrastate business because the activity being regulated related to interstate commerce only indirectly. In doing so, the Court characterized the distinction between direct and indirect effects of intrastate transactions upon interstate commerce as "a fundamental one, essential to the maintenance of our constitutional system." *Id.,* at 548. Activities that affected interstate commerce directly were within Congress' power; activities that affected interstate commerce indirectly were beyond Congress' reach. *Id.,* at 546. The justification for this formal distinction was rooted in the fear that otherwise "there would be virtually no limit to the federal power and for all practical purposes we should have a completely centralized government." *Id.,* at 548.

Two years later, in the watershed case of *NLRB v. Jones & Laughlin Steel Corp.,* 301 U.S. 1 (1937), the Court upheld the National Labor Relations Act against a Commerce Clause challenge, and in the process, departed from the distinction between "direct" and "indirect" effects on interstate commerce. *Id.,* at 36-38 ("The question [of the scope of Congress' power] is necessarily one of degree"). The Court held that intrastate activities that "have such a close and substantial relation to interstate commerce that their control is essential or appropriate to protect that commerce from burdens and obstructions" are within Congress' power to regulate. *Id.,* at 37.

In *United States v. Darby,* 312 U.S. 100 (1941), the Court upheld the Fair Labor Standards Act, stating:

> "The power of Congress over interstate commerce is not confined to the regulation of commerce among the states. It extends to those activities intrastate which so affect interstate commerce or the exercise of the power of Congress over it as to make regulation of them appropriate means to the attainment of a legitimate end, the exercise of the granted power of Congress to regulate interstate commerce." *Id.,* at 118.

In *Wickard v. Filburn,* the Court upheld the application of amendments to the Agricultural Adjustment Act of 1938 to the production and consumption of homegrown wheat. 317 U.S. [111,] 128-129 [(1942)]. The *Wickard* Court explicitly rejected earlier distinctions between direct and indirect effects on interstate commerce, stating:

"[E]ven if appellee's activity be local and though it may not be regarded as commerce, it may still, whatever its nature, be reached by Congress if it exerts a substantial economic effect on interstate commerce, and this irrespective of whether such effect is what might at some earlier time have been defined as 'direct' or 'indirect.' " *Id.,* at 125.

The *Wickard* Court emphasized that although Filburn's own contribution to the demand for wheat may have been trivial by itself, that was not "enough to remove him from the scope of federal regulation where, as here, his contribution, taken together with that of many others similarly situated, is far from trivial." *Id.,* at 127-128. . . .

But even these modern-era precedents which have expanded congressional power under the Commerce Clause confirm that this power is subject to outer limits. In *Jones & Laughlin Steel,* the Court warned that the scope of the interstate commerce power "must be considered in the light of our dual system of government and may not be extended so as to embrace effects upon interstate commerce so indirect and remote that to embrace them, in view of our complex society, would effectually obliterate the distinction between what is national and what is local and create a completely centralized government." 301 U.S., at 37, see also *Darby, supra,* 312 U.S., at 119-120 (Congress may regulate intrastate activity that has a "substantial effect" on interstate commerce); *Wickard, supra,* at 125 (Congress may regulate activity that "exerts a substantial economic effect on interstate commerce"). Since that time, the Court has heeded that warning and undertaken to decide whether a rational basis existed for concluding that a regulated activity sufficiently affected interstate commerce. . . .

Consistent with this structure, we have identified three broad categories of activity that Congress may regulate under its commerce power. . . . First, Congress may regulate the use of the channels of interstate commerce. See, *e.g., Darby,* 312 U.S., at 114; [*Heart of Atlanta Motel v. United States,* 379 U.S. 241, 256 (1964)] ("[T]he authority of Congress to keep the channels of interstate commerce free from immoral and injurious uses has been frequently sustained, and is no longer open to question.") Second, Congress is empowered to regulate and protect the instrumentalities of interstate commerce, or persons or things in interstate commerce, even though the threat may come only from intrastate activities. *See, e.g., Shreveport Rate Cases,* 234 U.S. 342 (1914); *Southern R. Co. v. United States,* 222 U.S. 20 (1911) (upholding amendments to Safety Appliance Act as applied to vehicles used in intrastate commerce). Finally, Congress' commerce authority includes the power to regulate those activities having a substantial relation to interstate commerce, *Jones & Laughlin Steel,* 301 U.S., at 37, *i.e.,* those activities that substantially affect interstate commerce. . . .

[I]f §922(q) is to be sustained, it must be under the third category as a regulation of an activity that substantially affects interstate commerce.

[W]e have upheld a wide variety of congressional Acts regulating intrastate economic activity where we have concluded that the activity substantially affected interstate commerce. Examples include the regulation of . . . restaurants utilizing substantial interstate supplies, [*Katzenbach v. McClung,* 379 U.S. 294 (1964)], inns and hotels catering to interstate guests, *Heart of Atlanta Motel, supra,* and production and consumption of homegrown wheat, *Wickard v. Filburn,* [*supra*]. . . . [T]he pattern is clear. Where economic activity substantially affects interstate commerce, legislation regulating that activity will be sustained.

Even *Wickard,* which is perhaps the most far reaching example of Commerce Clause authority over intrastate activity, involved economic activity in a way that the possession of a gun in a school zone does not. . . . The Court said . . . :

> "One of the primary purposes of the Act in question was to increase the market price of wheat and to that end to limit the volume thereof that could affect the market. It can hardly be denied that a factor of such volume and variability as home-consumed wheat would have a substantial influence on price and market conditions. . . . Home-grown wheat . . . competes with wheat in commerce." 317 U.S., at 128.

Section 922(q) is a criminal statute that by its terms has nothing to do with "commerce" or any sort of economic enterprise, however broadly one might define those terms. . . . Section 922(q) is not an essential part of a larger regulation of economic activity, in which the regulatory scheme could be undercut unless the intrastate activity were regulated. It cannot, therefore, be sustained under our cases upholding regulations of activities that arise out of or are connected with a commercial transaction, which viewed in the aggregate, substantially affects interstate commerce. . . .

Although as part of our independent evaluation of constitutionality under the Commerce Clause we of course consider legislative findings, and indeed even congressional committee findings, regarding effect on interstate commerce, . . . the Government concedes that "[n]either the statute nor its legislative history contain[s] express congressional findings regarding the effects upon interstate commerce of gun possession in a school zone." . . . We agree with the Government that Congress normally is not required to make formal findings as to the substantial burdens that an activity has on interstate commerce. . . . But to the extent that congressional findings would enable us to evaluate the legislative judgment that the activity in question substantially affected interstate commerce, even though no such substantial effect was visible to the naked eye, they are lacking here. . . .

The Government's essential contention, *in fine,* is that we may determine here that §922(q) is valid because possession of a firearm in a local school zone does indeed substantially affect interstate commerce. The Government argues that possession of a firearm in a school zone may result in violent crime and that violent crime can be expected to affect the functioning of the national economy in two ways. First, the costs of violent crime are substantial, and, through the mechanism of insurance, those costs are spread throughout the population. Second, violent crime reduces the willingness of individuals to travel to areas within the country that are perceived to be unsafe. The Government also argues that the presence of guns in schools poses a substantial threat to the educational process by threatening the learning environment. A handicapped educational process, in turn, will result in a less productive citizenry. That, in turn, would have an adverse effect on the Nation's economic well-being. As a result, the Government argues that Congress could rationally have concluded that §922(q) substantially affects interstate commerce.

We pause to consider the implications of the Government's arguments. The Government admits, under its "costs of crime" reasoning, that Congress could regulate not only all violent crime, but all activities that might lead to violent crime, regardless of how tenuously they relate to interstate commerce. Similarly, under the Government's "national productivity" reasoning, Congress could regulate any activity that it found was related to the economic productivity of individual citizens: family law (including marriage, divorce, and child custody), for example. Under the theories that the Government presents in support of §922(q), it is difficult to perceive any limitation on federal power, even in areas such as criminal law enforcement or education where States historically have been sovereign. Thus, if we were to accept the Government's arguments, we are hard pressed to posit any activity by an individual that Congress is without power to regulate.

Although Justice Breyer argues that acceptance of the Government's rationales would not authorize a general federal police power, he is unable to identify any activity that the States may regulate but Congress may not. Justice Breyer posits that there might be some limitations on Congress' commerce power, such as family law or certain aspects of education. These suggested limitations, when viewed in light of the dissent's expansive analysis, are devoid of substance. . . .

[I]f Congress can, pursuant to its Commerce Clause power, regulate activities that adversely affect the learning environment, then, *a fortiori*, it also can regulate the educational process directly. Congress could determine that a school's curriculum has a "significant" effect on the extent of classroom learning. As a result, Congress could mandate a federal curriculum for local elementary and secondary schools because what is taught in local schools has a significant "effect on classroom learning," and that, in turn, has a substantial effect on interstate commerce. . . .

Under the dissent's rationale, Congress could just as easily look at child rearing as "fall[ing] on the commercial side of the line" because it provides a "valuable service—namely, to equip [children] with the skills they need to survive in life and, more specifically, in the workplace." . . .

To uphold the Government's contentions here, we would have to pile inference upon inference in a manner that would bid fair to convert congressional authority under the Commerce Clause to a general police power of the sort retained by the States. Admittedly, some of our prior cases have taken long steps down that road, giving great deference to congressional action. The broad language in these opinions has suggested the possibility of additional expansion, but we decline here to proceed any further. To do so would require us to conclude that the Constitution's enumeration of powers does not presuppose something not enumerated, and that there never will be a distinction between what is truly national and what is truly local. This we are unwilling to do. . . .

Justice Kennedy, with whom Justice O'Connor joins, concurring.

Of the various structural elements in the Constitution, separation of powers, checks and balances, judicial review, and federalism, only concerning the last does there seem to be much uncertainty respecting the existence, and the content, of standards that allow the Judiciary to play a significant role in maintaining the design contemplated by the Framers. . . .

There is irony in this, because of the four structural elements in the Constitution just mentioned, federalism was the unique contribution of the Framers to political science and political theory. Though on the surface the idea may seem counterintuitive, it was the insight of the Framers that freedom was enhanced by the creation of two governments, not one. . . .

To be sure, one conclusion that could be drawn from The Federalist Papers is that the balance between national and state power is entrusted in its entirety to the political process. Madison's observation that "the people ought not surely to be precluded from giving most of their confidence where they may discover it to be most due," The Federalist No. 46, p. 295 (C. Rossiter ed. 1961), can be interpreted to say that the essence of responsibility for a shift in power from the State to the Federal Government rests upon a political judgment, though he added assurance that "the State governments could have little to apprehend, because it is only within a certain sphere that the federal power can, in the nature of things, be advantageously administered," *ibid*. Whatever the judicial role, it is axiomatic that Congress does have substantial discretion and control over the federal balance. . . .

At the same time, . . . the federal balance is too essential a part of our constitutional structure and plays too vital a role in securing freedom for us to admit inability to intervene when one or the other level of Government has tipped the scales too far. . . .

The statute before us upsets the federal balance to a degree that renders it an unconstitutional assertion of the commerce power, and our intervention is required. . . .

Justice Thomas, concurring.

Although I join the majority, I write separately to observe that our case law has drifted far from the original understanding of the Commerce Clause. In a future case, we ought to temper our Commerce Clause jurisprudence in a manner that both makes sense of our more recent case law and is more faithful to the original understanding of that Clause. . . .

At the time the original Constitution was ratified, "commerce" consisted of selling, buying, and bartering, as well as transporting for these purposes. . . . As one would expect, the term "commerce" was used in contradistinction to productive activities such as manufacturing and agriculture. . . .

[I]nterjecting a modern sense of commerce into the Constitution generates significant textual and structural problems. For example, one cannot replace "commerce" with a different type of enterprise, such as manufacturing. When a manufacturer produces a car, assembly cannot take place "with a foreign nation" or "with the Indian Tribes." Parts may come from different States or other nations and hence may have been in the flow of commerce at one time, but manufacturing takes place at a discrete site. Agriculture and manufacturing involve the production of goods; commerce encompasses traffic in such articles. . . .

The Constitution not only uses the word "commerce" in a narrower sense than our case law might suggest, it also does not support the proposition that Congress has authority over all activities that "substantially affect" interstate commerce. The Commerce Clause does not state that Congress may "regulate matters that substantially affect commerce with foreign Nations, and among the several States, and with the Indian Tribes." . . . Clearly, the Framers could have drafted a Constitution that contained a "substantially affects interstate commerce" Clause had that been their objective.

In addition to its powers under the Commerce Clause, Congress has the authority to enact such laws as are "necessary and proper" to carry into execution its power to regulate commerce among the several States. But on this Court's understanding of congressional power under these two Clauses, many of Congress' other enumerated powers under Art. I, §8, are wholly superfluous. After all, if Congress may regulate all matters that substantially affect commerce, there is no need for the Constitution to specify that Congress may enact bankruptcy laws, cl. 4, or coin money and fix the standard of weights and measures, cl. 5, or punish counterfeiters of United States coin and securities, cl. 6. . . .

Put simply, much if not all of Art. I, §8 (including portions of the Commerce Clause itself), would be surplusage if Congress had been given authority over matters that substantially affect interstate commerce. An interpretation of cl. 3 that makes the rest of §8 superfluous simply cannot be correct. . . .

Apart from its recent vintage and its corresponding lack of any grounding in the original understanding of the Constitution, the substantial effects test suffers from the further flaw that it appears to grant Congress a police power over the Nation. . . . The substantial effects test suffers from this flaw, in part, because of its "aggregation principle." Under so-called "class of activities" statutes, Congress can regulate whole categories of activities that are not themselves either "interstate" or "commerce." In applying the effects test, we ask whether the class of activities *as a whole* substantially affects interstate commerce, not whether any specific activity within the class has such effects when considered in isolation. . . .

The aggregation principle is clever, but has no stopping point. Suppose all would agree that gun possession within 1,000 feet of a school does not substantially affect commerce, but that possession of weapons generally (knives, brass knuckles, nunchakus, etc.) does. Under our substantial effects doctrine, even though Congress cannot single out gun possession, it can prohibit weapon possession generally. But one *always* can draw the circle broadly enough to cover an activity that, when taken in isolation, would not have substantial effects on commerce. Under our jurisprudence, if Congress passed an omnibus "substantially affects interstate commerce" statute, purporting to regulate every aspect of human existence, the Act apparently would be constitutional. Even though particular sections may govern only trivial activities, the statute in the aggregate regulates matters that substantially affect commerce. . . .

At an appropriate juncture, I think we must modify our Commerce Clause jurisprudence. Today, it is easy enough to say that the Clause certainly does not empower Congress to ban gun possession within 1,000 feet of a school.

JUSTICE STEVENS, dissenting.

Guns are both articles of commerce and articles that can be used to restrain commerce. Their possession is the consequence, either directly or indirectly, of commercial activity. In my judgment, Congress' power to regulate commerce in firearms includes the power to prohibit possession of guns at any location because of their potentially harmful use; it necessarily follows that Congress may also prohibit their possession in particular markets. The market for the possession of handguns by school-age children is, distressingly, substantial. Whether or not the national interest in eliminating that market would have justified federal legislation in 1789, it surely does today.

JUSTICE SOUTER, dissenting.

[T]he period from the turn of the century to 1937 is . . . noted for a series of cases applying highly formalistic notions of "commerce" to invalidate federal social and economic legislation. . . . [T]he Commerce Clause cases turned on what was ostensibly a structural limit of federal power, but under each conception of judicial review the Court's character for the first third of the century showed itself in exacting judicial scrutiny of a legislature's choice of economic ends and of the legislative means selected to reach them. . . .

In the years following these decisions, deference to legislative policy judgments on commercial regulation became the powerful theme under . . . the . . . Commerce Clause[], . . . and in due course that deference became articulate in the standard of rationality review. . . . The . . . complete elimination of the direct/indirect effects dichotomy and acceptance of the cumulative effects doctrine, *Wickard v. Filburn*, 317 U.S. 111, 125, 127-129 (1942) . . . , so far settled the pressing issues of congressional power over commerce as to leave the Court for years without any need to phrase a test explicitly deferring to rational legislative judgments. The moment came, however, with the challenge to congressional Commerce Clause authority to prohibit racial discrimination in places of public accommodation, when the Court simply made explicit what the earlier cases had implied: "where we find that the legislators, in light of the facts and testimony before them, have a rational basis for finding a chosen regulatory scheme necessary to the protection of commerce, our investigation is at an end." [*Katzenbach v. McClung*, 379 U.S. 294, 303-304 (1964).] Thus, . . . adoption of rational basis review expressed the recognition that the Court had no sustainable basis for subjecting economic regulation as such to judicial policy judgments. . . .

There is today, however, a backward glance . . . , as the Court treats deference under the rationality rule as subject to gradation according to the commercial or noncommercial nature of the immediate subject of the challenged regulation. The distinction between what is patently commercial and what is not looks much like the old distinction between what directly affects commerce and what touches it only indirectly. . . . Thus, it seems fair to ask whether the step taken by the Court today does anything but portend a return to the untenable jurisprudence from which the Court extricated itself almost 60 years ago. The answer is not reassuring. . . .

Further glosses on rationality review . . . may be in the offing. Although this case turns on commercial character, the Court gestures toward two other considerations that it might sometime entertain in applying rational basis scrutiny (apart from a statutory obligation to supply independent proof of a jurisdictional element): does the congressional statute deal with subjects of traditional state regulation, and does the statute contain explicit factual findings supporting the otherwise implicit determination that the regulated activity substantially affects interstate commerce? Once again, any appeal these considerations may have depends on ignoring the painful lesson learned in 1937, for neither of the Court's suggestions would square with rational basis scrutiny. . . .

[A]s for the notion that the commerce power diminishes the closer it gets to customary state concerns, that idea has been flatly rejected, and not long ago. The commerce power, we have often observed, is plenary. . . .

[As for] legislative findings[,] . . . [t]he question for the courts, as all agree, is not whether as a predicate to legislation Congress in fact found that a particular activity substantially affects interstate commerce. The legislation implies such a finding, and there is no reason to entertain claims that Congress acted ultra vires intentionally. Nor is the question whether Congress was correct in so finding. The only question is whether the legislative judgment is within the realm of reason. . . . Congressional findings do not, however, directly address the question of reasonableness; they tell us what Congress actually has found, not what it could rationally find. If, indeed, the Court were to make the existence of explicit congressional findings dispositive in some close or difficult cases something other than rationality review would be afoot. The resulting congressional obligation to justify its policy choices on the merits would imply either a judicial authority to review the justification (and, hence, the wisdom) of those choices, or authority to require Congress to act with some high degree of deliberateness, of which express findings would be evidence. But review for congressional wisdom would just be the old judicial pretension discredited and abandoned in 1937, and review for deliberateness would be as patently unconstitutional as an Act of Congress mandating long opinions from this Court. Such a legislative process requirement would function merely as an excuse for covert review of the merits of legislation under standards never expressed and more or less arbitrarily applied. Under such a regime, in any case, the rationality standard of review would be a thing of the past. . . .

Because Justice Breyer's opinion demonstrates beyond any doubt that the Act in question passes the rationality review that the Court continues to espouse, today's decision may be seen as only a misstep, its reasoning and its suggestions not quite in gear with the prevailing standard, but hardly an epochal case. I would not argue otherwise, but I would raise a caveat. Not every epochal case has come in epochal trappings. . . .

Justice Breyer, with whom Justice Stevens, Justice Souter, and Justice Ginsburg join, dissenting.

[A] statute that makes it a crime to possess a gun in, or near, a school . . . falls well within the scope of the commerce power as this Court has understood that power over the last half century. . . .

[T]he specific question before us, as the Court recognizes, is not whether the "regulated activity sufficiently affected interstate commerce," but, rather, whether Congress could have had "*a rational basis*" for so concluding. . . .

[W]e must ask whether Congress could have had a *rational basis* for finding a significant (or substantial) connection between gun-related school violence and interstate commerce. Or, to put the question in the language of the *explicit* finding that Congress made when it amended this law in 1994: Could Congress rationally have found that "violent crime in school zones," through its effect on the "quality of education," significantly (or substantially) affects "interstate" or "foreign commerce"? As long as one views the commerce connection, not as a "technical legal conception," but as "a practical one," *Swift & Co. v. United States,* 196 U.S. 375, 398 (1905) (Holmes, J.), the answer to this question must be yes. Numerous reports and studies — generated both inside and outside government — make clear that Congress could reasonably have found the empirical connection that its law, implicitly or explicitly, asserts. . . .

For one thing, reports, hearings, and other readily available literature make clear that the problem of guns in and around schools is widespread and extremely serious. These materials report, for example, that four percent of American high school students (and six percent of inner-city high school students) carry a gun to school at least occasionally, . . . that 12 percent of urban high school students have had guns fired at them, . . . that 20 percent of those students have been threatened with guns, . . . and that, in any 6-month period, several hundred thousand schoolchildren are victims of violent crimes in or near their schools . . . . And, they report that this widespread violence in schools throughout the Nation significantly interferes with the quality of education in those schools. . . . Based on reports such as these, Congress obviously could have thought that guns and learning are mutually exclusive. . . . Congress could therefore have found a substantial educational problem — teachers unable to teach, students unable to learn — and concluded that guns near schools contribute substantially to the size and scope of that problem.

Having found that guns in schools significantly undermine the quality of education in our Nation's classrooms, Congress could also have found, given the effect of education upon interstate and foreign commerce, that gun-related violence in and around schools is a commercial, as well as a human, problem. . . .

In recent years the link between secondary education and business has strengthened, becoming both more direct and more important. Scholars on the subject report that technological changes and innovations in management techniques have altered the nature of the workplace so that more jobs now demand greater educational skills. . . . Increasing global competition also has made primary and secondary education economically more important. . . . Finally, there is evidence that, today more than ever, many firms base their location decisions upon the presence, or absence, of a work force with a basic education. . . .

The economic links I have just sketched seem fairly obvious. Why then is it not equally obvious, in light of those links, that a widespread, serious, and substantial physical threat to teaching and learning *also* substantially threatens the commerce to which that teaching and learning is inextricably tied? That is to say, guns in the hands of six percent of inner-city high school students and gun-related violence throughout a city's schools must threaten the trade and commerce that those schools support. The only question, then, is whether the latter threat is (to use the majority's terminology) "substantial." The evidence of (1) the *extent* of the gun-related violence problem, (2) the *extent* of the resulting negative effect on classroom learning, and (3) the *extent* of the consequent negative commercial effects, when taken together, indicate a threat to trade and commerce that is "substantial." At the very least, Congress could rationally have concluded that the links are "substantial."

Specifically, Congress could have found that gun-related violence near the classroom poses a serious economic threat (1) to consequently inadequately educated workers who must endure low paying jobs, and (2) to communities and businesses that might (in today's "information society") otherwise gain, from a well-educated work force, an important commercial advantage. . . . Congress has written that "the occurrence of violent crime in school zones" has brought about a "decline in the quality of education" that "has an adverse impact on interstate commerce and the foreign commerce of the United States." The violence-related facts, the educational facts, and the economic facts, taken together, make this conclusion rational. . . .

To hold this statute constitutional is not to "obliterate" the "distinction between what is national and what is local," nor is it to hold that the Commerce Clause permits the Federal Government to "regulate any activity that it found was related to the economic productivity of individual citizens," to regulate "marriage, divorce, and child custody," or to regulate any and all aspects of education. First, this statute is aimed at curbing a particularly acute threat to the educational process — the possession (and use) of life-threatening firearms in, or near, the classroom. . . . Second, the immediacy of the connection between education and the national economic well-being is documented by scholars and accepted by society at large in a way and to a degree that may not hold true for other social institutions. It must surely be the rare case, then, that a statute strikes at conduct that (when considered in the abstract) seems so removed from commerce, but which (practically speaking) has so significant an impact upon commerce.

In sum, a holding that the particular statute before us falls within the commerce power would not expand the scope of that Clause. Rather, it simply would apply preexisting law to changing economic circumstances. . . .

Although the majority today attempts to categorize . . . [*Katzenbach v. McClung*, 379 U.S. 294 (1964)] . . . and [*Wickard v. Filburn*, 317 U.S. 111 (1942)] as involving intrastate "economic activity," the Courts that decided each of those cases did *not* focus upon the economic nature of the activity regulated. Rather, they focused upon whether that activity *affected* interstate or foreign commerce. In fact, the *Wickard* Court expressly held that Filburn's consumption of home-grown wheat, *"though it may not be regarded as commerce,"* could nevertheless be regulated — *"whatever its nature"* — so long as "it exerts a substantial economic effect on interstate commerce." *Wickard, supra,* 317 U.S. at 125 (emphasis added).

More importantly, if a distinction between commercial and noncommercial activities is to be made, this is not the case in which to make it. . . . [I]f there is a principled distinction that could work both here and in future cases, Congress (even in the absence of vocational classes, industry involvement, and private management) could rationally conclude that schools fall on the commercial side of the line. . . . Why could Congress, for Commerce Clause purposes, not consider schools as roughly analogous to commercial investments from which the Nation derives the benefit of an educated work force? . . .

Upholding this legislation would do no more than simply recognize that Congress had a "rational basis" for finding a significant connection between guns in or near schools and (through their effect on education) the interstate and foreign commerce they threaten. . . .

[Appendix to Opinion of Breyer, J., omitted.]

UNITED STATES V. MORRISON

529 U.S. 598 (2000)

CHIEF JUSTICE REHNQUIST delivered the opinion of the Court.

In these cases we consider the constitutionality of 42 U.S.C. §13981, which provides a federal civil remedy for the victims of gender-motivated violence. . . .

I

Petitioner Christy Brzonkala enrolled at Virginia Polytechnic Institute (Virginia Tech) in the fall of 1994. In September of that year, Brzonkala met respondents Antonio Morrison and James Crawford, who were both students at Virginia Tech and members of its varsity football team. Brzonkala alleges that, within 30 minutes of meeting Morrison and Crawford, they assaulted and repeatedly raped her. . . . In December 1995, Brzonkala sued Morrison [and] Crawford, . . . alleg[ing] that Morrison's and Crawford's attack violated §13981. . . .

Section 13981 was part of the Violence Against Women Act of 1994. It states that "[a]ll persons within the United States shall have the right to be free from crimes of violence motivated by gender." 42 U.S.C. §13981(b). To enforce that right, subsection (c) declares:

> "A person (including a person who acts under color of any statute, ordinance, regulation, custom, or usage of any State) who commits a crime of violence motivated by gender and thus deprives another of the right declared in subsection (b) of this section shall be liable to the party injured, in an action for the recovery of compensatory and punitive damages, injunctive and declaratory relief, and such other relief as a court may deem appropriate."

Section 13981 defines a "crim[e] of violence motivated by gender" as "a crime of violence committed because of gender or on the basis of gender, and due, at least in part, to an animus based on the victim's gender." §13981(d)(1). . . .

Although the foregoing language of §13981 covers a wide swath of criminal conduct, . . . [s]ubsection (e)(4) further states that §13981 shall not be construed "to confer on the courts of the United States jurisdiction over any State law claim seeking the establishment of a divorce, alimony, equitable distribution of marital property, or child custody decree."

Every law enacted by Congress must be based on one or more of its powers enumerated in the Constitution. "The powers of the legislature are defined and limited; and that those limits may not be mistaken, or forgotten, the constitution is written." *Marbury v. Madison*, 1 Cranch 137 (1803) (Marshall, C.J.). . . .

II

Due respect for the decisions of a coordinate branch of Government demands that we invalidate a congressional enactment only upon a plain showing that Congress has exceeded its constitutional bounds. With this presumption of constitutionality in mind, we turn to the question whether §13981 falls within Congress' . . . power "[t]o regulate Commerce with foreign Nations, and among the several States, and with the Indian Tribes."

As we discussed at length in [*United States v. Lopez*, 514 U.S. 549 (1995)], our interpretation of the Commerce Clause has changed as our Nation has developed. We need not repeat that detailed review of the Commerce Clause's history here; it suffices to say that, in the years since *NLRB v. Jones & Laughlin Steel Corp.*, 301 U.S. 1, Congress has had considerably greater latitude in regulating conduct and transactions under the Commerce Clause than our previous case law permitted.

Lopez emphasized, however, that even under our modern, expansive interpretation of the Commerce Clause, Congress' regulatory authority is not without effective bounds.

> "[E]ven [our] modern-era precedents which have expanded congressional power under the Commerce Clause confirm that this power is subject to outer limits. . . ." [514 U.S.], at 556-557.

As we observed in *Lopez*, modern Commerce Clause jurisprudence has "identified three broad categories of activity that Congress may regulate under its commerce power." "First, Congress may regulate the use of the channels of interstate commerce." "Second, Congress is empowered to regulate and protect the instrumentalities of interstate commerce, or persons or things in interstate commerce, even though the threat may come only from intrastate activities." "Finally, Congress' commerce authority includes the power to regulate those activities having a substantial relation to interstate commerce, . . . i.e., those activities that substantially affect interstate commerce." [*Id.*], at 558-559.

Petitioners . . . seek to sustain §13981 as a regulation of activity that substantially affects interstate commerce. . . . *Lopez* . . . provides the proper framework for conducting the required analysis of §13981. . . .

[T]he proper resolution of the present cases is clear. Gender-motivated crimes of violence are not, in any sense of the phrase, economic activity. While we need not adopt a categorical rule against aggregating the effects of any noneconomic activity in order to decide these cases, thus far in our Nation's history our cases have upheld Commerce Clause regulation of intrastate activity only where that activity is economic in nature. . . .

In contrast with the lack of congressional findings that we faced in *Lopez*, §13981 *is* supported by numerous findings regarding the serious impact that gender-motivated violence has on victims and their families. But the existence of congressional findings is not sufficient, by itself, to sustain the constitutionality of Commerce Clause legislation. As we stated in *Lopez*, "[S]imply because Congress may conclude that a particular activity substantially affects interstate commerce does not necessarily make it so." 514 U.S., at 557, n.2. Rather, "'[w]hether particular operations affect interstate commerce sufficiently to come under the constitutional power of Congress to regulate them is ultimately a judicial rather than a legislative question, and can be settled finally only by this Court.'" 514 U.S., at 557, n.2.

In these cases, Congress' findings are substantially weakened by the fact that they rely so heavily on a method of reasoning that we have already rejected as unworkable if we are to maintain the Constitution's enumeration of powers. Congress found that gender-motivated violence affects interstate commerce

> "by deterring potential victims from traveling interstate, from engaging in employment in interstate business, and from transacting with business, and in places involved in interstate commerce; . . . by diminishing national productivity, increasing medical and other costs, and decreasing the supply of and the demand for interstate products." H.R. Conf. Rep. No. 103-711, at 385.

Given these findings and petitioners' arguments, the concern that we expressed in *Lopez* that Congress might use the Commerce Clause to completely obliterate the Constitution's distinction between national and local authority seems well founded. The reasoning that petitioners advance seeks to follow the but-for causal chain from the initial occurrence of violent crime (the suppression of which has always been the prime object of the States' police power) to every attenuated effect upon interstate commerce. If accepted, petitioners' reasoning would allow Congress to regulate any crime as long as the nationwide, aggregated impact of that crime has substantial effects on employment, production, transit, or consumption. Indeed, if Congress may regulate gender-motivated violence, it would be able to regulate murder or any other type of violence since gender-motivated violence, as a subset of all violent crime, is certain to have lesser economic impacts than the larger class of which it is a part.

Petitioners' reasoning, moreover, will not limit Congress to regulating violence but may, as we suggested in *Lopez*, be applied equally as well to family law and other areas of traditional state regulation since the aggregate effect of marriage, divorce, and childrearing on the national economy is undoubtedly significant. Congress may have recognized this specter when it expressly precluded §13981 from being used in the family law context. Under our written

Constitution, however, the limitation of congressional authority is not solely a matter of legislative grace.[7]

We accordingly reject the argument that Congress may regulate noneconomic, violent criminal conduct based solely on that conduct's aggregate effect on interstate commerce. The Constitution requires a distinction between what is truly national and what is truly local. In recognizing this fact we preserve one of the few principles that has been consistent since the Clause was adopted. The regulation and punishment of intrastate violence that is not directed at the instrumentalities, channels, or goods involved in interstate commerce has always been the province of the States. . . . Indeed, we can think of no better example of the police power, which the Founders denied the National Government and reposed in the States, than the suppression of violent crime and vindication of its victims. . . .

Petitioner Brzonkala's complaint alleges that she was the victim of a brutal assault. But Congress' effort in §13981 to provide a federal civil remedy can[not] be sustained . . . under the Commerce Clause. If the allegations here are true, no civilized system of justice could fail to provide her a remedy for the conduct of respondent Morrison. But under our federal system that remedy must be provided by the Commonwealth of Virginia, and not by the United States. . . .

JUSTICE THOMAS, concurring.

The majority opinion correctly applies our decision in *United States v. Lopez*, and I join it in full. I write separately only to express my view that the very notion of a "substantial effects" test under the Commerce Clause is inconsistent with the original understanding of Congress' powers and with this Court's early Commerce Clause cases. By continuing to apply this rootless and malleable standard, however circumscribed, the Court has encouraged the Federal Government to persist in its view that the Commerce Clause has virtually no limits. Until this Court replaces its existing Commerce Clause jurisprudence with a standard more consistent with the original understanding, we will continue to see Congress appropriating state police powers under the guise of regulating commerce.

---

7. No doubt the political branches have a role in interpreting and applying the Constitution, but ever since *Marbury* this Court has remained the ultimate expositor of the constitutional text. As we emphasized in *United States v. Nixon*, 418 U.S. 683 (1974): "In the performance of assigned constitutional duties each branch of the Government must initially interpret the Constitution, and the interpretation of its powers by any branch is due great respect from the others. . . . Many decisions of this Court, however, have unequivocally reaffirmed the holding of *Marbury* that '[i]t is emphatically the province and duty of the judicial department to say what the law is.'" *Id.*, at 703.

Contrary to Justice Souter's suggestion, [*Gibbons v. Ogden*, 22 U.S. (9 Wheat.) 1 (1824)] did not exempt the commerce power from this cardinal rule of constitutional law. His assertion that, from *Gibbons* on, public opinion has been the only restraint on the congressional exercise of the commerce power is true only insofar as it contends that political accountability is and has been the only limit on Congress' exercise of the commerce power within that power's outer bounds. As the language surrounding that relied upon by Justice Souter makes clear, *Gibbons* did not remove from this Court the authority to define that boundary. . . .

JUSTICE SOUTER, with whom JUSTICE STEVENS, JUSTICE GINSBURG, and JUSTICE BREYER join, dissenting.

Congress has the power to legislate with regard to activity that, in the aggregate, has a substantial effect on interstate commerce. *See Wickard v. Filburn*, 317 U.S. 111, 124-128 (1942). The fact of such a substantial effect is not an issue for the courts in the first instance, but for the Congress, whose institutional capacity for gathering evidence and taking testimony far exceeds ours. By passing legislation, Congress indicates its conclusion, whether explicitly or not, that facts support its exercise of the commerce power. The business of the courts is to review the congressional assessment, not for soundness but simply for the rationality of concluding that a jurisdictional basis exists in fact. Any explicit findings that Congress chooses to make, though not dispositive of the question of rationality, may advance judicial review by identifying factual authority on which Congress relied. Applying those propositions in these cases can lead to only one conclusion.

One obvious difference from *United States v. Lopez*, 514 U.S. 549, is the mountain of data assembled by Congress, here showing the effects of violence against women on interstate commerce. Passage of the Act in 1994 was preceded by four years of hearings, which included testimony from physicians and law professors; from survivors of rape and domestic violence; and from representatives of state law enforcement and private business. The record includes reports on gender bias from task forces in 21 States, and we have the benefit of specific factual findings in the eight separate Reports issued by Congress and its committees over the long course leading to enactment. . . .

Congress thereby explicitly stated the predicate for the exercise of its Commerce Clause power. Is its conclusion irrational in view of the data amassed? True, the methodology of particular studies may be challenged, and some of the figures arrived at may be disputed. But the sufficiency of the evidence before Congress to provide a rational basis for the finding cannot seriously be questioned.

Indeed, the legislative record here is far more voluminous than the record compiled by Congress and found sufficient in two prior cases upholding Title II of the Civil Rights Act of 1964 against Commerce Clause challenges. In *Heart of Atlanta Motel, Inc. v. United States*, 379 U.S. 241 (1964), and *Katzenbach v. McClung*, 379 U.S. 294 (1964), the Court referred to evidence showing the consequences of racial discrimination by motels and restaurants on interstate commerce. . . .

If the analogy to the Civil Rights Act of 1964 is not plain enough, one can always look back a bit further. In *Wickard*, we upheld the application of the Agricultural Adjustment Act to the planting and consumption of homegrown wheat. The effect on interstate commerce in that case followed from the possibility that wheat grown at home for personal consumption could either be drawn into the market by rising prices, or relieve its grower of any need to purchase wheat in the market. The Commerce Clause predicate was simply the effect of the production of wheat for home consumption on supply and demand in interstate commerce. Supply and demand for goods in interstate commerce will also be affected by the deaths of 2,000 to 4,000 women annually at the hands of domestic abusers, and by the reduction in the work force by the 100,000 or more rape victims who lose their jobs each year or are forced to quit. Violence against women may be found to affect interstate commerce and affect it substantially. . . .

Chief Justice Marshall's seminal opinion in [*Gibbons v. Ogden*, 22 U.S. (9 Wheat.) 1, 193-194 (1824)], construed the commerce power from the start with "a breadth never yet exceeded," *Wickard v. Filburn*, 317 U.S., at 120. In particular, it is worth noting, the Court in *Wickard* did not regard its holding as exceeding the scope of Chief Justice Marshall's view of interstate commerce; *Wickard* applied an aggregate effects test to ostensibly domestic, noncommercial farming consistently with Chief Justice Marshall's indication that the commerce power may be understood by its exclusion of subjects, among others, "which do not affect other States," *Gibbons*, 9 Wheat., at 195. This plenary view of the power has either prevailed or been acknowledged by this Court at every stage of our jurisprudence. And it was this understanding, free of categorical qualifications, that prevailed in the period after 1937 through *Lopez*, as summed up by Justice Harlan: "'Of course, the mere fact that Congress has said when particular activity shall be deemed to affect commerce does not preclude further examination by this Court. But where we find that the legislators . . . have a rational basis for finding a chosen regulatory scheme necessary to the protection of commerce, our investigation is at an end.'" *Maryland v. Wirtz*, 392 U.S. 183, 190 (1968) (quoting *Katzenbach v. McClung*, 379 U.S., at 303-304). . . .

[T]oday's attempt to distinguish between primary activities affecting commerce in terms of the relatively commercial or noncommercial character of the primary conduct proscribed comes with the pedigree of near tragedy. . . . [T]his Court from time to time created categorical enclaves beyond congressional reach by declaring such activities as "mining," "production," "manufacturing," and union membership to be outside the definition of "commerce" and by limiting application of the effects test to "direct" rather than "indirect" commercial consequences.

Since adherence to these formalistically contrived confines of commerce power in large measure provoked the judicial crisis of 1937, one might reasonably have doubted that Members of this Court would ever again toy with a return to the days before *NLRB v. Jones & Laughlin Steel Corp.*, 301 U.S. 1 (1937), which brought the earlier and nearly disastrous experiment to an end. And yet today's decision can only be seen as a step toward recapturing the prior mistakes. . . .

The Court finds it relevant that the statute addresses conduct traditionally subject to state prohibition under domestic criminal law, a fact said to have some heightened significance when the violent conduct in question is not itself aimed directly at interstate commerce or its instrumentalities. Again, history seems to be recycling, for the theory of traditional state concern as grounding a limiting principle has been rejected previously. . . .

The objection to reviving traditional state spheres of action as a consideration in commerce analysis . . . not only rests on the portent of incoherence, but is compounded by a further defect just as fundamental. The defect, in essence, is the majority's rejection of the Founders' considered judgment that politics, not judicial review, should mediate between state and national interests as the strength and legislative jurisdiction of the National Government inevitably increased through the expected growth of the national economy. . . . Madison . . . took care in The Federalist No. 46 to hedge his argument for limited power by explaining the importance of national politics in protecting the States' interests. The National Government "will partake sufficiently of the spirit [of the States], to be disinclined to invade the rights of the individual States, or the prerogatives of their governments." The Federalist No. 46, p. 319 (J. Cooke ed. 1961). . . . [T]his Court recognized the political component of federalism in the seminal *Gibbons* opinion. After declaring the plenary character of congressional power within the sphere of activity affecting commerce, the Chief Justice spoke for the Court in explaining that there was only one restraint on its valid exercise:

> "The wisdom and the discretion of Congress, their identity with the people, and the influence which their constituents possess at elections, are, in this, as in many other instances, as that, for example, of declaring war, the sole restraints on which they have relied, to secure them from its abuse. They are the restraints on which the people must often rely solely, in all representative governments." *Gibbons*, 9 Wheat., at 197, 22 U.S. 1.

Politics as the moderator of the congressional employment of the commerce power was the theme many years later in *Wickard*, for after the Court acknowledged the breadth of the Gibbons formulation it invoked Chief Justice Marshall yet again in adding that "[h]e made emphatic the embracing and penetrating nature of this power by warning that effective restraints on its exercise must proceed from political rather than judicial processes." *Wickard*, 317 U.S., at 120. Hence, "conflicts of economic interest . . . are wisely left under our system to resolution by Congress under its more flexible and responsible legislative process. Such conflicts rarely lend themselves to judicial determination. And with the wisdom, workability, or fairness, of the plan of regulation we have nothing to do." *Id.*, at 129.

JUSTICE BREYER, with whom JUSTICE STEVENS joins, and with whom JUSTICE SOUTER and JUSTICE GINSBURG join as to Part I-A, dissenting.

No one denies the importance of the Constitution's federalist principles. Its state/federal division of authority protects liberty — both by restricting the burdens that government can impose from a distance and by facilitating citizen participation in government that is closer to home. The question is how the judiciary can best implement that original federalist understanding where the Commerce Clause is at issue.

I

The majority holds that the federal commerce power does not extend to such "noneconomic" activities as "noneconomic, violent criminal conduct" that significantly affects interstate commerce only if we "aggregate" the interstate "effect[s]" of individual instances. . . . [T]he majority's holding illustrates the difficulty of finding a workable judicial Commerce Clause touchstone — a set of comprehensible interpretive rules that courts might use to impose some meaningful limit, but not too great a limit, upon the scope of the legislative authority that the Commerce Clause delegates to Congress.

A

Consider the problems. The "economic/noneconomic" distinction is not easy to apply. Does the local street corner mugger engage in "economic" activity or "noneconomic" activity when he mugs for money? Would evidence that desire for economic domination underlies many brutal crimes against women save the present statute?

The line becomes yet harder to draw given the need for exceptions. The Court itself would permit Congress to aggregate, hence regulate, "noneconomic" activity taking place at economic establishments. See *Heart of Atlanta Motel, Inc. v. United States*, 379 U.S. 241 (1964) (upholding civil rights laws forbidding discrimination at local motels); *Katzenbach v. McClung*, 379 U.S. 294 (1964) (same for restaurants). And it would permit Congress to regulate where that regulation is "an essential part of a larger regulation of economic activity, in which the regulatory scheme could be undercut unless the intrastate activity were regulated." [*United States v. Lopez*, 514 U.S. 549, 561 (1995).] Given the former exception, can Congress simply rewrite the present law and limit its application to restaurants, hotels, perhaps universities, and other places of public accommodation? Given the latter exception, can Congress save the present law by including it, or much of it, in a broader "Safe Transport" or "Workplace Safety" act?

More important, why should we give critical constitutional importance to the economic, or noneconomic, nature of an interstate-commerce-affecting *cause*? If chemical emanations through indirect environmental change cause identical, severe commercial harm outside a State, why should it matter whether local factories or home fireplaces release them? The Constitution itself refers only to Congress' power to "regulate Commerce . . . among the several States," and to make laws "necessary and proper" to implement that power. The language says nothing about either the local nature, or the economic nature, of an interstate-commerce-affecting cause.

This Court has long held that only the interstate commercial effects, not the local nature of the cause, are constitutionally relevant. . . . Nothing in the Constitution's language, or that of earlier cases prior to *Lopez*, explains why the Court should ignore one highly relevant characteristic of an interstate-commerce-affecting cause (how "local" it is), while placing critical constitutional weight upon a different, less obviously relevant, feature (how "economic" it is). . . .

The majority, aware of these difficulties, is nonetheless concerned with what it sees as an important contrary consideration. To determine the lawfulness of statutes simply by asking whether Congress could reasonably have found that *aggregated* local instances significantly affect interstate commerce will allow Congress to regulate almost anything. Virtually all local activity, when instances are aggregated, can have "substantial effects on employment, production, transit, or consumption." Hence Congress could "regulate any crime," and perhaps "marriage, divorce, and childrearing" as well, obliterating the "Constitution's distinction between national and local authority."

This consideration, however, while serious, does not reflect a jurisprudential defect, so much as it reflects a practical reality. We live in a Nation knit together by two centuries of scientific, technological, commercial, and environmental change. Those changes, taken together, mean that virtually every kind of activity, no matter how local, genuinely can affect commerce, or its conditions, outside the State — at least when considered in the aggregate. *Heart of Atlanta Motel*, 379 U.S., at 251. And that fact makes it close to impossible for courts to develop meaningful subject-matter categories that would exclude some kinds of local activities from ordinary Commerce Clause "aggregation" rules without, at the same time, depriving Congress of the power to regulate activities that have a genuine and important effect upon interstate commerce.

Since judges cannot change the world, the "defect" means that, within the bounds of the rational, Congress, not the courts, must remain primarily responsible for striking the appropriate state/federal balance. *Garcia v. San Antonio Metropolitan Transit Authority*, 469 U.S. 528, 552. Congress is institutionally motivated to do so. Its Members represent state and local district interests. They consider the views of state and local officials when they legislate, and they have even developed formal procedures to ensure that such consideration takes place. Moreover, Congress often can better reflect state concerns for autonomy in the details of sophisticated statutory schemes than can the Judiciary, which cannot easily gather the relevant facts and which must apply more general legal rules and categories. Not surprisingly, the bulk of American law is still state law, and overwhelmingly so. . . .

POINTS FOR DISCUSSION

1. In *Lopez* and *Morrison*, the Court explained that under the commerce power Congress may regulate *economic* intrastate activities that, in aggregate, substantially affect interstate commerce, but perhaps not such *noneconomic* intrastate activities. "We have upheld," the Court stated in *Lopez*, "a wide variety of congressional Acts regulating intrastate 'economic activity' where we have concluded that the activity substantially affected interstate commerce." In *Morrison*, the Court expressed that "[w]hile we need not adopt a categorical rule against aggregating the effects of any noneconomic activity in order to decide these cases, thus far in our Nation's history our cases have upheld Commerce Clause regulation of intrastate activity only where that activity is economic in nature." Do these statements accord with *Wickard v. Filburn*, 317 U.S. 111, 125 (1942), in which the Court stated, "even if [the] activity be local and though it may not be regarded as commerce, it may still, whatever its nature, be reached by Congress if it exerts a substantial *economic effect* on interstate commerce" (emphasis added)? Is the economic/non-economic distinction any more justified under the Commerce Clause than the Court's previous distinctions between "commerce" and "manufacturing," and "direct" and "indirect" effects on commerce?

2. Chief Justice Rehnquist and Justice Souter debated whether the Court's decisions in *Lopez* and *Morrison* are consistent with Chief Justice Marshall's opinion for the Court in *Gibbons v. Ogden*, 22 U.S. (9 Wheat.) 1 (1824). Are they?

3. In *Lopez* the Court refused to defer broadly to Congress on whether the Commerce Clause justified the regulation at issue, for "[t]o do so would require

us to conclude that the Constitution's enumeration of powers does not pre-suppose something not enumerated, . . . and that there never will be a distinction between what is truly national and what is truly local." In *Morrison* the Court recognized that Congress made extensive findings regarding the effects of gender-motivated violence on interstate commerce; nonetheless, the Court held that the regulation exceeded Congress's commerce power. In dissent, Justice Souter argued that Congress's findings provided a "rational basis" for upholding the statute as a proper regulation of interstate commerce. Justice Breyer argued in dissent, citing *Garcia v. San Antonio Metropolitan Transit Authority*, 469 U.S. 528 (1985), that Congress is better situated to protect state interests and autonomy than courts. How do the majority and dissenting opinions differ in how much deference each would give Congress in determining whether the Commerce Clause authorized the regulation? How much deference should courts give Congress in this regard? Consider these questions in light of the debates over the political safeguards of federalism and judicial review that you read in Chapter 4. What positions from those debates do the Justices espouse? Do the *Lopez* and *Morrison* Courts implicitly endorse St. George Tucker's strict construction theory of congressional power or the Marshall Court's broader constructions that you studied in Chapter 1?

4. In *Lopez* and *Morrison*, the Court rejected broad aggregation theories on the ground that, in principle, they would afford Congress limitless regulatory authority in areas that states traditionally have regulated, including crime and family law. Are *Lopez* and *Morrison* inconsistent, or in tension, with the Court's rejection of traditional state function analysis in *Garcia*?

5. In dissent in *Morrison*, Justice Breyer acknowledged the structural tension between the Constitution's establishment of dual sovereignty and the deference that dissenting justices would afford Congress to regulate under the Commerce Clause. He argued, however, that this tension "does not reflect a jurisprudential defect, so much as it reflects a practical reality." He observed, "[w]e live in a Nation knit together by two centuries of scientific, technological, commercial, and environmental change. Those changes, taken together, mean that virtually every kind of activity, no matter how local, genuinely can affect commerce, or its conditions, outside the State — at least when considered in the aggregate." Is Justice Breyer correct that the structural tension between judicial deference to Congress and dual sovereignty is more a reflection of "practical reality" than of "jurisprudential defect"?

6. How, if at all, should the theories of dual, cooperative, and dynamic federalism that you studied in Chapter 3 inform how judges resolve whether Congress has exceeded its powers under the Commerce Clause?

In the next case, *Gonzales v. Raich*, 546 U.S. 1 (2005), the Court upheld federal drug prohibitions as applied to marijuana that was grown intrastate and used intrastate for medicinal purposes. As you read this case, consider these questions:

- Does the Court define the commerce power in a manner consistent with *Lopez* and *Morrison*?

- Is the degree of deference the Court gives Congress consistent with *Lopez* and *Morrison*?
- What role, if any, does the Necessary and Proper Clause play in the Court's analysis? What role should it play?

GONZALES V. RAICH

545 U.S. 1 (2005)

JUSTICE STEVENS delivered the opinion of the Court.

California is one of at least nine States that authorize the use of marijuana for medicinal purposes. The question presented in this case is whether the power vested in Congress by Article I, §8, of the Constitution "[t]o make all Laws which shall be necessary and proper for carrying into Execution" its authority to "regulate Commerce with foreign Nations, and among the several States" includes the power to prohibit the local cultivation and use of marijuana in compliance with California law.

I

California has been a pioneer in the regulation of marijuana. In 1913, California was one of the first States to prohibit the sale and possession of marijuana, and at the end of the century, California became the first State to authorize limited use of the drug for medicinal purposes. In 1996, California voters passed Proposition 215, now codified as the Compassionate Use Act of 1996. The proposition was designed to ensure that "seriously ill" residents of the State have access to marijuana for medical purposes, and to encourage Federal and State Governments to take steps towards ensuring the safe and affordable distribution of the drug to patients in need. The Act creates an exemption from criminal prosecution for physicians, as well as for patients and primary caregivers who possess or cultivate marijuana for medicinal purposes with the recommendation or approval of a physician. . . .

[T]he federal Controlled Substances Act (CSA), 84 Stat. 1242, 21 U.S.C. §801 et seq., . . . prevents [respondents, individuals who desire to use marijuana for medical purposes under the 1996 California law,] from possessing, obtaining, or manufacturing cannabis for their personal medical use. . . . Respondents claimed that enforcing the CSA against them would violate the Commerce Clause. . . .

The case is made difficult by respondents' strong arguments that they will suffer irreparable harm because, despite a congressional finding to the contrary, marijuana does have valid therapeutic purposes. The question before us, however, is not whether it is wise to enforce the statute in these circumstances; rather, it is whether Congress' power to regulate interstate markets for medicinal substances encompasses the portions of those markets that are supplied with drugs produced and consumed locally. Well-settled law controls our answer. The CSA is a valid exercise of federal power, even as applied to the troubling facts of this case.

II

The main objectives of the CSA were to conquer drug abuse and to control the legitimate and illegitimate traffic in controlled substances. Congress was particularly concerned with the need to prevent the diversion of drugs from legitimate to illicit channels.

To effectuate these goals, Congress devised a closed regulatory system making it unlawful to manufacture, distribute, dispense, or possess any controlled substance except in a manner authorized by the CSA. . . .

In enacting the CSA, Congress classified marijuana as a Schedule I drug. . . . By classifying marijuana as a Schedule I drug, . . . the manufacture, distribution, or possession of marijuana became a criminal offense. . . .

III

Respondents in this case do not dispute that passage of the CSA . . . was well within Congress' commerce power. Nor do they contend that any provision or section of the CSA amounts to an unconstitutional exercise of congressional authority. Rather, respondents' challenge is actually quite limited; they argue that the CSA's categorical prohibition of the manufacture and possession of marijuana as applied to the intrastate manufacture and possession of marijuana for medical purposes pursuant to California law exceeds Congress' authority under the Commerce Clause.

In assessing the validity of congressional regulation, none of our Commerce Clause cases can be viewed in isolation. As charted in considerable detail in [*United States v. Lopez*, 514 U.S. 549 (1995)], our understanding of the reach of the Commerce Clause, as well as Congress' assertion of authority thereunder, has evolved over time. The Commerce Clause emerged as the Framers' response to the central problem giving rise to the Constitution itself: the absence of any federal commerce power under the Articles of Confederation. For the first century of our history, the primary use of the Clause was to preclude the kind of discriminatory state legislation that had once been permissible. Then, in response to rapid industrial development and an increasingly interdependent national economy, Congress "ushered in a new era of federal regulation under the commerce power." . . .

Cases decided during that "new era," which now spans more than a century, have identified three general categories of regulation in which Congress is authorized to engage under its commerce power. First, Congress can regulate the channels of interstate commerce. Second, Congress has authority to regulate and protect the instrumentalities of interstate commerce, and persons or things in interstate commerce. Third, Congress has the power to regulate activities that substantially affect interstate commerce. Only the third category is implicated in the case at hand.

Our case law firmly establishes Congress' power to regulate purely local activities that are part of an economic "class of activities" that have a substantial effect on interstate commerce. See, *e.g.*, *Wickard v. Filburn*, 317 U.S. 111, 128-129 (1942). As we stated in *Wickard*, "even if appellee's activity be local and though it may not be regarded as commerce, it may still, whatever its nature, be reached by Congress if it exerts a substantial economic effect on interstate commerce." *Id.*, at 125. We have never required Congress to legislate with scientific exactitude. When Congress decides that the " 'total incidence' " of a practice poses a threat to a national market, it may regulate the entire class. In this vein, we have reiterated that when " 'a general regulatory statute bears a substantial relation to commerce, the de minimis character of individual instances arising under that statute is of no consequence.' " *E.g.*, *Lopez*, 514 U.S., at 558.

Our decision in *Wickard*, 317 U.S. 111, is of particular relevance. In *Wickard*, we upheld the application of regulations promulgated under the Agricultural Adjustment Act of 1938, which were designed to control the volume of wheat moving in interstate and foreign commerce in order to avoid surpluses and consequent abnormally low prices[:] . . .

> "The effect of the statute before us is to restrict the amount which may be produced for market and the extent as well to which one may forestall resort to the market by producing to meet his own needs. That appellee's own contribution to the demand for wheat may be trivial by itself is not enough to remove him from the scope of federal regulation where, as here, his contribution, taken together with that of many others similarly situated, is far from trivial." *Id.*, at 127-128.

Wickard thus establishes that Congress can regulate purely intrastate activity that is not itself "commercial," in that it is not produced for sale, if it concludes that failure to regulate that class of activity would undercut the regulation of the interstate market in that commodity.

The similarities between this case and *Wickard* are striking. Like the farmer in *Wickard*, respondents are cultivating, for home consumption, a fungible commodity for which there is an established, albeit illegal, interstate market. Just as the Agricultural Adjustment Act was designed "to control the volume [of wheat] moving in interstate and foreign commerce in order to avoid surpluses . . ." and consequently control the market price, a primary purpose of the CSA is to control the supply and demand of controlled substances in both lawful and unlawful drug markets. In *Wickard*, we had no difficulty concluding that Congress had a rational basis for believing that, when viewed in the aggregate, leaving home-consumed wheat outside the regulatory scheme would have a substantial influence on price and market conditions. Here too, Congress had a rational basis for concluding that leaving home-consumed marijuana outside federal control would similarly affect price and market conditions.

More concretely, one concern prompting inclusion of wheat grown for home consumption in the 1938 Act was that rising market prices could draw such wheat into the interstate market, resulting in lower market prices. *Wickard*, 317 U.S., at 128. The parallel concern making it appropriate to include marijuana grown for home consumption in the CSA is the likelihood that the high demand in the interstate market will draw such marijuana into that market. While the diversion of homegrown wheat tended to frustrate the federal interest in stabilizing prices by regulating the volume of commercial transactions in the interstate market, the diversion of homegrown marijuana tends to frustrate the federal interest in eliminating commercial transactions in the interstate market in their entirety. In both cases, the regulation is squarely within Congress' commerce power because production of the commodity meant for home consumption, be it wheat or marijuana, has a substantial effect on supply and demand in the national market for that commodity. . . .

Findings in the introductory sections of the CSA explain why Congress deemed it appropriate to encompass local activities within the scope of the CSA. . . . [T]he national, and international, market for marijuana has dimensions that are fully comparable to those defining the class of activities regulated by the Secretary pursuant to the 1938 statute. Respondents nonetheless insist that the CSA cannot be constitutionally applied to their activities because Congress did not make a specific finding that the intrastate cultivation and possession of marijuana for medical purposes based on the recommendation of a physician would substantially affect the larger interstate marijuana market. Be that as it may, we have never required Congress to make particularized findings in order to legislate. . . . While congressional findings are certainly helpful in reviewing the substance of a congressional statutory scheme, particularly when the connection to commerce is not self-evident, and while we will consider congressional findings in our analysis when they are available, the absence of particularized findings does not call into question Congress' authority to legislate.

In assessing the scope of Congress' authority under the Commerce Clause, we stress that the task before us is a modest one. We need not determine whether respondents' activities, taken in the aggregate, substantially affect interstate commerce in fact, but only whether a "rational basis" exists for so concluding. *Lopez*, 514 U.S., at 557; *Katzenbach v. McClung*, 379 U.S. 294, 299-301 (1964); *Heart of Atlanta Motel, Inc. v. United States*, 379 U.S. 241, 252-253 (1964). Given the enforcement difficulties that attend distinguishing between marijuana cultivated locally and marijuana grown elsewhere, and concerns about diversion into illicit channels, we have no difficulty concluding that Congress had a rational basis for believing that failure to regulate the intrastate manufacture and possession of marijuana would leave a gaping hole in the CSA. Thus, as in *Wickard*, when it enacted comprehensive legislation to regulate the interstate market in a fungible commodity, Congress was acting well within its authority to "make all Laws which shall be necessary and proper" to "regulate Commerce . . . among the several States." U.S. Const., Art. I, §8. That the regulation ensnares some purely intrastate activity is of no moment. As we have done many times before, we refuse to excise individual components of that larger scheme.

IV

To support their contrary submission, respondents rely heavily on . . . *Lopez*, 514 U.S. 549, and [*United States v. Morrison*, 529 U.S. 598 (2000)]. As an initial matter, the statutory challenges at issue in those cases were markedly different from the challenge respondents pursue in the case at hand. Here, respondents ask us to excise individual applications of a concededly valid statutory scheme. In contrast, in both *Lopez* and *Morrison*, the parties asserted that a particular statute or provision fell outside Congress' commerce power in its entirety. . . .

At issue in *Lopez* was the validity of the Gun-Free School Zones Act of 1990, which was a brief, single-subject statute making it a crime for an individual to possess a gun in a school zone. The Act did not regulate any economic activity and did not contain any requirement that the possession of a gun have any connection to past interstate activity or a predictable impact on future commercial activity. Distinguishing our earlier cases holding that comprehensive regulatory statutes may be validly applied to local conduct that does not, when viewed in isolation, have a significant impact on interstate commerce, we held the statute invalid. We explained:

> "Section 922(q) is a criminal statute that by its terms has nothing to do with 'commerce' or any sort of economic enterprise, however broadly one might define those terms. Section 922(q) is not an essential part of a larger regulation of economic activity, in which the regulatory scheme could be undercut unless the intrastate activity were regulated. It cannot, therefore, be sustained under our cases upholding regulations of activities that arise out of or are connected with a commercial transaction, which viewed in the aggregate, substantially affects interstate commerce." 514 U.S., at 561.

The statutory scheme that the Government is defending in this litigation is at the opposite end of the regulatory spectrum. . . . [T]he CSA . . . was a lengthy and detailed statute creating a comprehensive framework for regulating the production, distribution, and possession of five classes of "controlled substances." . . .

Congress . . . identified 42 opiates, 22 opium derivatives, and 17 hallucinogenic substances as Schedule I drugs. Marijuana was listed as the 10th item in the third subcategory. That classification, unlike the discrete prohibition established by the Gun-Free School Zones Act of 1990, was merely one of many "essential part[s] of a larger regulation of economic activity, in which the regulatory scheme could be undercut unless the intrastate activity were regulated." *Lopez*, 514 U.S., at 561. Our opinion in *Lopez* casts no doubt on the validity of such a program.

Nor does this Court's holding in *Morrison*, 529 U.S. 598. The Violence Against Women Act of 1994 created a federal civil remedy for the victims of gender-motivated crimes of violence. 42 U.S.C. §13981. The remedy was enforceable in both state and federal courts, and generally depended on proof of the violation of a state law. Despite congressional findings that such crimes had an adverse impact on interstate commerce, we held the statute unconstitutional because, like the statute in *Lopez*, it did not regulate economic activity. We concluded that "the noneconomic, criminal nature of the conduct at issue was central to our decision" in *Lopez*, and that our prior cases had identified a clear pattern of analysis: " 'Where economic activity substantially affects interstate commerce, legislation regulating that activity will be sustained.' " *Morrison*, 529 U.S., at 610.

Unlike those at issue in *Lopez* and *Morrison*, the activities regulated by the CSA are quintessentially economic. "Economics" refers to "the production, distribution, and consumption of commodities." Webster's Third New

International Dictionary 720 (1966). The CSA is a statute that regulates the production, distribution, and consumption of commodities for which there is an established, and lucrative, interstate market. Prohibiting the intrastate possession or manufacture of an article of commerce is a rational (and commonly utilized) means of regulating commerce in that product. Such prohibitions include specific decisions requiring that a drug be withdrawn from the market as a result of the failure to comply with regulatory requirements as well as decisions excluding Schedule I drugs entirely from the market. Because the CSA is a statute that directly regulates economic, commercial activity, our opinion in *Morrison* casts no doubt on its constitutionality. . . .

JUSTICE SCALIA, concurring in the judgment.

I agree with the Court's holding that the Controlled Substances Act (CSA) may validly be applied to respondents' cultivation, distribution, and possession of marijuana for personal, medicinal use. I write separately because my understanding of the doctrinal foundation on which that holding rests is, if not inconsistent with that of the Court, at least more nuanced. . . .

[O]ur cases have mechanically recited that the Commerce Clause permits congressional regulation of three categories: (1) the channels of interstate commerce; (2) the instrumentalities of interstate commerce, and persons or things in interstate commerce; and (3) activities that "substantially affect" interstate commerce. The first two categories are self-evident, since they are the ingredients of interstate commerce itself. The third category, however, is different in kind, and its recitation without explanation is misleading and incomplete.

It is *misleading* because, unlike the channels, instrumentalities, and agents of interstate commerce, activities that substantially affect interstate commerce are not themselves part of interstate commerce, and thus the power to regulate them cannot come from the Commerce Clause alone. Rather, . . . Congress's regulatory authority over intrastate activities that are not themselves part of interstate commerce (including activities that have a substantial effect on interstate commerce) derives from the Necessary and Proper Clause. *Katzenbach v. McClung*, 379 U.S. 294, 301-302 (1964); *United States v. E. C. Knight Co.*, 156 U.S. 1, 39-40 (1895) (Harlan, J., dissenting). And the category of "activities that substantially affect interstate commerce," [*United States v. Lopez*, 514 U.S. 549, 559 (1995),] is *incomplete* because the authority to enact laws necessary and proper for the regulation of interstate commerce is not limited to laws governing intrastate activities that substantially affect interstate commerce. Where necessary to make a regulation of interstate commerce effective, Congress may regulate even those intrastate activities that do not themselves substantially affect interstate commerce.

I

Our cases show that the regulation of intrastate activities may be necessary to and proper for the regulation of interstate commerce in two general circumstances. Most directly, the commerce power permits Congress not only to devise rules for the governance of commerce between States but also to facilitate interstate commerce by eliminating potential obstructions, and to restrict it by eliminating potential stimulants. That is why the Court has repeatedly sustained congressional legislation on the ground that the regulated activities had a substantial effect on interstate commerce. *Lopez* and [*United States v. Morrison*, 529 U.S. 598 (2000),] recognized the expansive scope of Congress's authority in this regard: "[T]he pattern is clear. Where economic activity substantially affects interstate commerce, legislation regulating that activity will be sustained." *Lopez, supra*, at 560; *Morrison, supra*, at 610 (same).

This principle is not without limitation. In *Lopez* and *Morrison*, the Court — conscious of the potential of the "substantially affects" test to "obliterate the distinction between what is national and what is local," *Lopez, supra*, at 566-567; see also *Morrison, supra*, at 615-616 — rejected the argument that Congress may regulate *noneconomic* activity based solely on the effect that it may have on interstate commerce through a remote chain of inferences. "[I]f we were to accept [such] arguments," the Court reasoned in *Lopez*, "we are hard pressed to posit any activity by an individual that Congress is without power to regulate." *Lopez, supra*, at 564; *see also Morrison, supra*, at 615-616. Thus, although Congress's authority to regulate intrastate activity that substantially affects interstate commerce is broad, it does not permit the Court to "pile inference upon inference," *Lopez, supra*, at 567, in order to establish that noneconomic activity has a substantial effect on interstate commerce.

As we implicitly acknowledged in *Lopez*, however, Congress's authority to enact laws necessary and proper for the regulation of interstate commerce is not limited to laws directed against economic activities that have a substantial effect on interstate commerce. Though the conduct in *Lopez* was not economic, the Court nevertheless recognized that it could be regulated as "an essential part of a larger regulation of economic activity, in which the regulatory scheme could be undercut unless the intrastate activity were regulated." 514 U.S., at 561. This statement referred to those cases permitting the regulation of intrastate activities "which in a substantial way interfere with or obstruct the exercise of the granted power." [*United States v. Wrightwood Dairy Co.*, 315 U.S. 110, 119]; *see also United States v. Darby*, 312 U.S. 100, 118-119 (1941). As the Court put it in *Wrightwood Dairy*, where Congress has the authority to enact a regulation of interstate commerce, "it possesses every power needed to make that regulation effective." 315 U.S., at 118-119.

Although this power "to make . . . regulation effective" commonly overlaps with the authority to regulate economic activities that substantially affect interstate commerce, and may in some cases have been confused with that authority, the two are distinct. The regulation of an intrastate activity may be essential to a comprehensive regulation of interstate commerce even though the intrastate activity does not itself "substantially affect" interstate commerce. Moreover, as the passage from *Lopez* quoted above suggests, Congress may regulate even noneconomic local activity if that regulation is a necessary part of a more general regulation of interstate commerce. *See Lopez, supra*, at 561. The relevant question is simply whether the means chosen are "reasonably adapted" to the attainment of a legitimate end under the commerce power. See *Darby, supra*, at 121. . . .

II

Today's principal dissent objects that, by permitting Congress to regulate activities necessary to effective interstate regulation, the Court reduces *Lopez* and *Morrison* to "little more than a drafting guide." I think that criticism unjustified. Unlike the power to regulate activities that have a substantial effect on interstate commerce, the power to enact laws enabling effective regulation of interstate commerce can only be exercised in conjunction with congressional regulation of an interstate market, and it extends only to those measures necessary to make the interstate regulation effective. As *Lopez* itself states, and the Court affirms today, Congress may regulate noneconomic intrastate activities only where the failure to do so "could . . . undercut" its regulation of interstate commerce. *See Lopez, supra,* at 561. This is not a power that threatens to obliterate the line between "what is truly national and what is truly local." *Lopez, supra,* at 567-568.

Lopez and *Morrison* affirm that Congress may not regulate certain "purely local" activity within the States based solely on the attenuated effect that such activity may have in the interstate market. But those decisions do not declare noneconomic intrastate activities to be categorically beyond the reach of the Federal Government. Neither case involved the power of Congress to exert control over intrastate activities in connection with a more comprehensive scheme of regulation; *Lopez* expressly disclaimed that it was such a case, 514 U.S., at 561, and *Morrison* did not even discuss the possibility that it was. . . . To dismiss this distinction as "superficial and formalistic," *see post* (O'Connor, J., dissenting), is to misunderstand the nature of the Necessary and Proper Clause, which empowers Congress to enact laws in effectuation of its enumerated powers that are not within its authority to enact in isolation. See *McCulloch v. Maryland,* 4 Wheat. 316, 421-422 (1819).

And there are other restraints upon the Necessary and Proper Clause authority. As Chief Justice Marshall wrote in *McCulloch v. Maryland,* even when the end is constitutional and legitimate, the means must be "appropriate" and "plainly adapted" to that end. *Id.,* at 421. Moreover, they may not be otherwise "prohibited" and must be "consistent with the letter and spirit of the constitution." *Ibid.* These phrases are not merely hortatory. For example, cases such as *Printz v. United States,* 521 U.S. 898 (1997), and *New York v. United States,* 505 U.S. 144 (1992), affirm that a law is not "*proper* for carrying into Execution the Commerce Clause" "[w]hen [it] violates [a constitutional] principle of state sovereignty." *Printz, supra,* at 923-924; see also *New York, supra,* at 166.

III

The application of these principles to the case before us is straightforward. In the CSA, Congress has undertaken to extinguish the interstate market in Schedule I controlled substances, including marijuana. The Commerce Clause unquestionably permits this. The power to regulate interstate commerce "extends not only to those regulations which aid, foster and protect the commerce, but embraces those which prohibit it." *Darby,* 312 U.S., at 113. To effectuate its objective, Congress has prohibited almost all intrastate activities related to Schedule I substances — both economic activities (manufacture, distribution, possession with the intent to distribute) and noneconomic activities (simple possession). That simple possession is a noneconomic activity is immaterial to whether it can be prohibited as a necessary part of a larger regulation. Rather, Congress's authority to enact all of these prohibitions of intrastate controlled-substance activities depends only upon whether they are appropriate means of achieving the legitimate end of eradicating Schedule I substances from interstate commerce.

By this measure, I think the regulation must be sustained. . . . As the Court explains, marijuana that is grown at home and possessed for personal use is never more than an instant from the interstate market — and this is so whether or not the possession is for medicinal use or lawful use under the laws of a particular State. Congress need not accept on faith that state law will be effective in maintaining a strict division between a lawful market for "medical" marijuana and the more general marijuana market. "To impose on [Congress] the necessity of resorting to means which it cannot control, which another government may furnish or withhold, would render its course precarious, the result of its measures uncertain, and create a dependence on other governments, which might disappoint its most important designs, and is incompatible with the language of the constitution." *McCulloch, supra*, at 424.

Finally, neither respondents nor the dissenters suggest any violation of state sovereignty of the sort that would render this regulation "inappropriate," *id.*, at 421 — except to argue that the CSA regulates an area typically left to state regulation. That is not enough to render federal regulation an inappropriate means. The Court has repeatedly recognized that, if authorized by the commerce power, Congress may regulate private endeavors "even when [that regulation] may pre-empt express state-law determinations contrary to the result which has commended itself to the collective wisdom of Congress." *National League of Cities v. Usery*, 426 U.S. 833, 840 (1976). At bottom, respondents' state-sovereignty argument reduces to the contention that federal regulation of the activities permitted by California's Compassionate Use Act is not sufficiently necessary to be "necessary and proper" to Congress's regulation of the interstate market. For the reasons given above and in the Court's opinion, I cannot agree. . . .

JUSTICE O'CONNOR, with whom THE CHIEF JUSTICE and JUSTICE THOMAS join as to all but Part III, dissenting.

We enforce the "outer limits" of Congress' Commerce Clause authority not for their own sake, but to protect historic spheres of state sovereignty from excessive federal encroachment and thereby to maintain the distribution of power fundamental to our federalist system of government. *United States v. Lopez*, 514 U.S. 549, 557 (1995); *NLRB v. Jones & Laughlin Steel Corp.*, 301 U.S. 1, 37 (1937). One of federalism's chief virtues, of course, is that it promotes innovation by allowing for the possibility that "a single courageous State may, if its citizens choose, serve as a laboratory; and try novel social and economic experiments without risk to the rest of the country." *New State Ice Co. v. Liebmann*, 285 U.S. 262, 311 (1932) (Brandeis, J., dissenting).

This case exemplifies the role of States as laboratories. The States' core police powers have always included authority to define criminal law and to protect the health, safety, and welfare of their citizens. Exercising those powers, California (by ballot initiative and then by legislative codification) has come to its own conclusion about the difficult and sensitive question of whether marijuana should be available to relieve severe pain and suffering. Today the Court sanctions an application of the federal Controlled Substances Act that extinguishes that experiment, without any proof that the personal cultivation, possession, and use of marijuana for medicinal purposes, if economic activity in the first place, has a substantial effect on interstate commerce and is therefore an appropriate subject of federal regulation. In so doing, the Court announces a rule that gives Congress a perverse incentive to legislate broadly pursuant to the Commerce Clause — nestling questionable assertions of its authority into comprehensive regulatory schemes — rather than with precision. That rule and the result it produces in this case are irreconcilable with our decisions in *Lopez*, *supra*, and *United States v. Morrison*, 529 U.S. 598 (2000). . . .

Today's decision suggests that the federal regulation of local activity is immune to Commerce Clause challenge because Congress chose to act with an ambitious, all-encompassing statute, rather than piecemeal. In my view, allowing Congress to set the terms of the constitutional debate in this way, *i.e.*, by packaging regulation of local activity in broader schemes, is tantamount to removing meaningful limits on the Commerce Clause. . . .

Today's decision allows Congress to regulate intrastate activity without check, so long as there is some implication by legislative design that regulating intrastate activity is essential (and the Court appears to equate "essential" with "necessary") to the interstate regulatory scheme. Seizing upon our language in *Lopez* that the statute prohibiting gun possession in school zones was "not an essential part of a larger regulation of economic activity, in which the regulatory scheme could be undercut unless the intrastate activity were regulated," 514 U.S., at 561, the Court appears to reason that the placement of local activity in a comprehensive scheme confirms that it is essential to that scheme. If the Court is right, then *Lopez* stands for nothing more than a drafting guide: Congress should have described the relevant crime as "transfer or possession of a firearm anywhere in the nation" — thus including commercial and noncommercial activity, and clearly encompassing some activity with assuredly substantial effect on interstate commerce. Had it done so, the majority hints, we would have sustained its authority to regulate possession of firearms in school zones. Furthermore, today's decision suggests we would readily sustain a congressional decision to attach the regulation of intrastate activity to a pre-existing comprehensive (or even not-so-comprehensive) scheme. If so, the Court invites increased federal regulation of local activity even if, as it suggests, Congress would not enact a *new* interstate scheme exclusively for the sake of reaching intrastate activity.

I cannot agree that our decision in *Lopez* contemplated such evasive or overbroad legislative strategies with approval. . . . *Lopez* and *Morrison* did not indicate that the constitutionality of federal regulation depends on superficial and formalistic distinctions. Likewise I did not understand our discussion of the role of courts in enforcing outer limits of the Commerce Clause for the sake of maintaining the federalist balance our Constitution requires, as a signal to

Congress to enact legislation that is more extensive and more intrusive into the domain of state power. If the Court always defers to Congress as it does today, little may be left to the notion of enumerated powers.

The hard work for courts, then, is to identify objective markers for confining the analysis in Commerce Clause cases. . . . The task is to identify a mode of analysis that allows Congress to regulate more than nothing (by declining to reduce each case to its litigants) and less than everything (by declining to let Congress set the terms of analysis). The analysis may not be the same in every case, for it depends on the regulatory scheme at issue and the federalism concerns implicated.

A number of objective markers are available to confine the scope of constitutional review here. Both federal and state legislation — including the CSA itself, the California Compassionate Use Act, and other state medical marijuana legislation — recognize that medical and nonmedical (i.e., recreational) uses of drugs are realistically distinct and can be segregated, and regulate them differently. Respondents challenge only the application of the CSA to medicinal use of marijuana. Moreover, because fundamental structural concerns about dual sovereignty animate our Commerce Clause cases, it is relevant that this case involves the interplay of federal and state regulation in areas of criminal law and social policy, where "States lay claim by right of history and expertise." *Lopez, supra,* at 583; *see also Morrison, supra,* at 617-619. California, like other States, has drawn on its reserved powers to distinguish the regulation of medicinal marijuana. To ascertain whether Congress' encroachment is constitutionally justified in this case, then, I would focus here on the personal cultivation, possession, and use of marijuana for medicinal purposes. . . .

Having thus defined the relevant conduct, we must determine whether, under our precedents, the conduct is economic and, in the aggregate, substantially affects interstate commerce. Even if intrastate cultivation and possession of marijuana for one's own medicinal use can properly be characterized as economic, and I question whether it can, it has not been shown that such activity substantially affects interstate commerce. Similarly, it is neither self-evident nor demonstrated that regulating such activity is necessary to the interstate drug control scheme. . . .

In *Lopez* and *Morrison,* we suggested that economic activity usually relates directly to commercial activity. The homegrown cultivation and personal possession and use of marijuana for medicinal purposes has no apparent commercial character. . . .

[C]haracterizing this as a case about the Necessary and Proper Clause does not change the analysis significantly. Congress must exercise its authority under the Necessary and Proper Clause in a manner consistent with basic constitutional principles. [*Garcia v. San Antonio Metro. Transit Auth.,* 469 U.S. 528, 585 (1985)] (O'Connor, J., dissenting) ("It is not enough that the 'end be legitimate'; the means to that end chosen by Congress must not contravene the spirit of the Constitution."). As Justice Scalia recognizes, Congress cannot use its authority under the Clause to contravene the principle of state sovereignty embodied in the Tenth Amendment. Likewise, that authority must be used in a manner consistent with the notion of enumerated powers — a structural principle that is as much part of the Constitution as the Tenth Amendment's explicit textual command. Accordingly, something more than mere assertion is required when Congress purports to have power over local activity whose connection to an intrastate market is not self-evident. Otherwise, the Necessary and Proper Clause will always be a back door for unconstitutional federal regulation. *Cf. Printz v. United States*, 521 U.S. 898, 923 (1997) (the Necessary and Proper Clause is "the last, best hope of those who defend ultra vires congressional action"). Indeed, if it were enough in "substantial effects" cases for the Court to supply conceivable justifications for intrastate regulation related to an interstate market, then we could have surmised in *Lopez* that guns in school zones are "never more than an instant from the interstate market" in guns already subject to extensive federal regulation, recast *Lopez* as a Necessary and Proper Clause case, and thereby upheld the Gun-Free School Zones Act of 1990. . . .

We would do well to recall how James Madison, the father of the Constitution, described our system of joint sovereignty to the people of New York: "The powers delegated by the proposed constitution to the federal government are few and defined. Those which are to remain in the State governments are numerous and indefinite. . . . The powers reserved to the several States will extend to all the objects which, in the ordinary course of affairs, concern the lives, liberties, and properties of the people, and the internal order, improvement, and prosperity of the State." The Federalist No. 45. . . .

If I were a California citizen, I would not have voted for the medical marijuana ballot initiative; if I were a California legislator I would not have supported the Compassionate Use Act. But whatever the wisdom of California's experiment with medical marijuana, the federalism principles that have driven our Commerce Clause cases require that room for experiment be protected in this case. . . .

JUSTICE THOMAS, dissenting.

Respondents . . . use marijuana that has never been bought or sold, that has never crossed state lines, and that has had no demonstrable effect on the national market for marijuana. If Congress can regulate this under the Commerce Clause, then it can regulate virtually anything — and the Federal Government is no longer one of limited and enumerated powers. . . .

Respondents' local cultivation and consumption of marijuana is not "Commerce . . . among the several States." U.S. Const., Art. I, §8, cl. 3. By holding that Congress may regulate activity that is neither interstate nor commerce under the Interstate Commerce Clause, the Court abandons any attempt to enforce the Constitution's limits on federal power. . . .

As I explained at length in *United States v. Lopez*, 514 U.S. 549 (1995), the Commerce Clause empowers Congress to regulate the buying and selling of goods and services trafficked across state lines. *Id.*, at 586-589 (concurring opinion). . . . On this traditional understanding of "commerce," the Controlled Substances Act (CSA) regulates a great deal of marijuana trafficking that is interstate and commercial in character. The CSA does not, however, criminalize only the interstate buying and selling of marijuana. Instead, it bans the entire market — intrastate or interstate, noncommercial or commercial — for marijuana. Respondents are correct that the CSA exceeds Congress' commerce power as applied to their conduct, which is purely intrastate and noncommercial. . . .

More difficult, however, is whether the CSA is a valid exercise of Congress' power to enact laws that are "necessary and proper for carrying into Execution" its power to regulate interstate commerce. Art. I, §8, cl. 18. . . . The question is . . . whether the intrastate ban is "necessary and proper" as applied to medical marijuana users like respondents.

[N]either in enacting the CSA nor in defending its application to respondents has the Government offered any obvious reason why banning medical marijuana use is necessary to stem the tide of interstate drug trafficking. Congress' goal of curtailing the interstate drug trade would not plainly be thwarted if it could not apply the CSA to patients like [respondents]. That is, unless Congress' aim is really to exercise police power of the sort reserved to the States in order to eliminate even the intrastate possession and use of marijuana. . . .

Even assuming the CSA's ban on locally cultivated and consumed marijuana is "necessary," that does not mean it is also "proper." . . . Even if Congress may regulate purely intrastate activity when essential to exercising some enumerated power, Congress may not use its incidental authority to subvert basic principles of federalism and dual sovereignty. . . . Here, Congress has encroached on States' traditional police powers to define the criminal law and to protect the health, safety, and welfare of their citizens.

POINTS FOR DISCUSSION

1. In *Raich*, the Court analogized the CSA to the regulatory scheme at issue in *Wickard v. Filburn*, 317 U.S. 111 (1942). Specifically, the Court explained that the CSA regulates an interstate market and prohibits the intrastate use of homegrown marijuana to prevent frustration of the interstate market regulation. The Court distinguished the statutes at issue in *Lopez* and *Morrison* on the ground that they regulated only intrastate activities, not an interstate market. Is this a sound distinction? Would it be fair to characterize the statutes at issue in *Lopez* and *Morrison* as regulating an interstate market by removing obstructions to the movement of people and goods in commerce? Is it plausible that Congress enacted the Guns-Free School Zones Act or the Violence Against Women Act for these purposes? Should congressional purpose be relevant to whether an act of Congress comports with the commerce power?

2. The *Raich* Court explained that "Congress had a rational basis for concluding that leaving home-consumed marijuana outside federal control would . . . affect price and market conditions," undermining the interstate market regulations of the CSA. In performing rational-basis review, did the *Raich* Court give Congress more deference than the Court gave it in *Lopez* and *Morrison*?

3. Justice Scalia, concurring in *Raich*, would have sustained the regulation under the Necessary and Proper Clause. He argued that the Necessary and Proper Clause empowers Congress to regulate (1) *economic* activities that have a substantial effect on interstate commerce and (2) *noneconomic* intrastate activities as necessary to carry regulation of an interstate market into execution. Does Justice Scalia's understanding of the Necessary and Proper Clause reconcile *Lopez* and *Morrison* with *Wickard*? Does Justice Scalia implicitly endorse either St. George Tucker's theory of strict construction or the Marshall Court's broader construction of the Necessary and Proper Clause that you studied in Chapter 1? Does Justice Thomas implicitly endorse either theory in his dissent in *Raich*?

4. In dissent in *Raich*, Justice O'Connor argued that Congress may not regulate the intrastate use of intrastate-grown marijuana in California because such regulation falls within the state's "core police powers." Is this method of analysis consistent with *Garcia v. San Antonio Metro. Transit Auth.*, 469 U.S. 528 (1985), which held that the concept of traditional state functions does not limit Congress's enumerated powers? Justice O'Connor also argued that the Court's opinion gives Congress an incentive to regulate broadly. To reach intrastate activity, she contended, Congress now may enact broad interstate market regulations that incorporate the targeted intrastate activity. Do the political safeguards of federalism counteract this incentive? For example, regarding the Guns-Free School Zones Act, should the political safeguards of federalism, in theory or practice, counteract any incentive *Raich* might create for Congress to enact a broad interstate firearms market regulation as a means of constitutionally prohibiting the possession of guns near schools?

B. THE SPENDING POWER

Article I, §8 of the Constitution provides that "Congress shall have Power To lay and collect Taxes, Duties, Imposts and Excises, to pay the Debts and provide for the common Defence and general Welfare of the United States. . . ." The Supreme Court has long held that the General Welfare Clause authorizes Congress to *spend*, not generally regulate, for the general welfare.

The cases in this section address three important questions about the "spending power" of the General Welfare Clause. First, what limitations, if any, constrain Congress's power to spend for the general welfare? In particular, does the "general Welfare" include only ends within Congress's enumerated powers, or is the "general Welfare" a separate end in itself?

Second, to what extent may Congress impose conditions upon the receipt of federal funds by states or individuals? When Congress appropriates money for a purpose, that purpose itself reflects a condition on the appropriation. For example, an appropriation of money to states for highway construction is conditioned on the state's use of the appropriated money for highway construction. How far may Congress go in imposing conditions upon receipt of federal monies? For instance, may Congress condition receipt of federal highway money on a state's agreement to raise its legal drinking age to 21?

Third, what power does Congress have under the Necessary and Proper Clause to enact regulations ensuring that federal appropriations effectively serve their intended purposes? May Congress, for example, make it a crime to bribe an official of a state agency that receives federal money?

As you read the cases in this section, keep the following questions in mind:

- How does the Court define the spending power in each case?
- To what extent does the Court defer to Congress in determining whether the enactments at issue are constitutional?

In addition, keep in mind that conditional spending programs represent one form of "cooperative federalism." As you saw in Chapter 3, cooperative federalism envisions the federal government and the states working together to serve national policy ends in ways that account for differing local circumstances. Consider whether the idea of cooperative federalism informs (or should inform) judicial understandings of the spending power.

UNITED STATES v. BUTLER

297 U.S. 1 (1936)

Mr. JUSTICE ROBERTS delivered the opinion of the Court.

In this case we must determine whether certain provisions of the Agricultural Adjustment Act, 1933, conflict with the Federal Constitution.

[The purpose of the Act was to regulate agricultural prices by reducing agricultural production. The Act authorized the Secretary of Agriculture to make agreements with farmers to reduce production in exchange for benefit payments. The federal government was to make the payments from "processing taxes" that would be levied "upon the first domestic processing of the commodity." Butler and his co-receivers for a company challenged the tax as constitutionally invalid.] . . .

The Government asserts that . . . Article 1, §8 of the Constitution . . . authorizes the contemplated expenditure of the funds raised by the tax. This contention presents the great and the controlling question in the case. . . .

There should be no misunderstanding as to the function of this court in such a case. It is sometimes said that the court assumes a power to overrule or control the action of the people's representatives. This is a misconception. The Constitution is the supreme law of the land ordained and established by the people. All legislation must conform to the principles it lays down. When an act of Congress is appropriately challenged in the courts as not conforming to the constitutional mandate, the judicial branch of the Government has only one duty, — to lay the article of the Constitution which is invoked beside the statute which is challenged and to decide whether the latter squares with the former. All the court does, or can do, is to announce its considered judgment upon the question. The only power it has, if such it may be called, is the power of judgment. This court neither approves nor condemns any legislative policy. Its delicate and difficult office is to ascertain and declare whether the legislation is in accordance with, or in contravention of, the provisions of the Constitution; and, having done that, its duty ends.

The question is not what power the Federal Government ought to have but what powers in fact have been given by the people. It hardly seems necessary to reiterate that ours is a dual form of government; that in every state there are two governments; the state and the United States. Each State has all governmental powers save such as the people, by their Constitution, have conferred upon the United States, denied to the States, or reserved to themselves. The federal union is a government of delegated powers. It has only such as are expressly conferred upon it and such as are reasonably to be implied from those granted. In this respect we differ radically from nations where all legislative power, without restriction or limitation, is vested in a parliament or other legislative body subject to no restrictions except the discretion of its members.

Article 1, §8, of the Constitution, vests sundry powers in the Congress. . . . The clause thought to authorize the legislation . . . confers upon the Congress power "to lay and collect Taxes, Duties, Imposts and Excises, to pay the Debts and provide for the common Defence and general Welfare of the United States. . . ." It is not contended that this provision grants power to regulate agricultural production upon the theory that such legislation would promote the general welfare. The Government concedes that the phrase "to provide for the general welfare" qualifies the power "to lay and collect taxes." The view that the clause grants power to provide for the general welfare, independently of the taxing power, has never been authoritatively accepted. Mr. Justice Story points out that, if it were adopted, "it is obvious that under color of the generality of the words, to 'provide for the common defence and general welfare,' the government of the United States is, in reality, a government of general and unlimited powers, notwithstanding the subsequent enumeration of specific powers."[11] The true construction undoubtedly is that the only thing granted is the power to tax for the purpose of providing funds for payment of the nation's debts and making provision for the general welfare. . . .

The Congress is expressly empowered to lay taxes to provide for the general welfare. Funds in the Treasury as a result of taxation may be expended only through appropriation. They can never accomplish the objects for which they were collected unless the power to appropriate is as broad as the power to tax. The necessary implication from the terms of the grant is that the public funds may be appropriated "to provide for the general welfare of the United States." . . .

Since the foundation of the Nation, sharp differences of opinion have persisted as to the true interpretation of the phrase. Madison asserted it amounted to no more than a reference to the other powers enumerated in the subsequent clauses of the same section; that, as the United States is a government of limited and enumerated powers, the grant of power to tax and spend for the general national welfare must be confined to the enumerated legislative fields committed to the Congress. In this view the phrase is mere tautology, for taxation and appropriation are or may be necessary incidents of the exercise of any of the enumerated legislative powers. Hamilton, on the other hand, maintained the clause confers a power separate and distinct from those later enumerated, is not restricted in meaning by the grant of them, and Congress consequently has a substantive power to tax and to appropriate, limited only by the requirement that it shall be exercised to provide for the general welfare of the United States. Each contention has had the support of those whose views are entitled to weight. This court has noticed the question, but has never found it necessary to decide which is the true construction. Mr. Justice Story, in his Commentaries, espouses the Hamiltonian

---

11. Story, Commentaries on the Constitution of the United States (5th Ed.) vol. I, §907.

position. We shall not review the writings of public men and commentators or discuss the legislative practice. Study of all these leads us to conclude that the reading advocated by Mr. Justice Story is the correct one. While, therefore, the power to tax is not unlimited, its confines are set in the clause which confers it, and not in those of §8 which bestow and define the legislative powers of the Congress. It results that the power of Congress to authorize expenditure of public moneys for public purposes is not limited by the direct grants of legislative power found in the Constitution.

But the adoption of the broader construction leaves the power to spend subject to limitations. . . . We are not now required to ascertain the scope of the phrase "general welfare of the United States" or to determine whether an appropriation in aid of agriculture falls within it. Wholly apart from that question, another principle embedded in our Constitution prohibits the enforcement of the Agricultural Adjustment Act. The act invades the reserved rights of the states. It is a statutory plan to regulate and control agricultural production, a matter beyond the powers delegated to the federal government. The tax, the appropriation of the funds raised, and the direction for their disbursement, are but parts of the plan. They are but means to an unconstitutional end.

From the accepted doctrine that the United States is a government of delegated powers, it follows that those not expressly granted, or reasonably to be implied from such as are conferred, are reserved to the states or to the people. To forestall any suggestion to the contrary, the Tenth Amendment was adopted. The same proposition, otherwise stated, is that powers not granted are prohibited. None to regulate agricultural production is given, and therefore legislation by Congress for that purpose is forbidden.

It is an established principle that the attainment of a prohibited end may not be accomplished under the pretext of the exertion of powers which are granted.

"Should Congress, in the execution of its powers, adopt measures which are prohibited by the constitution; or should Congress, under the pretext of executing its powers, pass laws for the accomplishment of objects not intrusted to the government; it would become the painful duty of this tribunal, should a case requiring such a decision come before it, to say, that such an act was not the law of the land." *McCulloch v. Maryland*, 4 Wheat. 316, 423. . . .

These principles are as applicable to the power to lay taxes as to any other federal power. Said the court, in *McCulloch v. Maryland, supra*, 4 Wheat. 316, 421:

"Let the end be legitimate, let it be within the scope of the constitution, and all means which are appropriate, which are plainly adapted to that end, which are not prohibited, but consist with the letter and spirit of the constitution, are constitutional."

The power of taxation, which is expressly granted, may, of course, be adopted as a means to carry into operation another power also expressly granted. But resort to the taxing power to effectuate an end which is not legitimate, not within the scope of the Constitution, is obviously inadmissible.

"Congress is not empowered to tax for those purposes which are within the exclusive province of the States." *Gibbons v. Ogden*, 9 Wheat. 1, 199. . . .

If the taxing power may not be used as the instrument to enforce a regulation of matters of state concern with respect to which the Congress has no authority to interfere, may it, as in the present case, be employed to raise the money necessary to purchase a compliance which the Congress is powerless to command? The Government asserts that whatever might be said against the validity of the plan if compulsory, it is constitutionally sound because the end is accomplished by voluntary co-operation. There are two sufficient answers to the contention. The regulation is not in fact voluntary. The farmer, of course, may refuse to comply, but the price of such refusal is the loss of benefits. The amount offered is intended to be sufficient to exert pressure on him to agree to the proposed regulation. . . . The power to confer or withhold unlimited benefits is the power to coerce or destroy. If the cotton grower elects not to accept the benefits, he will receive less for his crops; those who receive payments will be able to undersell him. The result may well be financial ruin. . . .

But if the plan were one for purely voluntary co-operation it would stand no better so far as federal power is concerned. At best it is a scheme for purchasing with federal funds submission to federal regulation of a subject reserved to the states. . . .

We are not here concerned with a conditional appropriation of money, nor with a provision that if certain conditions are not complied with the appropriation shall no longer be available. By the Agricultural Adjustment Act the amount of the tax is appropriated to be expended only in payment under contracts whereby the parties bind themselves to regulation by the Federal Government. There is an obvious difference between a statute stating the conditions upon which moneys shall be expended and one effective only upon assumption of a contractual obligation to submit to a regulation which otherwise could not be enforced. Many examples pointing the distinction might be cited. We are referred to appropriations in aid of education, and it is said that no one has doubted the power of Congress to stipulate the sort of education for which money shall be expended. But an appropriation to an educational institution which by its terms is to become available only if the beneficiary enters into a contract to teach doctrines subversive of the Constitution is clearly bad. An affirmance of the authority of Congress so to condition the expenditure of an appropriation would tend to nullify all constitutional limitations upon legislative power. . . .

Congress has no power to enforce its commands on the farmer to the ends sought by the Agricultural Adjustment Act. It must follow that it may not indirectly accomplish those ends by taxing and spending to purchase compliance. . . .

[It is not true that] the makers of the Constitution . . . by a single clause gave power to the Congress to tear down the barriers, to invade the states' jurisdiction, and to become a parliament of the whole people, subject to no restrictions save such as are self-imposed. . . .

Mr. JUSTICE STONE, dissenting.

It is upon the contention that state power is infringed by purchased regulation of agricultural production that chief reliance is placed. It is insisted that, while the Constitution gives to Congress, in specific and unambiguous terms, the power to tax and spend, the power is subject to limitations which do not find their origin in any express provision of the Constitution and to which other expressly delegated powers are not subject.

The Constitution requires that public funds shall be spent for a defined purpose, the promotion of the general welfare. Their expenditure usually involves payment on terms which will insure use by the selected recipients within the limits of the constitutional purpose. Expenditures would fail of their purpose and thus lose their constitutional sanction if the terms of payment were not such that by their influence on the action of the recipients the permitted end would be attained. The power of Congress to spend is inseparable from persuasion to action over which Congress has no legislative control. Congress may not command that the science of agriculture be taught in state universities. But if it would aid the teaching of that science by grants to state institutions, it is appropriate, if not necessary, that the grant be on the condition . . . that it be used for the intended purpose. Similarly it would seem to be compliance with the Constitution, not violation of it, for the government to take and the university to give a contract that the grant would be so used. It makes no difference that there is a promise to do an act which the condition is calculated to induce. Condition and promise are alike valid since both are in furtherance of the national purpose for which the money is appropriated.

These effects upon individual action, which are but incidents of the authorized expenditure of government money, are pronounced to be themselves a limitation upon the granted power, and so the time-honored principle of constitutional interpretation that the granted power includes all those which are incident to it is reversed. "Let the end be legitimate," said the great Chief Justice, "let it be within the scope of the Constitution, and all means which are appropriate, which are plainly adapted to that end, which are not prohibited, but consist with the letter and spirit of the Constitution, are constitutional." *McCulloch v. Maryland*, 4 Wheat. 316, 421. This cardinal guide to constitutional exposition must now be re-phrased so far as the spending power of the federal government is concerned. Let the expenditure be to promote the general welfare, still if it is needful in order to insure its use for the intended purpose to influence any action which Congress cannot command because within the sphere of state government, the expenditure is unconstitutional. And taxes otherwise lawfully levied are likewise unconstitutional if they are appropriated to the expenditure whose incident is condemned. . . .

Such a limitation is contradictory and destructive of the power to appropriate for the public welfare, and is incapable of practical application. The spending power of Congress is in addition to the legislative power and not subordinate to it. This independent grant of the power of the purse, and its very nature, involving in its exercise the duty to insure expenditure within the granted power, presuppose freedom of selection among diverse ends and aims, and the capacity to impose such conditions as will render the choice effective. It is a contradiction in terms to say that there is power to spend for the national welfare, while rejecting any power to impose conditions reasonably adapted to the attainment of the end which alone would justify the expenditure.

The limitation now sanctioned must lead to absurd consequences. The government may give seeds to farmers, but may not condition the gift upon their being planted in places where they are most needed or even planted at all. The government may give money to the unemployed, but may not ask that those who get it shall give labor in return, or even use it to support their families. It may give money to sufferers from earthquake, fire, tornado, pestilence, or flood, but may not impose conditions — health precautions, designed to prevent the spread of disease, or induce the movement of population to safer or more sanitary areas. All that, because it is purchased regulation infringing state powers, must be left for the states, who are unable or unwilling to supply the necessary relief. . . . If the expenditure is for a national public purpose, that purpose will not be thwarted because payment is on condition which will advance that purpose. The action which Congress induces by payments of money to promote the general welfare, but which it does not command or coerce, is but an incident to a specifically granted power, but a permissible means to a legitimate end. If appropriation in aid of a program of curtailment of agricultural production is constitutional, and it is not denied that it is, payment to farmers on condition that they reduce their crop acreage is constitutional. It is not any the less so because the farmer at his own option promises to fulfill the condition. . . .

The power to tax and spend is not without constitutional restraints. One restriction is that the purpose must be truly national. Another is that it may not be used to coerce action left to state control. Another is the conscience and patriotism of Congress and the Executive. "It must be remembered that legislatures are ultimate guardians of the liberties and welfare of the people in quite as great a degree as the courts." Justice Holmes, in *Missouri, Kansas & Texas R. Co. v. May*, 194 U.S. 267, 270. . . .

[I]nterpretation of our great charter of government which proceeds on any assumption that the responsibility for the preservation of our institutions is the exclusive concern of any one of the three branches of government, or that it alone can save them from destruction is far more likely, in the long run, "to obliterate the constituent members" of "an indestructible union of indestructible states" than the frank recognition that language, even of a constitution, may mean what it says: that the power to tax and spend includes the power to relieve a nationwide economic maladjustment by conditional gifts of money.

Mr. Justice Brandeis and Mr. Justice Cardozo join in this opinion.

South Dakota v. Dole

483 U.S. 203 (1987)

Chief Justice Rehnquist delivered the opinion of the Court.

Petitioner South Dakota permits persons 19 years of age or older to purchase beer containing up to 3.2% alcohol. . . . In 1984 Congress enacted 23 U.S.C. §158, which directs the Secretary of Transportation to withhold a percentage of federal highway funds otherwise allocable from States "in which the purchase or public possession . . . of any alcoholic beverage by a person who is less than twenty-one years of age is lawful." The State sued in United States District Court seeking a declaratory judgment that §158 violates the constitutional limitations on congressional exercise of the spending power. . . .

Here, Congress has acted indirectly under its spending power to encourage uniformity in the States' drinking ages. . . . [W]e find this legislative effort within constitutional bounds even if Congress may not regulate drinking ages directly.

The Constitution empowers Congress to "lay and collect Taxes, Duties, Imposts, and Excises, to pay the Debts and provide for the common Defence and general Welfare of the United States." Art. I, §8, cl. 1. Incident to this power, Congress may attach conditions on the receipt of federal funds, and has repeatedly employed the power "to further broad policy objectives by conditioning receipt of federal moneys upon compliance by the recipient with federal statutory and administrative directives." *Fullilove v. Klutznick,* 448 U.S. 448, 474 (1980) (opinion of Burger, C.J.). . . . The breadth of this power was made clear in *United States v. Butler,* 297 U.S. 1, 66 (1936), where the Court, resolving a longstanding debate over the scope of the Spending Clause, determined that "the power of Congress to authorize expenditure of public moneys for public purposes is not limited by the direct grants of legislative power found in the Constitution." Thus, objectives not thought to be within Article I's "enumerated legislative fields," *id.,* at 65, may nevertheless be attained through the use of the spending power and the conditional grant of federal funds.

The spending power is of course not unlimited, *Pennhurst State School and Hospital v. Halderman,* 451 U.S. 1, 17, and n.13 (1981), but is instead subject to several general restrictions articulated in our cases. The first of these limitations is derived from the language of the Constitution itself: the exercise of the spending power must be in pursuit of "the general welfare." See *Helvering v. Davis,* 301 U.S. 619, 640-641 (1937); *United States v. Butler, supra,* at 65. In considering whether a particular expenditure is intended to serve general public purposes, courts should defer substantially to the judgment of Congress. *Helvering v. Davis, supra,* at 640, 645.[2] Second, we have required that if Congress desires to condition the States' receipt of federal funds, it "must do so unambiguously . . . , enabl[ing] the States to exercise their choice knowingly, cognizant of the consequences of their participation." *Pennhurst State School and Hospital v. Halderman, supra,* at 17. Third, our cases have suggested (without significant elaboration) that conditions on federal grants might be illegitimate if they are unrelated "to the federal interest in particular national projects or programs." *Massachusetts v. United States,* 435 U.S. 444, 461 (1978) (plurality opinion). Finally, we have noted that other constitutional provisions may provide an independent bar to the conditional grant of federal funds.

---

2. The level of deference to the congressional decision is such that the Court has more recently questioned whether "general welfare" is a judicially enforceable restriction at all. See *Buckley v. Valeo,* 424 U.S. 1, 90-91 (1976) (*per curiam*).

South Dakota does not seriously claim that §158 is inconsistent with any of the first three restrictions mentioned above. We can readily conclude that the provision is designed to serve the general welfare, especially in light of the fact that "the concept of welfare or the opposite is shaped by Congress. . . ." *Helvering v. Davis, supra,* at 645. Congress found that the differing drinking ages in the States created particular incentives for young persons to combine their desire to drink with their ability to drive, and that this interstate problem required a national solution. The means it chose to address this dangerous situation were reasonably calculated to advance the general welfare. The conditions upon which States receive the funds, moreover, could not be more clearly stated by Congress. . . . Indeed, the condition imposed by Congress is directly related to one of the main purposes for which highway funds are expended — safe interstate travel. . . . This goal of the interstate highway system had been frustrated by varying drinking ages among the States. A Presidential commission appointed to study alcohol-related accidents and fatalities on the Nation's highways concluded that the lack of uniformity in the States' drinking ages created "an incentive to drink and drive" because "young persons commut[e] to border States where the drinking age is lower." Presidential Commission on Drunk Driving, Final Report 11 (1983). By enacting §158, Congress conditioned the receipt of federal funds in a way reasonably calculated to address this particular impediment to a purpose for which the funds are expended. . . .

[T]he "independent constitutional bar" limitation on the spending power is not . . . a prohibition on the indirect achievement of objectives which Congress is not empowered to achieve directly. Instead, . . . the power may not be used to induce the States to engage in activities that would themselves be unconstitutional. Thus, for example, a grant of federal funds conditioned on invidiously discriminatory state action or the infliction of cruel and unusual punishment would be an illegitimate exercise of the Congress' broad spending power. But no such claim can be or is made here. Were South Dakota to succumb to the blandishments offered by Congress and raise its drinking age to 21, the State's action in so doing would not violate the constitutional rights of anyone.

Our decisions have recognized that in some circumstances the financial inducement offered by Congress might be so coercive as to pass the point at which "pressure turns into compulsion." *Steward Machine Co. v. Davis,* 301 U.S. [548,] 590 [(1937)]. Here, however, Congress has directed only that a State desiring to establish a minimum drinking age lower than 21 lose a relatively small percentage of certain federal highway funds. Petitioner contends that the coercive nature of this program is evident from the degree of success it has achieved. We cannot conclude, however, that a conditional grant of federal money of this sort is unconstitutional simply by reason of its success in achieving the congressional objective. . . .

Here Congress has offered relatively mild encouragement to the States to enact higher minimum drinking ages than they would otherwise choose. But the enactment of such laws remains the prerogative of the States not merely in theory but in fact. Even if Congress might lack the power to impose a national minimum drinking age directly, we conclude that encouragement to state action found in §158 is a valid use of the spending power. . . .

JUSTICE BRENNAN, dissenting.

[R]egulation of the minimum age of purchasers of liquor falls squarely within the ambit of those powers reserved to the States by the Twenty-first Amendment. Since States possess this constitutional power, Congress cannot condition a federal grant in a manner that abridges this right. The Amendment, itself, strikes the proper balance between federal and state authority. . . .

JUSTICE O'CONNOR, dissenting.

My disagreement with the Court is relatively narrow on the spending power issue: it is a disagreement about the application of a principle rather than a disagreement on the principle itself. I agree with the Court that Congress may attach conditions on the receipt of federal funds to further "the federal interest in particular national projects or programs." *Massachusetts v. United States,* 435 U.S. 444, 461 (1978). . . . I also subscribe to the established proposition that the reach of the spending power "is not limited by the direct grants of legislative power found in the Constitution." *United States v. Butler,* 297 U.S. 1, 66 (1936). Finally, I agree that there are four separate types of limitations on the spending power: the expenditure must be for the general welfare, . . . the conditions imposed must be unambiguous, . . . they must be reasonably related to the purpose of the expenditure, . . . and the legislation may not violate any independent constitutional prohibition. . . . Insofar as two of those limitations are concerned, the Court is clearly correct that §158 is wholly unobjectionable. Establishment of a national minimum drinking age certainly fits within the broad concept of the general welfare and the statute is entirely unambiguous. . . .

But the Court's application of the requirement that the condition imposed be reasonably related to the purpose for which the funds are expended is cursory and unconvincing. We have repeatedly said that Congress may condition grants under the spending power only in ways reasonably related to the purpose of the federal program. . . . In my view, establishment of a minimum drinking age of 21 is not sufficiently related to interstate highway construction to justify so conditioning funds appropriated for that purpose. . . .

[T]he Court asserts the reasonableness of the relationship between the supposed purpose of the expenditure—"safe interstate travel"—and the drinking age condition. . . . It hardly needs saying, however, that if the purpose of §158 is to deter drunken driving, it is far too over and under-inclusive. It is over-inclusive because it stops teenagers from drinking even when they are not about to drive on interstate highways. It is under-inclusive because teenagers pose only a small part of the drunken driving problem in this Nation. . . .

When Congress appropriates money to build a highway, it is entitled to insist that the highway be a safe one. But it is not entitled to insist as a condition of the use of highway funds that the State impose or change regulations in other areas of the State's social and economic life because of an attenuated or tangential relationship to highway use or safety. Indeed, if the rule were otherwise, the Congress could effectively regulate almost any area of a State's social, political, or economic life on the theory that use of the interstate transportation system is somehow enhanced. If, for example, the United States were to condition highway moneys upon moving the state capital, I suppose it might argue that interstate transportation is facilitated by locating local governments in places easily accessible to interstate highways—or, conversely, that highways might become overburdened if they had to carry traffic to and from the state capital. In my mind, such a relationship is hardly more attenuated than the one which the Court finds supports §158. . . .

[In] *United States v. Butler,* 297 U.S. 1 (1936), . . . the Court wrote that "[t]here is an obvious difference between a statute stating the conditions upon which moneys shall be expended and one effective only upon assumption of a contractual obligation to submit to a regulation which otherwise could not be enforced." *Id.,* at 73. The *Butler* Court saw the Agricultural Adjustment Act for what it was—an exercise of regulatory, not spending, power. The error in *Butler* was not the Court's conclusion that the Act was essentially regulatory, but rather its crabbed view of the extent of Congress' regulatory power under the Commerce Clause. The Agricultural Adjustment Act was regulatory but it was regulation that today would likely be considered within Congress' commerce power. See, *e.g., Katzenbach v. McClung,* 379 U.S. 294 (1964); *Wickard v. Filburn,* 317 U.S. 111 (1942).

While *Butler's* authority is questionable insofar as it assumes that Congress has no regulatory power over farm production, its discussion of the spending power and its description of both the power's breadth and its limitations remain sound. The Court's decision in *Butler* also properly recognizes the gravity of the task of appropriately limiting the spending power. If the spending power is to be limited only by Congress' notion of the general welfare, the reality, given the vast financial resources of the Federal Government, is that the Spending Clause gives "power to the Congress to tear down the barriers, to invade the states' jurisdiction, and to become a parliament of the whole people, subject to no restrictions save such as are self-imposed." *United States v. Butler, supra,* 297 U.S., at 78. This, of course, as *Butler* held, was not the Framers' plan and it is not the meaning of the Spending Clause. . . .

[A] condition that a State will raise its drinking age to 21 cannot fairly be said to be reasonably related to the expenditure of funds for highway construction. The only possible connection, highway safety, has nothing to do with how the funds Congress has appropriated are expended. Rather than a condition determining how federal highway money shall be expended, it is a regulation determining who shall be able to drink liquor. As such it is not justified by the spending power. . . .

SABRI V. UNITED STATES

541 U.S. 600 (2004)

JUSTICE SOUTER delivered the opinion of the Court.

Basim Omar Sabri is a real estate developer who proposed to build a hotel and retail structure in the city of Minneapolis. Sabri . . . offered three separate bribes to a city councilman, Brian Herron, according to the grand jury indictment that gave rise to this case. At the time the bribes were allegedly offered . . . , Herron served as a member of the Board of Commissioners of the Minneapolis Community Development Agency (MCDA), a public body created by the city council to fund housing and economic development within the city. . . .

The charges were brought under 18 U.S.C. §666(a)(2), which imposes federal criminal penalties on anyone who

> "corruptly gives, offers, or agrees to give anything of value to any person, with intent to influence or reward an agent of an organization or of a State, local or Indian tribal government, or any agency thereof, in connection with any business, transaction, or series of transactions of such organization, government, or agency involving anything of value of $5,000 or more."

For criminal liability to lie, the statute requires that

> "the organization, government, or agency receiv[e], in any one year period, benefits in excess of $10,000 under a Federal program involving a grant, contract, subsidy, loan, guarantee, insurance, or other form of Federal assistance." §666(b).

In 2001, the City Council of Minneapolis administered about $29 million in federal funds paid to the city, and in the same period, the MCDA received some $23 million of federal money.

Before trial, Sabri moved to dismiss the indictment on the ground that §666(a)(2) is unconstitutional on its face. . . .

Congress has authority under the Spending Clause to appropriate federal monies to promote the general welfare, Art. I, §8, cl. 1, and it has corresponding authority under the Necessary and Proper Clause, Art. I, §8, cl. 18, to see to it that taxpayer dollars appropriated under that power are in fact spent for the general welfare, and not frittered away in graft or on projects undermined when funds are siphoned off or corrupt public officers are derelict about demanding value for dollars. See generally *McCulloch v. Maryland*, 4 Wheat. 316 (1819) (establishing review for means-ends rationality under the Necessary and Proper Clause). Congress does not have to sit by and accept the risk of operations thwarted by local and state improbity. Section 666(a)(2) addresses the problem at the sources of bribes, by rational means, to safeguard the integrity of the state, local, and tribal recipients of federal dollars.

It is true, just as Sabri says, that not every bribe or kickback offered or paid to agents of governments covered by §666(b) will be traceably skimmed from specific federal payments, or show up in the guise of a *quid pro quo* for some dereliction in spending a federal grant. But this possibility portends no enforcement beyond the scope of federal interest, for the reason that corruption does not have to be that limited to affect the federal interest. Money is fungible, bribed officials are untrustworthy stewards of federal funds, and corrupt contractors do not deliver dollar-for-dollar value. Liquidity is not a financial term for nothing; money can be drained off here because a federal grant is pouring in there. And officials are not any the less threatening to the objects behind federal spending just because they may accept general retainers. It is certainly enough that the statutes condition the offense on a threshold amount of federal dollars defining the federal interest, such as that provided here.

For those of us who accept help from legislative history, it is worth noting that the legislative record confirms that §666(a)(2) is an instance of necessary and proper legislation. The design was generally to "protect the integrity of the vast sums of money distributed through Federal programs from theft, fraud, and undue influence by bribery," see S. Rep. No. 98-225, p. 370 (1983). . . . Congress's decision to enact §666 only after other legislation had failed to protect federal interests is . . . indication that it was acting within the ambit of the Necessary and Proper Clause.

Petitioner presses two more particular arguments against the constitutionality of §666(a)(2), neither of which helps him. First, he says that §666 is all of a piece with the legislation that a majority of this Court held to exceed Congress's authority under the Commerce Clause in *United States v. Lopez,* 514 U.S. 549 (1995), and *United States v. Morrison,* 529 U.S. 598 (2000). But these precedents do not control here. In *Lopez* and *Morrison,* the Court struck down federal statutes regulating gun possession near schools and gender-motivated violence, respectively, because it found the effects of those activities on interstate commerce insufficiently robust. The Court emphasized the noneconomic nature of the regulated conduct, commenting on the law at issue in *Lopez,* for example, "that by its terms [it] has nothing to do with 'commerce' or any sort of economic enterprise, however broadly one might define those terms." 514 U.S., at 561. The Court rejected the Government's contentions that the gun law was valid Commerce Clause legislation because guns near schools ultimately bore on social prosperity and productivity, reasoning that on that logic, Commerce Clause authority would effectively know no limit. Cf. *Morrison, supra,* at 615-616, (rejecting comparable congressional justification for Violence Against Women Act of 1994). In order to uphold the legislation, the Court concluded, it would be necessary "to pile inference upon inference in a manner that would bid fair to convert congressional authority under the Commerce Clause to a general police power of the sort retained by the States." *Lopez,* 514 U.S., at 567.

No piling is needed here to show that Congress was within its prerogative to protect spending objects from the menace of local administrators on the take. The power to keep a watchful eye on expenditures and on the reliability of those who use public money is bound up with congressional authority to spend in the first place, and Sabri would be hard pressed to claim, in the words of the *Lopez* Court, that §666(a)(2) "has nothing to do with" the congressional spending power. *Id.,* at 561.

Sabri next argues that §666(a)(2) amounts to an unduly coercive, and impermissibly sweeping, condition on the grant of federal funds as judged under the criterion applied in *South Dakota v. Dole,* 483 U.S. 203 (1987). This is not so. Section 666(a)(2) is authority to bring federal power to bear directly on individuals who convert public spending into unearned private gain, not a means for bringing federal economic might to bear on a State's own choices of public policy. . . .

[JUSTICE KENNEDY filed an opinion concurring in part, in which JUSTICE SCALIA joined.]

JUSTICE THOMAS, concurring in the judgment.

Title 18 U.S.C. §666(a)(2) is a valid exercise of Congress' power to regulate commerce, at least under this Court's precedent. I continue to doubt that we have correctly interpreted the Commerce Clause. But until this Court reconsiders its precedents, and because neither party requests us to do so here, our prior case law controls the outcome of this case.

I write further because I find questionable the scope the Court gives to the Necessary and Proper Clause as applied to Congress' authority to spend. In particular, the Court appears to hold that the Necessary and Proper Clause authorizes the exercise of any power that is no more than a "rational means" to effectuate one of Congress' enumerated powers. This conclusion derives from the Court's characterization of the seminal case *McCulloch v. Maryland,* 4 Wheat. 316 (1819), as having established a "means-ends rationality" test, a characterization that I am not certain is correct.

In *McCulloch,* the Court faced the question whether the United States had the power to incorporate a national bank. The Court was forced to navigate between the one extreme of the "absolute necessity" construction advocated by the State of Maryland, 4 Wheat., at 387 (argument of counsel), which would "clog and embarrass" the execution of the enumerated powers "by withholding the most appropriate means" for its execution, *id.,* at 408, and the other extreme, an interpretation that would destroy the Framers' purpose of establishing a National Government of limited and enumerated powers, see *id.,* at 423; cf. *Gibbons v. Ogden,* 9 Wheat. 1, 194-195 (1824). The Court, speaking through Chief Justice Marshall, carefully and effectively refuted Maryland's proposed "absolute necessity" test. "It must have been the intention of those who gave these powers, to insure, as far as human prudence could insure, their beneficial execution," the Court stated; "[t]his could not be done by confiding the choice of means to such narrow limits as not to leave it in the power of Congress to adopt any which might be appropriate, and which were conducive to the end." *McCulloch,* 4 Wheat., at 415. The Court opined that it would render the Constitution "a splendid bauble" if "the right to legislate on that vast mass of incidental powers which must be involved in the constitution" were not within the power of Congress. *Id.,* at 421.

But the Court did not then conclude that the Necessary and Proper Clause gives unrestricted power to the Federal Government. See *ibid.* ("[T]he powers of the government are limited, and . . . its limits are not to be transcended."). Rather, it set forth the following test:

> "Let the end be legitimate, let it be within the scope of the constitution, and all means which are appropriate, which are plainly adapted to that end, which are not prohibited, but consist with the letter and spirit of the constitution, are constitutional." *Ibid.*

"[A]ppropriate" and "plainly adapted" are hardly synonymous with "means-end rationality." Indeed, "plain" means "evident to the mind or senses: OBVIOUS," "CLEAR," and "characterized by simplicity: not complicated." Webster's Ninth New Collegiate Dictionary 898 (1991); see also N. Webster, American Dictionary of the English Language (1828) (facsimile edition) (defining "plainly" as "[i]n a manner to be easily seen or comprehended," and "[e]vidently; clearly; not obscurely"). A statute can have a "rational" connection to an enumerated power without being obviously or clearly tied to that enumerated power. To show that a statute is "plainly adapted" to a legitimate end, then, one must seemingly show more than that a particular statute is a "rational means" to safeguard that end; rather, it would seem necessary to show some obvious, simple, and direct relation between the statute and the enumerated power. . . .

Under the *McCulloch* formulation, I have doubts that §666(a)(2) is a proper use of the Necessary and Proper Clause as applied to Congress' power to spend. . . . All that is necessary for §666(a)(2) to apply is that the organization, government, or agency in question receives more than $10,000 in federal benefits of any kind, and that an agent of the entity is bribed regarding a substantial transaction of that entity. No connection whatsoever between the corrupt transaction and the federal benefits need be shown.

The Court does a not-wholly-unconvincing job of tying the broad scope of §666(a)(2) to a federal interest in federal funds and programs. But simply noting that "[m]oney is fungible," for instance, does not explain how there could be any federal interest in "prosecut[ing] a bribe paid to a city's meat inspector in connection with a substantial transaction just because the city's parks department had received a federal grant of $10,000," *United States v. Santopietro,* 166 F.3d 88, 93 (C.A.2 1999). It would be difficult to describe the chain of inferences and assumptions in which the Court would have to indulge to connect such a bribe to a federal interest in any federal funds or programs as being "plainly adapted" to their protection. And, this is just one example of many in which any federal interest in protecting federal funds is equally attenuated, and yet the bribe is covered by the expansive language of §666(a)(2). Overall, then, §666(a)(2) appears to be no more plainly adapted to protecting federal funds or federally funded programs than a hypothetical federal statute criminalizing fraud of any kind perpetrated on any individual who happens to receive federal welfare benefits.

Because I would decide this case on the Court's Commerce Clause jurisprudence, I do not ultimately decide whether Congress' power to spend combined with the Necessary and Proper Clause could authorize the enactment of §666(a)(2). But regardless of the particular outcome of this case under the correct test, the Court's approach seems to greatly and improperly expand the reach of Congress' power under the Necessary and Proper Clause. . . .

POINTS FOR DISCUSSION

1. In *Butler*, the Court rejected the Madisonian view of the spending power (that the power is "confined to the enumerated legislative fields committed to the Congress") in favor of the Hamiltonian view (that the power is not limited to Congress's enumerated powers). The Court held, however, that Congress's appropriation of money to farmers in exchange for their curtailing production exceeded its spending powers because Congress lacks power "to regulate agricultural production." Is this holding consistent with the Court's rejection of the Madisonian view in favor of the Hamiltonian view?

2. In *Dole*, the Court upheld the condition on a congressional appropriation of highway funds that states increase the legal drinking age to 21. The Court reasoned that the condition was reasonably related to one of the main purposes underlying the appropriation—safe interstate travel. In dissent, Justice O'Connor argued that the condition was so attenuated from the

purpose of the appropriation that Congress in fact was regulating who may drink liquor, not exercising the spending power. Thus, the Court afforded more deference to Congress in determining what conditions are necessary to effectuate the purposes of the appropriation than Justice O'Connor did. Which level of deference is more appropriate in this context?

3. *Sabri* involved not a condition on an appropriation, as *Butler* and *Dole* did, but a regulation of non-recipients of a federal grant. The Court held that, under the Necessary and Proper Clause, the regulation was a "rational means" for ensuring the effectiveness of the appropriation. Justice Thomas rejected "means-ends rationality" in this context, preferring somewhat more searching judicial review. Did the Court afford more deference to Congress in this context than it did under the Commerce Clause in *Lopez* and *Morrison*? Is more or less deference appropriate in this context? How, if at all, do the differences between the majority and Justice Thomas reflect the differences that you observed in Chapter 1 between St. George Tucker and the Marshall Court over the breadth of the Necessary and Proper Clause?

4. The conditional spending program at issue in *Dole* provides an example of a "cooperative federalism" program — one in which the federal government and the States cooperate to serve national policy ends in ways that account for differing local circumstances. What values do such programs advance? Does the idea of cooperative federalism inform how the Court resolved (or should have resolved) the constitutionality of the conditional spending program at issue in *Dole*?

C. THE SECTION 5 POWER

Section 1 of the Fourteenth Amendment provides:

> No state shall make or enforce any law which shall abridge the privileges or immunities of citizens of the United States; nor shall any state deprive any person of life, liberty, or property, without due process of law; nor deny to any person within its jurisdiction the equal protection of the laws.

Over time, the Court has held that the Due Process Clause of the Fourteenth Amendment incorporates most provisions of the Bill of Rights against the states. (Before Reconstruction, the Court had held that the Bill of Rights restrains the federal government, not the states. *See Barron v. Baltimore*, 32 U.S. (7 Pet.) 243 (1833).) Accordingly, states may be in violation of the Fourteenth Amendment when they violate provisions of the Bill of Rights that the Due Process Clause incorporates against them. Chapter 7, which addresses constitutional limitations on state power, provides a summary of incorporation.

Section 5 of the Fourteenth Amendment states that "[t]he Congress shall have power to enforce, by appropriate legislation, the provisions of this article." Because of incorporation, §5 authorizes Congress to enforce most of the Bill of Rights against the states. The cases in this section address the scope of Congress's power "to enforce, by appropriate legislation, the provisions" of the Fourteenth Amendment.

In the *Civil Rights Cases*, 109 U.S. 3 (1883), which you read in Chapter 2, the Supreme Court held that §5 does not empower Congress to prohibit private discrimination. Section 1 limits state action, not private action, and thus Congress has no authority under §5 to enact rules for "the conduct of individuals in society." *Id.* at 14. Rather, §5 enables Congress "to adopt appropriate legislation for correcting the effects of . . . prohibited state law and state acts." *Id.* at 11. Under the *Civil Rights Cases*, then, Congress may enforce the Fourteenth Amendment only against state violations.

The cases in this section address Congress's power under §5 to enforce the Fourteenth Amendment against the states. As you read them, consider these questions:

- How has the Court defined the §5 power?
- What degree of deference has the Court afforded Congress in determining whether federal statutes comply with the §5 power? Has the Court shown more or less deference in §5 cases than in commerce and/or spending cases?
- How workable is the Court's §5 jurisprudence? In other words, how easily and predictably is it administered by courts?

KATZENBACH V. MORGAN

384 U.S. 641 (1966)

Mr. JUSTICE BRENNAN delivered the opinion of the Court.

These cases concern the constitutionality of §4(e) of the Voting Rights Act of 1965. . . . That law, in the respects pertinent in these cases, provides that no person who has successfully completed the sixth primary grade in a public school in, or a private school accredited by, the Commonwealth of Puerto Rico in which the language of instruction was other than English shall be denied the right to vote in any election because of his inability to read or write English. Appellees, registered voters in New York City, brought this suit to challenge the constitutionality of §4(e) insofar as it *pro tanto* prohibits the enforcement of the election laws of New York . . . requiring an ability to read and write English as a condition of voting. . . . We hold that, in the application challenged in these cases, §4(e) is a proper exercise of the powers granted to Congress by §5 of the Fourteenth Amendment . . . and that by force of the Supremacy Clause, Article VI, the New York English literacy requirement cannot be enforced to the extent that it is inconsistent with §4(e). . . .

Under the distribution of powers effected by the Constitution, the States establish qualifications for voting for state officers, and the qualifications established by the States for voting for members of the most numerous branch of the state legislature also determine who may vote for United States Representatives and Senators. But, of course, the States have no power to grant or withhold the franchise on conditions that are forbidden by the Fourteenth Amendment, or any other provision of the Constitution. Such exercises of state power are no more immune to the limitations of the Fourteenth Amendment than any other state action. The Equal Protection Clause itself has been held to forbid some state laws that restrict the right to vote.

The Attorney General of the State of New York argues that an exercise of congressional power under §5 of the Fourteenth Amendment that prohibits the enforcement of a state law can only be sustained if the judicial branch determines that the state law is prohibited by the provisions of the Amendment that Congress sought to enforce. More specifically, he urges that §4(e) cannot be sustained as appropriate legislation to enforce the Equal Protection Clause unless the judiciary decides — even with the guidance of a congressional judgment — that the application of the English literacy requirement prohibited by §4(e) is forbidden by the Equal Protection Clause itself. We disagree. . . . A construction of §5 that would require a judicial determination that the enforcement of the state law precluded by Congress violated the Amendment, as a condition of sustaining the congressional enactment, would depreciate both congressional resourcefulness and congressional responsibility for implementing the Amendment. It would confine the legislative power in this context to the insignificant role of abrogating only those state laws that the judicial branch was prepared to adjudge unconstitutional . . . .

Thus our task in this case is not to determine whether the New York English literacy requirement as applied to deny the right to vote to a person who successfully completed the sixth grade in a Puerto Rican school violates the Equal Protection Clause. . . . [Rather,] the question before us here [is]: Without regard to whether the judiciary would find that the Equal Protection Clause itself nullifies New York's English literacy requirement as so applied, could Congress prohibit the enforcement of the state law by legislating under §5 of the Fourteenth Amendment? In answering this question, our task is limited to determining whether such legislation is, as required by §5, appropriate legislation to enforce the Equal Protection Clause.

By including §5 the draftsmen sought to grant to Congress, by a specific provision applicable to the Fourteenth Amendment, the same broad powers expressed in the Necessary and Proper Clause, Art. I, §8, cl. 18.[9] The classic formulation of the reach of those powers was established by Chief Justice Marshall in *McCulloch v. Maryland*, 4 Wheat. 316, 421:

> "Let the end be legitimate, let it be within the scope of the constitution, and all means which are appropriate, which are plainly adapted to that end, which are not prohibited, but consist with the letter and spirit of the constitution, are constitutional." . . .

Correctly viewed, §5 is a positive grant of legislative power authorizing Congress to exercise its discretion in determining whether and what legislation is needed to secure the guarantees of the Fourteenth Amendment.

We therefore proceed to the consideration whether §4(e) is "appropriate legislation" to enforce the Equal Protection Clause, that is, under the *McCulloch v. Maryland* standard, whether §4(e) may be regarded as an enactment to enforce the Equal Protection Clause, whether it is "plainly adapted to

---

9. In fact, earlier drafts of the proposed Amendment employed the "necessary and proper" terminology to describe the scope of congressional power under the Amendment. See tenBroek, The Antislavery Origins of the Fourteenth Amendment 187-190 (1951). The substitution of the "appropriate legislation" formula was never thought to have the effect of diminishing the scope of this congressional power.

that end" and whether it is not prohibited by but is consistent with "the letter and spirit of the constitution."

There can be no doubt that §4(e) may be regarded as an enactment to enforce the Equal Protection Clause. . . . More specifically, §4(e) may be viewed as a measure to secure for the Puerto Rican community residing in New York nondiscriminatory treatment by government — both in the imposition of voting qualifications and the provision or administration of governmental services, such as public schools, public housing and law enforcement.

Section 4(e) may be readily seen as "plainly adapted" to furthering these aims of the Equal Protection Clause. The practical effect of §4(e) is to prohibit New York from denying the right to vote to large segments of its Puerto Rican community. . . . This enhanced political power will be helpful in gaining non-discriminatory treatment in public services for the entire Puerto Rican community. Section 4(e) thereby enables the Puerto Rican minority better to obtain "perfect equality of civil rights and the equal protection of the laws." It was well within congressional authority to say that this need of the Puerto Rican minority for the vote warranted federal intrusion upon any state interests served by the English literacy requirement. It was for Congress, as the branch that made this judgment, to assess and weigh the various conflicting considerations — the risk or pervasiveness of the discrimination in governmental services, the effectiveness of eliminating the state restriction on the right to vote as a means of dealing with the evil, the adequacy or availability of alternative remedies, and the nature and significance of the state interests that would be affected by the nullification of the English literacy requirement as applied to residents who have successfully completed the sixth grade in a Puerto Rican school. It is not for us to review the congressional resolution of these factors. It is enough that we be able to perceive a basis upon which the Congress might resolve the conflict as it did. . . .

There remains the question whether the congressional remedies adopted in §4(e) constitute means which are not prohibited by, but are consistent "with the letter and spirit of the constitution." The only respect in which appellees contend that §4(e) fails in this regard is that the section itself works an invidious discrimination in violation of the Fifth Amendment by prohibiting the enforcement of the English literacy requirement only for those educated in American-flag schools (schools located within United States jurisdiction) in which the language of instruction was other than English, and not for those educated in schools beyond the territorial limits of the United States in which the language of instruction was also other than English. . . .

[I]n deciding the constitutional propriety of the limitations in such a . . . measure we are guided by the familiar principles that a "statute is not invalid under the Constitution because it might have gone farther than it did," *Roschen v. Ward*, 279 U.S. 337, 339, that a legislature need not "strike at all evils at the same time." *Semler v. Oregon State Board of Dental Examiners*, 294 U.S. 608, 610, and that "reform may take one step at a time, addressing itself to the phase of the problem which seems most acute to the legislative mind," *Williamson v. Lee Optical Co.*, 348 U.S. 483, 489. . . .

[T]he limitation on relief effected in §4(e) does not constitute a forbidden discrimination. . . . We therefore conclude that §4(e), in the application challenged in this case, is appropriate legislation to enforce the Equal Protection Clause. . . .

Mr. JUSTICE DOUGLAS joins the Court's opinion except for the discussion of the question whether the congressional remedies adopted in §4(e) constitute means which are not prohibited by, but are consistent with "the letter and spirit of the constitution." On that question, he reserves judgment until such time as it is presented by a member of the class against which that particular discrimination is directed.

Mr. JUSTICE HARLAN, whom Mr. JUSTICE STEWART joins, dissenting.

The Court declares that since §5 of the Fourteenth Amendment gives to the Congress power to "enforce" the prohibitions of the Amendment by "appropriate" legislation, the test for judicial review of any congressional determination in this area is simply one of rationality; that is, in effect, was Congress acting rationally in declaring that the New York statute is irrational? . . .

When recognized state violations of federal constitutional standards have occurred, Congress is of course empowered by §5 to take appropriate remedial measures to redress and prevent the wrongs. But it is a judicial question whether the condition with which Congress has thus sought to deal is in truth an infringement of the Constitution, something that is the necessary prerequisite to bringing the §5 power into play at all. . . .

The question here is not whether the statute is appropriate remedial legislation to cure an established violation of a constitutional command, but whether there has in fact been an infringement of that constitutional command, that is, whether a particular state practice or, as here, a statute is so arbitrary or irrational as to offend the command of the Equal Protection Clause of the Fourteenth Amendment. That question is one for the judicial branch ultimately to determine. Were the rule otherwise, Congress would be able to qualify this Court's constitutional decisions under the Fourteenth . . . Amendment[] let alone those under other provisions of the Constitution, by resorting to congressional power under the Necessary and Proper Clause. . . . In effect the Court reads §5 of the Fourteenth Amendment as giving Congress the power to define the *substantive* scope of the Amendment. If that indeed be the true reach of §5, then I do not see why Congress should not be able as well to exercise its §5 "discretion" by enacting statutes so as in effect to dilute equal protection and due process decisions of this Court. In all such cases there is room for reasonable men to differ as to whether or not a denial of equal protection or due process has occurred, and the final decision is one of judgment. Until today this judgment has always been one for the judiciary to resolve. . . .

To deny the effectiveness of this congressional enactment is not of course to disparage Congress' exertion of authority in the field of civil rights; it is simply to recognize that the Legislative Branch like the other branches of federal authority is subject to the governmental boundaries set by the Constitution. . . .

POINTS FOR DISCUSSION

1. In *Morgan*, the Court equated the scope of Congress's §5 power with its power under the Necessary and Proper Clause. The Court recited Chief Justice Marshall's analysis of the Necessary and Proper Clause in *McCullough v. Maryland*, 17 U.S. (4 Wheat.) 316 (1819), and examined whether the regulation at issue is "'plainly adapted' to furthering . . . aims of the Equal Protection Clause." Should the Court have equated the §5 power with the necessary and proper power? Is a power to "enforce" a constitutional provision (§5) the same as a power to "carry into execution" a constitutional provision (Necessary and Proper Clause)?

2. The Court further explained in *Morgan* that "[s]ince Congress undertook to legislate so as to preclude the enforcement of the state law, and did so in the context of a general appraisal of literacy requirements for voting, . . . to which it brought a specially informed legislative competence, . . . it was Congress' prerogative to weigh these competing considerations." Thus, "[i]t is enough that we be able to perceive a basis upon which the Congress might resolve the conflict as it did." What deference does the Court afford Congress in *Morgan* relative to the deference shown in *United States v. Lopez*, 514 U.S. 549 (1995), and *United States v. Morrison*, 529 U.S. 598 (2000) (commerce power)? In *South Dakota v. Dole*, 483 U.S. 203 (1987), and *Sabri v. United States*, 541 U.S. 600 (2004) (spending power)?

CITY OF BOERNE V. FLORES

521 U.S. 507 (1997)

JUSTICE KENNEDY delivered the opinion of the Court.* . . .

I

Situated on a hill in the city of Boerne, Texas, some 28 miles northwest of San Antonio, is St. Peter Catholic Church. Built in 1923, the church's structure replicates the mission style of the region's earlier history. . . . In order to meet the needs of the congregation the Archbishop of San Antonio gave permission to the parish to plan alterations to enlarge the building.

A few months later, the Boerne City Council passed an ordinance authorizing the city's Historic Landmark Commission to prepare a preservation plan with proposed historic landmarks and districts. Under the ordinance, the commission must preapprove construction affecting historic landmarks or buildings in a historic district.

Soon afterwards, the Archbishop applied for a building permit so construction to enlarge the church could proceed. City authorities, relying on the ordinance and the designation of a historic district (which, they argued, included the church), denied the application. The Archbishop brought this suit challenging the permit denial. . . . The Archbishop relied upon [the Religious Freedom Restoration Act of 1993 (RFRA)] as one basis for relief from the refusal to issue the permit. . . .

---

*Justice SCALIA joins all but Part III-A-1 of this opinion.

II

Congress enacted RFRA in direct response to the Court's decision in *Employment Div., Dept. of Human Resources of Oregon v. Smith,* 494 U.S. 872 (1990). There we considered a Free Exercise Clause claim brought by members of the Native American Church who were denied unemployment benefits when they lost their jobs because they had used peyote. Their practice was to ingest peyote for sacramental purposes, and they challenged an Oregon statute of general applicability which made use of the drug criminal. In evaluating the claim, we declined to apply the balancing test set forth in *Sherbert v. Verner,* 374 U.S. 398 (1963), under which we would have asked whether Oregon's prohibition substantially burdened a religious practice and, if it did, whether the burden was justified by a compelling government interest. . . . [Instead,] *Smith* held that neutral, generally applicable laws may be applied to religious practices even when not supported by a compelling governmental interest. . . .

Many [Members of Congress] criticized the Court's reasoning, and this disagreement resulted in the passage of RFRA. Congress announced:

> "(1) [T]he framers of the Constitution, recognizing free exercise of religion as an unalienable right, secured its protection in the First Amendment to the Constitution;
>
> "(2) laws 'neutral' toward religion may burden religious exercise as surely as laws intended to interfere with religious exercise;
>
> "(3) governments should not substantially burden religious exercise without compelling justification;
>
> "(4) in Employment Division v. Smith, 494 U.S. 872 (1990), the Supreme Court virtually eliminated the requirement that the government justify burdens on religious exercise imposed by laws neutral toward religion; and
>
> "(5) the compelling interest test as set forth in prior Federal court rulings is a workable test for striking sensible balances between religious liberty and competing prior governmental interests." 42 U.S.C. §2000bb(a).

The Act's stated purposes are:

> "(1) to restore the compelling interest test as set forth in Sherbert v. Verner, 374 U.S. 398 (1963) and Wisconsin v. Yoder, 406 U.S. 205 (1972), and to guarantee its application in all cases where free exercise of religion is substantially burdened; and
>
> "(2) to provide a claim or defense to persons whose religious exercise is substantially burdened by government." §2000bb(b).

RFRA prohibits "[g]overnment" from "substantially burden[ing]" a person's exercise of religion even if the burden results from a rule of general applicability unless the government can demonstrate the burden "(1) is in furtherance of a compelling governmental interest; and (2) is the least restrictive means of furthering that compelling governmental interest." §2000bb-1. The Act's mandate applies to any "branch, department, agency, instrumentality, and official (or other person acting under color of law) of the United States," as well as to any "State, or . . . subdivision of a State." §2000bb-2(1). . . .

III

A

Congress relied on its Fourteenth Amendment enforcement power in enacting the most far-reaching and substantial of RFRA's provisions, those which impose its requirements on the States. . . .

All must acknowledge that §5 is "a positive grant of legislative power" to Congress, *Katzenbach v. Morgan*, 384 U.S. 641, 651 (1966). . . . Legislation which deters or remedies constitutional violations can fall within the sweep of Congress' enforcement power even if in the process it prohibits conduct which is not itself unconstitutional and intrudes into "legislative spheres of autonomy previously reserved to the States." *Fitzpatrick v. Bitzer*, 427 U.S. 445, 455 (1976). For example, the Court upheld a suspension of literacy tests and similar voting requirements under Congress' parallel power to enforce the provisions of the Fifteenth Amendment, see U.S. Const., Amdt. 15, §2, as a measure to combat racial discrimination in voting, *South Carolina v. Katzenbach*, 383 U.S. 301, 308 (1966), despite the facial constitutionality of the tests under *Lassiter v. Northampton County Bd. of Elections*, 360 U.S. 45 (1959). We have also concluded that other measures protecting voting rights are within Congress' power to enforce the Fourteenth and Fifteenth Amendments, despite the burdens those measures placed on the States. *Katzenbach v. Morgan*, *supra* (upholding ban on literary tests that prohibited certain people schooled in Puerto Rico from voting).

It is also true, however, that "[a]s broad as the congressional enforcement power is, it is not unlimited." *Oregon v. Mitchell*, [400 U.S. 112, 128 (1970)] (opinion of Black, J.). In assessing the breadth of §5's enforcement power, we begin with its text. Congress has been given the power "to enforce" the "provisions of this article." We agree with respondent, of course, that Congress can enact legislation under §5 enforcing the constitutional right to the free exercise of religion. The "provisions of this article," to which §5 refers, include the Due Process Clause of the Fourteenth Amendment. Congress' power to enforce the Free Exercise Clause follows from our holding in *Cantwell v. Connecticut*, 310 U.S. 296, 303, (1940), that the "fundamental concept of liberty embodied in [the Fourteenth Amendment's Due Process Clause] embraces the liberties guaranteed by the First Amendment." . . .

Congress' power under §5, however, extends only to "enforc[ing]" the provisions of the Fourteenth Amendment. The Court has described this power as "remedial," *South Carolina v. Katzenbach*, *supra*, at 326. The design of the Amendment and the text of §5 are inconsistent with the suggestion that Congress has the power to decree the substance of the Fourteenth Amendment's restrictions on the States. Legislation which alters the meaning of the Free Exercise Clause cannot be said to be enforcing the Clause. Congress does not enforce a constitutional right by changing what the right is. It has been given the power "to enforce," not the power to determine what constitutes a constitutional violation. Were it not so, what Congress would be enforcing would no longer be, in any meaningful sense, the "provisions of [the Fourteenth Amendment]."

While the line between measures that remedy or prevent unconstitutional actions and measures that make a substantive change in the governing law is not easy to discern, and Congress must have wide latitude in determining where it lies, the distinction exists and must be observed. There must be a congruence and proportionality between the injury to be prevented or remedied and the means adopted to that end. Lacking such a connection, legislation may become substantive in operation and effect. History and our case law support drawing the distinction, one apparent from the text of the Amendment.

1

The Fourteenth Amendment's history confirms the remedial, rather than substantive, nature of the Enforcement Clause. The Joint Committee on Reconstruction of the 39th Congress began drafting what would become the Fourteenth Amendment in January 1866. The objections to the Committee's first draft of the Amendment, and the rejection of the draft, have a direct bearing on the central issue of defining Congress' enforcement power. In February, Republican Representative John Bingham of Ohio reported the following draft Amendment to the House of Representatives on behalf of the Joint Committee:

> "The Congress shall have power to make all laws which shall be necessary and proper to secure to the citizens of each State all privileges and immunities of citizens in the several States, and to all persons in the several States equal protection in the rights of life, liberty, and property." Cong. Globe, 39th Cong., 1st Sess., 1034 (1866).

The proposal encountered immediate opposition, which continued through three days of debate. Members of Congress from across the political spectrum criticized the Amendment, and the criticisms had a common theme: The proposed Amendment gave Congress too much legislative power at the expense of the existing constitutional structure. . . . Democrats and conservative Republicans argued that the proposed Amendment would give Congress a power to intrude into traditional areas of state responsibility, a power inconsistent with the federal design central to the Constitution. . . .

As a result of these objections having been expressed from so many different quarters, the House voted to table the proposal until April. . . . The Amendment in its early form was not again considered. . . .

Section 1 of [a] new draft Amendment imposed self-executing limits on the States. Section 5 prescribed that "[t]he Congress shall have power to enforce, by appropriate legislation, the provisions of this article." . . . Under the revised Amendment, Congress' power was no longer plenary but remedial. Congress was granted the power to make the substantive constitutional prohibitions against the States effective. . . . The revised Amendment proposal did not raise the concerns expressed earlier regarding broad congressional power to prescribe uniform national laws with respect to life, liberty, and property. . . . After revisions not relevant here, the new measure passed both Houses and was ratified in July 1868 as the Fourteenth Amendment. . . .

The design of the Fourteenth Amendment has proved significant . . . in maintaining the traditional separation of powers between Congress and the

Judiciary. The first eight Amendments to the Constitution set forth self-executing prohibitions on governmental action, and this Court has had primary authority to interpret those prohibitions. . . . The power to interpret the Constitution in a case or controversy remains in the Judiciary.

2

The remedial and preventive nature of Congress' enforcement power, and the limitation inherent in the power, were confirmed in our earliest cases on the Fourteenth Amendment. In the *Civil Rights Cases,* 109 U.S. 3 (1883), the Court invalidated sections of the Civil Rights Act of 1875 which prescribed criminal penalties for denying to any person "the full enjoyment of" public accommodations and conveyances, on the grounds that it exceeded Congress' power by seeking to regulate private conduct. The Enforcement Clause, the Court said, did not authorize Congress to pass "general legislation upon the rights of the citizen, but corrective legislation, that is, such as may be necessary and proper for counteracting such laws as the States may adopt or enforce, and which, by the amendment, they are prohibited from making or enforcing. . . ." *Id.,* at 13-14. The power to "legislate generally upon" life, liberty, and property, as opposed to the "power to provide modes of redress" against offensive state action, was "repugnant" to the Constitution. *Id.,* at 15. . . .

3

There is language in our opinion in *Katzenbach v. Morgan,* 384 U.S. 641 (1966), which could be interpreted as acknowledging a power in Congress to enact legislation that expands the rights contained in §1 of the Fourteenth Amendment. This is not a necessary interpretation, however, or even the best one. In *Morgan,* the Court considered the constitutionality of §4(e) of the Voting Rights Act of 1965, which provided that no person who had successfully completed the sixth primary grade in a public school in, or a private school accredited by, the Commonwealth of Puerto Rico in which the language of instruction was other than English could be denied the right to vote because of an inability to read or write English. New York's Constitution, on the other hand, required voters to be able to read and write English. The Court provided two related rationales for its conclusion that §4(e) could "be viewed as a measure to secure for the Puerto Rican community residing in New York nondiscriminatory treatment by government." *Id.,* at 652. Under the first rationale, Congress could prohibit New York from denying the right to vote to large segments of its Puerto Rican community, in order to give Puerto Ricans "enhanced political power" that would be "helpful in gaining nondiscriminatory treatment in public services for the entire Puerto Rican community." *Ibid.* Section 4(e) thus could be justified as a remedial measure to deal with "discrimination in governmental services." *Id.,* at 653. The second rationale, an alternative holding, did not address discrimination in the provision of public services but "discrimination in establishing voter qualifications." *Id.,* at 654. The Court perceived a factual basis on which Congress could have concluded that New York's literacy requirement "constituted an invidious discrimination in violation of the Equal Protection Clause." *Id.,* at 656. Both rationales for upholding §4(e) rested on unconstitutional discrimination by New York and Congress' reasonable attempt to combat it. As Justice Stewart explained in *Oregon v. Mitchell, supra,* at 296, interpreting *Morgan* to give Congress the power to interpret the Constitution "would require an enormous extension of that decision's rationale."

If Congress could define its own powers by altering the Fourteenth Amendment's meaning, no longer would the Constitution be "superior paramount law, unchangeable by ordinary means." It would be "on a level with ordinary legislative acts, and, like other acts, . . . alterable when the legislature shall please to alter it." *Marbury v. Madison,* 1 Cranch, at 177. Under this approach, it is difficult to conceive of a principle that would limit congressional power. . . .

We now turn to consider whether RFRA can be considered enforcement legislation under §5 of the Fourteenth Amendment.

B

Respondent contends that RFRA is a proper exercise of Congress' remedial or preventive power. The Act, it is said, is a reasonable means of protecting the free exercise of religion as defined by *Smith.* It prevents and remedies laws which are enacted with the unconstitutional object of targeting religious beliefs and practices. . . .

RFRA's legislative record lacks examples of modern instances of generally applicable laws passed because of religious bigotry. The history of persecution in this country detailed in the hearings mentions no episodes occurring in the past 40 years. . . . Rather, the emphasis of the hearings was on laws of general applicability which place incidental burdens on religion. . . . It is difficult to maintain that they are examples of legislation enacted or enforced due to animus or hostility to the burdened religious practices or that they indicate some widespread pattern of religious discrimination in this country. Congress' concern was with the incidental burdens imposed, not the object or purpose of the legislation. . . .

Regardless of the state of the legislative record, RFRA cannot be considered remedial, preventive legislation, if those terms are to have any meaning. RFRA is so out of proportion to a supposed remedial or preventive object that it cannot be understood as responsive to, or designed to prevent, unconstitutional behavior. It appears, instead, to attempt a substantive change in constitutional protections. Preventive measures prohibiting certain types of laws may be appropriate when there is reason to believe that many of the laws affected by the congressional enactment have a significant likelihood of being unconstitutional. . . . Remedial legislation under §5 "should be adapted to the mischief and wrong which the [Fourteenth] [A]mendment was intended to provide against." *Civil Rights Cases,* 109 U.S., at 13. . . .

The stringent test RFRA demands of state laws reflects a lack of proportionality or congruence between the means adopted and the legitimate end to be achieved. If an objector can show a substantial burden on his free exercise, the State must demonstrate a compelling governmental interest and show that the law is the least restrictive means of furthering its interest. Claims that a law substantially burdens someone's exercise of religion will often be difficult to contest. Requiring a State to demonstrate a compelling interest and show that it has adopted the least restrictive means of achieving that interest is the most demanding test known to constitutional law. . . . This is a considerable congressional intrusion into the States' traditional prerogatives and general authority to regulate for the health and welfare of their citizens. . . .

When Congress acts within its sphere of power and responsibilities, it has not just the right but the duty to make its own informed judgment on the meaning and force of the Constitution. . . . Were it otherwise, we would not afford Congress the presumption of validity its enactments now enjoy. . . .

It is for Congress in the first instance to "determin[e] whether and what legislation is needed to secure the guarantees of the Fourteenth Amendment," and its conclusions are entitled to much deference. *Katzenbach v. Morgan,* 384 U.S., at 651. Congress' discretion is not unlimited, however, and the courts retain the power, as they have since *Marbury v. Madison,* to determine if Congress has exceeded its authority under the Constitution. Broad as the power of Congress is under the Enforcement Clause of the Fourteenth Amendment, RFRA contradicts vital principles necessary to maintain separation of powers and the federal balance. . . .

JUSTICE STEVENS, concurring.

In my opinion, the Religious Freedom Restoration Act of 1993 (RFRA) is a "law respecting an establishment of religion" that violates the First Amendment to the Constitution. . . .

JUSTICE SCALIA, with whom JUSTICE STEVENS joins, concurring in part.

I write to respond briefly to the claim of Justice O'Connor's dissent . . . that historical materials support a result contrary to the one reached in *Employment Div., Dept. of Human Resources of Oregon v. Smith,* 494 U.S. 872 (1990). . . . The material that the dissent claims is at odds with *Smith* either has little to say about the issue or is in fact more consistent with *Smith* than with the dissent's interpretation of the Free Exercise Clause. . . .

JUSTICE O'CONNOR, with whom Justice BREYER joins . . . , dissenting.

I agree with the Court that the issue before us is whether the Religious Freedom Restoration Act of 1993 (RFRA) is a proper exercise of Congress' power to enforce §5 of the Fourteenth Amendment. But as a yardstick for measuring the constitutionality of RFRA, the Court uses its holding in *Employment Div., Dept. of Human Resources of Oregon v. Smith,* 494 U.S. 872 (1990), the decision that prompted Congress to enact RFRA as a means of more rigorously enforcing the Free Exercise Clause. I remain of the view that *Smith* was wrongly decided, and I would use this case to reexamine the Court's holding there. Therefore, I would direct the parties to brief the question whether *Smith* represents the correct understanding of the Free Exercise Clause and set the case for reargument. If the Court were to correct the misinterpretation of the Free Exercise Clause set forth in *Smith,* . . . [w]e would then be in a position to review RFRA in light of a proper interpretation of the Free Exercise Clause. . . .

JUSTICE SOUTER, dissenting.

To decide whether the Fourteenth Amendment gives Congress sufficient power to enact the Religious Freedom Restoration Act of 1993, the Court measures the legislation against the free-exercise standard of *Employment Div., Dept. of Human Resources of Oregon v. Smith,* 494 U.S. 872 (1990). . . . I have serious doubts about the precedential value of the *Smith* rule and its entitlement to adherence. . . . In order to provide full adversarial consideration, this case should be set down for reargument permitting plenary reexamination of the issue. Since the Court declines to follow that course, our free-exercise law remains marked by an "intolerable tension," and the constitutionality of the Act of Congress to enforce the free-exercise right cannot now be soundly decided. I would therefore dismiss the writ of certiorari as improvidently granted. . . .

JUSTICE BREYER, dissenting.

I agree with Justice O'Connor that the Court should direct the parties to brief the question whether *Employment Div., Dept. of Human Resources of Oregon v. Smith,* 494 U.S. 872 (1990), was correctly decided, and set this case for reargument. . . .

POINTS FOR DISCUSSION

1. In *Boerne*, the Court explained that, for an act to be within Congress's §5 power, "[t]here must be congruence and proportionality between the injury to be prevented or remedied and the means adopted to that end." Because the "legislative record lacks examples of modern instances of generally applicable law passed because of religious bigotry[,] . . . RFRA is so out of proportion to a supposed remedial or preventive object that it cannot be understood as responsive to, or designed to prevent, unconstitutional behavior." Does this analysis reflect the same standard that the Court applied in *Morgan*? If not, how does it differ? Is this standard meant to be the same standard that the Court applies under the Necessary and Proper Clause? If not, how does it differ?

2. The *Boerne* Court explained that §5 authorizes Congress to enforce the Fourteenth Amendment but not to define the substance of its prohibitions against the states. "Congress does not enforce a constitutional right by changing what that right is." The Court used the "congruence and proportionality" test to distinguish measures that "enforce" the Fourteenth Amendment from measures that "decree the substance" of constitutional rights that the Fourteenth Amendment protects. Is the congruence and proportionality test well suited to make this distinction? Was the act of Congress at issue in *Morgan* congruent and proportional to the equal protection principles Congress sought to enforce?

3. In *Boerne*, the Court again invoked the idea of traditional state prerogatives. RFRA, the Court explained, "is a considerable congressional intrusion into the States' traditional prerogatives and general authority to regulate for the health and welfare of their citizens." In light of *Garcia v. San Antonio Metropolitan Transit Authority*, 469 U.S. 528 (1985), should the Court have considered the idea of "the States' traditional prerogatives" in determining whether Congress exceeded its powers under §5?

UNITED STATES V. MORRISON

529 U.S. 598 (2000)

[The facts of this case appear on page 324.]

CHIEF JUSTICE REHNQUIST delivered the opinion of the Court.

The principles governing an analysis of congressional legislation under §5 are well settled. Section 5 states that Congress may " 'enforce' by 'appropriate legislation' the constitutional guarantee that no State shall deprive any person of 'life, liberty, or property, without due process of law,' nor deny any person 'equal protection of the laws.' " *City of Boerne v. Flores*, 521 U.S. 507, 517 (1997). Section 5 is "a positive grant of legislative power," *Katzenbach v. Morgan*, 384 U.S. 641, 651 (1966), that includes authority to "prohibit conduct which is not itself unconstitutional and [to] intrud[e] into 'legislative spheres of autonomy previously reserved to the States.'" *Flores, supra,* at 518 (quoting *Fitzpatrick v. Bitzer*, 427 U.S. 445, 455 (1976)). However, "[a]s broad as the congressional enforcement power is, it is not unlimited." *Oregon v. Mitchell*, 400 U.S. 112, 128 (1970). In fact, . . . several limitations inherent in §5's text and constitutional context have been recognized since the Fourteenth Amendment was adopted.

[T]he language and purpose of the Fourteenth Amendment place certain limitations on the manner in which Congress may attack discriminatory conduct. These limitations are necessary to prevent the Fourteenth Amendment from obliterating the Framers' carefully crafted balance of power between the States and the National Government. See *Flores, supra,* at 520-524 (reviewing the history of the Fourteenth Amendment's enactment and discussing the contemporary belief that the Amendment " 'does not concentrate power in the general government for any purpose of police government within the States' ") (quoting T. Cooley, Constitutional Limitations 294, n. 1 (2d ed. 1871)). Foremost among these limitations is the time-honored principle that the Fourteenth Amendment, by its very terms, prohibits only state action. "[T]he principle has become firmly embedded in our constitutional law that the action inhibited by the first section of the Fourteenth Amendment is only such action as may fairly be said to be that of the States. That Amendment erects no shield against merely private conduct, however discriminatory or wrongful." *Shelley v. Kraemer*, 334 U.S. 1, 13, and n. 12 (1948).

Shortly after the Fourteenth Amendment was adopted, we decided . . . the *Civil Rights Cases*. In those consolidated cases, we held that the public accommodation provisions of the Civil Rights Act of 1875, which applied to purely private conduct, were beyond the scope of the §5 enforcement power.

The force of the doctrine of *stare decisis* behind these decisions stems not only from the length of time they have been on the books, but also from the insight attributable to the Members of the Court at that time. Every Member had been appointed by President Lincoln, Grant, Hayes, Garfield, or Arthur — and each of their judicial appointees obviously had intimate knowledge and familiarity with the events surrounding the adoption of the Fourteenth Amendment. . . .

[W]e conclude that Congress' power under §5 does not extend to the enactment of §13981.

In the following two cases—*Board of Trustees of the University of Alabama v. Garrett*, 531 U.S. 356 (2001), and *Tennesee v. Lane*, 541 U.S. 509 (2004)—the Court considered the constitutionality of certain provisions of the Americans with Disabilities Act (ADA) under §5 of the Fourteenth Amendment. As you read these cases, you may question why the Court did not address the constitutionality of these provisions under the Commerce Clause. There is an important reason. *Garrett* and *Lane* were suits against states. Under principles of state sovereign immunity, which you will study in Chapter 6, a private litigant may not sue a state without its consent in federal or state court, with limited exceptions—one of which is when Congress legislates under §5 of the Fourteenth Amendment. *See Fitzpatrick v. Bitzer*, 427 U.S. 445 (1976). The Court has held that Congress may abrogate state sovereign immunity when legislating under §5 but not when legislating under the Commerce Clause. Accordingly, the lawsuits in *Garrett* and *Lane* could only proceed against the defendant states if Congress had authority under §5 to enact the ADA provisions at issue.

BOARD OF TRUSTEES OF THE UNIVERSITY OF ALABAMA v. GARRETT

531 U.S. 356 (2001)

CHIEF JUSTICE REHNQUIST delivered the opinion of the Court.

We decide here whether employees of the State of Alabama may recover money damages by reason of the State's failure to comply with the provisions of Title I of the Americans with Disabilities Act of 1990 (ADA or Act), 104 Stat. 330, 42 U.S.C. §§12111-12117.[1] ...

The ADA prohibits certain employers, including the States, from "discriminat[ing] against a qualified individual with a disability because of the disability of such individual in regard to job application procedures, the hiring, advancement, or discharge of employees, employee compensation, job training, and other terms, conditions, and privileges of employment." §§12112(a), 12111(2) (5) (7). To this end, the Act requires employers to "mak[e] reasonable accommodations to the known physical or mental limitations of an otherwise qualified individual with a disability who is an applicant or employee, unless [the employer] can demonstrate that the accommodation would impose an undue hardship on the operation of the [employer's] business." §12112(b)(5)(A). ...

---

1. ... Though the briefs of the parties discuss both sections in their constitutional arguments, no party has briefed the question whether Title II of the ADA, dealing with the "services, programs, or activities of a public entity,"42 U.S.C. §12132, is available for claims of employment discrimination when Title I of the ADA expressly deals with that subject. ... We are not disposed to decide the constitutional issue whether Title II, which has somewhat different remedial provisions from Title I, is appropriate legislation under §5 of the Fourteenth Amendment when the parties have not favored us with briefing on the statutory question. ...

Respondent Patricia Garrett, a registered nurse, was employed as the Director of Nursing, OB/Gyn/Neonatal Services, for the University of Alabama in Birmingham Hospital. In 1994, Garrett was diagnosed with breast cancer and subsequently underwent a lumpectomy, radiation treatment, and chemotherapy. Garrett's treatments required her to take substantial leave from work. Upon returning to work in July 1995, Garrett's supervisor informed Garrett that she would have to give up her Director position. Garrett then applied for and received a transfer to another, lower paying position as a nurse manager.

Respondent Milton Ash worked as a security officer for the Alabama Department of Youth Services (Department). Upon commencing this employment, Ash informed the Department that he suffered from chronic asthma and that his doctor recommended he avoid carbon monoxide and cigarette smoke, and Ash requested that the Department modify his duties to minimize his exposure to these substances. Ash was later diagnosed with sleep apnea and requested, again pursuant to his doctor's recommendation, that he be reassigned to daytime shifts to accommodate his condition. Ultimately, the Department granted none of the requested relief. Shortly after Ash filed a discrimination claim with the Equal Employment Opportunity Commission, he noticed that his performance evaluations were lower than those he had received on previous occasions.

Garrett and Ash filed separate lawsuits in the District Court, both seeking money damages under the ADA. . . .

I

Section 5 of the Fourteenth Amendment grants Congress the power to enforce the substantive guarantees contained in §1 by enacting "appropriate legislation." See *City of Boerne v. Flores,* 521 U.S. 507, 536 (1997). Congress is not limited to mere legislative repetition of this Court's constitutional jurisprudence. "Rather, Congress' power 'to enforce' the Amendment includes the authority both to remedy and to deter violation of rights guaranteed thereunder by prohibiting a somewhat broader swath of conduct, including that which is not itself forbidden by the Amendment's text." *City of Boerne, supra,* at 536.

City of Boerne also confirmed, however, the long-settled principle that it is the responsibility of this Court, not Congress, to define the substance of constitutional guarantees. Accordingly, §5 legislation reaching beyond the scope of §1's actual guarantees must exhibit "congruence and proportionality between the injury to be prevented or remedied and the means adopted to that end." *Id.,* at 520.

II

The first step in applying these now familiar principles is to identify with some precision the scope of the constitutional right at issue. Here, that inquiry requires us to examine the limitations §1 of the Fourteenth Amendment places upon States' treatment of the disabled. . . .

States are not required by the Fourteenth Amendment to make special accommodations for the disabled, so long as their actions toward such individuals are rational. They could quite hardheadedly — and perhaps hardheartedly — hold to job-qualification requirements which do not make allowance for the disabled. If special accommodations for the disabled are to be required, they have to come from positive law and not through the Equal Protection Clause. . . .

III

Once we have determined the metes and bounds of the constitutional right in question, we examine whether Congress identified a history and pattern of unconstitutional employment discrimination by the States against the disabled. Just as §1 of the Fourteenth Amendment applies only to actions committed "under color of state law," Congress' §5 authority is appropriately exercised only in response to state transgressions. . . . The legislative record of the ADA, however, simply fails to show that Congress did in fact identify a pattern of irrational state discrimination in employment against the disabled. . . .

Congress made a general finding in the ADA that "historically, society has tended to isolate and segregate individuals with disabilities, and, despite some improvements, such forms of discrimination against individuals with disabilities continue to be a serious and pervasive social problem." 42 U.S.C. §12101(a)(2). The record assembled by Congress includes many instances to support such a finding. But the great majority of these incidents do not deal with the activities of States.

Respondents in their brief cite half a dozen examples from the record that did involve States. . . . [E]ven if it were to be determined that each incident upon fuller examination showed unconstitutional action on the part of the State, these incidents taken together fall far short of even suggesting the pattern of unconstitutional discrimination on which §5 legislation must be based. . . .

Justice Breyer maintains that Congress applied Title I of the ADA to the States in response to a host of incidents representing unconstitutional state discrimination in employment against persons with disabilities. A close review of the relevant materials, however, undercuts that conclusion. Justice Breyer's Appendix C consists not of legislative findings, but of unexamined, anecdotal accounts of "adverse, disparate treatment by state officials." Of course, . . . "adverse, disparate treatment" often does not amount to a constitutional violation where rational-basis scrutiny applies. These accounts, moreover, were submitted not directly to Congress but to the Task Force on the Rights and Empowerment of Americans with Disabilities, which made no findings on the subject of state discrimination in employment.[7] . . . And, had Congress truly understood this information as reflecting a pattern of unconstitutional

---

7. Only a small fraction of the anecdotes Justice Breyer identifies in his Appendix C relate to state discrimination against the disabled in employment. At most, somewhere around 50 of these allegations describe conduct that could conceivably amount to constitutional violations by the States, and most of them are so general and brief that no firm conclusion can be drawn. The overwhelming majority of these accounts pertain to alleged discrimination by the States in the provision of public services and public accommodations, which areas are addressed in Titles II and III of the ADA.

behavior by the States, one would expect some mention of that conclusion in the Act's legislative findings. There is none. . . .

Even were it possible to squeeze out of these examples a pattern of unconstitutional discrimination by the States, the rights and remedies created by the ADA against the States would raise the same sort of concerns as to congruence and proportionality as were found in *City of Boerne, supra.* For example, whereas it would be entirely rational (and therefore constitutional) for a state employer to conserve scarce financial resources by hiring employees who are able to use existing facilities, the ADA requires employers to "mak[e] existing facilities used by employees readily accessible to and usable by individuals with disabilities." 42 U.S.C. §§12112(5)(B), 12111(9). The ADA does except employers from the "reasonable accommodatio[n]" requirement where the employer "can demonstrate that the accommodation would impose an undue hardship on the operation of the business of such covered entity." §12112(b)(5)(A). However, even with this exception, the accommodation duty far exceeds what is constitutionally required in that it makes unlawful a range of alternative responses that would be reasonable but would fall short of imposing an "undue burden" upon the employer. . . .

Congressional enactment of the ADA represents its judgment that there should be a "comprehensive national mandate for the elimination of discrimination against individuals with disabilities." 42 U.S.C. §12101(b)(1). Congress is the final authority as to desirable public policy, but in order to authorize private individuals to recover money damages against the States, there must be a pattern of discrimination by the States which violates the Fourteenth Amendment, and the remedy imposed by Congress must be congruent and proportional to the targeted violation. Those requirements are not met here, and to uphold the Act's application to the States would allow Congress to rewrite the Fourteenth Amendment. . . . Section 5 does not so broadly enlarge congressional authority. . . .

Justice Kennedy, with whom Justice O'Connor joins, concurring.

I do not doubt that the Americans with Disabilities Act of 1990 will be a milestone on the path to a more decent, tolerant, progressive society. . . . [But t]hat there is a new awareness, a new consciousness, a new commitment to better treatment of those disadvantaged by mental or physical impairments does not establish that an absence of state statutory correctives was a constitutional violation. . . .

[W]hat is in question is not whether the Congress, acting pursuant to a power granted to it by the Constitution, can compel the States to act. What is involved is only the question whether the States can be subjected to liability in suits brought not by the Federal Government . . . , but by private persons seeking to collect moneys from the state treasury without the consent of the State. The predicate for money damages against an unconsenting State in suits brought by private persons must be a federal statute enacted upon the documentation of patterns of constitutional violations committed by the State in its official capacity. That predicate, for reasons discussed here and in the decision of the Court, has not been established. . . .

JUSTICE BREYER, with whom JUSTICE STEVENS, JUSTICE SOUTER, and JUSTICE GINSBURG join, dissenting.

As the Court recognizes, state discrimination in employment against persons with disabilities might "run afoul of the Equal Protection Clause" where there is no "rational relationship between the disparity of treatment and some legitimate governmental purpose." . . . In my view, Congress reasonably could have concluded that the remedy before us constitutes an "appropriate" way to enforce this basic equal protection requirement. And that is all the Constitution requires.

I

Congress compiled a vast legislative record documenting "massive, society-wide discrimination" against persons with disabilities. S. Rep. No. 101-116, pp. 8-9 (1989). In addition to the information presented at 13 congressional hearings, and its own prior experience gathered over 40 years during which it contemplated and enacted considerable similar legislation, Congress created a special task force to assess the need for comprehensive legislation. That task force held hearings in every State, attended by more than 30,000 people, including thousands who had experienced discrimination first hand. The task force hearings, Congress' own hearings, and an analysis of "census data, national polls, and other studies" led Congress to conclude that "people with disabilities, as a group, occupy an inferior status in our society, and are severely disadvantaged socially, vocationally, economically, and educationally." 42 U.S.C. §12101(a)(6). As to employment, Congress found that "[t]wo-thirds of all disabled Americans between the age of 16 and 64 [were] not working at all," even though a large majority wanted to, and were able to, work productively. S. Rep. No. 101-116, at 9. And Congress found that this discrimination flowed in significant part from "stereotypic assumptions" as well as "purposeful unequal treatment." 42 U.S.C. §12101(a)(7).

The powerful evidence of discriminatory treatment throughout society in general, including discrimination by private persons and local governments, implicates state governments as well, for state agencies form part of that same larger society. . . . In any event, . . . [t]here are roughly 300 examples of discrimination by state governments themselves in the legislative record. I fail to see how this evidence "fall[s] far short of even suggesting the pattern of unconstitutional discrimination on which §5 legislation must be based." . . .

As the Court notes, those who presented instances of discrimination rarely provided additional, independent evidence sufficient to prove in court that, in each instance, the discrimination they suffered lacked justification from a judicial standpoint. . . . But a legislature is not a court of law. And Congress, unlike courts, must, and does, routinely draw general conclusions — for example, of likely motive or of likely relationship to legitimate need — from anecdotal and opinion-based evidence of this kind, particularly when the evidence lacks strong refutation. In reviewing §5 legislation, we have never required the sort of extensive investigation of each piece of evidence that the

Court appears to contemplate. [See] *Katzenbach v. Morgan,* 384 U.S. 641, 652-656 (1966) (asking whether Congress' likely conclusions were reasonable, not whether there was adequate evidentiary support in the record). Nor has the Court traditionally required Congress to make findings as to state discrimination, or to break down the record evidence, category by category. . . .

Regardless, Congress expressly found substantial unjustified discrimination against persons with disabilities. . . . Congress could have reasonably believed that these examples represented signs of a widespread problem of unconstitutional discrimination.

II

There is simply no reason to require Congress, seeking to determine facts relevant to the exercise of its §5 authority, to adopt rules or presumptions that reflect a court's institutional limitations. Unlike courts, Congress can readily gather facts from across the Nation, assess the magnitude of a problem, and more easily find an appropriate remedy. Unlike courts, Congress directly reflects public attitudes and beliefs, enabling Congress better to understand where, and to what extent, refusals to accommodate a disability amount to behavior that is callous or unreasonable to the point of lacking constitutional justification. Unlike judges, Members of Congress can directly obtain information from constituents who have firsthand experience with discrimination and related issues.

Moreover, unlike judges, Members of Congress are elected. . . . To apply a rule designed to restrict courts as if it restricted Congress' legislative power is to stand the underlying principle — a principle of judicial restraint — on its head. . . .

III

The Court argues . . . that the statute's damages remedy is not "congruent" with and "proportional" to the equal protection problem that Congress found. . . .

[W]hat is wrong with a remedy that, in response to unreasonable employer behavior, requires an employer to make accommodations that are reasonable? Of course, what is "reasonable" in the statutory sense and what is "unreasonable" in the constitutional sense might differ. In other words, the requirement may exceed what is necessary to avoid a constitutional violation. But it is just that power — the power to require more than the minimum that §5 grants to Congress, as this Court has repeatedly confirmed. . . .

In keeping with these principles, the Court has said that "[i]t is not for us to review the congressional resolution of . . . the various conflicting considerations — the risk or pervasiveness of the discrimination in governmental services . . . , the adequacy or availability of alternative remedies, and the nature and significance of the state interests that would be affected." [*Morgan,*] 384 U.S., at 653. "It is enough that we be able to perceive a basis upon which the Congress might resolve the conflict as it did." *Ibid.* . . .

[Appendices to Opinion of BREYER, J., omitted.]

TENNESEE V. LANE

---

541 U.S. 509 (2004)

JUSTICE STEVENS delivered the opinion of the Court.

Title II of the Americans with Disabilities Act of 1990 (ADA or Act), 104 Stat. 337, 42 U.S.C. §§12131-12165, provides that "no qualified individual with a disability shall, by reason of such disability, be excluded from participation in or be denied the benefits of the services, programs or activities of a public entity, or be subjected to discrimination by any such entity." §12132. The question presented in this case is whether Title II exceeds Congress' power under §5 of the Fourteenth Amendment.

I

[R]espondents George Lane and Beverly Jones . . . , both of whom are paraplegics who use wheelchairs for mobility, claimed that they were denied access to, and the services of, the state court system by reason of their disabilities. Lane alleged that he was compelled to appear to answer a set of criminal charges on the second floor of a county courthouse that had no elevator. At his first appearance, Lane crawled up two flights of stairs to get to the courtroom. When Lane returned to the courthouse for a hearing, he refused to crawl again or to be carried by officers to the courtroom; he consequently was arrested and jailed for failure to appear. Jones, a certified court reporter, alleged that she has not been able to gain access to a number of county courthouses, and, as a result, has lost both work and an opportunity to participate in the judicial process. Respondents sought damages and equitable relief.

II

Invoking "the sweep of congressional authority, including the power to enforce the fourteenth amendment and to regulate commerce," the ADA is designed "to provide a clear and comprehensive national mandate for the elimination of discrimination against individuals with disabilities." §§12101(b)(1), (b)(4). It forbids discrimination against persons with disabilities in three major areas of public life: employment, which is covered by Title I of the statute; public services, programs, and activities, which are the subject of Title II; and public accommodations, which are covered by Title III.

Title II prohibits any public entity from discriminating against "qualified" persons with disabilities in the provision or operation of public services, programs, or activities. The Act defines the term "public entity" to include state and local governments, as well as their agencies and instrumentalities. §12131(1). . . .

III

When Congress seeks to remedy or prevent unconstitutional discrimination, §5 authorizes it to enact prophylactic legislation proscribing practices that are discriminatory in effect, if not in intent, to carry out the basic objectives of the Equal Protection Clause.

Congress' §5 power is not, however, unlimited. While Congress must have a wide berth in devising appropriate remedial and preventative measures for unconstitutional actions, those measures may not work a "substantive change in the governing law." [*City of Boerne v. Flores*, 521 U.S. 507, 519 (1997).] . . . Section 5 legislation is valid if it exhibits "a congruence and proportionality between the injury to be prevented or remedied and the means adopted to that end." *Id.*, at 520. . . .

Applying the *Boerne* test in [*Board of Trustees of the University of Alabama v. Garrett*, 531 U.S. 356 (2001)], we concluded that Title I of the ADA was not a valid exercise of Congress' §5 power to enforce the Fourteenth Amendment's prohibition on unconstitutional disability discrimination in public employment. . . . In view of the significant differences between Titles I and II, however, *Garrett* left open the question whether Title II is a valid exercise of Congress' §5 enforcement power. It is to that question that we now turn.

IV

The first step of the *Boerne* inquiry requires us to identify the constitutional right or rights that Congress sought to enforce when it enacted Title II. . . . As we observed [in *Garrett*], classifications based on disability violate that constitutional command if they lack a rational relationship to a legitimate governmental purpose. *Garrett*, 531 U.S., at 366.

Title II, like Title I, seeks to enforce this prohibition on irrational disability discrimination. But it also seeks to enforce a variety of other basic constitutional guarantees, infringements of which are subject to more searching judicial review. These rights include some, like the right of access to the courts at issue in this case, that are protected by the Due Process Clause of the Fourteenth Amendment. The Due Process Clause and the Confrontation Clause of the Sixth Amendment, as applied to the States via the Fourteenth Amendment, both guarantee to a criminal defendant such as respondent Lane the "right to be present at all stages of the trial where his absence might frustrate the fairness of the proceedings." *Faretta v. California*, 422 U.S. 806, 819, n.15 (1975). The Due Process Clause also requires the States to afford certain civil litigants a "meaningful opportunity to be heard" by removing obstacles to their full participation in judicial proceedings. *Boddie v. Connecticut*, 401 U.S. 371, 379 (1971); *M. L. B. v. S. L. J.*, 519 U.S. 102 (1996). We have held that the Sixth Amendment guarantees to criminal defendants the right to trial by a jury composed of a fair cross section of the community, noting that the exclusion of "identifiable segments playing major roles in the community cannot be squared with the constitutional concept of jury trial." *Taylor v. Louisiana*, 419 U.S. 522, 530 (1975). And, finally, we have recognized that members of the public have a right of access to criminal proceedings secured by the First Amendment. *Press-Enterprise Co. v. Superior Court of Cal., County of Riverside*, 478 U.S. 1, 8-15 (1986). . . .

In the deliberations that led up to the enactment of the ADA, Congress identified important shortcomings in existing laws that rendered them "inadequate to address the pervasive problems of discrimination that people with disabilities are facing." S. Rep. No. 101-116, at 18. It also uncovered further evidence of those shortcomings, in the form of hundreds of examples of unequal treatment of persons with disabilities by States and their political subdivisions. As the Court's opinion in *Garrett* observed, the "overwhelming majority" of these examples concerned discrimination in the administration of public programs and services. *Id.,* at 371, n.7.

With respect to the particular services at issue in this case, Congress learned that many individuals, in many States across the country, were being excluded from courthouses and court proceedings by reason of their disabilities. . . . The conclusion that Congress drew from this body of evidence is set forth in the text of the ADA itself: "[D]iscrimination against individuals with disabilities persists in such critical areas as . . . education, transportation, communication, recreation, institutionalization, health services, voting, and *access to public services.*" 42 U.S.C. §12101(a)(3) (emphasis added). This finding, together with the extensive record of disability discrimination that underlies it, makes clear beyond peradventure that inadequate provision of public services and access to public facilities was an appropriate subject for prophylactic legislation.

V

The only question that remains is whether Title II is an appropriate response to this history and pattern of unequal treatment. . . . Title II — unlike RFRA . . . and other statutes we have reviewed for validity under §5 — reaches a wide array of official conduct in an effort to enforce an equally wide array of constitutional guarantees. . . . But nothing in our case law requires us to consider Title II, with its wide variety of applications, as an undifferentiated whole.[18] Whatever might be said about Title II's other applications, the question presented in this case is not whether Congress can validly subject the States to private suits for money damages for failing to provide reasonable access to hockey rinks, or even to voting booths, but whether Congress had the power under §5 to enforce the constitutional right of access to the courts. Because we find that Title II unquestionably is valid §5 legislation as it applies to the class of cases implicating the accessibility of judicial services, we need go no further. . . . Title II's requirement of program accessibility . . . is congruent and proportional to its object of enforcing the right of access to the courts. . . .

JUSTICE SOUTER, with whom JUSTICE GINSBURG joins, concurring.

[T]he judiciary itself has endorsed the basis for some of the very discrimination subject to congressional remedy under §5. . . . Laws compelling sterilization were often accompanied by others indiscriminately requiring institutionalization, and prohibiting certain individuals with disabilities from marrying, from voting, from attending public schools, and even from appearing in public. . . . In sustaining the application of Title II today, the

---

18. Contrary to The Chief Justice, *Garrett* [does not lend] support to the proposition that the *Boerne* test requires courts in all cases to "measur[e] the full breadth of the statute or relevant provision that Congress enacted against the scope of the constitutional right it purported to enforce." In fact, the decision in *Garrett*, which severed Title I of the ADA from Title II for purposes of the §5 inquiry, demonstrates that courts need not examine "the full breadth of the statute" all at once. . . .

Court takes a welcome step away from the judiciary's prior endorsement of blunt instruments imposing legal handicaps. . . .

JUSTICE GINSBURG, with whom JUSTICE SOUTER and JUSTICE BREYER join, concurring.

Legislation calling upon all government actors to respect the dignity of individuals with disabilities is entirely compatible with our Constitution's commitment to federalism, properly conceived. It seems to me not conducive to a harmonious federal system to require Congress, before it exercises authority under §5 of the Fourteenth Amendment, essentially to indict each State for disregarding the equal-citizenship stature of persons with disabilities. Members of Congress are understandably reluctant to condemn their own States as constitutional violators, complicit in maintaining the isolated and unequal status of persons with disabilities. I would not disarm a National Legislature for resisting an adversarial approach to lawmaking better suited to the courtroom. . . .

CHIEF JUSTICE REHNQUIST, with whom JUSTICE KENNEDY and JUSTICE THOMAS join, dissenting.

While the Court today pays lipservice to the "congruence and proportionality" test, it applies it in a manner inconsistent with our recent precedents.

In *Garrett,* we conducted the three-step inquiry first enunciated in *City of Boerne* to determine whether Title I of the ADA satisfied the congruence-and-proportionality test. . . .

The first step is to "identify with some precision the scope of the constitutional right at issue." *Garrett, supra,* at 365. This task was easy in *Garrett* . . . and *City of Boerne* because the statutes in those cases sought to enforce only one constitutional right. . . .

In this case, the task of identifying the scope of the relevant constitutional protection is more difficult because Title II purports to enforce a panoply of constitutional rights of disabled persons: not only the equal protection right against irrational discrimination, but also certain rights protected by the Due Process Clause. . . . The Court cites four access-to-the-courts rights that Title II purportedly enforces: (1) the right of the criminal defendant to be present at all critical stages of the trial; (2) the right of litigants to have a "meaningful opportunity to be heard" in judicial proceedings; (3) the right of the criminal defendant to trial by a jury composed of a fair cross section of the community; and (4) the public right of access to criminal proceedings.

Having traced the "metes and bounds" of the constitutional rights at issue, the next step in the congruence-and-proportionality inquiry requires us to examine whether Congress "identified a history and pattern" of violations of these constitutional rights by the States with respect to the disabled. *Garrett,* 531 U.S., at 368. . . . [T]he majority identifies nothing in the legislative record that shows Congress was responding to widespread violations of the due process rights of disabled persons. . . . [T]here is *nothing* in the legislative record or statutory findings to indicate that disabled persons were systematically denied the right to be present at criminal trials, denied the meaningful opportunity to be heard in civil cases, unconstitutionally excluded from jury service, or denied the right to attend criminal trials. . . .

The third step of our congruence-and-proportionality inquiry removes any doubt as to whether Title II is valid §5 legislation. At this stage, we ask whether the rights and remedies created by Title II are congruent and proportional to the constitutional rights it purports to enforce and the record of constitutional violations adduced by Congress. . . . By requiring special accommodation and the elimination of programs that have a disparate impact on the disabled, Title II prohibits far more state conduct than does the equal protection ban on irrational discrimination. . . .

The majority, however, claims that Title II also vindicates fundamental rights protected by the Due Process Clause — in addition to access to the courts — that are subject to heightened Fourteenth Amendment scrutiny. But Title II is not tailored to provide prophylactic protection of these rights; instead, it applies to any service, program, or activity provided by any entity. . . .

The majority concludes that Title II's massive overbreadth can be cured by considering the statute only "as it applies to the class of cases implicating the accessibility of judicial services." I have grave doubts about importing an "as applied" approach into the §5 context. While the majority is of course correct that this Court normally only considers the application of a statute to a particular case, the proper inquiry under *City of Boerne* and its progeny is somewhat different. In applying the congruence-and-proportionality test, we ask whether Congress has attempted to statutorily redefine the constitutional rights protected by the Fourteenth Amendment. This question can only be answered by measuring the breadth of a statute's coverage against the scope of the constitutional rights it purports to enforce and the record of violations it purports to remedy.

In conducting its as-applied analysis, however, the majority posits a hypothetical statute, never enacted by Congress, that applies only to courthouses. The effect is to rig the congruence-and-proportionality test by artificially constricting the scope of the statute to closely mirror a recognized constitutional right. But Title II is not susceptible of being carved up in this manner; it applies indiscriminately to all "services," "programs," or "activities" of any "public entity." Thus, the majority's approach is not really an assessment of whether Title II is "appropriate *legislation*" at all, U.S. Const., Amdt. 14, §5 (emphasis added), but a test of whether the Court can conceive of a hypothetical statute narrowly tailored enough to constitute valid prophylactic legislation.

Our §5 precedents do not support this as-applied approach. In each case, we measured the full breadth of the statute or relevant provision that Congress enacted against the scope of the constitutional right it purported to enforce. If we had arbitrarily constricted the scope of the statutes to match the scope of a core constitutional right, those cases might have come out differently. In *Garrett*, for example, Title I might have been upheld "as applied" to irrational employment discrimination. . . .

[E]ven in the courthouse-access context, Title II requires substantially more than the Due Process Clause. Title II subjects States to private lawsuits if, *inter alia,* they fail to make "reasonable modifications" to facilities, such as removing "architectural . . . barriers." 42 U.S.C. §§12131(2), 12132. Yet the statute is not limited to occasions when the failure to modify results, or will likely result, in an actual due process violation — *i.e.,* the inability of a disabled person to participate in a judicial proceeding. Indeed, liability is triggered if an inaccessible building results in a disabled person being "subjected to discrimination" — a term that presumably encompasses any sort of inconvenience in accessing the facility, for whatever purpose. §12132. . . .

Congress has authorized private damages suits against a State for merely maintaining a courthouse that is not readily accessible to the disabled, without regard to whether a disabled person's due process rights are ever violated. . . .

JUSTICE SCALIA, dissenting.

I joined the Court's opinion in *Boerne* with some misgiving. I have generally rejected tests based on such malleable standards as "proportionality," because they have a way of turning into vehicles for the implementation of individual judges' policy preferences. . . .

The "congruence and proportionality" standard, like all such flabby tests, is a standing invitation to judicial arbitrariness and policy-driven decision-making. Worse still, it casts this Court in the role of Congress's taskmaster. Under it, the courts (and ultimately this Court) must regularly check Congress's homework to make sure that it has identified sufficient constitutional violations to make its remedy congruent and proportional. As a general matter, we are ill advised to adopt or adhere to constitutional rules that bring us into constant conflict with a coequal branch of Government. And when conflict is unavoidable, we should not come to do battle with the United States Congress armed only with a test ("congruence and proportionality") that has no demonstrable basis in the text of the Constitution and cannot objectively be shown to have been met or failed. . . .

I would replace "congruence and proportionality" with another test — one that provides a clear, enforceable limitation supported by the text of §5. Section 5 grants Congress the power "to *enforce,* by appropriate legislation," the other provisions of the Fourteenth Amendment. U.S. Const., Amdt. 14 (emphasis added). [*Katzenbach v. Morgan,* 384 U.S. 641 (1966),] notwithstanding, one does not, within any normal meaning of the term, "enforce" a prohibition by issuing a still broader prohibition directed to the same end. One does not, for example, "enforce" a 55-mile-per-hour speed limit by imposing a 45-mile-per-hour speed limit — even though that is indeed directed to the same end of automotive safety and will undoubtedly result in many fewer violations of the 55-mile-per-hour limit. And one does not "enforce" the right of access to the courts at issue in this case by requiring that disabled persons be provided access to *all* of the "services, programs, or activities" furnished or conducted by the State, 42 U.S.C. §12132. That is simply not what the power to enforce means — or ever meant. The 1860 edition of Noah Webster's American Dictionary of the English Language, current when the Fourteenth Amendment was adopted, defined "enforce" as: "To put in execution; to cause to take effect; as, to *enforce* the laws." *Id.,* at 396. See also J. Worcester, Dictionary of the English Language 484 (1860) ("To put in force; to cause to be applied or executed; as, 'To *enforce* a law' "). Nothing in §5 allows Congress to go *beyond* the provisions of the Fourteenth Amendment to proscribe, prevent, or "remedy" conduct that does not *itself* violate any provision of the Fourteenth Amendment. So-called "prophylactic legislation" is reinforcement rather than enforcement.

Morgan asserted that this commonsense interpretation "would confine the legislative power . . . to the insignificant role of abrogating only those state laws that the judicial branch was prepared to adjudge unconstitutional, or of merely informing the judgment of the judiciary by particularizing the 'majestic generalities' of §1 of the Amendment." 384 U.S., at 648-649. That is not so. . . . Section 5 authorizes Congress to create a cause of action through which the citizen may vindicate his Fourteenth Amendment rights. . . . Section 5 would also authorize measures that do not restrict the States' substantive scope of action but impose requirements directly related to the *facilitation* of "enforcement"—for example, reporting requirements that would enable violations of the Fourteenth Amendment to be identified. . . . But what §5 does *not* authorize is so-called "prophylactic" measures, prohibiting primary conduct that is itself not forbidden by the Fourteenth Amendment.

The major impediment to the approach I have suggested is *stare decisis.* A lot of water has gone under the bridge since *Morgan,* and many important and well-accepted measures, such as the Voting Rights Act, assume the validity of *Morgan.* . . . However, . . . *Morgan* . . . , all of our later cases . . . , and all of our earlier cases that even suggest such an expansive meaning in dicta, involved congressional measures that were directed exclusively against, or were used in the particular case to remedy, *racial discrimination.*

Giving §5 more expansive scope with regard to measures directed against racial discrimination by the States accords to practices that are distinctively violative of the principal purpose of the Fourteenth Amendment a priority of attention that this Court envisioned from the beginning, and that has repeatedly been reflected in our opinions. . . .

Thus, principally for reasons of *stare decisis,* I shall henceforth apply the permissive [*McCulloch v. Maryland,* 17 U.S. 316 (1819),] standard to congressional measures designed to remedy racial discrimination by the States. . . . I shall . . . not subject to "congruence and proportionality" analysis congressional action under §5 that is *not* directed to racial discrimination. Rather, I shall give full effect to that action when it consists of "enforcement" of the provisions of the Fourteenth Amendment, within the broad but not unlimited meaning of that term I have described above. When it goes beyond enforcement to prophylaxis, however, I shall consider it ultra vires. The present legislation is plainly of the latter sort. . . .

Justice Thomas, dissenting.

I join The Chief Justice's dissent. I agree that Title II of the Americans with Disabilities Act of 1990 cannot be a congruent and proportional remedy to the States' alleged practice of denying disabled persons access to the courts. . . .

POINTS FOR DISCUSSION

1. In *Garrett* and *Lane,* the Court (a) identified the constitutional right or rights at issue and (b) determined whether the congressional act in question was a congruent and proportional response to a history or pattern of constitutional violations. What factors accounted for the Court's holdings that Congress lacked §5 power to enact Title I of the ADA (*Garrett*), but that Congress had §5 power to enact Title II (*Lane*)? Should the Court have decided these cases differently (as it did)?

2. The Commerce Clause, General Welfare Clause, and §5 cases that you have read have all involved the question of how much courts should defer to Congress's judgment that an exercise of its powers is warranted. Do *Garrett* and *Lane* differ in the degree of deference that the majority in each case showed Congress? If so, which majority showed Congress the more appropriate level of deference?

3. In *Lane*, Justice Scalia, dissenting, would have replaced the "congruence and proportionality" test with a test allowing Congress to remedy conduct that violates the Fourteenth Amendment, not to enact prophylactic legislation. Justice Scalia argued that the congruence and proportionality test is not workable, and he found no support for it in constitutional text. Recall that in *Garcia v. San Antonio Metropolitan Transit Authority*, 469 U.S. 528 (1985), the Court rejected the traditional state functions test of *National League of Cities v. Usery*, 426 U.S. 833 (1976), in part on the ground that it was unworkable. To what extent should the Court adopt or reject constitutional tests on grounds of their workability? On the basis of constitutional text, should courts understand §5 to provide Congress with the same of scope of power that the Necessary and Proper Clause provides?

CHAPTER 6

DOCTRINES OF STATE SOVEREIGNTY

The preceding chapter addressed certain enumerated powers of Congress under the Constitution. The Tenth Amendment, adopted as part of the Bill of Rights, provides that "[t]he powers not delegated to the United States by the Constitution, nor prohibited by it to the States, are reserved to the States respectively, or to the people." In light of Article I's enumeration of congressional powers and the Tenth Amendment, the Supreme Court has limited Congress's exercise of enumerated powers to protect certain prerogatives of state sovereignty. This chapter considers these limitations. The doctrines that this chapter considers involve contested questions of historical practice, constitutional structure, and judicial precedent. The doctrines fall into four categories.

First, the Supreme Court has considered whether the Constitution precludes Congress from regulating areas that, traditionally, states have enjoyed the prerogative to regulate. As you studied in Chapter 4, the Supreme Court held in *National League of Cities v. Usery*, 426 U.S. 833 (1976), that Congress may not exercise the commerce power to regulate certain areas that it has traditionally been the function of states to regulate. The Court overruled *Usery* in *Garcia v. San Antonio Metropolitan Transit Authority*, 469 U.S. 528 (1985), but the idea of traditional state regulatory functions has endured. For example, as you saw in Chapter 5, the Supreme Court expressed concern in *United States v. Lopez*, 514 U.S. 549 (1995), and *United States v. Morrison*, 529 U.S. 598 (2000), that if it upheld the regulations at issue in those cases, Congress would have broad power to regulate areas of traditional state concern. You will see the idea of traditional state functions arise in various contexts in this chapter.

Second, the Court has applied a "clear statement rule" to acts of Congress that regulate certain areas of traditional state concern. In *Gregory v. Ashcroft*, 501 U.S. 452 (1991), the Supreme Court held that if Congress wishes to exercise an enumerated power to regulate such a matter of traditional state function, Congress must do so clearly, expressly, and unequivocally. Under this "clear statement rule" of interpretation, the Court will not extend congressional regulation into areas of traditional state function without express direction from Congress to do so.

Third, the Court has held that Congress may not "commandeer" state governments to enact or enforce a federal regulatory program. In *New York v. United States*, 505 U.S. 144 (1992), the Court held that Congress may not compel state *legislatures* to enact legislation in service of federal regulatory goals. In *Printz v. United States*, 521 U.S. 898 (1997), the Court held that Congress may not require state *executive officials* to enforce a federal regulatory program. In both cases, the Court explained that the Constitution empowers the federal government to act directly upon individuals, not through the instruments of state government.

Fourth, the Supreme Court has held that the states have sovereign immunity from private suits in state and federal courts. In *Seminole Tribe of Florida v. Florida*, 517 U.S. 44 (1996), and other cases, the Court has determined that the Constitution, by establishing dual sovereignty between the federal government and the states, implicitly recognized in states the same sovereign immunity that nations traditionally enjoyed under the law of nations. The Court has recognized congressional power to abrogate this immunity in only limited instances.

Finally, this chapter revisits the Necessary and Proper Clause, which provides that Congress has power "[t]o make all Laws which shall be necessary and proper for carrying into Execution the foregoing Powers, and all other Powers vested by this Constitution in the Government of the United States, or in any Department or Officer thereof." In various cases presented in this and the previous chapter, the Court has described the Clause as incorporating doctrines of state sovereignty: If an act of Congress violates state sovereignty, it is not a "proper" federal enactment. As you have seen, judges and other public officials have debated the breadth of the Necessary and Proper Clause since the Founding. This chapter concludes by examining the ongoing state of this debate.

As you read this chapter, keep in mind the following questions:

- How do state sovereignty doctrines relate to Congress's enumerated powers? Do certain protections of state sovereignty inhere in Article I's enumeration of powers? Does the Tenth Amendment affirmatively protect certain aspects of state sovereignty?
- How does judicial review of whether an act of Congress violates state sovereign prerogatives relate to the political safeguards of federalism? Is such judicial review appropriate?
- By what methods of constitutional interpretation has the Court discerned the state sovereignty doctrines that this chapter considers? Are they appropriate methods? Has the Court properly employed them?
- What values, if any, do these state sovereignty doctrines advance?

A. TRADITIONAL STATE FUNCTIONS

In Chapter 4, you studied *National League of Cities v. Usery*, 426 U.S. 833 (1976), holding that Congress may not exercise its enumerated powers to perform certain traditional state regulatory functions. You also studied *Garcia v. San Antonio Metropolitan Transit Authority*, 469 U.S. 528 (1985), which overruled *Usery*. In *Garcia*, the Court explained in part that the political safeguards of federalism, not judicial review, appropriately protect state regulatory autonomy in areas of state concern. Keep *Usery* and *Garcia* in mind as you read the materials in this chapter.

NATIONAL LEAGUE OF CITIES V. USERY

---

426 U.S. 833 (1976)

See supra at page 244.

GARCIA V. SAN ANTONIO METROPOLITAN TRANSIT AUTHORITY

---

469 U.S. 528 (1985)

See supra at page 249.

B. CLEAR STATEMENT RULES

The Supreme Court held in 1992 in *Gregory v. Ashcroft*, 501 U.S. 452 (1991), that it will not read an act of Congress to exercise certain traditional state regulatory functions unless the act exercises them in clear terms. You saw judicial application of such a "clear statement rule" in Chapter 2 in the *Slaughter-House Cases*, 83 U.S. (16 Wall.) 36, 78 (1872). Justice Miller argued that the Court should not understand the Privileges or Immunities Clause of the Fourteenth Amendment to "radically change[] the whole theory of the relations of the State and Federal governments to each other and of both these governments to the people . . . in the absence of language which expresses such a purpose too clearly to admit of doubt." This section presents three excerpts that introduce you to historical and present-day applications of clear statement rules to federal enactments. The first selection is from St. George Tucker's edition of *Blackstone's Commentaries*. Tucker explained how, under the law of nations, one sovereign would not understand a written document to abridge the sovereign rights of another by implication only; rather, only express terms would abridge such rights. Tucker invoked this principle in examining whether federal courts had general jurisdiction in common law cases. In the first decades after ratification, public officials vigorously debated whether the United States has a "federal common law," as you will study in Chapter 8. Federal common law refers to a federal rule of decision that no enacted form of federal law—the Constitution, statutes, and treaties of the United States—provides. Some argued that a federal common law jurisdiction in federal courts was inconsistent with the Constitution's limitations on federal lawmaking power and would deprive states of sovereign governance prerogatives. Tucker argued that the Constitution should not be read to deprive the states of such prerogatives absent a clear expression of intent to do so. In the second selection, *United States v. Nicholls*, 4 Yeates 251 (Pa. 1805), a Pennsylvania court relied on Tucker's analysis to interpret a federal statute narrowly to respect certain state governance prerogatives. The final selection, *Gregory v. Ashcroft*, similarly applies a clear statement rule to limit application of a federal statute in 1992.

As you read these selections, consider the following questions:

- How do clear statement rules relate to early debates over whether courts should strictly or broadly construe federal power under the Constitution?
- Is judicial application of clear statement rules consistent with *Garcia*?
- What values do clear statement rules advance in this context?

St. George Tucker, Blackstone's Commentaries

App. Note E, at 412, 422-423 (reprint 1969)
(Phila., William Young Birch & Abraham Small 1803)

How far [has] that portion of the common law and statutes of England, which has been retained by the several states, respectively, has been engrafted upon, or made a part of the constitution of the United States[?] . . .

[I]t has . . . been said, that if . . . general jurisdiction in common law cases has not been granted to the federal government in express terms, yet it is given by *implication*. . . . This is probably the first instance in which it has been supposed that sovereign and independent states can be abridged of their rights, as sovereign states, by *implication*, only. . . . For, no free nation can be bound by any law but its own will; and where that will is manifested by any written document, as a convention, league, treaty, compact, or agreement, the nation is bound, only according as that will is expressed *in* the instrument by which it binds itself. And as every nation is bound to preserve itself, or, in other words, it's independence; so no interpretation whereby it's destruction, or that of a state, which is the same thing, may be hazarded, can be admitted in any case where it has not, in the *most express terms*, given its consent to such an interpretation. . . .

United States v. Nicholls

4 Yeates 251 (Pa. 1805)

[The question before the Supreme Court of Pennsylvania was whether a 1797 Act of Congress providing that "debts due to the United States, shall first be satisfied" relative to other creditors applied in cases where a state had a lien on the debtor's property.]

Yeates, J.

I cannot bring myself to believe, notwithstanding the generality of words used in the 5th section of the act of congress of 3d *March* 1797, "the debts due to the *United States*, shall be first satisfied," that the provision therein contained was ever intended to extend to cases where an individual state was a creditor, and *as such* was clearly entitled under its municipal laws to a *lien* on the estate real or personal, of the insolvent debtor. No section or clause in any part of the act respects in the most distant manner the several states in their political and corporate capacities, as competitors with the *United States*; but on the contrary, every regulation and provision in the act is confined to the settlement of accounts, between the *United States* and individual citizens.

It has been truly said, that the constitution of the *United States*, considered *as federal*, is to be construed *strictly* in all cases, when the antecedent rights of a state may be drawn in question, *Tuck. Bla.* Append. 151; and it is a maxim of political law, that sovereign states cannot be deprived of any of their rights by implication, nor in any manner whatever, but by their own voluntary consent, or by submission to a conqueror. *Ib.* 143. It would certainly require strong, clear, marked expressions, to satisfy a reasonable mind, that the constituted authorities of the union contemplated by any public law, the devesting of any pre-existing right or interest in a state; or that the representatives of any state would have agreed thereto, even supposing the legitimate powers of congress in such particular, to be perfectly ascertained and settled.

The members of this court were unanimously of opinion, in *Smith v. Nicholson, December* term 1803, that the provision of the general lien, created by the act of assembly of 18th *February* 1785, on the settlement of an account by the comptroller general, continued in full force, and was not repealed either by the express words of any subsequent law, or by necessary implication. . . .

The legislature of this commonwealth had the unquestionable right to make such a law in 1785, to secure the fiscal interest of the state. This power was not delegated to the *United States* amongst the other enumerated powers, nor prohibited to the state by the constitution of 1787. But congress was authorised by act 1, *s.* 8 of that instrument, "to make all laws which should be *necessary and proper* for carrying into execution the powers delegated to them, and all other powers vested in the government of the *United States*, or in any department or officer thereof." Hence it results that congress have the *concurrent* right of passing laws to protect the interest of the union, as to debts due to the government of the *United States* arising from the public revenue; but in so doing, they cannot detract from the uncontroulable power of individual states to raise their own revenue, nor infringe on, or derogate from the sovereignty of any independent state. Federalist Letters, No. 32, 33. The consequences of a contrary doctrine are too obvious to be insisted upon. . . .

Smith, J.
    I fully concur. . . .

Brackenridge, J.
    If even the power was constitutionally delegated to congress to make a law, giving to the *United States* a preference in payment of debts over individual states, I cannot conceive that this right has been exercised by the expressions of the act of 3d *March* 1797. . . .

Gregory v. Ashcroft

501 U.S. 452 (1991)

Justice O'Connor delivered the opinion of the Court.

Article V, §26, of the Missouri Constitution provides that "[a]ll judges other than municipal judges shall retire at the age of seventy years." We consider whether this mandatory retirement provision violates the federal

Age Discrimination in Employment Act of 1967 (ADEA or Act), 81 Stat. 602, as amended, 29 U.S.C. §§621-634. . . .

Petitioners are Missouri state judges. . . . Both are subject to the §26 mandatory retirement provision. . . . The ADEA makes it unlawful for an "employer" "to discharge any individual" who is at least 40 years old "because of such individual's age." 29 U.S.C. §§623(a), 631(a). The term "employer" is defined to include "a State or political subdivision of a State." §630(b)(2). . . .

As every schoolchild learns, our Constitution establishes a system of dual sovereignty between the States and the Federal Government. This Court also has recognized this fundamental principle. In *Tafflin v. Levitt*, 493 U.S. 455, 458 (1990), "[w]e beg[a]n with the axiom that, under our federal system, the States possess sovereignty concurrent with that of the Federal Government, subject only to limitations imposed by the Supremacy Clause." . . .

The Constitution created a Federal Government of limited powers. "The powers not delegated to the United States by the Constitution, nor prohibited by it to the States, are reserved to the States respectively, or to the people." U.S. Const., Amdt. 10. The States thus retain substantial sovereign authority under our constitutional system. As James Madison put it:

> "The powers delegated by the proposed Constitution to the federal govern-ment are few and defined. Those which are to remain in the State governments are numerous and indefinite. . . . The powers reserved to the several States will extend to all the objects which, in the ordinary course of affairs, concern the lives, liberties, and properties of the people, and the internal order, improve-ment, and prosperity of the State." The Federalist No. 45.

This federalist structure of joint sovereigns preserves to the people numer-ous advantages. It assures a decentralized government that will be more sen-sitive to the diverse needs of a heterogenous society; it increases opportunity for citizen involvement in democratic processes; it allows for more innovation and experimentation in government; and it makes government more respon-sive by putting the States in competition for a mobile citizenry. See generally McConnell, Federalism: Evaluating the Founders' Design, 54 U. Chi. L. Rev. 1484, 1491-1511 (1987).

Perhaps the principal benefit of the federalist system is a check on abuses of government power. "The 'constitutionally mandated balance of power' between the States and the Federal Government was adopted by the Framers to ensure the protection of 'our fundamental liberties.'" *Atascadero State Hospital v. Scanlon*, 473 U.S. 234, 242 (1985), quoting *Garcia v. San Antonio Metropolitan Transit Authority*, 469 U.S. 528, 572 (1985) (Powell, J., dissenting). Just as the separation and independence of the coordinate branches of the Federal Government serve to prevent the accumulation of excessive power in any one branch, a healthy balance of power between the States and the Federal Government will reduce the risk of tyranny and abuse from either front. Alexander Hamilton explained to the people of New York, perhaps opti-mistically, that the new federalist system would suppress completely "the attempts of the government to establish a tyranny":

> "[I]n a confederacy the people, without exaggeration, may be said to be entirely the masters of their own fate. Power being almost always the rival of power, the general government will at all times stand ready to check the usurpations of

the state governments, and these will have the same disposition towards the general government. The people, by throwing themselves into either scale, will infallibly make it preponderate. If their rights are invaded by either, they can make use of the other as the instrument of redress." The Federalist No. 28.

James Madison made much the same point:

"In a single republic, all the power surrendered by the people is submitted to the administration of a single government; and the usurpations are guarded against by a division of the government into distinct and separate departments. In the compound republic of America, the power surrendered by the people is first divided between two distinct governments, and then the portion allotted to each subdivided among distinct and separate departments. Hence a double security arises to the rights of the people. The different governments will control each other, at the same time that each will be controlled by itself." *Id.*, No. 51.

One fairly can dispute whether our federalist system has been quite as successful in checking government abuse as Hamilton promised, but there is no doubt about the design. If this "double security" is to be effective, there must be a proper balance between the States and the Federal Government. These twin powers will act as mutual restraints only if both are credible. In the tension between federal and state power lies the promise of liberty.

The Federal Government holds a decided advantage in this delicate balance: the Supremacy Clause. U.S. Const., Art. VI, cl. 2. As long as it is acting within the powers granted it under the Constitution, Congress may impose its will on the States. Congress may legislate in areas traditionally regulated by the States. This is an extraordinary power in a federalist system. It is a power that we must assume Congress does not exercise lightly.

The present case concerns a state constitutional provision through which the people of Missouri establish a qualification for those who sit as their judges. This provision goes beyond an area traditionally regulated by the States; it is a decision of the most fundamental sort for a sovereign entity. Through the structure of its government, and the character of those who exercise government authority, a State defines itself as a sovereign. "It is obviously essential to the independence of the States, and to their peace and tranquility, that their power to prescribe the qualifications of their own officers . . . should be exclusive, and free from external interference, except so far as plainly provided by the Constitution of the United States." *Taylor v. Beckham*, 178 U.S. 548, 570-571 (1900). . . .

Congressional interference with this decision of the people of Missouri, defining their constitutional officers, would upset the usual constitutional balance of federal and state powers. For this reason, "it is incumbent upon the federal courts to be certain of Congress' intent before finding that federal law overrides" this balance. *Atascadero State Hospital v. Scanlon*, 473 U.S. 234, 243 (1985). We explained recently:

"[I]f Congress intends to alter the 'usual constitutional balance between the States and the Federal Government,' it must make its intention to do so 'unmistakably clear in the language of the statute.'" *Atascadero, supra*, 473 U.S., at 242. . . .

This plain statement rule is nothing more than an acknowledgment that the States retain substantial sovereign powers under our constitutional scheme, powers with which Congress does not readily interfere.

In a recent line of authority, we have . . . recognized explicitly the States' constitutional power to establish the qualifications for those who would govern:

> "Just as 'the Framers of the Constitution intended the States to keep for themselves, as provided in the Tenth Amendment, the power to regulate elections,' *Oregon v. Mitchell*, 400 U.S. 112, 124-125 (1970) . . . , "[e]ach State has the power to prescribe the qualifications of its officers and the manner in which they shall be chosen." *Boyd v. Thayer*, 143 U.S. 135, 161 (1892). . . . Such power inheres in the State by virtue of its obligation, already noted above, 'to preserve the basic conception of a political community.' *Dunn v. Blumstein*, 405 U.S. [330, 344 (1972)]. And this power and responsibility of the State applies, not only to the qualifications of voters, but also to persons holding state elective and important nonelective executive, legislative, and judicial positions, for officers who participate directly in the formulation, execution, or review of broad public policy perform functions that go to the heart of representative government." [*Sugarman v. Dougall*, 413 U.S. 634, 647 (1973).] . . .

These cases stand in recognition of the authority of the people of the States to determine the qualifications of their most important government officials. . . . It is a power reserved to the States under the Tenth Amendment and guaranteed them by that provision of the Constitution under which the United States "guarantee[s] to every State in this Union a Republican Form of Government." U.S. Const., Art. IV, §4.

The authority of the people of the States to determine the qualifications of their government officials is, of course, not without limit. Other constitutional provisions, most notably the Fourteenth Amendment, proscribe certain qualifications; our review of citizenship requirements under the political function exception is less exacting, but it is not absent. Here, we must decide what Congress did in extending the ADEA to the States, pursuant to its powers under the Commerce Clause. . . . As against Congress' powers "[t]o regulate Commerce . . . among the several States," U.S. Const., Art. I, §8, cl. 3, the authority of the people of the States to determine the qualifications of their government officials may be inviolate.

We are constrained in our ability to consider the limits that the state-federal balance places on Congress' powers under the Commerce Clause. See *Garcia v. San Antonio Metropolitan Transit Authority*, 469 U.S. 528 (1985) (declining to review limitations placed on Congress' Commerce Clause powers by our federal system). But there is no need to do so if we hold that the ADEA does not apply to state judges. Application of the plain statement rule thus may avoid a potential constitutional problem. Indeed, inasmuch as this Court in *Garcia* has left primarily to the political process the protection of the States against intrusive exercises of Congress' Commerce Clause powers, we must be absolutely certain that Congress intended such an exercise. "[T]o give the state-displacing weight of federal law to mere congressional *ambiguity* would evade the very procedure for lawmaking on which *Garcia* relied to protect states' interests." L. Tribe, American Constitutional Law §6-25, p. 480 (2d ed. 1988). . . .

In 1974, Congress extended the substantive provisions of the ADEA to include the States as employers. Pub. L. 93-259, §28(a), 88 Stat. 74, 29 U.S.C. §630(b)(2). At the same time, Congress amended the definition of "employee" to exclude all elected and most high-ranking government officials. Under the Act, as amended:

> "The term 'employee' means an individual employed by any employer except that the term 'employee' shall not include any person elected to public office in any State or political subdivision of any State by the qualified voters thereof, or any person chosen by such officer to be on such officer's personal staff, or an appointee on the policymaking level or an immediate adviser with respect to the exercise of the constitutional or legal powers of the office." 29 U.S.C. §630(f). . . .

"[A]ppointee at the policymaking level," particularly in the context of the other exceptions that surround it, is an odd way for Congress to exclude judges; a plain statement that judges are not "employees" would seem the most efficient phrasing. But in this case we are not looking for a plain statement that judges are excluded. We will not read the ADEA to cover state judges unless Congress has made it clear that judges are *included*. This does not mean that the Act must mention judges explicitly, though it does not. . . . Rather, it must be plain to anyone reading the Act that it covers judges. In the context of a statute that plainly excludes most important state public officials, "appointee on the policymaking level" is sufficiently broad that we cannot conclude that the statute plainly covers appointed state judges. Therefore, it does not. . . .

In light of the ADEA's clear exclusion of most important public officials, it is at least ambiguous whether Congress intended that appointed judges nonetheless be included. In the face of such ambiguity, we will not attribute to Congress an intent to intrude on state governmental functions regardless of whether Congress acted pursuant to its Commerce Clause powers or §5 of the Fourteenth Amendment. . . .

The people of Missouri have established a qualification for those who would be their judges. It is their prerogative as citizens of a sovereign State to do so. [T]he ADEA [does not] prohibit[] . . . the choice they have made. . . .

JUSTICE WHITE, with whom JUSTICE STEVENS joins, concurring in part, dissenting in part, and concurring in the judgment.

I agree with the majority that . . . the Age Discrimination in Employment Act (ADEA) [does not] prohibit[] Missouri's mandatory retirement provision as applied to petitioners. . . . [But] I cannot agree with [the majority's] "plain statement" rule. . . .

The only question is whether petitioners fall within the definition of "employee" in the Act, §630(f), which contains exceptions for elected officials and certain appointed officials. If petitioners *are* "employee[s]," Missouri's mandatory retirement provision clearly conflicts with the antidiscrimination provisions of the ADEA. Indeed, we have noted that the "policies and substantive provisions of the [ADEA] apply with especial force in the case of mandatory retirement provisions." *Western Air Lines, Inc. v. Criswell*, 472 U.S. 400, 410 (1985). Pre-emption therefore is automatic, since "state law is pre-empted to the extent that it actually conflicts with federal law." *Pacific Gas & Elec. Co. v. State Energy Resources Conservation and Development Comm'n*, 461 U.S. 190, 204 (1983). The majority's federalism concerns are irrelevant to such "actual conflict" pre-emption. " 'The relative importance to the State of its own law is not material when there is a conflict with a valid federal law, for the Framers of our Constitution provided that the federal law must prevail.' " *Fidelity Federal Sav. & Loan Assn. v. De la Cuesta*, 458 U.S. 141, 153 (1982), quoting *Free v. Bland*, 369 U.S. 663, 666 (1962).

While acknowledging this principle of federal legislative supremacy, the majority nevertheless imposes upon Congress a "plain statement" requirement. The majority claims to derive this requirement from the plain statement approach developed in our Eleventh Amendment cases, see, *e.g., Atascadero State Hospital v. Scanlon*, 473 U.S. 234, 243 (1985). . . . The issue in . . . *Atascadero* . . . was whether States could be sued under §504 of the Rehabilitation Act of 1973, 29 U.S.C. §794. . . . In the present case, by contrast, Congress has expressly extended the coverage of the ADEA to the States and their employees. Its intention to regulate age discrimination by States is thus "unmistakably clear in the language of the statute." *Atascadero, supra*, 473 U.S., at 242. . . .

The majority's plain statement rule is not only unprecedented, it directly contravenes our decisions in *Garcia v. San Antonio Metropolitan Transit Authority*, 469 U.S. 528 (1985), and *South Carolina v. Baker*, 485 U.S. 505 (1988). In those cases we made it clear "that States must find their protection from congressional regulation through the national political process, not through judicially defined spheres of unregulable state activity." *Id.*, at 512. We also rejected as "unsound in principle and unworkable in practice" any test for state immunity that requires a judicial determination of which state activities are " 'traditional,' " " 'integral,' " or " 'necessary.' " *Garcia, supra*, 469 U.S., at 546. The majority disregards those decisions in its attempt to carve out areas of state activity that will receive special protection from federal legislation.

The majority's approach is also unsound because it will serve only to confuse the law. First, the majority fails to explain the scope of its rule. Is the rule limited to federal regulation of the qualifications of state officials? Or does it apply more broadly to the regulation of any "state governmental functions"? Second, the majority does not explain its requirement that Congress' intent to regulate a particular state activity be "plain to anyone reading [the federal statute]." Does that mean that it is now improper to look to the purpose or history of a federal statute in determining the scope of the statute's limitations on state activities? If so, the majority's rule is completely inconsistent with our pre-emption jurisprudence. . . . The vagueness of the majority's rule undoubtedly will lead States to assert that various federal statutes no longer apply to a wide variety of state activities if Congress has not expressly referred to those activities in the statute. Congress, in turn, will be forced to draft long and detailed lists of which particular state functions it meant to regulate. . . .

The majority asserts that its plain statement rule is helpful in avoiding a "potential constitutional problem." It is far from clear, however, why there would be a constitutional problem if the ADEA applied to state judges, in light of our decisions in *Garcia* and *Baker*, discussed above. As long as "the national political *process* did not operate in a defective manner, the Tenth Amendment is not implicated." *Baker, supra*, 485 U.S., at 513. There is no claim in this case that the political process by which the ADEA was extended to state employees was inadequate to protect the States from being "unduly burden[ed]" by the Federal Government. See *Garcia, supra*, 469 U.S., at 556. In any event, as discussed below, a straightforward analysis of the ADEA's definition of "employee" reveals that the ADEA does not apply here. Thus, even if there were potential constitutional problems in extending the ADEA to state judges, the majority's proposed plain statement rule would not be necessary to avoid them in this case. Indeed, because this case can be decided purely on the basis of statutory interpretation, the majority's announcement of its plain statement rule, which purportedly is derived from constitutional principles, *violates* our general practice of avoiding the unnecessary resolution of constitutional issues. . . .

I would hold that petitioners are excluded from the coverage of the ADEA because they are "appointee[s] on the policymaking level" under 29 U.S.C. §630(f).

JUSTICE BLACKMUN, with whom JUSTICE MARSHALL joins, dissenting.

For the reasons well stated by Justice White, the question we must resolve is whether appointed Missouri state judges are excluded from the general *prohibition* of mandatory retirement that Congress established in the . . . ADEA. I part company with Justice White, however, in his determination that appointed state judges fall within the narrow exclusion from ADEA coverage that Congress created for an "appointee on the policymaking level."

POINTS FOR DISCUSSION

1. In analyzing whether federal courts have a common law jurisdiction relative to state governance prerogatives, Tucker appealed to the rights of "sovereign and independent states," which may not be abridged "by *implication* only." In light of the Founding-era materials that you read in Chapter 1, did Tucker properly treat the states as "sovereign and independent states" in this context?

2. The clear statement rule applied in *Nicholls* and *Gregory* does not derive from any express constitutional text. In *Nicholls*, the Supreme Court of Pennsylvania stated, citing Tucker, that "[i]t has been truly said, that the constitution of the *United States*, considered as *federal*, is to be construed *strictly* in all cases, when the antecedent rights of a state may be drawn in question." Recall the tension you studied in Chapter 1 between Tucker's rule of strict construction and Marshall Court constructions of the Necessary and Proper Clause. Did the *Gregory* Court implicitly adopt Tucker's rule of strict construction? Does the structure of the Constitution support judicial application of such a rule?

3. In *Gregory*, the Court explained that a federal prohibition on mandatory retirement ages for state judges would go "beyond an area traditionally regulated by the States; it is a decision of the most fundamental sort for a sovereign entity." Accordingly, it would "upset the usual constitutional balance of federal and state powers." In *Garcia v. San Antonio Metropolitan Transit Authority*, 469 U.S. 528 (1985), however, the Court explained that Congress's enumerated powers are not limited by such doctrines of sovereignty. Thus, how does a federal prohibition on mandatory retirement of state judges "upset the usual constitutional balance of federal and state powers"?

4. The *Gregory* Court explained, moreover, that "[i]nasmuch as this Court in *Garcia* has left primarily to the political process the protection of the States against intrusive exercises of Congress' Commerce Clause powers, we must be absolutely certain that Congress intended such an exercise." Does *Gregory*'s clear statement rule reinforce the political safeguards of federalism by ensuring that Congress has squarely considered the effect of a federal regulation on state autonomy and interests? Or does it unduly burden Congress's ability to regulate matters within the federal legislative power?

5. The *Gregory* Court, citing the article by Professor Michael McConnell that you read in Chapter 3, states "[t]his federalist structure of joint sovereigns preserves to the people numerous advantages." In the Court's view, "[p]erhaps the principal benefit of the federalist system is a check on abuses of government power." Although "[o]ne fairly can dispute whether our federalist system has been quite as successful in checking government abuse as Hamilton promised, . . . there is no doubt about the design. If this 'double security' is to be effective, there must be a proper balance between the States and the Federal Government." What role do these statements about the benefits of the federal structure play in the Court's reasoning? What role should they play?

C. ANTI-COMMANDEERING PRINCIPLES

In 1992, the Supreme Court addressed what it described as "perhaps our oldest question of constitutional law" — whether Congress may compel state legislatures to enact a regulatory program to serve federal policies. On the basis of constitutional structure and history, the Court held in *New York v. United States*, 505 U.S. 144 (1992), that Congress lacks such power. In 1997, the Court likewise held in *Printz v. United States*, 521 U.S. 898 (1997), that Congress lacks power to require state executives to administer a federal regulatory program. Again, the Court largely rested its decision upon historical practice and constitutional structure. In both of these cases, the Court distinguished its 1947 decision in *Testa v. Katt*, 330 U.S. 386 (1947), which held that the Constitution generally requires state courts to adjudicate federally created actions. It is useful to read the Court's brief opinion in *Testa* before *New York* and *Printz*.

As you read *Testa*, *New York*, and *Printz*, consider these questions:

- By what methods of interpretation does the Court resolve the constitutional questions before it?

- What values do the Court's decisions advance?
- Do these cases involve the same questions of judicial deference to Congress that the commerce, spending, and §5 cases that you read in Chapter 5 involved?

TESTA v. KATT

330 U.S. 386 (1947)

Mr. JUSTICE BLACK delivered the opinion of the Court.

Section 205(e) . . . of the Emergency Price Control Act provides that a buyer of goods above the prescribed ceiling price may sue the seller "in any court of competent jurisdiction" for not more than three times the amount of the overcharge plus costs and a reasonable attorney's fee. Section 205(c) . . . provides that federal district courts shall have jurisdiction of such suits "concurrently with State and Territorial courts." . . .

The respondent was in the automobile business in Providence, Providence County, Rhode Island. In 1944 he sold an automobile to petitioner Testa, who also resides in Providence, for $1100, $210 above the ceiling price. The petitioner later filed this suit against respondent in the State District Court in Providence. Recovery was sought under §205(e). The court awarded a judgment of treble damages and costs to petitioner. . . . On appeal, the State Supreme Court reversed. It interpreted §205(e) to be "a penal statute in the international sense." It held that an action for violation of §205(e) could not be maintained in the courts of that State. . . . The State Supreme Court rested its holding on its earlier decision in *Robinson v. Norato*, 71 R.I. 256 (1945), in which it had reasoned that: A state need not enforce the penal laws of a government which is foreign in the international sense. . . . Whether state courts may decline to enforce federal laws on these grounds is a question of great importance. . . .

For the purposes of this case, we assume, without deciding, that §205(e) is a penal statute in the "public international," "private international," or any other sense. . . . [W]e cannot accept the basic premise on which the Rhode Island Supreme Court held that it has no more obligation to enforce a valid penal law of the United States than it has to enforce a penal law of another state or a foreign country. Such a broad assumption flies in the face of the fact that the States of the Union constitute a nation. It disregards the purpose and effect of Article VI of the Constitution which provides: "This Constitution, and the Laws of the United States which shall be made in Pursuance thereof; and all Treaties made, or which shall be made, under the Authority of the United States, shall be the supreme Law of the Land; and the Judges in every State shall be bound thereby, any Thing in the Constitution or Laws of any State to the Contrary notwithstanding." . . .

[S]tate courts do not bear the same relation to the United States that they do to foreign countries. The first Congress that convened after the Constitution was adopted conferred jurisdiction upon the state courts to enforce important federal civil laws, . . . and succeeding Congresses conferred on the states jurisdiction over federal crimes and actions for penalties and forfeitures. . . .

Enforcement of federal laws by state courts did not go unchallenged. Violent public controversies existed throughout the first part of the Nineteenth Century until the 1860's concerning the extent of the constitutional supremacy of the Federal Government. During that period there were instances in which this Court and state courts broadly questioned the power and duty of state courts to exercise their jurisdiction to enforce United States civil and penal statutes or the power of the Federal Government to require them to do so. . . . But after the fundamental issues over the extent of federal supremacy had been resolved by war, this Court took occasion in 1876 to review the phase of the controversy concerning the relationship of state courts to the Federal Government. *Claflin v. Houseman*, 93 U.S. 130. . . . It repudiated the assumption that federal laws can be considered by the states as though they were laws emanating from a foreign sovereign. Its teaching is that the Constitution and the laws passed pursuant to it are the supreme laws of the land, binding alike upon states, courts, and the people, "any thing in the Constitution or Laws of any State to the Contrary notwithstanding." . . .

The *Claflin* opinion thus answered most of the arguments theretofore advanced against the power and duty of state courts to enforce federal penal laws. And since that decision, the remaining areas of doubt have been steadily narrowed. . . . There have been statements in cases concerned with the obligation of states to give full faith and credit to the proceedings of sister states which suggested a theory contrary to that pronounced in the *Claflin* opinion. . . . But when in *Mondou v. New York, N.H. & H.R. Co.*, 223 U.S. 1 [(1912)], this Court was presented with a case testing the power and duty of states to enforce federal laws, it found the solution in the broad principles announced in the *Claflin* opinion.

The precise question in the *Mondou* case was whether rights arising under the Federal Employers' Liability Act could "be enforced, as of right, in the courts of the states when their jurisdiction, as fixed by local laws, is adequate to the occasion. . . ." Id. at 46. . . . [T]his Court held that the Connecticut court could not decline to entertain the action. The contention that enforcement of the congressionally created right was contrary to Connecticut policy was answered as follows:

> "The suggestion that the act of Congress is not in harmony with the policy of the State, and therefore that the courts of the state are free to decline jurisdiction, is quite inadmissible, because it presupposes what in legal contemplation does not exist. When Congress, in the exertion of the power confided to it by the Constitution, adopted that act, it spoke for all the people and all the States, and thereby established a policy for all. That policy is as much the policy of Connecticut as if the act had emanated from its own legislature, and should be respected accordingly in the courts of the State." [Id.] at 57.

So here, the fact that Rhode Island has an established policy against enforcement by its courts of statutes of other states and the United States which it deems penal, cannot be accepted as a "valid excuse." . . . For the policy of the federal Act is the prevailing policy in every state. . . .

It is conceded that this same type of claim arising under Rhode Island law would be enforced by that State's courts. . . . Thus the Rhode Island courts have jurisdiction adequate and appropriate under established local law to adjudicate this action. . . . Under these circumstances the State courts are not free to refuse enforcement of petitioners' claim. . . .

NEW YORK v. UNITED STATES

505 U.S. 144 (1992)

JUSTICE O'CONNOR delivered the opinion of the Court.

These cases implicate one of our Nation's newest problems of public policy and perhaps our oldest question of constitutional law. The public policy issue involves the disposal of radioactive waste: In these cases, we address the constitutionality of three provisions of the Low-Level Radioactive Waste Policy Amendments Act of 1985. The constitutional question is as old as the Constitution: It consists of discerning the proper division of authority between the Federal Government and the States. We conclude that while Congress has substantial power under the Constitution to encourage the States to provide for the disposal of the radioactive waste generated within their borders, the Constitution does not confer upon Congress the ability simply to compel the States to do so. . . .

I

[T]he Low-Level Radioactive Waste Policy Amendments Act of 1985 . . . directs: "Each State shall be responsible for providing, either by itself or in cooperation with other States, for the disposal of . . . low-level radioactive waste generated within the State," 42 U.S.C. §2021c(a)(1)(A). . . . The Act provides three types of incentives to encourage the States to comply with their statutory obligation to provide for the disposal of waste generated within their borders.

1. *Monetary incentives.* [Under these incentives, Congress authorized states with disposal sites to impose a surcharge on radioactive waste received from other states. The Secretary of Energy would collect a portion of this surcharge and distribute the funds to states achieving certain milestones relating to the disposal of waste.] . . .

2. *Access incentives.* [Under these incentives, Congress authorized states with disposal sites gradually to increase the cost of access to the sites, and then to deny access altogether, to radioactive waste generated in states not meeting federal deadlines.] . . .

3. *The take title provision.* [Under this provision, Congress offered state governments a choice of regulating for the disposal of radioactive waste according to the instructions of Congress, or taking title to and possession of the waste.] . . .

Petitioners — the State of New York and . . . two counties — filed this suit against the United States in 1990. They sought a declaratory judgment that the Act is inconsistent with the Tenth . . . Amendment[] to the Constitution. . . .

II

A

In 1788, in the course of explaining to the citizens of New York why the recently drafted Constitution provided for federal courts, Alexander Hamilton observed: "The erection of a new government, whatever care or wisdom may distinguish the work, cannot fail to originate questions of intricacy and nicety; and these may, in a particular manner, be expected to flow from the establishment of a constitution founded upon the total or partial incorporation of a number of distinct sovereignties." The Federalist No. 82. Hamilton's prediction has proved quite accurate. While no one disputes the proposition that "[t]he Constitution created a Federal Government of limited powers," *Gregory v. Ashcroft*, 501 U.S. 452, 457 (1991); and while the Tenth Amendment makes explicit that "[t]he powers not delegated to the United States by the Constitution, nor prohibited by it to the States, are reserved to the States respectively, or to the people"; the task of ascertaining the constitutional line between federal and state power has given rise to many of the Court's most difficult and celebrated cases. . . .

These questions can be viewed in either of two ways. In some cases the Court has inquired whether an Act of Congress is authorized by one of the powers delegated to Congress in Article I of the Constitution. See, *e.g.*, *McCulloch v. Maryland*, 4 Wheat. 316 (1819). In other cases the Court has sought to determine whether an Act of Congress invades the province of state sovereignty reserved by the Tenth Amendment. See, *e.g.*, *Garcia v. San Antonio Metropolitan Transit Authority*, 469 U.S. 528 (1985). In a case like these, involving the division of authority between federal and state governments, the two inquiries are mirror images of each other. If a power is delegated to Congress in the Constitution, the Tenth Amendment expressly disclaims any reservation of that power to the States; if a power is an attribute of state sovereignty reserved by the Tenth Amendment, it is necessarily a power the Constitution has not conferred on Congress.

It is in this sense that the Tenth Amendment "states but a truism that all is retained which has not been surrendered." *United States v. Darby*, 312 U.S. 100, 124 (1941). . . . Congress exercises its conferred powers subject to the limitations contained in the Constitution. Thus, for example, under the Commerce Clause Congress may regulate publishers engaged in interstate commerce, but Congress is constrained in the exercise of that power by the First Amendment. The Tenth Amendment likewise restrains the power of Congress, but this limit is not derived from the text of the Tenth Amendment itself, which, as we have discussed, is essentially a tautology. Instead, the Tenth Amendment confirms that the power of the Federal Government is subject to limits that may, in a given instance, reserve power to the States. The Tenth Amendment thus directs us to determine, as in this case, whether an incident of state sovereignty is protected by a limitation on an Article I power.

The benefits of this federal structure have been extensively cataloged elsewhere, see, *e.g.*, McConnell, Federalism: Evaluating the Founders' Design, 54 U. Chi. L. Rev. 1484, 1491-1511 (1987), but they need not concern us here. Our task would be the same even if one could prove that federalism secured no advantages to anyone. It consists not of devising our preferred system of government, but of understanding and applying the framework set forth in the Constitution. "The question is not what power the Federal Government ought to have but what powers in fact have been given by the people." *United States v. Butler*, 297 U.S. 1, 63 (1936).

This framework has been sufficiently flexible over the past two centuries to allow for enormous changes in the nature of government. The Federal Government undertakes activities today that would have been unimaginable to the Framers in two senses; first, because the Framers would not have conceived that *any* government would conduct such activities; and second, because the Framers would not have believed that the *Federal* Government, rather than the States, would assume such responsibilities. Yet the powers conferred upon the Federal Government by the Constitution were phrased in language broad enough to allow for the expansion of the Federal Government's role. Among the provisions of the Constitution that have been particularly important in this regard, three concern us here.

First, the Constitution allocates to Congress the power "[t]o regulate Commerce . . . among the several States." . . . The volume of interstate commerce and the range of commonly accepted objects of government regulation have, however, expanded considerably in the last 200 years, and the regulatory authority of Congress has expanded along with them. As interstate commerce has become ubiquitous, activities once considered purely local have come to have effects on the national economy, and have accordingly come within the scope of Congress' commerce power. See, *e.g.*, *Katzenbach v. McClung*, 379 U.S. 294 (1964); *Wickard v. Filburn*, 317 U.S. 111 (1942).

Second, the Constitution authorizes Congress "to pay the Debts and provide for the . . . general Welfare of the United States." As conventional notions of the proper objects of government spending have changed over the years, so has the ability of Congress to "fix the terms on which it shall disburse federal money to the States." *Pennhurst State School and Hospital v. Halderman*, 451 U.S. 1, 17 (1981). Compare, *e.g.*, *United States v. Butler*, *supra*, 297 U.S., at 72-75 (spending power does not authorize Congress to subsidize farmers), with *South Dakota v. Dole*, 483 U.S. 203 (1987) (spending power permits Congress to condition highway funds on States' adoption of minimum drinking age). While the spending power is "subject to several general restrictions articulated in our cases," *id.*, at 207, these restrictions have not been so severe as to prevent the regulatory authority of Congress from generally keeping up with the growth of the federal budget.

The Court's broad construction of Congress' power under the Commerce and Spending Clauses has of course been guided, as it has with respect to Congress' power generally, by the Constitution's Necessary and Proper Clause, which authorizes Congress "[t]o make all Laws which shall be necessary and proper for carrying into Execution the foregoing Powers." . . .

Finally, the Constitution provides that "the Laws of the United States . . . shall be the supreme Law of the Land . . . any Thing in the Constitution or Laws of any State to the Contrary notwithstanding." U.S. Const., Art. VI, cl. 2. As the Federal Government's willingness to exercise power within the confines of the Constitution has grown, the authority of the States has correspondingly diminished to the extent that federal and state policies have conflicted. We have observed that the Supremacy Clause gives the Federal Government "a decided advantage in th[e] delicate balance" the Constitution strikes between state and federal power. *Gregory v. Ashcroft*, 501 U.S., at 460.

The actual scope of the Federal Government's authority with respect to the States has changed over the years, therefore, but the constitutional structure underlying and limiting that authority has not. . . .

B

Most of our recent cases interpreting the Tenth Amendment have concerned the authority of Congress to subject state governments to generally applicable laws. The Court's jurisprudence in this area has traveled an unsteady path. See *National League of Cities v. Usery*, 426 U.S. 833 (1976) (state employers are *not* subject to Fair Labor Standards Act); *Garcia v. San Antonio Metropolitan Transit Authority*, 469 U.S. 528 (1985) (overruling *National League of Cities*). This litigation presents no occasion to apply or revisit the holdings of any of these cases, as this is not a case in which Congress has subjected a State to the same legislation applicable to private parties.

This litigation instead concerns the circumstances under which Congress may use the States as implements of regulation; that is, whether Congress may direct or otherwise motivate the States to regulate in a particular field or a particular way. Our cases have established a few principles that guide our resolution of the issue.

1

As an initial matter, Congress may not simply "commandee[r] the legislative processes of the States by directly compelling them to enact and enforce a federal regulatory program." [Here, the Court discussed two cases, *Hodel v. Virginia Surface Mining & Reclamation Assn., Inc.*, 452 U.S. 264, 288 (1981), and *FERC v. Mississippi*, 456 U.S. 742 (1982).] . . .

Indeed, the question whether the Constitution should permit Congress to employ state governments as regulatory agencies was a topic of lively debate among the Framers. Under the Articles of Confederation, Congress lacked the authority in most respects to govern the people directly. . . .

The inadequacy of this governmental structure was responsible in part for the Constitutional Convention. Alexander Hamilton observed: "The great and radical vice in the construction of the existing Confederation is in the principle of Legislation for States or Governments, in their Corporate or Collective Capacities, and as contradistinguished from the Individuals of whom they consist." The Federalist No. 15. As Hamilton saw it, "we must resolve to incorporate into our plan those ingredients which may be considered as forming the characteristic difference between a league and a government; we must extend the authority of the Union to the persons of the citizens—the only proper objects of government." The new National Government "must carry its agency to the persons of the citizens. It must stand in need of no intermediate legislations. . . . The government of the Union, like that of each State, must be able to address itself immediately to the hopes and fears of individuals."

The Convention generated a great number of proposals for the structure of the new Government, but two quickly took center stage. Under the Virginia Plan, as first introduced by Edmund Randolph, Congress would exercise legislative authority directly upon individuals, without employing the States as intermediaries. 1 Records of the Federal Convention of 1787, p. 21 (M. Farrand ed. 1911). Under the New Jersey Plan, as first introduced by William Paterson, Congress would continue to require the approval of the States before legislating, as it had under the Articles of Confederation. 1 *id.*, at 243-244. These two plans underwent various revisions as the Convention progressed, but they remained the two primary options discussed by the delegates. One frequently expressed objection to the New Jersey Plan was that it might require the Federal Government to coerce the States into implementing legislation. As Randolph explained the distinction, "[t]he true question is whether we shall adhere to the federal plan [i.e., the New Jersey Plan], or introduce the national plan. The insufficiency of the former has been fully displayed. . . . There are but two modes, by which the end of a Gen[eral] Gov[ernment] can be attained: the 1st is by coercion as proposed by Mr. P[aterson's] plan[, the 2nd] by real legislation as prop[osed] by the other plan. Coercion [is] *impracticable, expensive, cruel to individuals.* . . . We must resort therefore to a national *Legislation over individuals.*" 1 *id.*, at 255-256 (emphasis in original). Madison echoed this view: "The practicability of making laws, with coercive sanctions, for the States as political bodies, had been exploded on all hands." 2 *id.*, at 9.

Under one preliminary draft of what would become the New Jersey Plan, state governments would occupy a position relative to Congress similar to that contemplated by the Act at issue in these cases: "[T]he laws of the United States ought, as far as may be consistent with the common interests of the Union, to be carried into execution by the judiciary and executive officers of the respective states, wherein the execution thereof is required." 3 *id.*, at 616. This idea apparently never even progressed so far as to be debated by the delegates, as contemporary accounts of the Convention do not mention any such discussion. The delegates' many descriptions of the Virginia and New Jersey Plans speak only in general terms about whether Congress was to derive its authority from the people or from the States, and whether it was to issue directives to individuals or to States. See 1 *id.*, at 260-280.

In the end, the Convention opted for a Constitution in which Congress would exercise its legislative authority directly over individuals rather than over States; for a variety of reasons, it rejected the New Jersey Plan in favor of the Virginia Plan. 1 *id.*, at 313. This choice was made clear to the subsequent state ratifying conventions. Oliver Ellsworth, a member of the Connecticut delegation in Philadelphia, explained the distinction to his State's convention: "This Constitution does not attempt to coerce sovereign bodies, states, in their political capacity. . . . But this legal coercion singles out the . . . individual." 2 J. Elliot, Debates on the Federal Constitution 197 (2d ed. 1863). Charles Pinckney, another delegate at the Constitutional Convention, emphasized to the South Carolina House of Representatives that in Philadelphia "the necessity of having a government which should at once operate upon the people, and not upon the states, was conceived to be indispensable by every delegation present." 4 *id.*, at 256. Rufus King, one of Massachusetts' delegates, returned home to support ratification by recalling the Commonwealth's unhappy experience under the Articles of Confederation and arguing: "Laws, to be effective, therefore, must not be laid on states, but upon individuals." 2 *id.*, at 56. At New York's convention, Hamilton (another delegate in Philadelphia) exclaimed: "But can we believe that one state will ever suffer itself to be used as an instrument of coercion? The thing is a dream; it is impossible. Then we are brought to this dilemma — either a federal standing army is to enforce the requisitions, or the federal treasury is left without supplies, and the government without support. What, sir, is the cure for this great evil? Nothing, but to enable the national laws to operate on individuals, in the same manner as those of the states do." 2 *id.*, at 233. At North Carolina's convention, Samuel Spencer recognized that "all the laws of the Confederation were binding on the states in their political capacities, . . . but now the thing is entirely different. The laws of Congress will be binding on individuals." 4 *id.*, at 153.

In providing for a stronger central government, therefore, the Framers explicitly chose a Constitution that confers upon Congress the power to regulate individuals, not States. . . .

2

This is not to say that Congress lacks the ability to encourage a State to regulate in a particular way, or that Congress may not hold out incentives to the States as a method of influencing a State's policy choices. Our cases have identified a variety of methods, short of outright coercion, by which Congress may urge a State to adopt a legislative program consistent with federal interests. Two of these methods are of particular relevance here.

First, under Congress' spending power, "Congress may attach conditions on the receipt of federal funds." *South Dakota v. Dole*, 483 U.S., at 206. . . . Second, where Congress has the authority to regulate private activity under the Commerce Clause, we have recognized Congress' power to offer States the choice of regulating that activity according to federal standards or having state law pre-empted by federal regulation. This arrangement . . . has been termed "a program of cooperative federalism," *Hodel, supra*, 452 U.S., at 289, [and] is replicated in numerous federal statutory schemes. . . .

By either of these methods, as by any other permissible method of encouraging a State to conform to federal policy choices, the residents of the State retain the ultimate decision as to whether or not the State will comply. . . . Where Congress encourages state regulation rather than compelling it, state governments remain responsive to the local electorate's preferences; state officials remain accountable to the people.

By contrast, where the Federal Government compels States to regulate, the accountability of both state and federal officials is diminished. If the citizens of New York, for example, do not consider that making provision for the disposal of radioactive waste is in their best interest, they may elect state officials who share their view. That view can always be pre-empted under the Supremacy Clause if it is contrary to the national view, but in such a case it is the Federal Government that makes the decision in full view of the public, and it will be federal officials that suffer the consequences if the decision turns out to be detrimental or unpopular. But where the Federal Government directs the States to regulate, it may be state officials who will bear the brunt of public disapproval, while the federal officials who devised the regulatory program may remain insulated from the electoral ramifications of their decision. Accountability is thus diminished when, due to federal coercion, elected state officials cannot regulate in accordance with the views of the local electorate in matters not pre-empted by federal regulation.

With these principles in mind, we turn to the three challenged provisions of the Low-Level Radioactive Waste Policy Amendments Act of 1985.

III

Construed as a whole, the Act comprises three sets of "incentives" for the States to provide for the disposal of low level radioactive waste generated within their borders. We consider each in turn.

A

The first set of incentives works in three steps. First, Congress has authorized States with disposal sites to impose a surcharge on radioactive waste received from other States. Second, the Secretary of Energy collects a portion of this surcharge and places the money in an escrow account. Third, States achieving a series of milestones receive portions of this fund.

The first of these steps is an unexceptionable exercise of Congress' power to authorize the States to burden interstate commerce. While the Commerce Clause has long been understood to limit the States' ability to discriminate against interstate commerce, that limit may be lifted, as it has been here, by an expression of the "unambiguous intent" of Congress. . . .

The second step, the Secretary's collection of a percentage of the surcharge, is no more than a federal tax on interstate commerce, which petitioners do not claim to be an invalid exercise of either Congress' commerce or taxing power.

The third step is a conditional exercise of Congress' authority under the Spending Clause: Congress has placed conditions—the achievement of the milestones—on the receipt of federal funds. . . .

The Act's first set of incentives, in which Congress has conditioned grants to the States upon the States' attainment of a series of milestones, is thus well within the authority of Congress under the Commerce and Spending Clauses. Because the first set of incentives is supported by affirmative constitutional grants of power to Congress, it is not inconsistent with the Tenth Amendment.

B

In the second set of incentives, Congress has authorized States and regional compacts with disposal sites gradually to increase the cost of access to the sites, and then to deny access altogether, to radioactive waste generated in States that do not meet federal deadlines. . . .

The Act's second set of incentives thus represents a conditional exercise of Congress' commerce power, along the lines of those we have held to be within Congress' authority. As a result, the second set of incentives does not intrude on the sovereignty reserved to the States by the Tenth Amendment.

C

The take title provision is of a different character. This third so-called "incentive" offers States, as an alternative to regulating pursuant to Congress' direction, the option of taking title to and possession of the low level radioactive waste generated within their borders and becoming liable for all damages waste generators suffer as a result of the States' failure to do so promptly. In this provision, Congress has crossed the line distinguishing encouragement from coercion. . . .

The take title provision offers state governments a "choice" of either accepting ownership of waste or regulating according to the instructions of Congress. Respondents do not claim that the Constitution would authorize Congress to impose either option as a freestanding requirement. On one hand, the Constitution would not permit Congress simply to transfer radioactive waste from generators to state governments. Such a forced transfer, standing alone, would in principle be no different than a congressionally compelled subsidy from state governments to radioactive waste producers. The same is true of the provision requiring the States to become liable for the generators' damages. Standing alone, this provision would be indistinguishable from an Act of Congress directing the States to assume the liabilities of certain state residents. Either type of federal action would "commandeer" state governments into the service of federal regulatory purposes, and would for this reason be inconsistent with the Constitution's division of authority between federal and state governments. On the other hand, the second alternative held out to state governments — regulating pursuant to Congress' direction — would, standing alone, present a simple command to state governments to implement legislation enacted by Congress. As we have seen, the Constitution does not empower Congress to subject state governments to this type of instruction.

Because an instruction to state governments to take title to waste, standing alone, would be beyond the authority of Congress, and because a direct order to regulate, standing alone, would also be beyond the authority of Congress, it follows that Congress lacks the power to offer the States a choice between the two. . . .

No other federal statute has been cited which offers a state government no option other than that of implementing legislation enacted by Congress. Whether one views the take title provision as lying outside Congress' enumerated powers, or as infringing upon the core of state sovereignty reserved by the Tenth Amendment, the provision is inconsistent with the federal structure of our Government established by the Constitution.

IV

[T]he United States argues that the Constitution does, in some circumstances, permit federal directives to state governments. Various cases are cited for this proposition, but none support it. Some of these cases discuss the well established power of Congress to pass laws enforceable in state courts. See *Testa v. Katt*, 330 U.S. 386 (1947). These cases involve no more than an application of the Supremacy Clause's provision that federal law "shall be the supreme Law of the Land," enforceable in every State. More to the point, all

involve congressional regulation of individuals, not congressional requirements that States regulate. Federal statutes enforceable in state courts do, in
a sense, direct state judges to enforce them, but this sort of federal "direction"
of state judges is mandated by the text of the Supremacy Clause. No comparable constitutional provision authorizes Congress to command state legislatures to legislate. . . .

The sited state respondents focus their attention on the process by which
the Act was formulated. They correctly observe that public officials representing the State of New York lent their support to the Act's enactment. . . .
Respondents note that the Act embodies a bargain among the sited and unsited
States, a compromise to which New York was a willing participant and from
which New York has reaped much benefit. Respondents then pose what
appears at first to be a troubling question: How can a federal statute be
found an unconstitutional infringement of state sovereignty when state
officials consented to the statute's enactment?

The answer follows from an understanding of the fundamental purpose
served by our Government's federal structure. The Constitution does not protect the sovereignty of States for the benefit of the States or state governments
as abstract political entities, or even for the benefit of the public officials governing the States. To the contrary, the Constitution divides authority between
federal and state governments for the protection of individuals. State sovereignty is not just an end in itself: "Rather, federalism secures to citizens
the liberties that derive from the diffusion of sovereign power." *Coleman v.
Thompson*, 501 U.S. 722, 759 (1991) (Blackmun, J., dissenting). "Just as the
separation and independence of the coordinate branches of the Federal
Government serve to prevent the accumulation of excessive power in any
one branch, a healthy balance of power between the States and the Federal
Government will reduce the risk of tyranny and abuse from either front."
Gregory v. Ashcroft, 501 U.S., at 458 (1991).

Where Congress exceeds its authority relative to the States, therefore, the
departure from the constitutional plan cannot be ratified by the "consent" of
state officials. An analogy to the separation of powers among the branches
of the Federal Government clarifies this point. The Constitution's division
of power among the three branches is violated where one branch invades
the territory of another, whether or not the encroached-upon branch approves
the encroachment. . . . The constitutional authority of Congress cannot be
expanded by the "consent" of the governmental unit whose domain is thereby
narrowed, whether that unit is the Executive Branch or the States. . . .

VII

Some truths are so basic that, like the air around us, they are easily over-
looked. Much of the Constitution is concerned with setting forth the form of
our government, and the courts have traditionally invalidated measures
deviating from that form. The result may appear "formalistic" in a given
case to partisans of the measure at issue, because such measures are typically
the product of the era's perceived necessity. But the Constitution protects us
from our own best intentions: It divides power among sovereigns and among
branches of government precisely so that we may resist the temptation to

concentrate power in one location as an expedient solution to the crisis of the day. The shortage of disposal sites for radioactive waste is a pressing national problem, but a judiciary that licensed extraconstitutional government with each issue of comparable gravity would, in the long run, be far worse.

States are not mere political subdivisions of the United States. State governments are neither regional offices nor administrative agencies of the Federal Government. The positions occupied by state officials appear nowhere on the Federal Government's most detailed organizational chart. The Constitution instead "leaves to the several States a residuary and inviolable sovereignty," The Federalist No. 39, reserved explicitly to the States by the Tenth Amendment.

Whatever the outer limits of that sovereignty may be, one thing is clear: The Federal Government may not compel the States to enact or administer a federal regulatory program. The Constitution permits both the Federal Government and the States to enact legislation regarding the disposal of low level radioactive waste. The Constitution enables the Federal Government to preempt state regulation contrary to federal interests, and it permits the Federal Government to hold out incentives to the States as a means of encouraging them to adopt suggested regulatory schemes. It does not, however, authorize Congress simply to direct the States to provide for the disposal of the radioactive waste generated within their borders. While there may be many constitutional methods of achieving regional self-sufficiency in radioactive waste disposal, the method Congress has chosen is not one of them. . . .

Justice White, with whom Justice Blackmun and Justice Stevens join, concurring in part and dissenting in part. . . .

I

My disagreement with the Court's analysis begins at the basic descriptive level of how the legislation at issue in these cases came to be enacted. . . . The Low-Level Radioactive Waste Policy Act of 1980, and its amendatory 1985 Act, resulted from the efforts of state leaders to achieve a state-based set of remedies to the waste problem. They sought not federal pre-emption or intervention, but rather congressional sanction of interstate compromises they had reached. . . . Unlike legislation that directs action from the Federal Government to the States, the 1980 and 1985 Acts reflected hard-fought agreements among States as refereed by Congress. . . .

II

Congress could have pre-empted the field by directly regulating the disposal of this waste pursuant to its powers under the Commerce and Spending Clauses, but instead it *unanimously* assented to the States' request for congressional ratification of agreements to which they had acceded. As the floor statements of Members of Congress reveal, the States wished to take the lead in achieving a solution to this problem and agreed among themselves to the various incentives and penalties implemented by Congress to ensure adherence to the various deadlines and goals. The chief executives of the States proposed this approach, and I am unmoved by the Court's vehemence in taking away Congress' authority to sanction a recalcitrant unsited State now that New York has reaped the benefits of the sited States' concessions.

A

[T]he States — including New York — worked through their Governors to petition Congress for the 1980 and 1985 Acts. . . . [T]hese statutes are best understood as the products of collective state action, rather than as impositions placed on States by the Federal Government. . . .

The State should be estopped from asserting the unconstitutionality of a provision that seeks merely to ensure that, after deriving substantial advantages from the 1985 Act, New York in fact must live up to its bargain by establishing an in-state low-level radioactive waste facility or assuming liability for its failure to act. . . .

B

Even were New York not to be estopped from challenging the take title provision's constitutionality, I am convinced that, seen as a term of an agreement entered into between the several States, this measure proves to be less constitutionally odious than the Court opines. . . . [T]o say, as the Court does, that the incursion on state sovereignty "cannot be ratified by the 'consent' of state officials," is flatly wrong. In a case involving a congressional ratification statute to an interstate compact, the Court upheld a provision that Tennessee and Missouri had waived their immunity from suit. Over their objection, the Court held that "[t]he States who are parties to the compact by accepting it *and acting under it assume the conditions* that Congress under the Constitution attached." *Petty v. Tennessee-Missouri Bridge Comm'n*, 359 U.S. 275, 281-282 (1959) (emphasis added). In so holding, the Court determined that a State may be found to have waived a fundamental aspect of its sovereignty — the right to be immune from suit — in the formation of an interstate compact even when in subsequent litigation it expressly denied its waiver. . . .

III

The Court announces that it has no occasion to revisit such decisions as . . . *National League of Cities v. Usery*, 426 U.S. 833 (1976), because "this is not a case in which Congress has subjected a State to the same legislation applicable to private parties." Although this statement sends the welcome signal that the Court does not intend to cut a wide swath through our recent Tenth Amendment precedents, it nevertheless is unpersuasive. . . .

The Court's distinction between a federal statute's regulation of States and private parties for general purposes, as opposed to a regulation solely on the activities of States, is unsupported by our recent Tenth Amendment cases. In no case has the Court rested its holding on such a distinction. Moreover, the Court makes no effort to explain why this purported distinction should affect the analysis of Congress' power under general principles of federalism and the Tenth Amendment. The distinction, facilely thrown out, is not based on any defensible theory. Certainly one would be hard pressed to read the spirited exchanges between the Court and dissenting Justices in *National League of Cities, supra*, and in *Garcia v. San Antonio Metropolitan Transit Authority*,

[469 U.S. 528 (1985)], as having been based on the distinction now drawn by the Court. An incursion on state sovereignty hardly seems more constitutionally acceptable if the federal statute that "commands" specific action also applies to private parties. The alleged diminution in state authority over its own affairs is not any less because the federal mandate restricts the activities of private parties. . . .

In *Garcia*, we stated the proper inquiry: "[W]e are convinced that the fundamental limitation that the constitutional scheme imposes on the Commerce Clause to protect the 'States as States' is one of process rather than one of result. Any substantive restraint on the exercise of Commerce Clause powers must find its justification in the procedural nature of this basic limitation, and it must be tailored to compensate for possible failings in the national political process rather than to dictate a 'sacred province of state autonomy.'" 469 U.S., at 554. Where it addresses this aspect of respondents' argument, the Court tacitly concedes that a failing of the political process cannot be shown in these cases because it refuses to rebut the unassailable arguments that the States were well able to look after themselves in the legislative process that culminated in the 1985 Act's passage. . . . The Court rejects this process-based argument by resorting to generalities and platitudes about the purpose of federalism being to protect individual rights.

Ultimately, I suppose, the entire structure of our federal constitutional government can be traced to an interest in establishing checks and balances to prevent the exercise of tyranny against individuals. But these fears seem extremely far distant to me in a situation such as this. We face a crisis of national proportions in the disposal of low-level radioactive waste, and Congress has acceded to the wishes of the States by permitting local decisionmaking rather than imposing a solution from Washington. New York itself participated and supported passage of this legislation at both the gubernatorial and federal representative levels, and then enacted state laws specifically to comply with the deadlines and timetables agreed upon by the States in the 1985 Act. For me, the Court's civics lecture has a decidedly hollow ring at a time when action, rather than rhetoric, is needed to solve a national problem.

IV

Though I disagree with the Court's conclusion that the take title provision is unconstitutional, I do not read its opinion to preclude Congress from adopting a similar measure through its powers under the Spending or Commerce Clauses. . . . Congress could . . . condition the payment of funds on the State's willingness to take title if it has not already provided a waste disposal facility. . . . Similarly, should a State fail to establish a waste disposal facility by the appointed deadline . . . , Congress has the power pursuant to the Commerce Clause to regulate directly the producers of the waste. . . .

V

The ultimate irony of the decision today is that in its formalistically rigid obeisance to "federalism," the Court gives Congress fewer incentives to defer to the wishes of state officials in achieving local solutions to local problems. This legislation was a classic example of Congress acting as arbiter among the States in their attempts to accept responsibility for managing a problem of grave import. The States urged the National Legislature not to impose from Washington a solution to the country's low-level radioactive waste management problems. Instead, they sought a reasonable level of local and regional autonomy consistent with Art. I, §10, cl. 3, of the Constitution. By invalidating the measure designed to ensure compliance for recalcitrant States, such as New York, the Court upsets the delicate compromise achieved among the States and forces Congress to erect several additional formalistic hurdles to clear before achieving exactly the same objective. Because the Court's justifications for undertaking this step are unpersuasive to me, I respectfully dissent.

JUSTICE STEVENS, concurring in part and dissenting in part.

Under the Articles of Confederation, the Federal Government had the power to issue commands to the States. See Arts. VIII, IX. Because that indirect exercise of federal power proved ineffective, the Framers of the Constitution empowered the Federal Government to exercise legislative authority directly over individuals within the States, even though that direct authority constituted a greater intrusion on state sovereignty. Nothing in that history suggests that the Federal Government may not also impose its will upon the several States as it did under the Articles. The Constitution enhanced, rather than diminished, the power of the Federal Government. . . .

PRINTZ v. UNITED STATES

521 U.S. 898 (1997)

JUSTICE SCALIA delivered the opinion of the Court.

I

The Gun Control Act of 1968 (GCA), 18 U.S.C. §921 *et seq.*, establishes a detailed federal scheme governing the distribution of firearms. It prohibits firearms dealers from transferring handguns to any person under 21, not resident in the dealer's State, or prohibited by state or local law from purchasing or possessing firearms, §922(b). It also forbids possession of a firearm by, and transfer of a firearm to, convicted felons, fugitives from justice, unlawful users of controlled substances, persons adjudicated as mentally defective or committed to mental institutions, aliens unlawfully present in the United States, persons dishonorably discharged from the Armed Forces, persons who have renounced their citizenship, and persons who have been subjected to certain restraining orders or been convicted of a misdemeanor offense involving domestic violence. §§922(d) and (g).

In 1993, Congress amended the GCA by enacting the Brady Act. The Act requires the Attorney General to establish a national instant background-check system by November 30, 1998, and immediately puts in place certain interim provisions until that system becomes operative. Under the interim provisions, a firearms dealer who proposes to transfer a handgun must first: (1) receive from the transferee a statement (the Brady Form), §922(s)(1)(A)(i)(I), containing the name, address, and date of birth of the proposed transferee along with a sworn statement that the transferee is not among any of the classes of prohibited purchasers, §922(s)(3); (2) verify the identity of the transferee by examining an identification document, §922(s)(1)(A)(i)(II); and (3) provide the "chief law enforcement officer" (CLEO) of the transferee's residence with notice of the contents (and a copy) of the Brady Form, §§922(s)(1)(A)(i)(III) and (IV). . . .

[T]he CLEO must "make a reasonable effort to ascertain within 5 business days whether receipt or possession would be in violation of the law, including research in whatever State and local recordkeeping systems are available and in a national system designated by the Attorney General." §922(s)(2). . . .

Petitioners Jay Printz and Richard Mack, the CLEOs for Ravalli County, Montana, and Graham County, Arizona, respectively, filed separate actions challenging the constitutionality of the Brady Act's interim provisions. . . .

II

[T]he Brady Act purports to direct state law enforcement officers to participate, albeit only temporarily, in the administration of a federally enacted regulatory scheme. . . .

Petitioners here object to being pressed into federal service, and contend that congressional action compelling state officers to execute federal laws is unconstitutional. Because there is no constitutional text speaking to this precise question, the answer to the CLEOs' challenge must be sought in historical understanding and practice, in the structure of the Constitution, and in the jurisprudence of this Court. We treat those three sources, in that order, in this and the next two sections of this opinion. . . .

The Government contends . . . that "the earliest Congresses enacted statutes that required the participation of state officials in the implementation of federal laws[.]" The Government's contention demands our careful consideration, since early congressional enactments "provid[e] 'contemporaneous and weighty evidence' of the Constitution's meaning," *Bowsher v. Synar*, 478 U.S. 714, 723-724 (1986) . . .

The Government observes that statutes enacted by the first Congresses required state courts to record applications for citizenship, Act of Mar. 26, 1790, ch. 3, §1, 1 Stat. 103, to transmit abstracts of citizenship applications and other naturalization records to the Secretary of State, Act of June 18, 1798, ch. 54, §2, 1 Stat. 567, and to register aliens seeking naturalization and issue certificates of registry, Act of Apr. 14, 1802, ch. 28, §2, 2 Stat. 154-155. . . . Other statutes of that era apparently or at least arguably required state courts to perform functions unrelated to naturalization, such as resolving controversies between a captain and the crew of his ship concerning the seaworthiness of the vessel, Act of July 20, 1790, ch. 29, §3, 1 Stat. 132, hearing the claims of slave owners who had apprehended fugitive slaves and issuing certificates authorizing the slave's forced removal to the State from which he had fled, Act of Feb. 12, 1793, ch. 7, §3, 1 Stat. 302-305, taking proof of the claims of Canadian refugees who had assisted the United States during the Revolutionary War, Act of Apr. 7, 1798, ch. 26, §3, 1 Stat. 548, and ordering the deportation of alien enemies in times of war, Act of July 6, 1798, ch. 66, §2, 1 Stat. 577-578.

These early laws establish, at most, that the Constitution was originally understood to permit imposition of an obligation on state *judges* to enforce federal prescriptions, insofar as those prescriptions related to matters appropriate for the judicial power. That assumption was perhaps implicit in one of the provisions of the Constitution, and was explicit in another. In accord with the so-called Madisonian Compromise, Article III, §1, established only a Supreme Court, and made the creation of lower federal courts optional with the Congress — even though it was obvious that the Supreme Court alone could not hear all federal cases throughout the United States. And the Supremacy Clause, Art. VI, cl. 2, announced that "the Laws of the United States . . . shall be the supreme Law of the Land; and the Judges in every State shall be bound thereby." It is understandable why courts should have been viewed distinctively in this regard; unlike legislatures and executives, they applied the law of other sovereigns all the time. The principle underlying so-called "transitory" causes of action was that laws which operated elsewhere created obligations in justice that courts of the forum State would enforce. . . .

For these reasons, we do not think the early statutes imposing obligations on state courts imply a power of Congress to impress the state executive into its service. Indeed, it can be argued that the numerousness of these statutes, contrasted with the utter lack of statutes imposing obligations on the States' executive (notwithstanding the attractiveness of that course to Congress), suggests an assumed *absence* of such power.[2] The only early federal law the Government has brought to our attention that imposed duties on state executive officers is the Extradition Act of 1793, which required the "executive authority" of a State to cause the arrest and delivery of a fugitive from justice upon the request of the executive authority of the State from which the fugitive had fled. See Act of Feb. 12, 1793, ch. 7, §1, 1 Stat. 302. That was in direct

---

2. Bereft of even a single early, or indeed even pre-20th-century, statute compelling state executive officers to administer federal laws, the dissent is driven to claim that early federal statutes compelled state judges to perform executive functions, which implies a power to compel state executive officers to do so as well. Assuming that this implication would follow (which is doubtful), the premise of the argument is in any case wrong. None of the early statutes directed to state judges or court clerks required the performance of functions more appropriately characterized as executive than judicial (bearing in mind that the line between the two for present purposes is not necessarily identical with the line established by the Constitution for federal separation-of-powers purposes). Given that state courts were entrusted with the quintessentially adjudicative task of determining whether applicants for citizenship met the requisite qualifications, see Act of Mar. 26, 1790, ch. 3, §1, 1 Stat. 103, it is unreasonable to maintain that the ancillary functions of recording, registering, and certifying the citizenship applications were unalterably executive rather than judicial in nature.

The dissent's assertion that the Act of July 20, 1790, ch. 29, §3, 1 Stat. 132-133, which required state courts to resolve controversies between captain and crew regarding seaworthiness of a vessel, caused state courts to act "like contemporary regulatory agencies," is cleverly true — because contemporary regulatory agencies have been allowed to perform adjudicative ("quasi-judicial") functions. It is foolish, however, to mistake the copy for the original, and to believe that 18th-century courts were imitating agencies, rather than 20th-century agencies imitating courts. The Act's requirement that the court appoint "three persons in the neighbourhood . . . most skilful in maritime affairs" to examine the ship and report on its condition certainly does not change the proceeding into one "supervised by a judge but otherwise more characteristic of executive activity," that requirement is not significantly different from the contemporary judicial practice of appointing expert witnesses, see, *e.g.*, Fed. Rule Evid. 706. The ultimate function of the judge under the Act was purely adjudicative; he was, after receiving the report, to "adjudge and determine . . . whether the said ship or vessel is fit to proceed on the intended voyage. . . ." 1 Stat. 132.

implementation, however, of the Extradition Clause of the Constitution itself, see Art. IV, §2.

Not only do the enactments of the early Congresses, as far as we are aware, contain no evidence of an assumption that the Federal Government may command the States' executive power in the absence of a particularized constitutional authorization, they contain some indication of precisely the opposite assumption. On September 23, 1789 — the day before its proposal of the Bill of Rights, see 1 Annals of Congress 912-913 — the First Congress enacted a law aimed at obtaining state assistance of the most rudimentary and necessary sort for the enforcement of the new Government's laws: the holding of federal prisoners in state jails at federal expense. Significantly, the law issued not a command to the States' executive, but a recommendation to their legislatures. Congress "recommended to the legislatures of the several States to pass laws, making it expressly the duty of the keepers of their gaols, to receive and safe keep therein all prisoners committed under the authority of the United States," and offered to pay 50 cents per month for each prisoner. Act of Sept. 23, 1789, 1 Stat. 96. Moreover, when Georgia refused to comply with the request, Congress's only reaction was a law authorizing the marshal in any State that failed to comply with the Recommendation of September 23, 1789, to rent a temporary jail until provision for a permanent one could be made, see Resolution of Mar. 3, 1791, 1 Stat. 225.

In addition to early legislation, the Government also appeals to other sources we have usually regarded as indicative of the original understanding of the Constitution. It points to portions of The Federalist which reply to criticisms that Congress's power to tax will produce two sets of revenue officers — for example, "Brutus's" assertion in his letter to the New York Journal of December 13, 1787, that the Constitution "opens a door to the appointment of a swarm of revenue and excise officers to prey upon the honest and industrious part of the community, eat up their substance, and riot on the spoils of the country," reprinted in 1 Debate on the Constitution 502 (B. Bailyn ed. 1993). "Publius" responded that Congress will probably "make use of the State officers and State regulations, for collecting" federal taxes, The Federalist No. 36, p. 221 (C. Rossiter ed. 1961) (A. Hamilton), and predicted that "the eventual collection [of internal revenue] under the immediate authority of the Union, will generally be made by the officers, and according to the rules, appointed by the several States," id., No. 45, at 292 (J. Madison). The Government also invokes The Federalist's more general observations that the Constitution would "enable the [national] government to employ the ordinary magistracy of each [State] in the execution of its laws," id., No. 27, at 176 (A. Hamilton), and that it was "extremely probable that in other instances, particularly in the organization of the judicial power, the officers of the States will be clothed with the correspondent authority of the Union," id., No. 45, at 292 (J. Madison). But none of these statements necessarily implies — what is the critical point here — that Congress could impose these responsibilities *without the consent of the States*. They appear to rest on the natural assumption that the States would consent to allowing their officials to assist the Federal Government, an assumption proved correct by the extensive mutual assistance the States and Federal Government voluntarily provided one another in the early days of the Republic, including voluntary *federal implementation of state law*. . . .

Another passage of The Federalist reads as follows:

> "It merits particular attention . . . that the laws of the Confederacy as to the *enumerated* and *legitimate* objects of its jurisdiction will become the SUPREME LAW of the land; to the observance of which all officers, legislative, executive, and judicial in each State will be bound by the sanctity of an oath. Thus, the legislatures, courts, and magistrates, of the respective members will be incorporated into the operations of the national government *as far as its just and constitutional authority extends*; and will be rendered auxiliary to the enforcement of its laws." The Federalist No. 27, at 177 (A. Hamilton) (emphasis in original).

The Government does not rely upon this passage, but Justice Souter . . . makes it the very foundation of his position; so we pause to examine it in some detail. Justice Souter finds "[t]he natural reading" of the phrases " 'will be incorporated into the operations of the national government' " and " 'will be rendered auxiliary to the enforcement of its laws' " to be that the National Government will have "authority . . . , when exercising an otherwise legitimate power (the commerce power, say), to require state 'auxiliaries' to take appropriate action." There are several obstacles to such an interpretation. First, the consequences in question ("incorporated into the operations of the national government" and "rendered auxiliary to the enforcement of its laws") are said in the quoted passage to flow *automatically* from the officers' oath to observe "the laws of the Confederacy as to the *enumerated* and *legitimate* objects of its jurisdiction." Thus, if the passage means that state officers must take an active role in the implementation of federal law, it means that they must do so without the necessity for a congressional directive that they implement it. But no one has ever thought, and no one asserts in the present litigation, that that is the law. The second problem with Justice Souter's reading is that it makes state *legislatures* subject to federal direction. (The passage in question, after all, does not include legislatures merely incidentally, as by referring to "all state officers"; it refers to legislatures *specifically* and *first of all*.) We have held, however, that state legislatures are *not* subject to federal direction. *New York v. United States*, 505 U.S. 144 (1992).

These problems are avoided, of course, if the calculatedly vague consequences the passage recites — "incorporated into the operations of the national government" and "rendered auxiliary to the enforcement of its laws" — are taken to refer to nothing more (or less) than the duty owed to the National Government, on the part of *all* state officials, to enact, enforce, and interpret state law in such fashion as not to obstruct the operation of federal law, and the attendant reality that all state actions constituting such obstruction, even legislative Acts, are *ipso facto* invalid. This meaning accords well with the context of the passage, which seeks to explain why the new system of federal law directed to individual citizens, unlike the old one of federal law directed to the States, will "bid much fairer to avoid the necessity of using force" against the States, The Federalist No. 27, at 176. . . .

Justice Souter contends that his interpretation of The Federalist No. 27 is "supported by No. 44," written by Madison, wherefore he claims that

"Madison and Hamilton" together stand opposed to our view. In fact, The Federalist No. 44 quite clearly contradicts Justice Souter's reading. In that Number, Madison justifies the requirement that state officials take an oath to support the Federal Constitution on the ground that they "will have an essential agency in giving effect to the federal Constitution." If the dissent's reading of The Federalist No. 27 were correct (and if Madison agreed with it), one would surely have expected that "essential agency" of state executive officers (if described further) to be described as their responsibility to execute the laws enacted under the Constitution. Instead, however, The Federalist No. 44 continues with the following description:

> "The election of the President and Senate will depend, in all cases, on the legislatures of the several States. And the election of the House of Representatives will equally depend on the same authority in the first instance; and will, probably, forever *be conducted by the officers* and according to the laws *of the States.*" *Id.,* at 287 (emphasis added).

It is most implausible that the person who labored for that example of state executive officers' assisting the Federal Government believed, but neglected to mention, that they had a responsibility to execute federal laws. If it was indeed Hamilton's view that the Federal Government could direct the officers of the States, that view has no clear support in Madison's writings, or as far as we are aware, in text, history, or early commentary elsewhere.

To complete the historical record, we must note that there is not only an absence of executive-commandeering statutes in the early Congresses, but there is an absence of them in our later history as well, at least until very recent years. . . .

The Government points to a number of federal statutes enacted within the past few decades that require the participation of state or local officials in implementing federal regulatory schemes. Some of these are connected to federal funding measures, and can perhaps be more accurately described as conditions upon the grant of federal funding than as mandates to the States; others, which require only the provision of information to the Federal Government, do not involve the precise issue before us here, which is the forced participation of the States' executive in the actual administration of a federal program. We of course do not address these or other currently operative enactments that are not before us; it will be time enough to do so if and when their validity is challenged in a proper case. For deciding the issue before us here, they are of little relevance. Even assuming they represent assertion of the very same congressional power challenged here, they are of such recent vintage that they are no more probative than the statute before us of a constitutional tradition that lends meaning to the text. Their persuasive force is far outweighed by almost two centuries of apparent congressional avoidance of the practice. . . .

III

The constitutional practice we have examined above tends to negate the existence of the congressional power asserted here, but is not conclusive. We turn next to consideration of the structure of the Constitution, to see if we can discern among its "essential postulate[s]," . . . a principle that controls the present cases.

A

It is incontestible that the Constitution established a system of "dual sovereignty." Although the States surrendered many of their powers to the new Federal Government, they retained "a residuary and inviolable sovereignty," The Federalist No. 39, at 245 (J. Madison). This is reflected throughout the Constitution's text, including (to mention only a few examples) the prohibition on any involuntary reduction or combination of a State's territory, Art. IV, §3; the Judicial Power Clause, Art. III, §2, and the Privileges and Immunities Clause, Art. IV, §2, which speak of the "Citizens" of the States; the amendment provision, Article V, which requires the votes of three-fourths of the States to amend the Constitution; and the Guarantee Clause, Art. IV, §4, which "presupposes the continued existence of the states and . . . those means and instrumentalities which are the creation of their sovereign and reserved rights," *Helvering v. Gerhardt*, 304 U.S. 405, 414-415 (1938). Residual state sovereignty was also implicit, of course, in the Constitution's conferral upon Congress of not all governmental powers, but only discrete, enumerated ones, Art. I, §8, which implication was rendered express by the Tenth Amendment's assertion that "[t]he powers not delegated to the United States by the Constitution, nor prohibited by it to the States, are reserved to the States respectively, or to the people."

The Framers' experience under the Articles of Confederation had persuaded them that using the States as the instruments of federal governance was both ineffectual and provocative of federal-state conflict. Preservation of the States as independent political entities being the price of union, and "[t]he practicality of making laws, with coercive sanctions, for the States as political bodies" having been, in Madison's words, "exploded on all hands," 2 Records of the Federal Convention of 1787, p. 9 (M. Farrand ed. 1911), the Framers rejected the concept of a central government that would act upon and through the States, and instead designed a system in which the State and Federal Governments would exercise concurrent authority over the people — who were, in Hamilton's words, "the only proper objects of government," The Federalist No. 15, at 109. We have set forth the historical record in more detail elsewhere, *see New York v. United States*, 505 U.S., at 161-166, and need not repeat it here. It suffices to repeat the conclusion: "the Framers explicitly chose a Constitution that confers upon Congress the power to regulate individuals, not States." *Id.*, at 166. . . .

This separation of the two spheres is one of the Constitution's structural protections of liberty. "Just as the separation and independence of the coordinate branches of the Federal Government serve to prevent the accumulation of excessive power in any one branch, a healthy balance of power between the States and the Federal Government will reduce the risk of tyranny and abuse from either front." [*Gregory v. Ashcroft*, 501 U.S. 452, 458 (1991).] . . . The power of the Federal Government would be augmented immeasurably if it were able to impress into its service — and at no cost to itself — the police officers of the 50 States.

B

[F]ederal control of state officers . . . would also have an effect upon the second element: the separation and equilibration of powers between the three branches of the Federal Government itself. The Constitution does not leave to speculation who is to administer the laws enacted by Congress; the President, it says, "shall take Care that the Laws be faithfully executed," Art. II, §3, personally and through officers whom he appoints (save for such inferior officers as Congress may authorize to be appointed by the "Courts of Law" or by "the Heads of Departments" who are themselves Presidential appointees), Art. II, §2. The Brady Act effectively transfers this responsibility to thousands of CLEOs in the 50 States, who are left to implement the program without meaningful Presidential control (if indeed meaningful Presidential control is possible without the power to appoint and remove). The insistence of the Framers upon unity in the Federal Executive — to ensure both vigor and accountability — is well known. That unity would be shattered, and the power of the President would be subject to reduction, if Congress could act as effectively without the President as with him, by simply requiring state officers to execute its laws.

C

The dissent of course resorts to the last, best hope of those who defend ultra vires congressional action, the Necessary and Proper Clause. It reasons that the power to regulate the sale of handguns under the Commerce Clause, coupled with the power to "make all Laws which shall be necessary and proper for carrying into Execution the foregoing Powers," Art. I, §8, conclusively establishes the Brady Act's constitutional validity, because the Tenth Amendment imposes no limitations on the exercise of *delegated* powers but merely prohibits the exercise of powers "*not* delegated to the United States." What destroys the dissent's Necessary and Proper Clause argument, however, is not the Tenth Amendment but the Necessary and Proper Clause itself. When a "La[w] . . . for carrying into Execution" the Commerce Clause violates the principle of state sovereignty reflected in the various constitutional provisions we mentioned earlier, it is not a "La[w] . . . *proper* for carrying into Execution the Commerce Clause," and is thus, in the words of The Federalist, "merely [an] ac[t] of usurpation" which "deserve[s] to be treated as such." The Federalist No. 33, at 204 (A. Hamilton). . . .

The dissent perceives a simple answer in that portion of Article VI which requires that "all executive and judicial Officers, both of the United States and of the several States, shall be bound by Oath or Affirmation, to support this Constitution," arguing that by virtue of the Supremacy Clause this makes "not only the Constitution, but every law enacted by Congress as well," binding on state officers, including laws requiring state-officer enforcement. The Supremacy Clause, however, makes "Law of the Land" only "Laws of the United States which shall be made in Pursuance [of the Constitution]," Art. VI, cl. 2, so the Supremacy Clause merely brings us back to the question discussed earlier, whether laws conscripting state officers violate state sovereignty and are thus not in accord with the Constitution.

IV

Finally, and most conclusively in the present litigation, we turn to the prior jurisprudence of this Court. . . .

[O]pinions of ours have made clear that the Federal Government may not compel the States to implement, by legislation or executive action, federal regulatory programs. . . . At issue in *New York v. United States*, 505 U.S. 144 (1992), were the so-called "take title" provisions of the Low-Level Radioactive Waste Policy Amendments Act of 1985, which required States either to enact legislation providing for the disposal of radioactive waste generated within their borders, or to take title to, and possession of, the waste—effectively requiring the States either to legislate pursuant to Congress's directions, or to implement an administrative solution. *Id.*, at 175-176. We concluded that Congress could constitutionally require the States to do neither. *Id.*, at 176. "The Federal Government," we held, "may not compel the States to enact or administer a federal regulatory program." *Id.*, at 188. . . .

The Government purports to find support . . . in our decision[] in *Testa v. Katt*, 330 U.S. 386 (1947). . . . *Testa* stands for the proposition that state courts cannot refuse to apply federal law—a conclusion mandated by the terms of the Supremacy Clause ("the Judges in every State shall be bound [by federal law]"). As we have suggested earlier, that says nothing about whether state executive officers must administer federal law. . . .

The Government also maintains that requiring state officers to perform discrete, ministerial tasks specified by Congress does not violate the principle of *New York* because it does not diminish the accountability of state or federal officials. This argument fails even on its own terms. By forcing state governments to absorb the financial burden of implementing a federal regulatory program, Members of Congress can take credit for "solving" problems without having to ask their constituents to pay for the solutions with higher federal taxes. And even when the States are not forced to absorb the costs of implementing a federal program, they are still put in the position of taking the blame for its burdensomeness and for its defects. . . .

Finally, the Government puts forward a cluster of arguments that can be grouped under the heading: "The Brady Act serves very important purposes, is most efficiently administered by CLEOs during the interim period, and places a minimal and only temporary burden upon state officers." There is considerable disagreement over the extent of the burden, but we need not pause over that detail. Assuming all the mentioned factors were true, they might be relevant if we were evaluating whether the incidental application to the States of a federal law of general applicability excessively interfered with the functioning of state governments. See, *e.g.*, *National League of Cities v. Usery*, 426 U.S. 833, 853 (1976) (overruled by *Garcia v. San Antonio Metropolitan Transit Authority*, 469 U.S. 528 (1985)). But where, as here, it is the whole *object* of the law to direct the functioning of the state executive, and hence to compromise the structural framework of dual sovereignty, such a "balancing" analysis is inappropriate. . . .

We held in *New York* that Congress cannot compel the States to enact or enforce a federal regulatory program. Today we hold that Congress cannot circumvent that prohibition by conscripting the State's officers directly. The Federal Government may neither issue directives requiring the States to address particular problems, nor command the States' officers, or those of their political subdivisions, to administer or enforce a federal regulatory program. . . .

JUSTICE O'CONNOR, concurring.

Our precedent and our Nation's historical practices support the Court's holding today. . . . The provisions invalidated here, . . . which directly compel state officials to administer a federal regulatory program, utterly fail to adhere to the design and structure of our constitutional scheme.

JUSTICE THOMAS, concurring.

In my "revisionist" view, the Federal Government's authority under the Commerce Clause, which merely allocates to Congress the power "to regulate Commerce . . . among the several States," does not extend to the regulation of wholly *intra*state, point-of-sale transactions. Absent the underlying authority to regulate the intrastate transfer of firearms, Congress surely lacks the corollary power to impress state law enforcement officers into administering and enforcing such regulations. . . . [Moreover, if] the Second Amendment is read to confer a *personal* right to "keep and bear arms," a colorable argument exists that the Federal Government's regulatory scheme, at least as it pertains to the purely intrastate sale or possession of firearms, runs afoul of that Amendment's protections. As the parties did not raise this argument, however, we need not consider it here.

JUSTICE STEVENS, with whom JUSTICE SOUTER, JUSTICE GINSBURG, and JUSTICE BREYER join, dissenting.

When Congress exercises the powers delegated to it by the Constitution, it may impose affirmative obligations on executive and judicial officers of state and local governments as well as ordinary citizens. . . . Article I, §8, grants the Congress the power to regulate commerce among the States. . . . [T]he additional grant of authority in that section of the Constitution "[t]o make all Laws which shall be necessary and proper for carrying into Execution the foregoing Powers" is surely adequate to support the temporary enlistment of local police officers in the process of identifying persons who should not be entrusted with the possession of handguns. In short, the affirmative delegation of power in Article I provides ample authority for the congressional enactment. . . . [T]he Tenth Amendment . . . confirms the principle that the powers of the Federal Government are limited to those affirmatively granted by the Constitution, but it does not purport to limit the scope or the effectiveness of the exercise of powers that are delegated to Congress. Thus, the Amendment provides no support for a rule that immunizes local officials from obligations that might be imposed on ordinary citizens. Indeed, it would be more reasonable to infer that federal law may impose greater duties on state officials than on private citizens because another provision of the Constitution requires that "all executive and judicial Officers, both of the United States and of the several

States, shall be bound by Oath or Affirmation, to support this Constitution." Art. VI, cl. 3. . . .

[T]he historical materials strongly suggest that the founders intended to enhance the capacity of the Federal Government by empowering it — as a part of the new authority to make demands directly on individual citizens — to act through local officials. Hamilton made clear that the new Constitution, "by extending the authority of the federal head to the individual citizens of the several States, will enable the government to employ the ordinary magistracy of each in the execution of its laws." The Federalist No. 27, at 180. Hamilton's meaning was unambiguous; the Federal Government was to have the power to demand that local officials implement national policy programs. . . .

More specifically, during the debates concerning the ratification of the Constitution, it was assumed that state agents would act as tax collectors for the Federal Government. Opponents of the Constitution had repeatedly expressed fears that the new Federal Government's ability to impose taxes directly on the citizenry would result in an overbearing presence of federal tax collectors in the States. Federalists rejoined that this problem would not arise because, as Hamilton explained, "the United States . . . will make use of the State officers and State regulations for collecting" certain taxes. *Id.*, No. 36, at 235. Similarly, Madison made clear that the new central Government's power to raise taxes directly from the citizenry would "not be resorted to, except for supplemental purposes of revenue . . . and that the eventual collection, under the immediate authority of the Union, will generally be made by the officers . . . appointed by the several States." *Id.*, No. 45, at 318.

The Court's response to this powerful historical evidence is weak. The majority suggests that "none of these statements necessarily implies . . . Congress could impose these responsibilities without the consent of the States." No fair reading of these materials can justify such an interpretation. . . .

Bereft of support in the history of the founding, the Court rests its conclusion on the claim that there is little evidence the National Government actually exercised such a power in the early years of the Republic. . . . [But] we have never suggested that the failure of the early Congresses to address the scope of federal power in a particular area or to exercise a particular authority was an argument against its existence. . . .

More importantly, the fact that Congress did elect to rely on state judges and the clerks of state courts to perform a variety of executive functions is surely evidence of a contemporary understanding that their status as state officials did not immunize them from federal service. The majority's description of these early statutes is both incomplete and at times misleading.

For example, statutes of the early Congresses required in mandatory terms that state judges and their clerks perform various executive duties with respect to applications for citizenship. The First Congress enacted a statute requiring that the state courts consider such applications, specifying that the state courts "*shall* administer" an oath of loyalty to the United States, and that "the clerk of such court *shall* record such application." Act of Mar. 26, 1790, ch. 3, §1, 1 Stat. 103 (emphasis added). Early legislation passed by the Fifth Congress also imposed reporting requirements relating to naturalization on court clerks, specifying that failure to perform those duties would result in a fine. Act of June 18, 1798, ch. 54, §2, 1 Stat. 567. Not long thereafter, the Seventh Congress mandated that state courts maintain a registry of aliens seeking naturalization. Court clerks were required to receive certain information from aliens, record those data, and provide certificates to the aliens; the statute specified fees to be received by local officials in compensation. Act of Apr. 14, 1802, ch. 28, §2, 2 Stat. 154-155.

Similarly, the First Congress enacted legislation requiring state courts to serve, functionally, like contemporary regulatory agencies in certifying the seaworthiness of vessels. Act of July 20, 1790, ch. 29, §3, 1 Stat. 132-133. The majority casts this as an adjudicative duty, but that characterization is misleading. The law provided that upon a complaint raised by a ship's crew members, the state courts were (if no federal court was proximately located) to appoint an investigative committee of three persons "most skilful in maritime affairs" to report back. On this basis, the judge was to determine whether the ship was fit for its intended voyage. The statute sets forth, in essence, procedures for an expert inquisitorial proceeding, supervised by a judge but otherwise more characteristic of executive activity. . . .

We are far truer to the historical record by applying a functional approach in assessing the role played by these early state officials. The use of state judges and their clerks to perform executive functions was, in historical context, hardly unusual. As one scholar has noted, "two centuries ago, state and local judges and associated judicial personnel performed many of the functions today performed by executive officers, including such varied tasks as laying city streets and ensuring the seaworthiness of vessels." Caminker, State Sovereignty and Subordinacy: May Congress Commandeer State Officers to Implement Federal Law?, 95 Colum. L. Rev. 1001, 1045, n.176 (1995). And, of course, judges today continue to perform a variety of functions that may more properly be described as executive. The majority's insistence that this evidence of federal enlistment of state officials to serve executive functions is irrelevant simply because the assistance of "judges" was at issue rests on empty formalistic reasoning of the highest order. . . .

The Court's "structural" arguments [also fail]. . . . As we explained in *Garcia v. San Antonio Metropolitan Transit Authority*, 469 U.S. 528 (1985): "[T]he principal means chosen by the Framers to ensure the role of the States in the federal system lies in the structure of the Federal Government itself. It is no novelty to observe that the composition of the Federal Government was designed in large part to protect the States from overreaching by Congress." *Id.*, at 550-551. Given the fact that the Members of Congress are elected by the people of the several States, with each State receiving an equivalent number of Senators in order to ensure that even the smallest States have a powerful voice in the Legislature, it is quite unrealistic to assume that they will ignore the sovereignty concerns of their constituents. It is far more reasonable to presume that their decisions to impose modest burdens on state officials from time to time reflect a considered judgment that the people in each of the States will benefit therefrom. . . .

Perversely, the majority's rule seems more likely to damage than to preserve the safeguards against tyranny provided by the existence of vital state governments. By limiting the ability of the Federal Government to enlist state officials in the implementation of its programs, the Court creates incentives for the National Government to aggrandize itself. In the name of State's rights, the majority would have the Federal Government create vast national bureaucracies to implement its policies. This is exactly the sort of thing that the early Federalists promised would not occur, in part as a result of the National Government's ability to rely on the magistracy of the States. . . .

Finally, the majority provides an incomplete explanation of our decision in *Testa v. Katt*, 330 U.S. 386 (1947), and demeans its importance. In that case the Court unanimously held that state courts of appropriate jurisdiction must occupy themselves adjudicating claims brought by private litigants under the federal Emergency Price Control Act of 1942, regardless of how otherwise crowded their dockets might be with state-law matters. That is a much greater imposition on state sovereignty than the Court's characterization of the case as merely holding that "state courts cannot refuse to apply federal law." That characterization describes only the narrower duty to apply federal law in cases that the state courts have consented to entertain.

The language drawn from the Supremacy Clause upon which the majority relies ("the Judges in every State shall be bound [by federal law], any Thing in the Constitution or Laws of any state to the Contrary notwithstanding"), expressly embraces that narrower conflict of laws principle. Art. VI, cl. 2. But the Supremacy Clause means far more. As *Testa* held, because the "Laws of the United States . . . [are] the supreme Law of the Land," state courts of appropriate jurisdiction must hear federal claims whenever a federal statute, such as the Emergency Price Control Act, requires them to do so. Art. VI, cl. 2.

Hence, the Court's textual argument is quite misguided. The majority focuses on the Clause's specific attention to the point that "Judges in every State shall be bound." *Ibid*. That language commands state judges to "apply federal law" in cases that they entertain, but it is not the source of their duty to accept jurisdiction of federal claims that they would prefer to ignore. Our opinions in *Testa* rested generally on the language of the Supremacy Clause, without any specific focus on the reference to judges. . . .

Even if the Court were correct in its suggestion that it was the reference to judges in the Supremacy Clause, rather than the central message of the entire Clause, that dictated the result in *Testa*, the Court's implied *expressio unius* argument that the Framers therefore did *not* intend to permit the enlistment of other state officials is implausible. Throughout our history judges, state as well as federal, have merited as much respect as executive agents. The notion that the Framers would have had no reluctance to "press state judges into federal service" against their will but would have regarded the imposition of a similar — indeed, far lesser — burden on town constables as an intolerable affront to principles of state sovereignty can only be considered perverse. If such a distinction had been contemplated by the learned and articulate men who fashioned the basic structure of our government, surely some of them would have said so. . . .

If Congress believes that such a statute will benefit the people of the Nation, and serve the interests of cooperative federalism better than an enlarged federal bureaucracy, we should respect both its policy judgment and its appraisal of its constitutional power. . . .

JUSTICE SOUTER, dissenting.

In deciding these cases, which I have found closer than I had anticipated, it is The Federalist that finally determines my position. I believe that the most straightforward reading of No. 27 is authority for the Government's position here, and that this reading is both supported by No. 44 and consistent with Nos. 36 and 45.

Hamilton in No. 27 first notes that because the new Constitution would authorize the National Government to bind individuals directly through national law, it could "employ the ordinary magistracy of each [State] in the execution of its laws." The Federalist No. 27, p. 174 (J. Cooke ed. 1961) (A. Hamilton). Were he to stop here, he would not necessarily be speaking of anything beyond the possibility of cooperative arrangements by agreement. But he then addresses the combined effect of the proposed Supremacy Clause, U.S. Const., Art. VI, cl. 2, and state officers' oath requirement, U.S. Const., Art. VI, cl. 3, and he states that "the Legislatures, Courts and Magistrates of the respective members will be incorporated into the operations of the national government, *as far as its just and constitutional authority extends*; and will be rendered auxiliary to the enforcement of its laws." The Federalist No. 27, at 174-175 (emphasis in original). The natural reading of this language is not merely that the officers of the various branches of state governments may be employed in the performance of national functions; Hamilton says that the state governmental machinery "will be incorporated" into the Nation's operation, and because the "auxiliary" status of the state officials will occur because they are "bound by the sanctity of an oath," *id.*, at 175, I take him to mean that their auxiliary functions will be the products of their obligations thus undertaken to support federal law, not of their own, or the States', unfettered choices.[1] Madison in No. 44 supports this reading in his commentary on the oath requirement. He asks why state magistrates should have to swear to support the National Constitution, when national officials will not be required to oblige themselves to support the state counterparts. His answer is that national officials "will have no agency in carrying the State Constitutions into effect. The members and officers of the State

---

1. The Court offers . . . criticisms of this analysis. . . . [A]s the Court puts it, the consequences set forth in this passage (that is, rendering state officials "auxiliary" and "incorporat[ing]" them into the operations of the Federal Government) "are said . . . to flow *automatically* from the officers' oath"; from this, the Court infers that on my reading, state officers obligations to execute federal law must follow "without the necessity for a congressional directive that they implement it," *ibid.* But neither Hamilton nor I use the word "automatically"; consequently, there is no reason on Hamilton's view to infer a state officer's affirmative obligation without a textual indication to that effect. This is just what Justice Stevens says. . . .

The Court reads Hamilton's description of state officers' role in carrying out federal law as nothing more than a way of describing the duty of state officials "not to obstruct the operation of federal law," with the consequence that any obstruction is invalid. But I doubt that Hamilton's English was quite as bad as all that. Someone whose virtue consists of not obstructing administration of the law is not described as "incorporated into the operations" of a government or as an "auxiliary" to its law enforcement. One simply cannot escape from Hamilton by reducing his prose to inapposite figures of speech.

Governments, on the contrary, will have an essential agency in giving effect to the Federal Constitution." *Id.*, No. 44, at 307 (J. Madison). He then describes the state legislative "agency" as action necessary for selecting the President, see U.S. Const., Art. II, §1, and the choice of Senators, see U.S. Const., Art. I, §3 (repealed by Amdt. 17). The Federalist No. 44, at 307. The Supremacy Clause itself, of course, expressly refers to the state judges' obligations under federal law, and other numbers of The Federalist give examples of state executive "agency" in the enforcement of national revenue laws.[2] . . .

JUSTICE BREYER, with whom JUSTICE STEVENS joins, dissenting.

I would add to the reasons Justice Stevens sets forth the fact that the United States is not the only nation that seeks to reconcile the practical need for a central authority with the democratic virtues of more local control. At least some other countries, facing the same basic problem, have found that local control is better maintained through application of a principle that is the direct opposite of the principle the majority derives from the silence of our Constitution. . . . They do so in part because they believe that such a system interferes less, not more, with the independent authority of the "state," member nation, or other subsidiary government, and helps to safeguard individual liberty as well. . . .

POINTS FOR DISCUSSION

1. In *New York*, Justice O'Connor wrote for the Court that "[i]t makes no difference whether one views the question at issue in these cases as one of ascertaining the limits of the power delegated to the Federal Government under the affirmative provisions of the Constitution or one of discerning the core of sovereignty retained by the Tenth Amendment." Is this true? In *United States v. Lopez*, 514 U.S. 549 (1995), and *United States v. Morrison*, 529 U.S. 598 (2000), which appear in the preceding chapter, all justices agreed that courts may review federal legislation for whether it exceeds the commerce power. (They disputed, however, how much deference courts owe Congress in doing so.) In *Garcia v. San Antonio Metropolitan Transit Authority*, 469 U.S. 528 (1985), the Court suggested that judicial review is inappropriate for whether Congress has violated traditional sovereign prerogatives of a state. Should it

---

2. The Court reads Madison's No. 44 as supporting its view that Hamilton meant "auxiliaries" to mean merely "nonobstructors." It defends its position in what seems like a very sensible argument, so long as one does not go beyond the terms set by the Court: if Madison really thought state executive officials could be required to enforce federal law, one would have expected him to say so, instead of giving examples of how state officials (legislative and executive, the Court points out) have roles in the election of national officials. One might indeed have expected that, save for one remark of Madison's, and a detail of his language, that the Court ignores. When he asked why state officers should have to take an oath to support the National Constitution, he said that "several reasons might be assigned," but that he would "content [himself] with one which is obvious & conclusive." The Federalist No. 44, at 307. The one example he gives describes how state officials will have "an essential agency in giving effect to the federal Constitution." He was not talking about executing congressional statutes; he was talking about putting the National Constitution into effect by selecting the executive and legislative members who would exercise its powers. The answer to the Court's question (and objection), then, is that Madison was expressly choosing one example of state officer agency, not purporting to exhaust the examples possible. . . .

make a difference, for purposes of judicial review, whether the question at issue in *New York* and *Printz* is (a) whether Congress has exceeded the commerce power or (b) whether Congress has violated a core principle of state sovereignty protected by the Tenth Amendment?

2. In *Printz*, Justice Scalia began: "Because there is no constitutional text speaking to this precise question, the answer . . . must be sought in historical understanding and practice, in the structure of the Constitution, and in the jurisprudence of this Court." How does this methodology relate to methodologies employed by the Marshall Court in cases you studied in Chapter 1? Do historical practice and structural principle justify the anti-commandeering principles of *New York* and *Printz* absent constitutional text specifically providing them?

3. In dissent in *Printz*, Justice Stevens argued that "[b]y limiting the ability of the Federal Government to enlist state officials in the implementation of its programs, the Court creates incentives for the National Government to aggrandize itself." In other words, if Congress cannot use state officials to enforce federal laws, Congress will enforce them through federal bureaucratic means. Justice O'Connor made a similar argument in dissent in *Raich*—that, by upholding federal regulation of intrastate activity under the Commerce Clause so long as it is part of a broader interstate market regulation, the Court gave Congress incentives to regulate more broadly. In light of the political safeguards of federalism, do the Court's decisions in *Printz* and *Raich* generate the kind of incentives that Justices Stevens and O'Connor identify?

4. In *New York*, the Court recited various values of federalism, citing the article by Professor Michael McConnell that you read in Chapter 3. The Court went on, however, to explain that "[t]he benefits of this federal structure . . . need not concern us here. Our task would be the same even if one could prove that federalism secured no advantages to anyone." Should the Court resolve cases like *New York* and *Printz* without regard for the benefits or values of the federal structure? Did the Court in fact decide *New York* and *Printz* without regard for perceived benefits of the federal structure? Do theories of cooperative and dynamic federalism that you studied in Chapter 3 speak to the issues in *New York* and *Printz*?

5. Do *New York* and *Printz* involve the same questions of judicial deference to Congress that the commerce, spending, and §5 cases that you studied in Chapter 5 involve?

D. STATE SOVEREIGN IMMUNITY

One of the most difficult and contested federalism questions in U.S. constitutional history is when private litigants may bring suits against states in federal courts. The materials in this section address this question. Aspects of this question remain highly contested among judges and scholars to the present day.

To appreciate the origins and development of this question, you must understand the text of Article III of the Constitution. Article III limits the judicial power of the United States to an enumerated list of "cases" and "controversies":

> The Judicial Power shall extend to all Cases, in Law and Equity, arising under this Constitution, the Laws of the United States, and Treaties made, or which shall be made, under their Authority; — to all Cases affecting Ambassadors, other public Ministers and Consuls; — to all Cases of admiralty and maritime Jurisdiction; — to Controversies to which the United States shall be a Party; — to Controversies between two or more States; between a State and Citizens of another State; between Citizens of different States; — between Citizens of the same State claiming Lands under Grants of different States, and between a State, or the Citizens thereof, and foreign States, Citizens or Subjects.

U.S. CONST. art. III, §2. This provision is generally understood to provide a ceiling on federal court jurisdiction, under which Congress may define the specific jurisdiction of different Article III courts. The first clause authorizes federal court jurisdiction over cases arising under the Constitution, laws, and treaties of the United States. Under this clause, Congress may authorize federal court jurisdiction to ensure the proper judicial enforcement and uniform treatment of federal laws. Other clauses, such as those extending federal judicial power to ambassadorial and admiralty cases, enable Congress to empower federal courts to adjudicate disputes implicating foreign relations of the United States.

The provision extending the judicial power to "Controversies . . . between a State and Citizens of another State" (the so-called Citizen-State Diversity Clause) generated a singular dispute. Under the common law, which incorporated the law of nations, sovereign immunity shielded nations from suit without their consent. Some members of the Founding generation feared that the Citizen-State Diversity Clause authorized federal court suits by citizens of one state against another state without regard for sovereign immunity. Because states had amassed considerable debts during the Revolutionary War, there was opposition to the idea that private litigants could sue states in federal courts without state consent.

Prominent Anti-Federalists, such as Patrick Henry and George Mason, opposed ratification on the ground (among others) that the Citizen-State Diversity Clause would subject states to federal court suits without their consent. Three prominent Federalists — Alexander Hamilton, James Madison, and John Marshall — on the other hand, argued that the Citizen-State Diversity Clause did not abrogate state sovereign immunity from suit. Alexander Hamilton argued in *The Federalist No. 81*:

> It is inherent in the nature of sovereignty not to be amenable to the suit of an individual *without its consent.* This is the general sense, and the general practice of mankind; and the exemption, as one of the attributes of sovereignty, is now enjoyed by the government of every State in the Union. Unless, therefore, there is a surrender of this immunity in the plan of the convention, it will remain with the States, and the danger intimated must be merely ideal. . . . [T]here is no color to pretend that the State governments would, by the adoption of that plan, be divested of the privilege of paying their own debts in their own way, free from every constraint but that which flows from the obligations of good faith. The contracts between a nation and

individuals are only binding on the conscience of the sovereign, and have no pretensions to a compulsive force. They confer no right of action, independent of the sovereign will. To what purpose would it be to authorize suits against States for the debts they owe? How could recoveries be enforced? It is evident, it could not be done without waging war against the contracting State; and to ascribe to the federal courts, by mere implication, and in destruction of a pre-existing right of the State governments, a power which would involve such a consequence, would be altogether forced and unwarrantable.

In the Virginia ratifying convention, James Madison argued that the federal courts'

jurisdiction in controversies between a state and citizens of another state is much objected to, and perhaps without reason. It is not in the power of individuals to call any state into court. The only operation it can have, is that, if a state should wish to bring a suit against a citizen, it must be brought before the federal court . . . and if a state should condescend to be a party, this court may take cognizance of it.

James Madison, Address to the Virginia Ratifying Convention (June 20, 1788), *in* 10 The Documentary History of the Ratification of the Constitution 1412, 1414 (John P. Kaminski & Gaspare J. Saladino eds., 1993). Thus, Madison argued that the Citizen-State Diversity Clause authorized states to sue citizens of other states in federal court, but only authorized suits against states "if a state should condescend to be a party"—in other words, if a state should consent to suit.

Finally, John Marshall argued in the Virginia convention:

With respect to disputes between a State, and the citizens of another State, its jurisdiction has been decried with unusual vehemence. I hope no Gentleman will think that a State will be called at the bar of the Federal Court . . . It is not rational to suppose, that the sovereign power shall be dragged before a Court. The intent is, to enable States to recover claims of individuals residing in other States.

John Marshall, Address to the Virginia Ratifying Convention (June 20, 1788), *in* 10 *id.* at 1430, 1433.

Upon ratification, Article III took effect notwithstanding controversy over whether the Citizen-State Diversity Clause abrogated state sovereign immunity. In 1793, in *Chisholm v. Georgia*, 2 U.S. (2 Dall.) 419 (1793), the Supreme Court addressed the case that Anti-Federalists had feared: a federal court suit by a citizen of one state against another state to recover on a Revolutionary War debt. Writing seriatim, the Justices upheld their jurisdiction to hear the suit notwithstanding the state's sovereign immunity defense. As you read *Chisholm*, consider:

- What arguments do the Justices make regarding whether states have sovereign immunity in suits brought within the federal courts' Citizen-State Diversity jurisdiction?
- What interpretive presumptions do the Justices apply to the Citizen-State Diversity Clause?

CHISHOLM V. GEORGIA

2 U.S. (2 Dall.) 419 (1793)

[Chisholm, a citizen of South Carolina, filed an action in the Supreme Court against the State of Georgia to recover on a debt.]

IREDELL, JUSTICE.

The question . . . is, will an action of assumpsit lie against a State? . . .

The words of the general judicial act, conveying the authority of the Supreme Court, under the Constitution, so far as they concern this question, are as follow: Sect. 13. "That the Supreme Court shall have exclusive jurisdiction of all controversies of a civil nature, where a State is a party, except between a State and its citizens; and except also, between a State and citizens of other States, or aliens, in which latter case it shall have original, but not exclusive jurisdiction." . . .

A general question of great importance here occurs. What controversy of a civil nature can be maintained against a State by an individual? . . . [A]ll the Courts of the *United States* must receive . . . all their authority, as to the manner of their proceeding, from the Legislature only. This appears to me to be one of those cases, with many others, in which an article of the Constitution cannot be effectuated without the intervention of the Legislative authority. . . .

If therefore, this Court is to be (as I consider it) the organ of the *Constitution and the law*, not of the *Constitution* only, in respect to the manner of its proceeding, we must receive our directions from the Legislature in this particular. . . .

But the act of *Congress* has not been altogether silent upon this subject. The 14*th sect.* of the judicial act, provides in the following words: "All the before mentioned Courts of the *United States*, shall have power to issue writs of *feire facias*, *habeas corpus*, and all other writs not specially provided for by statute, which may be necessary for the exercise of their respective jurisdictions, *and agreeable to the principles and usages of law*." These words refer as well to the Supreme Court as to the other Courts of the *United States*. Whatever writs we issue, that are necessary for the exercise of our jurisdiction, must be *agreeable to the principles and usages of law*. . . .

[B]esides [this] express reference to principles and usages of law as the guide of our proceeding, it is observable that in instances like this before the Court, this Court hath a *concurrent jurisdiction* only; the present being one of those cases where by the judicial act this Court hath *original* but not *exclusive* jurisdiction. This Court, therefore, under that act, can exercise no authority in such instances, but such authority as from the subject matter of it may be exercised in some other Court. . . . It follows, therefore, unquestionably, I think, that looking at the act of *Congress*, which I consider is on this occasion the limit of our authority (whatever further might be constitutionally, enacted) we can exercise no authority in the present instance consistently with the clear intention of the act, but such as a proper State Court would have been at least competent to exercise at the time the act was passed. . . .

[W]e have no other rule to govern us but the principles of the pre-existent laws, which must remain in force till superceded by others[.] [I]t is incumbent upon us to enquire, whether previous to the adoption of the Constitution . . . an action of the nature like this before the Court could have been maintained against one of the States in the *Union* upon the principles of the common law. . . . [T]here are no principles of the old law . . . that in any manner authorise the present suit, either by precedent or by analogy. The consequence of which, in my opinion, clearly is, that the suit in question cannot be maintained. . . .

So far as this great question affects the Constitution itself, if the present afforded, consistently with the particular grounds of my opinion, a proper occasion for a decision upon it, I would not shrink from its discussion. But it is of extreme moment that no Judge should rashly commit himself upon important questions, which it is unnecessary for him to decide. My opinion being, that even if the Constitution would admit of the exercise of such a power, a new law is necessary for the purpose, since no part of the existing law applies, this alone is sufficient to justify my determination in the present case. So much, however, has been said on the Constitution, that it may not be improper to intimate that my present opinion is strongly against any construction of it, which will admit, under any circumstances, a compulsive suit against a State for the recovery of money. I think every word in the Constitution may have its full effect without involving this consequence, and that nothing but express words, or an insurmountable implication (neither of which I consider, can be found in this case) would authorise the deduction of so high a power. . . .

BLAIR, JUSTICE.

The Constitution of the *United States* is the only fountain from which I shall draw; the only authority to which I shall appeal. Whatever be the true language of that, it is obligatory upon every member of the *Union*; for, no State could have become a member, but by an adoption of it by the people of that State. What then do we find there requiring the submission of individual States to the judicial authority of the *United States*? This is expressly extended, among other things, to controversies between a State and citizens of another State. Is then the case before us one of that description? Undoubtedly it is. . . .

WILSON, JUSTICE.

This is a case of uncommon magnitude. One of the parties to it is a STATE; certainly respectable, claiming to be *sovereign*. The question to be determined is, whether this State, so respectable, and whose claim soars so high, is amenable to the jurisdiction of the Supreme Court of the *United States*? . . .

I am, first, to examine this question by the principles of general jurisprudence. . . . The only reason, I believe, why a free man is bound by human laws, is, *that he binds himself.* Upon the same principles, upon which he becomes bound *by the laws*, he becomes amenable to the *Courts of Justice*, which are formed and authorised by those laws. If one free man, an original sovereign, may do all this; why may not an aggregate of free men, a collection of original sovereigns, do this likewise? If the dignity of each *singly* is undiminished; the dignity of all *jointly* must be unimpaired. A State, like a merchant, makes a contract. A dishonest State, like a dishonest merchant, wilfully refuses to discharge it: The latter is amenable to a Court of Justice: Upon general principles of right, shall the former when summoned to answer the fair demands of its creditor, be permitted, proteus-like, to assume a new appearance, and to insult him and justice, by declaring *I am a* SOVEREIGN *State?* Surely not. . . .

I am . . . chiefly . . . to examine the important question now before us, by the Constitution of the *United States*, and the legitimate result of that valuable instrument. . . . In *despotic* Governments, the *Government* has usurped, in a similar manner, both upon the *state* and the *people*: Hence all arbitrary doctrines and pretensions concerning the Supreme, absolute, and incontrolable, power of *Government.* In *each*, *man* is degraded from the *prime* rank, which he ought to hold in human affairs. . . . A *State* I cheerfully fully admit, is the noblest work of *Man*: But, *Man himself*, free and honest, is, I speak as to this world, the noblest work of God.

Concerning the prerogative of *Kings*, and concerning the sovereignty of States, much has been said and written; but little has been said and written concerning a subject much more dignified and important, the majesty of the people. . . . [O]ur national scene opens with the most magnificent object, which the nation could present. "The PEOPLE of the *United States*" are the first personages introduced. Who were those people? They were the citizens of thirteen States, each of which had a separate Constitution and Government, and all of which were connected together by articles of confederation. To the purposes of public strength and felicity, that confederacy was totally inadequate. A requisition on the several States terminated its *Legislative* authority: *Executive or Judicial* authority it had none. In order, therefore, to form a more perfect union, *to establish justice*, to ensure domestic tranquility, to provide for common defence, and to secure the blessings of liberty, *those people*, among whom were the people of *Georgia*, ordained and established the present Constitution. By that Constitution Legislative power is vested, Executive power is vested, *Judicial* power is vested.

The question now opens fairly to our view, *could* the *people* of those States, among whom were those of *Georgia*, bind those *States*, and *Georgia* among the others, by the Legislative, Executive, and Judicial power so vested? If the principles, on which I have founded myself, are just and true; this question must unavoidably receive an affirmative answer. If those *States* were the *work* of those *people*; those people, and, that I may apply the case closely, the people of *Georgia*, in particular, could alter, as they pleased, their former work: To any given degree, they could *diminish* as well as enlarge it. *Any* or *all* of the former State-powers, they could *extinguish* or *transfer*. The inference, which necessarily results, is, that the Constitution ordained and established by *those* people; and, still closely to apply the case, in particular by the people of *Georgia*, *could* vest jurisdiction or judicial power over those States and over the State of *Georgia* in particular.

The next question under this head, is, —*Has* the Constitution done so? Did those people mean to exercise this, their undoubted power? . . . Whoever considers, in a combined and comprehensive view, the *general texture* of the

Constitution, will be satisfied, that the people of the *United States* intended to form themselves into a nation for *national purposes*. They instituted, for *such* purposes, a national Government, complete in all its parts, with powers Legislative, Executive and Judiciary; and, in all those powers, extending over the whole nation. Is it congruous, that, with regard to *such* purposes, any man or body of men, any person natural or artificial, should be permitted to claim successfully an entire exemption from the jurisdiction of the national Government? Would not such claims, crowned with success, be repugnant to our very existence as a nation? When so many trains of deduction, coming from different quarters, converge and unite, at last, in the same point; we may safely conclude, as the *legitimate result* of this Constitution, that the State of *Georgia* is amenable to the jurisdiction of this Court.

But, in my opinion, this doctrine rests not upon the legitimate result of fair and conclusive deduction from the Constitution: It is confirmed, beyond all doubt, by the *direct* and *explicit declaration* of the Constitution itself. . . . "The judicial power of the *United States* shall extend to controversies, between a *state* and *citizens* of another *State*." . . . [C]ould this strict and appropriated language, describe, with more precise accuracy, the cause now depending before the tribunal? *Causes*, and not *parties* to causes, are weighed by justice, in her equal scales: On the former *solely*, her attention is fixed: To the latter, she *is* . . . blind. . . .

CUSHING, JUSTICE.

The grand and principal question in this case is, whether a State can, by the Federal Constitution, be sued by an individual citizen of another State?

The point turns not upon the law or practice of *England*, although perhaps it may be in some measure elucidated thereby, nor upon the law of any other country whatever; but upon the Constitution established by the people of the *United States*; and particularly upon the extent of powers given to the Federal Judicial in the 2d section of the 3d article of the Constitution. . . . The judicial power . . . is expressly extended to "*controversies between a State and citizens of another State*." . . . The case, then, seems clearly to fall within the letter of the Constitution. . . .

JAY, CHIEF JUSTICE.

From the differences existing between feudal sovereignties and Governments founded on compacts, it necessarily follows that their respective prerogatives must differ. Sovereignty is the right to govern; a nation or State-sovereign is the person or persons in whom that resides. In *Europe* the sovereignty is generally ascribed to the *Prince*; here it rests with the people. . . . Even [a] cursory view of the judicial powers of the *United States*, leaves the mind strongly impressed with the importance of them to the preservation of the tranquility, the equal sovereignty, and the equal right of the people.

The question now before us renders it necessary to pay particular attention to that part of the 2d section, which extends the judicial power "*to controversies between a state and citizens of another state*." It is contended, that this ought to be construed to reach none of these controversies, excepting those in which a

State may be *Plaintiff.* The ordinary rules for construction will easily decide whether those words are to be understood in that limited sense.

This extension of power is *remedial*, because it is to settle controversies. It is therefore, to be construed liberally. It is politic, wise, and good that, not only the controversies, in which a State is *Plaintiff*, but also those in which a State is *Defendant*, should be settled; both cases, therefore, are within the reason of the remedy; and ought to be so adjudged, unless the obvious, plain, and literal sense of the words forbid it. If we attend to the *words*, we find them to be express, positive, free from ambiguity, and without room for such implied expressions: "*The judicial power of the United States shall extend to controversies between a state and citizens of another state.*" If the Constitution really meant to extend these powers only to those controversies in which a State might be *Plaintiff*, to the exclusion of those in which citizens had demands against a State, it is inconceivable that it should have attempted to convey that meaning in words, not only so incompetent, but also repugnant to it. . . . The exception contended for, would contradict and do violence to the great and leading principles of a free and equal national government, one of the great objects of which is, to ensure justice to all: To the few against the many, as well as to the many against the few. . . .

POINTS FOR DISCUSSION

1. Justice Iredell was the only justice who would have upheld the sovereign immunity of the state from suit. He rested his opinion on statutory grounds, finding that Congress had preserved state sovereign immunity from suit in defining the jurisdiction and powers of federal courts. Although Justice Iredell saw no need to resolve the constitutional question—*viz.* whether the Constitution authorizes Congress to confer Citizen-State Diversity jurisdiction over cases against state defendants—he was skeptical that Article III authorized federal court jurisdiction over suits against states. "Nothing," he explained, "but express words would authorize the deduction of so high a power." In present-day terms, Justice Iredell applied a "clear statement rule" to the Constitution. Chief Justice Jay, on the other hand, applied "the ordinary rules of construction," construing the Citizen-State Diversity Clause "liberally" as a "remedial" provision. Which, if either, was the more appropriate rule of construction to apply—the clear statement rule against federal power or the rule of liberal construction in favor of federal power?

2. The Justices who upheld the Court's jurisdiction, notwithstanding Georgia's assertion of sovereign immunity, argued, *inter alia*, (1) that the text of the Citizen-State Diversity Clause authorized jurisdiction, and (2) that sovereign immunity has no place in government where the People hold ultimate sovereignty. Critically evaluate both of these arguments.

The Supreme Court came to describe its decision in *Chisholm* as generating a "shock of surprise throughout the country." *Hans v. Louisiana*, 134 U.S. 1, 11 (1890). In response to *Chisholm*, Georgia's House of Representatives passed a bill providing that anyone who attempted to enforce the judgment in

Chisholm was "hereby declared to be guilty of a felony, and shall suffer death, without the benefit of clergy by being hanged." Bills to amend the Constitution were soon introduced in Congress, resulting in the Eleventh Amendment, which Congress passed in 1794 and the States ratified in 1795. The Eleventh Amendment provides:

> The Judicial power of the United States shall not be construed to extend to any suit in law or equity, commenced or prosecuted against one of the United States by Citizens of another State, or by Citizens or Subjects of any Foreign State.

Judges and scholars have long debated the status of state sovereign immunity following adoption of the Eleventh Amendment. By its terms, the Eleventh Amendment prohibits federal courts from hearing citizen-state diversity suits against states. Beyond that, judges and scholars intensely dispute several questions:

- Does the Eleventh Amendment prohibit citizen-state diversity cases that also "arise under" federal law? The Arising Under Clause of Article III authorizes federal court jurisdiction over cases "arising under" the Constitution, treaties, and laws of the United States. Does the Arising Under Clause authorize jurisdiction over cases arising under federal law by a citizen of one state against another state?
- Do principles of state sovereign immunity prohibit federal courts from exercising "arising under" jurisdiction over suits by citizens against their own states, a category of cases that the Eleventh Amendment does not address in terms?
- If states enjoy a general immunity from suit in federal court, may Congress abrogate that immunity in the exercise of any of its enumerated powers?
- May Congress exercise any of its enumerated powers to abrogate the immunity from suit that a state enjoys in *its own courts*?

The following cases consider these and other questions. As you read these cases, keep in mind the following two opposing views of how the Eleventh Amendment relates to *Chisholm* and general principles of state sovereign immunity:

1. *Sovereign Immunity as Background Structural Constitutional Principle.* At the Founding, principles of state sovereign immunity were understood to limit all categories of federal court jurisdiction under Article III. The writings of Hamilton, Madison, and Marshall exemplify this view. In *Chisholm*, the Justices erroneously deviated from this understanding. The adverse political reaction to *Chisholm* was swift and certain. The Eleventh Amendment corrected the error of *Chisholm*, providing that the federal judicial power "*shall not be construed* to extend" to Citizen-State Diversity cases against states. The Eleventh Amendment thereby clarified that the only constitutional provision that arguably abrogated state sovereign immunity—the Citizen-State Diversity Clause—in fact did not abrogate such immunity. The Eleventh Amendment thus fully restored state sovereign immunity as a structural constitutional limitation on the judicial power of the United States.

2. *Sovereign Immunity as Limited Provision of Eleventh Amendment.* At the Founding, there was not a general understanding that state sovereign immunity limited the jurisdictional grants of Article III. The views of Patrick Henry and George Mason, as well as the Justices in *Chisholm*, demonstrate that state sovereign immunity was not a generally understood limitation on federal power. The theory behind the Eleventh Amendment was that states should not be subjected to suits by citizens of other states for the collection of state debts. The Eleventh Amendment did not reflect a principle that federal courts could not enforce federal law against the states in their jurisdiction over cases arising under federal law. The Eleventh Amendment thus enacted a state immunity from suit in a limited category of cases but did not restore, as constitutional principle, state immunity from any suit in federal court.

Keep these theories in mind as you read the following cases.

HANS v. LOUISIANA

134 U.S. 1 (1890)

This is an action brought in the Circuit Court of the United States . . . against the State of Louisiana, by Hans, a citizen of that State, to recover the amount of certain coupons annexed to bonds of the State, issued under the provisions of an act of the legislature approved January 24, 1874. [Hans alleged that an amendment to the Louisiana Constitution that barred the State from paying interest due impaired the obligation of contract in violation of the Contracts Clause of the Constitution of the United States.] . . . [T]he attorney general of the State filed an exception . . . : ". . . Plaintiff cannot sue the state without its permission; the constitution and laws do not give this honorable court jurisdiction of a suit against the state; and its jurisdiction is respectfully declined. . . ."

Mr. JUSTICE BRADLEY . . . delivered the opinion of the court.

The ground taken is that under the Constitution, as well as under the act of Congress passed to carry it into effect, a case is within the jurisdiction of the federal courts, without regard to the character of the parties, if it arises under the Constitution or laws of the United States. . . . The language relied on is that clause of the third article of the Constitution, which declares that "the judicial power of the United States shall extend to all cases in law and equity arising under this Constitution, the laws of the United States, and treaties made, or which shall be made, under their authority;" and the corresponding clause of the act conferring jurisdiction upon the Circuit Court, which, as found in the act of March 3, 1875, 18 Stat. 470, c. 137, §1, is as follows, to-wit: "That the Circuit Courts of the United States shall have original cognizance, concurrent with the courts of the several states, of all suits of a civil nature, at common law or in equity, . . . arising under the Constitution or laws of the United States, or treaties made, or which shall be made, under their authority[.]" It is said that these jurisdictional clauses make no exception arising from the character of the parties, and, therefore, that a State can claim no exemption from suit, if the case is really one arising under the Constitution, laws or treaties of the

United States. It is conceded that where the jurisdiction depends alone upon the character of the parties, a controversy between a State and its own citizens is not embraced within it, but it is contended that though jurisdiction does not exist on that ground, it nevertheless does exist if the case itself is one which necessarily involves a federal question, and, with regard to ordinary parties this is undoubtedly true. The question now to be decided is, whether it is true where one of the parties is a State, and is sued as a defendant by one of its own citizens.

That a State cannot be sued by a citizen of another State, or of a foreign state, on the mere ground that the case is one arising under the Constitution or laws of the United States, is clearly established by the decisions of this court in several recent cases. . . .

In the present case the plaintiff in error contends that he, being a citizen of Louisiana, is not embarrassed by the obstacle of the Eleventh Amendment, inasmuch as that amendment only prohibits suits against a State which are brought by the citizens of another State, or by citizens or subjects of a foreign State. It is true, the amendment does so read and if there were no other reason or ground for abating his suit, it might be maintainable, and then we should have this anomalous result, that in cases arising under the Constitution or laws of the United States, a State may be sued in the federal courts by its own citizens, though it cannot be sued for a like cause of action by the citizens of other States, or of a foreign state, and may be thus sued in the federal courts, although not allowing itself to be sued in its own courts. If this is the necessary consequence of the language of the Constitution and the law, the result is no less startling and unexpected than was the original decision of this court, that, under the language of the Constitution and of the judiciary act of 1789, a State was liable to be sued by a citizen of another State, or of a foreign country[.] That decision was made in the case of *Chisholm v. Georgia*, and created such a shock of surprise throughout the country that, at the first meeting of Congress thereafter, the Eleventh Amendment to the Constitution was almost unanimously proposed, and was in due course adopted by the legislatures of the States. This amendment, expressing the will of the ultimate sovereignty of the whole country, superior to all legislatures and all courts, actually reversed the decision of the Supreme Court. It did not in terms prohibit suits by individuals against the States, but declared that the Constitution should not be construed to import any power to authorize the bringing of such suits. The language of the amendment is that "the judicial power of the United States *shall not be construed* to extend to any suit in law or equity, commenced or prosecuted against one of the United States by citizens of another State, or by citizens or subjects of any foreign state." The Supreme Court had construed the judicial power as extending to such a suit, and its decision was thus overruled. . . .

This view of the force and meaning of the amendment is important. It shows that, on this question of the suability of the States by individuals, the highest authority of this country was in accord rather with the minority than with the majority of the court in the decision of the case of *Chisholm v. Georgia*, and this fact lends additional interest to the able opinion of Mr. Justice Iredell on that occasion. The other justices were more swayed by a close observance of the letter of the Constitution, without regard to former experience and usage;

and because the letter said that the judicial power shall extend to controversies "between a State and citizens of another State;" and "between a State and foreign states, citizens or subjects," they felt constrained to see in this language a power to enable the individual citizens of one State, or of a foreign state, to sue another State of the Union in the federal courts. Justice Iredell, on the contrary, contended that it was not the intention to create new and unheard of remedies, by subjecting sovereign States to actions at the suit of individuals, (which he conclusively showed was never done before,) but only, by proper legislation, to invest the federal courts with jurisdiction to hear and determine controversies and cases, between the parties designated, that were properly susceptible of litigation in courts.

Looking back from our present standpoint at the decision in *Chisholm v. Georgia*, we do not greatly wonder at the effect which it had upon the country[.] Any such power as that of authorizing the federal judiciary to entertain suits by individuals against the States had been expressly disclaimed, and even resented, by the great defenders of the Constitution whilst it was on its trial before the American people. As some of their utterances are directly pertinent to the question now under consideration, we deem it proper to quote them.

The eighty-first number of the Federalist, written by Hamilton, has the following profound remarks[:]

". . . It is inherent in the nature of sovereignty not to be amenable to the suit of an individual *without its consent*. This is the general sense and the general practice of mankind, and the exemption, as one of the attributes of sovereignty, is now enjoyed by the government of every State in the Union. Unless, therefore, there is a surrender of this immunity in the plan of the convention, it will remain with the States, and the danger intimated must be merely ideal. . . . A recurrence to the principles there established will satisfy us that there is no color to pretend that the state governments would, by the adoption of that plan, be divested of the privilege of paying their own debts in their own way, free from every constraint but that which flows from the obligations of good faith. The contracts between a nation and individuals are only binding on the conscience of the sovereign, and have no pretension to a compulsive force. They confer no right of action independent of the sovereign will. To what purpose would it be to authorize suits against States for the debts they owe? How could recoveries be enforced? It is evident that it could not be done without waging war against the contracting State; and to ascribe to the federal courts by mere implication, and in destruction of a pre-existing right of the state governments, a power which would involve such a consequence, would be altogether forced and unwarrantable."

The obnoxious clause to which Hamilton's argument was directed, and which was the ground of the objections which he so forcibly met, was that which declared that "the judicial power shall extend to all . . . controversies between a State and citizens of another State, . . . and between a State and foreign states, citizens, or subjects." It was argued by the opponents of the constitution that this clause would authorize jurisdiction to be given to the federal courts to entertain suits against a State brought by the citizens of another State or of a foreign state. Adhering to the mere letter, it might be so, and so, in fact, the Supreme Court held in *Chisholm v. Georgia*, but looking at the subject as

Hamilton did, and as Mr. Justice Iredell did, in the light of history and experience and the established order of things, the views of the latter were clearly right, — as the people of the United States in their sovereign capacity subsequently decided.

But Hamilton was not alone in protesting against the construction put upon the Constitution by its opponents. In the Virginia convention the same objections were raised by George Mason and Patrick Henry, and were met by Madison and Marshall as follows. Madison said "Its jurisdiction [the federal jurisdiction] in controversies between a State and citizens of another State is much objected to, and perhaps without reason. It is not in the power of individuals to call any State into court. The only operation it can have is that, if a State should wish to bring a suit against a citizen, it must be brought before the federal court. This will give satisfaction to individuals, as it will prevent citizens on whom a state may have a claim being dissatisfied with the state courts.

["]It appears to me that this [clause] can have no operation but this — to give a citizen a right to be heard in the federal courts, and if a state should condescend to be a party, this court may take cognizance of it." 3 Elliott's Debates, 2d ed. 533. Marshall, in answer to the same objection, said: "With respect to disputes between a State and the citizens of another State, its jurisdiction has been decried with unusual vehemence. I hope that no gentleman will think that a State will be called at the bar of the federal court. . . . It is not rational to suppose that the sovereign power should be dragged before a court. The intent is to enable States to recover claims of individuals residing in other states. . . . But, say they, there will be partiality in it if a State cannot be a defendant — if an individual cannot proceed to obtain judgment against a State, though he may be sued by a state. It is necessary to be so, and cannot be avoided. I see a difficulty in making a State defendant which does not prevent its being plaintiff." [Id.] 555.

It seems to us that these views of those great advocates and defenders of the Constitution were most sensible and just, and they apply equally to the present case as to that then under discussion. The letter is appealed to now, as it was then, as a ground for sustaining a suit brought by an individual against a State. The reason against it is as strong in this case as it was in that. It is an attempt to strain the Constitution and the law to a construction never imagined or dreamed of. Can we suppose that, when the Eleventh Amendment was adopted, it was understood to be left open for citizens of a State to sue their own state in the federal courts, whilst the idea of suits by citizens of other states, or of foreign states, was indignantly repelled? Suppose that Congress, when proposing the Eleventh Amendment, had appended to it a proviso that nothing therein contained should prevent a State from being sued by its own citizens in cases arising under the Constitution or laws of the United States, can we imagine that it would have been adopted by the States? The supposition that it would is almost an absurdity on its face.

The truth is, that the cognizance of suits and actions unknown to the law, and forbidden by the law, was not contemplated by the Constitution when establishing the judicial power of the United States. . . . The suability of a State, without its consent, was a thing unknown to the law[.] This has been so often laid down and acknowledged by courts and jurists that it is hardly necessary to be formally asserted. It was fully shown by an exhaustive examination of the old law by Mr. Justice Iredell in his opinion in *Chisholm v. Georgia*, and it has been conceded in every case since, where the question has, in any way, been presented. . . . In all these cases the effort was to show, and the court held, that the suits were not against the State or the United States, but against the individuals, conceding that, if they had been against either the State or the United States, they could not be maintained. . . .

But besides the presumption that no anomalous and unheard-of proceedings or suits were intended to be raised up by the Constitution — anomalous and unheard of when the Constitution was adopted — an additional reason why the jurisdiction claimed for the Circuit Court does not exist, is the language of the act of Congress by which its jurisdiction is conferred. The words are these "The circuit courts of the United States shall have original cognizance, concurrent with the courts of the several States, of all suits of a civil nature at common law or in equity, . . . arising under the Constitution or laws of the United States, or treaties," etc. — "Concurrent with the courts of the several States." Does not this qualification, show that Congress, in legislating to carry the Constitution into effect, did not intend to invest its courts with any new and strange jurisdictions? The state courts have no power to entertain suits by individuals against a State without its consent. Then how does the Circuit Court, having only concurrent jurisdiction, acquire any such power? It is true that the same qualification existed in the judiciary act of 1789, which was before the court in *Chisholm v. Georgia*, and the majority of the court did not think that it was sufficient to limit the jurisdiction of the Circuit Court. Justice Iredell thought differently[.] In view of the manner in which that decision was received by the country, the adoption of the Eleventh Amendment, the light of history and the reason of the thing, we think we are at liberty to prefer Justice Iredell's views in this regard.

Some reliance is placed by the plaintiff upon the observations of Chief Justice Marshall in *Cohens v. Virginia*, 6 Wheat. 264, 410. The Chief Justice was there considering the power of review exercisable by this court over the judgments of a state court, wherein it might be necessary to make the State itself a defendant in error. He showed that this power was absolutely necessary in order to enable the judiciary of the United States to take cognizance of all cases arising under the Constitution and laws of the United States. He also showed that making a State a defendant in error was entirely different from suing a State in an original action in prosecution of a demand against it, and was not within the meaning of the Eleventh Amendment, that the prosecution of a writ of error against a State was not the prosecution of a suit in the sense of that amendment, which had reference to the prosecution, by suit, of claims against a State. . . .

After . . . showing by incontestable argument that a writ of error to a judgment recovered by a State, in which the State is necessarily the defendant in error, is not a suit commenced or prosecuted against a State in the sense of the amendment, he added, that if the court were mistaken in this, its error did not affect that case, because the writ of error therein was not prosecuted by "a citizen of another State" or "of any foreign state," and so was not affected by the amendment, but was governed by the general grant of judicial power, as extending "to all cases arising under the Constitution or laws of the United States, without respect to parties."

It must be conceded that the last observation of the Chief Justice does favor the argument of the plaintiff. But the observation was unnecessary to the decision, and in that sense *extra judicial*, and though made by one who seldom used words without due reflection, ought not to outweigh the important considerations referred to which lead to a different conclusion. With regard to the question then before the court, it may be observed, that writs of error to judgments in favor of the crown, or of the State, had been known to the law from time immemorial, and had never been considered as exceptions to the rule that an action does not lie against the sovereign. . . .

It is not necessary that we should enter upon an examination of the reason or expediency of the rule which exempts a sovereign State from prosecution in a court of justice at the suit of individuals. This is fully discussed by writers on public law[.] It is enough for us to declare its existence. The legislative department of a State represents its polity and its will, and is called upon by the highest demands of natural and political law to preserve justice and judgment, and to hold inviolate the public obligations. Any departure from this rule, except for reasons most cogent, (of which the legislature, and not the courts, is the judge,) never fails in the end to incur the odium of the world, and to bring lasting injury upon the State itself. But to deprive the legislature of the power of judging what the honor and safety of the State may require, even at the expense of a temporary failure to discharge the public debts, would be attended with greater evils than such failure can cause.

Mr. JUSTICE HARLAN, concurring.

I concur with the court in holding that a suit directly against a State by one of its own citizens is not one to which the judicial power of the United States extends, unless the State itself consents to be sued. Upon this ground alone I assent to the judgment. But I cannot give my assent to many things said in the opinion. The comments made upon the decision in *Chisholm v. Georgia* do not meet my approval. They are not necessary to the determination of the present case. Besides, I am of opinion that the decision in that case was based upon a sound interpretation of the Constitution as that instrument then was.

POINTS FOR DISCUSSION

1. In *Hans*, the Court relied on background principles of sovereign immunity to hold that a citizen of Louisiana may not bring a suit "arising under" federal law against the State of Louisiana. What is the precise basis of the Court's decision?

2. The Court in *Hans* relied in part on the ratification-debate statements of Hamilton, Madison, and Marshall. Should their statements have priority over the views of the *Chisholm* Justices, who included delegates to the Federal Convention and prominent ratification-debate participants? Did the Court adequately deal with Marshall's seemingly conflicting account of state sovereign immunity in *Cohens v. Virginia*, 19 U.S. (6 Wheat.) 264 (1821)?

3. The *Hans* Court argued that "to deprive the legislature of the power of judging what the honor and safety of the state may require, even at the expense

of a temporary failure to discharge the public debts, would be attended with greater evils than such failure can cause." What are those evils? What values, if any, does state sovereign immunity advance? What values, if any, does it hinder? What role, if any, should those values play in judicial analyses of whether the Constitution recognizes state sovereign immunity?

Hans held that states have sovereign immunity even from suits "arising under" federal law. Given *Hans*, are there any means by which courts may provide redress for state violations of federal law? There are, indeed, some. First, the Supreme Court has held that state sovereign immunity does not bar suits against states by the United States. In *United States v. Mississippi*, 380 U.S. 128 (1965), the Court explained that although the Eleventh Amendment "has been read to bar a suit by a State's own citizens as well" as citizens of a different state, "nothing in this or any other provision of the Constitution prevents or has ever been seriously supposed to prevent a State's being sued by the United States." *Id.* at 140. Second, the Court has held that state sovereign immunity does not bar suits by one state against another. Article III extends the federal judicial power "to Controversies between two or more States." In *Kansas v. Colorado*, 206 U.S. 46 (1907), the Court explained that

> to the Supreme Court is granted jurisdiction of all controversies between the States which are justiciable in their nature. 'All the States have transferred the decision of their controversies to this court; each had a right to demand . . . that we should do that which neither States nor Congress could do, settle the controversies between them.'

Id. at 84 (quoting *Rhode Island v. Massachusetts*, 37 U.S. (12 Pet.) 657, 743 (1838)). Third, the Supreme Court has determined that local governments do not enjoy state sovereign immunity. In *Lincoln County v. Luning*, 133 U.S. 529 (1890), the Court stated that while a municipality "is territorially a part of the State, yet politically it is also a corporation created by and with such powers as are given to it by the State." *Id.* at 530. Thus, "any city, town, or other municipal corporation may be said to be a part of the State" only in a "remote sense." *Id.* Fourth, the Supreme Court has held that suits by private individuals against state officers in their individual capacities are not suits against the state. In *Ex parte Young*, 209 U.S. 123 (1908), the Court determined that state officers who act in violation of the Constitution often stand before the court as individuals, not states, because, in acting unconstitutionally, officers are stripped of their state authority. In application, this doctrine has many complex permutations. Finally, a private litigant may sue a state for violating federal law if the state has waived its immunity.

In recent years, the Court has faced the question whether Congress may abrogate state sovereign immunity by specifically authorizing private suits against states for violating federal law. In *Fitzpatrick v. Bitzer*, 427 U.S. 445 (1976), the Court held that Congress may abrogate state sovereign immunity when it legislates under §5 of the Fourteenth Amendment:

> [W]e think that the Eleventh Amendment, and the principle of state sovereignty which it embodies, see *Hans v. Louisiana*, 134 U.S. 1 (1890), are

necessarily limited by the enforcement provisions of §5 of the Fourteenth Amendment. In that section Congress is expressly granted authority to enforce "by appropriate legislation" the substantive provisions of the Fourteenth Amendment, which themselves embody significant limitations on state authority. When Congress acts pursuant to §5, not only is it exercising legislative authority that is plenary within the terms of the constitutional grant, it is exercising that authority under one section of a constitutional Amendment whose other sections by their own terms embody limitations on state authority. We think that Congress may, in determining what is "appropriate legislation" for the purpose of enforcing the provisions of the Fourteenth Amendment, provide for private suits against States or state officials which are constitutionally impermissible in other contexts. *Id.* at 456.

The Court has held, however, that Congress lacks power to abrogate state sovereign immunity when legislating under the Commerce Clause. In *Seminole Tribe of Florida v. Florida*, 517 U.S. 44 (1996), the Court distinguished *Bitzer* on the ground that the §5 power is unique insofar as it specifically authorizes Congress to take corrective action against the states. In *Alden v. Maine*, 527 U.S. 706 (1999), the Court went on to hold that Congress lacks power under the Commerce Clause to abrogate state sovereign immunity in state court.

Seminole Tribe and *Alden* broadly address the place of state sovereign immunity in the United States constitutional structure. As you read them, focus on the interpretive methodologies the Justices apply, especially their use of historical evidence. Also, try to identify the exact interpretive disagreements between the Justices. Keep in mind, too, that these cases are of relatively recent vintage, resolved 5-4, with dissenting Justices predicting that the Court will eventually overturn them.

SEMINOLE TRIBE OF FLORIDA V. FLORIDA

517 U.S. 44 (1996)

CHIEF JUSTICE REHNQUIST delivered the opinion of the Court. . . .

I

Congress passed the Indian Gaming Regulatory Act in 1988 in order to provide a statutory basis for the operation and regulation of gaming by Indian tribes. See 25 U.S.C. §2702. The Act divides gaming on Indian lands into three classes—I, II, and III—and provides a different regulatory scheme for each class. Class III gaming—the type with which we are here concerned—is defined as "all forms of gaming that are not class I gaming or class II gaming," §2703(8), and includes such things as slot machines, casino games, banking card games, dog racing, and lotteries. It is the most heavily regulated of the three classes. The Act provides that class III gaming is lawful only where it is . . . [*inter alia*] "conducted in conformance with a Tribal-State compact entered into by the Indian tribe and the State. . . ." §2710(d)(1).

[Section] 2710(d)(3) describes the process by which a State and an Indian tribe begin negotiations toward a Tribal-State compact:

"(A) Any Indian tribe having jurisdiction over the Indian lands upon which a class III gaming activity is being conducted, or is to be conducted, shall request the State in which such lands are located to enter into negotiations for the purpose of entering into a Tribal-State compact governing the conduct of gaming activities. Upon receiving such a request, the State shall negotiate with the Indian tribe in good faith to enter into such a compact."

The State's obligation to "negotiate with the Indian tribe in good faith" is made judicially enforceable by §§2710(d)(7)(A)(i) and (B)(i):

"(A) The United States district courts shall have jurisdiction over —

"(i) any cause of action initiated by an Indian tribe arising from the failure of a State to enter into negotiations with the Indian tribe for the purpose of entering into a Tribal-State compact under paragraph (3) or to conduct such negotiations in good faith. . . ."

In September 1991, the Seminole Tribe of Florida . . . sued the State of Florida. . . . Invoking jurisdiction under 25 U.S.C. §2710(d)(7)(A), as well as 28 U.S.C. §§1331 and 1362, petitioner alleged that respondents had "refused to enter into any negotiation for inclusion of [certain gaming activities] in a tribal-state compact," thereby violating the "requirement of good faith negotiation" contained in §2710(d)(3). Respondents moved to dismiss the complaint, arguing that the suit violated the State's sovereign immunity from suit in federal court. . . .

The Eleventh Amendment provides:

"The Judicial power of the United States shall not be construed to extend to any suit in law or equity, commenced or prosecuted against one of the United States by Citizens of another State, or by Citizens or Subjects of any Foreign State."

Although the text of the Amendment would appear to restrict only the Article III diversity jurisdiction of the federal courts, "we have understood the Eleventh Amendment to stand not so much for what it says, but for the presupposition . . . which it confirms." *Blatchford v. Native Village of Noatak*, 501 U.S. 775, 779 (1991). That presupposition, first observed over a century ago in *Hans v. Louisiana*, 134 U.S. 1 (1890), has two parts: first, that each State is a sovereign entity in our federal system; and second, that " '[i]t is inherent in the nature of sovereignty not to be amenable to the suit of an individual without its consent,' " *id.*, at 13, quoting The Federalist No. 81 (A. Hamilton). . . . For over a century we have reaffirmed that federal jurisdiction over suits against unconsenting States "was not contemplated by the Constitution when establishing the judicial power of the United States." *Hans, supra*, at 15. . . .

II

Petitioner argues that Congress through the Act abrogated the States' immunity from suit. In order to determine whether Congress has abrogated the States' sovereign immunity, we ask two questions: first, whether Congress has "unequivocally expresse[d] its intent to abrogate the immunity," *Green v. Mansour*, 474 U.S. 64, 68 (1985); and second, whether Congress has acted "pursuant to a valid exercise of power," *ibid.*

A

Congress' intent to abrogate the States' immunity from suit must be obvious from "a clear legislative statement." *Blatchford, supra*, 501 U.S., at 786. . . . Congress has in §2710(d)(7) provided an "unmistakably clear" statement of its intent to abrogate. . . . [W]e think that the numerous references to the "State" in the text of §2710(d)(7)(B) make it indubitable that Congress intended through the Act to abrogate the States' sovereign immunity from suit. . . .

B

Having concluded that Congress clearly intended to abrogate the States' sovereign immunity through §2710(d)(7), we turn now to consider whether the Act was passed "pursuant to a valid exercise of power." *Green v. Mansour*, 474 U.S., at 68. . . .

[O]ur inquiry into whether Congress has the power to abrogate unilaterally the States' immunity from suit is narrowly focused on one question: Was the Act in question passed pursuant to a constitutional provision granting Congress the power to abrogate? See, *e.g., Fitzpatrick v. Bitzer*, 427 U.S. 445, 452-456 (1976). Previously, in conducting that inquiry, we have found authority to abrogate under only two provisions of the Constitution. In *Fitzpatrick*, we recognized that the Fourteenth Amendment, by expanding federal power at the expense of state autonomy, had fundamentally altered the balance of state and federal power struck by the Constitution. *Id.*, at 455. We noted that §1 of the Fourteenth Amendment contained prohibitions expressly directed at the States and that §5 of the Amendment expressly provided that "The Congress shall have power to enforce, by appropriate legislation, the provisions of this article." See *id.*, at 453. We held that through the Fourteenth Amendment, federal power extended to intrude upon the province of the Eleventh Amendment and therefore that §5 of the Fourteenth Amendment allowed Congress to abrogate the immunity from suit guaranteed by that Amendment.

In only one other case has congressional abrogation of the States' Eleventh Amendment immunity been upheld. In *Pennsylvania v. Union Gas Co.*, 491 U.S. 1 (1989), a plurality of the Court found that the Interstate Commerce Clause, Art. I, §8, cl. 3, granted Congress the power to abrogate state sovereign immunity, stating that the power to regulate interstate commerce would be "incomplete without the authority to render States liable in damages." 491 U.S., at 19-20. Justice White added the fifth vote necessary to the result in that case, but wrote separately in order to express that he "[did] not agree with much of [the plurality's] reasoning." *Id.*, at 57. . . .

Following the rationale of the *Union Gas* plurality, our inquiry is limited to determining whether the Indian Commerce Clause, like the Interstate Commerce Clause, is a grant of authority to the Federal Government at the expense of the States. The answer to that question is obvious. If anything, the Indian Commerce Clause accomplishes a greater transfer of power from the States to the Federal Government than does the Interstate Commerce Clause. This is clear enough from the fact that the States still exercise some authority over interstate trade but have been divested of virtually all authority over Indian commerce and Indian tribes. Under the rationale of *Union Gas*, if the States' partial cession of authority over a particular area includes cession of the immunity from suit, then their virtually total cession of authority over a different area must also include cession of the immunity from suit. . . .

Respondents . . . contend that if we find the rationale of the *Union Gas* plurality to extend to the Indian Commerce Clause, then "*Union Gas* should be reconsidered and overruled." Generally, the principle of *stare decisis*, and the interests that it serves, viz., "the evenhanded, predictable, and consistent development of legal principles, . . . reliance on judicial decisions, and . . . the actual and perceived integrity of the judicial process," *Payne v. Tennessee*, 501 U.S. 808, 827 (1991), counsel strongly against reconsideration of our precedent. Nevertheless, we always have treated *stare decisis* as a "principle of policy," *Helvering v. Hallock*, 309 U.S. 106, 119 (1940), and not as an "inexorable command," *Payne*, 501 U.S., at 828. "[W]hen governing decisions are unworkable or are badly reasoned, 'this Court has never felt constrained to follow precedent.'" *Id.*, at 827. Our willingness to reconsider our earlier decisions has been "particularly true in constitutional cases, because in such cases 'correction through legislative action is practically impossible.'" *Payne*, *supra*, at 828.

The Court in *Union Gas* reached a result without an expressed rationale agreed upon by a majority of the Court. . . . The plurality's rationale also deviated sharply from our established federalism jurisprudence and essentially eviscerated our decision in *Hans*. . . . It was well established in 1989 when *Union Gas* was decided that the Eleventh Amendment stood for the constitutional principle that state sovereign immunity limited the federal courts' jurisdiction under Article III. The text of the Amendment itself is clear enough on this point: "The Judicial power of the United States shall not be construed to extend to any suit. . . ." And our decisions since *Hans* had been equally clear that the Eleventh Amendment reflects "the fundamental principle of sovereign immunity [that] limits the grant of judicial authority in Art. III," *Pennhurst State School and Hospital v. Halderman*, 465 U.S. 89, 97-98 (1984). . . . As the dissent in *Union Gas* recognized, the plurality's conclusion—that Congress could under Article I expand the scope of the federal courts' jurisdiction under Article III—"contradict[ed] our unvarying approach to Article III as setting forth the *exclusive* catalog of permissible federal-court jurisdiction." *Union Gas, supra*, 491 U.S., at 39. . . .

The plurality's . . . reliance upon our decision in *Fitzpatrick v. Bitzer*, 427 U.S. 445 (1976), that Congress could under the Fourteenth Amendment abrogate the States' sovereign immunity was . . . misplaced. *Fitzpatrick* was based upon a rationale wholly inapplicable to the Interstate Commerce Clause, viz., that the Fourteenth Amendment, adopted well after the adoption of the Eleventh Amendment and the ratification of the Constitution, operated to alter the pre-existing balance between state and federal power achieved by Article III and the Eleventh Amendment. *Id.*, at 454. . . .

Reconsidering the decision in *Union Gas*, we conclude that none of the policies underlying *stare decisis* require our continuing adherence to its holding. . . . We feel bound to conclude that *Union Gas* was wrongly decided and that it should be, and now is, overruled. . . .

For over a century, we have grounded our decisions in the oft-repeated understanding of state sovereign immunity as an essential part of the Eleventh Amendment. . . . It is true that we have not had occasion previously to apply established Eleventh Amendment principles to the question whether Congress has the power to abrogate state sovereign immunity (save in *Union Gas*). But consideration of that question must proceed with fidelity to this century-old doctrine.

The dissent . . . disregards our case law in favor of a theory cobbled together from law review articles and its own version of historical events. The dissent cites not a single decision since *Hans* (other than *Union Gas*) that supports its view of state sovereign immunity, instead relying upon the now-discredited decision in *Chisholm v. Georgia*, 2 Dall. 419 (1793). Its undocumented and highly speculative extralegal explanation of the decision in *Hans* is a disservice to the Court's traditional method of adjudication.

The dissent mischaracterizes the *Hans* opinion. That decision found its roots not solely in the common law of England, but in the much more fundamental " 'jurisprudence in all civilized nations.' " *Hans*, 134 U.S., at 17; see also The Federalist No. 81 (A. Hamilton) (sovereign immunity "is the general sense and the general practice of mankind"). The dissent's proposition that the common law of England, where adopted by the States, was open to change by the Legislature is wholly unexceptionable and largely beside the point: that common law provided the substantive rules of law rather than jurisdiction. . . . It also is noteworthy that the principle of state sovereign immunity stands distinct from other principles of the common law in that only the former prompted a specific constitutional amendment.

Hans — with a much closer vantage point than the dissent — recognized that the decision in *Chisholm* was contrary to the well-understood meaning of the Constitution. The dissent's conclusion that the decision in *Chisholm* was "reasonable," certainly would have struck the Framers of the Eleventh Amendment as quite odd: That decision created "such a shock of surprise that the Eleventh Amendment was at once proposed and adopted." *Monaco, supra*, at 325. The dissent's lengthy analysis of the text of the Eleventh Amendment is directed at a straw man — we long have recognized that blind reliance upon the text of the Eleventh Amendment is " 'to strain the Constitution and the law to a construction never imagined or dreamed of.' " [*Principality of Monaco v. Mississippi*, 292 U.S. 313, 326 (1934).] The text dealt in terms only with the problem presented by the decision in *Chisholm*; in light of the fact that the federal courts did not have federal-question jurisdiction at the time the Amendment was passed (and would not have it until 1875), it seems unlikely that much thought was given to the prospect of federal-question jurisdiction over the States.

That same consideration causes the dissent's criticism of the views of Marshall, Madison, and Hamilton to ring hollow. The dissent cites statements made by those three influential Framers, the most natural reading of which would preclude all federal jurisdiction over an unconsenting State. Struggling against this reading, however, the dissent finds significant the absence of any contention that sovereign immunity would affect the new federal-question jurisdiction. But the lack of any statute vesting general federal-question jurisdiction in the federal courts until much later makes the dissent's demand for greater specificity about a then-dormant jurisdiction overly exacting.

In putting forward a new theory of state sovereign immunity, the dissent develops its own vision of the political system created by the Framers, concluding with the statement that "[t]he Framers' principal objectives in rejecting English theories of unitary sovereignty . . . would have been impeded if a new concept of sovereign immunity had taken its place in federal-question cases, and would have been substantially thwarted if that new immunity had been held untouchable by any congressional effort to abrogate it." This sweeping statement ignores the fact that the Nation survived for nearly two centuries without the question of the existence of such power ever being presented to this Court. And Congress itself waited nearly a century before even conferring federal-question jurisdiction on the lower federal courts.

In overruling *Union Gas* today, we reconfirm that the background principle of state sovereign immunity embodied in the Eleventh Amendment is not so ephemeral as to dissipate when the subject of the suit is an area, like the regulation of Indian commerce, that is under the exclusive control of the Federal Government. Even when the Constitution vests in Congress complete lawmaking authority over a particular area, the Eleventh Amendment prevents congressional authorization of suits by private parties against unconsenting States. The Eleventh Amendment restricts the judicial power under Article III, and Article I cannot be used to circumvent the constitutional limitations placed upon federal jurisdiction. Petitioner's suit against the State of Florida must be dismissed for a lack of jurisdiction. . . .

JUSTICE STEVENS, dissenting.

The importance of the majority's decision to overrule the Court's holding in *Pennsylvania v. Union Gas Co.* cannot be overstated. The majority's opinion . . . prevents Congress from providing a federal forum for a broad range of actions against States, from those sounding in copyright and patent law, to those concerning bankruptcy, environmental law, and the regulation of our vast national economy. . . .

As Justice Souter has convincingly demonstrated, the Court's contrary conclusion is profoundly misguided. . . .

While . . . there is no justification for permanently enshrining the judge-made law of sovereign immunity, I recognize that federalism concerns — and even the interest in protecting the solvency of the States that was at work in *Chisholm* and *Hans* — may well justify a grant of immunity from federal litigation in certain classes of cases. Such a grant, however, should be the product of a reasoned decision by the policymaking branch of our Government. For this Court to conclude that timeworn shibboleths iterated and reiterated by judges should take precedence over the deliberations of the Congress of the United States is simply irresponsible. . . . [T]he better reasoning in Justice Souter's far wiser and far more scholarly opinion will surely be the law one day.

JUSTICE SOUTER, with whom JUSTICE GINSBURG and JUSTICE BREYER join, dissenting.

[T]he Court today holds for the first time since the founding of the Republic that Congress has no authority to subject a State to the jurisdiction of a federal court at the behest of an individual asserting a federal right. . . . I part company from the Court because I am convinced that its decision is fundamentally mistaken. . . .

I

It is useful to separate three questions: (1) whether the States enjoyed sovereign immunity if sued in their own courts in the period prior to ratification of the National Constitution; (2) if so, whether after ratification the States were entitled to claim some such immunity when sued in a federal court exercising jurisdiction either because the suit was between a State and a non-state litigant who was not its citizen, or because the issue in the case raised a federal question; and (3) whether any state sovereign immunity recognized in federal court may be abrogated by Congress. . . .

A

The doctrine of sovereign immunity . . . limits . . . the jurisdiction of the courts. . . . While some colonial governments may have enjoyed some such immunity, . . . the scope (and even the existence) of this governmental immunity in pre-Revolutionary America remains disputed. . . . Whatever the scope of sovereign immunity might have been in the Colonies, however, or during the period of Confederation, the proposal to establish a National Government under the Constitution drafted in 1787 presented a prospect unknown to the common law prior to the American experience: the States would become parts of a system in which sovereignty over even domestic matters would be divided or parcelled out between the States and the Nation, the latter to be invested with its own judicial power and the right to prevail against the States whenever their respective substantive laws might be in conflict. With this prospect in mind, the 1787 Constitution might have addressed state sovereign immunity by eliminating whatever sovereign immunity the States previously had, as to any matter subject to federal law or jurisdiction; by recognizing an analogue to the old immunity in the new context of federal jurisdiction, but subject to abrogation as to any matter within that jurisdiction; or by enshrining a doctrine of inviolable state sovereign immunity in the text, thereby giving it constitutional protection in the new federal jurisdiction. . . .

The 1787 draft in fact said nothing on the subject, and it was this very silence that occasioned some, though apparently not widespread, dispute among the Framers and others over whether ratification of the Constitution would preclude a State sued in federal court from asserting sovereign immunity as it could have done on any matter of nonfederal law litigated in its own courts. As it has come down to us, the discussion gave no attention to congressional power under the proposed Article I but focused entirely on the limits of the judicial power provided in Article III. And although the jurisdictional bases together constituting the judicial power of the national courts under §2 of Article III included questions arising under federal law and cases between States and individuals who are not citizens, it was only upon the latter citizen-state diversity provisions that preratification questions about state immunity from suit or liability centered. . . .

B

The argument among the Framers and their friends about sovereign immunity in federal citizen-state diversity cases . . . was short lived and ended when this Court, in *Chisholm v. Georgia*, 2 Dall. 419 (1793), chose between the constitutional alternatives of abrogation and recognition of the immunity enjoyed at common law. The 4-to-1 majority adopted the reasonable (although not compelled) interpretation that the first of the two Citizen-State Diversity Clauses abrogated for purposes of federal jurisdiction any immunity the States might have enjoyed in their own courts, and Georgia was accordingly held subject to the judicial power in a common-law assumpsit action by a South Carolina citizen suing to collect a debt. The case also settled, by implication, any question there could possibly have been about recognizing state sovereign immunity in actions depending on the federal question (or "arising under") head of jurisdiction as well. . . .

C

The Eleventh Amendment, of course, repudiated *Chisholm* and clearly divested federal courts of some jurisdiction as to cases against state parties. . . . There are two plausible readings of this provision's text. Under the first, it simply repeals the Citizen-State Diversity Clauses of Article III for all cases in which the State appears as a defendant. Under the second, it strips the federal courts of jurisdiction in any case in which a state defendant is sued by a citizen not its own, even if jurisdiction might otherwise rest on the existence of a federal question in the suit. Neither reading of the Amendment . . . furnishes authority for the Court's view in today's case. . . .

The history and structure of the Eleventh Amendment convincingly show that it reaches only to suits subject to federal jurisdiction exclusively under the Citizen-State Diversity Clauses. In precisely tracking the language in Article III providing for citizen-state diversity jurisdiction, the text of the Amendment does, after all, suggest to common sense that only the Diversity Clauses are being addressed. If the Framers had meant the Amendment to bar federal-question suits as well, they could not only have made their intentions clearer very easily, but could simply have adopted the first post-*Chisholm* proposal, introduced in the House of Representatives by Theodore Sedgwick of Massachusetts on instructions from the Legislature of that Commonwealth. Its provisions would have had exactly that expansive effect:

> "[N]o state shall be liable to be made a party defendant, in any of the judicial courts, established, or which shall be established under the authority of the United States, at the suit of any person or persons, whether a citizen or citizens, or a foreigner or foreigners, or of any body politic or corporate, whether within or without the United States." Gazette of the United States 303 (Feb. 20, 1793). . . .

Congress took no action on Sedgwick's proposal, however, and the Amendment as ultimately adopted two years later could hardly have been meant to limit federal-question jurisdiction, or it would never have left the States open to federal-question suits by their own citizens. . . .

It should accordingly come as no surprise that the weightiest commentary following the Amendment's adoption described it simply as constricting the scope of the Citizen-State Diversity Clauses. In *Cohens v. Virginia*, 6 Wheat. 264 (1821), for instance, Chief Justice Marshall, writing for the Court, emphasized that the Amendment had no effect on federal courts' jurisdiction grounded on the "arising under" provision of Article III and concluded that "a case arising under the constitution or laws of the United States, is cognizable in the Courts of the Union, whoever may be the parties to that case." *Id.*, at 383. The point of the Eleventh Amendment, according to *Cohens*, was to bar jurisdiction in suits at common law by Revolutionary War debt creditors, not "to strip the government of the means of protecting, by the instrumentality of its courts, the constitution and laws from active violation." *Id.*, at 407. . . .

The good sense of this early construction of the Amendment as affecting the diversity jurisdiction and no more has the further virtue of making sense of this Court's repeated exercise of appellate jurisdiction in federal-question suits brought against States in their own courts by out-of-staters. Exercising appellate jurisdiction in these cases would have been patent error if the Eleventh Amendment limited federal-question jurisdiction, for the Amendment's unconditional language ("shall not be construed") makes no distinction between trial and appellate jurisdiction. . . .

In sum, reading the Eleventh Amendment solely as a limit on citizen-state diversity jurisdiction has the virtue of coherence with this Court's practice, with the views of John Marshall, with the history of the Amendment's drafting, and with its allusive language. . . .

Because the plaintiffs in today's case are citizens of the State that they are suing, the Eleventh Amendment simply does not apply to them. We must therefore look elsewhere for the source of that immunity by which the Court says their suit is barred from a federal court.

II

The obvious place to look elsewhere, of course, is *Hans v. Louisiana*, 134 U.S. 1 (1890), and *Hans* was indeed a leap in the direction of today's holding, even though it does not take the Court all the way. The parties in *Hans* raised, and the Court in that case answered, only . . . whether the Constitution, without more, permits a State to plead sovereign immunity to bar the exercise of federal-question jurisdiction. Although the Court invoked a principle of sovereign immunity to cure what it took to be the Eleventh Amendment's anomaly of barring only those state suits brought by noncitizen plaintiffs, the *Hans* Court had no occasion to consider whether Congress could abrogate that background immunity by statute. Indeed (except in the special circumstance of Congress's power to enforce the Civil War Amendments), this question never came before our Court until [*Pennsylvania v. Union Gas Co.*, 491 U.S. 1 (1989)], and any intimations of an answer in prior cases were mere dicta. In *Union Gas* the Court held that the immunity recognized in *Hans* had no constitutional status and was subject to congressional abrogation. Today the Court overrules *Union Gas* and holds just the opposite. In deciding how to choose between these two positions, the place to begin is with *Hans*'s holding that a principle of sovereign immunity derived from the common law insulates a State from federal-question jurisdiction at the suit of its own citizen. A critical examination of that case will show that it was wrongly decided. . . . It follows that the Court's further step today of constitutionalizing *Hans*'s rule against abrogation by Congress compounds and immensely magnifies the century-old mistake of *Hans* itself and takes its place with other historic examples of textually untethered elevations of judicially derived rules to the status of inviolable constitutional law.

A

Hans addressed the issue implicated (though not directly raised) in the preratification debate about the Citizen-State Diversity Clauses and implicitly settled by *Chisholm*: whether state sovereign immunity was cognizable by federal courts on the exercise of federal-question jurisdiction. According to *Hans*, and contrary to *Chisholm*, it was. But that is all that *Hans* held. Because no federal legislation purporting to pierce state immunity was at issue, it cannot fairly be said that *Hans* held state sovereign immunity to have attained some constitutional status immunizing it from abrogation.

Taking *Hans* only as far as its holding, its vulnerability is apparent. The Court rested its opinion on avoiding the supposed anomaly of recognizing jurisdiction to entertain a citizen's federal-question suit, but not one brought by a noncitizen. There was, however, no such anomaly at all. As already explained, federal-question cases are not touched by the Eleventh Amendment, which leaves a State open to federal-question suits by citizens and noncitizens alike. If Hans had been from Massachusetts the Eleventh Amendment would not have barred his action against Louisiana. . . .

Hans was one episode in a long story of debt repudiation by the States of the former Confederacy after the end of Reconstruction. . . . Contract Clause suits like the one brought by Hans thus presented this Court with "a draconian choice between repudiation of some of its most inviolable constitutional doctrines and the humiliation of seeing its political authority compromised as its judgments met the resistance of hostile state governments." . . . Given the likelihood that a judgment against the State could not be enforced, it is not wholly surprising that the *Hans* Court found a way to avoid the certainty of the State's contempt. . . .

B

The majority does not dispute the point that *Hans v. Louisiana* had no occasion to decide whether Congress could abrogate a State's immunity from federal-question suits. . . . The majority, however, would read the "rationale" of *Hans* and its line of subsequent cases as answering the further question whether the "postulate" of sovereign immunity that "limit[s] and control[s]" the exercise of Article III jurisdiction, [*Principality of Monaco v. Mississippi*, 292 U.S. 313, 322 (1934)], is constitutional in stature and therefore unalterable by Congress. It is true that there are statements in the cases that point toward just this conclusion. These statements, however, are dicta. . . .

If it is indeed true that "private suits against States [are] not permitted under Article III (by virtue of the understanding represented by the Eleventh Amendment)," *Union Gas*, 491 U.S., at 40 (Scalia, J., concurring in part and dissenting in part), then it is hard to see how a State's sovereign immunity may be waived any more than it may be abrogated by Congress. After all, consent of a party is in all other instances wholly insufficient to create subject-matter jurisdiction where it would not otherwise exist. . . .

III

Three critical errors in *Hans* weigh against constitutionalizing its holding as the majority does today. The first we have already seen: the *Hans* Court misread the Eleventh Amendment. It also misunderstood the conditions under which common-law doctrines were received or rejected at the time of the founding, and it fundamentally mistook the very nature of sovereignty in the young Republic that was supposed to entail a State's immunity to federal-question jurisdiction in a federal court. While I would not, as a matter of *stare decisis*, overrule *Hans* today, . . . the Court today . . . compounds already serious error in taking *Hans* the further step of investing its rule with constitutional inviolability against the considered judgment of Congress to abrogate it.

A

There is and could be no dispute that the doctrine of sovereign immunity that *Hans* purported to apply had its origins in the "familiar doctrine of the common law," *The Siren*, 7 Wall. 152, 153 (1869), "derived from the laws and practices of our English ancestors," *United States v. Lee*, 106 U.S. 196, 205 (1882). . . . Here, as in the mother country, it remained a common-law rule. . . . [T]he adoption of English common law in America was not taken for granted, and . . . the exact manner and extent of the common law's reception were subject to careful consideration by courts and legislatures in each of the new States. . . .

While the States had limited their reception of English common law to principles appropriate to American conditions, the 1787 draft Constitution contained no provision for adopting the common law at all. . . .

The Framers . . . recognized that the diverse development of the common law in the several States made a general federal reception impossible. . . . The Framers may, as Madison, Hamilton, and Marshall argued, have contemplated that federal courts would respect state immunity law in diversity cases, but the generalized principle of immunity that today's majority would graft onto the Constitution itself may well never have developed with any common clarity and, in any event, has not been shown to have existed. . . .

B

Given the refusal to entertain any wholesale reception of common law, given the failure of the new Constitution to make any provision for adoption of common law as such, and given . . . protests . . . that no general reception had occurred, the *Hans* Court and the Court today cannot reasonably argue that something like the old immunity doctrine somehow slipped in as a tacit but enforceable background principle. The evidence is even more specific, however, that there was no pervasive understanding that sovereign immunity had limited federal-question jurisdiction. . . . James Madison, John Marshall, and Alexander Hamilton all appear to have believed that the common-law immunity from suit would survive the ratification of Article III, so as to be at a State's disposal when jurisdiction would depend on diversity. . . .

As Hamilton stated in The Federalist No. 81:

> "It is inherent in the nature of sovereignty, not to be amenable to the suit of an individual *without its consent*. This is the general sense and the general practice of mankind; and the exemption, as one of the attributes of sovereignty, is now enjoyed by the government of every state in the Union. Unless therefore, there is a surrender of this immunity in the plan of the convention, it will remain with the states, and the danger intimated must be merely ideal." The Federalist No. 81. . . .

[T]he immediate context of Hamilton's discussion in Federalist No. 81 has nothing to do with federal-question cases. It addresses a suggestion "that an assignment of the public securities of one state to the citizens of another, would enable them to prosecute that state in the federal courts for the amount of those securities." The Federalist No. 81. Hamilton is plainly talking about a suit subject to a federal court's jurisdiction under the Citizen-State Diversity Clauses of Article III. . . . Thus, the Court's attempt to convert isolated statements by the Framers into answers to questions not before them is fundamentally misguided. . . .

Given the Framers' general concern with curbing abuses by state governments, it would be amazing if the scheme of delegated powers embodied in the Constitution had left the National Government powerless to render the States judicially accountable for violations of federal rights. And of course the Framers did not understand the scheme to leave the Government powerless. In The Federalist No. 80, Hamilton observed that "[n]o man of sense will believe that such prohibitions [running against the States] would be scrupulously regarded, without some effectual power in the government to restrain or correct the infractions of them," and that "an authority in the federal courts, to over-rule such as might be in manifest contravention of the articles of union" was the Convention's preferred remedy. By speaking in the plural of an authority in the federal "courts," Hamilton made it clear that he envisioned more than this Court's exercise of appellate jurisdiction to review federal questions decided by state courts. Nor is it plausible that he was thinking merely of suits brought against States by the National Government itself, which The Federalist's authors did not describe in the paternalistic terms that would pass without an eyebrow raised today. Hamilton's power of the Government to restrain violations of citizens' rights was a power to be exercised by the federal courts at the citizens' behest. . . .

C

The considerations expressed so far, based on text, *Chisholm*, caution in common-law reception, and sovereignty theory, have pointed both to the mistakes inherent in *Hans* and, even more strongly, to the error of today's holding. Although for reasons of *stare decisis* I would not today disturb the century-old precedent, I surely would not extend its error by placing the common-law immunity it mistakenly recognized beyond the power of Congress to abrogate. . . .

POINTS FOR DISCUSSION

1. What are the exact points of disagreement between the majority and dissenting Justices? How should they be resolved?

2. In *Seminole Tribe*, the Court concluded that state sovereign immunity from suit is a constitutional limitation on federal court jurisdiction, one that Congress may not abrogate in the exercise of the commerce power. As a matter of history, the Court relies on statements by Hamilton, Madison, and Marshall; the "shock" of *Chisholm*; the decisive enactment of the Eleventh Amendment; and *Hans v. Louisiana*, 134 U.S. 1 (1890). In dissent, Justice Souter relies on the text of the Eleventh Amendment, the Amendment's drafting history, judicial precedent, the "common law" nature of sovereign immunity, and the idea of sovereignty under the Constitution. What, as a matter of history, are the Justices attempting to discern? The most popular understanding of the relationship between the Constitution and state sovereign immunity at the Founding? The most reasonable understanding of the relationship between the Constitution and state sovereign immunity at the Founding? What should the Justices be attempting to discern? Which Justices provide the most compelling historical account of the Eleventh Amendment and state sovereign immunity?

3. As a matter of precedent, the Court relied on *Hans v. Louisiana*. Did *Hans*, fairly construed, resolve the question presented in *Seminole Tribe*?

4. Justice Souter discredited *Hans* by characterizing it as "one episode in a long story of debt repudiation by the States of the former Confederacy after the end of Reconstruction. Given the likelihood that a judgment against the State could not be enforced, it is not wholly surprising that the *Hans* Court found a way to avoid the certainty of the State's contempt." The Court characterized this account as an "undocumented and highly speculative extralegal explanation of the decision in *Hans*," which "is a disservice to the Court's traditional method of adjudication." To what extent, if any, should courts determine the precedential effect of cases according to the historical and political contexts in which they were decided?

ALDEN v. MAINE

527 U.S. 706 (1999)

JUSTICE KENNEDY delivered the opinion of the Court.

In 1992, petitioners, a group of probation officers, filed suit against their employer, the State of Maine, in the United States District Court for the District of Maine. The officers alleged the State had violated the overtime provisions of the Fair Labor Standards Act of 1938 (FLSA), 52 Stat. 1060, as amended, 29 U.S.C. §201 *et seq.* (1994 ed. and Supp. III), and sought compensation and liquidated damages. While the suit was pending, this Court decided *Seminole Tribe of Fla. v. Florida*, 517 U.S. 44 (1996), which made it clear that Congress lacks power under Article I to abrogate the States' sovereign immunity from suits commenced or prosecuted in the federal courts. Upon consideration of *Seminole Tribe*, the District Court dismissed petitioners' action. . . . Petitioners then filed the same action in state court. The state trial court dismissed the suit on the basis of sovereign immunity. . . .

We hold that the powers delegated to Congress under Article I of the United States Constitution do not include the power to subject nonconsenting States to private suits for damages in state courts. . . .

I

The Eleventh Amendment makes explicit reference to the States' immunity from suits "commenced or prosecuted against one of the United States by Citizens of another State, or by Citizens or Subjects of any Foreign State." U.S. Const., Amdt. 11. We have, as a result, sometimes referred to the States' immunity from suit as "Eleventh Amendment immunity." The phrase is convenient shorthand but something of a misnomer, for the sovereign immunity of the States neither derives from, nor is limited by, the terms of the Eleventh Amendment. Rather, as the Constitution's structure, its history, and the authoritative interpretations by this Court make clear, the States' immunity from suit is a fundamental aspect of the sovereignty which the States enjoyed before the ratification of the Constitution, and which they retain today . . . except as altered by the plan of the Convention or certain constitutional Amendments.

A

Although the Constitution establishes a National Government with broad, often plenary authority over matters within its recognized competence, the founding document "specifically recognizes the States as sovereign entities." *Seminole Tribe of Fla. v. Florida, supra*, at 71, n.15. . . . Various textual provisions of the Constitution assume the States' continued existence and active participation in the fundamental processes of governance. See *Printz v. United States*, 521 U.S. 898, 919 (1997) (citing Art. III, §2; Art. IV, §§2-4; Art. V). The limited and enumerated powers granted to the Legislative, Executive, and Judicial Branches of the National Government, moreover, underscore the vital role reserved to the States by the constitutional design, see, *e.g.*, Art. I, §8; Art. II, §§2-3; Art. III, §2. Any doubt regarding the constitutional role of the States as sovereign entities is removed by the Tenth Amendment, which, like the other provisions of the Bill of Rights, was enacted to allay lingering concerns about the extent of the national power. The Amendment confirms the promise implicit in the original document: "The powers not delegated to the United States by the Constitution, nor prohibited by it to the States, are reserved to the States respectively, or to the people." U.S. Const., Amdt. 10.

The federal system established by our Constitution preserves the sovereign status of the States in two ways. First, it reserves to them a substantial portion of the Nation's primary sovereignty, together with the dignity and essential attributes inhering in that status. . . . Second, even as to matters within the competence of the National Government, the constitutional design secures the founding generation's rejection of "the concept of a central government that would act upon and through the States" in favor of "a system in which the State and Federal Governments would exercise concurrent authority over the people—who were, in Hamilton's words, 'the only proper objects of government.'" *Printz, supra*, at 919-920 (quoting The Federalist No. 15). . . .

The States thus retain "a residuary and inviolable sovereignty." The Federalist No. 39. They are not relegated to the role of mere provinces or political corporations, but retain the dignity, though not the full authority, of sovereignty.

B

The generation that designed and adopted our federal system considered immunity from private suits central to sovereign dignity. When the Constitution was ratified, it was well established in English law that the Crown could not be sued without consent in its own courts. . . .

Although the American people had rejected other aspects of English political theory, the doctrine that a sovereign could not be sued without its consent was universal in the States when the Constitution was drafted and ratified. . . . The ratification debates, furthermore, underscored the importance of the States' sovereign immunity to the American people. . . . The leading advocates of the Constitution assured the people in no uncertain terms that the Constitution would not strip the States of sovereign immunity. . . .

Although the state conventions which addressed the issue of sovereign immunity in their formal ratification documents sought to clarify the point by constitutional amendment, they made clear that they, like Hamilton, Madison, and Marshall, understood the Constitution as drafted to preserve the States' immunity from private suits. The Rhode Island Convention thus proclaimed that "[i]t is declared by the Convention, that the judicial power of the United States, in cases in which a state may be a party, does not extend to criminal prosecutions, or to authorize any suit by any person against a state." 1 [Debates on the Federal Constitution] 336 [(J. Elliot 2d ed. 1854) (hereinafter Elliot's Debates)]. The convention sought, in addition, an express amendment "to remove all doubts or controversies respecting the same." *Ibid.* In a similar fashion, the New York Convention "declare[d] and ma[d]e known," 1 *id.*, at 327, its understanding "[t]hat the judicial power of the United States, in cases in which a state may be a party, does not extend to criminal prosecutions, or to authorize any suit by any person against a state," 1 *id.*, at 329. The convention proceeded to ratify the Constitution "[u]nder these impressions, and declaring that the rights aforesaid cannot be abridged or violated, and that the explanations aforesaid are consistent with the said Constitution, and in confidence that the amendments which shall have been proposed to the said Constitution will receive an early and mature consideration." *Ibid.*

Despite the persuasive assurances of the Constitution's leading advocates and the expressed understanding of the only state conventions to address the issue in explicit terms, this Court held, just five years after the Constitution was adopted, that Article III authorized a private citizen of another State to sue the State of Georgia without its consent. *Chisholm v. Georgia*, 2 Dall. 419 (1793). . . . The Court's decision "fell upon the country with a profound shock." 1 C. Warren, The Supreme Court in United States History 96 (rev. ed. 1926). . . .

The States, in particular, responded with outrage to the decision. The Massachusetts Legislature, for example, denounced the decision as "repugnant to the first principles of a federal government," and called upon the Common-wealth's Senators and Representatives to take all necessary steps to "remove any clause or article of the . . . Constitution, which can be construed to imply or justify a decision, that, a State is compellable to answer in any suit by an individual or individuals in any Court of the United States." 15 Papers of Alexander Hamilton 314 (H. Syrett & J. Cooke eds. 1969) (internal quotation marks omitted). Georgia's response was more intemperate: Its House of Repre-sentatives passed a bill providing that anyone attempting to enforce the *Chisholm* decision would be " 'guilty of felony and shall suffer death, without benefit of clergy, by being hanged.' " [D. Currie, The Constitution in Congress: The Federalist Period 1789-1801, p. 196 (1997).]

An initial proposal to amend the Constitution was introduced in the House of Representatives the day after *Chisholm* was announced; the proposal adopted as the Eleventh Amendment was introduced in the Senate promptly following an intervening recess. Currie, *supra*, at 196. Congress turned to the latter proposal with great dispatch; little more than two months after its intro-duction it had been endorsed by both Houses and forwarded to the States. 4 Annals of Congress 25, 30, 477, 499 (1794); 1 Stat. 402.

Each House spent but a single day discussing the Amendment, and the vote in each House was close to unanimous. . . .

The text and history of the Eleventh Amendment also suggest that Con-gress acted not to change but to restore the original constitutional design. Although earlier drafts of the Amendment had been phrased as express limits on the judicial power granted in Article III, see, *e.g.*, 3 Annals of Congress 651-652 (1793) ("The Judicial Power of the United States shall not extend to any suits in law or equity, commenced or prosecuted against one of the United States . . ."), the adopted text addressed the proper interpretation of that provision of the original Constitution, see U.S. Const., Amdt. 11 ("The Judicial power of the United States shall not be construed to extend to any suit in law or equity, commenced or prosecuted against one of the United States . . ."). By its terms, then, the Eleventh Amendment did not redefine the federal judicial power but instead overruled the Court. . . .

The text reflects the historical context and the congressional objective in endorsing the Amendment for ratification. Congress chose not to enact lan-guage codifying the traditional understanding of sovereign immunity but rather to address the specific provisions of the Constitution that had raised concerns during the ratification debates and formed the basis of the *Chisholm* decision. . . . Given the outraged reaction to *Chisholm*, as well as Congress' repeated refusal to otherwise qualify the text of the Amendment, it is doubtful that if Congress meant to write a new immunity into the Constitution it would have limited that immunity to the narrow text of the Eleventh Amendment. . . . The more natural inference is that the Constitution was understood, in light of its history and structure, to preserve the States' tradi-tional immunity from private suits. As the Amendment clarified the only pro-visions of the Constitution that anyone had suggested might support a contrary understanding, there was no reason to draft with a broader brush.

Finally, the swiftness and near unanimity with which the Eleventh Amendment was adopted suggest "either that the Court had not captured the original understanding, or that the country had changed its collective mind most rapidly." D. Currie, The Constitution in the Supreme Court: The First Hundred Years: 1789-1888, p. 18, n.101 (1985). The more reasonable interpretation, of course, is that regardless of the views of four Justices in *Chisholm*, the country as a whole—which had adopted the Constitution just five years earlier—had not understood the document to strip the States of their immunity from private suits. . . .

Although the dissent attempts to rewrite history to reflect a different original understanding, its evidence is unpersuasive. The handful of state statutory and constitutional provisions authorizing suits or petitions of right against States only confirms the prevalence of the traditional understanding that a State could not be sued in the absence of an express waiver, for if the understanding were otherwise, the provisions would have been unnecessary. . . .

The dissent's remaining evidence cannot bear the weight the dissent seeks to place on it. The views voiced during the ratification debates by Edmund Randolph and James Wilson, when reiterated by the same individuals in their respective capacities as advocate and Justice in *Chisholm*, were decisively rejected by the Eleventh Amendment, and General Pinkney did not speak to the issue of sovereign immunity at all. Furthermore, Randolph appears to have recognized that his views were in tension with the traditional understanding of sovereign immunity, see 3 Elliot's Debates 573 ("I think, whatever the law of nations may say, that any doubt respecting the construction that a state may be plaintiff, and not defendant, is taken away by the words *where a state shall be a party*"), and Wilson and Pinkney expressed a radical nationalist vision of the constitutional design that not only deviated from the views that prevailed at the time but, despite the dissent's apparent embrace of the position, remains startling even today. . . .

In short, the scanty and equivocal evidence offered by the dissent establishes no more than what is evident from the decision in *Chisholm*—that some members of the founding generation disagreed with Hamilton, Madison, Marshall, Iredell, and the only state conventions formally to address the matter. The events leading to the adoption of the Eleventh Amendment, however, make clear that the individuals who believed the Constitution stripped the States of their immunity from suit were at most a small minority. . . .

C

The Court has been consistent in interpreting the adoption of the Eleventh Amendment as conclusive evidence "that the decision in *Chisholm* was contrary to the well-understood meaning of the Constitution," *Seminole Tribe*, 517 U.S., at 69, and that the views expressed by Hamilton, Madison, and Marshall during the ratification debates, and by Justice Iredell in his dissenting opinion in *Chisholm*, reflect the original understanding of the Constitution. . . . As a consequence, we have looked to "history and experience, and the established order of things," *id.*, at 14, rather than "[a]dhering to the mere letter" of the Eleventh Amendment, *id.*, at 13, in determining the scope of the States' constitutional immunity from suit.

Following this approach, the Court has upheld States' assertions of sovereign immunity in various contexts falling outside the literal text of the Eleventh Amendment. In *Hans*, the Court held that sovereign immunity barred a citizen from suing his own State under the federal-question head of jurisdiction. The Court was unmoved by the petitioner's argument that the Eleventh Amendment, by its terms, applied only to suits brought by citizens of other States. . . .

Later decisions . . . reflect a settled doctrinal understanding, consistent with the views of the leading advocates of the Constitution's ratification, that sovereign immunity derives not from the Eleventh Amendment but from the structure of the original Constitution itself. . . .

II

In this case we must determine whether Congress has the power, under Article I, to subject nonconsenting States to private suits in their own courts. . . .

While the constitutional principle of sovereign immunity does pose a bar to federal jurisdiction over suits against nonconsenting States, see, *e.g.*, [*Principality of Monaco v. Mississippi*, 292 U.S. 313, 322-323 (1934)], this is not the only structural basis of sovereign immunity implicit in the constitutional design. Rather, "[t]here is also the postulate that States of the Union, still possessing attributes of sovereignty, shall be immune from suits, without their consent, save where there has been 'a surrender of this immunity in the plan of the convention.'" *Ibid.* (quoting The Federalist No. 81). This separate and distinct structural principle is not directly related to the scope of the judicial power established by Article III, but inheres in the system of federalism established by the Constitution. In exercising its Article I powers Congress may subject the States to private suits in their own courts only if there is "compelling evidence" that the States were required to surrender this power to Congress pursuant to the constitutional design. [*Blatchford v. Native Village of Noatak*, 501 U.S. 775, 781 (1991).]

A

Article I, §8, grants Congress broad power to enact legislation in several enumerated areas of national concern. The Supremacy Clause, furthermore, provides:

> "This Constitution, and the Laws of the United States which shall be made in Pursuance thereof . . . , shall be the supreme Law of the Land; and the Judges in every State shall be bound thereby, any Thing in the Constitution or Laws of any State to the Contrary notwithstanding." U.S. Const., Art. VI. . . .

As is evident from its text, however, the Supremacy Clause enshrines as "the supreme Law of the Land" only those Federal Acts that accord with the constitutional design. See *Printz*, 521 U.S., at 924. Appeal to the Supremacy Clause alone merely raises the question whether a law is a valid exercise of the national power. . . .

The Constitution, by delegating to Congress the power to establish the supreme law of the land when acting within its enumerated powers, does not foreclose a State from asserting immunity to claims arising under federal law merely because that law derives not from the State itself but from the national power. A contrary view could not be reconciled with *Hans, supra*, which sustained Louisiana's immunity in a private suit arising under the Constitution itself. . . .

Nor can we conclude that the specific Article I powers delegated to Congress necessarily include, by virtue of the Necessary and Proper Clause or otherwise, the incidental authority to subject the States to private suits as a means of achieving objectives otherwise within the scope of the enumerated powers. . . . As we have recognized in an analogous context:

> "When a 'La[w] . . . for carrying into Execution' the Commerce Clause violates the principle of state sovereignty reflected in the various constitutional provisions . . . it is not a 'La[w] . . . *proper* for carrying into Execution the Commerce Clause,' and is thus, in the words of The Federalist, 'merely [an] ac[t] of usurpation' which 'deserve[s] to be treated as such.'" *Printz, supra*, at 923-924 (quoting The Federalist No. 33).

The cases we have cited, of course, came at last to the conclusion that neither the Supremacy Clause nor the enumerated powers of Congress confer authority to abrogate the States' immunity from suit in federal court. The logic of the decisions, however, does not turn on the forum in which the suits were prosecuted but extends to state-court suits as well.

The dissenting opinion seeks to reopen these precedents, contending that state sovereign immunity must derive either from the common law (in which case the dissent contends it is defeasible by statute) or from natural law (in which case the dissent believes it cannot bar a federal claim). As should be obvious to all, this is a false dichotomy. The text and the structure of the Constitution protect various rights and principles. Many of these, such as the right to trial by jury and the prohibition on unreasonable searches and seizures, derive from the common law. The common-law lineage of these rights does not mean they are defeasible by statute or remain mere common-law rights, however. They are, rather, constitutional rights, and form the fundamental law of the land. . . .

Despite the dissent's assertion to the contrary, the fact that a right is not defeasible by statute means only that it is protected by the Constitution, not that it derives from natural law. Whether the dissent's attribution of our reasoning and conclusions to natural law results from analytical confusion or rhetorical device, it is simply inaccurate. We do not contend the Founders could not have stripped the States of sovereign immunity and granted Congress power to subject them to private suit but only that they did not do so. By the same token, the contours of sovereign immunity are determined by the Founders' understanding, not by the principles or limitations derived from natural law. . . .

B

Whether Congress has authority under Article I to abrogate a State's immunity from suit in its own courts is . . . a question of first impression.

In determining whether there is "compelling evidence" that this derogation of the States' sovereignty is "inherent in the constitutional compact," *Blatchford*, 501 U.S., at 781, we continue our discussion of history, practice, precedent, and the structure of the Constitution.

1

We look first to evidence of the original understanding of the Constitution. Petitioners contend that because the ratification debates and the events surrounding the adoption of the Eleventh Amendment focused on the States' immunity from suit in federal courts, the historical record gives no instruction as to the founding generation's intent to preserve the States' immunity from suit in their own courts.

We believe, however, that the Founders' silence is best explained by the simple fact that no one, not even the Constitution's most ardent opponents, suggested the document might strip the States of the immunity. In light of the overriding concern regarding the States' war-time debts, together with the well-known creativity, foresight, and vivid imagination of the Constitution's opponents, the silence is most instructive. It suggests the sovereign's right to assert immunity from suit in its own courts was a principle so well established that no one conceived it would be altered by the new Constitution. . . .

To read this history as permitting the inference that the Constitution stripped the States of immunity in their own courts and allowed Congress to subject them to suit there would turn on its head the concern of the founding generation—that Article III might be used to circumvent state-court immunity. In light of the historical record it is difficult to conceive that the Constitution would have been adopted if it had been understood to strip the States of immunity from suit in their own courts and cede to the Federal Government a power to subject nonconsenting States to private suits in these fora.

2

Our historical analysis is supported by early congressional practice, which provides "contemporaneous and weighty evidence of the Constitution's meaning." *Printz*, 521 U.S., at 905. Although early Congresses enacted various statutes authorizing federal suits in state court, see *id.*, at 906-907, (listing statutes); *Testa v. Katt*, 330 U.S. 386, 389-390 (1947), we have discovered no instance in which they purported to authorize suits against nonconsenting States in these fora. The "numerousness of these statutes [authorizing suit in state court], contrasted with the utter lack of statutes" subjecting States to suit, "suggests an assumed *absence* of such power." 521 U.S., at 907-908. It thus appears early Congresses did not believe they had the power to authorize private suits against the States in their own courts. . . .

3

The theory and reasoning of our earlier cases suggest the States do retain a constitutional immunity from suit in their own courts. We have often described the States' immunity in sweeping terms, without reference to whether the suit was prosecuted in state or federal court. . . .

4

Our final consideration is whether a congressional power to subject nonconsenting States to private suits in their own courts is consistent with the structure of the Constitution. We look both to the essential principles of federalism and to the special role of the state courts in the constitutional design.

Although the Constitution grants broad powers to Congress, our federalism requires that Congress treat the States in a manner consistent with their status as residuary sovereigns and joint participants in the governance of the Nation. . . .

Petitioners contend that immunity from suit in federal court suffices to preserve the dignity of the States. . . . In some ways, . . . a congressional power to authorize private suits against nonconsenting States in their own courts would be even more offensive to state sovereignty than a power to authorize the suits in a federal forum. Although the immunity of one sovereign in the courts of another has often depended in part on comity or agreement, the immunity of a sovereign in its own courts has always been understood to be within the sole control of the sovereign itself. . . . A power to press a State's own courts into federal service to coerce the other branches of the State, furthermore, is the power first to turn the State against itself and ultimately to commandeer the entire political machinery of the State against its will and at the behest of individuals. . . .

Underlying constitutional form are considerations of great substance. Private suits against nonconsenting States — especially suits for money damages — may threaten the financial integrity of the States. It is indisputable that, at the time of the founding, many of the States could have been forced into insolvency but for their immunity from private suits for money damages. Even today, an unlimited congressional power to authorize suits in state court to levy upon the treasuries of the States for compensatory damages, attorney's fees, and even punitive damages could create staggering burdens, giving Congress a power and a leverage over the States that is not contemplated by our constitutional design. The potential national power would pose a severe and notorious danger to the States and their resources. . . .

A general federal power to authorize private suits for money damages would place unwarranted strain on the States' ability to govern in accordance with the will of their citizens. Today, as at the time of the founding, the allocation of scarce resources among competing needs and interests lies at the heart of the political process. While the judgment creditor of a State may have a legitimate claim for compensation, other important needs and worthwhile ends compete for access to the public fisc. Since all cannot be satisfied in full, it is inevitable that difficult decisions involving the most sensitive and political of judgments must be made. If the principle of representative government is to be preserved to the States, the balance between competing interests must be reached after deliberation by the political process established by the citizens of the State, not by judicial decree mandated by the Federal Government and invoked by the private citizen. . . .

By " 'split[ting] the atom of sovereignty,' " the Founders established " 'two orders of government, each with its own direct relationship, its own privity, its own set of mutual rights and obligations to the people who sustain it and are governed by it.'" *Saenz v. Roe*, 526 U.S. 489, 504, n.17 (1999), quoting *U.S. Term Limits, Inc. v. Thornton*, 514 U.S. 779, 838 (1995) (Kennedy, J., concurring). "The Constitution thus contemplates that a State's government will represent and remain accountable to its own citizens." *Printz*, 521 U.S., at 920. When the Federal Government asserts authority over a State's most fundamental political processes, it strikes at the heart of the political accountability so essential to our liberty and republican form of government. . . .

Congress cannot abrogate the States' sovereign immunity in federal court; were the rule to be different here, the National Government would wield greater power in the state courts than in its own judicial instrumentalities. . . .

The resulting anomaly cannot be explained by reference to the special role of the state courts in the constitutional design. Although Congress may not require the legislative or executive branches of the States to enact or administer federal regulatory programs, see *Printz, supra*, at 935; [*New York v. United States*, 505 U.S. 144, 188 (1992),] it may require state courts of "adequate and appropriate" jurisdiction, *Testa*, 330 U.S., at 394, "to enforce federal prescriptions, insofar as those prescriptions relat[e] to matters appropriate for the judicial power," *Printz, supra*, at 907. It would be an unprecedented step, however, to infer from the fact that Congress may declare federal law binding and enforceable in state courts the further principle that Congress' authority to pursue federal objectives through the state judiciaries exceeds not only its power to press other branches of the State into its service but even its control over the federal courts themselves. The conclusion would imply that Congress may in some cases act only through instrumentalities of the States. Yet, as Chief Justice Marshall explained: "No trace is to be found in the constitution of an intention to create a dependence of the government of the Union on those of the States, for the execution of the great powers assigned to it. Its means are adequate to its ends; and on those means alone was it expected to rely for the accomplishment of its ends." *McCulloch v. Maryland*, 4 Wheat. 316, 424 (1819). . . .

The provisions of the Constitution upon which we have relied in finding the state courts peculiarly amenable to federal command, moreover, do not distinguish those courts from the Federal Judiciary. The Supremacy Clause does impose specific obligations on state judges. There can be no serious contention, however, that the Supremacy Clause imposes greater obligations on state-court judges than on the Judiciary of the United States itself. The text of Article III, §1, which extends federal judicial power to enumerated classes of suits but grants Congress discretion whether to establish inferior federal courts, does give strong support to the inference that state courts may be opened to suits falling within the federal judicial power. The Article in no way suggests, however, that state courts may be required to assume jurisdiction that could not be vested in the federal courts and forms no part of the judicial power of the United States. . . .

In light of history, practice, precedent, and the structure of the Constitution, we hold that the States retain immunity from private suit in their own courts, an immunity beyond the congressional power to abrogate by Article I legislation.

III

Sovereign immunity . . . does not bar all judicial review of state compliance with the Constitution and valid federal law. Rather, certain limits are implicit in the constitutional principle of state sovereign immunity.

The first of these limits is that sovereign immunity bars suits only in the absence of consent. Many States, on their own initiative, have enacted statutes consenting to a wide variety of suits. . . . The States have consented, moreover, to some suits pursuant to the plan of the Convention or to subsequent constitutional Amendments. In ratifying the Constitution, the States consented to suits brought by other States or by the Federal Government. . . . Suits brought by the United States itself require the exercise of political responsibility for each suit prosecuted against a State, a control which is absent from a broad delegation to private persons to sue nonconsenting States.

We have held also that in adopting the Fourteenth Amendment, the people required the States to surrender a portion of the sovereignty that had been preserved to them by the original Constitution, so that Congress may authorize private suits against nonconsenting States pursuant to its §5 enforcement power. *Fitzpatrick v. Bitzer*, 427 U.S. 445 (1976). . . .

The second important limit to the principle of sovereign immunity is that it bars suits against States but not lesser entities. The immunity does not extend to suits prosecuted against a municipal corporation or other governmental entity which is not an arm of the State. Nor does sovereign immunity bar all suits against state officers. Some suits against state officers are barred by the rule that sovereign immunity is not limited to suits which name the State as a party if the suits are, in fact, against the State. The rule, however, does not bar certain actions against state officers for injunctive or declaratory relief. Even a suit for money damages may be prosecuted against a state officer in his individual capacity for unconstitutional or wrongful conduct fairly attributable to the officer himself, so long as the relief is sought not from the state treasury but from the officer personally. . . .

IV

The sole remaining question is whether Maine has waived its immunity. . . . To the extent Maine has chosen to consent to certain classes of suits while maintaining its immunity from others, it has done no more than exercise a privilege of sovereignty concomitant to its constitutional immunity from suit. The State, we conclude, has not consented to suit.

V

We need not attach a label to our dissenting colleagues' insistence that the constitutional structure adopted by the Founders must yield to the politics of the moment. Although the Constitution begins with the principle that sovereignty rests with the people, it does not follow that the National Government becomes the ultimate, preferred mechanism for expressing the people's will. The States exist as a refutation of that concept. In choosing to ordain and establish the Constitution, the people insisted upon a federal structure for the very purpose of rejecting the idea that the will of the people in all instances is expressed by the central power, the one most remote from their control. The Framers of the Constitution did not share our dissenting colleagues' belief that the Congress may circumvent the federal design by regulating the States directly when it pleases to do so, including by a proxy in which individual citizens are authorized to levy upon the state treasuries absent the States' consent to jurisdiction. . . .

Justice Souter, with whom Justice Stevens, Justice Ginsburg, and Justice Breyer join, dissenting.

Today's issue arises naturally in the aftermath of the decision in [*Seminole Tribe of Florida v. Florida*, 517 U.S. 44 (1996)]. The Court holds that the Constitution bars an individual suit against a State to enforce a federal statutory right under . . . FLSA . . . when brought in the State's courts over its objection. In thus complementing its earlier decision, the Court of course confronts the fact that the state forum renders the Eleventh Amendment beside the point, and it has responded by discerning a simpler and more straightforward theory of state sovereign immunity than it found in *Seminole Tribe*: a State's sovereign immunity from all individual suits is a "fundamental aspect" of state sovereignty "confirm[ed]" by the Tenth Amendment. As a consequence, *Seminole Tribe*'s contorted reliance on the Eleventh Amendment and its background was presumably unnecessary; the Tenth would have done the work with an economy that the majority in *Seminole Tribe* would have welcomed. Indeed, if the Court's current reasoning is correct, the Eleventh Amendment itself was unnecessary. Whatever Article III may originally have said about the federal judicial power, the embarrassment to the State of Georgia occasioned by attempts in federal court to enforce the State's war debt could easily have been avoided if only the Court that decided *Chisholm v. Georgia*, 2 Dall. 419 (1793), had understood a State's inherent, Tenth Amendment right to be free of any judicial power, whether the court be state or federal, and whether the cause of action arise under state or federal law. . . .

I

The Court rests its decision principally on the claim that immunity from suit was "a fundamental aspect of the sovereignty which the States enjoyed before the ratification of the Constitution," an aspect which the Court understands to have survived the ratification of the Constitution in 1788 and to have been "confirm[ed]" and given constitutional status by the adoption of the Tenth Amendment in 1791. If the Court truly means by "sovereign immunity" what that term meant at common law, its argument would be insupportable. While sovereign immunity entered many new state legal systems as a part of the common law selectively received from England, it was not understood to be indefeasible or to have been given any such status by the new National Constitution, which did not mention it. Had the question been posed, state sovereign immunity could not have been thought to shield a State from suit under federal law on a subject committed to national jurisdiction by Article I of the Constitution. Congress exercising its conceded Article I power may unquestionably abrogate such immunity. . . .

The Court does not, however, offer today's holding as a mere corollary to its reasoning in *Seminole Tribe*, substituting the Tenth Amendment for the Eleventh as the occasion demands, and it is fair to read its references to a "fundamental aspect" of state sovereignty as referring not to a prerogative inherited from the Crown, but to a conception necessarily implied by statehood itself. The conception is thus not one of common law so much as of natural law, a universally applicable proposition discoverable by reason. This, I take it, is the sense in which the Court so emphatically relies on Alexander Hamilton's reference in The Federalist No. 81 to the States' sovereign immunity from suit as an "inherent" right, a characterization that does not require, but is at least open to, a natural law reading.

I understand the Court to rely on the Hamiltonian formulation with the object of suggesting that its conception of sovereign immunity as a "fundamental aspect" of sovereignty was a substantially popular, if not the dominant, view in the periods of Revolution and Confederation. There is, after all, nothing else in the Court's opinion that would suggest a basis for saying that the ratification of the Tenth Amendment gave this "fundamental aspect" its constitutional status and protection against any legislative tampering by Congress. The Court's principal rationale for today's result, then, turns on history: was the natural law conception of sovereign immunity as inherent in any notion of an independent State widely held in the United States in the period preceding the ratification of 1788 (or the adoption of the Tenth Amendment in 1791)?

The answer is certainly no. There is almost no evidence that the generation of the Framers thought sovereign immunity was fundamental in the sense of being unalterable. Whether one looks at the period before the framing, to the ratification controversies, or to the early republican era, the evidence is the same. Some Framers thought sovereign immunity was an obsolete royal prerogative inapplicable in a republic; some thought sovereign immunity was a common law power defeasible, like other common law rights, by statute; and perhaps a few thought, in keeping with a natural law view distinct from the common law conception, that immunity was inherent in a sovereign because the body that made a law could not logically be bound by it. Natural law thinking on the part of a doubtful few will not, however, support the Court's position. . . .

The only arguable support for the Court's absolutist view that I have found among the leading participants in the debate surrounding ratification was the one already mentioned, that of Alexander Hamilton in The Federalist No. 81, where he described the sovereign immunity of the States in language suggesting principles associated with natural law:

> "It is inherent in the nature of sovereignty, not to be amenable to the suit of an individual *without its consent.* This is the general sense and the general practice of mankind; and the exemption, as one of the attributes of sovereignty, is now enjoyed by the government of every state in the union. Unless therefore, there is a surrender of this immunity in the plan of the convention, it will remain with the states, and the danger intimated [that States might be sued on their debts in federal court] must be merely ideal. . . . The contracts between a nation and individuals are only binding on the conscience of the sovereign,

and have no pretensions to a compulsive force. They confer no right of action independent of the sovereign will." The Federalist No. 81, at 548-549.

Hamilton chose his words carefully, and he acknowledged the possibility that at the Convention the States might have surrendered sovereign immunity in some circumstances, but the thrust of his argument was that sovereign immunity was "inherent in the nature of sovereignty." The apparent novelty and uniqueness of Hamilton's employment of natural law terminology to explain the sovereign immunity of the States is worth remarking, because it stands in contrast to formulations indicating no particular position on the natural-law-versus-common-law origin, to the more widespread view that sovereign immunity derived from common law, and to the more radical stance that the sovereignty of the people made sovereign immunity out of place in the United States. . . .

In the Virginia ratifying convention, Madison was among those who debated sovereign immunity in terms of the result it produced, not its theoretical underpinnings. He maintained that "[i]t is not in the power of individuals to call any state into court," 3 Debates on the Federal Constitution 533 (J. Elliot 2d ed. 1863) (hereinafter Elliot's Debates), and thought that the phrase "in which a State shall be a Party" in Article III, §2, must be interpreted in light of that general principle, so that "[t]he only operation it can have, is that, if a state should wish to bring a suit against a citizen, it must be brought before the federal court." Elliot's Debates 533. John Marshall argued along the same lines against the possibility of federal jurisdiction over private suits against States, and he invoked the immunity of a State in its own courts in support of his argument:

> "I hope that no gentleman will think that a state will be called at the bar of the federal court. Is there no such case at present? Are there not many cases in which the legislature of Virginia is a party, and yet the state is not sued? It is not rational to suppose that the sovereign power should be dragged before a court." *Id.*, at 555.

There was no unanimity among the Virginians either on state- or federal-court immunity, however, for Edmund Randolph anticipated the position he would later espouse as plaintiff's counsel in *Chisholm v. Georgia*, 2 Dall. 419 (1793). He contented himself with agnosticism on the significance of what Hamilton had called "the general practice of mankind," and argued that notwithstanding any natural law view of the nonsuability of States, the Constitution permitted suit against a State in federal court: "I think, whatever the law of nations may say, that any doubt respecting the construction that a state may be plaintiff, and not defendant, is taken away by the words *where a state shall be a party*." 3 Elliot's Debates 573. . . .

At the furthest extreme from Hamilton, James Wilson made several comments in the Pennsylvania Convention that suggested his hostility to any idea of state sovereign immunity. First, he responded to the argument that "the sovereignty of the states is destroyed" if they are sued by the United States, "because a suiter in a court must acknowledge the jurisdiction of that court, and it is not the custom of sovereigns to suffer their names to be made use of in this manner." 2 *id.*, at 490. For Wilson, "[t]he answer [was] plain and easy: the government of each state ought to be subordinate to the government of the United States." *Ibid.* Wilson was also pointed in commenting on federal jurisdiction over cases between a State and citizens of another State: "When this power is attended to, it will be found to be a necessary one. Impartiality is the leading feature in this Constitution; it pervades the whole. When a citizen has a controversy with another state, there ought to be a tribunal where both parties may stand on a just and equal footing." *Id.*, at 491. Finally, Wilson laid out his view that sovereignty was in fact not located in the States at all: "Upon what principle is it contended that the sovereign power resides in the state governments? The honorable gentleman has said truly, that there can be no subordinate sovereignty. Now, if there cannot, my position is, that the sovereignty resides in the people; they have not parted with it; they have only dispensed such portions of the power as were conceived necessary for the public welfare." *Id.*, at 443. While this statement did not specifically address sovereign immunity, it expressed the major premise of what would later become Justice Wilson's position in *Chisholm:* that because the people, and not the States, are sovereign, sovereign immunity has no applicability to the States.

From a canvass of this spectrum of opinion expressed at the ratifying conventions, one thing is certain. No one was espousing an indefeasible, natural law view of sovereign immunity. The controversy over the enforceability of state debts subject to state law produced emphatic support for sovereign immunity from eminences as great as Madison and Marshall, but neither of them indicated adherence to any immunity conception outside the common law.

At the close of the ratification debates, the issue of the sovereign immunity of the States under Article III had not been definitively resolved, and in some instances the indeterminacy led the ratification conventions to respond in ways that point to the range of thinking about the doctrine. Several state ratifying conventions proposed amendments and issued declarations that would have exempted States from subjection to suit in federal court. The New York Convention's statement of ratification included a series of declarations framed as proposed amendments, among which was one stating "That the judicial power of the United States, in cases in which a state may be a party, does not extend to criminal prosecutions, or to authorize any suit by any person against a state." 1 Elliot's Debates 329. Whether that amendment was meant to alter or to clarify Article III as ratified is uncertain, but regardless of its precise intent, New York's response to the draft proposed by the Convention of 1787 shows that there was no consensus at all on the question of state suability (let alone on the underlying theory of immunity doctrine). There was, rather, an unclear state of affairs which it seemed advisable to stabilize.

The Rhode Island Convention, when it finally ratified on June 16, 1790, called upon its representatives to urge the passage of a list of amendments. This list incorporated language, some of it identical to that proposed by New York, in the following form:

"It is declared by the Convention, that the judicial power of the United States, in cases in which a state may be a party, does not extend to criminal prosecutions, or to authorize any suit by any person against a state; but, to remove all doubts or controversies respecting the same, that it be especially expressed, as a part of the Constitution of the United States, that Congress shall not, directly or indirectly, either by themselves or through the judiciary, interfere with any one of the states . . . in liquidating and discharging the public securities of any one state." *Id.*, at 336.

Even more clearly than New York's proposal, this amendment appears to have been intended to clarify Article III as reflecting some theory of sovereign immunity, though without indicating which one. . . .

This dearth of support makes it very implausible for today's Court to argue that a substantial (let alone a dominant) body of thought at the time of the framing understood sovereign immunity to be an inherent right of statehood, adopted or confirmed by the Tenth Amendment. . . .

[T]he Court [cannot] make good on its claim that the enactment of the Eleventh Amendment retrospectively reestablished the view that had already been established at the time of the framing (though eluding the perception of all but one Member of the Supreme Court), and hence "acted . . . to restore the original constitutional design." There was nothing "established" about the position espoused by Georgia in the effort to repudiate its debts, and the Court's implausible suggestion to the contrary merely echoes the brio of its remark in *Seminole Tribe* that *Chisholm* was "contrary to the well-understood meaning of the Constitution." 517 U.S., at 69. The fact that *Chisholm* was no conceptual aberration is apparent from the ratification debates and the several state requests to rewrite Article III. There was no received view either of the role this sovereign immunity would play in the circumstances of the case or of a conceptual foundation for immunity doctrine at odds with *Chisholm*'s reading of Article III. As an author on whom the Court relies has it, "there was no unanimity among the Framers that immunity would exist," D. Currie, The Constitution in the Supreme Court: The First Hundred Years: 1789-1888, p. 19 (1985). . . .

II

The Court . . . has a second line of argument looking not to a clause-based reception of the natural law conception or even to its recognition as a "background principle," see *Seminole Tribe*, 517 U.S., at 72, but to a structural basis in the Constitution's creation of a federal system. . . . [T]he Court believes that the federal constitutional structure itself necessitates recognition of some degree of state autonomy broad enough to include sovereign immunity from suit in a State's own courts, regardless of the federal source of the claim asserted against the State. . . . [T]he Court's argument that state-court sovereign immunity on federal questions is inherent in the very concept of federal structure is demonstrably mistaken.

A

Once "the atom of sovereignty" had been split, *U.S. Term Limits, Inc. v. Thornton*, 514 U.S. 779 (1995) (Kennedy, J., concurring), the general scheme of delegated sovereignty as between the two component governments of the federal system was clear, and was succinctly stated by Chief Justice Marshall: "In America, the powers of sovereignty are divided between the government of the Union, and those of the States. They are each sovereign, with respect to the objects committed to it, and neither sovereign with respect to the objects committed to the other." *McCulloch v. Maryland*, 4 Wheat. 316, 410 (1819).

Hence the flaw in the Court's appeal to federalism. The State of Maine is not sovereign with respect to the national objectives of the FLSA. It is not the authority that promulgated the FLSA, on which the right of action in this case depends. That authority is the United States acting through the Congress, whose legislative power under Article I of the Constitution to extend FLSA coverage to state employees has already been decided, see *Garcia v. San Antonio Metropolitan Transit Authority*, [469 U.S. 528 (1985),] and is not contested here.

Nor can it be argued that because the State of Maine creates its own court system, it has authority to decide what sorts of claims may be entertained there, and thus in effect to control the right of action in this case. Maine has created state courts of general jurisdiction; once it has done so, the Supremacy Clause of the Constitution, Art. VI, cl. 2, which requires state courts to enforce federal law and state-court judges to be bound by it, requires the Maine courts to entertain this federal cause of action. Maine has advanced no "valid excuse," *Howlett v. Rose*, 496 U.S. 356, 369 (1990), for its courts' refusal to hear federal-law claims in which Maine is a defendant, and sovereign immunity cannot be that excuse, simply because the State is not sovereign with respect to the subject of the claim against it. The Court's insistence that the federal structure bars Congress from making States susceptible to suit in their own courts is, then, plain mistake.

B

It is symptomatic of the weakness of the structural notion proffered by the Court that it seeks to buttress the argument by relying on "the dignity and respect afforded a State, which the immunity is designed to protect," . . . and by invoking the many demands on a State's fisc. . . . It would be hard to imagine anything more inimical to the republican conception, which rests on the understanding of its citizens precisely that the government is not above them, but of them, its actions being governed by law just like their own. Whatever justification there may be for an American government's immunity from private suit, it is not dignity.

It is equally puzzling to hear the Court say that "federal power to authorize private suits for money damages would place unwarranted strain on the States' ability to govern in accordance with the will of their citizens." So long as the citizens' will, expressed through state legislation, does not violate valid federal law, the strain will not be felt; and to the extent that state action does violate federal law, the will of the citizens of the United States already trumps that of the citizens of the State: the strain then is not only expected, but necessarily intended.

Least of all does the Court persuade by observing that "other important needs" than that of the "judgment creditor" compete for public money. The "judgment creditor" in question is not a dunning bill collector, but a citizen whose federal rights have been violated, and a constitutional structure that stints on enforcing federal rights out of an abundance of delicacy toward the States has substituted politesse in place of respect for the rule of law. . . .

III

The Court apparently believes that because state courts have not historically entertained Commerce Clause based federal-law claims against the States, such an innovation carries a presumption of unconstitutionality. . . . At the outset, it has to be noted that this approach assumes a more cohesive record than history affords. . . . But even if the record were less unkempt, the problem with arguing from historical practice in this case is that past practice, even if unbroken, provides no basis for demanding preservation when the conditions on which the practice depended have changed in a constitutionally relevant way.

It was at one time, though perhaps not from the framing, believed that "Congress' authority to regulate the States under the Commerce Clause" was limited by "certain underlying elements of political sovereignty . . . deemed essential to the States' 'separate and independent existence.'" *Garcia*, 469 U.S., at 547-548. On this belief, the preordained balance between state and federal sovereignty was understood to trump the terms of Article I and preclude Congress from subjecting States to federal law on certain subjects. (From time to time, wage and hour regulation has been counted among those subjects.) As a consequence it was rare, if not unknown, for state courts to confront the situation in which federal law enacted under the Commerce Clause provided the authority for a private right of action against a State in state court. The question of state immunity from a Commerce Clause based federal-law suit in state court thus tended not to arise for the simple reason that Acts of Congress authorizing such suits did not exist.

Today, however, in light of *Garcia, supra* (overruling *National League of Cities v. Usery*, 426 U.S. 833 (1976)), the law is settled that federal legislation enacted under the Commerce Clause may bind the States without having to satisfy a test of undue incursion into state sovereignty. "[T]he fundamental limitation that the constitutional scheme imposes on the Commerce Clause to protect the 'States as States' is one of process rather than one of result." *Garcia, supra*, at 554. Because the commerce power is no longer thought to be circumscribed, the dearth of prior private federal claims entertained against the States in state courts does not tell us anything, and reflects nothing but an earlier and less expansive application of the commerce power.

Least of all is it to the point for the Court to suggest that because the Framers would be surprised to find States subjected to a federal-law suit in their own courts under the commerce power, the suit must be prohibited by the Constitution. . . . The Framers' intentions and expectations count so far as they point to the meaning of the Constitution's text or the fair implications of its structure, but they do not hover over the instrument to veto any application of its principles to a world that the Framers could not have anticipated.

If the Framers would be surprised to see States subjected to suit in their own courts under the commerce power, they would be astonished by the reach of Congress under the Commerce Clause generally. The proliferation of Government, State and Federal, would amaze the Framers, and the administrative state with its reams of regulations would leave them rubbing their eyes. But the Framers' surprise at, say, the FLSA, or the Federal Communications Commission, or the Federal Reserve Board is no threat to the constitutionality of any one of them, for a very fundamental reason:

> "[W]hen we are dealing with words that also are a constituent act, like the Constitution of the United States, we must realize that they have called into life a being the development of which could not have been foreseen completely by the most gifted of its begetters. It was enough for them to realize or to hope that they had created an organism; it has taken a century and has cost their successors much sweat and blood to prove that they created a nation. The case before us must be considered in the light of our whole experience and not merely in that of what was said a hundred years ago." *Missouri v. Holland*, 252 U.S. 416, 433 (1920) (Holmes, J.).
>
> "'We must never forget,' said Mr. Chief Justice Marshall in *McCulloch*, [4 Wheat., at] 407, 'that it is a Constitution we are expounding.' Since then this Court has repeatedly sustained the exercise of power by Congress, under various clauses of that instrument, over objects of which the Fathers could not have dreamed." *Olmstead v. United States*, 277 U.S. 438, 472 (1928) (Brandeis, J., dissenting).

IV

In 1974, Congress . . . amended the FLSA, "extend[ing] the minimum wage and maximum hour provisions to almost all public employees employed by the States and by their various political subdivisions." *National League of Cities*, 426 U.S., at 836. . . . [I]n *National League of Cities*, the Court held the extension of the Act to these employees an unconstitutional infringement of state sovereignty, *id.*, at 852. . . . In *Garcia*, . . . the Court overruled *National League of Cities*, see 469 U.S., at 557, this time taking the position that Congress was not barred by the Constitution from binding the States as employers under the Commerce Clause, *id.*, at 554. . . . [T]he Court held that whatever protection the Constitution afforded to the States' sovereignty lay in the constitutional structure, not in some substantive guarantee. *Ibid. Garcia* remains good law, its reasoning has not been repudiated, and it has not been challenged here. . . .

The Court in *Seminole Tribe* created a significant impediment to the statute's practical application by rendering its damages provisions unenforceable against the States by private suit in federal court. Today's decision blocking private actions in state courts makes the barrier to individual enforcement a total one. . . .

It is true, of course, that the FLSA does authorize the Secretary of Labor to file suit seeking damages, see 29 U.S.C. §216(c), but unless Congress plans a significant expansion of the National Government's litigating forces to provide a lawyer whenever private litigation is barred by today's decision and *Seminole Tribe*, the allusion to enforcement of private rights by the National Government is probably not much more than whimsy. . . .

So there is much irony in the Court's profession that it grounds its opinion on a deeply rooted historical tradition of sovereign immunity, when the Court abandons a principle nearly as inveterate, and much closer to the hearts of the Framers: that where there is a right, there must be a remedy. Lord Chief Justice Holt could state this as an unquestioned proposition already in 1702, as he did in *Ashby v. White*, 6 Mod. 45, 53-54, 87 Eng. Rep. 808, 815 (Q.B.):

> "If an act of parliament be made for the benefit of any person, and he is hindered by another of that benefit, by necessary consequence of law he shall have an action; and the current of all the books is so" (citation omitted).

Blackstone considered it "a general and indisputable rule, that where there is a legal right, there is also a legal remedy, by suit or action at law, whenever that right is invaded." 3 Blackstone *23. The generation of the Framers thought the principle so crucial that several States put it into their constitutions. And when Chief Justice Marshall asked about Marbury: "If he has a right, and that right has been violated, do the laws of his country afford him a remedy?," *Marbury v. Madison*, 1 Cranch 137, 162 (1803), the question was rhetorical, and the answer clear:

> "The very essence of civil liberty certainly consists in the right of every individual to claim the protection of the laws, whenever he receives an injury. One of the first duties of government is to afford that protection. In Great Britain the king himself is sued in the respectful form of a petition, and he never fails to comply with the judgment of his court." *Id.*, at 163.

Yet today the Court has no qualms about saying frankly that the federal right to damages afforded by Congress under the FLSA cannot create a concomitant private remedy. . . .

V

The Court began this century by imputing immutable constitutional status to a conception of economic self-reliance that was never true to industrial life and grew insistently fictional with the years, and the Court has chosen to close the century by conferring like status on a conception of state sovereign immunity that is true neither to history nor to the structure of the Constitution. I expect the Court's late essay into immunity doctrine will prove the equal of its earlier experiment in laissez-faire, the one being as unrealistic as the other, as indefensible, and probably as fleeting.

POINTS FOR DISCUSSION

1. In *Alden*, the majority and dissenting Justices relied heavily upon historical practice and constitutional structure to decide whether Congress may abrogate state sovereign immunity in *state* court. What exactly are the points of disagreement between the majority and dissenting Justices? How should those points of disagreement be resolved?

2. In his opinion for the Court, Justice Kennedy stated: "In exercising its Article I powers Congress may subject the States to private suits in their own courts only if there is 'compelling evidence' that the States were required to surrender this power to Congress pursuant to the constitutional design." Did he apply a "clear statement rule" to the text of the Constitution along the lines that you saw Tucker advocate in the last section? Is such a rule of interpretation warranted in this context?

3. As a matter of history, Justice Souter charged the Court with having adopted a "natural law" conception of state sovereign immunity. The dissent defined "natural law" as "a universally applicable proposition discoverable by reason." Does the Court in fact adopt such a conception of state sovereign immunity? If not, what is the conception that it adopts?

4. Courts and scholars have struggled to make sense of the text of the Eleventh Amendment. Consider these observations on current theories of the Eleventh Amendment:

> Current theories of the Eleventh Amendment . . . all presuppose that the Amendment was poorly drafted and would produce anomalous or absurd results if applied as written.
>
> The traditional "immunity" theory, currently embraced by a majority of the Supreme Court . . . , argues that states enjoy broad constitutional sovereign immunity beyond the terms of the [Eleventh] Amendment. Proponents of broad immunity regard the Amendment's text as unacceptably underinclusive because it bars suits only by out-of-state citizens. . . .
>
> By contrast, the more recent "diversity" theory, endorsed by a minority of the Court . . . , regards the text of the Eleventh Amendment as unacceptably overinclusive. Diversity theorists insist that the Amendment's prohibition against "any suit" cannot be applied literally because it would lead to the anomalous conclusion that in-state citizens can invoke federal question jurisdiction to sue a state but out-of-state citizens cannot. The purpose of the Amendment, they say, was merely to prohibit those suits in which jurisdiction rests solely on the state-citizen diversity clauses of Article III, not to curtail jurisdiction over suits against states supported by any of Article III's other heads of jurisdiction.
>
> Ironically, both groups criticize each other for ignoring aspects of the constitutional text. For example, proponents of broad immunity argue that the diversity theory contradicts the Amendment's express prohibition against extending the judicial power to "any suit" by an out-of-state citizen against a state because the theory would allow just such suits under federal question jurisdiction. Conversely, diversity theorists charge that broad immunity disregards the Eleventh Amendment's precise terms, which preclude jurisdiction over suits by out-of-state citizens but say nothing to bar suits brought by citizens against their own states.
>
> The "compromise" theory of the Eleventh Amendment attempts to avoid these criticisms by accepting the Amendment as written. This theory suggests that the Amendment reflects an unrecorded, and less than fully coherent, compromise. On this view, courts should simply follow the text and ignore any resulting anomalies. According to the proponents of this theory, it is simply not possible to discover the original meaning of the Amendment or to identify its precise purpose.

Bradford R. Clark, *The Eleventh Amendment and the Nature of the Union*, 123 Harv. L. Rev. 1817, 1820-1821 (2010).

Do the Court's decisions in *New York v. United States*, 505 U.S. 144 (1992), and *Printz v. United States*, 521 U.S. 898 (1997), shed any light on why the

Eleventh Amendment may have been drafted as it was? In *New York* and *Printz*, the Court held that Congress may not commandeer state legislatures and executive officials to carry a federal regulatory program into execution. The Court reasoned in part, as you read, that the Constitution empowered Congress to exert its legislative power over individuals, not states. Does this line of reasoning shed any light on the original meaning of the Eleventh Amendment, and help to explain how it made sense to those who drafted and ratified it? See Clark, *supra*, at 1838-1918.

E. THE NECESSARY AND PROPER CLAUSE REVISITED

This section revisits congressional power under the Necessary and Proper Clause. The Clause empowers Congress "[t]o make all Laws which shall be necessary and proper for carrying into Execution the foregoing Powers, and all other Powers vested by this Constitution in the Government of the United States, or in any Department or Officer thereof." U.S. CONST. art. I, §8, cl.18. The Necessary and Proper Clause appears in Article I with Congress's other enumerated powers. As you have seen, however, the Court has understood the word "proper" to incorporate certain doctrines of state sovereignty that you have studied in this chapter. Thus, it is useful to reconsider the Clause in light of both Congress's enumerated powers and the state sovereignty doctrines you have studied in this chapter.

The following case, *United States v. Comstock*, 130 S. Ct. 1949 (2010), provides the Court's most recent explanation of what it means for a law to be "necessary and proper" for carrying the powers of Congress into execution. The Justices rely on both the Court's enumerated powers jurisprudence (Chapter 5) and state sovereignty doctrines (Chapter 6) in stating their various positions. As you read this case, consider these questions:

- Which of the Justices' various understandings of the Necessary and Proper Clause is most compelling?
- How should courts and other constitutional decision makers understand the Necessary and Proper Clause in light of the cases that you have read in this chapter and the previous one—and in light of the historical, judicial, and academic materials you read in Part I?

UNITED STATES V. COMSTOCK

130 S. Ct. 1949 (2010)

JUSTICE BREYER delivered the opinion of the Court.

A federal civil-commitment statute authorizes the Department of Justice to detain a mentally ill, sexually dangerous federal prisoner beyond the date the prisoner would otherwise be released. 18 U.S.C. §4248. . . . Here we ask whether the Federal Government has the authority under Article I of the Constitution to enact this federal civil-commitment program. . . .

I

The federal statute before us allows a district court to order the civil commitment of an individual who is currently "in the custody of the [Federal] Bureau of Prisons," §4248, if that individual (1) has previously "engaged or attempted to engage in sexually violent conduct or child molestation," (2) currently "suffers from a serious mental illness, abnormality, or disorder," and (3) "as a result of" that mental illness, abnormality, or disorder is "sexually dangerous to others," in that "he would have serious difficulty in refraining from sexually violent conduct or child molestation if released." §§4247(a)(5)-(6).

In order to detain such a person, the Government (acting through the Department of Justice) must certify to a federal district judge that the prisoner meets the conditions just described. . . .

Confinement in the federal facility will last until either (1) the person's mental condition improves to the point where he is no longer dangerous (with or without appropriate ongoing treatment), in which case he will be released; or (2) a State assumes responsibility for his custody, care, and treatment, in which case he will be transferred to the custody of that State. The statute establishes a system for ongoing psychiatric and judicial review of the individual's case, including judicial hearings at the request of the confined person at six-month intervals. . . .

II

The question presented is whether the Necessary and Proper Clause grants Congress authority sufficient to enact the statute before us. . . . [W]e conclude that the Constitution grants Congress legislative power sufficient to enact §4248. We base this conclusion on five considerations, taken together.

First, the Necessary and Proper Clause grants Congress broad authority to enact federal legislation. Nearly 200 years ago, this Court stated that the Federal "[G]overnment is acknowledged by all to be one of enumerated powers," [*McCulloch v. Maryland*, 4 Wheat. 316, 405 (1819)], which means that "[e]very law enacted by Congress must be based on one or more of" those powers, *United States v. Morrison*, 529 U.S. 598, 607 (2000). But, at the same time, "a government, entrusted with such" powers "must also be entrusted with ample means for their execution." *McCulloch*, 4 Wheat., at 408. Accordingly, the Necessary and Proper Clause makes clear that the Constitution's grants of specific federal legislative authority are accompanied by broad power to enact laws that are "convenient, or useful" or "conducive" to the authority's "beneficial exercise." *Id.*, at 413, 418. Chief Justice Marshall emphasized that the word "necessary" does not mean "absolutely necessary." *Id.*, at 413-415. In language that has come to define the scope of the Necessary and Proper Clause, he wrote:

> "Let the end be legitimate, let it be within the scope of the constitution, and all means which are appropriate, which are plainly adapted to that end, which are not prohibited, but consist with the letter and spirit of the constitution, are constitutional." *McCulloch, supra*, at 421.

We have since made clear that, in determining whether the Necessary and Proper Clause grants Congress the legislative authority to enact a particular federal statute, we look to see whether the statute constitutes a means that is rationally related to the implementation of a constitutionally enumerated power. *Sabri v. United States*, 541 U.S. 600, 605 (2004); see *Gonzales v. Raich*, 545 U.S. 1, 22 (2005) (holding that because "Congress had a rational basis" for concluding that a statute implements Commerce Clause power, the statute falls within the scope of congressional "authority to 'make all Laws which shall be necessary and proper' to 'regulate Commerce . . . among the several States'").

Of course, as Chief Justice Marshall stated, a federal statute, in addition to being authorized by Art. I, §8, must also "not [be] prohibited" by the Constitution. *McCulloch*, *supra*, at 421. . . . [T]he present statute's validity under provisions of the Constitution other than the Necessary and Proper Clause is an issue that is not before us. Under the question presented, the relevant inquiry is simply "whether the means chosen are 'reasonably adapted' to the attainment of a legitimate end under the commerce power" or under other powers that the Constitution grants Congress the authority to implement. *Gonzales*, *supra*, at 37 (Scalia, J., concurring in judgment).

We have also recognized that the Constitution "addresse[s]" the "choice of means"

> "primarily . . . to the judgment of Congress. If it can be seen that the means adopted are really calculated to attain the end, the degree of their necessity, the extent to which they conduce to the end, the closeness of the relationship between the means adopted and the end to be attained, are matters for congressional determination alone." *Burroughs v. United States*, 290 U.S. 534, 547-548 (1934).

Thus, the Constitution, which nowhere speaks explicitly about the creation of federal crimes beyond those related to "counterfeiting," "treason," or "Piracies and Felonies committed on the high Seas" or "against the Law of Nations," Art. I, §8, cls. 6, 10; Art. III, §3, nonetheless grants Congress broad authority to create such crimes. And Congress routinely exercises its authority to enact criminal laws in furtherance of, for example, its enumerated powers to regulate interstate and foreign commerce, to enforce civil rights, to spend funds for the general welfare, to establish federal courts, to establish post offices, to regulate bankruptcy, to regulate naturalization, and so forth.

Similarly, Congress, in order to help ensure the enforcement of federal criminal laws enacted in furtherance of its enumerated powers, "can cause a prison to be erected at any place within the jurisdiction of the United States, and direct that all persons sentenced to imprisonment under the laws of the United States shall be confined there." *Ex parte Karstendick*, 93 U.S. 396, 400 (1876). Moreover, Congress, having established a prison system, can enact laws that seek to ensure that system's safe and responsible administration by, for example, requiring prisoners to receive medical care and educational training, and can also ensure the safety of the prisoners, prison workers and visitors, and those in surrounding communities by, for example, creating further criminal laws governing entry, exit, and smuggling, and by employing prison guards to ensure discipline and security.

Neither Congress' power to criminalize conduct, nor its power to imprison individuals who engage in that conduct, nor its power to enact laws governing prisons and prisoners, is explicitly mentioned in the Constitution. But Congress nonetheless possesses broad authority to do each of those things in the course of "carrying into Execution" the enumerated powers "vested by" the "Constitution in the Government of the United States"—authority granted by the Necessary and Proper Clause.

Second, the civil-commitment statute before us constitutes a modest addition to a set of federal prison-related mental-health statutes that have existed for many decades. We recognize that even a longstanding history of related federal action does not demonstrate a statute's constitutionality. A history of involvement, however, can nonetheless be "helpful in reviewing the substance of a congressional statutory scheme," *Gonzales*, 545 U.S., at 21, and, in particular, the reasonableness of the relation between the new statute and pre-existing federal interests.

Here, Congress has long been involved in the delivery of mental health care to federal prisoners, and has long provided for their civil commitment. . . . In 2006, Congress enacted the particular statute before us. It differs from earlier statutes in that it focuses directly upon persons who, due to a mental illness, are sexually dangerous. Notably, many of these individuals were likely already subject to civil commitment under [18 U.S.C. §]4246, which, since 1949, has authorized the post-sentence detention of federal prisoners who suffer from a mental illness and who are thereby dangerous (whether sexually or otherwise). Aside from its specific focus on sexually dangerous persons, §4248 is similar to the provisions first enacted in 1949. In that respect, it is a modest addition to a longstanding federal statutory framework, which has been in place since 1855.

Third, Congress reasonably extended its longstanding civil-commitment system to cover mentally ill and sexually dangerous persons who are already in federal custody, even if doing so detains them beyond the termination of their criminal sentence. For one thing, the Federal Government is the custodian of its prisoners. As federal custodian, it has the constitutional power to act in order to protect nearby (and other) communities from the danger federal prisoners may pose. . . . If a federal prisoner is infected with a communicable disease that threatens others, surely it would be "necessary and proper" for the Federal Government to take action, pursuant to its role as federal custodian, to refuse (at least until the threat diminishes) to release that individual among the general public, where he might infect others (even if not threatening an interstate epidemic). And if confinement of such an individual is a "necessary and proper" thing to do, then how could it not be similarly "necessary and proper" to confine an individual whose mental illness threatens others to the same degree?

Moreover, §4248 is "reasonably adapted," *United States v. Darby*, 312 U.S. 100 (1941), to Congress' power to act as a responsible federal custodian (a power that rests, in turn, upon federal criminal statutes that legitimately seek to implement constitutionally enumerated authority). Congress could have reasonably concluded that federal inmates who suffer from a mental illness that causes them to "have serious difficulty in refraining from sexually violent conduct," §4247(a)(6), would pose an especially high danger to the public if released. And Congress could also have reasonably concluded . . . that a reasonable number of such individuals would likely *not* be detained by the States if released from federal custody, in part because the Federal Government itself severed their claim to "legal residence in any State" by incarcerating them in remote federal prisons. . . . [Section] 4248 satisfies "review for means-end rationality," *i.e.*, . . . satisfies the Constitution's insistence that a federal statute represent a rational means for implementing a constitutional grant of legislative authority. *Sabri*, 541 U.S., at 605.

Fourth, the statute properly accounts for state interests. Respondents and the dissent contend that §4248 violates the Tenth Amendment because it "invades the province of state sovereignty" in an area typically left to state control. *New York v. United States*, 505 U.S. 144, 155 (1992). But the Tenth Amendment's text is clear: "The powers *not delegated to the United States* by the Constitution, nor prohibited by it to the States, are reserved to the States respectively, or to the people." The powers "delegated to the United States by the Constitution" include those specifically enumerated powers listed in Article I along with the implementation authority granted by the Necessary and Proper Clause. Virtually by definition, these powers are not powers that the Constitution "reserved to the States."

Nor does this statute invade state sovereignty or otherwise improperly limit the scope of [state power]. To the contrary, it requires *accommodation* of state interests: The Attorney General must inform the State in which the federal prisoner "is domiciled or was tried" that he is detaining someone with respect to whom those States may wish to assert their authority, and he must encourage those States to assume custody of the individual. §4248(d). He must also immediately "release" that person "to the appropriate official of" either State "if such State will assume [such] responsibility." *Ibid.* And either State has the right, at any time, to assert its authority over the individual, which will prompt the individual's immediate transfer to State custody. §4248(d)(1). . . .

Fifth, the links between §4248 and an enumerated Article I power are not too attenuated. Neither is the statutory provision too sweeping in its scope. . . . [A]s we have explained, from the implied power to punish we have *further* inferred both the power to imprison, and . . . the federal civil-commitment power.

Our necessary and proper jurisprudence contains multiple examples of similar reasoning. For example, in *Sabri* we observed that "Congress has authority under the Spending Clause to appropriate federal moneys" and that it therefore "has corresponding authority under the Necessary and Proper Clause to see to it that taxpayer dollars" are not "siphoned off" by "corrupt public officers." 541 U.S., at 605. We then further held that, in aid of that implied power to criminalize graft of "taxpayer dollars," Congress has the *additional* prophylactic power to criminalize bribes or kickbacks even when the stolen funds have not been "traceably skimmed from specific federal payments." *Ibid.* . . .

Indeed even the dissent acknowledges that Congress has the implied power to criminalize any conduct that might interfere with the exercise of an enumerated power, and also the additional power to imprison people who violate those (inferentially authorized) laws, and the additional power to provide for the safe and reasonable management of those prisons, and the additional power to regulate the prisoners' behavior even after their release. . . . [T]he same enumerated power that justifies the creation of a federal criminal statute, and that justifies the additional implied federal powers that the dissent considers legitimate, justifies civil commitment under §4248 as well. . . .

Nor need we fear that our holding today confers on Congress a general "police power, which the Founders denied the National Government and reposed in the States." *Morrison*, 529 U.S., at 618. . . . [Section] 4248 is narrow in scope. It has been applied to only a small fraction of federal prisoners. And its reach is limited to individuals already "in the custody of the" Federal Government. §4248(a). . . . Thus, far from a "general police power," §4248 is a reasonably adapted and narrowly tailored means of pursuing the Government's legitimate interest as a federal custodian in the responsible administration of its prison system.

To be sure, as we have previously acknowledged,

"The Federal Government undertakes activities today that would have been unimaginable to the Framers in two senses; first, because the Framers would not have conceived that *any* government would conduct such activities; and second, because the Framers would not have believed that the *Federal* Government, rather than the States, would assume such responsibilities. Yet the powers conferred upon the Federal Government by the Constitution were phrased in language broad enough to allow for the expansion of the Federal Government's role." *New York*, 505 U.S., at 157.

The Framers demonstrated considerable foresight in drafting a Constitution capable of such resilience through time. As Chief Justice Marshall observed nearly 200 years ago, the Necessary and Proper Clause is part of "a constitution intended to endure for ages to come, and, consequently, to be adapted to the various crises of human affairs." *McCulloch*, 4 Wheat., at 415. . . .

We do not reach or decide any claim that the statute or its application denies equal protection of the laws, procedural or substantive due process, or any other rights guaranteed by the Constitution. . . .

JUSTICE KENNEDY, concurring in the judgment.

The Court is correct, in my view, to hold that the challenged portions of 18 U.S.C. §4248 are necessary and proper exercises of congressional authority. . . .

When the inquiry is whether a federal law has sufficient links to an enumerated power to be within the scope of federal authority, the analysis depends not on the number of links in the congressional-power chain but on the strength of the chain. . . . [U]nder the Necessary and Proper Clause, application of a "rational basis" test should be at least as exacting as it has been in the Commerce Clause cases, if not more so. . . . [Commerce Clause] precedents require a tangible link to commerce, not a mere conceivable rational relation . . . "[S]imply because Congress may conclude that a particular activity substantially affects interstate commerce does not necessarily make it so." *Lopez, supra*, at 557, n.2. The rational basis referred to in the Commerce Clause context is a demonstrated link in fact, based on empirical demonstration. . . .

A separate concern stems from the Court's explanation of the Tenth Amendment. I had thought it a basic principle that the powers reserved to the States consist of the whole, undefined residuum of power remaining after taking account of powers granted to the National Government. The Constitution delegates limited powers to the National Government and then reserves the remainder for the States (or the people), not the other way around, as the Court's analysis suggests. And the powers reserved to the States are so broad that they remain undefined. Residual power, sometimes referred to (perhaps imperfectly) as the police power, belongs to the States and the States alone.

It is correct in one sense to say that if the National Government has the power to act under the Necessary and Proper Clause then that power is not one reserved to the States. But the precepts of federalism embodied in the Constitution inform which powers are properly exercised by the National Government in the first place. It is of fundamental importance to consider whether essential attributes of state sovereignty are compromised by the assertion of federal power under the Necessary and Proper Clause; if so, that is a factor suggesting that the power is not one properly within the reach of federal power.

The opinion of the Court should not be interpreted to hold that the only, or even the principal, constraints on the exercise of congressional power are the Constitution's express prohibitions. The Court's discussion of the Tenth Amendment invites the inference that restrictions flowing from the federal system are of no import when defining the limits of the National Government's power, as it proceeds by first asking whether the power is within the National Government's reach, and if so it discards federalism concerns entirely. . . .

JUSTICE ALITO, concurring in the judgment.

I am persuaded, on narrow grounds, that it was "necessary and proper" for Congress to enact the statute at issue in this case in order to "carr[y] into Execution" powers specifically conferred on Congress by the Constitution. . . .

I entirely agree with the dissent that "[t]he Necessary and Proper Clause empowers Congress to enact only those laws that 'carr[y] into Execution' one or more of the federal powers enumerated in the Constitution," but §4248 satisfies that requirement because it is a necessary and proper means of carrying into execution the enumerated powers that support the federal criminal statutes under which the affected prisoners were convicted. The Necessary and Proper Clause provides the constitutional authority for most federal criminal statutes. In other words, most federal criminal statutes rest upon a congressional judgment that, in order to execute one or more of the powers conferred on Congress, it is necessary and proper to criminalize certain conduct, and in order to do that it is obviously necessary and proper to provide for the operation of a federal criminal justice system and a federal prison system. . . .

Just as it is necessary and proper for Congress to provide for the apprehension of escaped federal prisoners, it is necessary and proper for Congress to provide for the civil commitment of dangerous federal prisoners who would otherwise escape civil commitment as a result of federal imprisonment. . . .

The Necessary and Proper Clause does not give Congress *carte blanche*. Although the term "necessary" does not mean "absolutely necessary" or indispensable, the term requires an "appropriate" link between a power conferred by the Constitution and the law enacted by Congress. See *McCulloch v. Maryland*, 4 Wheat. 316, 415 (1819). And it is an obligation of this Court to enforce compliance with that limitation. *Id.*, at 423.

The law in question here satisfies that requirement. This is not a case in which it is merely possible for a court to think of a rational basis on which Congress might have perceived an attenuated link between the powers underlying the federal criminal statutes and the challenged civil commitment provision. Here, there is a substantial link to Congress' constitutional powers. . . .

JUSTICE THOMAS, with whom JUSTICE SCALIA joins in all but Part III-A-1-b, dissenting.

The Necessary and Proper Clause empowers Congress to enact only those laws that "carr[y] into Execution" one or more of the federal powers enumerated in the Constitution. Because §4248 "Execut[es]" no enumerated power, I must respectfully dissent.

I

"[O]ur Constitution establishes a system of dual sovereignty between the States and the Federal Government." *Gregory v. Ashcroft*, 501 U.S. 452, 457 (1991). In our system, the Federal Government's powers are enumerated, and hence limited. Thus, Congress has no power to act unless the Constitution authorizes it to do so. The States, in turn, are free to exercise all powers that the Constitution does not withhold from them. Amdt. 10. This constitutional structure establishes different default rules for Congress and the States: Congress' powers are "few and defined," while those that belong to the States "remain . . . numerous and indefinite." The Federalist No. 45, p. 328 (B. Wright ed. 1961) (J. Madison).

The Constitution plainly sets forth the "few and defined" powers that Congress may exercise. Article I "vest[s]" in Congress "[a]ll legislative Powers herein granted," §1, and carefully enumerates those powers in §8. The final clause of §8, the Necessary and Proper Clause, authorizes Congress "[t]o make all Laws which shall be necessary and proper for carrying into Execution the foregoing Powers, and all other Powers vested by this Constitution in the Government of the United States, or in any Department or Officer thereof." Art. I, §8, cl. 18. As the Clause's placement at the end of §8 indicates, the "foregoing Powers" are those granted to Congress in the preceding clauses of that section. The "other Powers" to which the Clause refers are those "vested" in Congress and the other branches by other specific provisions of the Constitution.

Chief Justice Marshall famously summarized Congress' authority under the Necessary and Proper Clause in *McCulloch*, which has stood for nearly 200 years as this Court's definitive interpretation of that text:

> "Let the end be legitimate, let it be within the scope of the constitution, and all means which are appropriate, which are plainly adapted to that end, which are not prohibited, but consist with the letter and spirit of the constitution, are constitutional." 4 Wheat., at 421.

McCulloch's summation is descriptive of the Clause itself, providing that federal legislation is a valid exercise of Congress' authority under the Clause if it satisfies a two-part test: First, the law must be directed toward a "legitimate" end, which *McCulloch* defines as one "within the scope of the [C]onstitution" — that is, the powers expressly delegated to the Federal Government by some provision in the Constitution. Second, there must be a necessary and proper fit between the "means" (the federal law) and the "end" (the enumerated power or powers) it is designed to serve. *Ibid. McCulloch* accords Congress a certain amount of discretion in assessing means-end fit under this second inquiry. The means Congress selects will be deemed "necessary" if they are "appropriate" and "plainly adapted" to the exercise of an enumerated power, and "proper" if they are not otherwise "prohibited" by the Constitution and not "[in]consistent" with its "letter and spirit." *Ibid.*

Critically, however, *McCulloch* underscores the linear relationship the Clause establishes between the two inquiries: Unless the end itself is "legitimate," the fit between means and end is irrelevant. In other words, no matter how "necessary" or "proper" an Act of Congress may be to its objective, Congress lacks authority to legislate if the objective is anything other than "carrying into Execution" one or more of the Federal Government's enumerated powers.

This limitation was of utmost importance to the Framers. During the State ratification debates, Anti-Federalists expressed concern that the Necessary and Proper Clause would give Congress virtually unlimited power. Federalist supporters of the Constitution swiftly refuted that charge, explaining that the Clause did not grant Congress any freestanding authority, but instead made explicit what was already implicit in the grant of each enumerated power. Referring to the "powers declared in the Constitution," Alexander Hamilton noted that "it is *expressly* to execute these powers that the sweeping clause . . . authorizes the national legislature to pass all *necessary* and *proper* laws." The Federalist No. 33, at 245. James Madison echoed this view, stating that "the sweeping clause . . . only extend[s] to the enumerated powers." 3 J. Elliot, The Debates in the Several State Conventions on the Adoption of the Federal Constitution 455 (2d ed. 1854) (hereinafter Elliot). Statements by delegates to the state ratification conventions indicate that this understanding was widely held by the founding generation.

Roughly 30 years after the Constitution's ratification, *McCulloch* firmly established this understanding in our constitutional jurisprudence. . . .

II

No enumerated power in Article I, §8, expressly delegates to Congress the power to enact a civil-commitment regime for sexually dangerous persons, nor does any other provision in the Constitution vest Congress or the other branches of the Federal Government with such a power. Accordingly, §4248 can be a valid exercise of congressional authority only if it is "necessary and proper for carrying into Execution" one or more of those federal powers actually enumerated in the Constitution.

Section 4248 does not fall within any of those powers. The Government identifies no specific enumerated power or powers as a constitutional predicate for §4248, and none are readily discernable. Indeed, not even the Commerce Clause — the enumerated power this Court has interpreted most expansively — can justify federal civil detention of sex offenders. Under the Court's precedents, Congress may not regulate noneconomic activity (such as sexual violence) based solely on the effect such activity may have, in individual cases or in the aggregate, on interstate commerce. *Morrison*, 529 U.S., at 617-618. That limitation forecloses any claim that §4248 carries into execution Congress' Commerce Clause power. . . .

This Court, moreover, consistently has recognized that the power to care for the mentally ill and, where necessary, the power "to protect the community from the dangerous tendencies of some" mentally ill persons, are among the numerous powers that remain with the States. *Addington v. Texas*, 441 U.S. 418, 426 (1979). . . . Section 4248 closely resembles the involuntary civil-commitment laws that States have enacted under their *parens patriae* and general police powers. Indeed, it is clear . . . that §4248 is aimed at protecting society from acts of sexual violence, not toward "carrying into Execution" any enumerated power or powers of the Federal Government.

To be sure, protecting society from violent sexual offenders is certainly an important end. Sexual abuse is a despicable act with untold consequences for the victim personally and society generally. But the Constitution does not vest in Congress the authority to protect society from every bad act that might befall it.

In my view, this should decide the question. Section 4248 runs afoul of our settled understanding of Congress' power under the Necessary and Proper Clause. Congress may act under that Clause only when its legislation "carr[ies] into Execution" one of the Federal Government's enumerated powers. Section 4248 does not execute any enumerated power. Section 4248 is therefore unconstitutional.

III

A

1

b

The Court observes that Congress has the undisputed authority to "criminalize conduct" that interferes with enumerated powers; to "imprison individuals who engage in that conduct"; to "enact laws governing [those] prisons"; and to serve as a "custodian of its prisoners." From this, the Court assumes that §4248 must also be a valid exercise of congressional power because it is "reasonably adapted" to those exercises of Congress' incidental—and thus unenumerated—authorities. But that is not the question. The Necessary and Proper Clause does not provide Congress with authority to enact any law simply because it furthers *other laws* Congress has enacted in the exercise of its incidental authority; the Clause plainly requires a showing that every federal statute "carr[ies] into Execution" one or more of the Federal Government's *enumerated* powers.

Federal laws that criminalize conduct that interferes with enumerated powers, establish prisons for those who engage in that conduct, and set rules for the care and treatment of prisoners awaiting trial or serving a criminal sentence satisfy this test because each helps to "carr[y] into Execution" the enumerated powers that justify a criminal defendant's arrest or conviction. . . . Civil detention under §4248, on the other hand, lacks any such connection to an enumerated power.

2

T]he Court analogizes §4248 to federal laws that authorize prison officials to care for federal inmates while they serve sentences or await trial. But while those laws help to "carr[y] into Execution" the enumerated power that justifies the imposition of criminal sanctions on the inmate, §4248 does not bear that essential characteristic for three reasons.

First, the statute's definition of a "sexually dangerous person" contains no element relating to the subject's crime. It thus does not require a federal court to find any connection between the reasons supporting civil commitment and the enumerated power with which that person's criminal conduct interfered. As a consequence, §4248 allows a court to civilly commit an individual without finding that he was ever charged with or convicted of a federal crime involving sexual violence. . . .

Second, §4248 permits the term of federal civil commitment to continue beyond the date on which a convicted prisoner's sentence expires or the date on which the statute of limitations on an untried defendant's crime has run. The statute therefore authorizes federal custody over a person at a time when the Government would lack jurisdiction to detain him for violating a criminal law that executes an enumerated power. . . .

Third, the definition of a "sexually dangerous person" relevant to §4248 does not require the court to find that the person is likely to violate a law executing an enumerated power in the future. . . .

B

I cannot agree with Justice Alito that §4248 is a necessary and proper incident of Congress' power "to protect the public from dangers created by the federal criminal justice and prison systems." A federal criminal defendant's "sexually dangerous" propensities are not "created by" the fact of his incarceration or his relationship with the federal prison system. The fact that the Federal Government has the authority to imprison a person for the purpose of punishing him for a federal crime—sex-related or otherwise—does not provide the Government with the additional power to exercise indefinite civil control over that person. . . .

The historical record . . . supports the Federal Government's authority to detain a mentally ill person against whom it has the authority to enforce a criminal law. But it provides no justification whatsoever for reading the Necessary and Proper Clause to grant Congress the power to authorize the detention of persons without a basis for federal criminal jurisdiction. . . .

[T]he Court submits that §4248 does not upset the balance of federalism or invade the States' reserved powers because it "requires accommodation of state interests" by instructing the Attorney General to release a committed person to the State in which he was domiciled or tried if that State wishes to "assume . . . responsibility" for him. This right of first refusal is mere window dressing. More importantly, it is an altogether hollow assurance that §4248 preserves the principle of dual sovereignty—the "letter and spirit" of the Constitution—as the Necessary and Proper Clause requires. For once it is determined that Congress has the authority to provide for the civil detention of sexually dangerous persons, Congress "is acting within the powers granted it under the Constitution," and "may impose its will on the States." *Gregory*, 501 U.S., at 460. Section 4248's right of first refusal is thus not a matter of constitutional necessity, but an act of legislative grace. . . .

Absent congressional action that is in accordance with, or necessary and proper to, an enumerated power, the duty to protect citizens from violent crime, including acts of sexual violence, belongs solely to the States. *Morrison*, 529 U.S., at 618. . . .

Not long ago, this Court described the Necessary and Proper Clause as "the last, best hope of those who defend ultra vires congressional action." *Printz*, *supra*, at 923. Regrettably, today's opinion breathes new life into that Clause, and . . . comes perilously close to transforming the Necessary and Proper Clause into a basis for [a] federal police power. . . . In so doing, the Court endorses the precise abuse of power Article I is designed to prevent—the use of a limited grant of authority as a "pretext . . . for the accomplishment of objects not intrusted to the government." *McCulloch*, *supra*, at 423. . . .

POINTS FOR DISCUSSION

1. What competing understandings of the Necessary and Proper Clause are in play in *Comstock*? How do they relate to early disputes over the meaning of the Necessary and Proper Clause that you studied in Chapter 1?

2. In light of all the cases you have read in Chapters 5 and 6—and the historical, judicial, and academic materials you read in Part I—what should it mean for a law to be "necessary and proper" for carrying a power of Congress into execution? What interpretive methodologies are you employing to answer this question? Why are you employing those particular methodologies?

CHAPTER 7

FEDERAL LIMITATIONS ON STATE POWER

The preceding two chapters explored constitutional limitations on the powers of the federal government. This chapter explores federal limitations on state power. Specifically, it considers how the Constitution and federal regulatory schemes preempt state law. Under the Supremacy Clause, "This Constitution, and the Laws of the United States which shall be made in Pursuance thereof; and all Treaties made, or which shall be made, under the Authority of the United States, shall be the supreme Law of the Land. . . . " U.S. CONST. art. VI, cl. 2. Thus, three sources of federal law — the Constitution, treaties, and laws of the United States — are the *supreme Law of the Land*. This chapter examines various ways in which the Constitution and laws of the United States limit state power.

A. CONSTITUTIONAL LIMITATIONS

The Constitution preempts state legislative and executive action in at least three ways — through (1) express limitations on state governing authority, (2) individual rights enforceable against the states, including those incorporated by the Due Process Clause of the Fourteenth Amendment, and (3) implied limitations on state governing authority. This section focuses primarily on the third category — implied limitations on state power — but it is important that you appreciate all three categories.

Express Limitations on State Power. The Constitution expressly limits state power in various ways. Article I, Section 10 provides:

> No State shall enter into any Treaty, Alliance, or Confederation; grant Letters of Marque and Reprisal; coin Money; emit Bills of Credit; make any Thing but gold and silver Coin a Tender in Payment of Debts; pass any Bill of Attainder, ex post facto Law, or Law impairing the Obligation of Contracts, or grant any Title of Nobility.
>
> No State shall, without the Consent of the Congress, lay any Imposts or Duties on Imports or Exports, except what may be absolutely necessary for executing its inspection Laws: and the net Produce of all Duties and Imposts,

> laid by any State on Imports or Exports, shall be for the Use of the Treasury of the United States; and all such Laws shall be subject to the Revision and Controul of the Congress.
>
> No State shall, without the Consent of Congress, lay any Duty of Tonnage, Keep troops, or Ships of War in time of Peace, enter into any Agreement or Compact with another State, or with a foreign Power, or engage in War, unless actually invaded, or in such imminent Danger as will not admit of delay.

Moreover, as you studied in Chapter 2, the Reconstruction Amendments expressly limit state power to allow slavery, U.S. CONST. amend. XIII, §1; to "abridge the privileges or immunities of citizens of the United States," "deprive any person of life, liberty, or property without due process of law," or "deny . . . any person . . . the equal protection of the laws," *id.* amend. XIV, §1; and to deny "[t]he rights of citizens of the United States to vote . . . on account of race, color, or previous condition of servitude," *id.* amend. XV, §1. In these ways, and others, the Constitution expressly limits state governing authority.

Incorporation. In addition to the express provisions of the Reconstruction Amendments, other provisions of the Constitution provide individual rights enforceable against the states. Notably, the Supreme Court has incorporated most provisions of the Bill of Rights to apply against the states through the Due Process Clause of the Fourteenth Amendment. Before the Fourteenth Amendment was ratified in 1868, the Supreme Court did not understand the Bill of Rights to operate as a limitation upon state power. *Barron v. Baltimore*, 32 U.S. 243 (1833). Following ratification of the Fourteenth Amendment, however, the Supreme Court began considering the extent to which, if at all, the Fourteenth Amendment incorporated the Bill of Rights to limit state power.

Originally, proponents of incorporation relied on the Privileges or Immunities Clause of the Fourteenth Amendment. As you read in Chapter 2, however, the Court narrowly interpreted the Privileges or Immunities Clause in the *Slaughter House Cases*, 83 U.S. (16 Wall) 36 (1872). The Court distinguished "the privileges or immunities of *citizens of the United States*" in the Fourteenth Amendment from the "Privileges and Immunities of Citizens *in the several States*" in Article IV. The Fourteenth Amendment, the Court held, prevents states only from curtailing the privileges and immunities of citizens of the *nation*. The Court understood the "privileges or immunities of citizens of the United States" under the Fourteenth Amendment to include (1) those that the Constitution originally specified as binding upon the states and (2) those that "arise out of the nature and essential character of the National Government." *Maxwell v. Dow*, 176 U.S. 581, 593 (1900). The first category includes, for example, Article I's prohibition on states passing *ex post facto* laws. And the second category includes "the right . . . to peaceably assemble and petition for a redress of grievances; the right to the writ of habeas corpus, and to use the navigable waters of the United States, however they may penetrate the territory of the several States; also all rights secured to our citizens by treaties with foreign nations; [and] the right to become citizens of any State in the Union by a bona fide residence therein." *Id.* at 591. The Supreme Court thus defined the privileges or immunities of citizens of the *United States* as a narrow category of rights, not generally inclusive of the Bill of Rights.

In the *Slaughter House Cases*, the Court expressed concern that if the Fourteenth Amendment were construed to protect more than these limited rights, "the effect [would be] to fetter and degrade the State governments by subjecting them to the control of Congress, in the exercise of powers heretofore universally conceded to them of the most ordinary and fundamental character." 83 U.S. at 78. Justice Miller wrote for the Court that such a reading would "radically change[] the whole theory of the relations of the State and Federal governments to each other and of both of these governments to the people." *Id.*

Notwithstanding Justice Miller's concerns, the Supreme Court has held over time that the Due Process Clause of the Fourteenth Amendment incorporates much of the Bill of Rights even if the Privileges or Immunities Clause does not. The Court has selectively incorporated most rights of the first eight amendments to apply against the states through the Due Process Clause.

Arguably, the first provision of the Bill of Rights that the Court incorporated against the states was the Fifth Amendment's guarantee of just compensation for any taking of private property for public use. In *Chicago, Burlington and Quincy Railroad Company v. City of Chicago*, 166 U.S. 226 (1897), the Court reasoned that a taking of property without just compensation fails to satisfy the requirements of due process. *Id.* at 236. As a state law provided the same guarantee, however, it is only arguable that this was the first case of incorporation.

The Court proceeded to apply other provisions of Bill of Rights to the states through the Due Process Clause, including First Amendment rights of speech, *Gitlow v. New York*, 268 U.S. 652 (1925); press, *Near v. Minnesota*, 283 U.S. 697 (1931); assembly, *DeJonge v. Oregon*, 299 U.S. 353 (1937); non-establishment of religion, *Everson v. Board of Education*, 330 U.S. 1 (1947); and free exercise of religion, *Cantwell v. Connecticut*, 310 U.S. 296 (1940). Additionally, the Court took its first steps toward incorporating the Sixth Amendment's right to counsel when it held that due process required the assistance of counsel in state capital cases in *Powell v. Alabama*, 287 U.S. 45 (1932).

As case-by-case incorporation proceeded, the Court declined to hold that the Due Process Clause required complete incorporation, stating in *Palko v. Connecticut*, 302 U.S. 319 (1937), that "[t]here is no such general rule." In 1947, the Court considered selective versus total incorporation in *Adamson v. California*, 332 U.S. 46 (1947). California law allowed a jury to hold criminal defendants' silence against them when they elected not to testify. In Adamson, the defendant argued that the California law denied him a fair trial in violation of the Due Process Clause. The majority, in upholding his conviction, explained that "[t]he due process clause of the Fourteenth Amendment . . . does not draw all the rights of the federal Bill of Rights under its protection." *Id.* at 53. In a concurring opinion, Justice Frankfurter critically evaluated selective incorporation. He argued that selective incorporation left courts "in the dark as to which are in and which are out." *Id.* at 65. Moreover, he deemed the selective process subjective. *Id.* Justice Frankfurter proposed that instead of selective incorporation, courts should examine the totality of circumstances of each case. *Id.* at 67. He urged review of "the whole course of the proceedings in order to ascertain whether they offended those canons of decency and fairness which express the notions of justice of English-speaking peoples even toward those charged with the most heinous offenses." *Id.* In dissent, Justice Black advocated total incorporation. *Id.* at 75. He argued that those who framed the Fourteenth Amendment "conclusively" sought full incorporation of the Bill of Rights against the states. *Id.*

Following *Adamson v. California*, piecemeal incorporation of various rights continued, including the right to a public trial and information, *In re Oliver*, 333 U.S. 257 (1948), and the right to be free from unreasonable searches and seizures, *Wolf v. Colorado*, 338 U.S. 25 (1949). In *Mapp v. Ohio*, 367 U.S. 643 (1961), the Court gave the rights guaranteed by *Wolf* greater force, holding that evidence obtained in violation of these protections was inadmissible in state court.

More incorporation followed in the 1960s. The Court incorporated additional Fifth Amendment rights, *Malloy v. Hogan*, 378 U.S. 1 (1964) (self-incrimination), *Benton v. Maryland*, 395 U.S. 784 (1969) (double jeopardy), but not the right to a grand jury indictment. The Court also incorporated the balance of Sixth Amendment rights. *Gideon v. Wainwright*, 372 U.S. 335 (1963) (right to assistance of counsel); *Pointer v. Texas*, 380 U.S. 400 (1965) (right to confront adverse witnesses); *Washington v. Texas*, 388 U.S. 14 (1967) (right to compulsory process for obtaining witnesses); *Klopfer v. North Carolina*, 386 U.S. 213 (1967) (right to speedy trial); *Duncan v. Louisiana*, 391 U.S. 145 (1968) (right to trial by impartial jury). Moreover, the Court incorporated the Eighth Amendment's prohibition on cruel and unusual punishment. *Robinson v. California*, 370 U.S. 660 (1962).

In 1968, in *Duncan v. Louisiana*, 391 U.S. 145, the Court reflected upon its practice of incorporation. Over the years, courts had invoked differing formulations in determining whether due process included certain criminal process rights. These differing formulations asked "whether a right is among those 'fundamental principles of liberty and justice which lie at the base of all our civil and political institutions,' *Powell v. Alabama*, 287 U.S. 45, 67 (1932); whether it is 'basic in our system of jurisprudence,' *In re Oliver*, 333 U.S. 257, 273 (1948); [as well as] whether it is 'a fundamental right, essential to a fair trial,' *Gideon v. Wainwright*, 372 U.S. 335, 343-344 (1963); *Malloy v. Hogan*, 378 U.S. 1, 6 (1964); *Pointer v. Texas*, 380 U.S. 400, 403 (1965)." *Duncan*, 391 U.S. at 149. Justice White, writing for the Court, explained that the relevant question had become whether a right is "fundamental in the context of the criminal processes maintained by the American States." *Id.* at 149 n.14.

In *McDonald v. City of Chicago*, 130 S. Ct. 3020 (2010), the Court, asking whether "the right to keep and bear arms is fundamental to *our* scheme of ordered liberty," *id.* at 3036, held that the Due Process Clause of the Fourteenth Amendment incorporates the Second Amendment right to keep and bear arms.

Today, nearly all of the provisions of the first eight amendments have been incorporated against the states through a process of selective incorporation. "[T]he only rights not incorporated are (1) the Third Amendment's protection against quartering of soldiers; (2) the Fifth Amendment's grand jury indictment requirement; (3) the Seventh Amendment's right to a jury trial in civil cases; and (4) the Eighth Amendment's prohibition on excessive fines." *Id.* at 3035 n.13.

To the extent that the Due Process Clause incorporates Bill of Rights provisions against the states, it preempts state governmental action that violates those provisions. The complex doctrines surrounding the Bill of Rights are largely beyond the scope of this book.

Implied Limitations on State Power. Finally, the Court has discerned implied constitutional limitations on state power. In *McCullough v. Maryland*, 17 U.S. (4 Wheat.) 316 (1819), the Supreme Court, in holding that states lacked power to tax the Bank of the United States, explained that "[i]t is of the very essence of supremacy, to remove all obstacles to its action within its own sphere, and so to modify every power vested in subordinate governments, as to exempt its own operations from their own influence." *Id.* at 427. Since *McCullough*, the Court has considered, in different contexts, when the Constitution implicitly pre-empts state action as a means of upholding the powers of the federal political branches.

Article I of the Constitution expressly makes some federal powers exclusive of the states. For example, Article I, Section 10 forbids states from coining money or entering treaties — both express federal powers under the Constitution. The District Clause of Article I, Section 8 gives Congress power "[t]o exercise *exclusive* Legislation in all Cases whatsoever, over such District (not exceeding ten Miles square) as may . . . become the Seat of Government of the United States" U.S. CONST. art. I, §8, c1. 17 (emphasis added). In other instances, however, the Constitution provides federal powers without stating that they are exclusive of state regulation. Where the Constitution does not expressly provide that a federal power is exclusive, do the states hold that power concurrently?

The Constitution empowers Congress to regulate interstate commerce but does not expressly forbid the states from making such regulations themselves (except that they may not, under Article I, Section 10, lay certain imposts or duties). May the states regulate interstate commerce concurrently with Congress? The Constitution confers various powers upon the Congress and the President to conduct the foreign relations of the United States. Article I, Section 10 expressly forbids states from engaging in certain acts relating to foreign relations but does not generally prohibit the states from engaging in activities that affect foreign relations. May the states conduct foreign relations concurrently with Congress?

The Court has held that the Commerce Clause implicitly prohibits certain state regulations involving interstate commerce. Likewise, the Court has held that the foreign relations powers of the national government implicitly prohibit certain state regulations involving foreign relations.

This section will consider two implied constitutional limitations on state power: (1) the so-called *negative* or *dormant* Commerce Clause and (2) so-called *dormant* foreign relations preemption. The Court has considered each of these limitations necessary to uphold the Constitution's allocation of national law-making power to the federal political branches.

1. THE NEGATIVE COMMERCE CLAUSE

In *Gibbons v. Ogden*, 22 U.S. (9 Wheat.) 1 (1824), the Supreme Court acknowledged, without resolving, the question whether the Constitution's conferral of power on Congress to regulate interstate commerce implicitly precludes the states from regulating acts that fall within Congress's commerce power. In *Cooley v. Board of Wardens*, 53 U.S. (12 How.) 299 (1852), the Court stated in dicta that the Commerce Clause might prohibit state regulation when the subject warrants a uniform national rule:

> [W]hen the nature of a power like this is spoken of, when it is said that the nature of the power requires that it should be exercised exclusively by Congress, it must be intended to refer to the subjects of that power, and to say they are of such a nature as to require exclusive legislation by Congress. Now the power to regulate commerce, embraces a vast field, containing not only many, but exceedingly various subjects, quite unlike in their nature; some imperatively demanding a single uniform rule, operating equally on the commerce of the United States in every port; and some, like the subject now in question, as imperatively demanding that diversity, which alone can meet the local necessities of navigation.
>
> Either absolutely to affirm, or deny that the nature of this power requires exclusive legislation by Congress, is to lose sight of the nature of the subjects of this power, and to assert concerning all of them, what is really applicable but to a part. Whatever subjects of this power are in their nature national, or admit only of one uniform system, or plan of regulation, may justly be said to be of such a nature as to require exclusive legislation by Congress. *Id.* at 319.

Subsequently, the Court has held that the Commerce Clause implicitly preempts certain state laws relating to interstate commerce. The Court has struggled, however, to draw workable distinctions between state regulation that the Commerce Clause preempts and that which the Commerce Clause allows. The Court has decided many negative Commerce Clause cases, developing complex and fact-specific doctrines. The following cases introduce you to the broad parameters of that doctrine and the kinds of issues that the Court has addressed. As you read these cases, consider the following questions:

- On what grounds has the Court held that the Commerce Clause implicitly preempts some state law?
- How broad is the scope of implied Commerce Clause preemption?
- Absent legislation by Congress regulating interstate commerce, should the Commerce Clause be held to preempt state law at all?

CITY OF PHILADELPHIA v. NEW JERSEY

437 U.S. 617 (1978)

Mr. JUSTICE STEWART delivered the opinion of the Court.

A New Jersey law [ch. 363 of the 1973 N.J. Laws] prohibits the importation of most "solid or liquid waste which originated or was collected outside the territorial limits of the State. . . ." In this case we are required to decide whether this statutory prohibition violates the Commerce Clause of the United States Constitution. . . .

[T]he operators of private landfills in New Jersey, and several cities in other States that had agreements with these operators for waste disposal . . . brought suit against New Jersey and its Department of Environmental Protection in state court, attacking the statute and regulations on a number of state and federal grounds. . . .

The dispositive question . . . is whether the law is constitutionally permissible in light of the Commerce Clause of the Constitution. . . .

Although the Constitution gives Congress the power to regulate commerce among the States, many subjects of potential federal regulation under that power inevitably escape congressional attention "because of their local character and their number and diversity." *South Carolina State Highway Dept. v. Barnwell Bros., Inc.,* 303 U.S. 177, 185. In the absence of federal legislation, these subjects are open to control by the States so long as they act within the restraints imposed by the Commerce Clause itself. The bounds of these restraints appear nowhere in the words of the Commerce Clause, but have emerged gradually in the decisions of this Court giving effect to its basic purpose. . . .

The opinions of the Court through the years have reflected an alertness to the evils of "economic isolation" and protectionism, while at the same time recognizing that incidental burdens on interstate commerce may be unavoidable when a State legislates to safeguard the health and safety of its people. Thus, where simple economic protectionism is effected by state legislation, a virtually *per se* rule of invalidity has been erected. The clearest example of such legislation is a law that overtly blocks the flow of interstate commerce at a State's borders. But where other legislative objectives are credibly advanced and there is no patent discrimination against interstate trade, the Court has adopted a much more flexible approach, the general contours of which were outlined in *Pike v. Bruce Church, Inc.,* 397 U.S. 137, 142:

> "Where the statute regulates evenhandedly to effectuate a legitimate local public interest, and its effects on interstate commerce are only incidental, it will be upheld unless the burden imposed on such commerce is clearly excessive in relation to the putative local benefits. . . . If a legitimate local purpose is found, then the question becomes one of degree. And the extent of the burden that will be tolerated will of course depend on the nature of the local interest involved, and on whether it could be promoted as well with a lesser impact on interstate activities."

The crucial inquiry, therefore, must be directed to determining whether ch. 363 is basically a protectionist measure, or whether it can fairly be viewed as a law directed to legitimate local concerns, with effects upon interstate commerce that are only incidental. . . .

The purpose of ch. 363 is set out in the statute itself as follows:

> "The Legislature finds and determines that . . . the volume of solid and liquid waste continues to rapidly increase, that the treatment and disposal of these wastes continues to pose an even greater threat to the quality of the environment of New Jersey, that the available and appropriate land fill sites within the State are being diminished, that the environment continues to be threatened by the treatment and disposal of waste which originated or was collected outside the State, and that the public health, safety and welfare require that the treatment and disposal within this State of all wastes generated outside of the State be prohibited." . . .

The appellants strenuously contend that ch. 363, "while outwardly cloaked 'in the currently fashionable garb of environmental protection,' . . . is actually no more than a legislative effort to suppress competition and stabilize the cost of solid waste disposal for New Jersey residents. . . ." . . . The appellees, on the other hand, deny that ch. 363 was motivated by financial concerns or economic protectionism. . . .

This dispute about ultimate legislative purpose need not be resolved, because its resolution would not be relevant to the constitutional issue to be decided in this case. Contrary to the evident assumption of the state court and the parties, the evil of protectionism can reside in legislative means as well as legislative ends. . . . [W]hatever New Jersey's ultimate purpose, it may not be accomplished by discriminating against articles of commerce coming from outside the State unless there is some reason, apart from their origin, to treat them differently. Both on its face and in its plain effect, ch. 363 violates this principle of nondiscrimination. . . .

The New Jersey law at issue in this case falls squarely within the area that the Commerce Clause puts off limits to state regulation. On its face, it imposes on out-of-state commercial interests the full burden of conserving the State's remaining landfill space. . . . [T]he State has overtly moved to slow or freeze the flow of commerce for protectionist reasons. . . . What is crucial is the attempt by one State to isolate itself from a problem common to many by erecting a barrier against the movement of interstate trade.

The appellees argue that not all laws which facially discriminate against out-of-state commerce are forbidden protectionist regulations. In particular, they point to quarantine laws, which this Court has repeatedly upheld even though they appear to single out interstate commerce for special treatment. In the appellees' view, ch. 363 is analogous to such health-protective measures, since it reduces the exposure of New Jersey residents to the allegedly harmful effects of landfill sites.

It is true that certain quarantine laws have not been considered forbidden protectionist measures, even though they were directed against out-of-state commerce. But those quarantine laws banned the importation of articles such as diseased livestock that required destruction as soon as possible because their very movement risked contagion and other evils. Those laws thus did not discriminate against interstate commerce as such, but simply prevented traffic in noxious articles, whatever their origin.

The New Jersey statute is not such a quarantine law. There has been no claim here that the very movement of waste into or through New Jersey endangers health, or that waste must be disposed of as soon and as close to its point of generation as possible. The harms caused by waste are said to arise after its disposal in landfill sites, and at that point, as New Jersey concedes, there is no basis to distinguish out-of-state waste from domestic waste. If one is inherently harmful, so is the other. Yet New Jersey has banned the former while leaving its landfill sites open to the latter. The New Jersey law blocks the importation of waste in an obvious effort to saddle those outside the State with the entire burden of slowing the flow of refuse into New Jersey's remaining landfill sites. That legislative effort is clearly impermissible under the Commerce Clause of the Constitution. . . .

Mr. Justice Rehnquist, with whom The Chief Justice joins, dissenting.

In ch. 363 . . . , the State of New Jersey legislatively recognized the unfortunate fact that landfills . . . present extremely serious health and safety problems. . . . The health and safety hazards associated with landfills present appellees with a currently unsolvable dilemma. Other, hopefully safer, methods of disposing of solid wastes are still in the development stage and cannot presently be used. But appellees obviously cannot completely stop the tide of solid waste that its citizens will produce in the interim. For the moment, therefore, appellees must continue to use sanitary landfills to dispose of New Jersey's own solid waste despite the critical environmental problems thereby created.

The question presented in this case is whether New Jersey must also continue to receive and dispose of solid waste from neighboring States, even though these will inexorably increase the health problems. . . . The Court answers this question in the affirmative. New Jersey must either prohibit all landfill operations, leaving itself to cast about for a presently nonexistent solution to the serious problem of disposing of the waste generated within its own borders, or it must accept waste from every portion of the United States, thereby multiplying the health and safety problems which would result if it dealt only with such wastes generated within the State. . . . [T]he Commerce Clause does not present appellees with such a Hobson's choice. . . .

The Court recognizes that States can prohibit the importation of items "which, on account of their existing condition, would bring in and spread disease, pestilence, and death, such as rags or other substances infected with the germs of yellow fever or the virus of small-pox, or cattle or meat or other provisions that are diseased or decayed or otherwise, from their condition and quality, unfit for human use or consumption." *Bowman v. Chicago & Northwestern R. Co.*, 125 U.S. 465, 489 (1888). . . .

In my opinion, these cases are dispositive of the present one. Under them, New Jersey may require germ-infected rags or diseased meat to be disposed of as best as possible within the State, but at the same time prohibit the *importation* of such items for disposal at the facilities that are set up within New Jersey for disposal of such material generated *within* the State. The physical fact of life that New Jersey must somehow dispose of its own noxious items does not mean that it must serve as a depository for those of every other State. Similarly, New Jersey should be free under our past precedents to prohibit the importation of solid waste because of the health and safety problems that such waste poses to its citizens. The fact that New Jersey continues to, and indeed must continue to, dispose of its own solid waste does not mean that New Jersey may not prohibit the importation of even more solid waste into the State. I simply see no way to distinguish solid waste, on the record of this case, from germ-infected rags, diseased meat, and other noxious items. . . .

According to the Court, the New Jersey law is distinguishable from these other laws, and invalid, because the concern of New Jersey is not with the *movement* of solid waste but with the present inability to safely *dispose* of it once it reaches its destination. But I think it far from clear that the State's law has as limited a focus as the Court imputes to it: Solid waste which is a health hazard when it reaches its destination may in all likelihood be an equally great health hazard in transit.

Even if the Court is correct in its characterization of New Jersey's concerns, I do not see why a State may ban the importation of items whose movement risks contagion, but cannot ban the importation of items which, although they may be transported into the State without undue hazard, will then simply pile up in an ever increasing danger to the public's health and safety. The Commerce Clause was not drawn with a view to having the validity of state laws turn on such pointless distinctions. . . .

TYLER PIPE INDUSTRIES, INC. v. WASHINGTON STATE DEPARTMENT OF REVENUE

483 U.S. 232 (1987)

JUSTICE STEVENS delivered the opinion of the Court.

The principal question . . . is whether Washington's manufacturing tax . . . violates the Commerce Clause of the Constitution because it is assessed only on those products manufactured within Washington that are sold to out-of-state purchasers. . . .

For over half a century Washington has imposed a . . . tax on "the act or privilege of engaging in business activities" in the State. The tax applies to the activities of extracting raw materials in the State, manufacturing in the State, making wholesale sales in the State, and making retail sales in the State. . . . [Under Washington law,] local manufacturers pay the manufacturing tax on their interstate sales and out-of-state manufacturers pay the wholesale tax on their sales in Washington. . . .

Today we . . . address the claim that this provision discriminates against interstate commerce. . . .

Th[e] statutory exemption for manufacturers that sell their products within the State has the same facially discriminatory consequences as the West Virginia exemption we invalidated in [*Armco Inc. v. Hardesty*, 467 U.S. 638 (1984).] . . .

In *Armco*, [w]e explained:

> "The tax provides that two companies selling tangible property at wholesale in West Virginia will be treated differently depending on whether the taxpayer conducts manufacturing in the State or out of it. Thus, if the property was manufactured in the State, no tax on the sale is imposed. If the property was manufactured out of the State and imported for sale, a tax . . . is imposed on the sale price. . . ." [*Id.* at 642.] . . .

We conclude that Washington's [tax scheme] discriminates against interstate commerce. . . . The [tax scheme] exposes manufacturing or selling activity outside the State to a . . . burden from which only the activity of manufacturing in-state and selling in-state is exempt. . . .

JUSTICE POWELL took no part in the consideration or decision of these cases.

JUSTICE O'CONNOR, concurring.

I do not read the Court's decision as extending . . . *Armco* to taxes that are not facially discriminatory, nor would I agree with such a result. . . .

JUSTICE SCALIA, . . . dissenting in part.

I dissent . . . from the [part] of the opinion, invalidating the State's manufacturing tax as unconstitutionally discriminatory under the Commerce

Clause. . . . [I]n the 114 years since the doctrine of the negative Commerce Clause was formally adopted as holding of this Court, and in the 50 years prior to that in which it was alluded to in various dicta of the Court, see *Cooley v. Board of Wardens*, 12 How. 299, 319 (1852); *Gibbons v. Ogden*, 9 Wheat. 1, 209 (1824); our applications of the doctrine have, not to put too fine a point on the matter, made no sense. . . .

That uncertainty in application has been attributable in no small part to the lack of any clear theoretical underpinning for judicial "enforcement" of the Commerce Clause. The text of the Clause states that "Congress shall have Power . . . To regulate Commerce with foreign Nations, and among the several States, and with the Indian Tribes." Art. I, §8, cl. 3. On its face, this is a charter for Congress, not the courts, to ensure "an area of trade free from interference by the States." [*Boston Stock Exchange v. State Tax Comm'n*, 429 U.S. 318, 328 (1977).] The pre-emption of state legislation would automatically follow, of course, if the grant of power to Congress to regulate interstate commerce were exclusive, as Charles Pinckney's draft constitution would have provided, and as John Marshall at one point seemed to believe it was. See *Gibbons v. Ogden*, *supra*, at 209. However, unlike the District Clause, which empowers Congress "To exercise exclusive Legislation," Art. I, §8, cl. 17, the language of the Commerce Clause gives no indication of exclusivity. Nor can one assume generally that Congress' Article I powers are exclusive; many of them plainly coexist with concurrent authority in the States[, for example, the patent, copyright, and bankruptcy powers.] Furthermore, there is no correlative denial of power over commerce to the States in Art. I, §10, as there is, for example, with the power to coin money or make treaties. And both the States and Congress assumed from the date of ratification that at least some state laws regulating commerce were valid. The exclusivity rationale is infinitely less attractive today. . . . Now that we know interstate commerce embraces such activities as growing wheat for home consumption, *Wickard v. Filburn*, 317 U.S. 111 (1942), . . . it is more difficult to imagine what state activity would survive an exclusive Commerce Clause than to imagine what would be precluded.

Another approach to theoretical justification for judicial enforcement of the Commerce Clause is to assert, as did Justice Curtis in dicta in *Cooley v. Board of Wardens*, *supra*, at 319, that "[w]hatever subjects of this power are in their nature national, or admit only of one uniform system, or plan of regulation, may justly be said to be of such a nature as to require exclusive legislation by Congress." That would perhaps be a wise rule to adopt (though it is hard to see why judges rather than legislators are fit to determine what areas of commerce "in their nature" require national regulation), but it has the misfortune of finding no conceivable basis in the text of the Commerce Clause, which treats "Commerce . . . among the several States" as a unitary subject. And attempting to limit the Clause's pre-emptive effect to state laws *intended* to regulate commerce (as opposed to those intended, for example, to promote health), see *Gibbons v. Ogden*, *supra*, at 203, while perhaps a textually possible construction of the phrase "regulate Commerce," is a most unlikely one. Distinguishing between laws with the *purpose* of regulating commerce and "police power" statutes with that *effect* is . . . more interesting as a metaphysical exercise than useful as a practical technique for marking out the powers of separate sovereigns.

The least plausible theoretical justification of all is the idea that in enforcing the negative Commerce Clause the Court is not applying a constitutional command at all, but is merely interpreting the will of Congress, whose silence in certain fields of interstate commerce (but not in others) is to be taken as a prohibition of regulation. There is no conceivable reason why congressional inaction under the Commerce Clause should be deemed to have the same preemptive effect elsewhere accorded only to congressional action. There, as elsewhere, "Congress' silence is just that — silence. . . ." *Alaska Airlines, Inc. v. Brock*, 480 U.S. 678, 686 (1987).

The historical record provides no grounds for reading the Commerce Clause to be other than what it says — an authorization for Congress to regulate commerce. The strongest evidence in favor of a negative Commerce Clause — that version of it which renders federal authority over interstate commerce exclusive — is Madison's comment during the Convention: "Whether the States are now restrained from laying tonnage duties depends on the extent of the power 'to regulate commerce.' These terms are vague but seem to exclude this power of the States." 2 M. Farrand, Records of the Federal Convention of 1787, p. 625 (1937). This comment, however, came during discussion of what became Art. I, §10, cl. 3: "No State shall, without the Consent of Congress, lay any Duty of Tonnage. . . ." The fact that it is difficult to conceive how the power to regulate commerce would *not* include the power to impose duties; and the fact that, despite this apparent coverage, the Convention went on to adopt a provision prohibiting States from levying duties on tonnage without congressional approval; suggest that Madison's assumption of exclusivity of the federal commerce power was ill considered and not generally shared.

Against this mere shadow of historical support there is the overwhelming reality that the Commerce Clause, in its broad outlines, was not a major subject of controversy, neither during the constitutional debates nor in the ratifying conventions. . . . "The records disclose no constructive criticisms by the states of the commerce clause as proposed to them." F. Frankfurter, The Commerce Clause under Marshall, Taney and Waite 12 (1937). In The Federalist, Madison and Hamilton wrote numerous discourses on the virtues of free trade and the need for uniformity and national control of commercial regulation, see The Federalist No. 7, pp. 62-63 (C. Rossiter ed. 1961); *id.*, No. 11, pp. 89-90; *id.*, No. 22, pp. 143-145; *id.*, No. 42, pp. 267-269; *id.*, No. 53, p. 333, but said little of substance specifically about the Commerce Clause. . . . Madison does not seem to have exaggerated when he described the Commerce Clause as an addition to the powers of the National Government "which few oppose and from which no apprehensions are entertained." The Federalist No. 45, p. 293. I think it beyond question that many "apprehensions" would have been "entertained" if supporters of the Constitution had hinted that the Commerce Clause, despite its language, gave this Court the power it has since assumed. As Justice Frankfurter pungently put it: "the doctrine that state authority must be subject to such limitations as the Court finds it necessary to apply for the protection of the national community . . . [is] an audacious doctrine, which, one may be sure, would hardly have been publicly avowed in support of the adoption of the Constitution." Frankfurter, *supra*, at 19.

In sum, to the extent that we have gone beyond guarding against rank discrimination against citizens of other States—which is regulated not by the Commerce Clause but by the Privileges and Immunities Clause, U.S. Const., Art. IV, §2, cl. 1 ("The Citizens of each State shall be entitled to all Privileges and Immunities of Citizens in the several States")—the Court for over a century has engaged in an enterprise that it has been unable to justify by textual support or even coherent nontextual theory, that it was almost certainly not intended to undertake, and that it has not undertaken very well. It is astonishing that we should be expanding our beachhead in this impoverished territory, rather than being satisfied with what we have already acquired by a sort of intellectual adverse possession.

WEST LYNN CREAMERY, INC. v. HEALY

512 U.S. 186 (1994)

JUSTICE STEVENS delivered the opinion of the Court.

A Massachusetts pricing order imposes an assessment on all fluid milk sold by dealers to Massachusetts retailers. About two-thirds of that milk is produced out of State. The entire assessment, however, is distributed to Massachusetts dairy farmers. The question presented is whether the pricing order unconstitutionally discriminates against interstate commerce. We hold that it does. . . .

The Commerce Clause vests Congress with ample power to enact legislation providing for the regulation of prices paid to farmers for their products. *United States v. Darby*, 312 U.S. 100 (1941); *Wickard v. Filburn*, 317 U.S. 111 (1942). An affirmative exercise of that power led to the promulgation of the federal order setting minimum milk prices. The Commerce Clause also limits the power of the Commonwealth of Massachusetts to adopt regulations that discriminate against interstate commerce. "This 'negative' aspect of the Commerce Clause prohibits economic protectionism—that is, regulatory measures designed to benefit in-state economic interests by burdening out-of-state competitors. . . . Thus, state statutes that clearly discriminate against interstate commerce are routinely struck down . . . unless the discrimination is demonstrably justified by a valid factor unrelated to economic protectionism. . . ." *New Energy Co. of Ind. v. Limbach*, 486 U.S. 269, 273-274 (1988).

The paradigmatic example of a law discriminating against interstate commerce is the protective tariff or customs duty, which taxes goods imported from other States, but does not tax similar products produced in State. A tariff is an attractive measure because it simultaneously raises revenue and benefits local producers by burdening their out-of-state competitors. Nevertheless, it violates the principle of the unitary national market by handicapping out-of-state competitors, thus artificially encouraging in-state production even when the same goods could be produced at lower cost in other States.

Because of their distorting effects on the geography of production, tariffs have long been recognized as violative of the Commerce Clause. In fact, tariffs against the products of other States are so patently unconstitutional that our cases reveal not a single attempt by any State to enact one. Instead, the cases are filled with state laws that aspire to reap some of the benefits of tariffs by other means. In *Baldwin v. G.A.F. Seelig, Inc.*, 294 U.S. 511 (1935), the State of New York attempted to protect its dairy farmers from the adverse effects of Vermont competition by establishing a single minimum price for all milk, whether produced in New York or elsewhere. This Court did not hesitate, however, to strike it down. Writing for a unanimous Court, Justice Cardozo reasoned:

> "Neither the power to tax nor the police power may be used by the state of destination with the aim and effect of establishing an economic barrier against competition with the products of another state or the labor of its residents. Restrictions so contrived are an unreasonable clog upon the mobility of commerce. They set up what is equivalent to a rampart of customs duties designed to neutralize advantages belonging to the place of origin." *Id.*, at 527.

Thus, because the minimum price regulation had the same effect as a tariff or customs duty — neutralizing the advantage possessed by lower cost out-of-state producers — it was held unconstitutional. . . .

Massachusetts' pricing order is clearly unconstitutional. Its avowed purpose and its undisputed effect are to enable higher cost Massachusetts dairy farmers to compete with lower cost dairy farmers in other States. The "premium payments" are effectively a tax which makes milk produced out of State more expensive. Although the tax also applies to milk produced in Massachusetts, its effect on Massachusetts producers is entirely (indeed more than) offset by the subsidy provided exclusively to Massachusetts dairy farmers. Like an ordinary tariff, the tax is thus effectively imposed only on out-of-state products. The pricing order thus allows Massachusetts dairy farmers who produce at higher cost to sell at or below the price charged by lower cost out-of-state producers. . . .

Finally, respondent argues that any incidental burden on interstate commerce "is outweighed by the 'local benefits' of preserving the Massachusetts dairy industry." In a closely related argument, respondent urges that "the purpose of the order, to save an industry from collapse, is not protectionist." If we were to accept these arguments, we would make a virtue of the vice that the rule against discrimination condemns. Preservation of local industry by protecting it from the rigors of interstate competition is the hallmark of the economic protectionism that the Commerce Clause prohibits. . . . Whether a State is attempting to "enhance thriving and substantial business enterprises" or to "subsidize . . . financially troubled" ones is irrelevant to Commerce Clause analysis. . . .

JUSTICE SCALIA, with whom JUSTICE THOMAS joins, concurring in the judgment.

In my view the challenged Massachusetts pricing order is invalid under our negative-Commerce-Clause jurisprudence. . . . [But] I do not agree with the reasons assigned by the Court. . . . Accordingly, I concur only in the judgment of the Court. . . .

"The historical record provides no grounds for reading the Commerce Clause to be other than what it says—an authorization for Congress to regulate commerce." *Tyler Pipe Industries, Inc. v. Washington State Dept. of Revenue*, 483 U.S. 232, 263 (1987) (Scalia, J., concurring in part and dissenting in part). Nonetheless, we formally adopted the doctrine of the negative Commerce Clause 121 years ago, and since then have decided a vast number of negative-Commerce-Clause cases, engendering considerable reliance interests. As a result, I will, on *stare decisis* grounds, enforce a self-executing "negative" Commerce Clause in two situations: (1) against a state law that facially discriminates against interstate commerce, and (2) against a state law that is indistinguishable from a type of law previously held unconstitutional by this Court. . . . Applying this approach—or at least the second part of it—is not always easy, since once one gets beyond facial discrimination our negative-Commerce-Clause jurisprudence becomes (and long has been) a "quagmire." *Northwestern States Portland Cement Co. v. Minnesota*, 358 U.S. 450, 458 (1959). The object should be, however, to produce a clear rule that honors the holdings of our past decisions but declines to extend the rationale that produced those decisions any further. . . .

The issue before us in the present case is whether [the Massachusetts regulatory scheme at issue] must fall [under the Court's negative Commerce Clause jurisprudence]. Although the question is close, I conclude it would not be a principled point at which to disembark from the negative-Commerce-Clause train. . . .

CHIEF JUSTICE REHNQUIST, with whom JUSTICE BLACKMUN joins, dissenting.

The Court is less than just in its description of the reasons which lay behind the Massachusetts law which it strikes down. The law undoubtedly sought to aid struggling Massachusetts dairy farmers, beset by steady or declining prices and escalating costs. . . .

Massachusetts has dealt with this problem by providing a subsidy to aid its beleaguered dairy farmers. In case after case, we have approved the validity under the Commerce Clause of such enactments. "No one disputes that a State may enact laws pursuant to its police powers that have the purpose and effect of encouraging domestic industry." *Bacchus Imports, Ltd. v. Dias*, 468 U.S. 263, 271 (1984). "Direct subsidization of domestic industry does not ordinarily run afoul of [the dormant Commerce Clause]; discriminatory taxation of out-of-state manufacturers does." *New Energy Co. of Ind. v. Limbach*, 486 U.S. 269, 278 (1988). . . .

Consistent with precedent, the Court observes: "A pure subsidy funded out of general revenue ordinarily imposes no burden on interstate commerce, but merely assists local business." And the Court correctly recognizes that "[n]ondiscriminatory measures, like the evenhanded tax at issue here, are generally upheld" due to the deference normally accorded to a State's political process in passing legislation in light of various competing interest groups. But the Court strikes down this method of state subsidization because the nondiscriminatory tax levied against all milk dealers is coupled with a subsidy to milk producers. . . . The Court concludes that the combined effect of the milk order "simultaneously burdens interstate commerce and discriminates in favor of local producers." . . .

More than half a century ago, Justice Brandeis said in his dissenting opinion in *New State Ice Co. v. Liebmann*, 285 U.S. 262, 311 (1932):

> "To stay experimentation in things social and economic is a grave responsibility. Denial of the right to experiment may be fraught with serious consequences to the Nation. It is one of the happy incidents of the federal system that a single courageous State may, if its citizens choose, serve as a laboratory; and try novel social and economic experiments without risk to the rest of the country."

Justice Brandeis' statement has been cited more than once in subsequent majority opinions of the Court. His observation bears heeding today, as it did when he made it. The wisdom of a messianic insistence on a grim sink-or-swim policy of laissez-faire economics would be debatable had Congress chosen to enact it; but Congress has done nothing of the kind. It is the Court which has imposed the policy under the dormant Commerce Clause, a policy which bodes ill for the values of federalism which have long animated our constitutional jurisprudence.

GRANHOLM V. HEALD

544 U.S. 460 (2005)

JUSTICE KENNEDY delivered the opinion of the Court.

These consolidated cases present challenges to state laws regulating the sale of wine from out-of-state wineries to consumers in Michigan and New York. . . . [T]he object and effect of the laws are the same: to allow in-state wineries to sell wine directly to consumers in that State but to prohibit out-of-state wineries from doing so, or, at the least, to make direct sales impractical from an economic standpoint. It is evident that the object and design of the Michigan and New York statutes is to grant in-state wineries a competitive advantage over wineries located beyond the States' borders.

We hold that the laws in both States discriminate against interstate commerce in violation of the Commerce Clause. . . .

I

From 1994 to 1999, consumer spending on direct wine shipments doubled, reaching $500 million per year, or three percent of all wine sales. . . . [M]any small wineries do not produce enough wine or have sufficient consumer demand for their wine to make it economical for wholesalers to carry their products. This has led many small wineries to rely on direct shipping to reach new markets. Technological improvements, in particular the ability of wineries to sell wine over the Internet, have helped make direct shipments an attractive sales channel.

Approximately 26 States allow some direct shipping of wine, with various restrictions. Thirteen of these States have reciprocity laws, which allow direct shipment from wineries outside the State, provided the State of origin affords similar nondiscriminatory treatment. In many parts of the country, however, state laws that prohibit or severely restrict direct shipments deprive consumers of access to the direct market. According to the Federal Trade Commission (FTC), "[s]tate bans on interstate direct shipping represent the single largest regulatory barrier to expanded e-commerce in wine."

The wine producers in the cases before us are small wineries that rely on direct consumer sales as an important part of their businesses. . . .

II

A

Time and again this Court has held that, in all but the narrowest circumstances, state laws violate the Commerce Clause if they mandate "differential treatment of in-state and out-of-state economic interests that benefits the former and burdens the latter." *Oregon Waste Systems, Inc. v. Department of Environmental Quality of Ore.*, 511 U.S. 93, 99 (1994). This rule is essential to the foundations of the Union. The mere fact of nonresidence should not foreclose a producer in one State from access to markets in other States. States may not enact laws that burden out-of-state producers or shippers simply to give a competitive advantage to in-state businesses. This mandate "reflect[s] a central concern of the Framers that was an immediate reason for calling the Constitutional Convention: the conviction that in order to succeed, the new Union would have to avoid the tendencies toward economic Balkanization that had plagued relations among the Colonies and later among the States under the Articles of Confederation." *Hughes v. Oklahoma*, 441 U.S. 322, 325-326 (1979).

The rule prohibiting state discrimination against interstate commerce follows also from the principle that States should not be compelled to negotiate with each other regarding favored or disfavored status for their own citizens. States do not need, and may not attempt, to negotiate with other States regarding their mutual economic interests. Rivalries among the States are thus kept to a minimum, and a proliferation of trade zones is prevented.

Laws of the type at issue in the instant cases contradict these principles. They deprive citizens of their right to have access to the markets of other States on equal terms. The perceived necessity for reciprocal sale privileges risks generating the trade rivalries and animosities, the alliances and exclusivity, that the Constitution and, in particular, the Commerce Clause were designed to avoid. State laws that protect local wineries have led to the enactment of statutes under which some States condition the right of out-of-state wineries to make direct wine sales to in-state consumers on a reciprocal right in the shipping State. . . . The current patchwork of laws—with some States banning direct shipments altogether, others doing so only for out-of-state wines, and still others requiring reciprocity—is essentially the product of an ongoing, low-level trade war. . . .

B

The discriminatory character of the Michigan system is obvious. Michigan allows in-state wineries to ship directly to consumers, subject only to a licensing requirement. Out-of-state wineries, whether licensed or not, face a complete ban on direct shipment. The differential treatment requires all out-of-state wine, but not all in-state wine, to pass through an in-state wholesaler and retailer before reaching consumers. These two extra layers of overhead increase the cost of out-of-state wines to Michigan consumers. The cost differential, and in some cases the inability to secure a wholesaler for small shipments, can effectively bar small wineries from the Michigan market.

The New York regulatory scheme differs from Michigan's in that it does not ban direct shipments altogether. Out-of-state wineries are instead required to establish a distribution operation in New York in order to gain the privilege of direct shipment. . . . The New York scheme grants in-state wineries access to the State's consumers on preferential terms. The suggestion of a limited exception for direct shipment from out-of-state wineries does nothing to eliminate the discriminatory nature of New York's regulations. In-state producers, with the applicable licenses, can ship directly to consumers from their wineries. Out-of-state wineries must open a branch office and warehouse in New York, additional steps that drive up the cost of their wine. . . . It comes as no surprise that not a single out-of-state winery has availed itself of New York's direct-shipping privilege. . . .

We have no difficulty concluding that New York, like Michigan, discriminates against interstate commerce through its direct-shipping laws.

III

State laws that discriminate against interstate commerce face "a virtually *per se* rule of invalidity." *Philadelphia v. New Jersey*, 437 U.S. 617, 624 (1978). The Michigan and New York laws by their own terms violate this proscription. The two States, however, contend their statutes are saved by §2 of the Twenty-first Amendment, which provides:

> "The transportation or importation into any State, Territory, or possession of the United States for delivery or use therein of intoxicating liquors, in violation of the laws thereof, is hereby prohibited."

The States' position is inconsistent with our precedents and with the Twenty-first Amendment's history. Section 2 does not allow States to regulate the direct shipment of wine on terms that discriminate in favor of in-state producers. . . .

[T]he Court has held that §2 does not abrogate Congress' Commerce Clause powers with regard to liquor. . . . [M]ost relevant to the issue at hand, the Court has held that state regulation of alcohol is limited by the nondiscrimination principle of the Commerce Clause. . . .

IV

Our determination that the Michigan and New York direct-shipment laws are not authorized by the Twenty-first Amendment does not end the inquiry. We still must consider whether either state regime "advances a legitimate local purpose that cannot be adequately served by reasonable nondiscriminatory alternatives." [*New Energy Co. of Ind. v. Limbach*, 486 U.S. 269, 278 (1988).] The States offer two primary justifications for restricting direct shipments from out-of-state wineries: keeping alcohol out of the hands of minors and facilitating tax collection. We consider each in turn.

The States . . . claim that allowing direct shipment from out-of-state wineries undermines their ability to police underage drinking. Minors, the States argue, have easy access to credit cards and the Internet and are likely to take advantage of direct wine shipments as a means of obtaining alcohol illegally.

The States provide little evidence that the purchase of wine over the Internet by minors is a problem. . . . Without concrete evidence that direct shipping of wine is likely to increase alcohol consumption by minors, we are left with the States' unsupported assertions. . . . Even were we to credit the States' largely unsupported claim that direct shipping of wine increases the risk of underage drinking, this would not justify regulations limiting only out-of-state direct shipments. As the wineries point out, minors are just as likely to order wine from in-state producers as from out-of-state ones. . . .

The States' tax-collection justification is also insufficient. Increased direct shipping, whether originating in state or out of state, brings with it the potential for tax evasion. . . . The States have not shown that tax evasion from out-of-state wineries poses such a unique threat that it justifies their discriminatory regimes.

Michigan and New York offer a handful of other rationales, such as facilitating orderly market conditions, protecting public health and safety, and ensuring regulatory accountability. These objectives can also be achieved through the alternative of an evenhanded licensing requirement. Finally, it should be noted that improvements in technology have eased the burden of monitoring out-of-state wineries. Background checks can be done electronically. Financial records and sales data can be mailed, faxed, or submitted via e-mail.

In summary, the States provide little concrete evidence for the sweeping assertion that they cannot police direct shipments by out-of-state wineries. Our Commerce Clause cases demand more than mere speculation to support discrimination against out-of-state goods. . . .

V

States have broad power to regulate liquor under §2 of the Twenty-first Amendment. This power, however, does not allow States to ban, or severely limit, the direct shipment of out-of-state wine while simultaneously authorizing direct shipment by in-state producers. If a State chooses to allow direct shipment of wine, it must do so on evenhanded terms. Without demonstrating the need for discrimination, New York and Michigan have enacted regulations that disadvantage out-of-state wine producers. Under our Commerce Clause jurisprudence, these regulations cannot stand. . . .

JUSTICE STEVENS, with whom JUSTICE O'CONNOR joins, dissenting.

The New York and Michigan laws challenged in these cases would be patently invalid under well-settled dormant Commerce Clause principles if they regulated sales of an ordinary article of commerce rather than wine. But ever since the adoption of the Eighteenth Amendment and the Twenty-first Amendment, our Constitution has placed commerce in alcoholic beverages in a special category. Section 2 of the Twenty-first Amendment expressly provides that "[t]he transportation or importation into any State, Territory, or possession of the United States for delivery or use therein of intoxicating liquors, in violation of the laws thereof, is hereby prohibited." . . .

Because the New York and Michigan laws regulate the "transportation or importation" of "intoxicating liquors" for "delivery or use therein," they are exempt from dormant Commerce Clause scrutiny.

JUSTICE THOMAS, with whom THE CHIEF JUSTICE, JUSTICE STEVENS, and JUSTICE O'CONNOR join, dissenting.

The Webb-Kenyon Act immunizes from negative Commerce Clause review the state liquor laws that the Court holds are unconstitutional. . . . The Michigan and New York direct-shipment laws are within the Webb-Kenyon Act's terms and therefore do not run afoul of the negative Commerce Clause. . . . There is no need to interpret the Twenty-first Amendment, because the Webb-Kenyon Act resolves these cases. . . .

POINTS FOR DISCUSSION

1. The Supreme Court has held that Congress has power to regulate economic intrastate activities that substantially affect interstate commerce, *United States v. Lopez*, 514 U.S. 549 (1995), *United States v. Morrison*, 529 U.S. 598 (2000), and other intrastate activities as necessary and proper to carry into execution a broader regulation of interstate markets, *Gonzales v. Raich*, 545 U.S. 1 (2005). Why does the "negative Commerce Clause" not forbid states from regulating any activity that Congress may regulate under the Commerce Clause? Should it? What, if anything, justifies the Court in forbidding states from regulating some, but not all, activities that Congress may regulate under the Commerce Clause?

2. In his opinion in *Tyler Pipe*, Justice Scalia argued that Congress, not the judiciary, has responsibility to enforce the Commerce Clause against the States. Accordingly, he rejected much of the Court's negative Commerce Clause jurisprudence. Critically evaluate his claims that the Court's negative Commerce Clause jurisprudence (a) is unworkable and (b) finds insufficient support in the historical record. If the Court adopted his position, how, as a practical matter, would the relationship between the federal government and the states change?

In light of the Court's negative Commerce Clause jurisprudence, consider this question: May Congress, in exercising its commerce powers, authorize a state to enact a regulation of interstate commerce that the dormant Commerce Clause would otherwise prohibit the state from enacting?

PRUDENTIAL INSURANCE CO. v. BENJAMIN

328 U.S. 408 (1946)

Mr. JUSTICE RUTLEDGE delivered the opinion of the Court.

South Carolina [lays a] tax . . . on foreign insurance companies[; the tax] must be paid annually as a condition of receiving a certificate of authority to carry on the business of insurance within the state. The exaction amounts to three per cent of the aggregate of premiums received from business done in South Carolina, without reference to its interstate or local character. . . . No similar tax is required of South Carolina corporations. . . .

Prudential insists that the tax discriminates against interstate commerce and in favor of local business, since it is laid only on foreign corporations and is measured by their gross receipts from premiums derived from business done in the state, regardless of its interstate or local character. Accordingly it says the tax cannot stand consistently with many decisions of this Court outlawing state taxes which discriminate against interstate commerce. . . . South Carolina . . . maintains that the tax is valid, more particularly in view of the McCarran Act, . . . by which it is claimed Congress has consented to continuance of this form of taxation and thus has removed any possible constitutional objection which otherwise might exist. . . .

That the [Commerce Clause] imposes some restraint upon state power has never been doubted. For otherwise the grant of power to Congress would be wholly ineffective. . . . We are not required however to consider whether, on that level, the authorities [outlawing state taxes found to discriminate against interstate commerce] would require invalidation of South Carolina's tax. For they are not in point. . . . No one of them involved a situation like that now here. In each the question of validity of the state taxing statute arose when Congress' power lay dormant. In none had Congress acted or purported to act, either by way of consenting to the state's tax or otherwise. . . .

Fundamentally [Prudential] maintains that . . . neither Congress acting affirmatively nor Congress and the states thus acting coordinately can validly impose any regulation which the Court has found or would find to be forbidden by the commerce clause, if laid only by state action taken while Congress' power lies dormant. In this view the limits of state power to regulate commerce in the absence of affirmative action by Congress are also the limits of Congress' permissible action in this respect, whether taken alone or in coordination with state legislation.

Merely to state the position in this way compels its rejection. So conceived, Congress' power over commerce would be nullified to a very large extent. . . . For in all the variations of commerce clause theory it has never been the law that what the states may do in the regulation of commerce, Congress being silent, is the full measure of its power. Much less has this boundary been thought to confine what Congress and the states acting together may accomplish. So to regard the matter would invert the constitutional grant into a limitation upon the very power it confers.

The commerce clause is in no sense a limitation upon the power of Congress over interstate and foreign commerce. On the contrary, it is, as Marshall declared in *Gibbons v. Ogden*, a grant to Congress of plenary and supreme authority over those subjects. The only limitation it places upon Congress' power is in respect to what constitutes commerce, including whatever rightly may be found to affect it sufficiently to make Congressional regulation necessary or appropriate. . . . This limitation, of course, is entirely distinct from the implied prohibition of the commerce clause. The one is concerned with defining commerce, with fixing the outer boundary of the field over which the authority granted shall govern. The other relates only to matters within the field of commerce, once this is defined, including whatever may fall within the "affectation" doctrine. The one limitation bounds the power of Congress. The other confines only the powers of the states. And the two areas are not coextensive. The distinction is not always clearly observed, for both questions may and indeed at times do arise in the same case and in close relationship. . . . But to blur them, and thereby equate the implied prohibition with the affirmative endowment is altogether fallacious. There is no such equivalence. . . .

[T]he McCarran Act [provides in pertinent part]:

> ". . . the Congress hereby declares that the continued regulation and taxation by the several States of the business of insurance is in the public interest, and that silence on the part of the Congress shall not be construed to impose any barrier to the regulation or taxation of such business by the several States. . . ." . . .

Congress [determined] that state taxes, which in its silence might be held invalid as discriminatory, do not place on interstate insurance business a burden which it is unable generally to bear or should not bear in the competition with local business. . . .

[The] plenary scope [of the commerce power] enables Congress not only to promote but also to prohibit interstate commerce, as it has done frequently and for a great variety of reasons. . . . That power does not run down a one-way street or one of narrowly fixed dimensions. Congress may keep the way open, confine it broadly or closely, or close it entirely, subject only to the restrictions placed upon its authority by other constitutional provisions and the requirement that it shall not invade the domains of action reserved exclusively for the states.

This broad authority Congress may exercise alone, subject to those limitations, or in conjunction with coordinated action by the states, . . . in which case limitations imposed for the preservation of their powers become inoperative and only those designed to forbid action altogether by any power or combination of powers in our governmental system remain effective. . . . Here both Congress and South Carolina have acted, and in complete coordination, to sustain the tax. It is therefore reinforced by the exercise of all the power of government residing in our scheme. . . . Clear and gross must be the evil which would nullify such an exertion, one which could arise only by exceeding beyond cavil some explicit and compelling limitation imposed by a constitutional provision or provisions designed and intended to outlaw the action taken entirely from our constitutional framework. . . .

For great reasons of policy and history not now necessary to restate, [the powers of Congress and the states] were separated. They were not forbidden to cooperate or by doing so to achieve legislative consequences, particularly in the great fields of regulating commerce and taxation, which, to some extent at least, neither could accomplish in isolated exertion. . . .

Mr. Justice Black concurs in the result.

Mr. Justice Jackson took no part in the consideration or decision of this case.

POINTS FOR DISCUSSION

1. Prudential asserted in this case that "neither Congress acting affirmatively nor Congress and the states thus acting coordinately can validly impose any regulation which the Court has found or would find to be forbidden by the commerce clause, if laid only by state action taken while Congress' power lies dormant." Did the Court adequately refute this assertion?

2. If Congress may authorize a state to regulate interstate commerce in a way the Commerce Clause *implicitly* forbids, may Congress authorize a state to regulate in a way that the Constitution *expressly* forbids — such as to make a treaty (prohibited by Article I, §10), to coin money (prohibited by Article I, §10), or to violate due process (prohibited by the Fourteenth Amendment)? If your answer is "no" with respect to any of these examples, what distinguishes the example from the congressional authorization at issue in *Prudential*?

2. DORMANT FOREIGN RELATIONS PREEMPTION

The Constitution assigns various foreign relations powers to the political branches of the federal government. Specifically, Article I gives Congress power to "regulate Commerce with foreign Nations," U.S. Const. art. I, §8, cl. 3; "establish an uniform Rule of Naturalization," *id.* art. I, §8, cl. 4; regulate the value "of foreign Coin," *id.* art. I, §8, cl. 5; "define and punish Piracies and Felonies committed on the high Seas, and Offenses against the Law of Nations," *id.* art. I, §8, cl. 10; "declare War, grant Letters of Marque and Reprisal, and make Rules concerning Captures on Land and Water," *id.* art. I, §8, cl. 11; "raise and support Armies," *id.* art. I, §8, cl. 12; "provide and maintain a Navy," *id.* art. I, §8, cl. 13; "provide for calling forth the Militia to . . . repel Invasions," *id.* art. I, §8, cl. 15; "provide for organizing, arming, and disciplining, the Militia," *id.* art. I, §8, cl. 16; and "make all Laws which shall be necessary and proper for carrying into Execution the foregoing Powers, and all other Powers vested by this Constitution in the Government of the United States, or in any Department or Officer thereof," *id.* art. I, §8, cl. 18.

In addition, Article II establishes that "[t]he executive Power shall be vested in a President of the United States of America," *id.* art. II, §1, cl. 1; that "[t]he President shall be Commander in Chief of the Army and Navy of the United States, and of the Militia of the several States, when called into the actual Service of the United States," *id.* art. II, §2, cl. 1; that "[h]e shall have Power, by and with the Advice and Consent of the Senate, to make Treaties," *id.* art. II, §2, cl. 2; that "he shall nominate, and by and with the Advice and Consent of the Senate, shall appoint Ambassadors [and] other public Ministers and Consuls," *id.*; and that "he shall receive Ambassadors and other public Ministers," *id.* art. II, §2, cl. 3.

Taken together, these provisions assign responsibility for conducting important aspects of foreign relations to the political branches of the federal government rather than to the states. Acting in various combinations, the President, the Congress, and the Senate itself are responsible for recognizing foreign governments and nations, making international agreements, regulating foreign commerce and intercourse, and making other fundamental decisions affecting war and peace.

Article I simultaneously restricts the states' ability to exercise certain of these foreign relations powers. Section 10 provides that "[n]o State shall enter into any Treaty, Alliance, or Confederation; [or] grant Letters of Marque and Reprisal." *Id.* art. I, §10, cl. 1. It also prohibits states, without the consent of Congress, from "lay[ing] any Duty of Tonnage, keep[ing] Troops, or Ships of War in time of Peace, enter[ing] into any Agreement or Compact with another State, or with a foreign Power, or engag[ing] in War, unless actually invaded, or in such imminent Danger as will not admit of delay." *Id.* art. I, §10, cl. 3.

Absent an express prohibition on state action, such as those provided in Article I, Section 10, to what extent, if any, may states enact laws or otherwise take actions affecting the foreign relations of the United States? Does the Constitution implicitly prohibit states from taking certain actions impacting the foreign relations of the United States? The following case, *Zschernig v. Miller*, 389 U.S. 429 (1968), considers this question. As you read *Zschernig*, keep these questions in mind:

- How workable is the test that the Court applies for determining when a state has impermissibly acted in foreign relations?
- How does the test differ, if at all, from the Court's negative Commerce Clause jurisprudence?
- Does the Constitution support any form of dormant foreign relations preemption?

ZSCHERNIG V. MILLER

389 U.S. 429 (1968)

Mr. JUSTICE DOUGLAS delivered the opinion of the Court.

[Under Oregon law, a foreign citizen may not take property from the estate of an Oregon decedent without first proving that the foreigner's country (1) grants a reciprocal right to United States citizens to inherit property in that country, (2) recognizes the right of United States citizens to receive payment in the United States from estates of decedents in that country, and (3) guarantees that its citizens will enjoy the benefit, use, and control of property inherited from an Oregon estate without confiscation by the foreign country.]

[W]e conclude that the . . . Oregon statute . . . is an intrusion by the State into the field of foreign affairs which the Constitution entrusts to the President and the Congress. . . . [S]tate involvement in foreign affairs and international relations—matters which the Constitution entrusts solely to the Federal Government—is . . . forbidden. . . .

In *Clostermann v. Schmidt*, 215 Or. 55, the court . . . held that . . . the purpose of the Oregon provision was to serve as "an inducement to foreign nations to so frame the inheritance laws of their respective countries in a manner which would insure to Oregonians the same opportunities to inherit and take personal property abroad that they enjoy in the state of Oregon." *Id.*, at 68. . . . Oregon judges . . . seek to ascertain whether "rights" protected by foreign law are the same "rights" that citizens of Oregon enjoy. If . . . the alleged foreign 'right' may be vindicated only through Communist-controlled state agencies, then there is no 'right' of the type [the Oregon law] requires.

The same seems to be true if enforcement may require approval of a Fascist dictator. . . . The statute as construed seems to make unavoidable judicial criticism of nations established on a more authoritarian basis than our own.

It seems inescapable that the type of probate law that Oregon enforces affects international relations in a persistent and subtle way. The practice of state courts in withholding remittances to legatees residing in Communist countries or in preventing them from assigning them is notorious. The several States, of course, have traditionally regulated the descent and distribution of estates. But those regulations must give way if they impair the effective exercise of the Nation's foreign policy. Where those laws conflict with a treaty, they must bow to the superior federal policy. Yet, even in absence of a treaty, a State's policy may disturb foreign relations. As we stated in *Hines v. Davidowitz*, [312 U.S. 52, 64 (1941)], "Experience has shown that international controversies of the gravest moment, sometimes even leading to war, may arise from real or imagined wrongs to another's subjects inflicted, or permitted, by a government." Certainly a State could not deny admission to a traveler from East Germany nor bar its citizens from going there. If there are to be such restraints, they must be provided by the Federal Government. The present Oregon law is not as gross an intrusion in the federal domain as those others might be. Yet, as we have said, it has a direct impact upon foreign relations and may well adversely affect the power of the central government to deal with those problems.

The Oregon law does, indeed, illustrate the dangers which are involved if each State, speaking through its probate courts, is permitted to establish its own foreign policy.

Mr. JUSTICE MARSHALL took no part in the consideration or decision of this case.

Mr. JUSTICE STEWART, with whom Mr. JUSTICE BRENNAN joins, concurring.

In my view, each of the three provisions of the Oregon law suffers from the same fatal infirmity. All three launch the State upon a prohibited voyage into a domain of exclusively federal competence. Any realistic attempt to apply any of the three criteria would necessarily involve the Oregon courts in an evaluation, either expressed or implied, of the administration of foreign law, the credibility of foreign diplomatic statements, and the policies of foreign governments. Of course state courts must routinely construe foreign law in the resolution of controversies properly before them, but here the courts of Oregon are thrust into these inquiries only because the Oregon Legislature has framed its inheritance laws to the prejudice of nations whose policies it disapproves and thus has trespassed upon an area where the Constitution contemplates that only the National Government shall operate. . . .

Mr. JUSTICE HARLAN, concurring in the result.

Although I agree with the result reached in this case [on the ground that the Oregon law conflicts with a treaty], I am unable to subscribe to the Court's opinion. . . .

[I]n the absence of a conflicting federal policy or violation of the express mandates of the Constitution the States may legislate in areas of their traditional competence even though their statutes may have an incidental effect on foreign relations. Application of this rule to the case before us compels the conclusion that the Oregon statute is constitutional. Oregon has so legislated in the course of regulating the descent and distribution of estates of Oregon decedents, a matter traditionally within the power of a State. . . . [T]here is no specific interest of the Federal Government which might be interfered with by this statute. The appellants concede that Oregon might deny inheritance rights to all nonresident aliens. Assuming that this is so, the statutory exception permitting inheritance by aliens whose countries permit Americans to inherit would seem to be a measure wisely designed to avoid any offense to foreign governments and thus any conflict with general federal interests: a foreign government can hardly object to the denial of rights which it does not itself accord to the citizens of other countries. . . .

Essentially, the Court's basis for decision appears to be that alien inheritance laws afford state court judges an opportunity to criticize in dictum the policies of foreign governments, and that these dicta may adversely affect our foreign relations. In addition to finding no evidence of adverse effect in the record, I believe this rationale to be untenable because logically it would apply to many other types of litigation which come before the state courts. . . . However, judges have been known to utter dicta critical of foreign governmental policies even in purely domestic cases, so that the mere possibility of offensive utterances can hardly be the test. . . .

Mr. Justice White, dissenting.

I would affirm the judgment below. Generally for the reasons stated by Mr. Justice Harlan . . . , I do not consider the Oregon statute to be an impermissible interference with foreign affairs. . . .

POINTS FOR DISCUSSION

1. The Court explained in *Zschernig* that the foreign relations powers of the federal political branches forbid states from enacting laws that "directly impact" foreign relations or that "impair the effective exercise of the Nation's foreign policy." Is it possible to distinguish, in any meaningful way, those state laws that impact or impair foreign relations from those that do not? As local activities have increasing global effects in light of advances in communications, transportation, and general economic interdependencies, should state regulatory power be understood to diminish correspondingly?

2. How, if at all, does the Court's formulation of dormant foreign relations preemption in *Zschernig* differ from the formulations of the negative Commerce Clause that you have read?

3. In *Customary International Law as Federal Common Law: A Critique of the Modern Position*, 110 Harv. L. Rev. 815 (1997), Professors Curtis Bradley and Jack Goldsmith argue that

> dormant foreign relations preemption is of questionable legitimacy from the perspectives of text and history. Although the Constitution gives the federal political branches full control over U.S. foreign relations, it does not follow

that it preempts state law in the foreign relations field in the absence of affirmative political branch action. Indeed, constitutional text suggests the opposite. In contrast to the Commerce Clause, no clause in the Constitution provides the federal government with a general "foreign relations" power. Article I, Section 8 of the Constitution authorizes Congress to "define and punish . . . Offences against the Law of Nations," but it was settled long ago that this clause does not of its own force preempt state authority to do so as well. In addition, Article I, Section 10 expressly prohibits state activity in certain specified foreign affairs contexts, and Article I, Section 8 and Article II authorize the federal political branches to act with supremacy in certain specified foreign affairs contexts. . . . [T]he natural inference is that Article I, Section 10's self-executing limitations on state power in foreign relations are exhaustive and that other foreign relations activities fall within the concurrent authority of the state and federal governments until the federal political branches exercise their foreign relations powers in a manner that preempts state law. This natural reading of constitutional text was, in fact, the law for the first 175 years of our history.

Modern case support for dormant foreign relations preemption is similarly uncertain. . . . In *Zschernig*, . . . the Court concluded that the [Oregon statute at issue] was an "intrusion by the State into the field of foreign affairs which the Constitution entrusts to the President and the Congress." Although the rationale for the Court's decision in *Zschernig* is notoriously uncertain, the decision suggests a [relatively broad] foreign relations preemption . . . because the preempted activity involved a traditional state function and because the Court never specified the manner in which the statute jeopardized political branch prerogatives.

Id. at 862-864. Does a natural reading of the Constitution's text support dormant foreign relations preemption? Does *Zschernig* establish a broad principle of dormant foreign relations preemption?

B. STATUTORY AND ADMINISTRATIVE PREEMPTION

This section considers preemption of state law by an act of Congress or federal administrative action. The Supreme Court has described at least three categories of preemption in this context. *Express* preemption occurs when Congress explicitly provides that a federal regulatory scheme preempts state law. *Field* preemption occurs when an act of Congress occupies a "field" of regulation to the exclusion of state regulation in that field. *Conflict* preemption occurs when enforcement of state law conflicts with federal law — because either compliance with both federal and state law is impossible, or state law obstructs congressional purposes (sometimes called *obstacle* preemption).

As you read the materials in this section, consider these questions:

- What distinguishes each category of preemption that the Court describes from the others?
- What distinct purpose, if any, does each category of preemption serve relative to the others?

- Why has the Court applied a "presumption against preemption"? Is this presumption justified?
- Could or should the Court simplify its preemption doctrines?

1. CATEGORIES OF PREEMPTION

In the following case, the Supreme Court describes and applies various doctrines of preemption. Pay careful attention to how the Court applies these doctrines—and to the various judgments that, in application, each requires.

PACIFIC GAS AND ELECTRIC CO. v. STATE ENERGY RESOURCES CONSERVATION AND DEVELOPMENT COMMISSION

461 U.S. 190 (1983)

JUSTICE WHITE delivered the opinion of the Court.

In 1974, California adopted the Warren-Alquist State Energy Resources Conservation and Development Act. . . . The Act requires that a utility seeking to build in California any electric power generating plant, including a nuclear power plant, must apply for certification to the State Energy Resources and Conservation Commission (Energy Commission). . . . The Warren-Alquist Act was amended in 1976 to provide additional state regulation of new nuclear power plant construction. . . .

Section 25524.2 deals with the long-term solution to nuclear wastes. This section imposes a moratorium on the certification of new nuclear plants until the Energy Commission "finds that there has been developed and that the United States through its authorized agency has approved and there exists a demonstrated technology or means for the disposal of high-level nuclear waste." . . .

In 1978, petitioners Pacific Gas and Electric Company and Southern California Edison Company filed this action in the United States District Court, requesting a declaration that numerous provisions of the Warren-Alquist Act, including the . . . sections challenged here, are invalid under the Supremacy Clause because they are pre-empted by the Atomic Energy Act. . . .

It is well-established that within Constitutional limits Congress may pre-empt state authority by so stating in express terms. Absent explicit pre-emptive language, Congress' intent to supersede state law altogether may be found from a "scheme of federal regulation . . . so pervasive as to make reasonable the inference that Congress left no room to supplement it, because the Act of Congress may touch a field in which the federal interest is so dominant that the federal system will be assumed to preclude enforcement of state laws on the same subject, or because the object sought to be obtained by the federal law and the character of obligations imposed by it may reveal the same purpose." *Fidelity Federal Savings and Loan Assn. v. De la Cuesta*, 458 U.S. 141, 153 (1982). . . . Even where Congress has not entirely displaced state regulation in a specific area, state law is pre-empted to the extent that it actually conflicts with federal law. Such a conflict arises when "compliance with both federal and state regulations is a physical impossibility," *Florida Lime & Avocado Growers, Inc. v. Paul*, 373 U.S. 132, 142-143 (1963), or where state law "stands as an obstacle to the accomplishment and execution of the full purposes and objectives of Congress." *Hines v. Davidowitz*, 312 U.S. 52, 67 (1941).

Petitioners . . . present three major lines of argument as to why §25524.2 is pre-empted. First, they submit that the statute — because it regulates construction of nuclear plants and because it is allegedly predicated on safety concerns — ignores the division between federal and state authority created by the Atomic Energy Act, and falls within the field that the Federal Government has preserved for its own exclusive control. Second, the statute, and the judgments that underlie it, conflict with decisions concerning the nuclear waste disposal issue made by Congress and the Nuclear Regulatory Commission. Third, the California statute frustrates the federal goal of developing nuclear technology as a source of energy. We consider each of these contentions in turn.

A

[P]etitioners argue that the [Atomic Energy] Act is intended to preserve the Federal Government as the sole regulator of all matters nuclear, and that §25524.2 falls within the scope of this impliedly pre-empted field. But as we view the issue, Congress, in passing the 1954 Act and in subsequently amending it, intended that the Federal Government should regulate the radiological safety aspects involved in the construction and operation of a nuclear plant, but that the States retain their traditional responsibility in the field of regulating electrical utilities for determining questions of need, reliability, cost and other, related state concerns.

Need for new power facilities, their economic feasibility, and rates and services, are areas that have been characteristically governed by the States. Justice Brandeis once observed that "the franchise to operate a public utility . . . is a special privilege which . . . may be granted or withheld at the pleasure of the State." *Frost v. Corporation Comm'n*, 278 U.S. 515, 534 (1929) (dissenting opinion). "The nature of government regulation of private utilities is such that a utility may frequently be required by the state regulatory scheme to obtain approval for practices a business regulated in less detail would be free to institute without any approval from a regulatory body." *Jackson v. Metropolitan Edison Co.*, 419 U.S. 345, 357 (1974). . . . As we noted in *Vermont Yankee Nuclear Power Corp. v. Natural Resources Defense Council*, 435 U.S. 519, 550 (1978), "There is little doubt that under the Atomic Energy Act of 1954, state public utility commissions or similar bodies are empowered to make the initial decision regarding the need for power." Thus, "Congress legislated here in a field which the States have traditionally occupied. . . . So we start with the assumption that the historic police powers of the States were not to be superseded by the Federal Act unless that was the clear and manifest purpose of Congress." *Rice v. Santa Fe Elevator Corp.*, [331 U.S. 218, 230 (1947)]. . . .

[F]rom the passage of the Atomic Energy Act in 1954, through several revisions, and to the present day, Congress has preserved the dual regulation of nuclear-powered electricity generation: the federal government maintains complete control of the safety and "nuclear" aspects of energy generation; the States exercise their traditional authority over the need for additional generating capacity, the type of generating facilities to be licensed, land use, ratemaking, and the like. . . .

The above is not particularly controversial. But deciding how §25524.2 is to be construed and classified is a more difficult proposition. At the outset, we emphasize that the statute does not seek to regulate the construction or operation of a nuclear powerplant. It would clearly be impermissible for California to attempt to do so, for such regulation, even if enacted out of non-safety concerns, would nevertheless directly conflict with the NRC's exclusive authority over plant construction and operation. . . . Respondents do broadly argue, however, that although safety regulation of nuclear plants by states is forbidden, a State may completely prohibit new construction until its safety concerns are satisfied by the Federal Government. We reject this line of reasoning. State safety regulation is not pre-empted only when it conflicts with federal law. Rather, the Federal Government has occupied the entire field of nuclear safety concerns, except the limited powers expressly ceded to the States. When the Federal Government completely occupies a given field or an identifiable portion of it, as it has done here, the test of pre-emption is whether "the matter on which the state asserts the right to act is in any way regulated by the Federal Act." *Rice v. Santa Fe Elevator Corp., supra,* 331 U.S., at 236. A state moratorium on nuclear construction grounded in safety concerns falls squarely within the prohibited field. Moreover, a state judgment that nuclear power is not safe enough to be further developed would conflict directly with the countervailing judgment of the NRC that nuclear construction may proceed notwithstanding extant uncertainties as to waste disposal. A state prohibition on nuclear construction for safety reasons would also be in the teeth of the Atomic Energy Act's objective to insure that nuclear technology be safe enough for widespread development and use — and would be pre-empted for that reason.

That being the case, it is necessary to determine whether there is a non-safety rationale for §25524.2. California has maintained . . . that §25524.2 was aimed at economic problems, not radiation hazards. . . .

[W]e should not become embroiled in attempting to ascertain California's true motive. First, inquiry into legislative motive is often an unsatisfactory venture. *United States v. O'Brien,* 391 U.S. 367, 383 (1968). What motivates one legislator to vote for a statute is not necessarily what motivates scores of others to enact it. Second, it would be particularly pointless for us to engage in such inquiry here when it is clear that the States have been allowed to retain authority over the need for electrical generating facilities easily sufficient to permit a State so inclined to halt the construction of new nuclear plants by refusing on economic grounds to issue certificates of public convenience in individual proceedings. In these circumstances, it should be up to Congress to determine whether a State has misused the authority left in its hands.

Therefore, we accept California's avowed economic purpose as the rationale for enacting §25524.2. Accordingly, the statute lies outside the occupied field of nuclear safety regulation. . . .

B

Petitioners' second major argument concerns federal regulation aimed at the nuclear waste disposal problem itself. It is contended that §25524.2 conflicts with federal regulation of nuclear waste disposal, with the NRC's decision that it is permissible to continue to license reactors, notwithstanding uncertainty surrounding the waste disposal problem, and with Congress' recent passage of legislation directed at that problem. [The Nuclear Regulatory Commission (NRC) has] promulgated extensive and detailed regulations concerning the operation of nuclear facilities and the handling of nuclear materials. . . . The regulations specify general design criteria and control requirements for fuel storage and handling and radioactive waste to be stored at the reactor site. In addition, the NRC has promulgated detailed regulations governing storage and disposal away from the reactor. . . .

Congress gave the Department of Energy the responsibility for "the establishment of temporary and permanent facilities for the storage, management, and ultimate disposal of nuclear wastes." No such permanent disposal facilities have yet to be licensed, and the NRC and the Department of Energy continue to authorize the storage of spent fuel at reactor sites in pools of water. In 1977, the NRC was asked by the Natural Resources Defense Council to halt reactor licensing until it had determined that there was a method of permanent disposal for high-level waste. The NRC concluded that, given the progress toward the development of disposal facilities and the availability of interim storage, it could continue to license new reactors. . . .

The NRC's imprimatur, however, indicates only that it is safe to proceed with such plants, not that it is economically wise to do so. Because the NRC order does not and could not compel a utility to develop a nuclear plant, compliance with both it and §25524.2 is possible. Moreover, because the NRC's regulations are aimed at insuring that plants are safe, not necessarily that they are economical, §25524.2 does not interfere with the objective of the federal regulation.

Nor has California sought through §25524.2 to impose its own standards on nuclear waste disposal. The statute accepts that it is the federal responsibility to develop and license such technology. As there is no attempt on California's part to enter this field, one which is occupied by the Federal Government, we do not find §25524.2 pre-empted any more by the NRC's obligations in the waste disposal field than by its licensing power over the plants themselves. . . .

C

Finally, it is strongly contended that §25524.2 frustrates the Atomic Energy Act's purpose to develop the commercial use of nuclear power. It is well established that state law is pre-empted if it "stands as an obstacle to the accomplishment of the full purposes and objectives of Congress." *Hines v. Davidowitz*, 312 U.S., at 67. . . .

There is little doubt that a primary purpose of the Atomic Energy Act was, and continues to be, the promotion of nuclear power. . . . [T]he promotion of nuclear power[, however,] is not to be accomplished at all costs. The elaborate licensing and safety provisions and the continued preservation of state regulation in traditional areas belie that. Moreover, Congress has allowed the States to determine—as a matter of economics—whether a nuclear plant vis-à-vis a fossil fuel plant should be built. The decision of California to exercise that authority does not, in itself, constitute a basis for pre-emption. Therefore, while the argument of petitioners and the United States has considerable force, the legal reality remains that Congress has left sufficient authority in the States to allow the development of nuclear power to be slowed or even stopped for economic reasons. Given this statutory scheme, it is for Congress to rethink the division of regulatory authority in light of its possible exercise by the States to undercut a federal objective. The courts should not assume the role which our system assigns to Congress. . . .

JUSTICE BLACKMUN, with whom JUSTICE STEVENS joins, concurring in part and concurring in the judgment.

I join the Court's opinion, except to the extent it suggests that a State may not prohibit the construction of nuclear power plants if the State is motivated by concerns about the safety of such plants. Since the Court finds that California was not so motivated, this suggestion is unnecessary to the Court's holding. . . .

POINTS FOR DISCUSSION

1. The *Pacific Gas* Court applied "field" and "conflict" preemption, including "obstacle" preemption, to determine whether California could enforce its moratorium on building nuclear facilities. In applying these doctrines, the Court invoked a "presumption against preemption": "We start with the assumption that the historic police powers of the States were not to be superseded by the Federal Act unless that was the clear and manifest purpose of Congress." Is this essentially the "clear statement rule" that the Court applied in *Gregory v. Ashcroft*, 501 U.S. 452 (1991), which you read in Chapter 6?

2. When a court applies the doctrine of "field" preemption, it must (a) identify the appropriate regulatory field and (b) determine whether Congress intended to occupy all or part of it. In *Pacific Gas*, the Court defined the field that the federal act exclusively regulated as the field of nuclear *safety* concerns. Because the California law regulated in the field of *economic* concerns with nuclear power, not *safety* concerns, it was outside the field that the federal law exclusively occupied—and was thus not preempted. By what methods did the Court identify the relative fields of federal and state regulation? In determining the field of state regulation, the Court accepted California's "avowed economic purpose" for the regulation. Should the motive or purpose of a statute define the field of regulation? Are there any alternatives?

3. Regarding conflict preemption, the *Pacific Gas* Court determined that federal law did not *compel* utilities to build nuclear plants. Thus, there was no logical conflict between the federal and state regulatory schemes, such that compliance with both was impossible. Should conflict preemption require such a logical impossibility of compliance? The Court determined, moreover, that the California act did not frustrate the federal act's purpose of promoting

nuclear power. Notably, the Court explained that "continued preservation of state regulation in traditional areas belies" any claim of obstacle preemption. Should the idea of traditional areas of state regulation, which you encountered in various contexts in Chapters 5 and 6, factor in preemption analyses?

2. EXPRESS STATUTORY PREEMPTION

In the following two cases, the Supreme Court applies the doctrine of "express" preemption. Pay careful attention to how the Court applies this doctrine—and to the various judgments that, in application, it requires. Also, consider the following specific questions:

- How should courts interpret express preemption provisions? According to a presumption against preemption?
- How should the existence of an express preemption provision affect the application of other forms of preemption, such as conflict preemption?

CIPOLLONE V. LIGGETT GROUP

505 U.S. 504 (1992)

JUSTICE STEVENS delivered the opinion of the Court, except as to Parts V and VI.

"WARNING: THE SURGEON GENERAL HAS DETERMINED THAT CIGARETTE SMOKING IS DANGEROUS TO YOUR HEALTH." A federal statute enacted in 1969 requires that warning (or a variation thereof) to appear in a conspicuous place on every package of cigarettes sold in the United States. The question[] presented [is] whether that statute . . . pre-empted petitioner's common-law claims against respondent cigarette manufacturers.

Petitioner is the son of Rose Cipollone, who began smoking in 1942 and who died of lung cancer in 1984. He claims that respondent [cigarette manufacturers] are responsible for Rose Cipollone's death because they breached express warranties contained in their advertising, because they failed to warn consumers about the hazards of smoking, [and] because they fraudulently misrepresented those hazards to consumers. . . .

I

As one of their defenses, respondents contended that the . . . Public Health Cigarette Smoking Act of 1969, protected them from any liability. . . .

II

[First,] the Public Health Cigarette Smoking Act of 1969 (1969 Act or Act) [required a warning label] that cigarette smoking "is dangerous". . . . Second, the 1969 Act banned [television] cigarette advertising. . . . Third, and related, the 1969 Act [provided a] pre-emption provision [in §5] . . . :

"(b) No requirement or prohibition based on smoking and health shall be imposed under State law with respect to the advertising or promotion of any cigarettes the packages of which are labeled in conformity with the provisions of this Act." . . .

III

Article VI of the Constitution provides that the laws of the United States "shall be the supreme Law of the Land; . . . any Thing in the Constitution or Laws of any state to the Contrary notwithstanding." Art. VI, cl. 2. Thus, since our decision in *McCulloch v. Maryland*, 17 U.S. (4 Wheat.) 316 (1819), it has been settled that state law that conflicts with federal law is "without effect." *Maryland v. Louisiana*, 451 U.S. 725, 746 (1981). Consideration of issues arising under the Supremacy Clause "start[s] with the assumption that the historic police powers of the States [are] not to be superseded by . . . Federal Act unless that [is] the clear and manifest purpose of Congress." *Rice v. Santa Fe Elevator Corp.*, 331 U.S. 218, 230 (1947). Accordingly, "[t]he purpose of Congress is the ultimate touchstone" of pre-emption analysis. *Malone v. White Motor Corp.*, 435 U.S. 497, 504 (1978).

Congress' intent may be "explicitly stated in the statute's language or implicitly contained in its structure and purpose." *Jones v. Rath Packing Co.*, 430 U.S. 519, 525 (1977). In the absence of an express congressional command, state law is pre-empted if that law actually conflicts with federal law, see *Pacific Gas & Elec. Co. v. State Energy Resources Conservation and Development Comm'n*, 461 U.S. 190, 204 (1983), or if federal law so thoroughly occupies a legislative field "as to make reasonable the inference that Congress left no room for the States to supplement it." *Fidelity Fed. Sav. & Loan Assn. v. De la Cuesta*, 458 U.S. 141, 153 (1982). . . .

In our opinion, the pre-emptive scope of the . . . 1969 Act is governed entirely by the express language in §5. . . . When Congress has considered the issue of pre-emption and has included in the enacted legislation a provision explicitly addressing that issue, and when that provision provides a "reliable indicium of congressional intent with respect to state authority," *Malone v. White Motor Corp.*, 435 U.S., at 505, "there is no need to infer congressional intent to pre-empt state laws from the substantive provisions" of the legislation. *California Federal Savings & Loan Assn. v. Guerra*, 479 U.S. 272, 282 (1987) (opinion of Marshall, J.). Such reasoning is a variant of the familiar principle of *expressio unius est exclusio alterius*: Congress' enactment of a provision defining the pre-emptive reach of a statute implies that matters beyond that reach are not pre-empted. . . .

V

Petitioner . . . contends that §5(b) . . . does not pre-empt *common-law* actions. He offers two theories for limiting the reach of the amended §5(b). First, he argues that common-law damages actions do not impose "requirement[s] or prohibition[s]" and that Congress intended only to trump "state statute[s], injunction[s], or executive pronouncement[s]." We disagree; such an analysis is at odds both with the plain words of the 1969 Act and with the general understanding of common-law damages actions. The phrase "[n]o requirement or prohibition" sweeps broadly and suggests no distinction between positive enactments and common law; to the contrary, those words easily encompass obligations that take the form of common-law rules. As we noted in another context, "[state] regulation can be as effectively exerted through an award of damages as through some form of preventive relief. The obligation to pay compensation can be, indeed is designed to be, a potent method of governing conduct and controlling policy." *San Diego Building Trades Council v. Garmon*, 359 U.S. 236, 247 (1959). . . .

Moreover, common-law damages actions of the sort raised by petitioner are premised on the existence of a legal duty, and it is difficult to say that such actions do not impose "requirements or prohibitions." . . . We therefore reject petitioner's argument that the phrase "requirement or prohibition" limits the 1969 Act's pre-emptive scope to positive enactments by legislatures and agencies.

Petitioner's second argument for excluding common-law rules from the reach of §5(b) hinges on the phrase "imposed under State law." This argument fails as well. At least since *Erie R. Co. v. Tompkins*, 304 U.S. 64 (1938), we have recognized the phrase "state law" to include common law as well as statutes and regulations. . . .

[W]e must fairly but—in light of the strong presumption against pre-emption—narrowly construe the precise language of §5(b) and we must look to each of petitioner's common-law claims to determine whether it is in fact pre-empted. The central inquiry in each case is straightforward: we ask whether the legal duty that is the predicate of the common-law damages action constitutes a "requirement or prohibition based on smoking and health . . . imposed under State law with respect to . . . advertising or promotion," giving that clause a fair but narrow reading. As discussed below, each phrase within that clause limits the universe of common-law claims pre-empted by the statute.

We consider each category of damages actions in turn. In doing so, we express no opinion on whether these actions are viable claims as a matter of state law; we assume, *arguendo*, that they are.

Failure to Warn

To establish liability for a failure to warn, petitioner must show that "a warning is necessary to make a product . . . reasonably safe, suitable and fit for its intended use," that respondents failed to provide such a warning, and that that failure was a proximate cause of petitioner's injury. In this case, petitioner offered two closely related theories concerning the failure to warn: first, that respondents "were negligent in the manner [that] they tested, researched, sold, promoted, and advertised" their cigarettes; and second, that respondents failed to provide "adequate warnings of the health consequences of cigarette smoking."

Petitioner's claims are pre-empted to the extent that they rely on a state-law "requirement or prohibition . . . with respect to . . . advertising or promotion." Thus, insofar as claims under either failure-to-warn theory require a showing that respondents' post-1969 advertising or promotions should have included additional, or more clearly stated, warnings, those claims are pre-empted. The Act does not, however, pre-empt petitioner's claims that rely solely on respondents' testing or research practices or other actions unrelated to advertising or promotion.

Breach of Express Warranty

Petitioner's evidence of an express warranty consists largely of statements made in respondents' advertising. . . . The appropriate inquiry is . . . whether the claim would require the imposition under state law of a requirement or prohibition based on smoking and health with respect to advertising or promotion.

A manufacturer's liability for breach of an express warranty derives from, and is measured by, the terms of that warranty. Accordingly, the "require-ment[s]" imposed by an express warranty claim are not "imposed under State law," but rather imposed *by the warrantor*. If, for example, a manufacturer expressly promised to pay a smoker's medical bills if she contracted emphysema, the duty to honor that promise could not fairly be said to be "imposed under state law," but rather is best understood as undertaken by the manufacturer itself. While the general duty not to breach warranties arises under state law, the particular "requirement . . . based on smoking and health . . . with respect to the advertising or promotion [of] cigarettes" in an express warranty claim arises from the manufacturer's statements in its advertisements. In short, a common-law remedy for a contractual commitment voluntarily undertaken should not be regarded as a "requirement . . . *imposed under State law*" within the meaning of §5(b). . . .

Accordingly, to the extent that petitioner has a viable claim for breach of express warranties made by respondents, that claim is not pre-empted by the 1969 Act.

Fraudulent Representation

Petitioner . . . alleges intentional fraud and misrepresentation both by "false representation of a material fact [and by] conceal[ment of] a material fact." The predicate of this claim is a state-law duty not to make false statements of material fact or to conceal such facts. Our pre-emption analysis requires us to determine whether such a duty is the sort of requirement or prohibition proscribed by §5(b). . . .

[P]etitioner's fraudulent-misrepresentation claims that . . . arise with respect to advertising and promotions (most notably claims based on allegedly false statements of material fact made in advertisements) are not pre-empted by §5(b). Such claims are predicated not on a duty "based on smoking and health" but rather on a more general obligation: the duty not to deceive. . . . [I]n the 1969 Act, Congress offered no sign that it wished to insulate cigarette manufacturers from longstanding rules governing fraud. . . .

Thus, we conclude that the phrase "based on smoking and health" fairly but narrowly construed does not encompass the more general duty not to make fraudulent statements. Accordingly, petitioner's claim based on allegedly fraudulent statements made in respondents' advertisements is not pre-empted by §5(b) of the 1969 Act. . . .

VI

To summarize our holding: . . . the 1969 Act pre-empts petitioner's claims based on a failure to warn and the neutralization of federally mandated warnings to the extent that those claims rely on omissions or inclusions in respondents' advertising or promotions; the 1969 Act does not pre-empt petitioner's claims based on express warranty, [or] intentional fraud and misrepresentation. . . .

Justice Blackmun, with whom Justice Kennedy and Justice Souter join, concurring in part, concurring in the judgment in part, and dissenting in part.

Our precedents do not allow us to infer a scope of pre-emption beyond that which clearly is mandated by Congress' language. In my view, . . . the federal legislation at issue . . . [does not provide] the kind of unambiguous evidence of congressional intent necessary to displace state common-law damages claims. I therefore . . . dissent from Parts V and VI. . . .

[T]he question whether common-law damages actions exert a regulatory effect on manufacturers analogous to that of positive enactments — an assumption crucial to the plurality's conclusion that the phrase "requirement or prohibition" encompasses common-law actions — is significantly more complicated than the plurality[] . . . suggest[s].

The effect of tort law on a manufacturer's behavior is necessarily indirect. Although an award of damages by its very nature attaches additional consequences to the manufacturer's continued unlawful conduct, no particular course of action (e.g., the adoption of a new warning label) is required. A manufacturer found liable on, for example, a failure-to-warn claim may respond in a number of ways. It may decide to accept damages awards as a cost of doing business and not alter its behavior in any way. Or, by contrast, it may choose to avoid future awards by dispensing warnings through a variety of alternative mechanisms, such as package inserts, public service advertisements, or general educational programs. The level of choice that a defendant retains in shaping its own behavior distinguishes the indirect regulatory effect of the common law from positive enactments such as statutes and administrative regulations. Moreover, tort law has an entirely separate function — compensating victims — that sets it apart from direct forms of regulation. . . .

In light of the recognized distinction in this Court's jurisprudence between direct state regulation and the indirect regulatory effects of common-law damages actions, it cannot be said that damages claims are clearly or unambiguously "requirements" or "prohibitions" imposed under state law. The plain language of the 1969 Act's modified pre-emption provision simply cannot bear the broad interpretation the plurality would impart to it. . . .

By finding federal pre-emption of certain state common-law damages claims, the decision today eliminates a critical component of the States' traditional ability to protect the health and safety of their citizens. Yet such a radical readjustment of federal-state relations is warranted under this Court's precedents only if there is clear evidence that Congress intended that result. Because I believe that neither version of the Federal Cigarette Labeling and Advertising Act evidences such a clear congressional intent to pre-empt state common-law damages actions, I respectfully dissent from Parts V and VI of Justice Stevens' opinion.

JUSTICE SCALIA, with whom JUSTICE THOMAS joins, concurring in the judgment in part and dissenting in part.

Today's decision announces what, on its face, is an extraordinary and unprecedented principle of federal statutory construction: that express pre-emption provisions must be construed narrowly, "in light of the presumption against the pre-emption of state police power regulations." The life-span of this new rule may have been blessedly brief, inasmuch as the opinion that gives it birth in Part I proceeds to ignore it in Part V, by adjudging at least some of the common-law tort claims at issue here pre-empted. In my view, there is no merit to this newly crafted doctrine of narrow construction. Under the Supremacy Clause, U.S. Const., Art. VI, cl. 2, our job is to interpret Congress's decrees of pre-emption neither narrowly nor broadly, but in accordance with their apparent meaning. If we did that job in the present case, we would find . . . pre-emption of petitioner's claims complete.

I

The Court's threshold description of the law of pre-emption is accurate enough: Though we generally "assum[e] that the historic police powers of the States [are] not to be superseded by . . . Federal Act unless that [is] the clear and manifest purpose of Congress," *Rice v. Sante Fe Elevator Corp.*, 331 U.S. 218, 230 (1947), we have traditionally not thought that to require express statutory text. Where state law is in actual conflict with federal law, *Pacific Gas & Elec. Co. v. State Energy Resources Conservation and Development Comm'n*, 461 U.S. 190, 204 (1983), or where it "stands as an obstacle to the accomplishment and execution of the full purposes and objectives of Congress," *Hines v. Davidowitz*, 312 U.S. 52, 67 (1941), or even where the nature of Congress's regulation, or its scope, convinces us that "Congress left no room for the States to supplement it," *Rice*, *supra*, at 230, we have had no difficulty declaring that state law must yield. The ultimate question in each case, as we have framed the inquiry, is one of Congress's intent, as revealed by the text, structure, purposes, and subject matter of the statutes involved.

The Court goes beyond these traditional principles, however, to announce two new ones. First, it says that express pre-emption provisions must be given the narrowest possible construction. This is in its view the consequence of our oft-repeated assumption that, absent convincing evidence of statutory intent to pre-empt, " 'the historic police powers of the States [are] not to be superseded.' " But it seems to me that assumption dissolves once there is conclusive evidence of intent to pre-empt in the express words of the statute itself, and the only remaining question is what the *scope* of that pre-emption is meant to be. Thereupon, I think, our responsibility is to apply to the text ordinary principles of statutory construction. . . .

[T]he second new rule that the Court announces [is]: "When Congress has considered the issue of pre-emption and has included in the enacted legislation a provision explicitly addressing that issue, . . . we need only identify the domain expressly pre-empted by [that provision]." Once there is an express pre-emption provision, in other words, all doctrines of implied pre-emption are eliminated. This proposition may be correct insofar as implied "field" pre-emption is concerned: The existence of an express pre-emption provision tends to contradict any inference that Congress intended to occupy a field broader than the statute's express language defines. However, with regard to implied "conflict" pre-emption — *i.e.*, where state regulation actually conflicts with federal law, or where state regulation "stands as an obstacle to the accomplishment and execution" of Congress's purposes, *Hines*, *supra*, at 67 — the Court's second new rule works mischief. If taken seriously, it would mean, for example, that if a federal consumer protection law provided that no state agency or court shall assert jurisdiction under state law over any workplace safety issue with respect to which a federal standard is in effect, then a state agency operating under a law dealing with a subject other than workplace safety (*e.g.*, consumer protection) could impose requirements entirely contrary to federal law — forbidding, for example, the use of certain safety equipment that federal law requires. To my knowledge, we have never expressed such a rule before, and our prior cases are inconsistent with it. . . .

The proper rule of construction for express pre-emption provisions is, it seems to me, the one that is customary for statutory provisions in general: Their language should be given its ordinary meaning. When this suggests that the pre-emption provision was intended to sweep broadly, our construction must sweep broadly as well. And when it bespeaks a narrow scope of pre-emption, so must our judgment. . . .

II
Breach-of-Express-Warranty Claims

In the context of this case, petitioner's breach-of-express-warranty claim necessarily embodies an assertion that respondents' advertising and promotional materials made statements to the effect that cigarette smoking is not unhealthy. Making such statements civilly actionable certainly constitutes an advertising "requirement or prohibition . . . based on smoking and health." The plurality appears to accept this, but finds that liability for breach of express warranty is not "imposed under State law" within the meaning of §5(b) of the 1969 Act. "[R]ather," it says, the duty "is best understood as undertaken by the manufacturer itself." I cannot agree.

When liability attaches to a particular promise or representation, it attaches *by law*. For the making of a voluntary promise or representation, no less than for the commission of an intentional tort, it is the background law against which the act occurs, and not the act itself, that supplies the element of legal obligation. Of course, New Jersey's law of express warranty attaches legal consequences to the cigarette manufacturer's voluntary conduct in making the warranty, and in that narrow sense, I suppose, the warranty obligation can be said to be "undertaken by the manufacturer." But on that logic it could also be said that the duty to warn about the dangers of cigarettes is undertaken voluntarily by manufacturers when they choose to sell in

New Jersey; or, more generally, that *any* legal duty imposed on volitional behavior is not one imposed by law. . . .

C

Fraud and Misrepresentation Claims

If I understand the plurality's reasoning, it proceeds from the implicit assumption that only duties deriving from laws that are specifically directed to "smoking and health," or that are uniquely crafted to address the relationship between cigarette companies and their putative victims, fall within §5(b) of the Act, as amended. Given that New Jersey's tort-law "duty not to deceive," is a general one, applicable to all commercial actors and all kinds of commerce, it follows from this assumption that §5(b) does not pre-empt claims based on breaches of that duty.

This analysis is suspect, to begin with, because the plurality is unwilling to apply it consistently. . . . [I]f New Jersey's common-law duty to avoid false statements of material fact — as applied to the cigarette companies' behavior — is not "based on smoking and health," the same must be said of New Jersey's common-law duty to warn about a product's dangers. *Each* duty transcends the relationship between the cigarette companies and cigarette smokers; *neither* duty was specifically crafted with an eye toward "smoking and health." None of the arguments the plurality advances to support its distinction between the two is persuasive. . . . [I]t is not true that the States' laws governing fraud and misrepresentation in advertising impose identical legal standards, whereas their laws "concerning the warning necessary to render a product 'reasonably safe' " are quite diverse. The question whether an ad featuring a glamorous, youthful smoker with pearly-white teeth is "misrepresentative" would almost certainly be answered differently from State to State.

Once one is forced to select a *consistent* methodology for evaluating whether a given legal duty is "based on smoking and health," it becomes obvious that the methodology must focus not upon the ultimate source of the duty (e.g., the common law) but upon its proximate application. Use of the "ultimate source" approach (i.e., a legal duty is not "based on smoking and health" unless the law from which it derives is directed only to smoking and health) would gut the statute, inviting the very "diverse, nonuniform, and confusing cigarette . . . advertising regulations" Congress sought to avoid. And the problem is not simply the common law: Requirements could be imposed by state executive agencies as well, so long as they were operating under a *general* statute authorizing their supervision of "commercial advertising" or "unfair trade practices." . . .

I would apply to all petitioner's claims what I have called a "proximate application" methodology for determining whether they invoke duties "based on smoking and health" — I would ask, that is, whether, whatever the source of the duty, it imposes an obligation in this case because of the effect of smoking upon health. On that basis, I would find petitioner's failure-to-warn and misrepresentation claims both pre-empted. . . .

Like Justice Blackmun, "I can only speculate as to the difficulty lower courts will encounter in attempting to implement [today's] decision." Must express pre-emption provisions really be given their narrowest reasonable construction (as the Court says in Part III), or need they not (as the plurality does in Part V)? Are courts to ignore all doctrines of implied pre-emption whenever the statute at issue contains an express pre-emption provision, as the Court says today, or are they to continue to apply them, as we have in the past? For pre-emption purposes, does "state law" include legal duties imposed on voluntary acts, or does it not? These and other questions raised by today's decision will fill the lawbooks for years to come. A disposition that raises more questions than it answers does not serve the country well.

MEDTRONIC V. LOHR

518 U.S. 470 (1996)

JUSTICE STEVENS announced the judgment of the Court and delivered the opinion of the Court with respect to Parts I, II, III, V, and VII, and an opinion with respect to Parts IV and VI, in which JUSTICE KENNEDY, JUSTICE SOUTER, and JUSTICE GINSBURG join.

Congress enacted the Medical Device Amendments of 1976, in the words of the statute's preamble, "to provide for the safety and effectiveness of medical devices intended for human use." 90 Stat. 539. The question presented is whether that statute pre-empts a state common-law negligence action against the manufacturer of an allegedly defective medical device. Specifically, we must consider whether Lora Lohr, who was injured when her pacemaker failed, may rely on Florida common law to recover damages from Medtronic, Inc., the manufacturer of the device.

I

[T]he Medical Device Amendments of 1976 (MDA or Act) . . . classifies medical devices . . . based on the risk that they pose to the public. . . . [D]evices that either "presen[t] a potential unreasonable risk of illness or injury," or which are "purported or represented to be for a use in supporting or sustaining human life or for a use which is of substantial importance in preventing impairment of human health," are designated Class III. [21 U.S.C. §360c(a)(1)(C).] Pacemakers are Class III devices.

Before a new Class III device may be introduced to the market, the manufacturer must provide the FDA with a "reasonable assurance" that the device is both safe and effective. See 21 U.S.C. §360e(d)(2). Despite its relatively innocuous phrasing, the process of establishing this "reasonable assurance," which is known as the "premarket approval," or "PMA" process, is a rigorous one. Manufacturers must submit detailed information regarding the safety and efficacy of their devices, which the FDA then reviews, spending an average of 1,200 hours on each submission.

Not all, nor even most, Class III devices on the market today have received premarket approval because of . . . important exceptions to the PMA requirement. . . . [T]o ensure that improvements to existing devices can be rapidly introduced into the market, the Act . . . permits devices that are "substantially equivalent" to pre-existing devices to avoid the PMA process. See 21 U.S.C. §360e(b)(1)(B).

Although "substantially equivalent" Class III devices may be marketed without the rigorous PMA review, such new devices . . . are subject to the requirements of §360(k). That section imposes a limited form of review on every manufacturer intending to market a new device by requiring it to submit a "premarket notification" to the FDA. If the FDA concludes on the basis of the §510(k) notification that the device is "substantially equivalent" to a pre-existing device, it can be marketed without further regulatory analysis. . . . The §510(k) notification process is by no means comparable to the PMA process; in contrast to the 1,200 hours necessary to complete a PMA review, the §510(k) review is completed in an average of only 20 hours. . . .

II

As have so many other medical device manufacturers, petitioner Medtronic took advantage of §510(k)'s expedited process in October 1982, when it notified the FDA that it intended to market its Model 4011 pacemaker lead as a device that was "substantially equivalent" to devices already on the market. (The lead is the portion of a pacemaker that transmits the heartbeat-steadying electrical signal from the "pulse generator" to the heart itself.) On November 30, 1982, the FDA found that the model was "substantially equivalent to devices introduced into interstate commerce" prior to the effective date of the Act, and advised Medtronic that it could therefore market its device subject only to the general control provisions of the Act, which could be found in the Code of Federal Regulations. The agency emphasized, however, that this determination should not be construed as an endorsement of the pacemaker lead's safety. . . .

Lora Lohr is dependent on pacemaker technology for the proper functioning of her heart. In 1987 she was implanted with a Medtronic pacemaker equipped with one of the company's Model 4011 pacemaker leads. On December 30, 1990, the pacemaker failed, allegedly resulting in a "complete heart block" that required emergency surgery. According to her physician, a defect in the lead was the likely cause of the failure.

In 1993 Lohr and her husband filed this action. . . . Their complaint contained both a negligence count and a strict-liability count. The negligence count alleged a breach of Medtronic's "duty to use reasonable care in the design, manufacture, assembly, and sale of the subject pacemaker" in several respects, including the use of defective materials in the lead and a failure to warn or properly instruct the plaintiff or her physicians of the tendency of the pacemaker to fail, despite knowledge of other, earlier failures. The strict-liability count alleged that the device was in a defective condition and unreasonably dangerous to foreseeable users at the time of its sale. . . .

Medtronic . . . filed a motion for summary judgment arguing that both the negligence and strict-liability claims were pre-empted by 21 U.S.C. §360k(a).

That section, which is at the core of the dispute between the parties in this suit, provides:

"§360k. State and local requirements respecting devices

"(a) General rule
"Except as provided in subsection (b) of this section, no State or political subdivision of a State may establish or continue in effect with respect to a device intended for human use any requirement—
"(1) which is different from, or in addition to, any requirement applicable under this chapter to the device, and
"(2) which relates to the safety or effectiveness of the device or to any other matter included in a requirement applicable to the device under this chapter."

III

As in *Cipollone v. Liggett Group, Inc.*, 505 U.S. 504 (1992), we are presented with the task of interpreting a statutory provision that expressly pre-empts state law. While the pre-emptive language of §360k(a) means that we need not go beyond that language to determine whether Congress intended the MDA to pre-empt at least some state law, see *id.*, at 517, we must nonetheless "identify the domain expressly pre-empted" by that language, *ibid.* Although our analysis of the scope of the pre-emption statute must begin with its text, our interpretation of that language does not occur in a contextual vacuum. Rather, that interpretation is informed by two presumptions about the nature of pre-emption.

First, because the States are independent sovereigns in our federal system, we have long presumed that Congress does not cavalierly pre-empt state-law causes of action. In all pre-emption cases, and particularly in those in which Congress has "legislated . . . in a field which the States have traditionally occupied," *Rice v. Santa Fe Elevator Corp.*, 331 U.S. 218, 230 (1947), we "start with the assumption that the historic police powers of the States were not to be superseded by the Federal Act unless that was the clear and manifest purpose of Congress." *Ibid.* . . .

Second, our analysis of the scope of the statute's pre-emption is guided by our oft-repeated comment . . . that "[t]he purpose of Congress is the ultimate touchstone" in every pre-emption case. See, *e.g.*, *Cipollone*, 505 U.S., at 576. As a result, any understanding of the scope of a pre-emption statute must rest primarily on "a fair understanding of congressional purpose." [*Id.*] at 530, n. 27 (opinion of Stevens, J.). Congress' intent, of course, primarily is discerned from the language of the pre-emption statute and the "statutory framework" surrounding it. [*Gade v. National Solid Wastes Management Assn.*, 505 U.S. 88, 111 (1992) (Kennedy, J., concurring in part and concurring in judgment).] Also relevant, however, is the "structure and purpose of the statute as a whole," *id.*, at 98 (opinion of O'Connor, J.) as revealed not only in the text, but through the reviewing court's reasoned understanding of the way in which Congress intended the statute and its surrounding regulatory scheme to affect business, consumers, and the law. . . .

IV

Medtronic argues that . . . the Lohrs' claims alleging negligent design were . . . pre-empted by 21 U.S.C. §360k(a). That section provides that "no State or political subdivision of a State may establish or continue in effect with respect to a device intended for human use any requirement (1) which is different from, or in addition to, any requirement applicable under this chapter to the device, and (2) which relates to the safety or effectiveness of the device or to any other matter included in a requirement applicable to the device under this chapter." Medtronic suggests that any common-law cause of action is a "requirement" which alters incentives and imposes duties "different from, or in addition to," the generic federal standards that the FDA has promulgated in response to mandates under the MDA. In essence, the company argues that the plain language of the statute pre-empts any and all common-law claims brought by an injured plaintiff against a manufacturer of medical devices.

Medtronic's argument is not only unpersuasive, it is implausible. Under Medtronic's view of the statute, Congress effectively precluded state courts from affording state consumers any protection from injuries resulting from a defective medical device. Moreover, because there is no . . . private cause of action against manufacturers contained in the MDA, . . . Congress would have barred most, if not all, relief for persons injured by defective medical devices. Medtronic's construction of §360k would therefore have the perverse effect of granting complete immunity from design defect liability to an entire industry that, in the judgment of Congress, needed more stringent regulation in order "to provide for the safety and effectiveness of medical devices intended for human use," 90 Stat. 539 (preamble to Act). It is, to say the least, "difficult to believe that Congress would, without comment, remove all means of judicial recourse for those injured by illegal conduct," *Silkwood v. Kerr-McGee Corp.*, 464 U.S. 238, 251 (1984), and it would take language much plainer than the text of §360k to convince us that Congress intended that result.

Furthermore, if Congress intended to preclude all common-law causes of action, it chose a singularly odd word with which to do it. The statute would have achieved an identical result, for instance, if it had precluded any "remedy" under state law relating to medical devices. "Requirement" appears to presume that the State is imposing a specific duty upon the manufacturer, and although we have on prior occasions concluded that a statute pre-empting certain state "requirements" could also pre-empt common-law damages claims, *see Cipollone*, 505 U.S., at 521-522 (opinion of Stevens, J.), that statute did not sweep nearly as broadly as Medtronic would have us believe that this statute does.

The pre-emptive statute in *Cipollone* was targeted at a limited set of state requirements—those "based on smoking and health"—and then only at a limited subset of the possible applications of those requirements—those involving the "advertising or promotion of any cigarettes the packages of which are labeled in conformity with the provisions of" the federal statute. See *id.*, at 515. In that context, giving the term "requirement" its widest reasonable meaning did not have nearly the pre-emptive scope nor the effect on potential remedies that Medtronic's broad reading of the term would have in this suit. The Court in *Cipollone* held that the petitioner in that case was able to maintain some common-law actions using theories of the case that did not run afoul of the pre-emption statute. Here, however, Medtronic's sweeping interpretation of the statute would require far greater interference with state legal remedies, producing a serious intrusion into state sovereignty while simultaneously wiping out the possibility of remedy for the Lohrs' alleged injuries. Given the ambiguities in the statute and the scope of the preclusion that would occur otherwise, we cannot accept Medtronic's argument that by using the term "requirement," Congress clearly signaled its intent to deprive States of any role in protecting consumers from the dangers inherent in many medical devices. . . .

An examination of the basic purpose of the legislation as well as its history entirely supports our rejection of Medtronic's extreme position. The MDA was enacted "to provide for the safety and effectiveness of medical devices intended for human use." Medtronic asserts that the Act was also intended, however, to "protect innovations in device technology from being 'stifled by unnecessary restrictions,'" and that this interest extended to the pre-emption of common-law claims. While the Act certainly reflects some of these concerns, the legislative history indicates that any fears regarding regulatory burdens were related more to the risk of *additional* federal and state regulation rather than the danger of pre-existing duties under common law. . . .

The legislative history also confirms our understanding that §360(k) simply was not intended to pre-empt most, let alone all, general common-law duties enforced by damages actions. There is, to the best of our knowledge, nothing in the hearings, the Committee Reports, or the debates suggesting that any proponent of the legislation intended a sweeping pre-emption of traditional common-law remedies against manufacturers and distributors of defective devices. . . .

V

Medtronic asserts several specific reasons why, even if §360k does not pre-empt all common-law claims, it at least pre-empts the Lohrs' claims in this suit. In contrast, the Lohrs argue that their entire complaint should survive a reasonable evaluation of the pre-emptive scope of §360k(a). . . .

[I]t is impossible to ignore [the statutory language's] overarching concern that pre-emption occur only where a particular state requirement threatens to interfere with a specific federal interest. State requirements must be "with respect to" medical devices and "different from, or in addition to," federal requirements. State requirements must also relate "to the safety or effectiveness of the device or to any other matter included in a requirement applicable to the device." . . . The statute . . . , therefore, require[s] a careful comparison between the allegedly pre-empting federal requirement and the allegedly pre-empted state requirement to determine whether they fall within the intended pre-emptive scope of the statute. . . .

Such a comparison mandates a conclusion that the Lohrs' common-law claims are not pre-empted by the federal labeling and manufacturing requirements. The generality of those requirements make this quite unlike a case in which the Federal Government has weighed the competing interests relevant to the particular requirement in question, reached an unambiguous conclusion about how those competing considerations should be resolved in a particular case or set of cases, and implemented that conclusion via a specific mandate on manufacturers or producers. Rather, the federal requirements reflect important but entirely generic concerns about device regulation generally, not the sort of concerns regarding a specific device or field of device regulation that the statute or regulations were designed to protect from potentially contradictory state requirements. . . .

JUSTICE BREYER, concurring in part and concurring in the judgment.

This action raises two questions. First, do the Medical Device Amendments of 1976 (MDA) to the Federal Food, Drug, and Cosmetic Act ever pre-empt a state-law tort action? Second, if so, does the MDA pre-empt the particular state-law tort claims at issue here?

I

[M]y answer to the first question is that the MDA will sometimes pre-empt a state-law tort suit. I basically agree with Justice O'Connor's discussion of this point and with her conclusion. . . .

II

[T]he answer to the second question turns on Congress' intent. Although Congress has not stated whether the MDA does, or does not, pre-empt the tort claims here at issue, several considerations lead me to conclude that it does not.

First, the MDA's pre-emption provision is highly ambiguous. . . . Second, this Court has previously suggested that, in the absence of a clear congressional command as to pre-emption, courts may infer that the relevant administrative agency possesses a degree of leeway to determine which rules, regulations, or other administrative actions will have pre-emptive effect. . . . Third, the FDA has promulgated a specific regulation designed to help . . . :

> "State . . . requirements are preempted only when . . . there are . . . *specific* [federal] requirements applicable to a particular device . . . thereby making any existing *divergent* State . . . requirements applicable to the device different from, or in addition to, the *specific* [federal] requirements." 21 CFR §808.1(d) (1995) (emphasis added). . . .

[T]he regulation's word "specific" does narrow the universe of federal requirements that the agency intends to displace at least some state law. Insofar as there are any applicable FDA requirements here, those requirements, even if numerous, are not "specific" in any relevant sense. . . . Fourth, ordinary principles of "conflict" and "field" pre-emption point in the same direction. . . .

I can find no actual conflict between any federal requirement and any of the liability-creating premises of the plaintiffs' state-law tort suit; nor . . . can I find any indication that either Congress or the FDA intended the relevant FDA regulations to occupy entirely any relevant field. . . .

Justice O'Connor, with whom The Chief Justice, Justice Scalia, and Justice Thomas join, concurring in part and dissenting in part.

[T]he pre-emption provision of the Medical Device Amendments of 1976 (MDA) . . . provides that no State may establish or continue in effect "any requirement" "which is different from, or in addition to," any requirement applicable under the Federal Food, Drug, and Cosmetic Act of 1938 (FDCA) to the device. As the Court points out, because Congress has expressly provided a pre-emption provision, "we need not go beyond that language to determine whether Congress intended the MDA to pre-empt" state law. We agree, then, on the task before us: to interpret Congress' intent by reading the statute in accordance with its terms. This, however, the Court has failed to do. . . .

I conclude that state common-law damages actions do impose "requirements" and are therefore pre-empted where such requirements would differ from those imposed by the FDCA. . . .

The language of §360k demonstrates congressional intent that the MDA pre-empt "any requirement" by a State that is "different from, or in addition to," that applicable to the device under the FDCA. The Lohrs have raised various state common-law claims in connection with Medtronic's pacemaker lead. Analysis, therefore, must begin with the question whether state common-law actions can constitute "requirements" within the meaning of §360k(a).

We recently addressed a similar question in *Cipollone*, where we examined the meaning of the phrase "no requirement or prohibition" under the Public Health Cigarette Smoking Act of 1969. *Cipollone v. Liggett Group, Inc.*, 505 U.S. 504 (1992). A majority of the Court agreed that state common-law damages actions do impose "requirements." As the plurality explained:

> "The phrase, '[n]o requirement or prohibition' sweeps broadly and suggests no distinction between positive enactments and common law; to the contrary, those words easily encompass obligations that take the form of common-law rules. As we noted in another context, '[state] regulation can be as effectively exerted through an award of damages as through some form of preventive relief. The obligation to pay compensation can be, indeed is designed to be, a potent method of governing conduct and controlling policy.' *San Diego Building Trades Council v. Garmon*, 359 U.S. 236, 247 (1959)." *Id.*, at 521.

That rationale is equally applicable in the present context. Whether relating to the labeling of cigarettes or the manufacture of medical devices, state common-law damages actions operate to require manufacturers to comply with common-law duties. As *Cipollone* declared, in answer to the same argument raised here that common-law actions do not impose requirements, "such an analysis is at odds both with the plain words" of the statute and "with the general understanding of common-law damages actions." *Ibid.* If §360k's language is given its ordinary meaning, it clearly pre-empts any state common-law action that would impose a requirement different from, or in addition to, that applicable under the FDCA — just as it would pre-empt a state statute or regulation that had that effect. . . .

I conclude that a fair reading of §360k indicates that state common-law claims are pre-empted, as the statute itself states, to the extent that their recognition would impose "any requirement" different from, or in addition to,

FDCA requirements applicable to the device. From that premise, I proceed to the question whether FDCA requirements applicable to the device exist here to pre-empt the Lohrs' state-law claims.

I agree with the Court that the Lohrs' defective design claim is not pre-empted by the FDCA's §510(k) "substantial equivalency" process. The §510(k) process merely evaluates whether the Class III device at issue is substantially equivalent to a device that was on the market before 1976, the effective date of the MDA; if so, the later device may be also be marketed. Because the §510(k) process seeks merely to establish whether a pre-1976 device and a post-1976 device are equivalent, and places no "requirements" on a device, the Lohrs' defective design claim is not pre-empted.

I also agree that the Lohrs' claims are not pre-empted by §360k to the extent that they seek damages for Medtronic's alleged violation of federal requirements. Where a state cause of action seeks to enforce an FDCA requirement, that claim does not impose a requirement that is "different from, or in addition to," requirements under federal law. To be sure, the threat of a damages remedy will give manufacturers an additional cause to comply, but the requirements imposed on them under state and federal law do not differ. Section 360k does not preclude States from imposing different or additional *remedies*, but only different or additional *requirements*.

I disagree, however, with the Court's conclusion that the Lohrs' claims survive pre-emption insofar as they would compel Medtronic to comply with requirements different from those imposed by the FDCA. Because I do not subscribe to the Court's reading into §360k the additional requisite of "specificity," my determination of what claims are pre-empted is broader. Some, if not all, of the Lohrs' common-law claims regarding the manufacturing and labeling of Medtronic's device would compel Medtronic to comply with requirements different from, or in addition to, those required by the FDA. The FDA's Good Manufacturing Practice (GMP) regulations impose comprehensive requirements relating to every aspect of the device-manufacturing process, including a manufacturer's organization and personnel, buildings, equipment, component controls, production and process controls, packaging and labeling controls, holding, distribution, installation, device evaluation, and recordkeeping. The Lohrs' common-law claims regarding manufacture would, if successful, impose state requirements "different from, or in addition to," the GMP requirements, and are therefore pre-empted. In similar fashion, the Lohrs' failure to warn claim is pre-empted by the extensive labeling requirements imposed by the FDA. See, *e.g.*, 21 CFR §801.109 (1995) (requiring labels to include such information as indications, effects, routes, methods, frequency and duration of administration, relevant hazards, contraindications, side effects, and precautions). These extensive federal manufacturing and labeling requirements are certainly applicable to the device manufactured by Medtronic. Section 360k(a) requires no more specificity than that for pre-emption of state common-law claims.

To summarize, I conclude that §360k(a)'s term "requirement" encompasses state common-law claims. Because the statutory language does not indicate that a "requirement" must be "specific," either to pre-empt or be pre-empted, I conclude that a state common-law claim is pre-empted if it would impose "any requirement" "which is different from, or in addition to," any requirement applicable to the device under the FDCA. . . .

POINTS FOR DISCUSSION

1. In *Cipollone*, the plurality applied a presumption against preemption — that courts should not hold an act of Congress to supersede the police powers of the states unless Congress had a clear and manifest purpose to do so. The *Medtronic* Court applied the same presumption. The *Cipollone* and *Medtronic* dissents rejected this presumption, arguing that the Court simply should interpret an express preemption provision in accord with its evident meaning.

Is there any principled reason for applying a presumption against preemption in *Cipollone* or *Medtronic* but rejecting a clear statement rule in the context of *Gregory v. Ashcroft*, 501 U.S. 452 (1991)? In *Cipollone* and *Medtronic*, Justice Stevens applied a presumption against preemption to acts of Congress claimed to preempt state law. In *Medtronic*, he wrote, "[i]n all pre-emption cases, and particularly in those in which Congress has legislated in a field which the States have traditionally occupied, we start with the assumption that the historic police powers of the States were not to be superseded by the Federal Act unless that was the clear and manifest purpose of Congress" (internal quotations marks, ellipses, and citations omitted). But in *Gregory*, Justice Stevens joined Justice White's dissent, which argued that "federalism concerns are irrelevant to . . . 'actual conflict' preemption. The relative importance to the state of its own law is not material when there is a conflict with a valid federal law, for the Framers of our Constitution provided that the federal law must prevail." *Gregory*, 501 U.S. at 475 (internal quotation marks and citations omitted).

Conversely, is there any principled reason for applying a clear statement rule in the context of *Gregory*, but not in context of *Cipollone* or *Medtronic*? For instance, Justice O'Connor wrote the majority opinion in *Gregory* applying a clear statement rule but in *Medtronic* wrote that "the task before us" is "to interpret Congress' intent by reading the statute in accordance with its terms."

What, if anything, distinguishes these cases?

2. The Justices disagreed in *Cipollone* over whether "conflict" preemption applies when Congress enacts an "express" preemption provision. Should "conflict" preemption apply in that context?

3. In *Cipollone*, the plurality led by Justice Stevens determined that an express preemption of state law "requirements" included state common law obligations. In *Medtronic*, Justice Stevens wrote for a plurality in Part IV of his opinion that an express preemption of state law "requirements" did not include all state common law obligations. Did the pluralities properly interpret the word "requirements" differently in these contexts? Should the Court have interpreted the word to have the same preemptive effect in both contexts?

3. ADMINISTRATIVE PREEMPTION

The Supreme Court has recognized that federal administrative action, like a federal statute, may preempt conflicting state requirements. Administrative preemption raises some federalism concerns that statutory preemption does not. Consider the observations of Professor Ernest Young on administrative preemption:

> Preemption of state regulatory authority by national law is the central federalism issue of our time. Most analysis of this issue has focused on the preemptive effects of federal statutes. But . . . the advent of the administrative state has profound implications for . . . preemption doctrine. . . . Specifically, preemption doctrine has yet to resolve the extent to which executive action should be treated differently from legislation, or to grapple with the considerable range of diverse governmental activities that march under the banner of executive agency action.
>
> Federal administrative action is, in important ways, considerably more threatening to state autonomy than legislation is. As the constitutional limits on national action fade into history, the primary remaining safeguards for state autonomy are political, stemming from the representation of the states in Congress, and procedural, arising from the sheer difficulty of navigating the federal legislative process. These safeguards have little purchase on executive action. The states have no direct role in the "composition and selection" of federal administrative agencies, and much of the point of such agencies is to be more efficient lawmakers than Congress. Agency action thus evades both the political and the procedural safeguards of federalism. . . .
>
> Preemption doctrine has developed primarily as a doctrine of statutory construction, focused on the intent of Congress, and transporting that doctrine into the administrative law context raises a number of difficult problems of translation. The Supreme Court's preemption jurisprudence, unfortunately, has tended to ignore these problems. . . .
>
> [T]wo basic sets of problems [arise in this context.] The first involves questions of interpretation arising from an agency's determination that congressional action has preemptive effect. The most prominent issue here is whether, where Congress's own preemptive intent is ambiguous, courts should defer to the agency's conclusion that a statute preempts state law under *Chevron U.S.A. Inc. v. Natural Resources Defense Council*[, 467 U.S. 837, 843-844 (1984)].
>
> The second set of issues arises when preemption is asserted on the basis of regulations, orders, or other agency activity, rather than grounded in the relevant statute itself. These instances of preemption are problematic because they seem to shift preemptive authority from Congress to the agency—a result that contravenes both the text of the Supremacy Clause and the structural safeguards of federalism and separation of powers. As a result, I suggest that we may wish to restrict the agencies' role in preemption to interpreting what Congress has done.

Ernest A. Young, *Executive Preemption*, 102 Nw. U. L. Rev. 868, 869-871 (2008) (footnotes omitted). Focus on the second set of issues Professor Young identifies— arising from preemption by agency action— as you read the following two cases. Each case involves preemption of state law by federal administrative action.

GEIER v. AMERICAN HONDA MOTOR CO.

529 U.S. 861 (2000)

JUSTICE BREYER delivered the opinion of the Court.

This case focuses on the 1984 version of a Federal Motor Vehicle Safety Standard promulgated by the Department of Transportation under the authority of the National Traffic and Motor Vehicle Safety Act of 1966, 80 Stat. 718, 15 U.S.C. §1381 et seq. (1988 ed.). The standard, FMVSS 208, required auto manufacturers to equip some but not all of their 1987 vehicles with passive restraints. We ask whether the Act pre-empts a state common-law tort action in which the plaintiff claims that the defendant auto manufacturer, who was in compliance with the standard, should nonetheless have equipped a 1987 automobile with airbags. We conclude that the Act, taken together with FMVSS 208, pre-empts the lawsuit.

I

In 1992, petitioner Alexis Geier, driving a 1987 Honda Accord, collided with a tree and was seriously injured. The car was equipped with manual shoulder and lap belts which Geier had buckled up at the time. The car was not equipped with airbags or other passive restraint devices.

Geier and her parents . . . sued the car's manufacturer, American Honda . . . , under District of Columbia tort law. They claimed . . . that American Honda had designed its car negligently and defectively because it lacked a driver's side airbag. . . .

II

We first ask whether the Safety Act's express pre-emption provision pre-empts this tort action. The provision reads as follows:

"Whenever a Federal motor vehicle safety standard established under this subchapter is in effect, no State or political subdivision of a State shall have any authority either to establish, or to continue in effect, with respect to any motor vehicle or item of motor vehicle equipment[,] any safety standard applicable to the same aspect of performance of such vehicle or item of equipment which is not identical to the Federal standard." 15 U.S.C. §1392(d) (1988 ed.). . . .

[In addition,] a "saving" clause[] says that "[c]ompliance with" a federal safety standard "does not exempt any person from any liability under common law." 15 U.S.C. §1397(k) (1988 ed.). The saving clause assumes that there are some significant number of common-law liability cases to save. . . .

III

[T]he saving clause . . . removes tort actions from the scope of the express pre-emption clause. Does it do more? In particular, does it foreclose or limit the operation of ordinary pre-emption principles insofar as those principles instruct us to read statutes as pre-empting state laws (including common-law rules) that "actually conflict" with the statute or federal standards promulgated thereunder? . . .

We . . . conclude that the saving clause (like the express pre-emption provision) does *not* bar the ordinary working of conflict pre-emption principles.

Nothing in the language of the saving clause suggests an intent to save state-law tort actions that conflict with federal regulations. . . . [T]he saving provision . . . makes clear that the express pre-emption provision does not of its own force pre-empt common-law tort actions. And it thereby preserves those actions that seek to establish greater safety than the minimum safety achieved by a federal regulation intended to provide a floor. . . .

[However,] we conclude that the saving clause foresees . . . the possibility that a federal safety standard will pre-empt a state common-law tort action with which it conflicts. . . . Why . . . would Congress not have wanted ordinary pre-emption principles to apply where an actual conflict with a federal objective is at stake? Some such principle is needed. In its absence, state law could impose legal duties that would conflict directly with federal regulatory mandates, say, by premising liability upon the presence of the very windshield retention requirements that federal law requires. Insofar as petitioners' argument would permit common-law actions that "actually conflict" with federal regulations, it would take from those who would enforce a federal law the very ability to achieve the law's congressionally mandated objectives that the Constitution, through the operation of ordinary pre-emption principles, seeks to protect. To the extent that such an interpretation of the saving provision reads into a particular federal law toleration of a conflict that those principles would otherwise forbid, it permits that law to defeat its own objectives. . . . We do not claim that Congress lacks the constitutional power to write a statute that mandates such a complex type of state/federal relationship. But there is no reason to believe Congress has done so here. . . .

IV

The basic question, then, is whether a common-law "no airbag" action like the one before us actually conflicts with FMVSS 208. We hold that it does. . . .

DOT's own contemporaneous explanation of FMVSS 208 makes clear that the 1984 version of FMVSS 208 reflected the following significant considerations. First, buckled up seatbelts are a vital ingredient of automobile safety. . . . Second, despite the enormous and unnecessary risks that a passenger runs by not buckling up manual lap and shoulder belts, more than 80% of front seat passengers would leave their manual seatbelts unbuckled. . . . Third, airbags could make up for the dangers caused by unbuckled manual belts, but they could not make up for them entirely. . . . Fourth, passive restraint systems had their own disadvantages, for example, the dangers associated with, intrusiveness of, and corresponding public dislike for, nondetachable automatic belts. . . . Fifth, airbags brought with them their own special risks to safety, such as the risk of danger to out-of-position occupants (usually children) in small cars. . . . Sixth, airbags were expected to be significantly more expensive than other passive restraint devices, raising the average cost of a vehicle price $320 for full frontal airbags over the cost of a car with manual lap and shoulder seatbelts (and potentially much more if production volumes were low). . . . And the agency worried that the high replacement cost—estimated to be $800—could lead car owners to refuse to replace them after deployment. . . . Seventh, the public, for reasons of cost, fear, or physical intrusiveness, might resist installation or use of any of the then-available passive restraint devices—a particular concern with respect to airbags. . . .

FMVSS 208 reflected these considerations in several ways. Most importantly, that standard deliberately sought variety—a mix of several different passive restraint systems. It did so by setting a performance requirement for passive restraint devices and allowing manufacturers to choose among different passive restraint mechanisms, such as airbags, automatic belts, or other passive restraint technologies to satisfy that requirement. And DOT explained why FMVSS 208 sought the mix of devices that it expected its performance standard to produce. DOT wrote that it had *rejected* a proposed FMVSS 208 "all airbag" standard because of safety concerns (perceived or real) associated with airbags, which concerns threatened a "backlash" more easily overcome "if airbags" were "not the only way of complying." It added that a mix of devices would help develop data on comparative effectiveness, would allow the industry time to overcome the safety problems and the high production costs associated with airbags, and would facilitate the development of alternative, cheaper, and safer passive restraint systems. And it would thereby build public confidence. . . .

The 1984 FMVSS 208 standard also deliberately sought a *gradual* phase-in of passive restraints. It required the manufacturers to equip only 10% of their car fleet manufactured after September 1, 1986, with passive restraints. It then increased the percentage in three annual stages, up to 100% of the new car fleet for cars manufactured after September 1, 1989. And it explained that the phased-in requirement would allow more time for manufacturers to develop airbags or other, better, safer passive restraint systems. It would help develop information about the comparative effectiveness of different systems, would lead to a mix in which airbags and other nonseatbelt passive restraint systems played a more prominent role than would otherwise result, and would promote public acceptance. . . .

Finally, FMVSS 208's passive restraint requirement was conditional. DOT believed that ordinary manual lap and shoulder belts would produce about the same amount of safety as passive restraints, and at significantly lower costs — *if only auto occupants would buckle up*. Thus, FMVSS 208 provided for rescission of its passive restraint requirement if, by September 1, 1989, two-thirds of the States had laws in place that, like those of many other nations, required auto occupants to buckle up (and which met other requirements specified in the standard). . . . In the end, two-thirds of the States did not enact mandatory buckle-up laws, and the passive restraint requirement remained in effect.

In sum, as DOT now tells us through the Solicitor General, the 1984 version of FMVSS 208 "embodies the Secretary's policy judgment that safety would best be promoted if manufacturers installed *alternative* protection systems in their fleets rather than one particular system in every car." Brief for United States as Amicus Curiae 25; see 49 Fed. Reg. 28997 (1984). . . .

In effect, petitioners' tort action depends upon its claim that manufacturers had a duty to install an airbag when they manufactured the 1987 Honda Accord. Such a state law — *i.e.*, a rule of state tort law imposing such a duty — by its terms would have required manufacturers of all similar cars to install airbags rather than other passive restraint systems, such as automatic belts or passive interiors. It thereby would have presented an obstacle to the variety and mix of devices that the federal regulation sought. It would have required all manufacturers to have installed airbags in respect to the entire District-of-Columbia–related portion of their 1987 new car fleet, even though

FMVSS 208 at that time required only that 10% of a manufacturer's nationwide fleet be equipped with any passive restraint device at all. It thereby also would have stood as an obstacle to the gradual passive restraint phase-in that the federal regulation deliberately imposed. In addition, it could have made less likely the adoption of a state mandatory buckle-up law. Because the rule of law for which petitioners contend would have stood "as an obstacle to the accomplishment and execution of" the important means-related federal objectives that we have just discussed, it is pre-empted. *Hines* [v. *Davidowitz*, 312 U.S. 52, 67 (1941)]. . . .

JUSTICE STEVENS, with whom JUSTICE SOUTER, JUSTICE THOMAS, and JUSTICE GINSBURG join, dissenting.

"This is a case about federalism," *Coleman v. Thompson*, 501 U.S. 722, 726 (1991), that is, about respect for "the constitutional role of the States as sovereign entities." *Alden v. Maine*, 527 U.S. 706, 713 (1999). It raises important questions concerning the way in which the Federal Government may exercise its undoubted power to oust state courts of their traditional jurisdiction over common-law tort actions. The rule the Court enforces today was not enacted by Congress and is not to be found in the text of any Executive Order or regulation. It has a unique origin: It is the product of the Court's interpretation of the final commentary accompanying an interim administrative regulation and the history of airbag regulation generally. . . .

I

The question presented is whether either the National Traffic and Motor Vehicle Safety Act of 1966 (Safety Act or Act), or the [1984] Standard 208 . . . pre-empts common-law tort claims that an automobile manufactured in 1987 was negligently and defectively designed because it lacked "an effective and safe passive restraint system, including, but not limited to, airbags." . . . The purpose of the Act, as stated by Congress, was "to reduce traffic accidents and deaths and injuries to persons resulting from traffic accidents." 15 U.S.C. §1381. The Act directed the Secretary of Transportation or his delegate to issue motor vehicle safety standards that "shall be practicable, shall meet the need for motor vehicle safety, and shall be stated in objective terms." §1392(a). The Act defines the term "safety standard" as a "minimum standard for motor vehicle performance, or motor vehicle equipment performance." §1391(2).

Standard 208['s] purpose "is to reduce the number of deaths of vehicle occupants, and the severity of injuries, by specifying vehicle crashworthiness requirements . . . [and] equipment requirements for active and passive restraint systems." 49 CFR. §571.208, S2 (1998). . . .

The 1984 standard provided for a phase-in of passive restraint requirements beginning with the 1987 model year. In that year, vehicle manufacturers were required to equip a minimum of 10% of their new passenger cars with such restraints. While the 1987 Honda Accord driven by Ms. Geier was not so equipped, it is undisputed that Honda complied with the 10% minimum by installing passive restraints in certain other 1987 models. This minimum passive restraint requirement increased to 25% of 1988 models and

40% of 1989 models; the standard also mandated that "after September 1, 1989, all new cars must have automatic occupant crash protection." 49 Fed. Reg. 28999 (1984). . . .

Although the standard did not require airbags in all cars, it is clear that the Secretary did intend to encourage wider use of airbags. One of her basic conclusions was that "[a]utomatic occupant protection systems that do not totally rely upon belts, such as airbags . . . , offer significant additional potential for preventing fatalities and injuries, at least in part because the American public is likely to find them less intrusive; their development and availability should be encouraged through appropriate incentives." The Secretary therefore included a phase-in period in order to encourage manufacturers to comply with the standard by installing airbags and other (perhaps more effective) nonbelt technologies that they might develop, rather than by installing less expensive automatic seatbelts. As a further incentive for the use of such technologies, the standard provided that a vehicle equipped with an airbag or other nonbelt system would count as 1.5 vehicles for the purpose of determining compliance with the required 10, 25, or 40% minimum passive restraint requirement during the phase-in period. 49 CFR §571.208, S4.1.3.4(a)(1) (1998). . . .

III

When a state statute, administrative rule, or common-law cause of action conflicts with a federal statute, it is axiomatic that the state law is without effect. U.S. Const., Art. VI, cl. 2; *Cipollone v. Liggett Group, Inc.*, 505 U.S. 504, 516 (1992). On the other hand, it is equally clear that the Supremacy Clause does not give unelected federal judges carte blanche to use federal law as a means of imposing their own ideas of tort reform on the States. Because of the role of States as separate sovereigns in our federal system, we have long presumed that state laws — particularly those, such as the provision of tort remedies to compensate for personal injuries, that are within the scope of the States' historic police powers — are not to be pre-empted by a federal statute unless it is the clear and manifest purpose of Congress to do so. *Medtronic, Inc. v. Lohr*, 518 U.S. 470, 485 (1996). . . .

When a federal statute contains an express pre-emption provision, "the task of statutory construction must in the first instance focus on the plain wording of [that provision], which necessarily contains the best evidence of Congress' pre-emptive intent." *CSX Transp., Inc. v. Easterwood*, 507 U.S. 658, 664 (1993). The Safety Act contains both an express pre-emption provision . . . and a saving clause that expressly preserves common-law claims. . . . It is perfectly clear . . . that the term "safety standard" as used in these two sections refers to an objective rule prescribed by a legislature or an administrative agency and does not encompass case-specific decisions by judges and juries that resolve common-law claims. . . .

It is true that in . . . recent cases we concluded that broadly phrased preemptive commands encompassed common-law claims. In *Cipollone v. Liggett Group, Inc.,* . . . we concluded that the . . . command . . . that "[n]o requirement or prohibition . . . shall be imposed under State law" did include certain common-law claims. *Id.*, at 548-549 (Scalia, J., concurring in judgment in part and dissenting in part). . . . And in *Medtronic, Inc. v. Lohr*, we recognized that the statutory reference to "any requirement" imposed by a State or its political subdivisions may include common-law duties. 518 U.S., at 502-503.

The statutes construed in those cases differed from the Safety Act in two significant respects. First, the language in each of those pre-emption provisions was significantly broader than the text of §1392(d). Unlike the broader language of those provisions, the ordinary meaning of the term "safety standard" includes positive enactments, but does not include judicial decisions in common-law tort cases.

Second, the statutes at issue in *Cipollone* . . . and *Medtronic* did not contain a saving clause expressly preserving common-law remedies. The saving clause in the Safety Act unambiguously expresses a decision by Congress that compliance with a federal safety standard does not exempt a manufacturer from *any* common-law liability. In light of this reference to common-law liability in the saving clause, Congress surely would have included a similar reference in §1392(d) if it had intended to pre-empt such liability. . . .

Given the cumulative force of the fact that §1392(d) does not expressly pre-empt common-law claims and the fact that §1397(k) was obviously intended to limit the pre-emptive effect of the Secretary's safety standards, it is quite wrong for the Court to assume that a possible implicit conflict with the purposes to be achieved by such a standard should have . . . pre-emptive effect. . . .

IV

Even though the Safety Act does not expressly pre-empt common-law claims, Honda contends that Standard 208 — of its own force — implicitly pre-empts the claims in this case.

> "We have recognized that a federal statute implicitly overrides state law either when the scope of a statute indicates that Congress intended federal law to occupy a field exclusively, or when state law is in actual conflict with federal law. We have found implied conflict pre-emption where it is impossible for a private party to comply with both state and federal requirements, or where state law stands as an obstacle to the accomplishment and execution of the full purposes and objectives of Congress." *Freightliner Corp. v. Myrick*, 514 U.S. 280, 287 (1995) [internal quotation marks and citations omitted].

In addition, we have concluded that regulations "intended to pre-empt state law" that are promulgated by an agency acting nonarbitrarily and within its congressionally delegated authority may also have pre-emptive force. *Fidelity Fed. Sav. & Loan Assn. v. De la Cuesta*, 458 U.S. 141, 153-154 (1982). In this case, Honda relies on the last of the implied pre-emption principles stated in *Freightliner*, arguing that the imposition of common-law liability for failure to install an airbag would frustrate the purposes and objectives of Standard 208.

Both the text of the statute and the text of the standard provide persuasive reasons for rejecting this argument. The saving clause of the Safety Act arguably denies the Secretary the authority to promulgate standards that would pre-empt common-law remedies. Moreover, the text of Standard 208 says nothing about pre-emption, and I am not persuaded that Honda has overcome our traditional presumption that it lacks any implicit pre-emptive effect.

Honda argues, and the Court now agrees, that the risk of liability presented by common-law claims that vehicles without airbags are negligently and defectively designed would frustrate the policy decision that the Secretary made in promulgating Standard 208. This decision, in their view, was that safety — including a desire to encourage "public acceptance of the airbag technology and experimentation with better passive restraint systems" — would best be promoted through gradual implementation of a passive restraint requirement making airbags only one of a variety of systems that a manufacturer could install in order to comply, rather than through a requirement mandating the use of one particular system in every vehicle. . . .

[D]espite its acknowledgment that the saving clause "preserves those actions that seek to establish greater safety than the minimum safety achieved by a federal regulation intended to provide a floor," the Court completely ignores the important fact that by definition all of the standards established under the Safety Act — like the British regulations that governed the number and capacity of lifeboats aboard the *Titanic* — impose minimum, rather than fixed or maximum, requirements. The phase-in program authorized by Standard 208 thus set minimum percentage requirements for the installation of passive restraints, increasing in annual stages of 10, 25, 40, and 100%. Those requirements were not ceilings, and it is obvious that the Secretary favored a more rapid increase. The possibility that exposure to potential tort liability might accelerate the rate of increase would actually further the only goal explicitly mentioned in the standard itself: reducing the number of deaths and severity of injuries of vehicle occupants. . . .

I conclude that the Government, on the Secretary's behalf, has failed to articulate a coherent view of the policies behind Standard 208 that would be frustrated by petitioners' claims. . . .

V

Our presumption against pre-emption is rooted in the concept of federalism. It recognizes that when Congress legislates "in a field which the States have traditionally occupied . . . [,] we start with the assumption that the historic police powers of the States were not to be superseded by the Federal Act unless that was the clear and manifest purpose of Congress." *Rice v. Santa Fe Elevator Corp.*, 331 U.S. [218,] 230 [1947]. The signal virtues of this presumption are its placement of the power of pre-emption squarely in the hands of Congress, which is far more suited than the Judiciary to strike the appropriate state/federal balance (particularly in areas of traditional state regulation), and its requirement that Congress speak clearly when exercising that power. In this way, the structural safeguards inherent in the normal operation of the legislative process operate to defend state interests from undue infringement. *Garcia v. San Antonio Metropolitan Transit Authority*, 469 U.S. 528, 552 (1985); see *United States v. Morrison*, 529 U.S. 598, 660-663 [(2000] (Breyer, J., dissenting); *Gregory v. Ashcroft*, 501 U.S. 452, 460-464 (1991). In addition, the presumption serves as a limiting principle that prevents federal judges from running amok with our potentially boundless (and perhaps inadequately considered) doctrine of implied conflict pre-emption based on frustration of purposes — *i.e.*, that state law is pre-empted if it "stands as an obstacle to the accomplishment and execution of the full purposes and objectives of Congress." *Hines v. Davidowitz*, 312 U.S. 52, 67 (1941).

While the presumption is important in assessing the pre-emptive reach of federal statutes, it becomes crucial when the pre-emptive effect of an administrative regulation is at issue. Unlike Congress, administrative agencies are clearly not designed to represent the interests of States, yet with relative ease they can promulgate comprehensive and detailed regulations that have broad pre-emption ramifications for state law. We have addressed the heightened federalism and nondelegation concerns that agency pre-emption raises by using the presumption to build a procedural bridge across the political accountability gap between States and administrative agencies. Thus, even in cases where implied regulatory pre-emption is at issue, we generally "expect an administrative regulation to declare any intention to pre-empt state law with some specificity." *California Coastal Comm'n v. Granite Rock Co.*, 480 U.S. 572, 583 (1987). . . .

When the presumption and its underpinnings are properly understood, it is plain that Honda has not overcome the presumption in this case. Neither Standard 208 nor its accompanying commentary includes the slightest specific indication of an intent to pre-empt common-law no-airbag suits. . . .

[T]he Court identifies no case in which we have upheld a regulatory claim of frustration-of-purposes implied conflict pre-emption based on nothing more than . . . inferences from regulatory history and final commentary. . . . [W]hen snippets from them are combined with the Court's broad conception of a doctrine of frustration-of-purposes pre-emption untempered by the presumption, a vast, undefined area of state law becomes vulnerable to pre-emption by any related federal law or regulation. In my view, however, "preemption analysis is, or at least should be, a matter of precise statutory [or regulatory] construction rather than an exercise in free-form judicial policymaking." 1 L. Tribe, American Constitutional Law §6-28, p. 1177 (3d ed. 2000). . . .

Because neither the text of the statute nor the text of the regulation contains any indication of an intent to pre-empt petitioners' cause of action, and because I cannot agree with the Court's unprecedented use of inferences from regulatory history and commentary as a basis for implied pre-emption, I am convinced that Honda has not overcome the presumption against pre-emption in this case. . . .

WYETH V. LEVINE

129 S. Ct. 1187 (2009)

JUSTICE STEVENS delivered the opinion of the Court.

Directly injecting the drug Phenergan into a patient's vein [IV-push] creates a significant risk of catastrophic consequences. A Vermont jury found that petitioner Wyeth, the manufacturer of the drug, had failed to provide an adequate warning of that risk and awarded damages to respondent Diana Levine to compensate her for the amputation of her arm. The warnings on Phenergan's label had been deemed sufficient by the federal Food and Drug Administration

(FDA) when it approved Wyeth's new drug application in 1955 and when it later approved changes in the drug's labeling. The question we must decide is whether the FDA's approvals provide Wyeth with a complete defense to Levine's tort claims. . . .

II

[We] must be guided by two cornerstones of our pre-emption jurisprudence. First, "the purpose of Congress is the ultimate touchstone in every pre-emption case." *Medtronic, Inc. v. Lohr*, 518 U.S. 470, 485 (1996). Second, "[i]n all pre-emption cases, and particularly in those in which Congress has legislated in a field which the States have traditionally occupied, we start with the assumption that the historic police powers of the States were not to be superseded by the Federal Act unless that was the clear and manifest purpose of Congress." [*Id.*] . . .

III

Wyeth first argues that Levine's state-law claims are pre-empted because it is impossible for it to comply with both the state-law duties underlying those claims and its federal labeling duties. The FDA's premarket approval of a new drug application includes the approval of the exact text in the proposed label. See 21 U.S.C. §355; 21 CFR §314.105(b). Generally speaking, a manufacturer may only change a drug label after the FDA approves a supplemental application. There is, however, an FDA regulation that permits a manufacturer to make certain changes to its label before receiving the agency's approval. Among other things, this . . . regulation provides that if a manufacturer is changing a label to "add or strengthen a contraindication, warning, precaution, or adverse reaction" or to "add or strengthen an instruction about dosage and administration that is intended to increase the safe use of the drug product," it may make the labeling change upon filing its supplemental application with the FDA; it need not wait for FDA approval. . . .

Wyeth could have revised Phenergan's label . . . in accordance with th[is] regulation. . . . [In particular,] Wyeth could have analyzed . . . accumulating data [about Phenergan injection risks] and added a stronger warning about IV-push administration of the drug. . . .

Impossibility pre-emption is a demanding defense. . . . Wyeth has failed to demonstrate that it was impossible for it to comply with both federal and state requirements. The [applicable] regulation permitted Wyeth to unilaterally strengthen its warning, and the mere fact that the FDA approved Phenergan's label does not establish that it would have prohibited such a change.

IV

Wyeth also argues that requiring it to comply with a state-law duty to provide a stronger warning about IV-push administration would obstruct the purposes and objectives of federal drug labeling regulation. Levine's tort claims, it maintains, are pre-empted because they interfere with "Congress's purpose to entrust an expert agency to make drug labeling decisions that strike a balance between competing objectives." We find no merit in this argument, which relies on an untenable interpretation of congressional intent and an overbroad view of an agency's power to pre-empt state law.

Wyeth contends that the [federal Food, Drug, and Cosmetics Act (FDCA)] establishes both a floor and a ceiling for drug regulation: Once the FDA has approved a drug's label, a state-law verdict may not deem the label inadequate, regardless of whether there is any evidence that the FDA has considered the stronger warning at issue. The most glaring problem with this argument is that all evidence of Congress' purposes is to the contrary. . . .

If Congress thought state-law suits posed an obstacle to its objectives, it surely would have enacted an express pre-emption provision at some point during the FDCA's 70-year history. But . . . Congress has not enacted such a provision for prescription drugs. Its silence on the issue, coupled with its certain awareness of the prevalence of state tort litigation, is powerful evidence that Congress did not intend FDA oversight to be the exclusive means of ensuring drug safety and effectiveness. . . .

Despite this evidence that Congress did not regard state tort litigation as an obstacle to achieving its purposes, Wyeth nonetheless maintains that, because the FDCA requires the FDA to determine that a drug is safe and effective under the conditions set forth in its labeling, the agency must be presumed to have performed a precise balancing of risks and benefits and to have established a specific labeling standard that leaves no room for different state-law judgments. In advancing this argument, Wyeth relies not on any statement by Congress, but instead on the preamble to a 2006 FDA regulation governing the content and format of prescription drug labels. In that preamble, the FDA declared that the FDCA establishes "both a 'floor' and a 'ceiling,'" so that "FDA approval of labeling . . . preempts conflicting or contrary State law." [71 Fed. Reg. 3922, 3934-3935 (2006).] It further stated that certain state-law actions, such as those involving failure-to-warn claims, "threaten FDA's statutorily prescribed role as the expert Federal agency responsible for evaluating and regulating drugs."

This Court has recognized that an agency regulation with the force of law can pre-empt conflicting state requirements. *See, e.g., Geier v. American Honda Motor Co.*, 529 U.S. 861 (2000). In such cases, the Court has performed its own conflict determination, relying on the substance of state and federal law and not on agency proclamations of pre-emption. We are faced with no such regulation in this case, but rather with an agency's mere assertion that state law is an obstacle to achieving its statutory objectives. Because Congress has not authorized the FDA to pre-empt state law directly, the question is what weight we should accord the FDA's opinion.

In prior cases, we have given "some weight" to an agency's views about the impact of tort law on federal objectives when "the subject matter is technica[l] and the relevant history and background are complex and extensive." *Geier*, 529 U.S., at 883. Even in such cases, however, we have not deferred to an agency's *conclusion* that state law is pre-empted. Rather, we have attended to an agency's explanation of how state law affects the regulatory scheme. While agencies have no special authority to pronounce on pre-emption absent delegation by Congress, they do have a unique understanding of the statutes they administer and an attendant ability to make informed determinations about how state requirements may pose an "obstacle to the accomplishment and execution of the full purposes and objectives of Congress." [*Hines v. Davidowitz*, 312 U.S. 52, 67 (1941)]; see *Geier*, 529 U.S., at 883; *Lohr*, 518 U.S., at 495-496. The weight we accord the agency's explanation of state law's impact on the federal scheme depends on its thoroughness, consistency, and persuasiveness. . . .

Under this standard, the FDA's 2006 preamble does not merit deference. When the FDA issued its notice of proposed rulemaking in December 2000, it explained that the rule would "not contain policies that have federalism implications or that preempt State law." In 2006, the agency finalized the rule and, without offering States or other interested parties notice or opportunity for comment, articulated a sweeping position on the FDCA's pre-emptive effect in the regulatory preamble. The agency's views on state law are inherently suspect in light of this procedural failure.

Further, the preamble is at odds with what evidence we have of Congress' purposes, and it reverses the FDA's own longstanding position without providing a reasoned explanation, including any discussion of how state law has interfered with the FDA's regulation of drug labeling during decades of coexistence. The FDA's 2006 position plainly does not reflect the agency's own view at all times relevant to this litigation. Not once prior to Levine's injury did the FDA suggest that state tort law stood as an obstacle to its statutory mission. To the contrary, it cast federal labeling standards as a floor upon which States could build and repeatedly disclaimed any attempt to pre-empt failure-to-warn claims. . . .

In keeping with Congress' decision not to pre-empt common-law tort suits, it appears that the FDA traditionally regarded state law as a complementary form of drug regulation. The FDA has limited resources to monitor the 11,000 drugs on the market, and manufacturers have superior access to information about their drugs, especially in the postmarketing phase as new risks emerge. State tort suits uncover unknown drug hazards and provide incentives for drug manufacturers to disclose safety risks promptly. They also serve a distinct compensatory function that may motivate injured persons to come forward with information. Failure-to-warn actions, in particular, lend force to the FDCA's premise that manufacturers, not the FDA, bear primary responsibility for their drug labeling at all times. Thus, the FDA long maintained that state law offers an additional, and important, layer of consumer protection that complements FDA regulation. The agency's 2006 preamble represents a dramatic change in position.

Largely based on the FDA's new position, Wyeth argues that this case presents a conflict between state and federal law analogous to the one at issue in *Geier*. There, we held that state tort claims premised on Honda's failure to install airbags conflicted with a federal regulation that did not require airbags for all cars. The Department of Transportation (DOT) had promulgated a rule that provided car manufacturers with a range of choices among passive restraint devices. Rejecting an "all airbag" standard, the agency had called for a gradual phase-in of a mix of passive restraints in order to spur technological development and win consumer acceptance. Because the plaintiff's claim was that car manufacturers had a duty to install airbags, it presented an obstacle to achieving "the variety and mix of devices that the federal regulation sought." [*Geier*, 529 U.S., at 881.] . . .

[T]he regulatory scheme in this case is quite different. In *Geier*, the DOT conducted a formal rulemaking and then adopted a plan to phase in a mix of passive restraint devices. Examining the rule itself and the DOT's contemporaneous record, which revealed the factors the agency had weighed and the balance it had struck, we determined that state tort suits presented an obstacle to the federal scheme. After conducting our own pre-emption analysis, we considered the agency's explanation of how state law interfered with its regulation, regarding it as further support for our independent conclusion that the plaintiff's tort claim obstructed the federal regime.

By contrast, we have no occasion in this case to consider the pre-emptive effect of a specific agency regulation bearing the force of law. And the FDA's newfound opinion, expressed in its 2006 preamble, that state law "frustrate[s] the agency's implementation of its statutory mandate" does not merit deference for the reasons we have explained. . . .

In short, Wyeth has not persuaded us that failure-to-warn claims like Levine's obstruct the federal regulation of drug labeling. Congress has repeatedly declined to pre-empt state law, and the FDA's recently adopted position that state tort suits interfere with its statutory mandate is entitled to no weight. Although we recognize that some state-law claims might well frustrate the achievement of congressional objectives, this is not such a case. . . .

JUSTICE BREYER, concurring.

I write separately to emphasize the Court's statement that "we have no occasion in this case to consider the pre-emptive effect of a specific agency regulation bearing the force of law." . . . The FDA may seek to determine whether and when state tort law acts as a help or a hindrance to achieving the safe drug-related medical care that Congress sought. It may seek to embody those determinations in lawful specific regulations describing, for example, when labeling requirements serve as a ceiling as well as a floor. And it is possible that such determinations would have pre-emptive effect. I agree with the Court, however, that such a regulation is not at issue in this case.

JUSTICE THOMAS, concurring in the judgment.

I agree with the Court that the fact that the [FDA] approved the label for petitioner Wyeth's drug Phenergan does not pre-empt the state-law judgment before the Court. . . . I write separately, however, because I cannot join the majority's implicit endorsement of far-reaching implied pre-emption doctrines. In particular, I have become increasingly skeptical of this Court's "purposes and objectives" pre-emption jurisprudence. Under this approach, the Court routinely invalidates state laws based on perceived conflicts with broad federal policy objectives, legislative history, or generalized notions of congressional purposes that are not embodied within the text of federal law. Because implied pre-emption doctrines that wander far from the statutory text are inconsistent with the Constitution, I concur only in the judgment.

I

A

In order "to ensure the protection of our fundamental liberties," *Atascadero State Hospital v. Scanlon*, 473 U.S. 234, 242 (1985), the "Constitution establishes a system of dual sovereignty between the States and the Federal Government." *Gregory v. Ashcroft*, 501 U.S. 452, 457 (1991). The Framers adopted this "constitutionally mandated balance of power," *Atascadero State Hospital*, supra, at 242, to "reduce the risk of tyranny and abuse from either front," because a "federalist structure of joint sovereigns preserves to the people numerous advantages," such as "a decentralized government that will be more sensitive to the diverse needs of a heterogeneous society" and "increase[d] opportunity for citizen involvement in democratic processes," *Gregory*, supra, at 458. Furthermore, as the Framers observed, the "compound republic of America" provides "a double security . . . to the rights of the people" because "the power surrendered by the people is first divided between two distinct governments, and then the portion allotted to each subdivided among distinct and separate departments." The Federalist No. 51, p. 266 (M. Beloff ed., 2d ed.1987).

Under this federalist system, "the States possess sovereignty concurrent with that of the Federal Government, subject only to limitations imposed by the Supremacy Clause." *Tafflin v. Levitt*, 493 U.S. 455, 458 (1990). In this way, the Supremacy Clause gives the Federal Government "a decided advantage in [a] delicate balance" between federal and state sovereigns. *Gregory*, 501 U.S., at 460. "As long as it is acting within the powers granted it under the Constitution, Congress may impose its will on the States." *Ibid.* That is an "extraordinary power in a federalist system." *Ibid.*

Nonetheless, the States retain substantial sovereign authority. In accordance with the text and structure of the Constitution, "[t]he powers delegated by the proposed constitution to the federal government, are few and defined" and "[t]hose which are to remain in the state governments, are numerous and indefinite." The Federalist No. 45, at 237-238. Indeed, in protecting our constitutional government, "the preservation of the States, and the maintenance of their governments, are as much within the design and care of the Constitution as the preservation of the Union and the maintenance of the National government." *Texas v. White*, 7 Wall. 700, 725 (1869).

As a result, in order to protect the delicate balance of power mandated by the Constitution, the Supremacy Clause must operate only in accordance with its terms. . . . With respect to federal laws . . . the Supremacy Clause gives "supreme" status only to those that are "made in Pursuance" of "[t]his Constitution."

Federal laws "made in Pursuance" of the Constitution must comply with two key structural limitations in the Constitution that ensure that the Federal Government does not amass too much power at the expense of the States. The first structural limitation, which the parties have not raised in this case, is "the Constitution's conferral upon Congress of not all governmental powers, but only discrete, enumerated ones." [*Printz v. United States*, 521 U.S. 898, 919 (1997).]

The second structural limitation is the complex set of procedures that Congress and the President must follow to enact "Laws of the United

States." . . . The Supremacy Clause thus requires that pre-emptive effect be given only those to federal standards and policies that are set forth in, or necessarily follow from, the statutory text that was produced through the constitutionally required bicameral and presentment procedures. . . .

B

Congressional and agency musings, however, do not satisfy the Art. I, §7 requirements for enactment of federal law and, therefore, do not pre-empt state law under the Supremacy Clause. . . . Pre-emption must turn on whether state law conflicts with the text of the relevant federal statute or with the federal regulations authorized by that text.

II

This Court has determined that there are two categories of conflict pre-emption, both of which Wyeth contends are at issue in this case. First, the Court has found pre-emption "where compliance with both federal and state regulations is a physical impossibility for one engaged in interstate commerce." *Florida Lime & Avocado Growers, Inc. v. Paul*, 373 U.S. 132, 142-143 (1963). Second, the Court has determined that federal law pre-empts state law when, "under the circumstances of [a] particular case, [state] law stands as an obstacle to the accomplishment and execution of the full purposes and objectives of Congress." *Hines v. Davidowitz*, 312 U.S. 52, 67 (1941). . . .

This Court's entire body of "purposes and objectives" pre-emption jurisprudence is inherently flawed. The cases improperly rely on legislative history, broad atextual notions of congressional purpose, and even congressional inaction in order to pre-empt state law. I, therefore, cannot join the majority's analysis of this claim, or its reaffirmation of the Court's "purposes and objectives" jurisprudence. . . .

The consequences of this Court's broad approach to "purposes and objectives" pre-emption are exemplified in this Court's decision in *Geier*. . . . The Court's decision in *Geier* to apply "purposes and objectives" pre-emption based on agency comments, regulatory history, and agency litigating positions was especially flawed, given that it conflicted with the plain statutory text of the saving clause within the Safety Act, which explicitly preserved state common-law actions by providing that "[c]ompliance with any Federal motor vehicle safety standard issued under this subchapter does not exempt any person from any liability under common law," 15 U.S.C. §1397(k) (1988 ed.). . . . This Court has repeatedly stated that when statutory language is plain, it must be enforced according to its terms. . . . With text that allowed state actions like the one at issue in *Geier*, the Court had no authority to comb through agency commentaries to find a basis for an alternative conclusion. . . .

III

The origins of this Court's "purposes and objectives" pre-emption jurisprudence . . . , and its broad application in cases like *Geier*, illustrate that this brand of the Court's pre-emption jurisprudence facilitates freewheeling, extratextual, and broad evaluations of the "purposes and objectives" embodied within federal law. This, in turn, leads to decisions giving improperly broad pre-emptive effect to judicially manufactured policies, rather than to the statutory text enacted by Congress pursuant to the Constitution and the agency actions authorized thereby. Because such a sweeping approach to pre-emption leads to the illegitimate—and thus, unconstitutional—invalidation of state laws, I can no longer assent to a doctrine that pre-empts state laws merely because they "stan[d] as an obstacle to the accomplishment and execution of the full purposes and objectives" of federal law. . . .

JUSTICE ALITO, with whom THE CHIEF JUSTICE and JUSTICE SCALIA join, dissenting.
  This case illustrates that tragic facts make bad law. The Court holds that a state tort jury, rather than the . . . FDA . . . , is ultimately responsible for regulating warning labels for prescription drugs. That result cannot be reconciled with *Geier v. American Honda Motor Co.*, 529 U.S. 861 (2000), or general principles of conflict pre-emption. I respectfully dissent.

I

  [T]he real issue is whether a state tort jury can countermand the FDA's considered judgment that Phenergan's FDA-mandated warning label renders its intravenous (IV) use "safe." . . .
  Federal law [relies] on the FDA to make safety determinations like the one it made here. The FDA has long known about the risks associated with IV push in general and its use to administer Phenergan in particular. Whether wisely or not, the FDA has concluded . . . that the drug is "safe" and "effective" when used in accordance with its FDA-mandated labeling. . . .

II

A

  To the extent that "[t]he purpose of Congress is the ultimate touchstone in every pre-emption case," *Medtronic, Inc. v. Lohr*, 518 U.S. 470, 485 (1996), Congress made its "purpose" plain in authorizing the FDA—not state tort juries—to determine when and under what circumstances a drug is "safe." . . .
  Under the . . . FDCA . . . , a drug manufacturer may not market a new drug before first submitting a new drug application (NDA) to the FDA and receiving the agency's approval. See 21 U.S.C. §355(a). An NDA must contain, among other things, "the labeling proposed to be used for such drug," §355(b)(1)(F), "full reports of investigations which have been made to show whether or not such drug is safe for use and whether such drug is effective in use," §355(b)(1)(A), and "a discussion of why the benefits exceed the risks [of the drug] under the conditions stated in the labeling," 21 CFR §314.50(d)(5)(viii) (2008). The FDA will approve an NDA only if the agency finds, among other things, that the drug is "safe for use under the conditions prescribed, recommended, or suggested in the proposed labeling thereof," there is "substantial evidence that the drug will have the effect it purports or is represented to have under the conditions of use prescribed, recommended, or suggested in the proposed labeling thereof," and the proposed labeling is not "false or misleading in any particular." 21 U.S.C. §355(d).

After the FDA approves a drug, the manufacturer remains under an obligation to investigate and report any adverse events associated with the drug, see 21 CFR §314.80, and must periodically submit any new information that may affect the FDA's previous conclusions about the safety, effectiveness, or labeling of the drug, 21 U.S.C. §355(k). If the FDA finds that the drug is not "safe" when used in accordance with its labeling, the agency "shall" withdraw its approval of the drug. §355(e). The FDA also "shall" deem a drug "misbranded" if "it is dangerous to health when used in the dosage or manner, or with the frequency or duration prescribed, recommended, or suggested in the labeling thereof." §352(j).

Thus, a drug's warning label "serves as the standard under which the FDA determines whether a product is safe and effective." 50 Fed. Reg. 7470 (1985). Labeling is "[t]he centerpiece of risk management," as it "communicates to health care practitioners the agency's formal, authoritative conclusions regarding the conditions under which the product can be used safely and effectively." 71 Fed. Reg. 3934 (2006). The FDA has underscored the importance it places on drug labels by promulgating comprehensive regulations—spanning an entire part of the Code of Federal Regulations, see 21 CFR pt. 201, with seven subparts and 70 separate sections—that set forth drug manufacturers' labeling obligations. Under those regulations, the FDA must be satisfied that a drug's warning label contains, among other things, "a summary of the essential scientific information needed for the safe and effective use of the drug," §201.56(1), including a description of "clinically significant adverse reactions," "other potential safety hazards," "limitations in use imposed by them, . . . and steps that should be taken if they occur," §201.57(c)(6)(i). Neither the FDCA nor its implementing regulations suggest that juries may second-guess the FDA's labeling decisions.

B

Where the FDA determines, in accordance with its statutory mandate, that a drug is on balance "safe," our conflict pre-emption cases prohibit any State from countermanding that determination. . . . [T]he ordinary principles of conflict pre-emption turn solely on whether a State has upset the regulatory balance struck by the federal agency. . . .

A faithful application of this Court's conflict pre-emption cases compels the conclusion that the FDA's 40-year-long effort to regulate the safety and efficacy of Phenergan pre-empts respondent's tort suit. Indeed, that result follows directly from our conclusion in *Geier*. . . . Through Phenergan's label, the FDA offered medical professionals a menu of federally approved, "safe" and "effective" alternatives—including IV push—for administering the drug. Through a state tort suit, respondent attempted to deem IV push "unsafe" and "ineffective." To be sure, federal law does not prohibit Wyeth from contraindicating IV push, just as [the] federal law [at issue in *Geier*] did not prohibit Honda from installing airbags in all its cars. But just as we held that States may not compel the latter, so, too, are States precluded from compelling the former. . . .

III

Given the "balance" that the FDA struck between the costs and benefits of administering Phenergan via IV push, *Geier* compels the pre-emption of tort suits (like this one) that would upset that balance. The contrary conclusion requires turning yesterday's dissent into today's majority opinion. . . .

[T]he *Geier* Court specifically rejected the argument (again made by the dissenters in that case) that the "presumption against pre-emption" is relevant to the conflict pre-emption analysis. Rather than invoking such a "presumption," the Court emphasized that it was applying "ordinary," "longstanding," and "experience-proved principles of conflict pre-emption." [529 U.S.,] at 874. Under these principles, the sole question is whether there is an "actual conflict" between state and federal law; if so, then pre-emption follows automatically by operation of the Supremacy Clause. Id., at 871-872. . . .

By their very nature, juries are ill-equipped to perform the FDA's cost-benefit-balancing function. . . . [J]uries tend to focus on the risk of a particular product's design or warning label that arguably contributed to a particular plaintiff's injury, not on the overall benefits of that design or label; "the patients who reaped those benefits are not represented in court." [*Riegel v. Medtronic, Inc.*, 552 U.S. 312, 325 (2008)]. . . .

In contrast, the FDA has the benefit of the long view. Its drug-approval determinations consider the interests of all potential users of a drug, including "those who would suffer without new medical [products]" if juries in all 50 states were free to contradict the FDA's expert determinations. [*Id.*, at 326.] . . . And the FDA conveys its warnings with one voice, rather than whipsawing the medical community with 50 (or more) potentially conflicting ones. After today's ruling, however, parochialism may prevail. . . .

To be sure, state tort suits can peacefully coexist with the FDA's labeling regime, and they have done so for decades. But this case is far from peaceful coexistence. The FDA told Wyeth that Phenergan's label renders its use "safe." But the State of Vermont, through its tort law, said: "Not so."

The state-law rule at issue here is squarely pre-empted. . . .

POINTS FOR DISCUSSION

1. How does preemption by administrative action raise different federalism concerns than preemption by federal statutes? Do the Justices adequately address these concerns?

2. In *Geier*, Justice Stevens wrote in dissent:

> The signal virtues of [the] presumption [against preemption] are its placement of the power of pre-emption squarely in the hands of Congress, which is far more suited than the Judiciary to strike the appropriate state/federal balance (particularly in areas of traditional state regulation), and its requirement that Congress speak clearly when exercising that power. In this way, the structural safeguards inherent in the normal operation of the legislative process operate to defend state interests from undue infringement.

How, in Justice Stevens' view, does the presumption against preemption relate to the political safeguards of federalism? Does the presumption against preemption unduly burden Congress in exercising its enumerated powers?

3. Are the different categories of preemption involved in these cases—including express, conflict, and obstacle preemption—unnecessarily complex? Is a simpler preemption doctrine possible or desirable? Keep this question in mind as you read the next section.

4. RETHINKING PREEMPTION

In the following selection, Professor Caleb Nelson argues that the Supremacy Clause, understood in historical context, provides for preemption when state law contradicts a valid federal law. He contends that this contradiction principle encompasses "express," "conflict," and "field" preemption, but that the Supremacy Clause does not itself establish a principle of "obstacle" preemption. Finally, Professor Nelson explains that the Supremacy Clause does not support a "presumption against preemption." As you read this article, consider:

- How would the contradiction principle that Professor Nelson advocates affect existing preemption law?
- How would the preemption cases you have read be decided under this contradiction principle?

CALEB NELSON, PREEMPTION

86 Va. L. Rev. 225, 232, 234-242, 245-247, 250-252,
254-256, 260-262, 303-305 (2000)

Most commentators who write about preemption agree on at least one thing: Modern preemption jurisprudence is a muddle. . . .

As the Supreme Court and virtually all commentators have acknowledged, the Supremacy Clause is the reason that valid federal statutes trump state law. For too long, though, courts have treated the Supremacy Clause chiefly as a symbol—a rhetorical expression of federal dominance, but a provision with little practical content of its own. . . .

[T]he Supremacy Clause supplies a concrete test for preemption: It requires courts to ignore state law if (but only if) state law contradicts a valid rule established by federal law, so that applying the state law would entail disregarding the valid federal rule. In this respect, questions about whether a federal statute preempts state law are no different from questions about whether one statute repeals another. . . . [I]ndeed, the Supremacy Clause explicitly draws upon the traditional framework for repeals. Although changes in the techniques of drafting laws have obscured this point, early courts, legislators, and commentators understood the connection between preemption and repeals: They routinely discussed preemption in terms of whether federal law "repealed" state law, and they used the established framework for repeals to analyze this question.

A. Some Background: How Legal Draftsmen Superseded Prior Laws
1. The Traditional Rule of Priority

To understand the Supremacy Clause, we first need to understand how legal draftsmen of the late eighteenth century superseded existing laws. If a state legislature was aware of a particular statute that it wanted to replace with a new law, it could include a clause in the new law expressly repealing the old one. But official records were often poor, and legislators might not be aware of all the existing laws on a particular subject.

To get around this problem, or to avoid the burden of having to list all repealed statutory provisions separately, legislatures sometimes enacted general clauses repealing all prior legislation within the purview of the new statute. Such clauses made clear that the new statute occupied the field. But they had their own drawbacks; the legislature might inadvertently be repealing a useful law that was perfectly consistent with the new statute.

Rather than enact such repealing clauses, legal draftsmen could simply take advantage of the hoary maxim *leges posteriores priores contrarias abrogant*— later laws abrogate contrary prior ones. As William Blackstone summarized the principle, "where words are clearly repugnant in two laws, the later law takes place of the elder: *leges posteriores priores contrarias abrogant* is a maxim of universal law, as well as of our own constitutions."[35]

This rule of priority grew out of necessity. When two statutes were "repugnant" within the meaning of the rule, it would have been logically impossible for courts to follow both; courts that gave effect to one would not be giving effect to the other. In the language of the day, "repugnant" and "contrary" (the English equivalent of *contrarias*) meant the same thing as "contradictory." Thus, Samuel Johnson defined "repugnant" to mean "contrary" and "repugnantly" to mean "contradictorily"; his definition of "contrary" included both "contradictory" and "repugnant," while his definition of "to contradict" included "to be contrary to" and "to repugn."[36] . . .

When two statutes were *contrariae* or "repugnant," then, some rule of priority was essential. Consider Blackstone's example: Statute #1 says that no one is qualified to be a juror unless he has an income of £20 per year, while Statute #2 (as construed by the courts) says that everyone with some smaller income is qualified to be a juror. Because these rules contradict each other, the statutes could not have what Blackstone called "a concurrent efficacy." After all, when presented with a prospective juror whose income was below what Statute #1 required but above what Statute #2 specified, a court that followed Statute #1 would be disregarding Statute #2 (and vice versa). Courts would have to choose between the two rules, and Blackstone's maxim told them how to do so: In the case of contradiction, the later statute prevailed. All of the leading authorities agreed.[41]

---

35. 1 William Blackstone, Commentaries 59 (1765). . . .

36. Samuel Johnson, A Dictionary of the English Language (London, W. Strahan 1755) (unpaginated).

41. See, e.g., 4 Matthew Bacon, A New Abridgment of the Law 638 (London, W. Strahan 4th ed. 1778); 4 Edward Coke, Institutes of the Laws of England 43 (London, M. Flesher 1644); 2 T. Cunningham, A New and Complete Law Dictionary (London, 2d ed. 1771), tit. Statute; see also The Federalist No. 78, at 468 (Alexander Hamilton) (Clinton Rossiter ed., 1961) (noting the traditional rule that "in determining between two contradictory laws," courts should prefer "the last in order of time").

2. "Non Obstante" *Clauses and the Traditional Rule of Construction*

The widespread acceptance of this principle creates a puzzle. Statutes enacted by the early state legislatures often specified that they applied notwithstanding any provisions to the contrary in prior laws. The precise wording of these clauses varied from state to state and from statute to statute. Many statutes provided that they applied "any law to the contrary notwithstanding" or "any law, usage or custom to the contrary notwithstanding." Others used some variation of the formulation "any thing in any law to the contrary notwithstanding." But in one form or another, such *"non obstante* clauses" (named after the Latin phrase for "notwithstanding") were ubiquitous in the session laws of every state.

The puzzle is this: What work did the *non obstante* clauses do? Given the well-established principle that a new statute would abrogate contrary prior statutes anyway, weren't later commentators on legislative drafting correct to dismiss such clauses as superfluous?

The answer lies in the equally well-established principle that a new statute should not be read to contradict an earlier one (or a common-law rule) if the two laws can possibly be harmonized. Then as now, courts and commentators unanimously agreed that "repeals by implication are not favoured in law." People gave various reasons for their reluctance to read a newer statute to contradict (and therefore impliedly repeal) an earlier one. But whatever the reason, courts hesitated to read one statute to abrogate another if a harmonizing construction was possible.

The presumption against reading a statute in a way that would contradict prior law (and the related presumption that statutes in derogation of common-law principles should be strictly construed) created an obvious problem for legislatures. Sometimes legislatures *wanted* a new statute to supersede whatever prior law it might contradict. But in the absence of some direction to the contrary, courts might give the new statute a strained construction in order to harmonize it with prior law. The presumption against implied repeals, then, might cause courts to distort the new statute.

The *non obstante* clause addressed this problem. Far from being superfluous, it established an important rule of construction: A *non obstante* clause in the new statute acknowledged that the statute might contradict prior law and instructed courts not to apply the general presumption against implied repeals. Rather than straining the new statute in order to harmonize it with prior law, courts were supposed to give the new statute its natural meaning and to let the chips fall where they may. . . .

B. Reading the Supremacy Clause as a Legal Provision

With this legal background in place, we are now in a position to understand the Supremacy Clause. The Clause declares that the Constitution, treaties, and valid federal statutes "shall be the supreme Law of the Land; and the Judges in every State shall be bound thereby, any Thing in the Constitution or Laws of any State to the Contrary notwithstanding." For present purposes, we can break the Clause down into three aspects: (1) the declaration that federal law is the "Law of the Land" and that "the Judges in every State shall be bound thereby"; (2) the further declaration that federal law is the "supreme" law of the land; and (3) the statement that federal law is binding "any Thing in the Constitution or Laws of any State to the Contrary notwithstanding."

I hope to persuade readers of two basic points. . . . First, the Supremacy Clause puts the doctrine of preemption within the same general framework as the traditional doctrine of repeals. . . . [T]his point has important implications for "obstacle" preemption. Second, the final portion of the Supremacy Clause is a *non obstante* provision. . . . [T]his point has important implications for the presumption against preemption.

1. The Rule of Applicability: Federal Law in State Courts

The first aspect of the Supremacy Clause may strike modern readers as highfalutin rhetoric. But it serves a straightforward function: It sets out what might be called a "rule of applicability," making clear that federal law applies even in state courts. At least as far as the courts are concerned, then, federal statutes take effect automatically within each state and form part of the same body of jurisprudence as state statutes. . . .

[T]his was an important point. Under prevailing conceptions of the law of nations, the laws of one country did not apply in another country's courts of their own force, but only as a matter of comity. The judges in each state therefore had discretion to refuse to apply foreign laws. . . . In the absence of something like the Supremacy Clause, state courts might have sought to analogize federal statutes to the laws of a foreign sovereign, which they could ignore under principles of international law. . . .

2. The Rule of Priority

It was not enough, however, simply to declare that federal laws take effect of their own force within each state. If federal laws were merely on a par with state statutes, then they would supersede whatever preexisting state laws they contradicted, but they might themselves be superseded by subsequent acts of the state legislature. When two statutes contradicted each other and courts had to decide which one to follow, the established rule of priority was that the later statute prevailed.

Not surprisingly, the second aspect of the Supremacy Clause substitutes a *federal* rule of priority for the traditional temporal rule of priority. The Supremacy Clause not only makes valid federal law part of the same body of jurisprudence as state law, but also declares that within that body of jurisprudence federal law is "supreme"—a word that mean[t] "highest in authority." Under this new rule of priority, when courts had to choose between following a valid federal law and following a state law, the federal law would prevail even if the state law had been enacted more recently. . . .

[W]hile the Supremacy Clause changes the old rule of priority, it does not change what *triggers* the rule of priority. To borrow Madison's words, the Supremacy Clause's rule of priority matters only when state law is "repugnant to" valid federal law; the rule of priority comes into play only when courts cannot apply *both* state law *and* federal law, but instead must choose between them.

When we work through the Supremacy Clause with preemption in mind, we notice a striking fact: Even though the Supremacy Clause is the reason why courts sometimes must ignore state law, the Clause actually says very little about state law. The doctrine of preemption — the displacement of state law by federal law — is instead derivative. Taken as a whole, the Supremacy Clause says that courts must apply all valid rules of federal law. To the extent that applying state law would keep them from doing so, the Supremacy Clause requires courts to disregard the state rule and follow the federal one. But this is the extent of the preemption it requires. Under the Supremacy Clause, any obligation to disregard state law flows entirely from the obligation to follow federal law. . . .

The constitutional test for preemption is thus the same as the traditional test for repeal: Can state and federal law stand together, or do they establish contradictory rules? . . .

3. The Rule of Construction

The Supremacy Clause's final phrase — which, as we shall see, is a *non obstante* provision — confirms the connection between preemption and repeals. Indeed, to overlook that connection is to make this phrase superfluous. The Supremacy Clause's final fourteen words explicitly draw on the framework of repeals, and they serve a function only within that framework.

Modern readers, who consider preemption outside of that framework, are left scratching their heads over the Supremacy Clause's alleged redundancy: Once we have been told that valid federal law is supreme and binding, we see no reason to be told that it applies "any Thing in the Constitution or Laws of any State to the Contrary notwithstanding." Understood in light of the prevailing conventions for repeals, however, these words addressed a specific problem that remained even after the Supremacy Clause established its rules of applicability and priority. The rule of applicability told state courts to treat the federal Constitution, treaties, and valid federal statutes as "in-state law," and the rule of priority told them that the federal portion of "in-state law" trumped (or impliedly repealed) whatever aspects of the state portion it contradicted. But if the relevant provision of federal law did not contain a *non obstante* clause, courts might hesitate to read it in a way that created such a contradiction. Applying the normal presumption against implied repeals, they might strain the federal law's meaning in order to harmonize it with state law.

To be sure, the reasons for reading one law to avoid contradicting another are weaker when the two laws were enacted by different legislative bodies; it makes more sense to presume that statutes enacted by the same legislature will be consistent with each other than that statutes enacted by Congress will always be consistent with statutes enacted by the states. But the Supremacy Clause did not rely upon state courts to reach this conclusion on their own. Instead, the final part of the Supremacy Clause is a global *non obstante* provision. This provision established a rule of construction, telling courts not to apply the traditional presumption against implied repeals in determining whether federal law contradicts state law. Thus, even if a federal statute or treaty did not itself contain a *non obstante* provision, the Supremacy Clause told courts not to strain its meaning in order to harmonize it with state law. . . .

Like the rest of the Supremacy Clause, the *non obstante* provision is carefully formulated. It does not affect the presumption against reading two *federal* statutes to contradict each other; in that situation, the normal presumption against implied repeals continues to apply in full force. But the *non obstante* provision does caution against straining the meaning of a federal law to avoid a contradiction with *state* law. Unless there is some particular reason (over and above the general presumption against implied repeals) to believe that Congress meant to avoid such a contradiction, the Supremacy Clause indicates that the content of state law should not alter the meaning of federal law. . . .

C. Simplifying the Analytical Framework for Preemption Cases

When we put the various aspects of the Supremacy Clause together, we can clear away the overgrowth created by the Supreme Court's existing analytical framework for preemption cases. As we have seen, the rule of applicability and the rule of priority combine to mean that courts must follow all valid rules of federal law. But if courts can follow state law too, the Supremacy Clause leaves them free to do so. Under the Supremacy Clause, then, the test for preemption is simple: Courts are required to disregard state law if, but only if, it contradicts a rule validly established by federal law. . . .

The logical-contradiction test is not confined to instances of what the Court calls "conflict" preemption. It also comfortably accommodates both "express" preemption and appropriate instances of "field" preemption. As Laurence Tribe has noted, rules established by federal law can be either "substantive" or "jurisdictional"; substantive rules tend to regulate conduct directly, while jurisdictional rules tend to say that states may *not* regulate certain areas of conduct (or at least may not do so in particular ways).[108] It is easy to see how a "substantive" rule of federal law can contradict a state-law rule: If state law purports to authorize something that federal law forbids or to penalize something that federal law gives people an unqualified right to do, then courts would have to choose between applying the federal rule and applying the state rule, and the Supremacy Clause requires them to apply the federal rule. But a "jurisdictional" rule of federal law — of the sort typically associated with "field" preemption, whether express or implied — can also contradict a state-law rule. After all, if a state purports to regulate the forbidden field, a court would have to choose between giving legal effect to the state regulation and giving legal effect to the federal rule depriving such regulations of authority. Again, the Supremacy Clause tells the court to resolve this contradiction in favor of the federal rule (if that rule is within Congress's power to promulgate).

Once we recognize that all preemption cases are about contradiction between state and federal law, we should begin to question the usefulness of dividing them into the separate analytical categories of "express" preemption, "field" preemption, and "conflict" preemption. The Supreme Court itself has been unable to keep these categories "rigidly distinct," and they only get in the way of its analysis. . . .

---

108. See 1 Laurence H. Tribe, American Constitutional Law 1177 (3d ed. 2000). . . .

The Supremacy Clause requires preemption only when the rules provided by state and federal law contradict each other, so that a court cannot simultaneously follow both.

It follows that the modern doctrine of "obstacle" preemption has no place as a doctrine of constitutional law. Some federal statutes may establish (or authorize courts to establish) a subconstitutional rule of obstacle preemption. But others do not. The general doctrine of obstacle preemption must therefore give way to a more careful analysis of the rules established by the particular federal statute in question.

The same is true of the general presumption against preemption. When understood in its historical context, the *non obstante* provision in the Supremacy Clause tells courts that the general presumption against implied repeals does not apply in preemption cases. The *non obstante* provision rejects an artificial presumption that Congress did not intend to contradict any state laws and that federal statutes must therefore be harmonized with state law. It also undermines the notion that courts should automatically give federal statutes "narrow" readings in order to preserve the maximum possible scope for state authority.

In a sense, my analysis of the Supremacy Clause points in two different directions. Recognizing that preemption is all about contradiction would tend to rein in the potential breadth of "implied" preemption. In the realm of "obstacle" preemption, for instance, courts could no longer find preemption simply because they think that state law hinders accomplishment of the "full purposes and objectives" behind a federal statute; courts would first have to determine that the federal statute expresses or implies a rule of obstacle preemption broad enough to cover the state law. . . . On the other hand, eliminating the general presumption against preemption would tend to cut in the opposite direction: Although courts would find preemption only when state and federal law contradict each other, they would not indulge an artificial presumption against reading federal statutes to establish rules that contradict state law. The net effect would probably be to reduce the scope of "implied" preemption and to expand the scope of "express" preemption.

Of course, if Congress *wants* the courts to continue applying a general doctrine of "obstacle" preemption, it is free to enact preemption clauses to that effect. In the absence of such legislation, however, the Court's current tests for "implied" preemption let judges infer obstacle-preemption clauses that are hard to attribute to Congress. Conversely, the Court's tests for "express" preemption encourage judges to give crabbed readings to the preemption clauses that Congress actually does enact. If one accepts the common premise that " '[w]hether latent federal power should be exercised to displace state law is primarily a decision for Congress,' not the federal courts,"[239] these results seem precisely backward.

---

239. Atherton v. FDIC, 519 U.S. 213, 218 (1997) (quoting Wallis v. Pan Am. Petroleum Corp., 384 U.S. 63, 68 (1966)).

POINTS FOR DISCUSSION

1. How would the contradiction principle that Professor Nelson identifies affect existing preemption law?

2. Assuming Professor Nelson's account of the original meaning of the Supremacy Clause is accurate, should courts adopt it as the law of preemption?

3. How would the cases you have read on preemption in this chapter be decided under the contradiction principle?

PART III

JUDICIAL FEDERALISM AND RULES OF DECISION

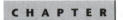

CHAPTER 8

FRAMING SOURCE OF LAW QUESTIONS IN FEDERAL COURTS

Thus far, you have extensively considered the regulatory powers of the federal and state governments. You now will consider the *judicial* powers of the United States. Questions of federal judicial power directly relate to many issues you have considered. Just as Article I limits congressional power by enumeration, Article III limits federal court jurisdiction by enumeration. Article III, Section 2 provides:

> The judicial Power shall extend to all Cases, in Law and Equity, arising under this Constitution, the Laws of the United States, and Treaties made, or which shall be made, under their Authority;—to all cases affecting Ambassadors, other public Ministers and Consuls;—to all Cases of admiralty and maritime Jurisdiction;—to Controversies to which the United States shall be a Party;—to Controversies between two or more States;—between a State and Citizens of another State;—between Citizens of different States;—between Citizens of the same State claiming Lands under Grants of different States, and between a State, or the Citizens thereof, and foreign States, Citizens or Subjects.

The Founders expressed various reasons for providing federal court jurisdiction over these particular categories of cases and controversies. The Arising Under Clause was meant—in tandem with the Supremacy Clause—to ensure the proper enforcement of federal law.

> The Founders of the Constitution adopted the Supremacy and Arising Under Clauses of the Constitution to prevent states from undermining the proper enforcement of enacted federal laws. Through these clauses, they designated the "Constitution," "Laws," and "Treaties" as supreme municipal law in the states, binding on state judges and enforceable in federal courts. . . .

Anthony J. Bellia Jr. & Bradford R. Clark, *The Federal Common Law of Nations*, 109 Colum. L. Rev. 1, 34 (2009) (footnotes omitted).

The Founders provided federal court jurisdiction over other categories of disputes—such as cases affecting ambassadors, cases of admiralty and maritime jurisdiction, and controversies between a state, or state citizen, and a foreign nation or its citizens-subjects—because they implicated foreign relations and commercial interests of the United States.

> The Convention . . . chose . . . to extend the judicial power to several types of cases in which the law of nations was likely to apply. Prominent Framers strenuously argued for federal jurisdiction over these categories . . . in order to prevent state courts from generating foreign conflict by disregarding such law. . . .
>
> The law merchant, or general commercial law, would often furnish the rule of decision in diversity suits involving both American and foreign citizens. . . . Likewise, the law maritime typically governed in private maritime cases. The Founders recognized that federal jurisdiction over such cases was necessary to encourage interstate and international trade and commerce.

Id. at 38, 42 (footnotes omitted).

Upon ratification, judges and other public officials struggled to understand the relationship between the Article III judicial power and the regulatory powers of the political branches. At the Founding, various sources of law provided rules of decision in cases within Article III's jurisdictional grant. Certainly, a validly enacted federal law—the Constitution, an act of Congress, or a treaty—could supply a rule of decision in federal court. But other sources of law could as well, including state law, the law of nations, the law maritime, or the law merchant. A question that arose early—and that continues to arise—is when, if ever, a federal court's application of a non-federally enacted rule of decision interferes with the lawmaking prerogatives of the political branches.

This question arose early with respect to "federal common law" as a potential source of law in federal courts. In England, the central courts exercised a general common law jurisdiction. The structure of government that the Constitution established for the United States differed, however, from the English structure in important respects. The Constitution both established a separation of powers among the three branches of the national government and recognized dual sovereignty between the national government and the states. Would a federal judicial power to develop common law for the United States comport with either the Constitution's allocation of federal lawmaking authority to the political branches (separation of powers) or its limitation of federal lawmaking authority to certain enumerated powers (federalism)? The concept of "federal common law"—a national common law for the United States—implicated both separation of powers and federalism. Members of the Founding generation came to debate the question of federal common law intensely, and such debates endure today.

To understand present-day source of law questions in federal courts, it is crucial to appreciate source of law questions as they arose historically. Accordingly, this chapter examines the development of source law questions from the Founding to the Supreme Court's landmark opinion in *Erie Railroad v. Tompkins*, 304 U.S. 64 (1938). The next chapter examines source of law questions as they have arisen after *Erie*.

In the Judiciary Act of 1789, Congress provided a general source of law rule for United States courts. Section 34, which came to be known as the Rules of Decision Act, provided:

> [T]he laws of the several states, except where the constitution, treaties or statutes of the United States shall otherwise require or provide, shall be regarded

> as rules of decision in trials at common law in the courts of the United States in cases where they apply.

Act of Sept. 24, 1789, ch. 20, §34 1 Stat. 73, 92. The Rules of Decision Act endures today, in somewhat different form, in 28 U.S.C. §1652:

> The laws of the several states, except where the Constitution or treaties of the United States or Acts of Congress otherwise require or provide, shall be regarded as rules of decision in civil actions in the courts of the United States, in cases where they apply.

To understand §34 of the Judiciary Act of 1789, it is necessary to appreciate the various sources of law that its drafters and other members of the Founding generation recognized.

First, its drafters recognized three forms of *United States* law — (1) the Constitution, (2) treaties, and (3) statutes of the United States ("where the *constitution*, *treaties* or *statutes* of the United States shall otherwise require or provide").

Second, its drafters recognized the existence of *state* law ("the laws of the several *states*"). State law assumed various forms. States had constitutions, and their legislatures enacted statutes. After the Declaration of Independence, states individually adopted the common law of England as state law. As adopted and subsequently developed, state common law was state law. Core areas of common law regulation included property, crime, and procedure.

Third, members of the Founding generation recognized the existence of *general* law. General law was distinguishable from *local*, or *municipal*, law. Local law was the law of a particular sovereign. Thus, the common law was local law of England, as were acts of Parliament. A state constitution, state statutes, and the common law adopted in a state were local laws of that state. The Constitution and acts of Congress were local laws of the United States. General law, in contrast to local law, was understood to be not the law of a particular sovereign but a transnational law — the law of civilized nations. Writers at the time described various categories of general law. They included (1) the law of nations, (2) the law maritime, and (3) the law merchant (the general commercial law). These categories were not always mutually exclusive, but they provide helpful categories for understanding the concept of general law. Section 34 specified that state law and federal law provided rules of decision in federal courts "in cases where they apply." This language may well have suggested that in cases where state law and federal law did *not* apply, general law applied.

As you read the materials that follow, bear in mind the distinction between *common law* and *general law*. There is a tendency to conflate all forms of unwritten law into the category "common law," generating confusion. Common law was local to a particular sovereign. General law was transnational in nature. It might well be that a state's common law incorporated general law as part of the state's local law. For example, English judges described the law of nations — a category of general law — as part of the common law of England. "Common law" and "general law" were not, however, interchangeable terms. Even if the common law (*viz.* local law) of a state recognized and incorporated general law, not all common law was general law. If you remain mindful of the distinction between common law and general law, you will better understand the development of source of law questions in the United States.

Under Article III, various sources of law could provide rules of decision in federal courts. Article III contemplated the Constitution, laws, and treaties of the United States as rules of decision in federal courts, especially in the "arising under" grant. In a controversy "between Citizens of different States," state law or general law (in particular the law merchant) might furnish a rule of decision. General law could provide rules of decision in various Article III "cases" and "controversies." The law of nations, one category of general law, could furnish a rule in "Cases affecting Ambassadors, other public Ministers and Consuls" — for example, a rule of ambassadorial immunity. The law maritime, another category of general law, could furnish a rule in "Cases of admiralty and maritime jurisdiction" — for example, a rule for interpreting marine insurance contracts. The law merchant, yet another category of general law, could furnish a rule of decision in controversies "between Citizens of different States" or between citizens of a state and citizens of another nation — for example, rules governing bills of exchange. These are only a few illustrative examples. The point is that each of these various sources of law could properly furnish a rule of decision in particular Article III cases and controversies.

This chapter examines source of law questions in United States courts before the 1938 *Erie* decision. First, it examines whether federal courts understood themselves to have power to apply "federal common law" as a rule of decision. In other words, it examines whether federal courts had authority to develop a "local" common law for the United States. Next, it examines how general law, as distinct from federal common law, operated in United States courts. You will see how, eventually, the distinction between common law and general law broke down, leading the Supreme Court to hold in *Erie* that "[t]here is no *federal general common law." Erie*, 304 U.S. at 78.

As you read the materials in this chapter, keep in mind the following questions:

- How was federal common law understood to differ from general law as a rule of decision in federal courts?
- How did the concepts of federal common law and general law implicate federalism?
- Why did the Supreme Court reject federal common law as a rule of decision in federal courts in 1812 but persist in applying general law?
- What blurred the distinction between federal common law and general law in the nineteenth and early twentieth centuries, generating a revival of federal common law?
- Why did the Supreme Court come to reject "federal general common law" in *Erie*?

In the next chapter, you will see how source of law questions endure in United States courts — and how federalism concerns continue to frame their consideration.

A. FEDERAL COMMON LAW AND GENERAL LAW BEFORE *ERIE*

In the first decades following ratification, the question whether federal courts had power to apply *federal common law* as a rule of decision was distinct from the question whether they had power to apply *general law*. The selections in this section describe (1) early debates over the legitimacy of federal common law and (2) the manner in which federal courts applied general law as rules of decision.

1. FEDERAL COMMON LAW

The first selection describes the early debate over whether federal courts could enforce a federal common law of crime. The next two selections are judicial opinions on this question. As you read these selections, consider how the early debate over federal common law implicated federalism concerns.

Anthony J. Bellia Jr. & Bradford R. Clark, The Federal
Common Law of Nations

109 Colum. L. Rev. 1, 47-48, 53-55 (2009)

Prior to ratification, states adopted the common law of England, which incorporated the law of nations. . . . After ratification, . . . [t]he question quickly arose whether the United States could prosecute individuals in federal court for committing common law crimes. The Judiciary Act of 1789 gave federal courts exclusive jurisdiction of crimes and offenses "cognizable under the authority of the United States."[233] For the next two decades, public officials in the United States debated whether federal courts had jurisdiction to define and punish common law offenses against the United States in the absence of further congressional action. In other words, they debated whether the United States had a *municipal* common law of crimes that incorporated, among other things, certain offenses against the law of nations. This debate was not limited to federal common law crimes, however, because its resolution turned on whether the United States (as opposed to the individual states) had received the common law of England.

To understand contemporaneous opinions of early executive branch officials and judges, one must appreciate their initial assumption that the United States — like the states — had received the common law and thus could prosecute and punish common law crimes, including offenses against the law of nations. Under English law, criminal penalties and private remedies were matters of municipal governance. . . .

[T]hroughout the 1790s, federal courts enforce[d] federal common law crimes on the assumption that the United States had received the common law. In 1798, Justice Chase, sitting on the circuit court, became the first judge to question this assumption. In *United States v. Worrall*, the defendant was

---

233. §9, 1 Stat. at 76-77 (providing district court jurisdiction); §11, 1 Stat. at 78-79 (providing circuit court jurisdiction).

indicted for attempting to bribe a federal Commissioner of Revenue.[269] Worall's counsel disputed "that the common law is the law of the United States, in cases that arise under their authority."[270] He argued that "[t]he nature of our Federal compact, will not . . . tolerate this doctrine."[271] Justice Chase agreed. An "indictment solely at common law," he declared, "cannot be maintained in this Court."[272] In his view, it was "essential, that Congress should define the offences to be tried, and apportion the punishments to be inflicted, as that they should erect Courts to try the criminal, or to pronounce a sentence on conviction."[273]

The issue soon resurfaced as part of a heated debate between incumbent Federalists and ascendant Jeffersonian Republicans over the constitutionality of the Sedition Act. The Act made it a crime to "write, print, utter or publish . . . any false, scandalous and malicious" statements about Congress, the government, or the President.[274] Republicans charged that the Act was unconstitutional because it was an exercise of "a power not delegated by the Constitution, but, on the contrary, expressly and positively forbidden by one of the amendments thereto."[275] Federalists responded that "the Act presented no 'constitutional difficulty' because the federal courts were already authorized to punish seditious libel as a common-law crime."[276] Republicans denied the central premise of the Federalists' defense: " 'that the common or unwritten law' . . . makes a part of the law of these States, in their united and national capacity."[277]

James Madison led the Republican attack and raised two powerful objections to the idea that the Constitution incorporated the common law. First, he specifically denied that the common law was adopted by the Constitution because the consequence would be that "the authority of Congress [would be] co-extensive with the objects of common law."[279] That conclusion would mean that Congress's power would be "no longer under the limitations marked out in the Constitution. They would be authorized to legislate in all cases whatsoever."[280] Second, Madison argued that federal incorporation of the common law "would confer on the judicial department a discretion little short of a legislative power."[281] He explained that such incorporation would

---

269. 2 U.S. (2 Dall.) 384, 384, 28 F. Cas. 774, 774 (C.C.D. Pa. 1798) (No. 16,766).

270. Id. at 391, 28 F. Cas. at 777 (emphasis omitted).

271. Id. ("[T]he very powers that are granted [to the central government] cannot take effect until they are exercised through the medium of a law.").

272. Id. at 393, 28 F. Cas. at 778.

273. Id. at 394, 28 F. Cas. at 779.

274. Ch. 74, §2, 1 Stat. 596, 596 (1798) (expired 1801).

275. James Madison, [Virginia] Resolutions of 1798, *in* 6 The Writings of James Madison 326, 328 (Gaillard Hunt ed., 1906).

276. William R. Casto, The Supreme Court in the Early Republic: The Chief Justiceships of John Jay and Oliver Ellsworth 149 (1995) (quoting Letter from Oliver Ellsworth to Timothy Pickering (Dec. 12, 1798)).

277. Letter from James Madison to Thomas Jefferson (Jan. 18, 1800), *in* 6 The Writings of James Madison, supra note 275, at 347, 372 [hereinafter Madison, Letter].

279. Id. at 380.

280. Id.; see also 9 Annals of Cong. 3012 (1799) (statement of Rep. Nicholas) ("The nature of the [common] law of England makes it impossible that it should have been adopted in the lump into such a Government as this is; because it was a complete system for the management of all the affairs of a country.").

281. Madison, Letter, supra note 277, at 380.

"present an immense field for judicial discretion" because it would require federal courts "to decide what parts of the common law would, and what would not, be properly applicable to the circumstances of the United States."[282] In his view, giving federal judges this degree of discretion "over the law would, in fact, erect them into legislators."[283]

The debate subsided in 1801 with Thomas Jefferson's election as President and the expiration of the Sedition Act. In 1806, however, federal prosecutors charged two Federalist editors with common law seditious libel. The case reached the Supreme Court in 1812, and the Court rejected federal common law crimes.[285] Because both the Attorney General and the defendant's counsel declined to argue the case, Justice Johnson issued a brief opinion on behalf of the Court.[286] He framed the question as "whether the Circuit Courts of the United States can exercise a common law jurisdiction in criminal cases."[287] Undoubtedly referring to the debate surrounding the Sedition Act, Johnson stated that the question had long been "settled in public opinion."[288] Before a federal court may exercise jurisdiction in such a case, "[t]he legislative authority of the Union must first make an act a crime, affix a punishment to it, and declare the Court that shall have jurisdiction of the offence."[289] . . .

UNITED STATES v. HUDSON & GOODWIN

11 U.S. (7 Cranch) 32 (1812)

[T]he following opinion was delivered by . . . JOHNSON, J.

The only question which this case presents is, whether the Circuit Courts of the United States can exercise a common law jurisdiction in criminal cases. . . .

Although this question is brought up now for the first time to be decided by this Court, we consider it as having been long since settled in public opinion. In no other case for many years has this jurisdiction been asserted, and the general acquiescence of legal men shews the prevalence of opinion in favor of the negative of the proposition.

The course of reasoning which leads to this conclusion is simple, obvious, and admits of but little illustration. The powers of the general Government are made up of concessions from the several states — whatever is not expressly given to the former, the latter expressly reserve. The judicial power of the United States is a constituent part of those concessions, — that power is to be exercised by Courts organized for the purpose, and brought into existence by an effort of the legislative power of the Union. Of all the Courts which the United States may, under their general powers, constitute, one only, the Supreme Court, possesses jurisdiction derived immediately from the constitution, and of which the legislative power cannot deprive it. All other Courts

---

282. Id. at 381.
283. Id. . . .
285. United States v. Hudson & Goodwin, 11 U.S. (7 Cranch) 32, 34 (1812).
286. Id. at 32.
287. Id.
288. Id.
289. Id. at 34.

created by the general Government possess no jurisdiction but what is given them by the power that creates them, and can be vested with none but what the power ceded to the general Government will authorize them to confer.

It is not necessary to inquire whether the general Government, in any and what extent, possesses the power of conferring on its Courts a jurisdiction in cases similar to the present; it is enough that such jurisdiction has not been conferred by any legislative act, if it does not result to those Courts as a consequence of their creation.

And such is the opinion of the majority of this Court: For, the power which congress possess to create Courts of inferior jurisdiction, necessarily implies the power to limit the jurisdiction of those Courts to particular objects, and when a Court is created, and its operations confined to certain specific objects, with what propriety can it assume to itself a jurisdiction — much more extended — in its nature very indefinite — applicable to a great variety of subjects — varying in every state in the Union — and with regard to which there exists no definite criterion of distribution between the district and Circuit Courts of the same district?

The only ground on which it has ever been contended that this jurisdiction could be maintained is, that, upon the formation of any political body, an implied power to preserve its own existence and promote the end and object of its creation, necessarily results to it. But, without examining how far this consideration is applicable to the peculiar character of our constitution, it may be remarked that it is a principle by no means peculiar to the common law. It is coeval, probably, with the first formation of a limited Government, belongs to a system of universal law, and may as well support the assumption of many other powers as those more peculiarly acknowledged by the common law of England.

But if admitted as applicable to the state of things in this country, the consequence would not result from it which is here contended for. If it may communicate certain implied powers to the general Government, it would not follow that the Courts of that Government are vested with jurisdiction over any particular act done by an individual in supposed violation of the peace and dignity of the sovereign power. The legislative authority of the Union must first make an act a crime, affix a punishment to it, and declare the Court that shall have jurisdiction of the offence.

Certain implied powers must necessarily result to our Courts of justice from the nature of their institution. But jurisdiction of crimes against the state is not among those powers. To fine for contempt — imprison for contumacy — inforce the observance of order, &c. are powers which cannot be dispensed with in a Court, because they are necessary to the exercise of all others[:] and so far our Courts no doubt possess powers not immediately derived from statute, but all exercise of criminal jurisdiction in common law cases we are of opinion is not within their implied powers.

The year after *Hudson & Goodwin* was decided, Justice Johnson, sitting as a Circuit Justice, concluded that the Constitution did not permit federal courts to punish an offense against the law of nations — namely piracy — in the absence of congressional authorization. (Justice Johnson is presumed to be the author of the William Butler opinion, though it is unsigned. *See* Gary

D. Rowe, *The Sound of Silence:* United States v. Hudson & Goodwin, *the Jeffersonian Ascendancy, and the Abolition of Federal Common Law Crimes*, 101 Yale L.J. 919, 926 n. 34 (1992)). In this opinion, Justice Johnson further developed the federalism and separation of powers implications of federal common law crimes. In 1813, Justice Story, sitting as a Circuit Justice, attempted to distinguish *Hudson & Goodwin* in a case involving prosecution of an individual for forcibly rescuing a prize—an offense against the law of nations. See *United States v. Coolidge*, 25 F. Cas. 619 (C.C.D. Mass. 1813). When *Coolidge* reached the Supreme Court, a majority declined "to review their former decision in [*Hudson & Goodwin*], or draw it into doubt." *United States v. Coolidge*, 14 U.S. (1 Wheat.) 415, 416 (1816).

THE TRIAL OF WILLIAM BUTLER FOR PIRACY (1813)

C.C.D. S.C. 1813

At a special Circuit Court for the Trial of Crimes against the United States, held at Charleston on the 22d June, 1813, William Butler, Captain of the Revenge Privateer, was indicted for Piracy, in robbing on the High-Seas a Spanish Vessel called the Inis, of a large Sum in Specie and Bullion.

[JOHNSON, CIRCUIT JUSTICE:]

The question whether the Courts of the United States possess common law jurisdiction in criminal cases, is one which about the year [1797] excited much interest throughout the United States. . . .

From that time the current of public opinion appears to have set so strongly against it, that we hear of no cases for a long time in which the Courts of the United States have persisted in this claim. . . .

It was not, as far as I can recollect, until the year 1811, that this claim to jurisdiction was again revived. This was in the Case of the United States *vs.* Hudson & Goodwin, which was an indictment for a Libel on the President, preferred in the State of Connecticut, and which was referred to the Supreme Court on a division of the Judges. In this Case a solemn and almost unanimous decision took place against the claim of jurisdiction. It has been said of this Case, that it was only decided by a majority; but I am confident that Judge Washington alone, if any one, at that time dissented from the opinion. It is true, it was not argued, but the true reason was, the universal conviction prevailing at the bar, that opinion had, in every department, settled down against it. And they had best reason for the conviction—for, in the Case of Boleman & Swartwont, . . . so explicit an opinion had been expressed by the Chief Justice [John Marshall] on this subject, as left no longer a doubt upon the mind of the Bar of what must be the decision of the Supreme Court on this subject, whenever it should be brought up distinctly for their determination.

The words of the Chief Justice to which I allude are the following:

"As a preliminary to any investigation of the merits of this motion, this Court deem it proper to declare, that it disclaims all jurisdiction not given by the Constitution or by the laws of the United States."

"Courts which originate *in the Common Law* possess a jurisdiction which must be regulated by the Common Law, until some statute shall change their established principles; but Courts which are created by *written law, and whose jurisdiction is defined by written law, cannot transcend that jurisdiction.* The reasoning from the Bar in relation to it may be answered by the single observation, that for the *meaning* of the term *habeas corpus* resort may unquestionably be had to the Common Law; but the power to award the writ by any of the Courts of the United States must be given by written law."

"This opinion is not to be considered as abridging the power of Courts over their own officers, or to protect themselves and their members from being disturbed in the exercise of their functions. It extends only to the power of taking cognisance of any question between individuals or *between the government and individuals.*" . . .

[Here is] a brief view of the ground on which rests the criminal jurisdiction of the United States generally and of this Court in particular.

Treason against the United States is the only offence which the Constitution defines, and it is remarkable, that the definition of this offence, as well as the clause which vests in Congress the power of declaring the punishment of it, is to be found in that article which relates to the judicial department. All the other penal powers of the United States, are to be found arranged under another article, having for its object the establishment of the legislative department of the general government.

Thus under the 8th Section of the 1st Article we find enumerated among the powers of Congress, the power "To provide for the punishment of counterfeiting the Securities, and current Coin of the United States."

"To define and punish Piracies and Felonies committed on the High-Seas, and offences against the Law of Nations."

"To exercise exclusive legislation in all cases whatsoever over such District (not exceeding ten miles square) as may be purchased for the Seat of Government and for Forts, Arsenals, &c."

And finally, "to make all laws which shall be necessary and proper for carrying into execution the foregoing powers, and all other powers vested by this Constitution in the government of the United States, or in any department or officer thereof."

Upon these four clauses of the 1st Article, and the second clause of the 3d Sect. 3d Article of the Constitution, are founded all the power over crimes which has been delegated to the general government. . . .

The last clause of the 1st Article is of a more comprehensive nature and is intended to enable Congress to enforce its legislative provisions by legal sanction. Laws, without a penalty or sanction, would be a dead letter, and the power of passing laws to carry into exercise their constitutional powers, was indispensably necessary to the exercise of those powers. Hence, under this head a discretion is vested in Congress of an extent which is only limited by certain restrictive clauses contained in the same Constitution. . . .

We maintain, that upon these clauses alone depend the criminal powers, which the general government may constitutionally exercise, — That the Article which establishes the judiciary, has nothing in it that adds to the criminal power of the United States, except the clause, which authorises Congress to declare the punishment of Treason, — That the sole object of the 3d Article is to establish a judiciary commensurate with the powers otherwise vested in Congress — to enforce the constitutional exercise of the powers of the United States on the one hand, and on the other, to protect the individual from the power of the general government, whenever the limits of constitutional power shall be transcended. The pretensions of the prosecuting officers of the United States, to implied Common Law jurisdiction over crimes, we consider an instance of this latter kind; and we maintain that the whole fabric of the Constitution is framed with sedulous care to preclude every department from the exercise of implied power.

The Convention was composed of men of the first order of talents, whose minds had been many years intently occupied with the enquiry — Whence arises it, that governments, although instituted solely for the security of the people, so generally terminate in their oppression? Equally unembarrassed by the reveries of wild theorists, and the manacled opinions of the antient world, their practical knowledge point out to them, that the evil existed in leaving to power the polypus-faculty of reproducing itself, lop it where you will. The lust of power is universal in man. . . .

Hence, the greatest excellence of every government is, the precise definite and obligatory assignment of limits to power in every department. With this view most sedulously and successfully has our Constitution been framed, and to this end, should the eye of every member in every department be indeviably directed, in every discussion which may arise upon the construction of any part of it.

It is sometimes asserted, that however applicable these observations may be to the other departments of government, they cannot be deemed so to the judiciary — that, that department has little inducement to arrogate power and is weakest in the use of it.

This opinion ought to be acted upon with great caution.

A judiciary, pure, enlightened, firm and patriotic, in unquestionably the greatest political blessing that a nation can enjoy. But, let it be ever remembered, that a judiciary must be composed of the same frail mortal materials with which every other department is filled — that it may become corrupt, weak, and luke-warm to the great interests of the State, and the security of the individuals who compose it, — and that constituted as ours is, accident by the death or removal of incumbents, may put it in the power of a corrupt executive, to model and mould it with a view to sinister purposes. And, what more powerful agent can be resorted to, to favor the views of a corrupt administration? Where are individuals to look for protection, if the judicial shield be withdrawn from between them and the arm of unprincipled power? On the other hand, suppose prejudices, or, if you will have it, virtuous error to preside at the consultations of your judiciary; and has not experience shewn us, how much administration may be embarrassed by judicial proceedings, without perhaps the possibility of effectually protecting itself against them? There is one remark on this subject which ought never to be lost sight of. Error in opinion is not punishable by impeachment. If other departments of government transcend their constitutional limits, the judiciary interposes, and possesses various methods of resisting or punishing the agents of government; by means of which unconstitutional laws are rendered inoperative. But, let the judiciary begin to assume jurisdiction by implication, and where is it to end? It necessarily possesses the right to declare laws unconstitutional — and how far in the exercise of this right may it not go, to nullify any attempts which may be made by the legislative power of the Union to check its career? It is truly appalling to reflect, when we pursue this idea, what an inundation may ensue from letting in the smallest rill of these judicial pretensions! Where would it end? . . .

[T]he advocates for this species of jurisdiction do not contend for adopting the entire system of the Common Law, but only so much of it as is essential to self-protection in the quality of a sovereign State. . . .

I think they can be shewn from their own reasoning to be incorrect. For, if the courts of the United States are to be at liberty to select such parts as in their judgment are applicable, what is this but giving as much force to one part as to another? By what rule or principle are they to be governed in the selection? I know of none; and the consequence is, either that they find the whole system in force, or what is worse, erect themselves into legislators in the selection. . . .

The reason for the adoption of the criminal Common Law into our juris-prudence, drawn from its having constituted the basis of the systems of all the individual States, we think on reflection will be found also inconclusive. . . .

[W]e find . . . every . . . State in the union, uniformly adopting, abrogating and amending the Common Law at their will. As they gradually advanced towards the right of self-government, most of them have thought the force of absolute constitutional or legislative provision necessary to give efficiency to the Common Law.

If the assertion be, that the individuals who composed these States, in their first establishment brought over with them the right of adopting the Common Law, the position, so far as they were not restrained by express stipulation, is incontestable. And, if it be further asserted, that they generally did adopt the Common Law as the foundation of their systems of jurisprudence, no one will deny it. But, in admitting the right to choose or refuse, the binding force and of consequence the penal part of that system is wholly rejected. And the conse-quence must be, that whether by constitutional provision, by statute or by early and continued practice, the adoption of the Common Law, depended upon the voluntary act of the legislative power of the several States, as much as the passage of any positive law.

The fact is, that their choice lay between the two great systems known to the civilised world, the Common and the Civil Law, either of which they might have adopted severally and entirely, or selected from both, and formed a sys-tem comprising the excellencies of both. They were best acquainted with the Common Law, were familiarised with the administration of it, and adopted it as the foundation of their respective systems, but generally have ingrafted upon it many very wise provisions drawn from the civil law; and it is a fact, that almost all the improvements in American jurisprudence are drawn from that excellent source. . . .

The many and radical discrepances which exist among the States as to the principles of the Common Law, retained in their jurisprudence, give rise to an argument against vesting the Courts of the United States with this implied jurisdiction now under consideration. Admitting the principle, upon which it is contended for, it is still necessary before any specific power is given, that it should be proven to be founded on the received law of every State in the

Union. But, who can doubt that such a point is fit only for legislative enquiry? Where is the boundary to the evil consequences arising from placing the liability of individuals to punishment upon such a footing? It would be worse than writing law in Cabalistic characters.

I have but one more remark to make on this point. Had Canada joined in the opposition to Great Britain, and become a member of the Confederation, how then would have stood the argument? The Civil Law was their birth-right, and the Common Law so far as it is now the law of that Province, was forced upon them by conquest: and, what good can there be at this day for our exercising Common Law criminal jurisdiction in our sister State of Louisiana? Perhaps I may be told that the principle is not applicable to that State, and she must be exempted from its operation. Admit it, but your government cannot go on without these implied powers, and we must at least take by implication the necessary reach of civil or Spanish criminal jurisdiction over that vast country. Surely it is wisest to reject a principle which in its application will involve us in the dilemma.

But, the advocates of this species of jurisdiction appear to be further in error, in supposing that the Constitution had left the general government under any necessity of resorting to implication for the powers necessary for its protection; and if it had, they are further in error in placing the general government in its relation to the several States on the ordinary footing of an independent sovereignty.

Where can be the necessity for resorting to Common Law jurisdiction over crimes affecting the sovereignty, rights, justice, peace, trade or police of the United States? Can any one doubt the power of the United States to pass laws which will amply serve all their purposes? What could have been the object of the Constitution in giving Congress the express power "to make all laws, which shall be necessary and proper, for carrying into execution the foregoing powers, and all other powers vested by this Constitution in the government of the United States, or in any department or officer there of?" It was evidently to take away every pretence for arrogating implied powers. The right to *pass laws* for the immediate purpose of laying and collecting duties &c. might have been claimed as necessarily resulting from the grant of those powers. But, in the exercise of that kind of collateral legislation, which might be necessary to protect herself and her officers in the exercise of her Constitutional powers, doubts and difficulties may have arisen, and to make provision against those doubts and difficulties, this general clause is inserted. Can any one doubt of the power of Congress under this clause, to pass laws, fully commensurate or even surpassing the Common Law provisions, for the punishment of offences against the sovereignty, rights, justice, peace, trade, or police of the United States? And why have they not done it in any particular case? Unquestionably, because they did not think it necessary. Why then should it be competent to the Courts of the United States, to assert that it is necessary, and proceed to punish offences against which Congress has not thought proper to legislate? Surely we should wait until summoned to the aid of the general government, or we may be deemed officious, forward and intrusive. . . .

All pretext then for arrogating jurisdiction by implication as an appendix to sovereignty, must be done away, when we find the most common and unquestionable cases to which the right of punishing is ascribed by the Common Law on the ground of sovereignty, given to the general government by express constitutional provision. Such are the cases of high treason, counterfeiting the current coin, offences on the high seas and against the law of nations. Surely the framers of the Constitution must have known best the nature of the political fabric they were about rearing—what was its inherent strength—and what were those powers which it must derive from express concession, and in thus particularising in making these concessions of power to punish, have declared that this is the power they shall exercise, and thus it shall be exercised but no otherwise. . . .

POINTS FOR DISCUSSION

1. In *Hudson & Goodwin*, the Court explained that for federal courts to have criminal jurisdiction, "[t]he legislative authority of the Union must first make an act a crime, affix a punishment to it, and declare the Court that shall have jurisdiction of the offence." In *William Butler*, Justice Johnson explained that rationale in more detail, relying in part on Article I's allocation of the power to define and punish certain crimes to Congress. Justice Johnson stated that if the judiciary selected what parts of the common law to apply, judges would "erect themselves into legislators in the selection." These are "separation of powers" arguments against federal court common law criminal jurisdiction. Are they "federalism" arguments as well? What aspects of the federal structure, if any, did these courts find, explicitly or implicitly, to preclude federal courts from exercising common law jurisdiction?

2. These cases raise interesting questions regarding the relevance of English practice to historical understandings of the U.S. Constitution. The central common law courts of Westminster in England possessed common law criminal jurisdiction. Is this fact relevant to the question whether Article III courts possess such jurisdiction? On the one hand, Article III recognizes a "judicial power of the United States." A natural referent for that power would be the judicial power of England is it existed at the Founding. On the other hand, the Constitution established a different structure of government than obtained in England, providing an explicit separation of powers among the Legislature, Executive, and Judiciary—and dual sovereignty between the federal government and the states. Moreover, it is unclear whether the proper English analogue of Article III courts would have been the central courts of Westminster. Article III courts, unlike the central courts of Westminster, were courts of limited jurisdiction. As such, they arguably were more akin to English courts of limited jurisdiction, which had only such jurisdiction as the common law or Parliament defined them to have. As Justice Johnson wrote in *William Butler*, "Courts which are created by *written law, and whose jurisdiction is defined by written law, cannot transcend that jurisdiction.*" In several cases, Article III courts analogized their jurisdiction not to English courts of general common law jurisdiction, but to English courts of limited jurisdiction. *See* Anthony J. Bellia Jr., *The Origins of Article III "Arising Under" Jurisdiction*, 57 Duke L.J. 263 273-284, 317-320 (2007). How, if at all, should courts determine what feature of historical practice and constitutional structure are *salient* to the question whether Article III courts have a common law jurisdiction?

3. In Chapters 1-3, you read various accounts of the values of dual sovereignty—historical and present day. Most of these accounts considered the value, if any, of limiting the *legislative* power of the national government to certain specified objects. In *William Butler*, Justice Johnson argued that limiting *judicial* power also serves certain values. The framers of the Constitution, he observed, were occupied with the question: "Whence arises it, that governments, although instituted solely for the security of the people, so generally terminate in their oppression?" The Constitution, he continued, was framed with the view in mind that "the greatest excellence of every government is, the precise definite and obligatory assignment of limits to power in every department." A judiciary, he asserted, may transcend limits on its authority, just as political branches may, to the detriment of "the great interests of the State, and the security of the individuals who compose it." What are the "great interests of the State, and the security of individuals" that Justice Johnson believed unauthorized judicial action threatened? How convincing are his arguments in this regard?

2. GENERAL LAW

The following selections concern not federal common law (local to the United States) but general law (transnational law). The first selection describes how general law provided rules of decision in federal courts after the Founding. The second selection—*Swift v. Tyson*, 41 U.S. (15 Pet.) 1 (1842)—is perhaps the Supreme Court's most famous case applying general law as a rule of decision. As you read these selections, consider whether judicial application of general law implicated the same federalism concerns as judicial application of federal common law.

WILLIAM A. FLETCHER, THE GENERAL COMMON LAW AND SECTION 34 OF THE JUDICIARY ACT OF 1789: THE EXAMPLE OF MARINE INSURANCE

97 Harv. L. Rev. 1513, 1517-1520, 1523-1525 (1984)

A modern reader may find it hard to understand the concept of general law employed by early nineteenth century lawyers and judges. The underlying premise was that the general law was not attached to any particular sovereign; rather, it existed by common practice and consent among a number of sovereigns. The group of relevant participants in the law-making and law-determining process varied depending on the category of general law at issue. The English common law was the law that prevailed in a single sovereignty, England. The law merchant, usually described as part of the common law, was the general law governing transactions among merchants in most of the trading nations in the world. The maritime law was an even more comprehensive and eclectic general law than the law merchant. The American courts resorted to this general body of preexisting law to provide the rules of decision in particular cases without insisting that the law be attached to any particular sovereign. . . .

During the first part of the nineteenth century, the federal courts often used the general law to supply the rule of decision. It was applied in a wide variety of cases, but most frequently and consistently in commercial cases. As an article of faith, and as a matter of substantial truth, jurisprudential writers from the middle of the eighteenth through the early nineteenth century reiterated that commercial transactions in all civilized trading countries were governed by a uniform set of commercial laws. For example, William Blackstone, a preeminently faithful reporter of the opinions of his time, referred to the law merchant in 1769 as a "great universal law," "regularly and constantly adhered to."[19]

The concept of a uniform law merchant was quite naturally imported into the treatment of commercial law by American courts. Justice James Wilson, in his Lectures on Law delivered in 1790 and 1791 in Philadelphia, referred to the law merchant as having "been admitted to decide controversies concerning bills of exchange, policies of insurance, and other mercantile transactions, both where citizens of different states, and where citizens of the same state only, have been interested in the event."[20] And he recited the ideal that "in commercial cases, all nations ought to have their laws conformable to each other."[21] The former chief justice of the Massachusetts Supreme Judicial Court, James Sullivan, in his 1801 treatise, *The History of Land Titles in Massachusetts*, wrote that the law of contracts depended on the "*jus gentium* (the general law of nations) for its origin and its expositions, rather than on any municipal regulations of particular countries."[22] Zephaniah Swift, justice and later chief justice of the Connecticut Supreme Court, wrote in his 1810 digest of the law of evidence and treatise on negotiable instruments, "In questions of commercial law, the decisions of Courts, in all civilized, and commercial nations, are to be regarded, for the purpose of establishing uniform principles in the commercial world."[23] And in the same volume, Swift wrote — somewhat optimistically, in light of the unsettled nature of some aspects of the law of negotiable instruments — that the law of bills "constitutes a branch of universal commercial law, to be governed by the customs and usages of nations, and not by municipal law."[24]

All American courts, state and federal, relied on the general law merchant in commercial cases. . . . The sense of adhering to and applying a "universal law" of commercial transactions persisted, to some degree, throughout the first half of the nineteenth century. . . .

Analytical difficulties in distinguishing between a supreme federal common law and the general . . . law are not altogether surprising . . . . [T]he general . . . law was assumed to provide the rule of decision in cases where it applied. [Virginian St. George] Tucker held this view notwithstanding his belief that such general . . . law was not a supreme federal law. In a long appendix to his edition of Blackstone published in 1803, Tucker argued vigorously that there was no national common law in the sense of a supreme

---

19. W. Blackstone, Commentaries *67.

20. 1 The Works of the Honourable James Wilson, L.L.D. 374-75 (B. Wilson ed. 1804) (footnote omitted).

21. *Id.* at 375 n.I.

22. J. Sullivan, The History of Land Titles in Massachusetts 337-38 (Boston 1801). . . .

23. Z. Swift, A Digest of the Law of Evidence, in Civil and Criminal Cases. And a Treatise on Bills of Exchange, and Promissory Notes at ix (Hartford 1810).

24. *Id.* at 245.

national law.[44] He noted that Supreme Court Justices Oliver Ellsworth and Bushrod Washington, among others, considered the common law of England to be the "unwritten law of the United States, in their national or federal capacity," and that the issue had been raised in the House of Representatives.[45] Arguing against this view of the common law, Tucker contended that, if it were adopted, the jurisdiction of the federal courts and the powers of the federal government would be unlimited:

> This question is of very great importance, not only as it regards the limits of the jurisdiction of the *federal courts*; but also, as it relates to the extent of the powers vested in the *federal government*. For, if it be true that the common law of England, has been adopted by the United States in their national, or federal capacity, the jurisdiction of the *federal courts* must be co-extensive with it; or, in other words, *unlimited*: so also, must be the jurisdiction, and authority of the *other branches* of the federal government; that is to say, their powers respectively must be, likewise, *unlimited*.[46]

But despite his argument against a *federal* common law, Tucker considered it appropriate — indeed, inescapable — that the federal courts should follow the general law . . . in cases where it applied. As he saw it, the United States circuit courts sitting in diversity should decide cases in the same way state courts would decide them — by applying whatever law was appropriate to those cases. The modern reader may be surprised by the many sources of law Tucker had in mind:

> In short, as the matters cognizable in the federal courts, belong . . . partly to the law of nations, partly to the common law of England; partly to the civil law; partly to the maritime law, comprehending the laws of Oleron and Rhodes; and partly to the general law and custom of merchants; and partly to the municipal laws of any foreign nation, or of any state in the union, where the cause of action may happen to arise, or where the suit may be instituted; so, the law of nations, the common law of England, the civil law, the law maritime, the law merchant, or the *lex loci*, or law of the foreign nation, or state, in which the cause of action may arise, or shall be decided, must in their turn be resorted to as the rule of decision, according to the nature and circumstances of each case, respectively.[47]

In other words, there were not only two categories of law, state and federal. There were also a number of categories that could be included under the term "general law" . . . . For Tucker, the notion of a federal common law was thus quite distinct from that of a general common law. The existence of the first was a matter of deep dispute, but the existence of the second was assumed. Most important, the obligation of the federal courts to apply the general law in appropriate cases was taken for granted even by those, like Tucker, who wished to limit the power of the national government. . . .

The dispute about the federal common law of crimes also illuminates early nineteenth century assumptions about the general . . . law. Reduced to its

---

44. Tucker, *Appendix to* I W. Blackstone, Commentaries at note E (S. Tucker ed. & comm. 1803).
45. *Id.* at 379-80 . . . .
46. *Id.* at 380 (emphasis in original).
47. *Id.* at 430; *see id.* at 421.

simplest terms, the question was whether the United States could prosecute crimes under the . . . common law of crimes or whether a federal statute declaring the conduct criminal was necessary for such prosecutions. Although it appears that the early sentiment of the Supreme Court was in favor of a federal common law of crimes, the issue was eventually settled the other way. But it is clear from the terms of the dispute about the federal common law of crimes that there was never any question about the existence of a general noncriminal . . . law or the ability of the federal courts to apply it. . . .

SWIFT v. TYSON

41 U.S. (16 Pet.) 1 (1842)

[Tyson bought land from speculators, Norton and Keith, using a bill of exchange. The speculators in turn gave Swift the negotiable instrument in satisfaction of a debt that they owed Swift. When Swift sought payment on the instrument from Tyson, Tyson refused to pay on the ground that the speculators had fraudulently induced him to buy land that the speculators did not own.

If Swift was a *bona fide* holder of the instrument, for a valuable consideration, Tyson had no defense to payment. Whether Swift was entitled to payment turned on whether the pre-existing debt that the speculators owed Swift was good consideration for the negotiable instrument.]

STORY, JUSTICE, delivered the opinion of the court. . . .

There is no doubt, that a bonâ fide holder of a negotiable instrument, for a valuable consideration, without any notice of facts which impeach its validity as between the antecedent parties, if he takes it under an endorsement made before the same becomes due, holds the title unaffected by these facts, and may recover thereon, although as between the antecedent parties the transaction may be without any legal validity. This is a doctrine so long and so well established, and so essential to the security of negotiable paper, that it is laid up among the fundamentals of the law, and requires no authority or reasoning to be now brought in its support. As little doubt is there, that the holder of any negotiable paper, before it is due, is not bound to prove that he is a bonâ fide holder for a valuable consideration, without notice; for the law will presume that, in the absence of all rebutting proofs, and therefore it is incumbent upon the defendant to establish by way of defence satisfactory proofs of the contrary, and thus to overcome the primâ facie title of the plaintiff.

In the present case, the plaintiff is a bonâ fide holder without notice for what the law deems a good and valid consideration, that is, for a preexisting debt; and the only real question in the cause is, whether, under the circumstances of the present case, such a pre-existing debt constitutes a valuable consideration in the sense of the general rule applicable to negotiable instruments. We say, under the circumstances of the present case, for the acceptance having been made in New York, the argument on behalf of the defendant is, that the contract is to be treated as a New York contract, and therefore to be governed by the laws of New York, as expounded by its Courts, as well upon general principles, as by the express provisions of the thirty-fourth section of the judiciary act of 1789, ch. 20. And then it is further contended, that by the law of New York, as thus expounded by its Courts, a pre-existing debt does not constitute, in the sense of the general rule, a valuable consideration applicable to negotiable instruments. . . .

[A]dmitting the doctrine to be fully settled in New York, it remains to be considered, whether it is obligatory upon this Court, if it differs from the principles established in the general commercial law. It is observable, that the Courts of New York do not found their decisions upon this point upon any local statute, or positive, fixed or ancient local usage; but they deduce the doctrine from the general principles of commercial law. It is, however, contended, that the thirty-fourth section of the judiciary act of 1789, ch. 20, furnishes a rule obligatory upon this Court to follow the decisions of the state tribunals in all cases to which they apply. That section provides "that the laws of the several states, except where the Constitution, treaties, or statutes of the United States shall otherwise require or provide, shall be regarded as rules of decision in trials at common law in the Courts of the United States, in cases where they apply." In order to maintain the argument, it is essential, therefore, to hold, that the word "laws," in this section, includes within the scope of its meaning, the decisions of the local tribunals. In the ordinary use of language it will hardly be contended that the decisions of Courts constitute laws. They are, at most, only evidence of what the laws are: and are not of themselves laws. They are often re-examined, reversed and qualified by the Courts themselves, whenever they are found to be either defective, or ill-founded, or otherwise incorrect. The laws of a state are more usually understood to mean the rules and enactments promulgated by the legislative authority thereof, or long established local customs having the force of laws. In all the various cases which have hitherto come before us for decision, this Court have uniformly supposed, that the true interpretation of the thirty-fourth section limited its application to state laws strictly local, that is to say, to the positive statutes of the state, and the construction thereof adopted by the local tribunals, and to rights and titles to things having a permanent locality, such as the rights and titles to real estate, and other matters immovable and intraterritorial in their nature and character. It never has been supposed by us, that the section did apply, or was designed to apply, to questions of a more general nature, not at all dependent upon local statutes or local usages of a fixed and permanent operation, as, for example, to the construction of ordinary contracts or other written instruments, and especially to questions of general commercial law, where the state tribunals are called upon to perform the like functions as ourselves, that is, to ascertain, upon general reasoning and legal analogies, what is the true exposition of the contract or instrument, or what is the just rule furnished by the principles of commercial law to govern the case. And we have not now the slightest difficulty in holding, that this section, upon its true intendment and construction, is strictly limited to local statutes and local usages of the character before stated, and does not extend to contracts and other instruments of a commercial nature, the true interpretation and effect whereof are to be sought, not in the decisions of the local tribunals, but in the general principles and doctrines of commercial jurisprudence. Undoubtedly, the decisions of the local tribunals upon such subjects are entitled to, and will receive, the most deliberate attention and respect of this Court; but they cannot furnish positive rules, or conclusive authority, by which our own judgments are to be bound up and governed. The law respecting negotiable instruments may be truly declared in the languages of Cicero, adopted by Lord Mansfield in Luke *v.* Lyde, 2 Burr. R. 883, 887, to be in a great measure, not the law of a single country only, but of the commercial world. . . .

It becomes necessary for us, therefore, upon the present occasion to express our own opinion of the true result of the commercial law upon the question now before us. And we have no hesitation in saying, that a pre-existing debt does constitute a valuable consideration in the sense of the general rule already stated, as applicable to negotiable instruments. Assuming it to be true, (which, however, may well admit of some doubt from the generality of the language,) that the holder of a negotiable instrument is unaffected with the equities between the antecedent parties, of which he has no notice, only where he receives it in the usual course of trade and business for a valuable consideration, before it becomes due; we are prepared to say, that receiving it in payment of, or as security for a pre-existing debt, is according to the known usual course of trade and business. And why upon principle should not a pre-existing debt be deemed such a valuable consideration? It is for the benefit and convenience of the commercial world to give as wide an extent as practicable to the credit and circulation of negotiable paper, that it may pass not only as security for new purchases and advances, made upon the transfer thereof, but also in payment of and as security for pre-existing debts. The creditor is thereby enabled to realize or to secure his debt, and thus may safely give a prolonged credit, or forbear from taking any legal steps to enforce his rights. The debtor also has the advantage of making his negotiable securities of equivalent value to cash. But establish the opposite conclusion, that negotiable paper cannot be applied in payment of or as security for pre-existing debts, without letting in all the equities between the original and antecedent parties, and the value and circulation of such securities must be essentially diminished, and the debtor driven to the embarrassment of making a sale thereof, often at a ruinous discount, to some third person, and then by circuity to apply the proceeds to the payment of his debts. What, indeed, upon such a doctrine, would become of that large class of cases, where new notes are given by the same or by other parties, by way of renewal or security to banks, in lieu of old securities discounted by them, which have arrived at maturity? Probably, more than one-half of all bank transactions in our country, as well as those of other countries, are of this nature. The doctrine would strike a fatal blow at all discounts of negotiable securities for pre-existing debts.

This question has been several times before this Court, and it has been uniformly held, that it makes no difference whatsoever as to the rights of the holder, whether the debt for which the negotiable instrument is transferred to him is a pre-existing debt, or is contracted at the time of the transfer. In each case he equally gives credit to the instrument. The cases of Coolidge *v.* Payson, 2 Wheaton, R. 66, 70, 73, and Townsley *v.* Sumrall, 2 Peters, R. 170, 182, are directly in point.

In England, the same doctrine has been uniformly acted upon. As long ago as the case of Pillans and Rose *v.* Van Mierop and Hopkins, 3 Burr. 1664, the very point was made and the objection was overruled. That, indeed, was a case of far more stringency than the one now before us; for the bill of exchange, there drawn in discharge of a pre-existing debt, was held to bind the party as acceptor, upon a mere promise made by him to accept before the bill was actually drawn. Upon that occasion Lord Mansfield, likening the case to that of a letter of credit, said, that a letter of credit may be given for money already advanced, as well as for money to be advanced in future: and the whole Court held the plaintiff entitled to recover. From that period downward there is not a single case to be found in England in which it has ever been held by the Court, that a pre-existing debt was not a valuable consideration, sufficient to protect the holder, within the meaning of the general rule, although incidental dicta have been sometimes relied on to establish the contrary, such as the dictum of Lord Chief Justice Abbott, in Smith *v.* De Witt, 6 Dowl. & Ryland 120 . . . .

Mr. Justice Bayley, in his valuable work on bills of exchange and promissory notes, lays down the rule in the most general terms. "The want of consideration," says he, "in toto or in part, cannot be insisted on, if the plaintiff or any intermediate party between him and the defendant took the bill or note bonâ fide and upon a valid consideration." Bayley on Bills, p. 499, 500, 5th London edition, 1830. It is observable that he here uses the words "valid consideration," obviously intended to make the distinction, that it is not intended to apply solely to cases, where a present consideration for advances of money on goods or otherwise takes place at the time of the transfer and upon the credit thereof. And in this he is fully borne out by the authorities. They go further, and establish, that a transfer as security for past, and even for future responsibilities, will, for this purpose, be a sufficient, valid and valuable consideration. Thus, in the case of Bosanquet *v.* Dudman, 1 Starkie, R. 1, it was held by Lord Ellenborough, that if a banker be under acceptances to an amount beyond the cash balance in his hands, every bill he holds of that customer's, bonâ fide, he is to be considered as holding for value; and it makes no difference though he hold other collateral securities, more than sufficient to cover the excess of his acceptances. The same doctrine was affirmed by Lord Eldon in Ex parte Bloxham, 8 Ves. 531, as equally applicable to past and to future acceptances. The subsequent cases of Heywood *v.* Watson, 4 Bing. R. 496, and Bramah *v.* Roberts, 1 Bing. New Ca. 469, and Percival *v.* Frampton, 2 Cromp. Mees. & Rose, 180, are to the same effect. They directly establish that a bonâ fide holder, taking a negotiable note in payment of or as security for a pre-existing debt, is a holder for a valuable consideration, entitled to protection against all the equities between the antecedent parties. And these are the latest decisions, which our researches have enabled us to ascertain to have been made in the English Courts upon the subject.

In the American Courts, so far as we have been able to trace the decisions, the same doctrine seems generally but not universally to prevail. In Brush *v.* Scribner, 11 Conn. R. 388, the Supreme Court of Connecticut, after an elaborate review of the English and New York adjudications, held, upon general principles of commercial law, that a pre-existing debt was a valuable consideration, sufficient to convey a valid title to a bonâ fide holder against all the antecedent parties to a negotiable note. There is no reason to doubt, that the same rule has been adopted and constantly adhered to in Massachusetts; and certainly there is no trace to be found to the contrary. In truth, in the silence of any adjudications upon the subject, in a case of such frequent and almost daily occurrence in the commercial states, it may fairly be presumed, that whatever constitutes a valid and valuable consideration in other cases of contract, to support titles of the most solemn nature, is held à fortiori to be sufficient in cases of negotiable instruments, as indispensable to the security of holders, and the facility and safety of their circulation. Be this as it may, we entertain no doubt, that a bonâ fide holder, for a pre-existing debt, of a negotiable instrument, is not affected by any equities between the antecedent parties, where he has received the same before it became due, without notice of any such equities. . . .

POINTS FOR DISCUSSION

1. As Judge William Fletcher observed in his article, St. George Tucker had this to say about federal common law in his edition of *Blackstone's Commentaries*:

> This question is of very great importance, not only as it regards the limits of the jurisdiction of the *federal courts*; but also, as it relates to the extent of the powers vested in the *federal government*. For, if it be true that the common law of England, has been adopted by the United States in their national, or federal capacity, the jurisdiction of the *federal courts* must be co-extensive with it; or, in other words, *unlimited*: so also, must be the jurisdiction, and authority of the *other branches* of the federal government; that is to say, their powers respectively must be, likewise, *unlimited*.

How does this view of federal common law relate to Tucker's theory you read in Chapter 1 that courts should strictly construe congressional power under the Constitution?

2. The issue before the Court in *Swift* was whether the "pre-existing debt" that Norton & Keith owed to Swift was "a valuable consideration, in the sense of the general rule applicable to negotiable instruments." The Court held that this issue was governed by "general commercial law," observing "that the Courts of New York do not found their decisions upon this point upon any local statute, or positive, fixed or ancient local usage; but they deduce the doctrine from the general principles of commercial law." English and American courts understood the law merchant to be subject to local deviations by statute or usage. *See* Anthony J. Bellia Jr. & Bradford R. Clark, *The Federal Common Law of Nations*, 109 Colum. L. Rev. 1, 20-22 (2009). Thus, it appears that if the New York court in *Swift* had founded its decision upon a New York statute or local usage deviating from general commercial law, the Court would have followed that New York deviation. The New York court, however, according to the *Swift* Court, founded its decision upon general commercial law. Accordingly, the *Swift* Court proceeded to determine whether the New York court correctly ascertained the governing rule of general commercial law. How does the question before the Court in *Swift* differ from the question before the Court in *Hudson & Goodwin*? What are the federalism implications, if any, of the *Swift* decision? Do they differ from the federalism implications of *Hudson & Goodwin*?

3. *Swift* interpreted §34 of the Judiciary Act of 1789, providing "that the laws of the several states, except where the constitution, treaties or statutes of the United States shall otherwise require or provide, shall be regarded as rules of decision, in trials at common law, in the courts of the United States, in cases where they apply." Justice Story famously wrote for the Court that

> [i]n the ordinary use of language, it will hardly be contended, that the decisions of courts constitute laws. They are, at most, only evidence of what the laws are, and are not of themselves laws. . . . The laws of a state are more usually understood to mean the rules and enactments promulgated by the legislative authority thereof, or long established local customs having the force of laws.

What did Justice Story mean by this statement? Had New York courts applied a New York statute or local usage as the rule of decision — instead of looking to general commercial law — what law would Justice Story have applied under the Rules of Decision Act?

4. At the time of *Swift*, a state court would not necessarily have deemed itself bound to follow a Supreme Court determination of general law. The state court would consider itself free to determine for itself the content of general law. Would the analysis differ if the Supreme Court styled its rule of decision "federal common law" instead of "general law"?

B. *ERIE* AND THE REJECTION OF FEDERAL GENERAL COMMON LAW

After *Swift v. Tyson*, the line between "general law" and "local law" became increasingly blurred. States began enacting principles of general law into state law and otherwise incorporating them into the "local" common law of the state. At the same time, federal courts increasingly described certain principles of local (state) law as general law and general law as "federal law." By describing state law as general law, federal courts independently determined the content of such law, rather than looking to state sources. Moreover, by describing general law as federal law, federal courts suggested that such law was preemptive of state law — and thus applicable in state and federal courts alike:

> As the positivistic thinking that culminated in *Erie* came to prevail, courts began a process of attributing matters of general law to either state or federal law. For example, in *Southern Railway Co. v. Prescott*, [240 U.S. 632 (1916),] the Supreme Court determined that the Interstate Commerce Act "manifest[ed] the intent of Congress that the obligation of the carrier with respect to the services within the purview of the statute shall be governed by uniform rule in the place of the diverse requirements of state legislation and decisions." As Congress had set forth no such uniform rule, general principles had to govern. To generate uniformity, the Court characterized the operation of general principles in this area as a federal matter: "[T]he measure of liability under [the Act] must . . . be regarded as a federal question. . . . And the question . . . is none the less a Federal one because it must be resolved by the application of general principles of the common law."

Anthony J. Bellia Jr., *State Courts and the Making of Federal Common Law*, 153 U. Pa. L. Rev. 825, 897-899 (2005) (footnotes omitted).

State courts responded differently to the "federalization" of general law by federal courts:

> Where the Supreme Court "federalized" general . . . law, state courts as a standard practice claimed to follow Supreme Court determinations of those principles. In other matters, general law remained distinct from federal law. It is interesting to observe how state courts treated Supreme Court precedent on general law regarding such matters. In countless cases, state courts simply explained how their determinations of federal law were "affirmed by" or "supported under" Supreme Court decisions. In other cases (fewer and more far between), state courts voluntarily overturned their own precedents on matters of general law in light of Supreme Court precedent on such matters, or deemed themselves compelled to follow such Supreme Court precedents. . . . In other cases, state courts rejected Supreme Court determinations of general principles.

Id. at 899-900. In *Erie Railroad v. Tompkins*, 304 U.S. 64 (1938), the Supreme Court came to hold that "[t]here is no federal general common law." As you read *Erie*, carefully identify the federalism issues that its analysis implicates.

Erie Railroad Co. v. Tompkins

304 U.S. 64 (1938)

Mr. Justice Brandeis delivered the opinion of the Court.

The question for decision is whether the oft-challenged doctrine of *Swift v. Tyson* shall now be disapproved.

Tompkins, a citizen of Pennsylvania, was injured on a dark night by a passing freight train of the Erie Railroad Company while walking along its right of way at Hughestown in that State. He claimed that the accident occurred through negligence in the operation, or maintenance, of the train; that he was rightfully on the premises as licensee because [he was] on a commonly used beaten footpath which ran for a short distance alongside the tracks; and that he was struck by something which looked like a door projecting from one of the moving cars. To enforce that claim he brought an action in the federal court for southern New York, which had jurisdiction because the company is a corporation of that State. It denied liability; and the case was tried by a jury.

The Erie insisted that its duty to Tompkins was no greater than that owed to a trespasser. It contended, among other things, that its duty to Tompkins, and hence its liability, should be determined in accordance with the Pennsylvania law; that under the law of Pennsylvania, as declared by its highest court, persons who use pathways along the railroad right of way — that is, a longitudinal pathway as distinguished from a crossing — are to be deemed trespassers; and that the railroad is not liable for injuries to undiscovered trespassers resulting from its negligence, unless it be wanton or willful. Tompkins denied that any such rule had been established by the decisions of the Pennsylvania courts; and contended that, since there was no statute of the

State on the subject, the railroad's duty and liability is to be determined in federal courts as a matter of general law.

The trial judge refused to rule that the applicable law precluded recovery. The jury brought in a verdict of $30,000; and the judgment entered thereon was affirmed by the Circuit Court of Appeals, which held that it was unnecessary to consider whether the law of Pennsylvania was as contended, because the question was one not of local, but of general, law and that "upon questions of general law the federal courts are free, in absence of a local statute, to exercise their independent judgment as to what the law is; and it is well settled that the question of the responsibility of a railroad for injuries caused by its servants is one of general law. . . . Where the public has made open and notorious use of a railroad right of way for a long period of time and without objection, the company owes to persons on such permissive pathway a duty of care in the operation of its trains. . . . It is likewise generally recognized law that a jury may find that negligence exists toward a pedestrian using a permissive path on the railroad right of way if he is hit by some object projecting from the side of the train."

The Erie had contended that application of the Pennsylvania rule was required, among other things, by §34 of the Federal Judiciary Act of September 24, 1789, c. 20, 28 U.S.C. §725, which provides:

> "The laws of the several States, except where the Constitution, treaties, or statutes of the United States otherwise require or provide, shall be regarded as rules of decision in trials at common law, in the courts of the United States, in cases where they apply."

Because of the importance of the question whether the federal court was free to disregard the alleged rule of the Pennsylvania common law, we granted certiorari. . . .

First. Swift v. Tyson . . . held that federal courts exercising jurisdiction on the ground of diversity of citizenship need not, in matters of general jurisprudence, apply the unwritten law of the State as declared by its highest court; that they are free to exercise an independent judgment as to what the common law of the state is — or should be; and that, as there stated by Mr. Justice Story,

> "the true interpretation of the thirty-fourth section limited its application to state laws strictly local, that is to say, to the positive statutes of the state, and the construction thereof adopted by the local tribunals, and to rights and titles to things having a permanent locality, such as the rights and titles to real estate, and other matters immovable and intraterritorial in their nature and character. It never has been supposed by us, that the section did apply, or was intended to apply, to questions of a more general nature, not at all dependent upon local statutes or local usages of a fixed and permanent operation, as, for example, to the construction of ordinary contracts or other written instruments, and especially to questions of general commercial law, where the state tribunals are called upon to perform the like functions as ourselves, that is, to ascertain upon general reasoning and legal analogies, what is the true exposition of the contract or instrument, or what is the just rule furnished by the principles of commercial law to govern the case."

The Court in applying the rule of §34 to equity cases, in *Mason v. United States*, 260 U.S. 545, 559, said: "The statute, however, is merely declarative of the rule which would exist in the absence of the statute." The federal courts assumed, in the broad field of "general law," the power to declare rules of decision which Congress was confessedly without power to enact as statutes. Doubt was repeatedly expressed as to the correctness of the construction given §34, and as to the soundness of the rule which it introduced. But it was the more recent research of a competent scholar, who examined the original document, which established that the construction given to it by the Court was erroneous; and that the purpose of the section was merely to make certain that, in all matters except those in which some federal law is controlling, the federal courts exercising jurisdiction in diversity of citizenship cases would apply as their rules of decision the law of the State, unwritten as well as written.[5] . . .

Second. Experience in applying the doctrine of *Swift v. Tyson*, had revealed its defects, political and social; and the benefits expected to flow from the rule did not accrue. Persistence of state courts in their own opinions on questions of common law prevented uniformity; and the impossibility of discovering a satisfactory line of demarcation between the province of general law and that of local law developed a new well of uncertainties. . . .

On the other hand, the mischievous results of the doctrine had become apparent. Diversity of citizenship jurisdiction was conferred in order to prevent apprehended discrimination in state courts against those not citizens of the State. *Swift v. Tyson* introduced grave discrimination by noncitizens against citizens. It made rights enjoyed under the unwritten "general law" vary according to whether enforcement was sought in the state or in the federal court; and the privilege of selecting the court in which the right should be determined was conferred upon the non-citizen. Thus, the doctrine rendered impossible equal protection of the law. In attempting to promote uniformity of law throughout the United States, the doctrine had prevented uniformity in the administration of the law of the State.

The discrimination resulting became in practice far-reaching. This resulted in part from the broad province accorded to the so-called "general law" as to which federal courts exercised an independent judgment. In addition to questions of purely commercial law, "general law" was held to include the obligations under contracts entered into and to be performed within the State, the extent to which a carrier operating within a State may stipulate for exemption from liability for his own negligence or that of his employee; the liability for torts committed within the State upon persons resident or property located there, even where the question of liability depended upon the scope of a property right conferred by the State; and the right to exemplary or punitive damages. Furthermore, state decisions construing local deeds, mineral conveyances, and even devises of real estate were disregarded.

In part the discrimination resulted from the wide range of persons held entitled to avail themselves of the federal rule by resort to the diversity of citizenship jurisdiction. Through this jurisdiction individual citizens willing to remove from their own State and become citizens of another might avail themselves of the federal rule. And, without even change of residence,

---

5. Charles Warren, *New Light on the History of the Federal Judiciary Act of 1789* (1923) 37 HARV. L. REV. 49, 51-52, 81-88, 108.

a corporate citizen of the state could avail itself of the federal rule by reincorporating under the laws of another State . . . .

The injustice and confusion incident to the doctrine of *Swift v. Tyson* have been repeatedly urged as reasons for abolishing or limiting diversity of citizenship jurisdiction. Other legislative relief has been proposed. If only a question of statutory construction were involved, we should not be prepared to abandon a doctrine so widely applied throughout nearly a century. But the unconstitutionality of the course pursued has now been made clear and compels us to do so.

Third. Except in matters governed by the Federal Constitution or by Acts of Congress, the law to be applied in any case is the law of the State. And whether the law of the State shall be declared by its Legislature in a statute or by its highest court in a decision is not a matter of federal concern. There is no federal general common law. Congress has no power to declare substantive rules of common law applicable in a State whether they be local in their nature or "general," be they commercial law or a part of the law of torts. And no clause in the Constitution purports to confer such a power upon the federal courts. As stated by Mr. Justice Field when protesting in *Baltimore & Ohio R.R. Co. v. Baugh*, 149 U.S. 368, 401, against ignoring the Ohio common law of fellow servant liability:

> "I am aware that what has been termed the general law of the country — which is often little less than what the judge advancing the doctrine thinks at the time should be the general law on a particular subject — has been often advanced in judicial opinions of this court to control a conflicting law of a State. I admit that learned judges have fallen into the habit of repeating this doctrine as a convenient mode of brushing aside the law of a State in conflict with their views. And I confess that, moved and governed by the authority of the great names of those judges, I have, myself, in many instances, unhesitatingly and confidently, but I think now erroneously, repeated the same doctrine. But, notwithstanding the great names which may be cited in favor of the doctrine, and notwithstanding the frequency with which the doctrine has been reiterated, there stands, as a perpetual protest against its repetition, the Constitution of the United States, which recognizes and preserves the autonomy and independence of the States — independence in their legislative and independence in their judicial departments. Supervision over either the legislative or the judicial action of the States is in no case permissible except as to matters by the Constitution specifically authorized or delegated to the United States. Any interference with either, except as thus permitted, is an invasion of the authority of the State and, to that extent, a denial of its independence."

The fallacy underlying the rule declared in *Swift v. Tyson* is made clear by Mr. Justice Holmes.[23] The doctrine rests upon the assumption that there is "a transcendental body of law outside of any particular State but obligatory within it unless and until changed by statute," that federal courts have the power to use their judgment as to what the rules of common law are; and that in the federal courts "the parties are entitled to an independent judgment on matters of general law":

---

23. *Kuhn v. Fairmont Coal Co.*, 215 U.S. 349, 370-372; *Black & White Taxicab Co. v. Brown & Yellow Taxicab Co.*, 276 U.S. 518, 532-536.

"but law in the sense in which courts speak of it today does not exist without some definite authority behind it. The common law so far as it is enforced in a State, whether called common law or not, is not the common law generally but the law of that State existing by the authority of that State without regard to what it may have been in England or anywhere else. . . .

"the authority and only authority is the State, and if that be so, the voice adopted by the State as its own [whether it be of its Legislature or of its Supreme Court] should utter the last word."

Thus the doctrine of *Swift v. Tyson* is, as Mr. Justice Holmes said, "an unconstitutional assumption of powers by the Courts of the United States which no lapse of time or respectable array of opinion should make us hesitate to correct." In disapproving that doctrine we do not hold unconstitutional §34 of the Federal Judiciary Act of 1789 or any other Act of Congress. We merely declare that in applying the doctrine this Court and the lower courts have invaded rights which in our opinion are reserved by the Constitution to the several States.

Fourth. The defendant contended that by the common law of Pennsylvania as declared by its highest court the only duty owed to the plaintiff was to refrain from willful or wanton injury. The plaintiff denied that such is the Pennsylvania law. In support of their respective contentions the parties discussed and cited many decisions of the Supreme Court of the State. The Circuit Court of Appeals ruled that the question of liability is one of general law; and on that ground declined to decide the issue of state law. As we hold this was error, the judgment is reversed and the case remanded to it for further proceedings in conformity with our opinion.

Mr. Justice Cardozo took no part in the consideration or decision of this case.

Mr. Justice Butler.

No constitutional question was suggested or argued below or here. And as a general rule, this Court will not consider any question not raised below and presented by the petition. . . .

So far as appears, no litigant has ever challenged the power of Congress to establish the rule [of §34] as [long] construed. It has so long endured that its destruction now without appropriate deliberation cannot be justified.

Mr. Justice McReynolds concurs in this opinion.

Mr. Justice Reed.

I concur in the conclusion reached in this case, in the disapproval of the doctrine of *Swift v. Tyson*, and in the reasoning of the majority opinion except in so far as it relies upon the unconstitutionality of the "course pursued" by the federal courts.

POINTS FOR DISCUSSION

1. In *Erie*, the Court rejected "the rule of *Swift*." According to the *Erie* Court, "*Swift* . . . held that federal courts exercising jurisdiction on the ground

of diversity of citizenship need not, in matters of general jurisprudence, apply the unwritten law of the state as declared by its highest court; that they are free to exercise an independent judgment as to what the common law of the state is — or should be." The *Swift* doctrine, the Court continued, "rests upon the assumption that there is a transcendental body of law outside of any particular State but obligatory within it unless and until changed by statute." Are these characterizations of *Swift* consistent with each other? Do either or both of these statements fairly characterize the *Swift* opinion?

2. The *Erie* Court relied on scholarship by Charles Warren — *New Light on the History of the Federal Judiciary Act of 1789*, 37 Harv. L. Rev. 49 (1923) — to reject *Swift*'s understanding of the Rules of Decision Act:

> [I]t was the more recent research of a competent scholar, who examined the original document, which established that the construction given to it by the Court was erroneous; and that the purpose of the section was merely to make certain that, in all matters except those in which some federal law is controlling, the federal courts exercising jurisdiction in diversity of citizenship cases would apply as their rules of decision the law of the state, unwritten as well as written.

Recall that §34 of the Judiciary Act of 1789 provided:

> The laws of the several States, except where the Constitution, treaties, or statutes of the United States otherwise require or provide, shall be regarded as rules of decision in trials at common law, in the courts of the United States, in cases where they apply.

A prior draft had provided — instead of "[t]he laws of the several States" — "the Statute law of the several states in force for the time being and their unwritten or common law now in use." Warren argued that "[t]he meaning of this change was probably as follows: that the word 'laws of the several states' was intended to be a concise expression and a summary of the more detailed enumeration of the different forms of state law, set forth in the original draft." Warren, *supra*, at 86. The *Erie* Court agreed that "laws of the several States" included both state statutes and state common law. Is this the only plausible inference to be drawn from the change in language from the prior draft to the enacted statute? Assuming that "laws of the several States" described both state statutes and state common law, did the Rules of Decision Act still leave room for the application of general law principles, "in cases where they apply"?

3. Perhaps the most famous and controversial passage of *Erie* is this:

> Except in matters governed by the Federal Constitution or by acts of Congress, the law to be applied in any case is the law of the State. And whether the law of the State shall be declared by its Legislature in a statute or by its highest court in a decision is not a matter of federal concern. There is no federal general common law. Congress has no power to declare substantive rules of common law applicable in a state whether they be local in their nature or "general," be they commercial law or a part of the law of torts. And no clause in the Constitution purports to confer such a power upon the federal courts.

What did the Supreme Court mean in this passage? (a) That federal courts have no power to provide a rule of decision governing tort duties owed by railroads because Congress lacks power to provide such a rule? (Today—if not at the time of *Erie*—the Supreme Court likely would find Congress to have such power under the Commerce Clause.) Is the breadth of congressional power to prescribe a rule determinative of the federal courts' power to prescribe the same rule? (b) That federal courts have no power to provide a rule of decision governing tort duties owed by railroads regardless of whether Congress has power to prescribe such a rule? If so, what was the Court saying about congressional power? That Congress has no power to declare the law of a particular state, as opposed to national law?

In *Erie*, the Court determined that "[t]here is no federal general common law." If this language abolished all general law and federal common law as rules of decision in federal courts, what source of law would govern disputes previously governed by general law—such as maritime disputes and controversies between states—absent a controlling state law or federal statute, treaty, or constitutional provision? After *Erie*, the Court came to resolve certain such disputes according to "federal common law." In fact, on the day that the Court decided *Erie*—in the very next case in the U.S. reports—the Court used "federal common law" to resolve a dispute over water rights in a river flowing from Colorado into New Mexico. *See Hinderlider v. La Plata River & Cherry Creek Ditch Co.*, 304 U.S. 92 (1938). Justice Brandeis, the author of *Erie*, explained for the Court that "whether the water of an interstate stream must be apportioned between two States is a question of 'federal common law' upon which neither the statutes nor the decisions of either State can be conclusive." *Id.* at 110. Moreover, Justice Brandeis continued, "[j]urisdiction over controversies concerning rights in interstate streams is not different from those concerning boundaries. These have been recognized as presenting federal questions." *Id.* Thus, although the *Erie* Court held that there is no "federal general common law," the Court applied "federal common law" in *Hinderlider*. Since *Erie*, the Court has invoked federal common law as a rule of decision in various categories of cases, including disputes between states, admiralty cases, and cases involving the rights and duties of the United States, to name a few. In defining enclaves of cases governed by federal common law, the Court has not merely applied general law by a different name. Whereas general law was not usually understood to preempt state law, federal common law—as understood by courts and scholars—preempts contrary state law (and possibly gives rise to federal court "arising under" jurisdiction). Present-day applications of federal common law have renewed debates—harking back to the Founding—about the legitimacy of federal common law as a rule of decision in federal courts.

The next chapter examines the nature and scope of (1) federal common law and (2) general law—and the implications of each for federalism—in the aftermath of *Erie*.

CHAPTER 9

RULES OF DECISION AFTER ERIE

In 1938, the Supreme Court declared in *Erie Railroad v. Tompkins*, 304 U.S. 64, 78 (1938), that "[t]here is no federal general common law." As you studied in the last chapter, "general law" and "federal common law" were distinct concepts in the early years of the Union. The Court held in *United States v. Hudson & Goodwin*, 11 U.S. (7 Cranch) 32 (1812), that federal courts lacked jurisdiction to apply a federal common law of crime, but federal courts regularly applied general law as rules of decision without apparent controversy for decades. In the late nineteenth and early twentieth centuries, the Court expanded the scope of general law to encompass matters previously governed by state law. In doing so, the Court increased the power of federal courts relative to states to define the content of rules of decision that federal courts would apply. In rejecting "federal general common law," the *Erie* Court used a phrase that seemingly encompassed both general law and federal common law. The Court explained that "[e]xcept in matters governed by the Federal Constitution or by acts of Congress, the law to be applied in any case is the law of the State." *Erie*, 304 U.S. at 78. Thus, *Erie* recognized two operative sources of law in federal courts—enacted federal law and state law.

In other cases, however, the Court also recognized that in certain Article III disputes, previously governed by general law, no enacted federal law—*viz.* the Constitution, statutes, and treaties of the United States—provided a rule of decision, and state law was incompetent to supply one. In *Hinderlider v. La Plata River & Cherry Creek Ditch Co.*, 304 U.S. 92 (1938), for example, the Court found that state law could not conclusively resolve a dispute over water rights in an interstate stream. In such cases, the Court came to recognize discrete "enclaves" of federal common law rules of decision. In some cases, state law was available as a rule of decision but, if applied, might frustrate perceived national interests in uniformity or outcome. Accordingly, the Court began applying federal common law in order to advance certain perceived national interests, including in cases involving commercial rights and duties of the United States. Before *Erie*, federal courts applied general law in cases involving commercial rights and duties of the United States, absent an applicable act of Congress. In concept, general law supplied a rule of decision that (1) was nationally uniform and (2) served the interests of the United States insofar as, absent an act of Congress to the contrary, it served the United States' interests to abide by transnational commercial rules. After *Erie* rejected general law, the Supreme Court began applying "federal common law" as the rule of decision in such disputes to uphold perceived interests of the United States.

Although the Supreme Court described federal common law as serving national interests, its application after *Erie* generated tension with structural constitutional principles. Federal common law differs in concept from general law. Federal common law is generally understood to be preemptive of state law and a sufficient predicate for federal court "arising under" jurisdiction. General law, in concept, was neither. As you read in the preceding chapter, the Supreme Court rejected the application of federal common law in *United States v. Hudson & Goodwin*, 11 U.S. (7 Cranch) 32 (1812), on grounds that it interfered with "[t]he legislative authority of the Union." The concern was that, if federal courts applied federal common law, they would be usurping the prerogatives of Congress to make law for the United States and the prerogatives of the states to regulate where Congress had not made federal law through constitutional lawmaking procedures in the exercise of its enumerated powers. These concerns involved both separation of powers (the relationship between federal courts and Congress) and federalism (the relationship between federal and state law-making authority). Tension endures between the principles on which the Court rejected federal common law jurisdiction in *Hudson & Goodwin* and the Court's continued application of federal common law in various enclaves of cases.

In this chapter, you will study how the Supreme Court has applied non-state customary law after *Erie*, and analyze its federalism implications. This chapter takes up three categories of customary law: (1) federal common law, (2) customary international law, and (3) general law. "Federal common law" is commonly described as "federal rules of decision whose content cannot be traced directly by traditional methods of interpretation to federal statutory or constitutional commands." Richard H. Fallon, Jr. et al., Hart and Wechsler's The Federal Courts and the Federal System 607 (6th ed. 2009). "Customary international law" is understood to "result[] from a general and consistent practice of states followed by them from a sense of legal obligation." *Restatement (Third) of the Foreign Relations Law of the United States* §102(2) (1987). "General law" historically encompassed general legal principles recognized by civilized nations, including the law of nations. These categories are not meant to be mutually exclusive. Traditionally, the customary law of nations was one category of general law. In the present day, there is vigorous debate over whether customary international law qualifies as federal common law. Some scholars recently have argued that general law endures notwithstanding its rejection in *Erie*, an observation not without controversy. Rather than describe mutually exclusive categories of customary law, the categories federal common law, customary international law, and general law will help facilitate your understanding of how federal court source of law questions are, in some measure, federalism questions.

As you read the materials in this chapter, consider the following questions:

- What justifies federal court application of federal common law in the aftermath of *Erie*? What about the application of general law?

- Does the application of federal common law undermine the political and procedural safeguards of federalism? What about the application of general law?
- Does the application of federal common law in the cases below advance or frustrate normative values of federalism?
- Is it possible to square present-day application of federal common law with historical practice? What about the application of general law?

A. FEDERAL COMMON LAW

Courts and scholars generally regard *Clearfield Trust Co. v. United States*, 318 U.S. 363 (1943), as a seminal case applying federal common law as a rule of decision in federal court. The year after *Erie* was decided, the United States filed suit against Clearfield Trust Co. to resolve a dispute over commercial paper. Under *Erie*, general commercial law could not supply the rule of decision. The *Clearfield Trust* Court applied federal common law instead. Note carefully both (1) how the Court justified the application of federal common law and (2) how the Court gave content to federal common law in *Clearfield Trust*.

CLEARFIELD TRUST CO. V. UNITED STATES

318 U.S. 363 (1943)

Mr. JUSTICE DOUGLAS delivered the opinion of the Court.

On April 28, 1936, a check was drawn on the Treasurer of the United States through the Federal Reserve Bank of Philadelphia to the order of Clair A. Barner in the amount of $24.20. It was dated at Harrisburg, Pennsylvania and was drawn for services rendered by Barner to the Works Progress Administration. The check was placed in the mail addressed to Barner at his address in Mackeyville, Pa. Barner never received the check. Some unknown person obtained it in a mysterious manner and presented it to the J.C. Penney Co. store in Clearfield, Pa., representing that he was the payee and identifying himself to the satisfaction of the employees of J.C. Penney Co. He endorsed the check in the name of Barner and transferred it to J.C. Penney Co. in exchange for cash and merchandise. Barner never authorized the endorsement nor participated in the proceeds of the check. J.C. Penney Co. endorsed the check over to the Clearfield Trust Co. which accepted it as agent for the purpose of collection and endorsed it as follows: "Pay to the order of Federal Reserve Bank of Philadelphia, Prior Endorsements Guaranteed."[1] Clearfield Trust Co. collected the check from the United States through the Federal Reserve Bank of Philadelphia and paid the full amount thereof to J.C. Penney Co. Neither the Clearfield Trust Co. nor J.C. Penney Co. had any knowledge or suspicion of the forgery. Each acted in good faith. On or before May 10, 1936,

---

1. Guarantee of all prior indorsements on presentment for payment of such a check to Federal Reserve banks or member bank depositories is required by Treasury Regulations. 31 Code of Federal Regulations §102.32, §202.33.

Barner advised the timekeeper and the foreman of the W.P.A. project on which he was employed that he had not received the check in question. This information was duly communicated to other agents of the United States and on November 30, 1936, Barner executed an affidavit alleging that the endorsement of his name on the check was a forgery. No notice was given the Clearfield Trust Co. or J.C. Penney Co. of the forgery until January 12, 1937, at which time the Clearfield Trust Co. was notified. The first notice received by Clearfield Trust Co. that the United States was asking reimbursement was on August 31, 1937.

This suit was instituted in 1939 by the United States against the Clearfield Trust Co., the jurisdiction of the federal District Court being invoked pursuant to the provisions of §24(1) of the Judicial Code, 28 U.S.C. §41(1). The cause of action was based on the express guaranty of prior endorsements made by the Clearfield Trust Co. J.C. Penney Co. intervened as a defendant. The case was heard on complaint, answer and stipulation of facts. The District Court held that the rights of the parties were to be determined by the law of Pennsylvania and that since the United States unreasonably delayed in giving notice of the forgery to the Clearfield Trust Co., it was barred from recovery under the rule of *Market Street Title & Trust Co. v. Chelten Trust Co.*, 296 Pa. 230. It accordingly dismissed the complaint. On appeal the Circuit Court of Appeals reversed. . . . .

We agree with the Circuit Court of Appeals that the rule of *Erie R. Co. v. Tompkins*, 304 U.S. 64, does not apply to this action. The rights and duties of the United States on commercial paper which it issues are governed by federal rather than local law. When the United States disburses its funds or pays its debts, it is exercising a constitutional function or power. This check was issued for services performed under the Federal Emergency Relief Act of 1935, 49 Stat. 115. The authority to issue the check had its origin in the Constitution and the statutes of the United States and was in no way dependent on the laws of Pennsylvania or of any other state. The duties imposed upon the United States and the rights acquired by it as a result of the issuance find their roots in the same federal sources.[2] In absence of an applicable Act of Congress it is for the federal courts to fashion the governing rule of law according to their own standards. . . .

In our choice of the applicable federal rule we have occasionally selected state law. But reasons which may make state law at times the appropriate federal rule are singularly inappropriate here. The issuance of commercial paper by the United States is on a vast scale and transactions in that paper from issuance to payment will commonly occur in several states. The application of state law, even without the conflict of laws rules of the forum, would subject the rights and duties of the United States to exceptional uncertainty.

---

2. Various Treasury Regulations govern the payment and endorsement of government checks and warrants and the reimbursement of the Treasurer of the United States by Federal Reserve banks and member bank depositories on payment of checks or warrants bearing a forged endorsement. See 31 Code of Federal Regulations §§202.0, 202.32-202.34. Forgery of the check was an offense against the United States. Criminal Code §148, 18 U.S.C. §262.

It would lead to great diversity in results by making identical transactions subject to the vagaries of the laws of the several states. The desirability of a uniform rule is plain. And while the federal law merchant developed for about a century under the regime of *Swift v. Tyson*, 16 Pet. 1, represented general commercial law rather than a choice of a federal rule designed to protect a federal right, it nevertheless stands as a convenient source of reference for fashioning federal rules applicable to these federal questions.

United States v. National Exchange Bank, 214 U.S. 302, falls in that category. The Court held that the United States could recover as drawee from one who presented for payment a pension check on which the name of the payee had been forged, in spite of a protracted delay on the part of the United States in giving notice of the forgery. . . .

The *National Exchange Bank* case went no further than to hold that prompt notice of the discovery of the forgery was not a condition precedent to suit. It did not reach the question whether lack of prompt notice might be a defense. We think it may. If it is shown that the drawee on learning of the forgery did not give prompt notice of it and that damage resulted, recovery by the drawee is barred. See *Ladd & Tilton Bank v. United States*, 30 F.2d 334; *United States v. National Rockland Bank*, 35 F. Supp. 912; *United States v. National City Bank*, 28 F. Supp. 144. The fact that the drawee is the United States and the laches those of its employees are not material. *Cooke v. United States*, 91 U.S. 389, 398. The United States as drawee of commercial paper stands in no different light than any other drawee. As stated in *United States v. National Exchange Bank*, 270 U.S. 527, 534, "The United States does business on business terms." It is not excepted from the general rules governing the rights and duties of drawees "by the largeness of its dealings and its having to employ agents to do what if done by a principal in person would leave no room for doubt." *Id.*, at p. 535. But the damage occasioned by the delay must be established and not left to conjecture. Cases such as *Market St. Title & Trust Co. v. Chelten Trust Co.*, *supra*, place the burden on the drawee of giving prompt notice of the forgery-injury to the defendant being presumed by the mere fact of delay. See *London & River Plate Bank v. Bank of Liverpool*, [(1896)] 1 Q.B. 7. But we do not think that he who accepts a forged signature of a payee deserves that preferred treatment. It is his neglect or error in accepting the forger's signature which occasions the loss. See *Bank of Commerce v. Union Bank*, 3 N.Y. 230, 236. He should be allowed to shift that loss to the drawee only on a clear showing that the drawee's delay in notifying him of the forgery caused him damage. See Woodward, Quasi Contracts (1913) §25. No such damage has been shown by Clearfield Trust Co. who so far as appears can still recover from J.C. Penney Co. The only showing on the part of the latter is contained in the stipulation to the effect that if a check cashed for a customer is returned unpaid or for reclamation a short time after the date on which it is cashed, the employees can often locate the person who cashed it. It is further stipulated that when J.C. Penney Co. was notified of the forgery in the present case none of its employees was able to remember anything about the transaction or check in question. The inference is that the more prompt the notice the more likely the detection of the forger. But that falls short of a showing that the delay caused a manifest loss. *Third National Bank v. Merchants' National*

Bank, 76 Hun 475, 27 N.Y.S. 1070. It is but another way of saying that mere delay is enough. . . .

Mr. JUSTICE MURPHY and Mr. JUSTICE RUTLEDGE did not participate in the consideration or decision of this case.

POINTS FOR DISCUSSION

1. The Court explained in *Clearfield Trust* that "[t]he rights and duties of the United States on commercial paper which it issues are governed by federal rather than local law." Although the Court noted connections between the issuance of commercial paper by the United States and certain federal statutes and regulations, none of these federal laws supplied the rule of decision that the Court applied. Should the Court have applied state law to the question before it? Can the Court's application of federal common law be reconciled with the Constitution's delegation of federal lawmaking power to Congress and prescription of bicameralism and presentment as federal lawmaking procedures?

2. Having determined that federal common law would govern, the Court asserted that "[i]n the absence of an applicable Act of Congress it is for the federal courts to fashion the governing rule of law according to their own standards." The Court went on to explain that, in an appropriate case, it might select state law as the "federal rule." Why would the Court ever choose to apply state law as the "federal common law" rule rather than apply state law as state law? In *Clearfield Trust*, the Court did not adopt state law as federal common law; rather, it looked to "general commercial law . . . as a convenient source of reference for fashioning federal rules applicable to these federal questions." Why did the Court look to "general commercial law" as a source of reference for fashioning federal common law? In what circumstances might pre-existing general commercial law not be an appropriate source of reference for fashioning federal common law? Are there any limitations on how federal courts should proceed to fashion federal common law where it governs? Or should courts make federal common law on the basis of the same kinds of policy judgments that Congress makes when it enacts a federal statute?

BOYLE v. UNITED TECHNOLOGIES CORP.

487 U.S. 500 (1988)

JUSTICE SCALIA delivered the opinion of the Court.

This case requires us to decide when a contractor providing military equipment to the Federal Government can be held liable under state tort law for injury caused by a design defect.

I

On April 27, 1983, David A. Boyle, a United States Marine helicopter co-pilot, was killed when the CH-53D helicopter in which he was flying crashed off the coast of Virginia Beach, Virginia, during a training exercise. Although Boyle survived the impact of the crash, he was unable to escape from the helicopter and drowned. Boyle's father, petitioner here, brought this diversity action in Federal District Court against the Sikorsky Division of United Technologies Corporation (Sikorsky), which built the helicopter for the United States.

At trial, petitioner . . . alleged that Sikorsky had defectively designed the copilot's emergency escape system: the escape hatch opened out instead of in (and was therefore ineffective in a submerged craft because of water pressure), and access to the escape hatch handle was obstructed by other equipment. The jury returned a general verdict in favor of petitioner and awarded him $725,000. . . .

The Court of Appeals reversed and remanded with directions that judgment be entered for Sikorsky. . . . It . . . found, as a matter of federal law, that Sikorsky could not be held liable for the allegedly defective design of the escape hatch because, on the evidence presented, it satisfied the requirements of the "military contractor defense," which the court had recognized the same day in *Tozer v. LTV Corp.*, 792 F.2d 403 (CA4 1986).

Petitioner . . . contends that there is no justification in federal law for shielding Government contractors from liability for design defects in military equipment. . . .

II

Petitioner's broadest contention is that, in the absence of legislation specifically immunizing Government contractors from liability for design defects, there is no basis for judicial recognition of such a defense. We disagree. In most fields of activity, to be sure, this Court has refused to find federal pre-emption of state law in the absence of either a clear statutory prescription, or a direct conflict between federal and state law. But we have held that a few areas, involving "uniquely federal interests," *Texas Industries, Inc. v. Radcliff Materials, Inc.*, 451 U.S. 630, 640 (1981), are so committed by the Constitution and laws of the United States to federal control that state law is pre-empted and replaced, where necessary, by federal law of a content prescribed (absent explicit statutory directive) by the courts — so-called "federal common law." See, *e.g., United States v. Kimbell Foods, Inc.*, 440 U.S. 715, 726-729 (1979); *Banco Nacional v. Sabbatino*, 376 U.S. 398, 426-427 (1964); *Clearfield Trust Co. v. United States*, 318 U.S. 363, 366-367 (1943); *D'Oench, Duhme & Co. v. FDIC*, 315 U.S. 447, 457-458 (1942).

The dispute in the present case borders upon two areas that we have found to involve such "uniquely federal interests." We have held that obligations to and rights of the United States under its contracts are governed exclusively by federal law. See, *e.g., United States v. Little Lake Misere Land Co.*, 412 U.S. 580, 592-594 (1973); *Clearfield Trust, supra.* The present case does not involve an obligation to the United States under its contract, but rather liability to third persons. That liability may be styled one in tort, but it arises out of performance of the contract — and traditionally has been regarded as sufficiently related to the contract that until 1962 Virginia would generally allow design defect suits only by the purchaser and those in privity with the seller.

Another area that we have found to be of peculiarly federal concern, warranting the displacement of state law, is the civil liability of federal officials for actions taken in the course of their duty. We have held in many contexts that the scope of that liability is controlled by federal law. See, *e.g., Westfall v. Erwin,* 484 U.S. 292, 295 (1988). The present case involves an independent contractor performing its obligation under a procurement contract, rather than an official performing his duty as a federal employee, but there is obviously implicated the same interest in getting the Government's work done. . . .

We think the reasons for considering these closely related areas to be of "uniquely federal" interest apply as well to the civil liabilities arising out of the performance of federal procurement contracts. . . . [I]t is plain that the Federal Government's interest in the procurement of equipment is implicated by suits such as the present one—even though the dispute is one between private parties. It is true that where "litigation is purely between private parties and does not touch the rights and duties of the United States," *Bank of America Nat. Trust & Sav. Assn. v. Parnell,* 352 U.S. 29, 33 (1956), federal law does not govern. Thus, for example, in *Miree v. DeKalb County,* 433 U.S. 25, 30 (1977), which involved the question whether certain private parties could sue as third-party beneficiaries to an agreement between a municipality and the Federal Aviation Administration, we found that state law was not displaced because "the operations of the United States in connection with FAA grants such as these . . . would [not] be burdened" by allowing state law to determine whether third-party beneficiaries could sue, *id.,* at 30, and because "any federal interest in the outcome of the [dispute] before us '[was] far too speculative, far too remote a possibility to justify the application of federal law to transactions essentially of local concern.'" *Id.,* at 32-33, quoting *Parnell, supra,* at 33-34, see also *Wallis v. Pan American Petroleum Corp.,* 384 U.S. 63, 69 (1966). But the same is not true here. The imposition of liability on Government contractors will directly affect the terms of Government contracts: either the contractor will decline to manufacture the design specified by the Government, or it will raise its price. Either way, the interests of the United States will be directly affected.

That the procurement of equipment by the United States is an area of uniquely federal interest does not, however, end the inquiry. That merely establishes a necessary, not a sufficient, condition for the displacement of state law.[3] Displacement will occur only where, as we have variously described, a "significant conflict" exists between an identifiable "federal policy or interest and the [operation] of state law," *Wallis, supra,* at 68, or the application of state law would "frustrate specific objectives" of federal legislation, *Kimbell Foods,* 440 U.S., at 728. The conflict with federal policy need not be as sharp as that which must exist for ordinary pre-emption when Congress legislates "in a field

---

3. We refer here to the displacement of state law, although it is possible to analyze it as the displacement of federal-law reference to state law for the rule of decision. Some of our cases appear to regard the area in which a uniquely federal interest exists as being entirely governed by federal law, with federal law deigning to "borro[w]," *United States v. Little Lake Misere Land Co.,* 412 U.S. 580, 594 (1973), or "incorporat[e]" or "adopt" *United States v. Kimbell Foods, Inc.,* 440 U.S. 715, 728, 729, 730 (1979), state law except where a significant conflict with federal policy exists. We see nothing to be gained by expanding the theoretical scope of the federal pre-emption beyond its practical effect, and so adopt the more modest terminology. If the distinction between displacement of state law and displacement of federal law's incorporation of state law ever makes a practical difference, it at least does not do so in the present case.

which the States have traditionally occupied." *Rice v. Santa Fe Elevator Corp.,* [331 U.S. 218, 230 (1947)]. Or to put the point differently, the fact that the area in question *is* one of unique federal concern changes what would otherwise be a conflict that cannot produce pre-emption into one that can. . . . But conflict there must be. In some cases, for example where the federal interest requires a uniform rule, the entire body of state law applicable to the area conflicts and is replaced by federal rules. In others, the conflict is more narrow, and only particular elements of state law are superseded. . . .

In *Miree, supra,* the suit was not seeking to impose upon the person contracting with the Government a duty contrary to the duty imposed by the Government contract. Rather, it was the contractual duty *itself* that the private plaintiff (as third-party beneficiary) sought to enforce. Between *Miree* and the present case, it is easy to conceive of an intermediate situation, in which the duty sought to be imposed on the contractor is not identical to one assumed under the contract, but is also not contrary to any assumed. If, for example, the United States contracts for the purchase and installation of an air-conditioning unit, specifying the cooling capacity but not the precise manner of construction, a state law imposing upon the manufacturer of such units a duty of care to include a certain safety feature would not be a duty identical to anything promised the Government, but neither would it be contrary. The contractor could comply with both its contractual obligations and the state-prescribed duty of care. No one suggests that state law would generally be pre-empted in this context.

The present case, however, is at the opposite extreme from *Miree.* Here the state-imposed duty of care that is the asserted basis of the contractor's liability (specifically, the duty to equip helicopters with the sort of escape-hatch mechanism petitioner claims was necessary) is precisely contrary to the duty imposed by the Government contract (the duty to manufacture and deliver helicopters with the sort of escape-hatch mechanism shown by the specifications). Even in this sort of situation, it would be unreasonable to say that there is always a "significant conflict" between the state law and a federal policy or interest. If, for example, a federal procurement officer orders, by model number, a quantity of stock helicopters that happen to be equipped with escape hatches opening outward, it is impossible to say that the Government has a significant interest in that particular feature. That would be scarcely more reasonable than saying that a private individual who orders such a craft by model number cannot sue for the manufacturer's negligence because he got precisely what he ordered. . . .

There is . . . a statutory provision that demonstrates the potential for, and suggests the outlines of, "significant conflict" between federal interests and state law in the context of Government procurement. In the FTCA, Congress authorized damages to be recovered against the United States for harm caused by the negligent or wrongful conduct of Government employees, to the extent that a private person would be liable under the law of the place where the conduct occurred. 28 U.S.C. §1346(b). It excepted from this consent to suit, however,

> "[a]ny claim . . . based upon the exercise or performance or the failure to exercise or perform a discretionary function or duty on the part of a federal

agency or an employee of the Government, whether or not the discretion involved be abused." 28 U.S.C. §2680(a).

We think that the selection of the appropriate design for military equipment to be used by our Armed Forces is assuredly a discretionary function within the meaning of this provision. It often involves not merely engineering analysis but judgment as to the balancing of many technical, military, and even social considerations, including specifically the trade-off between greater safety and greater combat effectiveness. And we are further of the view that permitting "second-guessing" of these judgments through state tort suits against contractors would produce the same effect sought to be avoided by the FTCA exemption. The financial burden of judgments against the contractors would ultimately be passed through, substantially if not totally, to the United States itself, since defense contractors will predictably raise their prices to cover, or to insure against, contingent liability for the Government-ordered designs. To put the point differently: It makes little sense to insulate the Government against financial liability for the judgment that a particular feature of military equipment is necessary when the Government produces the equipment itself, but not when it contracts for the production. In sum, we are of the view that state law which holds Government contractors liable for design defects in military equipment does in some circumstances present a "significant conflict" with federal policy and must be displaced.

We agree with the scope of displacement adopted by the Fourth Circuit here. . . . Liability for design defects in military equipment cannot be imposed, pursuant to state law, when (1) the United States approved reasonably precise specifications; (2) the equipment conformed to those specifications; and (3) the supplier warned the United States about the dangers in the use of the equipment that were known to the supplier but not to the United States. The first two of these conditions assure that the suit is within the area where the policy of the "discretionary function" would be frustrated — *i.e.*, they assure that the design feature in question was considered by a Government officer, and not merely by the contractor itself. The third condition is necessary because, in its absence, the displacement of state tort law would create some incentive for the manufacturer to withhold knowledge of risks, since conveying that knowledge might disrupt the contract but withholding it would produce no liability. We adopt this provision lest our effort to protect discretionary functions perversely impede them by cutting off information highly relevant to the discretionary decision.

We have considered the alternative formulation of the Government contractor defense, urged upon us by petitioner. . . . That would preclude suit only if (1) the contractor did not participate, or participated only minimally, in the design of the defective equipment; *or* (2) the contractor timely warned the Government of the risks of the design and notified it of alternative designs reasonably known by it, *and* the Government, although forewarned, clearly authorized the contractor to proceed with the dangerous design. While this formulation may represent a perfectly reasonable tort rule, it is not a rule designed to protect the federal interest embodied in the "discretionary function" exemption. The design ultimately selected may well reflect a significant policy judgment by Government officials whether or not the contractor rather than those officials developed the design. In addition, it does not seem to us sound policy to penalize, and thus deter, active contractor participation in the design process, placing the contractor at risk unless it identifies all design defects.

III

It is somewhat unclear from the Court of Appeals' opinion, however, whether it was in fact deciding that no reasonable jury could, under the properly formulated defense, have found for the petitioner on the facts presented, or rather was assessing on its own whether the defense had been established. . . . Accordingly, the judgment is vacated and the case is remanded. . . .

JUSTICE BRENNAN, with whom JUSTICE MARSHALL and JUSTICE BLACKMUN join, dissenting.

If respondent's immunity "bore the legitimacy of having been prescribed by the people's elected representatives," we would be duty bound to implement their will, whether or not we approved. *United States v. Johnson,* 481 U.S. 681, 703 (1987) (dissenting opinion of Scalia, J.). Congress, however, has remained silent—and conspicuously so, having resisted a sustained campaign by Government contractors to legislate for them some defense. The Court—unelected and unaccountable to the people—has unabashedly stepped into the breach to legislate a rule denying Lt. Boyle's family the compensation that state law assures them. This time the injustice is of this Court's own making.

Worse yet, the injustice will extend far beyond the facts of this case, for the Court's newly discovered Government contractor defense is breathtakingly sweeping. It applies not only to military equipment like the CH-53D helicopter, but (so far as I can tell) to any made-to-order gadget that the Federal Government might purchase after previewing plans—from NASA's Challenger space shuttle to the Postal Service's old mail cars. The contractor may invoke the defense in suits brought not only by military personnel like Lt. Boyle, or Government employees, but by anyone injured by a Government contractor's negligent design, including, for example, the children who might have died had respondent's helicopter crashed on the beach. It applies even if the Government has not intentionally sacrificed safety for other interests like speed or efficiency, and, indeed, even if the equipment is not of a type that is typically considered dangerous; thus, the contractor who designs a Government building can invoke the defense when the elevator cable snaps or the walls collapse. And the defense is invocable regardless of how blatant or easily remedied the defect, so long as the contractor missed it and the specifications approved by the Government, however unreasonably dangerous, were "reasonably precise."

In my view, this Court lacks both authority and expertise to fashion such a rule, whether to protect the Treasury of the United States or the coffers of industry. . . . I would leave that exercise of legislative power to Congress, where our Constitution places it. . . .

I

Before our decision in *Erie R. Co. v. Tompkins,* 304 U.S. 64 (1938), federal courts sitting in diversity were generally free, in the absence of a controlling state statute, to fashion rules of "general" federal common law. See, *e.g., Swift v. Tyson,* 16 Pet. 1 (1842). *Erie* renounced the prevailing scheme: "Except in matters governed by the Federal Constitution or by Acts of Congress, the law to be applied in any case is the law of the State." 304 U.S., at 78. The Court explained that the expansive power that federal courts had theretofore exercised was an unconstitutional " 'invasion of the authority of the State and, to that extent, a denial of its independence.' " *Id.,* at 79 (citation omitted). Thus, *Erie* was deeply rooted in notions of federalism, and is most seriously implicated when, as here, federal judges displace the state law that would ordinarily govern with their own rules of federal common law.[2]

In pronouncing that "[t]here is no federal general common law," 304 U.S., at 78, *Erie* put to rest the notion that the grant of diversity jurisdiction to federal courts is itself authority to fashion rules of substantive law. See *United States v. Little Lake Misere Land Co.,* 412 U.S. 580, 591 (1973). As the author of today's opinion for the Court pronounced for a unanimous Court just two months ago, "we start with the assumption that the historic police powers of the States were not to be superseded . . . unless that was the clear and manifest purpose of Congress." *Puerto Rico Dept. of Consumer Affairs v. Isla Petroleum Corp.,* 485 U.S. 495, 500 (1988) (citations omitted). Just as "[t]here is no federal pre-emption *in vacuo,* without a constitutional text or a federal statute to assert it," *id.,* at 503, federal common law cannot supersede state law *in vacuo* out of no more than an idiosyncratic determination by five Justices that a particular area is "uniquely federal."

Accordingly, we have emphasized that federal common law can displace state law in "few and restricted" instances. *Wheeldin v. Wheeler,* 373 U.S. 647, 651 (1963). "[A]bsent some congressional authorization to formulate substantive rules of decision, federal common law exists only in such narrow areas as those concerned with the rights and obligations of the United States, interstate and international disputes implicating conflicting rights of States or our relations with foreign nations, and admiralty cases." *Texas Industries, Inc. v. Radcliff Materials, Inc.,* 451 U.S. 630, 641 (1981) (footnotes omitted). "The enactment of a federal rule in an area of national concern, and the decision whether to displace state law in doing so, is generally made not by the federal judiciary, purposefully insulated from democratic pressures, but by the people through their elected representatives in Congress." *Milwaukee v. Illinois,* 451 U.S. 304, 312-313 (1981). See also *Wallis v. Pan American Petroleum Corp.,* 384 U.S. 63, 68 (1966); *Miree v. DeKalb County,* 433 U.S. 25, 32 (1977). State laws "should be overridden by the federal courts only where clear and substantial interests of the National Government, which cannot be served consistently with respect

---

2. Not all exercises of our power to fashion federal common law displace state law in the same way. For example, our recognition of federal causes of action based upon either the Constitution, see, *e.g., Bivens v. Six Unknown Fed. Narcotics Agents,* 403 U.S. 388 (1971), or a federal statute, see *Cort v. Ash,* 422 U.S. 66 (1975), supplements whatever rights state law might provide, and therefore does not implicate federalism concerns in the same way as does pre-emption of a state-law rule of decision or cause of action. Throughout this opinion I use the word "displace" in the latter sense.

for such state interests, will suffer major damage if the state law is applied." *United States v. Yazell,* 382 U.S. 341, 352 (1966).

II

Congress has not decided to supersede state law here . . . and the Court does not pretend that its newly manufactured "Government contractor defense" fits within any of the handful of "narrow areas," *Texas Industries, supra,* 451 U.S., at 641, of "uniquely federal interests" in which we have heretofore done so, 451 U.S., at 640. Rather, the Court creates a new category of "uniquely federal interests" out of a synthesis of two whose origins predate *Erie* itself: the interest in administering the "obligations to and rights of the United States under its contracts," and the interest in regulating the "civil liability of federal officials for actions taken in the course of their duty." This case is, however, simply a suit between two private parties. We have steadfastly declined to impose federal contract law on relationships that are collateral to a federal contract, or to extend the federal employee's immunity beyond federal employees. . . .

A

[I]t is . . . established that our power to create federal common law controlling the *Federal Government's* contractual rights and obligations does not translate into a power to prescribe rules that cover all transactions or contractual relationships collateral to Government contracts.

In *Miree v. DeKalb County, supra,* for example, the county was contractually obligated under a grant agreement with the Federal Aviation Administration (FAA) to "restrict the use of land adjacent to . . . the Airport to activities and purposes compatible with normal airport operations including landing and takeoff of aircraft." *Id.,* at 27 (citation omitted). At issue was whether the county breached its contractual obligation by operating a garbage dump adjacent to the airport, which allegedly attracted the swarm of birds that caused a plane crash. Federal common law would undoubtedly have controlled in any suit by the Federal Government to enforce the provision against the county or to collect damages for its violation. The diversity suit, however, was brought not by the Government, but by assorted private parties injured in some way by the accident. We observed that "the operations of the United States in connection with FAA grants such as these are undoubtedly of considerable magnitude," *id.,* at 30, and that "the United States has a substantial interest in regulating aircraft travel and promoting air travel safety," *id.,* at 31. Nevertheless, we held that state law should govern the claim because "only the rights of private litigants are at issue here," *id.,* at 30, and the claim against the county "will have *no direct effect upon the United States or its Treasury,*" *id.,* at 29 (emphasis added).

Miree relied heavily on [*Bank of America National Trust and Savings Association v. Parnell,* 352 U.S. 29 (1956),] and *Wallis v. Pan American Petroleum Corp., supra,* the former involving commercial paper issued by the United States and the latter involving property rights in federal land. . . . Here, as in *Miree, Parnell,* and *Wallis,* a Government contract governed by federal common law looms in the background. But here, too, the United States is not a party to the suit and the suit neither "touch[es] the rights and duties of the United States," *Parnell, supra,* at 33, nor has a "direct effect upon the United States or its Treasury," *Miree,* 433 U.S., at 29. The relationship at issue is at best collateral to the Government contract. . . .

That the Government might have to pay higher prices for what it orders if delivery in accordance with the contract exposes the seller to potential liability does not distinguish this case. Each of the cases just discussed declined to extend the reach of federal common law despite the assertion of comparable interests that would have affected the terms of the Government contract — whether its price or its substance — just as "directly" (or indirectly). Third-party beneficiaries can sue under a county's contract with the FAA, for example, even though — as the Court's focus on the absence of "*direct* effect on the United States or its Treasury," 433 U.S., at 29 (emphasis added), suggests — counties will likely pass on the costs to the Government in future contract negotiations. . . . As in each of the cases declining to extend the traditional reach of federal law of contracts beyond the rights and duties of the *Federal Government,* "any federal interest in the outcome of the question before us 'is far too speculative, far too remote a possibility to justify the application of federal law to transactions essentially of local concern.'" *Miree, supra,* at 32-33, quoting *Parnell,* 352 U.S., at 33-34.

B

Our "uniquely federal interest" in the tort liability of affiliates of the Federal Government is equally narrow. The immunity we have recognized has extended no further than a subset of "officials of the Federal Government" and has covered only "discretionary" functions within the scope of their legal authority. Never before have we so much as intimated that the immunity (or the "uniquely federal interest" that justifies it) might extend beyond that narrow class to cover also nongovernment employees whose authority to act is independent of any source of federal law and that are as far removed from the "functioning of the Federal Government" as is a Government contractor, [*Howard, v. Lyons,* 360 U.S. 593, 597 (1959)].

The historical narrowness of the federal interest and the immunity is hardly accidental. A federal officer exercises statutory authority, which not only provides the necessary basis for the immunity in positive law, but also permits us confidently to presume that interference with the exercise of discretion undermines congressional will. In contrast, a Government contractor acts independently of any congressional enactment. Thus, immunity for a contractor lacks both the positive law basis and the presumption that it furthers congressional will.

. . . The extension of immunity to Government contractors skews the balance we have historically struck. On the one hand, whatever marginal effect contractor immunity might have on the "effective administration of policies of government," its "harm to individual citizens" is more severe than in the Government-employee context. Our observation that "there are . . . other sanctions than civil tort suits available to deter the executive official who may be prone to exercise his functions in an unworthy and irresponsible manner," [*Barr v. Matteo,* 360 U.S. 564, 576 (1959),] see also *id.,* at 571, offers little deterrence to the Government contractor. On the other hand, a grant of immunity to Government contractors could not advance "the fearless, vigorous, and effective administration of policies of government" nearly as much as does the current immunity for Government employees. *Ibid.* In the first place, the threat of a tort suit is less likely to influence the conduct of an industrial giant than that of a lone civil servant, particularly since the work of a civil servant is significantly less profitable, and significantly more likely to be the subject of a vindictive lawsuit. In fact, were we to take seriously the Court's assertion that contractors pass their costs—including presumably litigation costs—through, "substantially if not totally, to the United States," the threat of a tort suit should have only marginal impact on the conduct of Government contractors. More importantly, inhibition of the Government official who actually sets Government policy presents a greater threat to the "administration of policies of government," than does inhibition of a private contractor, whose role is devoted largely to assessing the technological feasibility and cost of satisfying the Government's predetermined needs. Similarly, unlike tort suits against Government officials, tort suits against Government contractors would rarely "consume time and energies" that "would otherwise be devoted to governmental service." 360 U.S., at 571.

In short, because the essential justifications for official immunity do not support an extension to the Government contractor, it is no surprise that we have never extended it that far. . . .

III

[T]he Court invokes the discretionary function exception of the Federal Tort Claims Act (FTCA), 28 U.S.C. §2680(a). The Court does not suggest that the exception has any direct bearing here, for petitioner has sued a private manufacturer (not the Federal Government) under Virginia law (not the FTCA). . . .

Moreover, . . . the Government's immunity for discretionary functions is not even "a product of" the FTCA. Before Congress enacted the FTCA (when sovereign immunity barred any tort suit against the Federal Government) we perceived no need for a rule of federal common law to reinforce the Government's immunity by shielding also parties who might contractually pass costs on to it. Nor did we (or any other court of which I am aware) identify a special category of "discretionary" functions for which sovereign immunity was so crucial that a Government contractor who exercised discretion should share the Government's immunity from state tort law. . . .

IV

At bottom, the Court's analysis is premised on the proposition that any tort liability indirectly absorbed by the Government so burdens governmental functions as to compel us to act when Congress has not. That proposition is by no means uncontroversial. The tort system is premised on the assumption that the imposition of liability encourages actors to prevent any injury whose expected cost exceeds the cost of prevention. If the system is working as it should, Government contractors will design equipment to avoid certain injuries (like the deaths of soldiers or Government employees), which would be certain to burden the Government. The Court therefore has no basis for its assumption that tort liability will result in a net burden on the Government (let alone a clearly excessive net burden) rather than a net gain.

Perhaps tort liability is an inefficient means of ensuring the quality of design efforts, but "[w]hatever the merits of the policy" the Court wishes to implement, "its conversion into law is a proper subject for congressional action, not for any creative power of ours." [*United States v. Standard Oil Co. of Cal.*, 332 U.S. 301, 314-315 (1947).] It is, after all, "Congress, not this Court or the other federal courts, [that] is the custodian of the national purse. By the same token [Congress] is the primary and most often the exclusive arbiter of federal fiscal affairs. And these comprehend, as we have said, securing the treasury or the Government against financial losses *however inflicted*. . . ." *Ibid.* (emphasis added). . . .

Were I a legislator, I would probably vote against any law absolving multi-billion dollar private enterprises from answering for their tragic mistakes, at least if that law were justified by no more than the unsupported speculation that their liability might ultimately burden the United States Treasury. Some of my colleagues here would evidently vote otherwise (as they have here), but that should not matter here. We are judges not legislators, and the vote is not ours to cast. . . .

JUSTICE STEVENS, dissenting.

When judges are asked to embark on a lawmaking venture, I believe they should carefully consider whether they, or a legislative body, are better equipped to perform the task at hand. There are instances of so-called interstitial lawmaking that inevitably become part of the judicial process. But when we are asked to create an entirely new doctrine—to answer "questions of policy on which Congress has not spoken," *United States v. Gilman*, 347 U.S. 507, 511 (1954)—we have a special duty to identify the proper decisionmaker before trying to make the proper decision.

When the novel question of policy involves a balancing of the conflicting interests in the efficient operation of a massive governmental program and the protection of the rights of the individual—whether in the social welfare context, the civil service context, or the military procurement context—I feel very deeply that we should defer to the expertise of the Congress. . . .

POINTS FOR DISCUSSION

1. The *Boyle* Court justified its use of federal common law on the grounds that it was necessary to serve "uniquely federal interests." Justices Brennan and Stevens, however, argued in dissent that the question of immunity for military contractors is for Congress, not courts, to decide. Justice Brennan explained that "*Erie* was deeply rooted in notions of federalism, and is most seriously implicated when, as here, federal judges displace the state law that would ordinarily govern with their own rules of federal common law." *Erie*, he continued, "put to rest the notion that the grant of diversity jurisdiction to federal courts is itself authority to fashion rules of substantive law." How did the Court's application of federal common law in *Boyle* "seriously implicate[]" federalism? Does the Court's opinion properly account for the Constitution's federal structure?

2. Having determined that federal common law should displace state law in *Boyle*, the Court proceeded to give content to federal common law. It explained that courts may not impose liability for design defects in military equipment under state law "when (1) the United States approved reasonably precise specifications, (2) the equipment conformed to those specifications, and (3) the supplier warned the United States about dangers in the use of the equipment that were known to the supplier but not to the United States." Of all the rules the Court may have adopted, why did it adopt this one? What constraints, if any, exist on a federal court's authority to fashion a rule of federal common law?

3. In *United States v. Hudson & Goodwin*, 11 U.S. (7 Cranch) 32 (1812), the Court held that federal courts lack common law criminal jurisdiction. Nonetheless, courts continue to apply federal common law in certain enclaves of cases, such as in *Boyle*. Are *Hudson & Goodwin* & *Boyle* consistent?

In light of *Erie*—and cases such as *Clearfield Trust* and *Boyle*—scholars have vigorously debated the propriety of federal common law as a rule of decision in federal courts. Scholars have articulated various theories of federal common law. Most theories "fall into two categories: first, theories that argue that federal courts have *inherent* power to make federal common law in certain circumstances; and, second, theories that argue that federal courts may make federal common law when the Constitution or Congress has *delegated* power to them to do so." Anthony J. Bellia Jr., *State Courts and the Making of Federal Common Law*, 153 U. Pa. L. Rev. 825, 853 (2005). Inherent power theories argue that federal courts have a prerogative to make federal common law. For instance, Dean Larry Kramer has

> articulated an inherent power theory of the making of federal common law by federal courts. He argues that the effectiveness of such lawmaking justifies recognition of a "judicial prerogative" to make federal common law whenever it is "necessary and proper" to implement a congressional act. He describes the limits of this judicial prerogative as follows: "[T]he occasion for making federal common law must be to improve the effectiveness of a statute, but the court need not locate the source of its rules 'in' the statute"; rather, the "lawmaking power" of the federal courts is "broad enough to encompass any rule consistent with the general purposes of the statute on which it is based." The justification for this judicial prerogative, as he explains it, lies in "what works." As an empirical matter, he claims that the making of federal common law in this way is "exceedingly useful" insofar as it: (1) expands the governing capacity of the federal government; (2) resolves hard questions that Congress might otherwise avoid; and (3) involves another lawmaker in the resolution of societal problems.

Id. at 858-859 (discussing Larry Kramer, *The Lawmaking Power of the Federal Courts*, 12 Pace L. Rev. 263 (1992)) (footnotes omitted).

In contrast, delegated power theories argue that federal courts may make federal common law only when the Constitution or Congress has delegated power to them to do so. For instance,

> [Professor] Thomas Merrill has argued that federal courts have power to make federal common law "when Congress or the framers of the Constitution have conferred power on the federal courts to fashion federal rules of decision in order to round out or complete a constitutional or statutory scheme." [Professor] Martha Field has articulated a theory of federal common law that similarly is grounded in the need for an authoritative legal source to have enabled federal courts to make federal common law. She argues that a court may make federal common law if it can "point to a federal enactment, constitutional or statutory, that it interprets as authorizing the federal common law rule." "Deciding whether common law can be made in any given case," she explains, "is a matter of interpreting each possible enabling authority to see whether or not it supports federal common law." Both claims view the legitimacy of federal common law to be a matter of delegated power.
>
> In Merrill's view, "the question of the *power* of federal courts to make law should precede questions about the content of that law." For him, constitutional principles of federalism, separation of powers, and electoral accountability require a delegation of power to federal courts for their making of federal common law to be justified. In Field's view, "there must be a source of authority for any given exercise of federal common law power." "This limit," she explains, "flows from the proposition that authority must exist for any exercise of federal power, coupled with the proposition that there is no enactment giving federal courts power to make common law generally." . . .
>
> [Their] theories differ significantly[, however,] over when there has been a legitimate delegation of power to federal courts to make federal common law. Merrill argues that a legitimate delegation must be "specifically intended" and the scope of the delegation "reasonably circumscribed." Field takes a broader approach, one that "does not in fact require any particular form of authorization." Her theory leaves it to courts to decide "whether a directive is implicit in any particular enactment."

Bellia, 153 U. Pa. L. Rev. at 863-865 (discussing Martha A. Field, *Sources of Law: The Scope of Federal Common Law*, 99 Harv. L. Rev. 881 (1986), and Thomas W. Merrill, *The Common Law Powers of Federal Courts*, 52 U. Chi. L. Rev. 1 (1985)) (footnotes omitted).

With this background in mind, consider the following two competing accounts of federal common law. Professor Bradford Clark argues that the Constitution constrains federal courts' authority to apply federal common law. When federal courts make federal common law, he contends, they circumvent federal lawmaking procedures and assume lawmaking power that the Constitution assigns to the political branches, which are subject to the political safeguards of federalism. Professor Louise Weinberg, in contrast, argues that federal courts have broad power to make federal common law. Within their jurisdiction, she claims, federal courts have power to make law when it serves the national interest. As you read these two accounts, consider the following questions:

- What weight does each ascribe to constitutional structure, historical practice, national interests, and normatives value of federalism?
- How does each interpret the Supreme Court's opinion in *Erie*?

BRADFORD R. CLARK, SEPARATION OF POWERS AS A SAFEGUARD OF FEDERALISM

79 Tex. L. Rev. 1321, 1323-1325, 1328-1331, 1342-1343, 1403, 1412-1419 (2001)

During the last century, courts and commentators have accepted various forms of unconventional federal lawmaking—that is, lawmaking that appears to yield "the supreme Law of the Land,"[3] but fails to comply with the procedures established by the Constitution for adopting the "Constitution," "Laws," and "Treaties" of the United States.[4] Examples include . . . federal common law. Opponents of these innovations generally rely on the constitutional separation of powers to question the legitimacy of unconventional federal lawmaking. Proponents counter that such reliance is excessively formal, and urge courts to employ a more flexible, functional approach. Both sides, however, have failed to recognize that unconventional federal lawmaking implicates not only separation of powers, but also federalism—at least to the extent that such lawmaking purports to displace state law. . . .

The Founders understood that the means established for adopting federal law would have a direct impact on federalism. Some of the most potent safeguards of federalism, for example, derive from a surprising source: the Supremacy Clause. Although the Supremacy Clause performs the familiar function of securing the primacy of federal law over contrary state law, it also necessarily constrains the exercise of federal power by recognizing only three sources of law as "the supreme Law of the Land." These sources are the "Constitution, and the Laws of the United States which shall be made in Pursuance thereof; and all Treaties made, or which shall be made, under the Authority of the United States." The Founders, in turn, prescribed "finely wrought and exhaustively considered"[8] procedures elsewhere in the Constitution to govern the adoption of each type of law recognized by the Supremacy Clause. Although federal lawmaking procedures are generally regarded as "integral parts of the constitutional design for the separation of powers,"[9] they also preserve federalism both by making federal law more difficult to adopt, and by assigning lawmaking power solely to actors subject to the political safeguards of federalism. The text, structure, and history of the Constitution, moreover, suggest that these procedures were meant to be the exclusive means of adopting "the supreme Law of the Land." Permitting the federal government to avoid these constraints would allow it to exercise more power than the Constitution contemplates, at the expense of state authority. Accordingly, "federal law" adopted outside these procedures does not clearly fall within the terms of the Supremacy Clause, and thus provides a questionable basis for displacing state law.

---

3. U.S. CONST. art. VI, cl. 2.
4. *Id.*
8. INS v. Chadha, 462 U.S. 919, 951 (1983).
9. *Id.* at 946.

In this sense, federal action that violates the Constitution's separation of powers may also "invade[] rights which . . . are reserved by the Constitution to the several states."[11] For example, some of the Supreme Court's most prominent separation-of-powers decisions have invalidated attempts by each branch of the federal government to circumvent constitutionally prescribed lawmaking procedures. These decisions also safeguard federalism by permitting designated agents of the federal government to adopt federal law only if they employ procedures that "impose burdens . . . that often seem clumsy, inefficient, even unworkable."[13] In other words, enforcement of federal lawmaking procedures not only implements the Constitution's formal separation of powers, but also functions to preserve "the governance prerogatives of state and local institutions."[14]

Although the Supreme Court's recent decisions enforcing the limits of Congress's commerce power have understandably received considerable attention, strict adherence to federal lawmaking procedures arguably has a "larger influence upon the working balance of our federalism"[17] than the formal "distribution of authority between the nation and the states."[18] The reason is that decisions under the Commerce Clause serve only to police the outer boundaries of federal power—boundaries that have proven difficult to draw and enforce. Federal lawmaking procedures, by contrast, establish clear constraints on the federal government's ability to exercise power *within* these limits, wherever drawn. Each year, for example, thousands of bills are introduced in Congress, but only a small number pass both Houses and are signed into law by the President. Thus, even when national power is "quite unquestioned in a given situation,"[20] constitutionally prescribed lawmaking procedures frequently operate to screen out attempts by the federal government to exercise such authority. The states are the direct beneficiaries of this screening mechanism because the federal government's inability to adopt "the supreme Law of the Land" leaves states free to govern. . . .

Supremacy, Federal Lawmaking Procedures, and Federalism

In several prominent cases, the Supreme Court has strictly enforced federal lawmaking procedures, especially the bicameralism and presentment requirements of Article I, Section 7. It is common ground that the Founders regarded such procedures as a principal means of maintaining the constitutional separation of powers. The text, history, and structure of the Constitution, however, reveal that the Founders also used federal lawmaking procedures to safeguard federalism.

---

11. Erie R.R. v. Tompkins, 304 U.S. 64, 80 (1938).

13. *Chadha*, 462 U.S. at 959.

14. Larry D. Kramer, *Putting the Politics Back into the Political Safeguards of Federalism*, 100 COLUM. L. REV. 215, 222 (2000) (emphasis omitted).

17. Herbert Wechsler, *The Political Safeguards of Federalism: The Role of the States in the Composition and Selection of the National Government*, 54 COLUM. L. REV. 543, 544 (1954).

18. *Id.* at 543-44.

20. *Id.* at 545.

With respect to separation of powers, Madison explained that "[a]fter discriminating . . . in theory, the several classes of power, as they may in their nature be legislative, executive, or judiciary, the next and most difficult task is to provide some practical security for each, against the invasion of the others."[28] Madison distinguished between theory and practice because the Founders believed that "a mere demarcation on parchment of the constitutional limits of the several departments" would not be "a sufficient guard against those encroachments which lead to a tyrannical concentration of all the powers of government in the same hands."[29]

The Founders decided that "the defect must be supplied, by so contriving the interior structure of the government as that its several constituent parts may, by their mutual relations, be the means of keeping each other in their proper places."[30] For example, the Constitution first divides Congress into two Houses and then requires it to submit proposed "Laws" to the President for his approval.[31] Similarly, the Constitution conditions the President's power to make "Treaties" upon the advice and consent of the Senate.[32] By requiring the assent of more than one branch to adopt "Laws" and "Treaties," federal lawmaking procedures furnish each participant with "constitutional arms for its own defense."[33] The Founders considered such checks and balances necessary to maintain in practice "the degree of separation which the maxim requires."[34]

Federal lawmaking procedures safeguard federalism as well. The Founders designed "the interior structure of the government" not only to empower the political branches to check each other, but also to ensure that they would consider state prerogatives in performing their functions. As Madison explained, "each of the principal branches of the federal government will owe its existence more or less to the favor of the State governments."[35] The President, he remarked, "cannot be elected at all" without "the intervention of the State legislatures." The Senate, moreover, "will be elected absolutely and exclusively by the State legislatures." "Even the House of Representatives, though drawn immediately from the people, will be chosen very much under the influence of that class of men . . . elect[ed] into the State legislatures." Thus, by design, "each of the principal branches of the federal government . . . must consequently feel a dependence, which is much more likely to beget a disposition too obsequious than too overbearing towards" the states.[39]

Under the original Constitution, this structurally inspired concern for state prerogatives would encourage participants in the federal lawmaking process to withhold their consent from proposals objectionable to the states. Because federal lawmaking procedures give the House, the Senate, and the President

---

28. THE FEDERALIST No. 48, at 308 (James Madison) (Clinton Rossiter ed., 1961).
29. *Id.* at 313.
30. THE FEDERALIST No. 51, at 320 (James Madison) (Clinton Rossiter ed., 1961).
31. *See* U.S. CONST. art. I, §7, cl. 2.
32. *See Id.* art. II, §2, cl. 2.
33. THE FEDERALIST No. 73, at 442 (Alexander Hamilton) (Clinton Rossiter ed., 1961).
34. THE FEDERALIST No. 48, at 308 (James Madison) (Clinton Rossiter ed., 1961).
35. THE FEDERALIST No. 45, at 291 (James Madison) (Clinton Rossiter ed., 1961).
39. *Id.*

each at least a qualified veto, rejection by any of these institutions ordinarily prevents a proposal from becoming law. The Founders understood that these procedures — like the participants themselves — were "calculated to restrain the excess of lawmaking, and to keep things in the same state in which they happen to be at any given period."[40] This structural bias in favor of the status quo would necessarily defeat "a few good laws," but would "amply compensate[]" for this flaw by "preventing a number of bad ones."[41] In either event, the federal government's unwillingness or inability to adopt federal law would leave the states free to govern.

The Supremacy Clause effectively incorporates federal lawmaking procedures designed to safeguard federalism. The Clause provides as follows:

> This Constitution, and the Laws of the United States which shall be made in Pursuance thereof; and all Treaties made, or which shall be made, under the Authority of the United States, shall be the supreme Law of the Land; and the Judges in every State shall be bound thereby, any Thing in the Constitution or Laws of any State to the Contrary notwithstanding.[42]

By its terms, the Supremacy Clause recognizes only the "Constitution," "Laws," and "Treaties" of the United States as "the supreme Law of the Land." Although the Clause performs the familiar function of securing the supremacy of these sources of federal law over state law "to the Contrary," the negative implication of the Clause is that state law remains in full force in the absence of such law. . . . Because the Supremacy Clause designates only three sources of law as "the supreme Law of the Land," determining whether a particular legal text constitutes one of these sources is an essential predicate to every application of the Clause.

The Constitution establishes detailed procedures to govern the adoption of each type of law recognized by the Supremacy Clause. These procedures safeguard federalism on one level simply by requiring agreement among multiple actors, thus making the "Constitution," "Laws," and "Treaties" of the United States relatively difficult to adopt. In this sense, "the ultimate political safeguard may be the procedural gauntlet that any legislative proposal must run and the concomitant difficulty of overcoming legislative inertia."[46] Federal lawmaking procedures safeguarded federalism on another level by assigning power to adopt "the supreme Law of the Land" solely to entities subject to "the political safeguards of federalism" — that is, the states' "strategic role to the selection of Congress and the President."[47] These procedures enhanced the influence of the states by giving federal institutions designed to represent state interests — such as the Senate — a veto over all forms of federal lawmaking, and thus suggest that the Founders understood constitutionally prescribed lawmaking procedures to establish the exclusive means of adopting "the supreme Law of the Land." Although the direct election of Senators under

---

40. The Federalist No. 73, at 444 (Alexander Hamilton) (Clinton Rossiter ed., 1961).
41. *Id.*
42. U.S. Const. art. VI, cl. 2.
46. Ernest A. Young, *Constitutional Avoidance, Resistance Norms, and the Preservation of Judicial Review*, 78 Texas L. Rev. 1549, 1609 (2000).
47. Wechsler, *Political Safeguards, supra*, at 544.

the Seventeenth Amendment and other changes in the law have diminished the states' influence in the lawmaking process, federal lawmaking procedures continue to safeguard federalism by constraining the federal government's ability to displace state law. . . .

Restricting federal lawmaking to entities structured to be sensitive to state prerogatives served the ends of federalism by "retarding or restraining new intrusions by the center on the domain of the states."[107] Federal lawmaking procedures, moreover, maximized state influence by singling out the Senate — the federal institution in which the states had the greatest influence — to participate in all forms of federal lawmaking. . . .

Judicial Compliance With Federal Lawmaking Procedures

From Swift to Erie: *The Demise of General Common Law*

Erie Railroad Co. v. Tompkins represents perhaps the most significant effort by the Supreme Court to prevent judicial lawmaking and uphold federal lawmaking procedures. *Erie* overruled *Swift v. Tyson* and its progeny, which permitted federal courts to resolve the rights and duties of parties before the court according to so-called "general common law," notwithstanding contrary law. In its place, *Erie* recognized the principle that "[e]xcept in matters governed by the Federal Constitution or by Acts of Congress, the law to be applied in any case is the law of the State."[575] The shift from *Swift* to *Erie* reflects the Court's recognition — supported by the negative implication of the Supremacy Clause — that state law governs under the constitutional structure unless and until affirmatively displaced by federal law adopted in accord with the lawmaking procedures prescribed by the Constitution.

1. Erie *and Judicial Evasion of Federal Lawmaking Procedures.* Although the Supreme Court's decision in *Swift* (resolving a question of general commercial law) was arguably defensible when decided, the federal courts' continued adherence to — and expansion of — the *Swift* doctrine raised increasing constitutional concerns over time. First, at some point, "[s]tate courts no longer conceived of their task in commercial cases as applying a [customary] body of law common to many jurisdictions. Rather, they increasingly claimed or exercised authority to formulate commercial doctrines as a matter of state law."[577] Thus, the federal judiciary's continued application of the *Swift* doctrine in commercial cases to displace otherwise applicable state law lacked a clear constitutional foundation. Second, federal courts "vastly expanded the range of legal questions subject to the *Swift* doctrine" to include "such historically local matters as punitive damages, property, and torts."[578] Unlike commercial law, these matters were traditionally governed by local law. "These two developments created an ever-widening legitimacy gap"[580] by replacing large portions of state law with federal judge-made law in diversity

---

107. *Id.* at 558.
575. Erie R. Co. v. Tompkins, 304 U.S. 64, 78 (1938).
577. Bradford R. Clark, *Federal Common Law: A Structural Reinterpretation*, 144 U. Pa. L. Rev. 1245, 1290 (1996).
578. *Id.*
580. *Id.* at 1291.

cases. As Professor Lessig has observed, by the time *Erie* was decided, changing conceptions of state law revealed "the fundamental political reality" that "what a judge was doing when he decided an open question of common law was making law rather than finding law."[581] As discussed more fully below, such open-ended lawmaking by federal courts under *Swift* was constitutionally problematic because it allowed the federal government, through its courts, to displace state law without adhering to constitutionally prescribed lawmaking procedures designed to safeguard federalism.

Commentators have long pondered the precise nature of the constitutional defect found by the Supreme Court in *Erie*. Careful analysis reveals that *Erie*'s constitutional holding is best understood as an attempt to enforce federal lawmaking procedures and the political safeguards of federalism they incorporate. In other words, *Erie* reflects the idea that the Constitution not only limits the *powers* granted to the federal government, but also constrains the *manner* in which the federal government may exercise those powers to displace state law. *Erie* demonstrates that federal courts — no less than Congress and the President — must respect federal law-making procedures.

An essential predicate of the Court's decision in *Erie* was its recognition that state courts — no less than state legislatures — make law on behalf of the states. According to the Court, "whether the law of the state shall be declared by its Legislature in a statute or by its highest court in a decision is not a matter of federal concern."[585] Thus, the constitutional question before the Court in *Erie* was whether a federal court — in the absence of an applicable provision of the "Constitution," "Laws," or "Treaties" of the United States — may disregard "the law of the state" and apply its own conception of "general common law." The Court held this practice to be unconstitutional.

Erie began its constitutional analysis with the proposition that "[e]xcept in matters governed by the Federal Constitution or by Acts of Congress, the law to be applied in any case is the law of the State."[587] It follows that "[t]here is no federal general common law."[588] The Court supported these propositions with two observations. First, "Congress has no power to declare substantive rules of common law applicable in a state whether they be local in their nature or 'general,' be they commercial law or a part of the law of torts. And [second,] no clause in the Constitution purports to confer such a power upon the federal courts."[589]

The first observation is unsurprising if the Court merely meant to suggest that Congress lacks power to replace state common law en gros with a comprehensive federal code. If, on the other hand, the Court meant that Congress lacks power to enact a specific rule of decision for cases like *Erie*, then this observation is questionable in light of the Court's contemporaneous decisions broadly interpreting the scope of congressional power under the Commerce

---

581. Lawrence Lessig, *Understanding Changed Readings: Fidelity and Theory*, 47 Stan. L. Rev. 395, 431 (1995).
585. *Erie*, 304 U.S. at 78.
587. *Id.*
588. *Id.*
589. *Id.*

Clause. In any event, *Erie*'s suggestion regarding the lack of *congressional* power was unnecessary to the decision because no federal statute purported to prescribe a federal rule of decision applicable to the case. For these reasons, "the constitutional argument of *Erie* has since been reinterpreted to emphasize the distinction — at least implicit in the opinion — between the power of Congress and the power of the federal courts." In other words, as Professor Currie has observed, "on the facts of the case the more serious objection seemed to be one less of federalism than of separation of powers: whether or not Congress could make rules to govern the particular case, it had not done so; and the federal courts had only those powers given them by the Constitution or statute."[592]

This was the point of the Court's second observation: that "no clause in the Constitution purports to confer . . . power upon the federal courts" "to declare substantive rules of common law applicable in a State."[593] This observation, read in light of the Court's holding, necessarily presupposes that the lawmaking procedures established by the Constitution are the exclusive means by which agents of the federal government can adopt "law applicable in a State." When the federal government follows these procedures to adopt "the Federal Constitution," "Acts of Congress," and presumably treaties, then *Erie* acknowledges that federal courts must apply such law notwithstanding state law to the contrary. On the other hand, in the absence of federal law adopted according to these procedures, the Constitution requires federal courts to apply "the law of the State." In such cases, *Erie* instructs that " 'the authority and only authority is the State, and if that be so, the voice adopted by the State as its own (whether it be of its Legislature or of its Supreme Court) should utter the last word.' "[596]

The federal courts' strict adherence to the lawmaking procedures established by the Constitution necessarily constrains the exercise of federal power, and thus preserves state governance prerogatives. By design, none of the lawmaking procedures prescribed by the Constitution either requires or permits participation by the federal judiciary. As Todd Peterson has observed, "[t]he framers did not grant [federal] judges the right to exercise their own unlimited discretion or will instead of judgment."[598] Rather, they specifically "relied on the fact that [federal] judges [would] *not* possess the same kind of primary discretion as legislators."[599] Thus, the Constitution's general separation of legislative and judicial powers, and its specific imposition of federal lawmaking procedures, support the Supreme Court's assessment that "federal courts, unlike their state counterparts, are courts of limited jurisdiction that have not been vested with open-ended lawmaking powers."[601]

The reason for this disparity between state and federal courts is that lawmaking by state courts "is not a matter of federal concern,"[602] whereas

---

592. DAVID P. CURRIE, THE CONSTITUTION IN THE SUPREME COURT: THE SECOND CENTURY 1888-1986, at 243 (1990).

593. *Erie*, 304 U.S. at 78.

596. *Id.* at 79.

598. Todd D. Peterson, *Restoring Structural Checks on Judicial Power in the Era of Managerial Judging*, 29 U.C. DAVIS L. REV. 41, 53 (1995) (citing THE FEDERALIST No. 78, at 469 (Alexander Hamilton) (Clinton Rossiter ed., 1961)).

599. *Id.*

601. Northwest Airlines v. Transp. Workers Union, 451 U.S. 77, 95 (1981).

lawmaking by federal courts necessarily circumvents federal lawmaking procedures. Allowing federal courts unilaterally to fashion and apply "substantive rules of common law applicable in a State"—even rules like those applied during the *Swift* era that are not binding in state court—would enable federal courts to evade the "finely wrought" procedures that the Constitution established to govern the federal government's adoption of "the supreme Law of the Land." Such lawmaking by federal courts threatens the constitutional " 'autonomy and independence of the States' "[603] by depriving the states of their right to govern matters within their territory unless and until constitutionally designated actors agree to displace state law using constitutionally prescribed procedures.

Erie thus supports the view that strict adherence to the Constitution's lawmaking procedures is necessary to ensure that the political safeguards of federalism serve their intended function. The political safeguards of federalism are designed to constrain the exercise of federal lawmaking power by Congress and the President. These safeguards cannot similarly constrain lawmaking by federal courts because "the States are represented in Congress but not in the federal courts."[605] If the political safeguards of federalism are to check the exercise of federal power, then the federal government—including its courts—must adhere closely to the federal lawmaking procedures that incorporate those safeguards. As Henry Monaghan put it, *Erie* "recognizes that federal judicial power to displace state law is not coextensive with the scope of dormant congressional power. Rather, the Court must point to some source, such as a statute, treaty, or constitutional provision, as authority for the creation of substantive federal law."[606] The reason is that, unlike federal judge-made law, such sources are adopted in accordance with constitutionally prescribed lawmaking procedures. Seen in this light, *Erie* seems justified in concluding that "the doctrine of *Swift v. Tyson* is, as Mr. Justice Holmes said, 'an unconstitutional assumption of powers by the courts of the United States which no lapse of time or respectable array of opinion should make us hesitate to correct.'"[607]

Louise Weinberg, Federal Common Law

83 Nw. U. L. Rev. 805, 805-806, 809-816 (1989)

Introduction: A Paradox

In this fifty-first year of *Erie Railroad Co. v. Tompkins*, the legitimacy and the propriety of federal common law remain uncertain. The current debate is as vigorous—and inconclusive—as it has ever been.

I take it that there are no fundamental constraints on the fashioning of federal rules of decision. I will call this "the true position." I hasten to

---

602. *Erie*, 304 U.S. at 78.

603. *Id.*

605. City of Milwaukee v. Illinois, 451 U.S. 304, 317 n.9 (1981).

606. Henry P. Monaghan, *The Supreme Court, 1974 Term—Foreword: Constitutional Common Law*, 89 Harv. L. Rev. 1, 11-12 (1975).

607. *Erie*, 304 U.S. at 79 (quoting Black & White Taxicab & Transfer Co. v. Brown & Yellow Taxicab & Transfer Co., 276 U.S. 518, 534 (1928) (Holmes, J., dissenting)).

acknowledge that national policies of comity, federalism, and deference to the legislature are rightly (and as a matter of course) taken into account when federal questions are decided. But these burdens upon the decision of federal questions, however distinct from analogous burdens upon the decision of state questions, seem to me not disqualifyingly heavier ones.

My difficulty lies elsewhere. What I have just called "the true position" is indeed the clarified modern position, "so beautifully simple, and so simply beautiful." But it is not the actual position. Almost, but not quite. The problem is that "the true position" is not the *official* position of the Supreme Court. Like that favorite of logicians, the liar who insists he cannot speak truth, judge-made federal law tells us that judges cannot make federal law. . . .

(1) Empowerment and Interest

What empowers a sovereign to make and apply laws on a particular subject matter? Set to one side, for the moment, the question of legislation versus case law. Let us focus on the nature of lawmaking power itself. We can then begin to think about the lawmaking power of the nation on the one hand and of a state on the other.

The Supreme Court has recognized for at least half a century that the raw lawmaking power of a sovereign is coextensive with the sovereign's sphere of interest. In this sense, the *source* of sovereign lawmaking power — not the limits on that power — is the sovereign's sphere of legitimate governmental interest. Whether the Court reasons under the commerce clause, the due process clause, the equal protection clause, the contract clause, or the full faith and credit clause, the requirement remains constant. A state has presumptive power to govern a matter by its laws if it has an interest in doing so. It is the state's governmental interest that the Court refers to when it finds the "rational basis" that enables a law to survive minimal constitutional scrutiny.

A state lacking the requisite governmental interest in an issue has no power to govern it. Justice Brandeis, the author of *Erie*, was among those clarifying this modern position. A state attempting to govern a matter in which it has no legitimate governmental interest acts arbitrarily, irrationally, and without due process. Thus, those who insist that federal lawmaking requires special justification in the clear requirements of national policy are, of course, correct. But they should understand that state lawmaking also requires special justification in the clear requirements of state policy.

We can take other insights gleaned from our consideration of state power and apply them to the problem of national power. What is within the sphere of legitimate national governmental interest? The preamble to the Constitution of the United States, as it happens, makes that plain. The nation is empowered to provide for the general welfare (which seems logically to include, as well as be given direction by, the other concerns of the preamble — the goals of a more perfect union, and the securing of the blessings of liberty). The reference, importantly, is to our general welfare, "We the People of the United States." Thus, Congress is not authorized to make a law that does not provide for our general welfare.

Suppose, to take a too-well-known example, that to provide for the welfare of potential tort victims in Pennsylvania, Congress enacted a statute purporting to regulate the Pennsylvania tort duties of railways operating in Pennsylvania. Unless the statute were grounded on some national policy, the law would be unconstitutional. Congress lacks power to create rules of decision applicable in a state. Congress can provide only for the general welfare of the people of the United States.

Or, to take another example, suppose Congress enacted a law purporting to regulate the landscaping by English companies of English government buildings in England. That law, too, would be prima facie beyond the power of Congress. Congress is given power to provide for the general welfare of "the People of the United States." Just as in the example of a Congressional statute governing torts in Pennsylvania, it is hard to see how the English landscaping law comes within the terms of national empowerment.

But it must be equally evident that the legislature of Pennsylvania can no more sit as a little Congress, enacting laws purporting to govern the nation or any other country or state, than Congress can sit as a legislature of Pennsylvania or England. In the nature of things, Pennsylvania has no power to provide for the general welfare of non-Pennsylvanians.

What has been said thus far is sufficient to answer one of the oddly persistent questions in the ongoing debate. No one with a basic grasp of the essentials of empowerment would question that *Erie* was constitutionally required. *Erie*'s holding in chief was about the fundamental empowerment of the nation, not of its courts. *Erie* held, precisely, that the nation lacks power to make state law. State law is reserved to the states. The power of the nation is to make federal law only.

There was, of course, no conflict between federal and state law in *Erie*. The Court struck down no federal law or rule. It struck down only an independent view of what state law ought to be. Nothing in that holding qualifies national power to make federal law. For example, once Congress federalizes the tort duties of railroads, Congress has every relevant power. Congress has used part of that power to address the tort duties of railroads, as employers, in interstate commerce. We now understand, after *The Wheat Case* and *Heart of Atlanta Motel*, that Congress has extensive power even over intrastate commerce, power it exercises in a variety of other contexts. This power is evident in laws forbidding discrimination in employment, or regulating labor.

If there is a national interest in the regulation of English landscaping of English government buildings in England, Congress could act in that interest as well. Consider this: "If a foreign government denies landscaping contracts to lowest-bidding landscaping contractors who are United States nationals, landscaping contractors who are nationals of that government shall not be eligible to bid on public landscaping contracts offered by the United States."

So, deferring the questions of courts versus legislatures and of the nation versus the states, we can at least be somewhat clearer about national lawmaking power. We will not be misled by lists of "federal enclaves" chronically offered by courts and writers, lists of discrete topics upon which the nation's lawmaking power is supposedly confined in its courts. We are told that federal common law may legitimately arise when the government is a party; in cases involving the foreign relations of the nation; in admiralty; and in a few other areas of uniquely federal concern. Yet, as we have seen, the lawmaking power of a sovereign is coextensive with its sphere of governmental interest. Where a sovereign's interest ends its power ends, but obviously that will not hamper it in any area of concern to itself.

These truisms leave open, then, for the credulous, only the familiar but bizarre question whether there is any peculiar infirmity that disables *courts* from ruling in the national interest—and then, only from ruling on un-"listed" topics. The rest of us have always understood that our courts are, and must be, courts of coordinate powers. The judiciary must have presumptive power to adjudicate whatever the legislature and the executive can act upon. Without this principle we cease to be a nation of laws.

Despite these broad understandings of the lineaments of empowerment, occasionally one finds reference in the literature to discredited older doctrines. One hopes that few today think that since the nation is one of expressly delegated powers it can act only within the confines of an express Constitutional grant of power and not upon its perceived needs. It is too well understood by now that when the national interest so requires, national lawmaking power will be implied.

Recently, a new confidence seems to inform the literature that there is a need for some sort of authorization before federal common law can be fashioned. Some find this requirement in the structure of a government of separated powers; others find it in the structure of our federalism, in which residual governance is left to the states, and national powers are enumerated.

In every case, however, given the fundamentals of empowerment, what justifies an exercise of national lawmaking power is the existence of a legitimate national governmental interest. Courts must act, of course, within their constitutional and statutory jurisdiction. But no other "authorization" is required. . . .

(2) Federalism

I have said that *Erie* was not a limit on national lawmaking power. No national rule was in conflict with state law there. Congress was said to lack power to make rules of decision applicable in a state, rather than in the nation. We can also see that the power of the states does not significantly limit the lawmaking power of the nation—certainly not under *Erie*. Justice Brandeis' holding in *Erie* was premised on the lack of power in Congress to make state law, not on the tenth amendment. The problem was Congress' sheer lack of power to act in the interest of some state rather than of the nation.

Nor is the tenth amendment itself necessarily a limit on national power. Obviously, the Supreme Court could make it one again, despite the decision in the *Garcia* case. But nothing in the amendment, with its grand tautology, will give the Court any guidance. The problem is that nothing can actually be "reserved" to exclusive state governance that lies inside the sphere of national policy concern and outside any governmental interest of some state.

Yet rather than reasoning from the actual desiderata of governmental power, courts and writers will rely on all sorts of irrelevancies. It will be said that federal courts, unlike state courts, are courts of limited jurisdiction and therefore of limited lawmaking power. This is a *non sequitur*; but even if it were not, it should be obvious that there is no jurisdictional defect unique to the power of the *federal* sovereign. State courts, like federal courts, are limited in their jurisdictions — sometimes even by Congress. A state court, like a federal court, will feel a general obligation of deference to its legislature and indeed to Congress. State judges also can, do, and must fashion federal answers to federal questions and state answers to state questions.

Commentators continue to say (although the debate on this is so stale that sheer boredom ought to have put a stop to it) that there remain constitutional and statutory problems. The argument is that constitutional or statutory constraints, grounded in concerns of federalism, inhibit courts confronted with federal questions from fashioning federal answers. The trouble with this view has always been that none of the legal materials so relentlessly adverted to seem to matter. . . .

All the relevant materials are, for starters, tautological. The tenth amendment says that powers not granted to the nation are reserved to the states. But what about powers granted to the nation? *Erie* says that except in matters governed by federal law, state law governs. But what about matters governed by federal law? The Rules of Decision Act says that state law shall furnish the rules of decision in federal civil actions, in cases in which they apply. But what about cases in which they do not apply?

It might be argued that the asserted tautologies vanish when one recognizes that all of these materials reserving federal lawmaking power — *Erie*, the tenth amendment, the Rules of Decision Act — do not, in fact, expressly reserve federal case law. The national law that is held in reserve is the Constitution, treaties, or "laws" — i.e., statutes — of the United States. But because we now understand that the supremacy clause compels the application of federal case law where it applies, these omissions cannot have any modern meaning, no matter what they may have meant to those who made them. . . .

POINTS FOR DISCUSSION

1. Professors Clark and Weinberg each consider, in varying degrees, how federal common law relates to national interests, constitutional structure, historical practice, and federalism values. On what grounds should their differences of opinion be resolved?

2. Professor Clark understands *Erie* to preclude federal courts from applying a federal common law rule of decision regardless of whether Congress would have constitutional power to enact that rule of decision. Professor Weinberg, on the other hand, understands *Erie* to limit neither Congress's power to enact national laws nor federal courts' power to apply federal common law rules of decision. Which reading of *Erie*, if either, is more persuasive?

B. CUSTOMARY INTERNATIONAL LAW

Customary international law, as described in the *Restatement*, "results from a general and consistent practice of states followed by them from a sense of legal obligation." *Restatement (Third) of the Foreign Relations Law of the United States* §102(2) (1987).

> This sort of law is generally thought to have two components: the state practice itself, which must be assessed in terms of its generality, duration, and consistency; and *opinio juris*, that is, the psychological belief of states engaged in the relevant practice that their action is required by international law. Because states frequently do not explain why they take or refrain from taking particular actions, *opinio juris* has most often been inferred from practice. Evidence of state practice is itself derived from a wide variety of sources, including
>
> > diplomatic correspondence, policy statements, press releases, the opinions of official legal advisers, official manuals on legal questions, e.g., manuals of military law, executive decisions and practices, orders to naval forces etc., comments by governments on drafts produced by the International Law Commission, state legislation, international and national judicial decisions, recitals in treaties and other international instruments, a pattern of treaties in the same form, the practice of international organs, and resolutions relating to legal questions in the United Nations General Assembly.
>
> [T]here is considerable controversy about the relative merits and weights of these different sources.
>
> Unlike treaties, which bind only their parties, customary norms are presumed to be universally binding on all the world. Customary international law thus takes on particular importance in areas where important nations — such as the United States — have not agreed to be bound by treaties articulating the norm in question. It is true that in principle a state that indicates its dissent from a practice while the law is still in the process of development is not bound by that rule even after it matures. Nonetheless, a nation must take active steps to avoid becoming bound by an evolving customary norm. "[H]istorically," according to the authors of the *Restatement*, "such dissent and consequent exemption from a principle that became general customary law has been rare." . . .

Ernest A. Young, *Sorting Out the Debate over Customary International Law*, 42 Va. J. Int'l L. 365, 372-374 (2002) (internal quotation marks and footnotes omitted).

Traditional examples of customary international law include diplomatic and foreign sovereign immunity. More recently, customary international law has been understood to proscribe certain conduct by a nation against individuals, including, for example, certain aspects of capital punishment such as executing juveniles. This section presents three key Supreme Court cases implicating the status of customary international law in the U.S. federal system. Most of the cases in this chapter arose after the Court decided *Erie* in 1938. Because, however, it is useful to consider the span of cases implicating customary international law together, this section includes two pre-*Erie* cases — *Murray v. The Charming Betsy*, 6 U.S. (2 Cranch) 64 (1804), and *The Paquete Habana*, 175 U.S. 677 (1900) — in addition to the post-*Erie* case *Banco Nacional de Cuba v. Sabbatino*, 376 U.S. 398 (1964). Once you have read these cases, you will be prepared to engage more fully the debate among scholars over customary international law and its federalism implications. This section concludes by exploring that debate.

As you read these materials, consider the following questions:

- What is the status of customary international law in American courts — federal common law, state law, general law, or something else?
- Why is the debate over the status of customary international law in the federal system, in part, a debate about federalism?

MURRAY v. THE CHARMING BETSY

6 U.S. (2 Cranch) 64 (1804)

[During a period marked by undeclared hostilities with France, Congress enacted the Non-Intercourse Act of 1800, prohibiting commercial intercourse between residents of the United States and residents of any French territory. The question before the Court was whether this Act authorized an American frigate, under orders of Captain Murray, to capture an American-built vessel that an American captain sold at a Dutch Island to an American-born Danish burgher, who proceeded to carry the vessel for trade to a French island.]

MARSHALL, CHIEF JUSTICE, delivered the opinion of the court: —

It is contended on the part of the captors in substance,

1st. That the vessel *Charming Betsy* and cargo are confiscable under the laws of the *United States*. . . .

1st. Is the *Charming Betsy* subject to seizure and condemnation for having violated a law of the *United States*?

The libel claims this forfeiture under the act passed in *February*, 1800, further to suspend the commercial intercourse between the *United States* and *France* and the dependencies thereof.

That act declares "that all commercial intercourse," &c. It has been very properly observed, in argument, that the building of vessels in the *United States* for sale to neutrals, in the islands, is, during war, a profitable business, which Congress cannot be intended to have prohibited, unless that intent be manifested by express words or a very plain and necessary implication.

It has also been observed that an act of Congress ought never to be construed to violate the law of nations if any other possible construction remains, and consequently can never be construed to violate neutral rights, or to affect neutral commerce, further than is warranted by the law of nations as understood in this country.

These principles are believed to be correct, and they ought to be kept in view in construing the act now under consideration.

The first sentence of the act which describes the persons whose commercial intercourse with *France* or her dependencies is to be prohibited, names any person or persons, resident within the *United States* or under their protection. Commerce carried on by persons within this description is declared to be illicit.

From persons the act proceeds to things, and declares explicitly the cases in which the vessels employed in this illicit commerce shall be forfeited. Any vessel owned, hired or employed wholly or in part by any person residing within the *United States*, or by any citizen thereof residing elsewhere, which shall perform certain acts recited in the law, becomes liable to forfeiture. It seems to the court to be a correct construction of these words to say, that the vessel must be of this description, not at the time of the passage of the law, but at the time when the act of forfeiture shall be committed. The cases of forfeiture are, 1st. A vessel of the description mentioned, which shall be voluntarily carried, or shall be destined, or permitted to proceed to any port within the *French* Republic. She must, when carried, or destined, or permitted to proceed to such port, be a vessel within the description of the act.

The second class of cases are those where vessels shall be sold, bartered, entrusted, or transferred, for the purpose that they may proceed to such port or place. This part of the section makes the crime of the sale dependent on the purpose for which it was made. If it was intended that any American vessel sold to a neutral should, in the possession of that neutral, be liable to the commercial disabilities imposed on her while she belonged to citizens of the *United States*, such extraordinary intent ought to have been plainly expressed; and if it was designed to prohibit the sale of *American* vessels to neutrals, the words placing the forfeiture on the intent with which the sale was made ought not to have been inserted.

The third class of cases are those vessels which shall be employed in any traffic by or for any person resident within the territories of the *French* Republic, or any of its dependencies.

In these cases too the vessels must be within the description of the act at the time the fact producing the forfeiture was committed.

The [vessel] having been completely transferred in the island of *St. Thomas*, by a *bona fide* sale to *Jared Shattuck*, and the forfeiture alleged to have accrued on a fact subsequent to that transfer, the liability of the vessel to forfeiture must depend on the inquiry whether the purchase was within the description of the act.

Jared Shattuck having been born within the *United States*, and not being proved to have expatriated himself according to any form prescribed by law, is said to remain a citizen, entitled to the benefit and subject to the disabilities imposed upon *American* citizens; and, therefore, to come expressly within the description of the act which comprehends *American* citizens residing elsewhere.

Whether a person born within the *United States*, or becoming a citizen according to the established laws of the country; can divest himself absolutely of that character otherwise than in such manner as may be prescribed by law, is a question which it is not necessary at present to decide. The cases cited at bar and the arguments drawn from the general conduct of the *United States* on this interesting subject, seem completely to establish the principle that an *American* citizen may acquire in a foreign country, the commercial privileges attached to his domicil, and be exempted from the operation of an act expressed in such general terms as that now under consideration. Indeed the very expressions of the act would seem to exclude a person under the circumstances of *Jared Shattuck*. He is not a person under the protection of the *United States*. The *American* citizen who goes into a foreign country, although he owes local and temporary allegiance to that country, is yet, if he performs no other act changing his condition, entitled to the protection of our government; and if, without the violation of any municipal law, he should be oppressed unjustly, he would have a right to claim that protection, and the interposition of the *American* government in his favor, would be considered a justifiable interposition. But his situation is completely changed, where by his own act he has made himself the subject of a foreign power. Although this act may not be sufficient to rescue him from punishment for any crime committed against the *United States*, a point not intended to be decided, yet it certainly places him out of the protection of the *United States* while within the territory of the sovereign to whom he has sworn allegiance, and consequently takes him out of the description of the act.

It is therefore the opinion of the court, that the *Charming Betsy*, with her cargo, being at the time of her recapture the *bona fide* property of a *Danish* burgher, is not forfeitable in consequence of her being employed in carrying on trade and commerce with a *French* island.

POINTS FOR DISCUSSION

1. In *The Charming Betsy*, Chief Justice Marshall "observed that an act of Congress ought never to be construed to violate the law of nations if any other possible construction remains, and consequently can never be construed to violate neutral rights, or to affect neutral commerce, further than is warranted by the law of nations as understood in this country." What relationship does Marshall describe between acts of Congress and the law of nations? How, if at all, does the Court's use of the law of nations in this opinion serve the national interests? According to this opinion, what status does the law of nations appear to have within the U.S. federal system?

2. Assume that this case had arisen in state court. Would the state court have been free to read the unclear act of Congress as authorizing seizure of the vessel in violation of the law of nations?

THE PAQUETE HABANA

175 U.S. 677 (1900)

Mr. JUSTICE GRAY delivered the opinion of the court:

These are two appeals from decrees of the District Court of the United States for the Southern District of Florida condemning two fishing vessels and their cargoes as prize of war.

Each vessel was a fishing smack, running in and out of Havana, and regularly engaged in fishing on the coast of Cuba; sailed under the Spanish flag; was owned by a Spanish subject of Cuban birth, living in the city of Havana; was commanded by a subject of Spain, also residing in Havana; and her master and crew had no interest in the vessel, but were entitled to shares, amounting in all to two thirds, of her catch, the other third belonging to her owner. Her cargo consisted of fresh fish, caught by her crew from the sea, put on board as they were caught, and kept and sold alive. Until stopped by the blockading squadron she had no knowledge of the existence of the war or of any blockade. She had no arms or ammunition on board, and made no attempt to run the blockade after she knew of its existence, nor any resistance at the time of the capture. The Paquete Habana was . . . captured by the United States gunboat Castine. The Lola was . . . captured by the United States steamship Dolphin.

Both the fishing vessels were brought by their captors into Key West. A libel for the condemnation of each vessel and her cargo as prize of war was there filed on April 27, 1898; a claim was interposed by her master on behalf of himself and the other members of the crew, and of her owner; evidence was taken, showing the facts above stated; and on May 30, 1898, a final decree of condemnation and sale was entered, "the court not being satisfied that as a matter of law, without any ordinance, treaty, or proclamation, fishing vessels of this class are exempt from seizure."

Each vessel was thereupon sold by auction; the Paquete Habana for the sum of $490; and the Lola for the sum of $800. There was no other evidence in the record of the value of either vessel or of her cargo. . . .

[T]he question [is] whether, upon the facts appearing in these records, the fishing smacks were subject to capture by the armed vessels of the United States during the recent war with Spain.

By an ancient usage among civilized nations, beginning centuries ago, and gradually ripening into a rule of international law, coast fishing vessels, pursuing their vocation of catching and bringing in fresh fish, have been recognized as exempt, with their cargoes and crews, from capture as prize of war.

This doctrine, however, has been earnestly contested at the bar; and no complete collection of the instances illustrating it is to be found, so far as we are aware, in a single published work although many are referred to and discussed by the writers on international law, notably in 2 Ortolan, Régles Internationales et Diplomatie de la Mer (4th ed.) lib. 3, 2, pp. 51-56; in 4 Calvo, Droit International (5th ed.) §§2367-2373; in De Boeck, Propriété Privée Ennemie sous Pavillon Ennemi, §§191-196; and in Hall, International Law (4th ed.) §148. It is therefore worth the while to trace the history of the rule, from the earliest accessible sources, through the increasing recognition of it, with occasional setbacks, to what we may now justly consider as its final establishment in our own country and generally throughout the civilized world. [The Court proceeded to trace that history.]

International law is part of our law, and must be ascertained and administered by the courts of justice of appropriate jurisdiction as often as questions of right depending upon it are duly presented for their determination. For this purpose, where there is no treaty and no controlling executive or legislative act or judicial decision, resort must be had to the customs and usages of civilized nations, and, as evidence of these, to the works of jurists and commentators who by years of labor, research, and experience have made themselves peculiarly well acquainted with the subjects of which they treat. Such works are resorted to by judicial tribunals, not for the speculations of their authors concerning what the law ought to be, but for trustworthy evidence of what the law really is. *Hilton v. Guyot*, 159 U.S. 113, 163, 164, 214, 215.

Wheaton places among the principal sources international law "Textwriters of authority, showing what is the approved usage of nations, or the general opinion respecting their mutual conduct, with the definitions and modifications introduced by general consent." As to these he forcibly observes: "Without wishing to exaggerate the importance of these writers, or to substitute, in any case, their authority for the principles of reason, it may be affirmed that they are generally impartial in their judgment. They are witnesses of the sentiments and usages of civilized nations, and the weight of their testimony increases every time that their authority is invoked by statesmen, and every year that passes without the rules laid down in their works being impugned by the avowal of contrary principles." Wheaton's International Law (8th ed.), §15.

Chancellor Kent says: "In the absence of higher and more authoritative sanctions, the ordinances of foreign States, the opinions of eminent statesmen, and the writings of distinguished jurists, are regarded as of great consideration on questions not settled by conventional law. In cases where the principal jurists agree, the presumption will be very great in favor of the solidity of their maxims; and no civilized nation that does not arrogantly set all ordinary law and justice at defiance will venture to disregard the uniform sense of the established writers on international law." 1 Kent Com. 18.

It will be convenient, in the first place, to refer to some leading French treatises on international law, which deal with the question now before us, not as one of the law of France only, but as one determined by the general consent of civilized nations.

"Enemy ships," say Pistoye and Duverdy, in their Treatise on Maritime Prizes, published in 1855, "are good prize. Not all, however; for it results from the unanimous accord of the maritime powers that an exception should be made in favor of coast fishermen. Such fishermen are respected by the enemy so long as they devote themselves exclusively to fishing." 1 Pistoye et Duverdy, tit. 6, 1, p. 314.

De Cussy, in his work on the Phases and Leading Cases of the Maritime Law of Nations — *Phases et Causes Célèbres du Droit Maritime des Nations* — published in 1856, affirms in the clearest language the exemption from capture of fishing boats, saying, in lib. 1, tit. 3, §36, that "in time of war the freedom of fishing is respected by belligerents; fishing boats are considered as neutral; in law, as in principle, they are not subject either to capture or to confiscation"; and that in lib. 2, chap. 20, he will state "several facts and several decisions which prove that the perfect freedom and neutrality of fishing boats are not illusory." 1 De Cussy, p. 291. . . .

Ortolan, in the fourth edition of his *Règles Internationales et Diplomatie de la Mer*, published in 1864, after stating the general rule that the vessels and cargoes of subjects of the enemy are lawful prize, says: "Nevertheless, custom admits an exception in favor of boats engaged in the coast fishery; these boats, as well as their crews, are free from capture and exempt from all hostilities. . . . " 2 Ortolan, 55.

No international jurist of the present day has a wider or more deserved reputation than Calvo, who, though writing in French, is a citizen of the Argentine Republic, employed in its diplomatic service abroad. In the fifth edition of his great work on international law, published in 1896, he observes, in §2366, that the international authority of decisions in particular cases by the prize courts of France, of England, and of the United States is lessened by the fact that the principles on which they are based are largely derived from the internal legislation of each country; and yet the peculiar character of maritime wars, with other considerations, gives to prize jurisprudence a force and importance reaching beyond the limits of the country in which it has prevailed. He therefore proposes here to group together a number of particular cases proper to serve as precedents for the solution of grave questions of maritime law in regard to the capture of private property as prize of war. Immediately, in §2367, he goes on to say: "Notwithstanding the hardships to which maritime wars subject private property, notwithstanding the extent of the recognized rights of belligerents, there are generally exempted, from seizure and capture, fishing vessels." In the next section he adds: "This exception is perfectly justiciable — *Cette exception est parfaitement justiciable"* — that is to say, belonging to judicial jurisdiction or cognizance. Littré, Dict. *voc.* Justiciable; *Hans v. Louisiana*, 134 U.S. 1, 15. . . .

The modern German books on international law, cited by the counsel for the appellants, treat the custom by which the vessels and implements of coast fishermen are exempt from seizure and capture as well established by the practice of nations. Heffter, §137; 2 Kaltenborn, §237, p. 480; Bluntschli, §667; Perels, §37, p. 217.

De Boeck, in his work on Enemy Private Property under Enemy's Flag — *De la Propriété Privée Ennemie sous Pavillon Ennemi* — published in 1882, and the only continental treatise cited by the counsel for the United States, says in §191: "A usage very ancient, if not universal, withdraws from the right of capture enemy vessels engaged in the coast fishery. The reason of this exception is evident; it would have been too hard to snatch from poor fishermen the means of earning their bread. . . . The exemption includes the boats, the fishing implements, and the cargo of fish." . . . And in §196 he defines the limits of the rule as follows: "But the immunity of the coast fishery must be limited by the reasons which justify it. The reasons of humanity and of harmlessness — *les raisons d'humanité et d'innocuité* — which militate in its favor do not exist in the great fishery, such as the cod fishery; ships engaged in that fishery devote themselves to truly commercial operations, which employ a large number of seamen. And these same reasons cease to be applicable to fishing vessels employed for a warlike purpose, to those which conceal arms, or which exchange signals of intelligence with ships of war; but only those taken in the fact can be rigorously treated; to allow seizure by way of preventive would open the door to every abuse, and would be equivalent to a suppression of the immunity."

Two recent English text-writers cited at the bar (influenced by what Lord Stowell said a century since) hesitate to recognize that the exemption of coast fishing vessels from capture has now become a settled rule of international law. Yet they both admit that there is little real difference in the views, or in the practice, of England and of other maritime nations; and that no civilized nation at the present day would molest coast fishing vessels so long as they were peaceably pursuing their calling and there was no danger that they or their crews might be of military use to the enemy. Hall, in §148 of the fourth edition of his Treatise on International Law, after briefly sketching the history of the positions occupied by France and England at different periods, and by the United States in the Mexican war, goes on to say: "In the foregoing facts there is nothing to show that much real difference has existed in the practice of the maritime countries. England does not seem to have been unwilling to spare fishing vessels so long as they are harmless, and it does not appear that any State has accorded them immunity under circumstances of inconvenience to itself. It is likely that all nations would now refrain from molesting them as a general rule, and would capture them so soon as any danger arose that they or their crews might be of military use to the enemy; and it is also likely that it is impossible to grant them a more distinct exemption." So, T. J. Lawrence, in §206 of his Principles of International Law, says: "The difference between the English and the French view is more apparent than real; for no civilized belligerent would now capture the boats of fishermen plying their avocation peaceably in the territorial waters of their own state; and no jurist would seriously argue that their immunity must be respected if they were used for warlike purposes, as were the smacks belonging to the northern ports of France when Great Britain gave the order to capture them in 1800."

[The Court proceeded to digest the "writers of various maritime countries, not yet cited, too important to be passed by without notice," who stated an exception of fishing vessels from the custom or usage of capturing an enemy's private vessels.]

This review of the precedents and authorities on the subject appears to us abundantly to demonstrate that at the present day, by the general consent of the civilized nations of the world, and independently of any express treaty or other public act, it is an established rule of international law, founded on considerations of humanity to a poor and industrious order of men, and of the mutual convenience of belligerent states, that coast fishing vessels, with their implements and supplies, cargoes and crews, unarmed and honestly pursuing their peaceful calling of catching and bringing in fresh fish, are exempt from capture as prize of war.

The exemption, of course, does not apply to coast fishermen or their vessels if employed for a warlike purpose, or in such a way as to give aid or information to the enemy; nor when military or naval operations create a necessity to which all private interests must give way.

Nor has the exemption been extended to ships or vessels employed on the high sea in taking whales or seals or cod or other fish which are not brought fresh to market, but are salted or otherwise cured and made a regular article of commerce.

This rule of international law is one which prize courts administering the law of nations are bound to take judicial notice of, and to give effect to, in the absence of any treaty or other public act of their own government in relation to the matter. . . .

In *Brown v. United States*, 8 Cranch, 110, there are expressions of Chief Justice Marshall which, taken by themselves, might seem inconsistent with the position above maintained, of the duty of a prize court to take judicial notice of a rule of international law, established by the general usage of civilized nations, as to the kind of property subject to capture. But the actual decision in that case, and the leading reasons on which it was based, appear to us rather to confirm our position. The principal question there was whether personal property of a British subject, found on land in the United States at the beginning of the last war with Great Britain, could lawfully be condemned as enemy's property, on a libel filed by the attorney of the United States, without a positive act of Congress. The conclusion of the court was "that the power of confiscating enemy property is in the legislature, and that the legislature has not yet declared its will to confiscate property which was within our territory at the declaration of war." 8 Cranch, 129. In showing that the declaration of war did not, of itself, vest the Executive with authority to order such property to be confiscated, the Chief Justice relied on the modern usages of nations, saying: "The universal practice of forbearing to seize and confiscate debts and credits, the principle universally received that the right to them revives on the restoration of peace, would seem to prove that war is not an absolute confiscation of this property, but simply confers the right of confiscation," and again: "The modern rule, then, would seem to be that tangible property belonging to an enemy, and found in the country at the commencement of war, ought not to be immediately confiscated; and in almost every commercial treaty an article is inserted stipulating for the right to withdraw such property." 8 Cranch, 123, 125. The decision that enemy property on land, which by the modern usage of nations is not subject to capture as prize of war, cannot be condemned by a prize court, even by direction of the Executive, without express authority from Congress, appears to us to repel any inference that coast fishing vessels, which are exempt by the general consent of civilized nations from capture, and which no act of Congress or order of the President has expressly authorized to be taken and confiscated, must be condemned by a prize court, for want of a distinct exemption in a treaty or other public act of the Government. . . .

The position taken by the United States during the recent war with Spain was quite in accord with the rule of international law, now generally recognized by civilized nations, in regard to coast fishing vessels.

On April 21, 1898, the Secretary of the Navy gave instructions to Admiral Sampson, commanding the North Atlantic Squadron, to "immediately institute a blockade of the north coast of Cuba, extending from Cardenas on the east to Bahia Honda on the west." The blockade was immediately instituted accordingly. On April 22 the President issued a proclamation declaring that the United States had instituted and would maintain that blockade, "in pursuance of the laws of the United States, and the law of nations applicable to such cases." And by the act of Congress of April 25, 1898, chap. 189, it was declared that the war between the United States and Spain existed on that day, and had existed since and including April 21, 30 Stat. 364.

On April 26, 1898, the President issued another proclamation, which, after reciting the existence of the war, as declared by Congress, contained this further recital: "It being desirable that such war should be conducted upon principles in harmony with the present views of nations and sanctioned by their recent practice." This recital was followed by specific declarations of certain rules for the conduct of the war by sea, making no mention of fishing vessels. But the proclamation clearly manifests the general policy of the Government to conduct the war in accordance with the principles of international law sanctioned by the recent practice of nations. . . .

The Paquete Habana . . . had no arms or ammunition on board; she had no knowledge of the blockade, or even of the war, until she was stopped by a blockading vessel; she made no attempt to run the blockade, and no resistance at the time of the capture; nor was there any evidence whatever of likelihood that she or her crew would aid the enemy. . . . [T]he Lola [presents an indistinguishable case.] Each vessel . . . was engaged in the coast fishery, and not in a commercial adventure, within the rule of international law. . . .

Upon the facts proved in either case, it is the duty of this court, sitting as the highest prize court of the United States, and administering the law of nations, to declare and adjudge that the capture was unlawful and without probable cause. . . .

Mr. CHIEF JUSTICE FULLER, with whom concurred Mr. JUSTICE HARLAN and Mr. JUSTICE McKENNA, dissenting:

The District Court held these vessels and their cargoes liable because not "satisfied that as a matter of law, without any ordinance, treaty, or proclamation, fishing vessels of this class are exempt from seizure."

This court holds otherwise, not because such exemption is to be found in any treaty, legislation, proclamation, or instruction granting it, but on the ground that the vessels were exempt by reason of an established rule of international law applicable to them, which it is the duty of the court to enforce.

I am unable to conclude that there is any such established international rule, or that this court can properly revise action which must be treated as having been taken in the ordinary exercise of discretion in the conduct of war.

It cannot be maintained "that modern usage constitutes a rule which acts directly upon the thing itself by its own force, and not through the sovereign power." That position was disallowed in *Brown v. United States*, 8 Cranch, 110, 128, and Chief Justice Marshall said: "This usage is a guide which the sovereign follows or abandons at his will. The rule, like other precepts of morality, of humanity, and even of wisdom, is addressed to the judgment of the sovereign; and although it cannot be disregarded by him without obloquy, yet it may be disregarded. The rule is, in its nature, flexible. It is subject to infinite modification. It is not an immutable rule of law, but depends on political considerations which may continually vary."

The question in that case related to the confiscation of the property of the enemy on land within our own territory, and it was held that property so situated could not be confiscated without an act of Congress. The Chief Justice continued: "Commercial nations, in the situation of the United States, have always a considerable quantity of property in the possession of their neighbors. When war breaks out, the question, what shall be done with enemy property in our country, is a question rather of policy than of law. The rule which we apply to the property of our enemy, will be applied by him to the property of our citizens. Like all other questions of policy, it is proper for the consideration of a department which can modify it at will; not for the consideration of a department which can pursue only the law as it is written. It is proper for the consideration of the legislature, not of the executive or judiciary."

This case involves the capture of enemy's property on the sea, and executive action, and if the position that the alleged rule *proprio vigore* limits the sovereign power in war be rejected, then I understand the contention to be that, by reason of the existence of the rule, the proclamation of April 26 must be read as if it contained the exemption in terms, or the exemption must be allowed because the capture of fishing vessels of this class was not specifically authorized.

The preamble to the proclamation stated . . . that it was desirable that the war "should be conducted upon principles in harmony with the present views of nations and sanctioned by their recent practice." . . . The language of the preamble did not carry the exemption in terms, and the real question is whether it must be allowed because not affirmatively withheld, or, in other words, because such captures were not in terms directed. . . .

I come then to examine the proposition "that at the present day, by the general consent of the civilized nations of the world, and independently of any express treaty or other public act, it is an established rule of international law, founded on considerations of humanity to a poor and industrious order of men, and of the mutual convenience of belligerent states, that coast fishing vessels, with their implements and supplies, cargoes and crews, unarmed, and honestly pursuing their peaceful calling of catching and bringing in of fresh fish, are exempt from capture as prize of war."

This, it is said, is a rule "which prize courts, administering the law of nations, are bound to take judicial notice of, and to give effect to, in the absence of treaty or other public act of their own government."

At the same time it is admitted that the alleged exemption does not apply "to coast fishermen or their vessels, if employed for a warlike purpose, or in such a way as to give aid or information to the enemy; nor when military or naval operations create a necessity to which all private interests must give way;" and, further, that the exemption has not "been extended to ships or vessels employed on the high sea in taking whales or seals, or cod or other fish which are not brought fresh to market, but are salted or otherwise cured and made a regular article of commerce."

It will be perceived that the exceptions reduce the supposed rule to very narrow limits, requiring a careful examination of the facts in order to ascertain its applicability. . . .

[W]ere these two vessels within the alleged exemption? . . . They were engaged in what were substantially commercial ventures, and the mere fact that the fish were kept alive by contrivances for that purpose—a practice of considerable antiquity—did not render them any the less an article of trade than if they had been brought in cured.

I do not think that, under the circumstances, the considerations which have operated to mitigate the evils of war in respect of individual harvesters of the soil can properly be invoked on behalf of these hired vessels, as being the implements of like harvesters of the sea. Not only so as to the owners, but as to the masters and crews. The principle which exempts the husbandman and his instruments of labor, exempts the industry in which he is engaged, and is not applicable in protection of the continuance of transactions of such character and extent as these.

In truth, the exemption of fishing craft is essentially an act of grace, and not a matter of right, and it is extended or denied as the exigency is believed to demand.

It is, said Sir William Scott, "a rule of comity only, and not of legal decision."

The modern view is thus expressed by Mr. Hall: "England does not seem to have been unwilling to spare fishing vessels so long as they are harmless, and it does not appear that any State has accorded them immunity under circumstances of inconvenience to itself. It is likely that all nations would now refrain from molesting them as a general rule, and would capture them so soon as any danger arose that they or their crews might be of military use to the enemy; and it is also likely that it is impossible to grant them a more distinct exemption." . . . In his Lectures on International Law at the Naval Law College the late Dr. Freeman Snow laid it down that the exemption could not be asserted as a rule of international law. . . .

It is needless to review the speculations and repetitions of the writers on international law. Ortolan, De Boeck, and others admit that the custom relied on as consecrating the immunity is not so general as to create an absolute international rule; Heffter, Calvo, and others are to the contrary. Their lucubrations may be persuasive, but not authoritative.

In my judgment, the rule is that exemption from the rigors of war is in the control of the Executive. He is bound by no immutable rule on the subject. It is for him to apply, or to modify, or to deny altogether such immunity as may have been usually extended. . . .

POINTS FOR DISCUSSION

1. In *The Paquete Habana*, the Court explained: "International law is part of our law, and must be ascertained and administered by courts of justice. . . ." During the first decades following ratification, several judges and other public officials described the law of nations as "part of the law of the land" or "part of the law of the United States." What do these phrases mean? That customary international law is federal common law? That it is state law? That it is general law? That it has some other status? Had this case arisen in state court, would the court have been obliged to treat international law as the Supreme Court did? Why or why not?

2. Is there any reason, on federalism grounds, why the Supreme Court should not have applied customary international law as it did in *The Paquete Habana*? Did the Court's application of customary international law circumvent the procedural and political safeguards of federalism? If not, why not?

Banco Nacional de Cuba v. Sabbatino

376 U.S. 398 (1964)

Mr. Justice Harlan delivered the opinion of the Court.

The question which brought this case here . . . is whether the so-called act of state doctrine serves to sustain petitioner's claims in this litigation. . . . The act of state doctrine in its traditional formulation precludes the courts of this country from inquiring into the validity of the public acts a recognized foreign sovereign power committed within its own territory.

I

[Farr, Whitlock & Co., a U.S. commodities broker, contracted to buy sugar from a subsidiary of Compania Azucarera Vertientes (CAV), a corporation organized under Cuban law but whose capital stock was owned principally by Americans. The Cuban government expropriated the sugar, effectively requiring Farr, Whitlock to enter into a second contract with the Cuban government, the new "owner" of the sugar, in order to procure it. Farr, Whitlock promised to pay petitioner Banco Nacional de Cuba, a Cuban governmental agency, to which the Cuban government had given the right to payment. After Farr, Whitlock exported the sugar, it made payment to respondent Sabbatino, a receiver for CAV, rather than to Banco Nacional de Cuba. Banco Nacional de Cuba brought a diversity action in federal district court against Farr, Whitlock and Sabbatino for the proceeds of the sale.]

Proceeding on the basis that a taking invalid under international law does not convey good title, the District Court found the Cuban expropriation decree to violate such law in three separate respects: it was motivated by a retaliatory and not a public purpose; it discriminated against American nationals; and it failed to provide adequate compensation. Summary judgment against petitioner was accordingly granted.

The Court of Appeals, affirming the decision on similar grounds, relied on two letters (not before the District Court) written by State Department officers which it took as evidence that the Executive Branch had no objection to a judicial testing of the Cuban decree's validity. . . .

IV

The classic American statement of the act of state doctrine . . . is found in *Underhill v. Hernandez*, 168 U.S. 250, p. 252, where Chief Justice Fuller said for a unanimous Court:

> "Every sovereign State is bound to respect the independence of every other sovereign State, and the courts of one country will not sit in judgment on the acts of the government of another, done within its own territory. Redress of grievances by reason of such acts must be obtained through the means open to be availed of by sovereign powers as between themselves."

Following this precept the Court in that case refused to inquire into acts of Hernandez, a revolutionary Venezuelan military commander whose government had been later recognized by the United States, which were made the basis of a damage action in this country by Underhill, an American citizen, who claimed that he had been unlawfully assaulted, coerced, and detained in Venezuela by Hernandez.

None of this Court's subsequent cases in which the act of state doctrine was directly or peripherally involved manifest any retreat from *Underhill*. . . .

In deciding the present case the Court of Appeals relied in part upon an exception to the unqualified teachings of *Underhill* . . . which that court had earlier indicated. In *Bernstein v. Van Heyghen Freres Societe Anonyme*, 163 F.2d 246, suit was brought to recover from an assignee property allegedly taken, in effect, by the Nazi Government because plaintiff was Jewish. Recognizing the odious nature of this act of state, the court, through Judge Learned Hand, nonetheless refused to consider it invalid on that ground. Rather, it looked to see if the Executive had acted in any manner that would indicate that United States Courts should refuse to give effect to such a foreign decree. Finding no such evidence, the court sustained dismissal of the complaint. In a later case involving similar facts the same court again assumed examination of the German acts improper, *Bernstein v. N.V. Nederlandsche-Amerikaansche Stoomvaart-Maatschappij*, 173 F.2d 71, but, quite evidently following the implications of Judge Hand's opinion in the earlier case, amended its mandate to permit evidence of alleged invalidity, 210 F.2d 375, subsequent to receipt by plaintiff's attorney of a letter from the Acting Legal Adviser to the State Department written for the purpose of relieving the court from any constraint upon the exercise of its jurisdiction to pass on that question. . . .

This Court has never had occasion to pass upon the so-called *Bernstein* exception, nor need it do so now. For whatever ambiguity may be thought to exist in the two letters from State Department officials on which the Court of Appeals relied . . . is now removed by the position which the Executive has taken in this Court on the act of state claim; respondents do not indeed contest the view that these letters were intended to reflect no more than the Department's then wish not to make any statement bearing on this litigation.

The outcome of this case, therefore, turns upon whether any of the contentions urged by respondents against the application of the act of state doctrine in the premises is acceptable: (1) that the doctrine does not apply to acts of state which violate international law, as is claimed to be the case here; (2) that the doctrine is inapplicable unless the Executive specifically interposes it in a particular case; and (3) that, in any event, the doctrine may not be invoked by a foreign government plaintiff in our courts.

V

We do not believe that this doctrine is compelled either by the inherent nature of sovereign authority . . . or by some principle of international law. . . . If a transaction takes place in one jurisdiction and the forum is in another, the forum does not by dismissing an action or by applying its own law purport to divest the first jurisdiction of its territorial sovereignty; it merely declines to adjudicate or makes applicable its own law to parties or property before it. The refusal of one country to enforce the penal laws of another is a typical example of an instance when a court will not entertain a cause of action arising in another jurisdiction. While historic notions of sovereign authority do bear upon the wisdom or employing the act of state doctrine, they do not dictate its existence. . . .

The traditional view of international law is that it establishes substantive principles for determining whether one country has wronged another. Because of its peculiar nation-to-nation character the usual method for an individual to seek relief is to exhaust local remedies and then repair to the executive authorities of his own state to persuade them to champion his claim in diplomacy or before an international tribunal. Although it is, of course, true that United States courts apply international law as a part of our own in appropriate circumstances, . . . *The Paquete Habana*, 175 U.S. 677, 700, the public law of nations can hardly dictate to a country which is in theory wronged how to treat that wrong within its domestic borders. . . .

[I]t cannot of course be thought that "every case or controversy which touches foreign relations lies beyond judicial cognizance." *Baker v. Carr*, 369 U.S. 186, 211. The text of the Constitution does not require the act of state doctrine; it does not irrevocably remove from the judiciary the capacity to review the validity of foreign acts of state.

The act of state doctrine does, however, have "constitutional" underpinnings. It arises out of the basic relationships between branches of government in a system of separation of powers. . . . The doctrine as formulated in past decisions expresses the strong sense of the Judicial Branch that its engagement in the task of passing on the validity of foreign acts of state may hinder rather than further this country's pursuit of goals both for itself and for the community of nations as a whole in the international sphere. Many commentators disagree with this view; they have striven . . . to stimulate a narrowing of the apparent scope of the rule. Whatever considerations are thought to predominate, it is plain that the problems involved are uniquely federal in nature. If federal authority, in this instance this Court, orders the field of judicial competence in this area for the federal courts, and the state courts are left free to formulate their own rules, the purposes behind the doctrine could be as effectively undermined as if there had been no federal pronouncement on the subject.

We could perhaps in this diversity action avoid the question of deciding whether federal or state law is applicable to this aspect of the litigation. New York has enunciated the act of state doctrine in terms that echo those of federal decisions decided during the reign of *Swift v. Tyson*, 16 Pet. 1. . . .

However, we are constrained to make it clear that an issue concerned with a basic choice regarding the competence and function of the Judiciary and the National Executive in ordering our relationships with other members of the international community must be treated exclusively as an aspect of federal law. It seems fair to assume that the Court did not have rules like the act of state doctrine in mind when it decided *Erie R. Co. v. Tompkins*. Soon thereafter, Professor Philip C. Jessup, now a judge of the International Court of Justice, recognized the potential dangers were *Erie* extended to legal problems affecting international relations. He cautioned that rules of international law should not be left to divergent and perhaps parochial state interpretations. His basic rationale is equally applicable to the act of state doctrine.

The Court in the pre-*Erie* act of state cases, although not burdened by the problem of the source of applicable law, used language sufficiently strong and broad-sweeping to suggest that state courts were not left free to develop their own doctrines (as they would have been had this Court merely been interpreting common law under *Swift v. Tyson, supra*). The Court of Appeals in the first *Bernstein* case, *supra*, a diversity suit, plainly considered the decisions of this Court, despite the intervention of *Erie*, to be controlling in regard to the act of state question, at the same time indicating that New York law governed other aspects of the case. We are not without other precedent for a determination that federal law governs; there are enclaves of federal judge-made law which bind the States. A national body of federal-court-built law has been held to have been contemplated by §301 of the Labor Management Relations Act, *Textile Workers v. Lincoln Mills*, 353 U.S. 448. Principles formulated by federal judicial law have been thought by this Court to be necessary to protect uniquely federal interests, *D'Oench, Duhme & Co. v. Federal Deposit Ins. Corp.*, 315 U.S. 447, *Clearfield Trust Co. v. United States*, 318 U.S. 363. Of course the federal interest guarded in all these cases is one the ultimate statement of which is derived from a federal statute. Perhaps more directly in point are the bodies of law applied between States over boundaries and in regard to the apportionment of interstate waters.

In *Hinderlider v. La Plata River Co.*, 304 U.S. 92, 110, in an opinion handed down the same day as *Erie* and by the same author, Mr. Justice Brandeis, the Court declared, "For whether the water of an interstate stream must be apportioned between the two States is a question of 'federal common law' upon which neither the statutes nor the decisions of either State can be conclusive." Although the suit was between two private litigants and the relevant States could not be made parties, the Court considered itself free to determine the effect of an interstate compact regulating water apportionment. The decision implies that no State can undermine the federal interest in equitably apportioned interstate waters even if it deals with private parties. . . . The problems surrounding the act of state doctrine are, albeit for different reasons, as intrinsically federal as are those involved in water apportionment or boundary disputes. The considerations supporting exclusion of state authority here are much like those which led the Court in *United States v. California*, 332 U.S. 19, to hold that the Federal Government possessed paramount rights in submerged lands though within the three-mile limit of coastal States. We conclude that the scope of the act of state doctrine must be determined according to federal law.[25]

VI

If the act of state doctrine is a principle of decision binding on federal and state courts alike but compelled by neither international law nor the Constitution, its continuing vitality depends on its capacity to reflect the proper distribution of functions between the judicial and political branches of the Government on matters bearing upon foreign affairs. It should be apparent that the greater the degree of codification or consensus concerning a particular area of international law, the more appropriate it is for the judiciary to render decisions regarding it, since the courts can then focus on the application of an agreed principle to circumstances of fact rather than on the sensitive task of establishing a principle not inconsistent with the national interest or with international justice. It is also evident that some aspects of international law touch much more sharply on national nerves than do others; the less important the implications of an issue are for our foreign relations, the weaker the justification for exclusivity in the political branches. The balance of relevant

---

25. Various constitutional and statutory provisions indirectly support this determination, see U.S. Const., Art. I, §8, cls. 3, 10; Art. II, §§2, 3; Art. III, §2; 28 U.S.C. §§1251(a)(2), (b)(1), (b)(3), 1332(a)(2), 1333, 1350, 1351, by reflecting a concern for uniformity in this country's dealings with foreign nations and indicating a desire to give matters of international significance to the jurisdiction of federal institutions.

considerations may also be shifted if the government which perpetrated the challenged act of state is no longer in existence, as in the *Bernstein* case, for the political interest of this country may, as a result, be measurably altered. Therefore, rather than laying down or reaffirming an inflexible and all-encompassing rule in this case, we decide only that the (Judicial Branch) will not examine the validity of a taking of property within its own territory by a foreign sovereign government, extant and recognized by this country at the time of suit, in the absence of a treaty or other unambiguous agreement regarding controlling legal principles, even if the complaint alleges that the taking violates customary international law. . . .

The possible adverse consequences of a conclusion to the contrary . . . is highlighted by contrasting the practices of the political branch with the limitations of the judicial process in matters of this kind. Following an expropriation of any significance, the Executive engages in diplomacy aimed to assure that United States citizens who are harmed are compensated fairly. Representing all claimants of this country, it will often be able, either by bilateral or multilateral talks, by submission to the United Nations, or by the employment of economic and political sanctions, to achieve some degree of general redress. Judicial determinations of invalidity of title can, on the other hand, have only an occasional impact, since they depend on the fortuitous circumstance of the property in question being brought into this country. Such decisions would, if the acts involved were declared invalid, often be likely to give offense to the expropriating country; since the concept of territorial sovereignty is so deep seated, any state may resent the refusal of the courts of another sovereign to accord validity to acts within its territorial borders. Piecemeal dispositions of this sort involving the probability of affront to another state could seriously interfere with negotiations being carried on by the Executive Branch and might prevent or render less favorable the terms of an agreement that could otherwise be reached. Relations with third countries which have engaged in similar expropriations would not be immune from effect.

The dangers of such adjudication are present regardless of whether the State Department has, as it did in this case, asserted that the relevant act violated international law. If the Executive Branch has undertaken negotiations with an expropriating country, but has refrained from claims of violation of the law of nations, a determination to that effect by a court might be regarded as a serious insult, while a finding of compliance with international law would greatly strengthen the bargaining hand of the other state with consequent detriment to American interests.

Even if the State Department has proclaimed the impropriety of the expropriation, the stamp of approval of its view by a judicial tribunal, however, impartial, might increase any affront and the judicial decision might occur at a time, almost always well after the taking, when such an impact would be contrary to our national interest. Considerably more serious and far-reaching consequences would flow from a judicial finding that international law standards had been met if that determination flew in the face of a State Department proclamation to the contrary. When articulating principles of international law in its relations with other states, the Executive Branch speaks not only as an interpreter of generally accepted and traditional rules, as would the courts, but also as an advocate of standards it believes desirable for the community of nations and protective of national concerns. In short, whatever way the matter is cut, the possibility of conflict between the Judicial and Executive Branches could hardly be avoided. . . .

Against the force of such considerations, . . . [respondents contend] that United States courts could make a significant contribution to the growth of international law, a contribution whose importance, it is said, would be magnified by the relative paucity of decisional law by international bodies. But given the fluidity of present world conditions, the effectiveness of such a patchwork approach toward the formulation of an acceptable body of law concerning state responsibility for expropriations is, to say the least, highly conjectural. Moreover, it rests upon the sanguine presupposition that the decisions of the courts of the world's major capital exporting country and principal exponent of the free enterprise system would be accepted as disinterested expressions of sound legal principle by those adhering to widely different ideologies. . . .

It is suggested that if the act of state doctrine is applicable to violations of international law, it should only be so when the Executive Branch expressly stipulates that it does not wish the courts to pass on the question of validity. We should be slow to reject the representations of the Government that such a reversal of the *Bernstein* principle would work serious inroads on the maximum effectiveness of United States diplomacy. Often the State Department will wish to refrain from taking an official position, particularly at a moment that would be dictated by the development of private litigation but might be inopportune diplomatically. . . . We do not now pass on the *Bernstein* exception, but even if it were deemed valid, its suggested extension is unwarranted. . . .

Mr. JUSTICE WHITE, dissenting.

I am dismayed that the Court has, with one broad stroke, declared the ascertainment and application of international law beyond the competence of the courts of the United States in a large and important category of cases. I am also disappointed in the Court's declaration that the acts of a sovereign state with regard to the property of aliens within its borders are beyond the reach of international law in the courts of this country. However clearly established that law may be, a sovereign may violate it with impunity, except insofar as the political branches of the government may provide a remedy. This backward-looking doctrine, never before declared in this Court, is carried a disconcerting step further: not only are the courts powerless to question acts of state proscribed by international law but they are likewise powerless to refuse to adjudicate the claim founded upon a foreign law; they must render judgment and thereby validate the lawless act. Since the Court expressly extends its ruling to all acts of state expropriating property, however clearly inconsistent with the international community, all discriminatory expropriations of the property of aliens, as for example the taking of properties of persons belonging to certain races, religions or nationalities, are entitled to automatic validation in the courts of the United States. No other civilized country has found such a rigid rule necessary for the survival of the executive branch of its government; the executive of no other government seems to require such insulation from international law adjudications in its courts; and no other judiciary is apparently so incompetent to ascertain and apply international law.

I do not believe that the act of state doctrine, as judicially fashioned in this Court, and the reasons underlying it, require American courts to decide cases in disregard of international law and of the rights of litigants to a full determination on the merits. . . .

POINTS FOR DISCUSSION

1. The customary international law rule at issue in *Sabbatino* was that a taking invalid under international law does not convey good title to goods. The Court, however, refused to apply this rule, applying instead the act of state doctrine, which restrains courts from judging acts of another government committed within the territory of that government. If "international law is part of our law," as the Court asserted in *The Paquete Habana*, on what grounds could the Court refuse to apply it in *Sabbatino*? What values did applying the act of state doctrine advance relative to the rule of customary international law at issue in the case?

2. The *Sabbatino* Court stated that neither international law nor the Constitution compelled it to apply the act of state doctrine. Nonetheless, it explained, the act of state doctrine has "constitutional underpinnings" and its scope must be determined according to federal law. Under this reasoning, had *Sabbatino* arisen in state court, the state court likewise would have been bound to apply the act of state doctrine. Why, in this context, is the act of state doctrine a preemptive federal rule of decision if Congress has not enacted it into law? Does the Court's description and use of the act of state doctrine undermine the political and procedural safeguards of federalism? Does it undermine other state interests?

Scholars have extensively debated the place of customary international law within the U.S. federal system.

> Two diametrically opposed approaches have emerged. The "modern" position asserts that federal and state courts should recognize and enforce customary international law as supreme federal law whether or not the political branches have incorporated it through constitutional lawmaking processes. Proponents of this position maintain that courts should recognize customary international law as a form of federal common law and treat it as both preemptive of state law and sufficient to establish federal "arising under" jurisdiction. The "revisionist" position, by contrast, asserts that customary international law is federal law only to the extent that the political branches have properly incorporated it; otherwise, it may operate as state law if a state has incorporated it.
>
> No consensus has emerged from this impressive body of scholarship, and the Supreme Court has not recently addressed the issue. Adherents of the modern and revisionist positions dispute what historical practice evinces and what the constitutional structure requires regarding the role of customary international law in the federal system. Critics of the modern position

maintain that it is in tension with basic notions of American representative democracy because when a federal court applies [customary international law] as federal common law, it is not applying law generated by U.S. law-making processes. These critics contend that the modern position disregards the historical reality that before the Supreme Court decided *Erie Railroad Co. v. Tompkins* in 1938, customary international law was not regarded as federal law, but as a species of nonpreemptive "general law." *Erie*, they say, banished general law from federal courts and established that state law applies "[e]xcept in matters governed by the Federal Constitution or by Acts of Congress."

In response, critics of the revisionist position argue that it fails to account for the Constitution's assignment of foreign relations authority to the federal government rather than the states. In their view, the revisionist position contravenes the Constitution's basic allocation of foreign affairs power by allowing states to determine the force and effect of customary international law. In addition, they contend that the revisionist position disregards a long line of statements, stretching back to the founding, by federal judges and public officials that the customary law of nations—today known as "customary international law"—is "part of the law of the land." The critics argue that these public actors necessarily understood the law of nations to be preemptive of state law (and perhaps even federal statutes) as well as sufficient to generate Article III arising under jurisdiction. In light of the vast gap between these competing claims and critiques, the debate over the role of customary international law in the American federal system has reached something of a stalemate.

Anthony J. Bellia Jr. & Bradford R. Clark, *The Federal Common Law of Nations*, 109 Colum. L. Rev. 1, 2-5 (2009) (internal quotation marks, brackets, and footnotes omitted). Recently, scholars have argued that federal courts traditionally have applied some aspects of customary international law as a means of upholding the foreign relations powers of the federal political branches.

The excerpts below describe these various positions. Carefully distinguish each position from the others and consider how each implicates the relative balance of power between the federal government and the states.

Harold Hongju Koh, Is International Law Really State Law?

111 Harv. L. Rev. 1824, 1824-1826, 1830-1835 (1998)

How should we understand the following passages?

[W]e are constrained to make it clear that an issue concerned with a basic choice regarding the competence and function of the Judiciary and the National Executive in ordering our relationships with other members of the international community *must be treated exclusively as an aspect of federal law.*[1]

Customary international law is federal law, to be enunciated authoritatively by the federal courts.[2]

---

1. Banco Nacional de Cuba v. Sabbatino, 376 U.S. 398, 425 (1964) (emphasis added).
2. Brief for the United States as Amicus Curiae at 1, Filartiga v. Pena-Irala, 630 F.2d 876 (2d Cir. 1980) (No. 79-6090) (emphasis added), reprinted in 19 I.L.M. 585, 606 n.49 (1980).

International human rights cases predictably raise legal issues—such as *interpretations of international law—that are matters of Federal common law* and within the particular expertise of Federal courts.[3]

Taking these passages at face value, most readers would understand them to mean just what they say: judicial determinations of international law—including international human rights law—are matters of federal law. That these three declarations emanate from the federal judicial, executive, and legislative branches, respectively, only confirms the unanimity of relevant opinion on the subject.

As so often happens, the hornbook rule—international law, as applied in the United States, must be federal law—makes obvious sense. Every schoolchild knows that the failures of the Articles of Confederation led to the framing of the Constitution, which established national governmental institutions to articulate uniform positions on such uniquely federal matters as foreign affairs and international law. Even as the new Constitution withheld foreign affairs powers from the states, it authorized a national institution, Congress, "[t]o define and punish . . . Offences against the Law of Nations." But Congress's authority to construe the law of nations was never exclusive. The early Supreme Court spent much of its time deciding cases under the law of nations. International law came to occupy "an existence in the federal courts independent of acts of Congress."[9] By 1981, the Supreme Court had come unanimously to "recogniz[e] the need and authority in some limited areas to formulate what has come to be known as 'federal common law'" in cases in which "a federal rule of decision is 'necessary to protect uniquely federal interests,'" including "international disputes implicating . . . our relations with foreign nations."[10] . . .

Until 1842, federal and state courts alike construed customary international law with little regard to its federal or state character. Both federal and state courts applied the private international law rules of the law merchant (*lex mercatoria*) in an effort to construct a uniform national commercial law. In cases involving admiralty and alien torts, customary international law directly provided the rules of decision for federal courts.

Swift v. Tyson clarified that the bill of exchange rules derived from *lex mercatoria* constituted part of the "general common law" to be interpreted by federal courts sitting in diversity jurisdiction. Thereafter, federal courts construed both commercial and noncommercial rules of customary international law so regularly that Justice Gray provoked no dissent when he wrote: "International law is part of our law, and must be ascertained and administered by the courts of justice of appropriate jurisdiction, as often as questions of right depending upon it are duly presented for their determination."[36]

---

3. S. Rep. No. 102-249, at 6 n.6 (1991) (emphasis added) (explaining the Torture Victim Protection Act (TVPA) of 1991, 28 U.S.C. §1350 note (1994)).

9. Filartiga v. Pena-Irala, 630 F.2d 876, 887 n.20 (2d Cir. 1980). . . .

10. Texas Indus. v. Radcliff Materials, Inc., 451 U.S. 630, 640-41 (1981) (quoting Banco Nacional de Cuba v. Sabbatino, 376 U.S. 398, 426 (1964)).

36. The Paquete Habana, 175 U.S. 677, 700 (1900). . . .

There matters stood until *Erie*, in which Justice Brandeis famously invoked federalism concerns to pronounce that "[t]here is no federal general common law." . . .

Erie held that the grant of diversity jurisdiction, standing alone, did not authorize the federal courts to make a general federal common law of tort. But customary international law differs from the state tort law at issue in *Erie* in at least three crucial respects. First, Justice Brandeis claimed, the federal courts lack power to fashion common law tort rules in part because "*Congress* has no power to declare substantive rules of common law applicable in a [s]tate." But given both Congress's enumerated authority to define and punish offenses against the law of nations and its affirmative exercise of that power in a range of statutes, no one could similarly claim that federal courts lacked power to make federal common law rules with respect to international law.

Second, as Justice Harlan later noted, *Erie* required that state law be the governing substantive law in diversity cases because "the scheme of our Constitution envisions an *allocation of law-making functions between state and federal legislative processes* which is undercut if the federal judiciary can make substantive law affecting state affairs beyond the bounds of congressional legislative powers in this regard."[41] But with respect to international and foreign affairs law, the Constitution envisions no similar role for state legislative or judicial process. Federal judicial determination of most questions of customary international law transpires not in a zone of core state concerns, such as state tort law, but in a foreign affairs area in which the Tenth Amendment has reserved little or no power to the states. It was precisely to preserve the federal common lawmaking power of the federal courts in such areas that Justice Brandeis acknowledged—on the very same day that *Erie* was decided—that federal judges may continue to make *specialized* federal common law regarding issues of uniquely federal concern.[42]

Third, to treat determinations of customary international law as questions of state law would have rendered both state court and federal diversity rulings effectively unreviewable by the U.S. Supreme Court. Such unreviewability would have raised the specter that multiple variants of the same international law rule could proliferate among the several states.

Writing only one year after *Erie*, Professor (later World Court Judge) Philip Jessup noted these three problems in arguing that "the holding of th[at] case has no direct application to international law":[44]

> If the dictum of Mr. Justice Brandeis in the *Tompkins* case is to be applied broadly, it would follow that hereafter a state court's determination of a rule of international law would be a finding regarding the law of the state and would not be reviewed by the Supreme Court of the United States.
>
> . . . . [A]ny attempt to extend the doctrine of the *Tompkins* case to international law should [thus] be repudiated by the Supreme Court.

---

41. Hanna v. Plumer, 380 U.S. 460, 474-75 (1965) (Harlan, J., concurring) (emphasis added).

42. See Hinderlider v. La Plata River & Cherry Creek Ditch Co., 304 U.S. 92, 110 (1938) (stating that the issue of interstate water apportionment "is a question of 'federal common law' upon which neither the statutes nor the decisions of either State can be conclusive"). . . .

44. Philip C. Jessup, *The Doctrine of Erie Railroad v. Tompkins Applied to International Law*, 33 Am. J. Int'l L. 740, 741-43 (1939).

Mr. Justice Brandeis was surely not thinking of international law when he wrote his dictum. *Any question of applying international law in our courts involves the foreign relations of the United States and can thus be brought within a federal power*. . . . The several states of the Union are entities unknown to international law. It would be as unsound as it would be unwise to make our state courts our ultimate authority for pronouncing the rules of international law.[45]

More than a quarter century would pass before the Supreme Court clarified whether customary international law rules should be characterized as state or federal law. In 1964, the Supreme Court took up each of Jessup's concerns in *Sabbatino*. First, Justice Harlan, writing for an 8-1 majority, did not shy away from interpreting questions of customary international law. . . . To the contrary, the Court *construed* customary international law to determine that international law neither compelled nor required application of the act of state doctrine.

Second, Justice Harlan recognized Jessup's distinction between cases that fall within zones of state and federal power. Given the mischief that would ensue if each state could formulate its own act of state rule, Justice Harlan concluded, any "issue concerned with a basic choice regarding the competence and function of the Judiciary and the National Executive in ordering our relationships with other members of the international community must be treated exclusively as an aspect of federal law."

Third and finally, the Court cited with approval Judge Jessup's recognition of "the potential dangers were *Erie* extended to legal problems affecting international relations." The Court noted Jessup's concern for maintaining national uniformity in interpretation of legal rules, and his "caution[] that rules of international law should not be left to divergent and perhaps parochial state interpretations." Jessup's "basic rationale," the *Sabbatino* Court concluded, "is *equally applicable* to the act of state doctrine."

The most plausible reading of this language is that the *Sabbatino* Court simply confirmed Jessup's understanding that "rules of international law should not be left to divergent and . . . parochial state interpretations." A fortiori, the same reasoning must be "equally applicable" to interpretation of the act of state doctrine, which the Court had not found to be compelled by customary international law. Far from denying the appropriateness of federal courts' making federal common law rules based on their interpretation of international law, Justice Harlan declared it "apparent that the greater the degree of codification or consensus concerning a particular area of international law, the *more appropriate* it is for the judiciary to render decisions regarding it, since the courts can then focus on the application of an agreed principle to circumstances of fact."

In the decades since *Sabbatino*, the Supreme Court has routinely held that a "few areas, involving 'uniquely federal interests,' are so committed by the Constitution and laws of the United States to federal control that state law is pre-empted and replaced, where necessary, by federal law of a content prescribed (absent explicit statutory directive) by the courts — so-called 'federal

---

45. *Id.* at 741-43 (emphasis added).

common law.' "[57] The Court has specifically found such a "distinctive federal interest in . . . 'the exterior relation of this whole nation with other nations and governments.' "[58]

The proper reading of this doctrine, in my view, is that even after *Erie* and *Sabbatino*, federal courts retain legitimate authority to incorporate bona fide rules of customary international law into federal common law. This judicial authority inheres not just in the distinct federal interest in foreign relations, but also in the explicit grant of authority in Article I, Section 8, Clause 10 of the Constitution to define and fashion federal rules with regard to the law of nations, various other constitutional provisions, and particular federal statutes. Once customary norms have sufficiently crystallized, courts should presumptively incorporate them into federal common law, unless the norms have been ousted as law for the United States by contrary federal directives. . . .

ERNEST A. YOUNG, SORTING OUT THE DEBATE OVER
CUSTOMARY INTERNATIONAL LAW

42 Va. J. Int'l L. 365, 366-369, 372, 374-375, 377-378, 382-384,
392-394, 400-404, 406-409, 413, 415-419, 421-423, 432-434 (2002)

Is customary international law federal law or state law? Are these the only choices? One of legal academia's more heated spats in recent years has concerned the domestic status of customary international law, that is, international law that derives from the general practice of nations rather than from formal treaties and other agreements. The conventional wisdom has been that such law is (or is equivalent to) federal common law for purposes of creating federal subject matter jurisdiction and preempting state law. Curtis Bradley and Jack Goldsmith shook up the international law community in 1997, however, by arguing that this received view—which they call the "modern position"—is unconstitutional and illegitimate.[2] Their initial salvo prompted angry responses from prominent figures in international law. Invoking the Supreme Court's famous statement in *The Paquete Habana* that "[i]nternational law is part of our law," the international lawyers insisted that the modern position is consistent with well-settled understandings and warned of dire consequences should it be abandoned.

Customary international law has been around for a long time, but its status in American law has become controversial only recently. Part of the explanation is that customary law's status became a puzzle only after the Supreme Court's decision in *Erie Railroad Co. v. Tompkins*; prior to that time, customary international law had the status of "general" law under *Swift v. Tyson*. In light of *Erie*'s apparent rejection of a "general" law regime, Professors Bradley and Goldsmith have argued, "federal courts [must] identify the sovereign source for every rule of decision. Because the appropriate 'sovereigns' under the U.S. Constitution are the federal government and the states, *all* law applied by

---

57. Boyle v. United Techs. Corp., 487 U.S. 500, 504 (1988) (citation omitted).
58. *Id.* at 508 n.4. . . .
2. *See* Curtis A. Bradley & Jack L. Goldsmith, *Customary International Law as Federal Common Law: A Critique of the Modern Position*, 110 HARV. L. REV. 815 (1997) (hereinafter Bradley & Goldsmith, *Critique of the Modern Position*). . . .

federal courts must be either federal law or state law."[9] Hence the dispute about which box customary international law fits into.

Although the potential for debate on this question arose with *Erie*, the issue became salient in the latter part of the last century as a result of three further developments: First, international law's concerns have shifted to emphasize not only the relations among states, but also the relationship between states and their citizens. This shift has substantially increased the potential for conflict between international law and state law, thus requiring a determination of international law's preemptive force. Second, the expansion of international law's concerns has encouraged a wave of "transnational public law" litigation in American federal courts. These cases — which generally involve violations of internationally-recognized human rights — have both increased the salience of customary international law and, more particularly, required judges to determine whether or not such disputes "arise under" federal law for purposes of subject matter jurisdiction. Finally, it is probably fair to say that the Supreme Court's recent "federalist revival" in domestic law — exemplified by cases like *United States v. Lopez* and *Printz v. United States* — has sparked increased interest in issues of federalism generally, including the interaction between federalism and international affairs. . . .

I. Customary International Law as Federal Common Law

Customary international law "results from a general and consistent practice of states followed by them from a sense of legal obligation."[32] . . .

A. The Modern Position

Almost all participants in current debates over customary international law appear to agree that, prior to the Supreme Court's decision in *Erie Railroad Co. v. Tompkins*, that law had the status of "general" law. Customary norms, in other words, were neither state nor federal and could therefore neither preempt state law nor create federal question or Supreme Court appellate jurisdiction. *Erie*, however, seemed to foreclose this sort of status when it held that "[e]xcept in matters governed by the Federal Constitution or by Acts of Congress, the law to be applied in any case is the law of the State. . . . There is no federal general common law." By apparently eliminating the category into which customary international law had previously been thought to fall, *Erie* set the stage for modern debates over the status of that law.

Erie's rejection of the "*general* federal common law" did not foreclose the possibility of federal common law altogether. As Judge Henry Friendly famously explained, *Erie*'s rejection of "the spurious uniformity of *Swift v. Tyson* . . . cleared the way for the truly uniform federal common law on issues of national concern."[46] This law is often thought to encompass such subjects as admiralty, interstate boundary disputes, the commercial relations of the United States government, and foreign affairs. The "modern position" attacked

---

9. Bradley & Goldsmith, *Critique of the Modern Position*, *supra* note 2, at 852.

32. RESTATEMENT (THIRD) OF THE FOREIGN RELATIONS LAW OF THE UNITED STATES §102(2) (1987) [hereinafter RESTATEMENT (THIRD)]. . . .

46. Henry J. Friendly, *In Praise of* Erie — *And of the New Federal Common Law*, 39 N.Y.U. L. REV. 383, 384 (1964). . . .

by Professors Bradley and Goldsmith is that customary international law now forms part of Judge Friendly's "new federal common law." As the *Restatement (Third) of Foreign Relations Law* put it, "the modern view is that customary international law in the United States is federal law and its determination by the federal courts is binding on the State courts."[49] . . .

All proponents of the modern position *do* seem to agree on [one] implication[] of the claim that customary international law "is" or "is like" federal common law: [C]ustomary international law is "supreme" in its relation to state law. It is this aspect of the modern position that raises the most serious constitutional objections, implicating the Supremacy Clause's quite specific requirements for the pedigree of supreme federal law[60] as well as basic questions of state regulatory autonomy. . . .

B. Some Examples

The view that customary international law is federal law . . . creates the potential for such law to trump domestic law in a variety of contexts. One example—which I note but do not discuss further here—is the claim that new norms of customary law supersede preexisting federal statutes. More plausible arguments hold that customary international law preempts contrary state law or provides defenses to state law claims.

The most prominent instance in which customary international norms have been asserted to preempt state law involves the issue of capital punishment. Current debates seem to focus on particular aspects of the death penalty, such as the execution of murderers for crimes committed as juveniles. The state of Texas, for example, recently executed Gerald Lee Mitchell for murders committed when he was only 17 years of age. In refusing to commute Mitchell's sentence, Governor Rick Perry rejected pleas from foreign leaders that Mitchell's execution violated norms of international law. . . .

Other commentators argue that customary international law will inevitably outlaw capital punishment altogether in the future. But whatever the scope of the customary norm asserted, the argument for preemption is straightforward: Because federal common law generally has the same preemptive effect as federal statutes and constitutional provisions, the modern position's view that customary international law is federal common law requires that such law preempt contrary state law. . . .

Internationalists are quick to acknowledge that this position . . . has not been widely adopted by the courts. Advocates who have argued to American courts that customary international law trumps domestic norms report a "blank stare phenomenon"—that is, extreme judicial skepticism about the domestic force of customary law. . . .

Customary international law has played a more important (and far less controversial) role in creating defenses to criminal prosecution or civil causes of action under state law. Traditional notions of diplomatic, consular, or foreign sovereign immunity all derive from customary international law,

---

49. RESTATEMENT (THIRD), *supra* note 32, §111 Reporters' Note 3.

60. *See, e.g.*, Bradford R. Clark, *Separation of Powers as a Safeguard of Federalism*, 79 TEX. L. REV. 1321, 1332-34 (2001) [hereinafter Clark, *Separation of Powers*].

although these issues are nowadays chiefly governed by statute or treaty. Some potentially important immunities in this area remain uncodified, such as the immunity of visiting heads of state; in these areas, the modern position that such customary norms trump state law retains substantial importance. . . .

[Moreover,] customary international norms can play an important persuasive role even where they do not apply of their own force. Under the *Charming Betsy* canon of interpretation, "an act of Congress ought never to be construed to violate the law of nations, if any other possible construction remains."[98] Under this canon, ambiguities in legislative enactments are resolved in favor of compliance with both treaties and customary international law. It has been invoked, for example, to construe ambiguous statutes not to have extraterritorial effects. . . .

II. Evaluating the Critique

The modern position claims that customary international law is federal in the sense, *inter alia*, that it preempts contrary state law. That claim ought to point us toward the Supremacy Clause, which sets out a categorical list of the types of law that have this effect:

> The Constitution, and the Laws of the United States which shall be made in Pursuance thereof; and all Treaties made, or which shall be made, under the Authority of the United States, shall be the supreme Law of the Land; and the Judges in every State shall be bound thereby, any thing in the Constitution or Laws of any state to the Contrary notwithstanding.

This listing, as Brad Clark has demonstrated, provides an exclusive set of means by which supreme federal law may be produced. It does not, of course, mention customary international law. That law is mentioned, however, in Article I, Section 8, where Congress is given the power "[t]o define and punish . . . Offenses against the Law of Nations." This placement among Congress's enumerated powers—which are subject to the lawmaking procedures set out in Article I, Section 7—indicates that Congress must incorporate customary norms by statute before those norms can be recognized, under the Supremacy Clause, as supreme federal law.

We know, nonetheless, that the courts of the early Republic applied international law and, indeed, that the Framers intended them to do so. That practice can be easily reconciled with the constitutional text once we recognize that the law of nations was *not* considered federal law in this period. Rather, as virtually all participants in the customary law debate agree, it had the status of "general" law: neither state nor federal, and not preemptive of contrary state norms. Indeed, the other sort of "general" law applied by both federal and state courts during the nineteenth century—the general commercial law of *Swift v. Tyson*—was simply a subset of customary international norms.

By the end of the nineteenth century, however, the general commercial law had become *de facto* preemptive of contrary state rules—as, in fact, had some of the more clearly "international" portions of the law of nations. This development created the pressure that led to *Erie*, and *Erie* can thus be seen as a

---

98. Murray v. The Schooner Charming Betsy, 6 U.S. (2 Cranch) 64, 118 (1804).

reaffirmance of the Supremacy Clause's exclusive recipe for supreme federal law. "Except in matters governed by the Federal Constitution or by Acts of Congress," Justice Brandeis wrote, "the law to be applied in any case is the law of the State. . . . There is no federal general common law." "After *Erie*," Professors Bradley and Goldsmith argue, "a federal court can no longer apply CIL in the absence of some domestic authorization to do so, as it could under the regime of general common law."[149] . . .

The . . . most important . . . set of arguments against the internationalists' view of federal common law rests on principles of federalism. . . . As international law became increasingly concerned with regulating the relationship between states and their citizens, . . . the potential for conflict with state law expanded exponentially. And as globalization further erodes the distinction between "foreign" and "domestic" affairs, the potential for conflict can only increase.

The federalism argument against the modern position ultimately rests on "[t]he Supreme Court's modern federalism jurisprudence." But the jurisprudence that Professors Bradley and Goldsmith have in mind is not the Court's most recent "Federalist Revival," exemplified by cases like *United States v. Lopez* or *Printz v. United States*. Rather, they emphasize *Garcia v. San Antonio Metropolitan Transit Authority*, which announced the primacy of "political safeguards" for federalism. As Justice Blackmun wrote for the majority, "the principal means chosen by the Framers to ensure the role of the States in the federal system lies in the structure of the Federal Government itself." The States are represented in Congress, and they participate indirectly in the selection of the President. As a result, the Court adopted Herbert Wechsler's influential assertion that "the Court is on weakest ground when it opposes its interpretation of the Constitution to that of Congress in the interest of the states, whose representatives control the legislative process and, by hypothesis, have broadly acquiesced in sanctioning the challenged Act of Congress."[190]

The *Garcia*/Wechsler model raises any number of difficulties and its adequacy as a protection for federalism has been seriously questioned. At the same time, a "political safeguards" model does seem to impose one irreducible minimum requirement: federal law must, in fact, be made in a way that respects the political and institutional safeguards for state autonomy built into the federal structure. As Brad Clark has demonstrated, the Supremacy Clause accords "supreme Law of the Land" status only to rules made by very specific procedures.[192] "Each set of procedures," he argues, "safe-guards federalism in two related ways":

> First, each procedure requires the participation and assent of multiple actors to adopt federal law. This creates the equivalent of a supermajority requirement and thus reinforces the burden of inertia against federal action, leaving states

---

149. Bradley & Goldsmith, *Critique of the Modern Position, supra* note 2, at 852-53.

190. Herbert Wechsler, *The Political Safeguards of Federalism: The Role of the States in the Composition and Selection of the National Government*, 54 COLUM. L. REV. 543, 559 (1954). . . .

192. See Clark, *Separation of Powers, supra* note 60, at 1332 (arguing that . . . the text of the Constitution limits "supreme" status to "the 'Constitution,' 'Laws,' and 'Treaties' of the United States adopted in accordance with the corresponding lawmaking procedures prescribed elsewhere in the Constitution"); *id.* at 1338 (observing that "the constitutional structure confirms that the federal lawmaking procedures prescribed by the Constitution are the exclusive means adopting 'the supreme Law of the Land' ").

greater freedom to govern. Second, each procedures limits participation to actors—such as the Senate—originally structured to be responsive to state prerogatives.[193]

On this view, any form of federal lawmaking that does not go through the specified procedures—either Article V's provisions for constitutional amendment, Article I's provisions for statutory enactment, or Article II's treaty-making procedures—is highly suspect. The implications for customary international law are obvious. As Professors Bradley and Goldsmith observe, "the interests of the states are neither formally nor effectively represented in the lawmaking process" that gives rise to customary law.[194] Nor is customary law subject to the procedural hurdles and burdens of inertia that tend to safeguard state regulatory autonomy even in the absence of effective political representation.

By circumventing the political and procedural safeguards of federalism entirely, a federalized customary international law flouts even the minimal protections for federalism left standing after *Garcia*. This is especially true where . . . customary international law rules are derived from sources that the political branches—who *are* subject to political safeguards—have declined to incorporate into American law explicitly, such as unratified multilateral treaties. . . . The system is designed to protect state autonomy by channeling federal lawmaking to the political branches, who are accountable to both the People and the States and who can act only after overcoming significant procedural hurdles.

Internationalists have responded to the federalism argument not by attempting to refute it, but by dismissing its importance. . . . The thrust of the internationalist view on federalism . . . is that the modern position *does* eliminate state authority in areas covered by customary international law—and rightly so. . . .

Professor Koh[] . . . gives three reasons why *Erie*'s insistence that state law applies absent a positive federal enactment should not apply to cases involving customary international law: First, Koh argues that Justice Brandeis's opinion rested on a lack of federal *legislative* power to create the federal norm applied by the lower courts in *Erie*; there is no such lack, Koh says, in international cases. Second, *Erie* also rested on "an allocation of law-making functions between state and federal legislative processes"—an allocation which Koh says is likewise missing in foreign affairs, where federal power is exclusive. Third, Koh argues that "to treat determinations of customary international law as questions of state law" would "have raised the specter that multiple variants of the same international law rule could proliferate among the several states." This is because such treatment "would have rendered both state court and federal diversity rulings effectively unreviewable by the U.S. Supreme Court." . . .

1. *Erie* and the Limits of Federal Legislative Power

Professor Koh's first point raises a well-known ambiguity in the *Erie* opinion. Justice Brandeis wrote that that the regime of *Swift v. Tyson* was

---

193. *Id.* at 1339. . . .
194. Bradley & Goldsmith, *Critique of the Modern Position*, *supra* note 2, at 868.

unconstitutional because "Congress has no power to declare substantive rules of common law applicable in a State whether they be local in their nature or 'general,' be they commercial law or a part of the law of torts." International law, Koh says, is different. "[G]iven both Congress's enumerated authority to define and punish offenses against the law of nations and its affirmative exercise of that power in a range of statutes, no one could similarly claim that federal courts lacked power to make federal common law rules with respect to international law."

The problem in *Erie*, however, was not Congress's lack of enumerated authority to reach the conduct at issue in that case. Tompkins had been injured traveling on foot along a railroad right of way, and the critical question in the case involved the duty of care owed by the railroad to persons like Tompkins. There is little doubt that Congress could have provided a federal answer to that question by statute under the Commerce Clause. After all, *Erie* was decided in 1938, hard on the heels of *Jones & Laughlin* and the Court's "switch in time."[214]

To be sure, the completeness of the Court's retreat from enforcing limits on Congress's commerce power did not become clear until the unanimous decisions in *United States v. Darby* and *Wickard v. Filburn*, three and four years after *Erie*, respectively. But a federal statute prescribing rules for railroads — classic "instrumentalities" of interstate commerce — would likely have passed muster even before the Court's 1937 change of course. . . . In any event, *Erie*'s constitutional holding is not generally thought to have become obsolete in our post-1941 world; it must rest, therefore, on something other than a lack of federal legislative power over the subject matter of the general common law.

That "something" is the lack of *judicial* power to act in the absence of prior congressional authorization. As Henry Monaghan has observed, *Erie* "recognizes that federal judicial power to displace state law is not coextensive with the scope of dormant congressional power. Rather, the Court must point to some source, such as a statute, treaty, or constitutional provision, as authority for the creation of substantive federal law."[220] *Erie* recognized, in other words, a principle of *judicial* federalism which denies to federal courts the power to "go first" in making federal law, even if the same law would not be beyond the legislative competence of Congress. Justice Brandeis reinforced this reading when he quoted Justice Holmes to the effect that *Swift* was "an unconstitutional assumption of powers *by courts* of the United States which no lapse of time or respectable array of opinion should make us hesitate to correct." . . .

The fact that *Congress* has broad power to legislate in the area of foreign affairs, including a specific grant of authority to define and punish violations of international law, thus proves nothing about the federal *judiciary's* authority to perform the same task. . . .

---

214. See NLRB v. Jones & Laughlin Steel Corp., 301 U.S. 1 (1937) (upholding the National Labor Relations Act as within Congress's commerce power and marking the end of aggressive judicial review of federal legislation under the Commerce Clause).

220. Henry Monaghan, *Foreword: Constitutional Common Law*, 89 HARV. L. REV. 1, 11-12 (1975). . . .

2. Is the Federal Foreign Affairs Power Exclusive?

Justice Harlan read *Erie* as resting on the principle that "the scheme of our Constitution envisions an allocation of law-making functions between state and federal legislative processes which is undercut if the federal judiciary can make substantive law affecting state affairs beyond the bounds of congressional legislative powers in this regard."[252] This statement is entirely consistent with the account of *Erie* I have urged in the preceding section, so long as we read "the bounds of congressional legislative powers" to include the Article I procedures that federal lawmaking must follow as well as the subjects that federal lawmaking can reach. Professor Koh argues, however, that "with respect to international and foreign affairs law, the Constitution envisions no similar role for state legislative or judicial process." As a result, "[f]ederal judicial determination of most questions of customary international law transpires not in a zone of core state concerns, such as state tort law, but in a foreign affairs area in which the Tenth Amendment has reserved little or no power to the states." Put more crudely, the modern position cannot violate "states' rights" because the states *have* no rights in this area. . . .

[I]n *United States v. Belmont*,[257] . . . [the] Supreme Court . . . assert[ed] that

> [p]lainly, the external powers of the United States are to be exercised without regard to state laws or policies. . . . In respect of all international negotiations and compacts, and in respect of our foreign relations generally, state lines disappear. As to such purposes the State of New York does not exist.[258]

As a result, "state constitutions, state laws, and state policies are irrelevant to the inquiry and decision" of cases like *Belmont*.[259]

With all respect to Mr. Justice Sutherland, that claim was silly when made — and it is even sillier today. A political community of 19 million people does not "cease to exist" simply because a lawsuit raises one particular kind of issue rather than another. The State of New York has the world's ninth largest economy; it now houses the United Nations and the world's most important financial center; it has commercial missions in nine countries and receives 150,000 immigrants each year. *Of course* the State of New York *exists* in international affairs. . . .

Consider, for example, some recent disputes involving the State of California. For some years, California has calculated its franchise tax on corporations doing business within the state on a "worldwide combined reporting method" that multinational businesses claim is unfair. Despite the fact that foreign nations had protested California's practice, the Supreme Court — without dissent — upheld the practice against a claim that it interfered with the federal government's ability to conduct foreign affairs. Similarly, California's Proposition 187 ballot initiative would have sharply curtailed the ability of the state government to provide social services to undocumented aliens, including a large group of Mexican immigrants. . . . [T]he passage of

---

252. Hanna v. Plumer, 380 U.S. 460, 474-75 (1965) (Harlan, J., concurring).
257. 301 U.S. 324 (1937).
258. *Id.* at 331.
259. *Id.* at 332. . . .

Proposition 187 drew protests and the implicit threat of trade sanctions — not against the United States as a whole, but against California directly — from the Mexican government.

In both these instances, the State of California did not "cease to exist" because foreign affairs were involved. . . .

Professor Koh acknowledges . . . that

> [i]n the modern era, situations increasingly arise in which state and national governments exercise overlapping authority, the federal government has arguably condoned state action inconsistent with customary norms of international law, or customary international law and state law rules are insufficiently contradictory for a court to give the former preemptive force.

This acknowledgement of "overlapping" state and federal authority and the potential legitimacy of state law rules even in areas where customary international law may operate calls into question the entire enterprise of trying to define and police exclusive "foreign" and "domestic" spheres of activity. . . .

[A] rule of exclusive federal power for everything "touching on" or "affecting" foreign affairs is simply unthinkable. Are we to oust the states from regulating family law simply because a state's compliance with so-far unratified provisions of the International Convention on the Rights of the Child (which may, under some theories, have already become "binding" customary law) may have an effect on American foreign relations? Surely not. The theory of federal exclusivity is implausible because it proves too much.

Just as the expansion of the federal interstate commerce power during the New Deal cemented the presumption that states exercise concurrent power over such commerce, so, too, the expansion of the "international" will require the recognition of concurrent state authority in many areas that now raise foreign affairs concerns. A growing political science literature on globalization thus reaches the somewhat counterintuitive conclusion that the role of subnational governments will likely *expand*, rather than contract, as more issues take on international overtones. To be sure, this overlap may lead to all sorts of confusion and coordination problems. But those problems will not be avoided by pretending that the world has not changed or that "foreign affairs" can be cabined to a manageable zone of federal exclusivity. . . .

4. Supreme Court Review and the Problem of Uniformity

Professor Koh's final argument for distinguishing *Erie* is not so much a claim about *Erie*'s meaning as a concern about the consequences of its application. Koh argues that "to treat determinations of customary international law as questions of state law would have rendered both state court and federal diversity rulings effectively unreviewable by the U.S. Supreme Court." "Such unreviewability," he worries, "would have raised the specter that multiple variants of the same international law rule could proliferate among the several states." This is not a stand-alone argument. It does not provide an account of *Erie*'s rationale that would render it inapplicable in cases involving customary international law; rather, it provides a policy justification for preferring such an account — if it is otherwise available and plausible in its own right — over one that would not accord federal-law status to customary international norms.

Nonetheless, a few observations about the uniformity argument are in order. First, it is undisputed . . . that the intolerable situation that Professor Koh posits was the law for much, if not all, of the nineteenth century. As Koh himself acknowledges, federal courts in that period "construed both commercial and noncommercial rules of customary international law" as "part of the 'general common law' to be interpreted by federal courts sitting in diversity jurisdiction.'" Part of what made this law "general" was that it did not create appellate jurisdiction in the Supreme Court. Judge Fletcher has observed, "[s]tate courts generally followed common law decisions by the United States Supreme Court, but they were quite explicit in stating that they did not do so because of any legal compulsion."[348] As a result, it is hard to believe that the unreviewability of state court decisions applying customary norms would "have raised [a] specter" that would have frightened the founding generation.

The second point is that Professor Koh's uniformity argument is similar to claims made in opposition to *Erie* itself. Prior to the Court's decision, the defenders of *Swift v. Tyson* praised the "general law" regime on the ground that it produced a uniform system of commercial rules for businesses operating throughout the country. As the notion that judges simply "found" the general common law became increasingly unpersuasive in the early twentieth century, defenders of that system "increasingly stressed *Swift*'s status as an established precedent and its practical role in unifying the national economy."[351] And after 1938, *Erie*'s critics worried that the decision "would prove 'very damaging' because it decentralized the law where national uniformity was required."[352] The similarity of Koh's argument to the claims of *Swift*'s defenders suggests that his overriding concern with uniformity across different state jurisdictions was considered and rejected in *Erie* itself. Moreover, the aftermath of *Erie* — which did not see the sky fall on enterprises subject to the rules of more than one state — suggests that the consequences of applying *Erie* in cases involving customary norms may not be as catastrophic as internationalists sometimes suggest. . . .

Professor Koh's concerns about Supreme Court review and uniformity are part and parcel of longstanding debates over *Erie*; they are not grounds to distinguish *Erie* away.

ANTHONY J. BELLIA JR. & BRADFORD R. CLARK,
THE FEDERAL COMMON LAW OF NATIONS

---

109 Colum. L. Rev. 1, 5-9, 47-48, 53-55 (2009)

[T]he law of nations has interacted with the American federal system in a way that neither the modern nor the revisionist position fairly captures. The Supreme Court has treated certain aspects of the law of nations as a set of

---

348. [William A.] Fletcher, [*The General Common Law and Section 34 of the Judicary Act of 1789: The Example of Marine Insurance*, 97 HARV. L. REV. 1513,] 1561 [(1984)].

351. [EDWARD] PURCELL, [BRANDEIS AND THE PROGRESSIVE CONSTITUTION: *ERIE*, THE JUDICIAL POWER, AND THE POLITICS OF THE FEDERAL COURTS IN TWENTIETH-CENTURY AMERICA] 69 [(2000)].

352. *Id.* at 217 (quoting Zechariah Chafee, Jr., *Do Judges Make or Discover Law?*, 91 PROCEEDINGS OF THE AM. PHIL. SOC. 405, 415 (1947)).

background rules to guide its implementation of the Constitution's allocation of powers. Specifically, the Court has respected foreign sovereigns' "perfect rights" (and close analogues) as a means of ensuring that any decision to commit the nation to war would rest exclusively with the political branches, and not with the judiciary or the states. Indeed, when application of other aspects of the law of nations would risk embroiling the nation in war, the Court has declined to apply them in order to preserve political branch authority. The current debate over the status of customary international law has paid insufficient attention to the relationship between the law of nations and the Constitution's allocation of powers. To be sure, scholars on either side look to the founding and early judicial precedent to evaluate whether, as a matter of original understanding, courts have authority to take the lead over the political branches in adopting customary international law as the supreme law of the United States. But their historical accounts are either incomplete or anachronistic, often recasting history in a post-*Erie* mold. After the founding, public officials and judges initially debated a question similar to the one that dominates customary international law debates today: whether federal courts have Article III power to adopt the law of nations as part of a preemptive, jurisdiction-triggering federal common law. They ultimately moved beyond this question, concluding that the constitutional structure precludes the existence of a federal municipal common law. Instead, they recognized the perfect rights of sovereigns as essential background for understanding the Constitution's allocation of powers.

[In light of] this lost context[, there is] a third way to conceptualize how important aspects of the law of nations have interacted with the federal system. Our account recaptures the Founders' understanding of core aspects of the law of nations and best describes the Supreme Court's reliance on such law in key cases throughout American history. This allocation of powers approach helps alleviate the apparent tension between federal control over foreign affairs (stressed by proponents of the modern position) and the Constitution's federal lawmaking procedures (emphasized by proponents of the revisionist position).

In the late eighteenth century, a foundational principle of the law of nations was that each nation should reciprocally respect certain perfect rights of every other nation to exercise territorial sovereignty, conduct diplomatic relations, exercise neutral rights, and peaceably enjoy liberty. The perfect rights of sovereigns were so fundamental that interference with them provided just cause for war. Thus, respect for these rights was essential to maintaining international peace. This idea was ubiquitous in English and American legal thought at the time of the founding.

The Founders understood the need to respect perfect rights of sovereigns in order to avoid embroiling the fledgling United States in foreign conflict. This background provides essential context for understanding the Constitution's allocation of powers to the federal political branches to recognize foreign nations and make war and peace. The Founders also authorized federal court jurisdiction over several categories of cases implicating the law of nations. By simultaneously allocating authority to the federal political branches over foreign relations and jurisdiction to the federal judiciary over cases likely to implicate the law of nations, the Founders established complementary, not conflicting, powers.

From ratification through the War of 1812, the Supreme Court employed the law of nations to respect perfect rights and, in the process, upheld constitutional prerogatives of the federal political branches in foreign relations. Over time, judges increasingly grounded their decisions in the Constitution's allocation of foreign relations powers to the political branches. In the twentieth century, the Court continued to respect what were historically considered perfect rights, but recognized that the Constitution's allocation of foreign relations powers also required the judiciary to apply at least some principles of modern customary international law as well.

It is not our purpose to settle all questions regarding the role of customary international law in the federal system. Rather, we seek to identify the role that certain aspects of the law of nations actually have played throughout American history in light of the constitutional structure. In context, historical practice does not evince a principle that all of the law of nations necessarily functioned as preemptive federal law. Much of what was regarded as part of the law of nations — the law merchant, for example — was never understood to operate as preemptive federal law, by incorporation or otherwise. But neither does historical practice evince a principle that rules derived from the law of nations could *never* trigger federal preemption. Instead, history and structure demonstrate that courts have applied certain principles derived from the law of nations as a means of upholding the Constitution's allocation of foreign affairs powers to Congress and the President — in particular, the powers to recognize foreign nations and decide questions of war and peace. . . .

Like English courts, state courts incorporated the law of nations into state law before ratification. But their violations of the law of nations were well known, as were the challenges that those violations posed for U.S. foreign relations. The Constitution was framed in part to better consolidate national political control over foreign relations. In Articles I and II, the Founders allocated foreign relations powers to Congress and the President, including powers to recognize foreign nations and make war. Prominent members of the founding generation understood that federal political power over war and peace would be effective only if states did not embroil the United States in war by violating these principles of the law of nations. Thus, judicial enforcement of the law of nations was necessary to sustain the foreign relations powers allocated to the federal government. To serve that end, Article III authorized federal jurisdiction over categories of cases — such as those involving admiralty and ambassadors — in which the law of nations would often supply rules of decision. In addition, the Arising Under Clause provided a judicial mechanism to ensure the effective enforcement of enacted federal municipal law, including treaties and statutes exercising foreign relations powers. Taken together, Article III jurisdiction was designed to facilitate judicial adherence to the law of nations, uphold the constitutional prerogatives of the political branches, and guard against state actions that would give other nations just cause for war against the United States. . . .

[E]arly executive and judicial officials understood the Constitution to require application of certain default rules derived from the perfect rights of sovereigns. It was clear at the founding that federal court jurisdiction over cases implicating this part of the law of nations would further federal authority over foreign relations. It would take a couple of decades, however, for the Court to clearly articulate that the Constitution's allocation of powers was the basis of its obligation to enforce, as the law of the land, an important subset of principles derived from the law of nations. The Justices realized that not only states but also federal courts could undermine the Constitution's allocation of foreign relations powers if either disregarded core principles of the law of nations. Given the Constitution's allocation of foreign affairs and war powers, the Court recognized that the political branches, rather than the judiciary, should decide whether to risk provoking conflict with foreign nations by interfering with traditional sovereign rights. For various reasons, the question whether states remained free to pursue their own path in such cases did not come before the Court in the nation's early years. But to the extent that the Court understood Articles I and II to require courts to apply certain rules derived from the law of nations, it applied a constitutional rule of decision that would ultimately override contrary state law under the Supremacy Clause.

[S]everal well-known federal cases have continued to apply principles derived from the law of nations to uphold the Constitution's allocation of powers. Scholars often cite *Banco Nacional de Cuba v. Sabbatino*, for example, for the proposition that federal courts should apply modern principles of customary international law as federal law. The decision is best read, however, to reflect adherence to the same allocation of powers principles recognized by the Marshall Court, under which the Court upheld the perfect rights of sovereigns as a means of preserving federal political branch authority over foreign relations. The *Sabbatino* Court applied the act of state doctrine — a traditional rule respecting a foreign nation's perfect right to territorial sovereignty — rather than a modern rule that would have compromised foreign territorial sovereignty. In so doing, the Court carried on a centuries-old tradition of upholding perfect rights in cases implicating the law of nations. It is tempting simply to characterize the Court's practice as applying "federal common law" — judicially crafted "rules of decision whose content cannot be traced by traditional methods of interpretation to federal statutory or constitutional commands."[23] This characterization, however, is both anachronistic and too simplistic. Rather than devising its own rules of decision out of whole cloth in cases like *Sabbatino*, the Court has applied constitutionally derived rules of decision that preserve federal political branch control over the conduct of foreign affairs. Taken in historical context, the best reading of Supreme Court precedent dating from the founding to the present is that the law of nations does not apply as preemptive federal law by virtue of any general Article III power to fashion federal common law, but only when necessary to preserve and implement distinct Article I and Article II powers

---

23. See Richard H. Fallon, Jr., et al., Hart and Wechsler's The Federal Courts and the Federal System 685 (5th ed. 2003).

to recognize foreign nations, conduct foreign relations, and decide momentous questions of war and peace.

POINTS FOR DISCUSSION

1. How does the debate over customary international law implicate the relative balance of power between the federal government and the states?

2. How does customary international law relate to the allocation of foreign relations powers to the federal government?

C. GENERAL LAW

Since *Erie Railroad v. Tompkins*, 304 U.S. 64 (1938), courts and scholars have largely regarded general law as an historical artifact. With the rise of legal positivism, the *Erie* Court endorsed the proposition that "law in the sense in which courts speak of it today does not exist without some definite authority behind it." *Id*. at 79 (internal quotation marks and citations omitted). In the United States, according to *Erie*, that law is federal or state. It is perhaps not surprising, then, that most writings on general law are historical.

Nonetheless, might general law persist in the American federal system? Since *Erie*, the Court arguably has invoked "general law" as a rule of decision in various cases. The Title VII context provides a good example. Title VII of the Civil Rights Act of 1964 prohibits "employers" from discriminating on several bases, including the basis of sex, in the terms and conditions of employment. See 42 U.S.C. § 2000e, et seq. The Court has long held that sexual harassment constitutes a form of discrimination on the basis of sex in violation of Title VII. Consider the following question: If one *employee* sexually harasses *another employee*, has the *employer* discriminated on the basis of sex in violation of Title VII? In determining whether an "employer" is liable under Title VII for sexual harassment committed by an employee, the Court has looked in part to general principles of agency, including respondeat superior liability. *See Faragher v. City of Boca Raton*, 524 U.S. 775 (1998); *Burlington Industries, Inc. v. Ellerth*, 524 U.S. 742 (1998). In such cases, it might be argued, the Court is not applying general principles of law as independent rules of decision but rather is interpreting statutes in light of such principles. Either way, the Court appears to presume the existence of general legal principles, against which Congress legislates, that transcend state lines. As applied to interpret or enforce a federal statute, such principles are federal law: A state court could not ignore them in applying the same federal statute in the same context. But, beyond that context, such principles are not uniquely federal law. In using general agency principles to interpret or enforce a federal statute, the Supreme Court has not purported to establish a federal law of agency, preemptive of each state's law. Rather, it has invoked a general law of agency for interpreting a federal statute, otherwise leaving state agency law intact. Consider, as you read the following materials (1) whether general law in fact persists as a source of law in the U.S. federal system, and (2) whether the apparent persistence of general law comports with the U.S. federal structure.

CALEB NELSON, THE PERSISTENCE OF GENERAL LAW

106 Colum. L. Rev. 503, 503-505 (2006)

Studies of American federalism have elegantly catalogued the ways in which federal law can interact with the local law of individual states. Many federal rules of decision address only a few discrete questions, leaving each state free to regulate related matters as it sees fit. Other federal rules themselves incorporate local law in certain respects, so that their substance differs in different states.

Modern scholars, however, have been slower to acknowledge a different way in which federal law can piggyback on state law. Within the interstices of written federal law, courts often articulate federal rules of decision that again draw their substance from state law. Rather than tracking the local law of any single state, though, these federal rules reflect state law *in general*; what matters is how *most* states do things, not whatever the policymakers in one particular state have said.

To take just one example, consider the legal rules that determine the federal government's rights and obligations under contracts to which it is a party. Under current doctrine, no individual state is in charge of those rules; in the absence of relevant federal legislation, the governing rules are instead a matter of "federal common law." But the substance of those rules nonetheless reflects a multijurisdictional form of general American jurisprudence. As Judge Posner puts it, courts derive the legal rules applicable to government contracts from "the core principles of the common law of contract that are in force in most states" (tweaked where necessary to reflect "special characteristics of the federal government as a contracting partner").[3]

The Supreme Court has taken much the same approach to a variety of federal statutes that implicate background concepts of agency law, tort law, contract law, or the like. When the Bankruptcy Code refers to "fraud," for instance, the Court has understood it to be incorporating "the general common law of torts, the dominant consensus of common-law jurisdictions."[4] Likewise, the Court has assumed that various modern federal statutes implicitly draw their rules of vicarious liability from "the general common law of agency, rather than . . . the law of any particular State."[5]

For scholars who assume that the Court's landmark decision in *Erie Railroad Co. v. Tompkins* marked the end of the very concept of "general" law, this theme in modern jurisprudence is hard to fathom—which may be why it has largely escaped comment. Properly understood, however, *Erie* does not deny the ability of lawyers and judges, drawing upon precedents and practices followed in diverse jurisdictions, to distill rules that are available for legal recognition and that are sufficiently determinate to be "law-like." *Erie* simply altered prior views of the relationship between state and federal courts that engage in this process.

---

3. United States v. Nat'l Steel Corp., 75 F.3d 1146, 1150 (7th Cir. 1996). . . .

4. Field v. Mans, 516 U.S. 59, 70 n.9 (1995) (citations omitted).

5. Kolstad v. Am. Dental Ass'n, 527 U.S. 526, 542 (1999) (internal quotation marks omitted) (quoting Burlington Indus., Inc. v. Ellerth, 524 U.S. 742, 754 (1998) (quoting Cmty. for Creative Non-Violence v. Reid, 490 U.S. 730, 740-41 (1989))).

Indeed, our federal system all but requires continuing recourse to rules of general law. There are many situations in which courts and Congress alike will want to refer to some sort of national law on topics that typically are handled at the state level. Although the law of each state addresses these topics, one can certainly imagine questions as to which no individual state's law deserves controlling weight, and on which it seems more sensible to refer to a species of general law.

OUBRE v. ENTERGY OPERATIONS

---

522 U.S. 422 (1998)

JUSTICE KENNEDY delivered the opinion of the Court.

An employee, as part of a termination agreement, signed a release of all claims against her employer. In consideration, she received severance pay in installments. The release, however, did not comply with specific federal statutory requirements for a release of claims under the Age Discrimination in Employment Act of 1967 (ADEA), 81 Stat. 602, 29 U.S.C. §621 *et seq.* After receiving the last payment, the employee brought suit under the ADEA. The employer claims the employee ratified and validated the nonconforming release by retaining the moneys paid to secure it. The employer also insists the release bars the action unless, as a precondition to filing suit, the employee tenders back the moneys received. . . .

The Older Workers Benefit Protection Act (OWBPA) imposes specific requirements for releases covering ADEA claims. OWBPA, §201, 104 Stat. 983, 29 U.S.C. §§626(f)(1)(B) (F) (G). In procuring the release, Entergy did not comply with the OWBPA in at least three respects: (1) Entergy did not give Oubre enough time to consider her options. (2) Entergy did not give Oubre seven days after she signed the release to change her mind. And (3) the release made no specific reference to claims under the ADEA. . . .

The employer rests its case upon general principles of state contract jurisprudence. As the employer recites the rule, contracts tainted by mistake, duress, or even fraud are voidable at the option of the innocent party. See 1 Restatement (Second) of Contracts §7, and Comment *b* (1979). The employer maintains, however, that before the innocent party can elect avoidance, she must first tender back any benefits received under the contract. If she fails to do so within a reasonable time after learning of her rights, the employer contends, she ratifies the contract and so makes it binding. 1 Restatement (Second) of Contracts, *supra,* §7, Comments *d, e.* The employer also invokes the doctrine of equitable estoppel. As a rule, equitable estoppel bars a party from shirking the burdens of a voidable transaction for as long as she retains the benefits received under it. Applying these principles, the employer claims the employee ratified the ineffective release (or faces estoppel) by retaining all the sums paid in consideration of it. The employer, then, relies not upon the execution of the release but upon a later, distinct ratification of its terms.

These general rules may not be as unified as the employer asserts. See generally Annot., 76 A.L.R. 344 (1932) (collecting cases supporting and contradicting these rules); Annot., 134 A.L.R. 6 (1941) (same). And in equity, a person suing to rescind a contract, as a rule, is not required to restore the consideration at the very outset of the litigation. See 3 Restatement (Second) of Contracts, *supra*, §384, and Comment *b*; Restatement of Restitution §65, Comment *d* (1936); D. Dobbs, Law of Remedies §4.8, p. 294 (1973). Even if the employer's statement of the general rule requiring tender back before one files suit were correct, it would be unavailing. The rule cited is based simply on the course of negotiation of the parties and the alleged later ratification. The authorities cited do not consider the question raised by statutory standards for releases and a statutory declaration making nonconforming releases ineffective. It is the latter question we confront here.

In 1990, Congress amended the ADEA by passing the OWBPA. The OWBPA provides: "An individual may not waive any right or claim under [the ADEA] unless the waiver is knowing and voluntary. . . . [A] waiver may not be considered knowing and voluntary unless at a minimum" it satisfies certain enumerated requirements, including the three listed above. 29 U.S.C. §626(f)(1).

The statutory command is clear: An employee "may not waive" an ADEA claim unless the waiver or release satisfies the OWBPA's requirements. The policy of the OWBPA is likewise clear from its title: It is designed to protect the rights and benefits of older workers. The OWBPA implements Congress' policy via a strict, unqualified statutory stricture on waivers, and we are bound to take Congress at its word. Congress imposed specific duties on employers who seek releases of certain claims created by statute. Congress delineated these duties with precision and without qualification: An employee "may not waive" an ADEA claim unless the employer complies with the statute. Courts cannot with ease presume ratification of that which Congress forbids.

The OWBPA sets up its own regime for assessing the effect of ADEA waivers, separate and apart from contract law. The statute creates a series of prerequisites for knowing and voluntary waivers and imposes affirmative duties of disclosure and waiting periods. The OWBPA governs the effect under federal law of waivers or releases on ADEA claims and incorporates no exceptions or qualifications. The text of the OWBPA forecloses the employer's defense, notwithstanding how general contract principles would apply to non-ADEA claims.

The rule proposed by the employer would frustrate the statute's practical operation as well as its formal command. In many instances a discharged employee likely will have spent the moneys received and will lack the means to tender their return. These realities might tempt employers to risk noncompliance with the OWBPA's waiver provisions, knowing it will be difficult to repay the moneys and relying on ratification. We ought not to open the door to an evasion of the statute by this device. . . .

The statute governs the effect of the release on ADEA claims, and the employer cannot invoke the employee's failure to tender back as a way of excusing its own failure to comply. . . .

Justice Breyer, with whom Justice O'Connor joins, concurring.

I believe it important to specify that the statute need not, and does not, thereby make the worker's procedurally invalid promise totally void, *i.e.*, without any legal effect, say, like a contract the terms of which themselves are contrary to public policy. See 1 Restatement (Second) of Contracts §7, Comment *a* (1979); 2 *id.,* §178. Rather, the statute makes the contract that the employer and worker tried to create voidable, like a contract made with an infant, or a contract created through fraud, mistake, or duress, which contract the worker may elect either to avoid or to ratify. See 1 *id.,* §7, and Comment *b.* . . .

JUSTICE SCALIA, dissenting.

I agree with Justice Thomas that the Older Workers Benefit Protection Act (OWBPA), 29 U.S.C. §626(f), does not abrogate the common-law doctrines of "tender back" and ratification. Because no "tender back" was made here, I would affirm the judgment.

I do not consider ratification a second basis for affirmance, since ratification cannot occur until the impediment to the conclusion of the agreement is eliminated. Thus, an infant cannot ratify his voidable contracts until he reaches majority, and a party who has contracted under duress cannot ratify until the duress is removed. See 1 E. Farnsworth, Contracts §4.4, p. 381, §4.19, p. 443 (1990). Of course for some contractual impediments, discovery itself is the cure. See 12 W. Jaeger, Williston on Contracts §1527, p. 626 (3d ed. 1970) (ratification by a defrauded party may occur "after discovery of the fraud"); 2 Farnsworth, *supra,* §9.3, at 520 (ratification by party entitled to avoid for mistake may occur after "that party is or ought to be aware of the facts"). The impediment here is not of that sort. OWBPA provides that "[a]n individual may not waive any right or claim under th[e] [Age Discrimination in Employment Act of 1962] unless the waiver is knowing and voluntary," 29 U.S.C. §626(f)(1), and says that a waiver "may not be considered knowing and voluntary" unless it satisfies the requirements not complied with here, *ibid.* That a party later learns that those requirements were not complied with no more enables ratification of the waiver than does such knowledge at the time of contracting render the waiver effective *ab initio.*

JUSTICE THOMAS, with whom THE CHIEF JUSTICE joins, dissenting.

The Older Workers Benefit Protection Act (OWBPA), 29 U.S.C. §626(f), imposes certain minimum requirements that waivers of claims under the Age Discrimination in Employment Act of 1967 (ADEA), 29 U.S.C. §621 *et seq.,* must meet in order to be considered "knowing and voluntary." The Court of Appeals held that petitioner had ratified a release of ADEA claims that did not comply with the OWBPA by retaining the benefits she had received in exchange for the release, even after she had become aware of the defect and had decided to sue respondent. The majority does not suggest that the Court of Appeals was incorrect in concluding that petitioner's conduct was sufficient to constitute ratification of the release. Instead, without so much as acknowledging the long-established principle that a statute "must 'speak directly' to the question addressed by the common law" in order to abrogate it, *United States v. Texas,* 507 U.S. 529, 534 (1993), the Court holds that the OWBPA abrogates both the common-law doctrine of ratification and the doctrine that a party must "tender back" consideration received under a release of legal claims before bringing suit. Because the OWBPA does not address either of these common-law doctrines at all, much less with the clarity necessary to abrogate them, I respectfully dissent.

It has long been established that " '[s]tatutes which invade the common law . . . are to be read with a presumption favoring the retention of long-established and familiar principles, except when a statutory purpose to the contrary is evident.' " *United States v. Texas, supra,* at 534. . . . Congress is understood to legislate against a background of common-law principles . . . and thus "does not write upon a clean slate," [*Id.*] As a result, common-law doctrines " 'ought not to be deemed to be repealed, unless the language of a statute be clear and explicit for this purpose.' " *Norfolk Redevelopment and Housing Authority v. Chesapeake & Potomac Telephone Co. of Va.,* 464 U.S. 30, 35-36 (1983).

The only clear and explicit purpose of the OWBPA is to define "knowing and voluntary" in the context of ADEA waivers. . . . I . . . agree with the Court that the OWBPA abrogates the common-law definition of a "knowing and voluntary" waiver where ADEA claims are involved.

From this rather unremarkable proposition, however, the Court leaps to the conclusion that the OWBPA supplants the common-law doctrines of ratification and tender back. The doctrine of ratification (also known in contract law as affirmation) provides that a party, after discovering a defect in the original release, can make binding that otherwise voidable release either explicitly or by failing timely to return the consideration received. See 1 Restatement (Second) of Contracts §7, Comments *d, e* (1979); 1 E. Farnsworth, Contracts §§4.15, 4.19 (1990). The tender back doctrine requires, as a condition precedent to suit, that a plaintiff return the consideration received in exchange for a release, on the theory that it is inconsistent to bring suit against the defendant while at the same time retaining the consideration received in exchange for a promise *not* to bring such a suit.

The OWBPA simply does not speak to ratification. It is certainly not the case — notwithstanding the Court's statement that the OWBPA "governs the effect under federal law of waivers or releases on ADEA claims" — that ratification can *never* apply in the context of ADEA releases. There is no reason to think that releases voidable on non-statutory grounds such as fraud, duress, or mistake cannot be ratified: The OWBPA merely imposes requirements for knowing and voluntary waivers and is silent regarding fraud, duress, and mistake. Further, the statute makes no mention of whether there can ever be a valid ratification in the more specific instance, presented by this case, of a release of ADEA claims that fails to satisfy the statute's requirements. Instead, the statute merely establishes prerequisites that must be met for a release to be considered knowing and voluntary; the imposition of these statutory requirements says absolutely nothing about whether a release that fails to meet these prerequisites can ever be ratified.

Not only does the text of the OWBPA make no mention of ratification, but it also cannot be said that the doctrine is inconsistent with the statute. . . . Ratification *necessarily* applies where a release is unenforceable against one party at its adoption because of some deficiency; the whole point of ratification is to give legal effect to an otherwise voidable release.

By defining the requirements that must be met for a release of ADEA claims to be considered knowing and voluntary, the OWBPA merely establishes one of the ways in which a release may be unenforceable at its adoption. The OWBPA does not suggest any reason why a noncomplying release cannot be made binding, despite the original defect, in the same manner as any other voidable release.

Nor does ratification conflict with the purpose of the OWBPA. Ratification occurs only when the employee realizes that the release does not comply with the OWBPA and nevertheless assents to be bound. See 12 W. Jaeger, Williston on Contracts §1527 (3d ed. 1970) (ratification may occur only after defect is discovered); 3 Restatement (Second) of Contracts §381 (same). This is surely consistent with the statutory purpose of ensuring that waivers of ADEA claims are knowing and voluntary. . . .

For many of the same reasons that the OWBPA does not abrogate the doctrine of ratification, it also does not abrogate the tender back requirement. Certainly the statute does not supplant the tender back requirement in its entirety. Where a release complies with the statute but is voidable on other grounds (such as fraud), the OWBPA does not relieve an employee of the obligation to return the consideration received before suing his employer; the OWBPA does not even arguably address such a situation. And in the more specific context of a release that fails to comply with the OWBPA, the statute simply says nothing about whether there can ever be an obligation to tender back the consideration before filing suit.

Nor is the tender back requirement inconsistent with the OWBPA. Although it does create an additional obligation that would not exist but for the noncomplying release, the doctrine merely puts the employee to a choice between avoiding the release and retaining the benefit of his bargain. . . .

Finally, it is clear that the statutory requirements have no application to the tender back requirement. The tender back doctrine operates not to make the voidable release binding, as does ratification, but rather precludes a party from simultaneously retaining the benefits of the release and suing to vindicate released claims. That is, the requirement to tender back is simply a condition precedent to suit; it has nothing to do with whether a waiver was knowing and voluntary. Nothing in the statute even arguably implies that the statutory requirements must be met before this obligation arises.

In sum, the OWBPA does not clearly and explicitly abrogate the doctrines of ratification and tender back. Congress, of course, is free to do so. But until it does, these common-law doctrines should apply to releases of ADEA claims, just as they do to other releases. . . .

POINTS FOR DISCUSSION

1. The employer in *Oubre* argued that, to avoid the release, the employee had to "tender back" amounts previously received. As authority for the tender back doctrine, the employer relied upon general contracts principles as described in the *Restatement (Second) of Contracts*. The Court refused to require the employee to tender back, relying on the requirements of the statute. The dissent, however, would have required the employee to tender back amounts received as a matter of general contract principles. Justice Thomas wrote in dissent that the OWBPA "does not abrogate the doctrines of ratification and tender back." What is the source of these doctrines? Why does Justice Thomas consider general state law instead of the law of the particular state that otherwise would govern the dispute? Would applying the governing law of *a* state be more consistent with the procedural and political safeguards of federalism? What values does looking to *general* contract law, rather than to the law of a particular state, advance? Is looking to such law in tension with any features of the American federal system?

2. In *Erie Railroad v. Tompkins*, 304 U.S. 64, 78 (1938), the Court declared that "[t]here is no federal general common law," explaining that "[e]xcept in matters governed by the Federal Constitution or by acts of Congress, the law to be applied in any case is the law of the State." If this is true, by what authority do *general* contract principles of ratification and tender back exist?

TABLE OF CASES

Principal cases are indicated by italics.

TABLE OF AUTHORITIES

Italics indicate reprints in text.

TABLE OF STATUTES, ACTS, AND REGULATIONS

INDEX